MW00860677

Shinto

Shinto

A History

HELEN HARDACRE

OXFORD
UNIVERSITY PRESS

OXFORD
UNIVERSITY PRESS

Oxford University Press is a department of the University of Oxford. It furthers the University's objective of excellence in research, scholarship, and education by publishing worldwide. Oxford is a registered trade mark of Oxford University Press in the UK and certain other countries.

Published in the United States of America by Oxford University Press
198 Madison Avenue, New York, NY 10016, United States of America.

© Oxford University Press 2017

All rights reserved. No part of this publication may be reproduced, stored in a retrieval system, or transmitted, in any form or by any means, without the prior permission in writing of Oxford University Press, or as expressly permitted by law, by license, or under terms agreed with the appropriate reproduction rights organization. Inquiries concerning reproduction outside the scope of the above should be sent to the Rights Department, Oxford University Press, at the address above.

You must not circulate this work in any other form
and you must impose this same condition on any acquirer.

Library of Congress Cataloging-in-Publication Data
Names: Hardacre, Helen, 1949–
Title: Shinto : a history / Helen Hardacre.
Description: New York : Oxford University Press, 2016. | Includes bibliographical references and index.
Identifiers: LCCN 2016021265 (print) | LCCN 2016024681 (ebook) | ISBN 9780190621711 (cloth : alk. paper) | ISBN 9780190621728 (updf) | ISBN 9780190621735 (epub)
Subjects: LCSH: Shinto—History.
Classification: LCC BL2218 .H37 2016 (print) | LCC BL2218 (ebook) | DDC 299.5/6109—dc23
LC record available at https://lccn.loc.gov/2016021265

7 9 8

Printed by Sheridan Books, Inc., United States of America

For Linda

CONTENTS

ACKNOWLEDGMENTS

While conducting research for this book, I accumulated numerous, heavy debts. I received extensive financial support and collegial encouragement from the Edwin O. Reischauer Institute of Japanese Studies, Harvard University. The Reischauer Institute enabled me to have the manuscript read and critiqued by specialists. I would like to thank Gary Ebersole for his comments on chapters regarding the ancient period, Fabio Rambelli for his critique of the chapters concerning the medieval age, Anne Walthall for her comments on the chapters about the early modern period, and Inoue Nobutaka for his critique of the chapters on the modern period. Joan Piggott, Susan Napier, and Alexander Zahlten also took the time to comment on portions of the text. Each of these colleagues made extensive comments that enabled me to redraft the material and avoid a variety of errors. Those that remain are my responsibility, it goes without saying.

The Reischauer Institute's provisions for faculty exchange with Kokugakuin University have brought Shinto specialists to Harvard annually, and the chance to learn from them has been tremendously helpful to me. I am especially indebted to the late Abe Yoshiya, who originally proposed the exchange, as well as Miyake Hitoshi, Suga Kōji, Hoshino Seiji, and Daitō Takaaki. Besides their many kindnesses to me, Professors Suga, Hoshino, and Daitō have continued to guide Harvard students since their time in residence.

From May 2003 through May 2004, I had the opportunity to conduct participant observation research at the Ōkunitama Shrine, Fuchū City, Tokyo Prefecture, supported by a John Simon Guggenheim Fellowship. This research period at the shrine came after earlier visits in 1998 and 1999, and was followed by several subsequent opportunities to observe the shrine's rituals and festivals. My long-term mentor, Professor Miyake Hitoshi of Keiō and Kokugakuin Universities, kindly arranged an introduction to the shrine's Head Priest Sawatari Masamori. My year at the Ōkunitama Shrine was crucially important in affording me many opportunities to interact with the full range of people who support community shrines, including priests, shrine stewards, community groups that manage the shrine's eight *mikoshi* and their huge drums, the decorated floats maintained by young men and children who dance and play festival music (*hayashi*) on the float stages, related shrines that have various roles in Ōkunitama Shrine's Annual Festival, numerous officials of Fuchū City who regard the shrine as the town's public face, and local businessmen who provide the core of the shrine's support. I am particularly grateful to Head Priest Sawatari and his colleague Matsumoto Masashi, now Negi, at the shrine, for their generosity of spirit, as well as the many hours they spent with me, and their permission for me to observe and document so many aspects of shrine life.

I am likewise indebted to Kurozumi Muneharu, Patriarch of Kurozumikyō. His permission for me to research Kurozumikyō early in my studies of Shinto gave me an unparalleled opportunity to understand the devotional aspects of Shinto and to understand how new religious movements derived from Shinto relate to other sectors of the tradition. Reverend Kurozumi, his mother, wife, and sons, and the Fukumitsu family of the Ōi Church of Kurozumikyō have my deepest gratitude for thirty-five years of an extraordinary friendship and for their many kindnesses to Harvard students.

Many librarians contributed to my research, beginning with Kuniko Yamada McVey and James Cheng of the Harvard-Yenching Library. I also received significant assistance from the librarians of Kanagawa, Tokyo, Yamagata, Hokkaidō, Shimane, Okayama, Fukui, Ishikawa, Toyama, Shiga, Kyoto, Osaka, Shizuoka, Yamaguchi, Fukuoka, Nagasaki, Saga, Oita, Mie, Aichi, Wakayama, Nara, and Hiroshima Prefectures. I would also like to acknowledge the kindness of the Shinto Museum at Kokugakuin University in allowing me to reprint items from its holdings, as well as Paul Swanson, Editor of *Japanese Journal of Religious Studies* and Bettina Gramlich-Oka, Editor of *Monumenta Nipponica,* for their kind permission to use images from these journals. In addition, I am most grateful to Sarah Thompson, Curator, Japanese Art, of the Museum of Fine Arts, Boston, who helped me identify the images from the museum's collections that appear in this book, and Rachel Saunders, Abby Aldrich Rockefeller Associate Curator of Asian Art, Harvard Art Museums, who helped me acquire several illustrations from Harvard's collections.

Opportunities to co-teach seminars with Harvard colleagues and historians of art, Melissa McCormick and Yukio Lippit, gave me many new insights into the importance of the arts and aesthetics in Shinto. Their work continues to inspire me.

I also wish to acknowledge my reliance on the work of Kuroda Toshio, Allan Grapard, and Mark Teeuwen. Each of them has set tremendously challenging standards for research on Shinto.

Over the years of working on this book, many Harvard students contributed to my research. Discussions with the students in a 2010 course on Japanese folk religious traditions were especially important, and I would like to thank Ben Cox, Christina Fanciullo, Christian Greer, Harry Huberty, Tim Lehmann, Ariane Mandell, and Naoyuki Ogi. Likewise, opportunities to work with students and auditors in a seminar on State Shinto that same year, including Professor Komamura Keigo (Keiō University), Nishitakatsuji Nobuhiro, and Adam Lyons. In a variety of discussions, I benefited from talking with Hwansoo Kim, now Professor at Duke University, Maeda Hiromi, and Eric Swanson.

Suemoto Yōko assisted in every aspect of basic research for this book, including my fieldwork at Ōkunitama Shrine. She helped me survey, photograph, interview, and acquire historical documents concerning dozens of shrines throughout Japan, to say nothing of providing me with a room in her house, and her confidence in the value of my project. She helped me maintain relations with a variety of shrines, other religious organizations, scholars, libraries, museums, and publishers. In addition, she helped me collect statistics regarding public funding of shrines before 1945 at twenty-five prefectural libraries and negotiated extensively to secure permissions to reprint illustrations. She encouraged me tirelessly and never gave up in the search to round up the last possible detail on every issue. Her accounting skills came in handy time and again, as did her perseverance, determination, and love of a good laugh.

My assistant Ruiko Connor spent hundreds of hours preparing the final version of the text and greatly assisted me in proofreading, preparing illustrations, the index, and many other aspects of assembling a book manuscript. With her customary kindness, attention to detail, and unfailing good humor, she helped me cross the finish line in good spirits.

I would also like to thank Cynthia Read and Marcela Maxfield of Oxford University Press, Diem Bloom, as well as two anonymous readers who provided invaluable comments and suggestions for improving this study. Cartographer Scott Walker of the Harvard Libraries and indexer David Prout also have my heartfelt thanks.

Friends and family gave me much encouragement. They know who they are, and how much their support has meant to me.

I first met Hayashi Makoto at Tokyo University's Department of Religious Studies forty years ago, when he was pursuing his doctoral studies, and I was a visiting graduate student. In 2005 he published a study of On'yōdō, *Kinsei On'yōdō no kenkyū* (Tokyo: Yoshikawa Kōbunkan). As this book goes to press, I recall his preface to that work, where he wrote of his hopeful feeling upon releasing his book, like sending off a small boat one has carved by hand onto the immense ocean that is the history of research. Like him, I look forward to following the voyage, curious to know how this work will ply the waves.

NOTES FOR THE READER

Romanization of Japanese terms follows the Hepburn system, and Japanese names are written with the surname first, followed by the personal name. This study capitalizes terms for major deities and other supernatural beings. Thus the terms *Kami* and *Buddha* are both capitalized.

Shinto

Introduction

From earliest times, the Japanese people have worshipped Kami. Kami may be the spirits of a particular place or natural forces like wind, rivers, and mountains. Kami such as these would neither be regarded anthropomorphically nor be seen as embodying moral principles. Some are intimidating, and not all of them are good to humans. Only under Buddhist influence did the Kami come to be conceptualized anthropomorphically. Figures of myth, such as the Sun Goddess Amaterasu Ōmikami, make up a distinctive group of Kami. Other Kami, such as Inari, associated with agriculture and commercial success, grew out of communal customs and have no textual basis. Some Kami originated as the deified spirits of human beings, such as the Heian period courtier Sugawara no Michizane (845–903), apotheosized as Tenjin. In the early modern era, feudal lords, peasant martyrs, and founders of new religious movements were deified as Kami. In the modern period, the spirits of the war dead were apotheosized, and the idea of the emperor's divinity was promoted, not only by Shinto but also through such influential institutions as the schools and the military.

Wherever new settlements are founded, a shrine (often very small and not necessarily a permanent structure) would be erected for the spirits of that place, as a way of honoring them and soliciting their benevolence and protection. The motivation to build a shrine wherever people live stems from the idea that Kami are everywhere, or could be anywhere, that there is no place in Japan that is not under their dominion. If people plan to disturb their domain by digging in the earth, planting crops, and erecting buildings, it is "only proper" to begin by asking permission from the Kami, with prayer, food, drink, gifts, and a place for them to receive these offerings, or in which to dwell ongoingly, that is, a shrine. Without a shrine, a place is "unfit for human habitation," because proper relations with the Kami have not been established.

Shinto encompasses doctrines, institutions, ritual, and communal life based on Kami worship, including representations of Kami in the arts. In particular, this study investigates the history of an ideal of Shinto that has structured its internal debates, social roles, and politics. In this construct, a divinely descended monarch rules through rituals for the Kami, including his ancestral deities and all the Kami of heaven and earth. A priestly order assists the sovereign by coordinating rituals for the Kami in shrines across the realm, so that they mirror the ruler's ceremonies. The priesthood unifies the people with imperial rule, uniting them through the power of solemn rituals and joyous festivals. Center and periphery join together in untroubled harmony through this theater of state. The Kami bless and protect the people, who attain their greatest self-realization through fulfilling their obligations to the collective.

While this ideal has operated with greatest clarity in the modern period, its constituent elements have much longer histories. They did not all appear at once or emerge as whole cloth. The basic building blocks include concepts of imperial rule associating it with ritual, a government unit devoted to coordinating ritual throughout the nation's shrines, a code of law mandating an annual calendar of Kami ritual, the claim that rituals for the Kami are public in character, and the assertion that this complex of ideas and institutions devoted to the Kami embodies Japan's "indigenous" tradition. This study addresses the story of the emergence and development of these elements and debate concerning them. It is structured around two themes, the idea of Shinto as belonging to the "public," and the idea that it represents the "indigenous." In addition, it examines a variety of materials that shed light on Shinto's devotional aspects in order to show how Shinto acquired personal significance and achieved motivational power.

Because Shinto has Kami at its center, it might be assumed that it is a religion, but this study resists starting out with that assumption. Instead, I question the character of the tradition at each stage of its history and ask how Shinto was regarded at the time. Even today, the question whether Shinto should be considered a religion remains controversial. Shinto is highly diverse and stratified in every historical era. It is never "just one thing." In some respects and some eras, the concept of religion is not particularly helpful in understanding it. Government figures administering the shrines from the late 1860s to the end of World War II argued that Shinto was not a religion, then or in previous epochs. They claimed that Shinto is so inextricable from Japanese identity that it must not be debated in the manner of "mere" theological wrangling. Unlike religion, they claimed, it is not something individuals are free to choose.

Writing the History of Shinto

Through most of the twentieth century and especially up to Japan's surrender in 1945, a variety of taboos surrounded academic research on Shinto. Before the surrender, the Japanese government administered Shinto shrine ceremonies, using them to unite the people behind the regime, specifying minutely what rites were to be performed, when, by what rank of priests, at what kinds of shrines, and with what kind of offerings. Some of the rites were structured to mirror the emperor's rituals for his ancestors, traced back to the age of the Kami, from whom he was believed to be descended. Academics who questioned the historical premise of Shinto ceremonies or hesitated to participate in them could—and did—lose their jobs. Even after the war's end, unspoken taboos remained, into the 1970s. These sensitivities made it difficult, for example, for scholars to research the obvious connections between ancient Japan and the Asian continent, since to do so would inevitably reveal the Japanese imperial cult's many borrowings from China and Korea, and hence undermine the notion of its uniqueness. Postwar Shinto scholars who are also Shinto priests tended to write from the perspective of engaged proponents, or as Shinto theologians. The result was a perspective portraying Shinto ahistorically, as something that has existed unchanged since the beginning of time, or as the essence of Japanese ethnicity.

Shinto, The Kami Way: An Introduction to Shrine Shinto, published in 1962 by Ono Sokyō, a celebrated professor of Kokugakuin University, exemplifies the point. He writes here as a Shinto partisan or theologian, addressing non-Japanese readers.[1]

> Shinto [is] the indigenous faith of the Japanese people.... From time immemorial the Japanese people have believed in and worshipped kami as an expression of their native racial faith which arose in the mystic days of remote antiquity. To be sure, foreign influences are evident. This kami-faith cannot be fully understood without some reference to them. Yet it is as indigenous as the people that brought the Japanese nation into existence and ushered in its new civilization.[2]

Ono structures this description around a dichotomy of the indigenous and the foreign, aligning Shinto with something native to Japan and the ethnic identity of the Japanese people, calling it their "racial faith." He insists on the remote origins of Shinto, beginning in "the mystic days of remote antiquity," as if it would be improper to pin it down to a particular time. Ono also asserts that the Japanese people are unified in their worship of the Kami, even though he was undoubtedly aware that many Japanese reject Shinto entirely, on the basis of their affiliations with Buddhism, Christianity, new religious movements, or disinterest in religion of any kind. Ono goes on to enlarge Shinto beyond the category of religion:

> Shinto is more than a religious faith. It is an amalgam of attitudes, ideas, and ways of doing things that through two millenniums and more have become an integral part of the *way* of the Japanese people. Thus, Shinto is both a personal faith in the kami and a communal way of life according to the mind of the kami, which emerged in the course of the centuries as

> various ethnic and cultural influences, both indigenous and foreign, were fused, and the country attained unity under the Imperial Family.[3]

Whatever is meant by the "*way* of the Japanese people," it is clear that it trumps religion, based on the assertion that Shinto is both an individual faith and a communal way of life that somehow accords with or perhaps responds to "the mind of the kami," which is not further defined. Above all, Shinto is said to have emerged with or through the unification of the people under the Yamato dynasty. This mystifying unity seems to be promoted here in order to insulate Shinto from closer historical investigation. Long after the restoration of academic freedom, the idea that Shinto's ancient ties to the imperial institution place the tradition off limits for historical scholarship has been a constraint.

Theological slants, idealization, and willful falsification of historical reality caused many secular historians to criticize Shinto scholarship for failing to distinguish between theological and historical standards. Perhaps we should understand works like *Shinto: The Kami Way*, written for non-Japanese readers on the eve of Japan's rehabilitation into the company of nations against which it had fought in World War II, as part of the aestheticization of Japanese culture typical of that time. Certainly, we can also see the English-language works of D. T. Suzuki on Buddhism as similarly idealizing, essentialist, and concerned to paper over Japanese Buddhism's recent history as enthusiastic cheerleader for empire and war.[4] By contrast, when Ono wrote in Japanese as an historian of Shinto for an audience of Japanese scholars, as in his encyclopedic work of 1963, *Basic Knowledge and Problems of Shinto*, romanticizing and idealizing were absent. His empirical scholarship is sober, balanced, and authoritative.[5]

Medieval historian Kuroda Toshio (1926–1993) unapologetically ripped through the obfuscation in the late 1970s, continuing into the 1980s, in studies that subjected Shinto to historical analysis with no holds barred. Among researchers working in Western languages, his essay, "Shinto in the History of Japanese Religion" was especially influential.[6] He demonstrated persuasively that conceptualizing Shinto as Japan's timeless, indigenous faith cannot be sustained. He saw a covert ethnic nationalism in ahistorical studies of Shinto. In place of romanticized images, he proposed instead that from ancient times Shinto had been cocooned within Japanese Buddhism, so much so that it is nearly impossible to discern its separate existence for most of Japanese history. Shinto, in Kuroda's judgment, comes into view only as one way of promoting theories that are fundamentally Buddhist.

So electrifying, refreshing, and liberating was Kuroda's stance that it instantly garnered widespread support. Shinto became a respectable subject for historical inquiry, while those in the Shinto universities were challenged to reorient their research in light of Kuroda's work.

Kuroda was at Osaka University in the 1980s, and it was there that I encountered him when he was my mentor during a study of the religious life of Japan's Korean minority in 1981. I asked him what reactions he was receiving to his insistence on treating Shinto like any other subject of historical inquiry. He told me that he had anticipated a far more hostile reception. It seemed strange to him that the ahistorical view of Shinto should be abandoned so easily, given the persistence with which it had been asserted. He was surprised, he said, having fully expected that many questions would be raised about his work. He found it odd that his perspective should easily find so much support and be so little criticized. That was in 1981; Kuroda died in 1993.

Kuroda influenced Shinto scholarship profoundly. Though there may be some lingering resistance, respected scholars of Shinto have left behind the ahistoricism and veiled nationalism of earlier generations. Since Kuroda, it has become conventional to hold that Shinto only becomes institutionally independent of Buddhism with the 1868 government order for a "separation of Buddhas from Kami," regularly referred to as the "Separation of Buddhism from Shinto." More recently, medieval historians identify the beginning of Shinto thought in the work of Yoshida Kanetomo (1435–1511). In convincing a generation of researchers so completely of Shinto's envelopment within Buddhism until such late dates in history, Kuroda may have succeeded too well. In place of the rhetoric of Shinto as "the indigenous religion of Japan," now it has become difficult to perceive meaningful continuity from the ancient period to the present, or to discuss Shinto's early history without "scare quotes." This study tries to address the issue of continuity in Shinto history from a new vantage point.

The Organization of This Study

One of the most enduring themes running through Shinto's history is the rhetoric of the "indigenous," identifying Shinto with that which is native (*koyū,* and other terms) to Japan. But how can "the indigenous" be discerned in Kami worship when it is so clear that so much has been absorbed from so many other places and traditions, including Buddhism, Daoism, and Confucianism? Debates about the indigenous and the foreign, and shifting definitions of both, constitute a core issue. This study does not champion the notion that Shinto *is* "indigenous." Instead, it tries to analyze the rhetoric of Shinto as Japan's "indigenous tradition" and its relation to the "foreign."

A second dichotomy that structures Shinto is that between the "public" (*kō, ōyake*) and the "private" (*shi, watakushi*). Like the indigenous and the foreign, "public" and "private" are wide-ranging terms that have been understood differently in different epochs. From the ancient period until the present, we find the assertion that shrines and their rituals are or should be "public" in character. Preeminently, this contention holds that shrine rites are necessary to the emperor and governance, but the assertion has assumed various forms and nuances at different times. I do not argue that Shinto is, in fact, rightfully "public" in any sense; instead, I seek to understand the variety of claims to that effect and how they have changed over time.

I do not mean to suggest that indigenous/foreign and public/private are the only lenses by which we can make sense of Shinto's history. In the course of this study, I have encountered many phenomena that do not fit the framework adopted here, and I have tried to make clear the limitations of my approach. I have struggled to find a way to discuss Shinto in the eras before the term comes into widespread use, but I am under no illusion that I have overcome all the challenges involved. I adopt this framework of rhetorical distinctions because I believe that it helps us to grasp the origins and formation of powerful ideas about Shinto, and to see continuity from ancient times to the present, but I make no grand claims for my approach, anticipating that future researchers will supersede it with more precise analytic tools.

Chapter 1, the first of four treating the ancient period, begins with the flow of knowledge into Japan from the Asian continent, its influence on ancient Kami worship and concepts of rulership. The idea of *jingi* arose to distinguish the sovereign's worship of Kami, regarded as "indigenous," from his court's Buddhist rites. An annual calendar of Kami rituals was embodied in a distinct law code called Jingiryō, while separate codes governed Buddhism. A branch of government called the Jingikan, literally the *jingi* ministry, or Ministry of Divinities, was formed to oversee Kami-related affairs at court and at provincial shrines. I argue that although the term *Shinto* scarcely appears, we can identify Shinto's institutional origins in the late seventh- and early eighth-century coordination of Kami worship, regarded as embodying indigenous tradition, by a government ministry following legal mandates.

Chapter 2 examines two eighth-century compilations of myth and history, *Kojiki* (712) and *Nihon shoki* (720), provincial gazetteers and alternative myth-histories composed by clans outside the ruling dynasty. Both *Kojiki* and *Nihon shoki* expounded the dynasty's divine origins and claimed that the heavenly deities had charged their scions to rule eternally. *Nihon shoki*, the more immediately influential of the two, described the dynasty as eminently strong, in a message meant to impress continental rulers with Yamato mastery of Chinese statecraft and its patronage of arts, culture, and learning. *Kojiki* is more concerned to assert the sovereign's support for the "indigenous" tradition of Kami worship, never mentioning Buddhism (the preeminent embodiment of the "foreign" at the time), though Buddhism had been a part of the realm for centuries. *Kojiki* upholds the indigenous by erasing the foreign. The monarch is positioned as the arbiter of different social groups' claims to public status, funding, and patronage. The official histories portray major political antagonism between the champions of the "indigenous" (clans particularly specializing in Kami worship) and the "foreign" (those promoting Buddhism's expanded presence). The main elements of the "indigenous" consist of the Kami, a divine monarch, and a publicly authorized corps of Kami ritualists. Variants of this scheme can be seen in the alternate narratives of the Inbe and Nakatomi clans, which stress their own divine descent and legacy of assisting the sovereign.

Chapter 3 examines the Jingikan's coordination of provincial shrines' rites with the sovereign's Kami worship in the capital, under the Ritsuryō system of government, from the seventh through the ninth centuries. The push-pull between center and periphery revealed the provinces' determination to maintain maximum autonomy in all things, including their distinctive deities, even as they coveted the benefits of connections with the court. While the Jingikan enjoyed only limited success, the court emerged as the preeminent patron of shrines. Annual Kami rituals at court, enthronement rites, and the Vicennial Renewal of the Ise Shrines took shape during this era. Jingikan practice clarified that Kami ritualists would not debate matters of theology but instead would rely on the theater of ritual to embody the indigenous tradition. Meanwhile, at a popular level, a variety of institutional combinations of temples and shrines appeared. Buddhist scholarship explained the relation between Kami and Buddhas in several different ways.

Chapter 4 examines Shinto from the tenth through the twelfth centuries. The Jingikan's ability to coordinate shrine rites was so weakened that by the tenth century, provincial shrine priests treated the ministry contemptuously, with impunity. While the older calendar of annual *jingi* ritual continued, courtiers routinely ignored ceremonies required by their official appointments. A new group of twenty-two shrines emerged as the shrunken focus for *jingi* ritual. At the same time that the Ritsuryō system was disintegrating, however, the pantheon was expanding to encompass a variety of new supernaturals, including "vengeful spirits" (*goryō*), and the scope of "public rites" (*kōsai*) widened to include them. The court's anxiety concerning wrathful spirits led it to sponsor many ad hoc performances of the Great Purification Rite (Ōharae), originally a biannual observance of the yearly *jingi* calendar, for such purposes as purifying the imperial residence or exorcising ghosts. The aristocracy rapidly followed suit, with the result that many "private" elements became part of Shinto. These new ritual performances also revealed changing conceptions of Kami, now upholding moral principles, rather than merely striking down those who transgressed taboos. As the Kyoto populace began celebrating ceremonies for vengeful spirits, they staged large festivals with music, dancing, and parades of gorgeous floats, establishing a prototype for urban shrine festivals. These trends intensified during the era of cloister government (eleventh and twelfth centuries), when we find the court and the aristocracy increasingly worshipping specific Kami on a personal basis, not merely in fulfillment of their official duties or familial obligations. Meanwhile, pairing the Kami with various Buddhist supernaturals in the *honji-suijaku* theory, and the claim that the two were ultimately identical, undermined the image of the Kami's unique embodiment of the indigenous, even as it projected the new idea of the Kami as agents of salvation.

Chapter 5 is the first of three chapters concerning the medieval period (thirteenth through sixteenth centuries); it examines the esotericization of Shinto. I use this expression to refer to the development of thought about the Kami within the philosophical framework of esoteric Buddhism. Medieval Shinto esoteric thought was propounded both by Buddhist thinkers and within shrines' sacerdotal lineages. Both camps created distinctive rituals of rich symbolism and complex correspondences between the Kami and Buddhist divinities, such as Kami initiations culminating in the initiate's "enthronement," making him symbolically equivalent to an emperor. The Jingikan, such as it was at the time, was powerless to resist this encroachment on its turf. Esotericism called for secret transmissions from master to disciple, valorizing a privatized understanding of knowledge over public exposition. Esotericism's claim that the Kami and Buddhas were ultimately one and undifferentiated vitiated any sense of the superiority of the indigenous.

Oaths sworn to the Kami show that the Kami were increasingly perceived as requiring people to conform to a moral code. The Great Purification Prayer was fully loosed from its original moorings in annual *jingi* rites. It came to be used in shortened form for all manner of personal, individual, and private devotional purposes. Even as it continued to be seen as embodying something quintessentially "Shinto," it acquired an ecumenical character as it was appropriated by all manner of practitioners. Newly formed lineages of Shugendō, the cult of sacred mountains, practiced myriad ceremonies for mountain deities, who came to be roughly classed with the Kami, contributing to the ongoing diversification of the pantheon. In the late thirteenth century, the Mongol invasions threatened to destroy Japan entirely, but typhoons called "Kamikaze" (divine winds) diverted them. The popular sense that the Kami had delivered Japan greatly strengthened ideas of Japan as a divine land (*shinkoku*). Tens of thousands flooded the Ise Shrines in 1287 to give thanks to the Kami for Japan's deliverance.

Chapter 6 examines Shinto art, literature, dance-drama, and aspects of architecture to uncover medieval Shinto's devotional patterns. New architectural spaces were created for encountering "foreign," violent, or malevolent supernaturals who had not appeared in *Kojiki* or *Nihon shoki*, and who were outside the *honji-suijaku* framework. Through these encounters, threatening forces could be "domesticated," transformed into beneficent Kami, and practitioners could absorb some of their power. New interpretations of *Nihon shoki* myth produced many popular tales in several genres. Tale literature, shrine mandalas, and the monumental work of twenty illustrated scrolls called "Kasuga Gongen Genki-e" portrayed the Kami as compassionately leading humanity to salvation, blessing, protecting, and ultimately guiding them to the Pure Land. Shrines were pictured as Pure Lands on earth, and the idea of Kami and Buddhas as ultimately the same was given pictorial form. Humanity and the Kami are bound together in reciprocity. Not only do the Kami bless their human devotees, but also, when humanity builds shrines to reverence the Kami, the Kami are glorified and revivified, so that a circle of mutual benefit is formed. The *shinkoku* idea assumed a personal guise in this connection. All those living in the divine land were believed descended from the Kami, and to live in the divine land was to lack for nothing that might be required to attain salvation. Moreover, those who trust completely in the Kami could eventually become Kami themselves.

Chapter 7 treats the late medieval period (end of the fifteenth century through the sixteenth century), emphasizing the work of Yoshida Kanetomo, a courtier serving in the Jingikan. Kanetomo initiated revolutionary changes, producing the first structured exposition of Shinto, creating rituals for initiation into his secret teachings, and laying the groundwork for a system coordinating shrines nationwide. Kanetomo's use of the term *Shinto* for his philosophical system was virtually the first use of the word in that way. After the Jingikan burned down in the Ōnin War (1467–1477), Kanetomo appropriated its functions for an eccentric shrine of his own design, meant to be the symbolic center for all Kami worship, even securing imperial recognition for it as a substitute Jingikan. In Kanetomo's philosophical system, Shinto was essential to imperial rule. He reversed the *honji-suijaku* theory to present the Kami as the primal deities, with Buddhist figures as their traces. He asserted that the Kami and humanity are united through the heart-mind. Kanetomo's descendants perpetuated his doctrinal and ritual systems, providing instruction and initiations for priests, licensing them to recruit others, and thereby creating regional networks of shrines and priests linked through Yoshida affiliation.

Chapter 8 is the first of four chapters dealing with the early modern period (seventeenth through mid-nineteenth centuries). It investigates Confucianism's influence on Shinto in the seventeenth century, when Confucianism experienced a revival. The early modern term for legally constituted public authority, *kōgi*, encompassed the imperial court, shogunal government, and provincial rulers called *daimyō*. In fact, however, the shogunate completely overshadowed the monarchy. The shogunate provided the court's material support, revived its ceremonial life, and underwrote the Vicennial Renewals of the Ise Shrines. But while the shogunate was the major power, it lacked a correspondingly magnificent legitimation. Originally intended as a temporary military force, from the mid-seventeenth century there were few uprisings for it to quell, and as a result, erstwhile warriors were transformed into bureaucrats.

Hayashi Razan (1583–1657), Yoshikawa Koretaru (1616–1694), and Yamazaki Ansai (1616–1657) launched new Shinto theories, asserting the oneness of Shinto and Confucianism, and offering legitimating rationales to the shogunate. They stressed such ideas as the unity of Kami and Principle (a central term in Confucianism), the virtue of loyalty, and the symbol of the Heavenly Jeweled Spear as the emblem of benevolent shogunal rule. The spear was the instrument of creation in myth, and because it appeared before the Sun Goddess or the imperial regalia were created, temporal priority subtly validated shogunal rule as having originated before imperial rule. Razan, Koretaru, and Ansai consistently asserted that Shinto is an essential element of governance and a precious embodiment of indigenous tradition. They recommended purifications as a way to regain humanity's primordial union with Kami, primarily conceived of not as a vast pantheon, but focusing on a single, ultimate deity. Ansai taught his theories openly, and while Razan and Koretaru perpetuated esoteric transmission, Koretaru also breached that custom, teaching the Yoshida lineage's secret doctrines to outsiders. The Yoshida house secured the legal authority to spread their licensing system, though it caused much resentment in some quarters and inflamed critics to expose the deficiencies of Yoshida sacred texts.

To understand the devotional character of early modern Kami worship, Chapter 9 examines veneration of the Kami Inari and pilgrimage to the Ise Shrines. Both were concerned with the pursuit of happiness, elevating the value of ordinary people and validating their desire for well-being and abundance. Inari, who is not mentioned in ancient myth, began as a food god or Kami of rice, with foxes for messengers. By the early modern period, either the Kami Inari or its messengers could be referred to by the name "Inari." Shrines for Inari proliferated, so that by the 1830s there were over one hundred of them in Edo. Short-lived fads for particular Inari shrines sprang up repeatedly. Urban commercialism colored Inari worship pervasively. A variety of figures like *miko* and "Shintoists" (*Shintōsha*) promoted Inari fads, spread the tales that sparked them, and then found ways to make a living from the devotees.

Pilgrim masters (*onshi* or *oshi*) from the Ise Shrines developed village networks covering most of the country, compiling and spreading miracle tales about the Ise Kami to stimulate pilgrimage. Ise mandalas and travel guides instructed pilgrims how to travel to Ise and worship there. Village-based pilgrimage was a regular occurrence, but in addition, mass pilgrimage occurred many times. Often, pilgrims threw off all the restraints of ordinary life, dancing ecstatically in a carnival atmosphere, but mass pilgrimage seemed ominous to its observers. Pilgrims frequently traveled without money, became separated from their companions, or fell victim to sickness or thieves. Many could not explain why they were walking to Ise, only that they felt an overwhelming compulsion to go. No one spoke of these popular observances as "Shinto"; instead, they were regarded as expressions of "faith" (*shinkō*). Nevertheless, the term "Shintoist" began to be used as a term of self-reference, a significant change in popular usage.

Chapter 10 addresses the appearance within Shinto of three religious movements, each based on a regimen of self-cultivation, seeking salvation through uniting oneself with Amaterasu. The three groups, Kurozumikyō, Misogikyō, and Uden Shinto, arose in the early to mid-nineteenth century. These movements built on the foundation laid by Shinto popularizers, active from the sixteenth century, who spread recitation of the Great Purification Prayer. Popularizers encouraged ordinary people outside the shrine priesthood to recite this prayer daily. If they or a loved one were ill, it should be recited many times—as often as possible. The ancient prayer that began as a pillar of annual *jingi* ritual monopolized by priests was transformed into a means of self-cultivation for all, bringing healing and revealing Amaterasu's boundless power. The popular dissemination of Shinto prayers and communal worship before scrolls of The Oracle of the Three Shrines, as well as Ise pilgrimage and Inari faith, were part of a matrix of popular Kami worship, transformed by the founders of new religious movements into functional monotheisms devoted to Amaterasu. Revelation, preaching, healing, and frequent communal meetings for chanting and sermons characterized these groups. Kurozumikyō was founded in the Okayama domain in Western Japan, a prosperous area with a tradition of commoner education. The founder, Kurozumi Munetada, was a samurai shrine priest before his revelations, and his followers included samurai as well as farmers. Misogikyō and Uden Shinto were established in Edo, but both founders' concerns for the urban poor were taken as veiled criticism of the shogunate, leading to their suppression. By contrast, village headmen found Kurozumi's teachings useful in maintaining the social order. The three groups' early histories diverged significantly, in spite of important similarities among their teachings and practices.

Chapter 11 examines nativist thought, Kokugaku, in relation to Shinto. Calling for wholesale rejection of foreign influence in thought, culture, and politics, nativist scholars idealized the mythical Age of the Gods. Motoori Norinaga, Hirata Atsutane, and their students tried to recover a time before Japanese life had been corrupted by foreign influence, and openly denounced what they saw as the excessive rationalism of Confucianism and Buddhism. Kokugaku scholars elevated emotion above analytic thought as a positive, defining quality of human life. In his scholarship on the *Kojiki*, Norinaga declared that the text originally had been spoken by the emperor and was a true account of actual events. Read correctly, he believed, *Kojiki* would reveal a golden age when the Kami, the emperor, and his people were united in complete harmony. Atsutane, who also upheld this ideal, composed prayers that specified more minutely how people should worship the Kami and the emperor. He conceived of the ancestors as Kami, though the prevalent understanding at the time called for ancestors to be memorialized in Buddhist style, starting with Buddhist funerals. While Atsutane was critical of both the Yoshida and Shirakawa lineages, he accepted employment as a Yoshida teacher, subsequently using its shrine networks to promote his own teachings. He and Norinaga both attracted shrine priests as students. Late Edo period Kokugaku texts portray the cosmos as having been created by Kami, who entrust the imperial line with rule over the human world. Humanity will find its ultimate fulfillment in self-sufficient villages, where all residents farm the land, have many children, and assist fellow villagers.

At the end of the period, Japan was threatened by Western powers that successfully pressured the shogunate to sign humiliating trade treaties. With that, Kokugaku's definition of the foreign switched from China to the West, and nativism became an anticolonialist discourse seeking to replace the shogunate with direct imperial rule. Emperor Kōmei frequently appealed for divine assistance in expelling the foreigners, and in the process re-established palace ties to the Ise Shrines, as well as instituting novel ceremonies. Nativists called for restoration of the Jingikan as a central unit of government. Those in service to the monarch should utterly devote themselves to their official appointments, eliminating all trace of the private, so that Japan could be delivered from the foreign threat and recreate the way of life it had had in the Age of the Gods.

Chapter 12 is the first of five chapters examining modern Shinto. The term *State Shinto* has often been used, including by myself, to describe the modern Japanese government's takeover of shrine affairs that began in the Meiji period, but a variety of problems have been raised regarding the term. An alternative, "state management," has been proposed, and in this chapter I experiment with it, to question its usefulness and limitations as an alternative to State Shinto. This chapter examines the period from the Meiji Restoration of 1868 to the creation in 1900 of a branch of government solely dedicated to shrine administration. In 1868, Shinto finally achieved independence from Buddhism through a government-mandated separation of shrines from temples, and the Jingikan was briefly reinstated. It was downgraded and then abolished, however, as provisions were made for the emperor to begin performing rites based on ancient *jingi* in the new palace in the capital Tokyo.

The government initiated a campaign to unite the nation behind a state-authored creed, to be promulgated by Buddhist and Shinto priests, among others. Shinto-derived associations like Kurozumikyō, Misogikyō, and a variety of newly founded religious movements were involved in the campaign, but cordoned off from the shrines in a separate administrative category. Far from uniting the populace, however, the campaign was a spectacular failure.

A new formula holding that shrines represent "the nation's rites and creed" (*kokka no sōshi*) explained that shrines are not religious. A powerful ideal of Shinto providing state ritual through which the populace would unite to glorify the nation and its sovereign emerged. Shrines were ranked according to a unitary hierarchy with the Ise Shrines at the apex, though they had never before all been put beneath a single umbrella. Shrines devoted to Kami other than those connected to the throne found their deities replaced by government decree. Temples' and shrines' land was commandeered, and shrines had to scramble for popular support. Measures for supporting the shrines from public funds placed Shinto explicitly and unmistakably in the public realm, even though the actual amounts were mostly tokens of recognition, insufficient to maintain shrines or provide the priests a livelihood.

Many new shrines were built with popular support, some for imperial loyalists from history, the Yasukuni Shrine for the war dead of the Restoration, and numerous shrines in Hokkaidō, which was being settled on a large scale by Japanese pioneers from the main islands. The post-Restoration creation of these shrines initiated new relations among shrines, government, and the people, depending heavily on local fundraising, burnishing the image of local boosters, and producing significant business opportunities. These new relationships, as well as government administration of shrines, went considerably beyond the parameters of "state management," involving the people much more, and extending further into the realm of ideology than that bland phrase suggests.

Chapter 13 treats Shinto from the early twentieth century until the end of World War II, the heyday of the Japanese empire, when shrines were built in overseas colonies to assimilate colonial subjects, and Shinto observances were often given a compulsory character. I examine ideological campaigns mediated by shrines and explain how the term "State Shinto" can be employed to understand them. The Shrine Bureau within the Home Ministry oversaw shrine affairs until the Shrine Institute (Jingiin) superseded it in 1940. While the state shaped Shinto in numerous ways in this period, however, Shinto scholars freely disputed the government position that Shinto is not a religion. Tanaka Yoshitō and Katō Genchi articulated a distinctive concept of Kami and of Shinto as a religion, which embodies the essence of Japan's "national polity" (*kokutai*) and epitomizes Japan's indigenous tradition. Their ideas aimed, in part, to expand the foregoing understanding of Shinto to include the colonies, albeit in draconian ways. Mammoth new shrines were built during this era, both in the inner territories and the colonies. Those in the inner territories were created through partnerships between the Shrine Bureau and local-level promoters, who often represented business interests. Successful high-ranking shrines came to be managed more like corporations, while the priests of smaller low-ranking shrines pleaded for resources to fulfill the national project of uniting the people through shrine worship.

Local government campaigns succeeded in normalizing daily worship at home altars (*kamidana*). School administrators, who often held office in shrine associations, enforced compliance with school ceremonies, required pupils to participate in visits to local shrines where they performed volunteer labor, and from the 1930s orchestrated school trips to the Ise Shrines. School ceremonial became a focus for stigmatizing—sometimes violently—anyone who dissented from the required observances, especially Christians. The war dead were memorialized at the Yasukuni Shrine and its provincial outposts, divinized as Kami whom the emperor himself honored personally. Survivors traveled to Yasukuni to mourn and honor the fallen. The combination of these and other compulsory or semi-compulsory ceremonies resulted in the permeation of daily life with Shinto ritual. Shrines became potent symbols of home, duty, ethnic identity, the nation, and self-sacrifice.

Public funding of shrines doubled between 1931 and 1945, though Japan was continually at war. Shrine construction projects reached a peak in 1940, when Japan celebrated the 2600th anniversary of its legendary founding by Emperor Jinmu. Massive new shrine construction projects continued into the last year of the war, even when food and building materials were being rationed. These huge investments show that the hope of uniting the empire through common Shinto worship had become an essential element of imperial rule.

Chapter 14 examines Shinto from 1945 to 1989. The Allied Occupation of Japan ended government administration of shrines and had them classified as religious corporations (*shūkyō hōjin*). This policy squelched Shinto's claim to any role in governance and abruptly aligned it with religion. The Shinto Directive of December 1945 decreed a total separation of religion from state, ending all public funding and formal connections with government at any level. In its ignorance of similar enthusiasm for empire and war in virtually all sectors of Japanese religions, the Occupation singled out Shinto as responsible for the militarism and ultranationalism that it credited for leading Japan to war. Shinto figures were embittered when Occupation censorship (an ironic policy for an ostensibly democratizing force) prevented them from responding to this humiliating charge.

A national organization was formed, the Association of Shinto Shrines, to coordinate the shrines and to negotiate with the Occupation. It successfully persuaded the Occupation to allow most shrines to keep the land they had customarily held. This effective lobbying convinced the great majority of shrines to join the association. After censorship ended in 1952, the association entered the public sphere in a new way, using its newspaper to critique the Occupation as a vengeful conqueror bent on destroying "the Japanese spirit." The newspaper bitterly deplored the emperor's forced renunciation of divinity, Shinto's severance from public status under the postwar constitution (which the association believed had been wrongfully imposed on the Japanese people), the Tokyo War Crimes Trials, the loss of Yasukuni Shrine's status as the national war memorial, and much more.

The association became involved in politics, successfully lobbying for the creation of a national holiday renaming the pre-surrender ceremony commemorating the first emperor Jinmu's coronation as National Foundation Day. In the process, the association became a prominent patron of the Liberal Democratic Party's most right-leaning factions, forming a League of Shinto Politicians. The association campaigned long and hard for a bill returning Yasukuni Shrine to public status, only to find that politicians could not be trusted. Thereafter, the association modified its strategies, continuing to act as a political lobby for conservative causes. Among them are campaigns to promote respect for the monarchy, to ensure that school textbooks present a positive view of the imperial period, and for treatment of the war dead as national heroes, countering what it calls the "Tokyo War Crimes Trials view of history." It encourages prime ministers and their cabinets to patronize the Yasukuni Shrine, bemoans the cessation of imperial visits to Yasukuni, and criticizes Japan's former colonies for their objections to politicians' patronage of Yasukuni. The association likewise denounces government statements apologizing to other Asian nations for Japan's treatment of them during colonial rule. It continues to mourn Shinto's loss of public status and to call for legislative changes to elevate popular regard for Japan's "indigenous tradition." The politicization of Shinto through its national association set it on a new course as a rightist interest group.

Chapter 15 investigates postwar shrine festivals, engaging contemporary Shinto's affective, aesthetic, and social dimensions. Since 1945, shrines must negotiate with local government for use of public space and compete with civic pageants for a community's attention. No longer universally recognized as having preeminent claim to community resources, shrine festivals can suffer if they do not exert popular appeal. In order to prosper, shrines must respond to their communities' changing concerns and demographics. Civic pageants unconnected to temples and shrines are generally more adroit at including a wide range of participants, including women. By contrast, historic taboos have generally made it much harder for women to assume visible roles in shrine festivals, other than preparing food or costumes.

In my study of the Darkness Festival of the Ōkunitama Shrine (Fuchū City, Tokyo Prefecture), I found that the festival's dance, drama, music, and contests of strength have been added rather recently, to attract newcomers to the town, as urban sprawl turned Fuchū into a suburb of Tokyo. The ritual rationale of the Darkness Festival is that the Kami are reborn through returning to the spot where they originally manifested, paraded in gorgeous palanquins borne by young men inspired with the spirit of the Kami, who whirl the palanquins in a colorful procession. The motif of a return to primeval chaos is unmistakable. However, postwar Japanese society is focused on work and school, and has only limited patience for disturbance to the social order, especially on a school night. After a death at the festival in 1969, the local Parent Teacher Association (PTA) put its collective foot down and forced the festival to adopt a daytime schedule, playing havoc with the underlying religious rationale.

Since 1999, however, a new Head Priest rose to prominence, even becoming head of the PTA. He overcame the community's anxiety and reinstated the nighttime format, emphasizing ceremonies that symbolically promote an image of the shrine's "public" nature. In his view, shadow, mystery, and darkness, combined with beautiful rituals and elaborate offerings, are essential to the Kami's annual rebirth and the community's regeneration. City officials and civic groups are satisfied with the change, and the city now advertises the Darkness Festival as its official "face," a new kind of public presence.

Chapter 16 examines Shinto since the 1989 death of Hirohito. His successor, Emperor Akihito, has set a new tone in the palace, one which gives no encouragement to the Association of Shinto Shrines's backward-looking perspective, though the association continues to exert significant political influence. Following the 1995 sarin gas attack on the Tokyo subway system by a religious group called Aum Shinrikyō, Japanese society severely criticized religion, across the board. Moves to tax religious corporations arose, intimidating all of them. Society demanded that religious organizations explain what they contribute to the public good (*kōeki*). In response, a new line of Shinto scholarship arose, asserting that Shinto's greatest contribution lies in shrine rituals and festivals, which enhance communal solidarity. This argument is a contemporary expression of the venerable claim that communities are unified through shared worship of the Kami.

After the triple disaster of March 11, 2011, when an earthquake, tidal wave, and nuclear meltdown devastated northeastern Japan, religions of all kinds, including Shinto, began sustained relief campaigns in the region. It seems now that the combination of scholarship and recovery projects has restored some measure of trust in religions' contributions to the public good. We find Shinto leaders now calling on the priesthood to embrace the idea of Shinto as a religion, to renounce nostalgic longing for prewar mores, and recognize that Shinto priests live in a pluralistic society in which they cannot hope to monopolize the worldview.

If we judge Shinto's strength based only on statistical data concerning numbers of adherents and expressions of belief, we find the picture of decline common to all branches of religion in Japan. It is apparent that many smaller shrines in depopulating areas face an uncertain future. We also find, however, that shrines attract huge numbers of people each New Year's, and that the 2013 Vicennial Renewal of the Ise Shrines drew more than fourteen million visitors.

Surveys reveal that shrine priests perceive a growing gap between shrines' economic situations and the professional association's rigid traditionalism. Many have decided to strike out in new directions in order to guarantee the economic viability of their shrines and to appeal more persuasively to a changing clientele. The rising number of women priests contributes to diversifying relations between shrines and their community supporters. While recent legal verdicts suggest ongoing judicial ambivalence about connections between shrines and local government, increasing scope has opened for Shinto ceremonies in public settings. Popular culture shows a fascination with images drawn from Shinto, seen in youth culture, best-selling novels, manga, live action film, and anime. All this suggests that while it faces significant challenges, Shinto today is a vital force in Japanese society and culture.

1

Shinto in the Ancient Period

Introduction

By the end of the Yayoi period (400 BCE–300 CE), the Japanese archipelago was populated by a variety of ethnic groups originating in the East Asian continent and island Southeast Asia. Small "states" (C: *guo*; J: *kuni*) emerged and entered into trading and tributary relations with China and the three Korean kingdoms of Silla, Paekche, and Koguryŏ. The Korean kingdoms also maintained relations with China.

In Japan, a ruler styling himself "Great King" (*daiō*) emerged as a hegemon and began to extend his influence in a system of hierarchical relations called "Yamato kingship" (*Yamato ōken*). In the course of its diplomatic relations and military alliances with other East Asian states, the Yamato adopted Chinese models of governance. These models were introduced alongside older patterns in which rulers' authority was expressed through agricultural rites and the worship of ancestral deities. In part because all the major political entities in East Asia had accepted Buddhist rites, the Japanese did likewise in the sixth century. This decision proved highly controversial with groups that had developed specialized roles in performing Kami worship. A coup resulted in the defeat of the opponents of Buddhism and the intensification of broad Chinese influence in culture, society, and politics. Significant influence from Confucianism, Buddhism, and Chinese lore regarding astrology, a cult of immortality, and yin and yang (which in later ages would be called Daoism) flowed into the archipelago and colored concepts of rulership and the conduct of state ritual. Meanwhile, Japanese sovereigns struggled to subdue tribal peoples, who had settled earlier in the islands. Wars against these indigenes continued into the eighth century and after.[1]

In the mid-seventh century, a legal code called Ritsuryō was adopted to establish a Chinese-style centralized government. The Council of Divinities (Jingikan) was established as part of the new system. The Jingikan was charged with conducting rites of state and coordinating the provinces' ritual practices with those in the capital and the palace, based on a code of Kami Law (*Jingiryō*). An annual calendar of state ritual was created, based on an ideal of uniting the realm through Kami worship, with the sovereign at its head, aligning his earthly rule with that of his divine ancestors in heaven. The instantiation of this ideal within government gave Kami affairs an eminently public character, and its differentiation from a parallel apparatus to administer Buddhist matters cast the Council of Divinities as the keeper of the "indigenous" tradition.

I will argue that the Ritsuryō system represents the institutional origin of Shinto, based on the concept of *jingi*, the instantiation through Kami Law (*Jingiryō*) of an annual calendar of state ritual, and the establishment of the Council of Divinities (Jingikan) to administer the rites. This position is consonant with recent studies by Inoue Nobutaka, Mitsuhashi Tadashi, Itō Satoshi, Endō Jun, and Mori Mizue[2] while departing to some extent from the views of Kuroda Toshio, Inoue Hiroshi, Mark Teeuwen, Fabio Rambelli, and others. There are strong counterarguments to be considered, however, based on the almost complete absence of the term *Shinto* from the vernacular language and from documents of the ancient period. For Teeuwen and Rambelli, the absence of the term is decisive, whereas for me, structured institutions aiming to coordinate Kami affairs from the center weigh more heavily.

This study's thesis arguing for the coalescence of Shinto's institutional basis by the eighth century will be laid out in this and the following two chapters. Chapter 1 traces the development of Kami worship from prehistory through the early eighth century, emphasizing the gradual emergence of the *ideal* of a realm united in coordinated rites for the Kami. Chapter 2 examines the eighth-century texts *Kojiki* and *Nihon shoki*, in which enduring charters of ritual and rulership are set out in mythic form. Chapter 3 returns to the Jingikan's coordination of rites at provincial shrines across the realm to examine how the ideal of uniting the realm through the worship of the Kami was realized.

The Yayoi Period (400 BCE–300 CE)

The Yayoi period is the first to leave artifacts that can reasonably be linked to the later development of Shinto. Named for the area of Tokyo where the pottery of this age was first discovered, Yayoi society practiced rice agriculture and metalworking in bronze and iron. Ritual utilized bronze bells (*dōtaku*) and mirrors, as well as comma-shaped, pierced jasper and jade jewels called *magatama*. Burial customs differed regionally. Especially in southwestern Honshū and Kyūshū, there was much contact with China and Korea.[3]

Archaeological evidence suggests that religious life developed in connection with rice cultivation. One type of Yayoi ritual site centers on large rocks or boulders, some with food containers, wooden fetishes, and such precious objects as jewels.

Many such sites were located near springs, waterfalls, and riverbanks or hills and mountains, suggesting a focus on water and its importance to agriculture. It is believed that boundaries were created around ritual sites, and that spirits called Kami were invited to descend into some object, such as a tree, pillar, animal, waterfall, island, or mountain. Once the Kami had entered a tangible object (generically called *yorishiro*), ritual was performed for them, relating to the fertility of crops. The discovery of large numbers of *dōtaku* at ritual sites, along with bronze weapons and polished metal mirrors, suggests that these objects had a central role in ritual. It may be that their shiny surfaces or the sounds made by striking them were believed to be capable of calling the Kami to the site.[4]

The Kami were strongly identified with natural forces governing the crops. Kami were not originally imagined as having anthropomorphic form or as dwelling permanently in a single place. Instead, they were believed to respond to human invitations to manifest. Otherwise, they remained formless and invisible. The Kami's association with natural forces gave them an unpredictable quality. Just as nature can produce floods, drought, and epidemic disease, the Kami were not necessarily always beneficent to humanity. They could make erratic appearances, conceptualized as anger or wrath. For this reason, worship mainly took the form of beseeching and placating them, or seeking to avoid their anger. It was only much later that they came to be seen as having compassion for humanity.[5]

Hierarchically structured villages led by chiefs evolved. The chief performed ritual for the spirits of rice either at his dwelling or at the rice storehouse, where rice and the seeds for the next year's crop were stored, ensuring the continuity of the seasons and the success of agriculture. Chiefs and others associated with ritual were considered to be closely connected with the Kami or Kami-like themselves. Great caches of swords and other weapons too large to have actually been used functionally are found at some sites, such as Kōjindani in the Izumo area.[6] These finds suggest that symbols of political or military rule, such as swords, merged with religious symbols of power like jewels and mirrors in a concept of leadership that fused religious and secular elements.

By around 200 BCE Japanese rulers were seeking investiture (*sakuhō*) from Chinese monarchs to elevate their status and enable them to enter into international trade along the sea routes linking China, Korea, and Japan, as did Korean rulers (see Map 1.1). Japanese chieftains traded along the Inland Sea from the Asian continent to Kyūshū and eastward into Honshū. Trade in iron ingots was critical to Japanese society at this time, making possible the manufacture of metal weapons and tools that transformed warfare and agriculture. Iron axes and daggers were imported to Japan, and some Kyūshū sites have remains of small-scale ironworking, but Japan was almost entirely dependent on imported sources of iron ore.[7]

The Han dynasty fell in the third century, destabilizing the Korean Peninsula and apparently throwing the Yayoi chiefdoms into turmoil as well. Remains from this period show signs of warfare, with new defensive fortifications, including

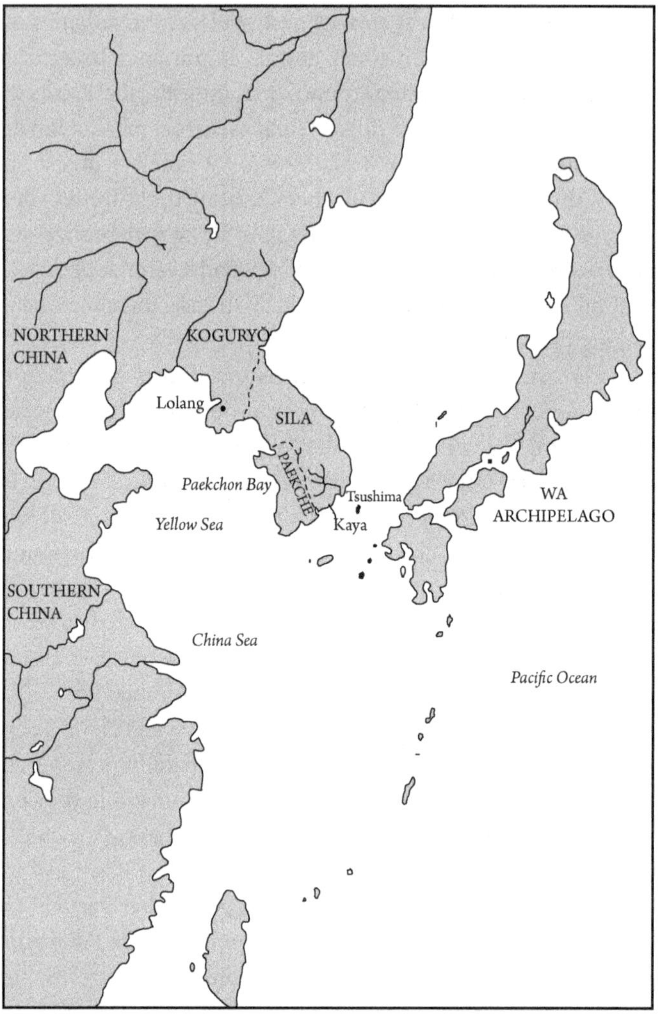

Map 1.1 The East China Sea Interaction Area. Source: Joan R. Piggott, *The Emergence of Japanese Kingship* (Stanford, CA: Stanford University Press, 1997), 2.

watchtowers and moats. Commoner burials include skeletons shot through by arrows or with the skull detached, suggesting violent death in battle.

The late third-century Chinese work *Records of Wei* (*Weizhi*, 297) is one of our earliest written records about Japan, which the Chinese called "Wa."

> The country formerly had a man as ruler. For some seventy or eighty years after that there were disturbances and warfare. Thereupon the people agreed upon a woman for their ruler. Her name was Pimiko. She occupied herself with magic and sorcery, bewitching the people. Though mature in age, she remained unmarried. She had a younger brother who assisted

> her in ruling the country. After she became the ruler, there were few who saw her. She had one thousand women as attendants, but only one man. He served her food and drink and acted as a medium of communication. She resided in a palace surrounded by towers and stockades, with armed guards in a state of constant vigilance.[8]

This text's statement that Pimiko, or Himiko, was chosen after a period of warfare, and that previously a man had been chieftain, broadly accords with instability that followed the fall of the Han. The text states further that soon after being made queen, Himiko sent a mission with gifts to the Chinese Wei emperor, who responded by bestowing on her the title "Queen of Wa." He also sent her one hundred polished bronze mirrors, writing that she should "exhibit them to your countrymen in order to demonstrate that our country thinks so much of you as to bestow exquisite gifts upon you." This imprimatur sealed Himiko's rule as both approved by her own people and confirmed by the ruler of the most advanced civilization.[9]

Himiko ruled over a land in Wa called Yamatai, composed of twenty-two chiefdoms. Although the exact location of Himiko's chiefdom has not yet been conclusively identified, if she was attended by a retinue of one thousand female servants, she must have resided in a large ceremonial center and ruled over an impressive territory. It would appear that Himiko's rule was largely peaceful, and that the constituent *kuni* formed an exchange network based on trading in iron and solidified by the distribution of ceremonial goods like the mirrors received from China.

The Kyūshū archaeological site called Yoshinogari, active from the first century BCE to the fourth century CE, gives us some idea of the ceremonial centers in Himiko's age. Yoshinogari was the pinnacle of a chiefdom that engaged in diplomacy, trade, metallurgy, and weaving. Its buildings were surrounded by a double moat and further protected by watchtowers. Yoshinogari monopolized the *kuni*'s metallurgy, and the subordinate hamlets did not have metalworking of their own. Yoshinogari's grain storehouses were significantly larger than those in the surrounding area, enabling the ruler to store the rice collected as tribute from the smaller settlements. Burials differed in size and grave goods, according to the social hierarchy, and commoner and elite burial grounds were separated from each other. The largest grave, reserved for the leader, was a great, mounded tomb. The tomb contained precious jewels, bronze daggers resembling those found in Korea, and glass beads imported from south China.[10]

The *Records of Wei* state that Himiko practiced a "spirit way" (*kidō*), and although we have too little evidence to determine exactly what that meant, we can turn for suggestive hints to comparative sources regarding Korean chiefdoms. A section of *Records of Wei* regarding Korea in the same period portrays chieftains holding communal rites for planting and harvesting crops and worshipping in ritual sites, where they erected pillars on which they hung bells and drums to commune with spirits. They performed rites for bygone heroes, the sun, moon, stars, and the directions. Divination using animal bones and tortoise shells was practiced, as was purification with water. Women often delivered oracles in divination rites. Other rites for healing, lifting, or imposing curses and taboos or to expel evil spirits also existed. From these records, we know that rulers were believed to control natural forces based on an ability to know the will of deities. Ancient rule was closely connected with shamanism, a religious practice in which a person in a state of spirit possession becomes a mouthpiece for a deity and communicates the spirit's will to a community of people. The *Records of Wei* states that after she became Queen, Himiko remained concealed from the people and occupied with ritual. Her invisibility to the people no doubt contributed to the aura of the supernatural that she cultivated. Himiko probably practiced some method of communicating with spirits. The man's role was to interpret Himiko's utterances and communicate the will of the Kami to the people.[11]

Religious beliefs evolved within a shared sphere of trade, diplomacy, and culture that encompassed parts of China, Korea, and the Japanese islands. In investiture, a Chinese sovereign confirmed lesser rulers by permitting trade relations and exchanging gifts, while the lesser rulers accepted the Chinese figure's dominant status. Distribution of gift mirrors was a means of incorporating regional chieftains. Although they cannot be definitively linked to Himiko, some 329 mirrors of a similar type have been found from the far West to Eastern Japan. These mirrors have rims decorated with triangles and images of gods and animals. The deities are in pairs: the Great King Father of the East and the Great Queen Mother of the West, associated with the contemporary Chinese cult of immortality.[12] Ideas of yin and yang, astrological lore, a cult of immortality, and Chinese divinities began to be absorbed into concepts of Kami and rulership.[13]

When Himiko died, according to *Records of Wei*, a great tomb was built, and more than one hundred attendants were buried with her. There is no archaeological evidence for human sacrifice in Japan, and thus this part of the text is not credible, but the report that Himiko's tomb was more than a hundred paces in diameter is quite compatible with others of the period, such as the largest, Nishitani Sangō in Yayoi Izumo, at forty-seven meters on a side.[14] After Himiko's death, war again erupted and was quelled only when Himiko's niece was installed as the new chieftain.[15]

Early references to the Yamato are linked to Mount Miwa and its Kami Ōmononushi, its divine ancestor and protector, who, as a "spirit of the land" (*kunitama*), was worshipped to secure good harvests and predictable weather. Ōmononushi was believed to appear in snake form, and later myths describe the Kami's ability to appear also in human form. As Yamato hegemons allied with other peoples, shrines dedicated to Ōmononushi were built in the allies' territories. Ōmononushi began to take on martial characteristics in addition to the earlier association with agriculture and ancestral or protective features. The characteristics of the Kami were augmented through this historical evolution, adding layers of meaning, but since structure and coordination were absent, it is not appropriate to label Kami worship at this time "Shinto." The Yamato rulers were closely linked to the Mononobe, who were located to the north of Mt. Miwa, at Isonokami. Following the Yamato consolidation of power, the Mononobe assumed important roles in court ritual.

The Kofun Period (300–700)

This era is named for the large tumuli or tomb mounds (*kofun*, literally, "old tomb") that characterize the era. *Kofun* from the late third century, such as Makimuku Ishizuka in Miwa, evidently served as the tomb for the leader of a local confederacy of chiefdoms. Makimuku contained pottery and grave goods from many other places, especially the rising Kibi center of power in present-day Okayama Prefecture, suggesting a wide network of trade and influence. The early fourth-century Hashihaka *kofun* is 275 meters long, more than three times the size of Makimuku, suggesting a much more powerful leader. The placement of the corpse in a stone chamber enclosed by earth follows Chinese practice, with the head facing north, suggesting that burial practices were absorbing Chinese influence. Clusters of tombs of the same shape but smaller size around the Hashihaka *kofun* suggest that subordinates' loyalty to the leader buried at Hashihaka was expressed by the building of tombs of the same shape but smaller scale. A variety of tomb shapes prevailed in different regions.[16]

In the late fourth century, eastern regions came under Yamato influence and adopted the keyhole tomb, forsaking earlier regional styles. We see a growing uniformity of grave goods: bronze mirrors, swords, halberds, stone bracelets, beads, flint, and iron tools. The separate regions were bound to the center at Miwa by gift-giving, trading, and marital exchange. In contrast, Izumo, an area on the Sea of Japan that did not immediately come under Yamato hegemony, continued to build tombs in a distinctive square shape.[17]

A Division Emerges between "the Indigenous" and "the Foreign" as Buddhism Enters Japan

In the mid-fourth century, the three Korean kingdoms went to war with each other. Wa allied with Paekche, against Koguryŏ, to ensure continuation of trade in iron ingots. War persisted into the fifth century, and emigrants fleeing the wars in Korea poured into Japan, bringing with them valuable metallurgic skills, hydraulic skills needed to open new irrigated fields, literacy, and their own patterns of religious life, including Buddhism. The immigrants included Confucian scholars, scribes (*fuhito*), interpreters, and administrators. They were called *kikajin*, or "naturalized subjects," and they formed distinct clans, such as the Hata, the Aya, and the Soga. Their foreign origins and foreign religion disinclined them to accord great status and deference to the "indigenous" clans, who prided themselves on genealogies going back to the mythical Age of the Kami.[18]

Siddhartha Gautama, also known as Shakyamuni, who lived between the sixth and fourth centuries BCE in India, had founded Buddhism around a thousand years before it reached Japan, the religion having traveled from India to China, and into the Korean peninsula, acquiring many elements from those places. The advent of Buddhism initiated profound changes in all aspects of Japanese life and greatly impacted the cults of the Kami. Buddhism was inseparable from continental culture, and it was closely associated with literacy, medicine, the arts, and many technical skills. Buddhism's acceptance by the court created a rivalry between the champions of the Kami and Buddhism's advocates. It also helped to define Kami cults as "indigenous," though they were diverse and specific to particular clans, some of which comprised recent immigrants. They came to be connected only through coordination from the center, which was bent on extending the Yamato court's territorial control.

Uji, often translated "clan," were the main units of the Yamato court from the late fifth century to the early seventh century. *Uji* leaders received titles (*kabane*) from the Great King that specified their relation to him and recognized them as his retainers. *Uji* were composed of a head or chiefly lineage, linked to subordinate groups, called *be* or *tomo*, who owed the chief specific duties. The whole corporate group was known by the same surname, though not all the members were actually related by kinship. *Uji* chiefs presided over ritual for their ancestral Kami, called *ujigami*, described in myth as having had some relation to the ancestral Kami of the Great King. *Uji* ritual presupposed that the entire corporate group of head lineage plus all the subordinate service groups shared a common descent from the *ujigami*.[19]

The tide of immigrants produced a division within Japan between clans with chieftains whose spiritual authority rested upon continental (including Buddhist) rites, and "native" groups whose leadership rested on the performance of rites for the Kami. Immigrants were associated with advanced Chinese techniques of construction, the technology for making iron tools and weapons, and the bureaucratic skills necessary to manage large estates and governmental affairs. These groups took the lead in introducing and supporting Buddhism, which provided the religious basis for their own authority. By contrast, the "native" clans were associated with agriculture and drew their religious legitimation from the performance of agriculturally based rites for the Kami. The immigrant clans increasingly built Buddhist temples and sponsored Buddhist rites there, while the native clans worshipped the Kami in shrines, built in imitation of Buddhism's permanent structures. This division of society, combined with the determination of the Yamato rulers to remain in control of the whole, lay in the background of the late sixth-century struggle over the official adoption of Buddhist ritual into the court, to be discussed later.

The "Great King" (*daiō* or *ōkimi*) as the late fifth-century Yamato ruler Yūryaku called himself, ruled over the Nara-Osaka area by military force, and outside that sphere made alliances with lesser rulers, who were by no means completely subdued. In forming alliances, the Great King married their daughters and began to extend his influence over the conduct of ritual in their territories. The Great King formed many marriage alliances, as allied groups vied to place their women in the court in the hope that an heir born to one of them would be chosen as the next king. Gift exchange cemented ongoing relations of specialized services, and clan laborers provided the workforce to clear new rice fields and build monumental *kofun* or cast iron tools, weapons, and ceremonial goods in bronze.[20]

The titles bestowed by the Great King upon allies, local generals, and military deputies were inherited by succeeding generations, giving them status in the Yamato retinue based on their clan ancestor's service to the Great King. The famed Inariyama sword, found in a round keyhole tomb in Musashi, bears a genealogy in Chinese characters cut into both sides of the blade and inlaid with gold as testament to the owner's entitlement to rank. The growing use of weaponry among grave goods attests to the increasingly martial character of *uji*. For example, in the case of the 250 objects found with the Inariyama sword, there was a quantity of other swords, armor, halberds, daggers, knives, and many iron arrowheads, as well as *magatama* jewels and a mirror.[21]

A number of ritual sites along the trade routes emerged at Naniwazu (contemporary Osaka) and on the small island Okinoshima in the narrow straits between Japan and the Korean peninsula. A sea god or protector of seafarers called Sumiyoshi was worshipped at Naniwazu. Between the fourth and tenth centuries, the Yamato offered thousands of ritual objects at Okinoshima to protect its trading vessels.[22]

By Yūryaku's day, kings increasingly delegated ritual functions to allies who specialized in ceremonial affairs. Besides the Mononobe, the Nakatomi (some of whom later took the name Fujiwara) specialized in the recitation of prayers to the Kami and were said to be the descendants of the Kami Ame no Koyane no Mikoto. The Sarume claimed descent from the female Kami Ame no Uzume no Mikoto. It is believed that the Sarume women, who took important roles in Enthronement Rites and in later eras performed ritual dances (*kagura*) as a part of court ritual, were originally seers and healers practicing spirit possession. The Inbe (or Imibe) claimed descent from the Kami Ame no Futodama no Mikoto. They were charged with procuring many of the materials used in the Great King's rituals, as well as the performance of abstinence rites. The Urabe were diviners who used tortoise shells and deer scapulae to predict the future, heating these objects over a fire until cracks appeared and then uttering prophesies based on the pattern of cracks.

Later, they claimed descent from Ame no Koyane (also, Amenokoyane) and took the surname Yoshida.[23]

Mt. Miwa had been the original Yamato ritual site, but for reasons that remain unclear, they disengaged from the Miwa deity in favor of a cult of a solar deity at Ise. The shift created a sacred site in the direction of the sun's rising; thereafter the sun deity was treated as a "universal" Kami who illuminates everything under Heaven, and whose worship was the exclusive prerogative of the Yamato. Although the timing and the reasons for the choice of Ise remain a tantalizing, much-debated puzzle, the shrine built at Ise was styled the "original" place of worship for the Yamato ancestor Kami, Amaterasu Ōmikami, while a shrine within the palace provided a place for the ruler's diurnal worship. But Ise was also home to a food deity named Toyouke no Ōkami. With the Yamato cult setting up nearby, Ise came to have a dual character, later described as the Inner and Outer Shrines, with the Inner Shrine, or Naikū, dedicated to Amaterasu Ōmikami, and the Outer Shrine, or Gekū, dedicated to Toyouke no Ōkami, called a servant of the sun deity.[24]

Yamato claims to rule "all under Heaven" (*tenka*) matched the choice of the sun as the clan's ancestral deity. The term *tenka*, "all under Heaven," which we can gloss as "the realm," conveys a distinctive Chinese concept of the polity and the world. The concept was known in Japan from at least the late fifth century and is found in the inscription on the Inariyama sword, which bears the date for 471, and on another sword of the late fifth century found at the Eta Funayama *kofun* in Kumamoto Prefecture. The term casts the realm as an area of 3,000 square *ri* (equivalent to 1,540,000 square kilometers) that was entrusted by Heaven to the ruler, who was styled the "Great King." The realm came to be regarded as a unified cultural sphere encompassing the civilized world, which was surrounded by barbarian lands and oceans. The Great King ruled over the realm and the people. The people were deemed incapable of ruling themselves, but they were equal in their relation to the ruler, regardless of wealth or status. The beneficent ruler maintained a stable social order that gave them peace and order. The realm was divided into "nine states" (*kyūshū*). The ruler established an administrative center called the *kinai*, where the palace was located, and which contained a shrine (*sōbyō*) for the worship of his ancestors.[25]

After the death of a Great King, his or her body was interred in a temporary burial on the palace grounds based on Chinese patterns seen in the *Book of Rites*. Rites were performed there to pacify the King's spirit, presided over by an elder prince, including the recitation of a eulogy, the deceased's genealogy, and posthumous title, with oaths of continuing allegiance. Later the body would be permanently interred in a *kofun*. Some larger *kofun* were surrounded by moats, defining them as sacred spaces. Each level of the mound under which the body was interred was carved into multiple levels, each of which might be decorated with large clay figurines called *haniwa*. These figurines had hollow cylindrical bases, fitted over wooden pillars that had been sunk into the mound to keep it from falling down. *Haniwa* were shaped into animals, warriors, female shamans called *miko*, or as buildings like a mansion or grain storehouse, arranged so that the human shapes formed a spirit army to protect the deceased. Sometimes there were clay tables and chairs placed outside the mansion to simulate ritual feasts offered to the dead. The burial chamber was lined with stone, and it was here that the grave goods were placed, including shield and quiver figurines at the corners, and a clay model of a mansion at the center.[26]

Succession rites began with the choice of a site by divination, construction of an enthronement platform, and carrying out of accession ceremonies there. Since the Great King took many wives, there could be many candidates to succeed him, and succession disputes frequently erupted. Integration of the country, which had grown under Yūryaku, fell apart after his death in 479, and the end of the Kofun period was characterized by warfare.

The Yamato began to influence provincial Kami worship beginning in the sixth century. Great King Keitai initiated a custom of sending offerings and priestly ritualists to distant shrines to coordinate their rites with palace ritual. A group called the Hiokibe, associated with worship of solar deities, was sent out from Yamato to coordinate regional Kami rites with those of the court, spreading the Yamato clan's style of ritual far from the center of the country. The Hiokibe were also engaged in irrigation works and iron production.[27]

By the middle of the sixth century, the Yamato purported to rule from Kyūshū through the Kantō Plain, based on their headship of an alliance stretching to those boundaries. Their "conquest" of this territory is recounted in myths compiled in the eighth-century *Kojiki* and *Nihon shoki* (see chapter 2). Ninigi's descendant Jinmu leaves Kyūshū and travels eastward, conquering the peoples who had not yet yielded, eventually settling in the Yamato area. In later myths, the hero Yamato Takeru, an imperial prince, conquers Kyūshū, Izumo, and the Kantō. These stories relate how other powerful groups supposedly submitted to Yamato rule and were appointed provincial chieftains. Local leaders were gradually incorporated into an expanding bureaucracy for ruling the land. They collected taxes, sent special products to the court, and led armies in expeditions against tribal peoples.[28]

Political Struggle Casts the Kami as "Indigenous" and the Buddhas as "Foreign"

According to the *Nihon shoki*, in 552 a gold and copper image of Shakyamuni and some scriptures were presented to the court by the King of Paekche, who sought Japanese military assistance against his neighboring states. The powerful groups around the throne quarreled about whether these gifts should be accepted. While the *Nihon shoki* account is undoubtedly stylized and considerably altered by editing, we can discern that the debate posed the question of which kind of Kami—the "indigenous" or the "foreign"—would bring the greatest material benefit to the ruler and his people.[29]

The Soga clan argued that Buddhism should be accepted because all the neighboring countries had accepted it, and Japan should not be left behind. The Mononobe and Nakatomi violently opposed the Soga position, predicting that the Kami would react violently if a "foreign" god was accepted. These two represented the view that kingship should continue to be based on the ruler's performance of rites for ancestral and agricultural spirits.

The sovereign decided in favor of the Soga position and commissioned the Soga to commence appropriate ritual for the statue. The Soga converted a dwelling into a kind of chapel and set up worship for the statue there. Soon afterward, however, an epidemic broke out, whereupon the Mononobe and the Nakatomi blamed the acceptance of Buddhism and demanded that the temple be burned and the statue thrown into the Naniwa canal. This indicates that they understood the Kami as being fully endowed with the power to affect events in the human world directly and immediately.

In 584, Soga Umako (551?–626), a powerful court minister under the monarch Bidatsu, built a Buddhist chapel, installed a statue of Maitreya, Buddha of the Future, and had two women "ordained" as nuns.[30] That the first people to take Buddhist ordination in Japan were women probably reflects an understanding that the statue required women to serve it by leading a life of purity, much like the pattern of service to the Kami at Ise that was developing at the same time.

However, as before, an epidemic broke out and was attributed to the wrath of the Kami. This time, the Nakatomi and Mononobe alliance persuaded the court that it had to stop, and again the chapel was burned and the statue thrown in the canal, and the nuns were publicly flogged. A new twist occurred when a third epidemic broke out, interpreted as the wrath of the Buddhas. Soga Umako was directed to resume worship of the Buddhist statue and reinstate the nuns.

The Court's Adoption of Buddhism

According to the *Nihon shoki*, in 587 Great King Yōmei (r. 585–587) converted to Buddhism, with Soga encouragement, and a priest was installed in the palace. It appears that the Soga then began a campaign of war and assassination against the Nakatomi and Mononobe, eventually prevailing. Thereafter, there was no serious opposition to state sponsorship of Buddhism, which spread rapidly, due to the belief that Buddhist rites were highly effective in producing this-worldly benefits. The Soga put Suiko (r. 592–628) on the throne, a woman of both Yamato and Soga descent. In 593, her nephew Shōtoku Taishi (whose actual historicity is debated) was made regent. Shōtoku is credited with taking many measures to unify the court and to raise the level of culture.[31] In addition to building important temples, he imported the Chinese calendar and was said to have composed the Seventeen Article Constitution, protocols for courtiers. While Tsuda Sōkichi and numerous other scholars have disputed the attribution of this document to Shōtoku,[32] the so-called constitution's cultural influence is not in doubt. Article 2 of this document reads:

> Sincerely revere the Three Treasures of Buddhism. In all four types of life and in all countries they are the ultimate truth. Any person of any age should revere Buddhist law.

Although the court advocated Buddhist teachings, however, it was not opposed to rites for the Kami. Under Suiko and Shōtoku, a new Chinese-style of government was introduced. The court was reorganized in 603 into a ranking system based on the Confucian virtues of benevolence, propriety, loyalty, justice, and knowledge.

Legal codes issued during Tenmu's reign (673–686) defined the sovereign as being above the law, and not subject to it. Tenmu portrayed himself as a descendant of the Kami Takamimusubi (see chapter 2) and Amaterasu, and he was referred to as a living god (*akitsumikami*) and an Immortal (*senjin*). The sovereign was portrayed as having the power to communicate or intercede with deities. He or she issued the annual calendar, though of course yin-yang masters made the necessary mathematical calculations and astronomical observations. He or she regulated the social hierarchy of prestige by assigning the ranks of officials. Either Tenmu or his widow and successor Jitō was the first sovereign to be called *tennō*. In modern times, this term is translated as "emperor," but the question of whether this is correct for early Japan is hotly debated. Although the change in terminology from Great King to *tennō* is significant, Japanese sovereigns of the ancient period were hardly on a par with Chinese monarchs, nor did Japanese monarchs preside over an empire before the late nineteenth century. After Kanmu (r. 781–806) and up to Meiji (r. 1868–1912), they "reigned" through a regent or a shogun, the position of the actual political power, but did not rule directly.[33]

The Ritsuryō Jingikan

The Ritsuryō system was built on penal codes (*ritsu*) and administrative law (*ryō*) adopted from China. The "Ritsuryō era" refers to the period when a system of governance based on these laws was dominant, particularly from the seventh through the ninth centuries, and thus differs from periodization based on the location of the capital (such as the Nara period, 710–794) or imperial reign names stipulating the time when a particular sovereign occupied the throne.[34] See Map 1.2 for the ancient provinces.

The Jingikan, the Council of Divinities, was one of two councils created by the Ritsuryō codes, the other being the Council of State (Dajōkan, Daijōkan). Although

Map 1.2 The Provinces of Ancient Japan. Source: Created by C. Scott Walker of the Harvard Map Collection.

the Jingikan was theoretically superior, in fact it operated according to royal orders transmitted by the Council of State, instead of acting autonomously. Although many elements of the Ritsuryō system were directly borrowed from China, the Jingikan had no Chinese precedent but was a new creation originating in Japan. It was charged with making sure that official Kami rites were performed in accordance with the Kami Law (*Jingiryō*).[35]

The term *Jingikan* is composed of 官-*kan*, "Council," and 神祇—*jingi*, originally a shortened form of *tenjin chigi*, "deities of heaven and earth." The "heavenly deities" (*tenjin, amatsukami*) meant the Kami in Takamagahara (heaven), from whom the imperial line supposedly descended, while "earthly deities" (*chigi, kunitsukami*) was a collective term for all other Kami, especially those like the Izumo Kami, who had not immediately submitted to Yamato rule. The term *jingi* also came to refer to ritual performed for the gods of heaven and earth, as well as to the deities themselves.[36]

Early uses of *jingi* did not refer to rites stipulated in law, nor did it necessarily imply elaborate state ritual. During Tenmu's reign (673–686), according to *Nihon shoki, jingi* applied to Tenmu's rites to stop or start rain, with the apparent intent to portray the monarch as having magical powers. In preparation for worshipping the Kami of heaven and earth, Tenmu is said, in *Nihon shoki*, to have decreed purifications throughout the land and to have had an "abstinence palace" erected.[37] While there were performances of the Daijō, Niiname, and Ōharae rites in Tenmu's day, his involvement was largely a matter of sending tribute to the relevant shrines, on the same level as his patronage of Buddhism.[38]

Jingiryō mandated that twenty annual rites be performed for the peace and prosperity of the realm. These rites were the content of Kami Law. The appearance of Kami Law represented a break from former sporadic attempts by the court to consolidate and control provincial ritual for the Kami. Kami Law demonstrated a new determination to assert the court's authority, analogous to its will to bring the provinces under its political control.[39]

These rites were stipulated in the Yōrō Code (718) and then considerably expanded in the *Jōgan gishiki* (ca. 872) and in the *Engi shiki* of 927. The Yōrō Code enumerated legally mandated rites, while later texts specified the procedures and the offerings for each ceremony, as well as for others that had been added by the mid-tenth century.[40] The Yōrō Code includes some thirty sections, each comprising laws governing different aspects of government and society. Two sections govern religious affairs. One of these is called *Jingiryō* and sets out rites for the Kami, to be administered by the Jingikan.[41] The other (the Laws for Monks and Nuns, or *Sōniryō*), governed Buddhist monks and nuns and was administered by a different branch of government, called the Genbaryō. The Jingiryō were clearly modeled on the Chinese ritual classic *The Book of Rites*, but Jingiryō did not include a number of rites that were central to the Chinese system, such as the worship of Confucius, or cattle sacrifice.[42]

Jingiryō consists of twenty articles, beginning with the prescription that the worship of the gods of heaven and earth is to be performed by the Jingikan. This stipulation accords the Jingikan the specific and apparently exclusive prerogative of worshipping the Kami on behalf of the emperor and his court. Other sections of the Yōrō Code allocate about one hundred official positions to the Jingikan.[43] The rites themselves are set out in articles 2 through 9 and article 18, producing the annual calendar shown in Table 1.1. The sovereign is absent from most of these rites, but he shares a meal with the Kami (*jinkonjiki*) in Tsukinamisai, Niinamesai, and Ainamesai.

Table 1.1 ***Jingi* Rites Mandated by the Yōrō Code**

	Ritual
1	Toshigoi no Matsuri (also pronounced Kinensai, in early spring), prayers for a good harvest.
2	Hanashizume no Matsuri (end of the 3rd month), prayers for freedom from illness.
3	Kamu miso no Matsuri (middle of 4th month), offerings of summer vestments at Ise.
4	Saigusa no Matsuri (4th month), the festival of the Isakawa Shrine in Yamato, a subshrine of the Miwa Shrine.
5	Ōmi no Matsuri (4th day of 4th month), the festival of the Hirose Shrine, for the Kami of rain.
6	Kaze no Kami no Matsuri (4th day of 4th month), the festival of the Tatsuta Shrine, for the Kami of wind.
7	Tsukinami no Matsuri (also, Tsukinamisai, 11th day of the 6th month), prayers for a good harvest.*
8	Michiae no Matsuri (last day of the 6th month), performed at a crossroads outside the capital, to prevent evil spirits from entering.
9	Hoshi shizume no Matsuri (follows Michiae no Matsuri on the last day of the 6th month), prayers to prevent fires at the palace.
10	Great Purification (Ōharai), purifies the emperor and the people of the transgressions and defilements of the first half of the year.
11	Ōmi no Matsuri (7th month, 4th day), repeating the spring festival of the same name.
12	Kaze no Kami no Matsuri (7th month, 4th day), repeating the spring festival of the same name.
13	Kamu miso no Matsuri (autumn repetition of the spring festival of the same name).
14	Tsukinami no Matsuri (autumn repetition of the spring festival of the same name).
15	Michiae no Matsuri (winter repetition of the summer festival of the same name).

(*continued*)

Table 1.1 **Continued**

	Ritual
16	Hoshi shizume no Matsuri (winter repetition of the summer festival of the same name).
17	Kanname-sai (9th and 10th months), special offerings at the Ise Shrines of the wine and food made from the new rice crop.
18	Ainame-sai (11th month), emperor shares a meal made from the first fruits of the new crop with the Kami of select shrines.
19	Niiname-sai (11th month), emperor shares a meal made from the first fruits of the new crop with the Kami, extending the sharing to a larger group of Kami than in Ainame-sai.
20	Great Purification (Ōharai, last day of the 12th month), purifies the emperor and the people of the transgressions and defilements of the second half of the year.

*It appears that this observance began as a monthly thanksgiving to the Kami, but by the early eighth century, had become a twice-yearly rite resembling the Toshigoi rite.

Source: Adapted from Felicia Bock, trans. *Engi-Shiki, Procedures of the Engi Era*. 2 vols. A Monumenta Nipponica Monograph. Tokyo: Sophia University, 1970, 1972.

One very striking feature of this annual ritual calendar is its bifurcation at mid-year, so that most of the rites are performed not once but twice annually, once in spring or summer and again in autumn or winter. We can also see that a significant number of these rites are closely linked to agriculture and either express prayers for a good harvest or thanksgiving for the harvest (numbers 1, 5, 6, 7, 11, 12, 14, 17, 18, 19). Apotropaeic rites (to ward off or prevent some misfortune) form another category (2, 8, 9, 15, 16). Purification rites at the end of each half-year are another distinctive component (10, 20). In addition, there are rites directed to the Ise Shrines (3, 13, 17) that can overlap with agricultural ritual. Finally, the Saigusa rite (4) at the Isakawa Shrine, a subshrine of the Miwa Shrine, consists of offering lilies arranged in a large barrel for sake brewing. The origins and significance of this rite are not well understood.[44]

The Jingikan was located within the palace precincts, and it also had provincial branches (see Figure 1.1).[45]

The Jingikan's overall coordination of shrine rites consisted of several main functions. First, it provided a corps of ritualists who assisted the sovereign and his court in the performance of palace ceremonies. Second, in a shrine within its compound, called the Hall of the Eight Deities (Hasshinden), it enshrined eight Kami who protected the imperial house.[46] Third, when misfortune struck or to determine the cause of ominous events, it performed divination to determine the identity of the responsible Kami. Fourth, the Jingikan conducted the distribution of tribute offerings (*heihaku*) to shrines for four annual rituals: Kinensai (Toshigoi no Matsuri), the spring and autumn Tsukinamisai, and Niinamesai.

The Jingikan maintained a register of shrines (*jinmyōchō*), shrine households (*kanbe*),[47] and shrine priests. The court designated some shrines as Official Shrines

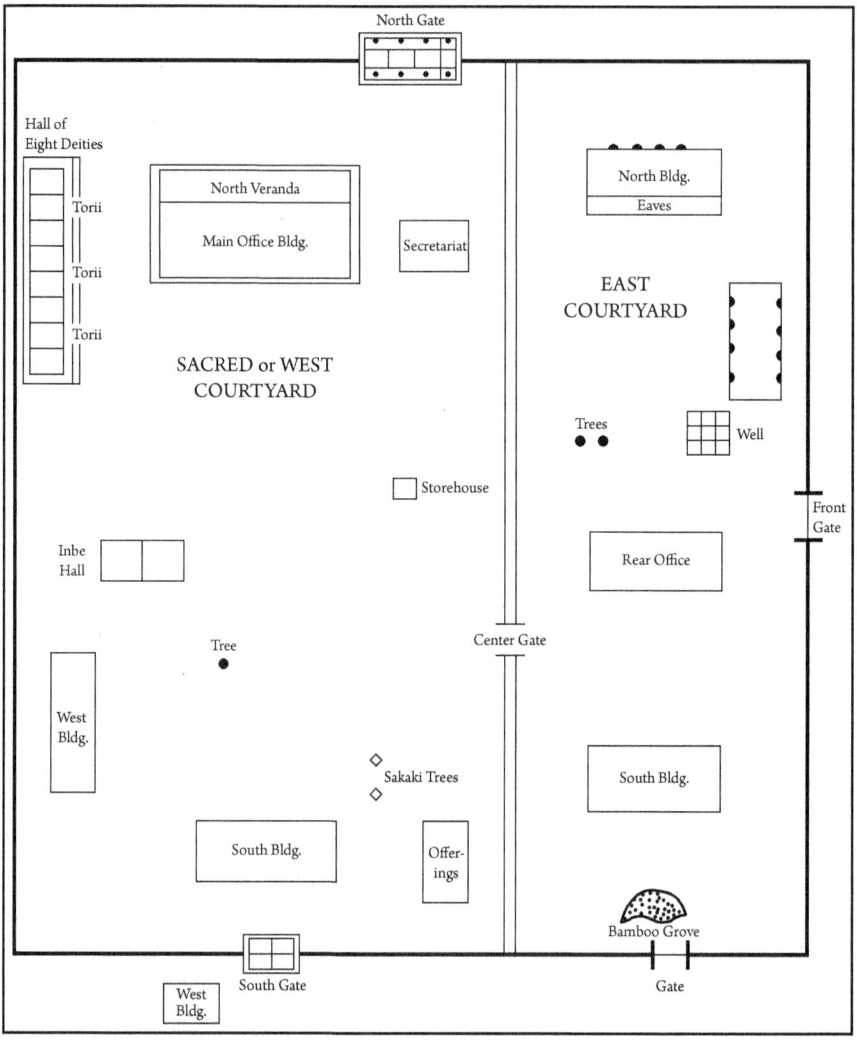

Figure 1.1 Ground Plan of the Jingikan. Source: Bock, *Engi-Shiki*, 1:23.

(*kansha*), meaning that they would receive tribute offerings from the emperor, through the Jingikan. In return, the Kami of those shrines would, it was hoped, guarantee abundant crops and cause the realm to flourish. In accepting the honor of being designated an Official Shrine, each one began to perform annual rituals for the protection of the state, orchestrated by the Jingikan.

The Official Shrines were further subdivided, in the late eighth century, into Imperial Shrines (*kanpeisha*) and National Shrines (*kokuheisha*). Each of these categories was further divided into Major and Minor categories. Ranking shrines paralleled the ranking of the Kami themselves. The emperor bestowed court ranks and high titles on Kami, and designated some Kami "Renowned Kami"

Table 1.2 **The Official Shrines, circa 927**

Official Shrines (Kansha)	*Shrines*	*Kami*	*Myōjin Shrines*
	2,861	*3,132*	*306*
Overseen by Jingikan	198	737	
Overseen by Provincial Governors	2,395	2,395	
Imperial Shrines (Kanpeisha)	573	737	
Major Imperial Shrines (Kanpei Taisha)	198	304	127
Minor Imperial Shrines (Kanpei Shōsha)	375	433	
National Shrines (Kokuheisha)	2,288	2,395	
Major National Shrines (Kokuhei Taisha)	155	188	179
Minor National Shrines (Kokuhei Shōsha)	2,133	2,207	

Source: Umeda Yoshihiko, "Kanpeisha," SSDJ, 264.

(*myōjin*). These honors were frequently bestowed on Kami who were believed to have brought about military victories. The fact that ranks for both shrines and Kami were bestowed in the sovereign's name positioned him as the highest Kami and entailed the implication that the highest authority over Kami affairs rested with him.[48]

Engi shiki (927), a compilation of *jingi* rites, enumerates 3,132 Kami in 2,861 shrines. All those shrines were considered Official Shrines (*kansha*), and all of their Kami received official tribute offerings. While the Jingikan was originally responsible for all these shrines, as of 798 it began delegating responsibility for the National Shrines to provincial governors. Thereafter the Jingikan took charge of 737 Kami, while the provincial governors were responsible for the rites for 2,395 of them. Table 1.2 sets out the system of shrine ranks as reflected in *Engi shiki*.

The Jingikan was staffed by a group of *jingi* families, based on the mythic deeds of their Kami ancestors. Chapter 2 examines these in detail. In brief, the Nakatomi specialized in the recitation of prayers (*norito*)[49] and monopolized the head position, called Jingihaku.[50] This sounded very grand; however, the post carried the fourth rank minor, just above the rank of a provincial governor. Still, the relatively small size of the staff (about one hundred in total, smaller by far than in some other ministries) showed that the Jingikan was subordinate to the Dajōkan.[51] Within the Jingikan, the Inbe family conducted the distribution of tribute offerings. Women of the Sarume family performed sacred dance. The Tamatsukuri manufactured jewels, while the Kagamitsukuri made bronze mirrors used in shrine rites. The Urabe, a relatively low-ranking group, performed divination.

Under the Jingihaku were two assistant heads, two scribes or recorders, and two clerks. The Minister could also call on the services of thirty families of priests (*hafuri* or *hafuri be*), twenty diviners, thirty attendants, and two servants. In addition, there were musicians who played the flute and *koto* during ritual, shrine maidens (*mikannagi*), dancers, and diviners' assistants. The thirty families of priests developed specializations.

The Jingikan played an important role in structuring the shrine priesthood in the Ritsuryō era. It recruited priests and maintained a register of them. There were many different, overlapping terms for shrine priests during this time, but those recruited and supervised by the Jingikan to serve at Official Shrines were called *hafuri*. (Confusingly, low-ranking priests at nonofficial shrines could also be called *hafuri*.) The priests with Jingikan appointments were allowed to dress as court officials and to carry a wooden staff of office called a *shaku*. Female priests were banned from these honors.

Although their tasks are not minutely specified, women ritualists of the Jingikan, called *mikanko* or *mikannagi*, worked in several capacities. Thought to date from before the emergence of anthropomorphic Kami, the rites in which they appear are closely related to the sovereign. While there is a tendency to assume that they must have been shamanic mediums, the *Engi shiki* depicts them as a regular component of Jingikan's ritualists. They conducted rites for twenty-three Kami who protect the emperor's person and the realm in general, including the Eight Deities of the Hasshinden. In the eighth and ninth centuries, they conducted purifications of the emperor's body.[52]

Engi shiki specifies that "all officials" (*hyakkan*) should be present at the Jingikan for eight of the twenty rites set out in Kami Law.[53] The Official Shrines should each send a representative to receive official tribute offerings four times a year: for use in the Kinensai, the two Tsukinamisai, and Niinamesai rites. These ceremonies followed the Kinensai pattern[54] as follows: prior to the ceremony itself, the Jingikan ritualists and attending officials practiced abstinence for four days, to ensure their purity and that of the ritual site. They were required to avoid all filth, the sick, and funerals. Officials were prohibited from signing orders for executions and from proclaiming criminal verdicts. The offerings were assembled, inspected by the Inbe, and placed in the Jingikan's West Courtyard.[55] Ceremonial headdresses of bark cloth were prepared for the ritualists, and seats of leaf matting were set out.

The distribution was conducted in the West Courtyard of the Jingikan. The participating ritualists formed a procession with the males in the lead, followed by the *mikannagi* and lesser officials, entering from the Center Gate and lining up in front of the West Building, facing east. The eight Imperial Advisors (*sangi*) then entered and awaited the arrival of the other participants. A group of high officials of the Council of State and the Jingikan processed into the West Courtyard through the South Gate and were seated according to rank in the South Building. The participating shrine priests who had come to receive offerings followed them and stood to the south of the West Building. The Imperial Advisors then took their seats.[56]

When all were in their assigned places, the Nakatomi officials recited a *norito*. The *norito* offered praise to the Kami and prayers that they would grant a bounteous harvest. If these prayers were answered, all manner of abundant tribute would be offered up. The prayers beg also,

> May this age of the divine descendant of heaven be an everlasting age, as firm as solid rock,...that it may flourish and be a happy reign.... [W]e humbly bow our necks way down like the cormorant in obeisance to the mighty ancestral gods and goddesses, and offer up the choice offerings from the divine descendant as we raise our words of praise.[57]

Each stanza of the *norito* specifies that the sovereign is the source of the offerings. After each stanza, the assembled shrine priests responded in assent, saying, "Ooh!" Then the Inbe, their sleeves tied back with magical sleeve-ties to enhance the potency of the offerings, distributed the offerings. That concluded the ceremony.[58]

Conducting distributions of offerings from the sovereign to the Kami and shrines of the realm through the Jingikan provided four annual occasions to assert symbolically that the ultimate authority over Kami affairs rested with the monarch, and that all other Kami were subordinate to his divine ancestors. Conveyed as it was in ritual form, this assertion was not open for debate. Presentation of this claim through ritual placed it above the discursive mode and made it immune to argument. In fact, remaining aloof from discussion came to be regarded as a virtue of the so-called indigenous tradition. *Man'yōshū* (an eighth-century poetry collection) put it this way, "The 'Land of the Plentiful Reed Plains and of the Fresh Rice-ears'[59] has been created by the Kami as a country which does not dispute with words" (*kamunagara kotoage o senu kuni*). The sovereign's realm receives the divine will just as it is and does not require explanation or justification. Rather, it is a country that refrains from debate.

One implication of this claim is that deeds are to be more highly respected than words. Another is the idea that a magical potency (*kotodama*) resides in words; hence they are not to be lightly bandied about.[60] Privileging ritual symbolism above discourse and argumentation, the Jingikan devoted itself to perpetuating ritual of the great solemnity and complexity seen in Kinensai and the other rites specified by Kami Law.

Table 1.3 compares the offerings at Kinensai (Toshigoi) to those at Tsukinamisai and Niinamesai. In addition to the offerings seen here, a further twenty-eight white horses, one white boar, and one white cock were required for special presentation to the Ise Shrines and other select shrines, and were to be conveyed to them separately by an Imperial Emissary.[61] As the table shows, the offerings consisted of different kinds of cloth, weaponry, antlers, tools, sake, salt, meat and sea products, and leaf matting. The number of shrines given tribute at Tsukinamisai and Niinamesai was

Table 1.3 **Kinensai, Tsukinamisai, and Niinamesai Offerings Compared (Measurements Approximate)**

	Kinensai (Toshigoi)		*Tsukinamisai*	*Niinamesai*
	Jingikan Offerings for 737 Kami	*Provincial Governments' Offerings to 2,395 Kami*	*Jingikan Offerings for 304 Kami*	*Jingikan Offerings for 304 Kami*
Cloth, in yards				
Pongee	1,167	0	629	410
Thin pongee	632	0	632	410
Hemp cloth	82	0	126	82
Tax cloth	3,321	0	1,148	1,148
Cloth and thread, by weight, in pounds				
Bark-cloth	122	0	50	33
Hemp	304	0	126	82
Silk thread	0	411	0	0
Floss silk	0	380	0	0
Weapons and tools				
Shields	737	0	304	198
Sword cases	912	0	594	0
Spearheads	737	0	304	198
Mattocks	291	0	198	0
Bows	198	0	198	0
Quivers	266	0	198	0
Food and liquor				
Sake, in gallons	317	0	792	0
Sake, in wine jars	198	0	0	0
Abalone and bonito, in pounds	163	0	163	0
Dried meat, in pounds	158	0	158	0
Seaweed, in pounds	196	0	196	0
Salt, in gallons	79	0	79	0

(*continued*)

Table 1.3 **Continued**

	Kinensai (Toshigoi)		*Tsukinamisai*	*Niinamesai*
	Jingikan Offerings for 737 Kami	*Provincial Governments' Offerings to 2,395 Kami*	*Jingikan Offerings for 304 Kami*	*Jingikan Offerings for 304 Kami*
Miscellaneous				
Offering tables	1,474	0	608	396
Leaf matting, in yards	1,167	0	629	410
Deer antlers	198	0	198	0

Source: Bock, trans. *Engi-Shiki, Procedures of the Engi Era*, vol. 1, 59–65, 80–81, 97.

one-tenth of the number at Kinensai, showing that Kinensai was the most important of these rites.[62]

The annual requirements of these four ceremonies (Tsukinami was performed twice annually), fulfilled through levies on the provinces, were staggering. The cloth products alone consumed over ten thousand yards of fabric, in an age when hand weaving represented one of the highest technologies. Brewing sake subtracted great quantities of rice from the food supply. Salt had to be made through a laborious process of condensing seawater. Hundreds of pounds of seaweed had to be gathered, dried, wrapped, and conveyed to the Jingikan, to say nothing of the antlers from almost six hundred deer. One cannot help wondering whether it was permissible to "recycle" the offerings rather than assemble a new set four times a year, but the *norito* disallows that, specifying twice that anything left over should go to the sovereign.

Struck by the huge investment in Kami ritual these offerings represent, scholars have queried whether these ceremonies were actually carried out as specified in *Engi shiki*. For example, Mitsuhashi Tadashi emphasizes the importance of recognizing that Kami Law represents an *ideal* and should not be assumed to reflect historical reality. Historical investigation is required to establish whether and how the ideal became reality.[63] Okada Seishi holds that the shrines receiving offerings at Tsukinamisai or Niinamesai must actually have been limited to the great shrines in Kinai, Ise, and Kii, or to shrines connected with the Nakatomi, Inbe, or Urabe.[64] In a separate work, he interpreted Ritsuryō ritual as ancient politics, asserting that in the ancient period all forms of coercion were expressed as divine will, whether control of persons or appropriation of economic resources. Political submission was expressed as subordination to the protective gods of the overlord; that was also true for taxes, which were represented as the subordinated people's offerings to the deities of the overlord.[65] Morita Tei questioned whether the Jingikan really was big enough to accommodate all those who were supposed to attend the main ceremonies, suggesting that they might have been conducted in a larger palace area.[66] A recent history of Shinto holds that while provincial priests actually used the tribute received from the Jingikan at their own shrines' performances of Kinensai, the tribute played only a secondary role there, since they had their own agricultural ceremonies unrelated to imperial myths.[67] Ogura Shigeji partially endorses the view that the effectiveness of the Jingikan declined over time, but stresses the importance of petitions from ninth-century shrines and their affiliates hoping to join the tribute system and gain recognition as Official Shrines.[68]

Summarizing the wide-ranging research on the Jingikan, Nishinomiya Hideki writes that while the system was challenged by natural disasters and epidemic disease in 733 and 737, and though there were cases of provincial governors substituting for shrine priests from the 730s, the Jingikan seems to have functioned effectively in the first half of the eighth century.[69] In the latter half of the eighth century, however, problems arose. In 775 the *hafuri* failed to appear for the Kinensai distribution, and many were removed from their posts as a result. Commuting four times a year to the Jingikan presented a hardship for more distant priests, because of bad roads and the dangers of travel. Fighting with aboriginal peoples continued, making travel unsafe and exposing shrines and priests to wartime damage and injury. There were reports of several shrines burning down in the fighting. With the 798 designation of National Shrine (*kokuheisha*), responsibility for the upkeep and offerings for those shrines shifted to provincial government. About two-thirds of the Official Shrines came to receive their offerings from provincial governors rather than the Jingikan directly, meaning that Jingikan's control over them became indirect, mediated by the governors. Between 810 and 824, there were repeated complaints that the *hafuribe* were refusing to assemble as directed. New measures to strengthen the system took effect in 821 and 822, and in those same years there were numerous appeals from shrines outside the ranks of the Official ones seeking entry to the system. As of 875, new provisions allowed for sending tribute to those shrines unable to send a representative to the Jingikan to receive offerings, showing a determination to maintain the system in spite of difficulties. From around 850, there were instances of emperors missing ceremonies they were supposed to conduct; but in all cases a substitute was appointed, and the rites were performed. In the later ninth century, petitions from provincial shrines for recognition as Official Shrines or Myōjin Shrines increased again. Nishinomiya concludes that while the Jingikan's tribute distributions became attenuated and formalistic, they were never abolished, and new petitions to join the system created a countervailing pressure to maintain the system.[70]

The Term *Shinto*

Does the creation of system and structure linking the ceremonial center in the palace with the ritual performance of shrines in the provinces allow us to speak of *Shinto* as the name for a unified framework of Kami worship from the late seventh century? Certainly, the *ideal* of structure and unity is made clear in the early eighth-century Jingiryō, but code and reality are rarely identical. While the establishment of the Jingikan as a government office charged with performing these rites represents an ideal of unity and coordination, the Jingikan was a minor unit, with limited geographical reach. Some provincial shrines and priests resisted its attempts to make them conform to a national system. Provincial shrines and the people they represented had their own traditions and interests. They would not have willingly ceded any more autonomous control of their own *jingi* affairs than was necessary to secure the benefits of ceremonial connections to the court.[71]

Beyond these considerations, if Shinto had become a distinctive element of classical life, we would expect that the term would assume a clear definition, and that it would appear with some frequency. The word *jingi* had come to be used to refer to the Kami and rites for them, but was the word *Shinto* used synonymously with *jingi*?

In fact, the term *Shinto* was not consistently used to designate Kami worship in early texts. It is not used at all in *Kojiki*, the *Man'yōshū*, *Kogoshūi* (807; see chapter 2), or the *fudoki* (chapter 3). *Shinto* appears only four times in the *Nihon shoki*.[72] The first occurrence is seen in the chapter on Great King Yōmei (r. 585–587), where it is stated that he "believed in (*shin*) the teachings [or Law, Dharma] of the Buddha (*buppō*) and reverenced (*son*) the Way of the Kami (*Shinto*)." As used here, the term distinguishes a "way" of the Kami from the "teachings" or Law of Buddhism, which sets out the inexorable, universal law of karma. In later eras the concept of a "way" came to be theorized in analytic and aesthetic terms, but we do not see such elaborations in this text or at this time.[73]

At the beginning of the chapter on Kōtoku's reign (645–654), we find the second occurrence: "He [the sovereign] honored the teachings of Buddha but scorned the Way of the Kami [Shinto]. He cut down the trees at Ikukunitama Shrine." The sovereign's preference for Buddhism is presented as motivating his disrespect for Shinto. This passage forms the opening of the chapter on Kōtoku's reign and is offered without context, so it is impossible to derive much content for the word *Shinto* as it appears here.

The third and fourth occurrences are linked to an edict of 647, also in Kōtoku's reign, in which the related term *kamunagara* "as a Kami would" or "while as a deity," is explained: "The expression "as a Kami would" (*kamunagara*) means to conform to Shinto. It also means in essence to possess oneself of Shinto." According to Edo-period scholars, this passage was inserted sometime after a later retranscription of the *Nihon shoki*; in other words, we cannot be certain that it reflects the period of *Nihon shoki*'s compilation.[74]

The compilers of the *Nihon shoki* were doubtless familiar with Chinese usage of the term *Shinto* (*shendao*), meaning miscellaneous folk practices, occasionally Buddhism, and even religious life generally. Thus the word as used in *Nihon shoki* probably means popular beliefs about Kami in general, as contrasted with the more structured *teachings* of Buddhism. The term refers to the activities of unspecified spirits, who are distinguished from Buddhist divinities, but not explicitly defined as indigenous to Japan. In none of these cases does *Shinto* refer to an organized institution.[75]

One influential interpretation of the term *Shinto* in *Nihon shoki* holds that it should be understood as meaning Daoism, itself a highly problematic term. This is the position of Fukunaga Mitsuji and Shimode Gyōseki, and also held by Kuroda Toshio.[76]

On the basis of these considerations, several tentative conclusions emerge: (1) the term *Shinto* was not always a synonym for *jingi* rites; (2) *Shinto* was an uncommon term associated with miscellaneous popular beliefs originating in China; and (3) it could be used to distinguish Kami-related phenomena from Buddhism. Beyond that, *Shintō* seems to have had little defined content in the period of the establishment of the Jingikan. Furthermore, one searches the official histories and classical Japanese literature in vain for uses of the term *Shintō*. Tsuda Sōkichi scoured texts dating through the end of the eleventh century and discovered only eleven instances of the term *Shinto*.[77] The term did not become common until the fifteenth century, stimulated by Yoshida Kanetomo, as subsequent chapters will show, and as Mark Teeuwen has cogently argued.[78]

Teeuwen argues that *Nihon shoki*'s use of the term *Shintō*—more properly *jindō*—the probable pronunciation of the term in the eighth century, reflects the hand of a Buddhist monk involved in the compilation.[79] If that is so, however, it seems odd that the monk's influence would be seen only in the accounts of the thirty-first and thirty-fifth sovereigns, out of a total of forty-one covered in *Nihon shoki*. Citing later Buddhist texts, Teeuwen claims that *jindō* occurs "relatively frequently" in discussions of Buddhism's "domestication of local Japanese deities" *after Nihon shoki*. On that basis, he concludes that *Shinto* should be understood as "Buddhist jargon," and that "*Shintō* plays second fiddle in what is basically an account of the establishment of Japanese Buddhism."[80] Hirai Atsuko takes issue with Teeuwen's assessment, however, writing of *Nihon shoki* that "the chronicle never used words that suggested denigration of the native *kami*."[81] Indeed, Teeuwen's idea that *Nihon shoki* is basically an account of Buddhism goes in quite a different direction than prior understandings of this text.

Teeuwen's stance is broadly congruent with a view of Shinto history that is favored among specialists of Japanese medieval religious history. Inoue Hiroshi's *Japan's Shrines and Shinto* (*Nihon no jinja to Shintō*) expounds this perspective in detail. Inoue begins by disassociating himself from recent publications portraying Shinto as Japan's primordial, indigenous religion, noting that such works often turn out to be nationalist screed masquerading as religious history. He notes that this characterization of Shinto has its roots in the views of Motoori Norinaga and other nativist scholars of the eighteenth and nineteenth centuries. In the twentieth century, it has been championed by Tsuda Sōkichi, Asoya Masahiko, and Mitsuhashi Tadashi, but without an underlying nationalist agenda.[82]

Inoue emphasizes changes in the meanings attributed to the term *Shintō* introduced by Yoshida Kanetomo. Kanetomo no longer used the word vaguely, as a foil to Buddhism, or to refer to religious life in general. Instead, in Inoue's opinion,

> [Shinto] functioned as a term and concept that encompassed an extremely ideological and political assertion upholding the secular order of Japan's nationhood and royal authority (*kokka ya ōken no arikata*).... Precisely this is the independently established concept that we must recognize as incorporating the meaning of something indigenous to Japan but also with new historical content... Shinto thus begins not in the ancient period but was fully established for the first time in the medieval period.[83]

To define Shinto history solely in terms of its doctrinal or philosophical dimension is understandably appealing to medievalists, since it is that aspect of the tradition that comes into focus so conspicuously in that era. It is a reasoned position, and its proponents have contributed immensely to our understanding of Shinto's history. It seems to me, however, that it privileges the doctrinal and conceptual aspects of Shinto at the expense of the institutional, and that it ignores more enduring continuities in institutional, ritual, and social history that are arguably as important and definitely more influential in society than medieval doctrines and philosophy.

It is undoubtedly true that Kanetomo used *Shintō* with much greater clarity and precision than we see before the fifteenth century. He provided the intellectual and conceptual basis for Shinto's subsequent history. But it would be a mistake to portray his achievements in this domain as appearing suddenly and de novo. As chapters 5 through 7 will show, he built on the work of numerous forebears. His intellectual authority rested in no small part on his position as de facto leader of the Jingikan. Moreover, Kanetomo's treatment of his doctrines as secrets to be disclosed only in esoteric initiations, and their dependence on the intellectual paradigm of esoteric Buddhism were decisively rejected (though not yet completely eliminated) in the early modern period. The same is true of other medieval Shinto theories arising within the Ise shrines and Buddhist monastic circles, and of the esoteric initiations to which they gave rise. When the Meiji government forcibly separated shrines from temples in 1868, the model it took for its new creation of an independent Shinto was the Ritsuryō Jingikan.

That being said, however, it remains extremely difficult to discuss Shinto in the ages before the term itself is widely used, that is, from the fifteenth century on. Up to that point, *Shinto* is a collective designation for *jingi*, state-sponsored Kami rites, and miscellaneous Kami cults. This usage is inevitably imprecise and unsatisfactory in various ways. To uphold the significance of institutional, social, and ritual continuities forces one to struggle for clarity where little is to be found, but others have also accepted this challenge.

Numerous historians of Shinto see its origins as stemming from the ancient court, Jingiryō, and the Jingikan, and that is the position of this study. Two recent examples of this perspective may be seen in Itō Satoshi, Endō Jun, Matsuo Kōichi, and Mori Mizue, *Shintō*[84] as well as in *Shinto: A Short History,* edited by Inoue Nobutaka, who writes in the book's introduction,

> The classical system of kami worship clearly possessed all the elements of a fully fledged religious system. Its origin is difficult to date, but it was completed as a system after the establishment of a central imperial state governed by an adapted version of Chinese law (J. *ritsuryō*). Shrines all over the country were included in a system of "official shrines" (*kansha*). This network of official shrines formed the *network* of kami worship's religious system. Also, the *constituents* [the people who maintain the system] of kami rituals were clearly identified, and their message (the system's *substance*) was transmitted... through ritual prayers (*norito*) and imperial decrees (*senmyō*). It is not possible to identify a religious system that might be described as "Shinto" before the systematization of kami worship by the new imperial state during the classical period, because the constituents, network, and substance of kami cults... were too ill-defined.[85]

In a chapter of this work edited by Inoue, titled "Ancient and Classical Japan: The Dawn of Shinto," Mori Mizue further clarifies the point of origin. Referring to the late seventh century, she writes, "It is at this point that, for the first time, we can speak of 'Shinto' as a religious system that is linked directly (if remotely) to the Shinto of today."[86] It seems to me also that once system and centralization emerge in the late seventh century, it is reasonable to speak of *Shinto* in recognition of the watershed represented by the Jingikan, a structured ritual calendar, Kami Law, and the incorporation of Kami priests into the government. By comparison with this ritual, institutional, and social system, doctrinal and philosophical expositions came later and were transmitted in esoteric frameworks restricting their transmission to initiates.

Moreover, the appearance of more consistent usage of terminology from the medieval period did not mean that Shinto suddenly became independent of Buddhism, a process that was not launched in earnest until the late nineteenth century. The precedent to which the late nineteenth-century bureaucrats looked as they sought to create an independent Shinto was the Ritsuryō-era Jingikan. If we want to understand Shinto's history from the ancient period until the present, the Jingikan in its early form provides an essential point of origin.

But what of the warning implicit in Inoue Hiroshi's specification of Kanetomo as the origins of Shinto? He implies that to place Shinto's origins earlier than the fifteenth century is to promote a crypto-nationalist view to the effect that Shinto is the essence of Japanese ethnicity or culture, that it is timeless and quintessentially indigenous. By contrast, I have tried to show that while the court's promotion of Kami rites as part of its drive to extend its territorial control involved a *rhetoric* of indigeneity as a means to distinguish Kami ritual from its parallel promotion of Buddhism, the ingredients of its Kami rites were drawn from a variety of continental sources. I reject the idea that Shinto is the basis of an essentialized notion of Japanese ethnicity.

Conclusions

This chapter has traced the beginnings of Shinto through the development of Kami worship down to the early eighth century, beginning with unsystematic, clan-based cults that were greatly influenced by religious beliefs and customs from the Asian continent. Daoist ideas permeated virtually all expressions of religious ideas, and Buddhism began to combine with Kami worship intellectually and institutionally. Religious conceptions of rulership were pervasively colored by all the traditions concerned. After a period of fluidity and mutual influence, in the late seventh and early eighth centuries a concept of *jingi* emerged as a name for the Kami of Heaven and Earth and rituals particular to them. Under the influence of the court's adoption of Buddhism, a corpus of rites understood as "indigenous" was separately embodied in the Jingiryō. It mandated the performance of Kami rites, while separate provisions structured Buddhist and yin-yang rites. The Jingikan, a new branch of government not taken from Chinese models, was established to manage the performance of Kami ritual. Court sponsorship of *jingi*, Kami Law, and the Jingikan lent a "public," official character to Kami worship and a further association with the indigenous. With the creation of the Jingikan and Jingiryō, we have the institutional beginnings of Shinto. Yet the Yamato court's claims to represent an indigenous tradition through Jingikan rites was precisely that: a *claim*, not a fact. We shall see in the next chapter that other clans maintained their own accounts of genealogy and tales that contested the Yamato account.

2

The Kami in Myth

Introduction

This chapter examines myths of the Kami in *Kojiki* (712), *Nihon shoki* (720), and the provincial gazetteers called *fudoki*. It seeks to place these tales in the historical context laid out in the previous chapter, addressing the ways they express ancient understandings of the Kami, the indigenous and the foreign, and the public versus the private.

Compilation of the *Kojiki*

According to the preface of *Kojiki*, a no-longer-extant genealogy of the imperial line called the *Teiki* had been drawn up in the late sixth century. It combined tales of the divine descent of the imperial clan with the myths of the origins of its allied clans. By the late seventh century, however, multiple discrepant versions had come into being, leading to conflicting claims to rank and title that could not be decisively adjudicated.

Emperor Tenmu (r. 673–686) commissioned a compilation of the genealogies and legends of the clans, resulting in the *Kojiki* (712). Having come to power through the Jinshin War (672), Tenmu required validation of his qualifications as well as accurate genealogies of allied clans, since court rank was partly based on genealogical connection to the throne. According to the work's preface, Tenmu commissioned a courtier named Hieda no Are to memorize the genealogies and legends of the major clans.[1] That material was committed to writing by Ō no Yasumaro and eventually presented after Tenmu's death to Empress Genmei, in 712, as *The Record of Ancient Matters* (*Kojiki*).[2] The compilation in writing "fixed" these tales that had previously circulated orally.[3]

Given the circumstances and motivations of its compilation, *Kojiki* cannot be taken as reflecting the beliefs and worldview of all the peoples of ancient Japan in any straightforward way. First, *Kojiki* consists in large part of the genealogies and narratives of the powerful clans around the court, while peripheral groups and their deities are dismissed as barbarians to be conquered. Even from the perspective of the allied clans, some were dissatisfied because *Kojiki* did not give sufficient emphasis to their particular traditions. In response, they compiled their own competing works. For example, the Inbe clan composed the *Kogoshūi*, and the remnant of the Mononobe compiled the *Sendai kuji hongi* to promote their own ancestors and traditions; these texts will be discussed in more detail later in the chapter. Second, it is important to be aware that although modern scholarship regards the content of *Kojiki*, particularly Book I: "The Age of the Gods" as myth, it was commissioned as a work of history.

Third, Confucian influence evident in *Kojiki's* depictions of the Kami suggests that popular understandings of the sacred would have differed considerably.[4] Fourth, as will be explained, *Kojiki* constitutes—in part—an elaborate legitimation of the ruling dynasty, treating their hegemony as a fait accompli, even though various clans and tribes continued to rebel for centuries.[5] *Kojiki*'s (and *Nihon shoki*'s) portrait of an untroubled, unified cosmos produces an artificial image of unity where precious little existed. In these circumstances we cannot assume that all the concepts, phenomena, and deities glossed as *Kami* shared a common essence.

Although by the time of *Kojiki*'s compilation, the Great Kings were deeply involved in Buddhist rites, philosophy, and scholarship, the work entirely omits any reference to Buddhism. Buddhism was sufficiently established in Japan by the time of *Kojiki*'s compilation that the omission of any reference to it must represent the compilers' decision. The absence of references to Buddhism cannot, however, be taken to mean that *Kojiki* is a "Shinto" text, since the word *Shinto* does not occur in it. The first use of the word *Shinto* occurs in *Nihon shoki* (720).

Book I of *Kojiki*, "The Age of the Gods," contains the most significant mythic material.[6] It can be divided into several sequences or cycles of related tales. Let us examine each sequence and then place this work in the context of other writings vying to be recognized as "official" and "indigenous."[7]

Cosmogony Sequence, Chapters 1–2

The original coming into existence of the universe is the *cosmogony*. The first chapter of *Kojiki* opens when heaven and earth divided,[8] and three invisible deities came into existence in heaven: Takamimusubi no kami, Amenominakanushi no kami, and Kamimusubi no kami. The land was unformed and resembled floating oil. Reed shoots appeared, and more invisible deities were born, including the male deity Izanagi no kami and the female deity Izanami no kami.

Until recently, research on *Kojiki* and *Nihon shoki* has tended to assume that they reflect a broadly shared worldview, but in fact they adopt different positions on important questions.[9] *Nihon shoki* contains several accounts of the cosmogony, all of which differ significantly from that of *Kojiki*. *Nihon shoki* opens with a version asserting that originally heaven and earth were not separated, nor had the principles of yin and yang yet come to exist. Heaven and earth together formed an undifferentiated mass resembling an egg. The pure, clear elements formed heaven. Subsequently the turbid, heavy elements formed earth. Heaven and earth joined (copulated), producing a reed-shoot that became the primal Kami Kunitokotachi no Mikoto.[10]

Nihon shoki's cosmogonies accord preeminence to Kunitokotachi rather than the triumvirate of *Kojiki*. Does this difference indicate an early theological debate on the nature of Kami? Both works clearly relied on earlier written records that are no longer extant. If we had access to them, perhaps we could attempt to answer this question. Moreover, *Nihon shoki*'s cosmogonies are couched in imagery seen in such Chinese texts as the "Youshi" chapter of the *Lushi chunqiu* (ca. 240 BCE): "Heaven and Earth had a beginning. Heaven was subtle so as to complete, and Earth blocked so as to give form. Heaven and Earth combining and harmonizing is the great alignment of generation."[11] In this text, heaven and earth emerge spontaneously, and "their mating gives birth to the myriad things." Or again, from the "Jingshen" chapter of the *Huainanzi* (ca. 139 BCE): "Long ago, in the time before there existed Heaven and Earth, there was only figure without form. . . . There were two spirits (*shen*; J: *Kami*) born together; they aligned Heaven, they oriented Earth."[12] According to Sinologist Michael J. Puett, the appearance of spirits who "align" the cosmos conceals a claim: human ability to become a spirit and thus gain control over the cosmos.[13] As we saw in chapter 1, Tenmu is believed to have undertaken austerities in a quest for immortality. In China there was a long history of cosmological debate, from as early as the fourth century BCE. Was *Nihon shoki* part of this debate? Was comparable debate in early eighth-century Japan the reason for different accounts of the cosmogony? Although there is no definitive answer to this question, it arises naturally when the accounts are viewed side by side. I believe that such questions help us escape from outdated assumptions of a unitary, seamless worldview of ancient Japan.

Izanagi and Izanami Sequence, Chapters 3–13

The heavenly deities commanded Izanagi and Izanami to make the land solid.[14] The pair then stood on the Heavenly Floating Bridge, lowered a jeweled spear into the brine beneath them, and stirred. The drops that fell from the spear's tip coagulated and formed an island called Onogoro. The pair then descended from the bridge to the island, where they set to work to "give birth to the land," by engaging in sexual intercourse. To seal their union, they agreed to walk separately around a pillar that joined heaven and earth, one going clockwise and the other counterclockwise. Meeting each other, Izanami spoke words of praise to Izanagi, and he responded in kind. He also admonished her, however: "It is not proper that the woman speak first." Nevertheless, they were united, but their first offspring was a "leech child," which they abandoned in a reed boat.

Seeking the reason for this failure to produce viable offspring, they went back up to heaven, called Takamagahara, literally, the "high fields of heaven," and took counsel with the other heavenly deities. The problem lay, they determined, in the female Izanami having spoken first. The two Kami went back down to earth and repeated the walk around the heavenly pillar, and this time Izanagi spoke first. They succeeded, and many islands were born. After this, Izanagi and Izanami gave birth to many pairs of male and female deities, who ruled the rivers, seas, winds, and fire. But Izanami was mortally burned when she gave birth to the fire deity. As she lay dying, other deities were born from her vomit, urine, and feces.

Izanagi grieved deeply for Izanami, regretting that in exchange for his beloved he had nothing but the child whose birth had killed her. Another deity was born from his tears. Izanagi buried Izanami. In anger at the fire deity, Izanagi hacked him to pieces with his sword. The blood dripping from Izanagi's sword brought numerous deities into existence as it spilled onto rocks, and other deities were born from the fire child's head, chest, belly, genitals, hands, and feet.

Determined to bring Izanami back from the dead, Izanagi traveled to the land of Yomi, the world of the dead, which he reached by crossing a "pass" and moving aside a great boulder. Izanagi met Izanami there and begged her to return with him so that they could continue with their creation of the land. Izanami wished to accompany him, but feared that she could not, because she had "eaten at the hearth of Yomi." She left Izanagi to wait while she took counsel with the gods of Yomi to see what could be done, telling Izanagi that he must not look at her. It was dark there, and after waiting a long time, Izanagi lit a fire with the comb he wore in his hair. To his horror, the light shone on Izanami's corpse, where "maggots were squirming and roaring." Many kinds of thunder deities were in the different parts of her body. He turned and ran.

Izanami was angry that he had seen her shame, and her love turned to fury. She sent the "hags of Yomi" to kill Izanagi. Izanagi could only escape by throwing down the vine that bound up his hair, which turned into grapes. The hags stopped to eat them, as well as the bamboo shoots that sprouted from his comb, but they pursued Izanagi all the way to the pass, where Izanami caught up with him. Izanagi rolled a boulder into the pass to block Izanami, and there they spoke an oath of divorce. Izanami promised that she would strangle one thousand people every day, to which Izanagi replied that he would build 1,500 parturition huts a day. The pass where they broke their troth is said to be in Izumo. Izanami drops out of the story at this point.

Let us pause in the narrative to notice several important aspects of the myths concerning Izanagi and Izanami. These tales portray a *vertical cosmology*, an image of the universe organized in vertical planes. This world is described as coming into existence by the separation of heaven from earth, as if they had once been joined and inseparable. As heaven and the earth separate, invisible deities come into existence and remain in the High Fields of Heaven. These deities call upon the seventh generation of deities, a visible male-female pair, Izanagi and Izanami, to solidify the earth, which is like floating oil. Heaven and earth are connected by the floating bridge on which they stand holding a spear. Drops falling from the spear create islands, and the pair descends to the earth, which is now sufficiently solid to support them. They circumambulate a "heavenly pillar" connecting heaven and earth, a second connector, in addition to the Heavenly Floating Bridge. Izanagi and Izanami can ascend to heaven and return to earth, showing that movement between the two planes is possible. Later we learn that a third territory exists, Yomi the world of the dead. It is dark and shadowy, and Izanagi reaches it by following a pass. Izanami had gone there in death, and so cannot come back to earth, but Izanagi, who has not died, can go there and return. Izanami's fate is sealed, because she had eaten food in Yomi and thus became a part of it. After Izanagi returns to the earth, he rolls a boulder into the pass, making it impossible for anyone who has gone to Yomi to return. This story can be taken as a myth of the origin of death.

Heaven is spoken of as the High Fields of Heaven, a place above the earth covered in fields, presumably of rice. The earth is named the Central Land of the Reed Plains, a place that does not yet know rice agriculture. Later chapters give us a fuller picture of heaven and earth. *Kojiki*'s main description of Yomi appears in these chapters. Yomi is rocky, dark, and a place of putrefaction. Although it is the realm of death, some kind of life goes on there, in shadow. Izanami originally appears as she had been in life, suggesting a view of death as a kind of shadowy semblance of life on earth. But the element of rottenness also makes it a place of horror and revulsion. It has maggots and ugly, horrible females called the "hags of Yomi." It seems at once to be a stone-lined chamber resembling the construction of the burial room within a *kofun* and to open onto a broader expanse, the area through which the hags pursue Izanagi.

Motoori Norinaga (1730–1801), the eighteenth-century scholar of the *Kojiki* who revived this work after centuries of its being virtually ignored and overshadowed by the *Nihon shoki*, took the view that Yomi is a third vertical plane beneath the Central Land of Reed Plains. In fact, however, the text does not specify exactly where Yomi lies in relation to the human world. As we have seen, it is reached by a pass, but the text does not actually depict anyone going up or going down. This has led some scholars, such as Kōno Takamitsu, to hold that Yomi is at the far edges of the plane of human life, not below it.[15] Let us note also that while the dead are said to live in Yomi, the text does not suggest that humans ascend to Takamagahara after death.

This sequence is notable for specifying that in many cases deities were created in male-female pairs, and of course, Izanagi and Izanami are the prototype. Some of the paired deities are further distinguished as one being a "heavenly Kami" (*amatsu kami*) and the other being an "earthly Kami" (*kunitsu kami*). We note that whereas the deities mentioned first in the text are invisible, Izanagi and Izanami have human form, and they are subject to death. Sexual intercourse is portrayed in neutral language, and both sexes engage in it straightforwardly. The body of the male is said to be "formed to excess," while the female body has a place that is "insufficiently formed." When Izanagi suggests joining these two "places," Izanami assents willingly, saying, "That would be good." The joining of their bodies thus makes a complete whole, in the sense that the female is completed by the male, continuing the sense of the female as being lacking or insufficient on her own. The myths portray the couple working in tandem to create deities, islands, and other things, but the narrative of their circumambulation of the heavenly pillar shows that their union is only productive when the male takes the lead. In other words, within a relation in which the two sexes complement or complete each other, which we can call a relation of *gender complementarity*, the male should take initiative, and the female should yield and assent. When those conditions are met, their union is successful, but when the female usurps male prerogatives, deformities or incomplete creations are the result. This construction assumes that the female is incomplete without the male, and that female initiative lacking male guidance is doomed to failure.[16]

Izanagi and Izanami are spoken of as Kami, but as we have seen, they closely resemble humans. They are not omniscient, omnipresent, or eternal, nor are they identified with wisdom or any special virtue. The original pair came into existence in the process of the separation of heaven and earth, but many of their progeny are born as a result of sexual intercourse. They express great grief in the face of death, and when Izanami dies, Izanagi "crawled around her head and around her feet, weeping." Izanagi feels rage so great that he kills the fire child whose birth had killed Izanami. Izanagi begs Izanami to return to him, and she responds lovingly, but her love changes to hatred when she is shamed by Izanagi's revulsion at the sight of her rotting corpse. Thus the Kami are portrayed as experiencing emotions and acting emotionally. There is no implication in the text that they are moral exemplars or symbols of ethical principles.

These chapters emphasize the idea of creation or generation (*musubi*), and the sheer numbers of deities, islands, and natural forms that Izanagi and Izanami create is staggering. Fertility comes from every imaginable source. Besides the process of separation of heaven and earth and sexual intercourse, new beings arise from reeds sprouting out of liquid, from liquid coagulating as it fell from the spear, and deities are born from vomit, urine, and feces. Blood dripping from a sword portrays the sword as an instrument of creation and destruction, while other deities are born from dismembered or rotting body parts. Plants sprout from a comb, and maggots become thunder deities. Although these Kami are the "parents" of all they create, however, they are not depicted in nurturing attitudes toward their offspring.

Sequence in Heaven, Takamagahara, Chapters 14–17

Izanagi was polluted by contact with death, so he purified himself by diving into a river.[17] As he threw down his bag and stick, and as he removed his clothing, new deities were born. As he washed himself, three deities were born: washing his left eye, the deity Amaterasu Ōmikami was born; washing his right eye, the deity Tsukiyomi no Mikoto was born; washing his nose, the deity Susanoo no Mikoto was born. Izanagi gave important missions to these three: Amaterasu was to rule Takamagahara; Tsukiyomi was to rule the night (this deity disappears thereafter); Susanoo was to rule the sea. Susanoo, however, refused this mission, leading Izanagi to expel him.

Claiming that he wished to bid farewell to Amaterasu, Susanoo ascended to Takamagahara, bearing a sword ten-hands-width long. Sensing danger, Amaterasu attired herself in male battle dress and wrapped her arms in long strings of *magatama* beads. Susanoo protested that he meant her no harm, and he proposed that they exchange oaths to prove the purity of their motives toward each other. Each chewed up the other's emblem—Amaterasu chewed up Susanoo's sword, and Susanoo chewed up Amaterasu's *magatama* beads—and spewed out a misty spray from which deities were born. The deities produced in this way by Amaterasu were all male, while those produced by Susanoo were all female. Susanoo claimed that he had won the contest.[18]

Proclaiming his triumph, Susanoo "raged with victory," defiling heaven by defecating in Amaterasu's sacred hall. This ritual hall was the place where on the following day Amaterasu was to have celebrated the harvest festival, Niinamesai. Susanoo broke down the barriers between the heavenly rice fields. When he threw a dead pony that had been skinned backward into the weaving hall, one of Amaterasu's heavenly weaving maidens was so frightened that she struck her genitals with the shuttle and died.[19] Seeing these outrages, Amaterasu was frightened and hid herself away in the Heavenly Rock Cave. Her seclusion plunged heaven and earth into complete darkness: "constant night reigned, and the cries of the myriad deities were everywhere abundant, like summer flies, and all manner of calamities arose."

Historian of religions Gary Ebersole views the cave myth as depicting the double burial system of the ancient court. This practice included a period of temporary interment before a final burial. It included practices attempting to "recall" the soul to the body, as well as elaborate mourning rites and the recitation of elegies for the deceased. These practices indicate the beliefs that the soul could leave the body but perhaps be recalled, and that death is the result of the permanent separation of the two.[20]

The heavenly deities led by Ame no koyane no Mikoto (ancestral deity of the Nakatomi clan, later called Fujiwara) took counsel about how to restore Amaterasu. They caused birds to cry. They brought iron to a smith and had him make a mirror. They had *magatama* beads made. They performed a divination with the shoulder bone of a deer. They uprooted a great *sakaki* tree and hung the beads and mirror in its branches, along with blue and white cloth. They made offerings, and Ame no koyane intoned a liturgy to soften Amaterasu's heart. Finally, a female deity named Ame no Uzume (ancestral deity of the Sarume clan) bound up her sleeves and headband with vine, took bunches of bamboo leaves in her hands, overturned a bucket and stood upon it, stomping. She became possessed and in that state exposed her breasts and genitals to the assembled deities, who all broke out laughing.[21] Amaterasu's curiosity was aroused. She opened a crack in the cave entrance, whereupon the other deities claimed that they were rejoicing that there was a deity superior to her. They showed her the mirror to prove their point, and when she ventured part way out to look, they pulled her out of the cave altogether. Then the deities imposed a fine on Susanoo for disrupting the heavenly peace. Cutting his hair, nails, and beard, they expelled him from heaven.[22]

The scene in which the Kami prepare a pure space for the performance of Ame no Uzume's dance became a template for Kami ritual. The preparation of a pure space and the needed items (mirror, jewels), divination, a *sakaki* tree decorated with streamers, intoning a prayer or liturgy, and the performance of dance are central elements in rites for the Kami. Further, the Kami who figure here become the ancestors of clans granted special privileges in the performance of imperial ritual: the Nakatomi, the Sarume, and others, such as jewel- and mirror-makers.

These chapters concerning Amaterasu and Susanoo contain very significant ideas, images, and motifs. Let us note first, however, that Izanagi disappears from the narrative once he creates the pair Amaterasu and Susanoo. Amaterasu accepts her assignment to rule over the heavens, but Susanoo rejects his task of ruling over the sea, which brings on his first expulsion. He wept and howled incessantly, which caused the mountains to wither and the rivers and seas to dry up, precipitating chaos comparable to what happened when Amaterasu hid in the cave. Malevolent deities proliferated, and many "calamities" arose. He complained to Izanagi that he wanted to go and visit his "mother," though Izanagi was his only parent. This detail reinforces the portrayal of Susanoo as willful and obstreperous. Susanoo is portrayed in later chapters as the ancestor of the Izumo clan, one of the last to accept the "sun line's" rule; thus, this story seeks to establish Izumo's disobedient and unruly nature.

This mythic sequence portrays heaven as presided over by Amaterasu, and Amaterasu as its rightful ruler. This is one conclusion that the compilers of *Kojiki* were most concerned to assert forcefully, since later sections claim the imperial clan's descent from the sun goddess. When the sun goddess's rule is unchallenged, heaven flourishes with effective ritual, rice, weaving, and metallurgy. Without her, heaven is dark and chaotic. This tale probably had a separate existence as a story explaining that eclipses happen when the sun is hidden in a cave. As when Susanoo refused to rule the seas, when Amaterasu temporarily abandoned the mission of ruling over heaven, malevolent deities threatened, and calamities arose.

Izumo Sequence, Chapters 18–31

Once Susanoo is expelled from heaven, he travels to Izumo, and chapters 18 to 31 relate myths about him and his descendant Ōkuninushi.[23] These chapters collect the myths of this important rival to the ruling dynasty and include them in the *Kojiki* narrative, though their content is so different from the preceding and subsequent chapters that the political intent to include but subordinate is very clear. Susanoo and Ōkuninushi are culture heroes of this area, which has its own account of the creation of the land, by Ōkuninushi and a small, "stranger god" Sukunabiko, who disappeared after helping Ōkuninushi.

Susanoo finds an old couple weeping by a stream, because every year a voracious dragon comes and demands one of their daughters to eat. The dragon had eaten seven daughters, and they had only one remaining. They promised this maiden to Susanoo if he would slay the dragon, whose fearsome appearance was described like this:

> His eyes are like red ground cherries; his one body has eight heads and eight tails. On his body grow moss and cypress and cryptomeria trees. His length is such that he spans eight valleys and eight mountain peaks. If you look at his belly, you see that blood is oozing out all over it.[24]

Susanoo then had the couple brew strong drink, which the dragon came and drank, promptly falling asleep. Susanoo then slew it, cutting it to pieces. In one of the tails, he discovered the great sword of Kusanagi, which he subsequently presented to Amaterasu, symbolizing the peaceful relations between his land and hers.

Several stories recount the struggles of Ōkuninushi against his eighty elder brothers, who force him to carry their bags wherever they go. On one such journey, he encountered a weeping rabbit, who had been skinned by crocodiles. Knowing full well how much it would hurt, Ōkuninushi's brothers had told the rabbit to bathe in salt water and let the wind blow on his cracked skin. Writhing in agony, the rabbit recounted his pitiful tale to Ōkuninushi, who healed the rabbit with pollen, in a demonstration of his magical healing powers. The grateful rabbit predicted that Ōkuninushi would prevail over his cruel siblings, and that a supremely desirable woman would choose him over them. Eventually, the prophecy came true, and the rabbit was called the White Rabbit of Inaba, one of the areas eventually incorporated into Izumo.

Ōkuninushi journeyed to Ne no Katasu Kuni, where Susanoo ruled. This seems not to be another name for the underworld, Yomi, though the two share an entrance. We recall that the pass through which Izanagi had entered the underworld was also in Izumo. Ne no Katasu Kuni is unlike the tomb-like Yomi in that it has fields and is light, not dark. Ōkuninushi had fallen in love with Susanoo's daughter, Suserihime, and the two were soon married. Susanoo then made numerous attempts on his son's life, having him sleep in a chamber of snakes, centipedes, and bees. Each time, Suserihime gave Ōkuninushi a magical scarf to repel them, and he was saved. When Susanoo tried to trap Ōkuninushi by surrounding him with a ring of fire, Ōkuninushi was saved by a mouse, who showed him how to hide in a hole while the fire passed over.

These chapters contain beautiful poetry in which Ōkuninushi and his consorts express their love for each other, as in these lines spoken by Suserihime:

> My breast, alive with youth
> Soft as the light snow
> You will embrace
> With your arms
> White as a rope of taku fibers.
> We shall embrace and entwine our bodies;
> Your jewel-like hands
> Will entwine with mine.
> With your legs outstretched,
> O come, my lord, and sleep!

These myths establish a connection between Izumo and Kamimusubi no kami, one of the first invisible deities to be created. Before we encounter him in Ne no Katasu Kuni, Susanoo murders a grain goddess, Ōgetsuhime, when he discovers that the food she had offered him was actually taken from her nose, mouth, and rectum; from her corpse grew silkworms, rice seeds, millet, red beans, wheat, and soybeans. Kamimusubi had these taken and used as seeds. In other words, the murder of this grain goddess produces the original stock of seeds for the cultivation of these grains and also silkworms. This tale must have been a freestanding myth about the origins of grain and sericulture. Perhaps it was incorporated here to stress Susanoo's violent nature.[25] Kamimusubi appears again in the Izumo cycle of myth when Ōkuninushi's mother ascends to heaven to revive him after his eighty evil brothers have slain him. Kamimusubi sends two female deities to save him. Finally, Sukunabiko, who joins Ōkuninushi in solidifying the land, is revealed to be Kamimusubi's child.

The Land-Ceding Sequence, Chapters 32–37

These chapters recount how the offspring of the heavenly deities takes command of the Central Land of the Reed Plains, that is, the human world.[26] Amaterasu decrees that the land is to be ruled by her progeny. She sent two emissaries to negotiate with the earthly deities, but they failed to return. On the third attempt, Amaterasu sent two deities to confront Ōkuninushi about yielding control to her. Ōkuninushi deferred to his son, Kotoshironushi. Later known as the deity of oracles (*takusen*),

Kotoshironushi agreed to yield the land to Amaterasu's descendants. After a struggle, Ōkuninushi's second son also agreed to cede the land. Ōkuninushi agreed that rebellion would cease if a shrine were built for him: "[I]f you will worship me, making my dwelling-place like the plentiful heavenly dwelling where rules the heavenly sun-lineage of the offspring of the heavenly deities, firmly rooting the posts of the palace in the bedrock below, and raising high the crossbeams unto [heaven] itself."[27] These myths mark the decisive subordination of Izumo.

The Heavenly Descent Sequence, Chapters 38–46

With all rebellious elements subdued, Amaterasu entrusted her grandson Ninigi with the Land of the Central Reed Plains and dispatched him to descend and rule over it.[28] She had Ame no Uzume (the deity whose comic dance had earlier enticed Amaterasu out of the Heavenly Rock Cave) accompany him as a guide along the way. She entrusted Ninigi with the *magatama* beads and the mirror she had used when she hid herself in the cave, as well as the sword that Susanoo had given her, named Kusanagi. These items later became the imperial regalia. Of the mirror she said, "This mirror—have [it with you] as my spirit, and worship it just as you would worship in my very presence."[29]

Just as Ninigi is about to descend, a mysterious deity appears. Ame no Uzume went out to confront him, and learned that he was Sarutahiko, an earthly god come to serve as a guide, having heard that the scion of the heavenly deities was about to descend. He and Ame no Uzume were the earthly diety and heavenly deity ancestors of the Sarume clan.[30] Then Ninigi pushed through the clouds, descended to a mountaintop in Tsukushi (in Kyūshū), and built a palace there.

A comparison of *Kojiki*'s and *Nihon shoki*'s accounts of the land-ceding and heavenly descent narratives reveals important differences, summarized and abbreviated in Table 2.1.[31] The two versions seen in *Nihon shoki* are arranged to make it clear that the first one (referred to hereinafter as the "first version") is the "main one," while the second is introduced as "another writing," indicating the priority accorded the first one.

Comparative study has shown that Japanese versions of these tales share a general outline with North Asian and Korean myths: bearing sacred regalia and a mandate from heavenly deities, their descendant, the original ruler, descends to the top of a mountain to take possession of the earth. Those who accompany him on the descent, or who are present to swear fealty upon his arrival, are the divine ancestors of those clans privileged to serve the ruler's descendants in perpetuity.[32]

Different deities are portrayed as being in charge of the events leading to the heavenly descent. Amaterasu appears alongside Takamimusubi in *Kojiki*, but not in version one of *Nihon shoki*. In fact, Amaterasu takes no prominent role in the first version of *Nihon shoki*, though she is definitely the main Kami in charge of the second version. Historian of Shinto Mark Teeuwen has noted a tendency in *Nihon*

Table 2.1 **Comparison of *Kojiki* and *Nihon shoki* Versions of the Land-Ceding and Heavenly Descent Narratives**

Item	***Kojiki*, Philippi translation, chapters 32–39, pp. 120–41.**	***Nihon shoki* Version 1, Aston, *Nihongi*, bk.1, 64–73; NKBT 67 *Nihon shoki jō*, 134–42.**	***Nihon shoki* Version 2, Aston, *Nihongi*, bk.1, 73*ff.*; NKBT 67 *Nihon shoki jō*, 142*ff.***
Who is in charge?	Amaterasu and Takamimusubi	Takamimusubi	Amaterasu
Who is sent after the failure of the original messengers?	Takemikazuchi (chapter 35: 5; p. 129), in a Heavenly Bird Boat (referred to as a second Kami). They sit on the points of swords and interrogate Ōkuninushi.	Futsunushi, Takemikazuchi; descending to the earth, they sit on their sword points and interrogate Ōnamuchi.	Futsunushi, Takemikazuchi; they interrogate Ōnamuchi.
What implements is Ninigi given?	Magatama, sword, jewels	Takamimusubi wraps Ninigi in a coverlet.	Amaterasu gives Ninigi the mirror, sword, and jewel.
Who accompanies Ninigi in the descent?	Ame no Uzume, Sarutahiko, Ame no Koyane, Futodama, Ishikori dome, Tamanoya	No one	Ame no Uzume, Ame no Koyane, Futodama, Ishikoridome, Tamaya
What happens after the descent?	Ninigi is received by various clan-ancestor Kami, who pledge to serve him. He built a palace and began to marry the daughters of various clans, including Kono Hana Sakuya Hime.	Ninigi traveled and married Kono Hana Sakuya Hime, who bore the ancestors of the Hayato and other clans. Ninigi died and was buried in Hyūga.	Ninigi conferred the titles Lords of Sarume on Ame no Uzume and Sarutahiko, who then took up residence in Ise.

shoki, seen here, to "tone down" *Kojiki*'s solar imagery and to relegate Amaterasu to a secondary position behind Takamimusubi and Kunitokotachi.[33]

All three accounts relate imbricated stories about messengers who were sent to negotiate with the descendants of Susanoo to induce them to yield the land to the heavenly deities. In all cases they failed, leading the heavenly deities to send Takemikazuchi, god of thunder, to remonstrate with Ōkuninushi in *Kojiki*, called Ōnamuchi in *Nihon shoki*.[34] In both versions in *Nihon shoki*, but not in *Kojiki*, Futsunushi, a sword deity, accompanied Takemikazuchi; both these deities later were installed at shrines closely associated with the Fujiwara clan. *Kojiki* and the first version in *Nihon shoki* depict these messengers as displaying magical power by sitting cross-legged atop sword points as they remonstrate with the recalcitrant Ōkuninushi/Ōnamuchi, who yields after consulting with his two sons.[35]

All three versions agree that it was Ninigi, the "Heavenly Grandson," who was sent down to rule the earth. Ninigi is the son of Amaterasu's son Ame no Oshihomimi, who had been born when Amaterasu chewed up her heavenly implements in her contest with Susanoo. Ninigi's mother was the daughter of Takamimusubi. The obvious question of why Ninigi was sent instead of Oshihomimi has no satisfactory answer.

In the first *Nihon shoki* version the account of the sacred implements given to Ninigi stands out from the other versions in three respects: Amaterasu has no role in the giving; Takamimusubi alone wraps Ninigi in a coverlet. In the other two versions Ninigi receives a sword, jewels, and a mirror, but there is no mention of a coverlet. Further, *Nihon shoki*'s first version depicts Ninigi as descending to earth unaccompanied. According to *Kojiki* translator Donald Philippi, "In Korea the Heavenly Being always descends alone,"[36] suggesting a Korean derivation for this account. By contrast, both *Kojiki* and *Nihon shoki*'s second version name a list of the heavenly deities who accompany Ninigi on his descent, tabulated in Table 2.2.

Inclusion of a clan-ancestor Kami on this list was the key to prestige and ongoing favor at court. As we will see below, clans who believed that they had been deprived of rightful privileges would return to these mythic accounts to justify their claims. These accounts became a paramount source of social capital.[37]

Following the heavenly descent, chapters 41 through 46 incorporate a variety of stories that show a strong resemblance to myths found in or near Indonesia. The

Table 2.2 **Clans Descended from Kami Accompanying Ninigi**

Kami Accompanying Ninigi	Clan
Ame no Uzume	Sarume
Sarutahiko	Sarume (according to *Nihon shoki* version 2)
Ame no Koyane	Nakatomi (later called Fujiwara)
Futodama	Inbe
Ishikori dome	Mirror Maker Clan
Tamanoya	Jewel Maker Clan

genealogy connecting Ninigi to the first emperor Jinmu is woven through these stories, each of which probably existed as a separate tale. Their stories are included by *Kojiki*'s compiler, but in a subordinate position and in a form adapted to advance the narrative's central point, which is the establishment of dynastic rule under Ninigi's great-grandson, Jinmu. They exhibit a *horizontal cosmology* that is quite distinct from the vertical cosmology we examined earlier.

Chapter 41 recounts how a local chief offered Ninigi his two daughters. The chief was greatly shamed when Ninigi accepted only the younger one, Konohana Sakuyahime (Blooming Flower Maiden), who was beautiful, and rejected Iwanagahime (Narrow [or long] Rock Maiden), the ugly elder daughter. He then placed a curse on Ninigi, saying that had he chosen the "rock" (the elder daughter) he would have enjoyed immortality, but because he chose the "flower" (the younger daughter), he and his descendants would only live a short time. This story closely resembles a myth of the Indonesian culture region, in which a choice of a banana instead of a stone is advanced as the reason for the brevity of human life.

Konohana Sakuyahime became pregnant after only one night with Ninigi, raising his suspicions that she might have had relations with some earthly deity. She swore to give birth in fire to prove her innocence of the charge. She built a sealed parturition palace, closed herself up in it, and as she was about to give birth, she set fire to it. Her delivery was successful. We will consider myths of this type more closely in what follows.

Konohana Sakuyahime bore Poderi and Powori, two male deities closely associated with the sea. Chapters 42 through 45 recount a struggle between these two, in which the younger brother Powori, grandfather of Jinmu, was ultimately victorious. Each owned a lucky fishhook, an implement that embodied their fortunes in life. Powori suggested that they exchange hooks and test the result. Poderi at first refused to relinquish his hook, and when it turned out that neither of them caught fish using the other's hook, it became clear that the luck attaching to the hooks cannot be transferred to another user. Poderi was right to be reluctant; he demanded that Powori return his hook, but the younger brother had lost it. When Poderi insisted, Powori had no choice but to go in search of the hook. He traveled out to sea and then descended beneath the waves to an undersea kingdom. There he met the sea deity's daughter Toyotamahime, whom he married. At the end of three years in the undersea palace, he recalled that he was searching for the fishhook and explained his dilemma to the sea deity. The sea deity called all the fishes together, and the fishhook was discovered stuck in the throat of the sea bream. The sea deity helped Powori return to earth on a crocodile's back and subdue his elder brother by making him lose his luck and almost drowning him several times.

Toyotamahime was about to give birth, but since it would not have been proper to deliver the child of heavenly deities in the ocean, she joined Powori. She was thatching the roof of a parturition hut on the shore with cormorant feathers when she was overtaken by birth pangs. Entering the hut, she said to Powori,

> All persons of other lands, when they bear young, revert to the form of their original land and give birth. Therefore, I too am going to revert to my original form and give birth. Pray do not look upon me![38]

But Powori was overcome with curiosity and broke the taboo. Peeking into the hut, he saw that his wife had turned into a giant crocodile and was "crawling and slithering about." He ran away in shock. Toyotamahime was so shamed by being seen in her true form as a giant reptile that she left the child behind and went back to the sea, saying, "I had always intended to go back and forth across the pathways of the sea; however, now that my form has been seen, I am exceedingly shamed. Then, closing the sea border, she went back into the sea."[39] The son of the child she left behind was Jinmu.

In the horizontal cosmology of these stories, there is a division between the human world and an undersea kingdom ruled over by a sea deity who lives in an underwater palace, reached by traveling out to sea. Up to the point of Toyotamahime's return to the ocean, it had been possible for land-dwellers to travel back and forth, but after she closed the way between the two realms, two-way passage became impossible. Thus the *Kojiki* encompasses both a vertical and a horizontal cosmology, based on the incorporation of peoples from two different culture areas, some from North Asia where the vertical model originated, and some from Southeast Asia where the horizontal form prevailed.

The *Kojiki* and *Nihon shoki* are inexhaustible sources for religious ideas in ancient Japan and its shared cultural sphere extending beyond the islands. In addition, these texts also can be examined for what they reflect of ancient society. In what follows, I have chosen a single example out of many possibilities in order to begin a discussion of the dichotomy of private versus the public at this early time.

Interpreting Ancient Japanese Myth in Terms of the Public and the Private

Shōtoku Taishi (who may or may not have been an historical personage) famously expressed Chinese thinking about the public and the private in his 604 "Constitution."

> *Article 15*: To subordinate private interests to the public good—that is the path of a vassal. Now if a man is influenced by private motives, he will be resentful, and if he is influenced by resentment he will fail to act harmoniously with others. If he fails to act harmoniously with others,

> the public interest will suffer. Resentment interferes with order and is subversive of law.[40]

The public is presented as the sphere of broad, collective interest, while the private refers to the narrow concerns of the individual or some limited group. The implication is that government officials (the "vassals") should put aside their personal or familial interests in favor of service to the greater good, the public. This Chinese framework of thought has been tremendously influential throughout Japanese history, though Japanese thought developed distinctive interpretations.

The "public" is rendered with this character: 公 (*kō, ōyake, kimi,* and other readings) and the "private" with 私 (*shi* and other readings). Both characters have been given different pronunciations and different nuances at different times. For example, the character 私 as it appears in the mythic compilations can mean "secret" or "hidden," though these meanings have dropped out in contemporary usage. Likewise, the most common use of 私 today is as a personal pronoun, meaning "I," but that usage did not arise until the medieval period and is not found in texts before that time.[41] Both characters can be used in combination with others, producing compounds of meaning and sound. For example, a variety of ancient texts refer to 公民 (*kōmin*), combining the character for "public" with that for "people," in the sense of "the people," members of some collectivity. Much academic debate surrounds the question of the exact meaning of *kōmin* and related terms. Does it mean all the people, or only those in service to the Great King—that is, government officials? While that question is still debated, it is clear that 公 is associated with officialdom, while 私 is associated with those outside government, those people who are to be governed by the officials.[42]

The Taika Reforms spelled drastic changes for the provincial clans. Deprived of their land and their weapons, and also made subject to a new system of taxation and land distribution, their status plummeted. They were no longer allowed to conduct burials in a style rivaling Yamato rulers. Yet the sun line was allied to these clans by complex marriage ties and had depended on them for most aspects of provincial rule. While the clans could be subordinated, they could not be banished altogether.

That it was not a simple matter to disengage from old customs and initiate new relationships with the clans can be seen in several myths of the *Kojiki* and *Nihon shoki* that use the language of 公 and 私. In the two works there are four appearances of the term 私.[43] They occur in myths of birth in fire or in secret, and we have already examined one example, the myth of Powori and Toyotamahime. The character 私 is pronounced *hisoka* in these cases, meaning "in secret." All four texts concern a male Kami who marries a female Kami, who becomes pregnant after a single night. When the male expresses doubt that he is the father, the female either gives birth in fire to prove that he is the father or, like Toyotamahime, reverts to a bestial form to give birth, making a parturition hut to hide herself from view and charging her husband not to look inside under any circumstances. It goes without saying that the male Kami can never resist the temptation to look. After giving birth, she leaves the child with the husband and withdraws.

In the seventh century, marriage patterns were in flux. Some marriages were uxorilocal, which is to say that the woman remained with her natal family after the marriage. The man would come to her there, retaining a separate residence for himself. After some years, the couple might set up an independent dwelling of their own. But such unions were not always exclusive, giving rise to questions about paternity. The children of these marriages were generally raised by the mother, but they were also claimed by the husband's kin, creating a bilateral tendency in the system of kinship.

According to Yoshie Akiko, the eighth century represented a turning point in marriage patterns. Patriarchal society had not yet displaced the earlier fluidity, but the higher levels of society were already beginning to change. We can see the beginnings of the patriarchalism that would eventually result in the ejection of women from the public sphere and from state ritual. Thereafter in marriage and in relations between families, women's position changed. Familial relations took on a much more political character in the process of the consolidation of national control, so that men monopolized positions in the bureaucracy and women were gradually excluded.[44]

The myths of giving birth in fire or in secret held particular significance. Because princes formed multiple marriages with different clans, and because the women involved might also have had multiple partners, the social system created questions of legitimate succession in the royal line. So long as the mother's kin had a claim to any children who might become the heir to the throne, they were in a position to challenge the imperial clan. But in the myths, the female Kami's leaving the child behind effectively terminates her "private" claim (and her family's) to the child. The mother's renunciation of the child provides a kind of resolution to the problems that the social system posed for the imperial clan, suggesting that these particular myths presented the imperial perspective and their image of themselves as embodying "the public." Indeed, one ancient reading of the character 公 is *kimi,* meaning "lord" or "the lord."

Another relevant tale recounts events during the reign of Suinin. His consort Sahohime had a half brother named Sahohiko, born of the same mother. Sahohiko plotted against Suinin and tried to recruit his sister Sahohime to betray Suinin. Sahohime could not bear the thought that Suinin would be killed, so she told him about the plot. But neither could she renounce her brother, so she went to join Sahohiko, to share his fate. The king surrounded Sahohiko's castle, with Sahohime inside. At just that time Sahohime was about to give birth. She begged Suinin to recognize the child as his heir. But the king's soldiers set fire to the castle, and Sahohime gave birth inside it as it burned. The child was saved to be raised by the king, but Sahohime and Sahohiko both perished.[45]

The resemblance of this story to myths of giving birth in fire is unmistakable. In this case the woman gives birth in a barricaded castle rather than a parturition hut, but the result is the same: the woman leaves the child behind for the man to raise, conveniently dying alongside her treacherous brother. This story clarifies what the dynasty feared from the clans: challenges to their authority and plots against them based on marriage ties.[46]

The Taika Reforms tried to put the provincial clans on equal footing in terms of their relation to the imperial line. If all of them had the same odds of producing potential heirs to the throne, they would have a stake in orderly succession to the throne. In other words, they would develop a commitment to 公, in the senses of both "the lord" and "the public," a collectivity that included many like themselves. The collectivity would transcend the 私 "private" or "secret" interests that they all had. It would be in their interest to see that all eligible clans were maintained on an even level in relation to the imperial clan.

If this interpretation of myths of giving birth in fire or "in secret" can be sustained, then we see how myth can be interpreted in the context of seventh-century society and politics. For our purposes in the present study, the appearance in myth of the public and the private is a signal development. We can regard the myths examined here as exploring the dynamic between the public and the private through narratives about the Kami. We note that in all cases, the male is associated with the public and the female with the private. The public-private dichotomy conveys a conception of gender in which the feminine is lesser and the female must renounce her children and her kin's claims in favor of the higher good represented by the male and the public. Since these messages are conveyed through narratives about the Kami, Kami concepts absorb these ideas about the gendered character of public and private.

Comparing *Kojiki* and *Nihon shoki*

Many questions about the relation between these two texts remain unanswered, including why *Nihon shoki* should have been compiled so soon after *Kojiki*, and why *Kojiki* was virtually ignored for so long. The two can be compared from many different perspectives, but the most important task for the present work is to understand their differing contributions to Shinto. It seems highly significant that *Kojiki*, unlike *Nihon shoki*, entirely omits any references to Buddhism, while *Nihon shoki* is replete with detailed discussions of it. Both works aim to establish the descent of the imperial clan from Amaterasu Ōmikami and the Kami's mandate that the clan should rule for all eternity. How should we understand the relation between these two works? Let us begin by noting that they were by no means the only mythic compilations of the period.

Sendai kuji hongi (often referred to as *Kujiki*), and *Kogoshūi*, believed to have been compiled by the Mononobe and Imibe (or Inbe) clans, respectively, contained material overlapping with *Kojiki* and *Nihon shoki*, but arranged to highlight each clan's divine origins and contributions to the imperial clan. For example, *Sendai kuji hongi,* which until the Edo period rivaled *Nihon shoki* in the high regard in which it was held, portrays a union between Amaterasu Ōmikami and Takamimusubi no Kami that produced a son, Osiho Mimi (or Masaka Akatu). Osiho Mimi had two sons, named Nigi Hayahi and Ninigi. In other words, while Ninigi is the sole grandchild of Amaterasu Ōmikami recognized in *Kojiki* and *Nihon shoki, Sendai kuji hongi* portrays Amaterasu as the wife of Takamimusubi, and as having not one grandchild, but two.

Nigi Hayahi is heir to the goddess' shamanic powers. She gives him medicines, magical formulae, and powerful emblems: a Mirror of the Ocean, a Mirror of the Shore, a Sword of great length, a Jewel of Life, a Jewel of Resurrection, a Jewel of the Foot, a Jewel of Return, a Ceremonial Cloth of the Serpent, a Ceremonial Cloth of the Bee, and a Ceremonial Cloth of Various Things. Upon imparting these magical implements to Nigi Hayahi, Amaterasu said to him, "If some part of the body is in pain, take these ten symbols and utter these words, 'hito, huta, mi, yo, itu, mu, nana, ya, kokono, tō.'" This formula counts the numbers one to ten; in other words, when in trouble he should grasp his regalia and count from one to ten.

While Ninigi descends to Kyūshū and then advances to Yamato by conquering the peoples in his path, Nigi Hayahi descends directly to Yamato. The Mononobe are prominent among Nigi Hayahi's attendants as he descends from Heaven in the Heavenly Rock Boat, flying in the sky until he reaches the Ikaruga Peak, gradually moving to Yamato. He takes a wife but dies before the child is born. His grandfather Takamimusubi has the body brought back to heaven, where it is buried, first in a temporary place and then permanently.[47]

The reputation of *Sendai kuji hongi* was ruined when Tokugawa Mitsukuni (1628–1700) judged it to be a forgery in the early Edo period. Motoori Norinaga accepted Mitsukuni's judgment. Both viewed the text as a glorification of the Mononobe, because that family's genealogy is laid out in such detail that it takes up half a chapter. Motoori was appalled by the idea of Ninigi having an elder brother and could not accept that Nigi Hayahi was a descendant of Amaterasu.[48]

Kogoshūi (807) by Inbe Hironari (dates uncertain) is regarded as containing significant material not included in *Nihon shoki,* but because its principle aim is to raise the fortunes of the Inbe family, its descriptions of that family's accomplishments are magnified. The text sets out the origins of Kami rituals at court, based on its account of the cooperation of the ancestors of the Nakatomi, Inbe, and Sarume families in enticing Amaterasu Ōmikami from the cave where she had fled after Susanoo's depredations. The text asserts that Ame no Koyane, Futotama, and Ame no Uzume, ancestral Kami respectively to the Nakatomi, Inbe, and Sarume clans, were equally essential to the desired restoration of light to the world. In spite of this harmonious beginning, however, the court ceased to show respect for the Inbe. The author expressed deep disappointment with the poor treatment of his family and called on the court to remedy the situation.[49]

Another rich source of myth are the works known as *fudoki*, "records of wind and water." A government order of 713 required each province to compile a record of its products, the quality of land in each settlement, the origins of the names of mountains and rivers, and distinctive tales. Most of the *fudoki* were compiled by around 750, but only a few are extant today, the ones from Izumo, Harima, Hizen, Hitachi, and Bungo provinces.[50]

While these works contain some of the same material related in *Kojiki* or *Nihon shoki*, they also relate purely local tales. For example, *Hitachi no Kuni Fudoki* tells how local people subdued an evil crowd of horned serpent deities. It also describes why the Kashima deity, the province's main deity, was sent down from heaven:

> The local people say that when at first Toyo Ashiwara no Mizuho no Kuni [i.e., the human world] was entrusted [to the Kashima deity], the unruly deities as well as the rocks on the ground, the standing trees, and even the single blades of grass uttered words, during the day making clamorous noise like flies in summer, and at night making the land bright as flames. For this reason the great deity was sent down from Heaven to subjugate the land.[51]

Like *Kojiki*, the *fudoki* of Hitachi Province posits an ancient time when many things in the natural world could speak. Silencing them was regarded as a step toward making a place fit for human habitation.

Izumo Fudoki contains a great deal of highly distinctive material, for example, this passage:

> Once again [the God Omidzunu] said mightily, "As I gaze toward the cape of Tsutsu in Koshi, in my search for spare land, I see more land to be spared." He grasped the wide spade shaped like a maiden's chest, thrust it into the land as though he plunged it into the gill of a large fish, and broke off a piece. Then he tied a three-ply rope around the land and began to pull it. He pulled the rope as if [he were] reeling in [a fishing line]. It looked like a huge riverboat [being] pulled by his mighty power. This additional land is the cape of Miho. The rope used to pull the land is the Isle of Yomi. The stake to which the rope was firmly tied is Mt. Fire God in the province of Hahaki.[52]

This myth tells how the Izumo Kami Ōmononushi, referred to here by one of his several other names, spied land across the sea in Korea and hauled it to his territory, where he attached it to Izumo. Anders Carlqvist has recently analyzed this story as an attempt by Izumo to increase its autonomy vis-à-vis the central government.[53]

Let us compare the way *Kojiki* and *Nihon shoki* were recorded. The two works were compiled using different techniques of adapting Chinese characters to the Japanese language, described in *The Encyclopedia of Shinto* as follows:

> There were many difficulties in recording an oral tradition preserving the Yamato (native Japanese) vocabulary, without losing the *kotodama* (the spirit power of the word) inherent in the lexicon of the myths when converting these words to [Chinese characters], a foreign orthography. In order to overcome this difficulty, *Kojiki* is written in a hybrid script, fusing the use of a Chinese graph for its phonetic value with the use of a graph for its semantic value. When recording song, the former (phonetic script) is used, while the latter forms the basis of prose, with phonetic script mixed in—this was an attempt to preserve the orality of the spoken traditions of mythology. To those courtiers well-versed in Chinese at the time, *Kojiki* was certainly much more difficult to read than *Nihon shoki*, but rather than being compiled for a wide readership, *Kojiki* was compiled to preserve the language of the myths, so the court did not consider the difficulty of reading the text a problem.... And regardless that Emperor Genmei, to whom *Kojiki* was presented, was a fervid believer in Buddhism, *Kojiki* consciously refrains from making any mention of Buddhism. These characteristics show that *Kojiki* is grounded in the timeless and repetitive world of mythology, and because of this it originated from a "closed" and self-contained structure of myth-history.[54]

The content of the *Nihon shoki* is far more voluminous than in *Kojiki*. *Nihon shoki* contains multiple variants of many narratives, whereas *Kojiki* presents only a single version. Sometimes the accounts of significant events differ completely between the two works, as we saw in the Cosmogony and Heavenly Descent Sequences.

Although *Nihon shoki* contains a great deal of mythic material that overlaps with and supplements material found in *Kojiki*, *Nihon shoki* is much more concerned with presenting the country in terms that would be recognized as dynastic history. In fact, it was the first of six official projects of dynastic histories.[55] But whereas it was regarded as "history," *Kojiki* was not. Although *Nihon shoki* was modeled on Chinese chronological records, it rejected the Chinese term for Japan, *Wa*, substituting the term *Nihon*, "sun-origin," or the place where the sun rises. *Nihon shoki* is much more preoccupied than *Kojiki* with presenting Japan to those outside the country in historical terms. While the chronology of *Kojiki* is often unclear, and sometimes goes back and forth, *Nihon shoki* strictly adheres to a precise chronology. It is written in classical Chinese. The compilers dated Jinmu's enthronement as occurring in 660 BCE. With this as the starting point, they presented a timeline leading back to the creation and forward to the reign of Jitō, ending in 697. It took a further twenty-three years to complete the work. *Nihon shoki* presents the country's administrative structure and its foreign diplomacy with the Asian continent, such as missions to China and the Korean kingdoms, and comments extensively on the introduction of Chinese culture and Buddhism.

We can regard these two works as adopting opposite positions toward Japan's situation in Northeast Asia in the late seventh century. Having suffered a great defeat by China and its ally Silla in the late seventh century, Japan arguably needed to present itself as a formidable country led by a mighty dynasty, unified under a strong government, and capable of dealing constructively with foreign countries. The national histories, including *Nihon shoki,* accept the need to communicate in Chinese and to adopt the strictly chronological framework expected, based on prior Chinese works. The preface of *Nihon shoki* even opens by listing the written sources on which it is based. *Nihon shoki* seeks to engage an external audience by adopting the language and written format accepted in the Chinese cultural sphere. By contrast, *Kojiki* adopted an idiosyncratic orthography, ignored conventional expectations, and proceeded as if Japan were alone in the cosmos.

Kojiki seems to represent a defiant assertion of the indigenous, rejecting classical Chinese in favor of a mixed script, and ignoring Japan's history of absorbing continental influence. The "indigenous" is constructed through extensive discussion of the Kami and their rites, emphasis on Japanese sovereigns as if they were the only ones in the world, and by expunging the record of contact with other countries and religions. In effect, the indigenous becomes an idealized portrait of Japan as the center of its own universe, communing with the Kami through the mediation of a divinely descended emperor, assisted by officials who specialize in ritual.

Although the paucity of extant sources regarding the differing motivations in the background of *Kojiki* and *Nihon shoki* prevents us from reaching firm conclusions, Mitani Eiichi has asserted a persuasive interpretation. Mitani believes that *Kojiki* was compiled with significant influence from the Jingikan. The overriding circumstance pointing to Jingikan involvement is the absence of any reference to Buddhism. Who, Mitani asks, had a vested interest in portraying Japan as a land from which Buddhism is absent? The Jingikan, is his answer. The Nakatomi, Inbe, Sarume, and Urabe families held positions in the Jingikan, but the Nakatomi were by far the most powerful. Mitani points to stories in *Kojiki* that present the origins of prayers and other features of ritual, noting that such elements are not much addressed in *Nihon shoki.* Mitani also sees strong support in *Kojiki,* but not in *Nihon shoki,* for the ritual roles performed by women, which leads him to propose that palace women, including Empress Jitō and her female attendants, also exerted influence over the work's final form. Mitani's point can perhaps never be proven entirely, but his thesis of strong Jingikan involvement makes sense of this greatest difference between *Kojiki* and *Nihon shoki.*[56]

Another major difference in the content of the two works lies in *Kojiki's* inclusion of much more material on Izumo than *Nihon shoki,* a point that Miura Sukeyuki has explored at length. According to Miura's calculation, around

40 percent of *Kojiki* is devoted to tales about Izumo. While *Nihon shoki* includes the story about Susanoo slaying a creature in whose tail he finds the Kusanagi sword, the creature is described merely as a "big snake," while the *Kojiki* magnifies it as a "great monster of Koshi," enhancing Susanoo's heroism in killing it. In *Kojiki*'s rendition, Susanoo arrives in Izumo having slain a grain goddess and thus possessing the seeds needed to create a new order of plenty, which he brings about after dispatching the monster.[57] Further, *Nihon shoki* omits most of the tales concerning the adventures of Ōnamuchi/Ōkuninushi, the sixth-generation descendant of Susanoo.[58]

Examining the later history of the two texts makes clear that the "internationalist" perspective represented by *Nihon shoki* won out over the nativism of *Kojiki*. *Kojiki* was superseded by *Nihon shoki*, which appeared a mere eight years later. Not only that, *Kojiki* received little attention for almost a millennium. Knowledge of how to read *Kojiki*'s idiosyncratic mixture of Chinese and phonetic script was lost until the eighteenth century. By contrast, *Nihon shoki* was highly regarded, and lectures on it were held at court until the late tenth century. These lectures included banquets and poetry composition. Urabe Kanekata compiled these proceedings in 1274, in a work called *Shaku nihongi*. In the medieval period *Nihon shoki* was interpreted according to the paradigms of esoteric Buddhism. When Motoori Norinaga's scholarship enabled his contemporaries to read *Kojiki*, the text came to be regarded as a classic of Shinto thought and has retained that status down to the present.[59]

Conclusion

The compilation of myth by the court and at least two major clans, as well as the collection of tales by the provinces in response to government order, was made possible by the growing unification of the country following the Taika Reforms. Japan's official compilations of myth and history codified the status of the dynasty as divine rulers charged to rule by heavenly deities. This message was directed not only to the other clans within Japan, but, at least in the case of *Nihon shoki*, also to the foreign powers that had soundly defeated Japan in its alliance with Paekche, that is, T'ang China and the Silla Kingdom in Korea. These works projected an image of Japan as unified and strong, not as a small, weak country that could easily be conquered.

Kojiki stands out for its nativist projection of the country as if it had never been involved with any outside power, and as if Buddhism had not already become one of two ritual traditions recognized by the court and massively subsidized by it. Indeed, the work presents the imperial clan as if it never had anything to do with Buddhism. *Kojiki*'s pride in the Kami and the ritual style in which they were worshipped upholds the clans that had become associated with the performance of Kami worship.

We see here the basic units of a conception of "the indigenous": the Kami, a ruler authorized by them, and a corps dedicated to performing Kami rituals. The indigenous in *Kojiki* could be projected as a coherent image only by erasing the historical reality of Japan's equally long and deep involvement with the foreign. We will see in the next chapter how Kami worship comes to be seen as belonging to "the public," setting the stage for the conceptualization of Shinto as representing the indigenous tradition as part of the public, as an essential element of governing the realm.

3

The Coalescence of Early Shinto

Introduction

This chapter examines Shinto during the Nara period (710–794) and the early Heian period (794–1185), addressing the Jingikan's influence over provincial shrines. Several large-scale rituals of state were especially important: the harvest festival (Niinamesai), enthronement ritual (Daijōsai), and imperial mortuary ritual. The chapter also discusses the Bureau of the Consecrated Imperial Princess (the *saiō*) and the Vicennial Renewal of the Ise Shrines. Later sections address uneasy relations between the Kami and emperors, the incorporation of Buddhist New Year's rites into the palace ritual, combinations of temples and shrines, and the Dōkyō Incident. Lastly, we examine portrayals of the Kami in early Buddhist tales called *setsuwa*.

The Jingikan and Shrine Priests

Ritual coordination by the Jingikan put the provincial shrines on a completely different basis than before. In the pre-Ritsuryō practice of independent, clan-based Kami worship, the clans had complete control of the worship of their deities, linked to the understanding that it was not possible or meaningful to worship Kami other than one's own. But because acceptance of the designation of Official Shrine implied that the provincial shrines would participate in the worship of the Kami upheld in the Jingikan, including those of the imperial family, the concept holding it meaningless to worship the deities of another kin group had to shift. The provinces were now symbolically united in a new way with the court, and their worship of the imperial deities could be construed as a form of symbolic submission to it. Acquiring rank within this system appeared to do great honor to the Official Shrines by the presentation of imperial tribute, but at the same time it subordinated them to imperial authority by incorporating them into a hierarchy that they had no role in defining. The ideal of rites coordinated throughout the realm depended on the center's ability to tax the provinces and extract their resources, ostensibly for use as "offerings" in the rites themselves. The provinces indicated their submission to the authority of the court by supplying those offerings and accepting imperial tribute.[1]

While the Jingikan was principally concerned that Jingiryō ritual be correctly observed, priests who were not a part of that system were focused on the traditions of their particular shrines, performing rites to ensure the prosperity and well-being of the communities around them. This dynamic of central structuring and local autonomy made for a layered quality of ritual life and priestly perspective. The differences between Official Shrines and priests and those who were not grew to immense symbolic significance.[2]

Niinamesai

More clearly than any other rites, the Niinamesai and Daijōsai illustrate the connection between the Kami and the emperor, excluding reference to Buddhism in any form. Notwithstanding this, the emperor and his court also performed many Buddhist rites from ancient times until the late nineteenth century.

Niinamesai, the New Food Festival of the eleventh month, was first standardized in the tenth-century *Engi shiki*, but it is thought to be more ancient. It is paired with Kinensai, held in the second month. While Kinensai's purpose is to pray for bounteous crops, Niinamesai's purpose is to give thanks for a good harvest. The emperor personally offers new rice, the first fruits, to the imperial ancestors and the deities of heaven and earth by making offerings of steamed rice, rice porridge, and sake. He makes these offerings before the altars for the Sun Goddess and the Kami of heaven and earth in the Shinkaden (a ritual hall within the palace) at dusk, and, following purifications and a change of garments, again at dawn on the following day. During the Ritsuryō era, the day following the ceremony was devoted to gift giving and feasting. A group of four dancers called Gosechi dancers, composed of two daughters of noble families and two daughters from the provincial officials' families, performed. The emperor's gifts to his ministers and provincial officials tacitly underlined their subordination to him.[3] Niinamesai serves as a prototype for many other shrine rituals. The format is that of a host inviting divine guests to share a meal. The "guests" are the Kami, of course, and the "entertainment" offered to them includes food and drink as well as prayers of praise and thanks. The "host," the emperor, acts as priest on behalf of the realm as a whole, qualified for this role by his descent from the Kami.

Enthronement Rites

The rites transforming the heir to the throne from designated successor to the new emperor are divided into two parts: accession (divided into Senso and Sokui) and succession (the Daijōsai). While enthronement rites are patterned on Niinamesai, their function is not to give thanks for the harvest but to transform the emperor into a living deity.[4]

Accession

In the Senso ritual the new emperor receives the imperial regalia, and the Sokui rite publicly proclaims that a new emperor has acceded to the throne. From the time of Empress Jitō through premodern times, the new emperor received the regalia from his or her ministers before a limited audience of high-ranking courtiers, but the timing for transmission of the regalia, as well as the particular items entrusted to the emperor, have varied. Also, in addition to the sword-jewel-mirror regalia, at some point it became customary to transmit official seals, following the Chinese custom. The seal is set to official documents to certify imperial approval or authorship. In the Senso rite, a proclamation by the previous emperor bequeathing rulership to the successor was read. A few days later, the Sokui rite was held before a much larger audience. As of the eighth or ninth century, the new emperor ascended to a throne on an elevated stage wearing ritual headgear and robes patterned on the Chinese practice, and the accession was announced throughout the land. The use of an octagonal, canopied throne dates from the Heian period, and in modern times the empress appears in enthronement rites alongside the emperor.[5]

The rites of enthronement represent an enlarged and more elaborate version of Niinamesai, lasting four days. Also performed in the eleventh month, the core of this ritual is a presentation of the first rice of the new harvest. It is performed only once in any emperor's reign, and in the year that the Daijōsai is held, no Niinamesai is held. Up until the eighth century, the Niinamesai and the Daijōsai were not always strictly separated, and the provision that the Daijōsai would be performed only once in an emperor's reign had not yet been established.[6]

The Daijōsai, Great New Food Festival, is composed of many purifications, offerings, and ceremonies. At the core is a meal prepared from the first fruits of the harvest, shared between the emperor and the heavenly deities. Extensive preparations lasting several months, including specially prepared rice, sake, and other foodstuffs in great quantities, are required, as well as many preparatory ritual observances. Communing with the deities in this way symbolically imbues the emperor with the power of the Kami as a living god. Enthronement rites communicate the emperor's transcendent status based upon a cosmological role of mediator between the human and divine worlds, descendant of the gods, uniquely unified with them. The ceremonies culminate with two days of feasting among the members of the court, when the emperor confers new ranks and titles upon them.

According to *Kojiki* myth, Emperor Jinmu originally observed the Niinamesai in his fourth year on the throne, 660 BCE. The ceremony was mandated by the *Jingiryō, Jōgan gishiki*, and the *Engi shiki*. The Daijōsai has been carried out for each of the historical sovereigns, except for a hiatus from 1466 to 1687. It is thus one of the world's oldest coronation rituals. But while its early codification makes it feasible to replicate ancient precedent accurately, the scale of the rites declined with the end of direct imperial rule, and the court frequently found it difficult to conduct even a modest version of the ceremonies.[7]

Imperial emissaries (chosen by divination) were dispatched to the various shrines with elaborate offerings to inform the Kami of the upcoming Daijōsai. Offerings were presented at several points in the lead-up to the enthronement itself. Because everything used for the Daijōsai had to be new, unsullied by prior mundane uses, a vast array of utensils, tools, clothing, and furnishings had to be produced. Extensive construction of buildings was also necessary. Everything created for the enthronement rites had to be disposed of afterward, so that nothing used in this most sacred rite would ever be tainted by ordinary use. Thus all the buildings were razed.

The fields selected to produce the rice used in the ceremony were chosen by Jingikan divination, and the fields themselves were called Yuki and Suki, believed to mean "pure and consecrated "(*yuki*) food offerings, and "next" or "succeeding" (*suki*). The fields were usually located to the East and West of the capital. Jingikan officials purified the fields and supervised the growing of the rice. A person titled "Lord (or Lady) of the Rice-Ears," was appointed to observe the crop ripening, and various lesser functionaries were also appointed. Shrine compounds for the eight deities who protect the emperor were constructed at these fields in the eighth month, along with auxiliary administrative buildings. The *Engi shiki* provides detailed specifications for the materials (various kinds of cloth, rice, sake, salt, seafood, etc.) to be used in offerings to the eight deities and the robes to be worn by the officiants.

The Jingikan officials presided over the ritual harvesting of the rice, and the provincial governors, district prefects, and other administrators all participated. Thereafter, the harvested rice was gathered into the shrine compounds for the eight deities and transported near the end of the ninth month from there to the capital in a stately procession led by the Lord or Lady of the Rice-Ears. Two unmarried daughters of the prefects of the Yuki and Suki districts were appointed *sakatsuko,* to brew black and white sake from the rice. Black sake is opaque, made by adding ashes to unstrained sake, while white sake is clear. These women were chosen by divination and assisted by others who were specially chosen for the task.

The emperor began preparatory abstinences during the tenth month, and his officials also began to observe taboos. Meanwhile, the mountain areas where the timbers required for the ceremonial buildings would be cut were selected by divination, and the place where the buildings would be set up was prepared. With great ceremony and under the watchful gaze of Jingikan officials, the provincial governors, and lesser officials, the necessary trees were cut and transported to the capital in a procession.

Chinkonsai

The first stage of the enthronement rites proper is Chinkonsai, held in the palace on the first of the four days, a ceremony to prevent the emperor's soul from leaving his body, literally, to "pacify the soul" of the new emperor. The emperor's robe, regarded as a symbol of his person, and a box called the "soul box" (*mitama hako*) were placed upon a table by a male officiant. At the same time, a female ritualist stood upon an overturned rectangular wooden box, holding a stalk of bells and a black lacquered halberd wrapped with vine. As the male officiant tied each of ten knots in a white cord binding the soul box, the female struck her overturned box with the halberd. This is believed to recapitulate the dance of Amenouzume when Amaterasu was enticed out of the Heavenly Rock Cave. Next, the male ritualist shook the emperor's robe ten times to the right and ten times to the left to imbue him with new vitality.

Spirit calming is based on ancient beliefs about the soul or spirit that it could separate from the body and wander away, and that the soul served as a person's guardian spirit. To calm the spirit and fix it within the body is the object of this rite. Besides the enthronement ceremony, spirit calming was also performed annually in the eleventh month for the emperor, empress, and the crown prince. Shinto thought identifies four aspects of the soul or spirit (*mitama* or *tamashii*). The "rough spirit" (*ara-mitama*) refers to action, courage, and initiative, the active side of life, while the "soft spirit" (*nigi-mitama*) refers to benign, gentle, or passive qualities. The "soft spirit" can be divided into two facets, the "joyous spirit" (*saki-mitama*) and the "wondrous spirit" (*kushi-mitama*). The "joyous spirit" is the contentment or happiness arising from gathering sustenance, while the "wondrous spirit" refers to the intellect, health, and the power to overcome illness.

Ceremonies of the Enthronement Palace

Enthronement ceremonies are held in an enclosed area called the Enthronement Palace (Daijōkyū or Daijōgū), entered through a shrine gate (*torii*), that marks it as sacred space. The location of the Enthronement Palace changed frequently. During the eighth century, enthronement palaces were erected in a variety of locations within the city of Nara.[8] Likewise, after the capital was transferred to Kyoto in 798, the enthronement palace would be set up in front of the palace building called the Daigokuden, with other sites established within the city, allowing the populace to see the processions and other ritual.[9] The main buildings are two virtually identical halls enclosed by brushwood fences, with gates on each side, and such auxiliary constructions as a bathhouse; two wells and several board shelters with thatched roofs for the serving personnel, the sake, offerings, cooks, and utensils. (See Figure 3.1.) The two halls were called the Yuki and Suki Halls, identical in their construction save for the angle on which the projecting roof beams are cut, horizontally in the case of the Yuki Hall and vertically in the case of the Suki Hall. The significance of

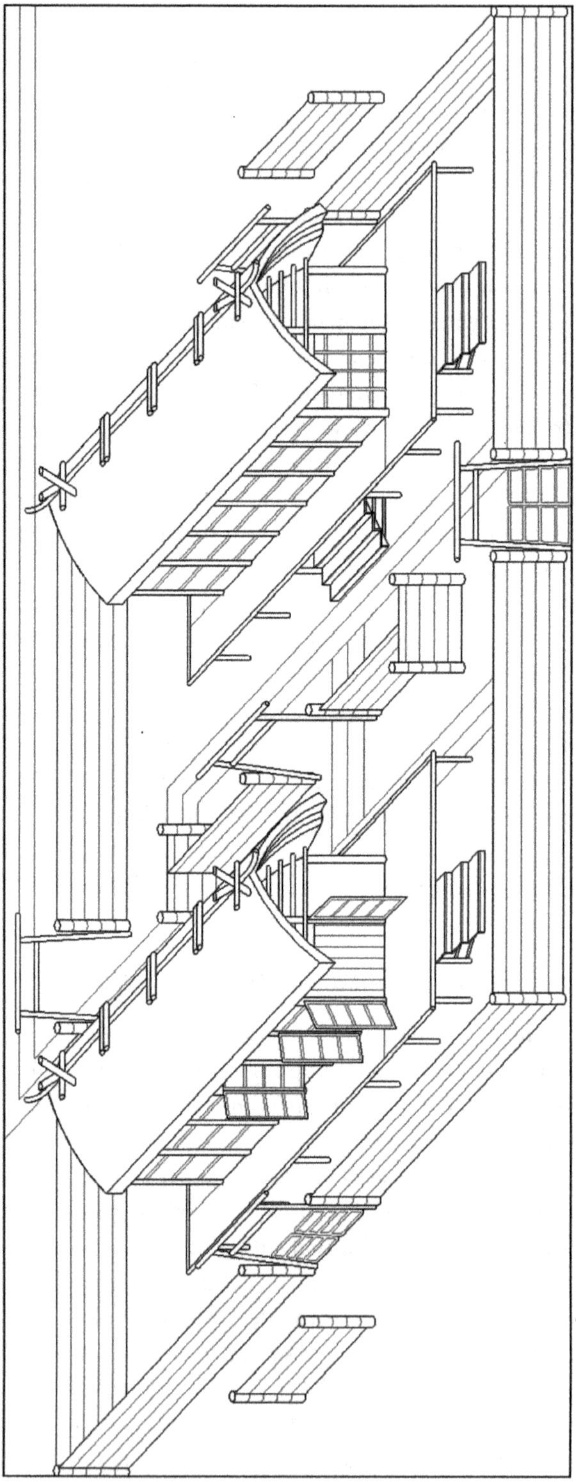

Figure 3.1 The Enthronement Palace (Daijōgū). Source: Bock, *Engi-Shiki*, 2:49. Reprinted by permission of *Monumenta Nipponica*, Sophia University, Tokyo, Japan.

this difference is not explained by extant texts, but it is found also at the Ise Inner and Outer Shrines, where it is believed to signal a difference in the gender of the Kami enshrined, female in the case of the horizontal and male in the case of the vertical. The two halls were constructed of unpeeled pine logs, with cypress beams, and thatched with fresh green miscanthus. The Yuki and Suki Halls were each composed of an inner and outer compound, the outer for the preparation of food and the inner for the use of the emperor to commune with the Kami. No metal is used in the construction.

Inside, the two halls are identically furnished with straw matting on the walls, floors, and ceilings, and in the inner compound white-edged *tatami* mats are laid out with a triangular pillow. The *tatami* mats form a bed called the "god seat" (*shinza*). Seven mats are laid out on top of each other in a complex manner, so that the lowest three (which are longer than the others) project out at the bottom (or North), forming a small platform for a pair of purple slippers. The second layer of two mats projects to the right (or East), forming a ledge for a comb and fan. The top layer of two *tatami* mats has the triangular pillow at the South end, and over both the pillow and the top mat are laid eight layers of reed matting, and above that, a white silk coverlet, called *ofusuma*. See Figure 3.2. In the same chamber are arranged baskets of soft and rough cloth on a table, as well as black and white lamps, each set on an eight-legged table.

The ceremonies of the Ḍaijōkyū are held on the night of the second day, continuing into the morning of the third. After the emperor takes a purifying bath, he dons a white silk robe and processes into the Yuki Hall. With each step, the mat on which he is walking is rolled forward so that he may pass, while behind him it is rolled up so that no one else treads on it. An umbrella is held above his head, and the sword and jewels of the imperial regalia are carried before him. He pauses in the outer compound to listen to music, played while the ceremonial meal is laid out. The meal is presented in unglazed red earthenware dishes by ten *uneme*, young women chosen for their beauty to be the sovereign's personal servants. The meal includes

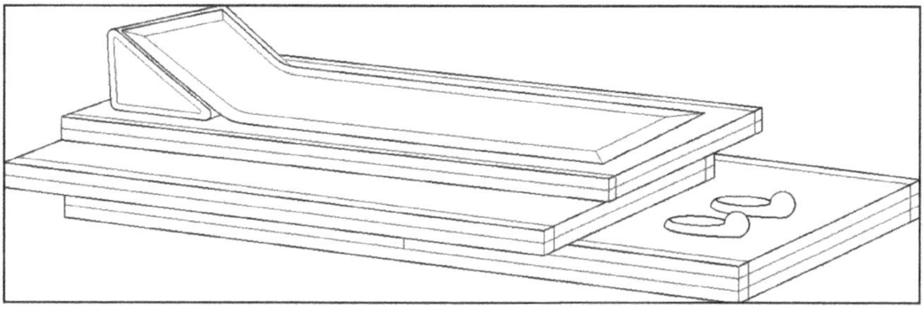

Figure 3.2 The Shinza. Source: Carmen Blacker, "The *Shinza* in the *Daijōsai:* Throne, Bed, or Incubation Couch?" *JJRS* 17, no. 2/3 (1990): 184. Reprinted by permission of *Japanese Journal of Religious Studies*.

steamed rice and millet, boiled rice and millet, abalone broth, seaweed broth, fresh and dried fish, fruit, and two kinds of sake. Five chefs are also present, as are sake brewers, a diviner, water carriers, and a small number of lesser functionaries, as well as Jingikan officials to oversee the proceedings. It should be noted, however, that extant texts do not describe the emperor's activities inside the Daijōkyū once he enters either the Yuki or Suki Hall. In the absence of an explicit account, however, the texts of prayers offered on the occasion make it clear that a meal is to be shared between the emperor and his divine ancestors:

> By the divine command of the mighty ancestral gods and goddesses abiding in the Plain of High Heaven, we humbly speak before the presence of the mighty Kami who dwell in heaven and earth. On this day . . . of the heavenly food, the food partaken eternally over the ages, the divine food partaken of by the divine descendant, may the mighty Kami consent to partake thereof with him. May his reign be a prosperous and happy one, lasting five hundred, yea a thousand autumns in peace and tranquility. With resplendent brightness may he glow as he partakes, the divine descendant, whose choice offerings we prepare for presentation: the bright cloth, the shining cloth, soft cloth, and coarse cloth; at this moment of the majestic and resplendent rising of the morning sun, we raise our words of praise.[10]

What is known about what the emperor actually does in the Yuki and Suki Halls has remained a secret tradition known through participants' accounts. According to them, the emperor's portion of rice and millet is formed into small balls. The emperor enters the inner compound and sits on a mat to the northeast of the *shinza*. Before him are two mats, one prepared with food for the Kami and a second mat with food for himself. He offers food to the Kami and then eats three of the rice and millet balls, picking up each one with chopsticks and placing it on his left hand. He then takes four sips of each of the two kinds of sake. He washes his hands and withdraws. This ceremony in the Yuki Hall ends around midnight. At two o'clock the next morning, he repeats exactly the same procedure in the Suki Hall, ending before sunrise, changing from his ritual attire and returning to the palace. This concludes the rites of the Daijōkyū.[11]

Ceremonies to permit the land to be returned to ordinary use were carried out, and in ancient times some of the emperor's ceremonial garments and even his ritual bath water were bestowed on the ritual officiants. The remaining implements and equipment are buried in the grounds of the Kamigamo Shrine in Kyoto.

The Third and Fourth Days

Following the conclusion of the Daijōkyū ceremonies, abstinences and taboos were lifted, and two days of feasting and celebration began. Officials from the Yuki and Suki districts hung colorful curtains and banners in the palace to greet the sovereign. The crown prince, officials, and the nobles convened in the palace grounds to await the emperor's appearance. The Jingikan officials bore auspicious *sakaki* branches, kneeling to recite congratulations to the deities. The emperor was borne in a carriage to the Yuki Curtain. Coming to rest there, he conferred promotions in rank. Priests of the Inbe clan then entered and presented the imperial regalia in the presence of this large audience. Tribute goods from the Yuki province were presented, and officials inspected the feast and sake that was prepared in an adjacent garden. The audience proceeded to the garden, where the highest ranking among them enjoyed a feast and songs performed by singers from the Yuki province. When the Yuki feast concluded, the emperor moved to the Suki Curtain and a second presentation of the regalia, tribute, and feasting began, matching the preceding Yuki celebration.

On the fourth and final day, the nobles and officials consumed another round of Yuki and Suki feasts and were entertained by music and dance. Special emoluments were provided to officials of the Yuki and Suki provinces, and their governors and noble families were granted court ranks. The lesser officials and the ordinary workers who participated in the ceremonies were all given gifts and entertained with court singing and dancing. The consecrated areas of the Yuki and Suki provinces were ceremonially de-consecrated and returned to ordinary use, and the fields were burned over.

The Meaning of the Daijōsai

The Daijōsai raises many tantalizing questions of religious meaning. For example, what is the significance of the pervasive doubling of Yuki and Suki provinces, of the parallel and nearly identical Yuki and Suki Halls, and of the doubled feasts linked to them on the third and fourth days? What is the meaning of the *shinza*, and what, if anything, is its role in the emperor's actions within the Yuki and Suki Halls? Why do the texts not spell out what he does there and elucidate its meaning? Why should the buildings and most of their equipment be destroyed at the end of the ceremonies? Why do the enthronement rites become the occasion for such a wide-scale presentation of ranks and titles by the emperor? These are only a few of the questions to which we most urgently want answers. In fact, however, although scholars have speculated for centuries on the meaning of these complex rites, all interpretation is destined to remain speculative to a degree.[12]

The doubling of elements seen in the architecture and furnishings of the Daijōkyū bears a general similarity to the twenty-year renewal of the Ise Shrines. At Ise the shrine buildings are enclosed within double fences, and adjacent to each main sanctuary is an identical plot of land where the buildings and all their contents are made entirely new, whereupon the old ones are razed. We recall that the annual calendar of official rites for the Kami established in the Jingiryō also had a doubled character.

The conjunction of the Daijōsai and harvest rites conveyed the idea that the emperor's behavior and purity ensured the fertility of crops, and that the correct performance of imperial ritual guaranteed material survival for those under his rule. It is also significant that the harvest rites occur near the winter solstice, when the powers of the sun are at an ebb, a propitious and appropriate time for the emperor's powers to be renewed in the spirit calming sequence.

Beds made from stacked *tatami* mats, spread with a coverlet, and topped by a pillow, have been found in several shrines of the Nara period. These beds seem to have been part of the equipment that shrines were expected to possess. The *shinza* is literally the "Kami seat," a place for the deity to rest after the meal. The reason that no extant text speaks of the emperor lying upon or even touching the *shinza* is most likely that the bed is for the Kami exclusively. There are two halls because respect for the Kami requires that the morning meal be served in a different place than the evening one. The Kami return to the heavenly world once night has ended and dawn comes. The coverlet of the *shinza* is mentioned in *Nihon shoki*, as we saw in chapter 2.[13] Takamimusubi no Kami wrapped Amaterasu's grandson in such a coverlet. The presence of this element in enthronement rites casts the new emperor as the Kami's descendant and rightful heir to rule of the land.

Why should the regalia be presented more than once to the sovereign? On the face of it, once should be enough, but in fact the regalia are presented to the emperor during the Senso and Sokui rituals and again on the third and fourth days of the Daijōsai. The new emperor's court and ministers are the main audience for the Senso-Sokui rites, while the provincial officials and participants from the Yuki and Suki provinces are the main audience for the feasting on the third and fourth days. Most likely, the purpose of these multiple presentations of the regalia was not merely to transmit them to the new emperor (because a single presentation would accomplish that goal), but also to display the transmission before multiple constituencies, making clear to each of them the myth of divine descent and mandate.[14]

We can uncover political dimensions of the meaning of the Daijōsai by examining Tenmu's performance of it. The regional elites played an important role in putting Tenmu on the throne, and he understood that he owed his victory largely to them. It was Tenmu who commissioned the compilation of the *Kojiki* and *Nihon shoki*, enabling the establishment of new official genealogies, no doubt favoring the local chieftains who had come over to his side in the Jinshin War. He also granted new titles to 177 families and then reorganized the order of precedence among the titles to place his supporters at the top of the hierarchy.[15]

These circumstances undoubtedly influenced Tenmu's decision to create a large, impressive, and inclusive court and to conduct ritual in a way that drew widely upon the regions. The Daijōsai conferred honorable roles on the provinces, especially those chosen as Yuki and Suki provinces, asserting imperial sovereignty over them by requiring them to make significant economic contributions to the enthronement rites. Enthronement ritual also elevated the regions by conferring gifts, ranks, and titles upon their noble families, and by making magnificent offerings to regional shrines where their ancestors were deified. Since all this also contributed to the emperor's own majesty, self-interest was also served, a situation in which all concerned were magnified and their importance enlarged.

The scale of the Daijōsai and the obvious expense it entailed, not only for the court, but also for the Yuki and Suki provinces is overwhelming. It is easy to draw the conclusion that these rites must have been the court's preeminent and continual preoccupation, but as we shall see, from the late eighth century, emperors were also engaging in rites that made them Buddhist monarchs, *cakravartin* or "Wheel-Turning King," protector of the Buddhist order, and exemplars of Buddhist virtue. Medieval emperors also underwent parallel Buddhist rites of enthronement called *sokui kanjō,* in which they symbolically took Buddhist vows and were presented as Buddhist monarchs. Tenmu undertook a massive sutra-copying project, and Buddhism was a central part of his court's cultural life.[16]

Because enthronement ritual was so complex and composed of so many disparate elements, it was possible to orchestrate it in a variety of ways that emphasized different ideas or aspects of the concept of the sovereign. Not surprisingly, the emphasis of these rites has changed significantly over time. For example, by the time of Emperor Shōmu's reign, the banquets of the third and fourth days greatly overshadowed the transmission of regalia, a trend that continued into Emperor Kanmu's reign (r. 781–806). This change disadvantaged the Inbe family, whose job it was to transmit the regalia. They were so aggrieved that in 807 Inbe Hironari complained to the court in the *Kogoshūi* that his family had been wrongfully relegated to obscurity. Furthermore, Kanmu adopted a much more Sinified style that sat uneasily alongside the old *jingi* families' desire to choreograph enthronement ritual as the maximal expression of indigenous tradition.[17]

Imperial Mortuary Ritual

Kofun ceased to be built after the Taika Reform of 645; thereafter, imperial mausolea took their place. Mausolea for emperors and empresses were built in the form of large mounded hills that outwardly resemble *kofun,* marked by the characteristic shrine gate (*torii*) and surrounded by dense forest. It was also from around the time of the Taika Reform that we see increasing concern that the Kami and shrines be protected from the pollution of death. For most of Japanese history, shrines and their priests have not been involved in imperial mortuary rites. For this reason, it is difficult to isolate a distinctively Shinto element in imperial mortuary rites before Emperor Meiji's funeral in 1912.

The mortuary rites for Tenmu were performed under the strong influence of ancient Chinese imperial ritual of the Han (206 BCE–220 CE) and T'ang (618–907) dynasties. Tenmu's corpse first rested in a mortuary hall constructed in the palace grounds, and formal mourning was carried out there. Female mourners wept, lamented, and offered food to the corpse daily. Speeches were delivered before it, as if the emperor could still hear. The funeral was held twenty-six months after the emperor's death, and the corpse was buried.[18]

Empress Jitō, who died in 702, was the first sovereign to be cremated, the preferred form of corpse disposition in Buddhism.[19] Full Buddhist mortuary rites were adopted for Emperor Shōmu, who died in 756, but the mourning practices seen in Tenmu's time were also observed. In the ninth century, however, such mourning observances were replaced by the Buddhist practices of sutra chanting and the offering of incense before the corpse, based on the idea that the dead can attain Buddhahood in the afterlife. Through the tenth century, cremation remained the preferred form of disposing of the imperial corpse, though there were also the cases of Emperors Daigo (885–930) and Murakami (926–967), who were buried. Beginning with Emperor Go-Ichijō (1008–1036), it became customary to construct Buddhist meditation halls and stupas near imperial mausolea. Emperor Go-Horikawa (1212–1234) was the first sovereign to have mortuary rites performed by the Kyoto Shingon Buddhist temple Sen'yūji. Sen'yūji performed the mortuary ritual for all subsequent emperors down through Emperor Kōmei (1831–1866). However, while the Buddhist rites at Sen'yūji were performed with the assumption that the corpse would be cremated, beginning with Emperor Go-Kōmyō (1633–1654), he and all following emperors were actually buried. Thus imperial cremation came to an end in the seventeenth century.[20]

The Bureau of the Consecrated Imperial Princess

According to *Nihon shoki*, the legendary Emperor Suinin entrusted the worship of his divine ancestor Amaterasu Ōmikami to a female shaman called Yamato Hime, who received an oracle from the sun goddess: "The province of Ise, of the divine wind, is the land whither repair the waves from the eternal world, the successive waves. It is a secluded and pleasant land. In this land I wish to dwell." This account serves as the mythical prototype for the Consecrated Imperial Princess.[21]

Tenmu appointed an unmarried imperial princess to serve the Ise Shrines as Consecrated Imperial Princess (*itsuki no miya* or *saiō*).[22] This relieved him of the necessity of going to Ise personally, and after Jitō (r. 690–697) no emperor made the journey until the late nineteenth-century visit by Emperor Meiji. Although the princess's roles were not included in Jingiryō, the Jingikan administered the princess's preparation and service through the Bureau of the Consecrated Imperial Princess (Saigū-ryō, or Itsuki no Miya no Tsukasa). Each new emperor had a Consecrated Imperial Princess chosen by divination by the Bureau of Yin and Yang (On'yō-ryō). She had to complete a long process of purification before actually taking up her duties at Ise, undergoing a year of purifications and abstinences within the palace, and then a second year of additional purifications outside the palace, in a place called Nonomiya. Only in the ninth month of the third year of her appointment did the *saiō* actually move to Ise and begin her service, traveling in a procession with hundreds of attendants. Strict limits were placed on funerals in those areas she traversed, so that she would not be contaminated by the pollution of death. In Ise, the *saiō* occupied a palace near the Ise shrines, called the *saigū*. (Both the palace and the princess herself are sometimes referred to by the term for her residence, the *saigū*). She continued to observe abstinences and to avoid the mention of anything having to do with Buddhism. She performed rites for the Kami in her palace and also made offerings at the Ise Shrines three times per year. The *saiō* served in principle until the accession of a new emperor, but in fact they often stepped down upon the death of a close relative or their own illness. Some died in office. *Saiō* continued to be appointed for a period of about 660 years, until the reign of Emperor Godaigo (r. 1318–1339), the last emperor to appoint a *saiō*.[23]

The princess's palace served as a miniature court adjacent to the Ise Shrines, dedicated entirely to the maintenance of purity and the performance of ritual. It had a staff of over 500 people and occupied a large compound with numerous buildings. The system of appointing a Consecrated Princess in effect designated a virginal female of the imperial family whose life would be dedicated to the service of the Ise deities until the death of the emperor who appointed her, or her own death.[24]

The *saiō* conducted ritual at Ise three times a year: at the *Tsukinami-sai* in the sixth and twelfth months, and at the *Kanname-sai*, a harvest ritual distinctive of Ise. On the last day of the month preceding the ritual to be performed, she purified herself in a river. Then on the fifteenth day of the month in which the festival was to be held (this was also the day of the full moon by the lunar calendar), she purified herself again and moved to a detached palace at a midway point between her palace and Ise. On the sixteenth she went to the Outer Shrine and set up a *tamagushi* (apparently as a *yorishiro*). On the seventeenth she did exactly the same thing at the Inner Shrine. On the eighteenth she returned to her palace.

To maintain this system from the late seventh to the fourteenth century represented an immense economic obligation. The symbolism of dedicating the very life of an imperial princess to the service of the Ise deities implies the highest religious commitment. The court's dedication to maintaining the Bureau of the Consecrated Imperial Princess, like its dedication to the vicennial rebuilding of the

Ise Shrines, should be seen as part of its determination to sponsor and promote the Kami, even as it was simultaneously acting as a major patron of Buddhism. Both Ise's rebuilding and the activities surrounding the Consecrated Princess also provided the court tremendous pageantry and spectacle through which to project an image of its own authority and majesty.

The Vicennial Renewal of the Ise Shrines *(Shikinen Sengū)*

Located to the southeast of the Yamato imperial capitals (in present-day Mie Prefecture), the Ise Shrines eventually came to comprise two main shrines and over one hundred smaller, auxiliary shrines. The two main shrines are the Inner Shrine, whose principal Kami is the sun goddess and ancestral spirit of the imperial house, Amaterasu Ōmikami, and the Outer Shrine, whose principal deity is Toyouke no Ōkami, a food goddess serving the sun goddess. The Inner Shrine is situated on the banks of the Isuzu River, while the Outer Shrine is located about two and a half miles away, in Yamadahara. Because Ise is the main seat of the imperial ancestral deities, it became a major site for state ritual, a place to display the majesty of the "indigenous tradition." Having successfully kept Buddhist influence at a distance by resisting attempts to build a *jingūji* there, it was regarded as preserving the purest expression of Kami worship.

The two main sanctuaries at Ise face south and are enclosed by multiple, nested fences. Each one has beside it an alternate site for the construction of an exact replica at twenty-year intervals. The complex preserves Japan's earliest architectural forms, modeled on ancient granaries, in a style called *yuiitsu shinmei-zukuri*. In each sanctuary, polished metal mirrors represent the Kami. The buildings are raised off the ground by pillars placed directly into the earth. Beneath the center of each sanctuary is a "Heart Pillar," the most sacred element; it protrudes from the ground but is not a structural support. Interpretations of its significance have evolved over the centuries, and it is undoubtedly the most sacred element of the entire complex.

Tenmu decreed that the Ise shrines should be rebuilt once in every twenty years, supplanting an earlier practice of rebuilding at indeterminate intervals on adjacent sites of the same size. Why twenty years? There are numerous possibilities, including these two: Since the pillars are set directly into the earth, they would naturally deteriorate, as would the rush-thatched roofs. Also, twenty years is roughly a generation, the time required to pass the building techniques from one generation of carpenters to the next.

Each rebuilding displays the sovereign's majesty and power. Beginning in 690 and continuing until 2013, the shrines have been rebuilt sixty-two times, through a remarkable ceremonial sequence called Shikinen Sengū. Construction techniques have been recorded minutely since ancient times, resulting in the transmission of the ancient prototype down to the present. While there may have been occasional rebuilding of the Ise shrines even earlier, the ones recorded in *Nihon shoki* for the years 690 (Inner Shrine) and 692 (Outer Shrine) were the first ones to be documented. Except for a hiatus during the medieval period and a brief postponement in the immediate postwar years, this remarkable ritual complex has continued to the present, the most recent in 2013, making it one of the most enduring in human history.

The term *Shikinen Sengū* is most closely associated with the Ise Shrines, but they are not the only ones that came to be rebuilt at set intervals. *Sengū* means "moving a shrine," and *shikinen* refers to ceremonies carried out at set intervals. Similar rebuilding ceremonies are carried out at the Kamo, Kasuga, Izumo, and other shrines, at varying intervals.[25]

Like his systematization of coordinated ritual through the Jingikan and his proclamation ordering the compilation of the *Nihon shoki*, Tenmu's command that the Ise Shrines should be rebuilt was another measure intended to enhance the majesty and authority of the throne. The procedure for Shikinen Sengū was first codified in the *Kōtai jingū gishikichō* (804). Held in late autumn, the culminating rite of moving of the symbols of the Kami from the old to the new shrine coincides with the harvest festival at Ise called Kanname-sai. The religious rationale appears to be that the Kami, having been reinvigorated or "reborn" in the course of their installation into the new shrine buildings, receive the harvest offerings from Kanname-sai.[26] Table 3.1 shows the Shikinen Sengū rites.[27]

Table 3.1 **Shikinen Sengū Rites**

	Ceremony	*Timing / Year in the Cycle*	*Content*
1	Yamaguchi-sai 山口祭	12	Reverence for the Kami of the mountain where the trees used in the *Shikinen Sengū* will be cut
2	Konomoto-sai 木本祭	12	Reverence for the Kami of the tree that will serve as the "Heart Pillar" (*Shin no Mihashira*); held in conjunction with Yamaguchi-sai
3	Misoma hajime-sai 御杣始祭	12	Trees symbolically cut from three directions
4	Kozukuri hajime-sai 木造始祭	13	Prayers for protection during the coming construction
5	Jichinsai 地鎮祭	15	Prayers to calm the spirits of the earth on which the new shrines will be constructed

(continued)

Table 3.1 **Continued**

	Ceremony	*Timing / Year in the Cycle*	*Content*
6	Ritchū-sai 立柱祭	19	Erecting the standing pillars
7	Gogyō-sai 御形祭	19	Prayers for the protection of the pillars; held in conjunction with Ritchū-sai
8	Jōtō-sai 上棟祭	19	Raising the ridge beam
9	Kotsugi-sai 杵築祭	20	To "harden" the base of the pillars
10	Kawara Ōharai 川原大祓	20	Purification of the priests who will take part in the *sengyo* (see next), the newly made shrine treasures, and vestments
11	Sengyo 遷御	20	Moving the Kami from the old shrine to the new one
12	Ōmike 大御饌	20	First offering of food at the new shrine
13	Hōhei 奉幣	20	Imperial emissary dedicates tribute of cloth to the shrine as a gift from the imperial house; held in conjunction with Ōmike-sai

The offerings and furnishings to be presented at these ceremonies are enumerated in the *Engi shiki*, where it is evident that Imperial Emissaries oversaw the rebuilding of the main sanctuaries and the most important of the auxiliary shrines, and that the rebuilding was paid for from tax revenues. New wood was required for the main sanctuaries, whose pillars required whole trees, ceremonially cut in the Yamaguchi-sai and dried for several years. Special offerings of tools, cloth, rice, sake, sea products, and utensils were presented for the Yamaguchi-sai and each of the other component rites of the renewal, and new robes for the ritualists were also required.[28]

The mirror symbolizing the great Kami was housed in a wooden container called the "august boat shape" (*mifunashiro*), which was encased in a second wooden box. The shrine treasures (*shinpō*) and furnishings for the main sanctuary of the shrine for Amaterasu Ōmikami included weaving equipment (several spindles, shuttles, reels, and beaters in gilt-bronze and silver-copper); weaponry (swords, scabbards, shields, bows, quivers, thousands of arrows); and musical instruments. The largest of the swords required a great bejeweled scabbard with an elaborate handle wound with gold wire. In addition, the sanctuary required silk umbrellas hung with lavender braided tassels, fans, mosquito netting, a silk canopy, curtains, a bed, numerous silk and brocade quilts, jackets, scarfs, and skirts of various colors and fabrics, headbands, sashes, shoes, combs and cases,

Figure 3.3 The Procession Escorting Amaterasu Ōmikami to the Newly Rebuilt Inner Shrine at Ise. Source: Photograph © 2016, Museum of Fine Arts, Boston [accession no. 2009.5007.7]

mirrors, hair ribbons, pearls, and pillows. All these things were to be newly made for each renewal. The nighttime procession moving the Kami, concealed within a moving curtain borne by priests, from the old shrine to the new was the culmination of the Vicennial Renewal (see Figure 3.3).[29]

Uneasy Relations between the Kami and Emperors

Ritual prescriptions inevitably convey an image of the Kami and the emperors as if they were perpetually bound together in untroubled harmony, but other accounts give a different impression altogether. Incidents of uneasy relations between the Kami and the sovereign are based on *tatari,* the idea that the Kami react to the breaking of taboos, disrespect, failure to perform expected ritual, or improper ritual with punishments that might take the form of damaging storms, epidemics, and various misfortunes for the perpetrator.[30] In ancient Japan, the Jingikan or the Bureau of Yin and Yang dealt with *tatari* according to a regular process. If an unusual event or misfortune were suspected of resulting from *tatari,* the Jingikan (or the Bureau of Yin and Yang) would perform divination to reveal the cause. It was believed that *tatari* could be calmed or quieted through ritual means. Once the reason for the *tatari* was determined, measures were taken to assuage the offended deity, such as

Table 3.2 **Examples of *Tatari* Involving the Sovereign**

Year	*Outline of Incident*
*5th, 6th years, Emperor Sūjin	A huge epidemic killed over half the populace; the remainder became homeless and rebellious; the cause was determined by plastromancy. The cause was worship in the palace of two Kami together: Yamato no Ōkunidama and Amaterasu. The solution was to remove them both from the palace and set up worship for them elsewhere. In other words, these two Kami had expressed their displeasure through the *tatari* of epidemic and popular unrest (Aston, *Nihongi*, bk. 1, 151–52; NKBT 67, *Nihon shoki jō*, 238).
Emperor Suinin's reign	The son of Emperor Suinin was unable to speak; Suinin was told in a dream by the Kami of Izumo that this misfortune would be cured by building a great shrine for the Kami; i.e., the son's inability to speak was due to *tatari* from this Kami (Aston, *Nihongi*, bk. 1, 167; NKBT 67, *Nihon shoki jō*, 257).
9th year, 2nd month, Emperor Chūai	The empress became possessed by an unnamed Kami, telling Chūai that he should abandon his expedition against the Kumaso (a rebellious tribal people) and instead try to conquer Shiraki (Silla) on the Korean peninsula. The emperor was killed by the wrath of the Kami when he declined to obey (Aston, *Nihongi*, bk. 1, 221–23; NKBT 67, *Nihon shoki jō*, 327).
661	Empress Saimei had trees belonging to a shrine cut in order to build a new palace; the Kami demolished the building (5th month, 9th day). The empress died (7th month, 24th day) (Aston *Nihongi*, bk. 2, 271–72; NKBT 68, *Nihon shoki ge*, 349).
686	Emperor Tenmu's final illness was discovered by divination to be caused by a curse (*tatari*) from the Kusanagi sword, one of the imperial regalia. The sword was removed to Atsuta, to be worshipped there instead of in the palace (Aston, *Nihongi*, bk. 2, 377; NKBT 68, *Nihon shoki ge*, 478).
745, Tenpyō 17, 9th month	In response to Emperor Shōmu's illness, offerings were made at the Kamo, Matsunoō, and Hachiman Shrines; i.e., his illness was due to *tatari* from those Kami (*Shoku nihongi*, cited in Okada, "Circular System").
746, Tenpyō 18	In response to Emperor Shōmu's illness, the Kami Hachiman was promoted in rank, with offerings of land, fifty ordained monks to serve the Kami, and 400 households of peasants to support Hachiman's shrine (*Shoku nihongi*, cited in Okada, "Circular System").

(continued)

Table 3.2 **Continued**

Year	*Outline of Incident*
763, 9th month, 1st day	Strange fires, plague, and drought are attributed to Kami *tatari*, because of the "irreverence of the various provincial officials." An order calling for their rotation was issued (Okada, "Circular System").
770, 2nd month, 23rd day	Divination reveals that Empress Shōtoku's illness derived from a curse from a stone at the base of Saidaiji's eastern pagoda. Two years later, Saidaiji's western pagoda was struck by lightning. Divination revealed that the cause was a curse owing to cutting a tree from shrine land and using it to construct the pagoda. In response, servant households were bestowed on the shrine where the tree had been cut (*Shoku nihongi*, cited in Okada, "Circular System").
*782, 7th month, 29th day	Jingikan and the Bureau of Yin and Yang jointly report: "Although the state performed the customary rites and regular offerings, the world is filled with death. Fortune and misfortune are confused, and troubles have sprung up everywhere. These are the curses of the Kami of Ise and the various shrines . . . there is the fear that this curse may even threaten the emperor's physical well-being" (*Shoku nihongi*, cited in Okada, "Circular System").
792	Discovery of *tatari* emanating from the tomb of Emperor Sudō (Okada, "Circular System").
806, 3rd month, 23rd day	Jingikan and Bureau of Yin and Yang divinations yield conflicting results regarding the cause of calamities affecting the country. Jingikan divination (which ultimately was accepted) found that because Emperor Kanmu's tomb was located near the Kamo Shrine, the shrine's Kami were causing *tatari* (Okada, "Circular System").
809	Discovery of *tatari* emanating from the tomb of Kanmu's consort (Okada, "Circular System").
*816, 6th month, 22nd day	Divination was performed to discover the cause of *tatari*. Ise priest (*miyaji*) Ōnakatomi no Kiyomochi, was determined to have polluted the shrine by performing Buddhist rites. He was fined and fired from his post (*Nihon kōki*; Okada, "Circular System").
*824, 4th month, 6th day	A sword and offerings were presented to the Kami of the Ise shrines to dispel *tatari* (*Ruiju kokushi*; Okada, "Circular System").
827, 1st month, 19th day	Divination reveals that Emperor Junna's illness was due to *tatari*; cutting trees belonging to an Inari shrine in order to build the pagoda at Tōji caused the *tatari*. The Kami Inari was elevated to the ranks of official Kami, Junior Fifth Rank (Okada, "Circular System").

(continued)

Table 3.2 **Continued**

Year	*Outline of Incident*
831	Discovery of *tatari* emanating from the Sagara tomb (Okada, "Circular System").
832, 5th month	The Kami Mishima and Ikonahime are inducted into the ranks of the eminent shrines (*myōjin*) as a countermeasure to *tatari* (*Nihon kōki, Shaku Nihongi*; Okada, "Circular System").
840	Discovery of *tatari* emanating from the tomb of Emperor Kanmu (Okada, "Circular System").
841	Discovery of *tatari* emanating from the tomb of Emperor Kanmu; discovery of *tatari* emanating from the tomb of Empress Jingū (Okada, "Circular System").
*842, 7th month, 19th day	The *tatari* of a heat wave that withered all the crops was determined by divination to be caused by the Kami of Ise and Hachiman. Ōnakatomi no Fuchina was dispatched to conduct prayers on the emperor's behalf (*Shoku nihongi*; Okada, "Circular System").
843	Discovery of *tatari* emanating from the tomb of Empress Jingū (Okada, "Circular System").
*863, 7th month, 2nd day	Jingikan divination determined that a shooting star of the previous month was due to *tatari* from Amaterasu; prayers of placation were conducted (Okada, "Circular System").
*864, 7th month, 27th day	Unrest and calamity in Kinai, Iga, Ise, Shima, Ōmi, Sagami, and Kazusa is addressed by provincial governors (*kokushi*) paying respects to their Kami (Okada, "Circular System").
*960	The emperor's living quarters within the palace burned down. Jingikan divination determined that the fire was due to the wrath of the Ise Kami. They were angered that someone of the wrong surname had been appointed to the post of Saishu (Fujimori Kaoru, *Heian jidai no kyūtei saishi to Jingikan-jin* (Tokyo: Daimeidō, 2000), 261–62).

Note: Items marked with an asterisk (*) involve the Ise Shrines or the Ise Kami.

Source: Adapted from Okada Shōji, "Tennō to kamigami no junkangata saishi taikei—kodai no tatarigami" [The circular system of rites linking the emperor and the kami—menacing apparitions of the kami in antiquity] *Shintō shūkyō* 199/200 (2005): 73–88. English version available online at http://21coe.kokugakuin.ac.jp/articlesintranslation/pdf/okada.pdf.

making special offerings, raising the deity's rank, or instituting regulations to prevent a recurrence of the offensive deeds. Table 3.2 introduces notable cases.

As the table shows, twenty-five cases of sovereigns being visited with *tatari* were reported from prehistory through the late tenth century, about one quarter of them involving the Ise Kami, and about half were from the Heian period. For example, Suinin, legendary eleventh sovereign, was full of awe and fear of the mirror in the palace, the one supposedly received from the heavenly Kami when Ninigi descended to earth and then passed on to each emperor. He was so frightened of it that, according to *Nihon shoki*, he had it taken out of the palace and enshrined at Ise.

The legendary fourteenth sovereign, Chūai, was apparently killed by the Kami's wrath after he ignored their advice to conquer Korea. He would have had to give up a planned military campaign against the aboriginal people called the Kumaso in favor of an expedition to Korea, but he even doubted that such a land existed. The Kami spoke to Chūai through his consort, Jingū, saying,

> I see this country [the Korean peninsula] outstretched like a reflection from Heaven in the water. Why sayest thou that there is no country, and dost disparage my words? But as thou, O King! has spoken thus, and hast utterly refused to believe me, thou shalt not possess this land. The child with which the Empress has just become pregnant, he shall obtain it.

Thereafter Chūai died, and Jingū took her army across to Korea.

Saimei, the thirty-seventh sovereign (r. 655–661?), was killed by the wrath of the Kami after cutting down trees belonging to a shrine:

> [T]rees belonging to the Shrine of Asakura were cut down and cleared away in order to build this Palace. Therefore the Gods were angered and demolished the building. Some were also struck, and in consequence the Grand Treasurer and many of those in waiting took ill and died.

Shortly after, the empress herself passed away.[31]

In the sixth month of 686, according to *Nihon shoki*, divination determined that the fatal illness of Emperor Tenmu was due to "a curse from the Kusanagi sword. The same day it was sent to the shrine of Atsuta, in Wohari, and deposited there."[32] In other words, the sword of the imperial regalia had placed a curse on the emperor and therefore was removed to Atsuta, paralleling Suinin's removal of the mirror to Ise.

In a striking display of authority by a Kami, the deity Hachiman demanded of Empress Kōken (r. 749–758) that he be installed at the great Buddhist temple complex in Nara, Tōdaiji, in 749. She acquiesced. In the view of Michael Como, the case of Empress Kōken and the Kami Hachiman represents the power of the immigrant Hata clan in northern Kyūshū, depicted through its deity Hachiman, to intimidate the court even in the mid-eighth century. Binding dangerous Kami to monastic centers was a means to domesticate them, even as the technique underlined their subordination to Buddhist divinities.[33]

In these accounts we find two instances in which the emperor either was intimidated by the presence of an object of the imperial regalia (the mirror, in Suinin's case) or was cursed by one of them (the sword, in Tenmu's case). Jingikan divination resulted in decisions to remove the troublesome article from the palace and have it installed in a shrine where priests could assume the duty of appropriate worship. The regalia both represented the presence of the Kami and also were regarded as magical implements. The sword was even portrayed as having the power to place a curse on the emperor for no stated reason. Clearly these articles are potent, dangerous, and unpredictable—even toward emperors.

Saimei died as a result of breaking a taboo on cutting timber at a shrine; to do so was regarded as offensive to the Kami, a theft of their property and also an indignity to their dwellings. We recall that Great King Kōtoku is said to have shown his disrespect for Shinto by cutting trees at a shrine. Chūai died when he ignored the Kami's words as spoken through the mouth of the empress. These two cases reflect the belief that the Kami's words cannot be taken lightly nor their taboos broken without a heavy penalty.

These incidents convey a subtext about the importance of the Jingikan to the emperor. It was divination that revealed the cause of Tenmu's illness, and the Jingikan was charged with performing divination whenever it was needed. By contrast, the laws governing the Buddhist priesthood forbade them from performing divination. Kami affairs are portrayed in these narratives as full of magical power—emperors ignore it at their peril. Through divination, the Jingikan had a role to play in determining the will of the Kami or explaining strange events in terms of the will of the Kami. Although the Bureau of Yin and Yang also had authority in this area, these stories can be regarded as messages to the emperor and to competing religious traditions to beware of encroaching on Kami affairs, the Jingikan's turf. The following incident illustrates this dynamic.

In 960 the emperor's living quarters within the palace burned down for the first time since Kyoto had been established as the capital. Jingikan divination determined that the fire had been caused by the wrath of the Kami. The shrines suspected were the Ise, Iwashimizu, and Isonokami shrines. Further divination determined that the Ise Kami (Amaterasu, Toyouke, and others) were angry, because someone of the wrong surname had been appointed to the post of Saishu. The Nakatomi family repeatedly urged Emperor Murakami to accept this interpretation of the fire, and eventually he did so, after it was determined that a recent Saishu appointee had been adopted into the Nakatomi family rather than being born into it. Thereafter, appointees to the Saishu role were limited to direct descendants, and adoptees were excluded. This decision allowed one line of the Nakatomi family to monopolize a prestigious and lucrative post, often with concurrent appointments as highest official in the Jingikan, as well as concurrent posts in the Dajōkan.[34]

This story illustrates the fear of divine wrath that had become prominent by the mid-Heian period. Jingikan divination in this case asserted the pre-eminence of a specific line of the Nakatomi family and the potential for calamity if they were not treated with proper respect. The emperor's acquiescence in this interpretation ratified the implication that failure to accord due deference to the Nakatomi could cause harm to the sovereign, the palace, and the capital. The story is also a powerful reminder that in the ancient period all political and economic activity was refracted through a religious lens.[35]

Kami and Buddhas in Emperor Shōmu's Reign

Changes in the links between the emperor and the Kami cults stemming from the introduction of Buddhism can be seen in Emperor Shōmu's reign (724–749). Perhaps his greatest achievement was the construction of a nationwide network of temples headed by Tōdaiji in Nara, where a monumental statue of Vairocana Buddha was created through a massive program of public contributions. On a trip to the provinces, Shōmu had seen a statue of this Buddha, known in Japanese as Rushana, and had been exceedingly impressed by it and by the Kegon Sutra, in which Rushana was the central figure. In the scripture, Rushana is pictured as filling the cosmos, surrounded by enlightened beings, turning the Wheel of the Dharma in all directions, in short, as presiding over the universe beneficently, ruling through wisdom and compassion. Shōmu was so moved by this experience that he began to receive tutoring on the scripture, and in 743 he issued an edict, calling for construction of a fifteen-meter-high bronze sculpture of this Buddha. A large bureaucracy took charge of the project, and all the provinces contributed. Local elites sent gold, silver, iron, and timber for the temple. Their contributions both developed local industry and were keys to elevating their personal status. Not only elites, but ordinary people as well responded to a campaign spearheaded by the charismatic Buddhist preacher Gyōki (668–749), who traveled the countryside asking people to give whatever they could. In all, some 51,590 people donated lumber; 370,275 gave some form of metal, and 2,179,973 contributed their labor. The Great Buddha project suffered numerous setbacks, but when the statue was successfully completed in 749, Gyōki administered monastic vows to Emperor Shōmu and the empress.[36]

Such magnificent patronage of Buddhism could not but impact the foregoing discourse of imperial legitimation, adding to it the presentation of the sovereign as a Buddhist monarch. For Shōmu to commence presenting himself as a "servant of Buddha" and a protector of Buddhism did not, however, invalidate the former discourse of the sovereign as a living god, or as a descendant of the Kami, with whom he or she could commune in ritual. Instead, the new ideas added to the old ones, given that all of them were symbolically reiterated in court-sponsored ritual. Nothing Shōmu did pitted the Buddhas against the Kami but rather "meshed the Buddhist cult and the cults of the Kami into an expanded official cult of realm protection over which the *tennō* presided as principal ritual coordinator."[37] We can imagine, however, that this move did not gladden the hearts of Jingikan officials or the old *jingi* families.

Nevertheless, priests of the Usa Hachiman Shrine became deeply involved in the Tōdaiji project. Because Hachiman did not appear in historical records before the Nara period, or in *Kojiki* or *Nihon shoki*, it is impossible to know much about him before that time. It is known, however, that he was a regional deity in Kyūshū, having strong shamanic and continental associations but lacking connections to the court. The Usa Hachiman Shrine's founding legend claims that it was established in the mid-sixth century. During a 720 rebellion of the Hayato people, the Kami was taken in a palanquin to the area where fighting was going on, and thereafter a ceremony liberating birds and animals (*hōjō-e*) was conducted for the shrine to console the souls of the dead.[38] This suggests that Hachiman was originally a continental deity.

The Kami was closely associated with Buddhism and oracles from its earliest appearances in documents. Hachiman's oracles differed from those of other Kami, such as oracles found in *fudoki*, in that they contained numerous references to Buddhism and expressed the hope of Japan becoming a Buddhist realm. Emperor Shōmu requested that a temple dedicated to the future Buddha Maitreya be built in the precincts of the Usa Hachiman Shrine in 738. Buddhist sutras began to be read before the shrine's altar in 740. In 741 Emperor Shōmu raised the shrine's rank and provided Buddhist scriptures and a three-story pagoda for it. In 748 and 749, he raised the ranks of two female Hachiman priests and confered elevated titles upon them, undoubtedly in recognition for their work in promoting the completion of the Great Buddha.[39] It appears that Shōmu was not only cultivating the Kami Hachiman, but also doing so in a way that emphasized the deity's rapprochement with Buddhism.

Following the announcement of the plan to build Tōdaiji and the Great Buddha, a female priest (*negi-ni*) of the Usa Hachiman shrine, named Ōga no Morime, proclaimed an oracle in late 749, saying that Hachiman wished to assist in the Tōdaiji project. She traveled from Kyūshū to the capital in a procession, riding in a purple palanquin similar to that used by the sovereign's chief consort. Her title of *negi-ni* combined a word for a priest of the Kami, *negi*, with the word for Buddhist nun, *ni*. In 750, Emperor Shōmu granted Hachiman the rank of "most high" (*ippin*).[40] Hachiman received the court's formal thanks at the 752 Tōdaiji dedication ceremonies, possibly in recognition of the large contributions from Usa. Moreover, Hachiman was made Tōdaiji's official protector and a shrine was created for him just outside the main temple gate, called Tamukeyama Hachiman Shrine.

This famed incident has been interpreted in a variety of ways. In the view of Tsuji Zennosuke, it illustrates a stage in the rapprochement of Kami and Buddhas, in which the Kami are shown in the form of sentient beings who convert to Buddhism and then become its protectors. For Tsuji, this motif was characteristic of the Nara period (710–794).[41] Other scholars have seen in it a symbolic expression of the subordination of the Kami to the Buddhas.[42]

The event can also be understood in terms of the changing relations between the imperial court and the periphery of the realm. In the opinion of Ross Bender, one could regard these formal accolades for what had been a somewhat obscure Kami from Kyūshū as evidence of the court's "need to obtain the sanction of a native god for a state undertaking of such extensive religious and political implications."[43] The effort to cast the head of the Great Buddha had foundered, after several failed attempts. The court hoped to find the necessary expertise among immigrant groups worshipping Hachiman, according to Sugawara Ikuko, who cites this as a reason for the court's elaborate patronage of the Usa Hachiman Shrine.[44]

Hachiman shrines also were created at Daianji, Tōji, and Yakushiji temples. In 781 the court bestowed the title "great Bodhisattva" (*daibosatsu*) on Hachiman. One of the major rites for Hachiman is the release of living creatures, based on the Buddhist prohibition on taking life. Painting and sculpture representing Hachiman as a Buddhist monk were created. In these ways, the identity of the Kami Hachiman developed many Buddhist elements. In Bender's view, "[T]he context for Hachiman's rise was the Nara attempt to discover an acceptable political balance of native and Buddhist beliefs."[45]

The Tōdaiji project was linked to an even more ambitious plan. In 740 an imperial edict was promulgated, establishing *kokubunji* and *kokubunniji* (a monks' temple and a nuns' temple) in each province. Tōdaiji stood at the apex of this system, as the symbolic "head temple" over the whole. Shōmu's consort Kōmyō was also a great promoter of Buddhism, and she took a special role in sponsoring the building of these provincial temples.

The *kokubunji* contributed greatly to the spread of Buddhist culture. There were at least 136 such temples. There were to be twenty monks to a monks' temple and ten nuns to each nuns' temple. The monks and nuns were to promote the peace and prosperity of the realm by studying Buddhist teachings, copying scriptures, and performing rites on a set schedule, added to which they also prayed for rain or sought relief for crop failures, eclipses, and natural disasters. Like the shrines, the Buddhist temples also prayed for their patrons' health or recovery from illness. Like the Official Shrines, the temples were public extensions of government and were accorded a role in upholding the court. From the court's point of view, both traditions could be useful and should be pressed into service, given patronage, land, and tax exemption. From the perspective of the priests of both the shrines and the temples, court patronage represented the highest possible prestige, and both exerted themselves to the utmost to secure and maintain that patronage. In provincial society, both Kami and Buddhas received respect and were seldom in competition, both being sought after for the benefits they might provide in this life.

Buddhist New Years Rites

While the Daijōsai presented the majesty of the emperor in terms of his connections with the Kami, Buddhist rites were introduced that presented him as a universal Buddhist monarch, the "wheel-turning king" (J: *tenrin shōō*; Skt: *cakravartin*). We have just seen how attractive this idea was to Emperor Shōmu. The Buddhist teachings are symbolized as a wheel; the wheel-turning king protects and sponsors Buddhism in order to help all beings to attain salvation. The great Buddhist saint Kūkai (Kōbō Daishi, 774–835) in 834 encouraged Emperor Shōmu to erect a chapel in the palace compound, called the Shingon'in (Imperial Mantra Chapel), for the performance of the "Imperial Rite of the Second Seven Days of the New Year" (*goshichinichi mishuhō*, or *mishihō*), which began in 835. The significance of the rite's timing, after the first seven days of the New Year, derived from the court's ritual calendar in which the first seven days were devoted to rites for the Kami. These Buddhist rites came to be conducted regularly by the abbot of Tōji (established 796), the Kyoto temple that served as the head temple of the Shingon sect in the Heiankyō capital. The rite's purpose was to conduct prayers for the health and safety of the emperor and for the protection of the realm. From the late eighth century, the second seven days rite was held in conjunction with the "Rites of the Latter Seven Days", (*misai-e*), another set of esoteric Buddhist rites for the protection of the nation and a successful harvest that had begun around 766. The "latter seven days" rite followed the "second seven days rite"; together, these two Buddhist rites occupied the second half of the court's first month's ritual calendar. The latter seven days rite involved recitation of the Golden Light Sutra of Victorious Kings (J: Konkōmyō saishōō kyō; Skt: Suvarna prabhāsa sutra), a work that had long been associated with the idea of Buddhism as spiritual protector of the state. It also expounded the role of the wheel-turning monarch.[46]

The second seven days rite in the Imperial Mantra Chapel presented the emperor as a Buddhist monarch through a complicated assemblage of esoteric symbolism. The north wall of the chapel was hung with scrolls of the five Wisdom Kings, wrathful protectors of Buddhism. In the center hung a scroll of Fudō Myōō, the "Immovable One" (Skt: Ācala or Ācalanātha). On the east and west walls of the chapel hung scrolls of the diamond and womb world mandalas, with a great ritual altar before each one. The rite was conducted before one or the other of these altars, alternating each year. Atop the altar was placed a reliquary holding a Wish Fulfillment Jewel (J: *nyoihōju*; Skt: *cintāmani*), believed to have magical powers to grant wishes and to benefit all beings. Two seats were prepared before the altar, one for the presiding abbot and the other for the emperor's robes. The rites ended with the abbot sprinkling perfumed water upon the emperor's robes that were supposed to have absorbed the powers of the jewel. After the emperor donned these robes, the abbot sprinkled water onto him, which consecrated him as the wheel-turning king. These rites continued to be performed until the fifteenth century.[47]

Combinations of Temples and Shrines

In the first stage of Buddhism's introduction, Buddhist divinities were treated as "foreign Kami," and we have seen how Hachiman emerged as an example of a Kami protecting the Buddhas. Later on, a variety of new institutional combinations emerged. Temples began to incorporate altars to the Kami, and in some cases designated monks read sutras before them to instruct the Kami in Buddhist teachings. The court began authorizing ordinations for this purpose in 794. Some shrines built chapels for the worship of Buddhist divinities on their grounds. From the standpoint of one researching this history, these institutions seem to result from a process of combining one tradition with another. Indeed, it is important to understand that shrines and temples are distinct and separate entities conceptually. When we ask, however, *how the process occurred*, the terms "combining" or "adding" do not capture how these places developed. They developed in response to a *desire to discover* how the Kami and Buddhist figures were related. The *search for correspondences and connections* led to institutions that—in effect—amalgamated the worship of Kami and Buddhas.

A formula to express the connection between Buddhist figures and Kami was the idea that the Kami's spiritual level must be uplifted through Buddhist practices like sutra recitation, or that they are dangerous beings, who must be transformed so that they will not harm people. This idea emerged in the same time frame as the idea of Kami as protectors of the Buddhas and had important precedents in Buddhism's history prior to its entry to Japan. The Indian goddess Hariti is a good example. She had begun as an ogre who eats children, but through her conversion to Buddhism, she became a protector of children. This goddess was incorporated into the Buddhist pantheon and was brought to Japan. In Japan, she became known as Kishimojin, and women prayed to her to conceive and for safe childbirth.

In Japan the context for the emergence of the idea that Kami need Buddhist instruction arose when Buddhist clerics tried to establish themselves on sites that were sacred to the Kami. The Tado Shrine was originally a sacred mountain on which a small shrine had been built in the fifth century, according to legend. The shrine's Kami was an ancestral god of a local gentry family. The shrine was listed in the *Engi shiki* and came into contact with Buddhism when a monk named Mangan Zenji, who was practicing austerities on the mountain, received an oracle in 763:

> I am the kami of Tado. Because I have committed grave offenses over many kalpas, I have received the karmic retribution of being born as a kami. Now

> I wish to escape from my kami state once and for all, and take refuge in the Three Treasures of Buddhism.[48]

Mangan Zenji "received" an oracle from the Kami, which incorporated the key idea of karmic retribution. According to the law of karma, a being is born in a particular status as the result of actions accumulated in previous lives. The statement here is that evil deeds in former lives resulted in birth as a Kami, and that the Kami desires to shed its Kami form. In other words, Kami, like humans and all other sentient beings, are subject to the law of karma; this means that they are inferior to the Buddhas, who have transcended karma.

Buddhism envisioned a hierarchy of states of existence based on karma, in which the Buddhas occupied the highest position, with Bodhisattvas next, followed by gods, and then human beings. The Kami were, in effect, slotted into the "god" category. This statement of the implied inferiority of the Kami to Buddhas still placed them above humanity, in a place of honor. In that sense, the "inferiority" of the Kami to the Buddhas was a relative condition shared by the vast majority of all beings.

The Tado oracle presents the Tado Kami as confiding to a Buddhist cleric his wish to convert to Buddhism to expunge the sins and transgressions of eons of karma and his determination to devote himself thereafter to the Buddha, the Buddhist teaching, and the Buddhist community (the Three Treasures). This view of Kami as inferior to the Buddhist divinities on the hierarchy of states of existence became commonly accepted within Japanese Buddhism.

In response to this oracle, Mangan built a *jingūji*, or shrine-temple, which eventually grew into a large complex of seventy buildings, housing three hundred monks. Mangan also built several other *jingūji*, temples built near shrines, in which the Buddhist side effectively controlled the shrine. *Jingūji* began to be created from the seventh century and spread through the country in the eighth century. As at Tado, a Buddhist monk, frequently an ascetic practicing austerities in the mountains, secured the support of local notable families to build a temple alongside a preexisting shrine, on the rationale that the Kami desired this to liberate them from their miserable state.

If we consider *jingūji* from Buddhism's perspective, we can interpret their founding as a means of spreading the religion by connecting it to preexisting beliefs. It would appear that the better trained, more organized, and more frequently literate Buddhist clerics rather easily dominated cult sites of the Kami where there was no professional shrine priesthood to resist the creation of a temple. For example, Mangan attracted attention by delivering an oracle from the Tado deity. Had this shrine already developed an organized priesthood, female ritualists would undoubtedly have delivered any oracles. In their absence, Mangan could claim to have communicated with the Kami without fear of contradiction.

There were, however, numerous reports of resistance from shrines with an organized priesthood. For example, when a *jingūji* was founded at Ise and huge rainstorms arose in 772, the storms were understood as manifestations of the anger of the Kami at Buddhism's encroachment. As a result, the *jingūji* was moved. The same thing happened again in 780, and again the temple was moved. Records after that time show no evidence of an Ise *jingūji*, suggesting that it was abandoned after the second removal.[49] In this case it appears that the shrine priesthood prevailed, but only a minority of shrines had a strong priesthood, and Buddhism largely succeeded in gaining control of shrines and their lands where *jingūji* were founded.

The Dōkyō Incident

Empress Shōtoku (718–770) had first ruled as Empress Kōken, from 749 to 758. She then abdicated and took the tonsure as a Buddhist nun, re-ascending the throne as Empress Shōtoku in 764. She promoted Buddhism through an adviser, the monk Dōkyō (700–782), who earlier had reputedly cured her of illness by use of his magical powers. The empress granted Dōkyō a higher position than any previous Buddhist cleric, eventually making him "Dharma King" (*hōō*). Dōkyō built a *jingūji* at Ise, implying Buddhism's superiority over the imperial cult. The Dōkyō incident unfolded after Dōkyō asserted that the Kami of the Usa Hachiman Shrine had proclaimed that he would become the next emperor. In the end, another Hachiman oracle canceled the first one, decreeing that no one but a descendant of Amaterasu could become emperor. After Empress Shōtoku died, Dōkyō was banished and died in exile.[50]

The Dōkyō incident threatened to undermine the social order as a whole. The prospect of Dōkyō's enthronement endangered the principle of hereditary succession on which the royal lineage was based. The aristocracy was likewise intimidated, because their prerogatives rested on their mythical connections to the throne. The Jingikan opposed Dōkyō, and, according to Mori Mizue, its head played a central role in ousting him. The Jingikan subsequently instituted taboos on even the mention of anything Buddhist in court rites for the Kami. This prohibition was based on the notion that the Kami abhor anything that might be connected with blood or death, and Buddhism was closely associated with rites for the sick and the dead. A further ban prohibited any speech related to Buddhism at Ise. These measures strengthened the idea that Buddhism is alien to Japan, a foreign teaching that is offensive to the Kami, with the subtext that shrines embody indigenous tradition.[51]

Clan Deities and Clan Shrines

The late eighth and early ninth centuries brought complex changes to the ancient clans. The court made bureaucratic appointments based on genealogical hierarchy, compiling genealogies to justify its appointments. The clans did likewise, to justify their claims to ancient origins and maximize their chances for the best appointments. During this time, clans promoted their deities on a scale not seen before, as additional testaments to their greatness. The competition for influence with the newer clans, who were the purveyors of continental culture, was another impetus to glorify older clan deities. As the older clans felt themselves threatened, they shored up native traditions about their origins from deities closely linked to the imperial ancestors, calling their deities *ujigami* and building shrines for them.[52]

The term *ujigami* (in the sense of a clan deity, rather than as a clan leader as we saw in earlier chapters) first occurred in official sources in the late eighth century and began with the Fujiwara and their clan deities at the Kasuga Shrine, which originally was a sacred site with no permanent structures. The site was a large, sloping hill called Mikasayama in present-day Nara City. Shortly after 710, the Fujiwara literally invented their *ujigami*, constructing the Kasuga Shrine in 768. Soon it was functioning as their tutelary shrine. They worshipped a thunder god called Takemikazuchi (one of the Kami born from the blood of the Fire Deity slain by Izanagi), Futsunushi (a Kami of swords and lightning), the Kami Amenokoyane (who presented a prayer when Amaterasu was drawn out of the Heavenly Rock Cave, and later escorted Ninigi from heaven down to earth), and Amenokoyane's consort, Himegami. Amenokoyane became the primary deity of the Kasuga Shrine.[53]

In the ninth century, many other clans began to construct their own shrines for *ujigami*. Sometimes a clan would join the cult of its ancestors to that of local territorial deities, producing myths relating how a thunder deity (the clan ancestor) had married a local female Kami or a human woman (who emerged as the deity of the territory). Subsequently, the shrine would begin to worship a "family" of Kami based on this pair and their children. The consort representing an autochthonous tradition was called a *himegami*, while the "children" were called *miko gami*. Numerous eighth- and ninth-century shrines followed this pattern, such as the Hachiman, Hie, Hirano, and Kamo shrines. This development illustrates a theme of ancestor worship in ancient Shinto.[54]

In Emperor Kanmu's reign (781–806), the mausoleum aspect of Ise was made increasingly clear by new prohibitions on anyone but the emperor or his delegates presenting offerings at the Ise Shrines. The emperor's personal performance of rites in the palace and observance of taboos became central elements in legitimating him as a divine being. But as reference to myth became less important to the emperor's legitimation than personal deportment, the clans—whose claims to privilege relied solely on myth—were undermined.[55]

In the ninth century, most of the clans were displaced, as positions at court came to depend on personal ties to the imperial family. In particular, the Fujiwara family (the name bestowed on the Nakatomi family after the death of Kamatari, 614–669) dominated court society by marrying into the imperial family and by monopolizing the office of regent (*sesshō, kanpaku*). The court sponsored the rites and festivals of the Kasuga Shrine because of the imperial family's personal connections with the Fujiwara family.[56]

Provincial Shrine Priests during the Ritsuryō Era

The court allotted land and peasant households called *kanbe* to some Official Shrines. These households and their crops supported the shrine and its priests. Most shrines, however, had no *kanbe*, and some had only one or two. As of 806, there were around 6,000 *kanbe* households, of which the largest number were at the Usa Hachiman Shrine, which had 1,660, while the Ise Shrines had 1,130. Land belonging to temples and shrines was exempt from taxation, so the shrine would then be exempt from taxation and could tax the people living on its land (the "Kami households").[57]

The Ritsuryō government's appointment of provincial governors (*kokushi* or *kuni no tsukasa*) displaced an older stratum of local leadership centered on the old provincial governors, *kuni no miyatsuko* or *kokuzō*. The *kokuzō* represented the leading families of each area, and many of them were closely associated with shrine ritual. After the creation of the new system, the *kokuzō* were appointed to posts in provincial branches of the Jingikan, serving as subordinates to court-appointed provincial governors. The *kokuzō* posts became hereditary, and incumbents were expected to confirm their fealty to the central government by presenting horses to the court at each of the two annual Great Purification rites. The *kokuzō* were local gentry, and the rites they performed were regarded as vital to the local tradition.[58] The ritual life of provincial shrines came to incorporate a mixture of state rites created and maintained by the central government and its appointees, on the one hand, and the ongoing traditions of Kami worship that were distinctive of particular locales, on the other. The provinces maintained beliefs, rites, and festivals that were only loosely related to the court's rites and its ideal of coordinating all Kami worship within a single system.[59]

The organization of provincial shrines varied in complexity depending on size. In the large shrines of the Kinai, there was a tripartite structure in which there was one head priest, called a *gūji* or *kannushi*, and under him a *negi*, who also performed ritual as the second-in-command, and at the bottom was one or more *hafuri*. In this case, the term *hafuri* referred to a lower-ranking priest who assisted those above him, and not to those priests at Official Shrines with the same title. Many provincial shrines of the ninth century were led by a *negi*, with *hafuri* under him. The most frequent pattern, however, was shrines whose priests were simply called *hafuri*. Around all kinds of shrines there might be a number of households, called *shake* (literally, "shrine houses" or "shrine families") that participated in ritual and festivals in various capacities, including heritable roles like keeping the keys, preparing the food offerings used in ritual, or shooting off arrows at the conclusion of rites to warn off demons. At the Ise and Izumo shrines, these positions have been passed down over the generations, beginning in antiquity and continuing until today.[60]

The priesthood of the Ise Shrines had a unique structure seen nowhere else, including a distinctive priestly office called *Saishu*, responsible for the vicennial rebuilding of the shrines and the transfer of the mirror of Amaterasu from the old to the new shrine. In enthronement ritual, the *Saishu* recited invocations for the emperor's well-being. The character of this office changed in modern times, so that a female member of the imperial house performs it now.[61]

Local-level Kami ritual in nonofficial village shrines in the eighth century took place at an assembly area called a *yashiro*, not yet at a permanent shrine. There were spring and autumn rituals at which the local Kami were "invited" to descend for a feast. Afterward, the food that had been offered to the Kami was shared in a communal meal called a *naorai*. Priests officiating at these rites were usually a male-female pair chosen for the occasion, so that eventually everyone who lived to adulthood would serve. Men mainly gathered the food or prey used as offerings and prepared the site, while women were the cooks and brewers of sake. The resources necessary to stage these rituals were treated as a tax shared by the villagers.[62]

Ritual Coordination in Provincial Shrines

Let us examine the case of one provincial shrine and the process by which it was integrated into the national system, a shrine called Rokusho no Miya, located in Musashi Province in present-day Tokyo Prefecture, in Fuchū city. According to the shrine's founding legend (*engi*), it was originally established in 111. Local legends held that in antiquity people from Izumo took control of the area and instated worship of their god, Ōkuninushi, along with a group of local tutelary gods called *kunitama*.[63] A tale explaining how Ōkuninushi came to be worshipped in Fuchū related that the god came down from the heavens and began looking for a place to stay the night. His awesome presence so alarmed the people at the first house he visited that they refused him entry. The man of the next house was prepared to receive Ōkuninushi, but his wife was giving birth at that moment, and he was afraid of polluting the deity. Ōkuninushi told the man that he did not fear entering a house of childbirth, so the two shared a meal while the wife gave birth, and the Kami spent the night. A shrine for Ōkuninushi was built. The family that refused the Kami came to a bad end, while the one that had treated him as an honored guest prospered all their days.

Prior to the mid-seventh century, Musashi had been governed by *kokuzō*. Fuchū was made the seat of provincial government for Musashi Province after the Taika Reform of 645, and a provincial governor (*kokushi*) appointed by the court took control.[64] The *kokuzō* did not disappear, however, but was incorporated into the provincial administration and given important roles in rituals. Offices of the provincial government were established adjacent to the shrine.[65]

The local shrines and temples of Musashi served as nodes through which the court could strengthen its relations with the province. To demonstrate respect for local religious institutions was a significant part of the governor's job. Because the provincial Buddhist temple (*kokubunji*) was near the provincial government office, he had obligations to it as well as to the shrines. He was expected to pay tribute annually to six major Musashi shrines on the dates of their Annual Festivals, but since the shrines were spread over a very large territory, travel would have consumed an extraordinary amount of time.

The Annual Festival (now called *reitaisai*) of a shrine stands outside the court-centered rituals mandated by Kami Law. The Annual Festival is an occasion to retell or reenact the stories of how the shrine's Kami came to be worshipped there, to offer distinctive foods, and to entertain the Kami with local songs and dances. The persistence of these festivals signaled the determination of the local elites and communities to preserve their independence and autonomy, even as they found it advantageous in other contexts to accept "guidance" from the center.

To relieve the governor of the burden of attending the Annual Festivals of all the major shrines in his territory, in the early or mid-Heian period a "Comprehensive Shrine" (*sōja*) was built adjacent to the Musashi government offices, symbolically bringing together the Kami of the six far-flung shrines.[66] This Comprehensive Shrine was dedicated to the six deities of the province, and the governor henceforth conducted his official worship there instead of traveling to the original shrines. The original six shrines also began sending their portable shrines to the comprehensive shrine in an annual enactment of their allegiance.[67] In political terms, the merger of the six shrines under the administration of an imperial official signaled the submission and fealty of the provincial shrines and their followers to the imperial court.

In the ancient period Musashi's Comprehensive Shrine was not an Official Shrine, but it was granted that status during the Meiji period. Until then, it was known as the Rokusho no Miya, Rokushogū, or Rokusho Myōjin. In each of these names the particle *roku*, meaning "six," refers to the original six shrines represented in the Comprehensive Shrine. It is thought that eventually a Comprehensive Shrine was established for almost all of the ancient provinces, though not all of them are extant, and data are lacking in some cases. Interestingly, seven of them were called

"Rokusho," suggesting a general practice of identifying six as the number of shrines per province at which the governor should worship.

In addition to the roughly 3,000 Official Shrines, some 391 other shrines not mentioned in the *Engi shiki* can be identified from seventh- and eighth-century sources. According to eighth-century records, there were 4,012 villages. Scholars estimate that the number of shrines was roughly the same as the number of settlements. This estimate may be too conservative, however, as the following example suggests. According to the *Izumo fudoki*, besides the 184 Official Shrines identified in the *Engi shiki*, there were 215 other shrines, for a total of 399, located in 179 settlements, or more than twice as many shrines as villages. In other words, an estimate of numbers of shrines pegged to number of villages will probably be lower than was actually the case, though we do not know how much lower.

The court's original strategy was to incorporate local shrines into a centrally-orchestrated ritual system, but the scope of central direction declined along with the Ritsuryō system. Furthermore, paying respect to Kami on the basis of their connection to imperial Kami declined in importance as the political influence of the clans receded. In place of these older criteria came a new connection between Kami and miracles. This shift in perceptions and expectations of the Kami resulted from the increasing permeation of Buddhism in Japanese society.

If a shrine's Kami manifested especially impressive powers (*myōjin*), the court would designate it a Myōjin shrine. These shrines were counted among the Official Shrines, but their emergence signaled a different relation between the court and provincial shrines. Unlike the older practice of requiring provincial shrine representatives to come to it to receive tribute for regularly scheduled rituals, the Jingikan would directly petition the Kami of these shrines with offerings (called *hōhei*, rather than *hanpei*) and specific requests to end droughts, epidemics, and the like. The rites conducted for these Myōjin shrines included such Buddhist elements as sutra recitation and ordaining monks and nuns to serve the Kami.[68]

These official marks of praise added luster to the shrines and further assisted them in securing revenue. By the early Heian period, the provinces had established "First Shrines" (*ichinomiya*), shrines where the provincial governor was expected to pray for the peace and welfare of the people of the province. There was little overlap with the earlier Comprehensive Shrines, though they continued to exist. Whereas the Comprehensive Shrines seem to have been established as a matter of convenience, the First Shrines represented a semiformal system of ranking, based largely on the perception within a province of which was its most important shrine, based on its reputation for powerful, miracle-working deities. Beneath these First Shrines, there were also Second Shrines (*ninomiya*) and Third Shrines (*sannomiya*). Accompanying the collapse of the Ritsuryō system, however, provincial governors ceased conducting rites in these shrines. In substitution, the custom arose of presenting tribute to twenty-two powerful shrines of the

Kinki region (*nijūni-sha*); the list of these shrines was fixed by 1081 (see chapter 4 for further discussion).[69]

The Kami in Buddhist Tales, *Setsuwa*

Setsuwa are an important source of popular ideas about the Kami as well as Buddhist divinities. The category of tale literature (*setsuwa bungaku; setsuwa* means "tale," and *bungaku* means "literature") encompasses both Buddhist works and others lacking religious coloration. The individual tales may be no more than a few lines or a few pages long, and not all of them show evidence of literary qualities beyond a basic narrative. *Setsuwa* can include myth, legends, and folk tales, as well as some children's literature. Most commonly, the term applies to collections of tales of the Heian (784–1185) and Kamakura periods (1185–1333).[70] While *setsuwa* were recorded mainly to explain Buddhist concepts or to propagate Buddhism, they contain tales about the Kami and are an important source for understanding concepts of Kami and ideas about how Buddhist practitioners and divinities were related to them.

Nihon ryōiki is a collection of Buddhist *setsuwa*, compiled between 810 and 824 by the monk Kyōkai, in three volumes. It is the earliest extant *setsuwa* collection and has exerted a great influence on subsequent Buddhist literature. Kyōkai lived from the late eighth through the early ninth century and was a Buddhist monk of Yakushiji at the time of the work's composition.[71] Kyōkai emphasizes the miraculous and inevitably draws a moral lesson from each story to explain the workings of karma.[72]

One tale concerns an ascetic named En no Ubasoku (later known as En no Ozunu or En no Gyōja), thought to have lived in the Nara period. En desired to become able to fly and "play in the garden of immortality"—that is, to attain immortality. Retiring to a mountain cave, he

> wore clothing made of vines, drank the dewdrops on pine needles, bathed in pure spring water to rinse away the filth of the world of desire, and learned the formula of the Peacock to attain extraordinary power. Thus he could employ spirits and kami at his command.[73]

While the exact content of the "Peacock formula" is unclear, it was undoubtedly a powerful magical spell or *darani* derived from one of several Buddhist texts relating to the Peacock King Kujaku Myō-ō (Mahāmāyūri-vidyārājñi), a guardian deity. Although the invocation of the Peacock formula connects En with Buddhism, his cultivation of flight and immortality, as well as his ability to manipulate lesser spirits, strongly suggests the influence of Daoism.

> Once [En] summoned [the Kami] and ordered them, "Make a bridge between Kane-no-take (Mt. Golden Peak, the mountain Kinpusen in the Yoshino range in Nara Prefecture) and Kazuraki-no-take (Mt. Kazuraki, on the border of Nara and present-day Osaka Prefectures)." They were not happy about this, and in the reign of the emperor residing at Fujiwara Palace (that is, Emperor Monmu, r. 697–700), Hitokotonushi no Ōkami of Kazuraki-no-take was possessed and slandered him, saying, "[En] plans to usurp the throne." The emperor dispatched messengers to capture him, but they found it hard to take him due to his mysterious magical power, so they captured his mother instead. In order that his mother might be freed, he gave himself up. He was exiled to the island of Izu.... Hitokotonushi no Ōkami was bound with a spell by [En], and he has not escaped even to this day.[74]

In this story, a power struggle unfolds between the ascetic En and the Kami, led by Hitokotonushi (Lord of the One Word). En demonstrates the superiority of his magic over the Kami by successfully compelling them to build a bridge for his convenience between two mountains that were known as places for ascetic practice. En planned to appropriate one of these mountains, Mt. Kazuraki, which was Hitokotonushi's home. The story portrays Hitokotonushi as retaliating with a false accusation, turning to the greater authority of the emperor, because the Kami lacks the power to repel En's advance on his own. But En seals his triumph over Hitokotonushi by binding him with a magical spell, thus neutralizing him for all eternity. The tale depicts the Kami as both weak and devious and is an obvious piece of propaganda for Buddhism, as are many *setsuwa*.

A second story concerning the Kami is similarly unflattering to them. In this one a monk named Eshō was visiting a temple near a shrine in present-day Shiga Prefecture dedicated to a Kami called Taga no Ōkami. One night the monk had a dream in which a white monkey appeared. The monkey declared himself to be Taga no Ōkami and asked the monk to recite the Lotus Sutra for him, in order that he might be released from his humiliating simian form. To Eshō's query about how he had fallen into such a state, the monkey replied that in a previous life he had been an Indian king who had refused permission to one thousand men who sought to become Buddhist monks. For unjustly obstructing their desire to follow the Buddhist path, he had been reborn as a monkey and the Kami of the Taga Shrine.[75]

Up to this point in the story, we see three slanders on the Kami: first, the idea that they might actually be animals, subhuman creatures; second, the idea that they reaped the karmic retribution of animal birth *and* birth as a Kami as a result of suppressing those who would follow Buddhism; and third, the idea that they so lack the power to ensure their own salvation that they must beg a passing monk to recite sutras for them to raise themselves to a human level in some future rebirth.

The story portrays the state of being a Kami as not an elevated birth but bestial—beneath the state of human existence.

The tale goes on to recount that when the monkey said that he could not offer Eshō any rice in return for his rituals, the monk refused the monkey's request for sutra recitations. So much for the compassion of Buddhism! In the course of this interchange, the monkey revealed that although he had received rice for such purposes from the government, the shrine priest had appropriated it as his personal property and would not release it to the Kami. Here the tale portrays shrine priests as venal and corrupt and the Kami as powerless to punish them.

Rebuffed by Eshō, the monkey vowed to join a group of monks in another district who were soon to hold a sutra recitation. Nonplussed by his dream, Eshō consulted a colleague named Manyo, who was expected to participate in the recitation that the monkey planned to join. Manyo rejected Eshō's tale out of hand, saying, "These are merely the words of a monkey. I do not believe what you say. Nor will I accept nor admit the monkey into the group." But as Manyo was preparing for the recitation, his temple, all its buildings, and their Buddhist images collapsed. Recognizing this destruction to be the Kami's retaliation, Manyo and Eshō were horrified. They promptly rebuilt the temple and allowed the monkey to hear the sutras, but not to join those reciting them.

This phase of the story admits that the Kami are not without destructive power but emphasizes the monks' authority to refuse them permission to act as if they were on the same level as a Buddhist priest: they may attend as members of the audience, but they may not recite sutras. They can have sutras recited, but not unless they pay. Kami are among the objects of sutra recitation, and they may receive merit from such rites, but they are not authorized to join the monks. Thus the story ends by upholding the unique authority of the Buddhist priesthood over the Kami.

Conclusion

We have seen that the creation of the Jingikan grew from the unification of the realm in the Ritsuryō government and the political imperative to subordinate and control the provinces. Throughout this discussion, we have seen the tension between center and periphery as the center tried to impose unity, and the periphery strove to maintain autonomy while at the same time securing the advantages of connection to the center. The limited success the Jingikan enjoyed in the attempt to unify the shrines is an index of the vitality of the local traditions of Kami worship, of the determination of local elites and communities to preserve their own myths and rites. Yet the outlines of system, the undisputed highest prestige attaching to connection with the imperial court, the emergence of the court as the preeminent patron of the shrines, the establishment in this period of annual court rites, enthronement ritual, and the Vicennial Renewal of the Ise Shrines, lasting—albeit with interruptions in the medieval period—for over a millennium, identify this period as the originating point for a very strong set of enduring, interlocked traditions that linked Kami cults across the country. Though the word was not yet in use, this is the beginning of Shinto.

But while we can see the emergence of founding elements of Shinto at this early period, we do not find their full development until later ages. Several factors examined in this chapter worked against Shinto developing autonomously. Although *jingi* purported to represent the indigenous, it remained deeply influenced by Daoism, Buddhism, and miscellaneous continental religious elements. Buddhism strove to envelop and subordinate the Kami, just as it had done with the other deities in its path as it spread beyond India, a process we see unfolding institutionally in Japan in the emergence of combinatory temple-shrines and being reflected at a popular level in tale literature. The authority and prestige of early Shinto derived from the court and the Ritsuryō system of government, but these connections made it dependent and vulnerable. Although Shinto was tied to the court in ways that both defined and benefited it, it was hostage to court decisions and policies that it could not control. The position of the highest-ranking Kami priests within the Jingikan was prestigious, but because the priests were primarily government ritualists, they were limited in the scope of action they could take. To be a priest was to perform ritual, not debate with courtiers. Priests were mostly mute at court. It was unthinkable for Jingikan officials to criticize the court, even when the court acted in ways that diluted its "indigenous" ritual system, such as building Tōdaiji and instituting Buddhist rites presenting the monarch as a Buddhist king. The Dōkyō incident threatened to circumvent the Jingikan entirely and put a monk on the throne. The only permissible remonstrance in the latter situation was to secure a supplemental oracle from the Kami Hachiman, who in the course of Tōdaiji's construction had already been larded with Buddhist titles and symbolism. In spite of much rhetoric about the harmony of the two traditions, the potential for antagonism between them was significant, and sometimes erupted nakedly.

As we will see in chapter 4, the court became involved in a variety of ritual practices that blurred the distinction between public, "official" rites and private ceremonial rites. The Ritsuryō system began to fall apart by the ninth century, and the Jingikan's tribute offerings to the Official Shrines both lost prestige and proved too expensive and unwieldy to maintain. Direct imperial rule was replaced by a regency system under which the ritual practices of the aristocracy grew to rival those of the court, and in which the centrality of the Jingikan was greatly undermined. In these various ways, the path toward fuller intellectual and institutional development was obstructed.

4

Shinto during the Middle and Late Heian Period, Tenth through Twelfth Centuries

Introduction

This chapter examines the transformation of Shinto over the middle and late Heian period, roughly the tenth through the twelfth centuries. We begin by examining the declining influence of the Jingikan over Kami affairs and then turn to the emergence of a new order. A new set of shrines patronized by the court, sixteen at first, eventually increasing to twenty-two, superseded the older annual calendar of shrine rites decreed by Kami Law, though the older system continued on a reduced scale under the management of the Department of State.

Kami Law originally specified what counted as "official" or "public" ritual, but in the middle to late Heian period, imperial patronage expanded significantly beyond those rites. The shrines connected to the Fujiwara family, who were the emperors' regents, mothers, and highest officials, received lavish court tribute and imperial visits, as did the Kamo Shrines and Iwashimizu Hachimangū. These shrines were joined by those such as the Gion Shrine or the Kitano Tenmangū (Tenjin Shrine), which originated in the Heian period as places for the worship of new divinities. A chain of misfortunes was attributed to the wrath of plague deities and the souls of those who had been wrongfully punished. Such spirits were called *goryō* or *on'ryō*.[1] A growing number of observances at an expanding group of shrines were designated as "official rites" (*kōsai*) and thus widened the scope of public ritual. Eventually these official rites encompassed the ceremonies of some twenty-two shrines to which the emperor paid tribute and/or made personal visits in the form of grand imperial progresses, processions that became popular spectacles witnessed by the entire capital. Much of the court's ceremonial was motivated by new religious anxieties, such as fear of *goryō*, illness, or pollution that might cause *tatari*, divine retaliation in the forms of sickness, famine, and natural disaster.

While imperial patronage was the key to "official" status, not all the court's observances had national significance, nor was the Jingikan involved in all of them. In fact, the Department of State took over responsibility for supervising public ceremonies, and the Jingikan's scope of activity shrank. The Jingikan lost control over official public rites owing to the widened scope of imperial involvement in shrines to which the Jingikan had no connection. But whereas the court had formerly positioned itself as the authorizer and orchestrator of all public rites, its entry into the ceremonial life of a multiplicity of shrines of disparate origins caused it to lose its position as the linchpin of a single system. The court became instead one of myriad supplicants to the divinities of these various shrines, albeit the most important one. The transformation was complete by around 1070.[2]

This means that the distinction between public and private, official and nonofficial, that had structured the court's ritual life broke down for lack of a new rationale that could convincingly argue for the national significance of all court ceremonial. The systematic character of public rites for the Kami dissolved, even as the scope of Kami worship grew.

Shrine and temple combinations became the norm. Buddhist and Kami rites were coordinated within combinatory institutions in which the Buddhist clergy typically held greater authority and power over the complex's resources. Thus, the combinatory motifs that arose in institutional, intellectual, and popular forms were not equal partnerships but significantly imbalanced in Buddhism's favor.[3]

Aristocratic diaries of the period reveal important shifts in attitudes that were reflected in the choice of the shrines and festivals that the elites patronized. Official appointment entailed participation in the older system of shrine rites, but we find in addition to fulfilling such obligations, a growing tendency for aristocrats to express personal faith in particular Kami. In addition, that is, to the older idea of state rites as a quintessentially "public" phenomenon, we see a privatizing, individualizing tendency in enhanced devotional attitudes directed to the Kami. These religious attitudes were modulated by ideas characteristic of the era, such as the new anxieties regarding *goryō*, illness, pollution, and *tatari*, as well as Buddhist ideas of the Latter Days of the Dharma.

Changes in the way the Great Purification Rite was performed show clearly that the court and aristocracy utilized this ritual to expunge pollutions and avert *tatari* in a way unrelated to the twice-yearly performances of this ritual as set out in Kami Law. We find the court commanding the Jingikan to perform the rite in a manner lacking public or national significance, using it instead to purify the emperor's living quarters or even to exorcise ghosts. Meanwhile, the aristocrats hired yin-yang masters and Buddhist priests to perform the rite for similar purposes for themselves, lending the rite a generic religiosity alien to its origins. This transformation of the Great Purification Rite vividly illustrates the privatization of formerly public Shinto rites and the religious sentiments that came to motivate the court and aristocracy to perpetuate them in new forms for new purposes.

The pantheon expanded as new shrines were constructed for *goryō*, and spectacular festivals were held to appease them, in the hopes that they might be transformed into beneficent protectors—new Kami. The townspeople of Kyoto participated in these and other shrine festivals enthusiastically and creatively, parading symbols of the Kami in gorgeously decorated palanquins, while dressed in splendid, elegant robes. Shrine festivals became important vehicles for the development and preservation of arts and crafts of all kinds. Significantly, the Jingikan had little or no role in administering the affairs of these new shrines or the shrines of the great aristocratic families. *Dengaku*, artful mass dancing in the form of multiday processions to shrines, arose. These dances could be joyous and celebratory, but sometimes they expressed popular discontent. *Dengaku* was both appreciated and feared by the aristocracy.

The court and aristocracy bequeathed so much land to shrines that the largest ones became great landholders. As their holdings grew, shrines established priestly orders to administer their distant fiefs and branch shrines. These lesser priests were not under the Jingikan's supervision. Because shrines typically had administering temples, we can sometimes discern struggles between the two over land. As they acquired distant fiefs, shrines would construct branch shrines far from the home shrine, and those branch shrines would conduct rites and ceremonies patterned after the observances at the home shrine. By this means the ritual and festival styles originating in the capital were transmitted to the provinces.

Temple-shrine multiplexes acquired the potential to become cultic centers and to spawn the creation of regional cultic centers in their distant fiefs. In this way shrines came to transcend by far their original rationales as places for revering clan ancestors or local tutelary deities. They evolved into places of considerable wealth and power in their own right, not depending on the older rationale of *jingi* rites and Kami Law. We will consider whether *honji-suijaku* and the combinatory complexes encompassing temples and shrines should be regarded as evidence of syncretism.

New ideas about relations between Kami and Buddhist divinities emerged, structured by Esoteric Buddhism, expressed through new philosophical paradigms, rituals, and artistic forms. The idea of the Buddhas as the "original ground" (*honji*) and the Kami as the "manifest traces" (*suijaku*) remained influential for centuries. Concepts of the Kami enforcing a moral code—not merely the observance of taboos—emerged in classical literature such as the *Tales of the Heike*.

The Jingikan's Decline and the Twenty-Two Shrines

The national system of shrine rites that the Jingikan had orchestrated in the eighth century formed a lasting ideal, focused on a public role for shrines, shrine ritual, and shrine priests uniting the realm in reverence for the monarchy through reverence for the Kami, not as a matter of personal religious faith, but *as a necessary function of government.* The vision was shattered, however, when the Jingikan lost control over the shrines in the dissolution of the Ritsuryō system. A 914 memorial presented to Emperor Daigo (r. 897–930) by Imperial Adviser (*sangi*) Miyoshi Kiyoyuki (847–918), commenting on the Jingikan's distribution of tribute to the Official Shrines for the Kinensai and Tsukinamisai, dramatically exposed the agency's loss of authority:

> The procedure is that the Court Nobles, at the head of the Secretaries and the civil officials, come to worship in the Jingikan. For every individual shrine the Jingikan [officials] set up offerings: the symbolic ones, one bottle of clear sake, one iron spear, displayed upon the offerings tables. If shrines are accorded horses (one horse for the Toshigoi [Kinensai] and two for the Tsukinami festival), then the Left and Right Mount Bureaus lead the procession of sacred horses. Then [the liturgist of] the Jingikan recites the prayer for the festival. When that is done, the said festival offerings are distributed to the various representatives to present them at their own shrines. The priests should have performed purification and fasting and then reverently bear [the offerings] to present them each at his own shrine. But in the very presence of the high nobility, [the priests] proceed to take the offerings of silk and tuck them into their bosoms, they throw away the handle of the spear and take only the head, they tip up the bottles of sake and drain them in a single draught. Indeed, not one person has gone out of the gates of the Jingikan bearing the offerings intact! How much more so with the sacred horses! Straightaway traders outside the [gates] buy them all and take them and depart. In this situation can the festival deities rejoice in the sacrifices? If they do not rejoice in the [offerings], how can we expect abundance and prosperity?[4]

It is not difficult to imagine the court's reaction. The shrine priests' brazen disrespect revealed the Jingikan's inability to restrain them. And no wonder—in fact, there were few penalties for a shrine's failure to send a representative to these ceremonies or for selling the tribute received.[5] A shakeup was in order. From the mid-Heian period, the central government ceased supporting the Jingikan. Instead, shrines were taxed to support the Jingikan.[6] Although probably not as a direct consequence of the memorial, the Nakatomi family lost control of the headship of the Jingikan, which became hereditary in the Shirakawa family. A new Jingikan post called *miyaji* came to be monopolized by the Urabe family, who later came to be known by the name Yoshida. The office-holder performed prayers for the emperor's health and purifications for his person. By this means, the Urabe family rapidly gained influence from the mid-Heian period, though in earlier times their position had been rather low.[7] This reshuffling occurred as changes were upending the hierarchy among the old *jingi* families. Official appointments of all kinds were becoming hereditary entitlements in particular families from the late tenth to the eleventh century.[8]

We can see a definite shift in the court's outlook on Kami rites from the mid-Heian period, away from the Jingikan's rites as originally specified in Kami Law. A list of sixteen shrines under imperial patronage was issued in 966, and by 1039 the total had grown to twenty-two, giving rise to an expression, "Twenty-Two Shrines" (*nijūnisha*). The twenty-two shrines were divided into three groups, based upon their distance from the capital, as summarized in the Table 4.1.

Table 4.1 **The Twenty-Two Shrines and Their Administering Temples**

Shrine Grouping	*Shrine Name*	*Shikinaisha Status*	*Name of Administering Temple*
The Upper Seven Shrines	Ise	*Shikinaisha*	Ise Daijingūji
	Iwashimizu Hachimangū	Not a *Shikinaisha*	Gokokuji (Daijō-in)
	Kamo (includes the Upper and Lower Kamo Shrines)	*Shikinaisha*	Kamo Jingūji
	Matsuno'o	*Shikinaisha*	Mansekiji
	Hirano	*Shikinaisha*	Semuidera (Kannonji)
	Inari	*Shikinaisha*	Inari Jingūji
	Kasuga	*Shikinaisha*	Fukaiden (Kōfukuji)
Middle Seven Shrines	Ōharano	Not a *Shikinaisha*	Ōharano Jingūji
	Ōmiwa	*Shikinaisha*	Daigorinji
	Isonokami	*Shikinaisha*	Isonokami Jingūji
	Yamato	*Shikinaisha*	Yamato Jingūji
	Hirose	*Shikinaisha*	Hirose Jingūji
	Tatsuta	*Shikinaisha*	Tatsuta Jingūji
	Sumiyoshi	*Shikinaisha*	Shiragidera
Lower Eight Shrines	Hie	*Shikinaisha*	Yakuō-in (Enryakuji)
	Umenomiya	*Shikinaisha*	Umeminomiya Jingūji
	Yoshida	Not a *Shikinaisha*	Jingū-in
	Hirota	*Shikinaisha*	Hirota Jingūji

(continued)

Table 4.1 **Continued**

Shrine Grouping	*Shrine Name*	*Shikinaisha Status*	*Name of Administering Temple*
	Gion	Not a *Shikinaisha*	Kankeiji (Kanshin-in)
	Kitano	Not a *Shikinaisha*	Kannonji
	Nibunokawakami (includes the Upper, Middle, and Lower Nibu shrines)	*Shikinaisha*	Nibunokawakami Jingūji
	Kibune	*Shikinaisha*	Jizō-in

Source: Adapted from Allan Grapard, "Institution, Ritual, and Ideology: The Twenty-Two Shrine Temple Multiplexes of Heian Japan," *History of Religions* 27, no. 3 (1998): 253.

The court's shift toward these twenty-two shrines came about as the Jingikan ceased to function to unite the Official Shrines. Most of the twenty-two were *shikinaisha*, but Gion, Kitano Tenmangū, and Iwashimizu Hachimangū represented newer shrines that were outside the old system. Gion and Kitano represented the court's new interest in *goryō*. All twenty-two shrines functioned in combination with temples (though Ise's *jingūji* eventually disappeared).[9] It is not entirely clear why these particular shrines should have been singled out for court patronage, but two possibilities have been advanced in previous research. The shrines might have been singled out because they had conducted rites to make rain or to stop excessive rain, rites for agricultural fertility, and rites to respond to political crises. The group reveals a strong presence of Fujiwara influence, since Ōharano and Yoshida shrines were symbolic replicas of the Kasuga Shrine that were established in Kyoto; in essence, they were clan shrines for the Fujiwara.[10]

The shift in the court's attentions to different shrines and rituals does not fully account for priests' lack of respect for imperial tribute, nor does their disrespect sufficiently explain the decline in the Jingikan's position. The answer to the puzzle lies in the increasing influence of Buddhist ritual over the court and aristocratic society, especially esoteric rites associated with the Tendai and Shingon schools. Both schools were established after Japanese monks were sent to study in China to absorb current trends in Buddhism. With the dissolution of the Bureau of Yin and Yang in 820, they also became heavily involved in the knowledge and technologies in which the bureau had specialized. We saw earlier that from the sixth century, a variety of Buddhist rites had been incorporated into the court's calendar of annual observances. That trend continued and greatly intensified throughout the Heian period. Esoteric Buddhism appealed to the court and the aristocracy in its complex texts, doctrines, and symbolism expressed in a variety of artistic media as well as in manifold rituals.[11] By contrast, *jingi* rites did not offer comparable intellectual challenge or aesthetic complexity, nor did the Jingikan produce scholarship asserting the value of its guardianship of "indigenous tradition." The Jingikan's specialization in minute ritual protocols was unsuited to analytic refutation or philosophical exposition. These manifold changes of the late Heian period can be seen in the transformation of the Great Purification Rite.

The Great Purification Rite

Kami Law mandated two annual Great Purifications (Ōharai), the first scheduled for the last day of the sixth month, and the second for the last day of the twelfth month. These rites aimed to cleanse away the accumulated pollution of the previous half-year. Each province was required to furnish a horse and other offerings for the purifications, showing that the intention was that the purifying effects of the rites would extend to the country as a whole. Beyond the court's usual offerings of fabric, weaponry, tools, deer antlers, rice, salt, sake, dried meat, and sea products, the Great Purification Rite called for the use of gilded and silver effigies.[12] In addition, six "expiatory horses" (*harae uma*), free of any blemish, were offered to the Kami. The horses were to carry away all defilements. The effigies prescribed for this ritual were simple human shapes cut out of metal, to be held or rubbed in order to transfer the pollution of the person's body to the effigy, which would then be discarded, purifying the person. Scribes presented the swords and effigies to the emperor, who breathed on them in order to transfer any defilement or pollution, thus cleansing himself and the palace before the recitation of the *norito* read by the Nakatomi.[13]

The use of the metal effigies is regarded as a Daoist practice invoking a Daoist cosmology, according to David Bialock.[14] The formula recited by the Recorders of East and West when extending the effigies and the sword to the sovereign is full of Daoist language:

> We humbly beseech the Supreme Ruler of Heaven, the (Six) Great Lords of the Three Terraces, the sun, the moon, the stars, and planets, the hosts of gods in eight directions, the arbiters of human destiny and the keepers of records, the Father King of the East on the left, the Mother Queen of the West on the right, the five rulers of the five directions, the four climates of the four seasons, as we humbly present these silver effigies, we beseech ye, free us from calamities. As we humbly present the golden sword, we beseech ye, prolong the life of our Sovereign. We pronounce the charm: To the East as far as Fusō,[15] to the West as far as Yu-yen,[16] to the south as far as the burning tropics, to the north as far as the arctic, to a thousand cities, a hundred countries, let the eternal reign extend! Banzai! Banzai![17]

The formula addresses Heaven as the supreme deity, and also a variety of astral bodies conceived of as ruling the human life span, beginning with the "three terraces," three pairs of stars in the Ursa Major constellation, and continuing to the Father King of the East and the Queen Mother of the West. All these deities are implored to keep the realm free of disaster and to lengthen the monarch's life to ten thousand years (this is the meaning of *banzai*).[18]

Certainly, the presence of Daoist symbols in imperial rites in this period is striking, but they did not nullify the motif of divine descent or the power of *kotodama*. Instead, there seems to have been a layering of symbolism without an attempt to reconcile their varying implications or to weave them discursively into a single, coherent philosophy of sovereignty.[19]

The twenty-seven *norito* included in the *Engi shiki* were used in the imperial court and are thought to have been collected in the Kōnin era (810–824). They are still used in shrines and highly esteemed today. They build on the older religious idea of *kotodama*, that magical action can be effected through speech. These prayers presume that happiness and good fortune can be brought about by the manipulation of powerful, elegant words, and likewise, that curses can come true by the use of speech spelling out the desired outcome.[20] The *norito* for this rite, known as the Great Purification Prayer (Ōharai norito), has come to be widely used, not only at court but also in the shrines, as later chapters will explain. According to Shinto scholar Mitsuhashi Tadashi, there is nothing more "Shinto" than purification, and nothing more emblematic of purification than the Ōharai *norito*.[21]

Ritual of Great Purification

O, All ye assembled imperial princes and princesses, ye other princes, ministers, and all the host of officials, hearken unto the words which we pronounce. Commencing with His Sovereign Majesty's scarf-decked attendants, quiver-bearing attendants, and sword-wearing attendants, yea, all the multitude of attendants, from all of these and from the many persons of all the different offices, let the varieties of offenses unwittingly or willfully committed[22] be driven out, in this great driving-out of the last day of the sixth month [or twelfth month] of this year; let them all be driven out and washed away, hearken ye all unto these words.

At the command of the mighty ancestral gods and goddesses divinely abiding in the Plain of High Heaven, the many myriad *kami* were divinely gathered together to discuss and plan, and by their words entrusted to the divine descendant[23] the country of rich rice-ears growing in the abundant reedy plains as a pleasant land to rule in peace.

Lest there be any unruly *kami* (*araburu kamitachi*) in the midst of the land entrusted to him, the *kami* asked and inquired why they were thus, and caused them to be divinely cleansed and purged. The words of questioning from rocks and trees, and even the least blade of grass, were ended. Leaving the worthy throne of heaven, parting asunder the many-layered heavenly clouds, with awesome parting, he descended from heaven to the land entrusted to him.

In the land in the center of all lands which was entrusted to him, the land of Yamato where the sun shines high, a pleasant land, the columns of his palace auspiciously planted, the crossed gable-boards reaching up toward heaven. Here is built the splendid, august dwelling-place of the divine descendant, sheltered from the gaze of heaven and from the blazing sun. In the pleasant land which he rules in tranquility, from the many people who by divine grace are born into it, may the countless offenses unwittingly or willfully committed be purged; beginning with the heavenly offenses (breaking down the paddy dikes, filling in irrigation ditches, opening the sluice-gates, double planting, setting up stakes, flaying alive, flaying backwards, cursing with excrement, and many such, these are designated as heavenly offenses) and then earthly offenses—defilement due to cutting live flesh, cutting dead flesh; due to vitiligo, due to excrescences; defilement due to intercourse with one's own mother, or one's own daughter, due to cohabiting with a woman and then her daughter by previous marriage, or from cohabiting with a girl and then her mother; defilement due to copulation with an animal, due to attack from creeping things, due to calamity from the *kami* on high, or from birds overhead, due to having caused death to livestock or other evil magic—let all these defilements be purged.

And when these are purged, by the divine ceremonial, let the Ōnakatomi take the sacred branches and, cutting off the thick ends, cutting away the leaf ends, lay them upon the many offering-tables in ample numbers. Let them gather and cut the stalks of thatching reeds and, cutting off the thick ends, clipping the leaf ends, divide them finely, needle-like, and recite the solemn liturgy of the heavenly magic formula.[24] When he has thus recited, may the heavenly *kami* push open the worthy doors of heaven, and part with an awesome parting the many-layered heavenly clouds. May the terrestrial *kami* ascend to the summits of the high mountains and summits of the hills and may they clear away the mists from the high mountains and the mists from the hills.

If they vouchsafe to do this, commencing with the august palace of the divine descendant, throughout all the lands, let every last offense—just as the winds of the boundless skies blow away the many-layered clouds of heaven, just as the morning wind blows to dispel the mists of the morning and the evening wind blows to dispel the winds of the evening; just as at the harbor's edge by letting loose its prow and letting loose its stern a big ship is put afloat on the broad plain of the sea; and just as the long, young branches are cut from the tree trunk with the tempered blade of a sharp sickle—so let the offenses be driven out and be purged so that none remain. From the tops of the high mountains, from the tops of the hills, in the waters which tumble into churning rivers, may the *kami* called Seoritsu-hime, who dwells in the mainstream of swift rivers, carry them out to the broad sea-plain. When they are carried away thus, over the myriad routes of the tides, may the *kami* called Haya-akitsu-hime, who dwells in the currents of the wild tides, swirl them about and swallow them up. When they are thus swallowed up may the *kami* called Ibukido-nushi, who dwells in the place of

> blowing air, blow them out and away from the country beneath, from the nether regions. When they are thus blown away from the country beneath and from the nether regions, may the *kami* called Haya-sasura-hime carry them and as she wanders about dissipate them. When they are thus dissipated, commencing with all the people of the various offices serving the Court of the Sovereign, from this day forth in all regions under heaven, may the offenses and defilements disappear. Let the creatures in heaven lend their ears, as the horses are led forward. On this the last day of the sixth [or the twelfth] month of this year, at the great driving out, at the setting of the sun, we humbly pray that Ye cause the driving out and cleansing of all, so say we. And let the *urabe* of the four provinces carry these and withdraw to the stream of the great river and cast them all out, so we pray.[25]

Centuries of Shinto exegesis have been devoted to this *norito*. Its symbolism is rich and complex. Its language is elegant and beautiful even in translation. When recited in ringing tones by a priest with a sonorous voice, or by hundreds of congregants in a Shinto-derived new religious movement, its rhythmic, repeated phrases build to a moving climax, as all blemishes, faults, and transgressions are symbolically swept away. Or, rather, two female Kami associated with water, Seoritsu-hime and Haya-akitsu-hime loose the pollutions into the tides to be swallowed up; then the male Kami Ibukido-nushi blows them into the nether regions. Finally, another female Kami, Haya-sasura-hime, wanders off and—essentially—loses the pollutions. To drive the point home visually, the Urabe diviners took the effigies out of the palace and threw them into the river.

The object of purification in this prayer is *tsumi*, sometimes translated as "sin," but since that term is so redolent with associations from Western religions, it is probably better to think of it as meaning "transgressions." The transgressions are divided into "heavenly transgressions" (*amatsu tsumi*) and "earthly transgressions" (*kunitsu tsumi*). The heavenly ones are the ones committed by Susanoo, while the earthly ones are concerned principally with spilling blood, incest as defined at the time, contact with insects and reptiles, falling victim to some divine "attack," or using magic. The list is reminiscent of the taboos seen in preliterate societies more generally.[26]

Yet the prayer is not confined to the ostensible aim of purifying the realm of these transgressions. It recounts a purge of the "unruly" (*araburu*) Kami, those obstreperous provincial deities whom we have seen continuing to resist imperial authority throughout the sixth, seventh, and eighth centuries. Only when they have been "cleansed" does the heavenly grandchild descend to earth, a scenario that clearly represented wishful thinking.

The Great Purification Rite was first established under Emperor Tenmu, as a reconstitution of pillar rituals performed in the Kofun period. It is not clear that the ritual was performed twice each year in Tenmu's time, or that all the government officials attended, as the text suggests. In *Nihon shoki* the ritual first appears in a record for the eighth month of 686, when Tenmu was in his final illness, where Tenmu commands that a great purification be performed toward the four directions, using "purification pillars" (*haraibashira*) supplied by the provinces, consisting of horses, cloth, swords, deerskins, mattocks, knives, and servants of both sexes. In other words, the provinces were required to supply "purification pillars," which are offerings used in the performance of the rite at Tenmu's court. The political significance of holding the rite in this way is to dramatize the submission of the provinces to imperial authority. The 686 rite was accompanied by Buddhist healing rituals. The way it was performed at this time, in combination with the preceding formula to prolong the emperor's life and followed by Buddhist curing ritual, suggests that it combined elements of provincial submission ritual with healing, and that it was not unambiguously "Shinto" from the beginning.[27] In this case, "purification" seems to have implied healing as well as the pacification of unruly elements in the provinces.

The Great Purification Rite held a central position in the annual calendar of Jingikan ritual prescribed by Kami Law. It continued to be conducted in the Nara period, but its performance overflowed the bounds prescribed in Kami Law, coming to be staged at various times besides the occasions specified in Kami Law for the sixth and twelfth months, and for a variety of purposes. For example, we find multiple instances in which the rite was performed to signal the end of a period of mourning after the death of an emperor or following a rebellion, banishment, or punishment of a high official. For example, in 729 an anonymous informer accused Prince Nagaya, the Minister of the Left, of treason against Emperor Shōmu. The allegation held that the prince was secretly practicing an "evil way" (*sadō* [lit., "the left way"]), magical techniques associated with Daoism. Eventually, Prince Nagaya was forced to commit suicide. Following this incident, an imperial rescript was promulgated prohibiting sorcery and curses disguised as Buddhist practices.[28] In this instance the Great Purification Rite was performed with only a small number of people in attendance, at a different location than usual, and for the purpose of purifying the palace, not the nation as a whole. *Shoku nihongi* records performances of the Great Purification Rite in 707 and 775 to quell epidemics, storms, and earthquakes. There were many performances of the rite in response to strange occurrences during the reign of Emperor Kōnin (770–781). For example, in 776 it was conducted to rid the palace of a ghost (*yōkai*). The rite was generally performed along with Buddhist rituals in such circumstances.[29]

The Great Purification Rite and *Tatari*

During the Heian period, the desire to guarantee the purity of the palace increased. As of 830, the Great Purification Rite came to be performed in front of the Kenreimon Gate, the entry to the palace closest to the emperor's living quarters. As if to underscore some anxiety about the purity of the emperor himself, Emperor Montoku (r. 850–858) had the Great Purification Rite performed twice before his enthronement rites and a third time after its conclusion. We can discern rising apprehension about pollution in the subsequent reign of Emperor Seiwa (r. 858–876). In the year and a half between Montoku's death and Seiwa's enthronement rites in 859, the Great Purification Rite was performed no less than thirteen times.[30]

The ceremony was sometimes held when a person in a state of pollution inadvertently brought the taint into the palace, for example, a person who had encountered a dead dog on the way to the palace. Another performance in 862 was held after this odd event: a rat chewed on the cushion on which the imperial seal reposed. When the court had the Jingikan carry out divination to discover the meaning of this queer portent, the verdict was that someone in a state of pollution had participated in the recent Niinamesai, angering the Kami. If pollution were discovered before a scheduled ritual for the Kami, that ceremony might be postponed until the Great Purification Rite could be performed, as a way to forestall *tatari*. In these circumstances, performance of the Great Purification Rite arose from a concern that pollution would anger the Kami and provoke them to *tatari*.[31]

The emperor's body symbolized "the body of the imperial state," and to protect and heal any defect of his person was a matter of national significance. Thus when the emperor fell ill, shrines and temples across the country were called upon to pray for him as a matter of protecting the realm. This coalescence of the symbolism of the imperial body and of the realm is key to a defining rationale for ancient rites of all kinds: *chingo kokka*, protection of the realm.[32] Yet this rationale and the underlying claim of greater significance for rites focused on the emperor's person or dwelling seems to be vitiated by such frequent *ad hoc*-ery as the court's numerous appropriations of the Great Purification Rite for small-bore purposes.

In stark contrast to the fervor with which the Great Purification Rite was being performed for the palace, the diary of Fujiwara Sanesuke, *Shōyūki*, records, in the sixth month of 982, that not one member of the nobility turned up for the Jingikan's twice-yearly performance of the ritual. One might wonder whether the aristocrats had simply lost interest in this ritual, but apparently that was not the case. The aristocracy had begun engaging yin-yang masters to perform the Great Purification Rite for purely private purposes such as healing and safe childbirth. The yin-yang masters would carry an effigy, (a paper doll or piece of the client's clothing tied to a ring of reeds, to which pollution adhering to the client had been symbolically transferred) to a riverbank, recite the Great Purification Prayer over it, and float the effigy away upon the water. Buddhist priests also began to recite the Great Purification Prayer for clients, as did a low-ranking priestly order from the Ise shrines, called *onshi* (or *oshi*). In 1178, the man who held more control within the court than anyone else, Taira no Kiyomori (1118–1181), staged a mammoth performance of the Great Purification Rite as a ritual for safe childbirth when his daughter Tokiko (principal consort of Emperor Takakura, r. 1168–1180) was about to give birth to the future Emperor Antoku (r. 1180–1185). Kiyomori employed ten yin-yang masters, officials of the Jingikan, and priests of his tutelary shrine, the Itsukushima Shrine, as well as assorted other shrine priests to recite the Great Purification Prayer one thousand times. These miscellaneous appropriations of the Great Purification Rite suggest that its former significance as an expression of national authority was lost as it became available on a fee-for-services-rendered basis. The prayer became available commercially because the weakened Jingikan could no longer enforce its monopoly over the ritual.[33]

Faith in the Kami

Before the Heian period, there are very few documents that reflect the character of individual belief. Diaries of Heian aristocrats allow us to know what shrines the aristocracy patronized, how often they went there, on what occasions, and what they did there. Written exclusively by male aristocrats, they do not reflect the religious lives of the entire society, but examining their changing content over the tenth through the twelfth centuries affords us precious insights.

One such diarist was Fujiwara Tadahira (880–949), whose writing covers the years 907 to 948. Having ascended to the headship of the Fujiwara family in 909, Tadahira became regent to Emperor Suzaku (r. 930–946) in 909, and his diary thus reflects the religious life of a high-ranking aristocrat during the period of regency. Tadahira typically visited on the occasion of important rituals at shrines linked to the Fujiwara family. He regularly attended scheduled rites at Ōharano Shrine (fourth and eleventh months) and at Kasuga Shrine (second and eleventh months). Visiting these shrines fulfilled his duty to the Kami of his family. Tadahira also attended rites at the Iwashimizu Hachimangū and Kamo Shrines.[34] To understand why Tadahira esteemed these two shrines so highly, it will be useful to examine them separately.

Iwashimizu Hachimangū

We saw in chapter 3 that the court had heaped honors on the Kami Hachiman in the sixth century, following Hachiman oracles supporting the construction of Tōdaiji; that the title of "Great Bodhisattva" had been bestowed upon the Kami; that Hachiman had been adopted as the protector of several significant temples in Nara in addition to Tōdaiji; and that a Hachiman oracle had delivered the coup de grace to Dōkyō. In 859 a Buddhist monk named Gyōkyō (dates unknown) of Daianji (one of the Nara temples of which Hachiman was the tutelary Kami) established Iwashimizu Hachiman Shrine at a place about twenty kilometers southwest of the palace, called Yawata. There was a temple on the site called Gokokuji ("Nation Protecting Temple"), which had control of the Iwashimizu Hachiman Shrine. The shrine's deities were established there by "inviting" (*kanjō*) the three Kami of the Usa Hachiman Shrine: the deified Emperor Ōjin, his mother Empress Jingū, and his consort Hime Ōkami.[35]

Iwashimizu Hachimangū was in fact a *miyadera*, a "shrine temple," and at the time of its founding there were only Buddhist priests in charge. *Miyadera* were administered by noncelibate Buddhist priests called "shrine monks" (*shasō*), who could marry and pass on their positions to their sons, or by monks called *kengyō*, *bettō*, and other titles. The *miyadera* could also employ subordinate shrine ritualists. *Miyadera* were neither administered by the Jingikan nor recorded in the *Engi shiki*. By contrast, *jingūji* were formed by a merger process in which one or more temples were built alongside preexisting shrines, which the temples later came to control. *Miyadera* were formed as shrines controlled by Buddhist clerics, not through a process of merger. There were no shrine priests at Iwashimizu Hachimangū until a member of the Ki family was appointed *kannushi* in 876. The Buddhist side monopolized all the highest positions at Iwashimizu, and in this sense it was managed in a completely different way than the original shrine at Usa.[36]

By the ninth century, the belief had developed that the spirits of the divinized Empress Jingū and her son Emperor Ōjin were merged with Hachiman, giving rise to the idea that Hachiman was an ancestral deity to the imperial house, along with the Ise deities. In 869 the court issued a proclamation calling Hachiman "the great ancestor of our dynasty" (*waga chō no daiso*). On this basis the shrine came to be respected as the "second imperial ancestral shrine" (*sōbyō*), second only to Ise in importance. It received imperial patronage on a level with the Kamo and the Kasuga Shrines. In 876 the court bestowed land on the shrine, and by around 1070, it possessed some thirty-four fiefs.

Like the Hachiman shrine at Usa, Iwashimizu Hachiman held its Annual Festival in the eighth lunar month, fifteenth day, for the release of living creatures, *hōjō-e*, at which the shrine's founding legend (*engi*) was read and lectures on Buddhist scriptures were presented. In 948 this ceremony was styled a *chokusai*, meaning that it was performed in accordance with imperial decree. In 974 it became a regular observance of the imperial house, and as of 1070, it began to be held on a huge scale that included an imperial procession to the shrine for the emperor to worship there personally.

In addition to the Annual Festival, beginning in 942 the shrine also held an annual "Occasional Festival" (*rinji-sai*), held in the lunar third month to commemorate the suppression of a rebellion led by Taira Masakado (?–940). In effect, the "Occasional Festival" was a second annual festival, though the term *occasional* inevitably gives a confusing impression of something more sporadic. For each festival, the court sent a Grand Imperial Emissary (*daishinpōshi*) to present prayers, songs, dances, and gifts from the imperial house that included twenty horses.[37]

The Kamo Shrines

Regarded as the protector of the capital, the Upper and Lower Kamo Shrines were symbolic barriers to the entry of evil influence from the northeast, traditionally regarded as a source of malevolent effects. When the capital was established at Kyoto, Emperor Kanmu sent special tribute to the shrines and an emissary to their festivals, also raising their ranks. Thereafter, their status was raised to the level of the Ise Shrines.[38]

The Kamo family had fought on the side of Ōama (the future Emperor Tenmu) in the Jinshin War and had been rewarded with the title *asomi*. In the mid-Heian period, they became closely associated with yin-yang knowledge, astronomy, astrology, and hemerology. Eventually, they came to specialize in calendar-making and calendrical divinations. Along with the Abe family, they came to hold the main posts in the Bureau of Yin and Yang.[39]

Held in the fourth lunar month, the Annual Festival of the Kamo Shrines became the capital's greatest spectacle of the year. It began, however, with a ceremony closed to all but shrine priests, which re-enacted the original descent of the Kami to the shrine. Within a freshly cut brushwood fence, two large cones of sand were formed, and pillars of pine logs were erected as *yorishiro* for the Kami. Called the *miare shinji* at the Upper Kamo Shrine and *mikage matsuri* at the Lower Kamo Shrine, this ceremony was held in darkness. The priests would extinguish all lights and call down the Kami to enter the *yorishiro*. Then, the priests would transfer the Kami to smaller *sakaki* trees, which they carried into the main sanctuary, to install the Kami in the shrine. The lights were rekindled, and the public events of the festival that ensued on the following days were intended as entertainments for the Kami, renewed by their symbolic rebirth.[40]

The court sent a Grand Imperial Emissary to convey offerings, including horses, dances, and prayers. Following elaborate ceremonies in which the emperor formally dispatched him, the emissary traveled in a grand procession from the palace to the Lower Kamo Shrine and then to the Upper Kamo Shrine. At each of the shrines, the emissary would present the offerings to the shrine's Kami, after which equestrian spectacles were presented as entertainments for the Kami. The Upper Kamo Shrine had a ceremony of horse racing, while archery on horseback (*yabusame*) was presented at the Lower Kamo Shrine.

The court also dedicated a consecrated imperial princess (*saiin*) to worship at the Kamo Shrines, beginning in 810, during the reign of Emperor Saga, and continuing until the early thirteenth century. This practice was patterned after the *saiō* at Ise. The *saiin* also read an imperial proclamation before the sanctuaries of the Kami at the Annual Festival (Kamo sai). Her procession from the palace to the shrines was a great spectacle of gorgeously costumed attendants who conveyed her and her many ladies-in-waiting in ox carts decorated with hollyhocks, as was her crown, giving rise to the popular name for the festival as a whole, the Aoi (hollyhock) Festival

(*Aoi matsuri*). So splendid were these processions that the entire capital turned out to watch.

Aristocratic ladies had their attendants scout out a good place for them to view from behind the screens of their own ox carts (it would have been most unseemly for them to be recognized). So much competition was there for the best spots that brawls would break out among the attendants, and the ladies' carts would sometimes be rudely pushed about. One such incident at the Kamo Shrine provided the scene for a famous episode called "the Carriage Clash" in *The Tale of Genji*, when Genji's wife's cart was roughly shoved aside by the cart of one of his lovers, Lady Aoi. The public humiliation suffered on this occasion by Genji's wife, the Lady Rokujo, set the stage in the novel for the mysterious death of Lady Aoi, which was rumored to have been caused by the Lady Rokujo's vengeful spirit. The Kamo Festival is mentioned in many other works of classical literature as well.

The Annual Festival of the Kamo Shrines had been made an official public rite (*kōsai*) in 810. It is notable, however, that the Jingikan had no role in this, the most splendid annual festival of the Heian period. Instead, the Grand Imperial Emissary and the *saiin* conveyed the court's prayers and offerings. The Jingikan ceased to function as a counterpart to the Department of State (Dajōkan). Public rites came under the supervision of the Department of State, and the Jingikan was downgraded. Its leadership became hereditary (rather than official appointment of individuals) and closely associated with the performance of prayers-for-fees (*kitō*).[41]

Imperial Processions to Shrines

The first historical record of an imperial procession to a shrine documents a procession to the Kamo Shrines in 942, undertaken in thanksgiving for the suppression of the rebellion led by Taira Masakado. Beginning in the reign of Emperor En'yū (r. 969–984) and continuing through the reign of Emperor Go-Ichijō (r. 1016–1036) a custom of each emperor making imperial processions to the Iwashimizu, Kamo, Matsuo, Hirano, Ōharano, Hie, Kasuga, and Inari shrines was established. With each imperial procession, the people of Kyoto were treated to a great spectacle, including seeing the emperor's cart gaily decorated with flowers. Viewing stands were set up to allow the townspeople to enjoy the marvelous sight of the procession passing by. These processions are described in classical literature, for example, in the *Ōkagami*:

> [T]here was the Imperial visit to Kasuga Shrine, a custom inaugurated in the reign of Emperor Ichijō [r. 986–1011]. Since Emperor Ichijō's precedent was considered inviolable, our present sovereign [Emperor Go-Ichijō] made the journey in spite of his youth, with Senior Grand Empress Shōshi accompanying him in his litter. To call the spectacle brilliant would be trite. Above all, what can I say about the bearing and

> appearance of [Fujiwara] Michinaga, the Emperor's grandfather, as he rode in the Imperial train? It might have been disappointing if he had looked anything like an ordinary man. The crowds of country folk along the way must have been spellbound. Even sophisticated city dwellers, dazzled by a resplendence like that of the Wheel-Turning Sacred Monarchs, found themselves, in perfectly natural confusion, raising their hands to their foreheads as though gazing on a Buddha."[42]

During the two-century span from 979 to 1179, over two hundred imperial processions to shrines were carried out, in seventeen imperial reigns. There was an especially strong sense that in the year following enthronement the emperor should visit Iwashimizu Hachimangū and the Kamo Shrines.[43]

Aristocratic Shrine Visits

The aristocracy followed the court's lead and began visiting Iwashimizu Hachimangū and the Kamo Shrines, usually on the day before their Annual Festivals, so as not to conflict with the court's observances. Tadahira visited these shrines on the occasion of their Annual Festivals and made offerings, including horses, as well as praying for recovery from his own and family members' illness. He viewed shrine treasures, Nō performances, *kagura* dances, had divinations performed, saw horseracing, attended shrine banquets, and sponsored prayers for the success of imperial missions to China. His diary shows that he paid attention to shrine taboos and noted, for example, that a dead dog had polluted the shrine garden.

Outside the framework of scheduled rites and festivals, Tadahira recorded a total of seven shrine visits. Four of those were to pray for recovery from illness or to be purified following some transgression regarding taboos, and two visits were to pray for military victory. From this we can see that visits outside a shrine's scheduled rites were partly to pray for purely personal matters unrelated to family or professional obligations and partly for the safety of the reign.[44]

The diary of Fujiwara no Sanesuke (957–1046), titled *Shōyūki*, covers the years 978 to 1032 and is an excellent source on aristocratic religious observances during the regencies of Fujiwara no Michinaga (966–1027; regent 1015–1017) and Yorimichi (992–1074; regent 1017–1068), when the power of the Fujiwara was at its height. Ending as it does some eighty years after Tadahira's diary, *Shōyūki* reflects significant changes. In place of laborious and time-consuming trips to distant shrines, it had become customary to send a Buddhist monk as a proxy to present one's prayers. While offerings continued to be made at court-sponsored observances, private devotions had become much more common, both for the imperial family and the aristocracy. For example, after a recovery from illness that he attributed to divine favor, Emperor Go-Ichijō dedicated horseracing and displays of fine horses in thanksgiving. The aristocracy followed suit and dedicated other horseraces and displays, as well as sponsoring sutra readings at several shrines to give thanks for the emperor's recovery. Michinaga also dedicated equestrian events to shrines when Fujiwara women among the emperor's consorts failed to become pregnant. From early in the eleventh century, Michinaga and other aristocrats began regularly attending "*goryō* meetings" (*goryō-e*) at the Gion Shrine and the Kitano Tenmangū, though they were appalled at commoners' ecstatic *dengaku*. The number of these "private" religious observances increased greatly during Michinaga's time.

In the aristocracy's personal shrine visits during the period of regency government, we seldom detect the presence of a shrine priest. The nobility composed their own prayers and presented offerings personally before the altars of the Kami or had a Buddhist priest do it for them. Some accounts mention either that there was no shrine priest in attendance, or that the diarist chanced to see a shrine attendant. Either way, shrine personnel were not directly involved in or necessary to aristocratic shrine visits, and it was rare for them to encounter shrine priests.[45]

A study of shrine ritualists at the Ōharano, Umemiya, Hirano, and Yoshida Shrines before the twelfth century found that the person in charge of intoning formal prayers (*norito*) at the annual festival was typically chosen by divination shortly beforehand. At the Kasuga Shrine, the officiant arrived at the shrine two days before the Annual Festival, along with musicians and diviners. This situation persisted until 992, when a resident priest in charge of all shrine matters emerged. The position quickly became hereditary in the Nakatomi family.[46] At the Kamo Shrines as of 1095, only the Upper Shrine had a head priest (*kannushi*). There were nine priests in total there, and only five at the Lower Kamo Shrine.[47]

The Jingikan's earlier strict monitoring of priestly appointments was an index of the strength of central authority in the eighth century. The transformation of those appointments into hereditary entitlements in the tenth century indicated a weakening of central authority. It is abundantly clear that many "private" elements were rising in importance, and that the Jingikan was becoming irrelevant to the actual religious practice of court and aristocracy. Classical literature provides other perspectives on the private prayers that aristocrats put before the Kami.

"The Kami Reject Prayers That Are Contrary to Morality" (*Kami wa hirei o ukezu*)

The idea that the Kami refuse to answer prayers contravening morality became a proverb famously illustrated in an episode from *The Tales of the Heike*, recounting an event of 1177.[48] The story unfolds as the post of Captain of the Imperial Guards became available, following a resignation. Narichika was one of three men seeking the appointment.[49] If he were to secure the post, however, Narichika would have risen to a rank higher than his father had achieved, and that was considered unfilial.

Thus Narichika's ambition flouted contemporary understandings of morality from the outset, and the story presumes that Narichika is not entitled to the rank he seeks. Nevertheless, Narichika tried to improve his chances through religious ritual.

Narichika hired one hundred monks to recite the Greater Prajñāpāramitā Sutra[50] for seven days at Iwashimizu Hachimangū. Of course it would have cost quite a large sum to pay so many monks to recite sutras for a week, and those funds would have gone into the shrine's coffers. It was regarded as meritorious to sponsor such rites, and Heian-period aristocrats would have understood that Narichika was seeking Hachiman's aid in his hopes for the Captaincy.

One day while the monks were reciting the sutra, three doves flew to an orange tree in front of one of the sub-shrines of Iwashimizu, called Kōra Daimyōjin, where they attacked each other and fought until all three were dead. Because the dove or pigeon is the totemic messenger of Hachiman, this macabre event was seen as a sign of the Kami's displeasure. The Buddhist monk in charge of the Kōra Daimyōjin Shrine reported the ominous portent to the court, which had the Jingikan perform divination to discover its meaning. That the court referred the case to Jingikan divination shows the Jingikan in action as of the late twelfth century. The Jingikan's divinations determined that the emperor was not at fault, but rather one of his subjects.

The audience of this tale would instantly have grasped that Narichika was the one at fault. Hachiman's displeasure with Narichika was revealed through the inauspicious actions of the Kami's dove messengers. Evidently the implication was not lost on Narichika, either, because he gave up trying to secure Hachiman's aid.

Finding no comfort at Iwashimizu, Narichika next tried the Upper Kamo Shrine. The contemporary audience would have rolled their eyes at this turn of events, which is both humorous as well as foreboding—things are not going to turn out well. In Japanese society today, the person who perseveres against all obstacles tends to be admired, but in the ancient period a different attitude prevailed. According to the older understanding, there is a natural course of events, and if a cherished ambition is at odds with the tide, it is wise to relinquish the goal. To persist in the face of a divine warning from Hachiman would have been regarded as foolish and dangerous—far better to renounce the Captaincy, however much Narichika might have desired it.

But Narichika stubbornly laid his prayers before the Kami of the Upper Kamo Shrine. To display his sincerity, he walked to the shrine late at night, a distance of about two and a half miles each way, for seven nights in a row, to pray that he would achieve his ambition. Returning home on the final night, he had a dream in which he heard a mysterious voice coming from the shrine sanctuary, speaking to him in a poem. The poem warned him not to be "like a cherry blossom that resents the wind for scattering its petals." Here the Kami is speaking to Narichika and telling him that he will fail in his ambition, and that this outcome is as natural as the scattering of cherry petals. He should not harbor resentment. Divinely inspired dreams such as this are a frequent occurence in classical Japanese literature.

Still undeterred even by this unmistakable warning from the Kami, Narichika tried another approach. He hired an ascetic (*hijiri*) to perform rites for Dakini Shinten,[51] an unorthodox god that would only be approached for some devious purpose, to gain something to which one was not rightfully entitled. Narichika employed the ascetic to perform these rites for one hundred days before an altar erected in a hollow tree behind the main sanctuary of the Upper Kamo Shrine. In other words, after the Kami warned him off the sanctuary itself, Narichika had his hireling set up an ersatz, hidden worship space to petition a distaff god who is alien and inferior to the Kami of the Kamo Shrine, while still within the Kamo Shrine precincts. Bringing in a charlatan and setting him up to pray to Dakini Shinten right next door to the sanctuary was, however, immensely insulting to the Kami and the Kamo priests. The audience would have realized that divine punishment was now inevitable and inescapable, a prospect that Narichika's bone-headed stubborness entitled the tale's audience to anticipate with no little pleasure.

On the seventy-fifth day of the ascetic's prayers, fearsome lightning struck the tree, setting off such a conflagration that even at a distance of several miles, the palace was threatened. The Kami of the Kamo Shrine had unleashed *tatari*. The evil consequences of Narichika's misbegotten ambition now endangered the monarch himself. The shrine priests managed to put out the fire, which they attributed to the Kami's wrath at the ascetic's devious rites, commanding him to cease and desist, but he refused. Thereupon the shrine priests took the matter to the palace, and an imperial edict was promulgated, empowering the shrine priests to deal with the ascetic as they liked. The priests beat the ascetic with their staffs and drove him south, far away from the shrine. The tale ended with the enunciation of the proverb, that the Kami do not receive prayers and petitions that are contrary to morality (*Kami wa hirei o ukezu*).

Not only did Narichika not get the post he sought, but he came to a miserable end. After the discovery of his role in a coup attempting to overthrow the regent, he was exiled to a distant province. Assassins planted sharpened stakes at the bottom of a twenty-foot cliff and threw him over the precipice to die, impaled on the spikes.

This story shows how concepts of the Kami in the late Heian period had come to incorporate the idea that the Kami act in accord with morality, not merely in response to broken taboos or pollution. The Kami are invoked here as enforcing a moral code that reflects and upholds the status order of contemporary society. In the medieval period the moral component of concepts of the Kami was further elaborated, as we shall see in the chapter 5.

Fear of *Goryō*: The Kitano Tenmangū and Gion Shrines

Among the spirits first appearing in the Heian period, the *goryō*, literally, "honored spirits," became closely associated with shrines. The term *goryō* was used in two main ways: to refer to the spirits believed to cause contagious diseases such as smallpox, or to refer to the spirits of people who had died after being wrongfully dishonored; the latter might also be called *on'ryō*. These beliefs presumed that Kami can retaliate and cause misfortune—*tatari*—if they are not properly placated. Ritual assemblies called "*goryō* meetings" were held to honor the vengeful spirits with offerings and entertainments and then send them away, in the hope that the misfortunes they caused would cease. The first recorded *goryō* meeting was held in 863, to honor an exiled prince, whose spirit was believed to be the cause of an epidemic, and thereafter these ceremonies became part of the court's annual observances. The most famous case was that of Sugawara Michizane (845–903).

The Fujiwara were able to monopolize most official appointments and to shut out other candidates, even if supremely gifted. In a rare exception, the scholar Sugawara Michizane secured official appointment and was a brilliant success, rising to become Minister of the Right.[52] But in spite of a stellar record in service to Emperor Uda (r. 887–897), after Uda abdicated in favor of his son, Emperor Daigo (r. 897–930), Uda could no longer protect Michizane from his rivals. Daigo was most impressed with Michizane and had been so moved by one of Michizane's poems that he gave Michizane a robe. However, he was young, inexperienced, and easily influenced by his wily counselors, who sought Michizane's downfall.

Chief among these rivals was Fujiwara Tokihira (871–909), Minister of the Left. Tokihira did not want to share power with Michizane.[53] Miyoshi no Kiyoyuki (847–918) was a scholarly rival of Michizane, who hoped to better his own position by shunting Michizane aside. It was he who had reported the ineffectiveness of the Jingikan to Emperor Daigo, in the memorial examined earlier in this chapter. Kiyoyuki waited until Emperor Uda had abdicated and was away from the capital. Then he claimed that an esoteric Chinese divination text prophesied that a high minister would commit treason against the throne and named Michizane as the traitor. Emperor Daigo (not yet twenty) was persuaded in 901 to exile Michizane to far-away Dazaifu, where he died in 903, bitterly protesting his innocence.

Michizane had been buried in the precincts of a Dazaifu temple; a memorial altar was constructed at the gravesite in 905 that developed into the temple Anrakuji, where Buddhist rites were performed for him. In 909 Michizane's principal antagonist Tokihira died at the age of thirty-nine. Chronicles of the time reported that as Tokihira lay dying, Michizane's spirit slithered out of Tokihira's ears in the form of two green snakes. The only possible conclusion in the circumstances was that Michizane's unquiet spirit had become a *goryō* and taken revenge through the murder of his rival in this hideous, reptilian form. The idea of Michizane's vengeful ghost took on new life when the crown prince, Tokihira's nephew, died in 922 at the age of twenty-one, again recorded as the work of the *goryō*. The reports were apparently believed at court, because Michizane was posthumously pardoned and reinstated to high position in hopes of stemming the tide of retaliation.

The legend was revived again in 930, when social unrest and inauspicious events broke out in the capital. A major drought blighted the crops. Following prayers for rain, a bolt of lightning set fire to the palace, with Emperor Daigo inside. One of the conspirators against Michizane was killed in the conflagration, along with three other courtiers. Shocked to the marrow by these events, which contemporary accounts again blamed on Michizane's spirit, Emperor Daigo took sick and died. He was only forty-six.

Ten years later, in 940, in the wake of Taira Masakado's rebellion, shamans from the Kantō area of eastern Japan where Masakado had made his base issued oracles claiming that it was Michizane's will that Masakado be made emperor. That the oracle issued from the Kantō means that by this time Michizane's legend had spread from Kyūshū to the east, and that this *goryō* could credibly be portrayed as supporting a coup against the throne.

In 941, the monk Dōken, son of the conspirator Kiyoyuki, presented the court with a story of a journey to hell that he claimed to have made. Fantastic and unbelievable as this seems to the modern reader, contemporary chronicles reported Dōken's tales as credible accounts of actual experience. While in hell, Dōken met Michizane, who told Dōken that it was his messengers, the 105,000 Heavenly Kami (*tenjin*) of Fire and Thunder, who had attacked the palace. The implication of this was that Michizane himself was not a thunder god—the thunder gods were his creatures. Dōken claimed that while still in hell, he also met Emperor Daigo, wearing only a shirt while being tortured for his misdeeds toward Michizane, along with two of his ministers, who were naked. Daigo begged Dōken to pray for his forgiveness and salvation.

In 942, a female shaman named Tajihi no Ayako proclaimed in an oracle that Michizane was the Kami Tenjin, and that he wished to have a shrine built for him at Kitano, in the capital Kyoto. Three years later, mass dancing broke out in Settsu Province. Hundreds of dancing protestors set out for Kyoto, bearing three portable shrines. They presented one of these to Tajihi no Ayako, apparently treating her as a living deity. In 947, a Shinto priest named Miwa no Yoshitane came forward claiming that his seven-year-old son had received an oracle revealing more details about what kind of shrine Tenjin wanted: it should have pines and a Lotus Meditation Hall; in other words, it should incorporate Buddhist rites. That same year, the court posthumously granted Michizane the rank of Prime Minister and had him deified as the Kami Tenman Daijizai Tenjin at the Kitano Tenmangū in Kyoto. Previously, the site had been a place for rites to the Deities of Heaven and Earth (Tenjin-chigi), which incorporated the concept of Tenjin. The shrine was rebuilt and expanded by Fujiwara no Morosuke (908–960). The Thunder God was already worshipped there, as were miscellaneous *goryō*, in a ritual style incorporating both Buddhist rites and shrine ritual. With these new honors, it was believed, Michizane's spirit was transformed from a vengeful *goryō* to a patron god of scholarship, poetry, and calligraphy.

In 985, Retired Emperor En'yū experienced a divine oracle that moved him to send tribute to the shrine personally. As of 987 the shrine's festival was made an official rite. This accolade completed the transition from *goryō* to tutelary protector. Places that enshrined *goryō* were *miyadera*; besides Iwashimizu Hachimangū, Gion, and Kitano Tenmangū Shrines, other examples were found at such mountain worship sites as Kumano and Hakusan.

The Gion Shrine and its festival originated from "*goryō* meetings" that began in 970 to appease the gods of pestilence. The Gion Shrine installed "the Ox-headed Heavenly King" (Gozu Tennō), originally an Indian deity incorporated into the Buddhist pantheon as a protector against infectious disease. In painting he is usually pictured as a fierce deity with the head of an ox atop his own head. He may be portrayed with multiple faces and with many arms and weapons. An Annual Festival for this deity was held in the sixth month. The imperial court began sending offerings to the Gion Shrine in 975, and ordinary people also participated with music, dancing, and many popular entertainments. Later, this festival became a prototype of urban shrine festivals, adopted by the entire city of Kyoto. Its processions of floats and a portable shrine became one of the city's largest annual observances.[54]

In fact, many popular entertainments appeared first in some connection with "*goryō* meetings." Ritual to appease *goryō* shared the Buddhist inspiration behind most Kami ritual in the Heian period: Buddhist instruction is necessary in order to uplift the Kami, and to transform them from vengeful spirits to beneficent protectors. Therefore, recitation of the Heart Sutra by Buddhist priests was central to *goryō* rites. Once the formal ritual was concluded, however, popular entertainments at both temples and shrines attracted the people. Processions called *fūryū* were staged as part of the effort to appease vengeful spirits, and these included music, dancing, and splendid costumes. In the case of the Gion Festival, the court donated horses to the shrine, and they were incorporated into the processions, ridden by gorgeously costumed boys. Gion festivals spread to many other shrines in fiefs owned by the Gion Shrine outside the capital.[55]

There was such intense competition to present the most elegant and astounding displays at festivals that sumptuary laws limiting financial outlays on these events were repeatedly promulgated. They were rarely enforced, it seems, but in the Kamo festival of 1014, some twenty people were stripped of vestments regarded as too pretentious for their station. In the Kamo festival of 1032, the regent Yorimichi himself had children dress in brocade robes made from gold and silver threads, an unprecedented spectacle astonishing all who saw it. Frequent issue of sumptuary laws is a sure sign that they were not being obeyed, and with the regent flouting the rules so ostentatiously, who could blame the ordinary townspeople?[56]

Religious Change during the Era of Cloister Government

From the end of the eleventh to the beginning of the twelfth century, the system of regency came to an end. Fujiwara power had become so oppressive to the imperial family that numerous emperors had hoped to rule without a regent, but it was not until Emperor Go-Sanjō (r. 1068–1072) ascended the throne that this aspiration was realized. Go-Sanjō himself was not born from a Fujiwara mother, and though two of his consorts were Fujiwaras, he had no heir by either of them. He had no regent himself, and this allowed him to abdicate in favor of his young son and open an Office of the Retired Emperor (*in no chō*), from which he was able to determine that his sons who were unrelated to the Fujiwara would succeed him. Thus control of government passed out of Fujiwara hands and back to the imperial family, which, through the twelfth century was able to revive its fortunes and rule without a regent. Emperors Shirakawa (r. 1072–1086), Toba (r. 1107–1123), and Go-Shirakawa (r. 1155–1158) all ruled powerfully both as emperors and even more so as retired emperors. Upon their abdication, they took the tonsure and "retired" to a cloister, and thereafter were expected to rule in accord with Buddhist principles. The name for this period, the era of "cloister government," derives from this practice.

Emperor Go-Sanjō had already expanded the extent of imperial progresses to shrines, visiting Hirano, Kitano Tenmangū, Matsuo, Kasuga, Fushimi Inari, Hie, Gion, and Shira Myōjin. The reign of Emperor Shirakawa (1072–1086) marked a zenith. He made imperial progresses to no fewer than ten shrines in three years, visiting the shrines already mentioned above, and also Kamo, Iwashimizu Hachimangū, and after his abdication he made pilgrimages to Kōyasan, Mt. Kinpu, and Kumano.[57]

As imperial practice shifted, the nobility followed suit, and the changes can be traced in aristocrats' diaries, such as Fujiwara Munetada's (1062–1141) *Chūyūki*, covering the years 1087 to 1138. Munetada's diary shows that he frequently visited shrines and prayed for spiritual guidance at times unrelated to the shrine's scheduled rites. As Munetada was promoted, his shrine visits increased. He traveled most frequently to shrines connected with the Fujiwara clan, such as Kasuga, and also to the Yoshida Shrine. He also revered Tenjin. He dedicated sutras to shrines in large numbers, such as one hundred copies of the Heart Sutra. Munetada was mainly concerned with expressing his personal prayers. He did not neglect the rites expected of high-ranking Fujiwara family members, but his personal faith was more inclusive.[58]

The diary of Fujiwara Teika (also known as Sadaie, 1162–1241), called *Meigetsuki*, covers the years 1180 to 1235 and thus reflects aristocratic life around a century later than Munetada's diary. Although Teika was famed as a poet and was one of the compilers of the imperial anthology, *Shinkokinshū*, he was not granted high official appointments. Every time he was due for promotion, however, he visited the Hie Shrine to pray that he might advance. He prayed for his health and the success of his poetry, and his wife also visited the shrine frequently. On one occasion, he secluded himself at the shrine for five days to pray. He dedicated a horse and sutras in the hope that his prayers would be answered. He always purified himself for two days before each visit by eating only vegetarian food. In ten months during

1199, he made eleven visits to the Hie Shrine; if the remaining two months of that year's diary were extant, it is highly likely that we would know of even more visits. Throughout his lifetime, Teika showed little interest in other shrines, and even after taking the tonsure in 1233, he continued to visit the Hie Shrine.[59]

Teika's diary shows that by the beginning of the twelfth century, attendance at the *jingi* rites of the Ritsuryō era had been all but forgotten. During the era of cloister government, we see aristocrats increasingly visiting shrines for purely personal reasons, choosing particular shrines for their association with poetry or scholarship, rather than because of the specific Kami enshrined there. They began to emphasize the quantity of shrine visits as an expression of the depth of personal devotion, idealizing one hundred visits to the same shrine (*hyakudo mairi*). Emphasis on quantity probably developed under the influence of the growing popularity of *nenbutsu* (see below) recitation in staggering numbers. Aristocrats emphasized shrine visits at the beginning of the year but otherwise treated annual ritual calendars as less important.

From the late eleventh century, aristocrats' diaries show that shrine priests were taking over the rites of conveying aristocratic patrons' prayers and offerings to the Kami. The court appointed priests to the shrines as representatives of particular families, and those appointments then became hereditary in those families. It became customary for emperors making an imperial progress to shrines to reward the priests with advances in rank, monetary gifts, and sometimes even landed estates. This allowed shrines and their priests more economic stability. The priests could set out precedents for ritual and administer shrine affairs consistently, thus gradually establishing their work as a recognized occupation and profession.[60] At the same time, however, priests at shrines represented a variety of religious identities, and many shrines were controlled by Buddhist monks. This meant that shrine officiants remained a mixed group.

Dengaku

At the turn of the eleventh century, festival displays and dancing based on popular religious beliefs became mass phenomena. First popularized by the Buddhist monk Kūya (903–972), a dance called *nenbutsu odori*, based on recitation of the name of the Buddha Amida, Buddha of the Western Paradise, spread widely. Kūya preached that Amida guaranteed salvation to all, and that people need only recite the *nenbutsu*, the phrase, "Hail to the Buddha Amida" (*namu Amida butsu*), in order to be saved. Paintings and documents of the times show that great throngs poured into the streets to dance while reciting the *nenbutsu*. Similarly, shrine festivals frequently included dancing and music called *dengaku*. Originally, the term *dengaku* simply meant the music and dance that accompanied rice planting, but in the Heian period it developed into a kind of dance unrelated to planting, resembling *nenbutsu odori* in its mass popularity. *Dengaku* groups formed in the capital and in the villages and turned out when events moved popular sentiment, especially when *goryō* festivals were staged. Because *dengaku* was popular with the aristocracy no less than the common people, aristocrats wrote about it in their diaries, leaving us valuable written records. Many shrines adopted *dengaku* as part of their annual *goryō* festivals.[61]

It is apparent that the court and the aristocracy were not only fascinated by the new popular entertainments around temples and shrines but also were intimidated by the sight of the populace dancing in the streets. Clearly, mass dancing and singing held the potential to express dissatisfaction with the ruling order. In order to create the appearance of aligning itself with popular sentiment, the court sponsored the Gion festival and supported *dengaku* in the era of cloistered emperors.

Shrines, especially, were linked to *dengaku* disturbances. During the Sumiyoshi Shrine's festival in the third month of 1096, rioting broke out, and as the authorities tried to restore order, dozens of people drowned themselves in the shrine's pond. The suicides were apparently protesting against the shrine by polluting the pond. The authorities prohibited all activity at the Sumiyoshi festival and also canceled the Matsuo Shrine's festival. Commoners were so outraged at the cancellation that *dengaku* groups took to the streets singing protest songs, and although these protests were repeatedly prohibited, the prohibitions were ignored. *Dengaku* had become a protest movement against the shrines and civil authority.[62] Three months later in the sixth month of 1096, another mass *dengaku* at the Gion festival broke out and could not be controlled. Commoners took to the streets in such huge crowds that contemporary writers attributed the dancing to the work of some malignant spirit or interpreted it as an evil omen. On this occasion, priests made up part of the performers. An excerpt from a contemporary account conveys how compelling these displays were:

> In the summer of [1096], a great *dengaku* took place in [Kyoto]. [Some performers were on stilts while others beat drums hung from their waists, clanged copper cymbals, and shook rattles.] Rice-planting and rice-harvesting maidens [danced] ceaselessly, day and night. The tremendous noise greatly amazed the citizens. City and local officials, as well as soldiers, formed different groups, some visiting temples, others flooding the streets. All the citizens of the capital acted like madmen. It was probably the deed of a fox spirit. [At night various *dengaku* groups of priests and laymen even approached the palace.] Some people went almost naked, clad only in red loincloths; others, their hair unkempt...kept marching to and fro.[63]

In this account and others, it is difficult to identify the cause of popular discontent. Some aristocrats were appalled by the sight of large numbers of commoners who seemed to be so out of control. Others, however, were caught up in the frenzy and could scarcely get enough of *dengaku*. Officials—even librarians—as well as police and priests are all mentioned as taking part in *dengaku*, though we cannot always discern their motives. It is evident, however, that it would have been quite dangerous both for the court and for shrines to be seen to oppose these expressions of popular sentiment, and much safer to be in support.

Shrines as Landholders and the Rise of the *Jinin*

During the Ritsuryō era, all land was theoretically owned by the state, and was periodically redistributed, with individuals receiving parcels based on their age and sex. As we saw earlier, this system proved unworkable, and people sought ways to evade it. Gradually, landed estates called *shōen* replaced the older system. Appearing first in the eighth century, *shōen* lasted through the Sengoku (Warring States) era, 1467 to 1568, forming the major unit of economic production. The *shōen* also supported the rise of the warrior class, the samurai. Shrines and temples acquired extensive *shōen*, which allowed them to become self-sustaining and, in some cases, very rich.

Since rice served as the staple crop and substituted for currency, it was highly desirable to increase the land where it could be grown. The chief method for creating more paddy land was to reclaim uncultivated land and make it into rice fields by draining marshes or clearing forests. Reclamation projects required resources exceeding the assets of most individuals, who sought sponsors among the aristocracy or religious institutions. An eighth-century law had declared that reclaimed land would be removed from the Ritsuryō system of land distribution and instead be held by the person, temple, or shrine that had sponsored the reclamation. The proprietor could then administer the land, recruit cultivators to work it, and collect taxes from them. Once reclaimed land passed into the holdings of a temple or shrine, the religious institution would seek to make it exempt from taxes, by declaring it shrine land (*shinden*, literally "Kami fields") or temple land (*jiden*), or by petitioning for exemption. If approved, a charter would be granted, setting out the estate's location, size, and the extent to which it would be free of taxation. This system allowed the number and size of the *shōen* to increase dramatically and led to complex arrangements in which the largest proprietors, including temples and shrines, could hold multiple estates that were widely scattered across the country. In the tenth century, however, the government began seeking to limit the amount of land exempted from taxation and sent the provincial governors into the estates to inspect them and determine their tax status.

The practice of "commendation" (*kishin*) became a prominent method to secure immunity from taxation, and religious institutions were able to profit significantly from it. If a local proprietor "commended" a parcel of land to a temple or shrine, the land would pass into its control, typically leaving the original proprietor in place as the estate's manager. He would continue to oversee the land and derive income from it. This practice was a great boon to religious institutions, not only because it put land under their control, but also because it provided a means to establish new temples and shrines in distant locations, complete with a new group of supporters from among the cultivators.

Shrines' acquisition of *shōen* was closely linked to the formation of branch shrines. If a shrine acquired a distant estate, it would typically establish a new branch of the original shrine, dedicated to its original Kami, perhaps including also Kami associated with the new estate's locale. The ritual procedure called for creating a "divided spirit" (*bunrei*) of the original Kami and "inviting" (*kanjō*) it to the new shrine. The formation of branch shrines enabled the spread of the cults of many Kami throughout the land. Inari, Hachiman, Tenjin, and the Kami of the Kamo and Kasuga Shrines are among those that came to be worshipped throughout the country through this process. In an analogous development, Buddhist sects were able to develop temple networks in *shōen* across the country based on the same process of commendation. *Shōen* proprietors of the twelfth century increasingly commended their land to more powerful figures and institutions as a means to gain tax exemption in perpetuity and to be guaranteed immunity from government officials entering their estates. A *shōen* that was exempt both from taxation and officials entering it would be virtually independent from inspection by the provincial governors. The proprietor could then administer the land as he saw fit, generally taking between 25 and 35 percent of the annual income for himself. Given that the costs to temples and shrines were minimal, *shōen* allowed them to acquire great wealth.[64]

Shōen owned by shrines were called by a variety of terms, including *shinryō*, "shrine estates," *mikuriya*, and *misono*. In rare cases such as the Ise Shrines, which held estates so large that they corresponded to whole districts (*kōri, -gun*), the shrine's estate was called a "Kami district," *shingun*. Shrines that controlled extensive estates flourished more than those which did not. But while estates were an important key to economic stability, becoming economically independent weakened the shrines' connections to the imperial house and further blurred the distinction between them and temples. Shrines also became subject to shifting, destabilizing legal changes regarding land tenure, and without the oversight of the central government, shrines could fall into disrepair.[65]

From the late tenth- through the mid-eleventh century, we see new activism among shrine priests, who came to be referred to collectively as *jinin* (also, *jinnin*), literally "Kami people." Groups of *jinin* would go to the capital to complain, for example, about the provincial governor's administration of shrines and the land attached to them. The following examples are among the most striking:

987: Ise *jinin* carrying *sakaki* gathered at the Yōmei palace gate, to complain about their provincial governor. Similar protests were made by the *jinin* of Usa Hachimangū and Sumiyoshi Shrine.

995: The provincial governor of Dazaifu was removed as a result of complaints from *jinin* of Usa Hachimangū.

1003: Further complaints from *jinin* of Usa Hachimangū against the cruelty of the provincial governor.

1004: Some fifty *jinin* of the Sumiyoshi Shrine gathered at the Yōmei Gate to protest ill treatment by the provincial governor. In the same year several hundred people, including *jinin* from Usa Hachimangū, gathered at the Yōmei Gate to protest ill treatment by a provincial governor.

1017: A group of Ise Shrine *jinin* wearing yellow robes broke into an official's house.

1024: A group of *jinin* from the Kehi Shrine gathered at the Yōmei Gate to protest ill treatment by the provincial governor in Kaga.

1029: A group of Ise Shrine *jinin* gathered at the Yōmei Gate to protest ill treatment by the provincial governor.

1039: Ise Shrine's Negi brought a group of the peasantry living on shrine lands to Kyoto to protest new regulations.

1050: Priests from the Ise Shrines brought peasants to Kyoto to protest against the Saishu.[66]

Clearly, shrine personnel had sufficient strength to challenge the central government's representatives, the provincial governors. When they converged upon the capital bearing portable shrines and other sacred symbols, they intimidated the court, which feared the wrath of the Kami. *Jinin* concentration in shrine lands made those territories into a power base, allowing them economic stability and increasing independence from the central government. Often, a temple administered the shrine in question, and in that case power accrued also to the temple. In response, the court tried to limit shrine priests' ability to press their demands. Emperor Go-Shirakawa issued a seven-article edict in 1156, especially addressed to Ise, Iwashimizu Hachimangū, Kamo, Kasuga, Sumiyoshi, Hie, and Gion Shrines, seeking to restrict the number of *jinin* and bemoaning the fact that many were claiming that status merely to escape taxation.[67]

The priests of the Ise Shrines appear very prominently in these demonstrations. They made up a growing, diverse group, beginning with three clan lineages: the Arakida of the Inner Shrine, the Watarai of the Outer Shrine, and the Ōnakatomi, who acted as the court's overseer of both shrines and monopolized the position of *saishu,* the preeminent authority at Ise. Under the supervision of these lineages, a variety of subordinate priests were responsible for ritual and ritual-related labor. Young girls and women who brewed sake and performed sacred dance, and even mountain ascetics, were attached at the periphery. Some Ise priests were deployed as tax collectors and to encourage landholders to commend estates to the shrines. Once land was commended to Ise, priests had to work on acquiring and maintaining tax immunity. By the early thirteenth century, the Ise shrines had some 450 commended estates. This wealth afforded Ise an opportunity to extend its influence, gain a widespread following, and expand the clientele for its ritual services.

After the disintegration of the old system of Jingikan offerings, the vicennial rebuilding of the Ise shrines was supported by a national tax initiated in 1070. But imperial support had not entirely disappeared. The court directly funded the rebuilding of important sub-shrines at Ise called *betsugū*, which enshrined the "violent spirits" (*aramitama*) of Amaterasu and Toyouke. The number of these sub-shrines grew from seven in the late ninth century to eleven by the end of the Kamakura period. These shrines were guaranteed buildings of a certain size and their own priests.[68]

The *jinin* of the Ise Shrines and provincial governors were bound to clash, because governors were charged to maximize the amount of taxable land wherever possible, while *jinin* sought to minimize taxation and government intrusion. The interests of shrines and provincial governors could converge, however, if a shrine's supporters cherished hopes of higher rank. If there were still higher ranks to which a shrine could aspire, maintaining good relations with the provincial governor was prudent. Court accolades remained the highest form of prestige that could come to an individual, a shrine, or a territory.

But the situation of most provincial shrines was discouraging. The majority were in a damaged state and unrepaired at the end of the eleventh century. An imperial edict of 1096 had called for their repair, but it is apparent from aristocratic diaries that many provinces had failed even to pay the levies to support the Vicennial Renewal of the Ise Shrines. Only those shrines to which a Grand Imperial Emissary was dispatched received any support from the central government. The provincial governors were technically responsible for the upkeep of the rest, until another imperial edict of 1103, which made "shrine personnel" (*shashi, yashiro no tsukasa*) responsible for repairs, with penalties for failure to comply.

These edicts provided considerable incentive to shrine personnel and provincial governors to "advertise" shrines as an aid to soliciting the funds necessary for repairs. Shrine affiliates could seek the provincial governor's aid in approaching the Jingikan to encourage the court to bestow a title or rank on the Kami of their shrine. A shrine whose supporters succeeded in such a complex campaign—necessitating "gifts" to all the intermediaries—might thereafter be known as the such-and-such "Myōjin Shrine," "Ichinomiya," or similar high-sounding title that distinguished it from other area shrines, and a gift of land might accompany the honor. Possessing such a title had the potential to raise the reputation of the locale, call attention to the governor's credentials, assist the shrine and its supporters to solicit commendation of land, or raise the reputations of the shrine personnel in defense against Buddhist encroachment.[69]

It was in these circumstances that the provincial governors approached the Jingikan for help in securing the new designations of First Shrine, Second Shrine, or Third Shrine. The new honors were initially bestowed only in provinces where there was not already a shrine to which a Grand Imperial Emissary was dispatched. It appears that these new designations were mainly accorded to shrines that had little significance within the traditional *jingi* system of the Ritsuryō era, and that they were chosen based on different criteria that show little unity or clarity. In some cases, the quid pro quo for the Jingikan's assistance was an agreement that the Jingikan could levy a tax on the shrine for its own support.[70]

Changing Concepts of Kami

Buddhism had already developed rubrics for the incorporation of native deities as its protectors before arriving in Japan. For example, many Indian deities (*deva*) were incorporated into a large collectivity called the "Group of Celestial Beings" (*tenbu*). Some, such as the Four Heavenly Kings (*shitennō*), were represented as warriors protecting Buddhism from every direction. These Celestial Beings were believed subject to the law of karma and regarded as not fully perfected spiritual beings, in spite of widespread respect for their great martial prowess. The "Bright Kings" (*myōō*), Buddhist protective deities with a fearful appearance but believed capable of protecting people from all sorts of calamities, deities such as Fudō, Aizen, and Fugen were similar in their function, distinguished by their weapons and fierce expressions.

Because of the assumption that Kami inhabited all Japan, wherever Buddhism set up a monastic community it encountered the belief that the resident Kami must be placated and recompensed for the incursion on their territory. One way to show respect to the Kami was to incorporate them as protectors of the newly created Buddhist establishment alongside the Celestial Beings and the Bright Kings. This phenomenon arose prominently in the establishment of mountaintop monasteries, such as the Tendai temple complex Enryakuji on Mt. Hiei, or at Kōyasan, the Shingon sect monastery in present-day Wakayama Prefecture.

In 805, the Buddhist monk Saichō (767–822) founded a temple on Mt. Hiei that eventually grew into the massive Enryakuji complex, with hundreds of buildings and thousands of monks. Saichō provided for the worship of the Kami of Mt. Hiei, titling the principle Kami "Mountain King," (Sannō). Like the Kamo Shrines, the mountain itself was located to the northeast of Kyoto, a direction understood in geomantic lore as "the demon gate." Thus, the Kami of the mountain protected the capital from evil spirits who might enter from that direction, as well as protecting the monastery. Ultimately, seven major shrines and many small ones were established for the various Kami of the mountain, unified under the main shrine called Hiyoshi Taisha (also, Hie Taisha). From the year 887, the court began approving the ordination of two monks each year dedicated to the service of the Sannō deities, and it became customary among the aristocracy to dedicate Buddhist scriptures, images, and relics to the Hiyoshi Shrine. A philosophical system of correspondences between the Hiei Kami and Buddhist divinities, called "Shinto of the Single Reality" (Sannō Ichijitsu Shintō), developed as an element of Tendai philosophy.[71]

An analogous system called Ryōbu Shinto was established by the Shingon school of Buddhism, founded by Kōbō Daishi (Kūkai, 774–835), centering on Kōyasan. It likewise developed Shinto shrines regarded as protectors of the monastery and a philosophical theory relating the Kami to Shingon doctrine. Both systems assimilated the Kami to the Diamond and Womb World mandalas, pairing the Buddhist divinities in each of these realms with specific Kami. Both Tendai and Shingon Shinto theories found artistic expression in mandalas created in painting and sculpture from the late twelfth century and continuing through the medieval period. We will examine these theories and related works of art in detail in the next chapter.

During the Heian period, the number and type of deities worshipped in Japan increased markedly. One reason was the growing faith in Buddhist protective deities. We also find the appearance of deities with both Kami and Buddhist attributes, but which cannot easily be categorized as one or the other. Some of these emerged with the formation of the cult of sacred mountains, Shugendō, as the Avatars (*Gongen*). Zaō Gongen was a central figure in this category. En no Gyōja, the legendary founder of Shugendō, first worshipped Zaō Gongen on Mt. Kinpu, in the Yoshino range, where early bands of mountain ascetics trained. Zaō Gongen is represented with his hair standing on end and grimacing, with fangs bared, three eyes, and holding a *vajra* in one hand and the other forming the "sword mudra" on his hip, his right foot lifted as if he were leaping into the air. Many other *Gongen* developed as mountain ascetic groups formed around particular sacred mountains.

Alongside this proliferation of protective deities, we also find the appearance of witch animals associated with sorcery: magical white snakes, fox spirits, and such imaginary creatures as *Tengu*, winged figures with red faces and phallic noses or bird beaks seen in such literary works as *Konjaku monogatari*, a twelfth-century collection of popular tales (see Figure 4.1). There was also a rising interest in worship of the stars, especially the Pole Star and the stars of the constellation Ursa Major, the "big dipper," as well as astrology and divination based on lore concerning auspicious or inauspicious days and directions. Yin-yang philosophy and magic enjoyed great popularity through the fame of a wizard named Abe no Seimei (921–1005), who used animal familiar spirits and astrology to predict the future and work wonders.[72]

This focus on fierce supernatural protectors, witchcraft, astrology, and magic dovetailed with the advent of *Mappō*, the "Latter Days of the Dharma" believed to have begun in 1052. Following the Buddhist idea that human possibility declines after the death of a Buddha, the last age was to be a time when the conditions for achieving salvation have sunk to the nadir. With the approach of the Latter Days, Heian culture grew increasingly fatalistic, deterministic, and tended to assume that life is controlled by dark forces against which humanity must protect itself. Under

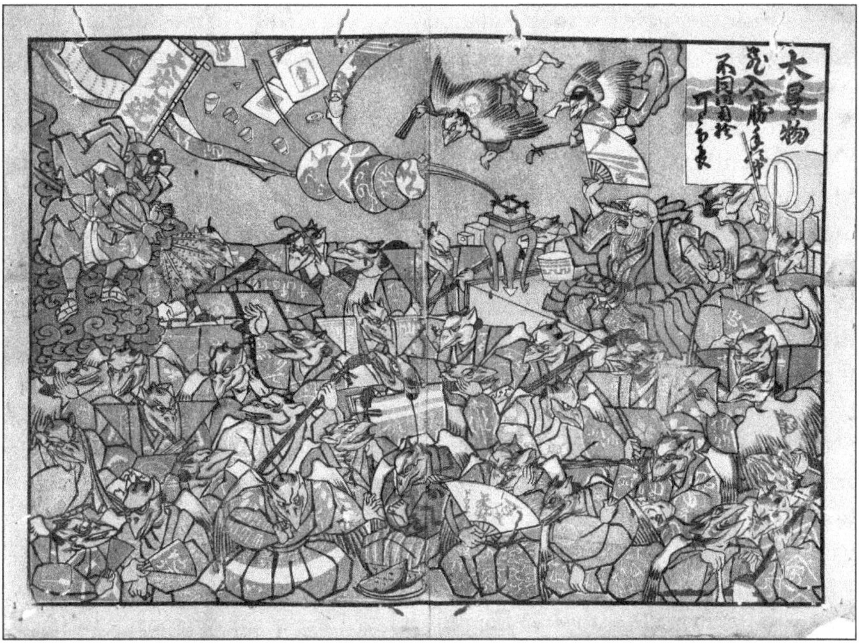

Figure 4.1 *Tengu.* Japanese, Edo period. Woodblock print (nishiki-e); ink and color on paper. 35.4 × 47 cm (13 15/16 × 18 1/2 in.). Source: Museum of Fine Arts, Boston/William Sturgis Bigelow Collection, 11.38609.

the influence of Chinese beliefs that located the realm of the dead either among the stars or on Mt. Taishan, Japanese aristocrats during the era of cloister government began to sponsor ritual offerings to stars believed capable of determining the fate of the dead. In a parallel development, from the late tenth century aristocrats sponsored offerings to the ruler of the realm of the dead, Enma-ō and a Daoist deity called Taizan Fukun, ruler of the Chinese Mt. Taishan and believed to keep records of human misdeeds to be punished in hell. We can see here a merging of beliefs concerning "fate-ordaining stars" and the rulers of the realm of the dead. At least one Ise text promoted the idea of Amaterasu as a judge of the dead, though it is difficult to discern how widely diffused this image was, given the esoteric context of textual transmission at Ise.[73]

The *honji-suijaku* paradigm provided a new means for interpreting the connection between Kami and Buddhist divinities in the Heian period. It was based on the idea of Kami as the "traces" or "emanations" (*suijaku*), the localized, phenomenal manifestations of the "original ground" (*honji*), the more universal and original Buddhist divinities. While a Buddhist philosophical framework distinguishing between "emanations" and "original ground" was much older, it was first applied to the relation between Kami and Buddhist figures in a document of 901, which stated that Buddhist divinities might take the form of Kami.[74]

This basic idea gave rise to speculation about the identity of the Buddhist figure standing behind the local Kami. By the thirteenth century, correspondences between Kami and Buddhas had been created across the country. The Buddhist divinities most frequently identified as the original form of Kami were those believed benefiting humanity: Kannon Bosatsu, an all-purpose savior; Yakushi, the Medicine Buddha; and Amida Buddha, who beckoned believers to his paradise, the Western Pure Land, after death. Different shrines produced varied pairings, and these sometimes changed over time. The Ise deities were regularly linked to Dainichi Nyorai, the supreme Buddha of esoteric thought. At mountain shrines the Kami were sometimes given the title "avatar" (*Gongen*), and in a few cases they were titled "Bodhisattva" (*Bosatsu*). In addition, sacred mountains were interpreted as emanations of Buddhist paradises, shrines were pictured as Buddhist *mandala*, shrine mirrors were cast with Buddhist figures represented on the backs, and *waka* poetry was understood to be analogous to Buddhist *darani* spells recited to gain specific benefits. Thus the search for correspondences extended far beyond pairings of deities.[75]

One particular formulation of *honji-suijaku* thought developed in connection with the belief in *mappō*. During the Latter Days of the Dharma, it was held, Buddhist divinities took pity on Japan, a place at the far periphery of the Buddhist world.[76] In a special dispensation, they "dimmed their light and mingled with the dust of the world" (*wakō dōjin*) in the form of Kami. In that form they could work for the salvation of the people. In other words, the Buddhas adopted Kami form as an expedient means (*hōben*). This interpretation promoted the idea that Kami are active agents of salvation. *Wakō dōjin* became a prominent element of tale literature in the medieval period, and we will examine examples in chapter 5.

Assimilations of Kami with Buddhist divinities suggested that there is no absolute distinction between the two, and if Buddhist divinities take Kami form to hasten the salvation of suffering humanity, then the place where Buddhism began becomes a peripheral matter of minor significance. Foreign origins became a distinction that only underscored the compassion of Buddhist divinities. No *jingi* theory emerged at this time to contradict the paradigm and insist on the continued relevance of indigeneity. In the absence of refutation, the *honji-suijaku* paradigm effectively neutralized a central claim regarding the Kami.

In the twelfth century we see the first assertion of "Shinto" or "Kami" as philosophical concepts. For example, a brief text associated with a *shōen* of the Ise Shrines, titled "Mitsunokashiwa denki" (1170), presents Kami as a cosmological force, a transformation of *ki*, "producing life from nothingness." The text describes Kami as operating to liberate all beings from karma. It equates Kami collectively with the cosmic Sun Buddha, Dainichi, transcending the earlier usage of Kami as referring to specific gods. The text also produced an influential categorization of specific Kami within the framework of the Buddhist concept of original enlightenment, schematized in Table 4.2.[77]

Table 4.2 **The Kami and Enlightenment**

Kami of Original Enlightenment	Amaterasu, who is unchanging and exists eternally, as a "primordial Kami of original enlightenment"
Kami of No Enlightenment	The Kami of Izumo and others, who are deluded and cannot escape rebirth in the four "evil realms"
Kami of Acquired Enlightenment	The Kami of Iwashimizu Hachimangū and others who, thanks to Buddhist teaching, have awakened from their delusion and returned to original enlightenment

This usage of "Shinto" and "Kami" as philosophical terms was a new and virtually unprecedented development. Since our knowledge of this new usage is based on a small number of documents primarily connected with the Ise Shrines, however, it is not clear how broadly accepted it was in the late Heian period. It is also important to bear in mind that the new departures in thought did not displace the older *honji-suijaku* paradigm, but developed within it. The court continued to refer to Kami rites and things having to do with the Kami as *jingi*. Aristocrats' writings only rarely used the term *Shinto* or *jindō*. Nevertheless, the appearance of this new usage can be seen as an important step in the development of new philosophical thought regarding the Kami.[78]

The Question of Syncretism

We have seen throughout this chapter that combinations, assimilations, and rapprochements between Buddhist divinities and the Kami, as well as between temples and shrines, intensified over the mid- to late Heian period. While the *jingūji* of the Ise Shrines disappeared, and these shrines preserved their autonomy, philosophical, ritual, and institutional combinations far outstripped the few cases of autonomous Kami, *jingi* rites, and shrines in this period. The question arises of whether we should consider the relation a case of syncretism.

Syncretism has been a key concept in religious studies, though there is little consensus regarding it. It has almost always been used with negative connotations, referring to some "attempted union or reconciliation of diverse or opposite tenets or practices," with the implication that such unions could only result in mongrelization.[79] Syncretism resulted, in the view of scholars such as Gerardus van der Leeuw, from a mixing of two or more religions, so that while each was originally a pure tradition, mixing produced an impure blend. This understanding has been criticized for its assumption that religions originally exist in a "pure" state; whereas in fact, they are always changing. As they change over time, they evolve into something different, and when they come into contact with other religions, mutual influence will inevitably occur.[80]

Assimilation of divinities, interpenetration of ritual systems, and combinatory institutions are the norm in Japan, not the exception. That being the case, using *syncretism* to describe the situation would not seem to enhance our understanding and could create mistaken assumptions. At minimum, we must keep uppermost in our minds that Buddhism and Shinto were not equally developed in the Heian period, and that Buddhism was much better equipped to exert a controlling influence. Whereas a system for coordinating Kami rites developed only in the late seventh century, Buddhism by that time had over a millennium of history and had spread from India to Sri Lanka, Tibet, China, the Three Korean Kingdoms, and Japan. Its doctrines were elaborate, complex, and highly developed. Its philosophy had been honed and advanced through its interactions with Confucian and Daoist thought. It had a sense of its own history and a vibrant, living tradition, with continual production of new schools of thought, texts, research, rituals, and proselytizing. Monks and nuns in Japan were ordained and educated in professionalized monastic settings that had no Shinto parallel.

By contrast, the *jingi* concept had not yet produced an awareness of Shinto as something that linked all the shrines apart from their connections to particular temples. Jingiryō was not formally abolished, but the respect that had originally been accorded it had faded, and the Jingikan was not producing scholarship to invigorate the idea of Shinto as guardian of the indigenous tradition. It is abundantly clear that the religious interests of the court and the aristocracy had shifted toward Buddhism and a new slate of official rites, imperial progresses, and miscellaneous practices, or changed uses of the original Jingiryō rites. Neither the Jingikan nor the court any longer coordinated the whole. The court had joined the ranks of worshippers, in place of the earlier portrayal of the emperor as a Kami or as the highest authority in Kami affairs. Thus Shinto remained philosophically underdeveloped in comparison with Buddhism, rarely able to assert autonomy intellectually or institutionally.

Yet the question of syncretism with respect to Shinto and Buddhism cannot be resolved in the abstract. We do not find that the Kami disappear in formulations dominated by Buddhist intellectual paradigms and divinities. Instead, the associations of particular Kami and Buddhas in specific sites defined the parameters of religious life there. When we examine religious life in terms of specific sites, we find a spectrum of relations, ranging from competition between sites to struggles for dominance within a single site to ceremonial and festivals that project an image of unity or harmony.

Allan Grapard, a pioneer of the perspective focusing on particular sites, describes the interactions of the Kasuga Shrine with its temple Kōfukuji in a way that shows how these relations operated.

> The multiplex was run by Fujiwara-born ecclesiasts and by Nakatomi sacerdotal lineages. Each major unit was further subdivided into halls run by various types of semiecclesiastic and semisecular people. . . . [Among them]

> the *shuto*, who in time became the most powerful leaders of the multiplex, earned a power base in the estates that they administered or protected in the name of the Kōfukuji [the temple administering the shrine]; in a parallel fashion, controllers who administered the estates of the Kasuga Shrine came to be known as *kokumin*, the Provincials. On the side of the shrines, the sacerdotal lineages governed a population of semireligious figures known as *jinin*, "*kami*-men," who were strictly organized and who specialized in varied duties related to the maintenance of the shrines, to the performance of rituals, or to armed protection of the multiplex. Whereas the *shuto* were directly related to specific temples of the Kōfukuji, while the *jinin* were directly related to the shrines of Kasuga, these two types of social body shared a unique culture based on the combinations of the *kami* with the buddhas or bodhisattvas. When the Wakamiya Shrine...was erected [under Kōfukuji] in 1135, the multiplex organized a festive rite known as *On-matsuri*. This rite, dedicated to a *kami* associated with the Bodhisattva of Wisdom Mañjuśrī, was ritually governed by the [abbot] but was in great part the responsibility of the *shuto* and *kokumin* of the province of Yamato, which the festive rite quickly came to symbolize. All classes of Yamato society participated in the rite, from the lowest class...who performed acrobatic tours to the highest levels of the priestly elite who were the guarantors of the power of the associated numinous entity said to govern the destiny of the province. As a result, the province was seen as sacred in its entirety, and the city of Nara itself achieved a sacred status.[81]

Here the Kasuga Shrine and the temple Kōfukuji each exhibit a high degree of internal differentiation and intense interaction with each other. They remain distinct entities, yet together they produce a festival that projects an image of the unity, not only of the two institutions, but also the city of Nara where they are located, and beyond its boundaries to encompass the entire province. The term *syncretism* not only fails to do justice to the complexity of this historical reality, but also obscures the variety of intellectual, religious, and institutional relations structuring religious life. For these reasons, the present study does not adopt that term.

Conclusion

Having examined the Jingikan in its Nara-period heyday in chapter 3 and seen its Heian-period decline in this chapter, I want to return to my claim that Shinto originates with the Jingikan. In chapter 3, I rejected the position that ties the beginning of Shinto to the medieval period, in part because of the repudiation of the medieval paradigm that occurred in the early modern period and the paradigm's absence from modern and contemporary Shinto. One could argue, however, that I have identified

Shinto's beginnings with something that remained in force for two centuries or less, and that my position should be rejected on the same grounds that I used in deciding against the position of Inoue Hiroshi and others. I believe that my position is preferable, however, because while the Jingikan lost effectiveness, it remained as an organ of the central government into the Meiji period. From the late seventh through the mid-nineteenth centuries, it was never abolished. One might add that Yoshida Kanetomo, who exemplifies the origins of Shinto as understood by Inoue, himself held high office within the Jingikan, and that without that position he would not have had the emperor's ear. In the late nineteenth and mid-twentieth centuries, the Shrine Bureau (Jinjakyoku, 1900–1940) and the Shrine Institute (Jingiin, 1940–1945) inherited the Jingikan's functions. The organization now purporting to unify the shrines in postwar Japan, the National Association of Shinto Shrines (Jinja Honchō), was formed explicitly for the purpose of continuing the functions of unifying the shrines and to lobby for their return to public status, demonstrating a determination to perpetuate the ideal of the Jingikan from 1946 to the present. In other words, the Jingikan and its successor organizations embodied an ideal that has continued from the late seventh century into the twenty-first century. The ideal is that shrines embody the "indigenous" tradition and unify the populace through ritual that is coordinated with the emperor's worship of his ancestors. Therefore, shrines should be administered and supported from the public purse as official sites for the performance of state rites. In my perspective, shrine ritual and the ideal of the Jingikan represent Shinto's most enduring elements of historical continuity, overshadowing doctrine and philosophy, which remain weak and underdeveloped even today, by comparison with Japanese Buddhism.

5

The Esotericization of Medieval Shinto

Introduction

The four centuries from the beginning of the Kamakura shogunate in 1192 until the establishment of the Tokugawa shogunate in 1600 are considered the medieval period of Japanese history. Warrior bands seized power as the court lost control over the countryside at the end of the Heian period. The Taira clan assumed control in the mid-twelfth century but was overthrown in 1185 by their rivals, the Minamoto clan under Yoritomo (1147–1199), whom the court granted the title, "Barbarian subduing Generalissimo" (*seitai shōgun*), and who subsequently formed a military government in Kamakura, in Eastern Japan, in 1192.

The dissolution of the system of central administration of shrines left a vacuum. Into it flowed a great outpouring of religious thought, rituals, institutions, and the creation of major works of art and literature about the Kami. Much of this cultural production sought to discover and elaborate hitherto unsuspected relations between the Kami and Buddhist divinities, or to understand the religious significance of historical events. In a separate development, the shogunate became a patron of religious institutions across the country, and a network of shrines and temples in Eastern Japan took shape around its tutelary shrine in Kamakura, the Tsurugaoka Hachiman Shrine (in fact, a *miyadera*). After the overthrow of the Minamoto, the shogunates of the Hōjō and Ashikaga families also became deeply involved in religious ceremonial, including for the Kami.

Chapters 5, 6, and 7 address the history of Shinto during the medieval period. They examine the evolving discourses regarding Shinto's rightful contributions to governance as well as its claims to represent Japan's indigenous traditions of Kami worship. During this era, significant changes in the concept of Kami occurred and were manifested in a variety of forms, including philosophical texts (composed within shrine lineages and within Buddhist schools of thought), literary works, shrine architecture, the visual and performing arts, and popular festivals. The most important changes in medieval concepts of Kami can be summarized for the sake of convenience under five major headings. First, we find that the Kami come to be portrayed as acting in accord with knowable principles, and thus they appear less unpredictable and arbitrary than in the ancient period. Second, the Kami come to be regarded as agents of salvation construed in Buddhist terms, and we find medieval people praying at the Iwashimizu Hachimangū, Hie, and Kumano shrines for rebirth in the Pure Land. Third, we find the Kami described as transcendent gods, in addition to their localized and limited forms that are more characteristic of the ancient period. Fourth, the idea of Kami becomes "internalized," believed to exist within the heart-mind (*kokoro*) of humanity. Fifth, while we have seen that the *honji-suijaku* paradigm had come to structure thought relating Kami to Buddhas, a variety of new (or newly prominent) supernaturals appear, classed roughly with the Kami, but who are outside the *honji-suijaku* framework. For the most part these divinities are perceived in negative terms as foreign, malevolent, or straightforwardly evil. Medieval religion developed a variety of ways of dealing with them.[1]

To understand this period, it is important to assess what I refer to as the *esotericization* of Shinto, Shinto thought as developed within esoteric Buddhism—that is, Buddhist theories of the Kami developing within the Tendai and Shingon schools, called Ryōbu Shinto. Those theories were closely linked to historical events surrounding the court and the Ise Shrines. The Outer Shrine at Ise was administered by the Watarai lineage, whose theologians advanced theories concerning that shrine's principal deity, and while Watarai Shinto was immersed in the esoteric Buddhist world, it also developed beyond that framework. Medieval Shinto theories were given symbolic expression through Kami Initiations, modeled on enthronement ritual, and also in the arts. Study of the *Nihon shoki* underwent a major revival. Oaths sworn to the Kami reveal how the Kami came to be associated with morality. The adoption of these oaths in a variety of contexts propagated evolving concepts of Kami. As the court weakened, the Great Purification Prayer continued to circulate independently of the ancient semiannual recitations formerly conducted by the Jingikan and came to be understood as *darani*, a magical formula. Shinto ideas were propagated in the newly forming lineages of the cult of sacred mountains, Shugendō, and in turn the mountain cult's diverse deities entered the stream of Shinto thought. When the country came under attack during the Mongol invasions, the idea of Japan as a divine land received new attention, and the virtues of the Ise deities were widely credited for Japan's salvation from annihilation.

The Esotericization of Shinto

In the early medieval period, the episteme of the Shingon school of Buddhism, especially, and also the esoteric aspects of Tendai Buddhism, came to structure thought and practice regarding the Kami pervasively. The basis for this development lay in the *honji-suijaku* thought we began to examine in chapter 4. It progressed markedly with the appearance of Ryōbu Shinto and the acquisition of fiefs by temples and shrines. These territories provided new bases for the spread of a seamless worldview of Kami and Buddhas working together to assist humanity to attain a Buddhist-conceived salvation.

In adopting the term *esotericization,* I refer particularly to the framework of the Diamond (or Vajra) and Womb world mandalas of esoteric Buddhism, standing for the principles of wisdom and compassion respectively. The cosmic Buddha Dainichi (Vairocana), also called Birushana (Rushana), represents the complete unity of wisdom and compassion. The Diamond and Womb world mandalas were represented pictorially in two complementary diagrams. Each component of the diagram could be symbolized by the figure of a Buddha, Bodhisattva, or other supernatural being. The two mandalas were hung in ritual spaces to represent the complete cosmos. The idea of the two mandalas was not, however, limited to pictorial representation but might take the forms of Siddham script, sculpture, calligraphy, or tapestry. In combination with the *honji-suijaku* paradigm, the paired mandalas were "mapped" onto the geography of sacred mountains and the architectural structures of shrines. Shrine mandalas resulting from that process symbolically attributed religious significance to particular Kami sanctuaries and shrine buildings, or to the geographical features of the land around shrines. The paired Inner and Outer Shrines at Ise were especially appealing for pairing with the mandalas. The idea of the ultimate unity of Amaterasu and Dainichi was promoted as the highest expression of the nature of the Kami as "one but dual."[2]

In Kuroda Toshio's evaluation, esoteric Buddhism dominated over ideas of the Kami.[3] Even figures championing the Kami and ideas of Japan as "the land of the Kami," such as Kitabatake Chikafusa (who was known as an imperial loyalist but also ordained as a Shingon monk) accepted an intellectual framework in which the Buddhas and Kami were ultimately united. The esoteric episteme also thoroughly colored palace ritual and the emerging thought regarding the regalia, as well as shrine rites. For these reasons, medieval Shinto is usually portrayed as thoroughly enveloped by Buddhism. More recent research, however, detects signs of a new direction in thought about the Kami in the Watarai Shinto and Buddhist preoccupation with supernaturals that were neither fully Buddhist or Kami. "[W]hile Buddhism exercised a sort of intellectual and ritual hegemony on *kami* matters during the [medieval] period, . . . non-Buddhist tendencies gradually developed and gained strength."[4]

The esoteric episteme of the age presupposed that knowledge of ultimate truth and correct ritual practice should be transmitted only by a master to a disciple through ritual; it was not suitable for wide consumption. It is tempting to conclude that the secrecy surrounding esoteric knowledge and rites would mean a turn toward the private, and that the public character and significance of Shinto was on the wane. There are elements of truth in this preliminary conclusion, and the close guarding of lineage secrets by the Watarai and the Yoshida, and their transmission through Kami Initiations, seems to confirm the image of privatization and loss of public significance for *jingi* rites and institutions. Subsequently, in the Edo period, Kokugaku thinkers criticized esoteric transmissions of Shinto thought as incompatible with the public character they idealized for Shinto, though they could not immediately dislodge the older pattern.

On the other hand, however, esoteric rites as performed at temples, shrines, and the palace often declared their public significance in terms of protection of the sovereign and the realm as a whole from foreign and domestic enemies. Receiving court or shogunal support obliged both temples and shrines to perform prayers for the peace and prosperity of the realm as a whole, whatever deities and doctrines they promoted. Moreover, as we will see in chapter 7, the Yoshida house devised mechanisms to enable the transmission of its esoteric knowledge to persons outside the lineage. Thus esotericization did not mean privatization, per se.

Interestingly, designations of particular forces as "foreign" shifted during this period. Warriors swore oaths to the Kami and to the Buddhist divinities of all Japan. The Kami became guardians of moral codes of allegiance and the values of truth, decisiveness, and compassion. No one would have disputed the designation of the Mongol invasions as a foreign threat, but in the chaos of the Ōnin War and subsequent warfare at the end of the period, all the partisans sought to legitimize themselves and appealed to the Kami as the legitimate forces of the true sovereign, even when there were multiple contenders for the throne.

In all, medieval esotericization of Shinto greatly complicated alignment of the *jingi* rites with the public and the indigenous. In one limited sense we can regard our difficulty applying these categories in this period as a reflection of Buddhism's intellectual hegemony, as a sign that it had succeeded completely in cocooning Kami cults of all kinds. We can, however, see other phenomena attesting to a widened scope for ideas and practices concerning the Kami in the visual and literary arts of the period, the subject of chapter 6. Some examples include shrine mandalas, magnificent illustrated scroll works, such as *Kasuga Gongen Genki-e*, that depicted the Kami in many forms, the dance and drama of *kagura* and Nōh theater in which dancers and actors took the roles of Kami, as well as the production of many tales about the Kami that were spread by popular preachers. All these show us that the Kami stimulated the age's creativity in myriad ways not bound by Buddhist doctrinal paradigms.

The Kamakura Shogunate and Hachiman

The Minamoto took Hachiman as their clan deity because their ancestor Minamoto Yoshiie (1039–1106) had had his coming-of-age ceremony (*genpuku*) performed at the Iwashimizu Hachiman Shrine in 1045, after which he took the name, "Hachiman

Tarō."[5] When Minamoto Yoritomo was raising his army to fight the Taira, he invariably worshipped at the shrines of the various groups whose allegiance he hoped to win. For example, in 1063, he paid respect to a Hachiman Shrine near Kamakura at Yuigahama, and in 1180, when he was raising troops in Eastern Japan, he gathered his soldiers at the Rokusho no Miya Shrine (the Comprehensive Shrine of Musashi Province) and dedicated horses and sacred arrows there as part of his prayers to the provincial Kami for military victory.[6] Similarly, he prayed for victory at the Mishima Shrine (1180.8.17) and rebuilt Hikawa Shrine, the "First Shrine" (*Ichinomiya*) of Musashi Province (1180.9). The next month, he arrived in Kamakura and moved the spirit of Hachiman from Yuigahama to the site where he would build a splendid new *miyadera*, the Tsurugaoka Hachiman Shrine, which became the shogunate's central ritual site. It incorporated many elements of Buddhist origin and was administered by Buddhist priests. It sought to unify the Comprehensive Shrines and *Ichinomiya*, while many other temples, shrines, and religious leaders sought to establish connections with it. (See Figure 5.1.)

In the 1180s, when the Minamoto were still at war against the Taira, Yoritomo patronized numerous shrines and temples in the hopes of securing troops from among the people on their estates. For example, he relied on the head of the Kumano Shrine to raise troops for him in late 1181; dedicated sacred horses to the Ise Shrines in prayers for victory in 1182; and dedicated estates to the Ise Shrines, the Hirota Shrine, and to the temples Jingoji and Onjōji in 1184.[7]

Yoritomo established his government, called a "tent government" (*bakufu*), based on the theory that the shogun ruled on behalf of the imperial court, which continued to exist in the capital Kyoto. In fact, however, the court's influence had weakened greatly. The early Kamakura period was a time of major temple and shrine construction by the shogunal order. Yoritomo gave sacred horses and monetary gifts to various shrines in appreciation for their role in destroying the Taira. For example, he had the Rokusho no Miya entirely rebuilt in 1186, so that it physically faced Kamakura, and issued orders that priests of various shrines in the province gather there in the seventh month of each year to pray for the peace of the realm. He made annual pilgrimages to the Izu, Hakone, and Mishima Shrines from 1188. He ordered his vassals to keep shrines and temples in their domains in good repair and to show respect for the Kami.[8]

Yoritomo built up the status of Tsurugaoka Hachiman through his personal patronage. Its principal festivals featured the liberation of living creatures (*hōjō-e*) and displays of archery on horseback (*yabusame*). Yoritomo personally attended these events, and his wife, Hōjō Masako, made a "hundred pilgrimages" (*hyakudo mairi*) to the shrine as an expression of her faith in Hachiman. Yoritomo had the shrine perform a great ceremony for recitation of the Larger Perfection of Wisdom Sutra. The shrine was expanded with the building of a five-story pagoda in 1189, and when it burned down in 1191, it was rebuilt within a year, and this time the spirit of Iwashimizu Hachiman was ceremonially installed. A *jingūji* was built at the shrine in 1208, and in 1216 a chapel for the Pole Star deity. In 1225, Yoritomo's widow initiated a lecture series at the shrine. In the same year, a great ceremony was held, in which 1,200 monks conducted ritual to quell an epidemic. In 1227, the shogunate sponsored 36,000 rites to the Kami to end a string of natural disasters and epidemics. Yoritomo's successors made offerings at many shrines, and continued his support for the Comprehensive Shrines. Yoritomo's vassals also contributed to the expansion of the shrine; for example, Ashikaga Yoshikane (1154–1199) dedicated mandalas of the Diamond and Womb Worlds in 1194.[9]

Yoritomo contributed generously to the rebuilding of Tōdaiji, which the Taira had burned down in 1180. The shogunate and the court collaborated in the reconstruction, and the Buddhist monk Chōgen (1121–1206) traveled the country to raise funds from the people. Yoritomo made a huge gift of money, great quantities of silk, and 10,000 *koku*[10] of rice. He made a further, massive contribution of gold when he attended the ceremonies marking the completion of the rebuilding in 1195, accompanied by tens of thousands of soldiers.[11]

After Yoritomo's death in 1199, his sons succeeded him as shogun, but in fact the Hōjō family controlled the shogunate by acting as regents. In 1221 Emperor Go-Toba (r. 1183–1198) attempted to overthrow the Kamakura shogunate in the Jōkyū War. It was also around this time that the imperial house made the Kyoto Shingon

Figure 5.1 Kōshun, Japanese, 1315–1328, *The Shinto Deity Hachiman in the Guise of a Buddhist Monk.* Japanese, Kamakura period, dated 1328, Japanese cypress (*Chamaecyparis obtusa*) with polychrome and inlaid crystal; joined woodblock construction. Overall: 81.3 × 93.3 × 61 cm (32 × 36 3/4 × 24 in.). Source: Museum of Fine Arts, Boston. Maria Antoinette Evans Fund and Contributions 36.413.

temple Sen'yūji an imperial prayer temple.[12] Subsequently, this temple began to perform imperial funerals, and imperial graves were located there. The shogunate defeated the court's forces, and thereafter installed deputies in Kyoto to ensure that no further coup attempts arose from the court. This incident marked the virtual end of the court's political power.

Revival of the *Nihon Shoki*

The court had held lectures on *Nihon shoki* through the ninth century, but those died out after 965, and the text remained unread for the rest of the Heian period. In the twelfth century, however, the text became an important source for poets and for scholars of ancient poetry. Fujiwara Michinori (also known by his clerical name, Shinzei, 1106–1159, a powerful politician allied with the Taira and also a close adviser to Emperor Nijō, who was also acclaimed as a scholar) lectured on the *Nihon shoki* and compiled a commentary titled *Nihongi shō* that served as a lexicon for *Nihon shoki*. The scope of this commentary extended to a larger corpus of mythic and poetic works. Because other scholars and poets adopted Michinori's enlarged perspective on ancient myth and history, the term *Nihongi* in the medieval period referred not only to *Nihon shoki* but also to myth as a whole. As the mythic corpus became more accessible, literary expression of its themes appeared. For example, an imperial poetry collection of the twelfth century was composed entirely of poems on *jingi* themes. Poetry celebrations and the dedication of poetry were held at such medieval shrines as Ise, Iwashimizu, Sumiyoshi, and others.[13]

Poetry played an important part in spreading esoteric thinking. Based on the idea that poems, *waka*, constitute the Japanese-language expression of Shingon mantras, the idea arose that *waka* are actually esoteric Buddhist spells (*darani*), with magical power to make actual events occur. Ultimately, *waka* and *darani* are one and the same, it was held, leading to the view that *waka* could substitute for *darani* in esoteric rites, especially Shugendō ritual.[14]

The Yoshida and Shirakawa families developed specializations in scholarship on the *Nihon shoki* and lectured at court. Drawing widely from the resuscitated *Nihon shoki* as well as *Sendai kuji hongi* (also known as *Kujiki*) and other ancient works, their studies created new myths and images not seen in the original texts. This research constituted one important basis for the Shinto theories of the medieval period. One significant commentary titled *Shaku nihongi*, by Urabe Kanekata (late thirteenth century, precise dates unknown), recorded the lectures on *Nihon shoki* that his father Kanefumi (thirteenth century, precise dates unknown) had delivered. *Shaku nihongi* is thus a compendium of the Yoshida lineage's scholarship on *Nihon shoki* that includes notes on the sources, suggested readings for difficult terms and passages, poetics, and esoteric interpretations linking the text to other ancient writings. Temples and shrines compiling their official histories (*engi*) drew on this expanded repository of myth, images, and ideas and also contributed to it based on their own legends. Buddhist esotericism provided the prevailing intellectual framework as well as ritual patterns.[15]

The *Nihon shoki* was transmitted through widespread copying projects based at temples and shrines. For example, *Nihon shoki* and many texts of Ryōbu Shintō and Watarai Shinto were copied at Kyōshōji and Kōkōji, temples located in Ise, by monks of the Saidaiji lineage of the Shingon-Ritsu sect, founded by Eison (1201–1290). A similar copying project was based in Shōmyōji in present-day Kanagawa Prefecture in Eastern Japan. In some cases, acquisition of a copy of the *Nihon shoki* became the occasion for conducting Kami Initiation rites at the temple where it was being copied. Copying projects such as these led to lectures on the text and the production of commentaries, mostly compiled by Tendai and Shingon clerics, who saw the tales of *Nihon shoki* as allegories of Buddhist doctrines. These Buddhist figures contributed very significantly to the development of medieval Shinto theories and theology and provided important conduits for the circulation of texts linking temples and shrines, as well as providing a channel for the communication of ideas among intellectuals, and mediating the transmission of texts between the Outer and Inner Shrines at Ise.[16]

Copying projects were not limited to the *Nihon shoki* but also included the reproduction of Buddhist scriptures to be dedicated to temples or shrines. A variety of organizations and groups produced texts in the medieval period, with the result that the age saw a dramatic output of new writings on religious subjects of all kinds. Buddhist temples, shrine lineages, and noble houses formed lineages for the ritual transmission of esoteric teachings that they claimed to possess. Each lineage promoted itself through claims of possessing unique authority to transmit its teachings. Their transmission rituals gave visual, symbolic form to each one's intellectual system. Transmission rites required the production of texts, and it was through this process that *jingi* texts came to be created in great number during this period.[17]

The Cosmology of Oaths

In the medieval period, the idea developed that the Kami demand moral behavior and faith. In addition to punishments, the Kami were also believed to *reward* people, and thus the term *punishment* is often coupled with the word for "reward" or "praise," producing the compound, "reward and punish" (*shōbatsu*).[18] The moral dimension of Kami was emphasized in a variety of medieval documents. The terms for "divine punishment" (*shinbatsu* and *myōbatsu*) in medieval oaths refer to Kami meting out punishments for moral transgressions. The term *tatari* does not appear in these oaths. The *idea* of *tatari* did not die out, but from around the beginning of the Kamakura period the terms *shinbatsu* and *myōbatsu* become much more prominent. For example, in 1160 Minamoto Yoshimune included a prayer in his land grant to the Ise Shrines, that the people of the shrine's lands be spared "divine punishment" (*shinbatsu*). In 1165 the Umenomiya Shrine of Yamashiro Province complained that the priest of Kōfukuji who was in charge of shrine rites had been negligent, and claimed that he had died as a result of divine punishment from the Kami. According to a tale in the *Konjaku monogatari*, a collection of popular morality tales from the twelfth century, the death by drowning of a provincial governor who had misappropriated wood intended for the Yakushiji temple was due to Hachiman's punishment.

A document titled *Goseibai shikimoku*, composed by Hōjō Yasutoki (1183–1242) in 1232 in response to the Jōkyū War, was the first law code for vassals of the Kamakura shogunate. Its first article required that warriors show respect for the Kami by keeping shrines in good repair and observing shrine rituals, stating also, "The dignity of the Kami is increased by the respect of humanity, and the good fortune of the people is increased by the virtue of the Kami." This introduced the idea that there exists a kind of reciprocity or mutuality between the Kami and humanity. This highly influential text became a set of precedents for the subsequent Muromachi (or Ashikaga) shogunate (1336–1573). A sacred character was ascribed to the document, and copies were placed inside cavities in Buddhist statues. In the Edo period it was used as a model for calligraphy practice and thus played an important role in education. *Goseibai shikimoku* concluded with a vow signed by Yasutoki and his vassals to uphold the code and calling upon a list of deities to punish them if they should disobey: Bonten, Taishaku-ten, the Four Heavenly Kings, the gods of heaven and earth of all Japan from the more-than-sixty provinces, especially the two avatars of Izu and Hakone, the Bright Deity of Mishima, the Great Bodhisattva Hachiman, and Tenman Daijizai Tenjin (that is, the divinized spirit of Sugawara Michizane).[19]

Oaths were known as *kishōmon*. The format of the oath seen in *Goseibai shikimoku* became a kind of template for the thousands of such documents produced in medieval Japan. At first written on white paper, they came to be composed on talismans issued from shrines and temples called Ox King Talismans (*go-ō hōin*), bearing a variety of esoteric symbols and images of a crow, the divine messenger of the Kumano Shrine. In a separate development, popular pilgrimage to the Kumano Shrine flourished in the twelfth century, and its Ox King Talismans spread through the country.[20] Vows were submitted in court proceedings and had legal standing. Warrior vassals pledged loyalty to their feudal lords in oaths, sometimes sealed with a bloody fingerprint.

A vow might be composed in the context of a mundane dispute. In an oath of the third month of 1325 the monk Shōson of Tōdaiji wrote to his superiors at the temple:

> Reverently I proclaim my vow. On the fourteenth of this month I was to have taken part in the Kegon ceremony, but my chronic illness flared up and I required moxibustion[21] treatment. For that reason I was unable to attend the ceremony. If I have fabricated this account of illness in order

> to evade participating in the ceremony, may I receive divine punishment (*shinbatsu, myōbatsu*) from the following divinities: Tenshō Daijin, the lord of all Japan; all the greater and lesser gods of heaven and earth from the more-than-sixty provinces, the Great Buddha, the Four Heavenly Kings, the Hachiman deities of the three places [Usa, Iwashimizu, and Tsurugaoka], all the Kami who "dim their light" [that we may be saved], especially Shōjin Kannon of the Nigatsudō.[22]

Shōson's superiors evidently suspected that he had absented himself from an important ritual, the Kegon ceremony, in which he had been expected to participate, not from genuine illness but for some other reason. Evidently Shōson composed this vow when called to account. Shōson calls on Kami and Buddhist divinities to bear witness to his honesty, indicating his belief that the Kami and Buddhas know what people do and their motives. All the divinities named are aligned with the principle of honesty, and all of them are prepared to punish Shōson if he should lie, his oath implies. Thus, the Kami and Buddhist deities enforce moral principles together.

If we compare the divinities invoked in these two vows, we find some significant differences, which we can represent schematically (see Table 5.1).

The order of categories of divinities seen in the two oaths varies significantly. Amaterasu/Tenshō Daijin is not mentioned at all in *Goseibai shikimoku*. The reason is that literate people in the thirteenth century knew of a tale holding that—out of compassion and the desire to spare Japan—this Kami had told a lie, and it would have been inappropriate to invoke her in a vow swearing to speak the truth.[23] This belief was based on tales about Tenshō Daijin and Enma-ō (judge of the dead) or Dairokuten Ma-ō (or Māra) that we will examine in more detail in chapter 6.

Table 5.1 ***Kishōmon* Divinities**

Goseibai shikimoku (1232)	*Shōson's Vow (1325)*
Bonten, Taishaku[-ten]	Tenshō Daijin, the lord of all Japan
The Four Heavenly Kings	The greater and lesser gods of heaven and earth from the more-than-sixty provinces
The gods of heaven and earth of all Japan from the more-than-sixty provinces	The Daibutsu (referring to the Great Buddha of Tōdaiji)
The two avatars of Izu and Hakone	The Four Heavenly Kings
The Bright Deity of Mishima	The Hachiman deities of the three places
Great Bodhisattva Hachiman	All the Kami who "dim their light" [*wakō dōjin*]
Tenman Daijizai Tenjin	Shōjin Kannon of the Nigatsudō

This legend was cited as the reason that Buddhist terminology was tabooed at Ise, and it circulated widely in the medieval period. We can also see, nevertheless, that people of Shōson's time had an image of Tenshō Daijin as standing at the top of the pantheon, as lord of all the Kami.[24]

The Heavenly Kings such as Bonten (Skt: Brahmā), Taishaku-ten (Skt: Indra), and the Four Heavenly Kings were typically invoked in vows. Compared to them, Kami other than Tenshō Daijin presided over a smaller portion of the cosmos. This understanding was based on a Buddhist image of the universe in which the divinities and nations are arranged around the cosmic mountain, Mt. Sumeru (J: Shumisen), the world center. At the top is the paradise of Taishaku-ten (Indra), and the Four Heavenly Kings live in its middle slopes. Eight seas surround Mt. Sumeru, and the sun, moon, and stars revolve around it.

The Indian origin of the Heavenly Kings was understood in medieval Japan, and India was regarded as a sacred and highly significant part of the cosmos, because the Buddha was born there. Japan, by contrast, was thought to be a tiny and insignificant land at the far margins of the known universe. Presiding over such inferior territory, its native gods were in a lesser category. As we will see below, this discourse of marginality was in tension with the triumphalism of Japan as "land of the gods."[25]

Finally, we can recognize the local specificity of each of these vows in the choice of divinities further down the list. The Izu and Hakone avatars and the Mishima deity were deities of eastern Japan, where the Kamakura shogunate was located, and Hachiman was the patron deity of warriors, enshrined by the shogunate at the Tsurugaoka Hachiman Shrine. In Shōson's vow we find divinities named that were in his immediate purview, such as the Great Buddha statue at his temple, Tōdaiji, here taken to be a *suijaku* of the Buddha represented by the statue. In other words, a statue was a tangible "trace" of the Buddha it represented, a living and powerful being once it was consecrated. In Shōson's case the "three Hachimans" include the Hachiman shrine immediately outside Tōdaiji's main gate, Tamuke Hachiman Shrine. The Kannon referred to is a statue in a chapel attached to Tōdaiji called the Nigatsudō. Thus, in both cases protector divinities close to the oath's author were prominently named.[26]

The Great Purification Prayer in the Medieval Period

We saw in the last chapter that the Great Purification ritual had come to be performed in private contexts by shrine attendants at Ise, Buddhist clerics, and yin yang masters during the late Heian period for individual purposes such as healing. A number of miscellaneous changes crept into the text as it became more widely distributed. Shortened forms of the Great Purification Prayer appeared, along with the practice of reciting it many times, giving rise to expressions like "one hundred purifications" or "one thousand purifications." These expressions assume the belief that multiple recitations would somehow be more effective, along the lines of *nenbutsu* recitation.

During the Muromachi period, the original form of the biannual court Great Purification ritual was lost, and the prayer became separated from the ancient rite. The prayer appeared in such new forms as the "Purification of the Six Roots," (*Rokkon shōjō harae*), in which the phrase "rokkon shōjō," "cleanse and purify the six roots," was repeated at the end, calling for purification of the five senses plus the mind. This turned the Great Purification Prayer into a device for purifying body and mind. The term "Nakatomi harae" came to be used as a general term for the Great Purification Prayer as used independently of the ancient court ritual. Yoshida Kanetomo, creator of the "Purification of the Six Roots" prayer (see chapter 7) frequently lectured at court on the Nakatomi no Ōharae and claimed that it had the power to grant all wishes, dispel all difficulties and misfortunes, and bring unlimited happiness. He also claimed that it epitomized Shinto.

As different kinds of religionists used the prayer in different forms for disparate purposes, commentaries were published. One of the most significant of these was *Nakatomi Harae Kunge*, examined below. Some of the common themes addressed in expositions of the prayer were the land of Japan, the myths of its founding, the emperor, and the regalia. The prayer acquired a kind of ecumenical character—in the sense that it was used by many different kinds of practitioners across traditions—even as it came to be regarded as embodying something essential to Shinto.[27]

Ryōbu Shinto

Based on the *honji-suijaku* paradigm, an explosive production of texts known as Ryōbu Shinto were compiled in the medieval era, beginning around 1150. The term *ryōbu*, meaning "both parts," refers to the Diamond and Womb World mandalas. Ryōbu Shinto was originally developed as a Shingon theory of the Kami in relation to the two mandalas. Its texts are thus heavily influenced by Shingon esotericism. They interrogate the relation of the Ise Kami to Buddhist figures, explain the taboos on words relating to Buddhism at the Ise Shrines, and relate the imperial regalia to the Wish-Fulfillment Jewel (*nyoi hōju*).[28]

The *Nakatomi Harae Kunge* was one of the most important commentaries on the Great Purification Prayer, as well as being a major text of Ryōbu Shinto. The date of the work as well as its authorship are unknown, but some part of the text was in existence by the late Heian period, and it shows signs of multiple authorship.[29] It asserts that the prayer is the ultimate *darani*, a powerful spell potent enough to dispel all demons blocking the path to salvation. It counters the text of the Great Purification Prayer, which itself begins with the statement that it is the words spoken by Izanagi when he purified himself after returning from the land of Yomi, claiming instead that it is also the words of a Buddhist tutelary deity Daijizaiten (Maheshvara). *Nakatomi*

Harae Kunge is one source of the idea that Amaterasu deceived Māra or Enma-ō with a lie. This text also contains a legend holding that Amaterasu revealed to the ascetic Gyōki that she is a *suijaku* of the cosmic Buddha Dainichi, in other words, the secret truth that her true nature is Buddhist.[30]

The *Nakatomi Harae Kunge* introduced the concept of original enlightenment to discussions of the Kami, and this remained a central element of Shinto thought until the Edo period. The work asserts that the Kami bestow compassion on all beings, that Japan is the land of the Kami, and is ruled over by an emperor descended from the Kami. The Kami are part of original enlightenment and are one with the three bodies of Buddha. Out of compassion for sentient beings, the cosmic Buddha Dainichi takes the form of Amaterasu, and although they may be different superficially, they are equally effective and powerful in salvation.[31]

Buddhist temples had begun to be constructed around the Ise Shrines, a trend that continued through the period. Already at the end of the tenth century, Ōnakatomi no Nagayori (exact dates unknown), who served as Saishu, had built a temple at Ise called Rendaiji and took the tonsure just before he died. The Arakida and Watarai families, head priests of the Inner and Outer Shrines, respectively, also built temples at Ise. As the temples became connected to the shrines, close personal relations among the priests were formed. Many Ise priests of both the Inner and Outer Shrines took the tonsure after their retirement, demonstrating their deep faith in Buddhism.[32]

In a related development, while fundraising to rebuild Tōdaiji, the celebrated monk Chōgen made a pilgrimage to Ise to pray for divine assistance, conducting a ceremony for the recitation of the Larger Perfection of Wisdom Sutra (1186.4.26). A record of his pilgrimage was compiled in the same year, and it became an inspiration for many other Buddhist figures to go to Ise as pilgrims and write accounts of their journeys. Ise became a sacred site for Buddhists, a development that led to the production of new texts concerning the unity of Dainichi and Amaterasu.[33]

In 1196, renewing the prayers for the rebuilding of Tōdaiji, sixty monks traveled to Ise. They carried out a major dedication of the Larger Perfection of Wisdom Sutra, which had been copied for this purpose by all the monks of Tōdaiji, at the Arakida and Watarai family temples. The dedicatory inscription makes clear that the retired emperor Go-Shirakawa had also been part of the project. The Inner Shrine priest Arakida Narinaga even took the monks into the shrine itself, in spite of taboos against this.[34]

A tax to support the vicennial rebuilding of the Ise Shrines had been established in 1193.[35] Ise's estates increased after the Jōkyū War, as the shogunate distributed new lands to encourage prayers for military victory.[36] Some temples on Ise lands, such as Yoshizu Sengūin, showed a strong influence from the Shugendō tradition of ascetic practice in the mountains. Mountain ascetics were probably among the first traveling proselytizers for the Ise Shrines.[37]

The creation of many Ryōbu Shinto texts continued throughout the medieval era, as more and more Buddhist temples were established on lands close to Ise or on estates belonging to the Ise Shrines. A great quantity of these texts was compiled at Shōmyōji, and the Ninnaji monk Shukaku (1150–1203) compiled a similarly impressive collection, which eventually was housed in the Owari temple Shinpukuji. A twelve-volume set within the Shinpukuji collection, known as the *Yaketsu*, illustrates the content of texts from the Sanbōin-Goryū lineage of Ryōbu texts, as well as providing a glimpse into the process of compilation.[38]

Yaketsu consists of the lineage's secret oral teachings to be transmitted through a series of rituals, based on the proposition, "Our kingdom is the land of the gods (*shinkoku*), and the most important thing is to learn about the Kami." The first step explains how to visualize the August True Bodies (*mishōtai*) of the Kami of the Inner and Outer Shrines, with lists of the proper *darani* recited when making "dharma enjoyment" (*hōe*) offerings to the Kami. A teaching about the *honji* of the Kami Hachiman follows. Teachings on the original construction of the Great Buddha at Tōdaiji include an oracle received by Emperor Shōmu from a figure called the Jade Maiden (*gyokunyo*), Gyōki's pilgrimage to Ise with an oracle from Amaterasu, and tales of Yamatohime's leading Amaterasu to Ise. The texts next turn to an account of the cosmogony, the separation of heaven from earth, teachings on the esoteric significance of the Ise Shrines' Heart Pillar (*shin no mihashira*), which is revealed to be a representation of the Heavenly Jeweled Spear of ancient myth. The text posits the existence of a primal deity called the "August Kami of Ultimate Origin" (Taigen sonshin), who is revealed to be identical to the "One Mind" (*isshin*). Turning to the "seven generations of heavenly Kami," the texts relate how Amaterasu bestowed the "divine soul" (*shinrei*) and three regalia upon the imperial dynasty. A secret oral teaching reveals that Kūkai is actually a manifestation of Amaterasu and identical with her.[39]

Shūkaku managed to collect all 180 fascicles composing the twelve volumes of *Yaketsu* in part through his position as a "Dharma Prince" (*hō shinnō*), a brother or other close male relative of the emperor who has taken the tonsure. Shūkaku sponsored a "cultural salon" in which he interacted with a variety of monks, secular scholars, and poets, who would relate their secret transmissions, texts, and other writings to him, when Shūkaku summoned them to present these treasures formally. As a member of the imperial family, of course Shūkaku was cognizant of the larger religious system of which the emperor was the center: the Twenty-Two Shrines around the capital, the First Shrines of each province, and the Comprehensive Shrines that coordinated the Kami cults of each locale. Shūkaku's compilation of the *Yaketsu*, as well as similar Ryōbu texts can be seen as a massive effort to integrate the esoteric paradigm with that system.[40]

Kami Initiations

Except for the Ise Shrines, in the medieval period Buddhist temples and their priests typically dominated shrines and the rituals that were conducted there. Temples and shrines existed together, either in the *jingūji* or *miyadera* forms we have examined earlier, or in close proximity on an estate. This usually meant that the Buddhist clergy largely controlled the proceeds of shrine estates. There was an understanding that the proceeds would be used to keep the shrines in good repair, to support the conduct of ritual, and to compensate ritualists. There were frequent disputes regarding the division of shrine estates' produce, however, with Buddhist clerics often accused by shrine personnel of taking the lion's share. However, it would be a misunderstanding to think of these conflicts as pitting "Buddhism" against "Shinto." One phenomenon that attests to this claim is the proliferation during the medieval period of "Kami Initiation" (*jingi kanjō*) rites in esoteric temple-shrine complexes. Let us examine one of these, the *Reikiki kanjō* performed within the Miwa Shrine lineage tradition, noting at the outset that there are many extant Kami Initiation texts, and not all of them follow the same format. In fact, at the present stage of research, the variety exceeds our ability to establish the boundaries of the phenomenon.[41]

The Shingon temple Ōmiwa-dera was the *jingūji* of the Ōmiwa Shrine. The Kami Initiation called *Reikiki kanjō* was performed primarily for Shingon monks and is based on the format of Shingon initiation rites. Thus it serves as a master's revelation of knowledge to a disciple, as the master leads the disciple through sacred spaces modeled on the Diamond World and Womb World mandalas. The content of the revealed knowledge was not necessarily hidden from the initiate before the ritual but was available in texts to be studied in preparation. Completing the initiation entitled the initiate to teach the doctrines and perform the rituals on which the initiation was based.[42]

The rite unfolded in four main steps:

Step 1: Initiate passes through three *torii*, representing heaven, man, and earth and each corresponding to five Kami. He purifies body and mind. The master asperses water on him, and they chant mantras and invocations to the Kami.

Step 2: *Rites of the Main Altar*. This altar is shaped like an eight-petaled lotus, with Tenshō Daijin at the center, surrounded by five Kami (those especially associated with Miwa). Around them are twenty-four Kami of major shrines (n.b.: these are *not* the Twenty-Two Shrines especially esteemed by the court).

First exposing his body to incense smoke, chanting mantras, and visualizing Sanskrit letters, the blindfolded initiate enters and throws a flower on the altar to establish a karmic connection with a Kami. The blindfold is removed, and the altar is revealed to him as the real world of the deities. He pays homage to them.

Step 3: Behind this altar is another sacred space, square in shape and encompassed by fences and *torii* on all four sides. At the center is a *sakaki* tree covered with a cloth. This represents Amaterasu in the cave. On the tree hangs a mirror. On the front is Tenshō Daijin and on the back is Toyouke Daijin. There is also a jewel and two swords. There are other objects in the space, such as flower garlands and copies of the Heart Sutra. This space represents the whole *honji-suijaku* universe in a mandala form. Taken together the two sacred spaces represent the Yuki and Suki halls of imperial enthronement.

Step 4: The master and initiate sit facing each other. The master leads the initiate in visualizing the emergence upon his head of a one-pronged *vajra*, which turns into Toyouke and then into Tenshō Daijin. At the conclusion of this step, the master gives the initiate the three regalia. The initiate pronounces a poem proclaiming that all his mind and action are the workings of the Kami. Here Kami is interpreted not as specific deities but as a "life force."

All this together is merely the first level of *jingi kanjō*. Beyond that are further levels revealing the initiate's Buddha nature and the disclosure that Tenshō Daijin is within the initiate's mind. In theory, undergoing this ritual made the initiate equivalent to an emperor. The whole procedure is a direct adaptation of esoteric Buddhist initiation practice, with a substitution of Kami-related elements for Buddhist imagery. The initiation process adopts the metaphor of "opening the cave." The content of the initiation is closely bound up with the imperial regalia, equating the two Ise deities with the regalia. The initiate recites a poem, substituting for a Buddhist magical formula (*darani*): "My body is the sacred space of the Kami; my breath is the Outer and Inner Shrines." Miwa commentaries state that in completing the initiation, the initiate has separated himself from life bound by karma and has attained the mind of Dainichi.[43]

There are so many layers of meaning to this extraordinary rite that it is hard to know where to start, but let us begin with some thoughts about the personnel. We know that at the very least, these rites were performed by and for Shingon clergy, and that in the Edo period, related rituals were made available to laity and to occupational groups, such as carpenters. We know from other contexts that Kami Initiations were increasingly being practiced for mountain ascetics, noncelibate shrine monks, and perhaps others, such as the associations for pilgrimage and popular worship, generically called *kō*, that proliferated around the shrines. Nothing is known of the motives people had for undergoing these rites in the medieval period, but the issue of acquiring new forms of licenses and credentials became very prominent in the Edo period. It may be anachronistic to apply this logic to understand why so many people in the medieval period desired to undergo Kami Initiation. But it is unlikely that the meaning of credentialing would be so radically different in the medieval period that there would have been no overlap at all. If we permit ourselves to speculate for a moment, some of the motives might have included the following. In the case of the Shingon monks assigned to serve at the Ōmiwa Shrine, they may have wished to achieve greater knowledge of the Kami they served, to discover how the Kami were related to Shingon divinities, to understand the true meaning behind appearances, or to find a link between the divine realm and the imperial house. In more prosaic terms, to be initiated might entitle the man to a higher rank, to greater religious authority, to authorization to teach. Having completed such an initiation might have been helpful to shrine personnel (whether or not their primary religious identity was as Buddhist clergy) in asserting their credentials against their competitors within a combinatory institution or to an outside institution seeking to assert its influence.

Let us focus on the way this ritual employed imperial symbolism. In steps 3 and 4, the initiate places himself within a space representing the mythic scene in which light returns to the world when Amaterasu is drawn out of the cave. We note that the initiation is symbolically likened to that scene, as an emergence from darkness into light, but also that the initiate is placed in the position of the great Kami. He is to regard his movement through the two ritual spaces as moving through the Yuki and Suki Halls of enthronement ritual, which makes him equal to an emperor. In the fourth step he receives the three regalia.

Clearly, for ritual such as this to emerge in the medieval period required an evolution (or a revolution?) in the conceptualization of Amaterasu/Tenshō Daijin. Let us notice, however, that there is no reference at all to the old state-controlled ritual order. Kami Initiations had entirely broken free of that or any other authorizing agency, and were developing through the elaboration of their own internal logic. In the absence of sanctions, and in the context of building networks of support through acquiring more land and new patrons, the extension of initiation ritual to ever-widening circles and groups outside the clergy is precisely what we would expect.

The Inner Shrine at Ise in the seventh century served as an imperial mausoleum, and no one outside the imperial family would have dared to worship there. Some scholars hold that Amaterasu's name was not widely known, even among courtiers of the ancient period, but in the medieval period knowledge of this Kami spread by a variety of routes in varied formulations. *Nakatomi Harae Kunge* had promoted the idea that the Inner and Outer Shrines are indivisible and analogous to the two esoteric mandalas. Protector Monks who had been appointed to serve in the imperial palace promoted the idea that Amaterasu is one with the cosmic Buddha. Temples established at Ise by the shrines' priests created new conduits for esoteric interpretations of Amaterasu. By the Kamakura period, Amaterasu was becoming accessible to a wider group, as Ise proselytizers (the *onshi* mentioned earlier) spread out to acquire new estates. By the middle of the Kamakura period, we find this Kami named as the "Lord of Japan," and a judge of the dead, meting out karmic rewards and punishment.[44]

A document from 1324 titled *Bikisho* provides a striking image of Amaterasu/Tenshō Daijin, offered in the course of arguing that everyone must make a pilgrimage to the Ise Shrines:

> [Tenshō Daijin] appears as King Enma after our fates have run out and our lives are over. He weighs the good and evil we have done and remonstrates

> [with] us.... It is for this reason that all sentient beings of our land, even if they have to cross the sea and split the clouds, must know of the meaning [of the Ise shrines] and make a pilgrimage there. Because they do not know of it and do not have faith in it, they fail to do so; but it is a natural principle that all those who have life will die, and it is the ultimate teaching of this shrine that all sentient beings of the trichilicosmos, without a single exception, will after their deaths appear in front of the deity of the Great Shrine of our land.[45]

As this passage makes clear, by the middle of the medieval period, Enma-ō, the king of the realm of the dead, had merged with Tenshō Daijin so thoroughly that the Ise shrines had become a palace where the dead would be judged. Everyone's destiny is to be judged at Ise, and for that reason everyone is encouraged to make a pilgrimage to the shrines while still in this life. It is notable also that this text's statements about Ise make no reference at all to its imperial connection, nor is Tenshō Daijin invoked as the force legitimating the imperial house. Finally, the use of the *honji-suijaku* paradigm that we see here does not in any way subordinate the Ise Kami to a Buddhist divinity but rather provides a vehicle with which to multiply associations and magnify their authority freely. *Bikisho* is thought to have originated with *onshi* of the Outer Shrine who were attempting to promote pilgrimage to Ise.[46] As we will see in chapter 9, Ise pilgrimage became a truly mass phenomenon in the Edo period. Clearly, the former prohibition on anyone outside the imperial family journeying to Ise had been completely overturned, and there seemed to be no constraints on the development of new interpretations of the Ise deities.

The Idea of Japan as the "Land of the Gods" *(Shinkoku)*

The idea of Japan as the Land of the Gods figured prominently in medieval Shinto thought. While earlier scholarship took the rise of *shinkoku* thought as evidence of opposition to Buddhism or attributed it to the Mongol invasions, more recent scholarship, led by historian Kuroda Toshio, has emphasized its roots in the dominant Buddhist discourse of the period. Indeed, we find Buddhist authors affirming it frequently, and there is little evidence of its use to critique or deny Buddhism. Instead, the idea of *shinkoku* was part and parcel of the Buddhist worldview in which, though Japan is situated at the periphery of the known universe, it is nevertheless a country where Buddhism has taken root and flourished. Japan is a land under the protection of the Kami; the land, the sovereign, and the people derive from the Kami. The Kami are so revered that Buddhism is subordinated at Ise, the original seat of all the Kami, and its characteristic terms are tabooed, but this is not because Buddhism is denied but is an expression of Buddhism's respect for the Kami.[47]

In Kuroda's view, *shinkoku* can be seen as a concept that arose in the mid-Kamakura period in response to popular interest, on the one hand, and as a response by elites to some of the reform movements among the new Buddhist groups, on the other. It was invoked by many varieties of thought, and it was also used to persuade commoner society not to become adherents of the Buddhist reformers Hōnen or Shinran, who developed paths to salvation that did not require the mediation of the Kami. While Hōnen and Shinran both envisioned roles for the Kami as protectors of *nenbutsu* practitioners, the implicit denial of the polytheism of medieval society provoked strong resistance. *Shinkoku*'s most distinctive aspects were its projection of the emperor as a divine being, a view of history as resulting from the actions of the Kami, and the quest to establish a unique status for Japan.[48]

The Impact of the Mongol Invasions

After the shogunate not only refused to submit to his authority but also beheaded his messengers, the Mongol emperor Kublai Khan sent naval expeditions against Japan in 1274 and 1281. The Mongols were vastly more powerful militarily, and Japanese islands and towns along their route were utterly destroyed in the attacks. It was only because of the typhoons that twice destroyed the Mongol fleet that Japan escaped greater devastation or even complete subjugation. The winds that spared Japan this horrible fate were widely regarded as *kamikaze*, "divine winds," literally, "the winds of the Kami." The belief arose that the Kami had protected Japan from the Mongols, and this undoubtedly deepened popular faith in them. At the same time, however, the costs of the effort to repel the Mongols were astronomical, leading to great dissatisfaction among the warrior class and ultimately to the downfall of the Kamakura shogunate in 1333.

All the temples and shrines of the country were called upon to pray for Japan's deliverance from the barbarians, and from as early as 1268, and lasting until at least 1293, such prayers were a major part of institutional religious life. (The Japanese had no way of knowing that the 1281 invasion would be the last.) Shogun and emperor alike sponsored prayers, ceremonies, and meritorious acts of piety, as well as going on pilgrimages and secluding themselves to pray for divine assistance in repelling the Mongols. The Kami of the Ise Shrines were frequently—but not uniquely—invoked in these appeals. In 1275 the court ranks of all the Kami were promoted one step.[49] In 1280, Emperor Kameyama sponsored the copying of the entire Buddhist canon and had it presented to the Ise Shrines with his prayers for the destruction of the enemy.[50] The monk Eison (1201–1290) traveled to Ise to perform prayers to the Ise deities for Japan's deliverance. The court and the shogunate were not alone in their appreciation of the Kami for repelling the Mongol foe. In 1287, on the occasion of the first vicennial rebuilding of the Outer Shrine following the Mongol invasions, tens of thousands of pilgrims poured into the shrine to give thanks. Evidently much of the credit for the *kamikaze* that destroyed the Mongols was due to the Ise Kami, in the popular view.[51]

Claiming a restoration of direct imperial rule, Emperor Go-Daigo (r. 1318–1339) overthrew the Kamakura shogunate in 1333, in the Kenmu Restoration (1333–1336). Go-Daigo himself was shortly overthrown by Ashikaga Takauji in 1336. Go-Daigo fled Kyoto and set up a separate court at Yoshino (the Southern Court) that persisted for almost a century, an era referred to as the Period of Northern and Southern Courts, (Nanbokuchō, 1336–1428). The Muromachi period (1333–1568) overlapped with it. The Muromachi period was named for the Muromachi area of Kyoto, where the Ashikaga established a new shogunate and controlled a separate, "Northern" imperial court.

Kitabatake Chikafusa

Given the great importance attached to the imperial house in theological reflections on the Kami, it is only to be expected that the splitting of the imperial line would provoke vigorous responses. Although Kitabatake Chikafusa (1293–1354) was not a shrine priest, his work titled *Jinnō Shōtōki* became extremely influential in the thought regarding the imperial house, the imperial regalia, and the religious meaning of imperial rule. Chikafusa served as an adviser to Emperor Go-Daigo during the Kenmu restoration, as well as leading Go-Daigo's military campaign to regain the throne. After Go-Daigo's death in 1339, Chikafusa sent copies of his major works to the young Emperor Go-Murakami (r. 1339–1368), then twelve years old, as a guide, and as a spirited defense of the Southern Court. In *Jinnō Shōtōki* (1339) he treated the reign of each emperor through Go-Daigo, the ninety-fourth. The work began with an idea that was widely held at the time:

> Great Japan is the divine land (*shinkoku*; *kami no kuni*). The heavenly progenitor founded it and the sun goddess bequeathed it to her descendants to rule eternally. Only in our country is this true; there are no similar examples in other countries. This is why our country is called the divine land.[52]

He also wrote, "The Kami have pledged to help the people. All the people of the empire are divine creatures."[53]

By placing Japan in a sphere where the Kami are active agents underwriting imperial rule and working to assist the people, who are described as divine, Chikafusa conceptualized the age in which he lived as sharing in the eternal perspective of the Kami. Even as he also described it as *masse*, the "last age," he nevertheless attributed the evils of his time to the actions of individuals rather than to the Buddhist law of historical decline seen in the concept of *mappō*. In his analysis of each emperor's reign, he pointed out both positive and negative aspects, showing how the choices made by the emperor and his ministers produced particular results. In this sense, he rejected the determinism of *mappō*.

Chikafusa wrote *Jinnō Shōtōki* in part to excoriate the Ashikaga shogunate for ousting Go-Daigo and setting up the rival Northern Court. While he did not regard shogunates as inevitably illegitimate, he regarded Ashikaga Takauji (r. 1338–1358), founder of the Ashikaga shogunate, as a great villain, and he called on the warrior class to recognize the court's preeminence and the legitimacy of the Southern Court.

Chikafusa saw imperial rule as legitimated by an unbroken line of succession (*bansei ikkei*), which for him was far more important than questions about whether a particular emperor's rule was good or bad, even if an emperor might have been incompetent or wicked. In fact, literate people were well aware that several emperors had fit that description. Emperor Yōzei (r. 876–884), for example, who may have been insane, was unspeakably cruel, fond of torturing both animals and humans, personally carrying out executions, and sadistically strangling women with the strings of musical instruments and then throwing their corpses into a lake. With such examples as Yōzei known well to medieval literati, to claim that the imperial line was legitimated by its supposed divine nature was not entirely convincing. Chikafusa attempted to overcome this contradiction through the imperial regalia. He saw the regalia as magical emblems with the power to legitimate an emperor's rule. At the same time, however, he imbued them with moral significance; he identified the mirror with the principle of honesty and straightforwardness (*shōjiki*), the sword with determination (*ketsudan*), and the jewel with compassion (*jihi*). Possession of the regalia constituted authority to govern, and also a divine guarantee that somehow things would turn out for the best. Not coincidentally, Go-Daigo claimed to have taken the regalia with him when leaving the capital, and at the end of his life, he transferred them to his intended successor, Go-Murakami.[54]

Written in 1339, while the Mongol invasions remained fresh in memory, *Jinnō Shōtōki* conveys great faith in the Kami and their determination to protect imperial rule and, indeed, all Japan. While it draws upon Buddhist and Confucian thought as well as Shinto, Shinto elements predominate and are expressed confidently, without any sense that the Kami are dominated by Buddhism or submerged within the *honji-suijaku* paradigm. Chikafusa's presentation of the divinity of the Japanese land and people, the identification of the regalia with moral principles, and his strong defense of the "unbroken line" of imperial succession left an enduring legacy of ideas drawn upon by Shinto thinkers of later ages.

Chikafusa had taken the tonsure and become a novice Shingon monk after the death of a young prince whom Chikafusa was grooming for succession to the throne. He retained his clerical status throughout his life, though it did not prevent him from taking the field of battle and leading the troops in defending Go-Daigo's ambition to regain the throne. Yet his Shingon affiliation was more than sentimental attachment to the departed prince. Chikafusa greatly esteemed Shingon, and in his 1346 "Doctrine of Inner Realization by Spiritual Words" (*Shingon naishōgi*), he praised Shingon as "a supreme form of esotericism that exceeds all other sects. It is noteworthy that the history of our country since the age of the gods accords with the teachings of Shingon."[55]

Chikafusa's military strategy reveals a significant aspect of the fusion of medieval Shinto and Buddhist thought. According to medieval historian Thomas Conlan, in the fourteenth century there was a widely shared image of central Japan as a kind of mandala of the realm as a whole, based on the presence there of the network of Twenty-Two Shrines. We recall from the previous chapter that the actual number varied in time; the fourteenth century referred to twenty-one shrines. Shingon palace ritual linked these sites to the idea of the emperor as Buddhist monarch. From the tenth century it had become customary to appoint seven Protector Monks (*gojisō*) to perform daily rites to protect the emperor's person. Because these monks were stationed in two small rooms adjacent to the emperor's sleeping quarters, they had exceptional access to the monarch and considerable influence over some of them. For example, Protector Monk Jiken is known to have discussed Buddhist enthronement ritual with Emperor Hanazono (r. 1308–1318) and to have cured him repeatedly of possession by evil spirits. Protector Monks performed prayers nightly, each night devoted to one of the shrines. Each completed cycle symbolically constructed a mandala of Japan and established the emperor as its Wheel-Turning Monarch.[56]

Because the Southern Court's forces were vastly outnumbered, they could not hope to subdue the realm as a whole. In those circumstances, their aspirations focused on the twenty-one shrines. In particular, Chikafusa was determined to occupy Ise, and he succeeded in doing so. While in Ise, Chikafusa established ties with the Watarai priestly lineage of the Outer Shrine; he studied Outer Shrine teaching with Watarai Ieyuki (1256–1351) and copied Ieyuki's 1330 work, *Ruijū jingi hongen* in 1337. In later years he also copied other writings by Ieyuki, showing that there was no contradiction for him in combining Shinto and Shingon learning.[57]

Chikafusa's theory of imperial legitimacy rested heavily on the symbolism of the imperial regalia, as we have begun to see. He wrote in *Jinnō Shōtōki*,

> The divine spirit of our country lies in the legitimate passage of the emperorship to the descendants of a single family. Transmission of the regalia through the generations is as fixed as the sun; the jewel possesses the essence of the moon; and the sword has the substance of the stars.[58]

Yet this assertion would seem to founder on significant difficulties, since we recall, and literate medieval people knew, that Emperor Suinin had banished the original mirror to the Ise Shrines because being under the same roof with it made him uncomfortable, and Emperor Tenmu had sent the original sword to the Atsuta Shrine after the sword had put a curse on him. Chikafusa was arguing that the legitimacy of the Southern Court was proven by its possession, not of the originals, but of "true copies" of the regalia. He believed that because the original mirror and sword were enshrined at the Ise and Atsuta Shrines, these items of the regalia did not need to be in the actual possession of the emperor. The emperor need only keep the jewels. Ideas about the regalia were in flux, and it had not yet become settled opinion that there are three and only three items that compose the regalia. *Sendai kuji hongi* remained authoritative, and it had specified ten items. The medieval court also included a set of musical instruments among the sacred treasures. Emperor Go-Uda believed that the jewels were at Ise, along with the mirror. It was also known that a palace fire of 960 had melted the copy of the mirror kept there, though Emperor Juntoku (r. 1210–1221) claimed that it had miraculously escaped destruction by flying to heaven, later descending to a cherry tree in the palace garden. Up through the eleventh century, emperors would inspect the palace's copies of the regalia, taking them out of their boxes and looking at them. However, in the twelfth century, the view emerged that emperors who looked upon the regalia would go mad. Emperor Reizei (r. 967–969) is said to have gone insane when he tried to open the box containing the jewels. Emperor Yōzei (r. 876–884) is said to have met the same fate. The palace copy of the sword had gone to the bottom of the sea at the Battle of Dan no Ura in 1185 with the child Emperor Antoku (r. 1180–1185), when he drowned in his nurse's arms while trying to escape the Minamoto troops. Taboos on viewing the regalia are seen in the historical chronicle compiled by the Kamakura shogunate from the late thirteenth to the early fourteenth century, *Azuma kagami*, which contains a tale recounting how a warrior was blinded and struck speechless when he tried to look upon the mirror. Thus Chikafusa's ideas about the regalia as key to imperial succession were in competition with other notions about the sacred articles and did not become widely accepted until the Edo period, when historians of the Mito school revived them.[59]

Watarai Shinto

Watarai Ieyuki (1256–1351) and other Watarai family priests at the Outer Shrine at Ise founded an influential school of medieval Shinto thought, known as "Ise Shinto" or "Watarai Shinto." Of the two terms, "Watarai Shinto" is the more accurate, since it emerged from the Outer Shrine specifically, and because to call it "Ise Shinto" suggests that both shrines were agreed in support of it, which most emphatically was not the case. From around the beginning of the Kamakura period, Watarai priests began compiling what they promoted as secret traditions from the ancient period concerning the true nature of the Kami of the Outer Shrine.

The deity of the Outer Shrine, Toyouke Daijin, originated as a local food goddess, who is not mentioned in the *Nihon shoki*. Lacking mythological pedigree meant that she was regarded as inferior to Amaterasu. When the Outer Shrine began to seek supporters from among the warrior class and through promoting popular pilgrimage to the shrine, it was necessary to justify upholding Toyouke as the equal of Amaterasu. The Outer Shrine priests began to claim that Toyouke was actually Amaterasu's ancestor, and hence superior to her. They also implied that Toyouke was an ancestor of the imperial house, based on secret books revealing these truths, which they claimed had been handed down in the Watarai family. The school went on to identify Toyouke with the primeval Kami at the time of the original creation, Ame no Minakanushi and Kunitokotachi, so that all three of them were names for the Kami of the Outer Shrine. This equation placed Toyouke in the imperial line, because Ame no Minakanushi was the great-grandfather of Ninigi.

By 1296 a group of five secret texts had been compiled, which later were collected and circulated as a set called the "Five Books of Shinto" (*Shintō gobusho*). They amounted to a rewriting of the sacred history (*engi*) of the Ise Shrines in order to elevate the Outer Shrine. They discuss such matters as the divine nature of the Ise deities and how they came to be enshrined at that place; the relation of the Inner and Outer shrines; mystical interpretations of the construction of the shrines; a biography of Yamato Hime no Mikoto, who had led Amaterasu to the Ise area when she was deciding on a place for her shrine; teachings on purification; and claims of the independence and originality of Shinto. The texts borrow heavily from esoteric Buddhism, Daoism, and Chinese theories of the five elements.

Along with the new theory came the invention of new rites to be offered to the new supporters. The Outer Shrine priests developed a kind of Kami Initiation based on esoteric Buddhism in which devotees could unite with the shrine's deities to experience their original enlightenment, which is further regarded as a state of absolute purity and a return to the moment of creation.

> Esoteric Buddhist doctrine explains that there exists an indestructible bond between man and the world-Buddha Dainichi. This bond is called *hongaku* or "[original] enlightenment." Every sentient being partakes of this innate enlightenment, and can activate it by attaining union, *kaji*, with Dainichi through meditation. Ise priests translated this idea into Shinto idiom. They came to the conclusion that the ritual purity which is required for the execution of Shinto ritual is in fact a mental state of union with the gods. Further, they argued that the gods are not external forces outside man, but in fact reside in the human mind itself. By attaining union with one's "mind-god," *shinshin*, man can reach a state of absolute purity which corresponds to the Buddhist idea of enlightenment. This "mind-god" corresponds to "[original] enlightenment" in Esoteric Buddhist doctrine. . . . [T]he state of union soon came to be described as a return to the moment of absolute unity which existed at the very beginning of the Age of the Gods: the time of "primeval chaos," *konton*, when "Yin and Yang had not yet separated."[60]

These theological innovations seen at the Outer Shrine bear the strong stamp of esoteric Buddhist thought, as does the initiation rite aiming for an experience of mystical union with the Kami. Watarai Shinto differed from Ryōbu Shinto by denying that Amaterasu is a *suijaku* or has a *honji* Buddha. Instead, in Watarai conception she is absolutely primal.[61] In addition, a highly significant feature of this school was the appearance of the idea of Shinto as a "way" or spiritual path that anyone may practice.

Watarai Shinto's determination to establish Toyouke's antiquity is linked to a widespread attention to cosmogony and a new need to re-examine the order of things during the Age of the Kami. As Fabio Rambelli writes, "[P]ervasive interest in cosmogony is one of the most significant aspects of the medieval Japanese intellectual arena and characterizes the entire contemporaneous discourse about the kami."[62] Over the course of the eleventh and twelfth centuries, according to Uejima Susumu, a revised understanding of historical chronology forced all branches of thought to review their timelines. The new view of history had emerged from efforts to resolve the discordant accounts of creation seen in *Kojiki, Nihon shoki*, and *Sendai kuji hongi*. According to the revised interpretation, Amaterasu emerged indisputably preeminent among the Kami, definitively erasing her ambiguous position in *Nihon shoki*. Moreover, subsequent attempts to integrate the genealogy of the Kami with the history of Buddhism and the imperial dynasty concluded that Shakyamuni had died in 949 BCE, and that Jinmu was enthroned in 660 BCE, both long after the time of Amaterasu. Understanding the history of Japan in this way was highly consequential. It drastically undermined the portrait of Japan as a peripheral speck at the edge of the cosmos. Instead, it allied Japan with India and lowered China to the position of tertiary antiquity and significance. Japanese monks traveling to Song China confidently reported what had become the conventional wisdom and received knowledge of the day: Japan is ruled by a line of sovereigns descended from the Age of the Kami; Japan's history is older than China's, and Amaterasu is one with Dainichi.[63]

Thus, the preoccupation with cosmogony and the order of precedence among the Kami seen in Watarai Shinto is part of a much broader reexamination of history that produced many new interpretations of the Ise deities and *Nihon shoki*. The overlapping attempts of Ryōbu and Watarai Shinto become intelligible in this larger context. While "Ryōbu Shinto texts still granted a sort of conceptual priority to Buddhism, [Watarai] Shinto texts tended instead to relativize the importance of Buddhism," relying on a wide variety of non-Buddhist texts, particularly Indian and Daoist sources. Watarai Ieyuki's "Ruiju jingi hongen," widely regarded as the finest expression of his philosophy, exemplifies his ability to circumvent Ryōbu dependence on Buddhism. In Fabio Rambelli's summation:

> It was perhaps the first time in premodern Japan that important philosophical discussions bypassed the Buddhist system. [I]t is thus necessary to revise the understanding that [Watarai] Shinto was essentially an offshoot of esoteric Buddhism—to which it can be reduced. Instead,

> [Watarai] Shinto, while sharing a general Buddhist framework, developed in ways that not only reduced the intellectual importance of Buddhism but also relativized its ethical and soteriological claims, thus opening the way for subsequent forms of thought of a non-Buddhist or even anti-Buddhist character.[64]

Watarai Shinto thus constitutes the beginnings of something quite new: a way of discussing the Kami that could challenge Buddhism. It opened the way for Yoshida Kanetomo and later thinkers to conceive of Shinto as an independent tradition wholly separate and independent of Buddhism.

Shinto and Shugendō

Shugendō is a tradition of beliefs regarding the sacrality of mountains and practices of mountain ascetics called *yamabushi* or *shugenja*, who seek to acquire magical powers through severe asceticism undertaken on sacred mountains, subsequently applying those powers to serve their followers. The term *Shugendō* is based on the idea of a "way" or "path" (*dō, michi*) of "mastering" or "cultivating" (*shū*) "spiritual powers" (*reiken*, and its shortened, elided form, *gen*). En no Gyōja (also known as En no Ozunu), who lived from the latter half of the seventh century to the early eighth century, is taken as its legendary founder. From as early as the tenth century, sacred mountains had been identified throughout Japan, and organizations for conducting ascetic practice in them had been established. Some of the more important mountains were Kinpusen and Ōminesan in the Yoshino Mountains; a mountainous area called Kumano; Katsuragisan, a peak on the border between the present-day Nara and Osaka Prefectures, where we recall that En no Gyōja bested the Kami Hitokotonushi; Hagurosan in the northeast; and Mt. Fuji in Eastern Japan. Many other, smaller mountains contained significant ascetic sites.

During the Muromachi period (1392–1573), the Tendai sect drew the *yamabushi* of the Kumano area into its organization. They were directly linked to two temples, Onjōji and its branch temple Shōgoin. *Yamabushi* organized in this affiliation with Tendai came to form the Honzan sect (Honzan-ha). The Tōzan sect (Tōzan-ha) is analogous to Honzan but affiliated with the Shingon sect. It centers on the Kyoto temple Daigoji Sanpōin and takes the figure Shōbō (832–909) as its founder. The Tōzan sect drew its followers from Kinpusen, Ōminesan, and Kumano. The doctrines and practices of both Shugendō sects were drawn from Tendai and Shingon esotericism, and they showed significant similarities. The two ascetic orders operated largely autonomously of their parent monastic orders, but unlike them were neither cloistered nor necessarily celibate.

Shugendō recognizes a number of divinities linked to sacred mountains, connected with certain spots within each mountain where specific ascetic exercises are performed. The divinity of each such location serves as the master of that place and the protector of those who train there, much like a tutelary Kami. Some, such as Hitokotonushi, are unambiguously Kami. The Tengu are winged, red-faced monsters with either a bird beak or a long, phallic nose, wearing *yamabushi* garb. Images of Tengu are believed to have originated in the medieval period and are depicted extensively in such works as the *Tengu zōshi*.[65] Other mountain deities are called "Avatars," Gongen, such as Zaō Gongen, Atago Gongen, Akiba Gongen, Izuna Gongen, and others. Their iconography typically depicts them as fearsome protectors of Buddhism like Fudō Myōō, often with fiery mandorla and weapons. Another category of Shugendō divinities are the "Princelings" (*ōji*) deities. The Eight Princelings, for example, represent the eight Kami (three female and five male children) produced by Amaterasu and Susanoo when they swore oaths to prove their sincerity. The Avatars and Princelings are sometimes informally classed with the Kami.

Important clerics of the esoteric schools made pilgrimages to Ise, such as Chōgen, and Gedatsu Shōnin (Jōkei, 1155–1213). As a result, branch temples of their home temples were opened in Ise, and the mountains around them began to attract *yamabushi* of their affiliated Shugendō lineages. The temples also had affiliated shrines, and those sites likewise came under esoteric influence as well as attracting *yamabushi*. Two of the more significant temples were Segiji and Jingūji, which began to flourish around the mid-thirteenth century. In the Muromachi period, a number of Kumano *bikuni* became known as accomplished Shugendō practitioners, made possible by the absence of any taboo on women entering the Kumano mountains. At the end of the medieval period, proselytizing nuns (Kumano *bikuni*) of Keikōin, a nuns' temple in Ise, campaigned very effectively to raise funds needed to stage the Vicennial Renewal rites at Ise after a century of desuetude.[66]

Shrines in Urban Society

Shrine-temple complexes were complicated economic and social organizations with growing populations. By the early thirteenth century, temple-shrine complexes had become the largest landowners in the country, and they rivaled the aristocratic and warrior houses in their power. Kyoto and Nara were the two main cities in the medieval period, and religious institutions were highly influential in both. In fact, the Kōfukuji/Kasuga complex controlled Yamato province as a whole, and Nara was believed to be under the protection of Kasuga Daimyōjin. Both temples and shrines developed intricate administrative organizations for Nara and their nearby and distant estate lands. Tōdaiji also exerted control in Nara as well. By the end of the period, there were about 35,000 people living in Nara, most of whom were under the control of one of the three institutions, and virtually all of whom were related to these institutions in some way.[67]

Temple and shrine lands were governed with considerable autonomy. As an example of the power of the largest temples, we can examine the case of Enryakuji, the head temple of the Tendai sect, located on Mt. Hiei, just north of Kyoto. Enryakuji had developed into a huge complex of more than 3,800 buildings, in an area of about twenty square kilometers, and had some 3,000 priests in residence. In addition, Enryakuji had no less than 370 branch temples (*matsuji*) around the country, which had been established through the proselytization tours of noted clerics over the centuries.[68]

In addition to a temple (or shrine) complex itself, large "towns before the gates" (*monzenmachi*) grew up around these cultic centers, providing goods and services to religious institutions and entrepreneurial opportunities for the personnel of temples and shrines, as well as the laity. These *monzenmachi* added to the economic resources, social influence, and cultural significance of religious institutions. Markets held periodically in or near the *monzenmachi* fostered the growth of merchants' associations and the circulation of goods and produce. In early fifteenth-century Nara, for example, there were around thirty such associations dealing in rice, yams, birds, fish, soybeans, pines, charcoal, paper, hats, buckets, nails, gold, kettles, arrows, and other items. In fact, the temple-shrine complexes and their surrounding districts were developing into cities.[69]

Shrine personnel played important roles in the development of medieval trade and industry. Most of the sake brewers of Kyoto were priests of the Hie Shrine or Enryakuji.[70] The *jinin* of Iwashimizu Hachiman Shrine were also intimately associated with trade, forming guilds to deal in fish and oil. They also traded in silk, cotton, cloth, cloth-dyeing, fresh produce, indigo, cakes, medicine, sesame, and salt. They were active as moneychangers and as tax collectors on the estates belonging to shrines.[71]

Conclusion

In this chapter we have begun to survey the ways in which esoteric Buddhism shaped medieval thought and practice regarding the Kami. In putting the matter this way, there is a danger of reifying the two traditions as if they were separate, freestanding religions, which was not the case. Without imagining things in that manner, however, it is important to ask where things stood for the people and institutions committed to the idea of Kami worship embodying an indigenous tradition whose ritual forms constituted an essential element of governance of the realm. It is likewise important to have a grasp of how Buddhism, considered for the moment as an umbrella term for the philosophical, instutional, and ritual systems centering on the worship of Buddhist divinities that encompassed many elements of Kami worship, was positioned.

Concepts of Kami presented in *honji-suijaku* pairings with Buddhist divinities were further transformed by their placement within esotericism, with its rituals aiming to unify the practitioner with divinities of the two mandalas and ultimately to attain to original enlightenment. The work of framing *honji-suijaku* within the paradigm of the Diamond and Womb World mandalas strengthened the idea of the oneness of Kami and Buddhist divinities, reducing any lingering sense of the foreignness of Buddhism. At the same time, esotericism's identification of Kami and Buddhas tended to neutralize the association between the Kami and "indigenous tradition," because the distinction between indigeneity and foreign origins was irrelevant to esotericism's ultimate aims.

As esoteric rites for the protection of the realm and the sovereign's person gained public significance, the *jingi* ritual system tended to be swallowed up within Buddhism. Esotericism's framework for the transmission of knowledge from master to disciple created a highly "private" construction of religious knowledge, sequestering it within a context valuing secrecy over public exposition. Kami Initiations within Buddhist esotericism led initiates through stages culminating in "enthronement," diluting *jingi* ritual's unique standing. Kami ritual's monopoly in this domain had already eroded due to the practice of Buddhist rites for the sovereign in the context of imperial succession. But the extension of ritual with an enthronement motif to Buddhist clerics and others widened the scope for those aspiring to some kind of "enthronement" without establishing any clear boundary or terms of eligibility. This challenge was started within Watarai Shinto and was eventually answered by Yoshida Kanetomo in the late medieval period, as we shall see in chapter 7.

The esoteric paradigm's influence upon concepts of Kami resulted in enhanced emphasis upon elements of morality, portraying the Kami as divinities who protect and punish. Oaths of the period show that Kami were regarded as having the power to discern and judge a person's character. In considerations of the regalia, Kami were identified with honesty, decisiveness, and compassion. As the equation of Kami with Buddhist divinities advanced, Kami were likewise invested with magnified powers. In Shugendō, the mountains of Japan and their Kami were drawn into esotericism and portrayed with heightened potency. The mountains themselves were transformed as actual Pure Lands through which ascetics could travel, absorbing the powers of mountain Kami as they moved through the landscape. Meanwhile, however, the esoteric framework also perpetuated earlier trends of negating or diminishing the Kami, as we saw in stories of Amaterasu as untruthful.

Buddhism's cosmology of a universe centered on Mt. Sumeru with Japan at the far periphery not only marginalized Japan, but also painted a picture of it as spiritually limited and limiting. The implications of this view for concepts of Kami were readily apparent. It was quite possible to draw the conclusion that Japan was stuck at the margins of the cosmos *because of* the impotence of the native deities. Or, that the native tradition provided no amelioration of the limitations imposed by geography. Against that, new understandings of the preeminence of Kami in the flow of cosmic time countered the cosmology suggested by the Mt. Sumeru image and promoted a view of the Kami and Japan as primal in the universal scheme of things.

As we will see in the next chapter, an allied claim presented in artistic form arose in the person of the Buddhist saint Myōe, and was given visible form in mandalas, illustrated scroll paintings, and narrative regarding the Kasuga Shrine.

Expanded approaches to *Nihon shoki* gave studies of the Kami a much broadened sphere of reference, encompassing myth as a whole, widening the scope to elevate the Kami and to encompass divinities originating in the local contexts of folk religion. The appearance of Shugendō contributed to this development.

The emergence of Watarai Shinto constituted a departure from the umbrella of Buddhist esotericism, even as it retained a framework much influenced by Buddhism, and while its leadership founded temples and hosted Buddhist monks. It created a foundation for later attempts to establish Shinto as a fully independent tradition.

While all the temples and shrines were called upon to pray and work magic for Japan's deliverance from the Mongol invasions, the people ultimately attributed their salvation mainly to the Kami. This development, encapsulated in the image of a divine wind protecting a sacred realm, again highlighted the Kami as Japan's final bulwark against decimation or enslavement. The Kami were seen to have fulfilled their promise of protecting the realm, the sovereign, and the people of Japan.

6

Medieval Shinto and the Arts

> For medieval people, the main actors in the world were not human beings, but the Kami and Buddhas at the source of the phenomenal world, who control it, and who were believed to move it. In this sense the medieval period is precisely "the age of the Kami and Buddhas." Kami and Buddhas frequently responded to human inquiries and gave indications of the path to be taken, it was believed. Medieval people always felt that they lived among the Kami and Buddhas, hearing their voices, feeling their gaze. Thus, if we hope to understand the worldview of medieval people and their concepts of the universe, it is not enough to look at the human creations of society or nation. We must broaden our view to include the entire structure of cosmology, including the Kami and Buddhas who transcend humanity.
>
> —Satō Hirō, *Kishōmon no seishinshi*, 25–26.

Introduction

This chapter explores ways in which the Kami were represented in the arts of medieval Japan. As the quotation above suggests, Kami and Buddhist divinities were deeply embedded in the thinking of medieval people, in ways that are unfamiliar to modern readers. By examining how the Kami were presented in painting, sculpture, and literary arts, as well as new spaces created for their rituals in temples and shrine architecture, we can see more directly into the worldview of medieval Japan. These materials reflect changes in concepts of the Kami, sometimes highlighting their association with "the indigenous," but seldom engaging questions of Shinto's roles in governance. While this chapter addresses many artistic expressions of Shinto ideas, however, it is not intended as a comprehensive survey of all forms of Shinto arts during the medieval period. The material addressed here has been chosen to reflect on the ways in which ideas concerning the Kami were expressed in artistic forms.

Medieval Changes in Shrine and Temple Architecture

Temple and shrine architecture became more complex in the medieval period, including the introduction of wooden flooring (instead of earthen floors) and "rear chambers" (*ushirodo*) or underground chambers (*geden*). In the ancient period, no particular significance was attributed to the space behind the main altars of shrines and temples, but this space was invested with a variety of meanings beginning in the twelfth century. Many temples began to add such chambers as places where rites might be performed. The temple Taima-dera is the earliest known example (1161).[1]

Rear or underground chambers were enclosed spaces at the rear of, or beneath a temple or shrine sanctuary. It was believed that by receiving a divinity in this closed space, one could absorb that being's powers. The rear or underground chamber could enshrine Buddhas or Kami, provide a space for esoteric ritual, contain a water source, provide a supplementary entrance and exit, and have other functions unrelated to ritual. In some cases, these chambers might be used simply to prepare or store items used in ceremonies. When used for ritual, the ritualist became the "receiving" party for a powerful visiting god.

A twelfth-century record shows that there was a rear chamber at Hōryūji that enshrined an image of Jizō, said to have been a gift from the King of Paekche. A twelfth-century document from Kōfukuji shows that the temple had a space beneath its Shaka triad where Ugajin, Daikoku, and other Kami who gained prominence in the medieval period were enshrined.[2] Neither Ugajin nor Daikoku appears in *Kojiki* or *Nihon shoki*. Ugajin is a food Kami represented as a white snake with the head of an old man. White snakes are widely associated in Japan with good luck and divine protection. Daikoku originated as an Indian deity, the male counterpart of the bloodthirsty Kali, but in Japan came to be associated with the spirit of rice. He holds a mallet which rains down coins. Daikoku is often represented alongside Ebisu, a sea god associated with success in fishing (see Figure 6.1). Both of them, as well as Ugajin, were associated with a newly popularized medieval cult of Happiness Gods, which we will examine later.

Mountain temples built remote Rear Chapels at their summits, called *Oku no In*, containing a hidden image as an object of worship. In some cases, such as at Enryakuji's Konpon Chūdō Hall and Ninnaji's Jōyuga-in Hall, the rear chamber might be a separate building directly behind the sanctuary of the main image, with a water source, illustrating a close connection between rear or underground chambers and the element of water. At the Gion Shrine and the Iwashimizu Hachiman Shrine, there were rear chambers where water and flowers used in ritual could be prepared.[3]

Much about these spaces remains unclear, and it seems unlikely that all such chambers were built for a common purpose. In some of them, a "foreign deity," a rough or violent Kami, devils (*oni*), and invisible maleficent spirits such as *mono* or *tama*, who were originally outside the *honji-suijaku* system, might be transformed

Figure 6.1 Daikoku and Ebisu. Attributed to Suzuki Harunobu, circa 1765–1769.
Source: Photograph © 2016, Museum of Fine Arts, Boston. Accession number 21.4637.

to benevolent, visible beings through rites conducted in these new chambers. Transforming these alien divinities in this way domesticated them and changed them into protectors.[4]

Different shrines showed a variety of constructions paired with their main halls in ways fitting the pattern of a rear chamber. At Ise, for example, a variety of ritual manuals attest to the existence of underground chambers at the main sanctuaries of both the Inner and the Outer Shrines. These chambers were apparently located beneath the main sanctuaries and the all-important Heart Pillar (*shin no mihashira*). Food-offering rites were held there seven times annually in a spatial arrangement suggesting that the offerings were made to the pillar. At Ise there is also a sub-shrine of the Inner Shrine, called the Aramatsuri no Miya, located to the north of the main sanctuary but separated by a small valley, which enshrines Amaterasu's "rough spirit" (*aramitama*). In relation to the Inner Shrine, the Aramatsuri no Miya served as the rear chamber, but in addition, it also contained an underground chamber. Sources from the tenth through the seventeenth centuries identify Aramatsuri no Miya as a place where oracles were delivered. Food offerings for the Aramatsuri no Miya were presented in the underground chamber seven times annually.[5]

The Hie Shrines comprised seven main shrines attached to the Tendai-sect monastic complex Enrakuji. The shrines were located on the slopes of Mt. Hiei, and were dedicated to the spirits of the mountain. They were counted among the Twenty-Two Shrines, and during the medieval period they became major pilgrimage sites for emperors, retired emperors, and commoners. By the mid-Kamakura period, there were underground chambers in several of the seven shrines, and eventually all of them incorporated such a chamber. These spaces were called *geden*, meaning literally "underground chamber." They appear in such literary classics as *Tales of the Heike* (*Heike monogatari*) and were used for a variety of rites. They contained altars and a water source and were used by low-ranking priests, blind monks, shamans, *miko* undertaking vigils, beggars, outcasts, and the sick. These places attracted shamans and healers, and the sick went there in search of cures. The practice of seclusion at a shrine for the purpose of prayer and ritual to achieve a goal like healing gave rise to the term "seclusion at a shrine" (*miyagomori*).[6]

Paired concepts of forward and behind, front and back, forward-facing movement and movement backward, and so on, became very important with the esotericization of Shinto. For example, the expression "advance and retreat procedure" (*shintai hō*) prescribed moving toward an altar by stepping forward with the right (yang) foot, and withdrawing by stepping back with the left (yin). Healing rites employed the idea of evil deities and spirits who could be contacted through spirit mediums, who could communicate oracles from those beings. Shamanistic mediums' names often incorporated the character for "left." Shugendō specialized in this type of knowledge, as well as in rites to exorcise spirits, prayer healings, and rites to alleviate calamities of all kinds. Buddhism and Shinto represented the "front," while Shugendō magic dealt with the rear, the reversed, the backward, and so forth. Such rites were held in rear and underground chambers, and the ritualists were not celibate clergy or representatives of shrines' sacerdotal lineages, but liminal figures such as *yamabushi*, shamans, blind or begging priests, and miscellaneous healers. Their deities were Matarajin and other "wild gods." A number of Kami associated with these developments were regarded as "foreign gods" (*ijin*) including Ugajin, Matarajin, Shinra Myōjin, and others.[7] While the exact nature of the link remains a subject for future research, there is a palpable connection among these gods, their hidden spaces, and the development of the arts of medieval masks, dance, and drama.[8]

The inclusion of a water source in nearly all the known underground chambers of medieval temples and shrines reflects the period's strong interest in water symbolism, as seen in new creation myths. The new myths we find in *Nakatomi no harae kunge* and the Five Books of Shinto composed by the Watarai lineage portray water as giving rise to a "spirit being" (*reibutsu*), which is revealed to be the Heavenly Jeweled Spear (*Ame no nuhoko*). From the drops of water falling from the spear's tip emerge the Kami, the Japanese islands, and all other things, each one paired with one of the five elements or an esoteric syllable. In this way, the Heavenly Jeweled Spear became a magical tool of creation. Whereas in *Kojiki* and *Nihon shoki* Izanagi and Izanami hold the spear, in medieval renditions of creation myth it is Amaterasu or Kunitokotachi who has the spear. We will examine an example later in discussing Mujū Ichien's *Collection of Sand and Pebbles.* Reflecting Shinto's esotericization during the medieval period, parallels were drawn between the spear and the *vajra,* an esoteric-Buddhist ritual implement.[9] Water sources in medieval underground chambers were often associated with a pillar, which is further linked to the Heavenly Jeweled Spear. Elaborate symbolism attached to the Heart Pillars at Ise, beneath which the underground chambers were located. The Heart Pillar was called the source of all creation, the source even of yin and yang, in *Hōki hongi,* one of the Watarai Five Books.[10]

The Tale of Gozu Tennō (*Gozu Tennō engi*) describes its central character, Gozu Tennō, the ox-headed deity of the Gion Shrine, riding on the Heavenly Jeweled Spear. According to this story, Gozu Tennō was the son of an Indian king, but because he was born with horns like an ox, he could not find a wife. Led by a dove, he journeyed to the Southern Sea, to the kingdom of the Sagara Dragon King. Along his journey, he sought lodging from a rich man of Khotan, but was refused. Then he went to the home of a poor man, Somin Shōrai, who took him in and treated him well. Gozu Tennō married the daughter of the Dragon King and had eight sons (identified as the Eight Princelings, the Hachiōji). When he returned to his kingdom, he destroyed the family of the rich man who had turned him away but spared the daughter of Somin Shōrai, giving her a talisman on which was written the expression, "the descendants of Somin Shōrai."[11]

An Expanding Pantheon

The appearance of new ritual spaces developed in parallel with novel deities. The Kami associated with the rear and underground chambers of medieval shrines differ from those found earlier in important ways. Most of the divinities worshipped at these new sites are not found in *Kojiki* or *Nihon shoki.* Some are regarded as "foreign," having been brought to Japan by Buddhist monks who had gone to China to study. Matarajin is a good example. This figure is found in *The Peacock Sutra* as a god who afflicts humanity with disease. By earnestly praying to him, one could avert sickness, according to the scripture. The Tendai monk Ennin (794–864) originally brought the worship of Matarajin to Japan. On Mt. Hiei, Matarajin was regarded as a protector of those who recite the *nenbutsu,* while in folk faith he became associated with a variety of other figures, such as Fudō, Daikoku, and others. He is pictured wearing Chinese headgear, holding a drum, and accompanied by two dancing children.[12] Kūkai is said to have established worship of Matarajin at Tōji, the Kyoto headquarters temple of Shingon, where Matarajin was regarded as a deity who could deliver oracles and predict good or bad fortune. Matarajin was sometimes depicted as having three faces in gold, white, and red.[13]

Matarajin was regarded as a *yasha* (Skt: *yaksa*), originally an Indian forest spirit with characteristics of a malevolent devil, who, if worshipped correctly can become a god of wealth. *Yasha* are frequently portrayed in Buddhist scriptures and adopted as protector deities of temples. They combine aspects of a devil who can do harm, and a benevolent god who can bring good fortune and happiness. The medieval period produced many different visual representations of Matarajin and rites for his worship in rear or underground chambers and other novel spaces.[14]

Matarajin became associated with androgyny, eroticism, song, and dance in a wide variety of settings beyond Mt. Hiei and Tōji. Following New Year's rites at medieval Tendai temples,[15] song, dance, and entertainments were performed as worship for Matarajin. Some of the songs and dances associated with the two children pictured with Matarajin contained veiled sexual references or mimed intercourse.[16] According to Suzuki Masataka, activating the divinities enshrined in the enclosed ritual spaces turned conventional morality upside down and could swiftly bring about dramatic changes in, or reversals of, perception. As a hidden god of the rear or that which lies behind, within whom is a dangerous power to change the world from its foundations, Matarajin's wild power could even be fundamentally evil. To awaken Matarajin's power, it is necessary to call on darkness, sound, smell, sensations, motility, and susceptibility to change. One arouses Matarajin through sound, voice, and song. The arts are the site of the sharpened sensitivity necessary to such transformation.[17]

The conception of Kami that are dangerous and to be avoided appears in the texts of the age as "real Kami" (*jissha, jisshajin,* or *jitsurui*). Some of them are outside the *honji-suijaku* framework, evil spirits or spirits of the dead, malevolent Kami who work *tatari,* animal spirits, and disembodied living spirits (*seirei* and other terms). These "real Kami" posed a new problem for Buddhist exegetes: "For the first time in Japan, some Buddhist authors envisioned deities who theologically resisted the incorporation within the Buddhist system because of their fundamentally evil nature—a dimension of the sacred that could not be integrated in Buddhism."[18]

In addition to the fearsome, powerful new Kami we have examined up to now, worship of the Seven Happiness Gods (Shichi Fukujin) developed in the medieval period (see Figure 6.2). This combination was popularized in Kyoto during the late fifteenth century as an amalgamation of faith in the deities at nearby shrines and temples frequented by the townspeople. Bishamonten was the principal deity at Kurama-dera, a temple associated with protection of the capital. Benzaiten was a goddess enshrined at Chikubushima, an island complex on Lake Biwa. The three-faced Daikoku was enshrined on Mt. Hiei, and Ebisu was the divinity of the Nishinomiya Shrine near Osaka. Daikoku was originally an Indian god ruling over food and drink, who became associated in Japan with agriculture and happiness. Ebisu protects a person's means of subsistence and brings happiness. In agricultural areas he came to be regarded as a deity of the rice field, while in fishing areas

Figure 6.2 The Seven Happiness Gods. Artist Unknown, Japanese. *The Social Reform Dance of the Seven Gods of Good Fortune (Fukujin yonaoshi odori)*, Japanese, Edo period–Meiji era, 1860s. Woodblock print (nishiki-e); ink and color on paper, vertical ōban diptych. Source: Museum of Fine Arts, Boston. William Sturgis Bigelow Collection 11.34998.16a–b. Photograph © 2016, Museum of Fine Arts, Boston.

he was understood as a god of plentiful catches. To these divinities were added Fukurokuju, Jurōjin, and Hotei. Fukurokuju and Jurōjin are different names for the same figure, who has a short body and an elongated head. He was regarded in China as a manifestation of a star believed to control the length of human life. Hotei originated as a humorous Zen monk, whose fat belly connoted plenitude. The names of these divinities make clear that they are not unambiguously Kami. Bishamonten and Benzaiten belong to the Buddhist category of *ten*, derived from the Indian *devas* and adopted as protectors of Buddhism. Bishamonten originated as one of the Four Guardian Kings (Shitennō), protectors of temples, and was associated with the North. Benzaiten originated as a river goddess in India, and was associated with water, the arts, and wealth. Despite their diverse origins and the fact that only Ebisu originated in Japan, in popular thought these seven deities came to be regarded as Kami.[19]

Shrine Kagura

Shrine personnel were important actors in the development of music, dance, and theatrical genres that gave birth to the art forms that later ages would see as most characteristically Japanese. During the Kamakura and Muromachi periods, the priests of the Kasuga Shrine were well known for performing *kagura* and Noh. While *miko* danced, male *jinin* accompanied them on flutes, drums, and other instruments. Originally *kagura* had developed as a form of offering to the Kami and was meant to be performed before an altar. *Kagura* might be a short set piece, or it could take the form of a divination for the ritual's sponsors, in which the *miko* used bells, or performed purifications while dancing around a boiling cauldron, dipping bamboo branches into it and flinging the water onto those in attendance to bless and purify them (this type was called "boiling water *kagura*," *yudate kagura*). Other forms of *kagura* developed in which the dance enacted episodes from myth or shrine tradition, including proclaiming oracles. There are twelfth-century records from the Kasuga Shrine showing that *kagura* was performed for aristocratic patrons of Kōfukuji, and Muromachi period records of a devotional group called a Benzaiten Kō meeting monthly to have *kagura* performed. *Miko* and *jinin* accompanists also performed outside shrines, for example, at rice planting.[20]

Taking sacred dance and music out of the shrines revealed their potential as entertainment. Records from the thirteenth century show complaints that the *jinin* or "Kagura men" (*kagura otoko*) were taking the *miko* to perform at private parties involving alcohol and vulgar dancing. In some cases, *jinin* were punished by losing their positions or, in extreme cases, by the destruction of their houses. It appears that Kōfukuji's critiques of the *jinin* were linked to the temple's displeasure at their impertinence, insulting the temple by sporting unauthorized vestments, brandishing swords, and declaiming miscellaneous vows (*kishōmon*) to the Kami.[21] It would seem, however, that Kōfukuji had some responsibility in the matter. Its priests had developed a custom of providing entertainment (generically called *ennen*) for sponsors and guests following the conclusion of formal rites, using *jinin*, *miko*, and beautiful young boys called *chigo*. Some of the racier material later developed into *kyōgen*, the comic dance-drama performed in the intermission at Noh performances.[22]

The Kami in Sculpture

Originally, there was a taboo against depicting the Kami in any representational form, and it was only under Buddhist influence and in the context of Buddhist worship that sculpted images of Kami were created. The earliest document mentioning a sculpture of the Kami concerns one placed at the *jingūji* of the Tado Shrine (discussed in chapter 1) and is dated 763. The oldest extant sculptures of Kami, generically called *shinzō*, date from the ninth century. The artists and the circumstances in which they were created are unknown. Many of the earliest examples were carved from single blocks of wood and easily cracked as a result. *Shinzō* included both male and female Kami. With the important exception of Hachiman in the guise of a monk, they were modeled on courtiers and are depicted in the clothing, hairstyles, and headgear characteristic of the early aristocracy. The posture of female Kami (seated, with one knee raised) is like that of Buddhist nuns. Unlike Buddhist iconography, however, *shinzō* did not bear distinctive characteristics that differentiate one Kami from another. In fact, it is only their placement in shrines that identifies them as Kami at all, rather than courtiers. Some, however, are shown in the posture used in the Heian period only when greeting the emperor, a gesture that makes sense in light of the custom of the emperor bestowing court ranks on Kami. In the absence of documents that would allow us to determine the matter with certainty, it is notable that Tsuda Sōkichi believed that *shinzō* showed the Kami in submissive gestures because they were believed to be converting to Buddhism and receiving the precepts. Both male and female deities' postures suggest a layperson receiving some transmission from a higher-ranking personage. *Shinzō* were not intended for viewing, nor did they serve as the main object of worship. They were generally placed in cabinets behind curtains, so that they shared the aura of "hidden Buddhas" (*hibutsu*). Little is known about how these ancient works came to be placed in shrines.[23]

From the mid-Kamakura period, a number of Kami sculptures were created as protectors of Buddhist temples (*garanjin*), including the seated statue of Shinra Myōjin at Onjōji and one representing the Izusan Gongen at Hannya-in.[24] Other sculptures were created for shrines. A sculpture of the seated Tamayori Hime was completed at the Mikumari Shrine in Yoshino in 1251, and a sculpture of Benzaiten for Tsurugaoka Hachiman Shrine was completed in 1266.[25]

Shrine Mandalas

Shrine mandalas (*miya mandara*) are among the most striking works of art of the period. They began to be produced in the late twelfth century, increasing in quantity through the end of the medieval age. A wide variety of types developed, depicting the sacred geography of specific shrines or their sacred symbols. Sometimes the Kami of the shrine were depicted along with their *honji* Buddha or Bodhisattvas, representing the shrine as an earthly paradise. They also served as pilgrims' guides (see Figure 6.3).[26]

Kasuga Shrine mandalas presented the shrine's sacred geography, a landscape rendered largely in green tones, with vermillion *torii* in the center, leading to numerous small buildings and a pagoda, and a grouping of shrine buildings in the upper section. Mt. Mikasa is depicted with the moon to its left, with five lunar discs in which the Buddhist *honji* of the shrine's Kami are depicted.[27] Some Kasuga

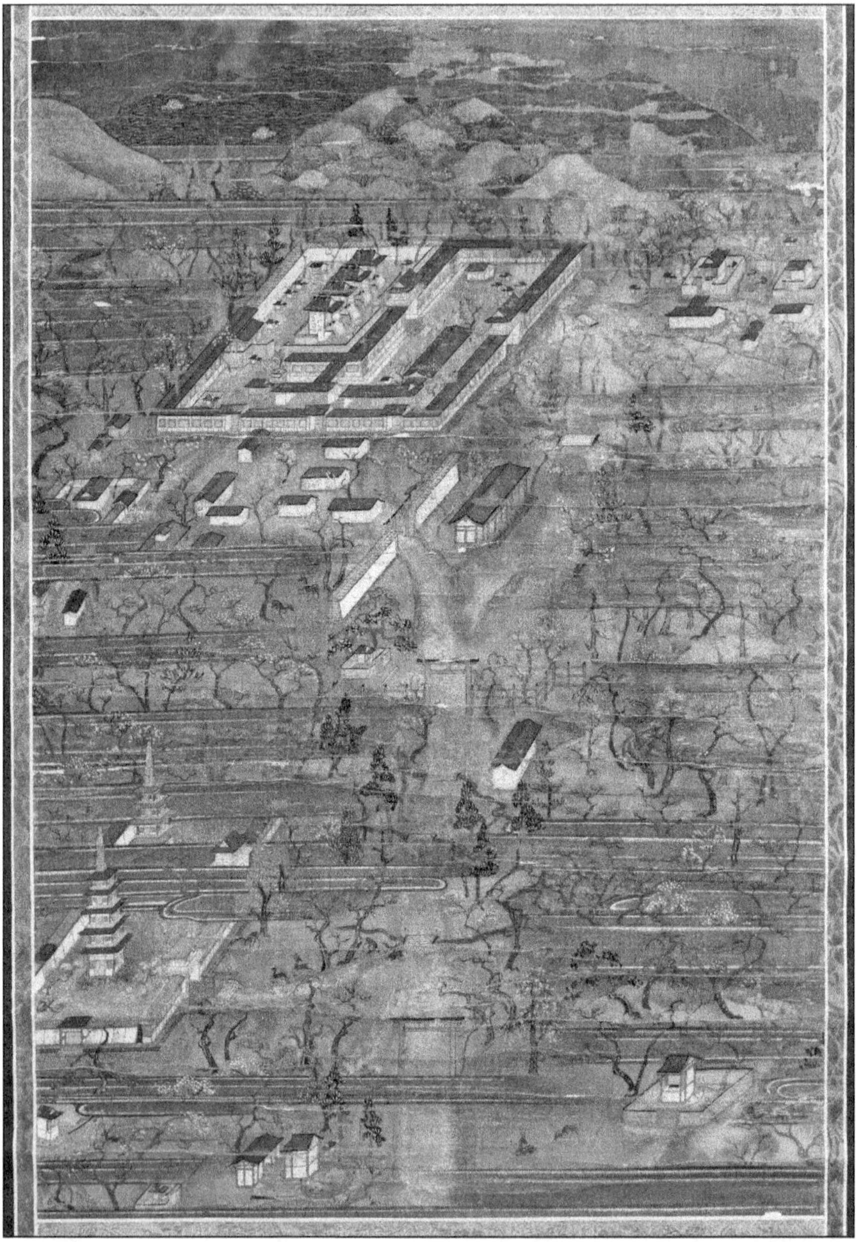

Figure 6.3 Mandala of Kasuga Shrine. Japanese, Muromachi period, 15th century. Hanging scroll; ink, color, and gold on silk, 58 × 39.1 cm (22 13/16 × 15 3/8 in.) (height × width). Source: Museum of Fine Arts, Boston, Special Chinese and Japanese Fund 20.752. Photograph © 2016, Museum of Fine Arts, Boston.

mandalas included representations of Kōfukuji. Many Kasuga mandalas carried the following text or a close approximation:

> In order to protect the true and perfect doctrine, He [the Kami] moved into a *sakaki* [tree] and rode forth from Kashima upon a stag. Out of compassion for the three thousand Hossō monks [of Kōfukuji], He tempered his light, manifested his trace, and lodged at the village of Kasuga.
>
> His original substance, Roshana [Vairocana],
> Perfectly enlightened for all eternity,
> In order to save sentient beings,
> Manifests the Daimyōjin.
>
> Thanks to the truth of the holy teaching, I have fully understood the *yuishiki* teaching. I hereby dedicate to all sentient beings the merit I have thereby acquired, and pray that together with them I shall speedily attain the highest enlightenment.[28]

The inscription conveys the legend that the Kasuga Kami came from Kashima riding upon deer, and that the original form was the Buddha Roshana (Rushana), who took Kami form as an expedient means to save all beings. A second type of mandala of the Kasuga Shrine depicted was a deer bearing a mirror hung in a *sakaki* tree on the animal's back (see Figure 6.4). After the poetic section, the text adopts the voice of the person sponsoring the creation of the mandala, saying that he/she/they have reached a full comprehension of the Consciousness-Only (*yuishiki*) doctrines of the Hossō sect of Kōfukuji, which controlled the Kasuga Shrine. Commissioning a mandala produced religious merit for the patron, which was dedicated to all beings in a prayer for their collective enlightenment.

The demand for shrine mandala paintings increased through the Kamakura period, becoming highly desired among the aristocracy and the court, as this passage from Emperor Hanazono's diary in 1325 attests:

> Kiyotsune told us that for the past three or four years, paintings of the Kasuga Shrine [have] been used to substitute for the rituals at the shrine. The painting depicting a view of the shrine is called *mandara*. Everyone seems to have one these days.[29]

Numerous shrine mandala paintings were created for a variety of shrines. In addition to those concerning the Kasuga Shrines, those concerning the Hie Shrines linked to the Tendai temple Enryakuji are particularly numerous and well known. Typically, shrines are shown linked to their associated temples. Similar mandala-like paintings of Kumano depicted a variety of shrines and temples in close association. While such paintings might begin with an aristocrat's commission to an accomplished painter, they were also copied in inexpensive forms and used by

Figure 6.4 Mandala of the Deer of Kasuga Shrine, *Kasuga shika mandara zu.*
Source: Photograph © 2016, Museum of Fine Arts, Boston. Accessions number 11.6288.

itinerant religious proselytizers, such as the "nuns of Kumano" (*Kumano bikuni*), to attract crowds. The proselytizer would exhibit such a painting and present a spoken explanation of its separate elements. These explanations helped pilgrims find their way through a complicated site, and they could also be used to explain doctrines and *honji-suijaku* associations.

In the late twelfth century, we can find evidence of devotions being performed before shrine paintings, which allowed worshippers to offer prayers to a shrine from a distance, without actually going there.[30] The Kasuga Shrine was known as the paradise of the *honji* of the Kami of the shrine, which were variously understood, not just as Roshana, but also as Kannon or Shaka for the Kami of the first sanctuary, Yakushi or Miroku for the Kami of the second sanctuary, and the Eleven-Headed Kannon or Dainichi for the Kami of the third sanctuary. The honji of the Wakamiya sanctuary was Monju (Manjusri Bodhisattva). Confusingly, these associations changed over time and were presented differently in different texts.[31] The identification of the shrine's sacred geography with these Buddhist paradises was not a metaphorical connection, but a literal equation, as this passage from a miracle tale about the shrine, *Kasuga Gongen Reigenki* (1309), makes clear:

> Since purity in accordance with the mind is itself the Pure Land, our own Kami are the Buddhas. How could the shrine not be the Pure Land? Jōruri [Skt., Vaidūrya] and Vulture Peak are present within the Shrine fence. Why seek Fudaraku [Skt., Potalaka] and Shōryōzan [another name for Mt. Wu-tai in China] beyond the clouds?[32]

The passage asserts that the shrine's sacred geography *is* the Pure Land, and thus a pilgrimage to the shrine is equivalent to a foretaste of paradise. The Buddhas reveal their Pure Lands to those whose minds are pure, and with a pure mind one realizes that the Kami and the Buddhas are identical. Thus, the shrine of the Kami is equivalent to the Pure Land of their *honji* Buddhas. The sanctuaries of the Kami and their *honji* Buddhas could be associated with a particular Pure Land paradise. These identifications of shrine sacred geographies with Pure Lands were seen in other shrines besides Kasuga. They acted as an encouragement to pilgrimage, and to organizing pilgrimage groups called *kō*. Some shrine mandalas were probably commissioned by such *kō* as a means to visualize their journey to the shrine.[33]

This idea of a shrine as earthly embodiment of paradise was asserted in numerous variant forms. The Noh play *The Dragon Deity of Kasuga* (*Kasuga Ryūjin*) presents arguments by the Kami to Myōe, a monk who wished to make a pilgrimage to India, saying that while the Buddha may have been born in India, now he resides on Mt. Mikasa, which is itself Vulture Peak. Therefore, Myōe need not journey to India but instead could accomplish the same religious goal by making a pilgrimage to Kasuga. Another version of this tale is included in the illustrated scroll we will examine in the next section, *Kasuga Gongen Genki-emaki*.[34]

In the several passages quoted above concerning the Kami of Kasuga, we notice a slippage between singular and plural usage. The Fujiwara clan originally emphasized a group of Kami as discussed previously, but in addition, by the mid-twelfth century we also find references to the Kasuga *Daimyōjin*, a "conglomerate" entity that could appear in a variety of forms. This transformation paralleled the extension of control over distant estates by Kōfukuji/Kasuga Shrine.[35]

Pilgrimage groups developed at the Hiei Shrines around the fourteenth century, composed of *jinin* and Enryakuji monks. Dressed in white, they were led through the shrine complex at night, in a manner suggesting their belief that the journey was a preview of the journey they would make to the Pure Land after death. Pilgrims' manuals specified the route and the places to stop and worship along the way. Manuals from the Edo period, when presumably there were lay members, show that the pilgrimage association held regular meetings, at which they recited the Heart Sutra before paintings that may have included shrine mandalas.[36]

Kasuga Gongen Genki-emaki

Many paintings of the Kami began to be produced from the thirteenth century, including illustrated scrolls highlighting the power of the Kami in the wake of the Mongol Invasions. In 1288 a set of scrolls relating the miracles of the Mt. Hiei Kami, titled *Sannō Reigenki* was created, and in 1299 the *Ippen Shōnin E-den*. In 1309 Saionji Kinhira dedicated perhaps the greatest work in the history of Shinto art to the Kasuga Shrine, the monumental illustrated scrolls of tales and paintings relating to the shrine, *Kasuga Gongen Genki-emaki*.

Kinhira commissioned the work to give thanks for being reinstated to his post after Retired Emperor Go-Uda (r. 1274–1287) had confiscated his estates and put him under house arrest in 1305.[37] This work followed in the tradition of Kasuga Shrine mandalas and built on miracle tales already in existence. The tales appearing in the work were compiled by a monk of Kōfukuji named Kakuen (1277–1304). Devotion to Kasuga by eminent Buddhist leaders of the period such as Jōkei (1155–1213, also known as Gedatsu Shōnin) and Myōe (1173–1232) had "given a new intensity to Kasuga faith."[38] Myōe was the first to encourage those outside the Fujiwara clan to worship at Kasuga, though we know that local groups had been worshipping at the site from ancient times. Gedatsu Shōnin identified Shakyamuni as the original form (*honji*) of Kasuga Daimyōjin.[39]

Kasuga Gongen Genki-emaki consists of twenty scrolls on silk cloth, presenting ninety-three sections of text (including poetry and prose) and pictures, plus an introductory text and a separate scroll for the contents and preface. The celebrated painter Takashina Takakane (dates unknown) painted the pictures at the Kōfukuji painting studio. There are fifty-six separate stories, though Royall Tyler's authoritative translation identifies seventy-two tales that "celebrate the enduring potency of the Kasuga deity, his readiness to chastise those who displease him, and, above all, the zeal with which he protects those who trust in him."[40]

According to Tyler, this work can be understood as addressing a major theme of religious life in the Kamakura period: how to respond to the idea that we live at the nadir of spiritual possibility, in a small, remote country on the outer edges of the cosmos, ages after the Buddha departed? Its response is the assertion that in reality Japan is blessed by divine favor delivered through the Kami of Kasuga. The land of this shrine grants access to paradise, and also to the hells, where the wicked will be punished. To devote oneself completely to Kasuga brings one into contact with the purest and fullest teaching, under the protection of loving, beneficent Kami who will show themselves to their devotees and soothe every pain, relieve every suffering.

A plethora of religious impulses were expressed at Kasuga. Mt. Mikasa, on whose slopes the shrine and temple were located, became identified with a variety of Pure Lands, and with the idea that the Daimyōjin would grant a devotee entrée to the paradise that was most pleasing to him or her, whichever that might be. Devotees sought visions and dreams of the Daimyōjin, in which the Kami would reveal his true form in response to the believer's unswerving faith. The Daimyōjin could heal any illness, but if displeased would threaten to depart. Gedatsu Shōnin believed that the Daimyōjin would appear before him at the moment of death:

> When the moment comes the August Deity will appear in my room, filling me, body and mind, with His deep peace, and producing for me much beneficial karma. Then He will make manifest those among the Three Treasures to whom I have a tie, and these will all grant me their aid. The [relics] I have will then, anew, reveal their wonders, and the True Teaching in which I take refuge will confer on me its power.[41]

Two tales from the seventeenth scroll recount events in which the Daimyōjin appeared to the monk Myōe in the form of "a lady of the Tachibana clan." Myōe, one of the most renowned clerics of the Kamakura period, was a monk of both the Kegon and Shingon schools of Buddhism. He was also a devotee of Kasuga and had recorded his first vision of the Daimyōjin in 1198. He preached to lay people in the provinces and became known as a healer. In 1201, he healed his aunt, who was pregnant, and she appears in these tales as the Tachibana lady, a medium of the Daimyōjin, a person through whom the Daimyōjin speaks to Myōe. These visitations occurred as Myōe was preparing to fulfill a cherished plan to travel to India in order to be closer to Shakyamuni by visiting his birthplace. Myōe's desire stemmed from the belief that Japan is a remote speck in the cosmic ocean, and that because Myōe lived in the Latter Days, his spiritual possibilities were limited as long as he remained in his own country. The Daimyōjin's appearances before him in the form of his aunt counter instead that the Kami cherish and protect Myōe, and that the Daimyōjin wishes him to remain in Japan to preach the teachings of Buddhism to the people. The second of the two tales begins when Myōe visits her with a group of many companions and is surprised to find a marvelous fragrance emanating from her room.

> "What is this scent?" [Myōe] asked.
>
> "I don't know," she answered, "but when I noticed how fragrant I was, I got ready to receive you. I want to be high, so I'll go up to the ceiling. Please close the doors."
>
> Myōe did so, and she immediately rose to the ceiling. When he opened the doors again one of the ceiling planks had been removed, and the unearthly fragrance was stronger than ever. Myōe and the others all gathered below her and prostrated themselves, saying, "Namu [Hail] Kasuga no Daimyōjin."
>
> The lady then began speaking in a soft, sweet voice. "It is rude of me to sit so high up," she said, "but as persons like me are used to being elevated, I have raised up the one through whom I am addressing you..."
>
> "There is not one of the Gods, good monk," she then continued, "who does not protect you. Sumiyoshi no Daimyōjin and I attend you particularly. And I, especially, am always with you in the center of your body [in the abdomen, the *hara*], so that even if you were across the sea we would not be parted, and I would not personally mind. But when I remember all the people who can be inspired by you to faith, as long as you are in Japan, [I am grieved] that you should mean to undertake so long a pilgrimage. I love all those who have faith in the Buddha's Teaching, and among them I think particularly of three: yourself, Gedatsu-bō, and another in the Capital.[42] But I am not as devoted to the other two as I am to you."
>
> Then she descended from the ceiling as silently as a swan's feather falling. The fragrance as she spoke had grown still more pronounced. Though not musk or any such scent, it was very rich, and quite unlike any fragrance of the human world. Transported with delight, those present licked her hands and feet, which were as sweet as sweetvine. One woman's mouth had been hurting for days, but when she licked her the pain was gone. Despite everyone pressing in to lick her, the lady kept her loving expression and seemed not to mind. She never moved. In color she was as bright as crystal, and every detail of her was beyond the ordinary. Her wide-open, unblinking eyes showed much less pupil than white. Everyone was weeping.
>
> "Never before have I shown my true form in this way and come down into human presence," she said, "and I never will again. I have done so now, good monk, because I have such supreme regard for you. That you should have your heart set on the mountains and forests of distant lands

> is wonderful as far as your own practice is concerned, but it makes those whom you would otherwise touch lose a chance to establish their link with enlightenment, and that is what distresses me...."
>
> "In your ardor to adore Lord Shaka where He actually lived, you are unique in all the world. This gives me particular pleasure.... Do not weep!" she said. "Ours is a latter age, when none give themselves heart and soul to practicing the Buddha's way... [S]tudy the sacred writings until you grasp their deep meaning!"... The tears streaming down her cheeks showed plainly her grief and pain. In her, the unspeakably moved company beheld inconceivable compassion.[43]

There are two paintings accompanying this tale. In one of them we see the Daimyōjin appearing in the form of Myōe's aunt in the rafters, speaking to Myōe and a group of monks and laypeople who look up to her adoringly. Curved lines indicate the unearthly fragrance signaling the presence of the Daimyōjin. In the second painting, we see a woman seeking healing licking the medium's feet. Myōe, a company of monks and laymen sit respectfully before the medium, the monks and the high-born inside the house or on the veranda, while the less exalted sit on the ground below. A woman and two children peer through the fence.

Much like the miracle tales of *Shintōshū* and *Shasekishū* that will be examined next, the tales in *Kasuga Gongen Genki-emaki* show a seamless unity of aspiration for Buddhist teachings, shared by the Kami and their followers as much as by monks like Myōe and Gedatsu Shōnin. The Kami protect the followers of Buddhism and encourage all to follow Buddhist teachings as the path to salvation. Moreover, the tale strongly affirms Japan as a sacred realm in which beneficent Kami respond lovingly to sincere devotees.

Depicting the Kami in Painting

A medieval convention held that the faces of the Kami should not be depicted in painting. There are many examples of scroll paintings in which clouds, a fan, or some other element obscures the face of a Kami or the Kami faces backward. There are other cases, however, in which the face of a Kami is shown facing forward. It remained unclear for a long time what criteria allowed a painter to depict Kami countenances. Understanding the logic of the medieval convention has been a significant issue in studies of Shinto arts.

According to the analysis of art historian Yamamoto Yōko, *Kasuga Gongen Genki-emaki* contains 2,046 painted images representing human forms. Thirty-three represent the Daimyōjin's messengers, and a further twenty represent people possessed by the Kami, such as the Tachibana Lady in the tale above. Other religious figures, such as devils or officials of hell, total seventy-three. There are twenty-seven representations of the Daimyōjin. Only five of them represent the Daimyōjin facing forward. What factors led the artist to depict some with their faces showing?[44]

Yamamoto determined that the face of the Kami is never visible when it appears in the form of an adult man in formal court dress. By the medieval period, both Buddhist divinities and Kami were represented having Japanese facial features. Yamamoto found that there are several instances in *Kasuga Gongen Genki-emaki* in which the Kami of the Third Sanctuary appears in the form of its *honji*, the Bodhisattva Jizō. In these cases, the face is shown, made up with white powder; the chest of the figure is exposed, wearing jewelry, and the Kami is sitting on a lotus seat. These features distinguish the figure from an ordinary monk. Thus, it appears to have been permissible to depict Kami faces when they appear in their Buddhist form.[45]

Apart from appearances in the form of mediums like Myōe's aunt, there are two paintings in which the Daimyōjin takes female form. Both of them occur in the first scroll, when the Daimyōjin appears as a shrine *miko* delivering an oracle, and the faces are shown in both cases. At this point in the story, the Kami appears in a bamboo grove, because the Kasuga Shrine has not yet been built. The Kami has not yet been enshrined to receive worship. Yamamoto discovered that timing—before or after the Kami's enshrinement—was the crucial criterion determining whether the face could be shown. She tested her theory through examination of other medieval scroll paintings that differ significantly from *Kasuga Gongen Genki-emaki* in style and provenance and found that this criterion operates in those other works as well. Thus the longstanding question seems to be settled. The faces of the Kami may be shown if they have not yet been enshrined.[46]

But what is the implication of this finding for our understanding of medieval concepts of Kami? It is the *human* action of enshrining the Kami that elevates them to such an eminence that their countenances must be hidden. The Kami are enhanced through their relation with humanity. Put another way, medieval people saw themselves as enmeshed in relations with the Kami, as if a kind of reciprocity bound the two. When humanity sincerely, purely worships the Kami by building a shrine and installing the Kami there, then surely the Kami will respond with beneficence.

Kasuga Gongen Genki-emaki was dedicated to the shrine and was unavailable for viewing except for the four times it was taken to Kyoto, once for a "picture-viewing party" (*e-awase*) and three times for imperial viewing.[47] In contrast, Kasuga Shrine mandalas and deer mandalas (*shika mandara*) were produced for worship. *Kō* formed around the shrine were called Shunnichi Kō, a title that gave an alternate reading to the characters used to write the word *Kasuga* (春日). One deer mandala produced for the Shunnichi Kō in the Muromachi era records the names of seven members, each beginning with the character for "spring," the first character in *Kasuga*. These must have been special names used within the group, or perhaps they were the names of *jinin*, lower-ranking shrine attendants.[48]

Shinto Themes in Tale Literature (*Setsuwa*)

Medieval *setsuwa*, compilations of morality tales incorporating elements of myth, legend, and popular tales, drew extensively on images of the Kami. Literature such as this had begun to appear even in the ancient period, with works such as *Nihon ryōiki*, increasing in the medieval period with such works as *Uji shūi monogatari* (1210–1221), *Zoku-kojidan* (1219), and *Shintōshū* (1352–1361) as representative examples. Collections of miracle tales about the Buddhas and Kami were also produced, such as *Hasedera reigenki* (1200–1219) and *Sannō reigenki* (1288).[49]

The monk Mujū Ichien (1226–1312), compiler of *Shasekishū* (*Collection of sand and pebbles*), was a priest of a Zen temple near the Atsuta Shrine in Owari Province, where the sword of the imperial regalia was believed to be enshrined. Mujū had studied in a variety of Buddhist sects before settling on Rinzai Zen. His temple was not far from the main road linking Kamakura and Kyoto, so it is likely that he collected some of his material from travelers' tales. His purpose was to lead people to Buddhism through sermons that incorporated popular stories. Starting with a familiar topic, he would develop a theme in a way that introduced an audience to doctrinal concepts and more difficult ideas.

From his location in Owari, it was possible to visit the Ise Shrines by ship. In fact, Mujū stated that a visit to the shrines sometime between 1261 and 1264 was his inspiration for compiling this work. *Shasekishū* is composed of ten "books," the first of which is devoted to tales of the Kami (and mountain deities) and their compassionate work for salvation.[50] It appears that in beginning his collection with these stories, Mujū may have planned to address those just beginning to grapple with more difficult Buddhist material through stories involving more familiar figures, the Kami. In one story, for example, he explains why the *honji-suijaku* paradigm is followed in Japan:

> [A]lthough the body of the Original Ground [*honji*] and the Manifest Traces [*suijaku*] are identical, their effects... vary.... As for its effects in our country, how superlative is the appearance of the Manifest Traces! This is because, in antiquity, when En no Gyōja was practicing austerities on Mt. Yoshino and the form of Sākyamuni appeared before him, the ascetic said: "In this august form it will be difficult to convert the people of this country. You should conceal yourself." Then the shape of Maitreya appeared to him, but En said: "This likewise will not do." However, when the Buddha manifested a fearsome shape as Zaō Gongen, En responded, "Truly, this is one who can convert our land to Buddhism." And today the Buddha manifests this Trace.[51]

Mujū's point is that in order to lead the people of Japan to Buddhism, the best form for Buddhist divinities to assume is a proximate one like the mountain deity Zaō Gongen.

Yet in the Kamakura period, it was understood that words related to Buddhism were forbidden at the Ise Shrines, an apparent contradiction. To explain this oddity, Mujū begins Book 1 with this tale about the Ise Shrines:

> In antiquity, when this country did not yet exist, the deity of the Great Shrine [the Sun Goddess, Amaterasu], guided by a seal of the Great Sun Buddha [Dainichi] inscribed on the ocean floor, thrust down her august spear. Brine from the spear coagulated like drops of dew, and this was seen from afar by Māra, the Evil One, in the Sixth Heaven of Desire. "It appears that these drops are forming into a land where Buddhism will be propagated and people will escape from the round of birth-and-death," he said, and came down to prevent it.
>
> Then the deity of the Great Shrine met with the demon king. "I promise not to utter the names of the Three Treasures, nor will I permit them near my person. So return quickly back to the heavens." Being thus mollified, he withdrew.
>
> Monks to this very day, not wishing to violate that august promise, do not approach the sacred shrine, and the sutras are not carried openly in its precincts. Things associated with the Three Treasures are referred to obliquely: Buddha is called "The Cramp-Legged One [*tachisukumi*]; the sutras, "colored paper" [*somegami*]; monks, "longhairs" [*kaminaga*]; and temples, "incense burners" [*koritaki*], etc. Outwardly the deity is estranged from the Law but inwardly she profoundly supports the Three Treasures. Thus, Japanese Buddhism is under the special protection of the deity of the Great Shrine.... Since all of this arose by virtue of the seal of the Great Sun Buddha on the ocean floor, we have come to identify the deities of the Inner and Outer Shrines with the Great Sun Buddha of the Two-Part Mandala.[52]

Mujū takes pain to provide an alternative to the view that the Ise deities reject Buddhist terms because they find such speech offensive. Rather, in the remote past Dainichi guided Amaterasu's formation of the Japanese islands as a place for Buddhism to flourish, by creating a target for the Heavenly Jeweled Spear on the seabed. But Māra, the incarnated principle of evil in Buddhism, who seeks always to prevent Buddhism's advance, swooped in to scotch this plan. Amaterasu cleverly deflected him by promising that Buddhism would never be mentioned near her. To uphold her honor in this ruse, Buddhist things are mentioned in Ise only by circumlocutions, and the take-home point for the audience is that Amaterasu reveres Buddhism even though it cannot be mentioned in Ise.

We note that Mujū grafts Dainichi onto the myth of creation with this story about an undersea target. He further alters the creation story seen in *Nihon shoki* by making Amaterasu rather than Izanagi and Izanami the principal actors in the creation of the land. In fact, medieval ideas of the cosmogony frequently ignored Izanagi and Izanami. These devices allow Mujū to make the Buddhist figure prior to the Kami, and to identify Dainichi as the *honji* and Amaterasu as the *suijaku*. In this way, he can both suggest that the Kami owe a debt to the Buddhas, and explain why Buddhism cannot be mentioned at Ise. It is also interesting to note that although Mujū served at a Zen temple, he invokes the mandalas of the esoteric tradition, showing that the framework of *honji-suijaku* was of greater concern to him than propagating Zen thought.

The Buddhas and Kami "Dim Their Light and Mingle with the Dust of the World" (*Wakō Dōjin*)

In the Heian period the idea had developed that the Buddhas and Kami "dim their light and mingle with the dust of the world" in order to save suffering humanity. The motif of Buddhist divinities "dimming their light" (*wakō*) became an important theme in explicating their relation to the Kami, finding some of its most celebrated expressions in medieval tale literature. If a person should encounter the Buddhist divinities in their true form, the light shining from them would be blinding. Out of compassion for human beings, the Buddhas "dim their lights" by provisionally adopting the form of Kami. In Kami form they can interact with humanity directly, thus "mingling with the dust of the world" (*dōjin*, literally, "same dust"). This theory shows a transcendent being, the Buddhist divinity, lowering itself to a worldly level in the form of a Kami, indirectly underscoring the difference in status between Kami and Buddhas.[53]

The *Shasekishū* expounded on the motif in numerous tales. In Mujū's accounts, both the Buddhas and the Kami can "dim their lights."

> The skillful means of the Blessed One [the Buddha] varies according to the country and occasion.... In our country, the land of the gods [*shinkoku*], the provisional manifestations of the Buddha leave their traces. Moreover, we are all their [the Kamis'] descendants.... If we pray to other blessed beings, their response will be ever so far distant from us. Consequently, there can be nothing so profitable as relying on the skillful means of the gods [the Kami], who soften their light in response to our potential for good, praying to them to lead us to the path essential for release from birth-and-death.[54]

Explaining why it is beneficial to worship the Kami, this passage suggests that the Buddhist teaching is expressed in different ways in different countries, and the character of each nation modulates the form that Buddhism takes. Japan's most distinctive characteristic in Mujū's view is that it is "the land of the Kami" (*shinkoku*).

The significance of the *shinkoku* idea in this passage is the assertion that *all* Japanese are the descendants of the Kami, that the people as a whole somehow share the monarch's divine descent. Based on this spiritual kinship, Japanese should pray to the Kami, rather than "other blessed beings." The people have a claim on the Kami as their descendants; it makes sense for the people to pray to the Kami rather than to any other kind of deity. The nature of the Kami is to have compassion for their descendants, and it is for that reason that they "dim their light" as one of their "skillful means," and lead suffering humanity toward release from the bonds of karma.

"Skillful means" (Skt., *upaya*, J: *hōben*), a concept propounded in many Buddhist works but, notably, in the Lotus Sutra, are provisional devices adopted by Buddhist divinities based on their perception of the intellectual and spiritual capacity of the person they seek to lead toward greater understanding. In one famed parable from the Lotus Sutra, a father coaxes his children out of a burning house by promising them three carts. When they emerge from the house, it is revealed that there is really only one cart. The meaning of the parable is that, because of humanity's limited understanding, it was provisionally stated that there are "three vehicles" to convey the devotee toward nirvana; but when greater understanding is achieved, it can be revealed that there was really only a "single vehicle" all along. It is in service to the task of leading humanity toward greater understanding and expanded spiritual capacity that the Buddhas employ "skillful means." Within the paradigm of the Kami "dimming their light and mingling with the dust of the world," the Kami are shown using skillful means in the same way as the Buddhas.

In another story in *Collection of Sand and Pebbles*, a monk named Jōganbō set out on pilgrimage to the Yoshino Shrine. He came upon two children, crying because their mother had died, and they were too small to bury her. Out of compassion for their plight, the monk buried the corpse, but in doing so became polluted by death. Based on the conventional wisdom of the day, he should have canceled his pilgrimage and returned home to purify himself before approaching the Kami at Yoshino. But when he set his feet toward home, he found himself inexplicably paralyzed. When he continued toward Yoshino, however, he had no trouble walking. Thinking this very strange, he stopped some distance from the shrine to recite sutras and consider what he should do.

> Presently a [female] attendant possessed by the deity [the Kami of the Yoshino Shrine] danced forth from the shrine and approached him. "What is the meaning of this, worthy monk?" she inquired. Jōganbō trembled with fear. "Alas, how short-sighted of me. I should not have come so far, and now I shall be chastised." "Why are you so late, worthy monk, when I have been expecting you for so long?" asked the deity as she approached. "I certainly do not abhor what you have done. On the contrary, I respect compassion." And taking the monk by the sleeve, she led him to the Worship Hall.[55]

As the story opens, the monk Jōganbō is on a pilgrimage to the Yoshino Shrine. In this story, the Kami of the Yoshino Shrine "dims its light" by speaking through a *miko,* one of its female "attendants," presumably one of the shrine ritualists. Compassion—a key Buddhist virtue—is invoked as a characteristic that the Kami "respect," despite their abhorrence for death pollution. The Kami had so eagerly anticipated the monk's pilgrimage that it "danced forth"—in the form of the *miko*—to meet the monk whose compassion for two pitiful children had compelled him to bury their mother. Moreover, far from keeping the monk at a distance, the Kami guides the monk into the shrine. Contrary to the monk's expectation that the Kami would be angry and punish him, the Kami's warm welcome rewards Jōganbō.

The idea of a divinity softening its blinding radiance so that it can interact with humanity to hasten salvation builds on and extends the *honji-suijaku* paradigm. When a Buddhist divinity takes the form of a Kami, a pairing like that of *honji-suijaku* is created. A further pairing is created when a Kami assumes the form of shrine personnel. When the Kami assumes human form, a chain linking Buddha to Kami to humanity is created. This chain is the rationale justifying the claim that by dimming their lights in this linked way, the Buddhas and the Kami work together for the salvation of humanity.

The image of the Kami dimming their lights and mingling with humanity illustrates the strengthened associations of the Kami with morality. The story of Jōganbō shows that the moral value of compassion trumps the taboo on death pollution at shrines. Through their association with Buddhist divinities, the Kami are shown placing a higher value upon elevated moral qualities than on observance of taboo. Taboos based on pollution notions, calendrical divinations, and yin-yang calculations are certainly not rejected entirely, but in this period we see a definite downgrading of them within the paradigm of *wakō dōjin.*

Engi and *Setsuwa: Shintōshū*

Tales of temples' and shrines' origins are called *engi. Engi* tales constitute an important form of medieval Shinto literature. The term *engi* derives from the Sanskrit word *pratitya samutpada,* twelve links in the chain of causation that explain the causes of suffering and the karmic relations that bind beings to the world of samsara. *Engi* literally means the "arising" (*ki, gi*) of [karmic] "relation(s)" (*en*). During the medieval period, legends of the founding of temples and shrines were composed in great numbers. A recent compilation includes some 279 separate *engi.*[56] A temple or shrine's *engi* served as its official history. Besides stories of a shrine's origin, *engi* generally included separate tales with moral lessons and thus overlapped with *setsuwa.* Often a list of the institution's material assets and treasures was appended. The standardization of these elements suggests that temples and shrines may have been under an obligation to submit them to government in loosely uniform format. In addition to any bureaucratic significance *engi* may have had, these tales were used as preaching texts by Buddhist clerics and the traveling *bikuni*, an informal order of proselytizers who traveled the country encouraging religious practice. *Bikuni* observed an abbreviated set of precepts and were distinct from cloistered nuns based at convents.[57]

Shintōshū, a later compilation of *engi* that is also regarded as an important source of *setsuwa*, was composed around 1358 by the Agui school of Tendai-sect preachers. This work contains many tales of the origins and history of temples and such famous shrines such as Kitano Tenmangū, Suwa Myōjin, Kumano, Nikkō, and other shrines. The following story from *Shintōshū* is the *engi* of a small shrine in Northern Japan called Kagami no Miya, or the Mirror Shrine.

The Mirror Shrine

These events happened in the time of Emperor Ankō [a legendary emperor of the mid-fifth century] in a village called Yamagata, in the Asaka District of Ōshū Province, a northern mountain village of about sixty peasant households. They chose a sensible old man to deliver the village's taxes to the capital. When he had completed his task, the man went along Fourth Avenue to buy souvenirs and saw a mirror in one of the shops. Looking into it, he saw a man of fifty-four or fifty-five. Curious, he asked the merchant what the strange object was. Realizing that this customer was a rustic from the mountains, the devious merchant set out to trick him into buying the mirror, saying, "This is a precious treasure. It is the mirror entrusted by Tenshō Daijin to her descendant, the Kami Ameno Oshihomimi no Mikoto, and it reflects the Kami's form. It is the same as the one in the palace sanctuary, the Kashikodokoro. It is the same as those hung in shrines to protect the country. It causes many treasures to manifest. Come with me, and I'll show you!"

Thereupon they set off to tour the capital. They saw the guilds that make armor, belly-bands, bows and arrows, long swords, and short swords, not to mention the guilds making brocade and saddles. Just then, an imperial procession was passing by. As people were scurrying hither and yon, fierce warriors, nobles, palanquins, carriages, and all sorts of elegantly dressed people passed by. The merchant showed each and every splendid sight to the old man from the north, reflecting each one in the mirror. Returning to the merchant's shop, the man made up his mind to buy the mirror. He asked, "If I buy the mirror, will everything it has shown me be mine? All the gold and silver, the many robes, the men and horses, the palanquins, and the carriages?" The merchant replied simply, "Of course." The merchant named a high price. The old man gave the merchant all the money he had, as well as all he could borrow from his comrades, amounting to a large sum many times the mirror's real worth. The merchant placed the mirror in a brocade bag, cautioning the man to hang it around his neck unopened until he returned home. The trusting old man did exactly as he was told and hurriedly returned home in great joy.

When his wife and family came out to meet him, he told them that because honored guests were coming, they should put out the *tatami* mats and make preparations.[58] When all was in readiness, he took the mirror out of the brocade bag and laid it on the *tatami* mat. But to his surprise, he could see nothing in the mirror but the face of an old man of fifty-four or fifty-five. When his wife looked into the mirror, she could see nothing but the face of a fifty-year-old woman. She burst into tears and cried, "Why have you brought home another wife, when you already have me?" When his grown sons and their wives looked into the mirror, they were all horrified at the thought that they were to be replaced by the people in the mirror.

Just then a traveling nun (*bikuni*) happened by and explained to them that the old man in the mirror was none other than the husband, and the woman reflected there was his wife, and likewise the younger generation. The nun continued, "This man once was young and had the face of a child, though he has now turned things over to his sons and grown old and ugly. This wife once had the pretty face of a bride, but now she is an old woman with white hair, and her once straight back is now bent and crooked. There are many people in this world who do not realize that this happens to everyone. Each of these signs is a messenger from the next world (*meido*). At the end we all go to the next world. We are astonished when we see in the mirror how much we have changed. One of the virtues of the mirror is to cause us to yearn for the next life. It is a precious treasure that joins together our present and our future."

Hearing these words, tears flowed from the old man's eyes as he exclaimed that the mirror was indeed a great treasure, leading humanity to the Buddhist path. Thereupon, he built a chapel to enshrine the mirror. From time to time, he would look into the mirror and cry. After a time, he took the tonsure and devoted himself to reciting the *nenbutsu*, never failing in his daily devotions. He was at peace when he died. Eventually both he and his wife appeared as Kami and bestowed many blessings on those in this world. The Asaka District tutelary shrine called the Mirror Shrine (Kagami no miya) is the place where they appeared as Kami. Thanks to the mirror, bought by this unfailingly honest man at such a great price, this man came to be called a Kami by later ages, and even now he brings blessings to the many. Even now the mirror is carefully preserved at the shrine.[59]

The story initially hinges on the fact that the rustic protagonist had never seen a mirror before his trip to Kyoto. His expectation that the mirror would magically give him everything reflected in its surface resembles ancient ideas of the magical properties of mirrors that were fading by the medieval period, remaining only in the backwoods. Meanwhile, the cunning shopkeeper sought to sell the mirror by equating it to the one that the Sun Goddess bestowed on her imperial descendants, as well as the one in the palace sanctuary, and to the mirrors in provincial shrines. That a merchant could credibly be depicted as having knowledge of the relevant myths and palace practices is significant in itself. The merchant obviously knew that the mirrors that could be bought and sold as souvenirs by vendors such as himself had little material value. He could only make a big profit if a hayseed such as the protagonist could be persuaded of the magical properties of mirrors to bring unimaginable wealth. Yet by the end of the story, it is clear that the protagonist's credulity was a sign of his honesty, a quality associated with mirrors in the context of the regalia in the medieval period.

When the protagonist and his family quarrel over the mirror, a *bikuni* intervenes to set them straight. The appearance of the traveling nun suggests that medieval audiences recognized the *bikuni* as preachers, and that *bikuni* transmitted tales like those in *Shintōshū* to the countryside. The nun's presentation of the mirror as awakening the desire for rebirth and leading to realization of the truth of impermanence resonates with ideas of the Kami as approachable objects of devotion who lead the faithful to more profound teachings and spiritual growth.

Yet there is no suggestion here of any antagonism between Shinto and Buddhism, or even that the two were conceptualized as separate traditions. Instead, the story illustrates the seamless organic unity of the two in the popular conception. The protagonist's Buddhist practice consists of *nenbutsu* recitation and contemplation of the mirror to deepen his sense of impermanence. Although he built a chapel and took the tonsure, by the end of the story the chapel has become a district tutelary shrine with the mirror as its object of worship. The protagonist and his wife have become blessing-bringing Kami. Thus the end result of Buddhist practice in this case was the appearance of Kami.

One important message of this story is the idea that ordinary people can become Kami through self-cultivation in virtue. The protagonist's honesty, which made him such easy prey for a crooked shopkeeper, links him and the mirror (symbol of honesty in this period) as figures of incalculable worth. The story attributes ultimate value to common people and suggests that their capacity for self-transformation through religious practice is unlimited. The story does not explore this idea in any detail, and the question of how or why the wife also became a Kami is not addressed. We note, however, that the old man suffered as part of his transformation. He cried as he looked into the mirror that he had enshrined. Was he crying at the loss he thought he had sustained in not being able to possess every wonderful thing the mirror showed him while he was touring Kyoto? Did he cry at the pathos of life, to which the *bikuni* had awakened him? The story does not give an explicit answer, but it is clear that he suffered on the way to his transformation to a Kami. The idea that ordinary people can become Kami was not widely taken up until the early modern period, most importantly among the new religious movements of the nineteenth century. It is clear, however, that medieval stories of becoming Kami constitute an important basis for the further development of the idea later on.

Shrine Priests and Power Politics in a Medieval Diary

A procession to the capital of shrine personnel bearing their sacred emblems and portable palanquins to protest something offensive to them was a common occurrence of medieval power politics. The *jinin* were active in these protests, but they were not alone. The specific composition of such protest demonstrations varied at different locations and could include monks and caretakers of estates dedicated to shrines and temples (*shuto*).

As the account below attests, the symbols of Kami paraded in these protests evoked awe in medieval Japan, even among the noble and powerful. The Kami could be evoked by a procession carrying a shrine palanquin or a large potted *sakaki* tree. These objects evoked fear and expressions of reverence because they were believed to embody the Kami. The provocations for marching into Kyoto bearing Kami symbols varied widely. In 1235, a man attached to Enryakuji had killed a *jinin* of Hie Shrine and had been exiled for his crime. Not satisfied with this punishment, the Hie *jinin* took the shrine's *mikoshi* into the capital to protest that the culprit should have been executed, but to no avail.[60] In 1283, Enryakuji monks carrying the *mikoshi* of the Hie Shrine, Gion Shrine, and other shrines, broke into the palace to press their demands.[61] In 1294, Tōdaiji followers bearing the *mikoshi* of the Tamuke Hachiman Shrine attached to the temple came to press their demands on the court. They remained in the capital for a year, returning home only when the court granted the temple a new estate.[62] Incidents like this continued throughout the period. It is evident that religious institutions relied on the court's fear of divine retribution in these displays of Kami symbols, and clear also that religious institutions were not afraid to brandish their sacred symbols to push their demands.

"The Sakaki Leaf Diary" (1366) by Nijō Yoshimoto (1320–1388) provides a detailed portrayal of the scale of the demonstrations mounted by shrines. In fact, this work is not a diary but an account of a dispute between the Kasuga Shrine and Kōfukuji, on the one hand, and a warlord named Shiba no Takatsune (1306–1367), on the other. Takatsune, a constable, had usurped the income of one of the fiefs belonging to Kasuga/Kōfukuji over a period of some years, making it impossible to perform important rituals. Shrine attendants took the sacred *sakaki* tree in procession to Takatsune's residence to protest against his unlawful appropriations, subsequently conducting the tree to its regular station while in Kyoto, the Rokujō Palace. To their great satisfaction, Takatsune's house burned to the ground as a result of the Daimyōjin's displeasure:

> They say the mind of the Gods is very like our own. The Kasuga God does not send instant chastisement, but surely there has never been a time when those who offend the Divine Will have not come in the end to grief.[63]

When Takatsune eventually relented and restored the income of the fief, it was decided to return the sacred tree to the shrine. The procession that conveyed it was a magnificent spectacle for the Kyoto townspeople, as well as a warning of the forces that the shrine could command: "In two or three days, some ten or twenty thousand *shuto* and shrine servants came up to the Capital. They filled all the roads." After numerous preparations, the procession set off. First came "several scores" of pages dressed in red and carrying white staffs. Then followed several hundred servants carrying *sakaki* branches. Next came the symbol of Isonokami Shrine, also associated with the Fujiwara ancestors. It was attended by several hundred shrine-servants in yellow robes. As it passed, "the Regent and all his gentlemen stepped down from their seats and knelt." Then came the *sakaki* and the mirrors of the five sanctuaries, borne by priests with their faces covered, and intoning eerie warning cries. At this, "the Regent and his nobles, and the monks themselves, all touched their foreheads to the ground and prostrated themselves full-length." The *sakaki* was followed by several hundred more shrine servants and musicians playing continuously. The procession continued with Ministers, Counselors, and other high officials, followed by high-ranking courtiers and senior monks. They were followed by "ten or twenty thousand *shuto*, blowing conches."

> At the hour of the Monkey (roughly, 3:00 to 5:00 pm), the sky cleared, and the late afternoon sun on the Sakaki displayed the mirrors just as they must have looked long ago, on Kagu-yama. The sight was unspeakably awe-inspiring, and the warning shouts of the shrine servants, too, filled one with eerie intimations. I have seen the gleaming [*mikoshi*] at Festival time, but now the intensely green, spreading Sakaki branches seemed the Mikasa Grove itself. The sight inspired holy dread, till all one's hair stood on end. The least serving girl wept to hear the music, which never paused as the cortege moved on.[64]

Conclusion

In this chapter we have examined medieval architectural, artistic, and literary expressions of ideas of the Kami. The changes in medieval shrine and temple architecture accommodated a broadening pantheon incorporating a widened spectrum of divinities. The creation of new spaces for interacting with these deities reflects the ongoing esotericization of Shinto that was characteristic of the period. The new spaces were intended to provide sites for rituals addressed to beings in a different class from those enshrined on the main altar. Some of the deities were regarded as "foreign" in origin, while others might be regarded as "indigenous" but requiring special treatment to make them approachable. They did not fit easily into the *honji-suijaku* paradigm, and in some cases the rites performed in the rear or underground chambers seem motivated by the intention to transform them so that they would conform to the paradigm better, so that they would somehow fit within a framework of salvation as conceived by Buddhism. Another implication was that the divinity would be "domesticated," both in the sense of being affirmed as having a rightful place within Japan, and also as affirming the preeminent importance of Buddhism. The creation of *kagura* performances beyond the shrines initiated a process of popularization of this dance-drama form. As representatives from Ise and other great shrines and temples began to perform *kagura* outside the context of formal ceremonies, their traditions spread to a wider clientele, both socially and geographically. As local forms of *kagura* developed, they incorporated local legends. They enacted stories of many wild and unruly gods and local heroes, both illustrating and promoting a broadened pantheon.

Shrine mandalas generally adopted the *honji-suijaku* framework, but their visual impact was achieved in large part by their depiction of shrine sanctuaries and the surrounding landscape as an earthly paradise. This is a visual affirmation of Japan as a space of salvation, in which all elements necessary for religious practice are fully present, and in which the Kami are powerful, active agents. Illustrated scrolls likewise portray the Kami as powerful guardians. *Kasuga Gongen Genki-emaki*'s presentation of the story of Myōe depicts Japan as protected by the Kami, under whose stewardship Japan is a moral realm in which the Kami will reveal themselves to sincere devotees and grant them protection.

Medieval *setsuwa* and *engi* literature include a vast array of tales about the Kami. Some, such as *Collection of Sand and Pebbles*, praise the Kami for making Japan a "land of the Gods," even as they propound images of the Kami as stymied in a confrontation with Māra. "The Mirror Shrine" tale from *Shintōshū* upholds the value of ordinary people and asserts that their sincere devotion to religious practice can even result in their transformation to Kami. This affirmation of the worth of ordinary people is also an affirmation of the Kami as representatives of an indigenous tradition that has no need of anything beyond itself. The depiction of awe and reverence in response to a procession of symbols of the Kami seen in "The Sakaki Leaf Diary" vividly portrays medieval responses to the Kami. In the next chapter we will see a new style of promotion of Shinto as Japan's indigenous tradition and of the Kami as the highest divinities.

7

The Late Medieval Period

Introduction

Although its headship had largely become a hereditary occupation monopolized by the Shirakawa House, the work of the Jingikan continued. At court and among the aristocracy, the Jingikan was greatly overshadowed by many kinds of ceremonial in which it had no role, but it remained a part of government, however tenuously. A basis still existed for reviving its claims to be an essential element of governance. A Hall of the Eight Deities (*hasshinden*) protecting the imperial house, where Jingikan officials performed rites for the protection of the emperor, had been built at the Jingikan in 1281.[1] Protection of the person of the emperor was equivalent to protection of the realm, as we saw in our discussion of analogous Buddhist ritual. In the late medieval period, maintaining the Hall of the Eight Deities was the Jingikan's main function.

The Ōnin War (1467–1477) ushered in a period of protracted warfare and disunity, the Period of Warring States (1467–1573). We can regard the years from the Ōnin War through the period of wars that ensued as the late medieval period. Much of the Ōnin War was fought in Kyoto, leaving the city destroyed. Emperor Go-Tsuchimikado fled to the shogun's residence in 1467, but he could only stay there around three months before fire forced him to flee to another temporary abode. The palace survived, but the times were too precarious to live there. It was not only the imperial family who suffered. Many high-ranking courtiers also saw their homes reduced to ashes, some as many as four times.

After the war, the Ashikaga shogunate was essentially taken over by the Hosokawa family, a situation that lasted until 1558. The demise of the Hosokawa touched off a power struggle that continued until the bloody struggles among three "unifiers" Oda Nobunaga (1534–1582), Toyotomi Hideyoshi (1537–1598), and Tokugawa Ieyasu (1542–1616) finally ended, and Ieyasu managed to unite the country again, inaugurating the Tokugawa shogunate in 1600.

The Ōnin War created chaos in Kyoto, at court, and in society as a whole. The niceties of ceremonial could hardly have been a high priority for the court at the time, but when peace returned, Jingikan officials called for the rebuilding of the organization. Moreover, a powerful Shinto figure within the Jingikan created a career outside it, carving out a novel role for himself and his family at court and in relation to provincial shrines. Yoshida Kanetomo upheld an ideal of Shinto as a "Way of *jingi*." He asserted that it is the Kami who are the cosmic, original beings (*honji*), while Buddhist figures are their phenomenal manifestations (*suijaku*). He claimed that Shinto—in its own right—as the country's "indigenous tradition" held public significance and should be supported from the public purse. Kanetomo set in place the elements for a new understanding of Shinto through his distinctive doctrines, the creation of a ceremonial space which he argued was a microcosm of the shrines of the realm and equivalent to the Jingikan, and a practice of issuing Kami ranks and priestly titles to shrines. Although these elements remained only loosely systematized in the late medieval period, they formed the basis for Kanetomo's promotion of himself and his lineage as the supreme leader of Shinto. Those ideas were incorporated into shogunal law in the seventeenth century.

Court Ceremonial during the Late Medieval Period

In late medieval Japan, the court consisted of about one hundred noble families, numbering around one thousand people. Before the Ōnin War, the imperial family had a "relatively robust income," from about two hundred estates. By the mid-sixteenth century, however, the court's income from these lands had declined as much as 90 percent. The imperial family lost control of their land when they became unable to manage it and oversee the process by which its produce was collected as tax and turned into cash.[2] The court nevertheless retained a valuable asset deriving from its relations with temples and shrines: it controlled the highest temple and shrine appointments. This meant that religious institutions seeking a raise in rank or title were required to present the court with lavish emoluments. Such gifts were required for both the initial approach and annually thereafter.[3]

Before the Ōnin War, the court had enjoyed a rich ceremonial life centering on a calendar of annual rites called *nenjū gyōji*. The annual observances had developed from the old Ritsuryō calendar of imperial ritual, and they still contained many of its highlights: the 1/1 Shihōhai, 2/4 Toshigoi (Kinensai), the Kamo Festival of the fourth month, the Niinamesai of the eleventh month, and Tsuina, an expulsion of demons at the end of the twelfth month. But after the Ōnin War, the annual ceremonies were cut back radically, and many ceremonies were "postponed," which sometimes turned out to be a euphemism for their abandonment. For example, Niinamesai was abandoned just before the Ōnin War and was not revived until the eighteenth century. Emperor Go-Tsuchimikado's funeral in 1500 had to be delayed for forty-four days for lack of funds, while his corpse remained in the palace. Emperor Go-Nara had to wait ten years for an enthronement ceremony in 1536. Since enthronement and related ceremonies cost between thirty and fifty times the court's annual income in this period, perhaps it is more remarkable that the ceremony ever *was* performed.[4]

In spite of the late medieval court's straitened circumstances, however, rites were sometimes *added* to its annual ceremonial calendar rather than subtracted, as in the case of the *tensō chifusai*, adapted from Chinese state rites. It was performed for shoguns as well as emperors, and was conducted consistently through the Edo period.[5] It is also notable that some imperial ritual began to be performed by the aristocracy and even commoners. Fujiwara Tadamichi (1097–1164) had noted in his twelfth-century diary that the aristocracy was performing the Rite of the Four Directions (*shihōhai*) along the lines favored among commoner society. In 1480, we find the courtier Nakamikado Nobutane (1442–1525) writing in his diary of his own elaborate performance of this rite on the first day of the New Year.[6]

We have seen that the imperial regalia were a focus of significant attention during the medieval period, but palace fires in 960, 1005, and 1040 had threatened them. The frequency of palace fires increased as rites came to be performed mainly at night from the late tenth century.[7] Miracle tales about the regalia came to be enacted in dance at the palace. Emperor Go-Toba had to be enthroned without the regalia in 1184, and as explained in chapter 5, the sword from the regalia had been lost in 1185. The Twenty-Two Shrines prayed for the recovery of the regalia, but to no avail. Perhaps it is no wonder that in the late medieval period, the court never legitimated itself by referring to the regalia.[8]

Ise in the Late Medieval Period

The Ise shrines suffered major damage in a typhoon of 1203, a huge fire destroying over fifty buildings in 1240, and another fire in 1262.[9] Ise had been a stronghold of support for the Southern Court, and its port city of Ōminato had seen many battles. After the reunification of the rival courts in 1392, Watarai Ieyuki was dismissed from his post, and Watarai theological writing ended. The transmission of Watarai initiations apparently also ended in the fourteenth century. The efforts of the Watarai to ally with the Southern Court had resulted in their alienation from the Ashikaga shogunate. Ashikaga Yoshimitsu (r. 1368–1394) underlined his military victories by staging grand displays of troops in areas formerly loyal to the Southern Court. Ostensibly as a pilgrimage to the Ise Shrines, Yoshimitsu paraded thousands of soldiers through Ise in 1393 and 1395, after which these exercises became almost annual events until 1441. These excursions helped popularize Ise pilgrimage among the warrior class.[10]

Because imperial proxies had long ceased conveying tribute from the court to provincial shrines, inevitably these shrines became dependent upon the peasantry living on their estates. That meant that the shrines increasingly had to adapt their practice to the religious needs and desires of local people. They had to offer commercialized ritual services even as they strove to retain the appearance of being above such "vulgarities" as healing rites and other ceremonies for "this-worldly-benefits." The shrines' ties to provincial rulers could be weakened by the appearance of pandering to the lowly. Overall, the loss of court support intensified the transformation of shrines from places performing rites to uphold the realm, to institutions embedded in the popular religious culture of the places where they were located. The "public" character of shrine rites was becoming thin and abstract, an ideal belonging to a past age rather than the pillar of contemporary practice. Not only at provincial shrines—even Ise was becoming increasingly dependent upon private patrons arriving as pilgrims.

The town of Uji had grown up around the Inner Shrine, while the town of Yamada had formed as the *monzen machi* of the Outer Shrine. Each was host to a growing pilgrimage business centering on inns, teahouses, and brothels. As in previous eras, pilgrims arrived at the Inner Shrine by roads that first passed the Outer Shrine. Inevitably, pilgrims spent most of their money at Yamada and the Outer Shrine, leaving less to spend at Uji and the Inner Shrine. The Inner Shrine complained repeatedly that the Outer Shrine deprived it of revenue.

Late Medieval Scholarship on *Nihon Shoki*

The production of commentaries on *Nihon shoki* was a major form of medieval Shinto scholarship, and one list of such works contains twenty-six medieval commentaries still extant, with many more composed in the early modern and modern periods.[11] Early medieval research on *Nihon shoki* was conducted by Buddhist priests, but in the late Muromachi period two new sources of scholarship on the text appeared: the Yoshida House and Ichijō Kanera (1402–1481), a great scholar who rose to become Minister of State. The Ichijō family had maintained connections with the Yoshida line since the Kamakura period and had studied the *Nihon shoki* with them, thereafter transmitting that text to others. Kanera composed a commentary on the section of *Nihon shoki* called "The Age of the Gods," the first portion of the work, devoted to mythological material preceding the appearance of historical emperors. Kanera's commentary, titled *Nihon shoki sanso* (ca. 1477), approached "The Age of the Gods" from the standpoint of a contemporary view, the "oneness of the three teachings" (*sankyō itchi*), to the effect that Buddhism, Confucianism, and Shinto are ultimately united.[12]

As we will see below, Yoshida Kanetomo conducted lectures on the *Nihon shoki* in the course of developing his own theories, and many extant documents record the content of his addresses. His descendants compiled commentaries on the text that influenced Edo-period Shinto thought. These works expressed a novel version of the "oneness of the three teachings," asserting that Shinto is the root, Confucianism the trunk, and Buddhism the fruits and flowers of a single tree. The intention was to promote the status of Shinto as the original source of the other two teachings, placing them in a dependent, derivative position.[13]

Yoshida Shinto

Yoshida Shinto refers to the doctrines, ritual practices, and the priestly organization established by the Yoshida lineage. As discussed in earlier chapters, this lineage, originally known as the Urabe, performed plastromancy and other kinds of divination in the ancient Jingikan. The lineage name was subsequently changed to Nakatomi and eventually to Yoshida. Yoshida Shinto is especially associated with Yoshida Kanetomo (1435–1511), who built on the family's heritage of ritual knowledge and scholarly interpretation of classical texts to create his own novel philosophical, ritual, and organizational system. Kanetomo's comprehensive doctrine encompassed the totality of Shinto, not merely the traditions of his own family and shrine. His writings, the distinctive ritual site and new rituals he created, and the organization he established for certifying shrine priests transcended and enveloped the teachings of other lineages. He conceived of Shinto not as a limited teaching comparable to Buddhism or Confucianism, but as a fundamental principle pervading the universe. Kanetomo consistently promoted his system of thought, ritual, and organization as an indigenous tradition essential to the rule of the realm and sought imperial and shogunal funds as proof of the public nature of his enterprise. On the basis of the groundwork Kanetomo laid, the Yoshida House exercised preeminent influence over the shrine priesthood, beginning in the late fifteenth century and enduring until the late nineteenth century, waning only with the ascendency of National Learning (Kokugaku). Yoshida Shinto marked a decisive departure from Shinto's former intellectual subordination to Buddhism, even as its doctrines and rituals showed marked Buddhist and Onmyōdō influence.

Because Kanetomo's theories, rituals, and organization were revolutionary in their day, the question arises how he acquired such authority in Shinto matters that his new creations could find broad acceptance. Kanetomo's authority depended in turn on a gradual elevation of his family during the Heian and Kamakura periods. In 859 the Urabe House was given supervision of a new shrine in the Yoshida district of Kyoto, the Yoshida Shrine, which was built by Fujiwara Yamakage (823–888). It enshrined the same deities as the Kasuga Shrine, and was intended to protect the capital and the Fujiwara lineage. It received court tribute as one of the Twenty-Two Shrines. As of 1001, the Urabe House was allocated the position of second-in-command at the Jingikan. In 1161, the Jingikan was changed so that its headship became hereditary within the Shirakawa family. The Shirakawa House's main responsibility in the Jingikan was to guard the palace sanctuary, the Kashikodokoro. They also performed "morning worship" (a daily obeisance to the Ise deities and the Kami of the four directions), in place of the emperor if he were ill or otherwise unavailable. The Yoshida, by contrast, had no role in palace ritual at this time, conspicuously marking their lower status relative to the Shirakawa.[14]

During the Kamakura period, the Urabe were granted the title Superior of Tortoise Shell Diviners (*Kiboku chōjō*), becoming experts in taboos and abstinences, so that courtiers consulted with them before important undertakings, to determine auspicious days and directions. To support their research into these matters, the family accumulated a huge library of classics and chronicles, called the Kaguraoka Library (*Kaguraoka bunko*). In 1375 the head of the Urabe family moved his residence near the Yoshida Shrine and took the surname "Yoshida," effectively dividing the House into two branches, the Yoshida and the Hirano. In 1383 Retired Emperor Go-Kameyama (r. 1383–1392) gave the Yoshida House the unique privilege of lecturing to emperors on *Nihon shoki*, in recognition of significant studies of the *Nihon shoki* and other classical texts by Yoshida scholars. In 1390, Shogun Ashikaga Yoshimitsu (r. 1368–1394) elevated Yoshida Kanehiro (1348–1402) to senior third rank, in recognition of his reputation as the *doyen* of *jingi* learning, marking the first time that the Yoshida ascended into the group of high courtiers.[15]

Meanwhile, however, as the Yoshida family's fortunes rose, the court's were falling. By the fifteenth century, court tribute to all shrines had ceased, though the Twenty-Two Shrines continued to be regarded as the most prestigious. [16]

Yoshida Kanetomo served as second-in-command at the Jingikan and also as the Head Priest of the Yoshida Shrine.[17] Kanetomo composed three "divine scriptures" that formed the basis for his esoteric teachings and rituals and built in his residence a ceremonial site, which he called Saijōsho. Unfortunately, in 1467 the residence burned to the ground, and during the following year the Yoshida Shrine burned as well. A lesser person might have been defeated by these setbacks, but Kanetomo began a period of tremendous creativity. The fact of the destruction of the Yoshida Shrine may actually have made it possible for Kanetomo to create something entirely new in place of the ruins.[18]

As he developed new theories of Shinto and the Kami, Kanetomo also collected information about local shrines around Kyoto at the request of the shogun Ashikaga Yoshimasa (r. 1449–1473), compiling records of the deities worshipped in each one, distinctive rites, and the name of the priest, if any.[19] Through this work, Kanetomo cultivated relations with the shogunate and powerful warrior families, as well as with priests of many shrines of no particular distinction. These latter connections became the basis for the priestly organization he founded. Kanetomo conducted prayers for Yoshimasa, and in 1470 Yoshimasa conferred public recognition on Kanetomo's Saijōsho, referring to it as if it were the Jingikan. On the basis of shogunal recognition of its contribution to the governance of the realm, Kanetomo petitioned for public funds for the Saijōsho.[20]

Since around 1470, Kanetomo had been issuing Daimyōjin certificates to shrines and persons wishing to promote their Kami in rank. Daimyōjin was the highest rank in that system. In 1469, Kanetomo issued a Daimyōjin certificate for a powerful Ashikaga vassal, Ōuchi Masahiro (1446–1495), whose father had been deified. This document certified that the deified man had been raised to the highest possible rank among the Kami. Kanetomo's issuance of the Daimyōjin certificate was a brash move that could be seen as usurping an imperial function.[21]

The original rationale for the court issuing such titles lay in a three-step process: (1) the emperor receives a communication of the will of the Kami about some matter; (2) the emperor issues a proclamation to that effect, addressed to the personnel of that Kami's shrine; (3) the shrine in question treats the proclamation as authorization to act accordingly. In the Yoshida case, however, they simply circumvented the step of imperial mediation and claimed instead that they had received a direct indication of the Kami's will themselves. This put the Yoshida house in the position of intermediary to the court, which in theory was the only agency with the authority to raise the rank of a Kami.[22]

Kanetomo also issued certificates raising the rank of a Kami in a way that differed from court practice. The court had previously raised ranks one step at a time, on the occasion of an imperial enthronement, or in thanks for shrines' prayers for some national project. Generally the ranks were bestowed on all shrines or a group of shrines. For example, as we saw in chapter 5, the court raised the ranks of all Kami by one step in 1275, in recognition of their role in warding off the first Mongol invasion through their "divine wind."

Kanetomo's practice differed from this in that he issued ranks in response to an individual's or a shrine's request. The request would be conveyed with lavish remuneration, so issuing certificates became a highly significant source of income. In the period of Northern and Southern courts, apparently there were so many such requests to the court, that it was actually relieved to be able to hand these over to the Yoshida, who were posing as specialists in such matters. The Shirakawa House had little involvement in the granting of shrine ranks at this time.[23]

As of 1470, Kanetomo established a mechanism allowing him to transmit secret lineage teachings and began conducting esoteric transmissions to selected courtiers, warriors, and Buddhist monks.[24] Kanetomo's opening of lineage secrets to outsiders was a significant departure from the usual practice of sacerdotal lineages. While the Watarai had occasionally made exceptions to the otherwise ironclad rule of restricing the lineage's esoteric teachings to its own members, Kanetomo began Kami Initiations as an adjunct to soliciting patronage and official recognition. Kanetomo's frequent transmissions of esoteric knowledge also indicate a change in the nature of shrines' participation in power politics. Unlike the practice of the early medieval period, Kanetomo could not muster a large number of *jinin* to press his claims, nor would it have been in his interests to oppose the court or warriors. He did not have extensive fiefs from which to recruit an army in any case. Instead, he cultivated relations with the court and warriors on all sides of any issue in order to protect and advance his interests.

After Kanetomo's request for public funds for the Saijōsho from Emperor Go-Tsuchimikado (r. 1464–1500) in 1470,[25] in 1473, the emperor issued an imperial proclamation (*rinshi*) granting funding for the renewal of the Saijōsho, in which he referred to it as "[t]he most exalted ceremonial hall for the worship of the Kami of heaven and earth in all Japan" (*Nihon saijō jingi saijō*) and "The Number-One Spiritual Place in the Land of the Gods" (*shinkoku dai-ichi no reijō*). The text of the proclamation described the Saijōsho as continuing Jinmu's achievements, as well as those of Amenokoyane and Amaterasu. It addressed Kanetomo as "The Superior of Jingi" (*jingi chōjō*). This indicates full public, national approval and recognition of the Saijōsho, and of Kanetomo's claim to be descended from Amenokoyane. This recognition greatly raised the respect of the aristocracy and the warriors for the Yoshida and the new ceremonial site Saijōsho. For example, in both 1478 and 1484, Hino Tomiko (1440–1496), wife of Ashikaga Yoshimasa, donated a huge sum for the Saijōsho. Imperial approval silenced anyone who might have criticized Kanetomo.[26]

Allotting public funding for Kanetomo's Saijōsho represented a major change in terms of the public character of shrines. It meant that for the first time, public funds were used to support a novel ritual site created by a living person. With imperial authorization secured, Kanetomo began to proclaim that the Saijōsho was the origin and foundation of all shrines in the nation.

From 1476 to 1480, Kanetomo frequently lectured at court on *Nihon shoki* and the Great Purification Prayer. While court lectures on *Nihon shoki* reinvigorated an ancient court practice, Kanetomo was apparently the first to lecture on the Great Purification Prayer. He was highly respected for his scholarship, though it goes without saying that Kanetomo's interpretations privileged his own lineage. He also performed rites at court in response to imperial requests. As of 1476, Kanetomo began to refer to himself publicly as the Superior of Shinto (Shintō chōjō), based on Emperor Go-Tsuchimikado's imprimatur. Unlike other shrine priests, he was both a theologian and a ritualist; he performed rites not simply to perpetuate past tradition but also to convey a novel religious message. While courtiers who heard his theories wrote that they were shocked at his idea that the Kami and Shinto are more ancient and fundamental than Buddhism and Confucianism, Kanetomo's views were highly influential. Kanetomo was already a revered teacher in the eyes of the court, the shogunate, and among courtiers. He was said to be a good speaker and an educated, cultivated person. Some courtiers, like Nakamikado Nobutane, were moved to receive Kami Initiations from Kanetomo. In a time when the court was in such distress and decline, Kanetomo seemed to offer a return to the court's past culture of elegance, so courtiers were well disposed toward him. Far from provoking serious opposition, Kanetomo gained a higher position, and the court began to patronize the rituals he offered.[27]

Kanetomo's position as second-in-command at the Jingikan was essential to his success. It was usual for the Head (the Jingihaku) to hand over the actual running of the organization to his immediate subordinate. At least one close relative of the Shirakawa family, Shirakawa Tadatomi, became Kanetomo's disciple. This is perhaps not too surprising, because Kanetomo allied with the Shirakawa in order to revive the Jingikan, allowing him to neutralize that potential source of opposition to his distinctive doctrines. To control the Jingikan's diurnal operations meant that Kanetomo held the actual power in the Jingikan, enabling him to widen his scope and to intervene deeply in court affairs, including commenting on the correct manner of conducting rites in the palace sanctuary, the Kashikodokoro. Holding an authoritative position in imperial rites enabled Kanetomo to recommend ritual protocols in his own distinctive style. Personal access to the throne was key to achieving an unassailable position.[28]

From 1484 to 1486, Kanetomo composed his major texts, *The Essentials of the Name and Law of the One and Only Shinto* (*Yuiitsu Shintō myōbō yōshū*) and *An Outline of Shinto* (*Shintō taii*). He composed the signature prayer that came to be recited by his disciples, *Purification of the Six Roots* (*Rokkon shōjō ōharai*), and created esoteric rites to initiate his affiliates into the esoteric teachings.[29] Perhaps most importantly, he reconstructed the Saijōsho on the top of Kagura Hill, to the northeast of the palace.

Kanetomo wrote in *Essentials* that Shinto contains the heart-mind of all beings, as well as animating all beings. Ultimately, it is the foundation of Heaven, Earth, and humanity:

> [T]here is nothing in the material world, nor in the worlds of life, of animate and inanimate beings, of beings with energy and without energy, that does not partake of this Shinto.
>
> Hence the verse:
>
> *Shin* is the heart-mind of all beings
> *Tō* is the source of all activities.
>
> All animate and inanimate beings of the triple world are ultimately nothing but Shinto only.[30]

This understanding of Shinto necessitated a corresponding change in the concept of Kami, which in Kanetomo's exposition became an animating force with a moral center based in the heart-mind.

Kanetomo called his doctrines "The One-and-Only Shinto" (Yuiitsu Shintō) and also "Shinto of the Original Foundation" (Genpon Sōgen Shintō). The characterization of his system as "one-and-only" did not exclude the other varieties of Shinto thought but instead recognized them as lower forms, subordinating them to Kanetomo's formulations. The "original foundation" constituted Kanetomo's assertion that Shinto is the "founding principle of the universe." Kanetomo regarded Shinto as universal, existing since the cosmogony. He compared Shinto to the roots of a tree, the source of all other teachings, which are like the trunk and branches. In like manner, he saw Japan as the primal nation, ruled over by a sacred emperor, and India and China as lesser countries.

Kanetomo claimed that his theories had been transmitted from Kunitokotachi, a creator deity appearing at the beginning of *Nihon shoki*, to Amenokoyane, the ancestral deity of the Yoshida House. Thereafter, Kanetomo claimed, a secret teaching had been faithfully transmitted to each generation of his family through the ages, in "an unbroken line of divination since the creation, an unbroken lineage since the age of the Kami, a lineage that has served the emperors without even a single gap of generation."[31]

In fact, however, Kanetomo had rewritten the lineage's genealogy to make it appear that the line originated with Amenokoyane. His textual evidence for this claim was so thin that some contemporaries and subsequent scholars regarded the new genealogy as an egregious falsification. Consider how Kanetomo promoted the deity Amenokoyane, purportedly the Yoshida lineage's divine ancestor. Kanetomo deleted a portion of the *Nihon shoki* text in order to prove that Amenokoyane was given authority over all divine matters:

The *Nihon shoki* text:

> Ame no koyane no mikoto had charge of the foundation of divine matters; therefore he was made to divine by means of the Greater Divination and thus to do his service.

Kanetomo's rendering:

> Ame no koyane no mikoto had charge of the foundation of divine matters.[32]

The original *Nihon shoki* text introduces Amenokoyane as supervisor of the minor task of divination, while Kanetomo presents him as overseer of all sacred affairs, thus inflating the importance of his ancestral deity.

Although *The Essentials of the Name and Law of the One and Only Shinto* bears a date of 1024, in fact it was written by Kanetomo and completed around 1484. He began by dividing Shinto into "light," or exoteric, and "dark," or esoteric, varieties. He also presented a separate tripartite division. The first division consisted of the secret transmissions of particular lineages at individual shrines. The second division was derived from associations between Kami and Buddhist divinities of the Diamond and Womb Mandalas, that is, various theories based on *honji-suijaku*. The third and highest was his own system, "Original and Fundamental Shinto" (*genpon sōgen Shintō*). Kanetomo's explication of this term proceeds from an etymological interpretation of the characters used to write "original" (*gen* and *pon*, or *hon*) and "fundamental" (*sō* and *gen*), summarizing each compound in verse, as follows:

> The term *gen* designates the origin of origins predating the appearance of Yin and Yang. The term *hon* designates the state predating the appearance of thought processes. Hence the following verse:
>
> Taking the Origin as Such, one penetrates the origin of origins;
> Taking the Original State as such, one sees the heart-mind.
>
> The term *sō* designates the original spirit predating the diversification of energy. All phenomena return to that single origin. The term *gen* designates the divine function referred to as "mingling with the dust and softening one's radiance." This provides the basis of benefit for all living beings. Hence the following verse:
>
> *Sō* indicates that all phenomena return to the One;
> *Gen* reveals the source of all bonds between living beings.[33]

The goal in this section is to establish that Shinto preached by the Yoshida was present already at the time of creation, as was the heart-mind. Shinto is both ancient and foundational; everything else springs from it and is bound to it. Thus, Shinto pervades the universe as a whole.

Kanetomo addressed a number of topics that would have been familiar to an educated audience, including the term *Shintō*, the imperial regalia, *honji-suijaku* thought, and the idea of Japan as a divine realm. Kanetomo identified three classical texts as the basis for his theory: *Kojiki*, *Nihon shoki*, and *Sendai kuji hongi*. In addition, he referred to Three Divine Scriptures, the three short works that he claimed had been revealed to Amenokoyane, but which in fact he had written himself between 1466 and 1470.[34]

Kanetomo addressed the concept of *shinkoku* in the following passage:

> This country is a Sacred Land (*shinkoku*). Its way is the Kami Way (*shintō*). The ruler of this country is the Sacred Emperor (*jinnō*). The Great Ancestor is Amaterasu Ō-kami. The awesome light of this one Kami pervades billions of worlds, and its will shall forever be transmitted along an imperial way laden with ten thousand chariots. Just as there are not two suns in heaven, there are not two rulers in a country.[35]

Kanetomo addressed contemporary anxieties about the imperial regalia, recognizing that the account of ten separate treasures in the *Sendai kuji hongi* contradicted that found in *Nihon shoki*, which enumerated only three. He spoke of the difference between the texts as relative rather than absolute and wrote that ultimately the ten are contained in the three, and that both together ultimately allow the emperor to govern.

> The ten kinds represent perfection, correspondence, completion,
> All contained within the three kinds, the ten and the three,
> Ultimately, a repository of divine presence, unsurpassable spiritual treasures.[36]

Kanetomo emphasized Shinto's connections to imperial rule. He wrote that it is "the main duty of a practitioner of Yuiitsu-Shinto to elucidate the foundation of the sacred character of this nation."[37]

Kanetomo adopted the *honji-suijaku* framework linking Kami and Buddhas but proclaimed that it is the Kami who are the primary and original deities, and the Buddhist divinities who are provisional and derivative. In answer to the question of whether the identification of a *honji* Buddha for each Kami is not a contradiction of the idea that Shinto is the origin while Buddhism is a later accretion, Kanetomo wrote:

> [W]hat one must understand as the real exoteric teaching is that buddhas and bodhisattvas are the Essence of the Kami, while the real esoteric teaching reveals that the Kami are the Essence of the buddhas and bodhisattvas. The Exoteric Teaching is shallow and simple; the Esoteric Teaching is most profound and secret. Consequently, to consider the buddhas and bodhisattvas as Essence is a shallow and simplistic view.[38]

In other words, Shinto represents an esoteric teaching, whereas Buddhism is a simple, accessible exoteric teaching. Here Kanetomo reversed the valences of the *honji-suijaku* framework and elevated the Kami above the Buddhas as the most fundamental existence, a position that later came to be called "reverse *honji-suijaku*."

The idea of the Kami as primary, and the Buddhist divinities as secondary was not completely new with Kanetomo. This idea was found in the writings of Jihen (dates unknown; active in the Kamakura and Nanbokuchō periods), who was born within the Yoshida family but became a Tendai monk. He wrote a number of influential works on Shinto topics that combined the perspectives of Sannō Ichijitsu Shinto and Watarai Shinto. Jihen had made a pilgrimage to Ise and developed a friendship with Watarai Tsuneyoshi. His 1332 work *Kuji hongi gengi* reversed the prevailing concept of Japan's relation to China and India, calling Japan the root, while the other two derived from Japan. He also proposed that Buddhist divinities derive from the Kami, rather than the reverse.[39]

An Outline of Shinto was composed in 1484 for shogun Ashikaga Yoshimasa. The *Outline* developed the idea that the "radiance of the Kami" (*shinmei*) dwells within the heart-mind, and that the heart-mind is the essence of Kami. Kanetomo wrote of Kami as preceding the appearance of Yin and Yang, as did Shinto as a whole. He treated Kami as a principle of existence, dwelling within each person in the heart-mind. The human senses, emotions, and the physical body have distinct Kami that oversee each organ and each of the senses, but Kami is more than these individual beings. Kami is both formless spirit, or soul, and it also may have form. Kami animates all existence. It is the spirit of all things and of human morality.

Kanetomo's system posited that Kami is a stable principle of continuity from the beginning of time to the present. Moreover, humanity shares the essence of Kami through the heart-mind. Therefore, Kami and humanity are ultimately one and united. The task for humanity is to realize that unity and live in accord with it. This was not, however, a teaching directed to the masses but only to an elite who would undergo the esoteric ritual transmissions at the Saijōsho necessary to give them full understanding.

Kanetomo's renewed Saijōsho comprised three main elements: the rebuilt Yoshida Shrine, where the Kasuga deities were enshrined; the supreme sanctuary Taigenkyū, an octagonal building occupying the center of the site; and the Sōgen Hall (Sōgenden), which housed three altars for the three main esoteric rites of Yoshida Shinto. The three main rites were the Eighteenfold Shinto transmission [an initiate's first major Kami Initiation], the Sōgen ritual [the initiate's second major transmission], and the Great Shinto Goma Ritual [the third major Kami Initiation]. Together these three constituted the Three Altars Rite (*sandan gyōji*). Near the Yoshida Shrine were three temples where Yoshida House personnel served as abbots: Shinryū'in, Shinon'in, and Shinkōji. Some Yoshida men like Bonshun took the tonsure to manage these temples, while continuing to promote Yoshida Shinto.[40]

The Taigenkyū could be entered by three staircases. The roof beams protruded with *chigi*, and the ridge beam was held in place by *katsuogi*. In the middle of the beam was a Wish Fulfillment Jewel. Except for its thatched roof, the Taigenkyū looked much like the octagonal buildings constructed within temples. The wood was painted red. The structure of the interior was to be kept secret, but it appears that there was a tubular pillar connecting the roof to an underground chamber where there was an earthen altar and a chamber for secret rites. The tube conducted rainwater from the sky into the ground, symbolically connecting Heaven and Earth. Attached to the middle of the pillar formed by the hollow tube was an octagonal structure, on which a round mirror was attached.[41]

The Taigenkyū was surrounded by smaller shrine buildings on left and right, each with separate enclosed altars under a single roof that were for the worship of all the Kami of Japan. Behind these were small shrine buildings representing the Outer and Inner shrines at Ise. There were also eight small sanctuaries representing the Hall of the Eight Deities. These facilities could be entered by one of two gates. When emissaries were dispatched to Ise, the ritual of sending them off would be performed before these sanctuaries.[42] Emperor Go-Tsuchimikado reportedly provided six portal inscriptions for the new site.[43] Near the Taigenkyū, Kanetomo built two platforms named after the *yuki*- and *suki*- fields appearing in imperial enthronement rites.[44]

The deity enshrined in the Taigenkyū was the Kami of Ultimate Origin (Daigen sonjin 大元尊神), the fundamental god of the universe. The Taigenkyū was supposed to encompass all the Kami and shrines of Japan. Accordingly, the Saijōsho made up the Ultimate Ritual Site. The Kami of Ultimate Origin might manifest as any of the Kami of Japan, but all of them were encompassed by the Kami of Ultimate Origin.

Ten Sacred Jewels enshrined in the Taigenkyū symbolized the imperial regalia as described in *Sendai kuji hongi*.[45] The shape of the Taigenkyū mirrored the octagonal seat used in imperial enthronement rites, and the term "cult site" (*saijō*) appropriated the same word used in enthronement ritual. A fourth element of imperial symbolism was the placement within the Saijōsho of its own Hall of the Eight Deities.[46]

Kanetomo's Claim That the Ise Kami Fled to the Saijōsho

Ongoing warfare at Ise provided Kanetomo an opportunity to consolidate his system further. Destruction was escalating, and there was a rumor that the Outer Shrine's objects of worship (*shintai*) had been lost. Competition between the two shrines erupted in a cycle of attacks and revenge assaults, beginning when the Outer Shrine blockaded the road to the Inner Shrine in 1449, continuing sporadically until 1486. In 1486 the towns' battles ended with the leader of the Outer Shrine forces setting it ablaze and committing suicide inside. In 1489 the Outer Shrine forces burned Uji, saving the Inner Shrine but killing all those who had taken refuge there. Then in revenge Uji sacked Yamada, leaving corpses strewn around the sanctuary of the Outer Shrine. In the sixth month of 1489, lightning and fire totally destroyed the building housing the treasures of the Outer Shrine.

Seen theologically, it would have been obvious to all that the Kami would be outraged by slaughter inside the sacred precincts, and logical in the medieval worldview to expect negative repercussions for the court. In the evening on the twenty-fifth day of the third month, 1489, Kanetomo wrote, eightfold dark clouds appeared over the Taigenkyū, with rain, wind, and thunder. Two terrifying lights appeared in the sky. Kanetomo saw a divine entity (*reibutsu*) on the ground between the Taigenkyū and the Hall of the Eight Deities. He picked it up and placed it on the altar. Then on the fourth day of the tenth month, he found a bright, round shape, which had come down out of the sky, and then precious objects manifested as before. He enshrined them all in the Taigenkyū.

On the nineteenth day of the eleventh month, Kanetomo delivered a "personal report" (*missō*) to Emperor Go-Tsuchimikado, claiming that the Ise deities and the shrines' treasures had flown to the Saijōsho.[47] In the twelfth month the emperor issued a proclamation ratifying Kanetomo's claim.[48] There were a few courtiers who protested against Kanetomo's assertion, but the Shirakawa did not.

Once an imperial proclamation had been issued, it was not possible to protest publicly.[49]

Kanetomo's account sounds preposterous to the modern reader, and the emperor's credulity seems equally absurd. Yet Kanetomo convinced the emperor and many others. How was this possible? It was believed that the Kami could move at will and come to rest at a location of their choosing.[50] We recall from chapter 5 that Emperor Juntoku had proclaimed in the thirteenth century that the mirror in the palace had flown to heaven to escape a palace fire. Given that this was accepted knowledge, anyone who knew of the desecration of the Ise Shrines could readily accept that the Kami might flee Ise. Second, Kanetomo must have cultivated relations with the court and his superior at the Jingikan, and perhaps even with some of the priests at Ise, to head off devastating protest.[51] To say that the deities had fled the sacrilege occurring in their shrines mirrored Go-Tsuchimikado's own flight in 1467 from the palace in the midst of the chaos in Kyoto, perhaps enhancing his openness to Kanetomo's claim. One could also ask, given the prevailing concepts of Kami, whether it was possible to believe that the Ise deities would have remained in the shrines as the sanctuaries burned, and killings were taking place in their presence. If we answer in the negative, then it made sense for someone in authority to assert that the Kami would move away from such a situation and find another place to dwell.

Kanetomo's Ritual System

Medieval Shinto writings were concerned with systematizing ritual by protecting and perpetuating ancient rites, while continually interpreting them in new ways. Kanetomo departed from this trend by portraying the new rituals he created as having ancient pedigrees and promoting them through his writings. One distinguished scholar of medieval Shinto, Ōsumi Kazuo, sees Kanetomo's thought as primarily structured by the rites he created, rather than the reverse.[52] In Ōsumi's view, *The Essentials of the Name and Law of the One and Only Shinto* can be read as a guide to Kanetomo's ritual system. Kanetomo's thought unfolded within and was structured by the Buddhist episteme discussed in the previous chapter. Yet while he imbibed many of its ritual forms such as "consecration rites" (*goma*) and "empowerment rites" (*kaji*), he invoked only Kami, never Buddhist figures, thus creating Shinto Initiations that did not rely on the power of Buddhist divinities. This was a dramatic, bold departure from the status quo.

Kanetomo imparted his teachings to initiates through three main rites of initiation (*sandan gyōji*). The first, the Eighteenfold Shinto, consisted of elaborate invocations of Kami and "empowerment" rites (*kaji*), using mudras, spells, and choreographed movement around an altar. Its triadic structure of Heaven, Earth, and Humanity, derived from Daoism.[53] This same structure was also adopted in the

Kami Initiations of the Ōmiwa Shrine lineage, discussed in chapter 5. Kanetomo explains in *Essentials* that Heaven, Earth, and Humanity are each endowed with a distinctive Shinto: Heaven is endowed with "a Shinto of perfect fundamental energy"; Earth is endowed with "a Shinto of perfect correspondence [to the energy of Heaven]"; and Humanity is endowed with "a Shinto of completion of life."[54] Each has five active aspects, considered in terms of the five elements, and each is linked to five Kami.[55] Numerically, the distinctive Shinto of Heaven, Earth, and Humanity equals three; adding the five aspects of each (fifteen in total) equals eighteen, and hence the name Eighteenfold Shinto. Those Kami connected to Heaven are the ancestors of the heavenly bodies, while those connected to Earth are the ancestors of the Earth spirits. Those connected to Humanity are the ancestors of those spirits that follow a person's "coarse spirit" (*aramitama*). The heart-mind transforms those spirits into all phenomena, thus proving that, "Outside the heart-mind there are no phenomena; all phenomena are issued from the heart-mind."[56] Among the benefits Kanetomo claimed for the Eighteenfold Shinto rite were longevity, good health, and spiritual and material well-being.[57]

The altar utilized in the Eighteenfold Shinto rite was a rectangular platform decorated with blue and white streamers and with a small *torii*, a gateway to the initiation, set directly in front of the initiate. The initiate sat on a round seat facing the *torii*. Drawn on the platform inside the *torii* was a four-pointed star-shaped form, with the point facing away from the ritualist elongated roughly one-third longer than the other three points. Inside the star were ritual tools, such as a stalk of bells. On either side of the ritualist's seat were small tables set with a bell and striker, a vessel of water, offering rice, and written directions for performing the rite. The rite consisted of eighteen separate stages; some of these were relatively simple steps like striking a bell or reciting a prayer. Others, however, were complex empowerment rites (*kaji*) calling for recitation of many Kami names and magical formulae. Existing texts remain silent on the ultimate purpose of the rite, but the central place given to empowerments suggests that the initiate was to absorb the powers of the Kami and align his heart-mind with theirs.[58]

The second main transmission was the Sōgen Shintō Rite (*sōgen Shintō gyōji*). While the Eighteenfold Shinto rite had focused on the active elements of the three foundations (Heaven, Earth, and Humanity), the Sōgen Shintō rite focused on their complementary "subtle" (*myō*) elements. Kanetomo provides a rationale for the ritual in *The Essentials*, writing,

> Shinto is the subtle activity of Heaven, Earth, and Humanity.... The subtle activity of Heaven is also called the realm of divine metamorphoses. The subtle activity of Earth is also called the realm of supernatural powers. The subtle activity of Humanity is also called the realm of divine power.... [Heaven's divine metamorphoses are to be found] in the sun, the moon, and the stars and the constellations.... [Earth's supernatural powers

> are to be found] in gas emanations from mountains and marshes, tides of the ocean, and energy of matter.... [Humanity's divine powers are to be found in] reverence, offering, and [mudras]... reading, reciting, and chanting... contemplation, memory, and thought."[59]

Following preparatory purifications, the rite was divided into three main stages, Empowerment of the Subtle Divine Powers of the Origin of Humanity, Empowerment of the Origin of the Subtle Shinto of the Earth, and Empowerment of the Origin of Heaven's Subtle Metamorphoses. Extant texts include no explication of the ritual's purpose, but within the first stage are prayers for purity, longevity, health, and elimination of all difficulties. The rite aimed at inner purification in order to activate the subtle forces with which the initiate would be empowered during the ritual, enabling him to internalize and use those powers in some way. Each stage is composed of numerous empowerment rites, including one empowering the ritualist with the virtues of the "Six Kami of yin and yang," utilizing mudras, spells, and chants, such as "Cleanse and purify!" (*harae tamae kiyome tamae*).[60]

The Sōgen Shintō Rite was performed before an elaborate altar, in which a *torii* formed the gate of initiation. Multiple elements were either octagonal or arranged by eights, invoking enthronement symbolism, like the Eighteenfold Shinto rite and the Kami Initiations discussed in chapter 5. Inside the *torii* was an octagonal shape referred to as a "palace," on which were set stalks of bells representing the Sun, the Moon, the pillars of Heaven and the realm, as well as a vessel representing the Great Origin, and a *himorogi* into which the Kami would enter. Behind this palace was a stand for jewels and more bells. Behind the stand was a potted *sakaki* tree. The rear of the altar was decorated with offering streamers in five colors and flowers in eight vases. The initiate sat upon an octagonal seat, with a low desk on either side set with items he would use in performing the rite.

The third main transmission was the Shinto *Goma* Rite (*Yui Shintō dai goma gyōji*). The term *goma* is derived from *homa*, a Sanskrit word meaning "consecration"; such rites are found in Hinduism, Jainism, and Buddhism. In *goma* rituals, offerings are cast into a consecrated fire. In Japan *goma* rites are a hallmark of esoteric Buddhism. In appropriating the *goma* ritual pattern, Kanetomo's intention was to show that Buddhism had borrowed it from Shinto.

The altar for the *goma* rite was considerably more complex than those used in the first and second transmissions. One notable difference is that the initiate was seated inside the *torii* gate, marking an elevated status achieved by undergoing the earlier rites. He is seated on a raised octagonal seat, before an octagonal altar, which had a fire pit in its center. The sun and moon were represented by stiff, standing representations of *hei* offerings, with tall cups set before them on a table directly across from the initiate but beyond the altar itself and separate from it. The octagonal altar seems to have been demarcated by poles decorated with paper streamers at each of the eight corners. Conducting the rite evidently required two assistants, whose seats were on either side of the altar, facing the fire pit. An incense urn is set out, as are offerings of cooked rice, rice porridge, different kinds of beans and grains, salt, sake, sesame, and tea. Vessels representing the Ultimate Origin are placed on the altar near the fire pit, as are tools for handling the fire, cups of oil, and a ladle for casting oil into the fire. Two small tables to the left and right of the initiate's seat are set with purifying wands, a fan to make the fire flame up, a bell, and striker. An additional two tables are set out for talismans. Their purpose is not specified, but it would appear that the initiate would cast them into the fire in order to convey to the Kami the requests or prayers inscribed on them.[61] (See Figure 7.1.)

The rite unfolds in twenty-nine steps. The first eighteen are drawn from the prior Eighteenfold Shinto and Sōgen Shinto rites and include purifications, such as the

Figure 7.1 Re-creation of Altar Used in the Shintō Goma. Courtesy of the Shinto Museum, Kokugakuin University.

Purification of the Six Roots Prayer, and various empowerment segments. The initiate begins to build a fire in a fire pit in the nineteenth step, and in step twenty recites a spell derived from a Daoist text, with prayers to the "nine spirits," seen only in the Shinto *Goma* Rite. From the twenty-first step, the initiate fans the flames while pronouncing a Sanskrit syllable and visualizing a wheel of fire, while forming mudras. One of the mudras is directed to the Seven Star spirits as a prayer for longevity. In subsequent steps, the initiate casts branches upon the fire while reciting verses. He casts oil on the fire as he forms ten mudras, invoking all Kami to come into the altar. He performs a spirit-calming empowerment (*chinkon kaji*) and ends with many mantras of the myriad Kami.[62] Marking the status of this rite as the culmination of esoteric knowledge that would be imparted to initiates in the Three Transmissions, *The Essentials* does not comment upon it. Apparently any explication provided to the initiate would have been communicated orally.

Kanetomo created an impressive set of complex Shinto rites that appropriated elements of Daoism and Buddhism but without invoking their deities. His rites depended entirely on invoking the power of the Kami and implicitly promised to empower the ritualist with all their potency.

Scholars have frequently remarked upon Kanetomo's intellectual dependence on Buddhism and Daoism. For example, Bernhard Scheid writes:

> Kanetomo obviously commanded an intimate knowledge of Chinese philosophy. On this knowledge he based his cosmogonic superstructure that included Shinto cosmology but excluded Buddhist notions of the cosmic order. He was equally well versed in the ritual system of esoteric Buddhism. This he took as a model for his system of Yuiitsu ritual, but only after having replaced a few crucial terms and explications according to his own Shinto conceptions. He combined these elements theoretically and symbolically by identifying the cosmogonic triad of Taoism with the ritual triadic symbolism of Buddhism [body, speech, and mind]. Further, he used the Buddhist notion of a double reality, secret and open, to explain (among other things) the coexistence of traditional and new elements in his teachings, and on a more general level, the compatibility of Yuiitsu Shinto with the common Buddhist world view.[63]

While Kanetomo's appropriations are undeniable, Kanetomo's Buddhist and Daoist references would have been fully apparent to his contemporaries as well. It is not that he borrowed elements covertly or hoped that no one would notice. Instead, he asserted that Shinto was prior to and thoroughly pervades all other teachings. He hoped to show through ritual that Shinto is ultimately the basis for Buddhism and Daoism, to show that they derive from Shinto, rather than the reverse. Kanetomo's intention was to display the Shinto origins of the other traditions symbolically by adopting their ritual forms as part of his claim of Shinto's priority.[64]

Changes in the Concept of Kami

In the early medieval period, the idea had developed in Buddhist writings about Shinto that humanity's original nature is steeped in greed, hatred, and desire, illustrating the era's preoccupation with salvation. Some Kami were portrayed as taking the form of evil deities in allegories of humanity's suffering under the weight of sin and evil karma. However, in the late medieval works of Yoshida Kanetomo, we find little anxiety about human evil, and he developed a more optimistic and affirmative concept of Kami, based on the idea that Kami dwell in the heart-mind (*kokoro*) of humanity. This development forms the basis for Shinto theories of the early modern period.[65]

How did this change come about? From the ancient period a distinction had existed between the Kami associated with rulership and others outside that group. As discussed in chapter 5, in the medieval period, numerous Buddhist writings about Shinto addressed a distinction between Kami who work for humanity's salvation as *suijaku* of Buddhist divinities and evil Kami, who are outside the *honji-suijaku* framework: evil spirits, ghosts, wandering spirits of the living and dead, and evil deities appearing in the form of poisonous snakes or ferocious beasts. We saw in chapter 6 how temples and shrines had developed enclosed spaces for dealing with these new supernaturals. It is easy to imagine how the horrors of protracted war during the late medieval period would have further stimulated new conceptions of evil beings abroad in the world.

Kamo no Chōmei and Mujū Ichien saw a connection between the problem of evil Kami and Japan's position at the furthest periphery of the cosmos. In the Latter Days of the Dharma, as a place so distant in time and space from Buddhism's origins, Japan was rife with evil spirits seeking to infiltrate Buddhism. Evil beings called *akurei, yōkai,* and *mono no ke* could even appear as beneficient Kami in order to deceive humanity into worshipping them, thus sinking humanity's already-minuscule chances for salvation. Moreover, the characteristics of good and evil Kami could even coexist in the same Kami. Buddhist writers of the Jōdo Shinshū school, such as Zonkaku, (1290–1373), a third-generation disciple of Shinran, strove to clarify the distinction between those Kami who are beneficial to humanity and the evil ones.[66]

It was widely acknowledged, however, that it was difficult to tell the difference. That being the case, what attitude should humanity take toward the Kami? Increasingly a trend emerged within Jōdo Shinshū of not worshipping the Kami at all, an attitude described as "non-worship of Kami" (*jingi fuhai*). Other Buddhists struggled to preserve Kami worship in some form. The difficulty of providing clear guidance on this crucial point is illustrated by the recommendation seen in *Shintōshū*, to adopt a worshipful attitude toward all the Kami, good or bad. But that advice was destined only to provoke further anxiety, since a person might end up worshipping one of the evil ones and thus invite *tatari*. This muddle derived from the problem of reconciling the idea of evil Kami with *shinkoku*. *Shintōshū* is at pains to explain that because Japan is the "Land of the Gods," all the Kami deserve respect and reverence, even if some of them are bent on humanity's destruction. No real resolution to this problem emerged within Buddhist theories of Shinto.[67]

Only with Kanetomo did a new concept of Kami appear. Assisting this change was his shift in the older Three Countries (*sangoku*) framework, in which India was the center and best place, to one in which Japan assumed the central position as the most important. Kanetomo equated spirit, the heart-mind, and Kami in his work *Shintō taii,* claiming that the Kami of heaven and earth are the spirit in all things. In humanity this spirit is called the heart-mind. The Kami also have the heart-mind, and it is ultimately identical with the heart-mind of humanity. The heart-mind is without form and is different from the organ that pumps blood through the body. It is associated with the lower abdomen, though not limited to that physical area. The heart-mind is the seat of the emotions, but in addition, it has aspects of "soul," because it is also concerned with moral character, a person's understandings of right and wrong, as well as the individual's feelings of duty and obligations to others. The Shinto theories of the Edo period drew out the full implications of the idea that the Kami are fundamentally united with humanity through the heart-mind, and this concept became a central element in Japanese conceptions of the human person.[68]

By equating Kami and the heart-mind, both of which he assumed were intrinsically good, Kanetomo's formulation simply bypassed the problem of evil and instead turned to a more optimistic orientation. Regarding the Kami as the original deities and Buddhist divinities as less fundamental allowed Kanetomo to pass over the problem of evil.

Contesting the Headship of the Jingikan

In 1495, the Yoshida and Shirakawa houses contested the headship of the Jingikan. There was a firm understanding at the time that this and other posts that had become hereditary since the breakup of the Ritsuryō system were now held legitimately by their incumbents. It was not acceptable to question the right of the Shirakawa House to the headship. Kanetomo was not trying to assert that he should be the head of the Jingikan in the sense of usurping this post from the Shirakawa. Instead, Kanetomo claimed that the Jingihaku post was "merely" technical and bureaucratic, and that a second post equivalent in status was required. The second post would be concerned with the "Way"—it would "transmit the way of *jingi*." Kanetomo's implication was that the Yoshida House was the custodian of the Way of Shinto and should be regarded as equal in station to the Shirakawa.[69]

The issue turned in part on Kanetomo's claim to the title Superior of Shinto, which had been confirmed by both emperor and shogun. Later emperors and shoguns were to approve the use of the title by Kanetomo's successors as well, giving the title a hereditary status. This put the head of the Yoshida House, as Superior of

Shinto, in a position of authority over Shinto affairs, but that authority was not necessarily accepted beyond the capital or at major shrines. Kanetomo's 1489 claim that the Ise deities had flown to the Saijōsho made enemies of the Watarai House, and other sacerdotal lineages were similarly ill-disposed to accept Kanetomo's views.

Kanetomo conceived of Shinto as a universal phenomenon underlying all religious teachings, but he conceptualized its administration within the lineage framework. This view carried important implications for the public nature of Shinto. In Miyaji Naokazu's view, up until Kanetomo's time, a priest's work at a shrine was a public service and treated as such, but with Kanetomo, priestly service moved into the private sphere of kinship. Posts in the Jingikan had been a part of a national bureaucracy, but in the late medieval period they became an inheritance to be handed on by the incumbent to his son or heir. Shrine administration should have been the court's unique prerogative, in Miyaji's view, but that privilege shifted to the Yoshida House. It was "as if" the Yoshida were acting on behalf of the court, and their orders were no more authoritative than any other issued by a private lineage, but in fact they were given public standing in Kanetomo's time.[70] Treating Shinto thought and ritual as esoteric knowledge belonging to a lineage, which was empowered to commodify and sell it in the form of ranks, titles, and licenses, blurred the line between public and private, tending to align Shinto with the private.

Yoshida Shinto after Kanetomo

After Kanetomo's death, his descendants perpetuated Yoshida Shinto through the twin strategies of cultivating connections with the court and the shogunate, on the one hand, and going on proselytizing tours of the countryside to recruit local priests to become initiated in the Three Altars Rites (*sandan gyōji*), on the other. Yoshida heirs after Kanetomo brought in shrine priests from a much wider territory than in Kanetomo's time, by making proselytizing tours and distributing certificates, ranks, and titles.

Kanetomo's son Kiyohara Nobutaka (1475–1550) went to Echizen and gave many lectures on *Nihon shoki* in 1550. He was the father of Kanemigi (1516–1573), who toured Echizen in 1569 and later traveled widely. He lectured, bestowed Shinto transmissions on local priests in that region, and performed prayer rites upon request. The burden of his lectures was the idea that the Buddhas are the *suijaku*, while Kami are the original form of deity.[71] He met with shrine priests, inspected the objects of worship in their shrines, composed *norito,* and gave advice on all kinds of shrine matters. He bestowed certificates on priests, *miko*, and also on Buddhist priests, receiving significant emoluments in return. The Yoshida usually dealt with priests whose positions were so humble that they were easily persuaded to accept Yoshida doctrines and rituals, using Yoshida affiliation to improve their positions on their home turf.[72]

In 1556, warlord and future shogun Tokugawa Ieyasu acquired Mikawa Province and applied for the title of Governor. Emperor Ōgimachi (r. 1557–1586) was reluctant to grant this high title to a provincial upstart until Kanemigi interceded and produced a genealogy that he claimed to have "discovered," ostensibly proving that Ieyasu was descended from the Fujiwara house as well as the Minamoto. The emperor relented and granted the governorship, and the Yoshida subsequently claimed this intercession as the basis of their tie to the Tokugawa shogunate.[73]

The Yoshida had maintained strong relations with the later Hōjō from the time of Kanemigi, and in 1559 received 3,000 pieces of gold from them for a *kitō* ceremony, later sending them purification and spirit pacification talismans on more than one occasion, as well as letters. But when the Hōjō castle fell, and Hōjō heads were publicly displayed on pikes, Kanemigi's diary betrayed no regret or sympathy for their fate. This attitude was found widely among aristocrats and Buddhist clerics of the age, who had to maintain good relations with all those in authority.[74] Since one never knew which way the winds might blow, it was unwise to show favoritism.

The Yoshida House's Impact on Regional Priestly Associations

In the medieval period, regional priestly associations formed around an area's most powerful shrine, grouping lesser shrines into a hierarchy. The head priest of the central shrine of such an association determined ranks, titles, and vestments that the subordinates could use. Several "comprehensive shrines" were at the center of such associations, and the head priest would typically insist that only he be allowed to use the title of Head Priest (*kannushi*), restricting his subordinates to lesser ranks. The subordinate shrines' priests would be required to serve at the central shrine when it performed major rites or festivals. The formation by the Yoshida House of its own, extensive network of priests challenged these regional associations by offering ranks and titles to lesser shrine priests who would not have been granted them in the older associations.[75]

Kanemigi was able to expand the network of shrines affiliated with the Yoshida House by offering the esoteric rituals devised by Kanetomo, modification of local shrine practices, bequeathing priestly titles, and granting permission to shrine priests to wear aristocratic vestments for shrine rites. The transmission of Yoshida House ritual was "revolutionary," inasmuch as ritual knowledge had heretofore been closely guarded as lineage secrets and restricted to those in a particular lineage, usually limited to an incumbent's transmission to his immediate successor. Kanemigi transmitted such rites much more widely than had Kanetomo, expanding his initiates to feudal lords and wealthy commoners, as well as shrine priests outside the Yoshida line. The titles and vestments were valued as a means of certifying that a priest was genuine and as a means of distinguishing himself among his peers. Another way in which Kanemigi's proselytizing undermined the authority of regional shrine associations was by granting indulgences to abrogate taboos or requirements of abstinences or ascetic exercises. For example, in 1589 one of the Shimazu vassals had Yoshida Kanemi (1535–1610) undertake intensive prayers to the mountain gods of the vassal's territory, to seek their permission for reclaiming forest land and turning it into fields.[76] Local priests and ritualists feared the Kami's wrath if they should fail to observe traditional requirements, but the Yoshida offered them indulgences that could shorten or limit these burdens, and thus were much sought after.[77]

Kanemi and his younger brother Bonshun (1553–1632) both cultivated ties with Nobunaga, Hideyoshi, and Ieyasu. Kanemi's diary, which covers the years 1575 to 1595, shows that Kanemi tried to form connections with Nobunaga but failed. Nevertheless, Kanemi formed significant bonds with powerful warriors, such as Shimazu Yoshihisa, Hosokawa Yūsai, Satake Izumo no Kami, Akechi Mitsuhide, and others. One of the Hosokawa married Kanemi's daughter.

Kanemi carried out all kinds of rites for warriors and commoners, from healing to *tatari* rites to rites for conjugal harmony, safe childbirth, undoing directional taboos, astral divinations, and issuing talismans. He visited the warlord Takeda Shingen (1521–1573) and other warriors at their battlefield encampments.[78] The Ikkōshū (later known as the True Pure Land Sect, Jōdo Shinshū) also was involved in medieval warfare, and in 1566 had Kanemi inscribe war banners for them. This means that the Yoshida were seen as possessing powerful magic that could help bring about military victory. Kanemi traveled and proselytized extensively, going to meet Hideyoshi at his encampment in 1573, and journeying to Iwami's silver mine and the gold mine in Sado, where he visited Ieyasu.[79]

In 1582, Emperor Ōgimachi had Kanemi take charge of sacred dance, candle lighting, and purification ritual at the palace. This was immensely significant for the House, because previously palace ritual had been the exclusive preserve of the Shirakawa.[80] Following this imperial recognition, in 1585 Hideyoshi recognized Kanemi's title as Superior of Shinto. Hideyoshi's 1587 expulsion edict directed to the Christian missionaries begins with a passage referring to Japan as *shinkoku* and criticizing Christianity for not conforming to the Way of the Kami. Hideyoshi may have had the edict composed as a result of his contact with the Yoshida.

Yoshida Shinto not only survived the era of warring states but actually seemed to thrive in the midst of chaos. According to Kanemi's diary, there was a huge earthquake in 1585, with endless aftershocks that terrified the people for over a month. During that time, Kanemi performed a huge Shintō Goma ceremony in the palace ritual hall, the Shishinden, with the emperor in attendance and a private audience following. This shows that Yoshida rites had taken on a public significance transcending lineage practices, much as Tendai and Shingon ceremonies had earlier.[81]

In 1585 Kanemi approached the future Emperor Go-Yōzei (r. 1586–1611) for permission to build a replica of the Hall of the Eight Deities at the Saijōsho. He received land worth 20 *koku* per annum for this purpose. The following year, in 1586, the Hasshinden was reconstructed inside the Yoshida Saijōsho. Also in 1586, Hideyoshi gave the land where the Jingikan had previously been located to his retainers, and the court had to suspend its rituals at this ruined site.[82] That left the Yoshida House's Hall of the Eight Deities as the only facility providing official worship of the tutelary Kami of the imperial house.[83] This made the Yoshida cult center equivalent to the Jingikan, whose main job during this era was to maintain rites for the imperial tutelary Kami.[84] However, the court was ambivalent about the significance of Kanemi's move, so much so that no public ceremonies were actually held at the Yoshida Hall of the Eight Deities until 1609.[85] Much later, in 1751, the Shirakawa House built its own Hall of the Eight Deities, but that did not mean that the one constructed by the Yoshida no longer operated. Instead, the Jingikan's functions were divided between the Yoshida and Shirakawa Houses.[86]

Hideyoshi and his son Hideyori were determined to deify Hideyoshi upon his death, and Hideyori put Kanemi in charge of the funeral and apotheosis rites, providing him land worth 10,000 *koku* per annum in return.[87] The Yoshida House had become known for Shinto funerals and deifications. Kanetomo, for example, had been deified as Shin'ryū Daimyōjin in a sub-shrine called Shin'ryūsha on the grounds of the Yoshida Shrine. When Hideyoshi died in 1598, he was deified as Toyokuni Daimyōjin. The Daimyōjin title was characteristic of the Yoshida House.

Groundbreaking began on the shrine dedicated to Hideyoshi's deified spirit, Hōkoku Jinja (also called Toyokuni Jinja). Kanemi's grandson Kaneyori (Hagiwara Kaneyori 1588–1660) was appointed the Head Priest of Hōkoku Shrine when he was only eleven years old, though Kanemi and Bonshun were actually in charge.[88] This shrine was paired with a grandiose temple that Hideoyshi had built nearby, called Hōkōji. Its Buddha Hall was the largest building in Japan at that time and housed a monumental bronze Buddha statue that was even larger than the one at Tōdaiji. The Hōkoku Shrine stood directly below a hill where a mausoleum for Hideyoshi was constructed. The mausoleum had an administering temple that was also Hōkoku Shrine's *jingūji*, where Bonshun served as abbot. Biannual festivals for Hideyoshi's deified spirit began, with a particularly spectacular pageant in 1604.

Reversal of Fortune under Tokugawa Ieyasu

After Ieyasu came to power, he swiftly annihilated the remaining Toyotomi clan. Since the Yoshida were closely associated with the Toyotomi, Ieyasu's rise was an ominous development, though its full implications unfolded only over time. After Kanemigi's death, leadership of the Yoshida House fell to Bonshun. Bonshun was the younger brother of Kanemi and the Intendant (*bettō*) of the *jingūji* of

Hōkoku Shrine, having taken the tonsure to serve in that post. He had frequently visited Hideyoshi in Ōsaka, but he was also friendly with Ieyasu and a number of other warriors and aristocrats. He wrote numerous commentaries on shrines and Shinto works.[89]

In 1610, the shogunate decided to fund the Vicennial Renewal of the Ise Shrines and directed that the Yoshida House should conduct the rite of dispatching an imperial emissary to Ise. This appointment transferred an important ritual responsibility from the Jingikan to the Yoshida House, which held the role until the end of the Edo period.[90] It also showed that Ieyasu was not bent on punishing the Yoshida for their close ties to the Toyotomi.

Unlike some of his illustrious forebears, however, Bonshun was not a celebrated scholar, and, according to what may be an apocryphal story, he was unable to read the *Nihon shoki*, as Ieyasu discovered when he asked Bonshun to read a portion for him. Ieyasu was very surprised that Bonshun couldn't do this, but he nevertheless questioned Bonshun on Shinto matters quite minutely on numerous occasions. Bonshun's relation with Ieyasu peaked around 1610, when the matter of Kami Initiations for Ieyasu arose. At that point Ieyasu seemed to put distance between them. Ieyasu decided not to undergo the initation, probably from the concern that any show of favoritism to Bonshun might damage his relations with other clerics.

Eventually, Bonshun lost out to the more powerful Buddhist clerics Tenkai (?–1643) and Sūden (1569–1633) in the competition for Tokugawa favor. Nevertheless, Bonshun gave Sūden a transmission of the Nakatomi Harae. It must have been a shock when in 1615 Ieyasu closed the Hōkoku Shrine where Hideyoshi had been deified. Bonshun's temple was also closed, and the Hōkoku Shrine's young Head Priest Hagiwara Kaneyori barely escaped being exiled.[91]

Bonshun maintained relations with Ieyasu, however. Bonshun visited Ieyasu in his home territory five times and performed purification prayers and *kitō* for him. But Tenkai succeeded in shunting Bonshun aside from any decisive role in Ieyasu's deification, and Ieyasu was eventually deified as a Gongen after the style of Sannō Shinto instead of as a Daimyōjin, as the Yoshida designation would have been.

Nevertheless, it was Bonshun who conducted Ieyasu's funeral, an early prototype for Shinto funerals.[92] The rites performed for Ieyasu took place after a temporary shrine-like hall had been constructed, equipped with a *torii*, lanterns, and fences, and curtained off by rolls of silk. In complete darkness, Ieyasu's spirit was symbolically transferred from the corpse into a mirror. Bonshun rang a bell in a procession of the ritualists carrying the mirror into the hall, flanked by attendants bearing weapons. There Bonshun installed the mirror as an object of worship, set many kinds of offerings before it, and intoned a prayer that Ieyasu's deified spirit would protect and bless the realm for all eternity.[93] Bonshun died in 1632, as the regional shrines set up as outposts of the Hōkoku Shrine were being destroyed, to prevent their attracting rebellious elements among Hideyoshi's remnant vassals.

Conclusion

Kanetomo emerged at a time when his competitors in the religious world were weak and ill-equipped to resist his claims. Imperial support enabled him to make great headway and achieve unparalleled influence. In the words of Shinto historian Endō Jun:

> Yoshida Shinto...had a forced, contrived quality, but [it] had the profoundest influence on the Shinto theories of later times since it was the first systematization of Shinto principles. Almost all early modern Shinto theories have Yoshida Shinto as their starting point, and one might go so far as to suggest that Yoshida Shinto doctrines as developed by Kanetomo marked not only the summation of medieval Shinto thinking, but the very origins of early modern Shinto thought.[94]

Yoshida Kanetomo's thought, the rituals he created, and his organizational strategies were revolutionary. He provided a conceptual basis for Shinto for the first time. This is the basis for the position that Shinto did not exist before him. However, Kanetomo did not "come out of nowhere," but built on the tendency seen in Watarai Shinto to depart from Buddhist frameworks, and on the work of Jihen and other earlier Yoshida scholars. Kanetomo's theories presumed the institutional basis of the Jingikan and *jingi* ritual that had existed since the ancient period. Had he not been in the position of de facto leader of the Jingikan, it is doubtful that he would have found a hearing. His dependence on those institutions is one basis for this study's position that we can trace the institutional history of Shinto to the Jingikan's beginnings in the ancient period.

Kanetomo's doctrines elevated Shinto above all other teachings and Japan above all other realms as primordial and foundational, the ultimate source of all other teachings and lands. No previous Shinto thinker had produced such a comprehensive understanding. His ritual system of sequential initiations built on a coherent doctrine and could stand alongside the Kami Initiations of esoteric Buddhism. While medieval Buddhism seemed unable to transcend the conundrums produced by the Latter Days of the Dharma, the problem of evil, and infinitely distant images of salvation, Kanetomo deftly sidestepped these issues. He proclaimed profound confidence in the Kami and created an image of humanity as basically good, unified with Kami through the heart-mind. He secured public status for the Saijōsho and his Hall of the Eight Deities through his arguments concerning the essential contributions of Shinto to the governance of the realm. In so doing, he elevated Shinto beyond its earlier submersion within Buddhist esotericism and promoted it as the embodiment of "the indigenous."

8

Early Edo-Period Shinto Thought and Institutions

Introduction

This is the first of four chapters concerning Shinto during the Edo period, also called the early modern or Tokugawa period, 1603–1867. This chapter focuses upon Shinto's institutional and philosophical development in the first half of the period, when Confucianism came to be heavily involved with Shinto. A variety of rapprochements arose, because Confucians appropriated Shinto in order to introduce a philosophy that was new to shogunal officials, and because Confucian rationalism was useful to Shinto thinkers. Chapters 9 and 10 mainly deal with the latter half of the period. Chapter 9 addresses popular shrine life, especially the rise of Inari devotionalism and Ise pilgrimage. Abundant records enable us grasp the significance of shrines in communal life, and what it meant to the common people to be able to travel on pilgrimage. Chapter 10 examines Shinto popularizers and the rise of new religious movements derived from Shinto. Recitation of the Great Purification Prayer spread to a popular level, and the idea arose that human happiness is a legitimate goal. Chapter 11 examines National Learning (Kokugaku) and its relation to Shinto. Kokugaku scholars came to promote a return to direct imperial rule, a complete separation of Buddhism from Shinto, and the idea of Shinto as the core of Japanese identity.

When Tokugawa Ieyasu (1542–1616) came to power, he established his base at Edo, which at the time was little more than a fishing village. Ieyasu's government, the shogunate established a broad legal framework to ensure social stability and economic productivity. Provisions governing religious institutions helped organize the people under the authority of the Buddhist temples, while other codes governed the court, the warrior class, and shrines. Political stability and shogunal support facilitated the revival of court ritual.

Enforcing a prohibition on Christianity was a major preoccupation in the early years of the period. Francis Xavier had established Catholic missions in Japan in the late fifteenth century, and Christianity had spread during the sixteenth century. The missionaries accompanying Portuguese and Spanish trading missions formed good relations with Nobunaga and Hideyoshi. After a trip to Nagasaki, where he saw the spread of Christian culture in the form of churches, hospitals, and schools, however, Hideyoshi came to fear that Christianity might represent a threat: if Japanese Christians formed an allegiance to the Pope in Rome, they might rise up against their secular rulers at home. Hideyoshi started issuing edicts against Christianity, and persecutions began, forcing Christians into hiding as the missionaries and many Japanese Christians were martyred. The Christian *daimyō* were defeated, and the foreign missions were stamped out. Christianity's last stand came in 1637 in the Shimabara Rebellion, which ended in the deaths of all the rebels. The remaining believers formed communities of "hidden Christians" in Kyūshū, on some offshore islands, and in other areas, where they practiced in secret until the ban on Christianity was lifted in the early Meiji period.

During the early Tokugawa period, 1600 to the Genroku era (1688–1704), the main features of the age were established. The country restricted foreign trade, except for a small station of Dutch traders on the island of Dejima, periodic visits by Korean missions, and some interaction with China through the Ryūkyū Islands. The land was divided into around two hundred fifty domains (*han*), whose rulers (the *daimyō*) were the shogun's vassals.[1]

In theory, society as a whole was divided into four status groups: warriors, farmers, artisans, and merchants. Since the country remained at peace after the Shimabara Rebellion, the warriors (the samurai), were transformed into bureaucrats to administer government. Despite the appearance of neat categories, however, there were numerous groups, including the Buddhist and Shinto priests, doctors, entertainers, and outcasts, who fell outside the four main groups. The crucial division was that between rulers and the commoners.

Toyotomi Hideyoshi had been posthumously deified in 1599 as Toyokuni Daimyōjin, and Ieyasu was likewise deified. After Ieyasu's death and initial interment in Shizuoka, Tenkai (1536–1643), one of Ieyasu's closest advisers, arranged for a great mausoleum to be built at Nikkō in 1617, long considered a sacred mountain. It was an important site for Shugendō practice and was regarded as an earthly manifestation of Kannon's Pure Land. Ieyasu was deified at Nikkō as Tōshō Daigongen. His mausoleum was called the Tōshōgū and was administered by a Tendai temple, Rinnōji. Rinnōji was a *monzeki* temple, meaning that its abbots were drawn from the imperial princes. The rationale for Nikkō's temple-shrine combination came from Sannō Shintō, attached to the Tendai school of Buddhism (see chapter 5). The shogunate promoted a cult of the deified Ieyasu, building a number of Tōshōgū shrines around the country.

The middle years of the Edo period began with a flowering of arts, literature, and urban culture in the Genroku era. By 1700 Kyoto and Osaka each had populations of around 400,000 people. Meanwhile, the population of Edo grew to more than a million by 1750, making it one of the largest cities in the world at that time, comparable to Paris or London not only in its population but also in the vibrancy of its cultural life, made possible by a concentration of wealth. The eighteenth century saw the spread of a currency-based economy to agricultural areas. Gold, silver, and copper were mined, though supplies were depleting. The domains developed specialized cottage industries in textiles, paper, lacquer goods, cloth, and such luxury products as silk, fine pottery, and sake. Markets that had begun to appear around temples and shrines in the medieval period increased and spread to castle towns.

A movement called National Learning (*Kokugaku*) developed in the eighteenth century from the study of ancient Japanese myth and literature into an anti-Buddhist discourse, and later—especially after the Opium Wars in China during the 1840s—into opposition to foreign influence and Western colonialism in the nineteenth century. Beginning as a scholarly endeavor, Kokugaku produced new ideas about the Kami and their worship that have continued to be influential until the present. As a social movement, Kokugaku galvanized the shrine priesthood for the first time to try to free Shinto from Buddhist control. Kokugaku thinkers like Motoori Norinaga and his successors called for a rejection of foreign thought and philosophy as a means to recover the mentality of ancient Japan. Motoori's life work, a philological study of the *Kojiki*, stimulated interest in this text for the first time in centuries.

Throughout the period, the development of society, especially the spread of literacy, expansion of publishing, growth of urban culture, and improved means of transportation, facilitated the growth of popular religion, manifested in the development of shrine festivals and pilgrimage to a variety of temples and shrines. Popular pilgrimage to Ise became a widespread phenomenon. Shinto popularizers spread recitation of the Great Purification Prayer to a popular level and, like shrine pilgrimage, built a new awareness of Shinto as something beyond local Kami cults. Several new religious movements emerged outside the priesthoods of Buddhism and Shinto from the beginning of the nineteenth century. Drawing on a host of Buddhist, Shinto, and folk ideas for their doctrines and practices, their egalitarian ethos and faith healing, as well as practical ethics emphasizing personal religious experience, attracted thousands of people. These early movements stand at the fountainhead of hundreds of such movements founded throughout the modern and contemporary periods.

The late Edo period (1800 to about 1850) saw the beginnings of a breakdown of shogunal control. The shogunate and the domains had to support the warrior class, but since samurai were not permitted to become cultivators or merchants, they were not economically productive. The samurai were given stipends in rice, but a stipend's value fluctuated greatly in accord with changes in the price of rice. The samurai were caught in the contradictions inherent in an economy that was theoretically based on rice but which actually operated on currency. The shogunate and the domains were perennially indebted to merchants. Squeezing the farmers to produce more and to pay more in taxes led to growing gaps between rich and poor, and to discontent. Famines exacerbated discontent, and some famines, such as the Tenpo famine that began in 1832, affected the entire country. There were many deaths, and the number of the poor increased. In 1837, Ōshio Heihachirō led a major uprising in Osaka that made clear the shogunate's weakness.[2]

Increasing knowledge of Western imperialism from the end of the eighteenth century and China's collapse in the Opium Wars made Japan acutely aware of Western powers' military might. From 1853, the American fleet under Admiral Matthew Perry began pressuring the shogunate to open Japan to trade with the United States. In 1854, the shogunate was forced to sign a treaty with the United States, and other Western powers rapidly followed suit in pressing for treaties granting them favorable conditions. The court reacted with calls to the shrines and temples for prayer ceremonies to expel the barbarians, increasingly involving itself in shrine affairs and becoming a magnet for a faction seeking to eject the foreigners and restore imperial rule. Ten years later, samurai from Western Japan's domains led a movement to overthrow the shogunate, though other factions sought to preserve shogunal rule.

The shogunate was eventually brought down by a coup spearheaded by the Satsuma and Chōshū domains in southern Japan. The throne provided a unifying symbol for them and other domains opposed to further shogunal capitulation to the foreigners. The samurai split into numerous factions, including those who defended the shogunate, those who called for the expulsion of foreigners and a restoration of direct imperial rule, and others who sat on the sidelines. Many Shinto priests joined the movement calling for the restoration of imperial rule, developing interpretations of the Kokugaku thought of Hirata Atsutane called Restoration Shinto (*fukko Shintō*).

Edo-Period Conceptions of "the Public"

Kōgi was an early-modern term for national or public authority or "authorities," "government," "public" as opposed to "private."[3] The particle *kō* (*ōyake*), "public," is identical with that examined in earlier chapters on the ancient period, contrasting with *shi* (*watakushi*), "private." Combined with *gi* (rule, affairs),[4] the compound can be understood as "public authority," "the authorities," "government," or "the public." In earlier usage during the Kamakura period, this term had referred to the court or the emperor; in the Sengoku era it had come to refer to the shogun, regional overlords, their exercise of political authority, or to the overlords themselves. For example, shogun Ashikaga Yoshiaki (r. 1568–1573) was referred to as *kōgi*. At this time, *kōgi* indicated a lesser scope of authority than *tenka*, which designated a seat of authority extending over the entire realm. In the Edo period, *kōgi* was distinguished from individual persons. Thus, the title that the emperor bestowed on Tokugawa Ieyasu in 1603, Barbarian-Subduing Generalissimo (Sei-i tai shōgun), lacked the term *kōgi*. *Kōgi* designated a legally constituted system of public authority. It encompassed the court, the shogunal government, and the *daimyō*. The *daimyō* represented themselves as acting in accord with public authority and required officials below them to know and abide by shogunal decrees (*hatto*) affecting their spheres of activity. The locus of *kōgi* could differ according to context, so that *kōgi* within a village could refer to the established rules of the area, while at the level of the domain it could refer to the public authorities' governance of the territory. At the highest level it referred to the shogunate, its laws, and legal system, or to the court.[5]

In terms of understanding how Shinto was positioned in relation to public authority, we should note that the scope of "the public" widened in the early modern period considerably beyond the court and the older Ritsuryō system that had established court- and shrine rituals and ceremonies, to encompass a sphere of authority governed by the shogunate and its officials. The laws that governed shrines issued from the shogunate, and Shinto figures strove to create strong ties to shogunal authority.

The Legal Framework Governing Religion during the Edo Period

Ieyasu crafted policies on religion so as to prevent religious insurrection and to shape religious institutions to monitor the populace. From 1608 to 1618, the government issued regulations to the major temples, demanding that they exercise strict discipline over the monks and occupy themselves with doctrinal study. By the mid-seventeenth century, an elaborate system for the administration and control of religious institutions was put in place, resting on four principal mechanisms: (1) absolute prohibition of Christianity (completed with the 1637 suppression of the Shimabara Rebellion), annual sectarian investigations to enforce the ban; (2) incorporation of all Buddhist temples and clerics into a fixed number of sects with rigid rules; (3) incorporation of the entire population into the Buddhist temples as their parishioners; (4) placing the Yoshida house in charge of certain shrine affairs. Taken together, these measures created a system in which Buddhism came to function as part of the framework of social control, and shrines remained largely overshadowed by the temples that administered them. Temple registration began to be enforced from the 1630s.

While the shogunate sought to adapt Buddhism to its purpose of enforcing the ban on Christianity, however, there were powerful figures who opposed official promotion of Buddhism. Such men as Hoshina Masayuki (1611–1672), Tokugawa Mitsukuni (1628–1700) of Mito, and Ikeda Mitsumasa (1609–1682) of Okayama, and others took a strong interest in Confucianism and Shinto.[6] They supported Neo-Confucian scholars and carried out separations of temples from shrines in their domains. Mitsumasa tried to create a system in which the population would register with shrines instead of temples, though the shogunate reversed him in a few years. He reduced the number of temples and Buddhist priests by about half.[7] He also called on the Yoshida house to assist him in eradicating some 10,527 "improper shrines" (*inshi*) and to merge some seventy more into larger shrines.[8] With the advice of the Confucian scholar Kumazawa Banzan (1619–1691), Mitsumasa also built a Confucian-style academy called the Shizutani Gakkō for the education of young samurai and began work on a network of Confucian-style schools for commoners. Mitsumasa and the others exemplified a current of anti-Buddhist sentiment among those in the ruling class that was linked to promotion of Confucianism and faith in the Kami. However, their patronage of shrines was selective and weighted toward older, established shrines.

In 1665 the shogunate issued "Regulations Governing All Shinto Shrines, Senior Priests, and Other Shrine Functionaries" (*Shosha negi kannushi hatto*) in five articles:

1. Senior priests and other shrine functionaries of all shrines nationwide shall devote themselves to studying "the Way of the Kami" (*jingidō, jingidōka*) and augment their understanding of the objects of worship at their respective shrines. They shall refrain from performing commonplace rituals and ceremonies. Those who are subsequently derelict in their duties shall be dismissed from their posts.
2. Those priests who have received court rank by means of their respective imperial mediators shall continue to conform to past procedure.
3. Shrine personnel without rank shall wear white robes. Other apparel may only be worn after obtaining a permit from the Yoshida family.
4. Land owned by a shrine must never be bought or sold.
   Addendum: Shrine land must not be used as collateral.
5. When a shrine is damaged, it should always be repaired as necessary.

   Addendum: Orders to clean a shrine shall be issued without delay.

The preceding articles shall be strictly observed. Anyone found in violation of these articles shall receive a ruling in accordance to the gravity of the offense.

7th month of 1665, Year of the Serpent.[9]

The first article recognized shrine priests as a group and assigned them the function of studying "the Way of the Kami." The word used was not Shinto, but *jingidō*, a Way of the Kami and the rites customarily performed for them. This provision was significant in creating a recognized status of "priest," implying the superiority of this position over other, lesser functionaries at shrines. Priests were to remain aloof from ritual that was devoted purely to the pursuit of individual gain or not properly part of authorized Kami ritual, such as rites of healing and exorcism.

The second article governed the issuance of ancient court ranks bestowed by the imperial house on some shrines. These ranks were regarded as prestigious and were widely sought in the Edo period by priests whose communities were prepared to back the necessary campaigning financially. Because shrine priests could not approach the imperial house directly, they used an intermediary noble house to "transmit" (*tensō, shissō*) their petition for the desired rank. These services were available for purchase from a number of noble houses, particularly the Shirakawa. While the wording suggests that those newly seeking certification should go through the Yoshida house, this article tacitly recognized the existing prerogatives of other aristocratic families, showing that the shogunate was content to let shrines and priests be administered through miscellaneous relationships established earlier.[10]

The third article was based on the idea that standard dress for shrine personnel should be white. Anyone wishing to use other colors would have to be authorized by seeking a license from the Yoshida house. We saw in our earlier discussion of Yoshida Kanetomo and his doctrine of "One-and-Only Shinto" that he and his descendants promoted his ideas by recruiting provincial priests and issuing licenses to them. In the Edo period this practice continued, with provincial priests traveling to Kyoto for a period of training at the Yoshida Shrine, after which they could receive a license for a fee, authorizing them to wear colored vestments.

The fourth and fifth articles perpetuated the status of shrines as semipublic institutions, which continued to perform prayers for the peace and prosperity of the realm and to receive public financial support on that basis. Shrines were not the private property of the priests or local supporters, and hence their lands should not be put up for sale or used as security in a loan. They should always be kept clean and in good repair.

The shogunate provided special courts for matters relating to religious institutions, overseen by the office of the Magistrate of Temples and Shrines (Jisha Bugyō), established in 1635. The Magistrate's judgments were treated as precedents in deciding subsequent cases. The domains also had such courts and magistrates. While a framework governing Shinto affairs was established through these mechanisms, however, administration was rather passive, not revealing any intention to use the shrines to indoctrinate the populace.

Yoshida Licenses and Certificates

It must have been chilling when in 1615 Ieyasu closed the Hōkoku Shrine where Hideyoshi had been deified. The shrine's Head Priest Hagiwara Kaneyori, who represented a collateral line of the Yoshida family, barely escaped being exiled. He became a kind of caretaker for the Yoshida line, living quietly in Kyoto, without ties to the shogunate.[11] The apparently precarious position of Kaneyori did not mean, however, that the Yoshida house had lost its influence among shrines. Its licensing system remained vital.

In theory, only the court had the authority to grant Kami ranks and titles, and only the court could take these away.[12] Nevertheless, the Yoshida family issued a variety of licenses and certificates that theoretically carried imperial authorization. Because licensing and certification implied that the receiving shrines accepted the doctrinal authority of the Yoshida house, many larger shrines such as the Twenty-Two Shrines, the Izumo Shrine, and others, disliked this implication and successfully petitioned to be exempted from the arrangement soon after the *hatto* was issued. In actuality, therefore, the law's provisions were mainly applied to smaller provincial shrines.[13]

The great majority of applicants for Yoshida credentials were actually Buddhist or Shugen priests of village shrines, since so many shrines lacked a professional shrine priest. In the first instance, securing these documents depended upon the approval of a village headman, since villagers would eventually bear the cost, which included the shrine priest or functionary traveling to Kyoto with appropriate gifts. Once the village head certified his approval, the priest needed a letter of reference from the domain lord (this also necessitated an appropriate gift). The *sōgen senji* was the type of Yoshida certification most frequently sought by provincial shrine priests. *Sōgen senji*, or Decree of the Utmost Origin, referred to the Yoshida house's ultimate origination (*sōgen*) from Amenokoyane, while *senji* referred to an imperial decree. These decrees conferred special ranks upon shrines in the name of the god Amenokoyane, as in the following example.

> Order of the Utmost Origin (*sōgen senji*)
> Senior First Rank Hachimangū Musashi Province, Sakitama District Hachijō Ward, Hon-Hachijō Village
> Hereby it is revealed that granting the utmost rank to this shrine is by divine order.
> Twenty-eighth day, eleventh month, Shōtoku 2 (1712).[14]

The decree was issued with a prayer sheet and gold-plated wand of streamers, in a box inscribed with the local shrine's deity's name, to be placed in the receiving shrine's sanctuary by a rite of installation. The receiving priest or functionary pledged to remove Buddhist items from the shrine and to make a clear distinction between offerings set before the Kami and those for Buddhist divinities.[15] Often the shrine's sacred history was rewritten, its enshrined gods changed to emphasize Kami mentioned in the *Nihon shoki*, and its ritual procedures might be changed to accord with Yoshida practice.[16]

While the certificate was issued to the shrine rather than to the priest per se, the priest's labor in securing this mark of recognition for the village shrine no doubt tended to increase his own authority as (one of) its managers. The decree itself was supposed to be issued with imperial approval, and since the same kind of paper used for imperial edicts was utilized, the Yoshida decrees looked as if they had come from the imperial house. But the Yoshida had been bypassing that step since Kanetomo's time and in actuality were issuing this and other certificates on their own authority.[17]

Provincial shrines had the option of applying for an actual imperial decree instead of the *sōgen senji*, but the imperial decree cost more than twenty times the price for a Yoshida document. In the case of the village whose certificate was introduced above, the total cost was 35 *ryō*, including the priest's travel costs, gifts, and a banner and plaque announcing the new rank and title.[18] Village records show that it took years to accumulate the necessary funds, indicating the scale of the undertaking and how far out of reach the imperial certificate was for most shrines of modest means. Especially considering that the Yoshida certificates were visually indistinguishable from the imperial ones, it is little wonder that villages most often opted for the Yoshida decree. The demand for Yoshida certificates was originally stimulated by the 1665 *hatto*, and the peak came between 1691 and the late 1710s, declining thereafter, and ceasing altogether in 1738, probably in response to rising criticism against the practice.[19] According to Shinto historian Inoue Tomokatsu, the *sōgen senji* were worthless after the mid-1740s.[20] Nevertheless, some shrine priests continued to seek ritual certification and court ranks from the Yoshida through the end of the period.[21]

The Revival of Shinto Ceremonies at Court

The shogunate neutralized any potential for the court to assert political power through an edict of 1615, "Regulations for the Emperor and the Court" (*Kinchū narabi ni kuge shohatto*). More remarkable than the edict itself was the painstaking study Ieyasu devoted to determining correct precedents in ancient records of court ceremony, vestments, and protocol. He directed scribes from five Kyoto Zen temples to assemble all the relevant documents, copy and compile them, and deliver the collection in a matter of months. One set required three large trunks. Based on this exhaustive collection, the edict called on the emperor to pursue scholarship and poetry, forbidding him to confer ranks and titles on warriors, or purple robes or titles of sainthood upon Buddhist abbots without the shogun's permission.[22] While Ieyasu surely intended to brook no political machinations from the court, his intention went beyond muscle flexing, to stabilizing the court after a long period of disruption, rehabilitating its ceremonial life and restoring it to an honored part of the realm.[23] Further, he required the wealthiest domain lords to contribute funds toward the performance of important court ritual, to periodic rebuilding of the palace, and for such rites for the emperor as coming-of-age, healing, and imperial funerals.[24]

While the court gradually re-established its Shinto rites, it also re-established Buddhist observances such as Buddhist enthronement rites, *sokui kanjō*, which all emperors of the period had performed.[25] Numerous annual rites stemming from On'yōdō were also staged.[26]

Imperial support for shrine ritual had declined dramatically after the Ōnin War. Court patronage of the Twenty-Two Shrines, provincial First Shrines (*ichinomiya*), and Comprehensive Shrines (*sōja*) came to an end. The shogunate confiscated their land, subsequently granting them smaller holdings. Imperial Emissaries were no longer sent to shrines bearing offerings for their annual festivals. The court ceased performing the annual harvest rite *Niinamesai*, and Emperor Go-Tsuchimikado (r. 1464–1500) was the last medieval emperor to have the *Daijōsai* enthronement rite performed.

Because the court was entirely dependent upon the shogunate for funds, its ceremonial life was restored at shogunal expense.[27] The Vicennial Renewal of the Ise Shrines had already recommenced in the late medieval period, in 1563 for the Outer Shrine (following a hiatus of 129 years) and in 1585 at the Inner Shrine (following a gap of 123 years).[28] The first Vicennial Renewal of the Edo period was held in 1610. In 1626 Emperor Gomizuno-o made an imperial progress to Nijō Castle.[29] In 1647 the custom of dispatching an Imperial Emissary to the Ise Shrines was revived, coinciding with the commencement of a parallel, annual dispatch of an Imperial Emissary to the Tōshōgū.[30] Requiring the court to send an Imperial Emissary to deliver ceremonial tribute to the Tōshōgū demonstrated the shogunate's ambition to raise the Tōshōgū's prestige to the same level as Ise and dramatized the court's subordination to the shogunate. The court's annual dispatch of an Imperial Emissary to Ise became its largest annual ceremony.[31] Tokugawa Hidetada, the second shogun (r. 1605–1623), revived the custom of requesting prayers from the Ise Shrines for healing or for overcoming an inauspicious year (*yakudoshi*). The fifth shogun, Tsunayoshi (r. 1680–1709), made these requests eleven times. Prayers for a shogun's recovery from illness bore a national, public character, as did similar rites performed for emperors. In some cases, all Twenty-Two Shrines were included in these requests, and sometimes an even larger number of shrines offered prayers.[32] In 1679 the Hōjō-e Ceremony of the Iwashimizu Shrine was revived, as was the festival of the Kamo Shrines, in 1694.[33] The Daijōsai was performed for Emperor Higashiyama in 1687 under Tsunayoshi, who also ordered a search to identify and refurbish the tombs of early emperors. By the end of the period, more shrine rites had been revived, especially under Emperor Kōmei, a subject taken up in chapter 10.

Jingikan functionaries provided the ritualists for these observances. However, while the Jingikan remained on the books, so to speak, as a recognized branch of government, it had been seriously undermined. The buildings of the Jingikan had not been rebuilt after their wartime destruction, and as described in the previous chapter, Hideyoshi had given its land to a vassal. Following the practice of the medieval period, the Jingikan's major posts and ceremonial responsibilities were divided between the Shirakawa and Yoshida Houses, both of which had their separate headquarters, conducting some rituals in the palace and others in their own facilities, such as the Hall of the Eight Deities maintained at the Yoshida headquarters. There was a division of labor between the two, with the Shirakawa holding the headship of the Jingikan, while the Yoshida held the position of second-in-command, an arrangement that had been established in the late Heian period. The Shirakawa House monopolized the roles requiring personal access to the emperor, conducting daily rites for protection of the palace and worship of the sun (*nippai*) on his behalf, and the Chinkonsai preceding the Niinamesai.[34] The Yoshida House performed divinations and supervised the dispatch of Imperial Emissaries to the Ise Shrines and the Tōshōgū.[35]

Confucian Shinto

The Tokugawa shogunate faced the task of transforming a tradition of military rule into a civilian government. By 1640, the Christians had been decisively expelled or forced underground, and as the threat of foreign invasion and civil war receded, a stable period of peace and order began. Creating a functional and centralized peacetime government necessitated new principles to replace reliance on military force, nothing less than a new rationale and ethic of governance. Buddhism was adopted for the usefulness of its networks of temples, as a framework for the social control of the farmers. But it did not commend itself in philosophical terms, and it was widely criticized as pessimistic, world-denying, and out of step with the needs of the new era. By the reign of the fourth shogun Ietsuna (r. 1651–1680), what was wanted was something more rational, more concerned with the ethics of this life than the next. This is the reason that Confucianism had an opportunity to be freed from its former status as a mere adjunct of Zen teaching and develop new scholarship. But at the beginning, Confucians were much divided among themselves. Their most widely shared element was dislike of Buddhism and Christianity, sentiments that Shinto also shared.[36]

Many Confucians absorbed Shinto elements; Fujiwara Seika (1561–1619) was one of these, equating Confucianism with Shinto, as a theory of government based on promotion of morality. The people should be honest and obedient to their rulers, and rulers should be moral exemplars. Nakae Tōju (1608–1648) also promoted Shinto, but he used the term to describe his notion of a universal teaching, thus blurring the link between it and Japan. He largely equated Shinto with shrine rites and customs until he visited the Ise Shrines for the first time in 1641. Having previously held that a true sage could appear only in China, he subsequently came to believe that Amaterasu was "the sage of Japan."[37]

Kumazawa Banzan (1619–1691) wrote of the "Heavenly Way" (*tendō*) that is manifest in different ways in different countries. It may be explained in different terms, according with the character of the people who arise to proclaim it, but it is one Way. Banzan inherited the medieval idea that Japan is one of the barbarian countries, but qualified that depressing view by claiming that it is the top-ranking one. Its people are endowed with a spiritual nature, and Amaterasu is a virtuous sage equal to the sages of China. Her teaching is manifest in the imperial regalia, which have the qualities of courage, benevolence, and wisdom. Banzan did not preach the identity of Shinto and Buddhism.[38]

All the early Confucians drew important links to Shinto and often identified Confucianism with it. But having done that, and having criticized Buddhism and Christianity as being "foreign," they had to show that Confucianism was not subject to the same critique, and that it meshed well with Shinto. They had to show further that while a merger of Shinto and Buddhism was a distortion of Shinto, a merger of Confucianism and Shinto was not. The key lay in the claim that Shinto and Confucianism were one, in the sense that Confucianism encompasses and incorporates Shinto. If that were true, then they could claim that Confucianism is Japan's original Way, or at least that was the attempt.[39]

Once Confucianism had a firm groundwork, Shinto could benefit from Confucianism's rationalism to systematize its own teachings. It was not difficult to defend the position, as Yoshida and Watarai Shinto both did, that Shinto should be independent of Buddhism. That was more or less assumed and accepted. However, in order to assist the political class of the times to understand Shinto, Shinto had to be explained rationally, in terms of universal concepts like the Way. Answers were needed to such questions as how the Kami of Japan related to other deities, and how Shinto related to the other established "Ways." Because criticism of Buddhism was so widespread, it was necessary to escape the framework in which Buddhism and its deities were inevitably linked with Shinto and the Kami.

We saw in the previous chapter that there was considerable fluidity and overlap in medieval Shinto thought, and that various tenets and ritual styles were shared across Ryōbu Shinto, Watarai Shinto, and Yoshida Shinto, these being the three great streams of thought regarding the Kami up to that time. According to Mark Teeuwen, so extensively had Watarai theologians borrowed Ryōbu Shinto ideas that it is almost impossible to tell the texts of the two schools apart.[40] While these schools of thought differed on significant points, they had produced a shared frame of reference.

Hayashi Razan's (1583–1657), "Shintō denju," (a title that could be construed as either *An Initiation to Shinto* or *Shinto Transmissions*) shows how Confucian thinkers took the medieval heritage as their point of departure. Written between 1645 and 1648, when Razan was between sixty-two and sixty-five years old, it represents his mature thought on Shinto, based on extensive research into Yoshida and Watarai texts. A colophon states that the work was compiled for Sakai Tadakatsu (1587–1662), the shogun's chief senior counselor from 1638 to 1660.[41]

Hayashi Razan was a Confucian scholar in service to the shogunate. "Razan" was his Confucian name; officially, he was referred to as Dōshun, his Buddhist name. He studied at the Kamakura Zen temple Kenninji from age thirteen, leaving two years later without being ordained. At twenty-two he began studying Confucianism with Fujiwara Seika. Wishing to form government connections, he went to serve Ieyasu in 1605. Since at the time there was no official recognition of Confucianism, he wore Buddhist monks' robes like other Buddhist advisers throughout his service to the first four Tokugawa shoguns. He inspected ancient works and published them, hosted the Korean missions, drafted documents for foreign relations, worked on court cases involving temple-shrine relations, and participated in public duties involving scholarship and ritual. His main Shinto works are "Shintō denju" and "Honchō jinja kō," a compilation of the traditions of major shrines completed several years before "Shintō denju."[42]

"Shintō denju" was originally prepared in the form of *kirigami,* literally, "cut paper," so that its eighty-nine separate sections might be ritually transmitted as "esoteric teachings" (one of the connotations of *denju*). *Kirigami* was a method of formal Buddhist transmission of esoteric knowledge, a certification or license for poetry, and Shinto learning, in use from the Muromachi period. Some sixty-nine *kirigami* roughly identical to "Shintō denju" are extant and should probably be considered the "original" of the manuscript in which all eighty-nine sections would have appeared seriatim, as a continuous text. In other words, "Shintō denju" was a set of teachings to be revealed in sequence, not all at once.[43]

Razan often attributed specific points to Yoshida teachings, but in fact he was launching a new way of expressing Shinto ideas. Razan begins by stating that "Kami are the spirits of Heaven and Earth," the spiritual powers causing the movements of the cosmos. Every occurrence results from their deeds. Razan wrote, "The heart-mind is the dwelling of Kami," that is, humanity and the Kami are united. The Kami behind the movements of Heaven and Earth is manifest in the heart-mind of the individual person. Up to this point, Razan was essentially restating ideas seen in Kanetomo's work.

Razan began a more original exposition when he expressed Yoshida positions on the Kami through Confucian concepts. He asserted that Kami is equivalent to *principle* (*ri*), claiming that Kami stands for a rational and ethical ideal that is fundamental to all reality.[44] Next, he transposed the Confucian idea that good action leads to good for the doer, while evil action leads to evil. To do good is to obey the Kami in the heart-mind; to do evil is to turn one's back on one's "mind-god" (*shinshin,* a combination of the characters for heart-mind and Kami). A pure heart-mind manifests Kami like a mirror. In later sections Razan distinguishes between inner and outer purification, the inner corresponding to the elimination of evil and illusion from the *kokoro,* the outer being a matter of physical cleanliness.[45]

Mention of a mirror provided Razan's segue to a discussion of the imperial regalia, which he linked to wisdom (the mirror), benevolence (the jewels), and courage (the sword), and also to the sun, the moon, and the stars. Received from Amaterasu, the regalia have been for each emperor the implements of governance. Shinto and "the Kingly Way" (*ōdō*, another hallmark concept of Confucian thought) are identical. Razan gave this point special emphasis, because he wanted to establish that Shinto contains a theory of governance identical to that found in Confucianism, "the Kingly Way," in which the ruler is first and foremost a moral exemplar who leads through law and personal example, educating the populace without resort to brute force.[46]

Razan's exposition next turned to the cosmogony, beginning with the time before the separation of Heaven and Earth. At that time of primeval chaos, there was one Kami without form, Kunitokotachi, the primal, original deity. The division of this Kami resulted in the myriad Kami and all beings, which accounts for the fundamental unity of Kami and humanity. Further remarks on the cosmogony in later sections clarified that Kunitokotachi and Toyouke are identical.[47]

Turning to the relation between Buddhas and Kami, Razan wrote that the two are ultimately one, and that in a mysterious appearance, the Buddhas "dim their light" to appear as Kami. The Buddhas are the Kami of India but are not, however, identical to the Kami of Japan. In Japan, the Kami are both *honji* and *suijaku*.[48]

In succeeding sections, Razan remarks on miscellaneous practices and concepts associated with the Kami, such as *torii* and *shimenawa*, purification prayers and spells, associations linking the Kami to the five elements, food offerings at shrines, the necessity of ancestor veneration, the oracles of Yamato Hime, and the Heavenly Jeweled Spear, among others. In fact, the majority of the eighty-nine sections are short and freestanding, appropriate to the intended method of transmitting them in sequence.

Razan's most distinctively Confucian assertion in this work is the idea of "Principle-is-the-mind Shinto" (*ritō shinchi Shintō*) in section 18:

> Principle-is-the-mind Shinto—this Shinto is the same as the kingly way (*ōdō*). There is no other kami, no other principle apart from the mind. The purity and brightness of the heart is the light of kami. Correct behavior is the form of kami. The enactment of government is by the virtue of kami, the ordering of the nation is by the power of kami. This has been transmitted from Amaterasu Ōmikami. It is what has been practiced by the emperors since the time of Jinmu. It is what has been carried on by the ministers of the left and right, the *sesshō* and *kanpaku* during reigns when the emperor has not yet attained his majority. It is said that in recent generations there are few people with knowledge of this Way.[49]

Razan uses the term *Shinto* frequently, as if it were a part of the vernacular. Adopting Yoshida Kanetomo's typology, Razan names three "streams" (*nagare, ryū*) of Shinto: Yuiitsu sōgen or Yoshida Shinto, Ryōbu Shinto in which Amaterasu is identified with Dainichi, and the combinatory practice of most shrines (*honji engi*). In the second paragraph of section 18, he emphasizes the importance of distinguishing Shinto as the Kingly Way from Shinto as a general name for things related to shrines:

> There is a secondary Shinto tradition of divination and ritualism. The *shake* (literally, "shrine families," attached to specific shrines and performing various services for them), *negi*, *kannushi*, and *hafuri* clean the shrines when rituals are to be performed, or they assist with prayers and purifications. The "Shinto" manifest by the emperor is hard to detect in this [secondary tradition]. For that reason, it should be understood that outside of Principle-is-the-mind Shinto, things related to the Kami belong to this secondary tradition.[50]

It is evident from "Shintō denju" that Shinto could be grasped in terms of religious concepts and ethics. Humanity has within it a spark of divinity, the "mind-god" (*shinshin*). To maintain it, one must seek to attain the undifferentiated state of the cosmos before the creation of Heaven and Earth, called *konton*. To attain such a state is to commune with the Kami, to be in union with them. Not coincidentally, because the primeval chaos is chronologically and cosmologically prior to Buddhism, Shinto trumps Buddhism. Union with the Kami became the aim of worship, and purification of body and mind the means to attain it. Because all people have the mind-god, worship theoretically became open to all.[51]

Razan's work emphasized Shinto's "public" character in the claim that it contains a rationale for governing the realm. Both Confucians and the political leaders whose patronage they sought struggled to make sense of shrines' unruly abundance of gods. Razan and others borrowed the language of Shinto in order to make Confucian ideas more familiar, less "foreign" to their intended sponsors. But this Confucian appropriation of Shinto discourse was largely a means to an end. The purpose was to put Confucianism across in a palatable way that the rulers could understand. This expedient use of Shinto was not central to Confucians' ongoing work. This is proven by the fact that their disciples did not bother to develop Confucian Shinto much further, and unsurprisingly the Shinto coloration of their Confucianism soon faded.

Shinto Adaptations of Confucianism

Shintoists adopted Confucian terms to explain Shinto logically. Two representatives of this approach came from the Watarai and Yoshida lineages: Watarai (Deguchi) Nobuyoshi (1615–1690) and Yoshikawa Koretaru (1616–1694). They both distinguished between Shinto as a transcendent "Way" and the miscellaneous practices of shrines. Nobuyoshi so seldom left Ise, however, that his influence did not extend very far beyond shrine priests there. By contrast, Koretaru had a great sense of mission that he must rebuild the Way and proclaim it widely, assiduously cultivating political patrons in Edo.[52]

Deguchi Nobuyoshi was the son of an *oshi* from Yamada. He was an autodidact in both Shinto and Confucianism, presenting his thought powerfully in "Yōfukki," written in 1650, when he was thirty-six. This work was a kind of manifesto outlining his principle concerns. He saw Shinto (especially at the Ise Shrines) as having declined due to Buddhist influence, and he wrote that it was crucial to establish Shinto's independence by ridding it of Buddhist elements. With its independence established, Shinto would be understood as a universal teaching for all peoples, something that they could practice in their daily lives. He wrote further that Shinto could be embodied at the individual level by adhering to Confucianism's five relations.

He particularly stressed the imperial connections of the Ise Shrines and the priority of the Outer Shrine. While affirming that the rituals performed at the Ise Shrines by their priests are exclusively for the imperial family, he wrote that lay people are free to pray to the Ise gods. Based on the idea that the Outer Shrine deity Toyouke is identical with Kunitokotachi, who existed prior to Amaterasu, he asserted the Outer Shrine's superiority. He founded a library at Yamada, the Toyomiyazaki Bunko, in 1648, through a subscription campaign so that Shinto texts could be accessible. Nobuyoshi's work stimulated the writing of many commentaries on the Five Books of Watarai Shinto (*Gobusho*), mainly philological explanations of their terms and phrases. Thus Nobuyoshi was responsible for a revival of Watarai Shinto that lasted until the 1730s and 1740s, when Yoshimi Yukikazu, a follower of Yamazaki Ansai and Suika Shinto, effectively destroyed claims of the Five Books' antiquity (see below).[53]

Tokugawa Ietsuna was only ten when his father Iemitsu, the third shogun, died in 1651. Five regents took charge until Ietsuna came of age in 1659. As half-brother to Iemitsu and uncle of Ietsuna, Hoshina Masayuki was chief among them. He was involved in the creation of significant law codes such as the *Codes of Warrior Conduct* (*Buke shohatto*), laws governing the Buddhist and Shugendō priesthoods, the shogun's harem, Nikkō Tōshōgū, and the establishment of the system of post stations linking Edo to every part of the realm. Besides being regent, Masayuki was the *daimyō* of the Aizu domain, which produced 23,000 *koku* annually, and also manager of shogunal lands worth another 55,000 *koku*.[54]

Becoming regent in 1651, Masayuki had to cope with problems associated with rebellious *rōnin*, "masterless samurai," displaced in the first years of the period. A *rōnin* plot to overthrow the shogunate was discovered in 1651, and an uprising by around 800 *rōnin* broke out in Sado Island in 1652. A devastating fire that killed 100,000 people in Edo and damaged the Edo castle occurred in 1657, the "Meireki Fire" (having occurred in the third year of the Meireki era). Masayuki built a nonsectarian temple in Edo called Ekōin for the victims of the fire and took extraordinary measures to ameliorate the widespread suffering caused by the fire, including the creation of a system of granaries for distributing grain in such disasters.[55]

Masayuki sought to rule through law and moral example. He had studied various philosophical systems in his youth, but seeing Confucianism as an intellectual basis for governance, he turned to it exclusively around 1650. Masayuki hoped to reconcile the samurai to their new role in society as salaried bureaucrats. He particularly sought to enforce a prohibition on *junshi*, the custom of warriors committing suicide to follow a deceased lord in death, which he regarded as a relic of wartime and also a violation of Confucian teaching. As lord of Aizu, Masayuki prohibited infanticide and cremation. He inveighed against religionists at newly established shrines and temples, whom he believed lacked any purpose beyond exploiting the gullible.[56]

Masayuki employed various scholar-lecturers. Among them were Koretaru and Yamazaki Ansai (1618–1682). It is largely thanks to Masayuki's patronage that either of them was able to attain a position of influence. Koretaru's father had died in battle in Ieyasu's army. His mother had Koretaru adopted by a merchant family in Edo, and though the nature of the business is unclear, the young Koretaru had access to books and opportunity to acquire a basic knowledge of Confucianism. He worked in this business until the age of thirty-nine, when his adopted father died and the business declined. Thereafter Koretaru retired and moved to Kamakura. He became interested in the *Nakatomi Harai* and went to Kyoto to study it with Hagiwara Kaneyori, who was regarded as the leading authority.[57]

Kaneyori was already quite elderly when Koretaru approached him, but he had not yet passed on the Yoshida secret teachings to a successor. Kaneyori was so impressed with Koretaru that he determined to transmit the teachings to him rather than to someone in the Yoshida family. Koretaru went to Kyoto repeatedly to receive lectures from Kaneyori, who had Koretaru instruct the young Yoshida heir and live on the Yoshida property while in Kyoto. Kaneyori called Koretaru to his deathbed in 1660 and charged him to transmit the lineage secrets to the Yoshida heir when the latter came of age. Kaneyori left management of the Yoshida house affairs in Kyoto to other disciples, including the lineage "business" (*kagyō*) of tending their own shrine and certifying provincial shrines, priests, and Kami. This means that the inheritance of the Yoshida house was split into two parts on a temporary basis, with the understanding that the two streams would be rejoined when the heir came of age.[58]

To initiate someone outside the Yoshida lineage was a major deviation from contemporary understanding about transmitting the teachings of the sacerdotal lineages. As it happened, the obvious candidates in the Yoshida line had either died young or were too sickly to serve effectively. The Fourfold Profound Secrets were supposed to be transmitted only once in a generation, ideally from father to son. Initiation would make the recipient the embodiment of the Yoshida ancestral Kami, Amenokoyane. While Kaneyori had written that Shinto's insistence on transmitting the teaching along kinship lines was a liability, it was unheard of to entrust the secrets to someone outside the Yoshida line. But the most important thing to Kaneyori was that the teachings not die out. On the other hand, although Koretaru was very keen, he had only been studying Shinto for five years and was considered lowborn by the rest of the Yoshida family. That such a man should be made the fifty-fourth incarnation of Amenokoyane by Kaneyori's unilateral decision enraged the Yoshida family.[59]

The main tenets of Yoshida Shinto as taught by Koretaru may be summarized as follows. Shinto is the origin of all teachings. Because Japan is the easternmost country and the first to be created, the Kami of Japan appeared before the creation of Heaven and Earth. The Kami of Japan created all countries, and all teachings, including Confucianism and Buddhism. It is not correct to hold that the three teachings are one. Kunitokotachi is the origin of all living things, all of whom have this Kami within them as the heart-mind (*kokoro*).[60]

Koretaru's thought shows strong influence from neo-Confucian thought. Kunitokotachi is principle, without form and eternal. Principle dwells within all humanity as their nature (*sei*) or heart-mind, which are equivalent to the *tama* of Kami. Thus we can say that the heart-mind is the seat of divine virtue (*shinmei*), or the "shrine of the primeval chaos" (*konton no miya*). Because Kami and humanity share this nature, Kami and humanity are originally one. But divine brightness becomes clouded by greed and desire. To return to the original brightness, it is necessary to be released from egotism, which is to become one with Kunitokotachi. The realization of this unity is the goal of Shinto.[61]

The way to realize the unity of Kami and humanity is through reverence (*tsutsushimi, kei*), sincerity (*makoto*), and uprightness (*shōjiki*). The method to attain reverence is through inner and outer purification, which remove sins and impurities and cleanses body and mind, allowing the inner divinity to manifest. Outer purification can be accomplished through the practice of ablutions (*misogi*). Inner purification comes about by banishing extraneous thoughts and practicing sincerity, returning to the undifferentiated state of *konton*.[62]

To fulfill the way of humanity is to fulfill the five relations, of which the most important is the relation between ruler and subject; the essence of Shinto lies in the preeminence of this relation. The relation between ruler and subject derives from Kunitokotachi and descends from him through Amaterasu and the lineage of human emperors.[63]

Koretaru returned to Edo and began cultivating patrons in government by proclaiming that Shinto's essence lies in its theory of governance. Koretaru's first opportunity to present his ideas to a high-ranking person was a lecture in 1657 before Tokugawa Yorinori (1602–1671, tenth son of Ieyasu and *daimyō* of the Kii domain). When Yorinori proposed to Koretaru that shrine priests manage shrines but seem to have no place in the governing of the country, Koretaru responded that Shinto is divided into Shinto of Ritual (*gyōhō jisō*) and Shinto of Principle (*rigaku Shintō*). The former has to do with shrine etiquette and the performance of ritual, which is the business of professional priests. Shinto of Principle (which Koretaru had obviously appropriated from Hayashi Razan) refers to matters of military force and the arts. From the divine age, Shinto of Principle has been transmitted to the descendants of the Kami Amenokoyane, that is, the Yoshida lineage. Japan is preeminent among all countries as the country richest in metal. Thus it is natural that the people as a whole take to the military arts and that Japan be called a military country (*bukoku*). Governance in the Age of the Gods rested on military force exerted through benevolence. This is the Way of the Heavenly Jeweled Spear, passed down from Izanagi to Amaterasu. Military preparedness is an exercise of benevolence, making the four seas calm and tranquil.[64]

The Confucian notion of benevolent rule emerged as a key element in the effort to guarantee social stability. Koretaru grasped the nature of the desired ideological transformation and succeeded in securing a political role for Shinto through Hoshina Masayuki's patronage. Since government had so obviously passed out of the hands of the emperor and his court, an emphasis on the imperial regalia alone could not have harmonized with the existence and preeminence of the shogunate. Thus Koretaru shifted his emphasis to the Heavenly Jeweled Spear and produced an image of benevolent government focused upon this symbol that originated even before the regalia. Koretaru provided a symbolic legitimation of shogunal rule, as well as incorporating an assertion of Japan's superiority and an individual ethic based on reverence, sincerity, and uprightness. In doing so, Koretaru imported Razan's ideas about Shinto as principle into the legacy of Yoshida Shinto.

Ietsuna's coming-of-age ceremony was held in 1659, and it was around that time that Masayuki withdrew from daily involvement with the shogunal government and turned his attention to his home domain. It was also from this time that Masayuki began to suffer frequently from an eye ailment. Throughout his illness, however, he had attendants read to him from Confucian texts, and if he did not agree with a particular point, he would stop the attendant mid-sentence and have him mark the passage. When the issue arose later, Masayuki would have the attendant return to the first section to compare the two and thus refine his understanding or strengthen his own argument against that point in the text. He had a retainer, Hattori Ankyū, study with Koretaru.[65]

Masayuki first had Koretaru lecture to him in 1661; the topic was the "Age of the Gods" section of the *Nihon shoki*. Koretaru asserted that loyalty is the most important virtue in Shinto, even more important than filial piety, and this impressed Masayuki very much. He began to involve Koretaru in policy deliberations. Since the shogunate continued to consult Masayuki even after his regency ended, his influence remained considerable. Koretaru lobbied successfully for inclusion of the provision in the 1665 code of law governing shrines that confirmed the privileges of the Yoshida house. Masayuki helped Koretaru promote the Yoshida house in this way and also by arranging a shogunal audience for the young Yoshida heir.[66]

The reason for Koretaru's success lay in the match between his teachings and the needs of the political class. He formed his connection to Masayuki after a stable peace had been established, and when the shogunate had determined to rule through peaceful means rather than force. Rulers were to manifest virtue, which the people would understand and emulate, an idea stemming from Confucianism. But in rulers' eyes there were problems with Confucianism. First, it was the teaching of another country, and they might have to adopt the worship of Confucius as a sage (which some, such as Ikeda Mitsumasa, did). Second, Confucian ethics upheld filial piety as the highest virtue, whereas Japanese rulers needed a teaching that would uphold loyalty as the supreme virtue. Koretaru proposed his version of Shinto as the answer to this conundrum.[67]

Masayuki involved Koretaru in governing Aizu, along with Yamazaki Ansai. Originally based in Kyoto, Ansai entered Masayuki's service in 1665. He was hired as a part-time advisor, spending spring and summer in Edo with Masayuki until 1672.[68] During this time, Ansai also formed an important connection with Koretaru. Ansai was a Confucian scholar in the first instance, and his first writing on Shinto (in 1655) was titled "The Lesser Learning of Yamato" (*Yamato shōgaku*).[69] Through his ties to Masayuki and Koretaru, Ansai became increasingly interested in Shinto and eventually became known as the founder of Suika Shinto, which remained highly influential throughout the era.

Through his connection with Koretaru, Ansai received initiation to Yoshida teachings. He was also very interested in Watarai teachings, and over the years 1657 to 1669, Ansai made six pilgrimages to Ise. On the last of these, Deguchi Nobuyoshi had him initiated in the Watarai esoteric teachings, another highly irregular transmission of lineage teachings outside kinship lines. Thus, Yamazaki Ansai was in the unique position of having received initiation to both the Yoshida and Watarai sacred teachings.[70]

Hoshina Masayuki involved both Koretaru and Ansai in developing his policies on religion in Aizu by having them survey the domain's *shikinaisha* in 1666. By undertaking this survey, Masayuki hoped to upgrade these ancient shrines relative to the temples that controlled them, and also to serve as a basis for distinguishing shrines with established histories from more recent shrines with unorthodox practices. In 1667, on the basis of Koretaru's and Ansai's survey, Masayuki abolished shrines and razed Buddhist temples and chapels established in the preceding twenty years, also closing temples that did not have a resident priest. Masayuki took these measures in the hope of directing popular religious faith toward institutions whose history was known, and whose practices were "authentic." These changes also strengthened the economic base of the remaining temples and shrines while sparing the people the burden of supporting too many of them. Masayuki was generous in his support of temples and shrines of which he approved.[71]

In 1669, Koretaru and Ansai compiled a historical survey of Aizu shrines titled *Aizu jinjashi* that combined shrine histories with information on their land holdings, treasures, and the Buddhist temples that administered them. Also in 1669, Koretaru conferred on Masayuki a "living shrine" title, "Hanitsu Reijin," which is to say apotheosis, and initiated him in the Fourfold Profound Secrets of the Yoshida house. Apparently Koretaru intended both the deification and the initiation as gestures of respect to Masayuki as his patron and had no expectation that Masayuki would take any role in the Yoshida house or transmit the teachings to anyone else. Thus Koretaru continued the unorthodox style of initiation that he himself had received, broadening the scope of eligibility to include a highly placed political patron. Koretaru also gave Ansai a "living shrine" name and an initiation a few days after Masayuki.[72]

Koretaru helped Masayuki identify a suitable location for his mausoleum on a mountaintop in Aizu, and both Ansai and Koretaru had roles in Masayuki's funeral. Only by aggressive lobbying of the shogunate was Koretaru able to secure permission for Masayuki to have a Shinto funeral from which all Buddhist elements were eliminated. After Masayuki's death, Ansai returned to Kyoto and did not visit Edo again. Koretaru campaigned for two years to have Masayuki's mausoleum built on a grand scale. He succeeded, and the Hanitsu Jinja was built on Mt. Minemi in Aizu, a huge construction project, in 1673.[73]

Masayuki had created the shogunate post of Shintōkata ("Shinto adviser") for Koretaru in 1666; Koretaru apparently took it up after Masayuki's death. "Shintokata" was to be a government post for a Shinto scholar-advisor to the Magistrate of Temples and Shrines on matters of Shinto ritual, whose advice would be based upon study of Shinto texts and rites. Through creating this post, Masayuki intended to give official standing to Koretaru and his descendants in perpetuity.[74] With Masayuki's death, however, Koretaru lost his patron, and neither he nor his descendants, who occupied the post, were able to achieve enough influence to use it to promote Shinto effectively. The salience of Koretaru's signature promotion of loyalty over filial piety receded as the threat of rebellion faded. The post was not always filled, and its stipend was far less than that granted to the Hayashi family. After the fifth shogun Tsunayoshi came to power, he promoted Confucianism enthusiastically, showing comparatively little interest in Shinto. Shinto became a peripheral philosophy as far as the government was concerned, though Koretaru's descendants tried to perpetuate his teachings by calling them Yoshikawa Shinto.[75] While Koretaru had inherited the legacy of Yoshida Shinto, he and his descendants emphasized the concept of Shinto as Principle, which was a departure from Kanetomo's teaching and a clear appropriation of Hayashi Razan's views in *Shintō denju*.[76]

Returning to Kyoto, Ansai collected disciples, his prestige elevated by his time in service to Masayuki. Some of his students specialized in Confucian learning; Ansai's school of Confucian thought was called Kimon. Other disciples emphasized Ansai's Shinto thought, which he dubbed "Suika Shinto," after the living-shrine name that Koretaru had bestowed on him.

Yamazaki Ansai and Suika Shinto

Ansai accepted that the cosmos and humanity are united by principle, which is a universal property of all existence, but it was important to identify what principle corresponds to in Japan. He concluded that the mind-god residing in each person is principle. Ansai described Shinto as a way of living in accord with the will of Kami. Prayer is the means to understand the will of the Kami and receive their favor, but in order to receive this divine favor, humanity must be upright and worship reverently.[77] Ansai attributed great significance to reverence (*kei, tsutsushimi*) as the proper attitude for worshipping the Kami and emphasized its importance for attaining union with Kami.[78]

In developing these ideas, Ansai clearly accepted important ideas from Yoshida Shinto, including the idea that Kunitokotachi is the primal deity of the universe, and that he is ultimately identical to Amenominakanushi. Ansai relied heavily on the "Yamato Hime seiki" of the Five Books of Watarai Shinto, the oracles of Yamato Hime. Ansai had secured a copy of this text through his brother-in-law, who was a priest at the Shimogamo Shrine.[79] Yamato Hime commanded "to keep right what is right and left what is left." Ansai used this formula to develop a key attitude: "to give in even one inch to evil will only lead to total disaster." He advocated cultivating an "ever-vigilant mind," unswerving in loyalty and selflessness.[80]

Ansai was determined to find Confucian principles in Japanese myth and took myth very seriously. Confucian tradition identified three types of sages: those possessing an innate understanding of morality and experiencing no difficulty in enacting it; the sort who comes to this understanding through learning and wisdom, and the kind of sage who comes to understanding through great effort in each action. Ansai sought a correspondence among the Kami for these types of sages and identified Amaterasu as the first, Sarutahiko as the second, and Susanoo and Ōnamuchi as the third. This exposition was meant to demonstrate that any kind of human being, of any disposition or intellectual endowments, could cultivate himself sufficiently to become united with Kami. Based on this theory, he explained Suika Shinto as the "Way of Amaterasu."[81]

Ansai identified the Way of Amaterasu with complete and unswerving loyalty to the emperor. Amaterasu is the ancestor of the imperial house and hence epitomizes the unity of humanity and the Kami. Unlike Confucianism's idea that an unsuitable emperor could legitimately be removed, Ansai stressed the absolute necessity of remaining loyal to such an emperor so as not to disturb the unity of humanity and the divine. To do otherwise would be to break the commandment of Yamato Hime, "to keep right what is right and left what is left."

Among the major works of Suika Shinto is Ansai's "Nakatomi no Harae fūsuisō," a compilation of foregoing commentaries on the Great Purification Prayer without significant original content. This work from Ansai's later years (the date is uncertain) is considered a basic text of the school, but only a small number of disciples were allowed access to it. Likewise, "Jijushō" was a set of the secret transmissions, intended solely for disciples, concerning the three regalia, and Yoshida secret traditions.[82] "Suika shagō" was an extended explanation of the name "Suika."[83]

Ansai lectured with passion, forcefully striking his lectern with a stick for emphasis. His disciples recorded these lectures, and these records also are regarded as central works of the school. "Jindai no maki fūyōshū" (also referred to as "Jindaimaki kōgi") was the major work of this kind, but it remained unfinished at Ansai's death and was a compilation of commentary on the first two chapters of *Nihon shoki*. In one passage, which Herman Ooms likens to "an evangelical sermon," Ansai discussed the mythological charter for the idea of "living shrine names" such as the ones he and Hoshina Masayuki had received from Koretaru.[84]

Japan's ancient tradition of deifying living human beings received new life in the Edo period from the Yoshida house, starting with Hideyoshi's deification as Toyokuni Daimyōjin. Kaneyori and Koretaru were regarded as incarnations of Amenokoyane in Yoshida house tradition. Koretaru's bestowing "living shrine names" (*reishagō*) on Masayuki and Ansai are only the best-known examples of a widespread phenomenon of ritual deifications that extended to *daimyō*, provincial shrine priests, and exemplary persons. All of Masayuki's *daimyō* descendants received these names, as did many of Ansai's disciples. The Yoshida house eventually worked out a tripartite ranking system for these names, which became a popular part of the "business" side of the house's influence over Shinto affairs. In 1674, one of Ansai's students built an altar in a Kyoto shrine where he served, Shimo Goryō Jinja, for the worship of the living Ansai's spirit, where Ansai's students regularly paid tribute. The symbol of deity was a pillar projecting from a copper box set in red earth (the favored combination of metal and earth), the pillar's dimensions proportionate to those of the sacred Heart Pillar at Ise. This practice of worshipping Ansai's spirit remained in effect until just before his death, when the city magistrate, acting on encouragement from the Yoshida house, had it removed to a side altar.[85]

Ansai continued to lecture on Confucianism even as his interest in Shinto deepened, and some of his disciples pursued the study of both traditions. Ansai designated the court noble Ōgimachi Kinmichi (1653–1733) his successor for Shinto matters, based on his belief that it was urgent that Shinto teachings be transmitted to the emperor. Kinmichi became Ansai's disciple in 1680 when his career at court was ascendant; he rose eventually to become Gon-dainagon in 1695. After Ansai's death, a group of forty-seven disciples signed an oath of allegiance to Kinmichi, who also inherited Ansai's library, including commentaries on the Great Purification Prayer. In 1684 Kinmichi transmitted a secret teaching to Ichijō Kaneteru (1652–1705), the regent for Emperor Reigen (r. 1663–1687), after which Kaneteru became a disciple of Suika Shinto and an important ally to Kinmichi in his quest to transmit Ansai's writings to the imperial family. Kinmichi and Kaneteru succeeded in showing a copy of "Nakatomi Harae Fūsuisō"[86] to Reigen's father, the retired emperor

Go-Sai (r. 1654–1663). Because Kinmichi had Ansai's books, he was able to give copies to Reigen's son, the crown prince and future Emperor Higashiyama (r. 1687–1709). On the basis of these contacts with the imperial house, Kinmichi began to speak of Ōgimachi Shintō, as if this were a new school distinct from Suika.[87]

In fact, however, the court was divided about accepting Suika Shinto, because many courtiers were already committed to Yoshida Shinto. Since Yoshida Shinto accepted Buddhist elements, it could not easily be reconciled with Suika when it came to the performance of court rites. To make matters more complicated, the Shirakawa family also held traditional prerogatives to perform court rites, and they tended to gravitate toward Kinmichi as an ally in resisting Yoshida authority in this area. Dislike of Yoshida prerogatives to issue licenses to provincial shrines provided common cause for important shrines to form connections with Kinmichi. The Twenty-Two Shrines, the Fushimi Inari Shrine, and other powerful shrines of the Kinai area, as well as the Izumo Shrine, the Atsuta Shrine, and others lobbied successfully for permission to receive licenses from court families other than the Yoshida. Together they formed a group of shrines outside the scope of Yoshida influence, and their opposition to the Yoshida encouraged them to gather around Kinmichi.[88]

The duality between Ansai's Confucianism and Shinto constituted a structural instability in the task of perpetuating his teachings. Even among the followers of Kinmichi, it was difficult to create unity. Only some of Ansai's Shinto teachings had been committed to writing, while the most important were transmitted either orally or using *kirigami*. Kinmichi is said to have stopped using *kirigami*, and he tried to systematize Ansai's Shinto teachings, but his own writing seemed less to develop Ansai's ideas than to open new lines of inquiry. His "Mukyūki," for example, upheld the legitimacy of the medieval Southern Court, based on its possession of the regalia. He also claimed that Amaterasu was the first human emperor. While Suika Shinto continued to stimulate loyalist thought into the twentieth century, as an active school of investigation into Shinto matters it came to an end with Kinmichi's death in 1733.[89]

Yoshimi Yukikazu (1673–1761)

As Kinmichi's followers coalesced in part out of dislike for the Yoshida certification system, another Suika follower arose to challenge the intellectual basis of Yoshida authority. Yoshimi Yukikazu was a scholarly follower of Yamazaki Ansai and priest at the Nagoya Tōshōgū. Under the terms of the 1665 shrine *hatto*, his shrine was under the authority of the Yoshida house, and he had to apply to the Yoshida for rank and title. He described Yoshida representatives as "empty" and evidently found them deficient in learning, unworthy to hold the authority given them by law. In his view, the Yoshida had wrongfully usurped a prerogative that belonged to the imperial court. Yoshimi had investigated the Yoshida claims to high status in antiquity, beginning with their claims to be descended from the Kami Amenokoyane. He concluded that the Urabe family, from whom the Yoshida family was descended, were no more than minor functionaries performing divination with tortoise shells. From his study of the Five Books of Watarai Shinto, upheld by the Yoshida as well as the Watarai, he concluded that these works could not possibly have been composed in antiquity, but in all likelihood were a product of the medieval period. Yoshimi's writings thus thoroughly undermined both the Yoshida and Watarai lineages. Various rebuttals were issued, but Yoshimi had the truth on his side, and others had shared his suspicions before he committed them to writing.[90]

Yoshimi marshaled his criticisms of the Yoshida in support of an unsuccessful petition to have his shrine exempted from Yoshida authority, as a number of larger, older shrines had done soon after the 1665 *hatto*'s original issuance. He did not publish his views, but they were widely known and circulated. Watarai figures themselves had found many of the ideas of the Five Books increasingly unsupportable. According to Mark Teeuwen, by the end of the period, they were almost relieved to relinquish the responsibility to uphold them any longer.[91] But while the Ise Shrines were enjoying great and growing popularity in these years and thus would certainly endure even if the intellectual rationale of the Outer Shrine were crippled, Yoshimi's criticisms had a more devastating effect on the Yoshida.

If the Yoshida were revealed as descended from a low-ranking family in antiquity that was responsible for plastromancy and not much else, then what was the value of the shrine ranks and certificates they issued? Why would any responsible government prop up such a group? These were among the practical questions that flowed from Yoshimi's writing. The number of certificates issued by the Yoshida suffered a major decline, and thereafter it seems that government pressure was also exerted to bring an end to Yoshida issuance of certificates recognizing particular Kami as holding certain ranks.[92] Another mark of official displeasure with the Yoshida came with the 1748 Daijōsai, when they were awarded only the job of divining the location of the Yuki and Suki fields and were pointedly excluded from taking any more important role, while the Ōgimachi house was given the plum job of overall orchestrating.[93] The Yoshida tried to recoup the situation by appointing a Suika Shinto figure, Matsuoka Obuchi (1701–1783), as their head of doctrine (*gakuto*), but this measure did not reap the intended results.[94]

The Yoshida family did, however, continue to issue licenses to shrine priests, and when the 1665 *hatto* was re-issued in 1782, it included a new provision allowing the Yoshida to certify village shrine guilds called *miyaza*.[95] The shogunate continued to find the social networks established by the Yoshida useful in organizing the shrines and creating a loose framework for their supervision, even if other Yoshida claims had been discredited. This utilitarian stance resembles the use of Buddhist temples by a government that had frequently shown contempt for the religion itself. Moreover, the provision for the Yoshida to issue licenses to shrine guilds throws into relief another feature of the licensing system: when both priests and lesser shrine functionaries were made eligible for the same licenses, that undermined the authority of the shrine priests in relation to others serving at their shrines. There were many instances of priests contending with the families around shrines entrusted with miscellaneous responsibilities (the *shake*) and other customary ritualists through the purchase of licenses.[96]

Later Suika Shintō and Imperial Loyalism

The idea developed within Suika Shinto that those who serve the emperor faithfully will become Kami after death and dwell in Takamagahara eternally. Later Suika figures argued forcefully that service to the throne is the purpose of existence, speaking of the emperor as *arahito gami*, a "manifest deity." Ansai's disciple Tamaki Masahide (1670–1736) called on everyone to protect the throne with their lives, believing that after death they would be rewarded by being accepted into the ranks of the Kami. He stressed that the moral character of any individual sovereign is immaterial to the duty of loyalty to the monarch. Another Suika disciple, Wakabayashi Kyōsai (1679–1731), promulgated the identical thesis in his work, *Shintō tai-i*. This doctrine linking the life after death to loyalism was seen at a popular level in the work of Tomobe Yasutaka (1667–1740), who wrote an introductory text, *Shinto nonaka no shimizu* (1732). Matsuoka Obuchi preached that it is the essence of "the Japanese soul" (*Nihon damashii*) to protect the emperor, extending this duty to the people as a whole.[97] These ideas of imperial loyalism that arose from within Suika Shinto later provided an important bridge from this school to Kokugaku.

In the Hōreki incident of 1758, Suika's theme of loyalism played a role in an incident that revealed antagonism between the court and the shogunate. A group of young courtiers who admired the work of a Suika Shinto follower named Takenouchi Shikibu (1712–1767) arranged for him to lecture before the young Emperor Momozono (1741–1762), who would have been seventeen at the time. The Yoshida House was very concerned lest Suika influence begin to spread through the court. Shikibu was acquiring a growing number of followers among young aristocrats, a trend that was worrying to the regent, who feared that the shogunate would take offense at Shikibu's emphasis on the theme of loyalty to the monarch as the supreme virtue. The regent complained to the shogun's deputy in Kyoto, and as a result Shikibu was interrogated for nearly a year, and then sentenced to banishment, dying on the road to exile.[98]

Conclusion

Hayashi Razan, Yoshikawa Koretaru, and Yamazaki Ansai shared a set of driving questions. Who is the original Kami? If the Kami and humanity were originally united but now have become separated, how can we recapture that lost harmony with deity? What can Shinto contribute to the governing of the realm? How can Shinto's tradition of monarchism be reconciled with the reality of shogunal power? How should we understand the relation between Shinto and foreign teachings? How can we both grasp Shinto as a unified Way and also take account of the multifarious devotional practices at shrines? How should knowledge of Shinto be transmitted?

Razan, Koretaru, and Ansai employed the Confucian idea of principle in their expositions of Kami. All three affirmed Kunitokotachi as the original Kami, sometimes identifying Kunitokotachi with Amenominakanushi. Identifying Kunitokotachi as the primal deity affirmed *Nihon shoki* as the most important source of knowledge about the Kami. This deity is not found in *Kojiki*. Outer purification cleanses the body, and inner purification dispels the ignorance, evil, and egotism that obstruct humanity's union with Kami. Both Razan and Koretaru retained the medieval idea of a return to the state of chaos prior to creation. Koretaru and Ansai especially emphasized reverence as an important key to attaining unity with Kami. Razan and Koretaru showed comparatively less interest in Amaterasu, while Ansai emphasized the Sun Goddess much more, even calling Shinto the "Way of Amaterasu," and identifying Amaterasu as one type of Confucian sage.

These ideas of an ultimate deity standing behind a vast, unorganized pantheon of lesser Kami, the assertion of humanity's oneness with the ultimate deity, the proposition that ignorance, evil, and egotism obstruct the original unity, and the recommendation to practice purification as the means to recover that oneness form the nucleus of a philosophical system. Both Razan and Koretaru lived in Edo and sought shogunal patronage, while Ansai was mainly based in Kyoto and, subsequent to his return from Aizu, concentrated on loyalty to the emperor. All three offered pleasing images of Shinto's harmonious contribution to government through symbolism (the regalia and the Heavenly Jeweled Spear).

Early Edo period formulations regarding Shinto's relation to "the public" emerged in Confucian frameworks casting Buddhism as "the foreign," while nervously dodging the accusation that Confucianism was no less alien. Symbolically aligning the shogunate with the Heavenly Jeweled Spear suggested more ancient origins and hence even greater primacy than the regalia, a welcome image of legitimacy at the beginnings of the Tokugawa shogunate. Over the course of the next one hundred fifty years, however, the salience of this symbolism faded, and Confucian Shinto failed to retain significant political influence. By contrast, the theme of imperial loyalism that emerged so prominently in Suika Shinto remained vital.

In spite of the weakening of Yoshida intellectual authority, mechanisms for the spread of Yoshida doctrines and rituals were strengthened, enabling them to permeate shrines across the country. But there was no provision compelling shrines to affiliate with the Yoshida or any other aristocratic house. This means that while all temples were pressed into a sectarian hierarchy, shrines were free to affiliate, or not. Thus the shrines and the priesthood remained less organized and professionalized than the Buddhist clergy. Those shrines that accepted Yoshida authority could find their names, deities, and rites shaped by that affiliation, but those outside the Yoshida network of shrines remained at liberty to develop through more localized influences.

Even as Shinto thought continued to be transmitted as esoteric knowledge, earlier limitations restricting its communication to specific lineages were overturned. Both Watarai and Yoshida figures breached these restrictions in the early Edo period, while Razan and Ansai, who also adopted esoteric forms of transmission, never observed such kinship restrictions in the first place. Shinto thought and practice became less limited by kinship and more broadly diffused. As we will see in chapter 10, Shinto popularizers further broadened the dissemination of Shinto knowledge, aided by the revolution in print culture. These developments created a wider social and geographical base for Shinto, inciting criticism of esotericism and lineage restrictions, and provoking calls to make Shinto "public" in the sense of "open to all."

9

Edo-Period Shrine Life and Shrine Pilgrimage

Introduction

This chapter turns from philosophical expressions of Shinto to shrine life at a popular level, where concern with custodianship of the indigenous, or with assertions of a public character, is absent. Instead, we find that widespread forms of Kami worship express more general social and cultural trends, especially commercialism and the quest for happiness. Becoming tremendously popular during the Edo period, the worship of Inari, the rice deity, coupled with its messenger the fox, represents the pursuit of happiness, long life, abundance, and wealth. Upholding the value of the individual person's happiness, Inari worship built on the foundation of the Seven Happiness Gods cult discussed in chapter 6. The transformation of Inari worship in the Edo period illustrates the development of popular Kami worship in urban culture. As mentioned in chapter 8, by 1750, Edo was the world's largest city, with a population of more than one million. Overall, about 10 percent of Japan's population (around thirty million) resided in cities of more than 10,000 people. The cities were home to the most cultured and wealthy of the population.[1]

The commercial and pleasure-seeking culture of the cities permeated religious attitudes. Guidebooks such as *A Treasury of the Kami and Buddhas of Edo* (*Edo shinbutsu gankake jūhōki*) presented lists of shrines and temples, categorized by the problems each cultic site specialized in. They allowed the reader to page through the city's richness of scenic sites, oddities, and urban legends. Talismans sold at shrines and temples allowed people to carry a magical charm on their persons for protection from specific maladies like smallpox, measles, or hemorrhoids. A person might pay a priest to conduct a prayer rite (*kitō*) on his or her behalf, or might pray without such mediation. Terms such as *gankake*, "prayer to Kami and Buddhas," appeared in the vernacular, referring to the prayer itself or to a regimen undertaken in the hopes that the prayer would be fulfilled. A *gankake* regimen might include giving up a favored food or drink (salt or tea), or making one hundred or one thousand visits to the shrine or temple. "One hundred visits" (*ohyakudo*) became a well-known term for making numerous visits in the hopes that a prayer would be answered, as proof of one's sincerity. While these ideas and practices were not unknown before the Edo period, they developed new variety and intensity during those years, particularly in Inari worship.[2]

In the late eighteenth century, a multivolume set of illustrated books by Toriyama Sekien (1712–1788), cataloging more than two hundred kinds of monsters (*yōkai*), called *Illustrated Parade of One Hundred Monsters* (*Gazu hyakki yakō*) appeared. There was a kind of *asobi* for telling such ghost stories.

> First, light one hundred lamps (wicks) with blue paper around them and hide all weapons. Now, for each frightening tale, extinguish one lamp... When all one hundred flames have been extinguished, a monster [*bakemono*] will most definitely appear.[3]

The writer clearly expects that those playing the game actually want to be scared out of their wits and encounter a monster. Obviously, this is a form of play.

Edo's culture of "prayer and play" was a characteristic combination of religious pursuits and an attitude of play.

> Japanese believed that they could achieve intimacy with a deity if they were able to "play [*asobi*] with" it and that they could even affiliate themselves with it if they were able to amuse it.... In other words, play was a religious act.[4]

Shrine visits offered many chances to play: to see something new and different outside one's usual habitat, to enjoy the vitality and infinite variety of the cities, to view a theatrical performance, to buy a souvenir, to have one's fortune told, to flirt, to display oneself in one's best clothes, to drink *sake*, to see the latest fashions, and to enjoy oneself away from the daily grind of making a living. Commerce and play are the dominant paradigms within which Inari worship developed during the Edo period.

The Transformation of Inari Worship

Inari devotion originated in the worship of a grain spirit that might be named Inari, Ugajin, Uka-jin, or Uga no mitama (and related names). These Kami were represented in various ways. Ugajin is typically portrayed as an old man, or as a snake (symbol of wealth) with the head of an old man. Inari is portrayed in many forms, but a common one is as a goddess, sometimes identified with Dakini Shinten, bearing a sheaf of rice or riding a white fox (see Figure 9.1). A common thread in rural

Figure 9.1 Dakini Shinten. Hanging Scroll Acquired at Toyokawa Inari (Myōgonji), Aichi Prefecture. Source: Courtesy of the author.

settings is the belief that a deity descends from a mountain to protect the fields in spring (around the First Horse Day of the second month, called Hatsu-uma) and after the harvest, ascends the mountain again, alternating its identity as the field god (*ta no kami*) and the mountain god (*yama no kami*). The belief that the god of the rice field is Inari is widespread. Inari's messenger is the fox, an animal admired for its cunning and intelligence, on the one hand, and disparaged for its supposed lack of virtue, its trickster-like character, on the other. In rural areas Inari functions as an agricultural deity. In the cities of the Edo period, Inari became a popular deity (*hayarigami*, see the next section for a discussion) with divine powers to bring commercial success and healing. This form of Inari worship is accompanied by a belief in a fox god or in spirit possession by a fox.[5]

The Inari Taisha, informally known as Fushimi Inari, is a major center for Inari worship in the Fushimi district of southern Kyoto. Its Annual Festival is held on the first Day of the Horse in the Second Month, by the lunar calendar. Founded in 711 by the Hata family, Fushimi Inari comprises five separate shrines and was known historically as a place to pray for rain. Imperial progresses to this shrine began in 1071, and from the Kamakura period each emperor made an imperial progress here. It acquired fiefs in Yamashiro, Mimasaka, Bingo, Kaga, Echizen, and Mino provinces in the Heian period, as well as many fields in its immediate vicinity, whose proceeds were dedicated to the shrine. From the late medieval period, a temple called Aisenji functioned as its intendant temple. Beginning in the Muromachi period, shoguns regularly bestowed fiefs on the shrine, a trend that continued in the Sengoku and Edo periods.

Many other major shrines to Inari had been established: Takekoma Inari Shrine in the north, Kasama Inari Shrine in the Kantō, Toyokawa Inari in central Japan, and Yūtoku Inari in Kyūshū. During the Edo period, both Aisenji and Fushimi Inari conducted enshrinements of Inari for fees, for those wishing to install this deity individually in their homes, or in chapels in existing temples or shrines. Today Fushimi Inari serves as the headquarters for the 30,000 Inari shrines across the country, or over one-third of the total number of all shrines. Belief in the divine powers of Inari spread rapidly in the mid-Edo period through the proliferation of small shrines to the deity brokered from Fushimi Inari. The popularity of Inari was promoted by a variety of folk religionists, called Inari Nenji, Odaisan, and other terms.[6]

Temples of the Tendai, Shingon, Jōdo, and Nichiren sects frequently constructed Inari chapels on their grounds, so Inari worship was by no means an exclusively Shinto phenomenon. The Main Hall of the great Edo temple Sensōji (also known as Asakusa Kannon) was surrounded by a number of smaller buildings, including the Sanja Daigongen Shrine. There were "invited deities" from Fushimi Inari, Kumano, Atago, and Tenmangū shrines on the grounds. Smaller temples established after the 1630s turned to commercialized ritual (*kitō*) as their major source of income, because they did not have funeral parishioners. Moreover, a law prohibiting the construction of new shrines was promulgated in 1685. Though the law did not stop the practice, shrines established after that time ran the danger of exposure and abolition by fiat. They filled their precincts with all kinds of small shrines and chapels for miscellaneous deities, advertising their miracles through rapidly fabricated *engi*. Inari purifications and exorcisms—among rites for various deities—were common at the many urban "prayer temples" (*kitōdera*). For example, a chapel in Kobinata (Bunkyō-ku, Edo) called Dainichi-dō was a veritable department store of miscellaneous deities: Fudō, an Amida triad, Shōtoku Taishi, Benten, Aizen, Izanagi, Izanami, 1,000-armed Kannon, Inari, Konpira Gongen, Sannō Gongen, Akiba Gongen, Hosso-gami (smallpox gods), and more.[7]

During the late medieval period, a number of Inari shrines had been established around Osaka as harvest deities and initially had an agricultural character (e.g., Kashima Inari Shrine, Tamatsukuri Inari Shrine). Many Tendai, Shingon, and Jōdo sect temples had Inari chapels with this same agricultural character. From the end of the seventeenth century to the beginning of the eighteenth century, a number of land reclamation projects were conducted. People started to believe that some of the newly cleared land was holy, especially if old tombs and fox dens were discovered on it. Ghost stories and urban legends about foxes spread. Woodblock prints familiarized city people with fox stories, and in the mid-eighteenth century, tales about uncanny foxes began to be performed in kabuki and the puppet theater.[8]

Inari shrines began to be founded in Eastern Japan in large numbers at the end of the medieval period, though there were some earlier examples. Before the seventeenth century, there were three notable Inari shrines in the area: Hibiya Inari, Karasumori Inari, and Yotsugi Inari. Thereafter, they proliferated in multifarious ways. In 1652 the operator of the new Tamagawa aqueduct established the Tamagawa Inari Shrine to protect the waterworks. In 1658 a townsman named Kurosuke moved an Inari shrine that had been in the middle of a paddy field into the new brothel district of Yoshiwara, where it was known as Kurosuke Inari. *Daimyō* moving to Edo often established Inari shrines inside their mansion compounds (*yashiki*), in small buildings that were separate from the domicile called *yashikigami*, literally "the Kami of the mansion." Some of these acquired a reputation for spiritual powers and attracted crowds of worshippers. Sometimes an entryway into the grounds would be constructed for the worshippers, and if that happened, a market was likely to set up nearby to attract the visitors to the shrine. *Ennichi* were announced, the days on which it was most auspicious to visit, and the markets coordinated with that schedule. An early example from 1697 concerned an Inari shrine that originated as a *yashikigami* for a *daimyō* mansion in Iidamachi. It was opened to the general public after the *daimyō* moved away, leaving the shrine behind. It became so popular that eventually a shrine priest was appointed, and a larger building was constructed.[9]

According to a gazetteer of 1662 called *Edo meisho ki*, the Ōji Inari Shrine was the "big boss" (*sō-tsukasa*) of all the Inari shrines around Edo. It is located near

Asukayama, a popular suburban spot for pleasure excursions from Edo. Visitors typically combined a visit to the shrine with lunch at one of the area's fine restaurants or a teahouse, a stroll by the Silent River (Otonashi Kawa), or cherry blossom viewing in spring. The teahouses rented out nets with which visitors could catch river fish and then either take them home to stock their own ponds or release them into the river as an act of merit.[10]

The area was home to many foxes, which were allowed to roam freely and were revered as divine messengers of Inari. Other gazetteers of the period preserve a story holding that on the last day of the year, innumerable foxes would gather at a certain hackberry tree to worship at the shrine, making foxfire, which could be seen from Edo. People would predict their fortunes for the coming year based on the appearance of the fire.[11]

Rakugo is a theatrical form of storytelling that developed in the Edo period, mainly to relate humorous stories drawn from popular social life. One *rakugo* tale is called "The Foxes of Ōji," and is set in the Ōji Inari Shrine. One day, a visitor encountered a very attractive woman. In fact, she was a fox in disguise. Realizing that the fox was about to seduce him, the visitor decided to play along. He took the fox-woman to an expensive restaurant, where the two of them ate and drank so much that the fox nodded off. They had also ordered takeout food, which was wrapped and waiting for them to take home. The man took the takeout food and sneaked away while the fox-woman was asleep, leaving her to pay the bill. When she awoke, she was so horrified that she couldn't keep her disguised fox ears from popping out, which brought the innkeeper and all the restaurant workers down on her, yelling, "It's a fox! It's a fox!" They chased her around the room with a broom, and she was only barely able to escape with her life. But the man who had tricked her began to have regrets, especially after someone told him that the fox was the Princess Messenger of Inari, and that he was liable to suffer the god's wrath if he failed to make amends. So he went back to the shrine, carrying the takeout food as a gift of apology. Later, the fox cubs presented it to their mother, who was in their den, still licking her wounds following her narrow escape.

> "Mom, that man who tricked you yesterday has come back."
>
> The mother fox replied, "What? He's back again? The nerve! Don't go out there!"
>
> "But he was apologizing all over the place and gave us this box. Hey! There could be rice cakes in here!"
>
> "Don't eat that! It could be horse shit!"[12]

The story's punch line hangs on the audience knowing that if a fox were going to trick someone with something appearing to be delicious food, it was likely to be equine excrement.

Inari Becomes a *Hayarigami*

In the mid-eighteenth century, a new belief emerged, holding that different manifestations of Inari had specific powers, and that ordinary people should pray to the manifestation most closely fitting their particular problems. Furthermore, people apparently began to worship Inari's messenger the fox itself, calling foxes Inari Myōjin. New forms of Inari worship appeared, with names in which the first part indicates the divine powers of that particular Inari. Well-known types include Flourishing Inari (*Sakae Inari*), Good Fortune Inari (*Kai-un Inari*), Happiness Inari (*Fuku Inari*), Successor Inari (*Yotsugi Inari*), Child-minder Inari (*Komori Inari*), Loving Wife Inari (*Tsumagoi Inari*), and Fire Extinguishing Inari (*Hikeshi Inari*).[13]

Sudden, short-lived fads or crazes for particular Inari began to appear, marking the deity's transformation to a *hayarigami*. Not limited to Inari, *hayarigami* refers to a sudden enthusiasm for a particular deity, followed by an equally sudden decline. The Tokoyo no Kami cult of the seventh century is an early example, and there were probably localized cases throughout history. The introduction into Kyoto of the cult of a previously unknown Kami called the Shidaragami in 945 touched off ecstatic dancing. In 1085, more ecstatic dancing broke out in Kyoto, stemming from enthusiasm for the Happiness Gods (Fukutoku-gami), later developing into *dengaku*, examined in chapter 4. In the early Edo period in the Chūbu and Tōkai regions, a cult of Shovel Gods (*kuwagami*) broke out. The shovel was made out of a mulberry branch supposedly used at the Ise Shrines in the divine rice fields there. The wooden shovels were passed from village to village as a symbol of the Kami. People passing these gods from one village to another would dance ecstatically, celebrating the fertility of the land that they hoped the Shovel Gods would bring. Ecstatic dance and prayers for this-worldly-benefits were regularly associated with *hayarigami*. In Edo people developed extensive knowledge of the *ennichi* schedules of temples and shrines and what kinds of benefits each one was known for. Searching for the right Kami or Buddhist figure to deal with one's problem gave rise to the proverb, "Kannon in the morning, Yakushi in the evening—even a sardine head becomes a charm if you believe in it" (*Asa Kannon, yū Yakushi, iwashi no atama mo shinshin kara*). The appearance of this attitude reflects the consumerism of the era and represents a distinctively urban shift in religious consciousness.[14]

Hayarigami cults show strong involvement in their promotion, transmission, and interpretation by miscellaneous religious figures like *miko, gyōja,* and "Shintoists" (*shintōsha*), who began to appear in the cities in the eighteenth century. Shinto scholars like Tada Yoshitoshi (1698–1750) recognized two types of *shintōsha,* scholars who taught students and lectured on such classics as the *Nihon shoki* and the Great Purification Prayer, and recently arisen urban shamans (*fugeki*), who deceive the people through spurious *kitō*.[15] Contemporary records attest to a blurred distinction between Shintoists in the sense of "orthodox" Shinto priests, on the one hand, and Shinto prayer healers and beggars, on the other. The Shintoists of the second kind mostly held no official positions or steady employment at shrines, other than at small facilities of their own devising, or at *yashikigami* shrines dedicated to Inari. They could be found sometimes, however, working on an informal basis at shrines, where they might assist in large-scale ceremonies requiring many ritualists.[16]

The Shrine Monk Shō-ō, of Ikutama Shrine (also known as Ikukunitama Shrine) in Osaka, whom Tada Yoshitoshi greatly respected, remarked in "Shintō benwaku" (1785):

> Lately many people called Shintoists have appeared. They live in rental housing in the backstreets of the cities and make a living by performing *kitō*. They wear white robes over pale yellow trousers, hanging offering boxes from their necks, and tying back their sleeves with a cotton sash. They stand outside a house ringing a bell, offering to purify it in exchange for rice or money offerings."[17]

In *Morisada Mankō* (1853), a book comparing the popular culture of Edo with that in Osaka and Kyoto, Kitagawa Morisada described Shintoists in much the same way, adding that in Osaka and Kyoto they had territories that they visited monthly, to purify the cooking pots and collect offerings. The bell-ringing Shintoists in Edo overlap with the people found serving at small Inari shrines, he noted. A satirical work (*kibyōshi*) of 1787 titled *Iro otoko tōde sanmon*, featured a protagonist named Hikaru Genji (after the hero of *The Tale of Genji*) who was comically mistaken for a Shintoist, meaning that in spite of his own high opinion of his looks and costume, he had been mistaken for a beggar who had lost his bell. This example illustrates how people of the time commonly understood the term Shintoist as connoting people who adopted the guise of religion and offered "purifications" as a way of begging for a living, ringing bells to attract attention. In *Ukiyo doko* (1813–1822), the author Shikitei Sanba (1776–1822) parodied Shintoists chanting purifications and called them "poverty-stricken shamans." In most of these references, the authors saw Shintoists as one element among the urban poor.[18]

Itō Wakasa was a Shintoist living in Edo, where he kept a small Inari shrine in his house. In 1744 a neighbor who operated an inn reported the theft of a huge sum of money. The innkeeper begged Wakasa to pray to Inari that the money be returned. Soon after Wakasa performed the prayers, he reported that the money had been miraculously found, wrapped in paper before his shrine. At first, Wakasa said, he thought the money had been left as an ordinary offering and was astonished when he opened the wrapping and found the stolen money. Everyone thought that the divine spirit of Inari had caused the return of the money. However, in the subsequent investigation, it turned out that Wakasa had colluded in the theft, hoping that his Inari shrine would become known as a place where one could pray for the return of stolen objects and thus make him rich.[19] This kind of story understandably gave Shintoists a bad name and reinforced the image of them as duplicitous.

It is impossible to pinpoint the cause for the sudden outbreaks of Inari crazes in each case, but there seems to be a loose connection with the process of urbanization, which caused the loss of forests as a result of intense building, and the transformation of rural areas into urban ones, so that city people were cut off from the countryside. Fox sightings came to be regarded as remarkable, mysterious apparitions of the natural world. One example is the "Oide Inari," a mysterious phenomenon recorded as having happened between 1772 and 1781 near the Shinzaki Inari Shrine of the Asakusa district. "*Oide*" is an informal command one might address to a child or a pet, meaning, "come here." The Oide Inari originated when an old woman spotted a fox and called it to her, saying, "*oide*" while holding out a piece of fried bean curd. She was amazed when the fox ate from her hand. The fox would come whenever she called, even in broad daylight, and no matter how many other people were around.

This fox's popularity was recorded in *Mimi-bukuro*, by Negishi Yasumori, compiled between 1785 and 1815, with a strange twist. A samurai visited the shrine after the Oide Inari fad had faded. When he asked a woman running a nearby teashop about the fox craze, she told him that right around the time it died down, her twelve-year-old daughter began to say strange things. The daughter spoke in an odd voice and said that in fact it was the fox talking. The fox was "under orders" (from whom?) to go somewhere "on official business." However, the fox wanted a rest and so had possessed the girl in order to hide out from its superiors. While possessed by the fox, the girl, who had no education, manifested a miraculous ability to compose poetry and write it on a fan with a brush.[20]

The Okina Inari *hayarigami* occurred in the Hōreki era, between 1751 and 1764. When workers were repairing a road leading out of Nihonbashi in central Edo, they dug up an antique bronze sculpture of an old man carrying rice on his shoulder. The local people thought it must be a sacred object and decided to use it as a protective deity that they called Okina Inari (Old Man Inari), placing the sculpture in the watchman's hut. Later a small shrine was built nearby. It was so small that people living nearby were scarcely aware of it. Its door was always shut, being opened only on the first Day of the Horse in the second month. Otherwise, the place was unused. The nearby residents hired a man named Uma-uemon to keep the place clean, but once he urinated there. His companion told him that he had better apologize and clean the place, but he refused and even cursed the god. Thereafter a fire broke out. Uma-uemon tried to put out the fire, but a piece of burning wood fell against his groin and he was gravely injured. He was scarcely breathing when he was pulled from the burning building. Despite his wounds, suddenly he opened his eyes wide and shouted, "You, Uma-uemon! How dare you pollute my dwelling? Not only that, you had the nerve to curse me as well! I'll punish you as a lesson to the world! Take this: *ara koko chi yo ya*!" (uttering a curse). Uma-uemon spun wildly while uttering these words and then collapsed. This happened time after time, until finally he died. His companions made an apology by cleaning up the shrine and dedicating a great stone water basin that worshippers could use to purify themselves. Everyone who heard the story was frightened by Okina Inari's awesome cursing powers, so visitors to the shrine suddenly started to come in droves to pray to the god. At first, the worshippers were just those living around Nihonbashi, but as the rumor spread they came from further and further away. The worshippers built a large stone *torii* and surrounded the grounds with a stone fence, making the place into a splendid shrine. They covered the grounds with fine stones, so that visitors could easily approach the shrine even in the rain. On Horse Days the place was packed. We can presume that Shintoists and other folk religious leaders came forth to proclaim the powers of Okina Inari and take a share of whatever wealth it generated. In spite of this sudden rise in popularity, however, in later years Okina Inari became deserted again when the novelty wore off.[21]

Inari worshippers formed confraternity (*kō*) groups that transcended established neighborhood and kinship groups, growing and transforming over time. Sometimes their leaders affiliated with one or another of the chapels at Fushimi Inari, and would guide members to various Inari shrines. Members gathered in house meetings to worship the various Inari they revered, conducting prayer sessions, divinations, purifications, exorcisms, and ablutions, seeking Inari's help in avoiding sickness and misfortune.[22] For example, a certain *yamabushi* named Sōgakubō lived in a village in Fukushima, where he worked witchcraft, using spirits called Izuna (imaginary spirit messengers resembling a weasel). After he died, white foxes took to prowling around the mound raised over him, so the local people started calling it Sōgaku Inari. In 1839 two ship captains bemoaning the recent poor catch of fish along the nearby coastline prayed at Sōgaku Inari and built a small shrine there. Despite their devotions, the catch remained poor, so the shrine fell apart and was forgotten until someone rebuilt it some years later. Then in 1852 the Sōgaku Inari exerted its divine powers and there was a huge fish catch, whereupon it was renamed the Great Catch Inari (Tairyō Inari). In 1859 the temple in charge of this Inari approached Aisenji, Fushimi Inari's intendant temple, and secured a ranking for the Great Catch Inari titling it "Most High" (Sei-Ichii), to enhance the site's prestige. In 1860 a worship hall was built for the shrine, and several festival days were added in addition to the first Horse Day of the Second Month. The place became wildly popular, and *kō* came from near and far to worship or perform vigils.[23]

Especially in Edo, the popularity of Inari worship rose to astonishing heights, as seen in *Shisō zasshiki*, compiled in 1834 by a clerk in the office of the Magistrate of Temples and Shrines under the pen name, the Old Fool of Asadani (Asadani Rōgu). This work helps make sense of a common expression in early nineteenth-century Edo, "The three things most often found in Edo are merchants, Inari shrines, and dog turds." The Old Fool wrote that there were so many new shrines to Inari springing up in Edo that he has no time even to record them all. Some of the examples he cited seem to be *yashikigami* that had evolved into popular cult sites, or new chapels at temples and shrines. The Old Fool noted that people had ranked the Inari shrines of Edo as if they were sumō wrestlers, in lists that gave the ranks for ninety-six of them, divided into East and West like a sumō tournament. The Old Fool identified the judges and other tournament officials with a further ten Inari shrines, for a total of 106 Inari shrines worth mentioning. He noted that there were many more *yashikigami* Inari in addition to these.[24]

Itinerant Inari Shintoists spread the fame of their particular Inari sites, benefitting from the proliferation of rumors and sometimes becoming quite wealthy. Most were from the lower ranks of society, and many of the women were the wives and daughters of miscellaneous folk religionists. One of their more popular practices was called "the descent of Inari" (*Inari oroshi, Inari sage*), in which clients could consult a male or female Shintoist possessed by Inari to communicate with the dead. "Orthodox" shrine priests kept aloof from dealings with the dead, because of the pollution that séances would bring upon the Kami of their own shrines.

The priest of the Ikota Shrine, now called Ikeda Shrine, near Osaka recorded in his diary of the twelfth month of 1833 that an old woman had set up shop at his shrine and was conducting a ceremony she identified as the Great Purification Prayer. Taking the position that the shrine was a public facility where all and sundry were free to worship, he wrote as if he were powerless to stop her. Her livelihood came from performing Inari divination and prayers at a variety of shrines. The shrine priest noted that there were other peasant women who took names like Sagami or Orie, that sounded like shaman names, and made themselves available at Inari shrines, at their own residences, or at patrons' homes to perform exorcisms, purifications, or séances. A troupe of women skilled in Inari possession began to frequent the shrine, conducting séances and leading prayers to Inari. They provided their services on shrine grounds, but without the approval of the priests. In other words, they were independent, itinerant religious entrepreneurs who made a living performing Inari rituals forbidden to the shrine priesthood itself.[25]

Some communal shrines in the cities or on the outskirts incorporated Inari worship by building an Inari chapel on their grounds in the hope of attracting the wealth of these new Inari cults. Shrine records from Ikeda, a village near Osaka, show that by the early nineteenth century the fortunes of the Ikota Shrine were in decline, probably because of a depression in the brewing business that many local households were involved in, as well as price increases across the board. The hereditary priests at the Ikota Shrine, the Kawamura family, had fallen on hard times. The shrine received a boost from the Ise pilgrimage (*okage mairi*) of 1830, which gave rise in Osaka to mass dancing, but the priest professed to be disgusted by the carnival atmosphere of the pilgrimage, and very disappointed when many of the shrine's supporters were seen among the dancers and revelers. Nevertheless, the priest lent the shrine's grounds as a place to stage dancing, only to be disappointed again by the paltry offerings the dancers made to the shrine.

Finally, the priests decided to allow supporters to enshrine Inari, Benzaiten, and the Seven Gods of Happiness on the shrine premises. There were already several noted Inari shrines nearby, as well as an Inari *kō*. The *kō* sponsored an annual celebration of the first Day of the Horse in the second month and a fire festival in the eleventh month to honor Inari. The Inari chapel at the Ikota Shrine was completed in 1811, built with contributions assessed on each neighborhood. An Ikkō-shū believer refused on religious grounds to donate money to the chapel, showing that not everyone was enthusiastic about the Ikota Shrine incorporating Inari worship. The Kawamura's lingering doubts about the propriety of installing this popular deity was symbolized by the placement of the chapel well away from the main hall.

A merchant parishioner, Aburaya Mohei, traveled to Fushimi Inari to receive the sacred objects that would be enshrined in the chapel: a paulownia box with an amulet of Inari and a Certificate of Authenticity authorizing the Kami's installation. Once the symbols of deity were installed, popular worship began:

> For the Hatsuuma Festival of the Second Month, for instance, the residential quarters donated banners and lanterns to decorate the chapel, and home owners donated *mochi* and *manjū* [the pounded rice cakes and steamed bean-jam buns that are a staple of cold-weather celebrations], for distribution to festival-goers and to the ordinary residents of the town. In sharp contrast to the ill-attended celebrations of recent years that had featured *kagura* dances at the main shrine, home owners and renters alike thronged to the Hatsuuma Festival, and the coins tossed into the offertory boxes at the Inari chapel piled higher and higher, growing into a small mountain in the eyes of the shrine's clerics."[26]

The proliferation of unorganized folk religionists practicing Inari divinations, purifications, and exorcisms attracted the attention of the Shugen sects, the Yoshida, Shirakawa, Tsuchimikado, and miscellaneous aristocratic households that were in the business of training and licensing shrine personnel. The Shirakawa House was particularly zealous in recruiting Inari *miko* and fortune tellers. The certifying lineages competed with each other and with Fushimi Inari Shrine to provide Inari enshrinements for the thousands of people seeking a certificate for a new Inari shrine in a house-lot shrine or a chapel within an existing shrine or temple grounds.

On the one hand, the established religious gatekeepers hoped to receive some of the wealth that independent religionists garnered. On the other, the entrepreneurs profited from the appearance of orthodoxy that gatekeepers' licenses and certificates represented. Over the years 1818 to 1830, the Shirakawa House tried to assert that it had an exclusive right to conduct Inari enshrinements, but this claim trod on the prerogatives of the Fushimi Inari Shrine, and it had been authorizing the erection of new Inari shrines for much longer. The Shirakawa House had previously been conducting some twenty or thirty Inari enshrinements per year, but in 1827 the number suddenly rose to 230. In reaction, the Yoshida House began to sponsor its own Inari enshrinements, also coming into conflict with Fushimi Inari. The Shirakawa House promoted its enshrinements by soliciting innkeepers on the routes to the Ise shrines to encourage Ise pilgrims to erect Inari chapels at their village shrines. The Shirakawa also offered incentives to shrines already affiliated with it to conduct these enshrinements, using the Inari *miko* they had certified as their agents.[27]

Gratified by the attention, some of the newly certified Inari shamans formed multiple affiliations with the aristocrats and displayed their personal wealth most conspicuously. The increase of unorthodox religionists stimulated the authorities to investigate and crack down, fearing that the unauthorized shrines might evolve into a unified movement with seditious tendencies. On the fifth day of the second month, 1804, the shogunate prohibited First Horse Day festivals. Two days later, it prohibited extravagant Inari ceremonies and festivals. In 1839, the shogunate prohibited the public from worshipping at *yashikigami* shrines and prohibited any new construction of such shrines or rebuilding existing ones. In 1842, many Shintoists promoting Inari worship were caught up in a general dragnet when the shogunate expelled folk religious leaders from Edo en masse as part of the Tenpo Reforms.[28]

Such measures were followed by prosecutions. Toyoda Mitsugi (?–1829) was an Inari diviner who was condemned to death for covertly promoting Christianity. Born into a lineage of poverty-stricken Shinto ritualists, she moved to Edo, where her elder brother was a Shintoist. Mitsugi was apprenticed as a maid at twelve. Her first husband sold her to a brothel. Her second marriage ended in divorce. She married a third time, but left her husband when she could no longer tolerate his womanizing. Ending up in Kyoto, she set herself up on the periphery of the Gion Shrine as a fortune teller and Inari exorcist. She took on female disciples, and together they practiced around the Fushimi Inari Shrine, conducting midnight ascents of the mountain and cold-water ablutions. She claimed to distinguish herself from others by adding Christian elements to Inari worship. Given the proscription on Christianity at the time, this strategy could only end badly.

Mitsugi gained enough wealth to affiliate to both the Shirakawa and Tsuchimikado Houses. She parleyed connections to become friendly with the Yoshida and other aristocrats as well. She "created an aura of prestige for herself by riding in a palanquin and surrounding herself with a retinue of sycophants when she visited the Tsuchimikado, Yoshida, and Yamanoi residential compounds in Kyoto." In 1827, the Osaka Magistrate Ōshio Heihachirō put her on trial as a Christian. The investigation was riddled with contradictory evidence, and some members of the court weren't convinced that Mitsugi was a Christian. To overrule the magistrate was regarded as setting such a bad precedent, however, that these judges nevertheless went along with a death sentence, though Mitsugi died in prison before the sentence could be carried out. In all, over one hundred people were punished along with her in this incident.[29]

On the face of it, the transformation of Inari worship doesn't seem immediately relevant to the issues structuring this study of Shinto's history: foreign versus indigenous and the public versus the private. The stories I have presented relate much more clearly to the hedonism and commercialism of the early modern cities. A colorful panorama of folk religionists responded to the populace's desire to "play" with Inari by offering a dazzling array of commercialized ritual services. Casual participants and observers seem to have enjoyed Inari shrines as part of the life of the city as well as places to pray for this-worldly benefits. The Shintoists were their neighbors. The parodies and satires inspired by Inari worship suggest that readers quite enjoyed the guilty pleasure of seeing other people's pretensions, foibles, and conniving schemes exposed. Yet people could only "play" at Inari shrines because there were so many for whom Inari represented the hope of deliverance from sickness, poverty, and shattered dreams. For the supplicants, no doubt, Inari was deeply serious. Their stories were potent sources of the miraculous tales of wealth bestowed, malfeasance punished, virtue rewarded, and reassurance that the dead were at peace.

The "proper" priesthood proved itself to be soaked in the same commercialism as the Shintoists whom they derided. Priests like the Kawamura elevated Inari worship by instantiating it within their shrines, whatever protestations of reluctance they made, and whatever their pretense of impotence to restrain the foolish masses. How much more so the greedy aristocrats, whose behavior conformed elegantly to the Japanese proverb of "wanting something so much, your hand nearly pops out of your throat to seize it." To issue licenses and certificates implied imparting prayers and sacred secrets to folk religionists like Toyoda Mitsugi, who presumably transmitted some version of that knowledge to their disciples and clients. In these various ways and by these circuitous routes, the "Shintoists" imbibed a version of Shinto "orthodoxy" even as wealth established new currents for them to influence a variety of shrines and priests.

Ise Pilgrimage

Shrine and temple pilgrimage was a central element of popular religious life in the Edo period, and Ise pilgrimage is one aspect of this larger phenomenon. Pilgrimage became feasible with the improvement of roads and the removal of many toll barriers. Although the development of inns, teahouses, palanquin carriers, ferry services, and passenger ships made pilgrimage easier than it had been previously, and more accessible to people at greater distances from Ise, however, pilgrimage was still arduous and dangerous. There were no provisions to assist those who might become ill or injured, as many did.[30]

Pilgrims during the Edo period might travel singly or in groups called *kō*, in this case, a pilgrimage association.[31] Groups such as these were typically organized by commoners and functioned without clerical direction, though in the case of Ise pilgrimage associations there were many Buddhist priests involved.

More influential than any other factor stimulating Ise pilgrimage were the organizing efforts of *oshi* (also called *onshi*) from Ise, beginning around 1605. *Oshi* were low-ranking staff at the Ise Shrines; the word *oshi* was a shortened form of "honored performer of prayers," (*o-kitōshi*), someone who conducts prayers at a client's request for a fee. The term *oshi* was also used more widely for the pilgrimage guides and proselytizers at other shrines. Eventually, hundreds of Ise *oshi* were active throughout the country, except for the far northeast. They organized pilgrimage associations that created enduring relations between the Ise Shrines and hundreds of villages, towns, and cities, establishing enduring beliefs about the Ise deities and about the duty of the Japanese people to support these shrines.

Individual locales (a village or town) entered into a relation with an individual *oshi* who made annual or twice-annual visits to collect funds for the shrines from each member household. Contributions might be in currency, but typically they were in rice or other produce. The households would enshrine an Ise talisman received from the *oshi*, who would perform religious services, such as purifying the dwelling, performing rites for safe childbirth, and so on, as requested. *Oshi* distributed religious goods and souvenirs from the shrines, such as tea, *obi* (the belts used to secure kimono), and many traditional foodstuffs, such as dried fish and seaweed; almanacs useful in agriculture; shrine talismans; and purifying wands (*harae no ōnusa*, a wooden wand with white streamers attached). These goods were presented in quantities and degrees of elaborate wrapping or packaging commensurate with the amount of the recipient's contributions. As the volume and weight of the gifts they gave and the contributions they received could be very considerable, *oshi* required horses and bearers to get from one village to the next. Villages provided horses and porters gratis, eventually delivering the accumulated tribute to a port, where it would be loaded on a ship to be transported back to Ise.

Typically, an Ise *oshi* traveled with several assistants. They lodged with village headmen or at houses called "Ise-ya" (Ise house). Sometimes these structures came to be regarded as sacred and developed into shrines for the Ise deities called Bright Kami/Shining Deity shrines (*shinmeisha*). The *oshi* were allowed to solicit donations freely, whatever the Buddhist sectarian affiliation of the village or of the member households. These "contributions," actually, an informal levy, were referred to as "first fruit offerings" (*hatsuho*) and were calculated in proportion to taxes paid. The notion arose that contributing donations to Ise *oshi* was a duty of all village residents, whatever a person's individual religious beliefs might be. In the process, residents as a whole were placed under a semiofficial obligation to support these shrines. Contributing to the Ise Shrines thus acquired a "public" character, separate from and unrelated to individual religious convictions. Proselytizers from a great many temples and shrines visited Edo period villages to raise funds, but only those from Ise, monks from Mt. Kōya, and the peregrinating head of the Jishū sect of

Buddhism were given such free access to the populace, and only they received such extensive public assistance.

When their organizing campaigns began in the early seventeenth century, *oshi* apparently established informal contracts first with the headman of the village or town, presenting him with expensive gifts. But residents were being pressed into a significant economic relation, and not everyone was equally willing to contribute. A collection of miracle tales about the Ise deities, Deguchi Nobuyoshi's "A Record of Divine Marvels of the Grand Shrine of Ise," composed in 1666, contains numerous stories reflecting local resistance to *oshi* networks. They show that many people did not particularly esteem the Ise deities nor wish to enshrine Ise talismans, and that *oshi* were often rejected in areas where the Jōdo Shinshū or Nichiren schools of Buddhism prevailed.[32]

These stories promoted the *oshi*, their talismans, purifying wands, and the boxes in which they were stored, as embodying the magical powers of the Ise Kami, warning that those who failed to revere them could expect to suffer divine wrath, especially by fire, as in the following story:

> In the ninth month of... [1650], the [*oshi*] Kubokura Hironobu [was]... staying in Utsunomiya as he distributed *ōnusa* [purification wands] to the vicinity. In a village called Okamoto the farmers all requested *ōnusa*, but the people from four or five homes made light of the Grand Shrine and said that the other villages must not receive the amulets. The priest let them have their way, but that very night, a fire broke out in one of those four or five houses, and three of them burned to the ground. As a result, the people of Okamoto Village were greatly astounded, saying that irreverence toward the Grand Shrine was the cause [of the fire], and they came all the way to Utsunomiya and begged fervently to receive the *ōnusa*."[33]

Deguchi relates a similar story about his father-in-law, who was an *oshi*. One night when he was visiting his territory in Musashi Province, a fire broke out and began moving toward the house where he was staying.

> The fire had spread as far as the building next door, when the master of the house in which he was staying cried out repeatedly, "May we be saved by the power of the [*oshi*] of the Grand Shrine!" My father-in-law was discouraged and wondered what could be done to combat such a fire, even by divine power. But he uttered a vow to the *shinmei*, raised up the purification wand, and when he paid distant worship to the Grand Shrine, the wind suddenly changed. The fire, which had reached the eaves of the house, went out, going on to burn in other places. It was an uncanny event.[34]

These stories show how the *oshi* were portrayed as capable of quelling fire by prayer and manipulating their wands. The persistent association between talismans, wands, and fire suggests the belief that when these articles were reverently accepted and enshrined, they protected the house against fire. Other stories relate how *oshi* performed rites of safe childbirth; in their absence, untying the cords binding the boxed purifying wands was believed to ease difficult births. It is notable also that the Ise deities appear in these stories not as individual Kami but as a collective called "bright deities" (*shinmei*), and that no distinction is made between Inner and Outer Shrines.[35]

When the association's members came as pilgrims to Ise, they would stay at their *oshi*'s inn, and nowhere else. Some of these inns could accommodate one hundred to two hundred people. The *oshi* guided pilgrims through the shrines, arranged for performances of shrine dance as an offering to the Kami, and conducted prayers for the prosperity and well-being of the members. *Oshi* provided talismans and souvenirs to be taken by the pilgrims back to the entire membership in the home village, firmly establishing the worship of the Ise Shrines at a popular level.

During the Edo period, *oshi* networks were the most pervasive type of organization linking people across domains to a shrine. Individual *oshi* carefully tended their collection routes and conceptualized groups of villages where they collected funds as their personal territories (*kasumi, dannaba,* and other terms). These territories were legally recognized as assets that could be bought, sold, or inherited. Possession of these territories could lead to great wealth, as in the case of one *oshi* of the Inner Shrine, who had territories encompassing one hundred thirty-one villages in three provinces, as well as urban territories in Kyoto and Osaka.[36]

The earliest known pilgrimage association was formed in 1417, a group of ten men from Kyoto who pooled their resources for five years and went on pilgrimage to Ise in 1422. Before departing, they purified themselves with a vegetarian diet, and after three days' journey arrived at Ise and stayed at an *oshi*'s inn. The next day they completed their pilgrimage, which included worshipping not only at the Inner and Outer Shrines but also at over one hundred lesser shrines attached to them, called *massha*. They also went up to a spot billed as the Heavenly Rock Cave behind the Outer shrine. The next day, they set off on their return journey, returning to Kyoto a few days later.[37]

The basic pattern seen here developed many elaborate variations. This fifteenth-century association sent all its members to Ise and dissolved after a single pilgrimage, but it became common for associations to send only a portion of the group, in rotation, so that over a period of years at least one representative from every member household was able to go. This kind of association was intended to continue over many trips. Pilgrimage associations bound for Ise began to extend the journey to include many other sites, as many as their funds would allow, so that, depending on their location, pilgrims to Ise also visited the great temples of Kamakura, Kyoto, and Nara; made the circuit of the thirty-three Kannon temples; and took in the cultural life of the cities, as well as including more remote sites like Mt. Kōya, Mt. Konpira, and Kumano. The most elaborate trips lasted several months and included a portion of sea travel and a land portion that alternated walking, riding rented horses, and being carried in palanquins.

Pilgrimage associations relied on diaries recording such practical information as the inns where their group had stayed in the past, fees, recommended tea houses and their prices, notes on the route to be traveled each day, and so on. Although these works were titled with one of several terms meaning "diary," they were not used for personal reflection so much as conveying factual information useful to future pilgrims. Hundreds of these pilgrimage diaries exist today. Pilgrims also could consult visual guides to the shrines in the form of shrine mandalas.

Ise Mandalas

Mandalas of the Ise shrines were produced from the sixteenth century, reaching a peak in the seventeenth century and continuing through the Edo period. These paintings provided pilgrims with information on how to worship at Ise, and they are an important resource for understanding how pilgrims actually moved through the shrines and the adjacent towns of Uji and Yamada. They serve as an important reminder that up until the Meiji period, the Ise Shrines were surrounded by temples, teahouses, shops, inns, and all manner of commercial activities, far from the austere, solemn, park-like setting one sees today. They remind us that the modern form of the Ise Shrines was achieved by removing much of the popular religious life surrounding the shrines in the Edo period. (See Figure 9.2.)

Ise mandalas were cheaply produced in quantity, using mainly primary colors on paper; they could be folded or mounted on scrolls. While they provided a kind of "map" for pilgrims, they did not attempt to capture actual scale. Ise mandalas squeezed the whole area of the shrines and parts of the adjacent towns into a large square or rectangular format, averaging about seventy inches (170 cm.) on a side, enlarging the most significant spaces and people beyond their actual scale, and covering connecting areas with mist or clouds. Painters' workshops in Kyoto produced these mandalas according to patrons' specifications and by consulting previous models rather than by observing the shrines as they were at the time. Thus the mandalas took on a standardized pattern, in which a sun hangs over the Inner Shrine and a moon over the Outer Shrine, corresponding to the Womb and Diamond Worlds of esoteric Buddhist thought. The pilgrim's journey begins at the lower right, first visiting the Outer Shrine.

In the Ise Sankei mandala shown in Figure 9.2, we see a group of male and female pilgrims crossing a bridge. Two of the men are *yamabushi*, distinguished by small, round black hats. To the right of the bridge we see a group of naked men purifying themselves in the river, and a veiled woman in red holding a purifying wand. She is

Figure 9.2 Ise Sankei Mandara. Source: Photo by Peter Knecht. From Peter Knecht, "*Ise sankei mandara* and the Image of the Pure Land," *Japanese Journal of Religious Studies* 33, no. 2 (2006): 223–248, on 226. http://www.onmarkproductions.com/assets/images/ise-sanzan-madala-Knecht-nanzan.jpg. Reprinted by permission from *JJRS* and Peter Knecht.

a stock figure, the first of many in the mandala demanding money from the pilgrims. In this case the scheme was to rush up to a naked man as he was getting out of the river, wave the wand over him, and demand money for this "purification." Entering the gate, the pilgrim comes to a small structure in which sit a florid-faced man and a haggard old woman holding a white cloth. They represent King Yama, lord of the underworld, and the Hag of Hades (Datsu-e Ba), a hideous old woman of folk belief who strips the dead on their way into the underworld, perpetuating older beliefs that the shrines are an earthly Pure Land. The pilgrims left coins here. Pilgrimage records of the Edo period do not refer to medieval ideas of Ise as an earthly paradise or as incarnating the Diamond and Womb world, suggesting that some elements of Ise mandalas were anachronisms perpetuated by the ateliers that produced them.

Proceeding towards the first shrine gate, the pilgrim passed shops run by the people of Yamada, the town attached to the Outer Shrine. Crossing a bridge, there is a temple to the right and two monks headed that way. To the left is a horse that has been dedicated to the shrine, and a small building, where one of the lesser priests sits with a shrine maiden, presumably offering prayers and sacred dance for fees. The Outer Shrine itself lies beyond these structures, and in the mandala we see a group of priests who have finished a ritual of some kind relaxing in the shrine precincts. They are depicted about one-third larger than other figures. The pilgrim worships outside the entrance to the shrine and then returns down the same path to cross a bridge at the bottom center of the painting into an area bounded by lines of trees on each side, separating the Inner and Outer Shrines, called Ai no Yama.

This middle portion of the mandala depicts a performance of Noh drama under a blossoming tree. Beyond lies a pavilion where a shrine maiden is performing sacred dance while lesser priests provide musical accompaniment. We see numerous subsidiary shrines (*massha*); there were some forty attached to the Outer Shrine and eighty at the Inner Shrine. Crossing a bridge, the pilgrim enters an area of teahouses, shops selling combs, for which the town was famous, and stalls for such entertainments as *nenbutsu* dance. As one Buddhist priest dances comically with a towel on his head, his comrade extends a bucket on a long pole for pilgrims to drop in coins. Just beneath the moon, a group of curious pilgrims examines the hollowed stump of an enormous tree.

Then we find a rock grotto and a group composed of a dancing shrine maiden, musicians, and some pilgrims. The mountain on which it was actually located (above Ai no Yama, but appearing in the mandala directly above the Outer Shrine) was called Mt. Takakura, and there were numerous small caves and grottos there. In ancient times these were used for burials, and hence the area was regarded as polluting to the Ise priests. If they went there, they could not participate in shrine rites for three days.[38]

Judging from contemporary diaries, a visit to this spot, which was called the Heavenly Rock Cave (*ame no iwato*), was the highlight of a pilgrimage to Ise. The mandala shows the re-creation in music and dance of the famous myth of the Sun Goddess who had plunged the world into darkness when she hid herself in the cave to flee the outrages of her brother Susanoo marauding in heaven (see chapter 2), returning light to the world by emerging from the cave. The diary of Tada Yoshitoshi (1698–1750), a theologian invited to lecture at the shrines, states that the Heavenly Rock Cave netted more revenue than any other site at Ise. He was outraged by the spectacle enacted at the cave, asking how Ise priests could possibly encourage pilgrims to visit a spot that they regarded as defiling, knowing full well that the pilgrims would go straight from there to the Inner Shrine, bringing with them the pollution of death.[39] But the scolding of purists aside, pilgrims evidently flocked to the place as their main destination.

Descending to the famous Uji Bridge, pilgrims threw coins to men waiting in the river below and entered the Inner Shrine grounds. Some bathed in the river and were accosted by more women claiming a fee for purifying them. Passing along a row of shops and inns on their right and a group of subsidiary shrines on their left, they entered the Inner Shrine, where priests cluster in and around the shrine. As we saw in the Outer Shrine grounds, there was another building where pilgrims could evidently pay to have offertory dance or personalized ritual performed. Continuing their ascent, pilgrims arrived at another area of subsidiary shrines by crossing another bridge. A Buddhist monk is pictured extending a bucket for coins. The pilgrimage concluded with a visit to the temple Kongōshōji, where pilgrims could see Mt. Fuji and the Futami Bay. The entire trip around the two Ise shrines could be concluded in one day, though some pilgrims chose to take two.

Travel Guides

The publishing boom beginning in the seventeenth century produced hundreds of travel guides for pilgrims.[40] Some were small enough for the traveler to carry on the journey, while others were multivolume works with copious illustrations. Let us examine an example of the larger variety, *An Illustrated Guide to the Famous Sites of a Pilgrimage to Ise* (*Ise sangū meisho zue*). This work was compiled in 1797 by Shitomi Kangetsu (1747–1797), an Osaka writer, painter, and calligrapher, who also wrote several other illustrated guides to famous places. It describes a pilgrimage route to Ise beginning in Kyoto and returning there.[41] Unlike the pilgrimage diaries examined earlier, the *Illustrated Guide* and works like it did not recommend particular inns and teahouses, nor did they record prices. Rather, they were gazetteers recording the history and traditions of each place along the route, including interesting legends, descriptions of noteworthy rites and festivals, and quotations from historical texts.

The *Illustrated Guide* states that the only reliable record of the events of myth is the "Age of the Gods" chapter of the *Nihon shoki*. Its account of the Inner Shrine begins by recapping *Nihon shoki*'s account of the cosmogony, proceeding to the story of Izanagi and Izanami giving birth to the land. In Shitomi's version, the Sun Goddess is their daughter, and Susanoo, described as a violent, evil Kami, is their son. His depredations in Heaven are recounted, as are Amaterasu's retreat to the cave, her return to the world (see Figure 9.3), Susanoo's expulsion and rule over Izumo, and Amaterasu's decision (in her 250,000th year) to send the heavenly grandchild (who also lived to an astronomical age) to rule the world, leading eventually to a line of human emperors.

Thus it is an indubitable truth, Shitomi writes, that the imperial line is directly descended from the Sun Goddess, and that the Ise Shrines are the nation's ancestral shrine, representing the union of Heaven and Earth. To worship there is to worship the parents of Heaven and Earth. The account finishes with remarks on the imperial regalia.[42]

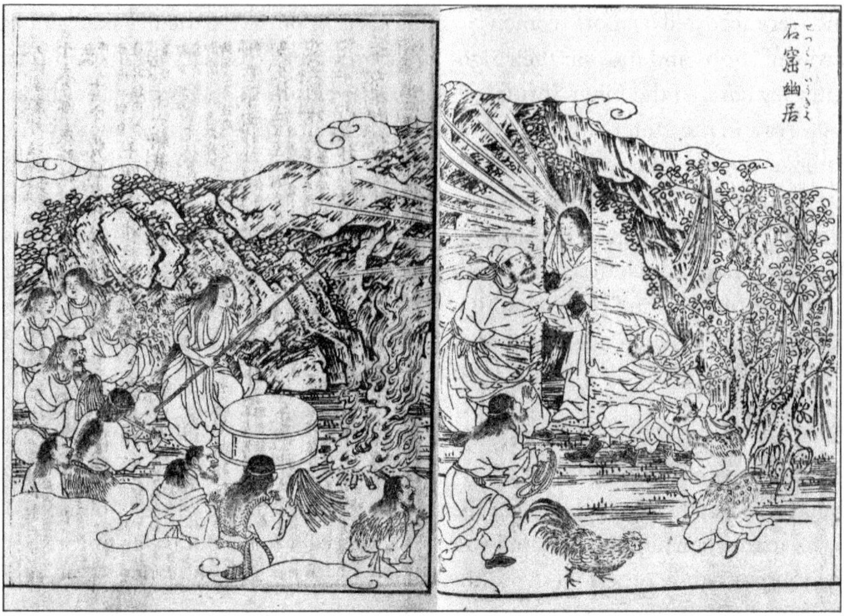

Figure 9.3 Seclusion in the Rock Cave (Sekkutsu yūkyo). By Shitomi Kangetsu.
Source: *Illustrated Guide to the Ise Pilgrimage* (Ise sangū meisho zue), vol. 5, part 1. Reprinted with permission from Harvard Art Museums / Arthur M. Sackler Museum. Bequest of the Hofer Collection of the Arts of Asia, 1985.671.5.

Here is what the *Illustrated Guide* has to say about the Kami of the Outer Shrine:

Watarai Shrine, Main Sanctuary: Toyoukesume Ōkami, one deity.

Attached Sanctuary: Amenohikohikohononinigi no mikoto, Amenofutotama no mikoto, Amenokoyanenomikoto, three deities.

[Ten poems on the site are recorded.]

The Outer Shrine was established during the reign of the twenty-second human emperor, Yūryaku, in the twenty-second year of his reign, ninth month, fifteenth day. In the tenth month of the twenty-sixth year of Emperor Suinin's reign, he had established a shrine [the Inner Shrine] for Amaterasu Ōmikami in this province on the banks of the Isuzu River. The two shrines were separate, but when they both began to be referred to as the Ise Daijingū, they took on the same name. Four hundred eighty-two years later, there was an oracle from Amaterasu Ōmikami, in which she stated that she had come from Yosa County in Tanba Province. Previously, the goddess Yamato Hime no Mikoto had served her there, having descended from Heaven to reside in the same hall. That is the origin of the shrine in Tango Province called the Inner and Outer shrines, and an oracle decreed that they be served their august meals together, morning and night... The

> two deities Amenokoyane no mikoto and Amenofutotama no mikoto also assist. Their shrines face south and have thatched roofs over standing pillars. This was the way houses were built after the ancient style of pit houses, employing bamboo tied with rope. They are topped with cross-beams and barrel-shaped roof-weights and are decorated with more kinds of materials than I can enumerate here.[43]

Clearly, the author of this passage anticipated an educated reader familiar with ancient history. The passage addresses questions that many pilgrims must have asked: Are the two shrines the same, or different? What deities are enshrined there? When and how were the shrines established? But while Ise Kami were named, beyond a list of impossibly long deity names, little detail is provided. Instead, the writer passes over them in favor of *another* Kami, Yamato Hime, who, in his retelling, quite overshadows the main deity Toyouke.

This travel guide and many more transmitted idiosyncratic accounts of ancient myth in vernacular Japanese, accessible even to those who could not decipher classical Chinese. Through these guides, readers were also instructed on such topics as the unbroken imperial line, the significance of the imperial regalia, and the meaning of Ise as a shrine that was at once the ancestral shrine of the imperial line and a place where all Japanese should worship. The travel guides on the Ise pilgrimage taught that the Japanese are all one people, based on their spiritual union in worship of the Ise deities, mediated by the imperial line.[44]

We also find that there were fifteen Buddhist temples within the area pictured in the mandalas, including such information as their sectarian affiliation, identity of their consecrated images, year of establishment, number of sub-temples and chapels, and so on. For example, Segiji, a *yamabushi* temple of the Shingon sect, consisted of nineteen chapels, whose priests served in rotation as Segiji's head priest. The temple's festival of the ninth month is described as involving the music of flutes and drums as the priests bore copies of sutras to a graveyard, scattering flowers on the path before the palanquin bearing the sutras.[45]

Second only to the experience of visiting the Heavenly Rock Cave for Edo-period Ise pilgrims was a tour of the subsidiary shrines (*massha*) arrayed around the main sanctuaries of both Inner and Outer Shrines. Whereas pilgrims were not permitted to enter the main sanctuaries, they were invited to go right up to the altars of the subsidiary shrines and leave "pigeon's eyes" there, coins perforated with a small hole that reminded people of a pigeon's eye. The *Illustrated Guide* notes that while popular usage mentions forty subsidiary shrines attached to the Outer Shrine and eighty at the Inner Shrine, there is no mention of these places in ancient records, and it ponders how they came to be here. The author refers to a work called the *Ritual Register of the Outer Shrine* (*Gekū gishikichō*), which states that originally there were more than two hundred of these shrines, but that in the century when the Vicennial Renewal of the shrines was not performed, the proper names for even

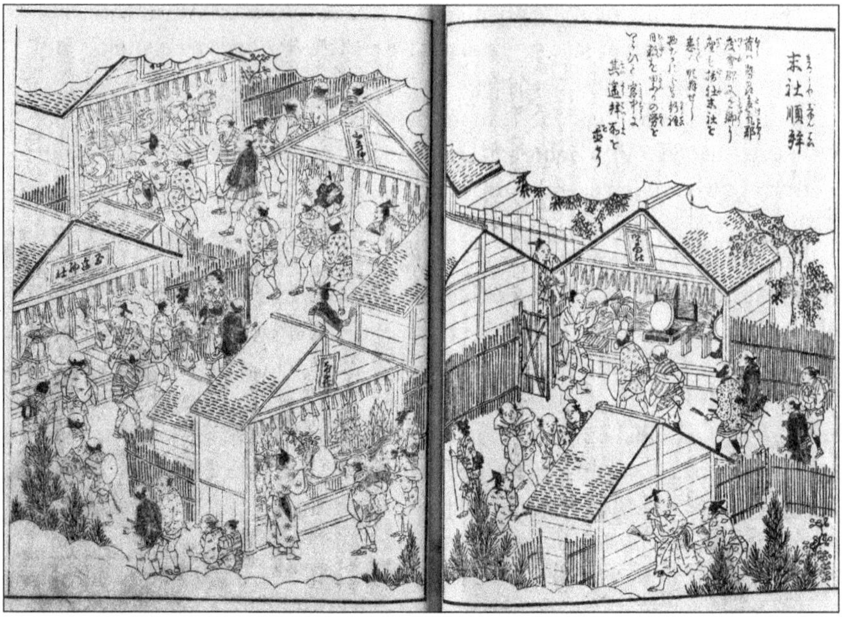

Figure 9.4 Massha Pilgrimage Circuit (*Massha junpai*) Source: *Illustrated Guide to the Ise Pilgrimage* (*Ise sangū meisho zue*), vol. 4. Reprinted with permission from Harvard Art Museums/Arthur M. Sackler Museum. Bequest of the Hofer Collection of the Arts of Asia, 1985.671.4.

these small shrines were lost, and some of them had burned down. In later ages, fortunately, people were able to reconstruct some of them.[46] Functionaries were on hand at each of these small shrines to solicit donations, explain the virtues of each one's deity (though in fact seventeen of the forty subsidiary shrines at the Outer Shrine and eight at the Inner Shrine were unable to identify their deity's name), and to display offerings and ritual equipment so that pilgrims could see them at close range. (See Figure 9.4.)

Organized by pilgrimage associations in the villages, towns, and cities, visually represented by shrine mandalas, and shaped by pilgrimage diaries and published travel guides, Ise pilgrimage spread through the country to become a widely shared experience. Guides and mandalas transmitted ancient myth in popular formats and conveyed the idea of the unity of the Japanese people, including the further stipulation that their unity had its axis mundi at Ise, mediated by the emperor. In the process, the Ise Shrines entered popular religious life as never before, along with the idea that everyone was obliged to support them. While the fact of the circulation of ideas of the people's unity and their alleged duty to support the Ise Shrines is significant in itself, we have no way of knowing how many people accepted them. But having begun with the idea that no one but the imperial family might rightfully visit, Ise became by the end of the Edo period a place that everyone was encouraged to visit at least once. Nevertheless, members

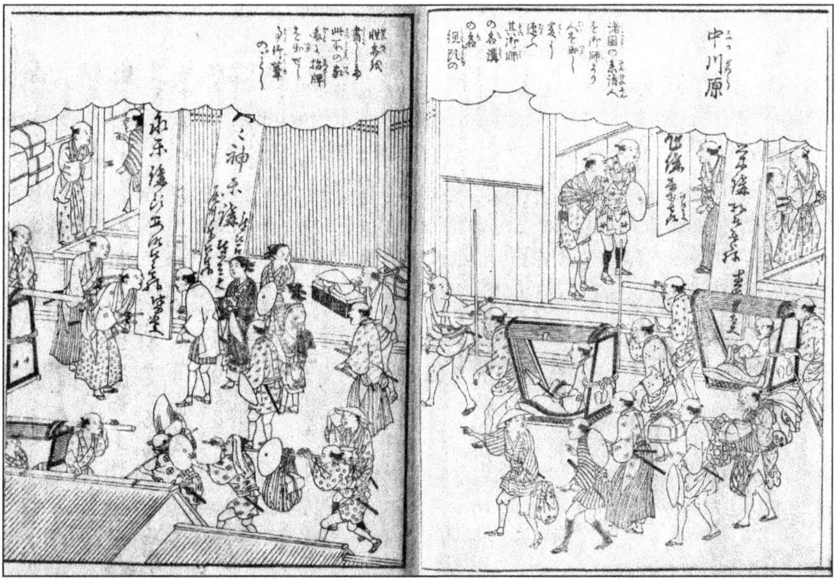

Figure 9.5 Inns at Nakagawara. Source: *Illustrated Guide to the Ise Pilgrimage* (Ise sangū meisho zue), vol. 4. Reprinted with permission from Harvard Art Museums/Arthur M. Sackler Museum. Bequest of the Hofer Collection of the Arts of Asia, 1985.671.4.

of some Buddhist sects, samurai, and aristocrats lacking permission to travel, as well as the poor, would not have had the opportunity. While Ise had no intendant temple like the combinatory institutions we have examined in earlier chapters, the shrines were enmeshed with numerous temples in and around their precincts. Pilgrims visited temples as a part of their pilgrimage in a style consonant with the combination of Kami worship and Buddhism that characterized religious life as a whole. The shrines themselves at this time were lively venues for commerce in religious ritual, entertainments, and souvenirs, through which people flowed in a highly structured way (see Figure 9.5). And when the regimented religious business of the journey was completed, pilgrims lodged at *oshi* inns, where the men with money among them could revel in the fleshpots of nearby Uji and Yamada. Popular pilgrimage thus also made Ise into a religious center, combining commerce, "play, and prayer."

Okage Mairi

While Ise pilgrimage "as usual" continued, mass pilgrimage also developed. The first of these occurred in 1457, when a group of around 5,000 pilgrims went to Ise. It is believed that during the Edo period, between 200,000 and 500,000 people visited the shrines annually,[47] and that number increased in years when the Vicennial

Renewal was held. Mass pilgrimage is believed to have occurred in 1650, 1705, 1718, 1723, 1771, 1830, 1863, and 1867; the ones in 1705, 1771, and 1830 are the best documented, while the pilgrimage of 1867 differs from the rest in important respects. It is known as the "Anything Goes" pilgrimage, after the pilgrims' chant, *ee ja naika*.[48]

The pilgrimage of 1705 is best known from a compilation of miracle tales by an Outer Shrine *oshi* named Watarai Hironori, *The Continuing Record of Divine Marvels of the Grand Shrine of Ise*, compiled in 1706. The 1705 pilgrims were largely young indentured domestic servants or agricultural workers, who reportedly went on pilgrimage on a sudden whim, without permission. In other words, they absconded and went to Ise without proper travel documents. Such pilgrims were known as *nuke mairi*.

> The term *nukemairi*...means literally one who has "slipped away" (*nuke*) on pilgrimage (*mairi*). The term was used to refer, primarily, to young persons who had gone to Ise without asking permission of their parents or masters, and by extension, it was also used to refer to the pilgrimage itself. While officially prohibited, the custom became widespread, and was a tacitly accepted means of making the pilgrimage for those (particularly the young) who could not otherwise receive official permission to leave their homes or occupations.[49]

According to Hironori, the pilgrimage began on the seventh or eighth day of the fourth intercalary month, which in the Western dating system corresponds to May 29 or 30, and saw staggering numbers of pilgrims over the next two months (see Table 9.1).

While the numbers shown in Table 9.1 are obviously impressionistic, they can be regarded as broadly indicative of an unprecedented number of pilgrims, with rises and falls within the period. The 1705 diary of the Head Priest of the Inner Shrine recorded his belief that most of the pilgrims were coming from Kyoto. Hironori's miracle tales tend to confirm the impression that most of the pilgrims were coming from within an area bounded by Kyoto on the north, Osaka to the West, with the Ise shrines at the easternmost extent, and only a handful from places further east, one from Edo having come the furthest. In other words, this pilgrimage was largely a phenomenon of that part of central Japan within a few days' walk of the shrines.[50]

Hironori describes the scale of the 1705 pilgrimage:

> Beginning the twenty-first day of the intercalary fourth month, children from throughout Osaka, between the ages of 7–8 and 14–15 began leaving on *nukemairi* in groups of two and three from each house. Even though their parents firmly prohibited them from leaving, since it was a busy time

Table 9.1 **Number of Pilgrims in the 1705 *Okage Mairi***

Dates	*Number of Pilgrims*
4.9	2,000–3,000
4.10	2,000–3,000
4.11	20,000–30,000
4.12	30,000–40,000
4.13	100,000
4.14–4.25	100,000 daily
4.26	50,000–60,000
4.27	70,000–80,000
4.28 and 4.29	120,000–130,000
5.1	70,000–80,000
5.2	40,000–50,000
5.3–5.7	120,000–130,000
5.8–5.10	140,000–150,000
5.11	70,000–80,000
5.12–5.14	100,000
5.15	150,000–160,000
5.16	220,000–230,000
5.17	70,000–80,000
5.19–5.20	50,000–60,000
5.21	40,000–50,000
5.22–5.23	20,000–30,000
5.24	10,000–20,000
5.25–5.28	10,000

before the seasonal festival [Boys' Day; 5th day, 5th month], it was to no avail. It was said that the children who left on *nukemairi* between morning and evening that day numbered more than ten-thousand.... Rain fell the next day, but they paid no heed, pouring out one after the other in a wave of chaos from the town wards, filling the roads and leaving not so much room as to stand a needle.... As a result, the wealthy of each town furnished assistance to *nukemairi* in various places, some donating copper money, some giving fans, others donating hand towels, red sacks, walking staffs, rush sandals, medicines, or tissue paper, while some others even gave out a piece of silver to each pilgrim. The giving responded to whatever each

> person desired and needed, so many things that my brush cannot do them justice. Then, some people began quarreling around the charity stands set up [in Osaka]; both sides had already created a great disturbance when amulets surprisingly rained into their midst![51]

Hironori's work was explicitly directed to the young and was intended to allay their fears. Most lacked the financial means to travel, the proper travel documents, a protector, access to medical care if they should become sick or injured, and knowledge of what to do in Ise. The solutions offered for these dilemmas include tales of divine aid; employers whose anger changed to compassion, or who were punished by divine wrath; stories of abundant alms, divine guidance and protection, kind people at Yamada (not Uji) this is definitely an Outer Shrine–centered text—who show compassion to young pilgrims; amulets miraculously falling from the sky, and stories of unscrupulous merchants punished by divine retribution.

Hironori was well aware of the labor relations problems posed by young servants and agricultural workers suddenly leaving their employers to go on pilgrimage: what happened if farm hands left during the busy planting or harvest seasons? Shouldn't the master be compensated, since he would have to hire substitute laborers? Shouldn't the absconders be punished, since they were causing economic harm to their employers and violating the terms of their employment? When absconder pilgrims return, what do they owe their masters, and how can good relations be restored after the breach of trust caused by an unexcused absence? As an example of the "inconvenience" that could be caused to a servant's employers by her sudden absconding, there was the case of a wet nurse who suddenly took off with the child she was tending. The masters were frantic with worry for the child. In general, the stories assert that the awesome Ise deities' miraculous protection of devout pilgrims trumps these mundane concerns.[52]

For child laborers, already in a weak position in relations with employers, the prospect of masters and mistresses furious upon the servant's return from an unauthorized pilgrimage to Ise was all too easy to imagine. Hironori took evident delight in portraying such ogre-ish employers as members of Buddhist sects that rejected worship of the Ise gods. Followers of Jōdo Shinshū and Nichiren sects were portrayed as especially unsympathetic masters of child pilgrims, for example, in story I.4 (86/21). When a serving girl left on pilgrimage without permission, her master and mistress were furious. He was a Nichiren believer, and his wife followed Jōdo Shinshū. Actually, it was not possible that a married couple be affiliated to different Buddhist sects, so this touch was a rhetorical flourish. Never dreaming that her employers would be so angry, the girl returned with amulets for them both, as well as seaweed and other gifts, but they threw the gifts into the fire and beat her mercilessly. To their horror, a small snake crawled out of a burning amulet box. After slithering around for a while, it grew larger and larger, coiling around the house pillar and glaring at the couple. Soon the wife came down with a raging fever; the man cried and apologized, but the snake was unmoved. The man sent a proxy on pilgrimage to Ise and repented for his sins, but the story does not record whether his wife was cured, or whether the snake went away.[53]

To encourage the young, Hironori offered tales of the compassion of the people of Yamada for pilgrims:

> At the height of this *nukemairi,* everyone through the districts, streets and byways of Yamada, even to the poorest widows who possessed only a single garment, was offering charitable lodgings to two or three pilgrims each.... There were many such offerings of charitable lodgings to the penniless pilgrims.[54]

While Hironori stresses the altruism of individual almsgivers, in fact many communities were required to contribute to a pilgrims' alms fund that was very burdensome and much disliked.[55]

Mass pilgrimage in 1771 and thereafter was referred to as *okage mairi,* literally, "thanks pilgrimage," following the expression *okage de* or *okagesama de,* meaning "thanks to [someone]." The expression referred to alms offered by merchants and ordinary people living along the routes to Ise; it was "thanks to" their charity that pilgrims could reach their goal and return home again. Documents on the 1771 *okage mairi* are very different from the rosy picture emerging from the miracle tales we examined earlier. Whether compiled by the Ise priests or by people living along the route, the overwhelming impression is that mass pilgrimage was a public health nightmare.

The 1771 diary of the Head Priest of the Inner Shrine recorded that the roads were choked with pilgrims, many of whom were children. People living along the roads to the shrines set up alms stalls, and the priests also set up alms stations inside the shrines. They gave money and a talisman to all, regardless of ability to pay. The priests feared that the crowds would cause a fire in the shrines, since these pilgrims were not being supervised by *oshi.* Uji and Yamada ran out of horses and oxen to transport firewood and other necessary supplies, and, at the same time, the animals used to transport pilgrims completely clogged the entrance to the shrine grounds. Palanquin bearers gouged the pilgrims on prices. There were pickpockets and thieves.[56]

Another document describes the sad case of a ship from Atsuta that went down in a storm, loaded with seventy-two *nuke mairi* pilgrims. Thirty perished, despite the best efforts of shore villages to rescue them. The villagers made a great effort to locate the bodies using nets, but they could only recover ten. The pilgrims themselves had come from various places in Eastern Japan, many from Owari (where they had boarded the boat), and some from Edo or nearby areas, traveling in small groups of two, three, or four.[57] It is apparent that the 1771 pilgrimage drew from a much wider area than the one in 1705, stretching from Kyūshū to the northeast.[58]

A diary of the 1771 pilgrimage by the otherwise unknown Tsuda Kin'uemon Norinao, "Ise mairi okage no nikki" (1771), uses the word *fushigi* (uncanny, incredible, unbelievable) to describe the events unfolding before him. He portrays the ceaseless tide of pilgrims as ominous, pitiful, and sometimes frightening. According to what he learned by talking to the pilgrims, many did not eat for days at a time and couldn't explain what they hoped to attain by going to Ise, except that they all hoped to receive a talisman. Rumors in Osaka and Nara of talismans falling from the sky sparked a wave of *nuke mairi*, about 70,000 to 80,000 (see Figure 9.6). Many pilgrims ended up sleeping outside or around the Great Buddha at Nara. Some fell ill or died, resulting in roadside villages having to foot the bill for medical treatment or to send the corpses home. Large groups, or people traveling with children, tied themselves together with rope so as not to be separated in the crowds. Even so, there were huge numbers of lost children and people separated from their fellow travelers. In the midst of all this misery, some pilgrims played music day and night, as if it were a festival. Many approached the shrines by lamplight, provoking great fear that the sanctuaries might catch fire, but pilgrims kept coming. In a complete absurdity, because Lord Matsudaira of Dewa was stopping over near the shrines, at Matsusaka, all alms-giving activity along his route was stopped so that he wouldn't be offended by sight of the rabble.[59]

Clearly, *okage mairi* was a mixed blessing for all concerned. Whereas the shrines at the beginning of the period were working hard to promote regularized, orderly pilgrimage, by the late eighteenth century, Ise pilgrimage had not only become self-sustaining, but had also completely overflowed the bounds of priestly control. The result was a volatile mixture of misery, crime, sickness, carnival, and religious enthusiasm.

The *okage mairi* of 1830 had many of the same features as in 1771: starving pilgrims, pilgrims sick and dead by the road, overwhelmed inns and teahouses, alms organized on a huge scale by merchants and others who undoubtedly participated out of fear that pilgrims could take what they wanted if the mood turned ugly. In addition, however, the fear of fire at the shrines came true when a huge conflagration burned down the Uji Bridge and the *torii* before it, all the homes of the Inner Shrine's *oshi*, and all the eighty *massha*. The main sanctuary was undamaged, but outlying sub-shrines burned down as the fire spread to the hills beyond, raging intensely, impossible to put out. The fire occurred just one year after the Vicennial Renewal; in mourning for the tragedy, all ringing of bells and boisterous entertainments in Kyoto were suspended for five days.[60]

But amid this misfortune, however, a different type of pilgrim, more stylish and wealthy, emerged in the nineteenth century from among those calling themselves

Figure 9.6 Talismans Falling from the Sky. Utagawa Yoshiiku, Japanese, 1833–1904. Publisher: Tsujiokaya Bunsuke (Kinshōdō), Japanese *Pilgrimage to the Ise Shrine (Hōnen okagemairi no zu)* Japanese, Edo period, 1867 (Keiō 3), 9th month, woodblock print (nishiki-e); ink and color on paper, vertical ōban. Source: Museum of Fine Arts, Boston, William Sturgis Bigelow Collection, 11.41238. Photograph © 2016, Museum of Fine Arts, Boston.

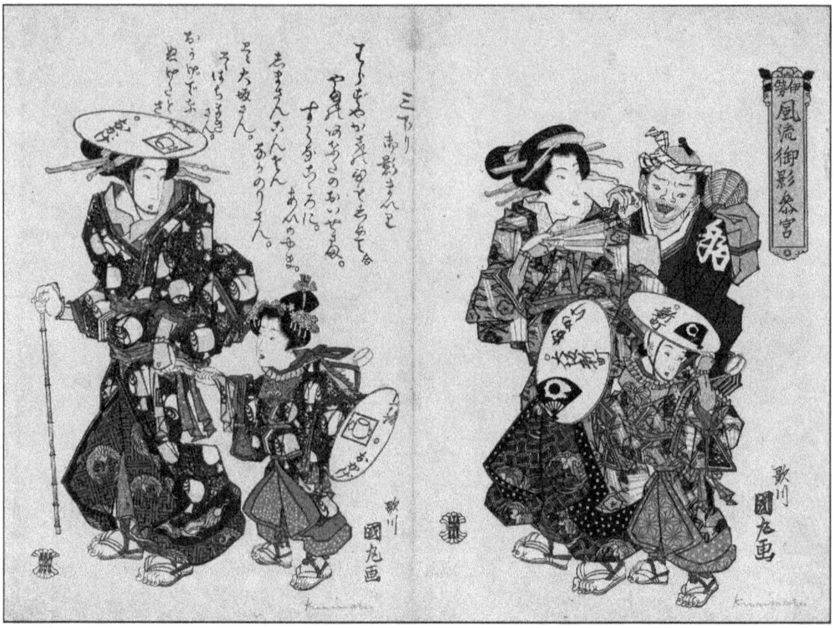

Figure 9.7 Fashionable Pilgrims. Utagawa Kunimaru, Japanese, 1793–1829. Publisher: Wataya Kihei (Wataki), Japanese *Fashionable Pilgrimage to the Ise Shrine (Ise fūryū okage sangū)*. Woodblock print (nishiki-e); ink and color on paper, vertical ōban; 38 × 25.5 cm (14 15/16 × 10 1/16 in.). Source: Museum of Fine Arts, Boston and Worcester Art Museum exchange, made possible through the Special Korean Pottery Fund, museum purchase with funds donated by contribution, and the Smithsonian Institution—MFA Chinese Expedition, 1923–24 RES.54.187.35a-b. Photograph © 2016, Museum of Fine Arts, Boston.

nuke mairi (see Figure 9.7). Groups of fifty or so young women from Osaka, each carrying a ladle and dressed alike, in white with white leggings, walked along in men's clothing, including loincloths and men's hairdos, gloves, and umbrellas and flags inscribed, "Okage mairi," and singing as they went, "Thanks be! We got away (*nuketa*)!" Another group of forty women from Osaka came, wearing elegant kimonos and beautifully made up. They carried ladles and were so beautiful that everyone came out to look. The gold thread with which they had embroidered "*oharai*" on their matching robes glittered in the sun. A mixed group of several hundred men and women from Himeji came, carrying ladles. Written on their matching umbrellas was, "How light our feet as we go to Ise / Thanks to your kindness, the blessings of Amaterasu upon our umbrellas." Another group of women from Osaka came dressed in men's clothing, with pale yellow *chirimen* cloth dyed with a pattern of red and white shrine talismans. They wore their hair in men's styles and were accompanied by men dressed in matching white silk with velvet pants. Others wore masks; there were people dressed entirely in red, others in high platform *geta* sandals.[61] They carried flags proclaiming that they were *nuke mairi*, but clearly the meaning of the phrase had changed drastically since 1771. The planning and construction of the costumes alone must have been exciting and time-consuming, a far cry from the earlier *nuke mairi* who took off in whatever they happened to be wearing at the time.[62]

Conclusion

Growing literacy spread knowledge of shrines and myth, while channeling popular thought, by, for example, making distinctions among different Kami and Buddhist figures based on their supposed specialties in dealing with different problems. Pilgrims' diaries and travel guides presented a variety of information about temples and shrines, especially the Ise Shrines, including accounts of myth in accessible language, often with odd interpretations. In none of these venues, however, do we see the systematic influence of the contemporary schools of thought about Shinto examined in chapter 8, probably because they continued to rely on esoteric transmissions limited to elites.

We know from Ise miracle tales that some schools of Buddhism rejected worship of the Ise deities, but we do not know how many of their parishioners took that position. Some pilgrimage guides claimed that all Japanese are linked to Ise through the emperor, suggesting the kernel of an expression of Japanese identity that would be greatly magnified in the modern period. Here again, we do not know whether such ideas took hold, or if they were significant factors motivating people to go to Ise on pilgrimage.

Inari devotion and Ise pilgrimage reflect on the question whether Shinto during the Edo period should be considered a religion. A religious system requires doctrines, institutions for their transmission and perpetuation, and practices (ritual, worship) embodying the system's ideas and symbols in collective action. Watarai Shinto and Ryōbu Shinto had also contributed significantly to the accumulation of a body of knowledge about Shinto, and doctrines specifically presented as "Shinto" teachings had existed since at least the time of Kanetomo. Shinto's philosophical dimension was further elaborated through Confucian Shinto and Yoshikawa Koretaru's formulation of Yoshida Shinto. Village *kō* were pilgrimage's institutional nodes, paralleling urban shrines' roles in Inari devotion. *Kō* worship practices, pilgrimage itself, and the plethora of commercialized rites available at shrines through the mediation of *oshi*, Shintōsha, and the other popular religionists belong to the dimension of worship and ritual.

In this rough-and-ready way, we can fill in the boxes belonging to doctrines, institutions, and practice that could conceivably constitute Shinto as a religion at this time. But this is insufficient. Just as we encountered considerable problems in adopting the term *Shintō* before it actually began to be used, the term *religion* (*shūkyō*) is likewise fraught with difficulties before it becomes a part of popular speech in the late nineteenth century, a subject taken up in detail in later chapters.

No one spoke of Shinto as a *religion* in the Edo period. The word most often used to describe popular devotions like those seen in Inari worship or Ise pilgrimage was "faith," or to "have faith in" (*shinkō*, the noun, and its verbal form, *shinkō suru*). *Shinkō* implies the action of believing in, revering, offering one's sincerity, trusting in, and relying upon without doubt. The term has a long history and is found in popular tales *Konjaku monogatari* (ca. 1120), *Shōbōgenzō* (1231–1253), the magnum opus of Dōgen, a major figure of Zen thought in the medieval period, *Tsurezuregusa* (ca. 1331), a literary commentary on social mores, war tales such as *Taiheiki* (fourteenth century), and many other works.[63]

The attitudes covered by *shinkō* seem to share much with devotional practices seen widely in many religious traditions, even though the terms *Shintō* and *shūkyō* were absent. Faith in Inari seems to have been spurred by rumor and the hope of securing answers to one's prayers. Authors of accounts of Ise pilgrimage were impressed by the rumors of talismans falling from the sky in sparking pilgrims' inarticulate urge to go to Ise. Mass pilgrimage was stimulated by the desire for an Ise talisman, though pilgrims could not always explain why.

None of the contemporary accounts that I have found attests to a sense among Inari devotees or Ise pilgrims that they were doing something specifically relating to Shinto. The authors of contemporary accounts did not record the influence of any particular doctrinal formulation of Shinto, most likely because they perceived none. Given the tradition of esoteric transmission, this is hardly surprising. In fact, the gap between Shinto's philosophical development, on the one hand, and the proliferation of popular faith and the development of institutions for its expression, on the other, is a conspicuous feature of Shinto in the Edo period.

What were the implications of this situation in terms of popular awareness of Shinto? Tada Yoshitoshi and others discussed "Shintoists," dividing them into two categories, those who teach and lecture on classic works versus "shamans" selling spurious rituals. Yoshitoshi clearly included himself in the first category, one that associated "Shinto" with a body of learning and its practitioners with scholarship and teaching. The distinction is reminiscent of those drawn by Hayashi Razan and Yoshikawa Koretaru, who upheld their own doctrinal-philosophical expressions while conceding that much of what went on at shrines was chaotic and unrestrained by any doctrinal system. *Hayarigami* and mass pilgrimage epitomized elite perceptions of popular Kami faith as undisciplined and vulgar.

This bifurcation reflects the mixed and as-yet unprofessionalized character of the ritualists involved. Yoshitoshi chided Ise *oshi* for their re-enactments of Amaterasu's emergence from a cave that in fact had been a burial site. As we have seen, many urban shrines were informally staffed—not by the representatives of venerable lineages. Since urban shrines frequently began as *yashikigami*, ritualists could be attached to them in fluid, casual ways. The Shintoists whom Tada Yoshitoshi disparaged as shamans seem to have been free from any restraints from the Yoshida, the Shirakawa families, or from larger shrines. We also saw families in service at Osaka shrines, such as the Kawamura, who regarded themselves as superior to the shaman Shintoists, even as they colluded in the latter's proliferation and instantiation at their own shrines. In fact, there was no single authorizing body training shrine priests, though the Yoshida licensing system functioned to structure the thought and practice of those who could afford to affiliate.

Nevertheless, by including himself among the scholar-teacher Shintoists, Yoshitoshi furnished an early example of *Shinto* as a term of self-reference. While there undoubtedly were examples of people associating themselves with Shinto prior to the Edo period, to refer to oneself and others as "Shintoists" was novel, a significant milestone toward a changed perception of Shinto. We will see in chapter 10 how proselytizers and new religious movements pushed further toward the recognition of Shinto as an element of personal identity.

10

Shinto and Revelation

Introduction

Religious revelation entered the history of Shinto at the end of the Edo period, when several figures came to believe that they had received a special mission and message from the Kami. While earlier eras had known of dreams or visions inspired by the Kami, in the mid-nineteenth century we find Kurozumi Munetada claiming that when he was at the point of death, Amaterasu, in the form of the sun, had come down from the sky, entered his mouth, and healed him. Likewise, Inoue Masakane believed that a mysterious female who came to him in a dream had passed a jewel into his mouth from hers, infusing him with great joy and certain knowledge of his life's mission. Both men fashioned their revelations into a Way of self-cultivation by which anyone could replicate their achievements, regardless of education, sex, or social position.

The nineteenth century saw a pervasive concern with "personal cultivation" (*mi o osameru, shūshin*; sometimes *gakumon*) crossing the boundaries of Shinto, Buddhism, and Confucianism. As explained by Janine Sawada, personal cultivation consisted of "the moral, ritual, physiological, and/or educational processes by which individuals were believed to attain well-being." Well-being meant peace of mind, health, peace within the family, economic stability, and harmony with the cosmos. Personal cultivation was based on the assumption that the "psychological, physiological, social, and cosmic conditions of an individual's existence" were intimately interrelated.[1] Thus to cultivate one's attitudes and state of mind would improve health, relations with others, social harmony, and ultimately, the cosmos. The matrix for personal cultivation was society as one found it—the goal was to achieve personal fulfillment within one's place in society as it is, not to try to change society to suit oneself. And while self-cultivation was intended to be transformative for the individual, there was no expectation that society would be upended. Instead, society would gradually improve as more people dedicated themselves to self-cultivation.

Shinto came under the influence of the widespread interest in self-cultivation, as nineteenth-century Japanese religious thinkers from diverse religious backgrounds developed novel programs of self-cultivation. Some of them came from a Shinto background and developed forms of personal cultivation that in the right circumstances could become new religious movements. The founders of these movements drew upon the religious enthusiasm seen in Inari faith and Ise pilgrimage and benefited from the work of popularizers to be examined in this chapter. But whereas the foregoing popular expressions of faith in the Kami were sporadic and lacked cohesion, new religious movements framed by self-cultivation regimens were more structured and encompassed all aspects of life.

New religious movements have appeared within all the major religions. Some evolved from within the parent tradition as a reconfiguration of existing themes. New religious movements generally build upon existing tradition even as they innovate.[2] They frequently experiment with novel ways of life, exhibiting unusual patterns of leadership, gender roles, and sexuality. While new religious movements often originate in an atmosphere of tension with the larger society, over time they may come to be quite compatible with the mainstream. This chapter addresses three new religious movements derived from Shinto, each of which was based on a distinctive program of self-cultivation: Kurozumikyō, Misogikyō, and Uden Shintō.[3]

New religious movements in Japan have arisen in clusters, first at the end of the Edo period (roughly 1800 to 1860), next during the 1920s, subsequently in the postwar period (1945 to around 1970), and most recently, a smaller cluster appeared in the mid-1980s. Their doctrines show great variety, but they generally uphold such traditional moral values as sincerity, frugality, diligence, filial piety, harmony, and family solidarity. The idea that anyone can perfect him- or herself is linked to a strong theme of human equality.[4]

New religious movements outside the Buddhist and Shinto priesthoods arose in the early nineteenth century. Their founders experienced religious revelations that became the basis for a comprehensive devotional life. Oracles or dreams inspired by the Kami served as the Shinto founders' touchstones for discerning their future course of action. These founders emphasized laity-based leadership and practices that could be carried out without clerical direction. The founders of new religious movements sometimes came to be regarded as living deities, and their life stories, writings, or recorded sayings, as divinely inspired. Members' daily observances focused on modeling oneself on the founder. Whatever their doctrinal basis, most Japanese new religious movements have practiced faith healing and believe that salvation is attainable by all, without respect to social class or sex. Their doctrines are promoted openly and universally, without respect to sex, kinship, territorial ties, religious lineage, or esotericism.

Edo-Period Shinto Popularizers

The Shinto-derived new religious movements did not arise in a vacuum but built on the groundwork laid by popularizers who spread foundational ideas and practices to ordinary society. From the sixteenth through the early nineteenth century, popularizers spread significant Shinto practices and knowledge, which had previously been restricted to the priesthood, into society at large. These men traveled the countryside, visiting shrines and their priests in an effort to disseminate reverence for the Great Purification Prayer, the Prayer for the Purification of the Six Roots, and the Oracles of the Three Shrines. These men can be regarded as popularizers of Shinto inasmuch as they spread easily grasped knowledge and practices among the ordinary populace, without attempting to convey rarefied doctrines or complicated ritual. A high degree of literacy was not required. Some of the things that the popularizers spread, such as the Oracle of the Three Shrines, were accompanied by artistic representations conveying teachings in a form that combined text and image. Some were loosely affiliated with the Yoshida House, or represented Suika Shinto; others were unaffiliated with any established school. Some of those working in the eighteenth and nineteenth centuries also took an active interest in Kokugaku and spread nativist ideas. In some cases, they urged a change in the shrine's name or deities to correspond to forms favored by Yoshida Shinto, or they claimed that the rightful deity of the shrine was in fact a Kami known from the *Nihon shoki*. The work of these popularizers gained increasing influence with the spread of literacy and print culture. Their appearance signifies that esoteric transmission of Shinto rites and doctrines was breaking down.

The Oracle of the Three Shrines (*sansha* [or the variant, *sanja*] *takusen*) was a powerful device for popularizing Shinto. The term *sansha takusen* refers to a hanging scroll on which images of, or the names of, Amaterasu, Hachiman, and Kasuga are inscribed vertically in calligraphy (or printing, in later examples), so that Amaterasu is in the center, Hachiman on the right, and Kasuga on the left (see Figure 10.1). The names of Amaterasu and the Kasuga deity are recorded in a way that makes clear that they are Kami, but in pre-Meiji examples Hachiman's name is often recorded as Hachiman Daibosatsu, his bodhisattva identity. If painted images are present, they may substitute for the written names. Amaterasu was pictured as a figure of ambiguous sex placed beneath a sun and moon, with a Buddhist halo, sometimes carrying a Wish-Fulfillment Jewel in the left hand and a jeweled staff in the right hand. She might have a five-story pagoda on top

Figure 10.1 Sansha Takusen. Source: The Petzold Collection, Harvard-Yenching Library, Harvard College Libraries.

of her head. The Kasuga deity and Hachiman are portrayed in court dress, with Hachiman sometimes holding a bow.

The text of the oracles is recorded in a lower register, generally beneath the calligraphic names or images. The text of the oracles is usually (but not in Fig. 10.1) as follows:

> AMATERASU: Though you may make a visible profit by sharp practice, inevitably retribution from the kami will follow. If you are honest, you may be shunned for a time, but in the end you will receive the blessing of the sun and moon.
>
> HACHIMAN: Though you may eat a ball of iron, accept nothing from a person with an impure heart. Though you may sit on blazing copper, do not approach the place of a person with an unclean heart.
>
> KASUGA: Though he may pull on the sacred rope [that is, ring the bells at a shrine to call the Kami's attention] for a thousand days, I will not approach the house of someone with perverted views. Even though you may be in deep mourning for your parents, I will come to a house where there is compassion.[5]

As the texts suggest, the oracles associate each of the Kami with a particular virtue, Amaterasu with *shōjiki*, meaning honesty, integrity, and uprightness; Kasuga with compassion; and Hachiman with purity. The scrolls were hung as devotional objects for group worship. While the original provenance of the scrolls remains uncertain, extant documents suggest that they were in existence by the beginning of the fifteenth century. Yoshida Kanetomo worked to promulgate them, and the Yoshida House began to dispense the scrolls to affiliates who visited its Kyoto headquarters. In 1832, for example, it distributed some 1,450 scrolls of the Oracles of the Three Shrines. It appears that the scrolls gained such esteem that they began to circulate independently of the Yoshida House. Independent proselytizers adopted them, and they were also adopted in Kurozumikyō.[6]

The Oracle of the Three Shrines stimulated awareness of the Kami as moral exemplars and as sources of oracular pronouncements. The oracles themselves positioned the three deities as claiming moral authority over all, not merely those within the geographical catchment area of a particular shrine or the members of a kinship group. Worship of this combination of deities was promoted as beneficial to the moral cultivation of the individual, regardless of location or social position. Shinto popularizers commonly employed the Oracle of the Three Shrines as a proselytizing tool.

Tachibana Mitsuyoshi (1635–1703) was an early Shinto popularizer who was loosely affiliated with the Yoshida House.[7] He began lecturing on Shinto in the Edo entertainment district called Asakusa, also developing his own formulation of essential Shinto doctrines, which he called The Fifty-Six Transmissions of Sōgen Shinto (*Sōgen Shintō gojūroku den*).[8] From 1675 to 1697, Tachibana traveled to the First Shrines of the country as well as hundreds of other shrines, dedicating a printed copy of the Great Purification Prayer, accompanied by his own commentary, to each of them.[9] He also lectured on this prayer as well as the Purification of the Six Roots Prayer and the Oracle of the Three Shrines. During this extraordinary journey of twenty-three years, he compiled a diary-like record called *A Record of Pilgrimage to the First Shrines* (*Ichinomiya sankeiki*), in which he occasionally commented on the contemporary hazards of travel, such as encountering bands of monkeys, boars, and badgers along the road. Upon meeting a local priest or official in charge of a shrine, he would ask to inspect its object of worship or historical documents. In many places, the people supporting such a shrine were uncertain of the identity of its Kami. Upon inspecting a sword or ridge beam inscription, Mitsuyoshi would draw connections between the object and some passage in *Nihon shoki*, authoritatively determining that the local deity was actually such-and-such a Kami in the classical text. Creating these connections tied the shrine and its supporters into an imagined community of a unified country with a divinely descended emperor at its head.[10]

Masuho Zankō (1655–1742) was an effective popularizer of Shinto, though very different in style and substance from Mitsuyoshi. Zankō had begun as a Buddhist priest, first in Pure Land Buddhism and later ordained in Nichiren Buddhism, and he may also have affiliated later to Tendai. He left the Buddhist priesthood at forty-three, and thereafter authored a popular book on "sensual matters in general and red-light districts . . . in particular," *Endō tsugan* (1715).[11] He later began a career as a popular lecturer on Shinto. Zankō apparently used his reputation as someone well acquainted with the sex trades to assemble audiences for lectures, then turned midway to a discussion of Shinto, mainly attacking Buddhism and Confucianism for their deleterious effects on Shinto. In Zankō's day, Buddhist preachers of the Jōdo Shinshū, Jōdo, and Nichiren schools were becoming known as great preachers. Zankō tried to refute them with blistering critique. To promote Shinto ritual, he would have his hosts build a *torii* in the room in which he would lecture, recite the Great Purification Prayer, and perform rites based on *goma* fire rituals. It is not clear whether Zankō was initiated in Yoshida House practices, but he spoke of the Threefold Purification (*sanshu no ōharai*) and the Oracles of the Three Shrines, seeming to have become strongly inclined toward Yoshida teachings in later life.[12]

Tomobe Yasutaka (1667–1740), a follower of Suika Shinto, wrote an introduction to Shinto for a popular audience, called *Shintō nonaka no shimizu* (1732), colored by distinctive Suika ideas. For example, he promoted the Suika idea that the highest duty is service to the emperor, linking this to a view of the afterlife in which the souls of those who serve the throne loyally will become Kami after death and live in Takamagahara.[13]

Tamada Naganori (1756–1836) was active after 1800. He was originally a samurai of Tokushima domain, but he lost his employment in the 1780s, made his way to Osaka, and became a professional lecturer. In 1791 he received initiation at the

Yoshida House, which proved to be a major turning point. In old age he was sufficiently wealthy to build a huge mansion near the Shimogamo Shrine in Kyoto, suggesting that his lectures must have been quite successful. Yoshida affiliation allowed Naganori a source of authority and permission to travel all around the country. When he entered a new locale, he would go to small shrines, inspect their objects of worship, and explain the nature of the Kami to the local people, who had mostly been worshipping the deity without knowing who it was. This technique, which Tachibana Mitsuyoshi had also adopted, allowed Tamada to link local shrines to classical myths and provide a "correct" historical interpretation of local deities. Local people accepted Naganori's interpretations because of his Yoshida authorization, allowing Yoshida teachings to permeate village shrines.[14]

Tachibana's and Tamada's work brought the Great Purification Prayer and other Shinto prayers to a popular level in their recommendations that everyone recite them. Apparently, the popularizers encouraged people to recite the Great Purification Prayer frequently, without restricting it to the ancient prescriptions for its use at the end of the sixth and twelfth months. People were encouraged to recite it in large numbers, similar to the way that the *nenbutsu* or *daimoku* were promoted in Japanese Buddhism. Tachibana and Tamada worked to link local shrines to the national history as it was understood at the time, as stretching back to an age of the Kami. They encouraged provincial shrine priests to understand their work as part of the flow of national life, not merely as perpetuating a local tutelary cult. Tachibana added his own intepretations of Yoshida Shinto in his "Fifty-Six Transmissions," though there is no extant evidence to suggest that these took root. Tamada's financial success suggests that he operated within the commercial framework dominant in the age. Masuho Zankō, who also promoted popular use of the Great Purification Prayer, borrowed from the Shinto *goma* rites known from the third stage of Yoshida Shinto's *Sandan gyōji,* no doubt making an impressive display at provincial shrines. His criticisms of Buddhism echoed a theme also developed by Kokugaku scholars, the assertion that breaking away from Buddhism was necessary to a correct grasp of Shinto. Tomobe Yasutaka popularized the Suika Shinto theme of monarchism as essential to Shinto.

The Shinto popularizers represented a new kind of figure in Shinto; they were independent operators who dedicated themselves to promoting Shinto as they personally understood it, making popularization their life's work, both an occupation and a calling. Although they all presented themselves as being qualified to perform Kami rituals, none of them were principally employed as shrine priests. Their promotion of Shinto consisted mainly of encouraging the recitation of Shinto prayers and the acceptance of an understanding that local tutelary gods were part of a larger national history. Where they advocated a particular understanding of morality, it was framed by the virtues recommended in the Oracle of the Three Shrines. They promoted their teachings universally, as relevant to all, without regard to class or social position.

The Life and Thought of Kurozumi Munetada

Kurozumi Munetada (1780–1850) was one of the most important founders of Shinto-derived new religious movement at the end of the Edo period. He was born December 21, 1780, into a samurai family of shrine priests of the Imamura Shrine, a tutelary shrine of the Okayama domain in Western Japan. Although he was the third son, one elder brother had died, and the other had declined to succeed his father, placing Munetada in line to become a shrine priest.

As a child, Munetada was devoted to his parents, and many hagiographical stories are told of his filial behavior. If one parent told him to wear sandals, and the other told him to wear wooden clogs, he wore one on each foot. He apparently acquired a Yoshida license by 1803 and made the first of six pilgrimages to Ise in that same year, at the age of twenty-four by the traditional way of counting age, in which a newborn baby is said to be one year old. The exact year of his marriage is not recorded, but his first daughter was born in 1807, so it must have occurred in his early twenties. His parents died of dysentery within a week of each other in 1812, plunging Munetada into such grief that he himself became ill. Believing that his death was near, on January 19, 1814, he had his pallet drawn to the verandah so that he could worship the rising sun one last time. This form of sun worship, called *nippai*, was a common observance in the region.[15]

To his astonishment, the sun came down from the sky and entered his mouth, pervading his entire body with its healing power. For Munetada this was a mystical experience of union with divinity, which he later called the "Direct Receipt of the Heavenly Mission" (*tenmei jikiju*). Munetada believed that he had become one with Amaterasu, whom he also referred to as Tenshō Daijin, or Tenshōkōtaijin. Munetada regarded Amaterasu Ōmikami as the creator of the universe and the parent of all living beings. He believed that each human being represents a "divided spirit" (*bunshin, wake mitama*) of Amaterasu, and that to attain and maintain a life of union with Amaterasu is the goal of human life. Munetada devoted the remainder of his life to preaching this message.

Though Munetada undertook religious exercises that appear to the modern reader "ascetic" in the extreme, to his followers he recommended simple practices of prayer and worship of the rising sun. In Munetada's understanding, union with Amaterasu could be accomplished in the present world—not after death—and in society as currently constituted. It did not require removing oneself from secular life or the customary obligations based on kinship and social location. Instead, he sought fulfillment of human potential through a life centered on gratitude to Amaterasu as the source of all life and happiness.

Munetada recognized the myriad Kami, and the Imamura Shrine apparently utilized the Oracle of the Three Shrines, but worship as it developed in the group Munetada founded did not single out the others, focusing on Amaterasu alone. As a shrine priest affiliated with the Yoshida House, Munetada was certainly aware of the significance of Amaterasu in the *Nihon shoki* and other classical texts. However, though he did not deny the existence of other Kami, he proceeded as if Amaterasu were the only one.

Munetada believed that the natural state of humanity is to be bright and joyous (*yōki*, a term formed by combining the word for the vital breath, *ki*, with yang, *yō*). When the heart is full of *yōki*, humanity and divinity are united. The natural result is good health. When the heart is full of sorrow or grief, however, it becomes *inki*, the opposite of *yōki*. In other words, if yin prevails in the equilibrium of yin and yang, the imbalance injures the divided spirit received from Amaterasu. The result is illness.

Munetada sought unity with Amaterasu by cultivating *yōki*. Building on the area's traditional practice of worshipping the rising sun, he developed a form of daily sun worship to enhance *yōki*; it combined deep breathing while facing the rising sun with recitation of the Great Purification Prayer. The deep breathing constituted drinking in the sun's yang essence, while the Great Purification Prayer dispelled pollution and enhanced purity. Good health would be the natural result. Munetada composed numerous poems to express this idea:

(1) The heart is the master, and the body is the servant. When we awaken, the heart commands the body, but when we are confused, the body commands the heart.
(2) The heart of Amaterasu Ōmikami is the heart of humanity, and when they are united, life is eternal.
(3) The heart of the ancients had no form, nor has ours today. When we forget the body and dwell in the heart, now is the Age of the Gods; the Age of the Gods is now![16]

Munetada began to preach soon after the Direct Receipt of the Heavenly Mission, making converts through faith healing. He cured a maidservant suffering from abdominal pains by applying his hand to her abdomen and blowing yang essence (which he had inspired through his daily worship) on the painful area, also reciting the Great Purification Prayer for her. He called this kind of curing "magic," *majinai* or *toritsugi*, vernacular terms already in use. Faith healing came to be a hallmark practice of the group that formed around Munetada, and people flocked to his lectures to be healed.

From 1815, Munetada began to issue certificates of discipleship (*shinmon*) to his more prominent followers, especially to the samurai among them. At first, the followers formed a confraternity of the Imamura Shrine, where Munetada had his official position, but his actions deviated from the duties of a shrine priest. Shrine priests did not usually preach, but Munetada was lecturing extensively. Shrine priests might conduct *kitō* for the purpose of healing, but their prayers would be performed for fees that contributed to the shrine's maintenance. By contrast, Munetada healed for free.

In 1816, the head priest of the Imamura Shrine directed Munetada to stop healing at the shrine, telling him to send anyone wanting healing to the other shrine priests for *kitō*. Moreover, Munetada was ordered to desist from distributing shrine talismans to his followers, because the practice suggested that the shrine endorsed his activities. Munetada also had to sign a pledge that he would not proclaim any new theories. Under these strained conditions, Munetada continued to serve as a priest at the Imamura Shrine until 1843, when he retired from his post in favor of his son Munenobu.

Despite the shrine's displeasure, Munetada pursued a novel course that bore little relation to the priesthood. He collected seventy-nine disciples between 1815 and 1824, an inner circle of those who received *shinmon* in Munetada's hand, mainly samurai and their family members residing in the domain's castle town of Okayama. Munetada wrote extensively to them when they accompanied the *daimyō* to Edo, and those letters later became part of the sacred texts of Kurozumikyō. The letters also reflect the key ideas and practices among Munetada's followers.

For example, a letter from 1821 shows that Ishio Kansuke had asked Munetada to paint a scroll of the Oracle of the Three Shrines for him, and that Munetada complied. We also learn that while Kansuke was in Edo, his father became a fervent believer and held meetings so Kurozumi could preach and heal.[17]

Munetada held meetings at his home or believers' homes six times monthly. His followers were called *michizure*, "those following the path." They assembled to recite the Great Purification Prayer together, to hear Munetada preach, and to witness or receive healing. Munetada spoke without notes, sometimes preaching for as long as eight hours at a stretch. The followers also hosted regular meetings, from 1815, in their homes, mainly in Bizen and Bitchū provinces. These meetings were initially regarded as *kō* of the Imamura Shrine.

A commoner follower described a meeting of the late 1840s as follows:

> The meetings held on the twenty-seventh were very well attended. We nearly always went, but there were others who came from even greater distances, only to return on the same day. In those days there was a sword-rack in the entry way, and there were many swords placed there. Everything was quite dignified, and as we left our umbrellas there and entered the house, there was a great crowd come to worship. Among them were such distinguished samurai as Lord Ishida, Lord Furuta, and others. They didn't receive seats of honor, however, just because they were samurai while farmers sat at the back. There were no such distinctions. Merchants, artisans, whoever came first, sat in the front. Some prominent people had to kneel on the ground all day while low-born women and children took the best seats. Even though those were days when the samurai held high status, they could neither see [to the front] nor move about.

> Once the meeting began, there was silence. The only sound was an occasional clap [not applause, but affirming what was being said]. No one so much as moved—not even the women and children. You might suppose that a stiff air of formality prevailed, but it wasn't that. Our Founder's voice seemed to penetrate into our very bones, and quite naturally our heads became heavy, and we knew nothing but the sense of gratitude. Once the meeting was over, I forgot entirely what had been said. I have such a good memory for other things that I have been called a "living calendar," and until I turned sixty or so I could remember events of the past down to the hour they happened. But I have never been able to recall the content of a sermon. I never tried to—I was simply grateful.
>
> After the sermon, people requested healing, also in the order of first-come-first-served. There were some who had been carried in to receive healing. After these healings, we took supper, and it was about [ten at night] when the meeting broke up.
>
> All the followers were kind and treated each other warmly, taking special care of the sick. Wherever we met fellow followers, it was like meeting a relative, and we had an unaccountable affection for each other. Once when I was returning home from a meeting, I chanced to meet five or six samurai ahead of me on the road. I was following along behind when they asked me politely how far I was going. When I replied that I was going to Shimo Yamada in Ōku County [about twenty-five kilometers away], they apologized for detaining me when I had so far to go and bid me go on before them. When they stood aside and let me pass, I knew they had acted this way because they were followers, and I was filled with gratitude.[18]

This description reveals key information about the sources of Munetada's appeal in late Edo society. In his focus on the "first-come-first-served" custom of Munetada's meetings, the writer marvels that the status hierarchy of the day was ignored. Normally, samurai were accorded precedence in every situation, but where Munetada preached, even women and children could remain seated in their presence. The writer returns to this theme, struck that out of consideration for the long journey ahead of him, samurai would stand aside and let him pass. In other circumstances when commoners encountered samurai on the roads, they would kneel to the ground as the warriors passed ahead of them. The customs observed in Munetada's meetings and among his followers established a principle of equality, based on the idea that everyone is equal in being a divided spirit of Amaterasu.

Munetada's seven closest disciples are known as the High Disciples. Furuta Masanaga was a high-ranking samurai of the Okayama domain who had received a certificate of discipleship in 1819. Ishio Kansuke (1775–1859) was likewise a samurai follower and was the most active proselytizer. About one-quarter of Munetada's correspondence was addressed to Ishio. Kawakami

Tadaaki (1795–1862) was a samurai scholar of Wang Yang Ming Confucianism employed by the domain who joined Munetada in 1822, after Munetada had healed Kawakami's mother, Tsuyako, of an eye ailment. Others among the High Disciples, such as Akagi Tadaharu (1816–1885) and Tokio Katsutarō, were more active after Munetada's death.

Women followers, such as Kawakami Tsuyako and Munetada's wife, Iku, were influential in spreading knowledge of Munetada's teachings among other women. Samurai women were unable to preach and proselytize, but they were nevertheless significant in recruiting. From an early time, there were both female and male ministers of the group, and we may presume that women were attracted by the principle of equality.

Munetada developed a creed for his followers in the form of the Seven Daily Household Rules (*Nichinichi kanai kokoroe no koto*):

1. Born in the Land of the Gods (*shinkoku*), you shall not fail to cultivate faith.
2. You shall neither become angry nor do harm.
3. You shall not give way to conceit nor look down upon others.
4. You shall not fix upon another's evil while increasing the evil in your own heart.
5. You shall not malinger in the work of your household except in illness.
6. While pledged to the Way of Sincerity (*makoto no michi*), you shall not lack sincerity in your own heart.
7. You must never stray from the spirit of gratitude. These rules must never be forgotten. The hearts of all you encounter shall be as mirrors to you, reflecting the face you have presented to them.

In combination with daily worship of the rising sun, deep breathing, and recitation of the Great Purification Prayer, the Seven Daily Household Rules formed the core of Munetada's distinctive regimen of self-cultivation. Munetada urged followers to deepen their faith in Amaterasu and to cultivate *yōki* and the attitude of constant gratitude. They should resist the negative emotions of anger and denigrating others. Sincerity should be demonstrated through diligence in work. Dedication to this regimen would ensure well-being and manifest each individual's original unity with Amaterasu.

Even as Munetada's leadership departed from the usual activities of a priest of a domain shrine, he remained connected to the Yoshida House. In 1824 he traveled to Kyoto to procure the court title Sakyō and the documents needed to complete his formal succession to his father's post at the Imamura Shrine, subsequently making another pilgrimage to the Ise Shrines. Later that year, he petitioned the Yoshida to grant a title of apotheosis (*reijingō*) to a deceased disciple. In 1833, he secured *reijingō* for each of his parents, and a third for the grandfather of one of his disciples. Though the extant records do not clarify Munetada's intention, a *reijin* was a healing Kami and a high-ranking posthumous title.

In 1834, he requested a talisman from the Yoshida House for safe travel for one of his disciples. Munetada seems to have reached an arrangement with the Yoshida that allowed him to manufacture and distribute protective talismans on his own. These talismans allowed Munetada's followers to own a tangible mark of Amaterasu's protection. A document describing Munetada's activities in 1834, *Michizure nen oboedome*, states that in that year he made and distributed some 44,861 talismans. The same work shows that Munetada was manufacturing *miso*, fermented beans, and various kinds of medicine to finance his religious activities. Other records show that he took out a number of loans. Giving away talismans, taking loans, and sporadically manufacturing miscellaneous goods suggest that Munetada lacked the entrepreneurial skills seen in the more commercially oriented sectors of religious life, and that he did not prosper economically from his religious activities.

During the years 1825 to 1835, Munetada undertook a strenuous regimen of pilgrimage, shrine vigils, recitation of the Great Purification Prayer in astronomical numbers, and one hundred sessions of shrine worship each month. He acted as leader for Ise pilgrimage associations and made three pilgrimages to Ise. Records of his Ise pilgrimages show that he did not follow the usual route that began with the Outer Shrine, but instead went straight to the Inner Shrine, the seat of Amaterasu Ōmikami, showing no particular interest in the Outer Shrine or its deities. A shrine vigil (*sanrō*) is a period of confinement in a shrine during which the person constantly prays or performs ritual, such as *goma*. Such regimens were undertaken in temples as well, but Munetada kept his vigils at the Imamura Shrine. It would appear that his vigils were restricted to nighttime, and that he performed ordinary activities during the day. His first recorded vigil began in the seventh month of 1825 and lasted until the end of the year. In 1826, he undertook a vigil of 309 nights, and by 1828, his total nights of shrine vigils had reached around 800. In the third month of 1829, Munetada recited the Great Purification Prayer 17,350 times over a period of twenty-one days. During the fourth month, he recited the prayer 19,740 times, while during a period of twenty-one days during the fifth month, he completed 9,510 recitations.[19] During a pilgrimage to the Ise Shrines during the third and fourth months of 1835, Munetada recited the prayer as many as 2,000 times a day, and during the fifth month, he recited the prayer some 7,600 times in the hopes of healing a disciple. Numbers like this suggest that Munetada was reciting at great speed, in an extraordinary state of mind beyond ordinary consciousness.[20] During a period of thirty-four months from 1830 to 1832, Munetada carried out a regimen of visiting a hundred shrines a month, presumably visiting many of the same shrines multiple times.[21] On a shrine visit in this sense, Munetada would have recited the Great Purification Prayer before the shrines' altars to the Kami and possibly made an offering of produce or cash.

Munetada did not record his reasoning for pursuing these regimens, but it seems likely that he was striving to enhance his purity and express his sincere devotion to Amaterasu Ōmikami. Vigils, prayers, and shrine visits in such huge numbers suggest an intention to attain an extraordinary state of mind in which there is no consciousness of self.

Munetada proselytized in and around his home in Okayama, in Bizen and Bitchū Provinces, an area within which he was free to travel without official permission. He lectured at the invitation of village headmen, who evidently hoped that he would preach traditional values and deflect any tendency to uprisings. Village headmen (*shōya*) were in charge of keeping order and delivering taxes to the domain lord. They were at the pinnacle of the village social organization and held broad powers at the local level. By the end of the period, however, increasing social mobility had begun to weaken the headmen's authority, and put them on the defensive, especially the "rich peasants" (*gōnō*). They sponsored morally edifying teachers as a way to prevent unrest.[22]

The Okayama domain operated a school for commoners called Tenshinkō, established in 1782. It was called a *kō* because it was modeled on a religious confraternity. Along with the "three Rs," it taught the Classic of Filial Piety and other recommendations to modesty, frugality, and obedience to authority.[23] Contemporary headmen's reports to the domain voiced fear that the peasantry were following strange gods and using the excuse of worship to take holidays from work. Because headmen had previously controlled village work schedules, these heterodox practices challenged headmen's authority. They hoped to use Tenshinkō as a way to reinforce subservience to authority.[24] But not only Tenshinkō—Ishida Baigan's Shingaku thought was likewise regarded as an acceptable popular version of Confucianism, and Shingaku preachers were frequent guests of headmen hoping to suppress rebellious tendencies in the people through moral edification.[25]

Munetada was evidently seen by village headmen as an appropriate lecturer. In 1846, he lectured at Tamaigū, a Bizen shrine, to calm the hearts of the people, who were bent on rebellion.[26] He was a priest in a domain shrine, and he was certified by the Yoshida House. The account provided above of one of his lectures suggests that his audience took away a sense of gratitude more than anything else. His emphasis on sincerity and his devotion to Amaterasu contained nothing for headmen to fear.[27]

Kurozumi and his followers reached an important milestone with the proclamation of a document called the "Rules of 1846" (*Kōka san-nen no go teisho*). From the early 1840s, there had been a new increase in those following Munetada's teachings. By this time there were too many followers in too many locations for all of them to have a personal connection with Munetada. Munetada referred to the increase in a letter to a follower from 1843, writing,

> The Way has come to prosper, and truly my hands and feet cannot keep up with it. Both day and night are joyous. I cannot say how things will turn out, but while I am awed to ask it of you, I hope that you will rejoice with me.[28]

As this letter makes clear, the group was becoming too large for Munetada to manage by himself. Many had been converted by his disciples' proselytizing, which raised the question whether disciples spoke in Munetada's name, and whether disciples' healings were as effective as Munetada's. It became necessary to establish rules for how the organization should be managed. The establishment of these rules marked the founding of Kurozumi's teaching as a new religious movement.

The "Rules of 1846" governed the behavior of those disciples acting in Munetada's name and specified that only those formally authorized by Munetada could preach in his name. Procedures were established for ensuring that talismans and offerings were properly handled, and that followers coming from great distances could be accommodated with all propriety. Munetada gave his last sermon at his home in the eleventh month of 1849 and died in the second month of 1850, at the age of seventy-one.

Propagating Munetada's Teachings after His Death

Munetada did not proselytize outside the provinces of Bizen, Bitchū, and Mimasaka, but his disciples spread the teachings further afield. After Munetada's death, the High Disciples drew lots to determine their ongoing assignments of proselytization locations. Akagi Tadaharu drew Kyoto, the location most important in securing the group's safety from suppression. After Munetada's death, his followers were in effect operating outside the law, as their association was not authorized by any recognized religious organization. In the situation, the best way forward was to cultivate the patronage of influential aristocrats, especially the Yoshida, who had already granted Munetada numerous marks of recognition and authorization.[29]

Kyoto in the 1850s was greatly affected by the perception of a foreign threat. The news of the Opium Wars in China reached Japan in 1840, and the prospect of China's loss of independence was terrifying. As a part of a general reform (the Tenpo Reforms) of the early 1840s, the shogunate advanced a plan to bolster coastal defenses and tighten social morality through a campaign of restricting luxury and (sporadically) restricting heterodox teachings. These measures were generally viewed as ineffective in protecting the country.

Religious affairs in Kyoto were much influenced by Emperor Kōmei, who had come to the throne in 1846 and soon began to seek divine protection for the nation. In 1847, Kōmei sent tribute to an annual festival of the Iwashimizu Hachiman Shrine and the Twenty-Two Shrines, a practice that had been in abeyance. In the sixth month of 1853, the court called for prayers to repel the foreigners, but Admiral Matthew Perry arrived in the same month, spurring the court to repeat the call again at the end of that year. In the second month of 1854, Kōmei sent tribute to the Twenty-Two Shrines. In the ninth month, Kōmei called on temples and shrines to pray for deliverance from the Russians, while in the twelfth month the court called on temples to donate their bells to be melted down for cannon. In the first month of 1856, Kōmei initiated a seven-day prayer ceremony for national deliverance, and in the ninth month the court requested prayers from the Twenty-Two Shrines. In the third and fourth months of 1863, Kōmei made an imperial progress to the Kamo Shrine and to Iwashimizu Hachimangū as a prayer for expulsion of the foreigners, who by that time had landed and were successfully forcing the shogunate to sign trade treaties. In the fourth month of 1864, Kōmei dispatched an Imperial Emissary with tribute to seven shrines, with prayers for victory over the foreigners.[30]

It was in this charged atmosphere that Akagi Tadaharu began his campaign to secure the survival of the group that Munetada had founded. In the fourth month of 1851, Tadaharu began proselytizing in Kyoto, hoping to secure ongoing Yoshida patronage. The Yoshida elders tested him by sending an old woman from among their relatives to Tadaharu for *majinai.* She was healed. Apparently, the Yoshida placed their trust in Tadaharu, because in the sixth month, they issued new posthumous titles for Munetada, first as a *reijin* (healing deity) and then as a *myōjin,* a higher title of apotheosis. Although records documenting the cost of these titles are lacking, a major fundraising campaign among Munetada's followers was necessary to raise the needed funds. In 1854 Tadaharu delivered a sermon to members of the Kujō aristocratic house, preaching the importance of hewing to the Way of Amaterasu in this time of national emergency.[31]

In the third month of 1856, the Yoshida House conferred on Munetada the coveted title of Daimyōjin, a major accomplishment for Tadaharu. The Daimyōjin title effectively completed Munetada's apotheosis as a Kami recognized within the legal structure of religious administration under the shogunate. There was no higher title, and its possession was sufficient to ensure that Munetada's followers would not be harmed. In the second month of 1862, under Tadaharu's direction, a new shrine honoring Munetada as a Kami, the Munetada Shrine, was built on the pinnacle of a prominent hill in Kyoto called Kagurayama, or Yoshidayama, near the Yoshida Shrine and the Daigenkyū. Further, the spatial proximity of the Munetada Shrine to the Yoshida headquarters gave visual reality to the idea that Munetada's teachings and followers enjoyed Yoshida support and authorization.[32]

The association with the Yoshida House led to significant accolades from other aristocratic houses. In the third month of 1862, Sanjō Sanemi dedicated a certificate of followership in his own hand, a significant show of respect for Munetada's teachings. In the same month, Nijō Nariyuki had a Kurozumi preacher conduct a healing for his son, and he also dedicated calligraphy to the Munetada Shrine. Tadaharu formed close connections with the Nijō family, conducting healing rites several times. They donated numerous gifts of rice, money, and stone lanterns to the shrine, and the Nijō House sponsored two rounds of seven-day prayers for the peace and prosperity of the country conducted by Tadaharu, in the second and third months of 1863. It is believed within Kurozumikyō that Tadaharu lectured before Emperor Kōmei at this time, and that this imperial connection led to the designation of the Munetada Shrine as an imperial prayer shrine (*chokugansho*) in the fourth month of 1865.[33]

The religion founded by Munetada went on to grow and prosper in the Meiji period, establishing churches across the nation. Yet this new religious movement followed a markedly different course from those of other associations that shared many traits with it. It is important for our understanding of Shinto-derived new religious movements at the end of the Edo period to contrast Kurozumikyō with others whose history turned out very differently.

Inoue Masakane (1790–1849), Founder of Misogikyō

Inoue Masakane was born into a samurai family, but was not connected with any shrine. In his youth he had practiced Zen meditation and learned medicine and physiognomy in Kyoto under Mizuno Nanboku (1757–1834). Masakane's father had been employed by the Tatebayashi domain and was involved in keeping its accounts. He was so disgusted by the era's commercialism and materialism that he secluded himself in an upstairs room from 1794 to 1803, trying fruitlessly to invent a pathway to save people from their unhappiness. He identified this pathway as Shinto. Masakane took on his father's quest as his own.[34]

Masakane went on pilgrimage to Ise at the age of twenty-four, the same age that Munetada went on his first Ise pilgrimage. Moving to Edo in 1815, he made a living by practicing medicine and hexagram divination. He also learned *shiatsu*, a therapeutic technique resembling massage, based on finger pressure applied to nerves and muscle.[35] Under Nanboku's direction, Masakane had studied breathing techniques, calling his style of breathing practice *Nagayo no den* (the eternal tradition). The practitioner should inhale deeply through the nose and draw the breath into the abdominal area below the navel. It was a calm practice, carried out seated before an altar for the length of time necessary to burn one stick of incense.[36]

After Masakane's father died in 1827, Masakane married his wife Itoko in 1828, later bestowing on her the name "Otoko nari" (Became a Man). He evidently intended this moniker as a compliment, meaning that she was as dedicated and as steadfast as his male followers. Itoko bore two children, but both died. In 1833 Masakane experienced an extraordinary spiritual dream:

> My father Magane was devoted to the study of National Learning (*Kokugaku*). Pursuing the learning of the heart-mind, he studied the Ways of Confucianism and Buddhism.... Rejoicing in [his] awakening to the Way, he bequeathed his teachings to me, bidding me deepen my understanding further.... I conceived the desire to follow in my father's footsteps. In spite of my ignorance, impotence, and lack of learning, I sought out teachers of Shinto, Buddhism, and Confucianism. I travelled the country searching for those who could reveal the innermost secrets to me. I gave everything to my singleminded pursuit of the Way. I spent some

> years unsatisfied, unable to achieve peace of mind, to train my body, to put my household in order. I gave up eating and drinking and fasted. I poured cold water over my body, I sat in meditation. But though I experienced visions, I achieved no enlightenment. All my efforts were in vain. Then in the spring of my forty-fourth year, I had a dream or vision. A young girl came and spoke to me, saying, "I have a Great Way to bequeathe to you, you who have sought so long for the Way and failed to achieve your goal. The Shinmei [the Ise deities] have responded to your wish and will bestow upon you a bright jewel enabling you to break through the darkness of your confused heart. Once it has come from my mouth and filled you, your mind will be free of perplexity for the first time.... When you awake from this dream, you will never forget this moment. You shall know that you have received a truly mysterious message, and you will be filled with gratitude and joy. Continue your training and never forget this practice. Know your ignorance and confusion up to now, protect the Kingly Way (*ōbō*) on which the teaching of the imperial country is based."[37]

In Masakane's vision, the young girl (or goddess?) passed a jewel from her mouth to his, inspiring him with knowledge and bliss. Believing in this mystical experience of revelation from a messenger from the Ise deities, Masakane embarked on further study while pursuing his distinctive method of self-cultivation. In 1834, he affiliated with the Shirakawa House, studying purification (*misogi* and *harae*) at their Kyoto headquarters.[38] He came to believe that chanting the phrase "*to ho kami emi tame harae tamae kiyome tamau*" in combination with his breathing method was the key to attaining a state of complete sincerity (*makoto*). The chant was not Masakane's invention but in fact had been devised by Yoshida Kanetomo as the highest distillation of the most profound secrets of his thought, which also has the function of purifying sins and pollution, while invoking happiness in everyday life.[39] Originally the chant had three sections and hence was known as the Threefold Purification (*sanshu no ōharae*).[40]

Masakane believed that chanting "*To ho kami emi tame*" would lead to a cathartic experience of gratitude, in which all consciousness of self would vanish, and the chanter would arrive at a state of complete sincerity.

> If you ask about *makoto* as I understand it, it means performing purification (*harae*) to the point of forgetting day and night, eating and sleeping, and by receiving the virtue of the Kami, reciting until you lose your voice and can no longer breathe in or out. At that point, you will have exhausted your body so completely that you will awaken to joy and forget all about regrets, attachments, and confusion—about eating, clothing, or a place to live. You will be conscious only of your debt to the country, to the lord, to teachers, and parents, and of the depth of your own mistakes.... Reaching

> this point, the heart of *makoto* arises for the first time, and you will be astonished. Thereafter, whenever you feel confusion or sloth or fear, if you chant "*to ho kami emi tame harae tamae kiyome tamau*," your bad thoughts will be dispelled, and thoughts of your great debt to the country will take their place.... This is the virtue of purification. Knowing the mysteries of the breath, the breath will become the basis of your body and your life. That is the reason that we die when we cease to breathe. When we die, the body decays, because the basis of life has ceased. But even if our hearts and actions are correct, if our breathing is incorrect, we will fall into pollution and the heart and actions will become disordered.[41]

Followers would recite the chant in rhythm with their breathing exercises, thus combining purification and breathing exercises. Masakane developed this practice in the course of his training with the Shirakawa, or shortly thereafter. He came to believe that those who followed his regimen would be freed from delusion, egotism, and self-doubt. Practitioners would be cleansed, and restored to a state of purity in which they could experience union with Amaterasu. They would achieve a "mind of faith" (*shinjin*), "a direct, personal experience of salvation, granted by Amaterasu to the individual." Further, chanting "activates *kotodama*," the power of words that could bring about such desired results as healing and rainmaking.[42]

Masakane had attracted followers as early as 1835, and in 1836 he took over as the priest of a shrine in the suburbs of Edo called the Umeda Shinmeigū, a post formerly held by a Yoshida-affiliated priest named Asahi Dewa. Among his followers there were doctors, samurai, and a large number of homeless people, whom he accommodated at the shrine.[43]

As Masakane became better known, his activities became known to the Magistrate of Temples and Shrines, especially the fact that crowds of homeless people were being lodged at the shrine. Arrests began in 1841; one follower died in jail. Officials of the Edo Office of the Shirakawa House sent a letter of support, and Masakane's followers raised money to secure his exoneration. While in detention, Masakane was required to set out in writing the relation between his practices and Shirakawa Shinto. In response he composed a work called *Shintō yuiitsu mondō sho*. Masakane was released for a time, but he was arrested again in 1842. Ultimately, he was convicted of preaching heterodox teachings and, in 1845, was banished to the remote island of Miyakejima.[44]

Similar Teachings, Different Outcomes

Kurozumi Munetada and Inoue Masakane both practiced a combination of breathing exercises and chanting prayers that they identified with Shinto. Both began to preach in the aftermath of a transformative religious experience in which they believed that they had been united with divinity. While Munetada believed that the sun had come down from the sky and entered into his mouth, Masakane believed that a goddess had passed a jewel to him from her mouth. Munetada held a license from the Yoshida House, while Masakane held a Shirakawa license; both were recognized as qualified to officiate at shrines. Both revered Amaterasu as if she were the only Kami. They both taught their followers to seek physical health, peace of mind, and trouble-free human relations. On the face of it, they seem to have much in common, but their treatment by the authorities was quite different. From 1842, Inoue was judged guilty of preaching novel doctrines and practices and using his shrine as an asylum for the old and the poor. Banished to a remote island in 1845, he died there four years later. By contrast, Munetada continued in service to the shrine where he had succeeded his father as *negi*, until his retirement. After that, while samurai were prohibited from becoming his followers, he preached and healed at the invitation of village headmen all over the provinces of Bizen, Bitchū, and Mimasaka.

Scholars seeking the reasons for Masakane's harsh treatment have looked to his thought but found little that would explain why he should have been singled out, rather than any of the many others in his day who were proclaiming novel theories and introducing distinctive worship practices. There is no denying that many of the banishments from Edo in the latter part of the period were arbitrary and lacked any clear rationale. We saw in chapter 9 that from the beginning of the nineteenth century there were many localized suppressions of religious activity in Edo for no very good reason. In the early 1840s, there was a general crackdown on assemblies for Shinto preaching and proselytizing (*Shintō kōshaku*) that was part of the Tenpo Reforms, an attempt to reinforce moral principles while stabilizing the economy and strengthening the country militarily. We will see in the next chapter that National Learning scholar Hirata Atsutane suffered banishment around the same time.

The practices Masakane recommended were part of an evolving repertoire that found wide acceptance, and his devotion to Amaterasu left no room for criticism. Like Munetada, he remained aloof from the political issues of his day and recommended adherence to conventional morality. Thus, the attempt to explain Masakane's banishment in terms of his thought or religious life produces no clear conclusion. If, however, we examine Masakane and Munetada in terms of the ways they interacted with society, we begin to see significant differences between them.

Munetada was born into the shrine priesthood, served at a domain shrine, and had among his followers a number of influential samurai and merchants of the castle town, Okayama. Munetada answered to the Imamura Shrine and ultimately to the domain authorities as his superiors. Although his critics accused Munetada of preaching new, heterodox doctrines, he did so for most of his life while serving at a domain shrine. Munetada was not causing problems for the domain, but was instead widely appreciated among the headmen for preaching conventional values. The domain could have silenced him at any time, yet chose not to. Should such a matter have been reported to the shogun's Magistrate of Temples and Shrines, the domain would have faced uncomfortable questions about why it had tolerated Munetada's novelties up to that point. In reporting a problem in the first instance, the domain would tacitly have admitted that it had failed to put its own house in order. In short, it was both possible and advantageous for the domain to regard Munetada's teachings as deviating only slightly from widely accepted ideas and practices and to turn a blind eye to his innovations.

By contrast, Masakane did not come from a shrine family; he was already middle-aged when the Shirakawa certified him as qualified to serve at a shrine in 1834. He apparently purchased the right to serve at the Shinmeigū in Umeda Village, located in the Adachi district some six miles from the center of Edo.[45] His claim to embody Shinto teaching was vulnerable. While Masakane was in detention, and later during his exile, he had plenty of leisure to write in essay form, while Munetada was so preoccupied with proselytizing and ministering to his followers that though he left poetry and letters, he did not compose essays. Masakane was convicted on the basis of what he had written as much as for the way he ran the Umeda Shinmeigū. The lack of doctrinal exposition in Munetada's case may actually have helped to insulate him from critique.

A gazetteer completed in 1826, called *Shinpen Musashi fudokikō,* describes Umeda Village and its religious institutions as they were shortly before Masakane took up residence. The village had 140 households at that time. The water supply was poor, which meant that the farmers had difficulty producing rice. They supplemented their income by producing paper called *Asakusa-gami.* Part of the village land belonged to the imperial house. Shogunal officials used the area for hunting, and one of the older families had established a restaurant to provide meals for hunting parties. The road from Edo to the shogunal mausoleum at Nikkō ran through Umeda.[46]

When the gazetteer was compiled, the Shinmeigū shrine was headed by a Yoshida priest named Asahi Dewa. A later history composed by the shrine states that it was a "new" shrine, founded in 1762 in the aftermath of a fire, on a spot where tutelary gods had previously been worshipped. Like all Shinmei shrines, it revered the Ise deities. While this shrine was relatively new to the area, Umeda's religious life had historically revolved around a temple of the Shingi-shingon school of Buddhism called Myōō-in. This temple had enjoyed the patronage of generations of local overlords, who had provided it with significant assets, such as a sub-shrine where Inari and Konpira were the main deities. Another shrine attached to Myōō-in was dedicated to Benzaiten, and it had a sculpture of the goddess, over three feet high. But the biggest attraction at Myōō-in was a Fudō chapel, which housed a large sculpture of the fierce deity holding a sword, said to have been carved by the great saint Kōbō Daishi at the age of forty-two. The forty-second year is believed to be fraught with danger for men, and the statue was meant to protect worshippers from all harm. Many came from far away to worship before the statue, turning the temple into a small-scale pilgrimage site in the suburbs of Edo, much as the Inari shrines of Asukayama had become. In addition to Myōō-in, there was a second Shingi-Shingon temple called Henshō-in, which incorporated the official tutelary shrine of the village (*mura chinju*), dedicated to Inari.

Considering Masakane's position when he moved into this village and took over the Shinmeigū, we assume that the Yoshida officials in Edo would not have been pleased to see a shrine that had so recently been under their control be taken over by a Shirakawa affiliate. Whereas the other shrines and temples of the village had a longer history of interconnection, the Shinmeigū was not attached to a temple, nor was it the village's official tutelary shrine, meaning that it had no clear-cut rationale, leaving it vulnerable to anyone pointing out that it had been built after the prohibition on new shrine construction. Others might have asked why villagers should be prevailed upon to support it. Masakane was new to the shrine world. He lacked longstanding relations with other religious figures in the village, who might otherwise have restrained his critics.

Myōō-in and Henshō-in had their own customs for operating shrines, in which Buddhist clerics were in charge of ritual. Myōō-in stood to profit from worshipers coming to the Fudō chapel. By contrast, Masakane operated the Shinmei-gū in a way that flew in the face of local custom, turning it into an asylum for the poor and the elderly. Today, we regard such religious "welfare" work positively, but the authorities in the Edo period would have seen things differently. Housing miscellaneous people having no visible means of support in a shrine would pollute the altars of the Kami and burden the local people who were expected to keep the shrines in good repair. Inviting the rabble from Edo to live in a village shrine would not have been well received by village officials or, necessarily, by Buddhist clerics, especially if they hoped to attract tourist-pilgrims from Edo.

But even if village officials refrained from complaining about Masakane, Umeda was in the shogun's back yard, and supervisors from Kyoto acting on behalf of the imperial house were also involved. There was no intermediate domain structure that might have benefited by keeping quiet. Masakane's deviance from law and custom was hard to ignore in these circumstances. His location made him vulnerable, even if his reverence for Amaterasu and his combination of breathing exercises and chanting differed little from Munetada's.

Umetsuji Norikiyo and the Case of Uden Shinto

Umetsuji Norikiyo (1798–1861), also known as Kamo no Norikiyo, had come from a family attached to the Kamo Shrine, one of the most powerful shrines of the period. During the early Edo period, distinctive theories of Shinto had developed at the shrine, purporting to represent the teachings of the ancestor of the Kamo family, Yatagarasu, the three-legged crow that had supposedly led the legendary Emperor Jinmu on his conquest of the islands for the Yamato clan. These theories had come to be referred to as Uden Shinto, meaning, "transmitted by the crow." Norikiyo was deeply attracted to the Confucian thought of Xu Hsi and proclaimed a theory of Shinto that was much influenced by Confucianism. Although he had been granted a court title, poverty forced him to leave the Kamo Shrine. He traveled for over ten years to improve his learning. He regarded Kami as the parent of all things. He strove to create an interpretation of Shinto that would prove to be of practical use in governing, referring to his ideas as Uden Shinto. In addition to his essays on Shinto, he wrote on poor relief, and his ideas were later interpreted as being critical of the government. He opened a facility that he called The Crow Garden (Sui-u-en) in the Ikenohata district of Edo in 1846, later expanding to a variety of locations in the city where he preached to the masses. His proselytizing attracted the shogunate's attention, and the government exiled him to Hachijōjima in 1847, after he was found guilty of proclaiming heterodox teachings. He died in exile in 1861.[47]

The verdict against Norikiyo is very informative regarding what constituted heterodoxy in Shinto at the end of the Edo period. Significantly, the official entrusted by the Magistrate of Temples and Shrines with determining Norikiyo's guilt or innocence was Yoshikawa Tominosuke, the Shintokata of the day, a descendant of Yoshikawa Koretaru. Norikiyo had adopted the position that purification (*harai*) is nothing more than clearing the heart-mind of egotism and miscellaneous preoccupations, an effect that results from the individual's self-cultivation, and not from a priest's magical ritual. Tominosuke took particular offense at Norikiyo's rationalism in denying the magical effectiveness of *kitō*. Tominosuke pointed out that the national histories refer many times to the effectiveness of prayer and spiritual power in ensuring the fertility of crops and thus concluded that Norikiyo was deeply mistaken. Tominosuke also disagreed with Norikiyo's interpretation that the myths of the *Nihon shoki* were allegories conveying moral lessons for the present. Tominosuke said that this interpretation reduced the status of *Nihon shoki* to nothing more than fiction and the Kami to made-up characters. The verdict also included citations from Norikiyo's writings regarding the poor and others in which he opined that the government was too generous to the Buddhist priesthood, which in his view was bloated with unnecessary persons whom the people had to support. The verdict condemned these writings for criticizing the government's policies.[48]

Conclusion

Comparing the fates of Inoue Masakane and Umetsuji Norikiyo to that of Kurozumi Munetada leaves the impression that the government regulation of religion at the end of the Edo period was most severe in Edo and considerably laxer in more distant locations. Munetada's status as a shrine priest bearing a Yoshida license before he began to preach and heal undoubtedly shielded him from his critics. Meanwhile, Inoue Masakane's teaching and religious experience resembled Munetada's in important respects yet met with very harsh punishment. The exile of Umetsuji Norikiyo seems to have resulted in large part from the bad luck of his case having been assigned to the Shintokata of the day.

Seen in its regional context, Kurozumi's movement emerged in a prosperous area with a tradition of commoner education and local authorities who found Munetada's teachings useful in preserving the status quo. While his combination of reciting the Great Purification Prayer with breathing exercises in the course of sun worship was Kurozumi's creation, its novelty did not fall afoul of the prohibition on new teachings. Unlike Inoue Masakane, Umetsuji Norikiyo, and the Shinto popularizers, Munetada did not stress the identification of his teaching with Shinto nor believe that he had to prove that point. He probably assumed that this was understood, because he had lived most of his life as a shrine priest promoting the worship of Amaterasu.

Kurozumi's teachings initiated a new kind of religious association based on Kami worship. Its concept of salvation was open to all and made no distinctions based on sex or class. All humanity is equal as "divided spirits" of Amaterasu. It was a universal teaching. Kurozumi's concept of Kami ignored the *honji suijaku* paradigm, and without denying the existence of Buddhist divinities, simply acted as if Amaterasu were the only divine being. Kurozumi's teaching made no particular reference to *Nihon shoki* or to Shinto scholarly writing. His teaching could be understood without prior knowledge of Shinto tradition.

The teachings of Kurozumi Munetada, Inoue Masakane, and Umetsuji Norikyo were principally concerned with the salvation of the individual through achieving spiritual union with Amaterasu. The injection into Shinto of a goal of salvation distinguished the Shinto-derived new religions from Shinto's previous forms, not only in terms of doctrine but also in ritual and communal life. We will see when we come to the Meiji period that the Shinto-derived new religious movements took on a distinctive position within the government-controlled administration of Shinto in the modern period and raised enduring questions regarding whether Shinto should be regarded as a religion or not.

11

Shinto and Kokugaku

The Rise of Nativist Thought

While Confucian ideas dominated seventeenth-century thinking about the Kami, that perspective was virtually swept away thereafter. In the eighteenth and nineteenth centuries, a reaction against Chinese influence arose in the form of nativist thought claiming the superiority of Japanese learning over Chinese and seeking to reclaim the life-ways of ancient Japan by eliminating foreign influence. The term *nativist* as used here is not a translation of a Japanese term but means an emphasis on the indigenous over the foreign, a sense of the superiority of the indigenous, and the expression of pride in that which is indigenous to one's country. For nativists, uplifting Japan entailed denigrating all things Chinese, especially Buddhism and Confucianism. Japanese nativists of the Edo period looked back to ancient Japan with longing and nostalgia, interpreting Japan's history from the moment of contact with China as a loss of purity and vitality. Japanese nativist thought took a variety of forms, and one stream that emerged in the Edo period was referred to as *Kokugaku*, "national learning."

Using the term *nativism* is complicated by the fact that while Japan had a long tradition of writings expressing pride in the indigenous and contrasting it with the perceived shortcomings of foreign countries, there was no single term that encompassed the endeavor as a whole. Also, the use of the term *Kokugaku* in the ancient period was completely different from the eighteenth- and nineteenth-century usage. In ancient Japan, *Kokugaku* referred to provincial institutions of learning, as opposed to the central Bureau of Education (Daigakuryō). Further, most Edo-period nativist writers did not use the term *Kokugaku* to name their scholarship, or did not use it exclusively. *Kokugaku* as used in scholarship about Edo-period nativism is thus mainly a historians' construction.

There was significant overlap between Kokugaku and Shinto, but Kokugaku was not only a type of Shinto thought; it also included studies of poetry and language that went beyond Shinto, not all of which concerned the Kami. Many shrine priests were among Kokugaku's most enthusiastic followers, but Kokugaku students came from many different quarters, and, as far as we know at the present stage of research, most shrine priests during the Edo period remained aloof from Kokugaku. People of all social classes and both sexes joined study circles and poetry groups based on the writings of the Kokugaku figures Kamo no Mabuchi, Motoori Norinaga, and Hirata Atsutane.

How should we understand the rise of Kokugaku? Various accounts have been advanced, but perhaps the most widely known is that by Maruyama Masao, eminent intellectual historian of Japan. Maruyama pointed out that Kokugaku advocated a return to the ancient texts in order to derive an integrated understanding of an ancient Japanese way of life before it became tainted or lost its vitality. Ironically, Edo-period Confucian thought—against which Kokugaku had arisen as a reaction—shares precisely this characteristic. Thus Kokugaku can appear to have adopted the fundamental position of Japanese Confucian thinkers, becoming almost a parallel "Japanese adaptation." Historian Matsumoto Sannosuke focused on Kokugaku's consistent rejection of the rationalism of Confucian thought. Unlike Confucians, Kokugaku thinkers tended instead to affirm emotion, to accept it as having an inherent validity, defining what it means to be human, which is not to be judged by moralism. Kokugaku thinkers pointed to the power and beauty of the emotions displayed by the Kami in myth, saying that it is not for humanity to judge the gods by human standards.[1]

Changes in society also facilitated the ascendance of Kokugaku, including the rise of literacy, the appearance of private academies, and a revolution in publishing. For many years, historians of Japan thought that during the Edo period, some 40 percent of men and perhaps 20 percent of women could read, write, and calculate. Recent scholarship has probed those figures and produced contradictory findings that have not yet been reconciled. Nevertheless, it is clear that the Japanese people were rapidly becoming more literate as early as the Genroku era (1688–1703). For example, the writer Ihara Saikaku portrayed a merchant father dismayed by his no-good son's inability to support himself, in spite of his education in the following skills: Nō chanting, poetry composition, flower arrangement, tea ceremony, Neo-Confucianism, *go*, archery, the courtier traditions of *kemari* kickball and incense appreciation, and playing the *biwa* and *koto* (stringed instruments). That a spoiled son of a merchant could credibly be depicted as trained in so many branches of art and knowledge represents a huge departure from the monopolization of learning by the few in the medieval period. Clearly, the late seventeenth century had a great thirst for knowledge. The private academy emerged as an important kind of school.[2]

The private academy catered to all classes, samurai, artisans, merchants, and even farmers. In their transformation from warriors to bureaucrats, samurai required education. Many had received the basics as children in schools operated by their domains, and then continued more specialized studies in private academies as adults. The fifth shogun, Tsunayoshi (r. 1680–1709) patronized Confucian scholars and conferred official status on the Hayashi school, the Shōheikō. Confucian scholar Nakae Tōju (1608–1648) had operated a small academy in Ōmi from the 1630s, while Itō Jinsai (1627–1705) opened a private academy in Kyoto for the study of "ancient learning" (*kogaku),* emphasizing the reading of Confucianism's primary texts on their own, without relying on the commentarial tradition. Around 40 percent of his students were samurai; the rest were from the merchant, artisan, or medical professions. The academies opened later by Kamo no Mabuchi, Motoori Norinaga, and Hirata Atsutane were part of this tradition of private academies.[3]

The Publishing Revolution and Its Impact on Shinto

In the seventeenth and eighteenth centuries, both literacy and publishing greatly expanded. As Peter Kornicki writes, by the eighteenth century, books had become "an everyday commodity." Between the 1730s and the 1770s, the volume of works published in Edo roughly doubled, and publishing in Kyoto and Osaka also expanded significantly. There were some 917 publishers in Edo by the early nineteenth century, and around 500 each in Kyoto and Osaka.[4]

Increased literacy and the publishing revolution both facilitated ancient studies by shrine priests and created a non-priestly readership for texts on Shinto, as shrines became important repositories for texts of all kinds. Many publishers treated shrines as libraries of deposit. Buddhist temples had maintained extensive libraries since antiquity, and temple complexes typically included a scriptorium. It is known that the Ise Shrines had a library in the eighth century, but at some point it disappeared. Although before the Edo period few shrines had significant libraries, they began to be founded in the seventeenth and eighteenth centuries. For example, shrine libraries were created (or in the case of Ise, re-established) in 1648 at the Outer Shrine, 1686 at the Inner Shrine, 1680 at the Kamigamo Shrine, 1688 at the Kitano Tenmangū, 1705 at the Kashima Shrine, and 1723 at the Osaka Sumiyoshi Shrine. Deguchi Nobuyoshi was a main force in re-establishing the Toyomiyazaki Library at the Outer Shrine. The collection of the monk Keichū formed the core of the holdings of the Kamigamo Shrine, where shrine priests created the library, also establishing an association for its ongoing support.[5]

Shrine libraries mainly preserved books instead of making them broadly accessible, although their collections routinely circulated among shrine priests. A Kyoto publishers' association attached to the Kitano Tenmangū constructed a book storage facility in 1702, where publishers deposited one copy of each publication, so that if the carved blocks held elsewhere were lost, this printed "master copy" could be used to create new ones. In 1730 a group of Osaka publishers formed a similar association at the Osaka Tenmangū, and there was another such association at the Sumiyoshi Shrine. The dedication of books to shrines had religious meaning for publishers, and the copy deposited often bore elaborate bindings or was printed on rare paper.[6]

The New Readership for Ancient Myth

The expansion of publishing helped produce what Susan Burns has called an "explosion of interest in the Divine Age narrative" of the *Kojiki* and *Nihon shoki*.[7] The boom began with the publication of the Divine Age narrative from *Nihon shoki* in 1599. We saw in our discussion of Confucian influences on Shinto that scholars, such as Hayashi Razan, approached mythic texts in order to discover Confucian ideas at work, such as principle. The *Kojiki* was newly published in 1644, in a version called the "Kan'ei version," so named after the Kan'ei era (1624–1644). The publication of these texts made them available to readers outside the court and the sacerdotal lineages. The texts presented significant difficulties for readers, however, especially the *Kojiki*. Publishers introduced markers into the text to make them more readable, but these inevitably introduced interpretive decisions that were to an extent arbitrary. To counteract this tendency, Mito scholars associated with the compilation of a huge historical project eventually called *The Great History of Japan* (*Dai Nihonshi*) created an unpunctuated version of *Kojiki*, but this left monumental problems for even the most determined readers, since the text's idiosyncratic orthography was not yet understood.

A number of scholars began to assert novel interpretations and approaches. Arai Hakuseki (1657–1725) claimed that the myths were allegorical expressions of real events and people in ancient times. Tayasu Munetake (1715–1771) interpreted the Divine Age tales as descriptions of ancient court life, asserting, for example, that a phrase likening the land to "floating oil" was meant to describe the unsettled state of society when the death of an emperor left the country ruled by a young son who was too immature to govern.

The Shingon priest Keichū (1640–1701) completed a critical commentary on the *Man'yōshū*, using methods developed for the study of Buddhist texts. This was a significant departure from foregoing approaches to ancient Japanese poetry, which had focused on finding analogies to Confucian or Buddhist teachings. Keichū is thought to have produced an annotated text of *Kojiki* with guides to pronunciation (it is not extant). In the process, he tried to recover the sounds of ancient Japanese language.

> [T]he reconstruction of the ancient orthography had "moral" as well as philological value. Keichū asserted that the ancient [syllabary] (*kana*) usage revealed the Japanese language in its pristine, original state, and he characterized the differences that separated the language of the past and that of the present not as the result of inevitable historical change but in terms of decline and loss.[8]

While Keichū's thought remained within a *honji-suijaku* framework, identifying Amaterasu with Dainichi, for example, he nevertheless concluded that Shinto is distinct from both Buddhism and Confucianism, and that Japan is a sacred realm.[9]

Kada no Azumamaro focused not on narrative but on specific words and phrases that he believed offered a glimpse of an ancient way of life. He produced a lexicon of terms used in the *Kojiki* that was based on etymology rather than connections at the level of "plot." Kamo Mabuchi (1697–1769), who had studied with Azumamaro, focused on the consequences he viewed as flowing from the "loss" of ancient ways, a distortion of society that he blamed on the introduction of the Chinese writing system. Mabuchi encouraged his students to study the language of *Kojiki* in order to recover the "spirit" of ancient Japan, and he produced two new versions of the text in order to reproduce what he believed was the correct pronunciation of it.

As this discussion suggests, by the mid-eighteenth century, a body of published research on the Divine Age narrative in the *Kojiki* had emerged, and a lively discussion was under way. This debate approached ancient literature as a repository of moral lessons, history, and as a window onto an ancient way of life that was in some ways more authentic than the contemporary world. Peering through this window, readers asked, "How can we return to that pristine era?"

Motoori Norinaga

Stimulated by this and related questions, Motoori Norinaga (1730–1801) developed radically new ideas and approaches to the Divine Age. In the process, he created a new theology of the Kami, and under his influence, some shrine priests embraced his vision of Shinto as the ancient Way. Norinaga was born in Ise Province, in a town called Matsusaka, to a relatively prosperous merchant family. He was educated in the Confucian classics and was drawn also to Japanese literature, especially *waka* poetry. Matsusaka was near the Ise Shrines, which Norinaga visited monthly as an adult. His family belonged to the parish of a Buddhist Pure Land (Jōdo) temple, and they were deeply committed believers. Norinaga himself received advanced Jōdo teachings and underwent the sect's "fivefold instruction" (*gojū sōden*). He read the scriptures daily, even in old age, as well as worshipping local tutelary Kami, *ubusunagami*. From 1752 to 1757 he studied in Kyoto, ostensibly to learn medicine, since he had proved to be unsuited to a merchant's life. He pursued Confucian studies and resided with his Confucian teacher for about half of his time there. He encountered the works of Ogyū Sorai, regarded at the time as avant-garde. He read widely and immersed himself in the vibrant intellectual life of the city, reading Keichū's work, studies of the *Nihon shoki*, and absorbed new currents of literary thought. Norinaga was drawn to Keichū's habit of quoting ancient literary sources at length, verbatim, and saw this as the optimum method to absorb the worldview of ancient Japan. He regarded Keichū as a master of linguistic scholarship. Norinaga also developed the persona of an eighteenth-century literatus while in Kyoto, composing verses with a wide circle of friends, taking excursions to famous sites in the area, enjoying theater, the festivals of temples and shrines, music, smoking, and drinking.[10]

Norinaga returned to Matsusaka, which he described as a prosperous and relatively cosmopolitan town, with access to a variety of commodities, entertainments, temples, and shrines. It had at least one bookstore in Norinaga's day. He participated in a poetry circle, these associations being an important social venue for cultured, educated persons. Shortly after his return to Matsusaka, Norinaga encountered the works of Kamo no Mabuchi, though the two did not meet until 1763. Mabuchi had dedicated his life to the study of the *Man'yōshū,* which he regarded as prerequisite to any study of more difficult texts like the *Kojiki.* He urged Norinaga to study the *Man'yōshū* deeply before taking up *Kojiki.* When Norinaga persisted in his determination to focus on the *Kojiki,* Mabuchi became critical of the younger man, and their relations soured.

In 1763, the same year as his meeting with Mabuchi, Norinaga completed two works, *Essentials of the Tale of Genji* (*Shibun yōryō*) and *Personal Views on Poetry* (*Isonokami no sasamegoto*). These works challenged Confucian literary criticism, in which the actions of characters were judged by the degree to which they conformed to a moral standard. Norinaga argued that literature should be evaluated by its capacity to inspire an emotional response.

Norinaga lectured on the great classic by Murasaki Shikibu, *The Tale of Genji,* developing an interpretation of its dominant aesthetic concept, *mono no aware,* or "the sadness of things" or "the profundity of things."[11] To respond to *mono no aware* requires empathy and the ability to enter into the emotional world of other people (or literary characters) sympathetically, understanding how they would have felt, and the constraints binding them.

> The term *mono no aware* defies satisfactory translation. In its most literal sense, it meant an awareness and appreciation of the "sadness" or "pity" (*aware*) of things (*mono*). Its implication, however, was one of an acute sensitivity to the affective and emotional qualities of life—the person who possesses *mono no aware* has a seemingly instinctive sympathy with human actions, a sympathy that transcends and obviates the passing of moral judgment upon the implications of those actions. . . . Norinaga . . . declared that what made the *Genji* a great work of literature was the author's ability to express *mono no aware* through her realistic depiction of those emotive elements that inspire and transfuse life's major events; and he asserted that this appreciation of *mono no aware* drew the reader into a state of sympathy with the novel's characters, which made didactic or moralistic interpretation of the work meaningless.[12]

With the *Kojikiden* (Commentaries on the *Kojiki*), parts of which began to circulate in the 1780s, Norinaga introduced radically new directions in the study of myth. He approached the *Kojiki* as a sacred text, which if read correctly, could reveal Japan in its pristine state as an ideal community in which Kami, the emperor, and his people lived in perfect harmony. Not only could the reader glimpse life in this sacred time, but could also hope to recover it by stripping away the alien way of thought that had obscured it for so long. He declared that the *Kojiki* was "the oral transmissions from the Divine Age" (*kamiyo kara no tsutaegoto*), which had originally been spoken by the emperor and imparted to Hieda no Are, who memorized it. The text had originated in an oral/aural social context, and its tales were true accounts of actual events. Norinaga's approach to ancient texts invited readers to respond to them emotionally, through the prism of *mono no aware*. This stance toward the classics implicitly encouraged readers to identify with the Kami in *Kojiki*, to regard them as if they were human characters in a cosmic drama. His perspective was "groundbreaking," inasmuch as it overturned the foregoing understanding that myth was the exclusive possession of the court, and that the people were connected to these tales only as objects of imperial will.[13]

Kojikiden was a massive work of forty-four volumes, not published until 1798. In it, Norinaga gave his account of each tale and explicated a huge number of terms and expressions. He introduced his concept of Kami, which became a famed touchstone for subsequent Shinto theology:

> I really do not claim to fully comprehend the meaning of the word *Kami*. Generally, *Kami* denotes, in the first place, the divine beings of heaven and earth that appear in the ancient texts and also the enshrined spirits that are revered in the nation's shrines; furthermore, among other beings, not only human but also animate and inanimate beings such as birds, beasts, trees, grass, seas, mountains, and the like. Any form of being whatsoever which possesses some unique and eminent quality, and is awe-inspiring, may be called Kami. "Eminent" does not refer simply to nobility, goodness, or special merit. Evil things or strange things, if they are extraordinarily awe-inspiring, may also be referred to as Kami.
>
> Needless to say, among the human beings who are called Kami, all the successive generations of emperors are the first to be counted, For, as is indicated by the fact that the emperors are called *totsu kami* (distant Kami), they are aloof, remote, august, and greatly worthy of human reverence. People who are referred to as Kami to a lesser degree can be found in former times as well as in modern times. There are also those who are respected as Kami, not universally, but locally, within a province, a village, or a family, according to their merits. The Kami in the Age of the Gods were for the most part human beings of that time, and the people of that time were all Kami.

> Such things as dragons, *tengu*, foxes, and the like, which are equally amazing and awe-inspiring, are Kami.... Furthermore, we can find frequent instances of rocks, stumps of trees, and leaves of plants speaking. All these were Kami.[14]

Norinaga's concept of Kami is notable for its descriptive approach and emphasis on awe—anything that inspires awe, in his view, might be regarded as Kami, whether good or bad. He is not concerned with prescribing what should or should not be called Kami; instead, he points out the wide range of things that had been regarded as Kami at some time or in some place. He does not pass judgment on whether it was correct to regard foxes as Kami; instead, he notes in a matter-of-fact way that they have been so regarded, along with all the emperors, all the people of ancient times, all the characters of ancient myth, imaginary beings like dragons and *tengu*, tree stumps, and others. His approach emphasizes emotion and human responses to unusual experience.

Norinaga developed the novel idea that all creation owes to a single, original Kami. *Kojiki* opens with the appearance of three deities, Amenominakanushi no Kami, Takamimusubi no Kami, and Kamimusuhi no Kami, who immediately disappear. Likewise, the main text of *Nihon shoki* also begins with three deities who have no connection to subsequent events, of whom the main one is Kunitokotachi (see chapter 2). Norinaga's innovation was to treat the three earliest Kami as a single entity, whom he named Musuhi-no-kami (or Musubi no Kami).[15]

Kojikiden included a separate section titled *The Rectifying Spirit* (*Naobi no Mitama*) that presented a concise summary of his views: The *Kojiki* is true and is the Way. The Way can be grasped by cleansing the mind of Chinese influence. The unbroken succession of imperial reign is proof of the narrative recounting that Amaterasu entrusted the Way to the imperial lineage. The Japanese people can conform themselves to the Way and live in peace and happiness by discarding Chinese thinking, worshipping the Kami, obeying their superiors, and maintaining a pure fire.

Let us examine these ideas.

> The meaning of the Way can be known now by studying *Kojiki* and other ancient texts. But the minds of the scholars are curdled by the evil Gods of Magatsubi and are smitten by the Chinese classics. All they think and say is derived from Buddhist and Chinese thought... In due course, Chinese books were introduced into Japan and the pursuit of learning began. People studied the customs of China and gradually these came to be employed in all aspects of Japanese life. It was at this time that the ancient manners and customs of Japan came to be specifically called "the Way of the Gods" [Shinto], lest our Way become confused with the Ways of China.... Even the hearts of the Japanese people changed to Chinese ways. Failure to

> identify one's own heart with the Emperor's and instead harbor personal desires means that the Chinese spirit has taken over.... Casting aside the superior Way of Japan, people copied and revered the superficially sophisticated and argumentative thought and behavior of the Chinese. Thus their minds and deeds, at one time so honest and pure, became contrived and filthy. In the end it became impossible to govern Japan without using the strict methods of China.[16]

In the beginning, Norinaga wrote, there was no need in Japan to speak of Shinto or a "Way," because it existed in the emperor's benevolent rule, and the people were so completely in harmony with him that they naturally followed the Way, having no need to analyze or even name it. This was the Age of the Gods. In a passage criticizing Yamazaki Ansai he wrote:

> In China they discuss formally the details of their Way because their Way is so shallow. The Japanese Confucians do not realize this and make light of our country, saying that there is no Way here. Their inability to understand arises because they regard everything of China as most lofty.... But this is just like monkeys laughing at humans for not having body hair. Feeling ashamed, the humans reply, "We do have hair," and strive to find and display their sparse hair in order to compete. Isn't this the action of fools who do not realize that being hairless is superior?[17]

Norinaga identified China or "the Chinese heart" (*karagokoro*) with logic chopping and excessive rationalism. The result for ancient Japan was that the harmony of the realm was lost and even knowledge of that time when the emperor ruled his people directly, in complete harmony and peace. The emperor is a linchpin between humanity and the divine world in Norinaga's thought, providing access to the Kami. This eternal truth is unaffected by the personality or actions of any living emperor:

> The decrees of the Sun Goddess do not state the Emperor should not be obeyed if he is evil, so no one should judge him as good or bad. As long as Heaven and Earth exist, as long as the Sun and the Moon emit their rays of light, the throne remains forever undisturbed. This is why the reigning Emperor was called a God in the ancient records. And because he is a God, disputes about his virtue or wrongdoings should be put aside, and we should revere and serve him unconditionally. This is the true Way.[18]

Norinaga envisioned Japan as rightfully ruled by the emperor, based on his divine descent, tracing back to the Sun Goddess, who had entrusted a sacred realm to her grandson Ninigi and thereafter to each succeeding emperor. The emperor's worship of his ancestral gods is the central element in his enactment of the Way of the Gods, and his worship ideally would be mirrored by the people's worship of their family ancestors.

> The Emperor worships and reigns in the presence of his great ancestor Gods. Similarly, the ministers, officials, subjects, and indeed the entire populace worship their respective ancestor gods. The Emperor enshrines the Gods of Heaven and Earth for the court and society. In the same manner, the subjects pray to the good Gods to attain happiness and placate the evil Gods to avoid disasters. If they sin or become defiled, they cleanse themselves. All such things are the natural actions of the human heart and should be performed without fail.[19]

In the passage immediately preceding this one, Norinaga noted the existence of evil Kami as well as good ones. He attributed all misfortune to these evil gods, the Magatsubi no Kami. Human reason is incapable of understanding why they do what they do; all we can do is accept it.

> Foulness and destruction exist in this world; it is not possible for everything to be in accord with just principles. Malice is also abundant, all of which can be attributed to these Gods. When they are extremely destructive, even the great power of the Sun Goddess and the God of Takami Musubi cannot control them, so human efforts accomplish nothing. The good are visited with calamity and the wicked lead happy lives. This and many other things that violate logical principles are all the doing of these gods.[20]

Norinaga used the term *Shintō* frequently, using it interchangeably in some cases with "the Way," but was highly critical of Ryōbu, Suika, and any form of Kami worship that had absorbed foreign influence. "[T]he common interpretation of Shinto so far has followed the twisted thought of Buddhism or Confucianism, and this has pushed the true Way to the brink of extinction."[21]

> From the Middle Ages down to the present people have industriously clothed themselves in the philosophy of Buddhism and composed poetry about things related to the [Shinto] deities, being deceived by the belief in "original substance and manifested traces" [*honji-suijaku*], where they identify with the concept that even the Shinto deities in the original land were all Buddhist entities, and using this terminology, even officials who serve the deities at the Ise Shrine commit this kind of blunder.[22]

Norinaga was very particular about the conduct of worship and ritual. He especially emphasized the importance of "pure fire," meaning that the food to be eaten by menstruating or postpartum women or by those in mourning should be cooked on a fire separate from that used to prepare food for anyone else or for cooking offerings for the Kami. If these precautions were not taken, the pollution of blood and death would be transferred, and the Kami would be offended.[23]

Some five hundred students gathered around Norinaga to pursue his insights, of whom around 14 percent were shrine priests.[24] Adults wishing to become a student of a teacher of some specialized branch of knowledge were said to have "entered the gate," becoming a *monjin* (*mon*: gate; *jin*: person) of the teacher, thus becoming members of his academy or school. Norinaga himself was a *monjin* of Kamo no Mabuchi; he did not terminate that relationship when he began teaching, so technically his students were indirectly linked to Mabuchi as well.

Having become a *monjin*, the student could receive instruction, whether through attending lectures or by correspondence. Norinaga gave themed lectures around seven, eight, or nine times a month at his home in Matsusaka, delivering a series of lectures devoted to a particular text, following a pre-announced schedule. He repeated his lectures on *The Tale of Genji* several times. Besides teaching on the upper floor of his home, called the Suzuya after a set of small bells (*suzu*) that he liked to ring when he was fatigued, he also traveled frequently to Kyoto and Wakayama to give lectures. And because many of his students lived too far away to attend the lectures, Norinaga exchanged letters with them. Perhaps the most frequent form of correspondence was students' requests for Motoori's comments on their poetry; students also wrote pamphlets and longer essays on literary texts for Norinaga's comments. Many students studied in poetry circles. While many of Norinaga's *monjin* devoted themselves to his teachings so fervently that they might be described as "disciples," not all were so dedicated, and Norinaga complained of a tendency to drop out after an initial period of interest. As a result, an entrance ceremony was created, and students took vows of faithful study. Students paid a fee, and study groups or poetry circles recruited new students and collected funds to publish Norinaga's works.[25]

Shrine priests became students of Norinaga for different reasons and by a variety of routes. There were forty-four priests of the Ise Shrines among the *monjin*, of whom twenty-six came from the Inner Shrine, ten from the Outer Shrine, and eight from Matsusaka. Another sizeable concentration of shrine priest *monjin* was found in Kii Province, where the castle town of Wakayama was located; they might have heard Motoori lecture there. Pilgrim masters from Ise (*oshi*) played an important role in recruiting students. As they traveled the country to visit their affiliates, they would exchange poetry with them and naturally learned of local poetry circles. For example, a group of four *monjin* from Iyo Province in Shikoku joined the Suzuya through their Ise Shrine pilgrim master. They were members of a poetry circle studying the *Man'yōshū* that included the local shrine priest. In a similar case, a shrine priest from the Nōtō area, Katō Yoshihiko, recorded that he learned of Norinaga from his Ise pilgrim master and then was attracted by Norinaga's personality and writings on

The Tale of Genji. In all, four members of Katō's poetry circle became *monjin*, hoping to deepen their understanding of classical literature.[26]

Norinaga believed that his quest to clarify the Ancient Way was the most important task for his followers, but after his death few of his students continued this emphasis. Instead, they pursued Norinaga's poetry studies in academies and informal circles around the country. Indeed, the practice of composing and exchanging poems was central to the reception of Norinaga's thought, including among shrine priests.

> The vast majority of the participants in the Kokugaku movement did not engage in scholarly pursuits, or at best regarded them as secondary to their real interest: the composition and exchange of poetry. At grassroots level, Kokugaku consisted of small, local gatherings of poetry lovers who wanted to improve their own writing by studying Japan's literary tradition.[27]

Shrine priests in the eighteenth and nineteenth centuries frequently belonged to the educated class that benefited most from the publishing revolution. They sought wide access to books and knowledge, beyond shrine lineage affiliations. They participated in poetry circles not only for the love of literature but also because these groups were the salons of the day, a venue in which educated men, and some women, could gather to develop their skills as poets and also to associate with others in responsible positions, such as the Buddhist priests and village headmen, to accrue social capital, authority, and reputation.

Returning to the concentration of Ise priests among Norinaga's *monjin*, it is notable that there were more than twice as many from the Inner Shrine (twenty-six) as the Outer Shrine (ten). The priests of the Inner Shrine among these *monjin* were mainly higher-ranked priests, *negi* or *gonnegi*. By contrast, the Outer Shrine *monjin* were mainly lower-ranked pilgrim masters, and there were only two *gonnegi*. One reason that fewer came from the Outer Shrine was that the Outer Shrine's distinctive theology centered on Toyouke, identified in Watarai thought with Kunitokotachi. Neither of these deities figured prominently in Norinaga's theology, which centered on the Musubi deities and Amaterasu. Thus there was a philosophical conflict between Outer Shrine theology and Norinaga's ideas, and this must have been a barrier to affiliation for the highest-ranking priests. By contrast, the Inner Shrine had no distinctive theology of its own; thus there was no philosophical barrier to affiliation with Norinaga. Not only that, Norinaga's understanding of Amaterasu "decoupled" her from Buddhist identifications with Dainichi and treated her as unambiguously the single most important deity, from whom the Way of the Gods had been entrusted to the imperial line. Norinaga's formulation implied the priority of the Inner Shrine over the Outer and thus must have been congenial to the Inner Shrine priests. For example, one of the first Inner Shrine priests to join sent

Norinaga a pamphlet, in 1773, upholding the superiority of the Inner Shrine; he became a *monjin* after receiving Norinaga's approving comments on his writing.[28] We notice, however, that not all the Inner Shrine priests were drawn to Norinaga, and that is because of another kind of barrier. Norinaga's concept of Amaterasu held that she is the sun, or that the sun is Amaterasu, but the Inner Shrine did not support that interpretation.[29]

So while we can identify clusters of shrine priests who became Norinaga's *monjin*, however, the vast majority of shrine priests did not do so, and that fact is as significant as exploring the motivations of those who did. First, we must recall that the Buddhist or Shugen priests administered many shrines, and they would not necessarily have found Norinaga's concept of the Kami—divorced from the *honji-suijaku* paradigm—acceptable. Others were already affiliated with the Yoshida or other sacerdotal lineage, and to affiliate with Norinaga would have been regarded as a defection. Those committed to Suika Shinto would have found Norinaga's views—especially his frequent excoriations of Confucianism—unacceptable philosophically. Still others guarded the autonomy of their shrines and resisted any outside authority. Affiliation with Norinaga carried no certification or authorization that made it easier for priests to rise in the estimation of fellow villagers or to assert themselves relative to other religionists, and hence was not necessarily a plus in raising one's status.

Another point on which Norinaga's concept of learning about the Kami conflicted with common patterns concerned the question of secret transmission, treating knowledge about the Kami as the private property of a particular group. Norinaga repeatedly inveighed against esotericism and advocated instead that such knowledge should be regarded as having a public character. As he wrote in *The Rectifying Spirit*:

> Detailed rituals became widespread and were regarded as the teaching of the Way of the Gods to be followed by individuals. But these are private inventions of recent years and arose out of envy for the teaching styles of the Chinese. In later years a custom of private initiation into arcane teachings arose, whereby knowledge is secretly transmitted to selected individuals. This is artificial and false, for in this world all good things should be disseminated in every possible way. To hide knowledge and not allow everyone to have access to it, trying to make it one's private possession, is deplorable. It is treasonous for the lowly to covet the awesome Way by which the Emperor governs this world and try to make it their private possession.[30]

The final sentence in this passage expresses Norinaga's view that all knowledge of the Kami is under imperial authority, and that the emperor's enactment of the

Way of the Kami is the ultimate source of true knowledge about the Kami, a point Norinaga addressed in a work of 1798, *First Steps into the Mountain* (*Uiyamabumi*):

> The Way is enacted by the ruler. It is bestowed on subjects from above, so subjects should not privately interpret and carry it out.... This is the just and public Way with which the Emperor governs the world. It is therefore repulsive and sad when people turn it into their private, individual possession, changing it into something narrow and small; performing unsound ritual like shamans, they call this the Way of the Gods. As far as subjects are concerned, the purpose of the ancient Way was for them to obey and behave in accordance with the laws of the government of the time, regardless of whether the laws were good or bad.[31]

As this passage makes clear, the role of the commoners in relation to the emperor is submissive and compliant in every respect, admitting no possibility of dissent or individual initiative respecting knowledge of the Kami. By contrast with the "public" character of the throne, popular initiative appeared "private" and selfish. All prerogative rests with the emperor, who "rules Japan as Akitsukami, or Manifest God."[32]

In addition, some shrine priests were critical of Norinaga based on their prior affiliation to Mabuchi or some other teacher of nativist thought. Arakida Hisaoyu (1746–1804), a poet and a pilgrim master at the Inner Shrine, is an example of someone in that position. Hisaoyu had become a disciple of Mabuchi in 1765, studied with him in Edo for a year, and later had some of Mabuchi's writings published. Returning to Ise after his stay in Edo, he showed his poems to Norinaga, whose home in Matsusaka was nearby, but while the two initially had friendly relations, Norinaga found Hisaoyu's poems deficient in several respects and wrote as much to other Inner Shrine priests. In spite of this incident, Norinaga and Hisaoyu exchanged poems when Norinaga later traveled to Ise to view the cherry blossoms, indicating that the two were on friendly terms.[33]

Hisaoyu's poetry ranged over many themes, often taking its inspiration from the *Man'yōshū*. The poems he composed for his affiliates might adopt a theme about the Kami, as in this poem: "The light of Amaterasu who illumines Heaven, high or low, who would not revere it?"[34]

Born into a family linked to the Outer Shrine but later adopted into one connected with the Inner Shrine, Hisaoyu was in a delicate position when it came to arguments over the relative status of the two. When Norinaga got involved in this debate and tried to steer a middle course, he prevailed upon Hisaoyu to make his views known. In doing so, Hisaoyu seems to have lost friends and supporters in both camps and came away deeply embittered against Norinaga, sentiments he vented in a letter to a student:

> Students of Ancient Learning all over the land praise every word Norinaga has uttered as a golden jewel, and even if my own theories are correct, they

> disregard them as nonsense without even giving them a thought. As you say, those "Ten Sages" [as they call the ten top students] of Norinaga's school are all great fools. Norinaga certainly did well, making a name for himself by surrounding himself with fools. . . . Just as Shinran and Nichiren spread the Law by drawing fools into it, so was Imperial Learning begun and spread by Norinaga; but those fools who study it are locked up in Norinaga's closet, and therefore Imperial Learning will also go down with Norinaga.[35]

Hisaoyu strove to write with flair, using words inventively chosen to honor a companion by placing him or her in an ancient lexicon, but he wanted the exercise to be fun, not a hard slog of reading texts, but an artful, spontaneous response to the moment. He finally concluded, "All this scholarship is completely useless."[36]

Hirata Atsutane, Overview of Life and Works

Born in 1776 to a mid-ranking samurai household of the Akita domain in northern Japan, Hirata Atsutane's education began with the Chinese classics, the typical pattern for male members of the samurai class. But as the fourth of five sons, Atsutane could not expect much family support. Moreover, the domain's finances were in a constant state of crisis, and samurai salaries were routinely "borrowed," that is, docked. Having little chance of advancement in Akita, the boy was apprenticed to a doctor, with the expectation that he could make his living by practicing medicine. At the age of twenty, Atsutane went to Edo and was adopted five years later by a samurai of the Matsuyama domain named Hirata Atsuyasu, after whom he took the name Hirata Atsutane. Later, he took the nom de plume Daikaku (or Daigaku). Ibukinoya (or Ibukisha) in time became the name of his academy. He continued his studies in Edo, supporting himself through his medical practice. He was poor much of the time, lived in straitened circumstances, and faced many difficulties accumulating the funds necessary to publish his written works. In 1801, he married the daughter of a samurai from Suruga named Orise, with whom he had three children; his two boys died very young, and only his daughter lived to adulthood. Around the same time, he became interested in Norinaga's writings and thereafter focused on nativist themes, rejecting Chinese learning, Buddhism, and foreign influence on Japan.[37]

A prolific writer, Atsutane developed a distinctive theology and eschatology. Like Norinaga, criticism of foreign influence was one of Atsutane's most frequent themes. The desire to somehow recover a time before Japanese ways were overlain with Chinese rationalism and Buddhist ideas pervades his works. Eventually, he came to accept a kind of ethnographic research in combination with textual scholarship, apparently believing that the common people were a living repository of Japan's Ancient Way, the beliefs and practices that must have prevailed before the advent of foreign influence. Beginning in 1820, he commenced interviewing a young shaman named Torakichi, who told him tales of supernatural travel to other worlds, meetings with *tengu,* and other "marvelous" events, later writing in *Senkyō ibun* as if the shaman's stories were empirical evidence regarding the supernatural world. These supernatural investigations were later incorporated into *Koshiden,* his magnum opus.[38]

It has long been recognized that Atsutane's reading of certain Christian writings influenced his views on the afterlife. He evidently read pamphlets by the Jesuit missionaries Matteo Ricci (1552–1610), Diego de Pantoja (1571–1618), and Giulio Aleni (1588–1642). Importing Christian writings into Japan was illegal at the time, and it is not known how Atsutane acquired them. Comparative study of the missionaries' tracts with an early work of 1806, *Honkyō gaihen,* has demonstrated conclusively, however, that Atsutane experimented with Christian ideas, substituting Amenominakanushi for God, and various other Kami for other Christian figures. His idea of Amenominakanushi as a creator deity paralleled Norinaga's construction of Musuhi no Kami as a single creator.[39]

Atsutane opened his academy, called Masugenoya (later called Ibukisha, then Ibukinoya), in 1806 in Edo. It was not only a classroom but also had a shrine, where Atsutane worshipped daily. Atsutane's son-in-law (and successor) Kanetane (1799–1880) managed the academy, answered students' doctrinal queries, and exchanged information with students in the provinces. Disciples identified three core texts among Atsutane's voluminous corpus as the most important: *Tama no Mihashira, Koshiden,* and *Tamatasuki.* In the discussion here, I focus on these works and try to derive the ideas and practices that were most significant for Atsutane's shrine priest followers.[40]

Atsutane looked to "ordinary people" (*bonjin, tadabito,* and related terms) as an invaluable source of knowledge about the Ancient Way, claiming that the language of the Kami was to be found among them. He spoke of the people as *aohitogusa,* literally "green grass people," in H. D. Harootunian's gloss: "diffuse, luxuriant, and dense with the growth of grass." This poetic expression evoked the creation of the people in the time of Izanami and Izanagi. Leaders should strive to learn from the people, not imagine themselves as overlords, entitled to rule as they pleased. Atsutane's openness to the varied beliefs of his day was spurned by the more orthodox of Norinaga's disciples, but it brought Atsutane many followers. Academies and study circles were formed around the country to pursue Atsutane's ideas.[41]

By the late eighteenth century, there were academies devoted to the pursuit of Norinaga's scholarship in all the major urban centers: Kyoto, Nagoya, Osaka, Edo, and Wakayama. Norinaga's followers in Edo other than Atsutane were few and mainly devoted to literary studies. They owed as much to Mabuchi and Azumamaro as to Norinaga. Their work presumed an ongoing connection to Chinese poetry and thus had an ambivalent relation to Norinaga's opposition to foreign influence.[42] Norinaga's son Haruniwa tragically had gone blind while Norinaga was still alive, so

Norinaga had adopted a man unrelated to him, Ōhira (1756–1833), as the one to keep the members of the school together and pursue scholarship on the *Kojiki*. As of 1811, when Atsutane compiled his *Tama no Mihashira,* he was only one of hundreds of Norinaga followers and enjoyed no exceptional status among them. Atsutane was a "posthumous disciple" who had not studied directly with the master. Ōhira, Ban Nobutomo (1773–1846), and other Norinaga followers found Atsutane's scholarship loose at best, and his interest in spirits and eschatology alien to Norinaga's focus on the Ancient Way.[43]

A rift opened between Atsutane and other nativist writers over a work by Hattori Nakatsune called *Sandaikō*, a cosmological text concerning the *Kojiki* chapters dealing with creation. Atsutane admired *Sandaikō*, but Ōhira denounced it, because it contradicted Norinaga on several important points. Nakatsune had concluded that Amaterasu resides in the sun, that Takamagahara *is* the sun, and that Tsukiyomi rules the land of the dead. Atsutane published *Tama no Mihashira* as a defense of Nakatsune. In this work he branched out to other texts besides the *Kojiki* and also ended up denying Norinaga's interpretations.[44]

In *Tama no Mihashira* Atsutane introduced a novel interpretation of the land of the dead, and this in turn was linked to a distinctive concept of death ritual and the nature of the ongoing relation between the living and the dead. While ancestral ritual was monopolized by Buddhism, and while ancestors were called *hotoke* ("Buddha"), Atsutane regarded ancestors as Kami. Atsutane's ideas about the afterlife provided theological support to shrine priests who were seeking liberation from the Buddhist temple-parish system. In his later work, *Tamatasuki,* Atsutane spoke of both emperors and the ancestors as "manifest deities" (*arahitogami*) or "distant Kami" (*totsu kami*), whereas Norinaga had reserved these terms for emperors. Clearly, Atsutane elevated the status of ancestors through his choice of terms.[45]

Norinaga had interpreted the *Kojiki* myths of Izanagi and Izanami to mean that upon her death, Izanami had traveled to a separate realm of the dead (*yomi*), which was a dark and polluted place. Atsutane asserted instead that the "spirit realm exists in this manifest realm and is not [in] a separate location. It is within the manifest realm simultaneously and is invisible; it cannot be seen from the manifest world." He spoke of the dead "concealing" or "hiding" themselves (*kakuru, kakureru,* and variations on this word), and he used the word *yūmei* "the hidden world" as his preferred term for the world of the dead.[46] This term was not chosen simply as a means to distinguish himself from Norinaga but was explicated over the course of Atsutane's career in a way that conveyed an entirely novel episteme, with its own worldview and politics, as H. D. Harootunian elegantly explains:

> The idea of a hidden world took on specific associations in the late-Tokugawa period when it became linked to the sanctuary of the ancestors. We know from Hirata's own studies of tutelary worship that this sanctuary of the spirits and ancestors was the village. But now, the original sense

> of a hidden world changed to overlap increasingly with the world of village, family, and household. In time, when the invisible realm was symbolized by the tutelary shrines (which themselves were associated with Ōkuninushi no kami, ruler of the invisible world), it became identical with the world of the village, concealed, powerless in the space of the visible, public authority, yet vibrant with real activity. Here, nativist discourse pitted a horizontal reality, close to nature, against the vertical world of the Tokugawa [deputy], daimyo, shogun, and even emperor, against the artifice of contemporary history itself. Hence, when Hirata argued that the living inhabited the visible world and the spirits and deities resided in the invisible realm, he suggested the possibility of an interesting dialectic between creation and custom. Each realm was separate but, nonetheless, related to the other; the living were the descendants of the ancestors and deities. And each bespoke the whole. Creation was, to be sure, the work of the gods, yet it was also a continuously productive act in which humans participated to literally reproduce the initial act of origins.[47]

Tama no Mihashira also has a more personal dimension. Written in the same year as the death of his wife Orise, this work conveys Atsutane's sense that she remained near him, guiding him as he composed the passages about the dead protecting and watching over those they have left behind. He wrote hopefully that while the dead must inevitably "return" to the world of the dead, each soul (*mitama*) becomes a Kami on a par with the Kami from the Age of the Gods. Ōkuninushi, lord of the *yūmei*, bestows good fortune on both the dead and the living.[48]

The dead remain near their graves, he wrote, and to build a shrine (*tamaya*) for them brings them peace and tranquility. Burial is the proper way to dispose of the body, which is but an "empty shell" (*nakigara*) that remains after the soul has separated from it. A further implication concerned imperial graves, many of which had become lost. Even where sites had been identified, many were overgrown, untended, and shabby. There was growing sentiment that all imperial tombs should be located, refurbished, and appropriate ritual for them be instituted.

Atsutane's understanding of the afterlife implicitly advocated an alternative eschatology, a substitute for Buddhist ideas. Edo-period Buddhism's institutional support, and many of its most deeply held convictions concerned death, the proper disposition of the body, memorial ritual, and the maintenance of gravesites. Japanese Buddhism conceived of an infinite number of heavens, Pure Lands, realms of rebirth, and hells, and presumed that the character of a person's conduct in this and previous lives determined the next "destination." These ideas coexisted uneasily with East Asian ideas about ancestors, their attachment to graves, their ongoing relations with their descendants, and descendants' obligations to conform to the conventional mores of society. Ancestors were mostly benevolent, but not always. In Atsutane's view, by contrast, all the dead, whether good or bad, would become concealed in the *yūmei*. But unlike in Norinaga's view, the dead were not in a dark or polluted place—they remain here among us, unseen, but powerfully present, always protecting and blessing their descendants.

Atsutane's discussion of the *yūmei* in *Tama no Mihashira* suggested that it was not primarily a place of judgment, punishment, or reward. Ōkuninushi, lord of the *yūmei*, was sometimes described in *Tama no Mihashira* as consoling the dead: "Ōkuninushi, who exists [in the *yūmei*] in his unseen form lovingly attends to them. Lords, parents, wives, and children all live in comfort and prosperity, just as they had in the revealed world." Elsewhere, however, he suggested that Ōkuninushi decided the fate of the dead. While not all points were resolved, Atsutane consistently stressed the continuity between the dead and the living.[49]

In 1823, Atsutane traveled to Kyoto, where he succeeded in presenting copies of his work to Emperor Ninkō (1800–1846), who sent commendations through Yoshida priests Mutobe Tokika and his son Yoshika (1806–1865), who later became Atsutane's disciples. Atsutane thus became the only nativist figure to secure "a kind of imperial sanction for his scholarship."[50] On his return, Atsutane visited the Ise Shrines, Norinaga's grave, and met with Ōhira, Haruniwa, and Nakatsune at the Suzunoya. Atsutane claimed to have received Norinaga's personal endorsement in a dream in which the master had appeared to him, and he later commissioned a painting of this dream meeting. While Ōhira remained critical of Atsutane, he presented Atsutane with one of three priests' staffs (*shaku*) that Norinaga had made; Ōhira and Haruniwa owned the other two. Haruniwa gave Atsutane a portrait of Norinaga and three of Norinaga's favorite brushes. Atsutane later used these items, along with a *norito* that he received from Nakatsune, as proof that he was Norinaga's successor.

Koshiden (*Treatise on Ancient History*), compiled between 1812 and 1826, was written in a style emulating that of the *Kojiki* and *Nihon shoki* and was intended as a "kind of scripture."[51] An immense work of twenty-eight fascicles, *Koshiden* incorporated the main ideas of *Tama no Mihashira* while also elucidating the cosmogony. Here Atsutane laid out his most distinctive theological positions. He described how Amenominakanushi had created the Musubi no Kami: Takamimusubi and Kamimusubi, who were male and female, respectively. He spoke of the three of them as the Three Gods of Creation (*zōka no sanshin*), who had created the cosmos, the Japanese islands, and the Japanese people.

Atsutane also accorded special importance to Izanagi, who created Amaterasu, and to Ōkuninushi, lord of the afterlife. Atsutane envisioned Ōkuninushi and the emperor as parallel rulers in the sense that Ōkuninushi ruled over the hidden world of the *yūmei* while the emperor rules over the manifest, visible world. *Koshiden*'s strong emphasis on Ōkuninushi tended to overshadow Amaterasu.

Koshiden's omission of Kunitokotachi from the account of creation was one step shy of denying the standing of this Kami's living champions, the Yoshida and Watarai lineages. The Watarai had identified their ancestor Toyouke with Kunitokotachi in order to elevate Toyouke's status. In Atsutane's work, Kunitokotachi was grouped with the underworld deities Tsukiyomi and Izanami. Atsutane's disciples regarded *Tamatasuki* as the crystallization of his thought. Written in a more accessible style than his earlier works, *Tamatasuki* circulated in draft from around 1811, was revised and expanded several times, and its first installment published with a preface by Motoori Ōhira in 1832. The work contains an extended explication of and exhortation to practice daily "Morning Prayers" (*maichō shinpai shiki*) for the Kami and the ancestors. The prayers provided a distinctive ritual that shrine priests could promulgate at their shrines. There were twenty-five or twenty-eight separate sections, depending on the edition; each section named specific Kami or shrines and set out a short *norito* to be recited. Some of the *norito* incorporate passages from ancient prayers such as the Great Purification Prayer and the Amatsu Norito. "Morning Prayers" included instructions for the proper direction to face, when to clap, and how to make offerings.[52] See Table 11.1.

Daily recitation of these prayers constituted the basis of Atsutane's practice of Shinto, revealing his style of worship and attitudes toward the Kami. The twenty-eight prayers can be divided into four sections. The first section includes prayers 1 through 16 and begins with praise and supplication of deities of the entire nation (#1–14), the worshipper's province (#15), and the worshipper's immediate community, whether hamlet, village, or town (#16). The second section (#17–26) is to be performed facing the domestic altar for the Kami, the *kamidana*. The third section is composed of a single prayer, the twenty-seventh, directed to the gods of learning, including Sugawara no Michizane, and the three nativist thinkers whom Atsutane recognized as the "orthodox" line: Mabuchi, Azumamaro, and Norinaga. The fourth section is the final prayer, which is directed to the household ancestors. The effect is to bind the worshipper into a hierarchy of Kami stretching from the emperor and the highest Kami down to the ancestors, from the beginning of time to the present, creating an image of a single community, including the ancestral Kami, united through worship of the Kami.[53]

Atsutane held that the soul is immortal, that the dead become Kami, and that the proper attitude toward ancestors is an extension of the filial piety a child has toward parents, who are to be regarded as "manifest deities" (*arahitogami*). The ancestors should not be worshipped in a Buddhist style. He spoke of ancestral souls as capable of dividing themselves so as to be simultaneously present in the ancestral altar (*tamaya*), at the grave, and always beside their descendants to bless and protect them.[54]

The Movement to Promote Shinto Funerals

Through the Ibukinoya and his connections with the Yoshida and Shirakawa Houses, Atsutane dealt with many shrine priests. His distinctive concepts of the afterlife gave new impetus to priests' desire for Shinto funerals. Because the

Table 11.1 **Hirata Atsutane's Morning Prayers ("Maichō shinpai shiki")**

Section/prayer number	*Location, direction, object faced by worshipper*	*Deities worshipped*
Section I		**National and Communal Deities**
1	Imperial palace	The reigning emperor
2	Yamato	Kami of Heaven and Earth (Amatsu kami, Kunitsu kami)
3	North	The Three Creator Kami (*zōka no sanjin*, Amenominakanushi, Takamimusubi, and Kamimusubi)
4	Sun	The Sun Goddess, her procreator Izanagi, and the myriad gods (Amaterasu, Izanagi, *yaoyorozu no kami*)
5	West	Underworld Kami (Kunitokotachi, Izanami, Tsukiyomi)
6	Hyūga	Ninigi and his consort Konohanasakuya Hime
7	Yamato	All generations of emperors and their consorts, including the reigning generation
8	Ise	All deities of the Inner, Outer, and subsidiary shrines at Ise
9	Hitachi	Takemikazuchi, Futsunushi (the Kashima and Katori Shrines)
10	Izumo	Ōkuninushi and his consort Suseribime
11	Yamato	Ōmononushi, Ōkunitama, Kotoshironushi
12	Hitachi	Ōnamochi, Sukunabiko (gods of medicine)
13	Izu	Kami of long life: Iwanagahime (ugly elder sister of Konohanasakuya Hime, whom Ninigi rejected as a consort)
14	Owari	Kami of the Atsuta Shrine
15	Ichinomiya of the worshipper's province	Provincial deities
16	Tutelary shrine of the worshipper's locale	Local tutelary Kami (*Ubusuna* deities)

(continued)

Table 11.1 **Continued**

Section/prayer number	*Location, direction, object faced by worshipper*	*Deities worshipped*
Section II	**Kamidana**	**Kami Protecting the Household**
17	"	The Kami of the Inner and Outer Shrines at Ise, the myriad Kami of Heaven and Earth, all Kami of all shrines
18	"	[redacted version of *Amatsu norito*, for the deities of No. 17]
19	"	Kami of the boundaries, Sae no Kami
20	"	Amenokoyane and others associated with thought
21	"	Amenouzume, the broom god, household gods
22	"	Yabune, a household god
23	"	Kami of the year
24	"	Kami of the cooking pot
25	"	Kami of the household water source
26	"	Toilet Kami
Section III	Kamidana	**Kami of Learning and Nativist Thought**
27	"	Sugawara no Michizane and the "great men" (*ushi*) of nativist thought, Kamo no Mabuchi, Kada no Azumamaro, and Motoori Norinaga.
Section IV	**Ancestral graves**	**Ancestral Kami**
28	"	Household Kami ancestors

Buddhist schools depended so heavily on funerals for revenue, they consistently opposed any attempt to perform non-Buddhist funerals. We saw in chapter 8 that Yoshikawa Koretaru had great difficulty arranging permission to perform the funeral of Hoshina Masayuki in a Shinto style. From the mid-eighteenth century, a growing number of shrine priests petitioned to have Shinto funerals performed for themselves. By this time, Shinto funerals conducted according to Yoshida Shinto had become more widely known. Both the Yoshida and Shirakawa acted as intermediaries endorsing priests' petitions. Permission was rarely granted, however, and even then, it usually applied only to the petitioner, not even extending to members of his immediate family, who remained under the requirement to receive Buddhist funerals. This stricture was increasingly viewed as oppressive, and as a strong reason for Shinto to break free from Buddhism. Movements to protest against Buddhist funerals arose in the Wakayama domain around 1795 and in the Hamada domain in 1838, but the requirement remained in place until the Meiji period.[55]

While this movement campaigned for legal reform, Atsutane's simple directions for ancestor worship addressed priests' concern to provide some alternative to Buddhism. Atsutane advocated having a domestic ancestral altar called a *tamaya* ("spirit dwelling"), for recitation of the last of the Morning Prayers, with offerings of water and *sakaki* branches. Graves should be carefully tended and visited periodically. Atsutane saw no harm in having Buddhist priests remain responsible for managing graveyards, but he did not think it was necessary for them to perform annual ceremonies. He proposed an "All Souls Festival" (*shoryō matsuri*) for ancestors, to replace the Buddhist *obon* ceremonies of the seventh month. While Atsutane regarded the ancestors as Kami, based on the emperor's worship of his ancestors in the form of Kami, Atsutane nevertheless maintained a distinction between the dead and the Kami where treatment of the corpse was concerned. He did not deny the idea of death pollution, and in that sense, the Kami status of the recently deceased remained unresolved, though the issue was less problematic in the case of more remote ancestors.[56]

Atsutane and the Yoshida and Shirakawa Houses

Atsutane's relations with the Yoshida and Shirakawa Houses unfolded in the context of rising competition between those two lineages, sparked in the Hōreki era (1751–1761) when the Shirakawa reasserted their claim to lead the Jingikan by rebuilding their Hasshinden, their altar for the eight protective deities of the imperial house. Thereafter, both lines sent representatives to tour regional shrines and solicit priests to affiliate with them.[57] Both opened offices in Edo, reflecting their competition for shrines in Eastern Japan, where many Yoshida-affiliated shrines were located.[58] Earlier in the period, the Yoshida had successfully solicited the heads of eastern regional shrine networks, such as that headed by the Rokushogū Shrine in Musashi Province. Its head priest had affiliated with the Yoshida, and through his mediation other Musashi priests acquired Yoshida licenses. In this way, regional networks of shrines had helped to expand Yoshida influence. The Shirakawa only began to recruit aggressively in the nineteenth century, but they could recruit more widely, because they were not subject to the same restrictions as the Yoshida. The Shirakawa began to issue licenses to a wide range of shrine personnel and others, apparently on a much more affordable basis.[59]

Both lineages sought connections with Atsutane, although he had written works criticizing esoteric transmission, which both lines practiced. In particular, Atsutane had described the Yoshida as part of "vulgar Shinto" (*zoku Shintō*).[60] Ikuta Yorozu

(1801–1837), a member of Atsutane's school, had also published a highly critical work. Thus the Yoshida had reason to fear that Atsutane and his followers might encourage shrine priests to defect. If that happened, they stood to be undermined in Eastern Japan, where Kokugaku had become the dominant trend of thought about Shinto. Yoshida thought at this time was heavily influenced by Suika Shinto, so the lineage faced a gap with the shrines of this area in thought and doctrine as well as competition from the Shirakawa.[61]

The Shirakawa wanted to claim Atsutane for themselves, since he had said nothing very critical about them, and because his scholarship was gaining recognition. To secure strong ties with Atsutane would help recruitment in the East. That possibility was important to them, because they could not rely on shrine networks comparable to those that the Yoshida had used to expand.

Atsutane could use the Yoshida networks to spread his thought and recruit affiliates for his school; expanding the number of his *monjin* would be the key to collecting the funds necessary to have his writings published. In these circumstances, and in spite of his earlier critique, Atsutane accepted a position as an instructor in the Yoshida Edo office in late 1822 and wrote two essays in defense of the Yoshida. In "Hitorigoto" (1822) he wrote that the Yoshida had only adopted Buddhist frameworks because that was common in the medieval period, while in "Kikke keifu den" (1823) he defended their claim to be the descendants of the Kami Amenokoyane. Atsutane was expected to give lectures and to tour the region's shrines where there were Yoshida affiliates, defusing any incipient defections. The experience deepened his understanding of shrine life and expanded his contacts among shrine priests.[62]

However, when the Yoshida passed him over for the overall head position of the Edo office several years later, Atsutane began to associate with the Shirakawa House. He actually composed the documents the Shirakawa submitted to the shogunate, vouching for their *monjin* Inoue Masakane when Masakane was under investigation (see chapter 10). Shortly before he left Edo, Atsutane had been in conversation with the Shirakawa regarding a post at their Edo office, but that idea was never realized. Later, the Shirakawa conferred divinization on Atsutane posthumously, as well as upon his ancestors and wives. Among Atsutane's followers were men involved in both Ibukinoya and the Shirakawa House, such as Furukawa Mitsura (also known as Miyuki, 1810–1883), who composed a memorial (*kenpakusho*) in 1862 calling for construction of shrines for imperial loyalists, re-establishing the Jingikan as the highest organ of government, and other key goals of Restoration Shinto.[63]

In 1841, Atsutane was banished from Edo, forced to return to Akita, and ordered to cease publishing. The reasons for this punishment are not clear, but he had criticized the shogunate's calendar-making in a work published that year titled *Tenchō mukyū reki*, a work that also criticized Confucianism and promoted direct imperial rule. In spite of his banishment, his followers continued to increase. They included Yano Harumichi (also known as Gendō, 1823–1887) and Ōkuni Takamasa (1792–1871), men who promoted and refined Atsutane's ideas after his death.

After Atsutane died in Akita in 1843, Kanetane, who had married Atsutane's daughter, succeeded him. Later in life, she took her mother's name, Orise, as Atsutane's second wife had done.

Atsutane's followers included over 1,300 members by the 1860s, including twenty-nine women. The more distant *monjin* held poetry meetings, exchanged nativist writings, and raised money to publish them. In these circles, *waka* poetry was the form in which one expressed "a person's deepest thoughts and strongest emotions." When Kanetane traveled to Kyoto in 1862 to investigate the city's political intrigues, his *monjin* followed him there. In 1863, a group of nine of them, one of whom was a shrine priest, beheaded three statues of the Ashikaga shoguns. The school regarded the Ashikaga as traitors because they had opposed Emperor Godaigo. Beheading the statues was intended to express reverence for the emperor and determination to expel the foreigners (*sonnō jōi*). These nine men were assisted by a female follower, Matsuo Taseko (1811–1894), who at fifty-two was already an old woman in the way of thinking at that time. In spite of her age, she was so inspired by Atsutane's thought that she defied her family in central Japan and traveled by herself to Kyoto in order to take part in the great cause of restoring direct imperial rule.[64]

Transmitting Atsutane's Thought to Rural Japan

Agricultural manuals and writings on agriculture served as important vehicles to propagate Atsutane's thought. Provincial scholars of agriculture and botany, who published their research in farm manuals (*nōsho*), approached Atsutane and Kanetane in the 1820s with the idea of collaboration. Atsutane and Kanetane realized that the manuals could serve as effective tools for transmitting Atsutane's teachings into the countryside. In these manuals, Atsutane provided theological explanations for agricultural practices, such as gender-based seed selection. In his thought, and in the writings of later Kokugaku figures, rice became a potent symbol. Ōkuni Takamasa asserted the superiority of Japan based in part on the prominence of rice. He described a mystical cycle of humanity's nurturance by heaven through the consumption of rice, further linking this to the *to ho kami emi tame* formula explained in the previous chapter. Publishing in farm manuals gave later Kokugaku writers access to farmers who might otherwise never have been exposed to these teachings, creating a wider audience than conventional publications.[65]

Sanctification of agricultural labor was a central theme, linked to concrete programs of action for avoiding rural unrest. Nativists converged with Shintoists like Kurozumi Munetada and others advocating self-cultivation regimens as the key to restoring village society's original harmony with the Kami. Analyzing a variety of nativist texts from the late Edo period, H. D. Harootunian shows how they are structured around these ideas: a portrayal of the universe as anchored by the role of the creation deities; Amaterasu's entrusting the imperial line with rule over the visible world; the sanctity of human reproduction; a model for self-sufficient villages united in reverence at village shrines for tutelary deities and the ancestors. People should dedicate themselves to agriculture, understanding that each task, from sexual intercourse to seed selection, and each step in growing rice, is grounded in divine precedent and has cosmic significance. They should have many children and provide mutual assistance to fellow villagers. Meanwhile, village officials and the affluent should regard their position and good fortune as an entrustment from the Kami that must be repaid to the community as a whole.[66]

Hirata Kokugaku after Atsutane: "Restoration Shinto"

The larger world of Kokugaku scholarship remained divided into multiple lineages in 1843, the year Atsutane died. Besides the followers of Kamo Mabuchi and Norinaga, Ban Nobutomo, and Kariya Ekisai (1775–1835) were also pursuing scholarship on the classics. Kanetane headed the followers of Atsutane, whose thought was referred to as "original teachings" (*honkyō*) or "original studies" (*hongaku*). The Hirata faction in later Kokugaku is referred to as Restoration Shinto (*fukkō Shintō*).[67]

Restoration Shinto was a grass-roots movement with a strong religious character, as Atsutane's followers disengaged from academism and brought the school's thought to a popular level. Their writings were close to everyday life, full of fertility imagery, idealizing a linked harmony between the earth, human fecundity, and fulfillment of the "imperial way." They wrote with palpable urgency during a period of increasing unrest in village society, and regarded Atsutane's ideas as directly applicable to restoring the villages to peace and harmony. In "Fundamentals for the Benefit of the Country" ("Kokueki honron," 1831), Miyaoi Sadao (or Yasuo, 1797–1858) wrote of the importance of providing the people with a "Way" whereby they could experience divine blessing through the sanctity of labor and dedicate themselves sincerely to communal life. Oka Kumaomi (1783–1851) further demanded that village elites provide assistance and relief to the poor. In his essay, "On the Traditions of Tutelary Shrines," ("Ubusuna shako denshō" [1857]), Mutobe Yoshika (1806–1863), a Shimōsa shrine priest, promoted communal worship of local tutelary Kami (*ubusunagami*), whom he described as constantly, zealously protecting the people. Mutobe produced a utopian synthesis of nativist ideas and symbols such as rice, the tutelary Kami, and Japan as a fertile land ruled over as a moral community by the emperor.[68]

By 1868, the Hirata school had 2,830 followers. Initially, most of the new members were merchants, farmers, and shrine priests. As the crisis caused by the foreign threat intensified in the 1850s, many came to view the country's problems as stemming not from moral deficiency but from the shogunate's inability to deal with foreign pressure. In the growing mood of national emergency, Kokugaku's anti-foreignism gained wider appeal, and samurai began to affiliate with Ibukinoya in growing numbers. Their presence politicized Restoration Shinto, including the shrine priests. The focus shifted to practical applications of *kannagara no michi*, a complex formula meaning "to follow the way of the Kami." The topics addressed included such questions as the sacred duty of service to the throne and clarifications of Japan's superior "national polity" (*kokutai*).[69]

As political issues became a more prominent concern, new teachers emerged, drawing on Atsutane's thought while striking out in new directions. Yano Harumichi, who was active in Kyoto, forged links with both the Shirakawa and Yoshida Houses, as well as the anti-foreign movement. Like many others, he enthusiastically anticipated the creation of a new government, in which the emperor would unify the people. Yano regarded a reconstituted Jingikan as essential to the new government. His essay, "A Fool's Humble Petition" (Kenkin sengo [1867]), set out the restoration faction's unique platform for a new government, centering on the ruler's performance of rites for the Kami. At the beginning of this essay, he wrote, "The most important duty in governing the realm is the performance of rites for the Kami of heaven and earth."[70]

Ōkuni Takamasa (1792–1871) founded what amounted to an independent school in the Tsuwano domain in Western Japan based on Hirata Kokugaku, which became a testing ground for policies seeking to make Shinto independent of Buddhism. Ōkuni had studied Dutch learning in Nagasaki and had learned Western principles of physics. In the process, he had come to think of Christianity as a potential threat to Shinto. He called on shrine priests to unite to prevent the spread of Christianity, in the event that foreigners should succeed in forcing the country open. From 1835 to 1853, he taught in Kyoto at his personal academy, called the True Learning School (Hō Hongaku Sha). In 1853, he returned to Tsuwano at the request of the domain lord, Kamei Koremi (1825–1885), to teach at the domain school. When Ōkuni realized that Christianity could not be kept out of the country, he shifted position to consider instead how it should be accommodated. He traveled and lectured widely throughout Western Japan, becoming, along with Yano, one of the Restoration faction's most influential thinkers.[71]

Hirata's followers agreed on the ideal of direct imperial rule, in which emperors would personally celebrate rites for the Kami. They idealized "unity of ritual and political rule" (*saisei itchi*), in which the emperor's personal worship of the Kami, complemented by Jingikan rites, would coordinate shrine ritual throughout the country. The concept of *saisei itchi*, discussed further in chapter 12, entailed the idea that those in service to the throne, including shrine priests, must submit to the ruler in a distinctive way. They should eliminate their own subjectivity, so that imperial rites would embody only the public, and all elements of the private would be eliminated. To submit in this way was regarded as the height of virtue. Ōkuni and his followers differed from Yano and Kanetane, however, on the position of the Yoshida and Shirakawa Houses. While Yano and Kanetane assumed that they would continue to play a central role, Ōkuni asserted instead that there would be no place for them.[72]

Reviving the Jingikan

The shogunate had asserted itself as an embodiment of "the public" at the beginning of the Edo period. Under the banner of "Restoration Shinto," the terms under which "public" versus "private" and "foreign" versus "indigenous" were debated at the end of the period differed greatly from the seventeenth-century discourse. Eighteenth-century Kokugaku's pervasive identification of Buddhism and China as the quintessential "foreign" influences obscuring the original unity between the emperor and his people was easily transposed to the Western powers pressuring Japan to open trade relations in the mid-nineteenth century. The Opium War made it clear to Japan that the Western powers were capable of subduing China, and that Japan was in the crosshairs as their next target of subjugation. It was a given in the thinking of the time that trade relations would be a mere prelude to colonial domination like that unfolding in China, and thus Restoration Shinto developed into an anticolonial discourse and a political practice. When the shogunate proved incompetent in dealing with the "foreigners," restorationists rejected it in favor of the ideal of direct imperial rule, upholding the emperor as the quintessential and absolute embodiment of both the public and the indigenous.

Reviving the Jingikan was a central goal of Restoration Shinto. Both the Yoshida and the Shirakawa claimed to be controlling the Jingikan, but concretely this only meant that each of them maintained an altar called the Hasshinden, where the protective deities of the imperial house were worshipped. This state of affairs was a far cry from the original idea of the Jingikan as a unified branch of government assisting imperial ritual and orchestrating complementary rites throughout the realm. The Yoshida and the Shirakawa both participated in palace ritual, but so did a number of other aristocratic houses and priests of a variety of Buddhist temples. The proximity of Buddhist monks to the throne was anathema to all branches of Kokugaku. In the emerging views of Ōkuni's followers, it was not appropriate for Shinto or imperial ritual to be split between two aristocratic Houses, or for licenses to perform Kami ritual to be sold for a fee. The competition between the two lineages was a disgrace to Restorationists' ideals regarding Shinto. The idea of a lineage "owning" knowledge about the Kami and parceling it out in esoteric transmissions went against the nativist idea that all the Japanese people have an obligation to serve the emperor and the Kami.[73]

Emperor Kōmei's intense attention to Kami rituals also stimulated the move to reinvigorate the Jingikan. Emperor Kōmei's frequent appeals to temples and shrines for divine assistance in repelling the foreigners increased after Perry's arrival, in some cases six times per year. The palace's ties to the Ise Shrines were renewed from 1855, when the court began sending Emissaries to Ise again after catastrophic earthquakes and a palace fire. From 1858, the emperor's prayers called for divine punishment of the disloyal, apparently referring to the shogunate. Prayers were held at the place that was supposed to be the grave of Emperor Jinmu, calling on him and later sovereigns to preserve and strengthen Japan in the face of the foreign threat. Kōmei made a point of worshipping in the direction of Jinmu's tomb, and from 1864, annuals rites for Jinmu were conducted at court.[74]

Aristocrat Sanjō Sanetsumu (1802–1859) and Hirata Kokugaku follower Furukawa Mitsura (introduced earlier) were significant figures in the move to renovate the Jingikan. They hoped to recreate its ancient form, based on Ritsuryō precedent. The Jingikan would stand above all the ministries of government to display the Way of *jingi* through the performance of Kami rites, replacing the facilities operated separately by the Yoshida and Shirakawa. Furukawa held that the Jingikan would be the basis for "the imperial nation," and display a model of loyalty and reverence for the Kami to the entire realm. This would require the abolition of all Yoshida influence and Buddhist elements from court ritual. Ōkuni Takamasa and Yano Harumichi envisioned the Jingikan as a central facility, where ceremonies for all the Kami connected with the imperial house would be performed. Work to set up the reconstituted Jingikan began in 1864, under Nakayama Tadayasu (1809–1888), maternal grandfather of Crown Prince Mutsuhito, who would become Emperor Meiji. In 1868, Nakayama was made Governor (*chiji*) of the Jingikan, a post he held until 1871. He worked to laicize the tonsured imperial princes, and to eliminate Buddhist elements from shrines. As of 1868, in the larger group directing the Jingikan preparations were Nakayama, Prince Arisugawa Takahito (1812–1886), Shirakawa Sukenori (1841–1906), and aristocrat Konoe Tadafusa (1838–1873). Up through that year, Yoshida and Shirakawa figures preserved positions in government.[75]

Meanwhile in Tsuwano, two powerful figures closely connected with shrines, the domain lord Kamei Koremi and Fukuba Bisei (1831–1907), engaged in an anti-Buddhism campaign to promote Shinto, expecting to spread their policies to the whole country. From the mid-1860s, the main roles in the administration and performance of Jingikan ritual were Kamei, Fukuba, and Nakayama. Gradually, the ideal of the Jingikan symbolizing Japan's superiority as a divinely protected nation (*shinkoku*) found widespread support among the domain lords, Kokugaku affiliates, and shrine priests. From 1866, Restoration Shinto allied with the faction bent on restoring direct imperial rule and forming a government with the Jingikan at its apex. The announcement of the imminent re-establishment of the Jingikan was promulgated in the third month, thirteenth day, of 1867. Five days later, a new law announced that all shrines and priests would be placed under the single authority of the Jingikan, marking the end of shrine priests' previous ties to the Yoshida, Shirakawa, or other aristocratic lineages.[76]

"Anything Goes!"

In the final months of the Edo period, an outbreak of carnival and revelry occurred, in which people danced through the streets singing, "Anything goes! Anything goes!" (*ee ja nai ka*). "Anything Goes!" erupted just before the shogunate's fall became official, and as the orders for the establishment of a new government were being issued. On 10.14.1867, the order returning all governing power to the imperial court was issued, and on 12.9.1867, the "restoration" of direct imperial rule was proclaimed. By the seventh or eighth month, people could sense that the shogunal order was passing away, and that a new order was being created. While "Anything Goes!" was not directly related to Shinto, except that rumors of shrine talismans falling from the sky had sparked the outbreaks, it reflected the mood of millenarian expectation surrounding the downfall of the shogunate. Like preceding episodes of mass pilgrimage to Ise, it evoked a mixture of hope and dread.[77]

Beginning in the seventh month of 1867 in Kyoto, Osaka, Mikawa, and Shikoku, rumors of falling talismans stimulated people to visit local temples and shrines. Because some of the revelers lived near the Ise Shrines and went there, the movement was originally mistaken for another outbreak of *okage mairi*. The majority involved in "Anything Goes!" went not to Ise but to shrines and temples near their homes. But, whereas in *okage mairi* the rumors of falling talismans only began after the pilgrimage was in full swing, in "Anything Goes!," the rumor of falling talismans was the trigger.[78]

A contemporary account from *Notes on Mysterious Happenings of Ise: Thanks Pilgrimage of the Keiō Era* described the scene:

> Wherever something was rumored to have fallen from the sky, the owners of the house would brew sake, as much as they could. The nearby people would take a holiday from work for four or five days, and the homeowner would have to treat them to sake, including his servants and apprentices, as well as anyone who was passing by. Everyone beat drums and gongs day and night, and everyone—male, female, young and old—caroused through the town. They would sing, "Stick paper over your privates, and if it falls off, just stick it on again. Who cares? Anything goes! This is the greatest!" Others would paint their faces so that men turned into women and women turned into men. Old granny would become a young girl. They played at all sorts of disguises and costumes in a huge dance, where the bad and the good were turned upside down, all the time singing, "Anything goes!" Some went on pilgrimage to the Ise shrines in a huge commotion.[79]

The following account describes how "Anything Goes!" unfolded in Kyoto:

> The dancers were strangely dressed, frantically dancing and singing, "Anything goes!" People didn't hesitate to push their way into the

> headman's house with their shoes on and dance around, going like this from house to house, beckoning to all and sundry to dance with them, so that a huge crowd of dancers would gather. If they were hungry, they helped themselves to rice cakes; if they were thirsty, they got drunk on sake and kept on dancing. If they got tired, they didn't care whose house they were in—they would just lie down on the spot, and when they woke up, they'd start dancing again. They threw their work aside and went around singing, "Anything goes!" The authorities who distributed rice and money garnered a good reputation, and some of them competed with their relatives and acquaintances to spread out the best banquet and the biggest mountains of presents. All the gifts made the dancers dance even more frenziedly.[80]

The Kyoto Magistrate outlawed "Anything Goes!" but with no effect. In some areas, farmers realized that the authorities were intimidated and used the occasion to redress old grievances.

> A dancer would boldly come into the house and seize clothing, tools, food or whatever and say to the owner, "Anything goes!," meaning, "Give this to me." The owner would respond, "Anything goes!," whereupon the dancer would take what he wanted and leave. Especially if it were the house of someone the dancer disliked, or someone in a position of authority, they would make a point of dancing into those houses singing, "Anything goes! Anything goes!," and make off even with whatever big tools they wanted, making sure to damage the furnishings as much as they dared.[81]

In modern understandings of Japan's religious history, it has come to be commonly assumed that "Anything Goes!" belongs to Shinto in some way, though we have seen that its revelries were as often carried out at temples, headmen's houses, and miscellaneous venues as at shrines. However we characterize it, "Anything Goes!" showed a widespread expectation that the Kami and Buddhas were about to enact some great change.

Conclusion

The Edo period ended with the term *Shinto* used more frequently than before, but with little agreement on its meaning. In Kokugaku writings it was most often raised in the course of criticizing Confucianism and Buddhism. It appeared most often, that is, in negative form, with the result that its actual content was left unspecified. The Kokugaku line of thought originating with Norinaga resolved itself into a focus on Amaterasu. Though not equivalent to the de facto monotheism of Kurozumi

Munetada, its focus on Ise was a natural result of Norinaga's understanding of the *Kojiki*, his location near the Grand Shrines, and his close association with its priests. The thought and religious practice stemming from Atsutane, on the other hand, held out for a more diffused form of Kami worship, as illustrated by his "Morning Prayers." There the Three Creator Deities (*zōka no sanshin*) stood out prominently and overshadowed Amaterasu. While Atsutane upheld the status of Ōkuninushi, this Kami played only a minor role in Norinaga's thought.

Concurrent with the emergence of such theological disparities, the urgency in invocations of Shinto at the end of the period nevertheless began to unite shrine priests around concrete political goals. Furukawa Mitsura, who had called for a new Jingikan in 1862, was an Atsutane *monjin* and closely associated with the Shirakawa, but his proposal was preceded by a similar proposition in 1858 from Sawatari Hiromori (1811–1884), head priest of the Rokushogū in Musashi, who was affiliated with the Yoshida and stood at the head of a regional network of Yoshida-affiliated shrines. They shared a number of goals. Furukawa urged upgrading the status of shrine priests, construction of shrines in the Ezo territories that would become Hokkaidō, transforming imperial graves into sites of national commemoration, and the establishment of shrines to honor imperial loyalists, past and future.[82] All these proposals were to be fulfilled in the Meiji period, when each of them came to be understood to be a part of Shinto. Thus Kokugaku of the late Edo period set the agenda for the next era of Shinto history.

12

Shinto and the Meiji State

Introduction

Scholarly debate concerning Shinto in the modern period has revolved around the idea of "State Shinto" since the publication of Murakami Shigeyoshi's influential book, *State Shinto* (*Kokka Shintō*, 1970).[1] Murakami regarded State Shinto as a state religion responsible for inculcating an attitude of unquestioning obedience to the state, which led the country into militarism, imperialism, and disastrous wars, culminating in Japan's 1945 defeat. In his view, Shinto was, in effect, taken over by the state and transformed into a tool of indoctrination in a manner and to an extent unparalleled in other Japanese religions. Shimazono Susumu, Inoue Hiroshi, Isomae Jun'ichi, and others have pursued Murakami's guiding questions, while qualifying his conclusions. Shimazono particularly emphasizes Shinto's influence in prewar education. He regards imperial rites as part of State Shinto and holds that as long as they persist, State Shinto has not yet truly been abolished.[2] Inoue Hiroshi writes:

> [State Shinto] was modern Japan's system of official religion.... It was through this ideology and system of shrines that "the Japanese people" were inculcated with emperor-system nationalism, which propelled their ideological and spiritual unification.[3]

Scholars of Shinto studies who were associated with the priesthood have criticized State Shinto on several counts. Ashizu Uzuhiko, an historian and official of the National Association of Shinto Shrines, denounced the postwar Occupation reforms that abolished public funding for Shinto as wrongfully depriving Shinto of its rightful place in the public realm.[4] Shinto historians Sakamoto Koremaru and Nitta Hitoshi have pointed out how little financial support prewar shrines actually received from the state and have also criticized broad uses of the term, extending it to imperial ritual and the education system. When the concept is extended so broadly, they write, it becomes vague and loses explanatory power. With the exception of the early Meiji attempt to create a state religion and the period from 1940 to 1945, Shinto historians who are also priests mostly reject the idea that a state religion that could be called State Shinto existed.[5]

Western scholarship up to the early postwar years, particularly that of Daniel Holtom (1884–1962), regarded State Shinto as a de facto religion that provided an engine of war. Researchers writing from the late 1970s to about 2000, including myself, tended to accept the concept of State Shinto, with qualifications. Western researchers generally treated State Shinto as an "invented tradition" but without attempting to identify Shinto as the central cause of imperialism, nationalism, and militarism.[6] Some German scholarship constitutes an exception to this generalization, however, and we can see a strong interest in Shinto's "war responsibility" in works by Klaus Antoni and Walter Skya.[7]

Western scholarship since 2000 reflects the ongoing controversy about State Shinto. John Breen and Mark Teeuwen, authors of *A New History of Shinto*, neither adopt the term nor explain why not, but they demonstrate that the history of modern Shinto can be written without it. Edited by Bernhard Scheid, *Kami Ways in Nationalist Territory*, a 2013 collection of essays on modern Shinto, questions how much responsibility can be attributed to Shinto for the various ideologies supporting the prewar regime. Trent Maxey argues for revising the concept of State Shinto based on a more precise understanding of the government's evolving interpretations of religion in relation to the imperial institution.[8]

The concept of State Shinto is frequently coupled with another historiographical paradigm, the "emperor system" (*tennōsei*). Sheldon Garon discusses the assumptions underlying the presumed connection between the emperor system and State Shinto: "Japanese leaders in the Meiji era [are said to have] created a new state orthodoxy centered around a sacrosanct emperor, who was to be worshipped by all subjects at government-sponsored shrines in a system of State Shinto."[9] Both the emperor system and State Shinto have been invoked as totalizing explanations of modern religious history, holding that the state made Shinto its puppet and ruthlessly suppressed anyone or any religious organization that contradicted its "orthodoxy," extending Shinto's influence into the educational system and over civil society broadly.

The emperor system and State Shinto share a number of conceptual weaknesses. As Garon writes, they tend to be used ahistorically, as if a blueprint had already existed in 1868 for everything that would unfold through 1945. They fail to elaborate what ideas constituted the supposed "orthodoxy" of State Shinto as a religion. These concepts obscure the enthusiastic participation of society and other religious groups in a variety of national projects, including the creation, funding, and governance of shrines, and the suppression of new religious movements. Research adopting these concepts presumes instead that the Japanese people were unknowing, easily led, and lacked self-awareness, a patronizing and unjustified generalization. Neither concept sets meaningful boundaries, and thus rituals of coerced expressions of reverence to the imperial portrait or the Imperial Rescript on Education in schools are regarded as part of Shinto, though shrine priests were rarely present. Emperor worship is assumed to belong uniquely to Shinto, though Buddhist sects, new religious movements, and some branches of Christianity were also fervid proponents. The idea of Shinto as the main "perpetrator" of emperor worship is mistaken and obscures the involvement of other religions, their scholars, and members.

In a recent review of State Shinto research in Japanese scholarship, Okuyama Michiaki suggests that the debate has reached a stalemate. On one side, he finds totalizing claims and, on the other, hyper-detailed parsing of government documents and ideological distinctions aiming to "whitewash" Shinto. Even the participants have come to find the debate "confusing and unproductive."[10] I have to agree.

In the meantime, however, a description of Shinto from 1868 to 1945 as "state managed" or under "state management" (*kokka kanri*) has emerged as a kind of compromise, recognizing the state's formidable influence without necessarily entering the debate about defining State Shinto. In fact, before "State Shinto" became contentious, priest-scholars such as Umeda Yoshihiko used "state managed" and "State Shinto" interchangeably.[11] Nowadays "state management" seems to have gained acceptance among scholars of Shinto studies.[12]

Clearly, "state management" is a circumlocution; yet because so much recent debate has been conducted at a conceptual level, there is something to be gained by stepping back from ideological commitments, to inquire what "state management" meant for shrine life. I hope to contribute to that endeavor in this chapter and the next by examining how Shinto formed new relations with government, and how those relations affected shrines, the priesthood, and shrine communities. Through that interaction, some of the most fundamental characteristics of modern Shinto were formed, including its politicization, its inextricable position in local social organization, the idea that it is a nonreligious tradition that has no doctrine, and the notion that it is the core of Japanese ethnicity.

This chapter deals with the bulk of the Meiji period, from 1868 to around 1900. These years are bounded at one end by a government fiat that suddenly "separated Kami from Buddhas" (1868) and gradually brought all the shrines under government administration and, at the other end, by creation of a government office dedicated solely to administering shrines, the Shrine Bureau (Jinjakyoku, 1900). These two events put Shinto in a position to develop independently of Buddhism for virtually the first time and established a place in national government for itself alone, distinguishing it from religion as a fundamentally nonreligious phenomenon. The shrine priesthood heartily welcomed these changes, though they precipitated unsuspected and unintended consequences.

Toward Restoration

Restoration Shinto had proposed fashioning shrines into bulwarks against an anticipated spiritual colonization by Christianity, as chapter 11 explained. "Return" to direct imperial rule, and imperial ritual as a means for indoctrinating the people in loyalty were widely accepted goals.[13]

Not all such ideas came from Restoration Shinto, however. Perhaps the most lastingly influential treatise of this kind was Aizawa Seishisai's (1782–1863) *New Theses* (*Shinron*, 1825). A Confucian scholar of the Mito domain, Aizawa had realized that Europeans were spreading Christianity in the countries they colonized, and he feared that the Japanese people could easily be converted and turned against their rulers.[14]

Mito Confucians took it for granted that rulers use religious policy to govern, and it seemed obvious to them that Christianity was a ruse used by the West to keep the people docile and loyal. They used the term *kokkyō* (national teaching) as a synonym for "state religion" in the sense in which they believed Western leaders manipulated Christianity to their own advantage.[15]

> They now endeavor to annex all nations of the world. The wicked doctrine of Jesus is an aid in this endeavor.... If a nation's defenses are weak, they will seize it by force but if there are no weaknesses to pounce on, they take it over by leading the people's minds astray with their wicked doctrine.[16]

Kokutai (literally, "nation-body," often translated as "national structure" or "national polity") was a key concept in *New Theses*. Aizawa used *kokutai* to refer to "national spiritual unity—the voluntary affection and trust that commoners felt for their rulers." He believed that in antiquity there had been a strong bond between rulers and the ruled, because ancient emperors used ritual to inspire the people with trust. He called this the "Way of Amaterasu," whose "mystical, suggestive power of ritual" was essential to uniting the nation. Aizawa saw this unity of ritual and government (*saisei itchi*) as the key to national unity, and after the publication of *New Theses*, the term gained widespread currency.[17]

The importation of foreign creeds had obscured and degraded the *kokutai*, raising the question of who was capable of promulgating a teaching that would restore it. Of course, nativists and shrine priests saw themselves as uniquely qualified, but few thinkers outside those circles viewed any of Japan's existing religious traditions as capable of uniting the people. Confucian scholar Yokoi Shōnan (1809–1869) summed up the common view of the ruling elite when he wrote in 1856,

> Although our land possesses Three Teachings, it is a [*kokutai*] lacking a [national] faith. The Way of the sages is an amusement for scholars; the

> Way of the kami is irrational and absurd; Buddhism deceives foolish commoners, but is not a Great Way that both high and low will accept.[18]

Mito scholar Fujita Tōko (1806–1855) thought Hirata Atsutane was doing something valuable by invigorating Kami worship, but he wrote of Atsutane to Aizawa, "I am embarrassed by his doubtful and random fabrications." When the proposal arose to give Atsutane an appointment in Mito, Aizawa commented acidly that if Hirata "died and journeyed to the underworld, it would not be such a lamentable thing."[19]

On the thirteenth day of the third month of 1868, the young Emperor Meiji issued a proclamation announcing that his new government would restore direct imperial rule (*ōsei fukko* 王政復古) and the unity of rites and government (*saisei itchi* 祭政一致).[20] This was the "restoration," though in fact the country was to be governed by an oligarchy, composed of men from Chōshū and Satsuma, until the promulgation of the constitution in 1889. The new government began trade and diplomatic relations with the West and inaugurated such sweeping reforms as universal compulsory education, military conscription, the eradication of the class system and hereditary social status, freedom of residence and occupation, and the end of compulsory affiliation with Buddhist temples.

The New Government's Understanding of State Ritual

The Meiji government at first consisted of two parts, the Council of Divinities (Jingikan) and the Council of State (Dajōkan), with the former as the top-ranking entity. It was understood, however, that these ancient names were provisional; a base upon which a new system adapted to contemporary circumstances would be built in time. Based on the thought of Ōkuni Takamasa, the Tsuwano domain's official ideology, Restoration Shinto thinkers from Tsuwano monopolized the Jingikan and swiftly ejected Yoshida and Shirakawa figures. The Council of Divinities could claim to "restore the ways of antiquity" in that it had public, official status that transcended rites previously performed separately by the Yoshida and Shirakawa families. However, in substituting samurai leadership for the aristocrats, the Meiji Council of Divinity differed significantly from the ancient model. The Meiji Jingikan also differed from the ancient prototype in its guiding values. Ōkuni declared that the Jingikan's main purpose was to uphold loyalty and filial piety, but inculcating those ideas had not been understood as the ultimate goal in the ancient Council of Divinities. Nevertheless, these values were the core of the samurai ethic, and samurai bureaucrats found it natural to remake the Jingikan accordingly.[21]

Ōkuni's followers, and Meiji Kokugaku figures more generally, idealized personal, unmediated imperial worship of the Kami (*tennō shinsai*). To realize the unity of rites and government, the sovereign should perform Kami rituals personally, without delegating the job to subordinates. On that view, the Council of Divinities was a provisional step on the path to the emperor taking charge of national ritual personally. Once the emperor took over the performance of state rites, the Jingikan would lose its rationale for existing and would be dissolved.[22] As we will see below, however, not everyone agreed that the Jingikan should work toward its own abolition.

Emperor Meiji began personally conducting ritual directly after his coming-of-age ceremony in the first month of 1868. On that occasion, he worshipped the grave of the legendary Emperor Jinmu from a ritual hall in the Kyoto palace. The 1868 imperial proclamations of *ōsei fukko* and *saisei itchi* took the form of oaths to the Kami of Heaven and Earth (*tenjin chigi*). This ceremony transcended the scope of traditional court ritual, compelling military commanders to sign an oath swearing loyalty to the emperor. It was widely expected that Mutsuhito would visit the graves of past emperors and the Ise Shrines personally to announce major events.[23]

It seems odd that the Niinamesai was not conducted until 1869, while Kinensai was not performed until 1870, and Mutsuhito's enthronement rites (Daijōsai) were not held until 1871, three years after his accession. In fact, the samurai who had dismissed the Yoshida and Shirakawa and taken charge of ritual affairs lacked the knowledge and facilities necessary to conduct these rites. The Niinamesai, Kinensai, and Daijōsai all had to be performed in Kyoto, since alternate facilities had not yet been created in Tokyo. Yoshida and Shirakawa figures were quietly reinstated and eventually came to serve in the Imperial Household Ministry as ritualists assisting the monarch in palace ceremonial, since the samurai who had replaced them did not know how to conduct state rites.[24]

It took some time for imperial ritual to supplant the Council of Divinities. The first order of business was to eradicate all Buddhist observances from the palace. When the capital was moved to Tokyo, the palace's Buddhist altar, the Okurodo, all imperial Buddhist memorial tablets (*ihai*), as well as Buddhist images and ritual facilities were entrusted to the Kyoto temple Sennyūji, where many imperial graves were located. Male members of the imperial house in Buddhist orders were laicized, and all *monzeki* posts were eliminated. The custom of naming temples "places of imperial prayer" (*chokugansho*) was abolished.[25]

Over the years 1868 to 1872, Konakamura Kiyonori (1821–1895), a Kokugaku scholar, played a central role in choreographing the 1871 enthronement rites for Emperor Meiji and composing the annual calendar of rites observed in the palace. When the emperor moved to Tokyo, three ritual halls were established within the palace: the Kashikodokoro, the Kōreiden, and the Shinden.[26] Around these three main halls a number of related ritual facilities were created (see Figure 12.1).

As Figure 12.1 shows, there were (and are) three main ritual halls, surrounded by auxiliary buildings in a walled compound that has five gates. The three main halls face south and are connected by corridors. The most important of these is the Kashikodokoro, located in the center of the complex. It houses a replica of the

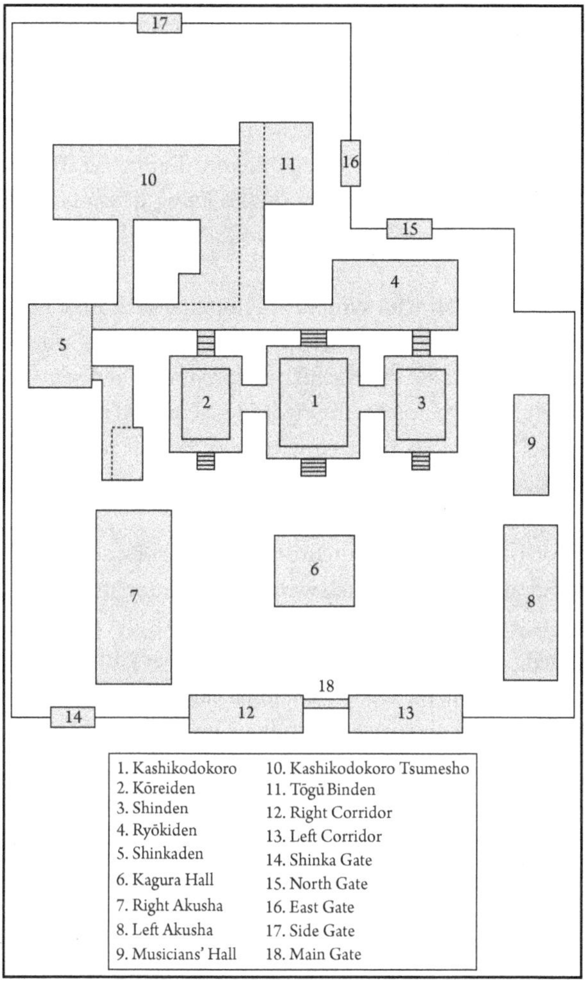

Figure 12.1 The Palace Shrines. Source: Nakazawa Nobuhiro, *Kyūchū saishi* (Tokyo: Dentensha, 2010).

sacred mirror of the Ise Shrines. Its floor is elevated higher off the ground than the two halls to its east and west, signaling its greater status. Immediately before the Kashikodokoro is the Kagura Hall, a roofed structure without walls, where sacred dance is performed as an offering to the Kami. To the east and west of the Kagura Hall are the Right and Left Akusha, two assembly halls for guests. Smaller structures are provided for the offerings used in ceremonies and for the use of musicians. To the west of the Kashikodokoro is the second most important structure, the Kōreiden, which enshrines the ancestral spirits of the imperial house. The third structure, to the east of the Kashikodokoro, is the Shinden, which enshrines the Kami of Heaven and Earth. In addition to these three main halls, the Shinkaden, an interior room adjacent to the Kōreiden and the open ground directly to the south of the room itself, called the Shinkaden Garden, are used for the monarch's performance of the Niinamesai, Ōharai, and Shihōhai. The Ryōkiden, an interior space behind the Shinden, is used for Chinkonsai and as a place for the emperor and empress to change vestments. The crown prince and princess change vestments in the Tōgū Binden, adjacent to the Kashikodokoro Tsumesho. The Kashikodokoro Tsumesho, to the rear of the Shinkaden, is the living quarters of the Naishōten, female ritualists who carry out twice-daily offerings to the enshrined deities and clean the halls.

The imperial regalia, powerful symbols of imperial authority, became more visible to the people through Emperor Meiji's numerous travels around the country. The mirror was never to leave the Kashikodokoro, but whenever the monarch left the palace for more than one night, the sword (a lacquered replica of the one at the Atsuta Shrine) and the jewels traveled with him. For all major ceremonies, both the sword and jewels accompany the emperor, carried by palace ritualists called Shōten.[27]

A proclamation of 1873.10.14 standardized palace rites, and in 1878 ceremonies for the spring and autumn equinoxes were added. Later still, others were added, such as a ceremony commemorating Emperor Meiji's death, and dates for some ceremonies were changed. Table 12.1 summarizes the types and timing of annual court ritual, which was made the basis for the annual calendar of all shrines in the Meiji period (see chapter 1 for comparison with the annual cycle of imperial ritual in the ancient period).[28]

This elaborate ritual calendar includes several types of ceremonies. Agricultural ritual forms one category: Kinensai, Kannamesai, and Niinamesai. Ancestral ritual forms the largest and most highly ranked component, including daily worship (Maichō Go-daihai) and annual observances for the founder of the imperial line, Emperor Jinmu (Kigensetsu and Jinmu Tennōsai), as well as memorial ceremonies for the four most recent generations of the reigning emperor's paternal ancestors and two generations of the female line. Astrological rites and those marking calendrical divisions included the Shihōhai, New Year's rites (Saitansai, Genshisai, and Matsurigoto-Hajime), the thrice-monthly Shunsai, the Ōharae and Yo-ori rites, ceremonies marking the spring and autumn equinoxes, and rites marking the end of the year (Kashikodokoro Mi-kagura, and Joya-sai). The ongoing significance of purification is evident in the Ōharae and Yo-ori rites, while the related phenomenon of spirit-calming is retained in the Chinkon-sai. The ranking of ceremonies as major, minor, or unranked corresponds to designated participants and to the display of the regalia. For major ceremonies, selected government officials are expected to attend, but in lesser numbers or not at all for the ceremonies designated as minor or unranked. On major ceremonies, the sword and jewels are both present, while for minor ceremonies only the sword accompanies the emperor.

With the emergence of structured imperial ritual, the Council of Divinities lost its rationale. The Jingikan remained in existence from the third month of 1868 until

Table 12.1 **Imperial Ritual during the Meiji period**

Schedule	*Rite*	*Rank (Major, minor, unranked)*	*Location*	*Participants*	*Purpose, etc.*	*Notes*
Daily	Maichō Go-Daihai		3 Main Halls	Shōten	Daily obeisance by a ritualist acting as the emperor's proxy.	
Monthly, On the 1st, 11th, and 21st days	Shunsai		3 Main Halls	1st: Emperor; 11th and 21st: Head Shōten	Three times per month the daily food offerings at the 3 Main Halls are presented in an augmented form.	Est'd. 1872
Annual 1.1	Shihōhai		Shinkaden Garden	Emperor	Prayers to the Kami of Ise, the imperial ancestors, and the Kami of the Four Directions for the peace of the nation and a bountiful harvest; the first ceremony of the New Year.	No one may serve as the emperor's proxy in this rite.
1.1	Saitansai	Minor	3 Main Halls	Emperor, Crown Prince	New Years prayers to the Kami of Heaven and Earth for the peace and prosperity of the nation.	
1.3	Genshisai	Major	3 Main Halls	Emperor, Empress, Crown Prince and Princess	New Years prayers for the nation's prosperity, celebration of the imperial house's origins.	Other members of the imperial house attend.

(continued)

Table 12.1 **Continued**

Schedule	*Rite*	*Rank (Major, minor, unranked)*	*Location*	*Participants*	*Purpose, etc.*	*Notes*
1.4	Matsurigoto Hajime		Hō-ō Audience Hall	Chief Palace Ritualist	The Chief Palace Ritualist (Shōten-chō) reports to the emperor on matters related to the Ise Shrines and Palace Ceremonial.	
1.11	Memorial Ceremony for Empress Dowager Eishō, wife of Emperor Kōmei	Minor	Kōreiden, gravesite	Emperor, Empress, Crown Prince and Princess	Held on the death anniversary of Emperor Meiji's mother.	
1.30	Memorial Ceremony for Emperor Kōmei	Minor	Kōreiden, gravesite	Emperor, Empress, Crown Prince and Princess	Held on the death anniversary of Emperor Meiji's father.	
2.11	Kigensetsu	Major	3 Main Halls	Emperor	Commemorates the enthronement of the legendary Emperor Jinmu.	Est'd. 1873; date and name subsequently changed.
2.17	Kinensai	Minor	3 Main Halls	Emperor and Crown Prince	Prayers for a good harvest, success in industry, the well-being of the nation and the imperial house.	Est'd. 1873

2.21	Memorial ceremony for Emperor Ninkō		Kōreiden, gravesite	Emperor, Empress, Crown Prince and Princess	Held on the death anniversary of Emperor Meiji's grandfather.	
Spring Equinox	Shunki Kōreisai, Shunki Shindensai	Major	Kōreiden, Shinden	Emperor and Shōten	2 ceremonies celebrating the equinox, dedicated to the imperial ancestors and to the Kami collectively.	
4.3	Jinmu Tennōsai	Major	Kōreiden, gravesite	Emperor, Empress, Crown Prince and Princess	Commemorates the death anniversary of Emperor Jinmu.	
6.30	Yo-ori no Gi		Takenoma Hall	Emperor, Chamberlain, Naishōten	Half-yearly purification of the emperor's person.	Est'd. 1871
6.31	Ōharai		Shinkaden Garden	Emperor, Shōten, representatives of the imperial house, the Imperial Household Ministry, and the imperial guards.	Half-yearly purification of the imperial family and the populace.	Includes recitation of the Ōharai Norito.
Autumn Equinox	Shūki Kōreisai, Shūki Shindensai	Major	Kōreiden	Emperor and Shōten	2 ceremonies celebrating the equinox, dedicated to the imperial ancestors and to the Kami collectively.	

(continued)

Table 12.1 **Continued**

Schedule	*Rite*	*Rank (Major, minor, unranked)*	*Location*	*Participants*	*Purpose, etc.*	*Notes*
10.17	Kannamesai	Major	Kashiko-dokoro	Emperor, Empress, Crown Prince and Princess	Offering first fruits of the harvest to Amaterasu.	
11.13	Tenchōsetsu	Minor	Various	Head Shōten	Celebration of the birthday of Emperor Meiji.	
11.22	Chinkonsai		Ryōkiden	Shōten, Naishōten	Calming the spirits of the emperor, empress, crown prince and princess, with prayers for their health and long life, directed to the Eight Deities.	Recreates the dance of Ame-no-uzume that drew Amaterasu out of the cave, performed by female ritualists called Naishōten.
11.23	Niinamesai	Major	Shinkaden Garden	Emperor and Shōten	Harvest rite and emperor's communal meal with Amaterasu.	
12.6	Memorial ceremony for Emperor Go-Momozono		Kōreiden	Emperor, Empress, Crown Prince and Princess	Commemorates the death anniversary of Emperor Meiji's great-great-grandfather.	

12.12	Memorial ceremony for Emperor Kōkaku		Kōreiden	Emperor, Empress, Crown Prince and Princess	Commemorates the death anniversary of Emperor Meiji's great-grandfather.	
12th month	Kashikodokoro Mikagura	Minor	Kagura Hall	Dancers, musicians	Offering sacred dance to the Kami of the Kashikodokoro.	All the furnishings of the building are renewed at this time.
12.31	Yo-ori no Gi		Takenoma Hall	Emperor, Chamberlain, Naishōten	Half-yearly purification of the emperor's person.	Est'd. 1871
12.31	Ōharai		Shinkaden Garden	Emperor, Shōten, representatives of the imperial house, the Imperial Household Ministry, and the imperial guards.	Half-yearly purification of the imperial family and the populace.	Includes recitation of the Ōharai Norito.
12.31	Joya-sai		3 Main Halls	Shōten	Final prayers of the year to give thanks to the Kami and to ask for their blessings in the New Year.	

Source: Yatsuka Kiyomi. "Kōshitsu saishi hyakunenshi." In *Meiji Ishin Shintō hyakunenshi*, vol. 1, edited by Shintō Bunkakai, 71–123 (Tokyo: Shintō Bunkakai, 1966).

the eighth month of 1871, when it was demoted to the status of a ministry and renamed the Ministry of Divinities (Jingishō). In the interval, Emperor Meiji made the first of four personal visits to the Ise Shrines, moved to Tokyo, and established the three main halls for palace rites. He visited the Jingikan to announce the policy of *saisei itchi* to his ancestors and the eight protective deities of the imperial house, since the altar of Eight Deities (Hasshinden) existed only within the Jingikan at that time. He also personally performed rites for Emperor Jinmu and sent emissaries to the purported site of Jinmu's grave.[29] The prominence of Jinmu in imperial rhetoric stimulated the creation of such works of art as Tsukioka Yoshitoshi's triumphal painting of Jinmu conquering "the East," led by a magical three-legged crow (see Figure 12.2).

A month after the demotion of the Council of Divinities to ministerial status, the emperor announced that his imperial ancestors would henceforth be worshipped at the new ritual halls in the palace. The ritual equipment necessary for that change was relocated from the Ministry of Divinities. When the Ministry of Divinities' last remaining ritual facilities, the symbols of the Eight Deities and the Kami of Heaven and Earth, were relocated to the palace, the Ministry was abolished, in the third month of 1872. With that, the palace became the sole and undisputed center of state ritual.[30] As we will see, however, not everyone was satisfied with the demise of the Jingikan.

The Separation of Buddhism from Shinto

Determined to rid the nation's shrines of Buddhist elements, and having already accomplished this in Tsuwano, Ōkuni Takamasa and his disciples Kamei Koremi (1824–1885) and Fukuba Bisei (1831–1907), the most influential bureaucrats for religious affairs in the early Meiji government, issued an edict in 1868 (tenth month, eighteenth day) ordering the "separation of Buddhas and Kami (*shinbutsu bunri rei*)."[31] The separation order initiated "state management" of Shinto. Their ultimate goal was to free Shinto from Buddhism.

As for specific measures, all Shinto priests were required to have Shinto funerals. Temples were to remove images of the Kami from their altars, and shrines likewise were to remove Buddhist images. Buddhist clerics were forbidden to recite sutras before Kami altars or to serve at shrines unless they renounced Buddhist orders and became Shinto priests, which many did. Beyond these general directions, Hachiman shrines were ordered to remove the "bodhisattva" title from the deity's name, and Nichiren-sect temples were ordered not to incorporate Amaterasu into their mandalas or into their "thirty protective deities" (*sanjūbanjin*).[32]

Shrines during the Edo period were so often managed by temples and Buddhist priests, and the people were so accustomed to the combination of Buddhas and Kami that the order was hard to comprehend. In some areas where Ōkuni's ideological

Figure 12.2 Emperor Jinmu Conquers the East. Tsukioka Yoshitoshi, Japanese, 1839–1892. Publisher: Funatsu Chūjirō, Japanese Emperor Jinmu (Jinmu tennō), from the series *Mirror of Famous Generals of Great Japan* (*Dai nihon meishō kagami*). Japanese, Meiji era, 1880 (Meiji 13), February 20, woodblock print (*nishiki-e*); ink and color on paper, Vertical ōban; 37.4 × 25.1 cm ($14\frac{3}{4} \times 9\frac{7}{8}$ in.). Source: Museum of Fine Arts, Boston. William Sturgis Bigelow Collection 11.18104. Photograph © 2016, Museum of Fine Arts, Boston.

vision was absent or weak, implementation was fairly mild, closing only those temples that had neither priests nor parishioners. Even there, however, ejecting Kami with Buddhist associations (Benzaiten, for example) was the rule. Some temples that had venerated Kami simply hid their paintings and sculptures for a while. In other areas, however, there was widespread plundering of temples and theft of their property. Many priests were forced to laicize, and temples' consecrated images and ritual gear were melted down for cannon. Across the country, many hundreds of temples were closed or destroyed, and Buddhism suffered great damage and loss, known as *haibutsu kishaku*, "destruction of Buddhism." Historian of religions Allan Grapard has likened the separation and ensuing destruction to a cultural revolution, and that is no exaggeration.[33]

By government order the deities at many shrines were changed, not only by removing Buddhist divinities, but also by eliminating Kami lacking any connection to the *Kojiki* and *Nihon shoki*. Miscellaneous Kami were typically replaced with Kami from those two texts, deified spirits of legendary figures like Yamato Takeru, or deified loyalists to the throne. Many case studies of *shinbutsu bunri* have been researched; what follows is a small sampling of what happened in different areas.[34]

Enoshima, an island pilgrimage site adjacent to Kamakura, was one of the most frequent pilgrimage destinations for people from Edo, because it was nearby and could be visited without official travel permits. During the Edo period there were three main shrines, each administered by an intendant temple of the Shingi Shingon sect. These three shrines venerated a staggering array of deities, including the Buddha Dainichi, various Buddhist protective deities, Inari, the Ise gods, the smallpox gods, Daikoku, the deified goddess of the island, and many others. After the Restoration, the deities were reduced to three female Kami only. The temples were closed, though some of their priests converted to Shinto and continued to serve in their former shrines. The pantheon was radically reduced, with the substitution of new gods not previously worshipped at the site.[35]

Public reaction was mixed. Sometimes shrine supporters took the substitution of nation-focused Kami for their unnamed tutelary deities as a "promotion." Wags sometimes lampooned the sudden changes, as seen in "The Idiot Sutra" (*Ahodarakyō*): "They say we can't mix up the Buddhas with the Kami, and it looks like Shaka, Amida, Jizō, and Fudō have all gotta go!"[36]

By contrast, domains ruled by anti-Buddhist followers of Hirata Atsutane were especially violent in implementing the separation of Buddhism from Shinto. The Naegi domain, in central Japan, is a good example. Naegi was a small fief ruled by a Hirata follower named Aoyama Naomichi. To implement the separation order, he effectively forced everyone in the domain to sever their ties with temples and "convert" to Shinto, including the requirement to have Shinto funerals. When adherents of the Jōdo Shinshū sect of Buddhism resisted, Aoyama personally went into their villages and forced them to burn their Buddhist altars, statues, scrolls, and other family treasures. In one case, a woman became so distraught that she tried to throw herself into the fire.[37]

The Shinto priesthood increased through Buddhist and Shugendo priests "converting" to Shinto. Large numbers of clerics who had previously served both at temples and shrines dropped their Buddhist affiliations and registered as shrine priests, which allowed them to remain in service at shrines.[38] In 1868, the Tōzan Daigoji sect of Shugendō ordered its priests who were connected with shrines to become certified as Shinto priests. They took the names of their former temples as their surnames and tried to continue performing the same kind of ritual as usual, only now serving exclusively at shrines. When the ruse was discovered, they were in many cases expelled, leading to the complete abolition of Shugendō in 1871. At the same time, however, it was declared that the characteristic deities of Shugendō, the *Gongen*, were actually Kami, though they had not previously been regarded as such. The hope was that Shugendō mountain pilgrimage sites such as Mt. Fuji, Yoshino, Haguro, Gassan, and Yudono could be transformed to shrines and their assets secured for Shinto.[39]

The separation order was a convenient excuse for shrine priests to vent their anger over centuries of subordination to Buddhist clergy, and for National Learning figures to try to re-enact the prototypical separation policies seen in Mito, Aizu, and Okayama early in the Edo period. Seizing Buddhism's wealth was the prelude to transferring it. The new government had decided to abolish the samurai class, and since the samurai would no longer be living on stipends, new ways to support them were vitally needed. An area like Shizuoka, for example, where there were many high-ranking samurai of the Tokugawa family, urgently needed to provide compensation to angry, dispossessed samurai. It is thus not surprising to find that significant destruction of Buddhist property happened there. Land and buildings belonging to shrines and temples were prime targets. Besides the ideological meaning of the separation edict, it was also a land grab, resulting in the confiscation of 87,200 *chō* from shrines and 52,800 from temples.[40]

I believe that the notion of "state management" is wholly inadequate to the analysis of the separation of Buddhism and Shinto. The separation was the most draconian change in Shinto's history up to that time. Carried out by determined Kokugaku ideologues in the Jingikan working with provincial partisans, it undid centuries of combinatory worship, setting the stage for massive reorganization of shrines and their Kami. The separation laid the groundwork for the entire populace to become involved in shrine life and for the government to manipulate shrines with unprecedented intensity.

The Ise Reforms

Of all the shrines, the Ise Shrines were most heavily "state managed." It was crucially important that these shrines should be showplaces of Shinto, separated from

Buddhism, and also exhibit unity of government and ritual. But at the beginning of the Meji period, Ise lacked unity and connection to the imperial institution. No reigning emperor since Jitō (r. 686–697) had ever actually visited the Ise Shrines. Control of the Outer and Inner shrines by the Watarai and the Arakita lineages, respectively, had obstructed the desired image of unity.

Reform at Ise began in 1868 with revival of the ancient custom of sending an Imperial Emissary to major Ise ceremonies. Temples near the shrines were razed. Local place-names that had incorporated some Buddhist-sounding element like "Yakushi" or "Gongen" were changed. The reforms gained new impetus in 1871, directed by Urata Chōmin (aka Nagatami, 1840–1893). Urata came from a family of pilgrim masters, but he had studied Kokugaku and also held appointment in the 1850s as a priest (*gon-negi*) at the Inner Shrine. In 1871 he was appointed to the Jingikan, and in 1872 he was appointed to serve concurrently as Vice Chief Priest at Ise.[41]

The next step was to oust the Watarai and the Arakita; they were out of their jobs overnight. A single administrative office for the Ise priesthood, the Jingūshichō, was established. The remaining priests were transferred—the former Inner Shrine priests to the Outer Shrine, and vice versa. By 1877, a single hierarchy of centrally appointed shrine priests had been established. Virtually all the women were fired. After the 1871 reform, there were a mere fifty-five shrine employees at Ise.[42] Because Urata found mass pilgrimage and the carnival atmosphere major embarrassments, he had the inns and houses of the pilgrim masters removed. After he argued for the abolition of the *oshi* post, several hundred pilgrim masters were terminated. Fully half the population of Uji and Yamada was left unemployed by Urata's reforms.[43]

Urata's draconian measures provoked an unexpected response. On the twenty-ninth day of the twelfth month of 1871, a group of about thirty men armed with repeating rifles arrived in Ise. The rebels decried the reforms and rumors that the emperor was to be taken abroad, and that the Ise Shrines were to be relocated to Tokyo. The threat of armed resistance was averted only by arresting the protestors.[44]

At Ise, state management meant the complete transfer of control from the former priestly lineages to agents of the central government and placing shrine assets under government oversight. The priests were paid a salary by the central government based on their rank. The shrine's land, which at the end of the Edo period had amounted to 13,000 *koku*, was "returned" to the throne, that is, confiscated. By the late 1870s, the land grant was replaced by an annual appropriation from the central government's budget.[45]

Ritual was another area of Ise reforms. Some ancient rites that had fallen into desuetude were reinstated, such as the Kinensai, reinstated in 1869. In other cases, rituals that had become customary at Ise but lacked ancient origins were eliminated. As part of a more general ousting of female ritualists and "masculinization" of the shrines, the Mono-imi and Kora roles were abolished, and the Saishu role was thereafter performed by a male member of the imperial family. Besides these various changes, entirely new rites were created, such as those for the mythical emperor Jinmu, performed from 1869. Overall, we can observe a pattern in which the former Inner Shrine began performing more rites than its Outer Shrine counterpart, illustrating the downgrading of the Outer Shrine.[46]

State management also targeted shrine architecture. Around 1875, a standard blueprint that had been developed by bureaucrats at the Ministry of Doctrine and the Finance Ministry was promulgated. Subsequently, village shrines began to adopt the *shinmeizukuri* style of the Ise Shrines, previously forbidden to lesser shrines, and to use mirrors as their consecrated objects of worship, whatever they might have used previously. They typically used unpainted cypress wood and simple braces, eschewing the elaborate styles associated with temples. Many shrines not built in the Ise style attached the billets and cross beams characteristic of Ise to their roofs, though they had no functional purpose.[47]

The Ise reforms took place alongside replacement of the Edo-period class system by a new social order in 1869. A new aristocracy, called *kazoku*, was formed from the old court nobles plus the former domain lords. The former samurai other than domain lords were called *shizoku* or elite samurai, and those who had been common soldiers, *sotsu*. Below them were the common people, *heimin*. The new aristocracy comprised some 427 families, including the Yoshida and Shirakawa families, along with the Fujinami family serving as the Ise Saishu, who were made Viscounts. Thirteen other shrine families were made Barons.[48]

The former samurai group felt itself greatly deprived and disadvantaged by the loss of its customary prerogatives, status, and economic support. The Edict Prohibiting the Wearing of Swords (March 1876) was the last straw. It touched off a series of uprisings by former samurai in Western Japan that ended in the Satsuma Rebellion (also referred to as the Seinan War) of 1877, led by Saigō Takamori (1827–1877). In the Shinpūren Rebellion, "Divine Wind Rebellion," of October 24, 1876, about one-quarter of the 127 men from the Divine Wind Brigade who died were shrine personnel.[49]

Shrines as the Nation's Rites and Creed

Adding to the rubrics of *saisei itchi*, a Council of State proclamation of 1871 declared shrines the "rites and creed of the nation" (*kokka no sōshi*). This phrase became a key element giving substance to the ideal of unity of rites and government. *Kokka no sōshi* meant "rites" (*-shi*) and "creed" (*-sō*) of the nation (*kokka*); in other words, the shrines were made public institutions for the performance of state ritual, by fiat. The "creed" would be clarified in the Great Promulgation Campaign (see below). The Ministry of Divinities (Jingishō, established in the eighth month of 1871) began to standardize shrine rites in 1871, expanding the list of ceremonies that shrines were required to perform, in tandem with the ongoing expansion of imperial rites, a process that gradually aligned all the shrines with the palace.[50]

The government created a ranking system for the shrines, and designated the Ise Shrines the most prestigious. This was the first time all shrines had been brought under a single "umbrella" and Ise officially accorded preeminence. The ranking system for shrines had three main tiers: official shrines (*kansha*), unofficial shrines (*minsha*), and unranked shrines (*mukakusha*). The official shrines were divided into Imperial (*kanpeisha*), National (*kokuheisha*), and Special shrines (*bekkakusha*); the Imperial and National Shrines were further subdivided into three grades: Major, Middle, and Minor. The official shrines were administered centrally, while the unofficial shrines were administered by regional and local-level administrations. Over time, lesser shrines might advance in rank through meritorious service to the country, which in practice meant monetary contributions. That gave local communities of shrine supporters something to aspire to, positioning shrines at the center of efforts to boost a town's image.[51]

Never since ancient times had court ritual been used as a standard for ordinary shrines, nor had Ise's rites been used in that way. In addition to centrally mandated rites, one or more Annual Festivals (*reitaisai*) commemorating the founding of a shrine or an important event in its history were authorized. The Annual Festivals were outside the calendar of state ritual and were particular to each shrine. Shrine priests and local governments were expected to assemble the entire community for the performance of both the official rites of the state and the shrine's Annual Festivals. While participants would typically make some offering on these occasions, the rites were not performed for fees. The requirement that shrines perform these state rites did not, however, preclude performance of customary prayers for safe childbirth, baby blessings, or other commercialized rites.

Having ejected the lineages that had controlled the major shrines and many of the regional and smaller ones, the government (central and regional) appointed new priests and paid them a salary and in many cases reinstated some of the priests who had initially been displaced. Others recruited to shrine service included former samurai. Declaring the shrines public facilities and confiscating shrines' land were central features of state management of Shinto. A new, unified ranking system for the priests based on examinations was created, making a career path based on common criteria of achievement. Thus, in theory, a merit system replaced customary ascriptions based on kinship and wealth. In fact, however, hereditary succession to the priesthood continued in many cases, and the government could not sustain its policy of paying priestly salaries; in 1873 the central government cut the salaries of all priests at the Prefectural Shrines and at lower-ranking shrines. Along with the ranking system for shrines and priests came standards for how many priests, of what rank, could be appointed to the shrines of a particular rank. Because many shrines of the preceding era had been landed properties—small fiefs, in some cases—the people involved in their rituals were typically drawn from the farmers who cultivated shrine land. These part-time shrine personnel (generically called *shake*, literally, "shrine family") could be quite numerous, and even a medium-sized regional shrine might have dozens of families attached to it, performing a variety of roles in ritual, from sacred dance to divination rites, and could be polishers of mirrors, those who prepared offerings or decorations, those who were entitled to beat drums or march in festival processions, to those who would shoot arrows off at the conclusion of a ceremony to ward off evil influence. The majority of these functionaries lost their official roles when the new priestly system was implemented. Buddhist priests who had formerly conducted rites at shrines could continue in service only if they shed their Buddhist affiliations and "converted" to being full-time shrine priests. Nearly all the women previously serving at shrines as dancers and diviners were dropped.

It is estimated that at the beginning of the Meiji period there were approximately 74,642 shrines and a total population of around thirty-five million people.[52] Obviously, the government could not underwrite the total expenses of all shrines. National, Imperial, and Special Shrines received "tribute" (*heihaku*) from the court. Lesser shrines received monetary contributions from the administrative unit to which they were assigned (prefecture, town, or village, for example). At the Annual Festivals of the most important shrines, an Imperial Emissary would be dispatched with the tribute. The appearance of the emissary, a symbolic proxy for the emperor himself, preceded by his entourage and a large wooden trunk containing offerings, was a most impressive sight. This mark of imperial regard was social capital, tremendously significant in strengthening a shrine's sense of its own importance, increasing its ability to call upon local people to respect and support it.

It is important to note, however, that "tribute" mainly consisted of small bolts of colored cloth or food offerings and covered virtually none of a shrine's ongoing expenses. This means that shrines necessarily operated on a combination of public funds and income generated locally. The extent of state monetary support for shrines was always a bone of contention, and shrine priests were consistently disappointed in the amount they received. For them it was not only a personal matter; it also limited their ability to meet the expectation that shrines function as public facilities. The necessity to depend significantly upon private support, especially income from commercialized religious rituals, could only blur the image of shrines as facilities for the performance of state-authorized ritual.

The people were brought into the new, nationalized shrine system by the practice of census registration at shrines, *ujiko shirabe*. In 1871, universal shrine registration was instituted in place of the former Buddhist temple registration system. Every subject at birth became a parishioner of a shrine by receiving a talisman from the local shrine near him or her. Everyone was to register with a new shrine upon a change of residence, and at death the talisman was to be returned. In addition, subjects were to enshrine a talisman of the Ise Grand Shrines in their homes. In this way, each household installed the "divided spirit" (*bunrei*) of the Ise deities in its domestic altar for the Kami (*kamidana*), as opposed to the simple purification talisman *oshi* formerly distributed.[53]

Shrine registration was clearly intended to unify the nation in the worship of the Ise deities. In fact, however, while registration was a boon to shrines, it did not work well as a census system. Shrine registration was dropped as a census mechanism, but shrines retained the practice of making everyone living nearby a shrine parishioner. This expanded shrines' base of support and broadened the sense of shrine affiliation based on place of residence. Shrines continued to place a talisman in each household *kamidana*. Prior to Meiji, the status of shrine parishioner (*ujiko*) had been limited to a few privileged families in a shrine's territory. A shrine could now assert that anyone living within its bailiwick was its parishioner and duty-bound to support it.[54] The full implications of universal membership in shrine parishes became evident in the twentieth century.

The Great Promulgation Campaign

An edict of 1870 announced that a Great Teaching (*taikyō*) would be promulgated throughout the land.[55] The Jingikan and the organizations that succeeded it, the Ministry of Divinities (Jingishō, 1871–1872), the Ministry of Doctrine (Kyōbushō, 1872–1877), and the Bureau of Temples and Shrines (Shajikyoku, 1877–1900) indoctrinated the people in new tenets through the Great Promulgation Campaign (*taikyō senpu undō*), lasting from 1870 to 1884.[56] An organization called the Great Teaching Institute (Daikyōin) was created as an extension to the Jingikan (and its successors). The Institute certified National Instructors and sent them out to teach the Great Teaching to all subjects. The Teachings were (1) respect for the gods, love of country; (2) making clear the principles of Heaven and the Way of Man; and (3) reverence for the emperor and obedience to the will of the court. The Three Great Teachings were not grounded in popular thought and were so vague even to the Instructors, in fact, that manuals explaining how to preach about them had to be issued. The manuals addressed taxation, conscription, compulsory education, and the solar calendar, as well as government slogans like *fukoku kyōhei* (rich country, strong army) and *bunmei kaika* (civilization and enlightenment). Thus Instructors were actually explaining the meaning of the Three Great Teachings in terms of the modernizing policies of the new government.[57]

As the Great Promulgation Campaign unfolded, the modern term for religion, *shūkyō*, was only just entering the Japanese language. The new term, and the necessity of accommodating foreign trading partners' demands to allow Christian missionaries to proselytize, generated much debate among Meiji intellectuals, in and out of government, concerning religion's role in a modern society. For example, the Meiroku Society published in its journal, *Meiroku zasshi*, a wide spectrum of views by Mori Arinori, Nishi Amane, Katō Hiroyuki, Shimaji Mokurai, and others, which eventually coalesced in support of the idea that Japan should not adopt a state religion, and that it should recognize religious freedom, to the extent that its exercise did not disturb public order. This was the understanding that was eventually codified in the Meiji constitution's provision for freedom of religion. As elite thinking began supporting religious freedom in some form, a widening gap opened between elite thinking on religion and the Great Promulgation Campaign. The result was that the clergies of Shinto, Buddhism, and a variety of new religious movements that became involved in the Campaign were expected to promote a state doctrine even as those in power were rejecting the idea of a state religion.[58]

The Great Teaching Institute was located in the Tokyo temple Zōjōji, formerly the Tokugawa family temple. The National Instructors (*kyōdōshoku*), composed of Buddhist and Shinto priests first and foremost, but also accompanied by traditional storytellers, actors, preachers of Shingaku, Kokugaku, and others drawn from the new religions, were graded into fourteen ranks by examinations. The head abbots of the Buddhist schools were automatically accorded high ranks.[59] The Institute's opening ceremony featured mirrors and a Shinto ritual style, and Buddhist priests were required to wear wigs. The Institute was both a government office and a religious institution, fitted with an altar enshrining Amaterasu and the "Three Deities of Creation" (*zōka sanjin*, discussed in chapter 11). Each prefecture was to have a Middle Teaching Institute (*chūkyōin*, usually housed in a prefecture's largest shrine), which administered the Instructors' examinations. The title of Small Teaching Institute (*shōkyōin*) was conferred upon participating temples and shrines. It is estimated that 100,000 temples and shrines participated in the system at its height, with a variety of management patterns.[60]

The Great Teaching Institute operated like a small seminary, training prospective Instructors in ritual and how to preach about the "Great Teaching." The plan was that the Instructors would transcend and subsume all their sectarian differences in support of a common creed for the nation. There was no explicit definition of this creed as "Shinto," but liturgy was based on the shrine rites, performed in shrine priests' vestments, Shinto prayers, and so on. Buddhist elements were disallowed. This unarticulated dimension of ritual gave Shinto symbolic preeminence.[61]

Institute staff reflected regional factionalism, so that those from Satsuma tended to oppose those from Chōshū. Among Institute administrators were former samurai such as Fukuba Bisei,[62] who had carried out the separation of Buddhism from Shinto.[63] Former samurai and aristocrats monopolized the higher-ranked posts but had little experience of shrine life, to say nothing of preaching. The shrine priests in the Campaign broke into factions based on a complex mix of regional and doctrinal commitments. Some Instructors unapologetically promoted their own interpretations of Shinto under the cover of a "national teaching." Those who joined the Campaign from a commitment to Kokugaku thought were predictably divided between followers of Motoori and Hirata, and not all of them were experienced in proselytizing. All non-Buddhist personnel distrusted the Buddhists and were jealous of Buddhism's stronger organization and greater wealth. The sectarian identities of the Instructors and their audiences proved to be irrepressible. The Buddhists were better preachers, and their audiences acted much as they would have at any temple sermon. People who came to hear Pure Land preachers commonly recited the *nenbutsu* and threw coins, as they were lectured on the Great Teachings.[64]

Tokoyo Nagatane (1838–1886), a teacher of the Instructors, composed the "The Tale of the Divine Teachings System" ("Shinkyō soshiki monogatari"), an intimate account of the Campaign. Tokoyo recounts that one Campaign official was promoting his own creed, referred to as "the Shinto Teaching" (Shintōkyō), and prevailed on junior staff to adopt his views. A group of Hirata followers wanted to emphasize their master's teachings about the afterlife, but they got bogged down in disputes over the location of Yomi, pressuring each other to sign oaths to adhere to particular interpretations of this matter.[65]

The Campaign's disarray was all too apparent. The first sign of the government's displeasure was staff cuts in 1871,[66] followed by the loss, in 1873, of official salaries for shrine priests at the Prefectural Shrine level and below, and also in 1873 came a significant uprising against the Campaign, called the Echizen Uprising to Uphold the Dharma.[67]

Echizen, on the Japan Sea coast, had a long history of near-total commitment to Jōdo Shinshū. Because virtually everyone who lived in Echizen belonged to this Buddhist sect, attitudes to the Campaign were shaped by this prior religious commitment. A Shinto Instructor named Ishimaru Hachirō had gone to Echizen representing the Great Promulgation Campaign in 1872 and proceeded to enact his idea of a "Three-Tenet Sect," precipitating the Echizen Uprising to Uphold the Dharma (Echizen gohō ikki) in March 1873. Because Ishimaru and other Campaign preachers adopted Western dress and imposed the Gregorian calendar, local people regarded the Campaign as a disguised version of Christianity. The preachers tried to make Jōdo Shinshū priests cease their sermons, called Dharma talks. The memory of the great destruction Buddhism had suffered in *shinbutsu bunri* was still fresh in local memory, because Echizen bordered on Toyama, where Buddhism had suffered some of its worst losses. All this being the case, it was hardly unreasonable that local people should conclude that the Campaign's covert goal was the destruction of Buddhism.

Resistance to the Campaign also incorporated other issues that were offensive to local people, such as compulsory education, the Gregorian calendar, and a new land tax. The new tax was payable only in cash, unlike the former system, which allowed payment in kind. The land tax exacerbated social inequalities and forced many independent farmers into tenancy. After burning the Campaign's branch office in Ōno Village, three to four thousand men bearing *nenbutsu* flags and bamboo spears went through the town attacking anything that appeared Western. After police detained five suspects, including a priest, rioters set fire to the village office and also damaged the mayor's house. Rioting spread to the surrounding counties. Prefectural officials were terrified and summoned troops to put down the riot, after the rebels torched several village officials' residences and large businesses. Probably unrelated to the Campaign, local officials removed the public notice boards inscribed with the prohibition on Christianity that had been in force since the early Edo period. The change only further confirmed local suspicions that the Campaign was promoting Christianity. Over a three-week period, several tens of thousands of people became involved in rioting. The end came when the leaders, "five or six priests," were executed by hanging.[68]

Above all, this uprising was a visceral, violent reaction to the Great Promulgation Campaign, based on the belief that the Campaign's true intent was the destruction of Buddhism. The rebels' solidarity was based on their determination to prevent that. The uprising belied the view that Japanese religions contained nothing capable of motivating people to sacrifice themselves for their beliefs, though the Campaign certainly failed to inspire anyone with such conviction.

The combined effort of Buddhist and Shinto clergy seen in the first few years of the Campaign ended when the Buddhist sects withdrew in 1875. Shimaji Mokurai (1838–1911), an elite Shinshū priest, had become convinced through his travel to Europe that the state should remain aloof from religion and tolerate a range of religious beliefs among the populace. He petitioned the government on this subject repeatedly, eventually concluding that his sect should withdraw from the Campaign.[69] In 1876, Kurozumikyō also received permission to withdraw, as did another new religious movement, Shintō Shūseiha.[70] Over the next few years, several other groups broke away from the Campaign, creating considerable resentment among the Campaign leadership, who viewed the sects as schismatics who undermined Shinto's image of a united front.[71] From that point on, the Buddhist sects and other religious organizations permitted to operate outside the Campaign began to function autonomously. By contrast, Shinto shrines remained under state management. With the departure of the Buddhists, the Campaign became for the first time unambiguously "Shinto" in character. In recognition of this change, a new government organization called the Shinto Office (Shintō jimukyoku) was established as a substitute for the Great Teaching Institute in 1875, with the Chief Priest of the Ise Shrines as its head.

By 1876, there were more than 10,000 National Instructors, but they were expected to finance their activities independently; the central government offered no financial support. This situation could not be sustained. The lack of public funding for the Campaign stimulated development of a new type of Shinto organization: a Shinto "church" (*kyōkai*) attached to a shrine, with members organized by territory-based parishes.[72] The church, led by priest-Instructors, then became the shrine's proselytizing division and tried to persuade parishioners to have Shinto funerals and ancestral rites performed by the church, cutting their ties with Buddhist temples. For Shinto clergy, however, funerals remained problematic. A priest who performed a funeral could bring the pollution of death in contact with Kami of his shrine. On the other hand, revenues that could come from funerals and ancestral rites were a considerable incentive to overcome such taboos. The churches were serendipitous in this connection, because priests leading a church ministered in their capacity as Instructors, a second identity with which to separate their funeral and shrine roles.[73]

The Ise Grand Shrines created a church attached to the shrines called Jingūkyōkai. Organized in 1872 by Urata Nagatami and Tanaka Yoritsune (1836–1897),[74] Jingūkyōkai drew its ministers largely from former pilgrim masters, who typically became Instructors as well. Ministers of the new religions and ordinary shrine priests frequently combined their roles with the Jingūkyōkai ministry and also became Instructors. By 1875, Jingūkyōkai claimed 304,704 members, meeting in a nationwide network of 1,600 preaching stations, often located in existing shrines. The believers were organized into parish confraternities called Jinpū Kōsha, "Divine Wind Associations." In many cases the pre-Meiji Ise confraternities formerly led by *oshi* were simply renamed "Jinpū Kōsha," and these groups continued to function under the new name much as they had before 1868. Jingūkyōkai tracts presented Amaterasu as an agricultural deity, and Jingūkyōkai distributed talismans and almanacs of the Ise Grand Shrines.[75] Jingūkyōkai ministers reportedly addressed audiences that routinely numbered in the several thousands.[76]

While the shrine priests struggled to establish these churches in order to support their proselytizing as Instructors, however, the absence of public funding revealed a contradiction with the rhetoric of shrines as *kokka no sōshi*, public facilities providing the nation's rites and creed. If the funding had to be arranged entirely on a private basis, then what foundation was there for claiming that shrines had a public status? The Shinto Office (Shintō jimukyoku) was supposed to smooth these bumps in the road, but the appointment of the Ise Shrines' Chief Priest as its head implied that Shinto as a whole should center on Ise. The Head Priest of the Izumo Shrine, Senge Takatomi (1845–1918), challenged that idea in the Pantheon Dispute.

The idea of "state management" is inadequate to the task of analyzing the Great Promulgation Campaign. Its purpose was manifestly ideological, not managerial. The Campaign operated for fourteen years through state agencies deriving from the Jingikan and thus can be regarded as a state project.

The Pantheon Dispute

The Pantheon Dispute (*saijin ronsō*) divided the Shinto world into two halves. On the face of it, the issue was whether to add to the pantheon enshrined in the Shinto Office (Amaterasu and the Three Creator Deities) the principal Izumo deity Ōkuninushi no Mikoto,[77] as the lord of the underworld. The Izumo faction wished to elevate this deity to national status, foreseeing advantages this would bring to Izumo Ōyashirokyō, popularly known as Taishakyō, the funeral-performing church attached to the Izumo Grand Shrine, headed by Senge. The Ise faction, led by Chief Priest Tanaka Yoritsune, opposed the proposed change, because adding a new deity would set a dangerous precedent for theological disunity, and also because Izumo's encroachment threatened Ise's preeminence.[78]

Beyond these considerations, the Pantheon Dispute exposed resistance to reducing all Kami faith to a single hierarchy topped by Ise. Amaterasu and the other "heavenly deities" (*tenjin*) had in ancient myth emerged preeminent over Ōkuninushi and the other "earthly deities" (*chigi*), but only with the consent of the latter. The Izumo partisans represented a distinct cosmology and worldview that could not be subsumed as subordinate to Amaterasu. They could justly point out that focusing exclusively on the imperial line of Kami failed (again) to provide people with any consolation regarding death and the afterlife.

The Instructors met repeatedly at local, prefectural, and national levels, each branch many times submitting its opinions to the central office,[79] but in the end no resolution was reached.[80] The dispute effectively came to a halt in 1882, when the matter was submitted to the imperial court for adjudication, and shrine priests were prohibited from becoming Instructors. This prohibition prevented shrine priests from performing funerals. Many shrine priest-Instructors stormed the Shinto Office to protest this prohibition, which pulled the rug from beneath the churches they had labored so hard to construct.[81] Some decided that if they could not minister freely to their followers within the Campaign, they would go it alone and form a Shinto "sect." The Campaign was ended by government order in 1884.[82]

Early Meiji Shinto "Sects" and Religious Movements

A large number of organizations related to Shinto were active in the early Meiji period. Table 12.2 presents a typology of the main ones. They shaped and channeled popular faith in the Kami, creating new creeds, uniting formerly disparate pilgrimage associations into religious movements, and perpetuating aspects of the Great Promulgation Campaign long after the government had given up on it.

We can divide these organizations into two main categories: Shinto-derived new religious movements and "sects" of Shinto. Shinto-derived new religious movements refers to those founded on the basis of a founder's revelations, leading to the development of distinctive doctrines, rituals, and patterns of communal life focused on worship of the Kami. While their doctrines varied considerably, they all aimed to alleviate poverty, sickness, and unhappiness in relations with others.[83]

Chapter 10 presented detailed discussion of three such groups, Kurozumikyō, Misogikyō, and Uden Shinto. Of these, Kurozumikyō was the largest, most organized, and best able to expand in the early Meiji period. Kurozumikyō benefited greatly from its participation in the Campaign, which facilitated its spread into new areas, allowing it to claim for the first time that it belonged to the "public." Ministers could—and did—present their teachings as one form of an officially recognized creed. By 1883, Kurozumikyō had a total of 1,744 ministers certified as National Instructors and would have had more, except for a quota imposed on it in 1879. By 1900 Kurozumikyō had fifty-two churches in Okayama and also proselytized vigorously in Kyoto, Shikoku, and western Japan.

Table 12.2 **The Early "Sects" of Shinto**

Type	*Sect*	*Founding Date*	*Founder*	*Notes*
Based on founder's revelations	Kurozumikyō	1814	Kurozumi Munetada (1780–1850)	See chapter 10 for detailed discussion of founding and early beliefs. Kurozumikyō became independent of government oversight in 1876.
	Misogikyō	Began between 1830–1844	Inoue Masakane (1790–1849)	See chapter 10 for detailed discussion of founding and early beliefs. Misogikyō became independent of government oversight in 1894.
	Tenrikyō	1838	Nakayama Miki (1798–1887)	Faith healing was a central practice.
	Konkōkyō	1858	Kawate Bunjirō (1814–1883)	Faith healing was a central practice.
	Shinrikyō	1875–1876	Sano Tsunehiko (1834–1906)	Following the founder's revelations, he began preaching and opened a church in Kokura in 1880. After a period of operations under Ontakekyō auspices, it gained recognition as a separate religious organization in 1894. Faith healing was a central practice.
Based on earlier mountain-worshipping groups	Fusōkyō	1873	Shishino Nakaba (1844–1884)	This organization initially promoted the teachings of Hasegawa Kakugyō (1541?–1646?), an ascetic who promoted faith in the deities of Mt. Fuji, but during the Meiji period it adopted worship of the Great Promulgation Campaign's Kami. It grew rapidly through a merger with Maruyamakyō, also focused on Mt. Fuji.
	Jikkōkyō	1878	Shibata Hanamori (1809–1890)	This group was formed by a schism from an earlier association based on worship of Mt. Fuji. Jikkōkyō preached that Fuji was a world center of spiritual power and promoted worship of the emperor.

	Shintō Taiseikyō	1882	Hirayama Seisai (1815–1890)	In 1879 Hirayama organized some followers of Misogikyō and members of Mt. Ontake pilgrimage associations into a group that received recognition as a sect of Shinto in 1882. Numerous groups, such as Shingaku associations and Renmonkyō, operated under its umbrella and later became independent religious associations. Taiseikyō had little clear-cut identity of its own and declined after Hirayama's death.
Formed to continue the work of the Great Promulgation Campaign	Shintō Shūsei-ha	1876	Nitta Kuniteru (1829–1902)	Nitta had become a National Instructor in 1872, beginning a preaching career at that time. He proselytized among shrine priests, and mountain ascetics of Mt. Ontake and Mt. Fuji. Nitta preached worship of the Three Creator Deities of the Great Promulgation Campaign.
	Shinshūkyō	1882	Yoshimura Masamichi (1839–1915)	Yoshimura came from a Tsuyama samurai family. He studied Confucianism and Kokugaku in Kyoto, also practicing austerities on Mt. Kurama. He became a National Instructor in 1880, meanwhile developing a unique doctrine purporting to perpetuate the Nakatomi lineage's practice of Shinto. His purpose was to provide a national religion based on ancient Shinto.
	Shintō Honkyoku, later known as Shintō Taikyō	1885	Inaba Masakuni (1834–1898)	Inaba had been a *daimyō* of the Yodo domain. The organization he founded was known before 1940 as Shintō Honkyoku, thereafter as Shintō Taikyō. Its leadership was drawn from the National Instructors of the Great Promulgation Campaign, whose work was terminated in 1884 with the end of the Campaign. Shintō Taikyō continued to preach the Three Great Teachings and functioned as an umbrella for other movements, such as Tenrikyō, Maruyamakyō, and Fujikō, until they could gain independence from government oversight.

(continued)

Table 12.2 **Continued**

Type	*Sect*	*Founding Date*	*Founder*	*Notes*
Based on a reorganization of former shrine pilgrimage assocations	Taishakyō	1878–1882	Senge Takatomi (1845–1918)	During the Edo period, the Izumo Shrine had a large group of pilgrim masters called *oshi*, who organized people to go on pilgrimage to the shrine, providing lodging, performing ceremonies, and maintaining distinct bailiwicks that they visited to distribute Izumo talismans. After the *oshi* profession was banned, Senge united the earlier pilgrimage associations into a single group. Senge had promoted the idea that the main Kami of the Izumo Shrine, Ōkuninushi, is the deity of the underworld, and in accord with that belief he developed the practice of enshrining the souls of the organization's deceased believers.
	Jingūkyō	1882	Tanaka Yoritsune (1836–1897)	This organization is not regularly regarded as one of the Shinto sects now, but up until the mid-Meiji period it was officially recognized as such. The group originated as the instructional branch of the Ise Shrines and was staffed with former pilgrim masters (*oshi*), whose profession had been banned. These local-level leaders then reorganized the members of their former pilgrimage associations into a unified religious organization providing funerals and other ceremonies. The group was dissolved in 1899, later to be reorganized as a fundraising organization for the Ise Shrines, continuing until the present, now known as Jingū Hōsankai.

Sources: Kokugakuin Daigaku Nihon Bunka Kenkyūjo, ed. *Shintō jiten* (Tokyo: Kōbundō, 1999), Murakami Shigeyoshi, *Nihon shūkyō jiten* (Tokyo: Kōdansha, 1978).

During the Campaign, Kurozumikyō meetings featured *norito* addressed to the national pantheon of Amaterasu and the Three Creator Deities, as well as the emperor. At each assembly, believers bowed for worship of the emperor and a reading of the Three Great Teachings. Ministers used the term *Shinto* to describe Kurozumikyō teachings, and cultivated friendships with shrine priests, who sometimes built Kurozumikyō churches in their shrine precincts. Many Kurozumikyō ministers also became shrine priests. Some ministers were also active in Jingūkyōkai, a natural association as both organizations focused on worship of Amaterasu. Ministers established deep roots in rural society, where they became local mayors, and served on school boards, town councils, and fire brigades.[84]

Sano Tsunehiko (1834–1906) founded Shinrikyō in 1880, following years of study, travel, and mystical dreams. He began to proselytize on the basis of his *Diagram of Divine Truth*, which among other things, propounded the idea that the sun revolves around the earth, and opened a church in Kokura. He continued to travel widely to visit shrines and Campaign officials. He was extremely disappointed in the quality of the people he met, but remained committed to the goal of adapting Shinto to prevent the spread of Christianity. In a typically vehement explosion, Sano said of the Office of Shinto Affairs:

> The whole Office of Shinto Affairs is rotten, like a pumpkin stuck full of needles. I feel helpless yet impelled to act when I see the spectacle, and I have not had a moment's peace since first seeing the priests and National [Instructors] of the capital. Because I have not met a single admirable person since coming here, my heart is now troubled; I want to say one thing to the priests and National [Instructors] here. Their "sermons" consist of nothing but the performance of ritual; the priests are simply imitating those imitating something they do not understand. Their so-called "confraternities" are full of displaced *yamabushi*. None of them knows anything about doctrine. They wipe the lips and asses of the unlearned with high talk about restoring Shinto to its proper estate, and from beginning to end not one can stand on his own.[85]

After a period of operations under Ontakekyō auspices, Shinrikyō gained recognition as an autonomous religious organization in 1894. Healing based on the founder's medical theories was a central practice.[86]

The founders of Tenrikyō and Konkōkyō repeatedly rejected the idea that their teachings were connected to Shinto as it had been promoted in the Great Promulgation Campaign. However, subsequent leaders in both groups decided to accept the label of *Shinto* in order to escape persecution, and both organizations were significantly changed by that decision.[87]

Tenrikyō was founded in 1838 by Nakayama Miki (1798–1887), a woman of the village headman class from Wakayama. Her revelations first led to her being regarded as a living deity of safe childbirth, and later to the development of a complex doctrine and way of life dedicated to a universal parent god. Faith healing remained a central practice. While Tenrikyō was small and disunited in early Meiji, in the twentieth century it grew to become one of the most important religious movements in Japanese history. Tenrikyō did not become officially affiliated with the Campaign, largely because of the founder's intransigent opposition. Nakayama did not regard her teaching as a part of Shinto. Partly as a result, early Meiji was a time of extreme suppression of this new religion. The police interrogated Nakayama seventeen times, and local churches were subject to suppression. Only after her death was a policy of compromise adopted, and the group adopted the label of Shinto, gaining freedom to proselytize in 1908.[88]

Konkōkyō's founder Akazawa Bunji (also known as Konkō Daijin and Kawate Bunjirō, 1814–1883) began life as a wealthy farmer in Bitchū Province. Following grave misfortunes, including the deaths of his children and cattle, Bunji experienced revelations leading him to attribute these hardships to mistaken beliefs about the deity Konjin. Konjin was commonly regarded as a malicious directional deity responsible for baleful influences from the northeast. Bunji came instead to regard Konjin as a universal deity, whom he called Tenchi Kane no Kami. Bunji taught that humanity can know the nature of deity and be in accord with its will through the mediation (*toritsugi*) of himself and his ministers. When Konkōkyō's followers were persecuted, the group sought refuge under the auspices of other, recognized groups, but this strategy led to schisms that threatened Konkōkyō's very existence. Bunji had become a Shinto priest, but he later repudiated this subterfuge, and his beliefs and practices bore little resemblance to Shinto. Bunji's closest disciple, Satō Norio (1856–1942), defied Bunji's protests and became a National Instructor in 1880, preaching throughout Okayama and Hiroshima, using the opportunity to bind Konkōkyō churches more closely to the headquarters. Satō thus aligned Konkōkyō with Shinto, and some 222 Konkōkyō ministers became National Instructors.[89]

The second major category, early Meiji Shinto sects, designates organizations that attempted to perpetuate the ideas of the Great Promulgation Campaign. The 1882 prohibition produced a legal distinction between the shrine priests and those who proselytize (the Instructors). In the bureaucratic terminology of the day, all the proselytizers were lumped together as "Shinto sects" (*kyōha Shintō*), religious organizations distinct from the shrines.[90] These organizations were mainly established by former samurai committed to Restoration Shinto thought, who built churches where they preached as National Instructors. They are more accurately viewed as "organizers" than as "founders."[91]

Among the early Meiji Shinto sects, we can discern three subcategories. The first is composed of those led by former samurai with little prior grounding in popular religious practices (Taiseikyō, Shintō Shūseiha, Shinshūkyō, and Shintō Taikyō). They lacked doctrines distinct from the Campaign. Taiseikyō and Shintō Taikyō acted as umbrella organizations providing legal protections to disparate smaller organizations—even the Buddhist healing group Renmonkyō—that had not yet gained official recognition.

The second subcategory is formed by those groups based on earlier pilgrimage associations of sacred mountains (Fusōkyō, Jikkōkyō, Ontakekyō). Fusōkyō and Jikkōkyō represented the "rebranding" and unification of various pilgrimage associations linked to Mt. Fuji, while Ontakekyō represented a similar unification and renaming of those affiliated with Mt. Ontake.

The third subcategory is composed of groups based on earlier shrine pilgrimage associations (Jingūkyōkai, Izumo Ōyashirokyō). As discussed above, Jingūkyōkai represented a renaming and unification of earlier pilgrimage associations linked to the Ise Shrines, while Taishakyō represented a similar transformation for associations linked to the Izumo Shrine.

The Shrine Priesthood in the Early Meiji Period

The shrine priesthood in the early Meiji period was composed of five main groups. First, were the Tokyo administrators of Shinto affairs, whom John Breen has described as "ideologues" seeking to enact an ideal of *saisei itchi* in which shrines would be public facilities engaged mainly in performing state rites, unifying the populace in support of the government.[92] Second, high-ranking figures of the Yoshida and Shirakawa Houses maintained important roles in imperial ritual. Third, priestly lineages of the National and Imperial Shrines usually managed to continue controlling those shrines and play important roles in local administration of shrine affairs. Fourth, local appointees to the priesthood—often former samurai—were chosen on the basis of local administrative needs, or the men themselves chose the priesthood as a supplementary or post-retirement occupation. Fifth, a number of "recycled religionists" entered the priesthood, persons whose religious allegiances, beliefs, and practices originated elsewhere: in Buddhism, the cult of sacred mountains, pilgrimage associations, and the new religious movements. These people became priests either because they were forced out of their former religious associations (*yamabushi, oshi,* and some Buddhist priests) or because certification as a shrine priest enabled them to practice their original religion without fear of persecution (ministers of the new religions).[93]

These five clusters were heterogeneous and overlapped. They were linked to central and local governments in a variety of ways. The nature of their religious experience and commitment varied widely. They were an uneasy coalition, united more by shared dislikes than positive aims: they disliked Buddhism and Christianity and believed that government did not support the shrines enough to make *saisei itchi* a reality. The forces drawing them together were counterbalanced by divisive attachments to specific shrines, birthplace, and varied doctrines.[94] Table 12.3 sets out the number of shrine priests in the early and mid-Meiji period.

Table 12.3 **Number of Shrines and Shrine Priests, 1868–1890**

Year	*"Official Shrines"* (Kansha)	*"Ordinary Shrines"* (Minsha)	*Total Number of Shrines*	*No.* Kansha *Priests*	*No.* Minsha *Priests*	*Total Number of Priests*
1868	–	–	74,642	–	–	–
1871	97	–	–	–	–	–
1873	–	–	123,705	–	–	–
1881	123	187,233	187,356	641	13,959	14,600
1885	151	192,024	192,175	881	13,731	14,612
1890	162	193,079	193,241	473	14,183	14,656

NB: The figures presented here do not include overseas shrines.

Sources: Umeda Yoshihiko, "Jinja seido enkakushi." In *Meiji ishin Shintō hyakunenshi*, vol. 1, edited by Shintō Bunkakai (Tokyo: Shintō Bunkakai, 1966), 227; Umeda Yoshihiko, *Nihon shūkyō seidoshi* (Tokyo: Tōsen shuppan, 1971), 3:38; Sonoda Minoru and Hashimoto Masanori, eds. *Shintōshi daijiten* (Tokyo: Yoshikawa kōbunkan, 2004), 1201–2.

The priesthood no longer always held the decisive voice in shrine management. When the shrines were forced to relinquish their land in 1868, they lost their main source of income and had to turn to the populace for support. The people who were registered as parishioners of the shrine came to be seen as responsible for keeping it in good repair and funding its main observances. As shrine parishioners shouldered the burden of supporting shrines, they gained a say in the way shrines operated. As of 1881, all shrines and temples were legally required to appoint a minimum of three stewards (*sōdai*) to assist the priest in the management of the institution's income and assets. The stewards signed all official documents and were supposed to be chosen from among public-spirited men of sufficient wealth to contribute financially to the institution's upkeep. The official shrines were not required to appoint stewards, but many did so. Stewards might number over a hundred at larger shrines. To be chosen was an honor.[95]

The diary of Tanaka Sen'ya (1826–1898) illustrates the life of a rural shrine priest in the Meiji period. Born in the Chichibu area of Saitama, Tanaka was in his late forties when the town mayor urged him to become certified as a shrine priest and take over the Muku Shrine. Tanaka had been active in shrine and temple affairs, had made pilgrimages to Kannon temples and to the Ise Shrines, and participated in various confraternities. He had a good living from his land and a small-scale money-lending business. People trusted him to keep money on deposit for them before the development of rural banking. Financial security was not an issue in his decision to become a shrine priest. Everyone understood that no one could make a living as a priest of a small village shrine.[96]

Tanaka was not a bureaucrat following orders from Tokyo but instead a dedicated and engaged resident of a small town, who became a priest in a spirit of public service. He did not change overnight as a result of the government's decree for separating worship of Kami and Buddhas. With no apparent sense of contradiction, he composed calligraphic scrolls for shrine parishioners that invoked the Buddhist deity Jizō. Far from indoctrinating the populace with Campaign rhetoric, he incorporated the worship of a local dog spirit into his shrine. He performed *kitō* for all manner of this-worldly benefits, such as making rain, stopping sleet, and protecting silkworms. He performed thirty-eight fox-spirit exorcisms, in spite of repeated prefectural and central prohibitions against exorcism. He performed many funerals and decried the government's 1882 prohibition on shrine priests' involvement with death rites.[97]

The example of Tanaka Sen'ya suggests that popular religious life was not transformed overnight in response to the rhetoric of administrators that shrines existed to enact "the nation's rites and creed." Instead, shrine life in rural communities developed in accord with local social dynamics and religious traditions. Various new shrine support groups were formed, some from occupational groups like sake brewers, silk producers, and carpenters. Their members gained access to roles previously monopolized by priests and the early-modern functionaries like *kagi-tori*, and the like, including permission to carry the portable shrines (*mikoshi*) paraded at shrine festivals. Local towns encouraged the expansion of shrine festivals to promote an image of communal vitality.[98]

Creating New Shrines

The construction of new shrines was a central feature of the meaning of "state management" for modern Shinto. Between 1868 and 1945, some 237 shrines were built with government assistance, not counting the overseas shrines to be discussed in the next chapter. Each one was a separate project in which residents of a particular area formed a partnership with government. Generally, the national and prefectural governments offered some level of support for the initial construction, but it was the local communities that raised the bulk of the necessary funds and bore the burden of maintaining these shrines, along with pre-existing ones.

According to Shinto historian Okada Yoneo, the new shrines were built to express the spirit of the restoration, to give substance to the idea of a nation centered on an emperor ruling directly over his people. The Kami of these shrines included former emperors, historic military leaders, loyalists of the restoration, the ancestors of domains that had fought on the imperial side, pioneers of newly settled areas like Hokkaidō, meritorious persons who had contributed significantly to society, and the war dead. New shrines were also built for the worship of Amaterasu and the mythical Emperor Jinmu. Shrines for Amaterasu, those for the restoration's war dead, deified domain ancestors, and those for pioneers were the most numerous.[99]

As part of the Ise reforms, Urata Nagatami helped establish some seventy prefectural branches of the Ise Shrines, known as the Daijingū or Kōtai Jingū of a locale.[100] Some Daijingū were entirely new, while others resulted from renaming existing shrines, and some were simply small spaces marked off in or near the precincts of a shrine and titled "places for worship from afar" (*yōhaisho*).[101] These new facilities linked provincial shrines to Ise, giving substance to the idea that Ise was the center of Shinto. The placement of some of them at port cities (Nagasaki, Kobe, Yokohama, and Niigata, for example) positioned the shrines to ward off foreign spiritual influence. These shrines also frequently played host to Jingūkyōkai.[102]

Minatogawa Shrine

Kusunoki Masashige (1294–1336) was a warrior of the Kenmu Restoration (1333–1336), Emperor Godaigo's quixotic attempt to overthrow the Ashikaga shogunate and return to direct imperial rule. Obeying Godaigo's order to make a doomed last stand, Kusunoki led the imperial troops at the Battle of Minatogawa (1336, near present-day Kobe) and died by his own hand. Fifteen members of his family followed him in death. Kusunoki's story was dramatized in literature and on the stage, elevating him to the status of a culture hero who epitomized loyalism, the nobility of self-sacrifice for the emperor. At the end of the Edo period, several domains held memorial ceremonies in his honor.[103] The idea to build a shrine where Kusunoki would be deified as a Kami arose with the man who would become the first Head Priest of the Minatogawa Shrine, Orita Toshihide (1825–1897), a Satsuma samurai. He had set up informal memorials for Kusunoki in Kyoto and Edo, where he performed commemorative ceremonies. He gained the imperial court's permission to establish a shrine, and as this plan progressed from 1868 to 1872, Orita inspired Fukuba Bisei, Kamei Koremi, and other officials of the Meiji government to lend their support to the project. The imperial court dedicated 4,000 yen, and the royal imprimatur spurred domains in Owari, Kaga, and Okayama to dedicate a further 2,000 yen plus shrine mirrors, stone basins where visitors might purify their hands and mouths, and lumber. Groups of villages in the shrine's vicinity gave land and construction stone. The largest share of the donations came from private persons, nearly four times the combined total from the court and the domains. In fact, donations raised exceeded the needed funds (23,860.136 yen). Public funding, funneled through the Ministry of Finance, amounted to only 119.382 yen, a mere 5 percent of the total and was limited to the 1872 installation ceremony (*chinzasai*).[104]

The case of Minatogawa Shrine exemplifies significant aspects of new shrine construction after 1868. Many new shrines adopted deified loyalists as their Kami, and Minatogawa was the preeminent example, becoming the first Special Shrine (Bekkaku Kanpeisha). Kusunoki's towering example had such inspirational potential that his story was incorporated into school curricula. Apotheosizing loyalists as Kami projected an image of shrines as places to express reverence for the emperor.[105]

Minatogawa Jinja arose from a partnership of government and local people. Government funding defined a shrine as having public status and brought it under state management. In this case, funding from the national government was very little, but any amount was sufficient to provide official authorization. From 1868 to 1945, regional funding typically far outstripped shrines' national level funding, meaning that local people bore the greater burden for shrines' upkeep. A further implication is that research in this area cannot rest solely on national-level data. (See Figure 12.3.)

The post-Restoration creation of shrines was fundamentally a new development, and established new relations among the state, religion, and society. Local participation was a key factor in securing the necessary land and raising the funds needed. Local notables would make large contributions, while others were assessed through taxation. People living on land allocated to shrines could be forced to relocate—a serious hardship—but business opportunities abounded. A large shrine produced employment in construction, interior decorating, landscaping, and related work. Participation in a government project created chances for businessmen to make connections with government officials beyond the local level. After completion, a

Figure 12.3 The Minatogawa Shrine. Source: Courtesy of the author.

new shrine became a symbol of the community. The businessmen who had contributed would become prime candidates to be appointed as shrine stewards. Large wooden walls listing the contributors and the amount of their donations were (and are) erected in shrines, making clear to all the hierarchy of the shrine's strongest supporters. On the occasion of shrine festivals, the stewards would be singled out, seated in the worship hall (closest to the Kami), invited to banquets, and generally given VIP treatment. Others would naturally regard them as meritorious examples of generosity and competence, as contributing to raising the community's reputation. Thus these building projects advertised the kind of man to admire and emulate, while the shrines themselves projected an image of community well integrated into national values, identity, and purpose.

New Shrines for Newly Settled Territory: The Shrines of Hokkaidō

While government policies could encounter opposition where prior religious commitments were strong, as in the case in the Echizen Uprising to Uphold the Dharma, Hokkaidō was closer to a blank slate where shrine construction was concerned. Here, the interests of post-Meiji settlers in establishing shrines as communal centers dovetailed smoothly with government initiatives to develop the territory and unify the people through shrine worship. Until the Meiji period, indigenous people called the Ainu composed the main population of Hokkaidō. Most of Hokkaidō's pre-Meiji shrines were located in and around Hakodate (see Map 12.1).[106] The Matsumae clan led early campaigns to push the Ainu into the interior and constructed shrines

Map 12.1 The Prefectures of Contemporary Japan. Source: Created by C. Scott Walker of the Harvard Map Collection.

in their military outposts, usually dedicated to Hachiman. These shrines later took on the character of tutelary shrines for settlers.[107] By 1718 there were 140 shrines, mostly on the coast, mainly focused on Kami linked to particular occupations. Inari shrines (agriculture, forestry, commerce in general) were the most numerous, and there were many shrines devoted to water deities like Konpira, Itsukushima, Funadama, and Sumiyoshi (fishing, shipping).[108]

The Matsumae domain formed the "Justice Corps" (Seigitai) to enact the separation of Kami from Buddhas. At that time, many shrines with Buddhist-influenced deities were destroyed or their deities changed. The Council of Divinities mandated that many of the remaining shrines should worship a group of deities that it had composed, called the Three Pioneer Deities (Kaitaku Sanjin), namely, Ōkunitama, Sukunabiko, and Ōnamuchi. Because there was little preexisting popular veneration for any of the three, there was little basis to object to this bland collectivity.[109] Settler-soldiers called Tonden-hei, who were mainly engaged in agriculture but also used as soldiers during times of war, had fought on the imperial side in the Boshin and Seinan Wars.[110] Those who died were deified and enshrined at the Hakodate Nation-Protecting Shrine (Hakodate Gokoku Jinja), which has a graveyard of some fifty settler-soldiers, separated from the main shrine precincts by a stone fence.[111]

Sapporo emerged as the island's main city, and the center of shrine life shifted there. The Hokkaidō Shrine (Hokkaidō Jinja, later, Hokkaidō Jingū), founded in 1871, began as a small shrine but by 1899, had become unquestionably the island's largest and most splendid shrine. It was the island's only Imperial Shrine, Major Grade (Kanpei Taisha, elevated to that status in 1899). Its Kami were the Three Pioneer Deities.[112]

Other major shrines of Sapporo founded in the Meiji period are mainly devoted to memorializing the pioneers and war dead of the area. The Sapporo Nation-Protecting Shrine (Sapporo Gokoku Jinja, founded 1879) originally enshrined Tonden troops killed in the Seinan War. It later added the war dead from Sapporo killed in Japan's subsequent wars, for a total of 25,518 Kami as of 2009. Each conflict is commemorated with a separate memorial. The prefecture promoted Shinto funerals for settlers and the Tonden troops; the Sapporo All-Spirits Shrine (Sapporo Sōreisha) was established as a Shinto funeral facility, combined with an ossuary.[113]

Over the years 1873 to 1883, the central government allocated an annual average of about 2,500 yen for shrines in Hokkaidō. Although statistics for regional and local governments' appropriations for shrines are not available until the early twentieth century, we may assume that this was a small fraction of the necessary funds, and that local people contributed much more than that in order to construct the island's shrines.[114] However small, an appropriation from the national budget was necessary, in order to give shrines a "public" status and uphold their raison d'être of *kokka no sōshi*.

However, not all Hokkaidō shrines were brought into the government ranking system. As later settlers moved to Hokkaidō from elsewhere, new residents set up informal shrines, usually beginning by enshrining the Kami of their original communities. Sometimes they added Amaterasu or a "divided spirit" (*bunrei*) from the Hokkaidō Jinja. These informal shrines were called "cut-bundle" shrines (*kirikabu jinja*), based on their use of bundles of tied rushes or grass (*kirikabu*), on which Kami name(s) had been written in ink, as symbols of the Kami. They had no formally consecrated object of worship, only this makeshift substitute. As of 1898, forty-three of Hokkaidō's shrines were of this type.

Memorializing the war dead of the imperial forces and the island's settlers was at the center of Meiji-period Hokkaidō shrines. The Jingikan-created Three Pioneer Deities supplanted the tutelary and occupational basis of earlier shrines, giving them a unified focus. Hokkaidō shrines thus came under heavy and pervasive state influence in the Meiji period, developing a strong emphasis on worship of the deified war dead. Government policy regarding Shinto had a freer hand here than perhaps anywhere else.

Creating New Kami: Gathering in the War Dead

In 1864 the Chōshū domain began establishing war memorial sites, literally, "spirit-calling places," (*shōkonjō*), reaching a total of twenty-three by 1870. Other domains followed suit, for a national total of 105. In 1868, military personnel killed on the imperial side going back to 1853 were divinized at a memorial in the Higashiyama district of Kyoto. In addition, various domains built their own war memorials in the district that were later merged with the Higashiyama "Nation-Protecting Shrine" (Gokoku Jinja). In 1869 came the establishment of Tokyo Spirit-Calling Shrine (Tokyo Shōkonsha, later renamed Yasukuni Jinja), enshrining 3,588 military dead.[115]

"Spirit calling" is based on the idea that the soul leaves the body at death, and that because it requires offerings, it remains for a time within reach of human agency. A priest "calls" the spirits to a place where they receive offerings and praise. Because the newly dead, especially those who perished violently, are tainted by the pollution of death, it is not appropriate that they be "called" directly into a shrine, whose consecrated object of worship would become polluted. Therefore, early maps showing the layout of Yasukuni Shrine incorporate a "spirit-calling garden" (*shōkontei*) adjacent to but clearly separated from the main shrine. The terminological change from *shōkonjō* to *shōkonsha*, signaled a change in conceptualization of war memorials from a "spirit-calling place" to a "spirit-calling *shrine*." Emperor Meiji visited the shrine seven times to pay tribute to the fallen in person. The Taishō emperor visited twice, and the Shōwa emperor visited twenty times up to the defeat in 1945. On each occasion, the emperor personally paid reverence by holding an offering (a sprig from a *sakaki* tree), which a priest subsequently placed on the altar, according Yasukuni a unique status.[116]

Figure 12.4 The Grand Festival at Yasukuni Shrine. Shinohara Kiyooki, Japanese, active 1895. Publisher: Takekawa Seikichi (Sawamuraya Seikichi), Japanese *The Grand Festival at Yasukuni Shrine (Yasukuni jinja daisai no zu)*. Japanese, Meiji era, 1895 (Meiji 28), printed December 2, published December 5. Woodblock print (nishiki-e); ink and color on paper, vertical ōban triptych; 35.7 × 71.5 cm (14 1/16 × 28 1/8 in.). Source: Museum of Fine Arts, Boston, Jean S. and Frederic A. Sharf Collection 2000.513a–c. Photograph © 2016, Museum of Fine Arts, Boston.

In 1875, the Tokyo Shōkonsha was elevated further by symbolically gathering into it all the war dead from all the other war memorial shrines, a total of 10,880. This did not mean that the other shrines were abolished, but that the same people were now honored in at least two places. In 1879, the Tokyo Shōkonsha was officially renamed Yasukuni Shrine. Its objects of worship were a sword, a mirror, and a register (*reijibo*) of the military dead recognized as Kami.[117] In 1882, the military museum of the Yasukuni Shrine, called Yūshūkan, was established, and the shrine was placed under the administration of the Army and Navy rather than the Home Ministry, which administered the other shrines. Thus from its beginnings in 1869 until the early 1880s, Yasukuni gradually emerged as the central shrine for divinization and memorialization of the war dead in Shinto form. Contemporary illustrations of the shrine stressed its military character, as seen in Figure 12.4.[118]

Yasukuni developed a ritual procedure to overcome the issue of death pollution. The Ministries of Army and Navy would forward the names of those to be enshrined; shrine priests would enter the names in the register, to be approved by the imperial house. Subsequently the priests would ritually transform the spirits into Kami and merge them into the consecrated sword. At that point, a spirit became part of the collectivity of Kami and had no further individual existence. These enshrined spirits are the shrine's Kami. Ceremonies adding new Kami were conducted at the Spring and Autumn Festivals.[119]

Yasukuni was one of twenty-eight designated "Special Shrines" (*bekkakusha*) dedicated to the worship of apotheosized people distinguished by their self-sacrifice for the throne. While the other Special Shrines, such as Minatogawa Shrine, were dedicated to the worship of individual loyalists from the past, however, Yasukuni and the prefectural Nation-Protecting Shrines were for the worship of expanding numbers of divinized military personnel from the nineteenth and twentieth centuries.

Yasukuni Shrine's practice (seen also at the regional Nation-Protecting Shrines) of continually enshrining the war dead over a period of more than seventy years created a new kind of Kami. There had been many divinizations of living human beings and many instances of the worship of their spirits after death, but the idea of a shrine having as its deities a continually expanding list of the dead was new. Yasukuni enshrines around two and one-half million Kami as of 2015.

Annual Army Ministry allocations for Yasukuni remained constant from 1876 well into the twentieth century at 7,550 yen.[120] However, dependence on this unchanging source forced Yasukuni to supplement public funding by instituting remunerative commercial entertainments at its Annual Festivals (*sumō*, geisha dancing, horse racing, etc.) as well as by offering commodified "masses" for sub-groups of the war dead to their survivors, all of which contrasted oddly with the shrine's rationale of solemn commemoration of the war dead as an undivided collectivity.[121] The Ise Shrines received their own allocation of 27,113 yen from the Home Ministry beginning in 1894, which rose to 230,000 yen by 1922. The Meiji Shrine similarly dwarfed Yasukuni's funding. While Yasukuni enjoyed distinction among war memorial shrines, the gulf between it and imperially connected shrines was clearly reflected in economic terms.

"Serious Money": Shrine Funding in Early Meiji

Records of public funding for shrines before 1900 are scarce but sufficient to provide some unexpected findings. During the years 1873 to 1876, prefectural governments collected a basic tax called *minhi*, from which they funded their appropriations for education, medical facilities, roads and other infrastructure maintenance, disaster relief, shrines, and many other items. Using *minhi* records, we can calculate the portion of tax revenue devoted to shrines and compare that to other categories of public funding. Also, from 1875 the national government issued statistics on its appropriations for shrines, allowing us to calculate shrines' total public funding from both levels of government.[122] See Table 12.4.

Prefectures mainly funded the National Shrines (Kokuheisha) and those below at first, while the central government funded the Imperial and Special Shrines. The prefectures provided funding for maintenance, ceremonies, and salaries, of which ceremonial regularly garnered the largest amount, followed by maintenance, with priestly salaries attracting only about half the funds for maintenance. Ceremonial expenses focused on state-mandated rites, which mirrored rituals performed in the palace or at the Ise Shrines, and a shrine's Annual Festival. It is likely

Table 12.4 **All Prefectures' and National Government Shrine Funding, with Comparison to Hospital Expenses, 1873–1876, in Yen**

Year	*Total Shrine Funding, National and All Prefectures*	*National Government's Shrine Funding, Based on* Nihon Teikoku Tōkei Nenkan.	*All Prefectures' Total Shrine Funding, Based on* Nihon fuken minpi hyō: Meiji 6–9 nen.			*All Prefectures' Total Minpi Tax Revenue*	*All Prefectures' Shrine Funding as % of Total Minpi Revenue*	*Annual Total Spent by All Prefectures on Hospitals*	*Hospital Funding as % of Total Minpi Revenue*	*Total Shrine Funding Divided by Hospital Funding*
1873 M6	NA	NA	455,187.92			16,238,455.22	2.803	60,668.63	0.373	7.503
				Maintenance	155,054.37					
				Ceremonial	215,023.28					
			plus grain–>	Salaries	85,110.27					
1874 M7	NA	NA	494,390.81			20,394,641.02	2.424	53,514.38	0.262	9.238
				Maintenance	181,040.49					
				Ceremonial	231,618.37					
				Salaries	81,731.95					
1875 M8	696,055.34	210,507.00	485,548.34			21,399,218.57	2.269	42,466.91	0.198	11.434
				Maintenance	179,309.66					
				Ceremonial	220,864.07					
				Salaries	85,374.61					
1876 M9	653,180.77	198,261.00	454,919.77			22,408,552.48	2.031	13,815.13	0.061	32.929
				Maintenance	172,951.74					
				Ceremonial	197,220.61					
				Salaries	84,747.42					
Average	674,618.05	204,384.00	472,511.71				2.382		0.224	15.276

Note: Maintenance is for National Shrines and those of lower rank. Salaries are for priests at Prefectural Shrines and lower-ranked shrines. The column at the far right shows that on average the amount spent annually by the prefectures on shrines was 15 times the amount spent on hospitals.

that these expenses included not only the costs a shrine incurred in the actual performance of ritual, but also the *naorai*, a post-ceremony party for visiting dignitaries, officials, and noteworthy local supporters. In 1873, priests' salaries were allocated in a combination of cash and grain (rice, wheat, and millet), changing after that to cash only.[123] Over these years, prefectural funding rose in 1874 and 1875, only to fall below the 1873 level in 1876.[124] All prefectures' average annual shrine funding from 1873 to 1876 was slightly more than the 1873 total for police salaries, and equivalent to twenty times the amount required to construct the Minatogawa Shrine. Shrine funding on average consumed 2.38 percent of the prefectures' total *minhi* revenue, but that figure could vary from less than one percent (Tokyo) to 4.1 percent (Nara). Another measure of the value attributed to shrines in prefectural budgets emerges from a comparison with appropriations for hospitals. All prefectures' shrine allocations in these years averaged fifteen times the amount spent on hospitals. When we compare the total national and prefectural levels of shrine funding, we find that the prefectures were providing more than twice the national amount. This means that the major weight of supporting shrines fell on the prefectures, with the further implication that when we seek to quantify the meaning of "state management" of shrines, using regional as well as national-level data is crucial. It would appear that it was never the intention of the central government to provide the total funding necessary to turn shrines into showplaces of *kokka no sōshi*. Instead, shrine parishioners were expected to bear that burden, an expectation that became clearer when the Shrine Bureau took over state management of shrines in 1900. See Map 12.1 for the modern prefectures.

The Home Ministry's Shrine Bureau

The Home Ministry's (Naimushō, or Ministry of Home Affairs) responsibilities encompassed police and law enforcement, construction and public works, public health, social welfare, disaster relief programs, repair and maintenance of the ports, and publications, as well as shrines. From 1877 to 1900, temple and shrine affairs had been administered together within its Bureau of Shrines and Temples (Shajikyoku). After promulgation of the Meiji constitution (1889), shrine administration had to conform to article 28:

> Japanese subjects shall, within limits not prejudicial to peace and order, and not antagonistic to their duties as subjects, enjoy freedom of religious belief.

This clause granted religious freedom, to the extent that there was no interference with imperial subjects' duties to the state. The constitution was silent on the topic of separation of religion from state. This formulation left unresolved the issue of how religion would relate to Shinto. However, the drafters generally understood

Shinto as belonging to a different sphere than religion, a view stated most clearly by Yamagata Aritomo (1838–1922, who served twice as Prime Minister, as Minister of the Army, and other influential positions). In his 1879 draft for a constitution, Yamagata specified that

> worship at Shinto shrines is the symbolic [acknowledgement of] civic obligations and human virtues, and shall not be understood as a matter of religious belief.[125]

As a member of the *genrō*, the seven most powerful political leaders and advisers to the emperor, Yamagata's statement represented the position of the Japanese state. The statement is ideological in character, not managerial. Shinto was being positioned in relation to the state in a new way that transcends the idea of "state management" of shrines. A different kind of concept is needed to grasp the ideological character of Yamagata's intervention.

By the early 1890s, shrine priests were beginning to cultivate patrons among Diet members. Ōtsu Jun'ichirō (1857–1932), a politician and newspaperman from Ibaraki, became their champion for a separate bureaucratic unit for shrines.[126] Shrine priests were very dissatisfied with the Home Ministry's combining temples and shrines in a single agency and lobbied to establish a separate unit for shrine affairs, in order to clarify the public, nonreligious character of shrines summed up in the expression *kokka no sōshi*.[127]

A bill establishing a separate unit for shrine administration in the Home Ministry was passed twice but was only implemented after extensive lobbying. The Ministry resisted creating a special bureau, because there was no purely bureaucratic rationale justifying it. If it were only a question of managing shrines' appropriations, that could have been done by the Finance Ministry; likewise, the Construction wing of the Home Ministry could have built new shrines and handled repairs or expansion projects; recordkeeping could have been handled by any of several existing units. The Shrine Bureau was an anomaly as the Ministry's smallest unit, and its substance continued to be regarded as belonging more to the areas of religion or education, in spite of determined rhetoric asserting the nonreligiosity of shrines.[128] We will examine the Shrine Bureau's actual management of shrines in the next chapter.

Conclusion

State management elevated Shinto to the realm of "the public," and newly strengthened connections with the imperial institution clarified Shinto's embodiment of "the indigenous." The Shinto world responded enthusiastically to the separation order, serving as National Instructors, coordinating shrine ritual with palace rites, establishing churches as adjuncts to shrines, and creating shrine parishes. In these and other ways, Shinto partisans supported the new government and greatly enhanced their own status in the process. The desire to be part of the national project was ubiquitous and demonstrated with great dedication and self-sacrifice. The years from the Restoration to 1900 set Shinto on a new course, in which the priesthood was charged to uphold the state silently, by ritual, so as to align the people with the throne. Shinto's reorganization did not, however, come about solely as a result of bureaucratic edicts, but more importantly as a result of partnerships between government and society in building, maintaining, and promoting shrines.

Although the government's rhetoric of *kokka no sōshi* implied a commitment to a creed, the creedal aspect evaporated in the 1880s. The Pantheon Dispute glaringly revealed doctrine's potential to undermine unity, and the idea of Shinto as something different from religion took hold. "It was natural that religious creed, secondary anyway, would be pushed aside when national identity became established as fundamental and the need for justification diminished."[129] Historian of nationalism Liah Greenfeld might have written these words about Japan, though in fact she was describing what happened in England.

Shinto's independence from Buddhism came at the price of accepting state intervention in virtually every aspect of shrine operation. A standard blueprint gradually homogenized shrine architecture. Shrines were drawn into a single hierarchy with the Ise Grand Shrines at the top, ranked in a single system for the first time. Customary deities were abruptly ejected and new ones installed. The new gods reoriented shrines to focus on the nation through the choice of Kami derived from ancient myth, newly apotheosized imperial loyalists, and the divinized war dead. Shrine rites were standardized to revolve around the emperor's performance of Kami rituals in the palace. Receiving official "tribute" at these ceremonies created social capital for shrines but did not pay their bills. Statistics from the 1870s show, however, that the greater burden for Shinto's material support consistently fell on the regions.

The priests were ranked and briefly put on government salaries, but these ended after only a few years, leaving priests dependent on popular support, since their land had also been confiscated in whole or in part. The short-lived system of shrine registration enabled shrines to create parishes as an alternative economic base. The claim that the people were universally *ujiko,* with a duty to support the shrines opened new roles in shrine life to the populace. The new format for shrine management, in which stewards shared authority with priests, inevitably diluted priestly authority. On the other hand, parishes could be prevailed upon to repair and maintain shrines, but they might not leap to the task if they themselves were poor, if the priest was uninspiring, or unsympathetic with the parish's vision of how the shrine should be run. Meanwhile, commoditized ritual for individual patrons relating to their personal well-being was another form of income. These rites were entirely unrelated to *kokka no sōshi,* however, and muddied the rhetorical waters regarding Shinto's coveted public status.

The idea of Shinto as the forum for the populace to worship in unison to glorify the nation and its monarch became firmly entrenched. Partnerships between government and local communities created hundreds of new shrines and refashioned older ones. Shrines became emblematic of community pride in a new way. The dynamics of state management established from 1868 to 1900, and their consequences for shrine life, would determine Shinto's stance until the defeat in 1945. Nevertheless, while the state was clearly "managing" shrines, its relations with Shinto went well beyond that notion into the dimension of ideology. The next chapter examines how that dimension developed and questions whether the idea of State Shinto helps deepen our understanding.

13

Shinto and Imperial Japan

Introduction

This chapter examines Shinto in the Japanese empire from the final years of the nineteenth century through 1945. The term "State Shinto" has most frequently been applied to this period, but I believe that our understanding of Shinto will not advance if we use the term merely to mark off a period, as if "State Shinto" were an adjective describing everything about Shinto at the time. Nor is it appropriate to think of State Shinto as "the religion of the state," because Japan had rejected the idea of a state religion. The constitution had neither designated a state religion nor made any explicit provisions for Shinto, and the Shrine Bureau denied that Shinto had doctrines. In law, Japan was and is a secular state.

While the state played a defining role in establishing the legal provisions for all aspects of shrine administration, the bureaucrats were not all-powerful, nor were they alone in shaping Shinto's development. All manner of self-described "Shintoists" claimed to act in the name of Shinto for a variety of purposes. Shinto scholars disputed the bureaucrats' position that Shinto is not a religion, in order to promote "Shinto Studies" (*Shintōgaku*) as an essential component of "national morality" (*kokumin dōtoku*). Politicians and shrine priests pressured the bureaucrats to provide more public funding for Shinto, but the Shrine Bureau was the smallest unit of the Home Ministry and lacked the necessary clout until the 1920s. Even when the Bureau began to secure significant funds for the Imperial and National Shrines, however, there was no law ensuring regular funding for lower-ranking shrines, which made up the vast majority. The Bureau could not enable all shrines to fulfill their rationale as sites of the rites of the state (*kokka no sōshi*). The journals of shrine priests show clearly that many felt alienated from the state bureaucracy, sometimes opposed its projects, and saw it as obstructing their desire to lead the people in reverence for the Kami. Hierarchies of rank and funding produced stark divisions within the priesthood.

Tokyo bureaucrats and Shinto partisans of all kinds aimed to permeate the home and the schools with Shinto ceremony, producing frequent clashes over the issue of religious freedom. With encouragement from the Shrine Bureau, local officials, who were frequently active in local Shinto associations, pressured people to install *kamidana* and attend shrine ceremonies. These observances were presented as nonreligious in character, something that all Japanese should follow as a "natural" demonstration of their love of country and community. Those who declined were marked, their authenticity and loyalty as Japanese called into question. It was not the Tokyo bureaucrats who carried out this coercion, however, but local society and officialdom. In the twentieth century, shrine management, local government, and local business became overlapping groups, taking their cues from central bureaucrats in formulating ideological rationales. The Tokyo bureaucrats could encourage the local level, but they could not back up the local level if coercive measures were challenged.

The empire added another dimension. Japanese emigrants built settler shrines throughout the empire and in other places where they settled, such as Hawaii, Brazil, and areas under Japanese control that were not technically colonies, such as Manchuria. Colonial administrators built huge shrines as symbols of Japanese rule and as places where colonial subjects could learn to act, feel, and think as Japanese—that is, to assimilate. As in the promotion of shrine ceremonies in the inner territories, dissenters found their "Japanese-ness" questioned, and faced a variety of sanctions.

The complexity of twentieth-century Shinto, its mediation of state-authorized ideological projects, its expanded intellectual, political, and social influence, its permeation of the educational system, and the imbrication of shrine management with local government and business overwhelm the simple descriptive device of "state management of shrines." In order to isolate one aspect of Shinto's changed character in the twentieth century, I use the term *State Shinto* to identify Shinto mediation of state-sponsored ideological campaigns. This usage takes into account the history of debate around this term discussed in chapter 12, while establishing limits to prevent it becoming vague, totalizing, or a veneer for my own ideological commitments. When limited in this way, State Shinto can help us better understand significant aspects of Shinto's development in the imperial period.

State Shinto was not all there was to Shinto between 1900 and 1945. In significant ways, the Shinto-derived new religious movements remained at a remove. They were outside the framework of public funding, and while they frequently accepted and promoted the Shrine Bureau's objectives, they were not empowered to implement them beyond their own organizations, unless the ministers were also civil servants, local mayors, or education officials.

The construction of new shrines continued in partnership with government, but in the twentieth century the partners were not only local communities but also business interests and corporate sponsors. New shrines constructed in this era were massive projects on an unprecedented scale. These shrines could never have been built solely on the basis of available public funding or local community support. Shrines profited greatly by adopting bureaucratized corporate-management styles, and by attracting businessmen and business organizations into their own managing groups. The histories of the most prosperous shrines clearly show that their success rested on this kind of integration into the modern economy. In the terms adopted here, these factors of modern shrine life are not aspects of State Shinto.

A Changed Context

Japan was at war for almost half of the years from 1900 to 1945. Following the first Sino-Japanese War, Japan acquired Taiwan as an overseas territory, becoming an empire. Following that war, Japan adopted an attitude toward China much like that taken by Western powers toward Japan a few decades earlier. In the 1895 Treaty of Shimonoseki, Japan required China to recognize Korea's independence, relinquish territory, and pay massive reparations. A decade later, when Russia refused to suspend its occupation of Manchuria, Japan formed a pact with Britain and went to war against Russia, in 1904. Emerging victorious, Japan acquired Karafuto (the southern half of Sakhalin Island) and the Liaotung Peninsula, later renamed the Kwangtung Leased Territories. After World War I, a conflict in which Japan was mainly a bystander allied with Britain, Japan acquired a group of South Sea islands from Germany, called the Southern Sphere (Nan'yō). The combined population of these new territories numbered about twenty-two million people as of 1920, or around 40 percent of Japan's "inner territory," while the land acquired amounted to about three-quarters the area of its original land.[1]

Japan's acquisition of these new peoples and lands forced it to confront the question whether they were to be treated as colonies or assimilated as part of Japan proper, and what "Japan" should mean in terms of personal and national identity. The empire produced distinctions between the "inner territory" (*naichi*) and the "outer territories" (*gaichi*). Were people in the outer territories to be considered Japanese, and if so, how were they to be integrated into the fabric of Japanese society? These were urgent questions, given that the new populations had been conquered militarily and were not all resigned to their incorporation into the Japanese Empire. These questions also extended—if less urgently—to Hokkaidō and Okinawa, at the borders of the "inner territory."

Japan's transformation precipitated long-running debates about Shinto's roles in assimilating the newly conquered peoples. The Taiwan Shrine (Taiwan Jinja; see Figure 13.1), established in 1900, was the first of several shrines constructed by a colonial governor. The shrine priesthood had little say in the decisions to build this shrine or determine its deities. An Imperial Shrine, Major Grade (Kanpei Taisha), the Taiwan Shrine's Kami were chosen by the colonial governor and did not

Figure 13.1 Taiwan Shrine. Source: Reproduced by Permission of the Research Center for Nonwritten Cultural Materials, Kanagawa University.

include any deities who were native to Taiwan. The Home Ministry spent 350,000 yen to construct the shrine, considerably more than its total annual allocation for all the shrines in the inner territory. The expenditure attests to the value placed on this shrine as an essential element of Japanese rule, though what the Taiwanese were supposed to learn from or experience at the shrine was not yet clear.[2]

The Meiji constitution provided a touchstone for discussion of the public realm, but debate over its key concepts intensified in the twentieth century, as ongoing war and expansion necessitated a rethinking of the basic terms. Not purely a matter of cerebral cogitation, this rethinking was channeled through the ambitions and emotions of nationalism and "ethnic imagination" regarding the relation of the political nation (*kokumin*) to the "ethnic nation" (*minzoku*, i.e., Japanese ethnicity) and questions of "race" (*jinshu*) in discussion of colonial peoples. It was a given that the emperor was the linchpin holding everything together. Through the first half of the century, the emperor was increasingly surrounded with a numinous aura, which sometimes identified him with the *kokutai*. New observances at shrines and schools created and supported an attitude of reverence to the throne. The constitution specified the emperor's position in articles 1 and 3:

> Article 1: The Empire of Japan shall be reigned over and governed by a line of emperors unbroken for ages eternal.
> Article 3: The Emperor is sacred and inviolable.

The 1889 Imperial Household Law (*Kōshitsu tenpan*) gave legal status to the transmission of the regalia and Enthronement Rites (Daijōsai). The imperial house became a source of charity in society at large and a major benefactor to shrines.[3]

The public realm continued to be described in terms using the -*kō* element that had structured discussion of "the public" since the ancient period, albeit with a variety of changed meanings. Several terms for "society" emerged, including *kōkyō* (bearing nuances of the public good or shared public interest), *shakai* (the collective population), and *seken* (the "world" of human life). The idea of a "home place" (*kyōdo, furusato*) was central to popular understandings of society. The home place was stereotypically imagined as a hamlet surrounded by an expanse of rice fields, with a hamlet shrine. Through this connection with the sentimentally charged image of a home place, shrines came to be laden symbols of home, family, and community. Shrines came to bear this emotional weight as a complicated result stemming from lived experience, bureaucratic campaigns to transform shrines into such symbols, and priests' efforts to instill the associated feelings.[4]

Shinto's position was not inscribed in the constitution, however, nor was the idea of its nonreligious nature, nor the touchstone, *kokka no sōshi*. Its position was relatively undefined and thus remained a subject of debate. Bureaucratic usage consistently referred to "shrines" (*jinja*) not "Shinto," and the term *jinja* became the common usage, replacing a spectrum of earlier terms.[5] In fact, however, the bureaucratic focus on "shrines" rather than "Shinto" resulted from fear of contradicting the constitution's provisions for freedom of religious belief. Shrine Bureau officials could mandate that "shrines" should do thus and so, but they could not be seen to tell the people as a whole that they must observe "Shinto," at least not publicly, since that stance had no legal basis.

Kokugaku and the Kume Affair

Kokugaku remained a significant paradigm for the discussion of shrines and Shinto in some academic societies, but the adoption of Western historiographical methods undermined the authority of the ancient texts, especially *Kojiki* and *Nihon shoki*. In the 1880s a number of scholars began to construct new chronologies of Japanese history that exposed inaccuracies in these revered texts and cast doubt on the historicity of early emperors. It became plain that these works, especially their chapters dealing with the Age of the Gods, could not be regarded as history.[6] Kokugaku scholars of the Meiji period, such as Konakamura Kiyonori, had, however, premised their work on the assumption of textual inerrancy. Moreover, since Konakamura regarded Westernization as the herald of Japan's decline, the appearance of Western scholars of the ancient texts must have been repellent. Two British scholars were at work on English translations. Basil Hall Chamberlain (1850–1935) published his translation of *Kojiki* in 1882, while W. G. Aston was at work on a translation of *Nihon shoki* that was published in 1896.[7] Academic historians at the imperial university, Kume Kunitake (1839–1931) and Shigeno Yasutsugu (1827–1910), were even more viperous. Kume, who had been the Iwakura Mission's official chronicler, had been commissioned along with Shigeno to edit a new history of Japan, to be titled *Dainihon hennenshi,* which they proposed to compile *in Chinese* (*kanbun*). Shigeno and Kume regarded much of the lore surrounding national heroes like Yamato Takeru and Kusunoki Masashige as fictional. Shigeno in particular sparked such anger in this connection that he was branded "Dr. Obliterator" (*massatsu hakase*).[8]

The Kume Affair of 1892 brought this antagonism to a head. In a journal that was read by only a handful of academics, Kume claimed that Shinto is a vestigial remnant of an ancient cult of Heaven.[9] Adopting the widely accepted evolutionary paradigm, Kume wrote that Heaven worship originated in humanity's childhood. Ise, he wrote, was not originally for the worship of the imperial ancestors but was the center of this cult of Heaven. Shinto originated with purification ceremonies adopted by ancient governments, but it cannot meet the needs of modern society, he concluded.[10] The article would probably have shared the fate of much scholarly writing, gathering dust in the archives, had it not been republished in a popular journal.

In the context of contemporary debates on Shinto's religiosity, Shinto partisans understood Kume to be implying that Shinto is inferior to religion, less "evolved," representing a more primitive society and intellect. According to contemporary press accounts, a group of four "self-appointed Shintoists" (*jika Shintōka*), from a little-known private Shinto academy called Dōseikan, confronted Kume at his home on February 28, 1892, and harangued him for five heated hours, at the end of which Kume agreed to retract the article. The "Shintoists" found Kume's treatment of the Kami as imaginary fictions and his idea that Amaterasu was not the original Kami at Ise to be particularly objectionable. They accused him of lacking reverence for the imperial institution and of hiding behind his professorial appointment to spread perverted views. In the days following this confrontation, the "Shintoists" went directly to the Home Ministry, the Ministry of Education, and the Imperial Household Ministry to demand Kume's immediate dismissal. Kume lost his post on March 4, 1892, a mere four days after the confrontation.[11]

Historian Margaret Mehl has shown that, in fact, Kume's article was not the kind of scholarship in which he specialized, and that it had a number of undeniable failings. She finds it peculiar, however, that Kume was dismissed so rapidly, that the university failed to come to his defense, and that otherwise unknown "Shintoists" should wield such influence over three cabinet ministries. Miyachi Masato, a historian of modern Japanese religions and the "emperor system," particularly stresses the ties that must have existed between the bureaucrats and Shinto ideologues outside the priesthood to effect the firing of a professor of the imperial university in less than a week. Akazawa Shirō, historian of religion and government "moral suasion campaigns" (*kyōka undō*), writes that Shinto groups like Dōseikan, though small in number, had an unshakable basis of support among the governing class, because the ideology they represented was directly related to the legitimation of imperial rule. Mehl points to Konakamura's influence behind the scenes and views the affair as—in part—a manifestation of the Kokugaku scholars' displeasure.[12]

The Shinto partisans mobilized a major lobbying campaign; shrine priests' associations from twenty-one prefectures sent over sixty memoranda to the Imperial Household Ministry, demanding the criminalization of disrespect toward shrines, creation of a historiographical institute within the Imperial Household Ministry, and restitution of the Jingikan to prevent further outrages. They also demanded that Shigeno be fired and that the institute of historical studies at the university be abolished. It was closed in 1893, and Shigeno lost his position.[13] The Kume Affair erupted into a broad debate in civil society about Shinto. The partisans claiming to represent Shinto managed to secure state support by means that remain unclear, resulting in the suppression of academic freedom. But there was no state-sponsored ideological campaign mediated by Shinto, and hence the Kume Affair cannot be described as State Shinto.

Shinto and National Morality

"National morality" (*kokumin dōtoku*) provided the focus for thinking through Japan's ideals as a state and nation in the first two decades of the twentieth century. One of the most authoritative spokesmen was Inoue Tetsujirō, whose 1911 work, *Edited Textbook for Moral Training* (*Shinhen shūshin kyōkasho*), was commissioned by the Ministry of Education. He portrayed national morality as distinct from religion, "an expression of the [Japanese] folk spirit (*minzoku teki seishin*)," and the morality of the *kokumin*, posing the state as the arena in which self-realization would take place. As the individual seeks perfection by enacting a moral life, the state will also be perfected, he opined. Another goal was to suppress disorder and divergent ideologies that were at odds with state policy, especially socialism and communism. "Subjects must first of all submit to the commands of the state. The state possesses an absolute and unlimited authority over the subject, and the subject may not defy it, whatever the situation might be."[14]

Inoue's government sponsors feared the social disorder associated with political dissent. The Hibiya Riot of September 1905 provided an early example, when crowds rioted to protest the terms of the treaty ending the Russo-Japanese War. Although Japan had won the war, it not only received no reparations, but was forced to relinquish territory it had captured. This incident and the growing influence of leftist activism prompted the Boshin Rescript of 1908, which called upon shrines to assist the throne in unifying the people. In the circumstances, it was a call to resist leftist thought of all kinds. Here the state sought to instigate Shinto mediation of its anti-leftist ideology, though little immediate reaction seems to have occurred. The

High Treason Incident of 1910 originated with a plot to assassinate the emperor and developed into a convenient pretext to suppress leftists.[15]

Although Inoue had official backing, numerous thinkers vigorously opposed him. Responding to the ongoing environmental disasters at the Ashio Copper Mine in Tochigi Prefecture, socialist writer and editor Arahata Kanson (1887–1981) criticized the state for moral failure. Arahata accused the state of colluding with capitalists in what he called "a well-organized crime," the ruination of villages so that a corporation could profit. The socialist Buddhist priest Uchiyama Gudō (1874–1911, executed in the High Treason Incident) placed the blame specifically on "the emperor, the wealthy, the large landowners—they are all blood-sucking ticks." In *An Inquiry into the Good,* Nishida Kitarō pointed out that the entire enterprise of "national morality" could hardly be called "moral," since it was premised on blind obedience rather than reasoned choice. These writers opposed any view of national morality that would impute absolute authority to the state, showing that the state did not hold ideological hegemony.[16]

New Perspectives on Shinto's Religiosity

The Shrine Bureau intended that the shrines should align themselves with the semi-official line set out by Inoue Tetsujirō, but Inoue held other views on Shinto that did not conform to the government's position. In his 1912 *Outline of National Morality* (*Kokumin dōtoku gairon*), Inoue had stated, "There is no doubt that Shinto is a religion." This view was also accepted by his protégé Tanaka Yoshitō (1872–1946), one of three men who took up professorial positions in "Shinto Studies" (*Shintōgaku*) at Tokyo Imperial University in 1921. Another of the three, Katō Genchi (1873–1965), also promoted Shinto as a religion.[17]

The constitutional settlement establishing that Japan would be a secular nation had been in effect for over twenty years by 1910. On the assumption of Japan's secularism, some of the same people who had earlier argued for Shinto's nonreligious status now began to promote it as either a religion or as something analogous to the state religions of Western countries. The redoubtable Ōtsu Jun'ichirō made this argument in the Diet. The eminent Waseda University professor Aruga Nagao (1860–1921), who had been General Secretary of the Genrōin and a legal adviser to Yuan Shikai, argued that Shinto should play a role similar to that of the state religions of the West. Some shrine priests echoed these views, though they were a minority.[18]

A gap opened up between government rhetoric and the larger intellectual debate about Shinto. Shrine Bureau officials could only have been discomfited by this muddying of the waters. The bureau had been established precisely on the basis of Ōtsu's earlier impassioned arguments to the effect that Shinto was a nonreligious phenomenon and hence required its own administrative unit separate from religious affairs.

The view of Shinto as religious was welcome at the imperial university's Department of Religious Studies, where noted scholar and intellectual Anesaki Masaharu (1873–1949), another student of Inoue Tetsujirō, was in charge. Anesaki participated enthusiastically in a series of consultations for representatives of "the three religions" (*sankyō*), beginning with meetings in 1904 and continuing through the Conference on the Three Religions (Sankyō Kaidō) of 1912. The three religions were Buddhism, Christianity, and Shinto. But in conformity with the Shrine Bureau's position that shrines are not religious, Shinto was represented by the Shinto-derived new religious movements, not shrine priests. These conferences were initiated within the Home Ministry, stemming from bureaucrats' hopes that religion could be used to promote popular allegiance to government policies. The 1912 meeting's final resolution promised to "raise the morality of the people" and improve social mores.[19] In this instance, the Home Ministry seemed almost to be working against its own Shrine Bureau, whose rationale depended on the idea of Shinto being nonreligious.

In the midst of this swirling debate, Tanaka Yoshitō championed "Shinto Studies" (*Shintōgaku*), a term suggesting a branch of empirical research, which, however, as practiced by Tanaka and Katō, was theological and prescriptive. Tanaka saw Shinto as a "Great Way" that stemmed from the will of the Kami. Tanaka believed that Shinto's essence could be expressed in a variety of ways and regarded the Shinto-derived new religious movements very positively, writing about them extensively in works that are still quoted a century later.[20] Tanaka wrote in *Outline of Shinto* (*Shintō gairon*),

> I firmly hold that Shinto and shrines are religion. [The point is that] Buddhism and Christianity are merely religions and nothing more; but Shinto and shrines are politics, as well as morality, as well as a great religion.[21]

Tanaka saw Shinto as a superordinate entity transcending the other religions, and Japan as a place where people might believe in (ordinary) religions like Buddhism but would first and foremost—as an automatic consequence of being Japanese—believe in Shinto. Thus in a sense Buddhism and Christianity were *encompassed within* Shinto, not in conflict or competition with it. While this might sound quite ecumenical, that was not the approach Tanaka took: "If there are believers of particular creeds who cannot tolerate this, . . . they will have to emigrate to another country."[22]

Katō Genchi pioneered the study of Shinto within a comparative religions framework, writing over thirty books and many articles. He was very much engaged with such foreign scholars of Shinto as Basil Hall Chamberlain and Ernest Satow (1843–1929), a British diplomat and Japanologist, and hoped to ensure that a "correct" view of Shinto would be purveyed to the West.[23] Western theories of the evolution of religion that categorized Shinto with the religions of primitive peoples or as "animism" understandably offended Katō.[24] Emphasizing the commonalities between Shinto and other religions, Katō wrote of Shinto's development from a religion of nature worship to become a "civilizational creed" (*bunmeikyō*).[25] As of around 1919, he identified Shinto with "Mikadoism," emperor worship. In this passage Katō elevates emperor worship to a religious sentiment:

> Shinto...has culminated in Mikadoism or the worship of the Japanese Emperor as a divinity, during his lifetime as well as after his death.... Herein lies...the life of Shinto, inseparably connected with the national ideal of the Japanese people. Japanese patriotism...is the lofty self-denying enthusiastic sentiment of the Japanese people toward their august Ruler, believed to be something divine, rendering them capable of offering up anything and everything, all dearest to them, willingly, that is, of their own free will; of sacrificing not only their wealth or property, but their own life itself, for the sake of their divinely gracious sovereign.[26]

At this stage, however, "Shinto Studies" did not yet have a firm institutional footing. It was a mere research office (*kenkyūshitsu*) at the imperial university, competing with Religious Studies, which had departmental status and a highly respected leader in Anesaki. Tanaka and Katō had to prove that Shinto Studies addressed a subject at least as important as religion, one that could contribute to national development. They argued that Shinto had much to contribute to raising the level of morality, and that its religiosity was not an obstacle but an advantage.

We seem to have arrived at a very strange place, having begun the Meiji period with a rejection of the idea of Shinto's religiosity, only to find a few decades later Shinto's most prominent spokespersons promoting it as a kind of über-religion. The key to this puzzling situation lies in the changed meanings surrounding "religion" in the interval. As long as Japan was subject to the unequal treaties (that is, until the promulgation of the constitution), "religion" appeared to be a tool of imperialism by which Western powers hoped to subjugate Japan. But once the constitution had declared Japan a secular nation, and Japan had an empire of its own, it no longer needed to regard religion merely as a threat. A new scope opened up in which it was possible to consider positive roles for religion, including Shinto.

Shrines and the World of Business

The 1881 legal requirement, mentioned in chapter 12, that shrines be managed by a priest and at least three stewards, bore fruit in the expansion of shrine festivals, new shrine construction, and a growing tendency for affluent shrines to be managed like corporations. Festivals expanded as a consequence of shrines losing their land in the early Meiji period. They had no choice but to look to local people for economic support, starting with the people living on the recently relinquished land. The example of the Ōkunitama Shrine in Fuchū City, in western Tokyo Prefecture, illustrates a more general development.

When this shrine lost its land, worth five hundred *koku*, the largest bequest to any shrine in Musashi Province during the Edo period, it prevailed on the four wards (*chōnai*) of Fuchū to maintain the portable palanquins (*mikoshi*) used in the Annual Festival. Assuming this economic burden, the wards gained a say in how the shrine would conduct the festival. Meanwhile, Fuchū and the wards in charge of the *mikoshi* prospered through the introduction of sericulture, raising silkworms and producing thread for the textile industry. In the 1880s, they began to compete among themselves to refurbish and enlarge their *mikoshi* in splendid style, also vying to make the biggest drum, so that each *mikoshi* would be preceded in the festival procession by a drum so massive that it would be drawn along on a cart by dozens of uniformly costumed men. The drums became so large with each new refurbishing that several men could stand atop them as they moved along the procession's route. Creating these drums meant searching far and wide for the largest trees, engaging special carpenters to hollow them out, fit them with hides for the drum heads, manufacture the carts, and fashion decorated bats to beat them with, investing increasing amounts of money to outdo the neighboring wards.

Since the wards were official units in local government, they could also assess all residents for contributions to the festival, meaning that not all the "contributions" were truly voluntary. The wards also solicited donations in neighboring towns, where new support groups were established. As these outsiders' donations grew, outsiders also acquired a voice in shrine affairs. Members of the various groups contributing to the festival earned permission to carry the *mikoshi* and beat the drums, illustrating a general principle of festival management: authority and privilege follow monetary contribution.[27] (See chapter 15 for illustrations of the Annual Festival of the Ōkunitama Shrine.)

At the end of the nineteenth century, we find a novel pattern in new shrine construction, in which supporters of the proposed Heian Shrine (Heian Jingū) regarded their project in terms of a business proposition. Founded in 1898 to commemorate the 1100th anniversary of the founding of Kyoto as the nation's capital, Heian Jingū enshrined the deified Emperor Kanmu as its principal Kami. Kanmu was the emperor who had moved the court to Kyoto and was the last to rule directly, without a regent, until Emperor Meiji. Not merely a set of ritual halls, the Heian Shrine replicated the ancient capital Heiankyō, with numerous pavilions connected by corridors and an extensive garden, on an eighteen-acre plot.[28]

The Heian Shrine began entirely through the initiative of Kyoto business interests, with no significant government support and without priestly direction. The idea originated in 1893 with a group of businessmen who thought that such a shrine would help promote the city. Their idea for a new shrine near the city center, the old imperial palace, and the city government offices began in conjunction with plans for an industrial exhibition in 1895. The plan called for the exhibit site to be turned over to the shrine project when the exhibition closed.[29]

The businessmen expected that a shrine dedicated to the deified emperor who had founded the city would attract visitors and business, that its planned garden would become a famed beauty spot, that its monumental architecture would be a new city landmark, and that its extensive open space would allow for huge assemblies in the city center. Unfortunately, however, the costs were projected to exceed available funds. The Kyoto City Council was wary of adopting the project, and there was no hope of national funding. A variety of other business associations joined the project, but while expanding the fundraising network was helpful, their various perspectives threatened to vitiate the project as a whole. Luckily, when competitors for hosting the industrial exhibition emerged in Tokyo and Osaka, the disparate Kyoto business groups were able to unite to overcome the competition.

After the site of the industrial exhibition was successfully decided in favor of Kyoto, the Imperial Household Ministry committed 20,000 yen to the project. The association still needed more allies, but to collect funds beyond Kyoto, the project would have to be promoted as having wider relevance. And in order to do that, it would be necessary to aim for a larger-scale project, which, in turn, would cost more.

In the end, this project succeeded through the creation of links with other business groups in Nagoya, Nara, Hiroshima, and Kobe. The sponsors held lectures for religious leaders in these cities and persuaded their famous temples and shrines to help. The priests of a group of prominent Kyoto temples that included Higashi Honganji, Tōji, Myōshinji, and Daikakuji formed a supporting organization, promising to add suitable Buddhist rites to the shrine's opening ceremonies. With this widened base of support, the businessmen prevailed, and the shrine was constructed successfully.[30]

The example of the Heian Shrine illustrates the process that resulted in a fuller integration of shrines into the modern economy. It made sense for a shrine to involve affluent businessmen in its managing group. Business acumen, along with wealth, connections, and social influence, became important keys to shrine economics and to maintaining a positive social profile. It was natural for shrines to seek stewards with these qualities, and for such men to gravitate toward prosperous shrines as places to display their social position and acquire new connections. Thriving shrines became more affluent in proportion to their ability to attract prosperous businessmen who could establish corporate sponsorship for shrine initiatives. One result was the tendency for prosperous shrines to be managed like the corporations their stewards commanded.

The Shrine Bureau through the 1920s

The Shrine Bureau was responsible for all matters regarding shrines and their priests, including the Ise Grand Shrines, the Imperial and National Shrines, the Prefectural Shrines and lesser grades of shrines, and the Special Shrines. It did not, however, administer the Yasukuni Shrine, which was overseen by the Ministries of Army and Navy, nor the overseas shrines, which were administered by the separate colonial authorities. While the Shrine Bureau controlled the national budget for Ise and the Imperial and National Shrines, it did not provide funding to shrines below those levels.

The Shrine Bureau's main responsibilities were to secure annual appropriations for shrines in the national budget, to regulate the shrine priesthood and the operation of shrines, and to continue standardizing shrine ritual, based on the model of palace rites. The Bureau provided programs of professional development through the Kōten Kōkyūjo, forerunner of Kokugakuin University, and made appointments to priestly positions in the Imperial and National shrines. The journals of the National Association of Shrine Priests (*Zenkoku shinshokukai*), called *Reports of the National Association of Shrine Priests* (*Zenkoku shinshokukai kaihō*, 1899–1920, hereinafter *Reports*) and *The Journal of the Shrine Federation* (*Jinja kyōkai zasshi*, 1902–26, hereinafter *The Journal*) provided for communication between the Bureau and the priesthood.[31]

Shrine Bureau officials were university-educated men whose first allegiance was to the bureaucracy itself, not to Shinto. The Restoration generation was gone. Shrine Bureau officials were career civil servants in the Home Ministry. In their twenties and thirties, Home Ministry appointees would be posted for short periods to various bureaus, including the Shrine Bureau, to give them wide experience covering the spectrum of the ministry's work, while frequent rotations prevented them from becoming beholden to extramural partisans lobbying for better treatment.

A career bureaucrat led the Shrine Bureau as its Chief (kyokuchō), sometimes holding this office concurrently with other appointments. Over the years 1900 to 1940, nineteen men served as Shrine Bureau Chief (Jinjakyoku kyokuchō).[32] There was no set term of office, but, generally, they served for two or three years. In exceptional cases they might serve four or five years; the longest term was seven years (Inoue Tomoichi, who served from 1908 to 1915). These men did not come from a shrine background, nor, with one exception, were they chosen on the basis of any particular knowledge of Shinto.[33] Only one Shrine Bureau Chief, Mizuno Rentarō (who served as Shrine Bureau Chief from 1904 to 1908) retained lasting ties with the shrine world after leaving office.[34]

Of the nineteen Shrine Bureau Chiefs, nine had come from positions as Prefectural Governor (*ken chiji*), and ten were assigned to governorships after their appointments as Shrine Bureau Chief.[35] "Prefectural Governor" was the title given to the heads of the Home Ministry's prefectural offices, an appointment usually held by men in their mid-thirties. In postwar Japan, prefectural governors are elected, but before 1945 these posts were appointments. The tendency for Shrine Bureau Chiefs to be appointed from and to be sent back to Prefectural Governor posts suggests that the two positions were roughly on a par. There was some limited overlap between these posts in that the Prefectural Governor (or his deputy) was expected to attend the Kinensai, Niinamesai, and the Annual Festival of the Prefectural Shrine(s) where he served, and to act as the government's messenger in conveying the official tribute (*shinsen-heihaku*) for these rites.[36]

The fact that almost none of the Bureau Chiefs returned to shrine-related work suggests that the Bureau's work was not especially appealing. According to Iinuma Kazumi, the last Shrine Bureau Chief, the talented and ambitious regarded assignment to the Shrine Bureau as undesirable because the Bureau Chief had to study *norito* and other shrine-related matters that contributed nothing to professional advancement.[37]

Shrine Mergers

As a result of forcible mergers from 1906 to 1912, about 44 percent of the total number of shrines existing in 1906 disappeared.[38] Mergers resulted in the closure of more than half of the Village Shrines and Unranked Shrines, a total of more than 83,000 shrines. Mergers were carried out unevenly, however, so that only four percent of shrines in Aomori Prefecture were merged, while eighty-nine percent were merged in Mie Prefecture.

Shrine mergers were part of a government program launched after the Russo-Japanese War known as the Local Improvement Movement (*chihō kairyō undō*), which aimed to integrate small-scale farmers into the national economy, encourage thrift and savings, improve tax collection, and redistrict the land in a more rational way. Model villages were rewarded for success in implementing agricultural reforms, including planting rice in straight rows and the introduction of cash crops that diversified their sources of income.[39]

Shrine mergers fit into the Local Improvement Movement as a means to refocus the sentiments of the people on the new districts that replaced the hamlets. Mergers were also supposed to produce more local-level funding for shrines, inasmuch as each prefecture would be funding a reduced number of shrines. The funding issue had become quite serious, because the national government provided no funding for the *minsha* shrines, those below the ranks of the Imperial and National Shrines, meaning that there was no national funding for the vast majority of shrines and their priests. This situation made a mockery of the notion of *kokka no sōshi*, as the priesthood repeatedly pointed out. In the absence of law clearly mandating public support for all shrines, the prefectures and lower levels of government followed a patchwork of funding arrangements that left the *minsha* in distress. Ōtsu Jun'ichirō had submitted a draft bill to the Diet in 1901 to address the problem, but it failed to pass. The Finance Ministry opposed the national funding of these shrines, proposing instead that they become self-supporting. The *minsha* were already so impoverished, however, that this proposal was unfeasible. The prefectures could not manage the kind of appropriations the national government made, in the form of "shrine fees" (*jinja hi*). As a substitute for shrine fees, the Diet had passed a bill in 1902 authorizing the prefectures and municipalities to pay annual "offering fees" (*shinsen heihakuryō*), but for lack of funds the bill was not actually implemented until 1906. At that time, there were no less than 50,000 *minsha*, and even though the "offerings" were token amounts, they were "permitted" rather than required, and for many prefectures they presented an impossible financial burden. To narrow the terms of eligibility, the Shrine Bureau introduced criteria by which shrines would be designated as candidates for the offerings. To enable some kind of mechanism to fund all shrines, however meagerly, Ōtsu proposed mergers.[40]

The Shrine Bureau explained the idea of shrine mergers to the priesthood as aiming to raise the dignity of shrines by eliminating places that were not worthy of the name. In 1906, Mizuno Rentarō said:

> In some places people have tied a *shimenawa* (a rope festooned with paper streamers, used to demarcate a sacred place) around a roadside tree and called that a shrine, but [such places] become the lairs of foxes and badgers.... What is to become of [shrines] in such circumstances?"[41]

When shrines were merged, the object of worship of the shrine to be abolished was moved to the shrine that would remain, whereupon the shrine to be merged ceased to exist. The parishioners of the merged shrine were expected to move their affiliation to the remaining shrine. Buildings of the shrine to be abolished were frequently razed or turned over to some public use. If the shrine had a sacred grove, the trees might be felled for timber and the land plowed over, with no compensation paid. The remaining shrine might appropriate the merged shrine's land and other property, also without compensation.[42] Besides land and lumber, the confiscated property might include altar equipment, palanquins (*mikoshi*) and other gear used in festivals, as well as lion masks or other costumes used in folk rites connected with shrines. Local people would have accumulated these items over generations, handing down the traditions that went with them. Their loss typically occasioned incomprehension and grief. Priests charged with justifying these mergers were put in the impossible position of telling bewildered parishioners, "We had to destroy your shrine to order to dignify the remaining shrine."

Shrine mergers show that neither the priesthood nor society at large moved in lock step with the bureaucracy's policies on Shinto. Shrine priests repeatedly complained that they disagreed with the policy's rationale, that bureaucrats provided no assistance to carry it out, and that they were at a loss how to integrate new parishioners. The assertion that shrine mergers only decreased respect for Shinto was frequently heard. One priest related a story from Hiroshima: after a group of men conveyed the object of worship from a merged shrine into the one it had been merged with, they all died sudden and mysterious deaths. The local people were so outraged that they lobbied successfully to re-establish their original shrine.[43]

With the rate of shrines merged ranging from 4 percent to 89 percent, it is clear that some prefectures dragged their feet, while zealotry reigned elsewhere. The Shrine Bureau mobilized a campaign to bring reluctant priests to heel. Mizuno Rentarō, Shrine Bureau staff, and officials of Mie Prefecture, seat of the Ise Shrines, joined forces to make Mie the "model merger prefecture." They instituted a "shrine patrol" system, in which all priests were required to go to each shrine they served daily, stamping their seals to attest that they had visited each and every day. Since it was common then, as now, for a single village shrine priest to serve no fewer than ten shrines, this requirement was so onerous that it became a motivation for shrine priests to support mergers. Over the years 1904 to 1910, a total of 5,561 Mie shrines were merged, three times the national average.[44]

However, though there were many signs of unhappiness, long-lasting resistance was rare. Azegami Naoki has shown that where the Local Improvement Movement succeeded, shrine mergers tended to be accepted. Conversely, where the broader reforms did not enhance economic stability, villagers resisted shrine mergers. Likewise, the longer the agricultural transformation took to produce good results, the longer resistance to shrine mergers lasted. Overall, acceptance rather than resistance prevailed.[45] While mergers were a Shrine Bureau project, because the aim was not primarily ideological, it is not appropriate to regard the mergers as a case of State Shinto.

Shinto and Moral Suasion

The Shrine Bureau Chiefs' speeches consistently sought to mobilize the priests to quell social unrest and promote conformity to national morality. Chief Tsukamoto Seiji pressed this demand urgently in response to the 1918 Rice Riots, mass demonstrations that erupted when the price of rice skyrocketed after World War I. Direct ideological injunction to the shrine priesthood was part of larger government campaigns of "moral suasion" (*kyōka*). These movements aimed to awaken the people to Japan's changed situation, urging them to depress consumption, particularly spending on festivals and funerals, to demonstrate their patriotism by observing the national holidays and flying the flag. Japan had fallen into economic depression after World War I, and in response the government promoted thrift and saving. Numerous new social groups were founded to promote these campaigns, such as self-government councils (*jichikai*), military reservists', women's, youth, and heads-of-household associations (*koshu kai*).[46]

Government-sponsored campaigns to promote new customs fit in with moral suasion. The modern custom of visits to shrines and temples at New Years (*hatsumōde*) began that way, with officials advocating it in the 1880s. Prior to the modern period, people typically remained at home at New Year's to receive the Kami of the New Year (Toshigami), sometimes visiting a shrine located in an auspicious direction (*ehō mairi*). By the 1890s, a New Year's ceremony had become mandatory at government offices, the courts, police stations, post offices, and schools. Municipal governments also encouraged *hatsumōde*, and as of this writing it is the most widespread custom in Japan (see chapter 16).[47]

In 1890 a practice began of placing the imperial portrait, a copy of the Imperial Rescript on Education, and other symbols of the emperor in each school. As the items increased, the need to protect them led to the proliferation of fireproof structures in schoolyards called *hōanden*. Assemblies and school ceremonies were held before them, and pupils were required to bow before them when entering or leaving the schoolyard, as if they were shrines.[48]

After World War I, the slogan "Shrines at the Center" (*jinja chūshin shugi*) provided the umbrella under which municipalities and the associations active in moral suasion campaigns promoted a variety of shrine-related practices. The principal goals were to install a *kamidana* in every home, furnished with a talisman from the Ise Shrines and one from the local *ujigami* shrine, and to strengthen links between shrines and schools. In Wakayama Prefecture, the head-of-household associations had so proliferated that 77 percent of the municipalities had them; women's groups, youth groups, and reservists' associations were similarly pervasive. To clarify the goal of "Shrines at the Center," these associations frequently held their meetings in shrines. These groups pushed to universalize *kamidana* and Ise talismans, on the theory that "dangerous thought" would be prevented by that means. The promoters enjoyed significant successes. Some 78 percent of Iwate Prefecture households had *kamidana* by around 1919, and by 1921, 84 percent of Tokyo households had one. New shrine ceremonies were created to announce the decisions of self-government associations to the Kami (*jichi hōkokusai*) or to announce the names of new military draftees or those returning from military service. Local people were pressured to attend these ceremonies, which were presented as nonreligious in nature, following a 1913 declaration that shrines down to the District Shrine level represented *kokka no sōshi*.[49]

The Shrine Bureau encouraged the local level to pursue these campaigns, saying that it was "desirable" for all households to have *kamidana* and Ise talismans. Nevertheless, there was considerable resistance by Christians and followers of the Jōdo Shinshū school of Buddhism. Opposition regularly turned out the same way, whether in Shimane, Fukuoka, Shiga, Shizuoka, Gifu, or Hiroshima prefectures, to name only a few of the places where resistance occurred. A group of Christians or Jōdo Shinshū followers would object to coercion, saying that their rights to religious freedom were being violated. The Shrine Bureau would repeat its position that shrines are not religious, but there was no legal basis requiring anyone to own a *kamidana*. In the end, local-level officials or groups would be forced to back down. As opponents' grievances were aired, new criticism of coercive practices would typically emerge: objections against making shrine festivals into school holidays, critique of enshrining in Yasukuni Shrine people convicted of criminal wrongdoing in life, and criticism of expensive shrine-construction projects where local people would have to foot the bill. No doubt local officialdom lost faith in state bureaucracy when the Shrine Bureau failed to support them effectively in these confrontations. In other words, whereas the Shrine Bureau's original intention was to use the shrines to unite the people, the coercion became a source of alienation.[50]

While localized disputes regarding *kamidana* and shrine talismans regularly ended up affirming that no one was legally required to possess and worship these things, local education officials enjoyed considerably more latitude in enforcing policies requiring students to visit shrines. School visits to shrines became widespread beginning around 1900, as an element of school discipline, to augment the effects of ceremonial surrounding the Imperial Rescript on Education. 1929 was the rescript's fortieth anniversary, and across the country new policies were being enacted to enhance its impact. Schoolteachers, disappointed that solemn assemblies for recitation of the rescript did not automatically produce orderly classrooms, expected shrine priests to help in the goal of enforcing discipline while boosting pupils' respect for the *kokutai*. During shrine visits, priests instructed pupils on the proper etiquette for worshipping the Kami, and afterward pupils frequently performed volunteer labor, such as cleaning the grounds.[51]

The Mino Mission is a group of Christian churches in Gifu Prefecture established in 1918 by the American missionary Sadie Lea Weidner (1875–1939). In 1929, a primary school in Ōgaki City planned a visit to Tokiwa Shrine (a Prefectural Shrine), to worship at its Annual Festival. The parents of four female pupils, members of the Mino Mission, requested permission for their daughters to be excused, on grounds of a conflict with their Christian faith. Three of them were excused, but Weidner's adopted daughter was forced to go. When Weidner confronted the principal, he responded that (1) shrines are not religious, (2) that the purpose of shrine visits is to inculcate respect for the *kokutai*, and (3) that shrine visits are an essential disciplinary measure from which no pupil could be excused. The mothers who had refused permission were interrogated by the police, who repeatedly called them traitors. The confrontation was widely reported in the newspapers over a six-month period.[52] The Reservists' Association, the PTA, Gifu politicians, Buddhist priests, and Christians not affiliated with the Mino Mission waged a fiery denunciation campaign against the Mission for its supposed lack of patriotism.[53]

With the Manchurian Incident of 1931, a sense of national emergency stimulated a policy of sending sixth-grade pupils throughout the empire to the Ise Shrines. See Table 13.1.

Ise Shrine trips began in Gifu in 1932, where Fujiwara Takao (dates unknown) was Head of Gifu Prefectural Educational Affairs (Gifu-ken gakumuchō) and Head of the Gifu Prefectural Educational Association (Gifu ken kyōikukai kaichō). He was also the Head of the prefectural Divine Virtue Association (Shintokukai kaichō), the local shrine supporters' organization. Fujiwara instituted new school policies of

Table 13.1 **School Trips and Pupil Visits to the Ise Shrines, 1934–1942**

Year	*Schools*	*Pupils*
1934	13,098	1,062,127
1936	16,232	1,456,348
1938	20,238	1,923,414
1939	24,902	2,200,173
1942	19,530	1,969,823

Source: Gomazuru Hiroyuki et al., "Jingū hyakunen no ayumi," in *Meiji ishin Shintō hyakunenshi*, ed., Shintō bunkakai (Tokyo: Shintō bunkakai, 1966), 1:495.

daily ceremonies for obeisance before the *hōanden*, and one shrine visit each term. Matriculation and graduation ceremonies were to be held at shrines. There should be a ceremonial reading of the Imperial Rescript on Education during each period of morality instruction (*shūshin*, a required course). Shrine priests were to lecture regularly at schools and attend teachers' meetings. Fujiwara's successors held the same overlapping appointments as prefectural officials and Shinto association heads.[54]

When the Mino Mission refused to send children on a planned trip to the Ise Shrines in 1933, the matter was widely reported in the newspapers. Prefectural officials withdrew the permits the Mission needed to continue operating its churches. The school held public meetings to condemn the church and urge parents to withdraw children from a nursery school run by the Mission. The PTA condemned the church with a song titled, "Defend the Kokutai! Bury the Evil Religion!" The parents who had refused to send their children to Ise were severely pressured. The children were beaten by other pupils and expelled from school. A wider campaign of public denunciation ensued, with Katō Genchi thundering that Mino Mission would be the ruination of the country (*kokka no annei chitsujo o bōgai suru saidai no mono*).[55]

The Mino Mission incidents are clear cases of the operation of State Shinto in violation of religious freedom. The state's "Shrines at the Center" campaign placed shrines between the state and the populace, casting the priesthood as ideological instructors. Katō's remarks suggest that Shinto academics felt a need to speak out. Overlapping ties between the priesthood and educators facilitated communication between the two in the area of policies on shrine visits, school ceremonial, and morality instruction, as well as placing priests in a position to monitor teachers. Moral suasion groups, religionists, and local society pressured the dissenters. The ideology underlying these practices was intimately connected with Shinto and was implemented coercively, as police interrogators said repeatedly to the refusniks: "Any Japanese who won't worship at shrines is a traitor!" (*Nihonjin de sanpai senu to... iu yatsu wa hikokumin da*).[56]

New Developments in the Shinto-derived New Religious Movements

By 1884, the original thirteen groups designated as "Shinto sects" by the early Meiji government had been granted autonomy, except for Shinrikyō, Misogikyō, Konkōkyō, and Tenrikyō. Of the thirteen, Kurozumikyō expanded most conspicuously through the Meiji period, based on its enthusiastic participation in the Great Promulgation Campaign and a growing number of its ministers who earned reputations as trusted community leaders. A federation of the sects was established; it encouraged each organization to adopt shared practices, such as conducting *yōhai* ceremonies toward the palace on the eleventh of each month. All thirteen, as well as newer Shinto-derived organizations, benefited from universal literacy, allowing them to proselytize through print media, publish and distribute their founders' writings, and coordinate through newsletters. Likewise, the expansion of rail transport facilitated use of the lecture circuit to proselytize. In 1893 a representative of Jikkōkyō traveled to Chicago to address the World Parliament of Religion in English, exemplifying the growing tendency for sect leaders to receive higher education.[57]

The founders of Tenrikyō and Konkōkyō had resisted the transformation of their teachings into a form of Shinto, though that might have saved them from localized suppression. But the founders' deaths (Konkō Daijin in 1883 and Nakayama Miki in 1887) cleared the way for a generation of pragmatic leaders. Konkōkyō lobbied bureaucrats and in 1899 presented a huge "donation" of 10,000 yen, demonstrating its sincere desire for autonomy, which it was granted the next year. Tenrikyō's path was considerably more difficult, and Nakayama was jailed and interrogated numerous times, but the group finally gained independence in 1908.[58]

While many Japanese religious organizations proselytized in the colonies, Tenrikyō's overseas missions were particularly extensive, having begun in Korea in 1893. By 1910, when Korea was formally "annexed" to Japan, there were thirteen Tenrikyō churches claiming 3,200 Japanese members and 1,300 Korean members, increasing by 1918 to 14,772 Japanese and 7,764 Koreans, on the eve of the March 1, 1919 Independence Movement. Tenrikyō proselytizers in Korea at the time wrote of the shock they experienced upon learning that Korean converts, even those deeply attached to Tenrikyō, felt deep grievances against Japanese rule. This confrontation stimulated Tenrikyō to train Koreans themselves as missionaries and ministers, providing them with Japanese language instruction, opportunities to travel to Japan, and other measures aimed as integrating them more deeply into the organization. The Independence Movement also opened Tenrikyō's eyes to the poverty of the Korean people and spurred missionaries to adopt humane standards for their Korean tenant farmers. Tenrikyō's reaction contrasted starkly with that seen in shrine priests' *Reports,* which blamed the uprising on American Christian missionaries.[59]

A number of new Shinto-style religious organizations were founded, and among them Ōmoto stands out as particularly active and provocative in the first two decades of the twentieth century. Founded by Deguchi Nao (1837–1918), the group was little known beyond its headquarters in rural Kyoto Prefecture until Nao was joined by the charismatic Ueda Kisaburō, who took the name Deguchi Onisaburō (1871–1948) when he married one of Nao's daughters. In 1914, Onisaburō formed an urban proselytizing corps called the Spirit Army (Shinreigun), which missionized in the cities among civil servants, intellectuals, and students, including those at the naval academy (Kaigun Kikan Gakkō), where Asano Wasaburō (1874–1937) taught. This was the group's first attempt to expand beyond its rural base. Onisaburō recruited Asano, who was attracted by *chinkon kishin,* an Ōmoto practice that dovetailed with a widespread popularity of spiritualist practices in Japan at that time. Asano and Onisaburō formulated a presentation of Nao's millenarian thought as an "Imperial Way" and a "Taishō Restoration." They published these beliefs and prophecies in an Osaka newspaper they purchased, *Taishō nichi-nichi shinbun,* which became a highly effective proselytizing tool. Both were arrested in 1921 and convicted of lèse-majesté (for doctrines seen to impugn the imperial dignity) and violating the Newspaper Law, under which millenarian prophecy was deemed a threat to public order.[60]

Shrine priests, as well as most of the Japanese religious world, applauded this first major twentieth-century suppression of a Shinto religious group.[61] The suppression of Ōmoto qualifies as an example of State Shinto because of the use of state ideology regarding the deified emperor as a means to enforce conformity.

Meiji Shrine

The Meiji Shrine was built through a combination of government funding and contributions from a nationwide range of civil society groups, religious associations, and private individuals. It stands alone as a shrine built largely by the people as an expression of their reverence for a widely respected emperor. Meiji was the first Japanese sovereign to be widely seen and to have his image distributed to the people, so that he was visible in a way that no previous emperor had been. When it was reported that his death was approaching, tens of thousands of people came to the palace grounds and knelt there in prayer for his recovery. When he died, the sense of the end of an era was pervasive, and it was inevitable that he would be deified and a great shrine built to worship his spirit. [62]

Construction had begun in central Tokyo, but the project faltered because of severe labor shortages and rising construction prices after World War I. Around 11,000 members of youth groups and uncounted numbers from women's groups;

professional groups of all kinds; religious associations, including not only the Meiji Shrine Support Association (Meiji Jingū Hōsankai) but also Buddhist groups; and such organizations as Tokyo Prefecture, Tokyo City, and the Tokyo Chamber of Commerce, mobilized to volunteer labor, timber, 95,000 seedlings for the gardens, and six million *yen* in donations to complete the shrine. With their aid, the shrine was completed in 1920. An extensive garden was planted on the land where Meiji's funeral had been held, and a museum of painting was constructed in the shrine precincts.[63]

Newspapers around the country covered the Meiji Shrine's opening ceremonies, with the result that the shrine became hugely popular nationwide. Katō Genchi and others established an academic society for the promotion of study and reverence regarding Emperor Meiji, the Meiji Japan Society (Meiji Seitoku Kinen Gakkai, literally, Association to Commemorate the Sacred Virtues of Meiji). Many *yōhaisho* were set up to worship the Meiji Shrine from a distance. In addition, Meiji was added to the deities of several overseas shrines at the behest of Japanese living in the colonies.[64]

While there was undoubtedly an ideological element in the founding of the Meiji Shrine, and no doubt an element of coercion in the supposedly volunteer labor, it seems to me that popular enthusiasm outweighed state ideology in this case. Thus while the shrine was to become a significant monument of state ideology, it is not useful to think of the shrine's original construction as a case in which State Shinto was the dominant factor.

The Shrine Priesthood during the Interwar Period

A new division appeared among shrine priests based on public funding, pitting priests of the lower-ranking *minsha* shrines against those of the Imperial and National Shrines. The Imperial and National Shrines received funding from the national government, in amounts that had been rising dramatically since 1913. Priests of the Imperial and National Shrines monopolized the leadership of the national and regional shrine associations. The examination system for entry to higher ranks was restricted to priests serving Imperial and National Shrines, meaning that examinations merely reproduced the existing hierarchy and suppressed meritocracy. In contrast, the *minsha* priests' funding was insufficient and precarious, based only on the largesse of individual prefectures and municipalities rather than legal mandate. Many felt consigned to a kind of limbo outside the realm of *kokka no sōshi*, since only shrines down to the District Shrine level had been formally given that designation.[65]

Minsha priests' activism emerged soon after the prefectures and municipalities began allocating "offering fees" to shrines. Around the country, *minsha* priests formed organizations to push their claim that they, more than the higher-ranking priests, carried the burden of realizing the ideal of *kokka no sōshi* and thus should be properly funded.[66] Activists tended to be young, and their zeal for change was part of a generational transition. A group founded in northern Okayama Prefecture had a poignant analysis of their situation. When they asked themselves, "why are we ridiculed?", their answer was that they were excessively conservative, even reactionary in their thinking, and uninformed about contemporary issues. Yet they burned to offer themselves in public service and contribute to the transformation of rural society. They pressured the Shrine Bureau to provide training that would help them implement the ideals of *kokka no sōshi*, "Shrines at the Center," and achieve a thoroughgoing *personal* renovation. Their movement spread and in some areas remained vital into the 1930s.[67]

In response, the Shrine Bureau began to provide training programs. Bureau Chief Inoue Tomoichi's (1871–1919) speech at the graduation ceremony of the fourth training class conveyed his ideals for graduates, asking them to become leaders of their communities and to assist the government in reforming society. The priests should not concern themselves with whether the government is giving shrines enough support, however, trusting that if they improve themselves, the system will gradually improve.[68]

The new training programs did not immediately produce the hoped-for results, however. The issue of priests' salaries presented a severe problem—the most frequently addressed topic in priestly journals—and it is clear that *minsha* priests could not make a living solely through their work at shrines.[69] Nevertheless, it was difficult to persuade government at any level to increase salaries, since it was known that the priesthood had become a haven for retirees from miscellaneous backgrounds, including the civil service, who were completely ignorant of shrines, and could not, if their lives depended upon it, read—let alone compose—a *norito*. Also, the sons of some priests were allowed to succeed their fathers without taking the examination. Therefore, any proposal to increase priestly salaries was a hard sell. In this situation, it was also difficult for earnest young priests to reverse the view that their profession was lacking in learning and virtue. The difficulty of making a living as a priest pushed the most talented into other professions or secondary employment, often in teaching or civil service, in which case, the priesthood became a by-employment.[70]

Shrine Funding

Shrine funding was a major preoccupation throughout the priesthood and at each level of government. The national government, prefectures, cities, towns, and villages, as well as the imperial house, provided funds to shrines. The national government and the prefectures began shrine funding in early Meiji, while lower levels of government started after 1906. First, let us examine shrine funds in

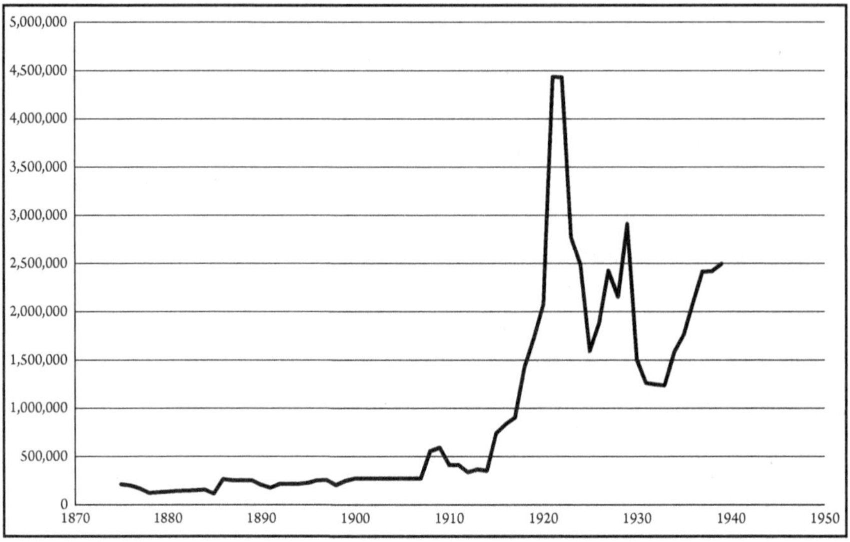

Chart 13.1 Shrine Funding from the National Budget, 1875–1939, in Yen.

the national budget for the years 1875 to 1939. (See Table A.1 in the Appendix and Chart 13.1.) Please note that these illustrations include the Ise Shrines, the Imperial, and National Shrines; they do not include funding for the overseas shrines, the Yasukuni Shrine, or *minsha* shrines.

Chart 13.1 shows that a huge spike begins in 1915, peaking in 1921. This jump in expenses went to the government's contributions to the enthronement ceremonies for Emperor Taishō (r. 1912 to 1926; enthroned in 1915) and to build the Meiji Shrine (see Columns F and G in Table A.1 in the Appendix). But the Shrine Bureau's budget did not return to the levels prevailing before 1915, but instead rose again when the Shōwa Emperor was enthroned in 1928, and the Ise Shrines performed the Vicennial Renewal of 1929 on an unprecedented scale. The budget dipped briefly in the early 1930s, but after 1933 rose steadily.

Preliminary research on shrine funding reveals a variety of patterns in prefectural and municipal budgets that did not always follow the rises and falls in national appropriations. As Chart 13.2 shows, there was no uniform standard governing shrine allocations at the lower levels of government. By 1915 the combined annual allocation for shrines from each prefecture's administrations at all levels (prefectural, city, town, and village) had come to exceed the amount provided to the prefecture from national funding. The exceptions were Hyōgo, where the balance tipped in 1926, and Kyoto, where national funding consistently exceeded that provided by lower levels of government. It appears that shrine funding followed a rising baseline established between 1906 and 1910. In addition, extra appropriations were occasionally provided to enable shrines to demonstrate their support for the monarchy. We find Kyoto Prefecture making a conspicuous appropriation in 1915, up almost

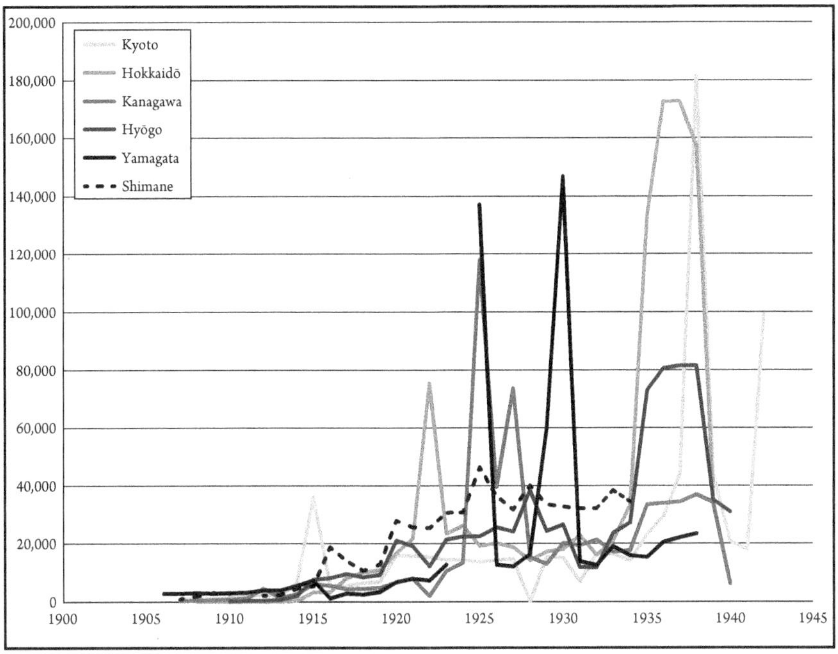

Chart 13.2 Selected Prefectures' Shrine Funding, 1906–1942, in Yen.

50 percent from the previous year, probably to celebrate the enthronement of Emperor Taishō that year. The spike in Yamagata and Kanagawa Prefectures' appropriations in 1924 likely celebrated the marriage of Hirohito, the future Shōwa emperor. Yamagata's spike in the late 1920s probably was to be a gift to the Ise Shrines for the Vicennial Renewal of 1929. All the prefectures represented here raised their allocations to prepare for the twenty-sixth centennial anniversary of the nation's founding in 1940 (except for Shimane, whose records had come to an end), but the amounts varied considerably. In addition to those prefectures represented in the Chart, Okayama provided a whopping 421,000 yen for the occasion, double that seen in Kyoto and Hokkaidō.[71]

Besides public funding in the form of "shrine fees" and "offering fees," in the national and prefectural budgets, the imperial house consistently provided funds to shrines during the years 1899 to 1914 (see Table 13.2). These contributions were the ultimate prize for shrines, cherished and commemorated with plaques and monuments. The funds had a semipublic status, since they were not explicitly part of the national shrine appropriations.

The imperial house's gifts to shrines have only been documented in this form for the fifteen-year period shown in Table 13.2, but it seems likely that such gifts originated before 1899 and continued after 1914. Other imperial gifts to shrines were frequently reported in priestly publications and focused on the Imperial Shrines.[72]

Table 13.2 **The Imperial Household's Gifts to Shrines, 1899–1914, in Yen**

Year	*Imperial House Funding for Shrines*
1899	9,218
1900	9,822
1901	10,041
1902	9,333
1903	11,633
1904	14,137
1905	14,041
1906	12,143
1907	12,904
1908	12,017
1909	12,040
1910	16,498
1911	19,252
1912	18,456
1913	2,867
1914	2,858

Which Shrines Prospered?

In 1933, *The Journal* published a report on how the assets of the Imperial and National Shrines (not counting the Ise and Atsuta Shrines) had changed over the period 1911 to 1931. From this, we can form an idea of which shrines were flourishing.[73] Assets were categorized in cash, stocks, and land, and the wealthiest had diversified their holdings so that they held strong positions in all three. As of 1932, public funding provided on average 18 percent of the expenses of Imperial and National Shrines.[74] While the donations of individual visitors to these shrines remained an important source of revenue, powerful twentieth-century shrines had developed a corporate management style. The assets of the top twenty-five in 1931 had multiplied over five times between 1911 and 1931, on average. The assets of the top ten had multiplied eight times. The richest shrines were concentrated in the old Kinai area, for a total of ten out of the top twenty-five (Kyoto: five; Nara: three; Osaka: two). None of the richest shrines was located in the Northeast. Rank was a significant but not determining factor. Of the top twenty-five wealthiest shrines, thirteen held the top rank, Imperial Shrine, Major Grade. Three were Special Shrines, and the remainder were

National Shrines. Thus the Imperial and Special Shrines together made up sixteen out of the top twenty-five, or 64 percent.

In spite of the evident significance of rank, the top three wealthiest shrines were all National Shrines. The wealthiest in 1931 was Iyahiko Shrine in Niigata Prefecture, a National Shrine, Middle Grade. Number two was Kotohiragū Shrine, also National Shrine, Middle Grade, located in Kagawa Prefecture, while the third, Hakone Shrine in Kanagawa Prefecture, was a National Shrine, Minor Grade. Up through the 1880s, Niigata Prefecture was the largest population center in the country, outstripping Tokyo and Aichi Prefectures.[75] This little-known fact is counterintuitive in our present context, in which Tokyo is *the* metropole. But Niigata is a major port linking Japan to the Asian continent, and in the early twentieth century it prospered as a petroleum production boom town (since dried up). Iyahiko Shrine is the only significant shrine in the prefecture. Its assets multiplied almost fifteenfold from 1911 to 1931.[76]

Kotohiragū, the former Konpira Gongen, had been the most significant shrine on the island of Shikoku since the Edo period and was indirectly linked to the cult of the Buddhist saint Kūkai, inasmuch as it was located in the same district as Zentsūji, the temple associated with the saint's birthplace, which was the starting point for the island's Eighty-eight Temple Pilgrimage Route. The shrine had flourished in the Edo period, specializing in the protection of seafarers and maritime business. In the modern period, it flourished as a result of the energetic work of Koto-oka Hirotsune, who renounced his Buddhist identity as Head Priest of the temple in early Meiji and became Head Priest of the shrine in 1886. Following the sale of many Buddhist art works from the former temple, he cultivated government patronage through heavy donations to the new regime. He formed a support group (*kō*) focused on the site's associations with seafaring, and it grew to three million members by 1889. This group cultivated the navy during the Sino-Japanese War, leading to corporate sponsorship by numerous shipbuilding companies.[77]

The third richest, Hakone Shrine (Hakone Jinja, the former Hakone Gongen), located in the foothills of Mt. Fuji, is easily accessible from Tokyo by car or rail, and had been a center of mountain worship. After 1868, it fell on hard times until an imperial detached palace (Hakone *rikyū*) was built in the vicinity in 1896, precipitating a large number of visits by members of the imperial family. Hakone became the focus of a major drive in the early twentieth century to promote overseas tourism as a source of foreign currency. Hakone's famous Fujiya Hotel saw its annual number of guests rise from 12,000 in the 1890s to 19,000 in 1915. In addition to foreign tourists, wealthy Tokyoites came to Hakone to escape the capital's summer heat and enjoy the natural beauty of its lakes, mountains, and hot springs. Politicians found it a convenient place for quiet consultations away from the prying eyes of the press. The combination of these factors brought Hakone Shrine unprecedented wealth.[78]

The wealthiest shrines were major landholders, a new factor given that all shrines and temples had earlier been required to relinquish their land. From around 1908 into the 1920s, *The Journal* published many articles about shrines that had secured forestland for preservation.[79] Some shrines successfully petitioned to have land they had owned before the Restoration returned to them, and that seems to be what happened at the Hakone Shrine, whose historical documents contain extensive records of repeated appeals to the government on this subject.[80] It is evident that the most prosperous shrines in imperial Japan were well integrated into the national economy and had diversified their assets and adopted corporate sponsorship as a major form of their support. It is likely that any state funding they received represented only a small part of their annual income.

The Vicennial Renewal of the Ise Shrines in the Modern Period

The Vicennial Renewal ceremonies held from the beginning of the Meiji period through 1929 (that is, the ones in 1869, 1889, 1909, and 1929) were all conducted under the authority of the national government. Ise had changed radically since the Restoration, as we saw in chapter 12, and these changes extended to the renewal ceremonies as well. The 1869 observance re-established the placement of wooden fences around the main sanctuaries, offering some protection against the crush of pilgrims, who tended to increase in Vicennial Renewal years. Jingūkyōkai tried to organize a mass pilgrimage for 1889, since 1890 would have been an *okage mairi* year, sponsoring huge *kagura* and displays of shrine treasures, as well as viewings of the old buildings before they were taken down. Rail transport was available for the first time for the 1909 pilgrimage, and discounted tickets were provided. An estimated 1,660,000 people visited the shrines that year. A wide variety of Shinto groups publicized the 1929 ceremonies, and it was the first one that people all across the country were aware of. The ceremonies of 1929 attempted a complete return to the most ancient form of each associated ritual, and the construction involved a more thorough-going renewal, replacing all the timber and furnishings, not only at the main sanctuaries but at all the associated shrines.[81]

The Committee to Investigate the Shrine System

In order to put an end to growing public questioning about shrines and religion, in the late 1920s, the government planned to enact two comprehensive bills, one on religion and one on shrines. The initiative toward a religions bill took place within the Ministry of Education, which administered religious affairs, while the one on shrines took place under the auspices of the Shrine Bureau. The strategy was to form a high-level committee to discuss the issues and make recommendations, so that the government could claim that a consensus favoring those recommendations had come into existence. That would clear the way to enact legislation even if opposition persisted.[82] A committee attached to the Shrine Bureau was formed in 1929, called the Committee to Investigate the Shrine System (Jinja seido chōsakai). The committee headship was an imperial appointment; Mizuno Rentarō was the last of four men to head it. Its membership, which could number as many as thirty, was appointed by the Cabinet and composed of Diet members from both Houses, staff from the Imperial Household Ministry, Vice Ministers of the Education and Finance Ministries, scholars, and representatives from the priesthood. But in spite of this august company's best efforts, discussion foundered on the question of the religious nature of shrines, and it was impossible to draft the desired legislation. The collapse of the proposed shrine law illustrates that the state was not all-powerful where Shinto was concerned.

To rescue the effort, the group turned instead to smaller questions and enacted such changes as drawing the various war-dead shrines into a single category called Nation-Protecting Shrines (Gokoku jinja) and recommending that they be made prefectural outposts of the Yasukuni Shrine in Tokyo. Their work ended in 1940, with a recommendation—responding to a groundswell of sentiment from shrine priests—to reinstate the Jingikan, in the form of a new organization to be called the Institute of Ceremonies (Jingiin). That recommendation was enacted.[83]

Overseas Shrines in the 1930s

The number and scale of shrines built in Japan's colonies is astonishing. Some 1,640 shrines were constructed in Taiwan, Korea, Manchuria, Sakhalin, the Kwangtung Leased Territories, the South Sea Islands, Singapore, Batavia, Thailand, and in the Republic of China. As Japanese from the inner territory emigrated to the colonies, they typically built shrines, often using a symbol from the home shrine to set up the new one. Settlers generally intended that they would use these shrines exclusively, and did not anticipate that colonial people would worship there. In addition, however, Japanese colonial administrations constructed shrines and war memorials, prevailing upon colonial subjects to pay obeisance. Thus the overseas shrines comprised two distinct types, settler shrines and government-constructed shrines.

The majority of the overseas shrines, some 1,163, or about 72 percent of the total, were built between 1931 and 1945. After 1931, Korea became the staging ground for Japan's war in China, while Taiwan played that role for Japan's war in Southeast Asia. The element of coercion in suppressing indigenous religious practices and making colonial subjects worship at these shrines intensified after the Manchurian Incident of 1931, continuing until the defeat in 1945. In Taiwan many buildings used by local religious associations were destroyed. In Korea, shrines visits were required of all school pupils after 1931, and after 1936 schools that rejected shrine visits were closed.

The character of the overseas shrines differed considerably between those areas where a policy of *kōminka*, or "Japanization," was enforced from 1937—that is, Taiwan and Korea—and areas where coercive policies of cultural assimilation were not enacted, such as Manchukuo. The term *kōminka* means "to transform [colonial people] into imperial subjects [*kōmin*]."[84] "Japanization" was implemented when Japan mobilized for "holy war" (*seisen*), beginning with the second Sino-Japanese War and included four main elements: (1) religious "reform" (meaning suppression of indigenous religious organizations and worship sites), (2) promotion of the Japanese language (and suppression of the indigenous language), (3) changing personal names to Japanese names, and (4) military recruitment. Colonial subjects were called on to dedicate themselves to winning Japan's "holy war" as fervently as Japanese in the inner territories, though not all enjoyed the rights guaranteed under the Meiji constitution.[85]

Colonials should become Japanese "in spirit," and "spirit" was at the center of *kōminka*. Promotion of Shinto by Japanese colonial administrations was part of this push for spiritual mobilization. Priests were recruited to go overseas to serve at colonial shrines, and military officers frequently officiated in shrine rites. After the colonization of Korea in 1910, Shinto priests were urged to become missionaries in Korea, but by the mid-1930s, there were only sixty-one Shinto priests in Korea, and by 1941, sixty-six in Taiwan. There were also many cases of settlers who acted as priests of settler shrines for ceremonies, but who were mainly engaged in some other occupation.[86] The use of shrines in campaigns to force colonial subjects to assimilate is this era's clearest example of State Shinto.

The military was in charge, and there is no evidence of the priesthood playing a role in decision-making. At most, priests could petition the military regarding the Kami to be enshrined, but we find no evidence that their views carried decisive weight. Like everyone else under military rule, the Shinto priests were expected to obey without question. When Koreans requested that their national founder be enshrined at the Korea Shrine (see Figure 13.2), the military governor rejected the idea, saying that they should be willing to worship the imperial ancestors of Japan. This decision flew in the face of the advice of the National Association of Shinto Priests and such Shinto scholars as Ashizu Kōjirō and Ogasawara Shōzō, who passionately advocated for the inclusion of native Korean deities.[87]

Ogasawara, a Kokugakuin graduate who traveled widely among the overseas shrines, from Brazil through Japan's colonies, had written a book on colonial shrines in 1933, warning against the coercive use of Shinto:

> Shinto shrines are "sites for the performance of State Ritual" (*Kokka no Sōshi*) of course, but forcibly maintaining entities alienated from peoples' actual lives through the state power would make shrines lose their religious nature, and make them something like a kind of monument. If this principle were to be disregarded, any shrine, not just the [Korea Shrine] but also

Figure 13.2 The Korea Shrine. Source: Reproduced by Permission of the Research Center for Nonwritten Cultural Materials, Kanagawa University.

> others in Korea and Manchuria, and even shrines in the mainland, would gradually come to lose their ties with the people's individual life, social life, and national life.[88]

As Ogasawara's prophetic example shows, many Shinto intellectuals regarded draconian administration of overseas shrines as deeply problematic and unlikely to win the respect of the colonials. Unfortunately, the administrators did not listen to them. It must be noted, however, that the priesthood did not recommend that colonials' desires in the matter should prevail, any more than the military governors did. Both groups assumed that shrine administration was to be decided by the regime, and that the colonials should abide by its decisions. The colonials predictably regarded this attitude as paternalistic, arrogant, and degrading.

When Korean teachers refused to worship at the Korea Shrine, they were sacked. In 1935, the Governor-General of Korea launched what he called a "movement to develop the 'field of the mind'" (*shinden kaihatsu*). In 1937, "The Oath as Subjects of the Imperial Nation" (*Kōkoku shinmin no seishi*) was introduced in Korea, and recitation of the oath (using different versions for children and adults) was made compulsory on "each and every public occasion," becoming "a daily ritual of indoctrination of Koreans in Japanese state ideology."[89] In 1938, a policy requiring one shrine per local district was instituted, resulting in a further increase in the number of shrines and considerable local resistance. After 1938, all Christians in Korea were forced to worship at shrines, sometimes at the point of a bayonet.

Beginning in 1922, the Governor-General of Taiwan ordered that representatives of all local religious groups attend the Taiwan Shrine for Kinensai, Niinamesai, the shrine's Annual Festival, and the anniversary of the beginning of Japanese rule in Taiwan. Each Taiwanese and Korean household was encouraged to set up a *kamidana* and to enshrine a talisman of the Ise Shrines and worship it daily. As of 1941, some 70 percent of Taiwanese households possessed Ise talismans; there are no reliable figures regarding the frequency of worship. The number of Japanese shrines in Taiwan increased during "Japanization," and thirty-eight of the total of sixty-eight were built between 1937 and 1943. In 1942 a record of 150,000 visitors attended the Taiwan Shrine's annual two-day festival. These measures accompanied a policy discouraging indigenous religious customs and the removal of statues of local gods. Under Governor-General Kobayashi Seizō, from 1936 to 1940, one-third of the Taiwanese temples practicing a hybrid mix of Buddhism, Daoism, and shamanism were destroyed.[90]

What did officials imagine the result of their draconian policies would be? Did they seriously think that colonial subjects would willingly come to shrines and worship? To the end, they knew that their policies were doomed to failure, *and* they kept enforcing them, seemingly incapable of changing course. When the defeat came, fleeing officials knew full well how colonials would relish the chance to rip these shrines to shreds. Officials belatedly tried to prevent desecration, either burying or taking mirrors and other altar gear with them as they fled. To no one's surprise, the colonials destroyed these shrines. Today virtually nothing remains of Shinto in Japan's former colonies, except where buildings have been preserved as monuments to anti-Japanese sentiment.

Shinto in Wartime and the Institute of Shinto Ceremonies (Jingiin)

We can observe a marked change in the character of Shinto from 1937, with the beginning of "total war" in China and the mobilization of the people to support it.

Kokutai rhetoric reached a fever pitch, and the Ministry of Education released a work of popular indoctrination called *The Essence of Kokutai* (*Kokutai no Hongi*, 1937). It was composed by a committee that included two prominent Shinto scholars, Kōno Seizō and Miyaji Naokazu. The work was distributed to schoolteachers so that they could counter "dangerous thought" among the young. The work addressed Japan's supposed mission to rule the world. To realize that ultimate purpose, all Japanese must submerge individual aspiration, of any kind, in the collective. The tone is fanatical and features passionate adulation of death in war. The subsequent publication in 1941 of *The Way of the Subject* (*Shinmin no Michi*) served up more of the same.[91]

At long last, the priesthood's hope to revive the Jingikan, for shrines to be administered by a special branch of government outside the cabinet ministries, came true. The Institute of Ceremonies was founded in 1940 with a mandate to spread respect for the Kami, and in 1944 it issued a work called *The Essence of Shrines* (*Jinja hongi*), with much the same content as the earlier ideological screeds. A recent history of the Home Ministry describes this work as completely rejecting rationality and labels it an example of "pathological nationalism" (*byōriteki nashonarizumu*).[92] While the Jingiin played the role of an ideology factory, it also secured unprecedented levels of shrine funding.

Table 13.3 and Chart 13.3 show the budget for shrine funding from 1931 to 1945. Although Japan was continually at war from 1931 to 1945, shrine funding more than doubled. The source was a dramatic fivefold increase in funding from

Table 13.3 **Total Shrine Funding from Imperial, National, Prefectural, and Municipal Budgets, 1931–1945, in Yen**

Year	*Imperial*	*National*	*Prefectural and Municipal*	*Total*
1931	NA	1,265,000	691,498	1,956,498
1935	NA	1,920,000	1,212,177	3,132,177
1945	52,355	1,041,550	3,418,668	4,512,573

Sources: For 1931 and 1935, see "Shiryō" *JKZ* 34, no. 8 (1935): 35–40; for 1945, see Okada Yoneo, *Jingiin shūsen shimatsu* (Tokyo: Jinja Honchō, 1964), 82–84.

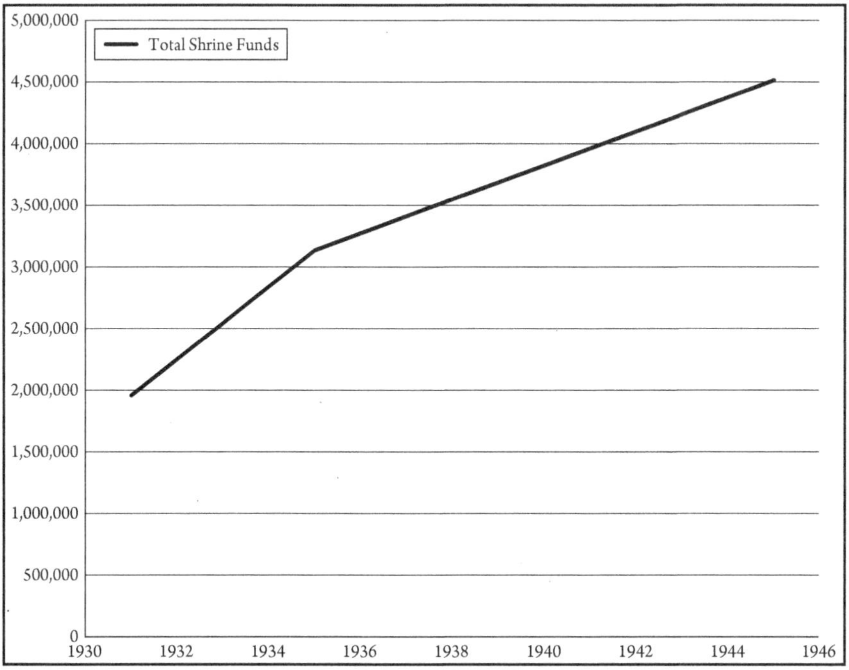

Chart 13.3 Total Shrine Funding from National Budget, Imperial Funds, Prefectural, and Municipal Budgets, 1931–1945, in Yen.

the prefectures and municipalities, even as national budget funding rose and fell.[93] Because statistics from the late 1930s are fragmentary, it is not easy to put these figures in context, but the amount of shrine funding per capita can serve as a rough yardstick. Matching the total appropriations for shrines in 1945 to the total population (72,147,000 people in the inner territories), the per capita expenditure for shrines was 16 yen. The last wage figures available in Japan's annual statistical yearbook are for 1939, when a male factory worker on average earned 255 yen annually. This means that an amount equivalent to 6.3 percent of his annual income was spent on shrines at the same time that food, paper, and gasoline were strictly rationed. In the latter years of the war, education had come to a halt so that pupils could be sent to the factories or evacuated to the countryside, home defense units were practicing with bamboo spears, the cities were being bombed, and the troops were making desperate last stands. Yet Japan continued to build, maintain, and expand the shrines. This fact testifies eloquently to the supreme value the empire placed on shrines and Shinto.

The Empire's 2600th Anniversary Celebrations

According to historian Kenneth Ruoff, imperial Japan reached its zenith in 1940, with the Celebration for the Empire's 2600th Anniversary (*kigen 2600 nen shikiten*). These empire-wide festivities also define State Shinto's zenith. Shrines were at the center of observances commemorating Emperor Jinmu's legendary founding of the country. Never before (or since) were so many drawn into shrines for such a spectacle of political theater uniting the empire in the worship of the Kami.

The 1940 anniversary celebrated the ideology of an unbroken imperial line as the center of Japan's incomparable *kokutai*, stretching back to Jinmu and ultimately to the Sun Goddess. Jinmu, who had supposedly been enthroned on February 11, 660 BCE on a hill called Unebiyama in present-day Nara Prefecture, mythically conquered the peoples from Kyūshū to his eventual capital in central Japan, "extending the blessings of imperial rule to them."[94]

Preparations for the 1940 celebrations had begun decades earlier. According to Okada Kaneyoshi, the Sacred Grove Society (Shin'en Kai) was already anticipating the 2600th anniversary when it purchased land adjacent to the Ise Shrines in 1886 to create a "Kami Capital" (*shinto*). The Society aimed to create a band of dignified sacred forest around the shrines, composed of dark, broad-leafed evergreen trees and gravel walkways. In effect, the Society furthered the transformation of Ise that had begun immediately following the Restoration. The Shrine Bureau and the imperial house continued the Society's work, funding expansions of the forest tracts around the Ise Shrines in 1912, 1922, and 1934. Ise's dark-forested landscape served as the model for sacred forests planted around the Meiji and Kashihara Shrines.[95]

Seven other places were planning "Kami Capital" projects in anticipation of the 1940 anniversary celebrations, but the one at Kashihara Shrine was undoubtedly the most ambitious and fully realized.[96] Founded in 1890 through the collaboration of local boosters and the Shrine Bureau, Kashihara Shrine (Kashihara Jingū, Imperial Shrine, Major Grade) enshrines Emperor Jinmu and his consort on a vast site where the main buildings alone occupy over twelve acres. The shrine achieved its present monumental scale in stages. First, to commemorate the 2550th anniversary of the nation's founding in 1890, the imperial family gave the shrine two buildings from the Kyoto palace to serve as the Main Sanctuary and Worship Hall. Later expansions in 1915 (commemorating Emperor Taishō's coronation) and 1940 increased its original land tenfold. The 1940 expansion, largely devoted to planting the sacred forest, involved volunteer labor by over 1.2 million people, including a brigade from Korea.[97]

The 2600th Anniversary Celebrations were coordinated with annual rites for Jinmu and performed on November 11 in the palace and at shrines nationwide. A massive pavillion called the Kōkaden was built on the outer grounds of the Tokyo palace. Some 50,000 invited guests assembled in orderly rows on the morning of November 10, to await the arrival of Emperor Hirohito and his wife (he in the austere costume of the Imperial Rule Assistance League, and she in Western dress). At precisely 11:00 am, they appeared standing on a dais behind brocade-wrapped desks some three meters or so above ground level. Prime Minister Konoe Fumimaro presented the nation's congratuations, and an imperial edict was read out, declaring the emperor's hope that Japan would contribute to the world through its "Great Way of the ancient Kami" (*kamunagara no ōmichi*). The national anthem and three *banzai* cheers completed that day's events. On the next day, following the emperor's performance of the annual rituals for Jinmu, he and the empress again took their places in the Kōkaden before their 50,000 guests, to whom commemorative medals were presented. Guests included Nazi officers in uniform and Ambassador Joseph Grew of the United States. Following the national anthem and another three *banzai* cheers, entertainments of ancient dance (*bugaku*) were presented. NHK Radio broadcast the ceremony live, and newspapers from around the country covered the celebrations extensively, as well as associated events like a review of battleships and troops, sports tournaments, martial arts competitions, art exhibits, and smaller celebrations across the empire.

Associated shrine ceremonies around the country were timed to coincide precisely with those at the palace. Those unable to attend shrine ceremonies were expected to observe one minute of silence at 11:00 am. In addition, a number of shrines in both the inner and outer territories were newly consecrated, rebuilt, or raised in rank as part of the 2600th Anniversary, including the new Ōmi Jingū in Ōtsu City, Shiga Prefecture, which enshrines Emperor Tenchi. The Heian Shrine was rebuilt, and Emperor Kōmei was installed as a second Kami of the shrine. The Foundation Shrine (Kenkoku Shinbyō) in Manchukuo was completed. The Nan'yō

Shrine in Palau added Amaterasu as one of its Kami, and the Beijing Shrine (Pekin Jinja) was founded.

Although recreational travel was discouraged as a wartime austerity measure, there were special promotions offering discounted train tickets to shrines with imperial connections, including Ise and Kashihara Shrines. Eight million people are said to have visited the Ise Shrines in 1940. On the 1940 observance of the annual rites for Jinmu at the Kashihara Shrine, some 1,100,000 people visited the shrine, and a further eight million or more visited during the year. A pillar was erected near the Miyazaki Shrine (Miyazaki Jingū, in the area where Jinmu's eastward conquest had begun), called "The Eight Corners of the World under One Roof." This phrase was thought to have originated with Jinmu but in 1940 also referred to Japan's territorial ambitions.[98]

The Denouement

Immediately following the cathartic release of the 2600th anniversary, the Imperial Rule Assistance League plastered the cities with posters reading, "The party's over; let's get back to work!" (*Iwai owatta—saa, hatarakō*!). The festive mood dissipated quickly. The celebrations had been a distraction from the quagmire of the long war in China, where 100,000 had already perished. When war with the United States and its allies began in December 1941, attention turned to war in all sectors of Shinto.

The Nation-Protecting Shrines acted as satellites of Yasukuni Shrine, to honor the war dead in each prefecture, while imperial visits to Yasukuni increased in proportion to the mounting numbers of the dead. At the shrine's fall festival in 1942, some 15,021 spirits were enshrined; the emperor and empress worshipped there as thousands of the bereaved knelt on the ground. The total would rise to two and one-half million spirits. When the emperor visited Yasukuni, everyone in the empire was expected to stop what they were doing, bow in the direction of Yasukuni, and observe a moment of silence at the precise moment of his worship, announced by radio.[99]

Nisshin, Kurozumikyō's monthly magazine, changed overnight from being an ordinary newsletter to being totally preoccupied with the war. Each issue bore fevered slogans, such as "the sovereign is divine; Japan is the Land of the Kami!" (Ō wa shinnō; kuni wa shinkoku!), followed by exposition of the emperor's unity with Amaterasu and Japan's mission of world rule, articles on heroes of loyalist sacrifice like Kusunoki Masashige, or the duties of youth in wartime. Vows to Amaterasu were announced, including the determination to fight to the death in the name of the Kami.[100]

Conclusion

The contemporary assumption that Shinto is a religion, widely shared among researchers today, is partly owing to Tanaka Yoshitō's and Katō Genchi's portrayal of Shinto in those terms. It was not a state religion, but if Shinto was a religion, what kind of religion was it in imperial Japan? Beneath the bureaucratic denial that Shinto has doctrines, the very existence of shrines and their rituals is meaningless without the tenet that the Kami exist and are powerful beings. In this era, a Kami was primarily a deified Japanese person who had made an extraordinary contribution to Japan. Linked assumptions include the idea that by worshiping at shrines, Japanese can experience an ongoing connection with those who have sustained Japan throughout history. Shrine worship allows the Japanese people to experience their oneness *as a people* (*minzoku*), mediated by the Kami. Shinto identifies these meritorious persons, past or present, ranks them as Kami, and honors them with appropriate ritual. Shinto preserves the places and things connected with the Kami, treating them as shrines and memorials. Shinto leads the people in expressing respect and reverence for the Kami and facilitates the spiritual relation between Kami and the Japanese people through beautiful, moving rituals, thereby edifying the whole society.[101]

It was important *not* to announce these unspoken tenets as "doctrines," however, for fear of contradicting the constitution's guarantee of religious freedom. But the potential for conflict with the constitution was not the only reason. A deeper rationale lay in the determination to treat ideas about the Kami as "natural," as givens that are not appropriate for debate, something that all Japanese should agree upon and take for granted. At the same time, Shinto thinkers of imperial Japan also seemed to regard Shinto as infinitely expansive, something capable of encompassing different religions, hence making it possible for a Buddhist to be a Shinto stalwart. Dissenters opened themselves to stigmatization and sanction, calling into question their identity as Japanese.

The theology of Shinto in imperial Japan was *kokutai* thought. Writers always explained *kokutai* as having originated in Amaterasu's charge to Ninigi and his descendants to rule eternally over Japan. Theories of *kokutai* equated it with Shinto, expounded imperial divinity, Japan's superiority, its mission to rule Asia (if not the whole world), and the idea of the family state.[102] In his work of 1913, *Research on the Nation* (*Kokka no kenkyū*), Kakei Katsuhiko (1872–1961, a legal scholar at the imperial university and a Shinto theorist who served on the Committee to Investigate the Shrine System) wrote, "The basis of the solidity and immovability of *kokutai* is based on... *kannagara no michi*, that is, ancient Shinto."[103] Kōno Seizō (1882–1963), the president of Kokugakuin University from 1935 to 1942, wrote, "[T]he Emperor is the reincarnation of Amaterasu Ōmikami [who] rules the empire of Japan according to the divine message of this ancestral deity."[104]

In *kokutai* theology the nation is one great family, but the family-state concept could founder on the question of the diverse "races" in the empire. Katō Genchi had a solution for this conundrum. So long as colonial subjects revere the emperor as their father, he wrote, all the peoples of the world will become the children of the empire. It will be as if the great Yamato race were adopting children from different places. Once they have become a part of the empire, "[a] great familial nation (*ichi dai-kazokuteki kokka*) will emerge."[105]

Shinto was deeply rooted in lived communities in imperial Japan. *Kamidana* marked the domicile as a Shinto space. Frequent obeisance at shrines started soon after birth and continued through a lifetime. Each year was punctuated with state mandated shrine ceremonies, as well as state-fabricated observances like *hatsumōde*. School life was permeated by shrine ceremonies, to say nothing of teaching myth as history. Twice daily obeisance at *hōanden* was complemented by participation in the imperial mystique through pupils' trips to the Ise Shrines. Participation in civic associations of all kinds was tied to shrine ceremonies. Each significant event of national life—state funerals, enthronement rites, and the 2600th Anniversary being only the most conspicuous—was marked by shrine ceremonies. Honoring the war dead as Kami assuaged bereaved families' grief and tied their sacrifice to the larger purpose of Japan's mission in Asia. The empire placed great value on shrines as a means to inculcate proper beliefs, attitudes, and behavior in *all* its subjects. Equally important was the frequent stigmatization of those who failed to absorb the right mix of emotions and action. The positive message that Shinto unites the life of each family and community with the nation's sacred mission included a duty to demonstrate one's heartfelt acceptance by rejecting dissenters.

In what way is the term *State Shinto* useful here? Without a doubt, the state played the central role in sustaining Shinto in imperial Japan. The state had given Shinto its institutional independence from Buddhism, established the rites to be performed at shrines, provided funding, and regulated new shrine construction and staffing through a designated office from 1900. Unquestionably, the state played the defining role in structuring Shinto from 1868 to 1945, but state-sponsored ideological projects mediated by Shinto began in the twentieth century.

Shinto's most influential academics rejected the state's line on Shinto's nonreligious nature with impunity, so the state did not enjoy hegemony in defining Shinto. Civic debate scotched the plan for a shrine law. The greatest monuments of Shinto in this period would have been impossible without the strong civic support that underwrote the expansion of festivals, the building of settler shrines in the colonies, the massive fundraising for the Vicennial Renewal ceremonies, and the construction of mammoth new shrines. Civic participation was essential to Shinto. The state alone could not have accomplished these undertakings.

"State Shinto" advances our understanding of religious life when used in a limited and specific way, to refer to Shinto's mediation of state-sponsored ideological campaigns. "State Shinto" should not be restricted to the imperial period, however, as that would assume that the state might never promote (or has never promoted) a similar dynamic after 1945. We will inquire in subsequent chapters whether revival of State Shinto remains a possibility.

14

Shinto from 1945 through 1989

Introduction

Japan's defeat in 1945 brought shattering changes for Shinto. Occupation reforms struck at the heart of modern Shinto's reason for being, abolishing its place in the public realm, repudiating imperial divinity, and depriving palace ritual (*kyūchū saishi*) of all public status. Shrines lost all public funding and were transformed into religious organizations. Their rationale as *kokka no sōshi* dissolved. A new organization, the National Association of Shinto Shrines (hereinafter, NASS), was founded to unify the shrines and negotiate with the Occupation (1945–1952). NASS's entry into party politics set postwar Shinto on a new course, making it a highly conservative interest group advocating for traditionalist causes. This chapter discusses the postwar history of Shinto, from 1945 to 1989, when the Shōwa emperor Hirohito died, emphasizing the process by which Shinto became politicized. Chapter 15 examines changes in shrine life, addressing how festivals have changed since 1945. Chapter 16 explores contemporary Shinto, especially in relation to Japan's changing demographics and popular culture.

Occupation Policies Regarding Shinto

The Potsdam Declaration of July 26, 1945 dictated the terms of Japan's unconditional surrender and announced that freedom of religion would be established. After the surrender, Shinto leaders were initially in shock and extremely fearful of the Occupation's intentions regarding Shinto. Many believed that the Occupation intended to abolish Shinto completely.[1]

The Occupation set up its Civil Information and Education Section (hereafter, CIE) on September 22, 1945, headed by Colonel (later, Brigadier General) Ken R. Dyke, which subsequently established internal divisions relating to religion and education. Lieutenant William Kenneth Bunce (1907–2008) headed the Religions

Division, serving until the end of the Occupation in 1952. Bunce was the official with whom Shinto representatives most closely interacted. Another central staff member of the Religions Division was William P. Woodward, who served from May 1946 through the end of the Occupation. Woodward had advanced training in religion from Union Theological Seminary and had been a missionary in Japan for the Congregational Christian Churches from 1921 to 1941.[2]

The work of the Religions Division was just beginning when John Carter Vincent, chief of the Division of Far Eastern Affairs in the State Department, stated in a radio broadcast, in Washington, DC, on October 6, 1945, that the Occupation would abolish Shinto as a state religion:

> Shintoism, insofar as it is a religion of individual Japanese, is not to be interfered with. Shintoism, however, insofar as it is directed by the Japanese Government, and is a measure enforced from above by the government, is to be done away with. People will not be taxed to support National Shinto and there will be no place for Shintoism in the schools. Shintoism as a state religion—National Shinto, that is—will go.[3]

Having introduced a distinction between "Shintoism" as a religion of the individual and "National Shinto" as a government-created phenomenon, the need for further clarification was self-evident. Dyke ordered Bunce to commence a study of Shinto that would become the basis for an Occupation directive to the government of Japan.

The Shinto world, still under the leadership of the Jingiin and its long-serving Vice Chief Iinuma Kazumi, immediately began preparing a response to the Vincent broadcast. No doubt Iinuma and the shrine priesthood were shocked, but they were certainly relieved to find that their worst fear—the total abolition of Shinto—was not even being contemplated. Iinuma prepared a memo on October 9, 1945, for the Occupation, assuming that the Jingiin would continue to exist.[4]

Probably realizing the memo would be regarded as insufficient, the Jingiin followed up three days later with further proposals to abolish the Jingiin and the laws providing public funding to shrines.[5] While these proposals were for public consumption, the Jingiin was also making its own internal plans for how to cope with the Occupation. Jingiin's most important goal was to preserve the idea of shrines as public establishments for the performance of state ritual, that is, *kokka no sōshi*.[6] But despite developing such detailed plans, Iinuma did not actually visit the Religions Division until November 28, 1945.[7]

Meanwhile, Bunce had begun intensive study of Shinto in order to prepare the directive. He drew considerably on the works of Daniel Holtom, George Sansom, and Basil Hall Chamberlain. At the time, Holtom was the most widely recognized scholar of Shinto writing in English, and Bunce was greatly influenced by his views. It seems likely that Bunce also read the English works of Katō Genchi and Kōno Seizō on "*mikadoism*" published in the English-language journal at Sophia University in Tokyo, *Monumenta Nipponica*. On numerous occasions he consulted with scholar of Zen Buddhism D. T. Suzuki and with Miyaji Naokazu of the Jingiin and the chair for Shinto Studies at Tokyo Imperial University. Bunce also consulted with professor of comparative religions Anesaki Masaharu, but he worked most closely with Kishimoto Hideo (1903–1964), son-in-law and former student of Anesaki, then an assistant professor at Tokyo Imperial University. Kishimoto, who had spent the years 1930 to 1934 at Harvard, had been drafted to facilitate the CIE's communications with Japanese experts, scholars, and government offices relating to education and religion.[8]

Historian Miyaji Naokazu (1886–1949) was extremely influential in determining the course of Shinto from the imperial era into the crucial early postwar years. His scholarship on the early history of Shinto resulted in the first systematic studies of this complex field. Having succeeded Katō Genchi and Tanaka Yoshitō at the imperial university's program on Shinto Studies in 1918, Miyaji was concurrently appointed to the faculty at Kokugakuin in 1922, even as he advised the Shrine Bureau in a variety of responsible positions, including several projects regarding the Meiji Shrine and the Taiwan Shrine. A postwar collection of Miyaji's major scholarly writings comprises eight volumes. Miyaji's scholarship was characterized by scrupulous fidelity to textual evidence and minutely detailed analysis, with emphasis upon court rites and shrines patronized by the court, as seen in his studies of the Hodaka Shrine and the Suwa Shrine in Nagano Prefecture, and in his studies of the Hachiman cult. His work established the topics now deemed essential to any study of ancient Shinto, including the history of the establishment of shrines, the influence of continental thought on early Shinto, and combinatory frameworks, such as *honji suijaku* thought, arising from Buddhist influence. Without a doubt, Miyaji's historical scholarship set the standard to which subsequent scholarship still aspires.[9]

On some ten occasions, Bunce had Kishimoto make presentations on Shinto, while Bunce put questions to him. Kishimoto also arranged visits for Bunce and Dyke to visit various sites to observe religious life in situ. It became clear to Bunce that Shinto was a wide-ranging, polymorphous tradition that could not be comprehended through slogans like militarism and nationalism. The question of the Yasukuni Shrine remained distinctly problematic, however, and there was an element in the Occupation that favored closing it. A Special Enshrinement Service was planned for November 20, 1945, to apotheosize around two million war dead. With Miyaji's and Kishimoto's mediation, Dyke and Bunce attended the ceremony, and found it entirely unproblematic.[10]

Wartime propaganda had doubtless prepared Dyke and Bunce to believe that Shinto might be equated with militarism and nationalism. Gradually, however, the occupiers' views became more nuanced and their understanding more sophisticated. Interaction among Occupation officials, Japanese scholars, and religious leaders was not always easy, but the results were generally positive.

The Occupation view of Shinto in relation to militarism or nationalism was, however, unbalanced and distorted. The Religions Division was so focused on Shinto, so intent on clarifying Shinto's contribution to militarism and nationalism, that it failed to realize that virtually all other branches of Japanese religions up to 1945 had similarly devoted themselves to prayers for military victory, exaltation of the martial spirit, and justification of Japan's supposed mission to rule all of Asia. In other words, the experience of single-minded focus on Shinto in these crucial weeks both underlined Shinto's connection with militarism and nationalism and also obscured that same connection in other branches of religion. The result, in Woodward's words, was that, "Shrine Shinto became the whipping boy of the Occupation."[11]

The staff study accompanying the Shinto Directive began by explaining why a directive regarding Shinto was necessary. "State Shinto has been used by militarists and ultranationalists in Japan to engender and foster a military spirit among the people and to justify a war of expansion," which will remain a danger until it is completely separated from the state and eliminated from the schools.[12] The staff study describes Shinto in several overlapping ways, as "a primitive religion put to modern uses"; a tradition lacking specific doctrines but identified with "the racial spirit of the Japanese people"; closely connected to the imperial house, nature worship, the worship of ancestors and national heroes; and "a system of patriotism and loyalty centering in emperor worship." The study particularly notes that militaristic elements were relatively subdued in Shinto's history before the Meiji period.[13]

The report introduces distinctions between "State Shinto" and "Sect Shinto," but for all practical purposes, *State Shinto* and *Shrine Shinto* were interchangeable terms in the Shinto Directive. The report states conclusively that State Shinto was a religion. Though it did not have specific doctrines, it stood for a belief in the superiority of Japan, the emperor, and the Japanese, worship of the emperor as a living god, and the belief that Japan had a mission to rule Asia. The report concluded with several specific recommendations for severing the relation between the state and Shinto and for eliminating Shinto teachings from the schools: ending shrines' public funding; eliminating the government administration of shrines, placing Shinto on an equal footing with other religions; eliminating the Jingiin; removing *kamidana* from schools and public offices; and abolishing compulsory school trips to shrines. The report further recommended that the emperor be prevailed upon to issue a rescript repudiating all notions of Japanese superiority and the idea that Japan has a mission to rule in Asia.

The Shinto Directive

The Shinto Directive served as the Occupation's fundamental charter on Shinto from the time of its issuance (December 15, 1945) until it was superseded by the postwar constitution of 1947. The directive began with an elaborate statement of purpose: "to lift from the Japanese people the burden of compulsory financial support of an ideology which has contributed to their war guilt, defeat, suffering, privation, and present deplorable condition," to "prevent a recurrence of the perversion of Shinto theory and beliefs into militaristic and ultranationalistic propaganda designed to delude the Japanese people and lead them into wars of aggression," and "to assist the Japanese people in a rededication of their national life to building a new Japan based on the ideals of perpetual peace and democracy."[14]

The directive required that the following cease immediately: all use of public funds for Shinto, all propagation and dissemination of militaristic ideology in Shinto—and all religions'—doctrines, practices, rites, and ceremonies, public educational institutions devoted to Shinto or to Shinto priests' training, and any dissemination of Shinto doctrines in schools. Circulation of *Kokutai no Hongi* was ordered stopped, and the use of terms such as "Greater East Asia War" (*dai tōa sensō*) or "the Whole World Under One Roof" (*hakkō ichiu*) were prohibited. *Kamidana* were ordered removed from public buildings of all kinds, especially schools. No person was to be discriminated against because of refusal to profess belief in Shinto or because of refusal to participate in any Shinto ceremony. Public officials were to cease the practice of visiting shrines to report their assumption of office. All religions were to be put "upon exactly the same basis, entitled to precisely the same opportunities and protection." Not only Shinto, but all religions were forbidden to affiliate with the government or to propagate "militaristic and ultra-nationalistic ideology." Any laws upholding any of these prohibited practices were to be repealed swiftly by the Japanese government.

No shrine was to be closed. Sect Shinto was not to be interfered with and would enjoy the same protections as any other branch of religion. "After having been divorced from the state and divested of its militaristic and ultranationalistic elements," shrine Shinto would be recognized as a religion "if its adherents so desire." The directive repeatedly forbade "militaristic and ultra-nationalist ideology," which it defined as doctrines of the superiority of the emperor, the Japanese people, and the Japanese islands, as well as any doctrine "which tends to delude the Japanese people into embarking upon wars of aggression or to glorify the use of war as an instrument for the settlement of disputes with other peoples."[15]

The directive went some distance toward a wider declaration of separation of religion from state, inasmuch as all religions (Shinto included) were prohibited from "affiliation with the government."[16] The Japanese government moved swiftly to comply with the Shinto Directive, issuing orders within days to the prefectures to suspend all the prohibited practices. By the end of February 1946, some thirty-four laws had been repealed. The ministries ordered prefectural governors to scrupulously abide by all the directive's provisions. The Ministry of Education removed *kamidana* from the schools and references to religion from textbooks. Ethics courses were suspended.[17] The chair of Shinto Studies at the imperial university was abolished. On March 15, 1946, the Japanese government reported that appropriate consultations at all levels had been held, and that public support for Shinto had been removed from the budget. The Occupation was satisfied with these measures.

The intentions behind the Shinto Directive were explained to the Japanese people in a radio broadcast by Kishimoto on December 17, 1945: "The spirit of religious freedom is being observed completely and freedom of belief in and respect for shrines is fully guaranteed," Kishimoto assured the people. While the faith of their adherents continues, "shrines face the necessity of developing their religious character and from now on may freely endeavor to make a new start in a new direction."[18]

Newspaper coverage of the Shinto Directive was minimal and showed the most interest in the question of whether the emperor would be forced to abdicate or the imperial system eliminated altogether. Certainly there were no protests, but since the directive was issued a mere four months after the surrender, concerns about surviving from one day to the next were still uppermost in everyone's mind. Moreover, the Occupation had imposed a policy of censorship beginning in September 1945, so that even if someone had violently disapproved of the Shinto Directive, protest was unlikely to see the light of day. It was forbidden to criticize the Occupation or its policies, an ironic stance for a regime that intended to democratize Japan.

The government and the military were identified as having misused Shinto, but without naming names or even a government ministry. Neither priests nor Shinto scholars were singled out for punishment, though some were briefly "purged," which is to say, required to refrain from public activity for a period of time. No specific blame was assigned for the twisting of Shinto that the directive claimed had been carried out from the Meiji period through 1945.

Both the Shinto Directive and the staff study that preceded it tacitly absolved the Shinto world of responsibility for its "misuse" and "perversion" by the government and the military. But what about the people's roles in Shinto's transformation? The directive treated the people as virtually passive onlookers or victims, as lacking the agency to change the course of events. No particular person seemed to bear any responsibility. The fuzzy image of a tradition seized upon by government and twisted to its ends, with no specific agency attributed to anybody in the bureaucracy, to the priesthood, or the people, became part of the popular narrative of Shinto's modern history. State Shinto was apparently something that had "just happened" to the priests and the people.

The Shinto Directive was not even mentioned in the Diet before 1949, suggesting that legislators did not find it problematic. However, especially early in the Occupation, Diet members' commentary on anything related to shrines was remarkably circumspect and brief. This suggests that even though the Diet was not subject to censorship, a sort of self-censorship was practiced. At any rate, if Diet members took exception to Occupation policies regarding shrines, they did not speak out. No one called on the government to resume national management of shrines.

The *Yomiuri* newspaper used its editorial on December 18, 1945, to declare that the Shinto Directive removed "a veil of mystery" from Shinto, shedding new light on the causes of Japan's deplorable condition. Although there were those in the educated classes who must have doubted Shinto's "mysticism" (*shinpisei*), no one had the "power" (*chikara*) to challenge it, from scholars to socialists to the labor unions. This passivity had allowed the bureaucrats and the military to twist Shinto into a philosophy of Japan's mission of world domination, which had led to war and utter defeat. Now that the veil has been lifted, however, the people should rebuild the country and "reform its history," beginning with the emperor system, since Shinto has taken the emperor as its head priest.[19] In this editorial as well, it appeared that the "veil of mystery" came out of nowhere and descended on Shinto in a way that made it impossible to question. No one was at fault. The newspaper certainly did not raise the possibility that the media bore any responsibility. Since everyone was equally a victim, there were no perpetrators.

Reception of the Shinto Directive by the shrine priesthood was overwhelmingly negative, and criticism of it remains a staple of Shinto scholarship even in the twenty-first century. The Shinto Directive absolved the shrine world of responsibility for Shinto's "perversion," but that left the clear implication that the priesthood had either been incapable of defending the tradition or complicit in its misuse.[20] Reception of the Shinto Directive in Japanese society revealed both that the attitudes the directive sought to eradicate were deeply rooted and not easily changed, and also that citizens quickly adopted the directive as a standard that could assist them in rejecting ongoing coercion to support shrines monetarily.

Local officials were not always able to compel reluctant people to contribute to shrines, but they had ways of exacting retribution. Woodward discusses a complaint from a farmer, writing to the *Yomiuri* newspaper in mid-1948, asserting that young men carrying a *mikoshi* during a festival had damaged the property of people who had not contributed. The writer stated that "in such cases few people talk for fear of further reprisals."[21] A similar article in the *Yomiuri* in late 1948, called "*Mikoshi* and Democracy," complained that attacks using *mikoshi* as battering rams showed that democracy remained a thin veneer over antidemocratic attitudes.[22]

The Shinto Directive revealed the existence of conflicting interests between shrines and other kinds of Shinto organizations, as seen in the following letter to the Occupation by Tsuchiya Chōichirō, president of the Society for Research on Izumo in the Age of the Gods (Jindai Izumo Chōsakai). Both Tsuchiya and his society are otherwise unknown.

> Dear Sir:
>
> I would like to express my heartfelt gratitude for the orderly manner in which the occupation program has progressed during the year since Japan's surrender.
>
> Some time ago, a directive was issued, whereby the state would be divorced from Shintoism, and, in general this objective has been attained. Nevertheless, I would like to report a regrettable incident, which has occurred in this vicinity.

> In 1926, we founded the Society for Research on Izumo in the Age of the Gods, as a scientific research body to clarify the status of the imperial ancestry, and have been publishing reports on our findings. Beginning with the publishing in 1943 of the report discussing the actual grave of Izanami no Mikoto, the mother of Amaterasu Ōmikami, supporters of the Society were solicited from the people and expenses were thus defrayed. However, since the legendary place is within the grounds of a shrine called the Kume Shrine, there was dissension between the plan for the soliciting of maintenance funds of this shrine and the soliciting of supporters for our Society. The shrine authorities requested the town and village mayors to stop the people from joining our Society. The mayors submitted to the request, and instructions were issued preventing the village and town associations from becoming affiliated with the Society.... This objective was achieved. However, it goes without saying that the act is clearly contrary to the directive ordering the divorce of Shinto from the state.
>
> However, an additional lamentable feature is that the policemen are participating in the individual investigation of the persons who had joined our Society, since this was disadvantageous to the welfare of the shrine. This was a psychological blow to our members. Recently, the police confiscated our membership roster. Several months ago, policemen... came on three separate occasions to our office and advised that we accede to the landlord's request that we vacate the house, which we were using as combined office and living quarters. However, we have not as yet complied with this request since at present there are no suitable houses in this vicinity.
>
> As mentioned above, I firmly believe that the vigorous abetting of the Shinto shrines by the government officials is extremely contrary to the objectives of the occupation. I beg of you to investigate these conditions.[23]

One of the concerned parties was the Kume Shrine, located in Shimane Prefecture, which maintained a legend to the effect that Izanami's tomb is there. The other party was a group devoted to researching the ancient history of the region. Although it called itself a research society, the fact that at least some of the membership seem to have been living communally at the time of the complaint suggests that it may have been a Shinto-derived new religious movement. At any rate, the Society and the shrine seem to have been depending upon the same population for their support, creating competition between them. The shrine was able to prevail upon the local mayors to prevent people from joining the Society. Not only that, the police intimidated the Society's members by interrogating them, confiscating the membership roster, and trying to evict them. Faced with united opposition from the shrine, the mayors, and the police, the Society turned to the Occupation for help, based on the Shinto Directive. This case represented exactly the kind of collusion between shrines and government authority that the Shinto Directive was intended to eradicate. It is equally clear both that the habit of such collusion was difficult to break, and that the people based their resistance—and their sense of a right to be free of coercion from shrines—on the Shinto Directive.

The Emperor, the Postwar Constitution, and the Religious Corporations Law

Shinto greatly esteems its relations with the imperial house, and the divinity of the emperor had become a central tenet. Thus when Hirohito denied his divinity in his New Years' rescript of 1946, Shinto received a tremendous shock. Occupation officials had drafted a text for Hirohito to read on the radio (it was only the second time his voice had been broadcast, the surrender announcement being the first). The cabinet and officials of the Imperial Household Ministry negotiated with Occupation drafters, burying a line in the middle referring to the "mistaken idea" that the emperor is a living deity. The address fell far short of a direct renunciation of divinity. Even so, since the end of censorship in 1952, Shinto publications have bitterly deplored the emperor's "declaration of humanity" (*ningen sengen*) as one of the Occupation's worst deeds, part of a three-pronged attack on the *kokutai*, the other two being the Shinto Directive and the abolition of the Imperial Rescript on Education.[24]

The constitution adopted the principle of popular sovereignty. Article 1 stated that "the Emperor shall be the symbol of the State and of the unity of the people, deriving his position from the will of the people with whom resides sovereign power." With respect to imperial ritual, the constitution stated in article 7 that the emperor would "perform ceremonial functions" (*gishiki o okonau*). The ceremonies referenced here included New Year's celebrations, accession rites (*sokui rei*), and imperial funerals (*taisō no rei*). Perhaps most devastating was the 1947 abolition of legal status for the annual calendar of palace ritual. With this, palace ritual (*kyūchū saishi*), that is, the rituals performed by the emperor in the three palace ritual halls, lost all public significance and became private observances of the imperial family. Society had no obligation to take notice of them. Palace rites were the core of *jingi*, the ancient rituals codified in Kami Law (*jingiryō*) in the eighth century, coordinated through the Jingikan to align the monarch's palace rituals with mirroring ceremonies at shrines. These were the rites through which modern shrines had sought to unify the people. This change dissolved the legal foundations for Shinto's rationale as assisting the sovereign in rituals deemed to be essential to governance. Like the imperial renunciation of divinity, the changed status of palace ritual undermined Shinto's very reason for being. *Jinja shinpō*, the newspaper of the newly established National Association of Shinto Shrines, has produced over fifty editorials on this topic, vilifying the Occupation for the change, and calling for these rites to be returned to public status.[25]

The postwar constitution of 1947 established a new framework for relations between religion and the state. The constitution's main provisions on religion are contained in articles 20 and 89:

> *Article 20*: Freedom of religion is guaranteed to all. No religious organization shall receive any privileges from the state, nor exercise any political authority. No person shall be compelled to take part in any religious act, celebration, rite, or practice. The State and its organs shall refrain from religious education or any other religious activity.
>
> *Article 89*: No public money or other property shall be expended or appropriated for the use, benefit or maintenance of any religious institution or association or for any charitable, educational or benevolent enterprises not under the control of pubic authority.

Related to these two main articles, article 14 forbids "discrimination in political, economic, or social relations because of . . . creed," and article 19 prohibits any violation of freedom of thought or conscience.

Although the Occupation had compiled the document in secret, the Diet discussed the draft constitution as if it were the work of the Japanese government, eventually adopting it with some changes—all of which had to be approved by Occupation officials. None of the changes concerned religion. The Diet adopted the constitution, and it was promulgated by the emperor as his gift to the people, ostensibly as an amended version of the Meiji constitution.[26]

Shinto reaction to the provisions on religion was mixed. On the one hand, Shinto leaders could agree with leaders of other traditions that an unconditional guarantee of religious freedom was highly beneficial, and they took no issue with articles 14 and 19. But because problems concerning shrine lands was under consideration at the same time, the wording of article 89 prohibiting religious organizations from receiving any privileges from the state seemed to suggest that shrines would have to relinquish their land. When it became clear that the Occupation did not intend that outcome, this anxiety evaporated.

By the end of the war, some 1,374 shrines, or around one percent of the total, had been destroyed. This number does not take account of the other Shinto organizations, in which some 15 percent of the total number of churches is estimated to have been destroyed. In order to rebuild and move forward, it was imperative that these institutions be permitted to incorporate, allowing them to own property and operate businesses. By passage of the Religious Juridical Persons Law (*Shūkyō hōjinhō*, replacing the 1945 ordinance of the same name), also known as the Religious Corporations Law, in 1951, some 80,000 to 100,000 shrines were allowed to register as corporations.[27] Together with the constitution, the Religious Corporations Law provided the most fundamental legal framework for the operation of religious bodies in Japan from its adoption in 1951 until its 1996 revision.[28]

The new law freed religious organizations from bureaucratic supervision; nevertheless, some Buddhist and Christian leaders disliked it. They wanted the government to authorize religions as "genuine," based on the proposition that the people of Japan are not capable of making that determination.[29] By contrast, *Jinja shinpō* showed a clear understanding of the law. While criticizing it for lacking a clear definition of religion, the paper affirmed the desirability of preventing the state from making value judgments about religions or discriminating among them. The state should not, the paper wrote, become involved in questions of the truth or falsity of religious doctrine. Editorials advised readers not to expect this law to establish guidelines for discerning true religious organizations from fraudulent ones, because that responsibility rightfully belongs to the individual.[30]

The Founding of the National Association of Shinto Shrines

As the Occupation began, it was clear that Shinto would be severed from the state, and that it would fall to the priesthood to unite the shrine world in some new form. Kōten Kōkyūjo (formerly responsible for the priesthood's professional development), Dai Nihon Jingikai (the name of the national priesthood association at the end of the war), and Jingū Hōsaikai (the principal support group for the Ise Shrines) were the most influential groups at the time. They were joined by the Shinto Youth Organization (Shintō Seinen Konwakai, which in fact was composed of middle-aged men) and its forceful leader Ashizu Uzuhiko (1909–1992) in deliberations on a new, comprehensive organization to unite the Shinto world. The organization that emerged in February 1946, the National Association of Shinto Shrines, was the first Shinto organization formed entirely by the priesthood and lay shrine supporters, independent of government for the first time. It has become a multifaceted organization that not only manages shrine appointments and sets standards for the way that shrine rites and festivals are performed, but also seeks consensus among the priesthood on the range of issues that affect them, and lobbies for an evolving agenda of conservative causes.

Early planning for a new shrine association had adopted the form of a religious group, based on the assessment that it would no longer be possible to position shrines under government management.[31] The Shinto Youth Organization objected, however, that Shinto had no doctrines or sacred scriptures. To claim that the shrines are united by doctrine would be false. Moreover, shrines should be understood as a manifestation of Japanese identity and thus embrace the whole populace. To describe the association as religious would inevitably alienate those with prior religious commitments. Ashizu emphasized that shrines historically had been independent of any central doctrinal authority, denying that shrines should be seen as offshoots of Ise. Therefore, the new association should not take the form of a religious organization but instead should be a central point of contact for all shrines, without imposing any sort of doctrinal orthodoxy or subordination to Ise.[32]

At the eleventh hour, on December 2, 1945, the newspapers published special issues to announce the Occupation's arrest of fifty-nine suspected war criminals, including several significant figures from the shrine world. The Saishu of the Ise Shrines, Prince Nashimoto Morimasa (1874–1951), Mizuno Rentarō (1868–1949, president of the Dai Nihon Jingikai), and Hiranuma Kiichirō (1867–1952, vice-director of the Kōten Kōkyūjo) were ordered to report to Sugamo Prison on suspicion of having committed Class-A war crimes. Their arrests added elements of confusion, scandal, and urgency to the ongoing discussions about a new organization for Shinto.[33]

Because Prince Nashimoto was a senior member of the imperial family, his arrest was especially electrifying. He had been appointed Saishu of the Ise Grand Shrines in 1937, but he was largely a figurehead whose role was to represent the imperial house. He was the only member of the imperial family to be jailed on suspicion of war crimes, and the press regarded him sympathetically. He was released without charge after four months in prison, in April 1946, but the taint of arrest forced him to relinquish the post of Saishu and made it impossible for him to assume office in the new shrine association.[34]

Mizuno Rentarō had served as head of the Shrine Bureau and as Home Minister in 1918, from 1922 to 1923, and again in 1924. He was Education Minister from 1927 to 1928. Although a warrant for his arrest for Class-A war crimes was issued, he was excused on account of illness and advanced age and was not prosecuted, but he relinquished his post as head of the Dai Nihon Jingikai.[35]

Of these three men, only Hiranuma was actually charged and tried for war crimes. He was among a larger group of defendants who had held high-level political, military, or bureaucratic posts, and who were thought to have made the decision to initiate Japan's wars in China and elsewhere. The designation of "Class A" was reserved for those centrally involved in the decisions leading Japan into wars of aggression, as distinguished from those charged with conventional war crimes or "crimes against humanity" (Class B), and the planning, ordering, or failure to prevent such crimes (Class C). The charges against Hiranuma stemmed from his involvement in decisions to go to war against China and the Allies.[36]

The charges against these men contained nothing regarding their participation in Shinto, and the Occupation drew no connection between Shinto and war crimes. Press coverage of these arrests carried no mention of Mizuno's and Hiranuma's Shinto affiliations. While Mizuno and Nashimoto arguably had the closest connections with Shinto, they were not even charged in the end.

For lack of any alternative, NASS elected to register as a religious corporation under the Religious Corporations Ordinance (*Shūkyō hōjin rei*) of December 28,

1945. The association's Charter identified the Ise Grand Shrines as the highest and most respected shrines. But while the decision to become a religious corporation allowed NASS to incorporate and enjoy corporate tax benefits, the old arguments about the religious character of shrines and the status of doctrine within Shinto continued. The proclamation issued on NASS's founding states:

> The ultimate meaning of reverence for shrines is to draw near to *kannagara no michi,* to clarify the Way of morality, to give thanks for divine favor, to preserve and practice the divine virtue of our ancestors, faithfully and with great care to invigorate the spiritual character of the Yamato people, and thus manifest, clarify, strengthen, and raise up our traditional faith of contribution to the welfare and peace of humanity.[37]

This passage appears to contain a host of doctrines: the existence and significance of the mysterious *kannagara no michi,* the existence of the Kami and the ancestors, and their power to bestow divine favor. Yet the insistence that Shinto has no doctrines persisted.

The purpose of the association is "to encourage Shinto rituals, promote the prosperity of Shinto shrines, and support the continuity of Japanese culture and traditions."[38] NASS assumed the responsibility of distributing talismans from the Ise Shrines nationwide. Branches of the association were established in each prefecture. Strong powers were vested in the association to appoint and remove priests from office, and to standardize shrine ritual, based on the presurrender system of shrine ranks and approved rites, as well as continuing to align shrine rites with those of the imperial house and the Ise shrines.[39]

NASS had no power to compel shrines to join it. As of 1955, there were 79,387 member shrines in the association. At the time, there were around 110,000 shrines. Thus by 1955, approximately 72 percent of all shrines had elected to join the association, meaning that a little over one-fourth had decided against joining.[40] It is not difficult to surmise which ones might have hesitated.

The association was formed in part to fill the vacuum left by the elimination of government supervision. NASS claimed authority to appoint or remove the Chief Priest of the former Imperial and National Shrines, a provision those shrines would surely have resisted. Likewise, those shrines not wishing to be governed by a novel association, those without a strong commitment to the presurrender ritual calendar, those wishing to return to customary rites unrelated to the nation, those not wishing to follow the practice of the Ise Shrines, and those lacking financial resources to support the association are the most obvious candidates to have rejected it. In 1948, new provisions limiting NASS intervention in personnel decisions in some shrines were introduced, mainly the former Imperial and National Shrines.[41]

The Issue of State-owned Shrine Lands

The new association campaigned intensively to assure that shrines be allowed to retain the land that they had customarily occupied, proving that it could lobby effectively for shrine interests. This early success went some distance toward overcoming resistance to the association.

In 1945 many shrines and temples were technically occupying public land without paying for it. They did not hold legal title to the land, though it could be argued that their customary stewardship was legitimate, based on a long history that had been interrupted by the state seizing their land in 1868.[42] Only a very small number of shrines were huge landholders. These were the shrines that stood to lose the most if they were forced to relinquish all the land that was either state-owned or subject to redistribution in the postwar land reform. There would have been a considerable overlap between these shrines and the former Imperial and National shrines, that is, those that were structurally positioned to resist the association's leadership of all shrines.

From the Occupation's point of view, the problem of shrine lands pitted the value of religious freedom against that of separation of religion from state. If the shrines were deprived of their land entirely, they would be unable to continue. They would be forced out of existence if, for instance, they had been compelled either to vacate all their land or buy it at market value. For the Occupation knowingly to place the shrines in such a position would have been an egregious violation of the right to religious freedom. On the other hand, if shrines were granted title to their lands with no compensation to the state, that would have violated the principle of separation of religion from state.[43]

NASS campaigned extensively for the passage of a bill providing a formula under which most shrines could keep their land. In 1946 the association had begun publishing a newspaper, *Jinja shinpō*, which ran numerous editorials on the land issue. The editorials argued strongly that revenue produced by land is integral to the religious function of temples as well as shrines, and that it would be an infringement of religious freedom to prevent them from drawing on that income.[44]

Occupation officials agreed that shrines had a rightful claim to their property. The Supreme Commander of the Allied Powers (SCAP) issued a directive on November 13, 1946, that gave shrines title to the land they needed for the performance of their religious functions, gratis.[45] A *Jinja shinpō* editorial of September 15, 1947, noted that an appropriate solution had been reached. By 1952, virtually all applications for title to customary land holdings had been approved. But shrines that lost considerable forest or agricultural land remained disgruntled, as did the shrines for the war dead, which were left out of the settlement.[46]

The Occupation reserved a decision on land held by shrines for the war dead until 1951. During the interval, the question was a matter of some anxiety, because without clear title to their land, those shrines could not move forward to rebuild or plan for the future. NASS developed proposals for reforming these shrines to remove militaristic elements by appointing Shinto priests to take over from the military officers who had customarily been appointed their Chief Priests.[47] *Jinja shinpō* had been calling for the end to military appointments from 1946:

> We hear that there are many cases in which former career military officers have been made Chief Priest of a shrine or Chief of Shrine Elders, or Chief of a support group... It goes without saying that it is inappropriate for shrines, which have only lately cast off the distortions of an exclusive nationalism, to be associated with former career military officers, whose war responsibility is now being investigated.[48]

As the Occupation was ending, in 1951, the Religions Division decided that shrines for the war dead would be allowed to purchase land on the same basis as other shrines, and with that, the matter came to a close.

The Tsu City Grounds Purification Case

The new constitution radically altered the configuration of "the public." After the end of Occupation censorship, the media was largely freed of restrictions (though taboos on topics connected with the emperor remained). The public sphere proliferated with print and broadcast media, including television, and debate flourished. Civil society grew with the end of prewar restrictions, and a great variety of new religious movements vied for new members. Shinto had to carve out a new place for itself in this changed public realm. Consequential lawsuits began to establish new parameters for Shinto ceremonial in public life.

In 1965 the city of Tsu (Mie Prefecture) held a grounds purification ceremony (*jichinsai*) to inaugurate construction of a city gymnasium. *Jichinsai* had originated in ancient Japan as a Daoist ritual to calm or pacify (*shizumeru*) the spirits of the earth in advance of construction. In modern times, shrine priests or the clergy of Shinto-derived new religious movements generally perform *jichinsai*, which can be relatively simple or quite elaborate, depending on the type and scale of the construction. *Jichinsai* requires marking off a sacred space within the construction site with four fresh bamboo poles, strung together by rope festooned with paper streamers (*shimenawa*). A portable altar is placed within this space, laden with fresh fruit offerings, sake, salt, and water. The property owners and representatives of the construction firm assemble inside the ropes, facing the altar. One or more priests intones a *norito* invoking the blessings of the earth spirits on the construction project to come, that it may be safe and successful. He, she (or they) sprinkle salt, sake, and small squares of colored paper at each corner, and bury a small quantity of five grains. After purifying those in attendance, priests and participants offer small sprigs of *sakaki* on the altar.[49]

It was quite common and unexceptional to perform *jichinsai* for civic buildings at the time of the Tsu case. Nevertheless, a member of the Tsu City Council raised a lawsuit, claiming violation of articles 20 and 89 of the constitution. One question was whether it is proper to regard *jichinsai* as a religious ritual, given that it had become widespread and seemed to carry no particular doctrinal message. The district court found for the plaintiff, but the appeals court reversed that verdict, and the case went to the Supreme Court. The high court's 1977 ruling, which has become a standard, ruled that no total separation of religion from state is possible, but that activity "whose purpose carries a religious meaning, and whose effect is to support, encourage, or promote religion, or to oppress or interfere with it" is prohibited. This is referred to as the "purpose and effect standard" (*mokuteki-kōka kijun*). By this understanding, there can exist "ceremonies" which are not "religious," because some rituals such as *jichinsai* have become more "customary" than religious in nature, the process of secularization having weakened their religious meaning.

The Tsu case introduced an important distinction between religious and customary ceremonies that allows local governments to use public funds to conduct rites performed by shrine priests. The case is particularly significant in opening a role for postwar public ceremonies deriving from Shinto and in rekindling ideas about the relevance of Shinto to all, regardless of religious belief. Subsequent lawsuits testing the meaning of the constitution's provisions on religion focused on the Yasukuni Shrine.

The Yasukuni Shrine in Postwar Japan

From 1946 until his death, Tsukuba Fujimaro (1905–1977) was the Head Priest of the Yasukuni Shrine, the first to have been appointed from the imperial family. Within a week of Tsukuba's appointment, the shrine lost its official status and funding, going on to become a religious corporation.[50] Not having a territory-based group of parishioners to support it, Yasukuni Shrine faced a dire financial situation after the surrender. The shrine had to open itself to a more diverse clientele, creating ceremonies and festivals with wider appeal, and cultivating groups to support it. Veterans' associations provided a natural clientele, and eventually the shrine came to host more than sixty such groups. The National Federation of War Comrades (Zenkoku sen'yū rengōkai) was founded in 1968 for the purpose of promoting the restoration of state support to Yasukuni. Composed of 212 veterans' groups from all branches of service, in 2002 it donated over $90,000 to Yasukuni. While veterans' groups are staunch supporters of Yasukuni, their advancing age and declining numbers indicate that the shrine cannot count on their support indefinitely.[51]

Since the surrender, Yasukuni has come to offer many of the same commodified rituals found at other shrines: New Years' rites, wedding ceremonies, Shichi-go-san (rites for the safety and untroubled growth of children), prayers for safety during astrologically inauspicious years (*yaku barai*), prayers for success in school entrance examinations, and a variety of other this-worldly benefits. Yasukuni initiated the Mitama Matsuri Festival in 1946, a nighttime festival of lanterns and dance to honor and comfort the dead, which has become a major summer event for the city of Tokyo. The spring and autumn festivals were the occasions when new spirits of the war dead were deified, and they inevitably carried military associations. By contrast, the Mitama Matsuri was intended to provide a time of remembrance of all the dead.[52]

Yasukuni Shrine had originally addressed only the collectivity of the war dead and did not cater to individual requests, consistent with the idea that the spirits had irrevocably merged into the shrine's object of worship through divinization rites. In 1950, however, the shrine began to offer Eitai Kagura or "eternal shrine dance" for specific spirits, starting at a price of 100,000 yen. Individual masses (*ireisai*) were also introduced, at 30,000 yen per ceremony. In 1982, spirit marriage ceremonies were created, allowing clients to bring dolls representing brides to stand in alongside photographs of the groom, so that men who had gone to their deaths unmarried could enjoy the benefits of marriage posthumously.[53] In these various ways, Yasukuni became much more like an ordinary shrine in terms of soliciting revenue through festivals and fee-based ceremonies, while retaining the character of a war memorial.[54]

The scope of spirits enshrined at Yasukuni has expanded over the postwar years. Head Priest Tsukuba had enshrined B- and C-class war criminals from 1959; when asked whether he would enshrine Class-A war criminals, he did not refuse, but said that the timing of such a move would be very sensitive and speculated that it could not happen during his lifetime.[55]

Returning from a 1963 trip to participate in the Religionists' Mission to Abolish Nuclear Weapons project, Tsukuba established a small sub-shrine, close by Yasukuni's main sanctuary, called the Chinreisha.[56] It enshrines two kinds of spirits that are not enshrined at the main sanctuary: first, the spirits of Japanese who have perished in pursuit of their professions since 1853, in war or international incidents, of illness, or from suicide; and second, the spirits of foreigners who have died in war or other military encounters. All of these spirits are to be "comforted" or consoled (*hō'i*), while those enshrined in Yasukuni's main sanctuary are to be "honored" (*kenshō*) as well as comforted or consoled. The Chinreisha is described as enshrining the victims of all wars.

Since Head Priest Tsukuba did not clarify why he established the Chinreisha, much speculation arose to ferret out his true purpose. One of the more plausible notions is that a shrine of this kind would allow for the enshrinement of those on the losing side of the Boshin War (some of whom had committed suicide) or others, such as Saigō Takamori, who are popularly regarded as heroes of the Meiji restoration, even though they perished opposing the imperial side. It has been noted also that the Chinreisha would include the victims of the firebombing of Tokyo. The inclusion of all victims of war from all nations substantiates the shrine's claims to offer prayers for peace. Beyond these reasons, the decision may have been related to the question of Class-A war criminals. Head Priest Tsukuba was undoubtedly aware that to enshrine them in an explicit way would place the emperor in a difficult position. Japan's acceptance of the San Francisco Treaty was interpreted by the government of Japan as accepting the verdicts of the Tokyo War Crimes Trials. The emperor could hardly pay respects at a shrine that deified the convicted without contradicting his government's position. Knowing this, Head Priest Tsukuba resisted the Stewards' call to enshrine those spirits in the Main Sanctuary, though the Chinreisha could be regarded as including them.

National Foundation Day

One of NASS's early political successes was the 1966 establishment of Kigensetsu, a renaming of the presurrender holiday commemorating the enthronement of the legendary first emperor, Jinmu. The Jinmu ceremony had been abolished by the Occupation for reeking of nationalism and militarism. There was widespread popular support for establishing a holiday to celebrate the birth of the nation, to be called Foundation Day, but deep-rooted division about *when* to celebrate it. February 11 was the date that Jinmu had supposedly ascended the throne. Other proposals included the anniversary of the postwar constitution (May 3), the anniversary of Prince Shōtoku's constitution in ancient times, or the anniversary of the San Francisco Peace Treaty (April 28). The point at issue was the date, not the holiday itself, because while a majority could agree on the idea of a national holiday to celebrate the nation's founding, different dates made a huge difference in the holiday's ideological associations. A decision for February 11 affirmed Japan's past, including the war, while a decision for April 28 affirmed Japan's postwar commitment to pacifism and the idea that the nation was born anew in 1947. For NASS it was axiomatic that the holiday should be set for February 11, to repudiate the Occupation and to affirm the monarchy and the role of shrine ritual in national life.

The campaign to establish Kigensetsu in law began in 1948, and in 1952, Liberal Democratic Party (hereinafter LDP) politicians adopted the issue. NASS expected that the bill would be docketed at that time, but it was crowded out by discussion of the peace treaty and other, weightier issues. Private celebrations of Kigensetsu were held in Tokyo in 1956, including a parade that drew much attention.[57] In 1959, NASS and the general public celebrated Kigensetsu again on a large scale. About 3,000 people attended ceremonies in Hibiya Hall. The Members of Parliament who attended signed a resolution calling for the day to be made a legal holiday. In 1959 the issue was again crowded out of Diet debate by other issues. In 1960, anticipating bitter opposition by the Socialist, Democratic, and other parties, the LDP delayed Diet discussion by creating a study group on the issue. NASS kept preparing pamphlets for the public on the holiday as well as many forms of advertising regarding the various observances around the country, continuing this campaign through 1966.[58]

The 1960 renewal of the US-Japan Security Treaty ushered in a new era of Japanese politics. New religions Sōka Gakkai and the ultraconservative Seichō no Ie jostled to make their voices heard. Sōka Gakkai formed its own political party in 1964, called the Clean Government Party (Kōmeitō), while other fast-growing new religious movements like Seichō no Ie, Reiyūkai Kyōdan, and some of the Shinto sects became reliable sources of block votes for the LDP. Having been suppressed before the surrender and with the experience of its founder having died in prison, Sōka Gakkai was adamantly opposed to any public role—much less public support—for anything related to Shinto. The League of New Religious Movements (Shin Nihon Shūkyō Dantai Rengōkai), led by a Buddhist laypersons' group, Risshō Kōseikai, not only opposed any public support for Shinto, but also was becoming involved in politics as a funder of many centrist politicians, including those in the LDP. Because the League included many fast-growing groups with an urban base, politicians eagerly vied for their support.

In 1966, rather than letting the issue die again, the LDP prime minister delegated the task of determining the date to an advisory council (*shingikai*), a strategy frequently used to circumvent contentious Diet debate when the government seeks an endorsement for some policy. When the committee eventually recommended February 11, Foundation Day was established for that date. *Jinja shinpō* expressed its elation in an editorial blaming the Occupation for society's lack of unanimity: "The Occupation forces, wielding absolute, limitless authority, ignored our opposition and the opinion of the majority of the people to snuff out and eradicate February 11." The Occupation's true aim, the paper wrote, was to crush the Japanese spirit and destroy the *kokutai*.[59]

As Japanese politics became increasingly polarized through opposition to renewal of the US-Japan Security Treaty, NASS's monarchism and nostalgia for presurrender Japan aligned it with the far right, giving the organization a reputation for ideological extremism. NASS undoubtedly realized that the Kigensetsu decision might easily have gone against it. Opposition to the measure in the legislature and in society remained strong and reflected the support of respected academics, religious groups, unions, and about half of the general public.

NASS's political influence was blunted by the rapid rise of new religious movements. NASS could not compete with them in terms of numbers, money, or commitment. Populated in large proportion by zealous recent converts, these movements were becoming active in politics, and they were highly attractive to politicians because of the promise of committed organizing and bloc voting. Their members could be counted on to vote for the candidates endorsed by their leaders. NASS could not deliver so many votes. Some of the new movements tithed and thus were accumulating funds at a rate that NASS could not match. The Kigensetsu campaign proved that NASS needed allies both inside and outside party politics. While those who had lived through the war favored NASS's stance, the new religions had a slice of that demographic sector and also a large youth membership to whom NASS appeared antiprogressive.

The Yasukuni Bill

The Occupation had banned public funerals for the war dead, but after 1952 Japan sought a dignified way to memorialize them. The task was made more difficult for the fact that the government of Japan had never issued its own statement on the war and its meaning. Yet the remains of the dead continued to be repatriated, as the last prisoners of war were not released from captivity in the Soviet Union until 1956, and thus the issue remained unresolved.

Although Yasukuni Shrine became a religious corporation, many people, politicians among them, continued to regard it as Japan's main war memorial. Ordinarily, foreign dignitaries could be expected to pay tribute at a national war memorial, but in 1953, the US vice president Richard Nixon canceled a planned trip to Yasukuni, hastening the Japanese government's efforts to provide a memorial that was not sectarian. At the same time, however, foreign military personnel as well as a small number of diplomats from foreign countries occasionally did visit Yasukuni. These events kept alive the hope that Yasukuni could become recognized as Japan's official national war memorial. These visits were also cited as evidence that such recognition already existed outside Japan.

The completion of the Chidorigafuchi National Cemetery (Chidorigafuchi Senbotsusha no Boen) in 1959, less than a mile away from Yasukuni, rekindled the issue. Chidorigafuchi was an ossuary, where the cremains of unidentified persons were held. NASS, Yasukuni Shrine, and the Association of Nation-Protecting Shrines grew anxious that Chidorigafuchi, which overlooked the moat of the imperial palace and was devoid of any symbolism glorifying war, could divert sentiment away from Yasukuni. The 1959 Chidorigafuchi completion ceremonies focused on interring the remains of 600 persons, and flowers were sent from the imperial house, the prime minister, the heads of both Diet houses, the Supreme Court, and the governors of each prefecture. The emperor and empress attended, and a stone stele was unveiled, on which a moving poem by the emperor commemorating the loss of the war dead had been carved. The emperor and empress continued to attend the ceremonies annually until 1964, after which a member of the imperial family attended on their behalf.[60]

The Izokukai, the country's largest association for the war bereaved, was a nationwide organization of eight million members, which could deliver so many votes that no politician could ignore it. Beginning in 1956, the Izokukai began lobbying for restoring state support to Yasukuni. In 1959, it collected 2,950,000 signatures for this cause. Many politicians were themselves among the bereaved, and a powerful alliance grew up between them and Izokukai. Yasukuni was a potent symbol for the Izokukai, channeling pain, grief, and loss into focused political action. As of 1962, when Kaya Okinori became the Izokukai president, the group added the aim of "honoring the glorious war dead" (*eirei no kenshō*) to their traditional slogans of world peace, social welfare, and the prevention of war. Serving until 1977, Kaya essentially turned the Izokukai into a support group for Yasukuni Shrine.[61] The Izokukai wanted to reconstitute the spectacle of the emperor worshipping there, surrounded by the leaders of his government and his armed forces.[62]

Yasukuni Shrine had developed its own draft for a "Yasukuni Bill" in 1957 and continued to issue calls for the shrine to remain a Shinto establishment under state support, but reclassified as a "special corporation." The draft held that Yasukuni Shrine's registration as a religious corporation was not binding. From 1964, Izokukai and Yasukuni Shrine began holding joint meetings to work toward the passage of legislation, hoping to accomplish this in time for the shrine's 100th anniversary in 1969.

In 1963, the government began holding an annual commemoration for all victims of war on August 15. Perhaps to test public sentiment, the LDP decided to hold the 1964 commemoration at Yasukuni Shrine. The Japan Socialist Party objected and questioned whether backdoor methods were being used to give Yasukuni Shrine some special status. Christian groups strongly objected. The commemoration was held as planned, but the LDP retreated from this public display of commitment to Yasukuni and in later years held the event at the Nippon Budōkan, a mammoth hall in central Tokyo.[63]

The LDP commissioned a study in 1963, calling on Yasukuni to essentially shed its Shinto identity: remove *torii*, swords, and mirrors; cease calling the ritualists "shrine priests" (*shinshoku*); delete Shinto prayer from ritual; cease performing purifications and *kagura*; and even cease invoking the Kami. Without such changes, the study stated, public funds could not be extended to the shrine, because to do so would conflict with article 89, the clause prohibiting state expenditure in support of religion.[64] Although the shrine could hardly agree to these conditions, politicians pushed ahead without its consent, proposing to dissolve the shrine as a religious corporation and reclassify it as a nonreligious body.[65]

Over the years 1969 to 1974, LDP politicians tried five times to pass the Yasukuni Bill.[66] In each case but the last, the bill was docketed but then nullified because the session ended before it was brought to the floor. In other words, the LDP was not so committed to the bill that it was prepared to move the Yasukuni Bill up the docket or extend the session in order to debate it. The failure of the bill in 1969 came as a particular disappointment, because 1969 was Yasukuni's centennial anniversary, and the shrine's supporters very much wanted to celebrate a legislative victory on that occasion. Several tens of thousands of people worshipped at Yasukuni on the surrender anniversary that year. *Jinja shinpō* wrote that the LDP had capitulated to religious organizations and also criticized Yasukuni for depending on the Izokukai to battle on its behalf.[67]

The bill was submitted each time without significant change. Diet debate centered on the question whether the shrine was religious and whether it would be unconstitutional to support it with public funds. The opposition parties and the press strongly objected to what they termed the LDP's "steamrollering" tactics. Legal scholars and historians prepared statements opposing the bill. Higashi Honganji, headquarters temple of one of the largest Buddhist sects, prepared a statement: "We demand that deliberations be conducted in a manner that does not infringe upon religious freedom." Shinshū Ōtani-ha, another large Buddhist sect, sent telegrams to the Diet opposing the bill. The Japan Religionists' Peace Council (Nihon Shūkyōsha Heiwa Kyōgikai) predicted that other Asian countries would be alarmed and intimidated if the bill were adopted. Several religious groups held hunger strikes against the bill. The Sōka Gakki Youth Group (2.5 million members) held mass meetings and distributed handbills across the country. A coalition of Christian, Buddhist, and new religious movements expressed unease with the idea that the shrine would become a different kind of entity *after* the bill passed; if the shrine truly had a will to transform itself, they asked, why did it not speedily do so? Many found the bill's presumption that there would be *future* war dead deeply troubling.[68]

Jinja shinpō, countered with the case of the Tokyoto Ireidō, a public memorial for the victims of the Taishō Earthquake of 1923 and the 1945 fire bombings, funded by the city of Tokyo. This facility was set up as a special corporation, but it nevertheless holds Buddhist memorial rites conducted by clergy. If no one objects to that, why should Yasukuni be any different?[69]

NASS had learned from its experience in the campaign to revive Kigensetsu that politicians could be fickle. In response, it began to cultivate LDP politicians individually, leading to the 1969 founding of the League of Shinto Politicians (Shinto Seiji Renmei; its preferred English translation is Shinto Association of Spiritual Leadership). This organization now has its offices in the NASS building. NASS expected League members to support its causes and, in consultation with the League, nominated thirteen candidates for the upper house elections of 1971. But it did not yet have enough members in 1974 to turn the tide in favor of the Yasukuni Bill.

During the period the bill was being debated, an interim verdict was rendered in the Tsu City case. The Nagoya District Court found, in 1971, that the use of public funds to pay for the grounds purification ceremony was unconstitutional. This ruling denied the old rhetoric holding that shrines are not religious, cross-cutting the Yasukuni Shrine Bill's presumption that the shrine could be made nonreligious, and underlining the constitution's prohibition on public expenditures for religious organizations.[70] This ruling undoubtedly caused LDP politicians to waver in their support for Yasukuni Shrine.

The LDP was not united in support of the bill, and as it faced increasing opposition, Nakasone Yasuhiro (later to become prime minister) suggested abandoning Yasukuni in favor of constructing an entirely new facility unhindered by Yasukuni's religious baggage. He said bluntly that the claims of the bill's supporters that Yasukuni was or ever could be nonreligious was a fabrication.[71] On the eve of the bill's final defeat, *Jinja shinpō* wrote that the annual submission of the Yasukuni Bill had become absolutely pointless. The editorial threatened, however, that if the party were to break its promise of support, shrine supporters would expose its treachery and seek a new approach.[72]

Lessons Learned

NASS's activism in the failed Yasukuni Bill campaign positioned it at the other end of the political spectrum from the True Pure Land Buddhist sects, Sōka Gakkai, and Christianity. NASS's politicization created popular associations with far-right politics, but many ordinary shrine priests were focused on developing positive images for their shrines, did not want to get involved in politics, and began to wonder why NASS did not accord them more importance. Put another way, it became clear that NASS did not necessarily represent the priorities of shrine priests as a group, exposing a gap between NASS and the people it supposedly represented. In NASS as in religious organizations generally, politics proved to be divisive.

As in the revival of Kigensetsu, the LDP had proved unreliable. Politicians could win the votes of the most conservative by appearing to back the Yasukuni Bill, without actually passing it. Those voters did not have alternative candidates in any other parties, so the LDP risked little by bringing up the measure repeatedly but failing to pass it. Also, the Yasukuni Bill campaign exposed division within the LDP between Yasukuni backers and Nakasone's faction, who wanted a new war memorial. While the LDP had been a disappointment, however, the Izokukai had proved to be a strong ally. The League of Shinto Politicians proved to be a good idea, but it did not yet function as a nationwide network rivaling the larger Buddhist organizations' political clout. The scholars supporting NASS's position were neither so numerous nor so persuasive as the liberal historians outside the Shinto universities who opposed NASS. Clearly, NASS needed academic heavyweights.

Official Prime Ministerial Visits to Yasukuni, 1974–1985

After the failure of the Yasukuni Bill, NASS pursued three main strategies toward its long-term goal of state support for Yasukuni: promotion of official visits to the shrine by the prime minister and his cabinet (*kōshiki sanpai*), countering lawsuits brought against the shrine, and cooperation with like-minded groups such as the Association to Answer the War Dead.

Most postwar prime ministers had visited Yasukuni during their term of office, the exceptions being the second postwar prime minister, Hatoyama Ichirō (1954–56) and his successor Ishibashi Tanzan (1956–57). A custom of prime ministers visiting on the spring and/or fall festivals had emerged by the time of Tanaka Kakuei (1972–74). Post-Occupation cabinets also revived another practice that the Occupation had forbidden, visiting the Ise Shrines to announce their assumption of office to the Kami.

Prime Minister Miki Takeo (1974–76) introduced a new nuance, visiting Yasukuni on August 15, the surrender anniversary. Subsequent prime ministers through Nakasone Yasuhiro (1982–1987), with the exception of Ōhira Masayoshi (1979–1980), a Christian, continued to visit Yasukuni on the surrender anniversary. Since the change came the year following the defeat of the Yasukuni Bill, it was widely interpreted as a reassertion of LDP determination to give the shrine official status in the future. In spite of these associations, and in spite of his initial assertions that he would visit the shrine in his official capacity, however, when August 15, 1975, came, Miki retreated, stating that he had visited as a private individual, not as prime minister (*kōshiki sanpai*).[73]

Beginning with this visit and continuing for a decade, the media, religious groups outside Shinto, liberal academics, and political activists on the left questioned the constitutionality of *kōshiki sanpai*. The indicators of an "official" visit included the source of any money offering the minister made to the shrine, or the source for a gift of *sakaki* plants, flowers or other offerings, whether he used his official car, and whether he signed the shrine register merely with his name, or his official title. All concerned appeared to assume that using any public funds would violate article 89. Alongside these developments, in 1975 Hirohito made his seventh and (as it turned out) final postwar visit to Yasukuni Shrine, despite strong protest from religious groups and extensive debate in the Diet.

NASS took a dim view of Prime Minister Miki's innovation, seeing it as muddying the waters by introducing an inappropriate distinction between "private" and "official" (*kōshiki*) visits:

> An "official visit to Yasukuni Shrine" (*Yasukuni Jinja kōshiki sanpai*) is the minimal form in which the country pays respect to the Yasukuni Shrine. In spite of this, for more than thirty years since the war, not even this has been done. Last year, in spite of announcing that he would visit Yasukuni Shrine in his capacity as prime minister, in the end, Prime Minister Miki visited as a private individual (*kojin*). The memory of his disgraceful behavior is still fresh.[74]

The year 1976 saw the formation of the Association to Answer the War Dead (Eirei ni Kotaeru Kai), a coalition of forty-plus right-wing groups, including NASS, sections of Izokukai, the far-right new religion Seichō no Ie, women's groups, veterans' groups, and educational groups. These groups were well established, and the major players already had a history of mutual cooperation. The first president of the association was Ishida Kazuto (1903–1979), a former Supreme Court justice known for his campaign to rid the Japanese courts of liberal judges. His remarks at the May 1978 ceremonies marking the founding of the Kagoshima branch of the Association to Answer the War Dead illustrate his thinking:

> The first thing the Occupation troops tried to do when they landed in Japan was get rid of Yasukuni Shrine. They hoped to rip out the soul of the Japanese. That war was one that Japan could not avoid fighting.... I revere those two million five hundred thousand glorious war dead who gave their lives so that Japan could live in peace, and I sincerely thank them.[75]

In September 1978 he wrote a letter to the magazine *Gekkan Keizai*:

> The Tokyo War Crimes Trials were the other side's trick.... They wanted to destroy the Japanese concept of *kokutai* and leave nothing for the Japanese soul to rely upon. The problem with the Yasukuni Shrine has the same origin.[76]

As these remarks make clear, the Association to Answer the War Dead claimed that Japan's postwar recovery owed to the sacrifice of the war dead. It repudiated the war crimes trials and charged that the Occupation tried to crush the defeated enemy by starving them of the spiritual sustenance they took from the Yasukuni Shrine and the *kokutai*.

The new Association hoped ultimately to bring Yasukuni official status and public funding, by building a broad consensus in society. NASS explained the aims of the new organization as follows:

> To hang our hopes [for official status for Yasukuni] on legislation is meaningless, as we painfully realize. The formation of the Association to Answer the War Dead comes from the belief that it would be better to form a movement that comes from the depths of national feeling.[77]

NASS also hoped to reverse its image of being made up of retrograde reactionaries trying to return Japan to the presurrender past. They wanted to make support for Yasukuni seem "natural" and unproblematic. They began a multifaceted public relations campaign that included the publication of books and even film production.[78] They also conducted pilgrimages to battlefields to collect the remains of the Japanese war dead. These moving journeys became an important means to transmit their view of history to a new generation. Press interviews provided opportunities to reassure the public; Ashizu Uzuhiko made this statement in one such interview: "State Shinto will not be revived. There is not one single shrine belonging to NASS . . . that wants to revive the State Shinto system."[79]

After the failure of the Yasukuni Bill, a host of civil society groups and private persons began to file lawsuits against officials who used public funds for shrine visits, mainly to Yasukuni but including other shrines as well. They hoped to secure a Supreme Court ruling that would determine that politicians' visits to Yasukuni Shrine were unconstitutional, as a preliminary step toward getting a verdict that would prevent the shrine being given public funding.[80] Thus the battle over Yasukuni opened a new front in the late 1970s, though the final verdicts on most of the cases did not emerge until after 2000.

In 1979, NASS rejoiced at the codification in law of the custom of recording dates according to imperial reigns (*gengō*). The legal basis for the use of reign names had been abolished as a result of 1947 revisions to the Imperial Household Law (*kōshitsu tenpan*). But the newspapers, textbooks, and media in general continued to use the system, under which 1979 was called "Shōwa 54," designating the fifty-fourth year of the rule of the Shōwa emperor, that is, Hirohito. The great majority of the Japanese people favored retaining the system rather than changing to the Western dating system, mainly because they were accustomed to it. The LDP prepared legislation, and after the usual processes, a bill was adopted without widespread opposition.

In the 1980s, NASS became involved in a debate regarding whether Japan's takeover of territory in Korea and China should be presented in textbooks as an *invasion* (*shinryaku*) or an *advance* (*shinshutsu*). A variant of the same issue queried whether Japan's military history from the Manchurian Incident of 1931 through the defeat was appropriately described as an "aggressive war" (*shinryaku sensō*).[81] The Ministry of Education had added a new standard for textbook review in 1982, calling for texts to "consider Japan's friendship with neighboring Asian countries from the perspective of international understanding and cooperation." NASS criticized the term *invasion* because of the effects it foresaw for Japanese youth. Citing a prime minister's survey on youth attitudes around the world, *Jinja shinpō* bemoaned the finding that only 70 percent of Japanese youth expressed pride in their country, while the number in the United States was in the high nineties. Whereas most other countries sampled showed that a majority of youth wished to be of service to their nation, that sentiment was expressed by less than 40 percent of Japanese youth.[82] By contrast, when asked what kind of life they wanted, most young Japanese said either that they wanted to be free to live as they pleased or that they wanted to be rich. *Jinja shinpō* regarded these aspirations as irresponsible, passive, and hedonistic and blamed the textbooks. The paper called for a robust, positive portrayal of Japan's past that could inspire youth to constructive ambition, warning that textbooks describing the Japanese empire in terms of imperialism encourage "masochistic" (*jigyaku-teki*) attitudes. The real source of the problem lies, the paper opined, in the "Tokyo War Crimes Trial view of history" (*Tokyo saiban shikan*), which led textbook writers to give young readers the impression that Japan's modern history was a series of unilateral, rapacious seizures.[83]

Enshrining Class-A War Criminals at Yasukuni Shrine

In 1978 Matsudaira Nagayoshi (1915–2005) succeeded Tsukuba Fujimaro as Head Priest of Yasukuni Shrine, adopting the slogan, "All Japanese are *ujiko* of Yasukuni," as a way of promoting popular support. He revived the shrine's museum, Yūshūkan, in 1986, using its exhibits to repudiate the Tokyo War Crimes Trials and to glorify the war dead. Soon after assuming office, Matsudaira performed rites to deify fourteen Class-A war criminals, who had been executed (or died in prison awaiting execution) following verdicts at the Tokyo War Crimes Trials, referring to them as the "Shōwa Martyrs."[84]

Cabinet Secretary Miyazawa Kiichi announced, in 1980, the LDP's position that an official visit (*kōshiki sanpai*) to the Yasukuni Shrine by the prime minister would be unconstitutional. Two years later, the LDP formed a committee to study the Yasukuni issue in the hopes of finding some interpretation of Prime Ministerial shrine visits that would not be unconstitutional. In defiance of the party's official position, however, prime ministers continued to visit Yasukuni each August 15 from 1980 to 1985. Their evident determination to persist in defiance of the party's position made clear again that the LDP was internally divided on the issue. Also clear was the fact that some in its most conservative wing found that patronizing the shrine was useful, even when, or perhaps especially when, they assumed a stance of resistance to the party's mainstream. To pose as patriots by going to Yasukuni on August 15 did not mean, however, that those politicians were necessarily reliable allies of the conservative groups that supported them. These dynamics were similar to those seen in the earlier controversy about the Yasukuni Bill, a fact that was not lost on NASS.

Prime Minister Nakasone proved to be especially problematic, because though he continued to visit Yasukuni, he had not repudiated his earlier statement that a completely new war memorial to supplant Yasukuni might be a better option. As Japan's relations with China had deepened, prime ministers before him increasingly paid attention to Chinese sentiments regarding the ongoing textbook debates. None of his predecessors had, however, gone so far as to admit that Japan had fought a "war of aggression" (*shinryaku sensō*). In 1983, in the face of opinion surveys showing rapidly declining popular support for his administration, and with the prospect of a visit to China by his cabinet secretary, Nakasone broke the taboo and characterized Japan's past actions as a war of aggression, stating that he accepted this international criticism humbly (*kenkyo ni uketomeru*).[85]

Jinja shinpō was outraged, attributing his attitude to the "Tokyo War Crimes Trials view of history" (*Tokyo saiban shikan*), and declaring that the Tokyo War Crimes Trials were nothing more than victors' justice.

> We do not claim that in the course of fifteen years of history following the Manchurian Incident, Japan did nothing regrettable in China or elsewhere. However, that does not mean that the whole fifteen years amounted to "aggression." When we consider that the majority of the Japanese people today, nearly forty years since the end of the war, still regard their own history along the lines of the judgments of the Tokyo War Crimes Trials, and that youth are still receiving that kind of education, Prime Minister Nakasone bears a heavy responsibility for his statement. We feel bitterly the need for a reconsideration of the verdicts of the Tokyo War Crimes Trials.[86]

On his 1983 visit to Yasukuni, Prime Minister Nakasone signed the register with his official title for the first time. This was widely seen as a signal to his most conservative supporters that he intended to make a new push toward restoring public funding to the shrine. In November that year, the LDP formed a new internal party committee; drawing on the Tsu City case, it issued a statement holding that cabinet tribute at the shrine would not violate the constitution. The party's 1980 position holding the opposite was, however, still in effect, again displaying the party's internal divisions.

In August 1984, Nakasone convened an advisory council (*shingikai*), expecting that it would issue a report citing a broad swell of public support for cabinet tribute to the shrine, which he could use to justify an official visit. Meanwhile, the opposition questioned what possibly could be the point of convening the committee, other than to give the prime minister "cover" for doing whatever he pleased.[87] Contrary to Nakasone's expectation, the advisory council deadlocked. On August 9, it submitted a report split three ways: those in favor of official cabinet tribute at Yasukuni Shrine, those opposed, and those advocating an entirely new war memorial.[88]

Ignoring the advisory council's internal divisions, however, Nakasone determined to forge ahead, appending to the report, "Based upon the findings of this Advisory Council, this government intends to take appropriate measures toward formal cabinet tribute at the Yasukuni Shrine."[89] Nakasone determined that he would visit Yasukuni on August 15, 1985, in a way that would not violate the constitution. In essence, he attempted to create a secular style by ignoring traditional shrine etiquette. He bypassed the *temizusha*, the trough where visitors wash the hands and rinse the mouth before approaching the shrine. He would not bow, accept purification, or offer the traditional *tamagushi*, bringing flowers instead. He was accompanied by four armed bodyguards, who carried loaded weapons into the presence of the Kami.

When the cabinet secretary visited Yasukuni Head Priest Matsudaira to inform him of the prime minister's intentions, Matsudaira was outraged. He thought Nakasone was unpardonably rude and refused to escort him during his visit. Thus Nakasone was met and escorted by Matsudaira's second-in-command (who turned up in informal dress to underline his displeasure), while Matsudaira had "shadow purification" performed in an effort to shield the Kami from the prime minister's insolence.

The press buildup to Nakasone's Yasukuni visit on the surrender anniversary provoked an unusually large wave of opposition from the various political parties, civil society groups, and religious organizations that regularly criticized government meddling at Yasukuni. But in addition, the recent resumption of relations with China injected a new dynamic into the Yasukuni issue. During the years 1980 to 1985, the *People's Daily* carried forty-five articles on Yasukuni, explaining the shrine's history and questioning politicians' motives for involvement with the shrine. Leading up to Nakasone's 1985 visit, the paper carried a number of critical articles, noting that other Asian countries were also distressed by the Japanese government's patronage of Yasukuni. The paper did not react very strongly, however, until Nakasone's visit on the surrender anniversary in 1985. On August 22, the paper printed this:

> Regrettably, when the Japanese government makes the decision to formally visit the Yasukuni Shrine, it states that "it deeply acknowledges the pain and damage it has inflicted"...on the one hand, while on the other hand, it states that "the purpose of worship is to mourn the war dead who have sacrificed their valuable lives for protecting their home country and fellow citizens." This kind of statement blurs the nature of the war of aggression launched by the Japanese militarists, and hurts the feelings of Chinese people and Asian people.[90]

Media coverage of Nakasone's visit to Yasukuni in the former colonies protested that the shrine is a symbol of Japanese militarism and aggression that has no other purpose than glorification of war and repudiation of Japanese war responsibility. Journalists in Korea and China wrote that the Japanese government's patronage of such a place could only mean that it intended to return to the policies of the past, repudiate its responsibility for war and the suffering of the colonies, and encourage reactionary elements to spread these poisonous sentiments. They were entirely unimpressed with Nakasone's gestures toward secularizing his visit.[91] In September 1985, student demonstrations broke out in several Beijing universities, and soon spread to other cities.

The Yasukuni issue had been offensive to China for some time before 1985, but it did not make a diplomatic issue of it. By 1985, however, China had emerged from its former alliance with the Soviet Union and was pursuing an independent course. The outbreak of student-led demonstrations made clear that Yasukuni had become symbolic of a variety of Chinese dissatisfactions with Japan that reached beyond government officials to the public. These were to deepen and become more complicated as time went on. After 1985, Japanese prime ministers were so cowed by international reaction to Nakasone's visit that they refrained from visiting the shrine again until 1996, when Hashimoto Ryūtarō broke the taboo with a visit on his birthday. After that, no prime ministers visited again until the administration of Koizumi Jun'ichirō (2001–2006). Thus the LDP retreated from the shrine almost completely during the years 1986 through 2000.

The Yamaguchi Self-Defense Force Case

In 1968 Nakaya Takafumi, an active-duty Self-Defense Force (hereinafter, SDF) member, was killed in a traffic accident. Several years later, the Yamaguchi Prefecture Veterans' Association, linked to the SDF but not a government agency, approached Nakaya Takafumi's widow Yasuko, about deifying his spirit as a Kami in the Yamaguchi prefectural Nation-Protecting Shrine. Takafumi would be deified through a rite called *gōshi*, patterned on Yasukuni ritual, which would join his spirit to the others already enshrined there. Yasuko protested that she did not wish her husband to be transformed into a Kami, since that would violate her beliefs as a Christian. The Veterans' Association went ahead over her objections, however, and had her husband deified. Yasuko sued the SDF and the Veterans' Association for violation of her freedom of religion and for violation of article 20, as an unlawful participation of the state in religious activity.

The Veterans' Association has its headquarters within the Ministry of Defense and is closely linked to it, and also to the Nation-Protecting Shrines. The SDF commonly supplied information regarding the deaths of troops for whom the Veterans' Association's prefectural branches would sponsor deifications at prefectural Nation-Protecting Shrines. These connections linking a government body to shrines through the mediation of a veterans' association led the district court to inquire whether in intention or effect (the standard established in the Tsu City case) the SDF was promoting a particular religion—namely, Shinto. They found that the SDF's actions constituted promotion of Shinto and therefore violated article 20. After the court awarded Nakaya Yasuko a sum of one million yen, the government appealed the case to the Supreme Court.

The Supreme Court ruled that the Veterans' Association had acted alone in sponsoring religious ceremonies, and therefore the SDF had not violated article 20. The court did not address the question of the propriety of the SDF assisting an intermediate organization whose purpose was to sponsor shrine rites. The court also ruled that the SDF had no intention to promote religion. Moreover, it was the Veterans' Association, not the SDF, that had liaised with the shrine and sponsored the ceremony. Since the SDF neither promoted nor harmed any religion by intention or in effect, it had not, the court ruled, violated article 20. On that basis the Supreme Court overturned the lower court's ruling.

But the court was divided. Three justices issued a minority opinion, in which they wrote that the SDF's assistance to the Veterans' Association for the performance of shrine ceremonies was exactly what article 20 prohibited. The court had interpreted the sphere of prohibited religious activity too narrowly. The majority opinion had sidestepped the question of the religiosity of deification ritual by focusing instead on the narrow question of responsibility for the ceremony and finding that it was the Veterans' Association, not the SDF, ignoring the conjoint nature of the two organizations. Had the court focused on the ceremony itself, based on any reading of the ritual's history, it could only have concluded that ritual to turn a dead person into a Kami is religious, in the view of the minority opinion. Later investigative reporting found that such ceremonies were widely conducted in Western Japan, resulting in the apotheosis of 465 veterans between 1945 and 1988, leading to several lawsuits against the Veterans' Association, which nevertheless continued to sponsor divinization rituals.[92]

Lastly, the Supreme Court found that Nakaya Yasuko's objection to the apotheosis impinged on the shrine's freedom of religion, saying that the shrine was free under the constitution "to make someone the object of one's faith or to memorialize someone or seek the tranquility of that person's soul through the religion that expresses one's faith." It also denied her claim that she was entitled to state protection of her "religious human rights" (*shūkyōteki jinkaku ken*).[93]

The idea of "religious human rights" amounted to an extension of the right to religious freedom to include an exclusive right to determine the religion(s) permitted to conduct memorializations. Nakaya Yasuko claimed that she not only had a right to memorialize her husband according to her Christian beliefs, but also that it was her right to prohibit his being memorialized according to any other beliefs. On that basis, she claimed that the shrine that divinized his spirit was violating her "religious human rights."

While "religious human rights" was a new legal argument, it engaged ancient ideas about the how the dead should be memorialized. Traditionally, no one but the actual members of a kinship group participated in worship of its ancestors. This understanding had been the basis for the medieval imperial court's exclusive worship at the Ise Shrines, and for the exclusion of the general population. To worship the ancestors of a conqueror was the mark of the submission of the conquered to their new overlord and of their incorporation into his people. The worship of ancestors is evidence of legitimate membership in a kin group, and on that basis, newly married women would begin worshipping their husband's ancestors. The lower court's award to Nakaya affirmed these widely held, if tacit, understandings.

In denying Nakaya Yasuko's claim to have such a right, the high court interpreted the problem as a conflict between her religious freedom and that of the shrine. This way of framing the question imputed personhood to the shrine and then reasoned that the shrine was free to memorialize anyone as it saw fit. For Nakaya to restrict the shrine's rights in this regard was a violation of its religious freedom.[94] The Supreme Court's verdict clarified that shrines are not obligated to curtail memorial rites for the war dead based on survivors' religious beliefs. The Supreme Court's failure to rule on the religious character of deification rites enabled politicians to continue to patronize Yasukuni and to lobby for the re-establishment of state support.

Conclusion

The Occupation unfairly blamed Shinto for the nationalism and imperialism that it believed had led Japan to war. The Occupation failed to realize that virtually every branch of Japanese religions promoted support for war and empire. Far less was it able to apportion blame among the many different forces in society beyond religion that had produced militarism and nationalism. The occupiers blithely ignored the fact that the religious institutions of their home countries had also been praying earnestly for victory, sending chaplains to bless and comfort the troops, and preaching that God was on their side. With justification, NASS came to blame the Occupation for many of the ills it saw in postwar Japan. The editorial pages of *Jinja shinpō* have also, however, perpetuated a "blame the Occupation" perspective that conveniently deflects self-criticism for whatever responsibility may rightly lie with Shinto.

Over the postwar decades, NASS has grown into a powerful political interest group. The cabinets formed by Prime Minister Shinzō Abe have drawn more than half their members from Shintō Seiji Renmei. No doubt politicians look at the network of 80,000 shrines as a potential vote-getting machine. But how do politicians' ambitions for shrines fit with the aspirations of shrine priests and their communities? As we will see in chapters 15 and 16, not all priests are happy to see NASS resources spent on political activism when so many shrines struggle even to keep their doors open. Furthermore, it is by no means the case that all those who dedicate themselves to shrine life share NASS's political stances. The potential for politics to divide Shinto has been amply demonstrated.

Occupation reforms quashed Shinto's claim to belong to the public realm. The people, not the emperor, define the public in postwar Japan. Nevertheless, NASS has argued tirelessly since the end of the Occupation for reinstating Shinto's lost public status, especially for palace rites and the Yasukuni Shrine. In terms of

Shinto's longtime claim to represent the indigenous, NASS continues to fight the Occupation as the embodiment of the foreign. Postwar legal judgments have slowly opened a path for Shinto ceremonies sponsored by government, but have not yet produced a way to return Yasukuni to official status. Imputing legal personhood to shrines has created grounds for shrines to repel charges of violating the religious freedom of individuals. Conversely, arming shrines with legal personhood has created a major hurdle for the individual challengers of shrine practices. Chapter 16 examines later development of these dynamics.

15

Shrine Festivals and Their Changing Place in the Public Sphere

Historian and folklorist of religion Sonoda Minoru described the original religious significance of shrine festivals, *matsuri*, as follows:

> *Matsuri* consist of ritual and festival components in a dramatic structure, set in a phase of extraordinary communitas, in which the cosmology of the group is symbolically actualized. Within this representation of the symbolized world concept, the group reconfirms the fundamental meaning of its continued existence and strengthens the ethos of each member. In summary, *matsuri* concern the symbolic rebirth of the group.[1]

Drawing on the work of anthropologist Victor Turner, Sonoda's interpretation regards *matsuri* as a kind of sacred drama, in which a myth of the community's origin is re-enacted. Such myths typically relate how the community shrine's Kami came to be worshipped there, and the *matsuri* act out an existence that human beings share with the deity. *Matsuri* are performed as if they defined the lifeworld of the community, a bounded space and time, in which all existence is imbued with a particular meaning. Within the time and space of the *matsuri*, participants are focused on symbols and do not concern themselves with questions of belief or unbelief. The individual man (the following does not truly apply to women) withdraws from the framework of ordinary life and enters the world of the *matsuri* by donning unusual clothing (and sometimes masks and makeup) that hides his ordinary identity, transforming himself in order to play his part. Young men who bear the *mikoshi* are expected to manifest ecstatic behavior, as the Kami within the sacred palanquin whirls it about according to divine will and irresistible sacred power. Through costume and ecstatic behavior, the individual becomes one with the group; this oneness is the meaning of "communitas." The structure of everyday life melts away. Collective fervor is heightened through dance, performance, competition, and imbibing copious amounts of alcohol, so that the individual forgets himself, becoming one with the group and its idealized image of human life vivified by the Kami. During the *matsuri*, society's rules are suspended and overturned. Unrestrained feasting, singing, dancing, violence, and sexual license are permitted—even expected. All these elements are regarded as contributing to the rebirth of the Kami, the community, and the life force of the individual. Society returns to primitive chaos, making possible a complete communication with a different world, with the Kami.[2]

Religious organizations of various kinds make claims on public space in carrying out their observances, but these claims have faced growing resistance since 1945. For example, in the early twentieth century, funerals (generally Buddhist) often incorporated a public procession. With the growth of motorized transport, civic administrations became less tolerant of requests to block off streets so that a procession could pass. The same is true of the processions accompanying *matsuri*. Local governments are increasingly likely to pressure shrines to limit the time when their processions and other observances will disrupt traffic, and also to minimize the violence, drunkenness, noise, and nighttime carousing that has traditionally been part of shrine festivals. Shrine support groups sponsoring large-scale festivals must negotiate with the police and fire departments each year, because local government is not at liberty to set aside its mandate to maintain safety and order to accommodate festivals.

Shrines' longstanding claims to be part of the public sphere and their appeals to be recognized as acting on behalf of all community residents are no longer reflected in government. Shrines are on the same footing as any other body that seeks to temporarily abrogate the routines structuring a local administration in order to carry out some observance. Shrines must request permission to take over public space, and if they violate communal norms and laws repeatedly, they risk being denied permission to hold their festivals. In other words, local governments treat shrines like any other private organization and do not accord them the public status that Shinto has historically claimed. That being said, however, elected officials and other civil servants participate in shrine support groups and festivals, including the rites inside a shrine's worship hall.

The heart of *matsuri* undoubtedly lies in a public, protean spectacle dramatizing communal origins, in which ecstatic behavior points toward a communion of Kami and humanity that is aimed at their shared revitalization. But in contemporary society, Shinto's claims on public funds, public space, and a public voice are dramatically reduced compared to the prewar era. How is it that many *matsuri* continue—even thrive—in these conditions? This chapter examines the concept of *matsuri*, their basis in society, their postwar history, and a case study of a thriving festival, the Darkness Festival of the Ōkunitama Shrine in Fuchū City (Tokyo Prefecture).

Introducing *Matsuri* and Related Terms

The term *matsuri* can be used in a broad sense to denote any shrine observance of a celebratory nature. The term has vernacular meanings that include festivals but also transcend the boundaries of the term's usage in academic Shinto circles. According to one etymological interpretation, *matsuri* is a noun derived from the verb *matsurau*, meaning "to submit to the will of the Kami." Humanity demonstrates its acceptance of that authority through ceremony collectively called *matsuri*. The verb *matsuru* means to serve the Kami by receiving them respectfully and reverently.[3] Another etymology of *matsuri* holds that it is an event in which people invite invisible Kami and "wait" (*matsu*) for them to manifest. There are many contemporary *matsuri* that in their names or associated activities refer to waiting for the Kami.[4]

Presentation of food offerings (*shinsen*) to the Kami is one essential component of *matsuri*. *Matsuri* conclude with a communal meal based on the offerings, shared by the Kami and those in attendance, celebrating the union of the Kami with the people under their protection. Food offerings thus maintain and mediate the relation between the Kami and humanity, renewing their bond through regular ceremony and communion.[5]

Dictionaries of Shinto define *matsuri* more narrowly than as festivals, using it as a collective noun for rites for the Kami, which might or might not be associated with a festival. The rites bring the divine spirits into harmonious connection (*musubi*) with humanity. The noun *musubi* means "connection" or "relation" in a Shinto context, and it also means the action of causing things to be born and grow, the creation of life and power, the formation of value, causing to mature and develop. Thus the ultimate aim of *matsuri* is to join humanity and the Kami together so that both can be revitalized. The themes of *musubi* and an associated idea of the rebirth of the Kami through *matsuri* give many shrine festivals an intense erotic charge.

To bring the Kami into this productive relation with humanity, the ritualist prepares for the *matsuri* as if preparing to receive an honored guest. The priest (or others who approach the altars of the Kami) must prepare for the event with a spirit of sincerity (*makoto*) and reverence (*tsutsushimi*), purifying body and mind (*misogi*). The words used in addressing the Kami must be carefully chosen, avoiding inauspicious or negative speech and choosing bright, positive, auspicious words.[6]

Matsuri may be performed for a variety of reasons: to present prayers, to offer thanks for prayers that have been fulfilled (as in seasonal agricultural fesivals), to comfort a spirit (such as spirits of the war dead), for magical purposes, and to divine the will of the Kami.[7] Examples of *matsuri* for magical purposes include rites seeking to avoid calamity such as fire, to keep children safe from misfortune and ensure their growth to maturity, or to avoid the misfortunes associated with inauspicious years in human life (*yakudoshi*). These inauspicious years differ between the sexes, with the forty-second year in the life of a man and the thirty-third for women being regarded as particularly inauspicious and requiring ritual to avoid misfortune. Divination rites principally attempt to predict whether the harvest will be good or bad. It is conceivable that a *matsuri* could be devoted to a single purpose, but it is usual for them to be combined. Thus a spring festival conveys prayers for a good harvest together with thanks for past protection and blessings, as well as praise for the Kami.[8]

Matsuri Typology

There are literally hundreds of different shrine festivals performed annually in Japan today. Based on shrines' historically local character, the festivals differ greatly in form. For example, there are *matsuri* that focus on preparation of distinctive food offerings and the communal meal in which they are shared; the Niinamesai is one well-known example of this type, but there are more localized versions in shrines around Japan. A second type is the procession form of *matsuri*, in which an Annual Festival (*taisai, reisai, reitaisai*) includes a procession where symbols of the Kami are carried in portable shrines (*mikoshi*) from the shrine sanctuary to a spot of special significance, such as the place where that Kami first manifested. A third type is *matsuri* based on a competition of some kind, which could be horse racing, *sumō* wrestling, archery, a tug-of-war, or a boating competition. *Yabusame*, or archery on horseback, performed at the Tsuruoka Hachiman Shrine in Kamakura, is a particularly well-known example of this type. A fourth type of *matsuri* is based on such artistic performances as dance in various forms or theater, such as Nō drama. At the Ōgi Matsuri of the Kasuga Shrine in Tsuruoka City (Yamagata Prefecture), Nō plays are performed by the Kurokawa Nō troops that began in the late Muromachi period. A fifth type is based on various divination practices seeking to know the will of the Kami and thereby foretell the future, for example, seeking to predict the harvest.[9] To this typology we could also add rites that seek to placate or expel an evil Kami from a community, such as the Gion Matsuri, which originated in ritual aiming to placate a disease god, or *matsuri* in which a person takes the role of scapegoat and is symbolically expelled from the community as a means of purifying it from evils of all kinds, such as the Kōnomiya Shrine's *Hadaka matsuri*.[10]

Nowadays, the term *matsuri* has a commercial usage in which it can mean a collective display intended to commemorate, celebrate, or promote something. Thus a "Harbor Matsuri" might mean a display of decorated boats, maritime skills, and a sale of marine products by the people who live and work around a particular harbor. A "Men's Suits Matsuri" would be a bargain sale of men's suits. While these uses of the term *matsuri* seem quite distant from shrine observances, their rationale derives from the historical practice of holding markets during the period when a festival was performed. People could buy things like agricultural tools, a year's supply of medicine, and many other goods at stalls set up during a *matsuri* as an added attraction to the shrine festival itself.

In contemporary Japan, the term *matsuri* is also applied to civic pageants that may have no connection to a shrine, or only a tenuous relation. The postwar appearance of such pageants is a major watershed in the history of *matsuri* and signals the growing separation of communal festivity from shrines in some places, especially the larger cities, where it is rare for a single shrine to command the allegiance of the whole population. These pageants include women and newcomers to the locale in a variety of public roles, a factor that conspicuously distinguishes them from the all-male gender order characteristic of traditional shrine *matsuri*.

Divisions of Labor

Shrine festivals reflect the hierarchy of local society through their criteria of eligibility for participation in certain roles. For example, it is common for men of middle age and older to form the planning groups that stage a shrine's Annual Festival, and to take responsibility for raising the necessary funds, as well as coordination with the police or fire departments to secure permission, for example, to block off traffic while a procession passes by, or to make arrangements for lost articles, lost children, medical treatment, etc. Men also are generally in charge of coordinating the activities of various groups, such as different neighborhood *mikoshi* carriers, to ensure that a procession is choreographed and timed smoothly. Young men have crucial roles in shouldering the *mikoshi* in processions taking the Kami through the territory over which they preside and in those *matsuri* that feature competitions. Both groups may be involved in teaching young children dance and music involved in festivals.

With some exceptions, women's roles are limited to behind-the-scenes work, like cooking food and serving it to male participants, preparing costumes, and the like. They are usually a small minority among the shrine supporters invited to enter the Worship Hall and witness the priest's performance of rites. In such cases, they may represent a husband who could not attend. Nowadays, *miko* are shrine employees. They principally perform *kagura* as part of the entertainment offered to the Kami during *matsuri*, but otherwise, the role of *miko* has become confined to general office work, selling talismans, guiding guests, and other roles under the direction of priests. Women may appear in shrine festivals as musicians. There are a small number of women shrine priests, a distinctly modern development treated in chapter 16. As discussed below, some shrines have started to allow young women to participate in festivals as *mikoshi* bearers. These gendered dynamics of *matsuri* make festivals into occasions for displays of masculinity and a traditional pattern of gender relations in which men hold the roles of dealing with the public or "outside," while women take charge of the private, or "inside."

Postwar Festival History

The history of festivals in the postwar era can be divided into several distinctive periods. The years 1945 to 1955 saw a revival of shrine festivals and the creation of civic pageants. To name only a few examples, in 1946, the Awa Odori Festival was revived, followed by the Gion Festival, Nagasaki Kunchi, and Sendai Tanabata in 1947. In 1949, the Osaka Tenjin Matsuri was revived, followed by the Aomori Nebuta Matsuri in 1950 and the Kanda Matsuri and the Sannō Matsuri in 1952. With the exception of the Awa Odori, a dance festival of Tokushima City, the others are connected with shrines in major cities. During this period, civic pageants, designed to attract tourists and mark the revival of cities, not based on shrine rites, were also created. Some of them were the Hiratsuka Tanabata (Kanagawa Prefecture), created in 1951, the Hyakuman Koku Matsuri (Kanazawa Prefecture) in 1952, the Yosakoi Matsuri (Kōchi Prefecture) in 1954, and the Nagoya Matsuri (Aichi Prefecture) in 1955.[11]

Civic Pageants

The Kobe Matsuri is one of the oldest and largest civic pageants. It was founded in 1967 through the initiative of the city government and does not stem from shrine ceremonial, in spite of its use of the term *matsuri*. Its main event is a parade that includes around one hundred different dance groups and bands in any given year, also including children's *mikoshi* (that have no symbol of divinity inside), baton twirling groups, and—the highlight—samba dancers, many of whom are foreigners. Women participate without restriction, as do nonresidents of the city. Groups from companies, schools, and miscellaneous associations are readily incorporated. There is even a parade of floats from foreign countries, highlighting Kobe's historical significance as a port for foreign vessels.[12]

As this description suggests, the sponsors of civic pageants can and have welcomed the participation of groups historically marginalized or excluded from shrine festivals.[13] The contrast between *matsuri* and civic pageants is stark. A variety of towns and cities have created civic pageants as a way to attract business and domestic tourism. A city can work freely with local civic groups to combine and shape their efforts to present the city in the most attractive light. By contrast, the constitution limits the ways that government can interact with shrines. Shrines have their own religious rationales for holding festivals, which would not ordinarily include polishing the city's image for outside consumption. Shrine organizers may be reluctant to set aside precedents or incorporate newcomers or outsiders. These conventions seem increasingly retrograde to city administrators hoping to project an image of modernity and openness.

The Osaka Exposition of 1970 proved to be a watershed event in the history of festivals. Festival groups from all over the country convened at the exposition grounds to display the ways they conducted *matsuri*. Previously it had not been common for festival ceremonies to be performed outside their home settings as "something to see," a spectacle detached from a shrine's religious rationale for conducting it. Following these displays, before audiences that included foreigners, however, many festival groups were invited to make overseas appearances, which gave organizers confidence to try to enlarge their festivals.

During the 1970s, the Japanese economy was greatly destabilized by the "oil shocks" of 1973 and 1976, when the price of petroleum quadrupled. Some shrine festivals had to be suspended for a time, but many *matsuri* were revived after the immediate economic crisis. *Mikoshi* clubs appeared, hobbyist groups formed to go around the country to participate in "other people's *matsuri*," by carrying *mikoshi*. Their emergence stimulated more general interest in "other people's festivals." This development is also related to increasing domestic tourism, and growing acceptance of outsiders coming as spectators to the festivals of shrines to which they have no personal or traditional relation.[14]

The stimulating effect of the Osaka Exposition on shrine festivals was greatest in urban festivals, because resources to revive and expand were larger in the cities than in rural areas. By the 1970s, the trend toward the depopulation of rural areas had already begun, and young men, traditionally an essential part of festival organizing, were increasingly moving to the cities. The festivals of the small rural shrines cannot usually compete with the urban pageants for scale, splendor, variety, and luxury.[15]

There are, however, some exceptions to this general trend, such as the Ōgi Matsuri for the performance of Kurokawa Nō. Kurokawa Nō is staged at the Kasuga Shrine of the Kurokawa district of Tsuruoka City (Yamagata Prefecture). It is thought to have begun with *daimyō* patronage as early as the late Muromachi period. There are two separate troupes of performers, whose complete repertory consists of about 510 pieces, of which around 100 are regularly performed, in addition to forty *kyōgen* pieces. Kurokawa Nō was designated an Intangible Folk Culture Asset in 1976. Kurokawa Nō performances attract large numbers from outside the prefecture, and the troops travel to perform. [16]

From 1980 to 1991, Japan experienced an economic "bubble" based on a rapid inflation of the price of land. Hyperinflation of real estate prices in the cities, especially Tokyo, had a deleterious effect on traditional urban festivals, because long-time residents increasingly sold their land to developers and moved away, causing a decrease in the population of resident shrine supporters. They were replaced by increasing numbers of weekday employees, who worked in the area but did not live there.[17]

Many *matsuri* that had excluded women from participating in the carrying of the *mikoshi* were gradually forced to relent for lack of manpower. The Kanda Matsuri provides a good example. Before the economic bubble, Sudachō, one of the central Tokyo neighborhoods that had managed a *mikoshi* for the Kanda Shrine's annual festival, had over 250 households, but by 1989, the number had plummeted to only seventy-six. There were too few young men to carry the *mikoshi.*

Faced with the possibility that they might have to cancel the Kanda Festival unless desperate measures were taken, shrine supporters began to advertise for women to shoulder a women's *mikoshi* in 1985, targeting the young female office workers in the buildings that had replaced the older residents' homes. They attracted about one hundred applicants, but then failed to train them in how to carry the *mikoshi* in good form. This first effort ended in failure, but shrine organizers persevered, improving their training, advertising, and costumes in the late 1980s. In 1990, a total of 148 women participated, the great majority drawn from the banks and other financial institutions that had come to dominate the area. Meanwhile, the shrine support group started incorporating the commuting population into its organization as officers or "advisers," thereby treating these outsiders as honorary residents.[18]

While women participate as *mikoshi* carriers much more frequently than in the past, male shrine supporters still resist their presence in some areas. One such case concerns the shrine festival of rural Iki Island (Nagasaki Prefecture), in which men traditionally pulled a float mounted with a giant phallus. On the one hand, women wanted to participate in the festival, but they were not attracted to the idea of pulling the phallic float. They decided to make their own float and took this idea to the local council. The men opposed them, but the women went ahead anyway. Thereafter, the men refused to participate any longer.[19]

Between 1986 and 1989, the number of civic pageants doubled. A new national development plan of 1987 called for creating novel regional festivals as a means of attracting tourism.[20] Festivals as a whole were canceled or held in a subdued way following the death of Emperor Hirohito in 1989.

In 1991, Japan entered a long economic recession from which, as of 2016, it has not yet fully emerged. The recession generally worsened the conditions for sponsorship of rural festivals, as the depopulation of the countryside continued, exacerbated by the aging of the population as a whole, a demographic change that is most conspicuous in rural Japan. Nevertheless, the "Matsuri Law" of 1992 stimulated the creation and maintenance of shrine festivals and civic pageants, including in rural areas, though some restrictions regarding parade routes and late-night events were also introduced.[21] Civic pageants increased greatly.

The Kurayami Matsuri: A Thriving Festival

We turn to a discussion of one shrine festival that stands in stark contrast to the trend of civic pageants overshadowing *matsuri,* the Darkness Festival (Kurayami Matsuri) of the Ōkunitama Shrine. Much of the information presented here is based on the author's fieldwork at the shrine, including observing the festival three times (2001, 2003, 2004) and a year's residence in Japan (2003–2004) to study the shrine and its annual ritual calendar.[22] This festival exemplifies the continued vitality of shrines' claims to public significance and to embodying indigenous tradition. Through its dramatization of the shrine's myth of origin and later historical events, the festival presents priests' and supporters' beliefs concerning the shrine's historic contributions to governance and society.[23]

The Darkness Festival at Ōkunitama Shrine begins on April 30, and officially concludes on May 6. Its central purpose is to effect the rebirth of the shrine's Kami, but in the process it dramatizes the shrine's myth of origin, the story of its connection to ancient government, and the community's significance as a place where fine horses were raised during the early modern period. The shrine originated as a Comprehensive Shrine, founded in 111, according to local tradition. The six Kami of the major shrines of ancient Musashi Province were gathered into one place for the convenience of the ancient provincial governor. The shrine also revered the Izumo deity Ōkuninushi, worshipped by local gentry, and an undifferentiated group of "spirits of the land" (*kunitama*). During the Kamakura period, the Comprehensive Shrines across the country were called upon by the shogunate to conduct rites to assuage the vengeful spirits of those who had died wrongful or violent deaths. These spirits were called *goryō*, and they came to be elided with the spirits of the land at this shrine. Based on their association with violent death, the *goryō* came to be distinguished from the other deities of the shrine.

Before looking further into the separate ceremonies, however, it is important to note a kind of slippage between the singular and the plural in references to "the Kami" involved in the festival. We noted a similar phenomenon in chapter 6, in a discussion of the *Kasuga gongen genki-e*, where we saw that the Kasuga Kami might be referred to in either the singular or the plural. In the Darkness Festival's separate ceremonies, "the Kami" can designate a particular Kami or all of them collectively; usually the context makes the distinction clear.

The expanding base of support for the Ōkunitama Shrine and its Darkness Festival parallels the expansion of Fuchū City. The city has expanded geographically far beyond the four wards around the shrine that assumed responsibility for the eight *mikoshi* and drums in the 1880s. Fuchū City now spreads east to west along the Tama River, bordering on Kokubunji City to the north, Chōfu City to the east, and Hino City and Tama New Town across the river to the south. A national racetrack has taken the place of the old horse market, and the town also incorporates a mammoth public cemetery, the Tama Rei-en, and a prison. Before 1945 it housed an army base. Now there are major "campuses" of such corporations as Toshiba and NEC in Fuchū. Fuchū is served by the Keiō Railway line and the Nanbu line of Japan Rail.

Probably the most important factor pressuring festival organizers to change their ways is the city's postwar transformation to a suburban area of Tokyo and rapid population increase. See Table 15.1.

Table 15.1 **Fuchū City Population, 1945–2015**

Year	*Population*
1945	40,987
1950	45,295
1960	82,098
1970	163,173
1980	192,198
1990	209,396
2000	226,769
2010	255,506
2015	256,930

Source: Fuchū City. 2004. *Fuchū shi tōkei sho*. Fuchū City; and the Fuchū City home page: http://www.city.fuchu.tokyo.jp (accessed January 6, 2013).

The city's steady growth began in the early postwar period and continues to the present writing. In the 1950s, the City Council called on the shrine to restrain the participants and transform the Annual Festival into something that could be enjoyed by all, starting by turning it into a daytime observance.[24] According to the *Mainichi shinbun*'s report on the 1955 festival, there was a major brawl in which someone almost died, three fights in which the victims sustained injuries requiring from one to three months' recuperation, and fifty-five lighter injuries. The local police recorded forty incidents of violence, one rape, one case of extortion, five violations of firearms laws, and a further five incidents involving the use of weapons.[25] Apparently, this level of violence had not been uncommon in the first half of the twentieth century, when shrines had a clear claim on the use of public space and *matsuri* displays of masculinity were not policed extensively.[26]

But after the war, Japanese society came to be oriented very tenaciously around salaried employment and school. Customs out of sync with that ordered lifestyle had to go. Shrines were no longer backed by the force of law in claiming special prerogatives that could make it hard for workers and pupils to follow their routines.

Fuchū's population roughly doubled in the 1960s, and it was in this decade that festival supporters' and the townspeople's different orientations came into conflict. As Fuchū expanded, the centrality of the four wards around the shrine contracted.[27] Most of Fuchū's population has moved there since 1945, and the people of the four wards now make up only about 10 percent of the town's population. Owing to the postwar constitution's separation of religion from the state, it is no longer possible to assess all residents of the town for contributions to the festival. The older residents are concentrated in the four wards, which form a center of small- to medium-sized local businesses around Fuchū Station on the Keiō Railway line. They are unlike Tōshiba and NEC, which are much larger and more integrated into the national economy. Since the inception of the long-lasting recession in 1991, however, it may be a blessing not to be too closely tied to the national economy. While no one would call Fuchū a boomtown, it seems unlikely to "bust," either.

Pressure to Adopt a Daytime Schedule

After the 1955 Darkness Festival, the local Parent Teacher Association (PTA) published a resolution requesting that the festival no longer be held at night. It had been customary for the *mikoshi* to depart the shrine around midnight, carousing through the town until they returned the next morning. There are eight *mikoshi* in total, six for the original six shrines brought together in the Comprehensive Shrine and two additional ones. The first six *mikoshi* and drums are referred to by a numbering system that combines a number with *-miya,* a word for "shrine," producing the names Ichinomiya (number one), Ninomiya (number two), Sannomiya (number three), Yonomiya (number four), Gonomiya (number five), and Rokunomiya (number six). The seventh *mikoshi,* called Goryōgū, is for the *goryō,* who are now regarded as the ancestors of the *ujiko* as a whole, and an eighth *mikoshi* of the whole shrine is called Gohonsha. Each of these *mikoshi* is linked to a neighborhood, where its supporters reside, and to *kō* composed of supporters who reside outside of Fuchū.[28] Each of these *mikoshi,* except for Ichinomiya, has its own drum, used symbolically to clear the path ahead with a booming sound that warns people to get out of the way. In addition to these eight *mikoshi* and seven drums, there is a great drum called Misakibarai Taiko, dedicated to the shrine by a *kō* in nearby Koganei and Chōfu Cities. The word *misakibarai* means "purifying the road ahead." Each of these drums rests on a mammoth silk cushion atop a wooden cart. Long ropes are attached to each cart for supporters to pull the drums along in the procession. The Misakibarai Taiko was created after the sponsors traveled to Cameroon and brought back the huge tree that was used to make the body. It was hollowed out, and two cowhide drumheads were attached. The circumference of the body measures 8 meters 38 centimeters. The drum weighs two and one-half tons (see Figure 15.1).

The shrine gave in to local pressure, and over the next few years the schedule was in flux. See Table 15.2 for a chronology of the changes that followed. Then, in 1969, a drunken spectator was killed when he slipped and was trampled after insisting on carrying the *mikoshi* in the dark. Thereafter, a new management organization was put in charge, eventually named the Festival Committee. In effect, the festival was taken away from the wards that had formerly been in command. It was decided that all persons carrying *mikoshi* would henceforth be required to wear white, to prevent accidents and deaths.[29]

Figure 15.1 Festival Drum. Source: Courtesy of the author.

Table 15.2 **Chronology of Changes in the Darkness Festival, 1955–2002**

1955	59 persons injured in a brawl during the festival; the PTA urges changing to a daytime schedule.
1957	Negative publicity about the festival appeared in the *Asahi* newspaper (April 23, 24).
1958	The festival schedule was arranged so that the *mikoshi* procession would begin at 11:00 pm.
1959	The festival schedule was arranged so that the *mikoshi* procession would begin at 9:00 pm.
1960	The festival schedule was arranged so that the procession would begin at 9:00 pm, but instead of *mikoshi,* only large boxes were used in the procession. When fifty or sixty men tried to take out the *mikoshi,* they got into a fight with the police. Five spectators were injured.
	The Festival Committee was established to deal with the issue.
1961	The *mikoshi* procession was reinstated, but Ninomiya and Sannomiya did not participate.
1962	The festival schedule was arranged so that the *mikoshi* procession would begin at 4:30 pm. Sannomiya reinstated its participation in the *mikoshi* procession.

(*continued*)

Table 15.2 **Continued**

1963	Ninomiya reinstated its participation in the *mikoshi* procession.
1964	Introduction of *dashi* to the festival.
1967	Spectators cause a major brawl at the festival.
1968	The Taisai Honbu was established to deal with the ongoing problem of violence at the festival.
1969	A drunken spectator pushed his way into the *mikoshi* bearers, slipped in the dark, and was trampled to death. Thereafter the Taisai Honbu was strengthened and systematized.
1970	Following a violent incident among those carrying the Sannomiya *mikoshi*, a rule was established requiring all *mikoshi* bearers to dress identically in white.
1973	The Gohonsha *mikoshi* was renewed.
1977	The Ninomiya drum was renewed.
1979	Introduction of the Mandō Contest.
1985	The *Misakibarai* drum was created to celebrate the emperor's sixtieth year on the throne.
1990	The Sannomiya drum was renewed.
1991	The Gonomiya and Rokunomiya *mikoshi* were renewed.
1993	The Taisai Honbu was renamed the Festival Committee.
	The drums of Gonomiya and Rokunomiya were renewed.

Source: Ōkunitama Jinja Taisai Kankei Nenpyō, received from Head Priest Sawatari Masamori.

In addition to the measures specifically undertaken to minimize violence, the four wards tried to incorporate newcomers. Newcomers complained about the noise of a nighttime festival, traffic jams, and the shadowy presence of organized crime controlling the food and game stalls that set up in the shrine precincts for the week-long duration of the festival each year. It is not unusual to see yakuza gangsters at larger festivals, and the Darkness Festival is no exception.[30]

Newcomers would like to restrict to weekends any event that suspends conventions regarding noise or the use of public space. They have little patience for the proposition that it is beneficial to experience a period of chaos, loosening of restrictions on dress, sex, food, manners, and violence on the occasion of the annual rebirth of the community's Kami. In reaction, the longstanding shrine supporters have tried to accommodate the newcomers, adding new activities to attract them, limiting violence and overnight revelry, and groping toward an expanded presentation of "community."[31]

For example, neighborhood-based shrine supporters incorporated a children's *mikoshi* parade, enabling young children, up to the age of eight or so, to participate

Figure 15.2 Festival Floats (*Dashi*). Source: Courtesy of the author.

in the festival. Now there are around twenty children's *mikoshi*, and the neighborhoods organize identically dressed groups of local children to carry these *mikoshi* (smaller than the real ones, and lacking any symbol of divinity) in a short procession ending with worship before the shrine. The introduction of decorated floats (*dashi*; see Figure 15.2) in 1964, managed by the neighborhoods, led to the formation of youth groups in which children from the age of nine or ten learn to play festival music (*hayashi*) on flutes, drums, gongs, and other instruments, as well as the dances that accompany the music. There are twenty-four *hayashi* groups, led by men who teach the children music and dance once a week, and some of these groups have performed abroad. The *dashi* engage children in the shrine festival at an early age, transmitting technical knowledge, artistic skills, ideas about serving the Kami, and the importance of maintaining a connection to the shrine. The *dashi* themselves are constructed by professionals, at prices exceeding one million dollars, from the funds raised in the neighborhoods. It requires from 100 to 150 people (adult men, mainly) to pull the *dashi*.[32] The *dashi* are paraded, on the evening of May 4, along the Old Kōshū Highway in front of the shrine's main *torii*, where they confront each other and engage in contests for the liveliest dance and music, and the most splendid costumes. After this parade, the *dashi* line up in the arcade of Zelkova trees between the Keiō Railway Fuchū Station and the shrine, performing for hours into the night, as crowds stroll from one to the other.

Figure 15.3 The *Mando* Contest. Source: Courtesy of the author.

A contest called Mando Taikai was introduced in 1979, in which young people in their teens and early twenties create huge decorated umbrella-like floats attached to a long pole, using different colors, materials, and designs of their own choosing (see Figure 15.3). *Mando* literally means "ten thousand lanterns," although no illumination element is actually used.[33] A contest is held to display the *mando*, twirled by the young men, in a show of strength, so that the decorations fly in a circle. The group of young men and women who have created each one appear together, identically dressed, cheering on two or three young men who take it in turn to twirl their *mando* with chants and rhythmic clapping.

Originally, neither the children's *mikoshi*, the *dashi*, nor the *mando* contest bore any relation to shrine ritual or had any religious significance. Nevertheless, these three activities now constitute the nucleus for a three-stage set of youth organizations that induct the young into participation in shrine life. These organizations are extremely significant for transmitting knowledge of shrine life from older to younger generations. It is also significant that these organizations were founded at the initiative of the neighborhoods and are all under neighborhood—not priestly—authority.

Inevitably, the character of the festival changed. Older men who recall the Darkness Festival before the 1960s are nostalgic for a time when it seemed that the festival belonged to them. They could lose themselves in it without worrying what anyone else thought. While they are now resigned that community life today will not tolerate the rowdiness they miss, they say—with a sense of loss—that the festival has changed from something the participants created to something staged for spectators to see. The men who now carry the *mikoshi* are from a different generation. They have little if any experience of losing oneself in a brawl, of exaltation at drawing blood, nor would most of them find that prospect attractive. Society has so successfully stigmatized *matsuri* masculinity that it lacks the attraction it once had for some of the older men. Nevertheless, as we shall see below, violence has not entirely disappeared, and there remains a desire to maintain *matsuri* as a social space where an older, less restrained image of manhood can be displayed unapologetically and with pride.

Changes Instituted by the Head Priest since 1999

In order to dramatize the significance of the separate ceremonies composing the festival, the Head Priest has instituted important changes that focus attention on the mystery and grandeur of the Kami. When Head Priest Sawatari Masamori took up his appointment in 1999, he moved to change the Annual Festival back to a nighttime schedule. By the time he took up his post, however, the festival had been a daytime event for decades, long enough for a generation of participants to grow up regarding the daytime schedule as the rightful, traditional way of doing things. Head Priest Sawatari pointed out, however, that it is traditional within Shinto to hold important ceremonies in which the Kami move from one place to another at night. Night, darkness, and shadow are important elements for portraying the mystery of the Kami. It is essential that people should know this and experience the festival in a way the puts the Kami at the center of the observance. Moreover, the daytime scheduling had made some of the customary elements nonsensical. For example, the continued use of large lanterns on poles during the daytime observances was out of place. It only makes sense to use them when it is dark. More importantly, however, the daytime schedule forces the priests to hurry, so that the individual ritual components were not performed correctly, and the overall meaning of the Annual Festival was obscured.[34] In his view, the religious meaning of the festival is a rebirth of the Kami and their reinstallation into the shrine. In his words,"We are receiving a new Kamisama, to whom we will pray throughout the year for the bounty of crops and the health of the *ujiko*. This should be the most important rite of the entire year."[35]

After three years of negotiation with the city and consultations with shrine support groups, Head Priest Sawatari succeeded in 2002 in moving the festival to a nighttime schedule.[36] Since that time, there have been no incidents provoking the community to criticize the shrine or try to force it back to a daytime schedule. Head Priest Sawatari has thus returned the festival's orientation to the annual renewal or rebirth of the Kami.

Rituals of the Kurayami Matsuri That Assert Public Significance

The Ōkunitama Shrine's Annual Festival follows an outline of ritual standardized by NASS. Table 15.3 shows the ritual procedures that constitute an Annual Festival (*reitaisai*).[37] These are the ceremonies performed between 10:00 am and 12:00 pm on May 5. However, a great deal more is involved in the Darkness Festival, because individual shrines augment the NASS-specified ceremonies with their own traditions.

The major ceremonies composing the Darkness Festival (and including the Annual Festival as specified by NASS) and the overall schedule are set out in Table 15.4. The locations relevant to the festival are noted on Map 15.1.

The events from April 30 through May 2 are small in scale and not attended by anyone other than actual participants. They are devoted to preliminary purifications and preparations. The Review of the Horses, held on the evening of May 3, is the first of four ceremonies that assert public significance for the shrine and its festival.[38] This observance dramatizes a practice of the Nara and Heian periods, in which the provincial governor (*kokuzō*) of Musashi would present forty to fifty fine horses to the Yamato court annually. The shrine is located adjacent to (what was) a large stretch of good pastureland along the Tama River, where there was a horse market.[39] In the Review of the Horses, the Head Priest in effect takes the role of the ancient provincial governor to make certain that they are superior animals, worthy of dedication to the court. The horses and riders are first presented before the Worship Hall, and then a procession is formed to walk out of the shrine grounds into the Zelkova tree arcade linking the shrine to the central business district. The procession incorporates hundreds of men bearing lanterns and others marking each step by striking the ground with a ringed metal staff, making a clanging noise that warns those in the road to move aside.

While the spectators wait for the procession to emerge from the shrine's *torii*, *hayashi* groups play music as costumed dancers perform on the stages of the *dashi*, which have been lined up on the east side of the Zelkova arcade. The dance and music are lively. The mood of tension and excitement among the spectators waiting in the arcade heightens palpably as the lanterns appear from out of the darkness, and as the ringing staffs are heard. The men with lanterns and staffs are followed by the horses and riders, and the Head Priest, accompanied by local officials and other shrine priests. The horses prance as they see the huge crowd and approach the noisy *dashi*. Although the total distance covered is only a few hundred meters, because the procession itself is over fifty meters long, it requires thirty minutes for it to reach the reviewing stand.

While the crowd is waiting, an announcer, using a loudspeaker, reviews the historical origins of the event for the crowd, most of whom do not appear to be

Table 15.3 **Ritual Constituting an Annual Festival (Reitaisai)**

	Ritual Activity
1	Participants process to the shrine (the Head Priest; lesser ritualists; musicians; the representative of NASS, called *kenpeishi*, the shrine stewards (*sōdai*); and representatives of the shrine's parishioners (*ujiko*).
2	Purification (*shubatsu*); the procession may stop at the shrine's *temizusha*, the roofed trough where each participant may rinse the mouth and hands. Typically, a subordinate priest purifies the entire group with a wand of paper streamers (*nusa*).
3	Once the ritualists and participants are assembled in the shrine's worship hall (*haiden*), the Head Priest approaches the altar and announces the commencement of the *matsuri* to the Kami.
4	Opening of the doors of the Kami. The priest intones a *keihitsu*, a long, drawn-out, loud "Ooooo" that invokes the Kami to be present.[40]
5	Presentation of offerings.
6	The Head Priest recites a *norito* that expresses the purpose of the *matsuri*, prayers, and thanks.
7	Presentation of offerings from NASS.
8	The NASS representative recites a *norito* praising the Kami.
9	Presentation of music, *kagura*.
10	The Head Priest and other ritualists offer *tamagushi*, sprigs of the *sakaki* plant decorated with paper streamers (*hei*).
11	The NASS representative offers *tamagushi*.
12	The shrine stewards offer *tamagushi*.
13	Removal of the NASS offerings.
14	Removal of other offerings.
15	Closing the doors of the sanctuary.
16	The Head Priest announces the conclusion of the *matsuri*.
17	*Naorai*: participants' communal meal, incorporating (some of) the offerings.[41]

Source: Yatsuka Kiyomi, "Shintō yōgo shū: Jinja saishiki," *Nihon bunka kenkyūjo kiyō* 14 (1964): 239.

paying attention. Anyone listening, however, would learn that in addition to the ancient origins, in the medieval period, Minamoto no Yoriyoshi (988–1075) and his son Yoshiie (1039–1106) stopped at the shrine before a battle of 1051 to pray for victory, and Yoshiie repeated such prayers before another battle of 1087. Returning victorious each time, the warrior(s) came again to the shrine to offer prayers and to express their gratitude with a gift of one thousand Zelkova seedlings.[42]

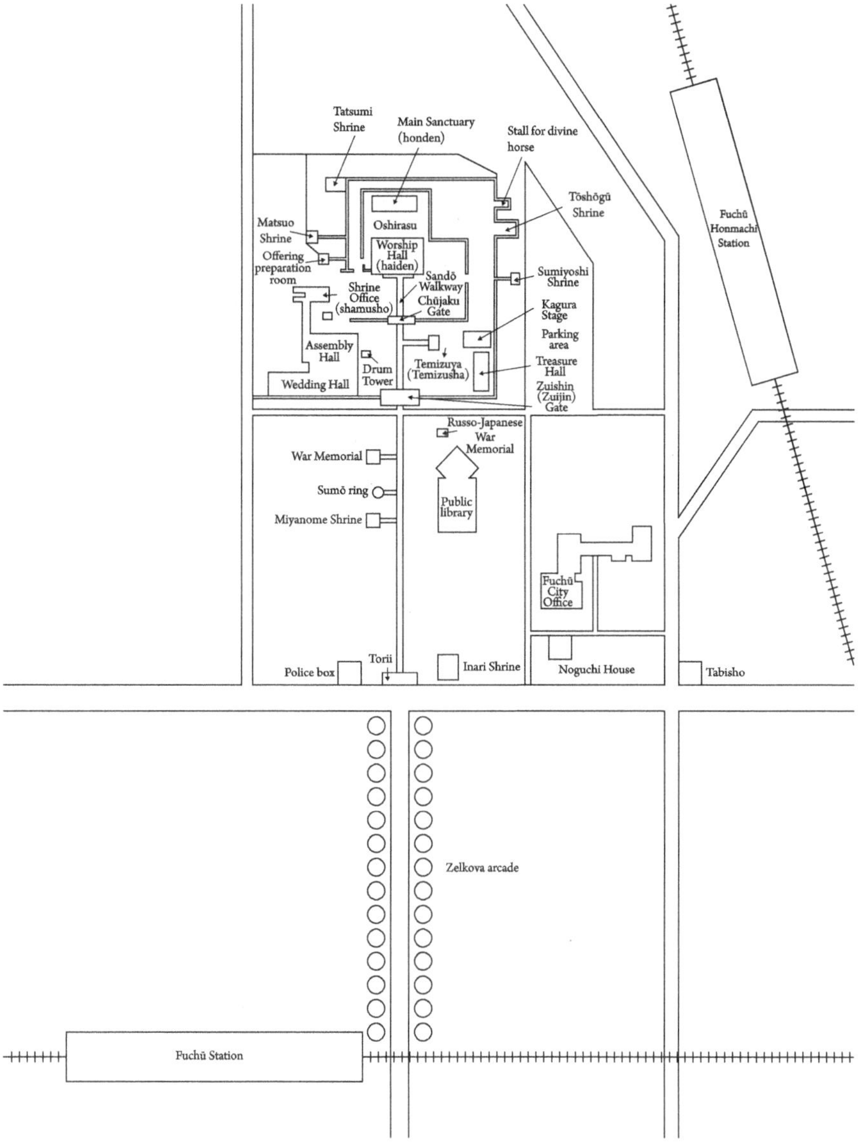

Map 15.1 Ōkunitama Shrine.

Arriving finally at the Zelkova arcade, the Head Priest and a variety of local officials and shrine supporters ascend into a reviewing stand, to watch as four horses and riders from a local college gallop up and down a specially prepared roadway, soft enough not to damage the horses' hooves and legs. The crowd cheers wildly, spooking the horses further with flash cameras. The Review of the Horses dramatizes the antiquity of Fuchū's importance to the court, the fertility of the land, and the town's ancient significance in national affairs. This event presents the festival as a whole as having public, communal, even national significance.[43]

Table 15.4 **Darkness Festival Schedule, 2003**

Day Time	*Event*	*Notes*
4/30 1:00 pm	Purification at Shingawa	(*Shinagawa kaijō keifutsu shiki*) Five priests from Ōkunitama Shrine, accompanied by officers of the Festival Committee, and 10 members of the Shiomori-Kō travel by car to the seashore at Shinagawa. They are met by the priest of Ebara Shrine and representatives of the Kō formed to assist in this observance. They board a boat and sail out to sea, changing into matching silk vestments. They purify their hands and mouthes with salt water, also collecting water for use in preparing offerings in the shrine for the duration the Annual Festival. They visit the Ebara Shrine and worship there before returning to Fuchū.
5/1 9:00 am	Prayers for good weather	(*Kiseisai*) Priests, *miko*, and *gagaku* musicians offer prayers in the Worship Hall for clear weather during the festival.
5/2 7:30 pm	Mirror polishing ceremony	(*Mikagami suri shiki*) Two *shinjin*, Mr. Noguchi and Mr. Horie, use salt and rice straw brushes to polish the mirrors to be used in the festival. The shrine priests and the *miko* attend.
5/3 8:00 pm	Review of the Horses	(*Koma kurabe shiki*) Held outside the shrine gates within an arcade of Zelkova trees extending toward the station of the Keio Railway line, this event is attended by a huge crowd, who watch as four horses and riders run back and forth in front of a reviewing stand, where the priests watch. This is the first ceremony in the festival to be attended by large crowds.
5/4 9:00 am	Ceremony to attach new silk cords to the *mikoshi*	(*Mitsuna sai*) Supporters from the four wards decorate their *mikoshi* with new silk cords in white, red, and purple silk.
1:00 pm	Mandō Contest	(*Mando taikai*) In front of the Kaguraden, thirteen troupes from the shrine's Youth Group display the *mando* they have made; a prize is given for the best performance.

(*continued*)

Table 15.4 **Continued**

Day Time	*Event*	*Notes*
6:00 pm	Dashi Parade	(*Dashi gyōretsu*) The *dashi* floats managed by separate neighborhoods process to the Old Kōshū Highway running in front of the shrine's main gates and then stop in the Zelkova arcade of trees for a display of music and dance.
5/5 10:00 am	Annual Festival	(*Reitaisai*) Priests and about 120 guests process to the Worship Hall, where the main ceremony is performed. The Head Priest and assistant priests open the doors of the three main sanctuaries to present offerings of food and dance. An emissary (*kenpeishi*) from NASS arrives with assistants, who carry a large wooden trunk of offerings for the festival.
1:30 pm	Purification of the Road	(*Michikiyome shuppatsu*) A group of young men bearing long bamboo poles walk along both sides of the road that the *mikoshi* will travel, striking it and using noisemakers called *sasara* to expel any malevolent influence.
2:00 pm	Presentation of Offerings at Miyanome Jinja	(*Miyanome Jinja hōhei*) The Miyanome Jinja is located where the ancient garrison of the central government (*kokufu*) was, according to local legend. It is within the precincts of Ōkunitama Shrine. It was traditionally a shrine at which women prayed for safe childbirth.
2:30 pm	Presentation of the *mikoshi*	(*Kaku mikoshi sashi komi*) The *mikoshi* assemble before the Worship Hall.
2:30 pm	Presentation of the Drums	(*Kaku taiko okuri komi*) The drums assemble before the Worship Hall; their attendants beat the drums loudly. Some stand on top of the drums, while others strike the drums with wooden bats. The attendant standing on top lowers a lantern to illumine the drumhead and cries, "O-rai" (the Kami is coming). Seeing the spot to aim for, the striker hits the drumhead with the bat.
3:00 pm	Ceremony of Completing the Offering Preparation	(*Misen saisoku no gi*) Offerings of cooked and raw food are prepared for presentation at the Tabisho. The *shinjin* Hosoya and Urano repeatedly announce that preparations are complete.

(*continued*)

Table 15.4 **Continued**

Day Time	*Event*	*Notes*
3:30 pm	The drums cease	(*Kaku taiko uchidome*) The drums, which had been sounded throughout the day, all cease.
3:30 pm	Presentation of the Ebara Shrine Shiomori Kō	(*Shiomori Kō okurikomi*) Representatives of the Shiomori Kō of the Ebara Shrine worship before the Worship Hall.
3:30 pm–5:20 pm	Announcement to the Kami of the imminent *mikoshi* procession	(*Dōzasai*) Priests make offerings at the three main sanctuaries and present seven dances.
4:00 pm	Presentation of the Divine Steed	(*Go jinme okuri komi*) The horse prepared for the Kami to ride in the procession of *mikoshi* is presented before the Worship Hall.
4:10 pm	Arrival of the Fireworks Handlers	(*Hanabi yaku okuri komi*) The fireworks handlers assemble in front of the Worship Hall before starting to work. Fireworks will be shot off when the *mikoshi* depart.
4:20 pm	Presentation of the Offering Chests	(*Misen nagamochi okuri komi*) The offerings prepared for presentation at the Tabisho are packed into chests carried on long poles (*nagamochi*) and presented at the Worship Hall.
4:30 pm	The drums are moved into place.	(*Kaku taiko idō kaishi, junji seiretsu*) Each of the drums is moved into the space between the Zuishinmon Gate and the Chūjakumon Gate and lined up in their traditional order.
5:20 pm	Distribution of the weapons used to guard the procession	(*Shinkō igibutsu juyō*) The weapons, swords, pikes, and other things, all wrapped in silk brocades, are distributed to the bearers. The bearers are shrine supporters dressed in brocade robes and hats.
5:20 pm	Symbols of divinity are moved into each *mikoshi*.	(*Goreisen no gi*) In the Oshirasu, the Head Priest moves symbols of the Kami in the sanctuaries into the *mikoshi*. The symbols are wrapped so that they cannot be seen, but participants say that the objects feel like large, round stones.

(*continued*)

Table 15.4 **Continued**

Day Time	*Event*	*Notes*
6:00 pm	*Mikoshi* departure	(*Mikoshi gohatsu*) Three fireworks are shot off, and then the *mikoshi* move one by one to the space before the Worship Hall, whirl around that area for about twenty minutes each, and then exit the area through the Zuijinmon Gate, and then process toward the Tabisho.
8:00 pm	Departure of the representative to the Kokuzō	(*Kokuzō dai hatsu*) A priest mounted on a horse departs to make offerings at the Tsubonomiya Shrine, where the first Provincial Governor (*kokuzō*) is enshrined as the shrine's deity. This shrine is located outside the precincts of the Ōkunitama Shrine. The procession there takes about fifteen minutes.
8:30 pm	Presentation of offerings at the Tsubonomiya Shrine	(*Tsubonomiya Jinja hōhei*) Arriving at the Tsubonomiya Shrine, the priest intones a *norito* and presents offerings before the spirit of the first Provincial Governor.
9:15 pm	Last *mikoshi* arrives at the Tabisho	(*Goryōgū mikoshi otabisho tōchaku*) Goryōgū, which travels by a separate route, arrives at the Tabisho, concluding the procession.
9:30 pm	Lifting of traffic restrictions	When all the *mikoshi* are safely inside the Tabisho, traffic restrictions are lifted, and normal traffic resumes along the Old Kōshū Kaidō. Restrictions are briefly reinstated on the morning of the next day, when the *mikoshi* tour their supporting neighborhoods and return to the shrine.
9:30 pm–10:20 pm	Offering rites for the *mikoshi* at the Tabisho	(*Otabisho shinji*) Offering tables are set out before each *mikoshi*, and the Head Priest presents prayers and the offerings that had been carried in the long trunks. Spectators are strictly forbidden from peeping through the fence to see this ceremony.
10:30 pm	Rites of the Noguchi Hut	(*Noguchi kariya no gi*) The Head Priest processes to the Noguchi House, riding on a horse. Arriving there, he and the head of the Noguchi family reenact the advent of the Kami to this area. The Head Priest takes the role of Ōnamuchi no Kami.

(*continued*)

Table 15.4 **Continued**

Day Time	*Event*	*Notes*
11:00 pm	Yabusame	(*Yabusame shiki*) The Head Priest shoots at a target with a bow and arrow in front of the Tabisho, to dispel evil spirits and malevolent influences. This marks the end of the observances of May 5, and three fireworks are shot off.
5/6 4:00 am–7:00 am	The *mikoshi* leave the Tabisho.	(*Mikoshi Otabisho hatsugyo*) Before dawn, the *mikoshi* depart the Tabisho to tour their sponsoring neighborhoods and return to the shrine. Three fireworks are shot off to mark the commencement of activities for May 6. The *mikoshi* return to the shrine through the main gate.
7:00 am–9:00 am	Final whirling before the Worship Hall	All the *mikoshi* at once whirl before the Worship Hall before being brought back to the main sanctuaries.
9:00 am	Replacing the symbols of deity in the sanctuaries	(*Chinzasai*) This rite removes the symbols of deity from the *mikoshi* and replaces them in the main sanctuaries.
9:30 am	Arrow-shooting	(*Hikime shinji*) One of the *shinjin*, Mr. Horie, shoots an arrow over the fence at each of the four corners of the Oshirasu, where the sanctuaries are located, to repel any evil spirits or malevolent influences.
9:40 am	Fireworks	A final blast of three fireworks announces the conclusion of the festival.

Note: This chart is based on the festival as it was performed in 2003. Minor variations in order or timing may occur from year to year.

From early in the morning on May 5, a large crowd strolls in the shrine grounds. The path leading from the *torii* on the Old Kōshū Highway up to the Worship Hall is lined with stalls selling food or offering games for children. The distant beating of the drums touring their home neighborhoods can be heard. Large numbers of men belonging to drum or *mikoshi* groups are dressed in decorated jackets (*hanten*), leggings, long, split-toed socks, and headgear identifying their group.

At 10:00 am, when the Annual Festival Rites (that is, the *reitaisai* proper) begin, the Head Priest leads a procession of about 120 people from the Assembly Hall to a small tent where they will be purified before proceeding to the Worship Hall. These people—almost entirely men—have been invited as official worshippers who will be seated in the Worship Hall to witness the rites before the shrine altars. (Hundreds of others will watch from outside.) They represent the many different supporting organizations attached to the shrine. During this writer's fieldwork, the group always included the mayor of Fuchū, who served as one of the shrine's stewards (*sōdai*). As the purification of the invited guests comes to an end, a smaller procession arrives. It is the official NASS emissary (*kanpeishi, kenpeishi*), dressed in priestly vestments and accompanied by several assistants carrying a long wooden trunk, slung from poles on the shoulders of a pair of priests. The trunks contain the "official tribute" (*kanpei*), offerings of food to be presented from NASS to the Kami of the Ōkunitama Shrine. The emissary follows the main group into the Worship Hall, so that the emissary is seated near the back. After Head Priest Sawatari opens the three doors of the Main Sanctuary, oversees the placement of offerings before each one, and offers a *norito*, the NASS emissary rises and proceeds to the Main Sanctuaries, where he also offers a *norito*. Each of these actions is announced to those within the Worship Hall, who also have printed programs. At the conclusion of these rites in the Worship Hall (not all of which are described here), the Ōkunitama Shrine priests and the NASS entourage depart together. This structure of ceremony dramatizes a provincial shrine's unity with the other shrines of the nation and is the second to assert public significance.

The third occurs on the afternoon of May 5, when a small procession of priests presents offerings at the Miyanome Shrine, located within the shrine's precincts, between the great *torii* and the Zuishin Gate. Based on local legend, this shrine is thought to have been founded in the same year as Ōkunitama Shrine, and to be located on the spot where the ancient provincial government (the *kokuga*) was situated. The actions of the ritualist in this ceremony, the ceremony at Tsubonomiya Shrine, and the rites of the Tabisho (both to be presented here) are the same. They are quite distinctive and not seen in other rites of this shrine. The ritualist seats himself before the shrine's altar, holding a large *sakaki* bough. Standing, he waves the bough in a broad left and right movement. He retreats three paces and repeats waving the bough. This sequence is performed three times, ending with his placing the *sakaki* on the altar.

The fourth is a presentation of offerings at the Tsubonomiya Shrine, where the spirit of the original provincial governor of Musashi Province is enshrined. This small shrine (technically a part of Ōkunitama Shrine) is located about a fifteen-minute walk from the main shrine. On the night of May 5, the Negi (second in rank among the shrine priests), mounted on a horse, heads a small procession of assistants to travel to the Tsubonomiya Shrine to present offerings and prayers announcing the Annual Festival. As before, the ritualist repeats the movements seen at the Miyanome Shrine. His procession does not return directly to the Ōkunitama Shrine, but instead goes to the Tabisho, to participate in the rituals there. With the Review of the Horses, the ceremonies at the Miyanome and Tsubonomiya Shrines set the festival in a context of ancient history when shrines were indeed an essential element in extending the control of the central government over its provincial frontiers.[44]

Ceremonies to Effect the Rebirth of the Kami

The Darkness Festival accomplishes the rebirth of the Kami by transporting them in *mikoshi* to the site where the original Kami first descended to Fuchū, offering them dignified, beautiful, and mysterious worship in that place, later returning them to the main shrine, where they remain until the next year's festival.

Map 15.2 presents an enlarged view of the spaces where the relevant events take place.

For most of the year, the *mikoshi* and drums are kept in the Treasure Hall (Hōmotsuden), a museum on the shrine premises. On the morning of May 4, the *mikoshi* are moved to the Oshirasu, a white-graveled area between the rear of the

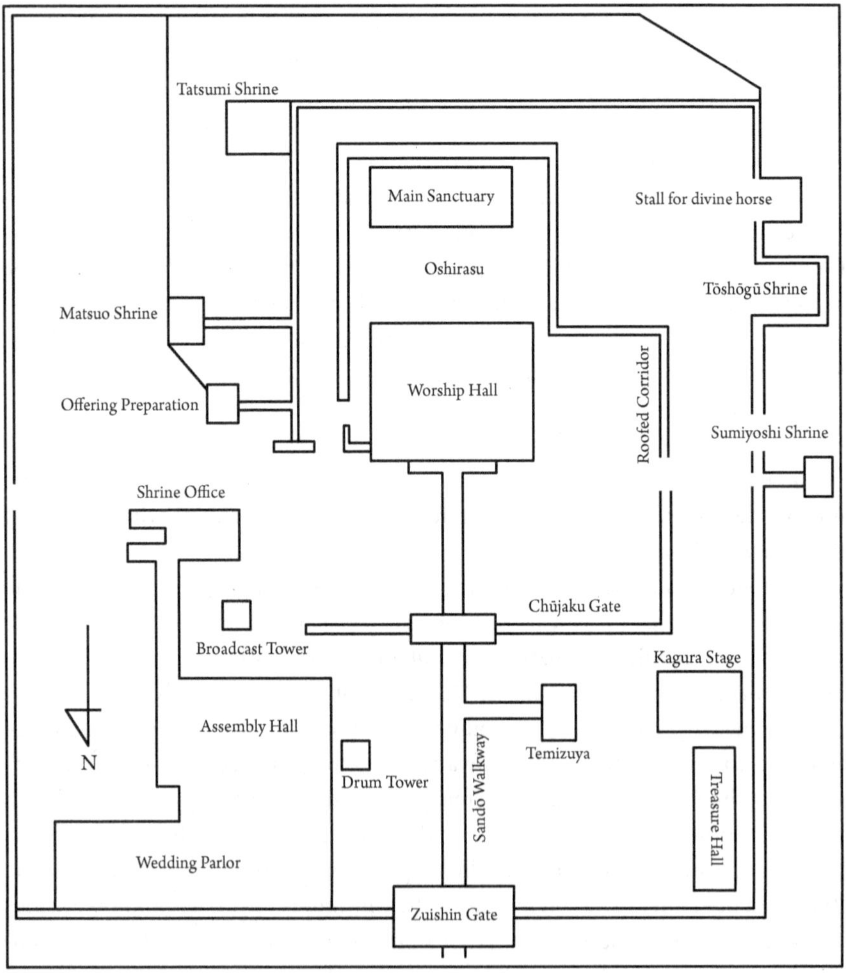

Map 15.2 The Principal Ritual Spaces of Ōkunitama Shrine.

Worship Hall and the Main Sanctuary, by men from the managing neighborhoods, for a ceremony—traditionally off limits to women—to attach new silken cords.[45] The *mikoshi* remain there until late afternoon on May 5, when they are presented before the Worship Hall as the vehicles that will be used to transport the Kami to the Tabisho.

In the interval, the *Dōzasai* is performed, a ceremony announcing the imminent procession to the Kami. When Shinto scholar Mogi Sakae observed the festival in 1989, under the former Head Priest, he noted that at a length of one hour and ten minutes, it was relatively long.[46] In changing back to a nighttime schedule, one of Head Priest Sawatari's main aims was to restore this ceremony to its original form. He lengthened it to nearly two hours, separating out miscellaneous minor ceremonies that had previously been crammed into it. He had the drums cease for the duration of the ceremony. In effect, he has transformed it into a series of seven dances performed by professional *kagura* dancers who soothe the Kami before the chaos that will ensue in the procession.

Animating the *Mikoshi*

Immediately upon the conclusion of the *Dōzasai*, the *mikoshi* are returned to the Oshirasu, where priests and leaders of the *mikoshi*-organizing groups move the symbols of deity into them from the sanctuary, in a secret ceremony that must not be seen except by the immediate participants.[47] Participants report that the objects are heavily wrapped in white cloth, and thus not visible, but feel like heavy stones. At this point, the Kami are now understood to be inside the *mikoshi*, which become their divine palanquins.

Formation of the Procession

As this ceremony is being performed, in the Sandō walkway, the leaders of the procession assemble. First come eight men in festival jackets, leggings, and black, numbered headgear, bearing long lanterns, one for each *mikoshi*, followed by two men with ringed metal staffs. They are followed by a *shinjin* dressed in a tall black hat with a white headband and silk robes, bearing a long bamboo pole, from which all but the leaves at the top have been stripped. The *shinjin* consist of fifteen families in which specific roles in shrine rites are passed down hereditarily. He waves this implement, called an *imi sasa*, broadly to right and left to ward off evil influences. Then comes another *shinjin*, bearing a large *sakaki* bough, decorated with paper streamers. Behind him come a group of musicians in silk vestments, playing *gagaku* music. Behind them is borne a *masakaki* (a large, potted *sakaki* plant), then lanterns on high poles, and a pair of huge lion masks. Next comes a long line of men bearing *igibutsu*, weapons to protect the procession; as these are all wrapped in brocade, naked blades are not displayed. They consist of four pikes, one long blade at the end of a pole, two named swords, a bow, an arrow, a shield, and three short swords.

The entourage of the Misakibarai Drum concludes this section of the procession, composed of forty or fifty men pulling the cart along with thick white ropes.[48] It inevitably astonishes the crowd by its great height, nine or ten feet from the ground, the many men riding atop it, and its great booming sound. All of these people pass through the Zuishin Gate to await the emergence of the *mikoshi*. The drums attached to each *mikoshi* are also waiting in that area.

The *Mikoshi* Whirl

When the signal is given, the Ichinomiya *mikoshi*, borne by forty men rhythmically calling "*Hoissa! Hoissa!*" bursts out of the Oshirasu into the area between the Worship Hall and the Chūjaku Gate, to tremendous applause from the spectators (see Figure 15.4). The bearers are in high spirits; their preparations have included drinking sake in great quantity. The drums beat continually, calling the *mikoshi* toward them. As soon as the *mikoshi* bearers appear, they are immediately surrounded by dozens of Ichinomiya men of middle age in *hanten* and hats inscribed with the number one, bearing lanterns, some blowing whistles, everyone shouting. Their function is to guide the *mikoshi* toward the Chūjaku Gate, but not immediately.

The *mikoshi* rise about four feet above the bearers' heads, borne aloft on two vertical poles. The *mikoshi* weigh around one ton each, making a considerable weight

Figure 15.4 Whirling *Mikoshi*. Source: Courtesy of the author.

on each bearer's shoulder. A cloud of dust rises as the bearers shouting "*Hoissa! Hoissa!*" move by shifting right, then left, so that the *mikoshi* rhythmically rocks back and forth with each step. The *mikoshi*'s movement speeds up, tracing random patterns in all directions. This is what the crowd has come to see. The *mikoshi*'s metal decorations flash and jingle, the silk cords fly back and forth, and the wings of the golden phoenix flap. The *mikoshi* appears to move of its own accord, with the bearers seeming to hang on to the poles to keep themselves upright, or to keep the *mikoshi* from ascending into the air. It is an ecstatic moment, melding Kami and humanity into one. The men surrounding the bearers crowd in, so that the *mikoshi* rocks and whirls through the area for twenty minutes or so in a pulsing rhythm punctuated by the "*Hoissa!*" chanting, whistle-blowing, the persistent beating of drums from beyond the gate, and the crowd's wild cheering.

Near the end, the group moves toward the broadcast tower (set up only during the Annual Festival), a sort of crows' nest where a police observer, an announcer, and a crew from the local cable TV station are set up. At this point, the bearers may exchange a few punches in order to get the spots at the end of the poles, and hence be visible on TV. The police announcer, always a woman, calls in a very nice voice for the ruffians to knock it off (*yamenasai*!), always to no avail. After this, the *mikoshi* moves toward the Chūjaku Gate, which means backing it up enough to approach it head on and "aiming" it to fit inside. It is also necessary at the last moment for the bearers to lower the *mikoshi* to thigh level, to enable it to squeeze through the narrow opening.

This sequence is repeated for each of the *mikoshi*. Once the convoy has passed through the Chūjakumon Gate, it is joined by another large group of men surrounding the *mikoshi*'s drum, pulled by forty or fifty men. More *mikoshi* bearers join the original men. Men bearing lanterns go in front, then the *mikoshi*, followed by a group of Ichinomiya supporters. The procession will travel through the Zuishin Gate, at which point two extra poles are attached to the *mikoshi* horizontally, so that more bearers can share the load, making four poles in all. The whole Ichinomiya entourage is now joined to the long line that began with lantern bearers and weapons bearers, and starts with the Misakibarai Drum.

The entire procession sets out for the Tabisho, turning left outside the main *torii*. The procession moves very slowly, taking a full three hours for all the *mikoshi* to arrive at the Tabisho. Along the way, there may be several changeovers of bearers, and some of the replacements may include *kō* members from outside Fuchū or *mikoshi* clubs who have negotiated an arrangement in advance. Goryōgū takes a different route, turning left outside the Zuishin Gate and meeting up with the main procession at the same time that Gohonsha is arriving. Also arriving at this time is the procession returning from Tsubonomiya Shrine.

The route is lined with crowds of spectators, who may total as many as 350,000 in the years when May 5 falls on Saturday or Sunday. At 9:00 pm. Gohonsha enters the Tabisho by the North Gate, and Goryōgū enters by the East Gate. Lastly, the

Priest who led the procession from Tsubonomiya Shrine enters from the North Gate. Both gates are then shut.

Rites of the Tabisho

The place identified as the spot where the Kami first descended is called the Tabisho. In this case, because the myth concerns the Kami Ōkuninushi or Ōnamuchi, the reference is to a single Kami. The Tabisho is a vermillion enclosure, walled by a high fence with two large gates, and open to the sky. Only a small number of bearers, the priests, and the *gagaku* musicians are allowed inside. Peeping is strictly forbidden. The Tabisho is specially prepared with eight roofed structures made from freshly cut tree limbs. Each *mikoshi* is placed within one of these. When all *mikoshi* are thus settled, all lights are extinguished.

Offerings are set out before each *mikoshi*, two dishes for each one, except for Goryōgū, which has eight. When these have been arranged and a *norito* is read to announce the event, the Negi who had led the procession to the Tsubonomiya Shrine, bearing a large *sakaki* bough, steps before each *mikoshi* in turn as *gagaku* music is played. He performs the same motions as at Tsubonomiya Shrine (and as had been performed at the Miyanome Shrine), waving the *sakaki* in broad motions to the right and the left, advancing and retreating three times. Only this time, the Negi represents the ancient provincial governor paying tribute to the main shrines of the province. His worship recreates the rationale for the existence of Ōkunitama Shrine as a Comprehensive Shrine and asserts again the shrine's significance in the scheme of ancient governance. After his worship concludes, the Head Priest of the Ōkunitama Shrine performs identical worship.

Everyone departs from the Tabisho, and it is sealed. After the rites have concluded, the Tabisho takes on the character of a womb. The *mikoshi* remain there overnight, symbolizing gestation in darkness and silence.

Rites of the Noguchi Hut

After honoring the Kami in the Tabisho, the Head Priest himself takes the role of the first Kami who sought lodging in the town. The shrine's myth of origin invokes a tale found widely among shrines, holding that in ancient times an unknown Kami came seeking lodging for the night.[49] He was refused at the first house. He tried again at the Noguchi house. The Noguchi man who answered the Kami's request said that he would gladly host the Kami, but that his wife was giving birth at that moment, and he was afraid of exposing the Kami to pollution. The Kami said that he had no fear of pollution, whereupon he entered the house and shared a meal with his host. In the Darkness Festival the Head Priest travels on horseback from the Tabisho to the descendants of that family, to re-enact the first interaction of Kami and humanity. This ceremony is held between 10:30 and 11:00 pm. The ceremony is held in a room with wide, detachable doors open to the street, exposing the three remaining walls. Its *tatami* flooring is covered with straw mats, with a large drum set out in the center, flanked by two large wooden candlesticks, and further lit by two large lanterns hung near the ceiling. Small tables for the meal are set at each place. The three walls are hung with dark blue curtains, decorated with two large, white wisteria crests on each wall. The head of the Noguchi family acts as host. The Head Priest, Negi, and attendants are seated, along with representatives of five *shinjin* families. Besides the Noguchi family, others take responsibility for preparation of some offerings, making and shooting arrows, polishing mirrors for the festival, and other tasks. When they are seated, an attendant strikes the drum three times, and the meal begins. Noguchi samples each item first, to show that each is free of poison. Noguchi and the Head Priest exchange cups of sake, after which the others are served. This sequence is repeated for each item on the menu, which includes two kinds of sake, steamed rice with red beans, and tea. At the conclusion, the Head Priest leads the group out.

Reinstalling the Reborn Kami

The next morning, at 4:00 am, the *mikoshi* are borne back through their sponsoring neighborhoods one more time, and then they return to the area between the Chūjaku Gate and the Worship Hall, where all of them at once are whirled for one final time. At 9:00 am, the Head Priest moves the symbols of the Kami from the *mikoshi* and replaces them in the sanctuary. This ceremony reinstalls the reborn Kami to bless and protect the community for the year to come.

The Darkness Festival Since Its Return to a Nighttime Schedule

This writer carried out interviews in 2004 that reflect on the way the festival is regarded within Fuchū since the changeover to a nighttime schedule. Officials of the Fuchū City Tourism Office (Fuchū Kankō Ka) expressed the view that the *matsuri* promotes bonds of friendship and solidarity among people, a sense of mutual aid, contribution to society, and civic pride. In the city's view, the festival also promotes the reputation of Fuchū City, spreads information about the city, and gives people self-confidence and pride. They showed me a variety of the city's promotional materials that feature the festival prominently.[50]

Nakasato Ryōhei described a fight that broke out at the Kurayami Matsuri in 2006 between members of two local youth groups. A young member of one youth group struck the leader of the second group, for reasons that were unclear. No one pressed for an explanation of the problem between the two men, and the ultimate cause of the blow was treated as unimportant. A local man of middle age was asked to intervene, and he called in a colleague to assist in the mediation. The ultimate solution was a declaration by the two groups that they would break off relations (*enkiri*). This resolution was regarded as appropriate, because it was not necessary in the end to expose the matter to the older men or outsiders.[51]

In 2007, a dispute occurred at the festival between a local young man and an outsider; the two were carrying a *mikoshi* together. The outsider had been granted the privilege of carrying the *mikoshi* by applying to a group of local men who were in charge of managing outsiders' participation; for convenience, let us call them Group A. The outsider had been lent a set of clothes identical to those of the local men. In the excitement of the moment, they did not immediately grasp that he was not one of them until he pushed his way to the front of the pole. From that position, he could be sure of being seen by the television cameras filming the festival, but this position was jealously guarded by the local men as a privilege exclusive to them. A fistfight broke out. After the fight ended, the local men took no further retribution on the outsider, nor did the outsider on them. Group A was found wanting in its management of outsiders, and apologized for its negligence. The Group A member who had lent *matsuri* clothing to the outsider without warning him to stay away from the end of the pole was expelled. In this case, too, it was possible to keep the incident from being taken up by the older men.[52]

A third example began as a fight of an unknown cause between a local young man and a spectator. In this case a policeman weighed in to stop the fight but was injured in the process. The injury of the police officer was considered very serious, and the elder men stepped in. They formed a special committee to deal with the problem; after meeting several times, they decided thereafter to engage a private security firm to keep spectators in line and also issued a written statement of procedures to be followed in the future. The police were satisfied with this, and the dispute was thus resolved.[53]

These examples provide insight into the unwritten rules of *matsuri*. Mild violence is seen as an appropriate means of resolving disputes among insiders. Violence is also permitted in disputes between insiders and outsiders, provided that it is not so extreme as to force the men of middle age to call in their elders. If a dispute can't be resolved on the spot, a middle-aged man of influence is called in, rather than taking it to the older men. If a spectator is involved, or the police, the elder men must ultimately resolve the problem. None of these incidents was regarded as sufficiently troubling to provoke calls that the Darkness Festival go back to a daylight schedule.

Conclusion

This chapter has examined postwar shrines' circumstances with regard to claims on public space. Study of the postwar history of shrine festivals produces two contrasting findings. On the one hand, civic pageants unaffiliated with shrines have grown and prospered. Local governments create and shape them in order to promote domestic tourism and positive images of the community. Local government can enjoy much more autonomy and meet less resistance, and can also incorporate a wider spectrum of the population than when it has to deal with shrines. The promotional aims motivating local government lie in another dimension from the religious rationales underlying traditional shrine festivals. On the other hand, despite shrines' limited postwar prerogatives in terms of the control of public space and access to public funds, many festivals are growing. We examined the Darkness Festival as one such example.

The confrontation with the residents of the surrounding community precipitated by violence constituted a major crisis for the Ōkunitama Shrine in the 1950s and 1960s. Violence at festivals is in part an outgrowth of the ethos common to *matsuri* as a whole, the idea that it is appropriate to overturn the ordinary social order and its restrictions. Violence is also associated with—but not caused by—the idea that men bearing a *mikoshi* are being moved by the Kami inside it, and that in that condition individuals cannot be held accountable for their actions. This impasse with the community was resolved for a period of about thirty years by moving the festival to a daytime format. That format became intolerable to the Head Priest appointed in 1999. The problem of violence had receded by that time, and to him it was important to reassert the festival's original religious rationale. The festival's rationale lies ultimately in effecting an annual revitalization of the Kami and the community. The separate ceremonies of which it is composed assert claims to public significance and a context of nation, in which observances originating in antiquity express the idea that Shinto contributes vitally to the life of the people.

The Head Priest's innovations were strengthened greatly by the creation before his appointment of new activities drawing a widened spectrum of Fuchū residents into the festival. The children's *mikoshi*, the *dashi* and their children's dance and music troops, and the *mando* contest have established important channels for transmitting the love of *matsuri* to future generations. Thus this festival continues to grow and flourish. The City Office is proud to adopt the Darkness Festival as the "face" of Fuchū, using photos of the festival in its many print and Internet promotional materials. Ongoing efforts to incorporate the community will undoubtedly remain crucial to maintaining the vitality of this festival.[54] The combined efforts of the Head Priest and shrine supporters have secured a central place for the Ōkunitama Shrine in Fuchū's public sphere. At the same time, the coherence of Shinto's religious rationales for the separate ceremonies composing the Darkness Festival has been re-established.

16

Heisei Shinto

Introduction

After Hirohito's death, major figures in the Shinto world began calling for change. Sonoda Minoru, a graduate in Religious Studies from Tokyo University, professor at Kyoto University, and Head Priest of the Chichibu Shrine (Saitama Prefecture), electrified readers of *Jinja shinpō* with a New Year's message in 1996.

> The year 1995 marks the end of an era. It is time for the Shinto world to shed its obstinate, rigid, defensive posture. Instead, we should positively, purposefully proclaim our ideal for shrines to a troubled society. That will require us to make fundamental changes. First, we must realize that Shinto is a religion, not a religion of salvation, but rather a "religion existing within the secular" (*sezoku-nai shūkyō*), a cultural religion (*bunkateki shūkyō*) that accommodates itself to contemporary society. Second, we must realize that Japan is no longer a village society. We must build a qualitatively new sense of community in an urban context. Third, it is essential that priests establish new, higher standards for themselves, ... realize that they are part of a religion, and that it is essential to associate with other religionists. No religion or worldview can expect to monopolize social values.... People in Japan are free to choose. The time has long gone when a traditional religion like Buddhism or Shinto could expect to command the allegiance of all the people. However, in calling on you to realize that you are part of a religion, I ask you to free yourselves of a narrow concept of religion based on individual faith as stipulated in the constitution or the Religious Corporations Law. Instead, you should think of religion more broadly, as a system of symbols incorporating traditional culture and society. Even if this religion doesn't have a concept of salvation, it supports the culture of daily life (*seikatsu bunka*) and supports the members

> of society. We must realize that this is the kind of religion Shinto is, and not a narrow-minded, intolerant religion. The basic character of Shinto is based on the living culture of the Japanese people, who have dwelt in this land in a way adapted to this country, [with] its own spiritual concepts of life. This is [Shinto's] basis, not a founder's teachings. Up to now, Shinto has idealized village society as providing our ideal community, [but] we can see from the persistence of *matsuri* that shrine communities can adapt to urbanization. Rather than becoming pessimistic at the loss of older ideas, we must recognize [contemporary society's] desire for qualitatively new images of community. If we cling to the old and merely try to operate shrines like businesses, then shrines will die out in the not too distant future. Allow the *ujiko* and stewards to play their part, open up responsibilities to them. Face up to the issues of contemporary society. Find peace and contentment in your way of life, knowing that in the past, present, and future, Shinto is a Way of worshipping the Kami and revering the ancestors.[1]

In essence, Sonoda called on the shrine priesthood to step back from NASS politics and focus instead on creating a new vision of Shinto that accepts it as a religion, understands how society is changing, and works with its lay supporters to establish new ideals for urban communities.

While Hirohito's death was widely seen as heralding a new era, however, NASS's politics since 1989 have been consistent with its earlier history. When protests erupted against the huge expense of Hirohito's state funeral and of the enthronement ceremonies for Emperor Akihito (who has ruled since 1989), NASS and other conservative groups denounced the protesters. NASS continues to condemn the Occupation and urge the eradication of the "Tokyo War Crimes Trial view of history," and to expand Shinto Seiji Renmei, press for a rosy view of the imperial period, and advocate revising the constitution to change article 9, the clause renouncing war and the maintenance of a military force, as well as revision of the clauses on citizen's rights, in the direction of expanding duties and curtailing rights.

As Japanese prime ministers have continued to issue apologies to the former colonies, followed by the predictable backlash from conservative groups, NASS has been sidelined on this issue by the one person it can never criticize—namely, the emperor. Emperor Akihito has made a number of apologies of his own, beginning only three months after Hirohito's death. He has expressed contrition on foreign trips to China, Korea, Southeast Asian nations, and on his visits to World War II battle sites in the Pacific and in Japan, where he and Empress Michiko have offered prayers for Allied soldiers, for the civilians who lost their lives as well as the colonial subjects dragooned into military service, and for Japanese soldiers. The emperor's statements have been widely received as utterly sincere and heartfelt. Hirohito's passing thus made way for an entirely new tone in the palace.[2]

I devote this final chapter to discussion of new directions that illustrate how Shinto has changed during the Heisei era, and how it is likely to develop in the future. Japanese attitudes toward religion have been powerfully affected by the Aum Shinrikyō incident of 1995, in which a religious group of that name carried out an attack on the Tokyo subway system using sarin gas. The incident resulted in the deaths of eleven people, injuries to hundreds of others, and led to a widespread condemnation of religion. In 1996, the Religious Corporations Law was revised, mandating greater state oversight of religion and requiring religions to reveal more information about their operations and assets. The most significant change, however, was the introduction of a perspective emphasizing government's responsibility to protect citizens from abusive practices by religious groups. The new perspective envisions regulating religious organizations along the lines of consumer-protection provisions, and the Japan Federation of Bar Associations has prepared guidelines for prosecuting abuses by religious groups. In the process, a marketplace framework has been introduced, in which religions are regarded as something people choose (or not), much like consumer goods.[3]

A vigorous debate has ensued, questioning whether religion contributes to the public good. Before its 1996 revision, the Religious Corporations Law prohibited government from judging whether a particular group qualifies as "authentically" religious and accorded religious organizations near-total autonomy to manage their internal affairs. Religious corporations are classified as public interest corporations (*kōeki hōjin*), along with foundations, schools, and medical- and social-welfare institutions, based on the assumption that religion contributes to the public good. The law also gives religions a privileged tax status; they are assessed a lower rate of taxation on their for-profit activities than ordinary businesses (22 percent versus 30 percent). Even when abuses were revealed, the disclosures did not produce sweeping demands to tax all religious organizations. But after the Aum incident, Japanese society began to question whether religion contributes to *kōeki,* "the public good," the "public interest," or "public welfare," all of which are possible translations, depending on the context. This term is not minutely defined either in law or vernacular usage.

Since 2007, the Diet, the media, and a wide variety of Internet sites have begun to debate the issue of imposing higher taxes on religious organizations. Not surprisingly, religious groups vigorously oppose the idea. Scholars warn that taxation should never be used for retribution.[4] Buddhist and Christian denominations can point to their schools, hospitals, and charitable foundations, and Japanese Christianity takes pride in its historical emphasis on education, altruism and charity. Numerous new religious movements operate schools, hospitals, and smaller medical facilities. The largest of them, such as Sōka Gakkai and Tenrikyō, even have universities. Sōka Gakkai and Risshō Kōseikai support international welfare programs through their affiliated non-governmental organizations (NGOs) to build schools, conduct reforestation, provide clean drinking water, and similar services.

Shinto's contributions to public welfare are less visible, in part because they tend to be channeled through community organizations located near particular shrines. On a broader scale, NASS has contributed to international aid efforts following the 2010 earthquake in Haiti, though this has not been widely publicized by the mainstream media. Shinto-derived new religious movements are typically involved in a variety of welfare projects, volunteering at local homes for the handicapped and the aged, as well as participating in relief work in the wake of natural disasters. Their efforts are likewise underreported.

Contemporary Debate

Public-opinion surveys on religion since 1995 reveal a steep increase in negative perceptions of religion among all age groups and both sexes. Negative perceptions have been intensified by recent revelations of misuse of religions' favorable tax provisions. For example, an inactive religious group can sell its incorporated name, and the buyer can operate a completely unrelated business under that umbrella, opening not only the possibility of tax fraud but also that criminal activity might be carried out using a religion's name.

Pet funerals performed by Buddhist temples have become an issue, rituals that seem absurd to many people, suggesting that clerics who advertise them are exploiting their clients by charging exorbitant fees for cremation, pet graves, and reciting sutras, as if pets were human beings. A 2007 Supreme Court case ruled against a temple called Jimyōin (Tendai sect, Kasugai City, Aichi Prefecture), requiring it to pay corporate income tax on fees from pet funerals, declaring in the process that such rituals are not religious. This verdict has been criticized for, in essence, defining religion, but there is no higher court of appeal. By contrast, another Supreme Court judgment, in a similar case about pet funerals, involving the Tokyo temple Ekōin (Jōdo sect), resulted in a verdict that the temple's long history of animal memorials was reason to excuse it from taxes on the land and structures used in pet funerals. These two irreconcilable verdicts suggest that Japanese legal thinking remains conflicted in this area.[5]

The triple disaster of March 11, 2011, was a watershed in the debate on religion's contribution to the public good. A massive earthquake of magnitude 9.0 in Northeast Japan touched off a huge tidal wave along the northern Pacific coast, and a nuclear reactor near Sendai experienced a meltdown, contaminating a wide area. The earthquake was the largest in Japan's history. In all, around 16,000 people died; thousands more were injured and displaced from their homes, and numerous towns and hamlets were utterly wiped out. Many thousands of buildings and businesses were destroyed or left structurally unsound. Railway lines, airports, nuclear and electrical power plants, roads, and dams were severely damaged. Schools, hospitals, homes for the aged, town offices, banks, retail businesses of all kinds, and virtually all social services were severely disrupted. Fishing fleets were lost, and farming was disrupted by the complete destruction of fields and irrigation works. Fish and other edible products of the area affected by the earthquake were contaminated with radiation. Thousands of people remain in temporary housing. Many have given up hope and have relocated to other areas of Japan. The government dithers over standards for compensation, and as of 2016, the seepage of nuclear waste into the air and water continues.

Hundreds of shrines, temples, Christian churches, and the churches of new religious movements were damaged or destroyed. Many of those remaining opened their doors to people who had lost their homes. Religious organizations, their clergy and members were among the first to distribute food, clothing, and to offer shelter, funeral rites, and counseling. The disaster offered religious groups of all kinds a chance to demonstrate their readiness to contribute to the public welfare.

Shinto in Contemporary Religious Culture

To interpret current debate in a broader context, it is useful to consider the place of religion in Japanese society as a whole, and to ask whether or in what ways the Japanese people are religious. This is a question that arises for anyone who has visited this vibrant country, where educators, government representatives, businessmen, and many educated persons are quite likely to remark that they personally do not regard religion as playing a central role in their own lives or in Japan's public life. Certainly, these attitudes reflect something important about contemporary Japan, but they may not reflect the whole society or tell the whole story. In many cases, these views reflect a pervasive secularism among elites, their opinions regarding how Japan *ought* to be, rather than the attitudes of society as a whole. Elites want the world to know that Japan is a modern nation, where people think rationally and reject superstition. They often try to make this point by denying that Japan is religious, but it is not the case that religion can be reduced to superstition and irrationality.

On the other hand, statistics on adherence to religious beliefs, membership in religious organizations, observance of traditional practices, and indicators of the influence of religious organizations in public life have been in decline since the 1950s. This trend is seen in all branches of Japanese religions, including Shinto.[6] Against this is the strong and rising presence of religious themes and motifs in popular culture, especially those derived from Shinto.

Table 16.1 introduces 2013 data from the Agency for Cultural Affairs of the Ministry of Education, Culture, Sports, Science and Technology (MEXT). Shinto shrines and Shinto-derived organizations together make up about 40 percent of all religious organizations in Japan. Shrines make up about 37 percent of the total. In MEXT's calculations, the Shinto-, Buddhist-, and Christian-derived new religious

Table 16.1 **Religious Organizations in Japan as of 2013**

	Religious Organization					
Religion/ Tradition	*Shrines*	*Temples*	*Churches*	*Proselytizing Stations*	*Other*	*Total*
Shinto	81,235	20	5,450	1,027	817	88,549
Buddhism	29	77,329	2,172	1,941	3,811	85,282
Christianity	0	2	7,051	856	1,438	9,347
Other	72	41	17,147	18,053	1,448	36,761
Total	81,336	77,392	31,820	21,877	7,514	219,939

Table 16.2 **Members and Clergy of Japanese Religious Organizations as of 2013**

Religion / Tradition	*Total Members and Clergy*	*Number of Members*	*Number of Clergy*	*Male Clergy*	*Female Clergy*
Shinto	91,341,359	91,260,343	81,016	49,955	31,061
Buddhism	87,279,911	86,902,013	377,898	196,114	181,784
Christianity	2,982,371	2,947,765	34,606	26,322	8,284
Other	9,269,592	9,066,141	203,451	78,687	124,764
Total	190,873,233	190,176,262	696,971	351,078	345,893

movements would be folded into each religion's total numbers for organizations and adherents, while the "other" category includes unaffiliated new religious organizations and their adherents, as well as minority traditions such as Judaism and Islam, in which the membership is composed largely of foreigners (plus Japanese spouses and children). As these figures suggest, Japan hosts a vibrant religious scene with temples, shrines, churches, and other religious organizations throughout the country.

Table 16.2 presents the number of clergy and adherents of the major branches of Japanese religions today. These numbers represent the figures submitted by the organizations to the Department of Religious Affairs, the government agency charged with administering religious affairs. This department belongs to the Agency for Cultural Affairs within MEXT. The Department of Religious Affairs does not investigate or confirm these self-reported statistics.

Combining the results seen in Tables 16.1 and 16.2 allows us to derive a rough set of statistics regarding Shinto. First, we note that there are around 81,000 shrines in Japan. This number includes shrines affiliated with NASS (around 79,000) and roughly 2,000 others. The others are roughly evenly divided between shrines established by Shinto-derived new religious movements and ordinary shrines not affiliated with NASS. The figures in Table 16.2 regarding Shinto clergy represent the total of shrine Shinto clergy and clergy of Shinto-derived new religious movements. The number of clergy in the Shinto-derived new religious movements far exceeds that of ordinary shrines. NASS estimates that there are around 20,000 shrine priests, of whom 2,678, or 13 percent, are women.[7] This finding shows that the proportion of women clergy in the Shinto-derived new religious movements is considerably higher than in shrine Shinto. No breakdown is available regarding the number of adherents of Shinto-derived new religious movements versus ordinary shrines.

Japan's population today is around 126 million, but Table 16.2 shows that the total number of adherents of religious organizations is far higher. This statistical paradox has been found since the country began collecting statistics on religion in 1945. It reflects the pattern of multiple religious affiliations, in which families are typically affiliated with both a temple and a shrine; but it should also be noted that because these statistics are compiled on the basis of numbers supplied by the various religious organizations themselves, there is a strong tendency for numerical inflation.

Changing Belief in the Kami and Buddhas

Surveys since the 1950s have asked respondents whether they believe in the existence of the Kami and the Buddhas. The results provide an important index of the vitality of religion in society (see Table 16.3).

If we compare the results of surveys from 1994 and 1995, we see a drop in affirmations of belief in the Kami and Buddhas, from 43.8 to 19.4 percent.[8] A decrease by more than half in a single year is monumental, even allowing for different surveying organizations with different techniques and slight differences of wording. This result should be attributed to the fact that respondents in 1995 were reacting to the Aum incident. When we focus on the questions asked in the NHK surveys from 1973 to 1988, however, we can see greater continuity. We observe an overall decline in expressions of belief, but the decline in belief in Buddhas is greater. Overall, it appears that about one-third of the Japanese people straightforwardly affirm the existence of the Kami, while around 40 percent affirm the existence of Buddhas.

Japanese Religiosity in International Perspective

Placing Japanese religiosity in a comparative framework helps us to see where the country fits among other developed nations. Table 16.4 shows that Japan ranks lowest in proportion of the population affiliated with a religious organization, at 44.4 percent. The nearest country on this index is France, at 57.5 percent. It is likely

Table 16.3 **Percentage Affirming Belief in the Kami and the Buddhas**

Survey	*Question*	*Year*								
		1952	*1973*	*1978*	*1983*	*1988*	*1993*	*1994*	*1995*	*1998*
Yomiuri Shinbun, "Zenkoku yoron chōsa"	Do you believe that the Kami and the Buddhas exist?	54.6						43.8		
NHK Hōsō yoron chōsajo, "Nihonjin no ishiki chōsa"	Do you believe in the Kami?		32.5	37.0	38.9	36.0	35.2			31.5
NHK Hōsō yoron chōsajo, "Nihonjin no ishiki chōsa"	Do you believe in the Buddhas?		41.6	44.8	43.8	44.6	44.1			38.7
Nihon Seron Chōsakai, "Shūkyō seron chōsa"	Do you believe that the Kami and the Buddhas exist?								19.4	

Source: Adapted from Ishii Kenji. "Gendai Nihonjin no kami kannen no ha'aku to yoron chōsa (Tokushū: Shintō to Nihon bunka no shosō)" *Kokugakuin zasshi*, 104, no. 11 (2003): 365–66.

that Japanese asked to respond to the question, "Do you belong to a religious organization?" may say "No," even though they could be members of a Buddhist temple parish and on the list of *ujiko* of their local shrine. These affiliations have acquired such a customary and traditional nature that many people would not immediately think of them as "religion" (*shūkyō*), a term that people tend to associate with a set of specific doctrines and a requirement to affirm a doctrinal creed.

The character of religious affiliation tends to be customary, based on location, family, and community more than on religious conviction. Shinto and Buddhism make only minimal demands on ordinary believers for time, money, and allegiance, though, of course, people who feel a stronger attachment will devote more resources and energy. By contrast, Japanese Christianity places much more emphasis on religious beliefs and conviction, and Christian ministers and priests provide much more religious education. Bible study and discussion are central in most churches, whether Protestant or Catholic, as are charitable activities.

Historical patterns of religious affiliation with Buddhism and Shinto, especially, have resulted in a merging of social and religious values, probably leading many stalwart members of Buddhist and Shinto congregations to deny that they belong to a religious organization. Religious education has not been a central element of Buddhist or Shinto affiliation, except in new religious movements. Thus, while significant proportions of the Japanese people engage in a variety of religious activities, participate in such daily religious observances as tending household altars, and visit temples and shrines for traditional observances throughout the year, they may not see these activities as "religious." Thus if we were to characterize the way in which people are religious in Japan, it would be closely linked to the family and to tradition, emphasizing the things that people do, rather than attention to doctrines.

We notice a big difference between the results seen in Table 16.2 and 16.4 regarding membership in religious organizations. How can it be true that the total number of people affiliated with religious ogranizations shown in Table 16.2 is higher than the national population, while in Table 16.4 we find the figure of 44.4 percent? This gap can be attributed to the tendency of religious organizations to inflate their membership numbers and the tendency of people not to regard traditional temples and shrines as religious. Several different surveys conducted between 1999 and 2009 found that over 70 percent of Japanese respondents had never participated in a religious organization.[9] The figures from Table 16.3 are based on surveys of individuals—not organizations.

France, Sweden, and Japan stand at the low end of countries where people attend monthly religious services. In the case of Japan, neither temple Buddhism nor shrine Shinto has typically held such services, and thus it is not surprising to find that only a minority, of 9.8 percent, attend services monthly. Even so, Japan's rate exceeds Sweden's, at 7.9 percent. Those attending monthly services in Japan are probably composed largely of Christians and members of new religious movements. In terms

Table 16.4 **Multinational Comparison of Religious Affiliation, Attitudes, and Beliefs**

Country	*Japan*	*Rep. of Korea*	*Singapore*	*France*	*Germany*	*Sweden*	*UK*	*Canada*	*USA*
% belonging to a religious denomination	44.4	63.2	80.3	57.5	60.4	75.8	83.1	68.6	78.5
% identifying as atheist or agnostic	13.1	1.6	4.7	20.5	24.2	31.2	14.4	15.3	12.6
% attending religious services at least once per month	9.8	39.1	44.1	11.0	18.9	7.9	23.5	34.2	49.0
% active in a religious organization	4.4	17.5	–	4.4	13.0	6.9	19.2	27.9	37.9
% that meditate or pray	40.5	46.6	69.6	41.1	47.0	46.7	49.9	76.7	84.0
% believing in life after death	50.8	52.2	74.0	44.9	29.5	46.0	58.2	72.7	81.2
% believing in the soul	70.9	72.7	91.5	55.3	77.2	68.8	69.9	91.2	95.6
% that think often of life's meaning and purpose	24.3	39.6	–	44.3	28.7	31.2	38.1	47.0	36.4
% finding comfort and strength in religion	31.5	67.1	76.7	34.7	41.5	31.1	37.5	63.1	79.5
% considering religion important	19.5	47.0	71.0	40.9	33.9	29.4	40.7	59.1	71.6
% confident in religious organizations	8.8	48.9	–	47.2	37.6	56.0	45.7	59.7	66.3
% believing that religious leaders should not influence people's vote	75.3	55.3	–	86.2	72.8	80.7	69.3	77.6	60.5

Note: These data are drawn from the Association of Religion Data Archives (http://www.thearda.com/internationalData), accessed March 13, 2012. For each case I used the most recent data available.

of the proportion of people who say that they are active in religious organizations, Japan, France, and Sweden are similar, with rates under 10 percent.

Another way to gauge religiosity is to ask how many people identify as atheist or agnostic. Japan, at 13.1 percent, has around the same proportion as the United Kingdom (14.4%), Canada (15.3%), or the United States (12.6%). Notably, France, Germany, and Sweden have significantly higher proportions of atheists and agnostics.

When we examine typical religious practices and widespread beliefs, we find again that Japan is broadly similar to Western European countries, though showing lower rates on some indicators. These include prayer and meditation, belief in the soul and the afterlife, thinking about life's meaning and purpose, and finding strength and comfort in religion. Among other Asian countries, apart from the last of these items, Japan and Korea are broadly similar, while Singapore shows higher rates. By contrast, Canada and the United States show higher rates on most of these items than the other countries surveyed here. Japan occupies the middle of the spectrum, at 75.3 percent believing that religious leaders should not try to influence people's vote, showing a higher rate than Korea, Germany, the United Kingdom, and the United States, but lower than France, Sweden, and Canada. One area in which Japan is exceptional concerns the questions of how many people consider religion important and how many regard religious organizations with confidence. Japan's lower rates may result in part from lingering distrust of religion stemming from the Aum incident.

Findings thus far suggest that while there has been a definite decline in some traditional religious beliefs and observances, nevertheless beliefs like the existence of the soul and the afterlife are as strong in Japan as in Western Europe. Moreover, the Japanese people express some of the same beliefs, regardless of vastly different religious histories. On most indicators, Japan is more like Western Europe than the United States. It is noteworthy that the United States generally shows higher levels of belief and participation in religion than the other developed countries. For that reason, it would be a mistake to use the United States as a yardstick for measuring the religiosity of other developed countries, including Japan.

Kamidana and *Butsudan* Ownership

One measure of traditional religiosity in Japan is seen in changing rates at which the Japanese people maintain *kamidana* and *butsudan*. It should be understood that these home altars are usually associated with families. While it is not unknown for single people to have them, it is not surprising that many young people living in apartments in the cities would not, either because they would think that these matters are taken care of by their parents, and/or because the small size of Japanese apartments makes it difficult to find space for them. Statistics on ownership of *kamidana* and *butsudan* collected since the 1960s consistently show higher rates in rural areas and lower rates in the cities. Some early surveys limited to small samples and small areas of the country are available. While differences in their samples makes it difficult to compare them minutely, they show that rates of ownership of home altars began to decline from the 1950s. It is only since the 1980s that surveys covering the entire country have been conducted. Table 16.5 summarizes some of the major findings.

These figures in Table 16.5 show that the rates of ownership of home altars have declined in both Shinto and Buddhism, and also that the rate of ownership tends to be lower in the cities. We note also that the rate of decline is steeper in the case of *kamidana,* and that the difference between city and countryside in owning *kamidana* is larger than the comparable gap in ownership of *butsudan.*

Shinto Observances and Attitudes

Statistical surveys of religious observances of all kinds consistently show that the main occasion on which people visit Shinto shrines is New Years. The custom of visiting a shrine at New Year's is called "First Shrine Visit" (*hatsumōde*). People of all religious affiliations as well as many with no affiliation perform "first visits" as a joyful part of ushering in a new year. The trains and subways run for free all night to carry the crowds out after midnight to make this traditional shrine visit. As Table 16.6 shows, literally millions of people visit a variety of shrines—large, small, famous, or not well known—to begin the year by ringing the shrine's bell, making a small offering, and praying that the New Year may bring happiness and well-being.

These numbers can be put into rough perspective by comparing the total population of the cities concerned to the number of "first visit" shrine visitors. For instance, the total population of Tokyo is presently 13.23 million, which means that about one person in four visited the Meiji Shrine at New Years. Osaka has a population of about 2.87 million, which means that the number of people visiting Sumiyoshi Taisha, its most popular shrine, was almost equal to the entire population. Kyoto's population is 2.54 million, which means that more people visited Fushimi Inari Taisha at New Years than live in the entire city. The scale of the movement of the Japanese people to visit shrines at New Years is reminiscent of the huge numbers that went on "Thanks Pilgrimage" (*okage mairi*) to the Ise Shrines in the Edo period. New Years visits to shrines represent a central element in Shinto's significance within Japanese religious culture.

Other occasions on which people visit shrines include baby blessings (*hatsu miya mairi*) and visits to pray for a child's safety while growing to maturity (*shichi-go-san*). Baby blessings originally marked communal recognition of the new child and the end of the period of pollution following childbirth. The newborn child

Table 16.5 **Percentage Possessing Kamidana and Butsudan, 1951–2009**

Survey	*Year*	*Kamidana*	*Butsudan*	*Notes*	
Ronald Dore	1951	53	80	Conducted in blue-collar areas of Tokyo	
Joseph Spae	1957	71	78	Conducted in urban areas	
Morioka Kiyomi	1964–65	96	92	Conducted in a rural area of Yamanashi Prefecture	
"	1964–66	61	69	Conducted in working class areas of Tokyo	
"	1964–67	43	45	Conducted in white collar areas of Tokyo	
Joseph Spae	1966	40	60	Conducted in urban areas	
		Kamidana All Japan	***Kamidana Largest 14 Cities***	***Butsudan All Japan***	***Butsudan Largest 14 Cities***
Asahi Shinbun	1981	62	–	63	–
NHK	1981	60	–	61	–
Asahi Shinbun	1995	54	–	59	–
NASS	1996	51.3	35.9	–	–
Shūkyō dantai chōsa	1999	49	29.5	57.1	48.3
NASS	2001	50.5	36.8	–	–
Kokugakuin University COE	2004	44	29.2	56.1	46.9
NASS	2006	43.8	26.4	–	–
Jujutsu ishiki chōsa	2006	–	25.8	–	47.0
Nihonjin no shūkyōsei chōsa	2008	42.0	27.5	55.0	46.7
Nihonjin no shūkyōsei chōsa	2009	43.1	28.0	52.1	48.0

Source: Adapted from Ishii Kenji, ed. *Shintō wa doko e iku ka?* Tokyo: Perikansha, 2010, 21.

Table 16.6 **Number of Visitors to Top Ten Shrines for New Years Visit (*Hatsumōde*)**

Popularity Rank	*Shrine*	*Location*	*Number of Visitors*
1	Meiji Jingū	Tokyo	3,190,000
2	Fushimi Inari Taisha	Kyoto	2,770,000
3	Sumiyoshi Taisha	Osaka	2,600,000
4	Tsuruoka Hachimangū	Kamakura	2,510,000
5	Atsuta Jingū	Aichi Pref.	2,350,000
6	Ōmiya Hikawa Jinja	Saitama Pref.	2,050,000
7	Dazaifu Tenmangū	Fukuoka	2,040,000
8	Ikuta Jinja	Hyōgo Pref.	1,550,000
9	Miyajidake Jinja	Fukuoka	1,080,000
10	Yasaka Jinja	Kyoto	1,000,000

Source: Police Agency statistics, cited in "Shirarezaru Shintō no Sekai," *Daiyamondo* 99, no. 26 (July 2, 2009), 98.

was traditionally believed to be affected by pollution for a period of thirty-three days, but since the child's parents remained under the taboo until the seventy-fifth day, the child was usually taken to the local tutelary shrine by the father's mother, sometimes accompanied by the midwife. Nowadays, however, the idea of childbirth pollution has declined so greatly that the parents take the child to the shrine as early as one week or so after the birth. Many regional customs may be combined with the visit, such as dressing the baby in an ornate robe or painting the character for "big" on the foreheads of boy babies and making them cry loudly when ringing the shrine bell, in order to impress the Kami with a big healthy baby.[10]

Shichi-go-san is a celebration for children at the ages of three, five, and seven. *Shichi-go-san* literally means "seven-five-three," referring to the custom of taking children of both sexes to the *ujigami* shrine at the age of three, with further visits for boys at the age of five, and girls at the age of seven. The visit occurs on the fifteenth of November or around that time. Children are dressed in festive attire, usually a *kimono* for girls and for boys the wide-legged trousers called *hakama* with a jacket called *haori*, over an under-robe. At the shrine the parents (and grandparents) may simply make their own prayers for the Kami's protection for the child, or they may have a priest perform formal prayers.[11]

Another occasion that brings people to shrines (and temples) is prayers to avoid misfortune in inauspicious years (*yakudoshi*). The folk idea of inauspicious years holds that people are liable to experience misfortune in certain years, differing by sex, with different observances in different areas. The ages of twenty-five and forty-two are widely thought to be inauspicious for men, and for women the inauspicious

Table 16.7 **Impressions of Tutelary Shrines (*Ujigami*)**

Impression/Year	*1996*	*2001*	*2006*
A place that gives me peace of mind	38.6	37.2	31.0
A shrine that protects the people living nearby	30.6	34.1	37.8
An historical place	28.6	26.5	22.6
A sacred place	21.0	24.4	23.5
No specific impression	18.2	17.9	20.9
A shrine with a lively festival	12.6	17.0	13.9
A place with an attractive forest	10.1	11.5	11.0

Source: NAAS surveys reported in Ishii Kenji, "Jinja Shintō wa suita shita no ka," in *Shintō wa doko e iku ka?*, edited by Ishii Kenji (Tokyo: Perikansha, 2010), 19.

years are nineteen and thirty-three. The ages of thirty-three for women and forty-two for men are regarded as the most inauspicious.[12] In recent years, shrines have begun to advertise that they offer special prayer services for inauspicious years, and these have become quite popular, particularly among women.[13]

Surveys of attitudes toward local tutelary shrines (*ujigami*) give an indication of the way people think about shrines. The respondents of these surveys were not chosen for their religious affiliations, and thus can be taken to represent the population as a whole. Table 16.7 suggests that images of shrines as historical places that provide peace of mind and protection for the local people are the most salient, and that around one-third of survey respondents hold such an image.

Issues Facing the Priesthood

A survey of some 500 shrines undertaken in 2003 elicited the following statements from priests.

> No matter how much I try, I can't make a living at this small, weak shrine. My family has been [serving the shrine] for a long time, but I don't think my son will become a priest. He says it's because he couldn't make a living.[14]
>
> No one wants to become a shrine priest, because they can't make a living at small shrines. NASS doesn't realize what a problem this is.[15]
>
> Most head priests of rural shrines draw so little income from the shrine that nearly all of them have secondary employment that they live on. Moreover, there are many priests who have to make up a shrine's expenses for ceremonies from their own pocket. It's the same for shrine repairs in many cases, which means that the shrine comes to be maintained on the funds provided individually by the priest.[16]

> At this shrine there is no salary... so all the electricity, gas, telephone, water and sewer costs are borne by the priest.... I resigned from the Hachiman Shrine where I worked previously to become head priest at my family shrine, but I've been hit with the effects of the depression, and my income has decreased radically. I started a parking lot two years ago.[17]

As these quotations make abundantly clear, many priests face great difficulties in making a living. Many must take secondary employment and pay the shrine's basic expenses themselves. Some are forced to start businesses using shrine assets, such as land for a parking lot, and others must accept that their sons will not succeed them because of anxiety about income. Some believe that NASS does not grasp the scale of the problem they face.[18] Table 16.8 provides figures on the annual income of shrines. Chart 16.1 shows how that income is distributed.

Table 16.8 **Annual Income of Shrines, in US Dollars, Calculated at the rate of US$1 = 100 yen**

Annual Income	*Percentage of Shrines*
Less than $50,000	31.0
$50,000–$100,000	14.3
$100,000–$500,000	27.6
$500,000–$1,000,000	13.7
$1,000,000–$5,000,000	9.9
More than $5,000,000	0.2
NA	3.2

Source: Adapted from Shūkyō jōhō risāchi sentā. *Jinja soshiki ni kansuru ankēto chōsa hōkokusho*. Tokyo: Shūkyō jōhō risāchi sentā, 2003, table 6, p.7.

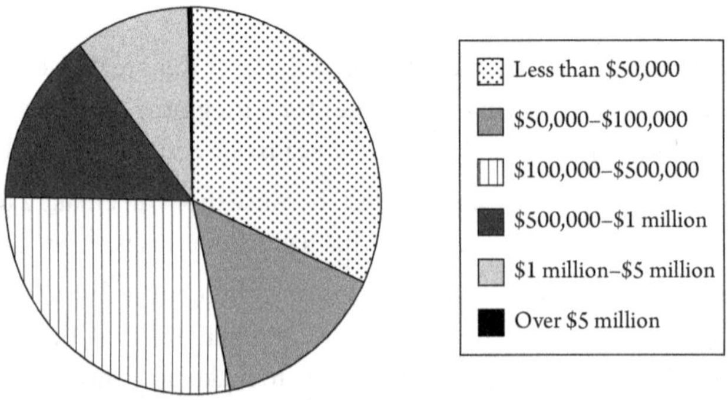

Chart 16.1 Distribution of Annual Shrine Income. *Source:* Bunkachō, *Shūkyō nenkan Heisei 25-nen* (2013), 34; *Shūkyō nenkan Heisei 26-nen* (2014), 35.

A shrine's income would have to cover the salary of any priests. In practice this probably means that the two lowest income categories, which together make up 45 percent of all shrines, face major difficulties in supporting the livelihood of a priest as well as paying for maintenance, routine repairs, and ceremonies, plus savings toward major repairs or rebuilding. On the other hand, over half of the shrines seem to have a reasonable income or to be receiving very impressive incomes. It goes without saying that we could only put these figures into proper perspective by matching them in each case with a shrine's expenses, which available statistics unfortunately do not permit. Nevertheless, we notice that there is a correlation between a shrine's income and its rank in the pre-1945 system. About half of the shrines ranked Village Shrine or District Shrine in the old system have annual incomes of less than $50,000. The former Prefectural Shrines usually have annual incomes of between $100,000 and $500,000. By contrast, two-thirds of the former National or Imperial Shrines have annual incomes of $500,000 or more.[19]

There is a correlation between the rank of a shrine under the old system and the likelihood that it will have corporations among its *ujiko*. This is significant, because corporations contribute more than an individual or family. The shrines with corporate supporters are most likely to be in the larger cities, and the larger the town or city where the shrine is located, the larger its annual income. Shrines in smaller towns are less likely to have corporate sponsors and are likely to have low income.[20]

Likewise, the higher the shrine's rank in the old system, the larger the proportion of its income that will be derived from the performance of ritual, by contrast with income from other sources. In the case of the former National and Imperial Shrines, fully eighty percent of their income is derived from the performance of ritual plus sale of talismans. This means that both individuals and corporate sponsors gravitate to larger shrines of more distinguished rank for ceremonies, undercutting the potential income that might otherwise go to smaller shrines.[21]

In addition to issues regarding income, shrine priests frequently experience difficulty in dealing with shrine stewards, *sōdai*. Shrines incorporated under the Religious Corporations Law are required to govern themselves through a group of three or more Responsible Officers (*sekinin yakuin*), which usually consists of the priest (if any) and the shrine stewards. The priest is typically elected as the Official Representative (*daihyō yakunin*) for the purpose of dealing with any legal or official matters. In practice this usually means that the priest and the shrine stewards manage the shrine's affairs together, each of them having equal authority, with decisions made by majority vote.[22] Problems arise from the gap between the law's specifications and priests' expectations, as the following comment by a priest makes clear.

> The stewards at my shrine are chosen by each neighborhood, and usually it's the same elderly men. With the decrease of population, it's difficult to get them to stand for office, so the selection process has become a revolving system where the steward's office passes from household to household,

> with the result that they don't show up for meetings. We're dealing with both the issue of aging and an automatic selection process, resulting in a system that can't respond to the changes in society. There is a rule that the priest doesn't comment on the Stewards' Association's personnel decisions. We preserve the appearance that the stewards are all volunteers who come forward of their own volition, but... it's far from being an active group. I would like to choose young and able *ujiko*, but they have their work, and there is only a slim chance of their being chosen by the neighborhood associations. The aging of the population is a serious issue all over this prefecture. To put it in an extreme way, the stewards are mainly old men alienated from their families, and few of them can appeal to women, youth, or men who are employed.[23]

Under the Religious Corporations Law, each shrine is free to decide how its stewards will be chosen, and at large shrines located in a town or city there may be dozens, even several hundred of them. In some cases, such as at the Ōkunitama Shrine in Fuchū City, Tokyo (discussed in chapter 15), the stewards make up the core of the Hōsankai, a generic term for a shrine-based fundraising organization, a group of several hundred men who manage the shrine's accounts, consult with the priest, publish a newsletter, and raise funds. This group raises funds not only for Ōkunitama Shrine but also for shrines damaged by natural disasters, and events observed by the shrine world as a whole, such as the Vicennial Renewal of the Ise Shrines.[24] Its level of engagement and activity is at the other end of the spectrum from the situation the priest just quoted is commenting on.

In other cases, custom dictates that some stewards are appointed by the priest, while others are chosen by neighborhood groups in the shrine's territory that maintain a *mikoshi* or other festival equipment, and/or from among nonresident support groups (*sūkeisha*). As the priest's comment suggests, where stewards are chosen solely from neighborhood groups, there is a tendency for the post to become a revolving door in which the same elderly men are chosen repeatedly, resulting in the fossilization of the group and frustration for the priest.

Stewards and priests are technically allotted equal authority under the Religious Corporations Law, but this arrangement accords no official recognition to the priest's greater knowledge and training with respect to Shinto. It is hardly surprising to find that the result is frustration for the priest. The following selection of comments from several different priests makes this clear:

> Because this is a rural shrine, the stewards frequently express their opinions. I have forty-five years' experience as a priest, and often they come up with things that I find hard to permit. It is difficult to avoid rifts.[25]
>
> I have doubts about the requirement that priests report the shrine's finances to the stewards.... The idea of opening the books to all and sundry

> means that leadership would pass to the stewards. They'll say things like,—"So little money in the offering box? Isn't the priest just pocketing it?" or "Isn't the priest just pocketing the money he receives for rituals he performs outside the shrine?" This is damaging to the dignity of priests.[26]
>
> Too many shrine priests everywhere are tied down by local customs and are suffering because they are forced to deal with stewards who have no understanding. There is a tendency for people to look down on shrine priests by comparison with temple priests.[27]

As these comments show, the close connection between shrines and neighborhood associations (*chōnaikai* or, informally, *jichikai*) that emerged in the prewar era persists, based on the role of the associations in choosing stewards. Some priests—especially at smaller shrines—find the relationship stifling, a hindrance to revitalizing shrine life, and sometimes personally undermining. The relation between shrines and neighborhood associations overlaps with the ties between shrines and their *ujiko,* who are likely to be the residents of those neighborhoods. The neighborhood associations used to have legal capacity before the end of the war, and some larger ones now are incorporated, though they are not technically part of the governing apparatus of villages, towns, and cities. Nevertheless, overlap between the stewards and elected officials is typical. Some priests are anxious that they may be criticized for not enforcing a strict separation between shrine officers and public officials.

> I'm worried, because our shrine has public officials for some of its officers, and I'm afraid that could become a problem.[28]
>
> The annual accounting for our shrine is managed by the head of the local Self Government Association (Jichi rengōkai).... Through this system the head priest maintains strong relations with the Self Government Association. We depend on it for all the funds needed for repairs or ceremonies. We don't yet plan on separation of religion from state. The fact that we have been able to maintain the shrine for many years is due to this underground (*chika*) system. The young people understand, but I'm worried whether it can continue.[29]

Clearly, lingering issues about public officials serving as shrine officers or using elected office to collect funds for shrines continue to cause anxiety. Priests feel vulnerable to public scrutiny, yet they also want to affirm the public character of shrines as central to communal life. This desire may be expressed with a variety of nuances, as in this statement: "In the old days, people used to think that the shrine here belonged to the priest, but now I'm glad to say that the *ujiko* have come to think that it belongs to them all."[30] In this case, the feeling among local people of shared ownership pleases the priest. That sense of the shrine's "public" character differs from what we see here: "Shrines have a strong public character (*kōkyōsei*), and even though they have been made religious corporations, their nature as an object of faith for a community and its local customs hasn't changed."[31] The priest who made that statement has a more politically inflected sense of the public nature of the shrine and harks back to a time before the postwar changes to shrines' legal status. A stronger version of the sentiment is seen in this comment: "We should be operating shrines on the principle of *saisei itchi* (unity of ritual and political rule)."[32]

As these comments suggest, priests interpret the public nature of shrines differently, and some are anxious whether their sentiments are shared by Japanese society as a whole. Since recent judgments by Japanese courts yield no single conclusion on this issue, this mixture of attitudes is only to be expected. Two cases decided in 2010 yielded conflicting verdicts.

The first arose when a Christian in Sunagawa City (Hokkaidō Prefecture) brought suit against the city for allowing a shrine to exist on public land without requiring it to pay rent. Through complicated events lasting from 1892 until 1994, the city ended up owning land where a meeting hall had been built with public funds. A small shrine called the Sorachita Jinja had been moved into the building, and someone had put up a *torii* for it, also on public land. The suit charged that this situation constituted a violation of the constitution's article 89, forbidding public funding of religious organizations. The shrine is very small, is not incorporated, and has no full time priest. It is managed by a group of nearby residents, who, in the course of the trial, testified that they regarded their service to the shrine as an element of communal life, not religious activity. All of them asserted that their religion is Buddhism. In spite of this, the court ruled that Sunagawa City had violated article 89.[33]

A second case arose in 2005 after the mayor of Hakusan (Shirayama) City (Ishikawa Prefecture) attended a party held by the Hōsankai of Hakusan Hime Jinja, which was celebrating its 2100th Annual Festival. Hakusan Hime Jinja is a religious corporation that stands at the head of about 2,000 Hakusan shrines nationwide. The party was not held at the shrine, nor did it involve Shinto ritual. The mayor used his official car and took his official secretary to the Hōsankai party, where he gave an address. The suit charged the mayor with violating article 89.

The mayor regarded the Hakusan Shrine's Annual Festival as the town's biggest annual tourist event and believed that he had a responsibility to cultivate good relations with all groups involved. From his point of view, to participate in the Hōsankai's party was to use his office to encourage tourism. He did not consider the matter in a framework of religious issues at all.

The Kanazawa District Court upheld the mayor in 2007, but he lost on appeal in 2008 when the Nagoya High Court ruled against him. The Nagoya court ruled that a violation of article 89 had occurred, because the mayor understood that the Hōsankai had been established for the purpose of supporting the shrine's Annual Festival. Therefore, he knew that his actions gave the impression of supporting the festival, and that he was supporting religious activity. The court deemed it irrelevant that the Hōsankai event was held outside the shrine, and that the meeting did not follow the form of a Shinto rite. It cannot be argued, the judges opined, that the mayor's address to the Hōsankai was merely a social observance lacking religious significance, because the party supported and promoted the shrine.[34]

At first, the mayor was resigned to the verdict, but he changed his mind after receiving an avalanche of telephone calls, emails, and letters, saying that if the Nagoya court's judgment were allowed to stand, local governments all over the country would be inundated with lawsuits. In other words, a lot of other towns were operating much as the mayor of Hakusan City had been. The mayor decided to appeal to the Supreme Court.

The Supreme Court upheld the mayor. It recognized the significance of the shrine as a source of tourist revenue. The Hōsankai event took place in a nonreligious venue, and the party was not a religious ritual. The mayor's intention was to perform an expected social function that was part of his job. His actions did not exceed the bounds of nonreligious ceremonial, nor did they result in promotion (or hindrance) of any religion. Therefore, there was no violation of article 89.[35] *Jinja shinpō* expressed satisfaction with this result in an editorial of August 2, 2010.

New Initiatives by the Priesthood

Under pressure both to contribute to the larger society and to tackle economic problems, some shrine priests are emphasizing the religious character of Shinto, much as Sonoda Minoru advocated in his 1996 article.

> It's a waste of energy for the shrine world's big men to keep telling us that no matter what it takes, we have to maintain the *ujiko* system. It is obvious that it won't last forever, whatever renaming might happen, and regardless whether these men really believe what they are saying. It would be much more worthwhile to direct that energy to securing non-resident worshippers (*sūkeisha*) with no territorial connection to the shrine. I don't believe that all shrines have to be based on territory. The future of the shrine world will start to open up precisely through gathering non-resident worshippers one by one. I think that true faith originally is a matter for the individual—whether it's shrine Shinto or Buddhism—it isn't something shared by a family and certainly not something that's the same across a whole region.... For the sake of Japan's rebirth, we need to abolish this system of stewards and *ujiko* that remains fixated on territory.[36]
>
> The gap between NASS' definition of *ujiko*, stewards, and *ujiko* territory and the reality on the ground grows bigger by the day... Most shrines actually operate like family businesses. Is it better to put shrines like that on the

> same incorporated basis as large shrines? And does it make sense for shrine organizations to operate solely on the basis of custom?[37]

As these striking statements make clear, there are priests who believe that shrines cannot be sustained by continuing to rely on the *ujiko* system. These priests associate the *ujiko* system with "tradition" and "custom" in the negative sense of things perpetuated without creative thinking. In their opinion, this is what NASS policy represents.

> Shinto and Buddhism both broke out of their original forms as religions of ritual. Considering the international situation today, from the perspective of educating youth, I think we should put much more energy into religious education. In the current circumstances, there is no future for shrine Shinto or Buddhism. We should look again at our tradition of combinatory worship of Kami and Buddhas (*shinbutsu shūgō*) and work toward a peaceful age of spiritual fulfillment.[38]

This priest thinks it would be a good idea to revive combinatory worship of Kami and Buddhas. An organization called Association of Sacred Sites of the Kami and Buddhas (Shinbutsu Reijōkai) is working toward this goal, encompassing a number of prominent temples and shrines in central Japan.[39]

> At present all shrines have to develop self-defense strategies. At our shrine, what we came up with was running a graveyard.... It is obvious that the *ujiko* system is falling apart.... We're going back to the original meaning of shrines as a place for individual believers of faith and building a system on that. I think we must rebuild shrines to take individual groups of believers as their basic building blocks.[40]
>
> I'd like to plan to expand Shinto funerals, expanding shrine management in a forward-looking way to a graveyard for those having Shinto funerals, a general graveyard, and a columbarium open to all supporters of the shrine.[41]
>
> At this shrine we collect no funds from the *ujiko* but depend for our religious activities entirely on the income from for-profit business. In two to three years, we expect to build a columbarium and a Japanese language school for foreigners.[42]

According to the three priests cited immediately above, the solution to shrines' economic woes is to offer funerals, graves, and memorials. Sonoda Minoru's remarks at the beginning of this chapter warn against this urge to commodify religious services, but it is evident that present circumstances leave some shrines few alternatives. Numerous shrines are now pursuing this course, and it is not uncommon for

Shinto-derived new religious movements to have facilities for honoring the souls of the ancestors, whether or not they operate graveyards. The Tsuruoka Hachiman Shrine in Kamakura operates a Shinto cemetery, as do numerous smaller shrines. The sites may be quite large, as at Tsuruoka Hachiman, which has space for over 800 graves.

A study published in 2010 listed forty-two Shinto graveyards in Japan as a whole,[43] but since that time the number has increased and the trend seems likely to continue. Shrines offering Shinto graveyards generally make available a separate, shrine-like building for the performance of funerals and memorials, so that a physical separation is maintained between these facilities and the shrine itself. Some of them offer columbaria and other memorial services, such as a memorial ceremony for dolls offered at Nishino Shrine.[44]

One might ask why enterprising priests would construct a graveyard rather than a wedding parlor. Some, for example, the Tsuruoka Hachiman Shrine and the Nishino Shrine mentioned here, already have wedding facilities. In the case of smaller, more remote shrines, the income potential of weddings may be limited, given the aging demographic trend in rural Japan, and the probability that most couples would probably prefer an urban setting and or a large shrine. Furthermore, the proportion of shrine weddings as a proportion of the total number of weddings (itself a declining figure) each year is only around 16 percent, suggesting a limited market for these services.[45]

Another reason why shrines might eschew an investment in an expensive wedding facility is seen in the example of the Yokohama Kōtai Jingū (also known as Iseyama Kōtai Jingū), which narrowly escaped its land being sold at auction after a business deal in this field went bad. The shrine built a lavish hotel and wedding parlor in 1991, but by 2001 it had become unable to repay the money it had borrowed, and the bank seized the land. The Kanagawa Prefectural Shrine Association was able to negotiate with the bank to prevent sale of the land, but the company the shrine had formed to manage the hotel was declared bankrupt and was dissolved in 2006. This was the first case of a shrine affiliated with NASS going bankrupt.[46]

Issues for Women Shrine Priests

Women priests face the same issues that male priests confront, with the addition of lingering gender discrimination. The first women priests, certified by Kokugakuin University in 1946, were a small group of twenty-nine. At first, women were not permitted to be appointed head priest (*gūji*), but that restriction was removed in 1948. A national group for women priests called the National Conference of Women Shrine Priests (Zenkoku joshi shinshoku kyōgikai) represents them.[47]

Whether male or female, a priest's life differs greatly depending on the shrine's status as a former National, Imperial, or Special Shrine, on the one hand, or some rank below that, on the other. Shrines below the first three ranks continue to be known informally as "unofficial shrines" (*minsha*). Most women priests serve at the former unofficial shrines. They may have the head priest title if no male relative performs the job, or, if a male relative has that title, they may be called on to help out at large-scale ceremonies or New Years. This is also the case if a woman marries into a shrine family of a *minsha*. In that case, helping out at ceremonies is part of the wife's role, and she is expected to seek certification enabling her to perform necessary ritual. Recent surveys of succession in shrines show that about 15 percent of designated successors are women.[48] This result suggests that the number of women priests will continue to increase. One projection is that in ten years, women will make up 20 percent of the priesthood, perhaps reaching 30 percent by around 2035.[49]

At these smaller shrines, being a woman can be an advantage, in that *ujiko* find it easy to approach women to discuss personal issues, and women priests usually have close personal relations with the *ujiko*. They would normally attend meetings of the Women's Group (Fujinkai), if there is one, and form relations with other nearby women shrine priests to practice dance and exchange information. Most women shrine priests did not choose the profession as the fulfillment of an ambition, but in order to perform their role as wife or daughter in a family. For this reason, they are not opposed by the shrine world, which holds that the ideal woman is a "good wife and a wise mother" (*ryōsai kenbo*). On this view, women should not be employed after marriage or the birth of children, or if they are employed, the job should take second priority after the roles of wife and mother. According to a recent study, women priests do not claim equal rights with men, nor do they aim to upgrade women's position as shrine priests. Instead, they rely on traditional ideals of femininity and stress women's advantages in dealing with *ujiko*, taking for granted that there will be a sex-based division of labor among priests.[50]

New graduates from the Shinto universities who will serve eventually at family shrines often seek apprenticeships at larger shrines. This training enables them to gain experience in a wide variety of ceremonies and to form connections with a large number of experienced priests. Women who lack shrine experience and marry into a shrine family may seek qualifications as a priest through attending summer courses at one of the Shinto-affiliated universities or through correspondence courses. They also seek apprenticeships at larger shrines.[51]

From the perspective of larger shrines, however, it is difficult to integrate women priests. Many shrines expect priests to rotate the duty of providing security for the shrine at night, having them stay overnight to patrol the grounds at intervals. It is difficult to integrate women priests into this routine, because shrine facilities are set up for the overnight team to stay in the same room and use the same bathroom. For reasons of propriety, the shrines find it difficult to have women share this duty. Also, women shrine priests' vestments are different from men's, and the etiquette they follow in ritual differs slightly from men's. Thus if the shrine does not already have women serving as priests, it must provide an expensive set of vestments; given the likelihood that women priests will not stay long, this is an economic burden. When a large-scale ceremony is held, women are conspicuous because of their different vestments and etiquette, and the appearance of all the priests acting in unison is disrupted by their presence.[52]

Beginning in 1996, issues regarding women priests have been named by NASS as one of the basic problems facing Shinto. Some of the issues addressed are whether women can serve as priests while menstruating, how to raise their position, whether their professional service can be reconciled with women's roles in the traditional family system, and how to reconcile their service with current laws on gender equality. Since that time, NASS has determined that menstruation is not an issue, but recognizes that there are prejudices among some *ujiko* regarding women in positions of leadership. The organization recognizes that there are male priests for whom it is emotionally difficult to accept women priests on an equal footing with them or in positions above them. NASS's position on reconciling professional and family roles is that women are suitable for performing shrine rites, but only to the extent that this does not conflict with their family roles. In the organization's opinion, this is not a question of equality of the sexes.[53]

The question of reconciling NASS's position with current laws regarding gender equality remains unresolved, due to the organization's adamant opposition to the Fundamental Law on Gender Equality. A current example of the organization's attitude is illustrated by a *Jinja shinpō* editorial of July 29, 2013, which criticized a recent government white paper for presenting lagging indicators of women's equality, and called on the government to recognize that the value of women's unpaid work in the home, including the job of nursing the elderly, accounts for fully one-third of Japan's annual gross domestic product (GDP), though women are not paid for this labor in the family. Notably, NASS was not proposing that such labor should be compensated.

Shinto's Contributions to the Public Good

Research on religion's contributions to society expanded after the Aum incident.[54] In 1998, Kōgakukan University established a Faculty of Social Welfare that conducts research on the history of social welfare in Shinto, citing the need to revise the common view that welfare work is not well developed in Shinto.[55] In 2009, an edited collection on religion's contributions was published,[56] as was a monograph on Shinto's "social enterprises" (*shakai jigyō*).[57] A journal for the study of religion's social contributions, *Shūkyō to shakai kōken*, commenced in 2011, and in the same year a second monograph on Shinto's contributions was published.[58]

Table 16.9 **Social Contributions of Japanese Religious Organizations**

Shrine Shinto	*Buddhist Temples*	*Christian Churches*	*New Religious Movements*
Fund drives and monetary contributions; Participation in local self-government association activities; Preservation of trees; Antiques bazaars; Offering grounds to sports teams; Offering space to clubs for the aged; Boy Scouts, Girl Scouts.	Fund drives and monetary contributions; Participation in local self-government association activities; Concerts; Bazaars; Residents' Groups' activities; Sponsoring children's clubs; Sponsoring tea ceremony; Sponsoring daily exercise programs on radio.	Fund drives and monetary contributions; Support groups for mothers; Volunteering at welfare facilities; Bazaars; Peace groups; Benefit sales for the disabled; Concerts; English education.	Fund drives and monetary contributions; Cleaning activities (eg, removing trash from public places); Disaster relief; Participating in ceremonies of neighborhood associations; Volunteering at welfare facilities.

Source: Adapted from Yoshino Kōichi and Terazawa Shigenori. "Chiiki shakai ni okeru shūkyō no shakai kōken katsudō." In *Shakai kōken suru shūkyō*, edited by Inaba Keishin and Sakurai Yoshihide, Tokyo: Sekai shisōsha, 2009, table 2, p. 166.

Researchers found that Japanese religious organizations engage in a wide variety of activities that contribute to society in various ways but that not all branches of religion are engaged in the same kind of activities. Table 16.9 summarizes the results of a survey undertaken in 2008.

This research shows that half of the shrines had helped collect money for public welfare, a larger proportion than seen in Christian churches but less than in temples and new religious movements. Seventy percent of shrines contributed to environmental movements or projects. Only 10 percent of shrines contributed to education, health, citizens' rights, or international exchange projects; Christian churches were the main participants in most of those projects, with lower numbers among the temples. There was no Shinto participation in projects relating to peace or medicine, categories in which only 10 percent of the organizations surveyed participated. By contrast, 70 percent of the shrines participated in projects to preserve traditional culture, which consisted of preserving historic sites or presenting traditional arts. Some of the reasons that religious organizations either do not engage in these activities or become unable to sustain them include lack of funds; demographic changes in their constituencies, such as the aging of society; the appearance of another organization that takes over the activity; or restrictions on religious organizations by welfare agencies, for fear that religious persons may use volunteering as an opportunity to proselytize.[59]

Recent publications on Shinto's social contributions reveal an anxiety that Shinto not be judged in this field on the same criteria as other traditions, because of Shinto's differences from other religions:

> Leading some special religious life, or putting some ethical way of life based on doctrine into practice—that's not Shinto. The religious role of Shinto lies in a consciousness of mutual understanding and respect, living creatively in peace and tranquility in daily life, as well as the awareness of having Japan as the space given to one.[60]

Fujimoto Yorio, a researcher in this field, argues that shrine priests' ordinary service at shrines contributes to social solidarity and thus should be considered the tradition's primary social contribution.

> When considering the issue of welfare in Shinto, especially the welfare of a geographical area, the first element to mention is shrine rites, which occur daily, as a religious form of folk culture that can ignite the development of the area. Shrine rites represent the perpetuation of traditional culture, and shrine life itself originally had a volunteer character. From ancient times, every shrine exists in a community where people help and support each other, praying for the happiness of their shared community, which deepens the ties of the community. In short, through shrine rites and the accumulation of shared, mutual service, people's varied ways of thinking and values are brought together. Shrines have performed the function of building spiritual unity. Across the country there are about 79,000 shrines under NASS' umbrella, and in each area hundreds of thousands, even millions of shrine rites, large and small, are performed. This shows that shrines are performing the role of building communities' spiritual unity, and this is the most important distinguishing characteristic of shrine Shinto.[61]

Some 141 shrine priests are acting as chaplains as of 2015, out of a total of 1,862 chaplains of all religions. There are also sixty-six chaplains from Konkōkyō.[62] In addition, shrine priests frequently act as mentors (*hogoshi*) for released prisoners or for juveniles released from reform school. The most recent statistics show that there were about 43,442 *hogoshi* as of 1999. Of them, about 5,000 were clergy of some religion; of these clergy, about 400 were shrine priests, or about 8 percent. Shrine priests make up about nine-tenths of one percent of all *hogoshi*. Shrine priests make up around eighteen percent of *minsei iin*, a type of welfare counselor. Neither of these positions carries significant monetary compensation. In addition, there are around

200 kindergartens and nursery schools operated by shrines, out of a total of some 35,500. The number of clinics or hospitals operated by shrines is less than ten.[63]

Disaster Relief after the Great East Japan Earthquake of March 11, 2011

Immediately after March 11, 2011, all branches of Japanese religions turned to relief work to aid Northeastern Japan. Virtually all major religious organizations participated in memorial ceremonies, donated money and rebuilding materials, and assisted displaced persons. Shrine Shinto and the Shinto-derived new religious movements were active on all these fronts. For example, in the first month alone, NASS, through the National Shinto Youth Council, sent truck caravans containing food and other goods to the area. Later NASS set up a three-million-dollar fund for the reconstruction of shrines.[64] Ōmoto sent around $15,000 and organized a volunteer corps to remove debris and provide food. Tenrikyō provided $10,000 to Miyagi, Iwate, and Fukushima Prefectures and sent a volunteer corps to provide water, distribute food, clothing, blankets, and remove debris. Many other Shinto-derived new religious movements contributed. Shrines across the area distributed food that would otherwise have been used in their daily offerings. The Asakusa Shrines and the Kanda Shrine in Tokyo canceled their Annual Festivals to provide funds to the relief effort. The Ise Shrines dedicated timber that would ordinarily have been used in the Vicennial Renewal. These early responses to the disaster unfortunately received minimal coverage in the mainstream papers.[65]

Damage to religious institutions was extensive. According to NASS statistics, 4,818 shrines were damaged; the Main Sanctuary was totally destroyed or swept away in ninety-nine shrines.[66] By comparison, some 3,200 temples were damaged; forty-seven temples were washed away, and another thirty were totally destroyed. About one-quarter of all Tendai temples were damaged or destroyed. Fifty-five Christian churches were damaged or destroyed.[67]

The national newspapers carried numerous articles or letters to the editor after the disastrous Hanshin-Awaji Earthquake of January 17, 1995, complaining that religions had not contributed to relief work. However, many religious persons active at that time were not wearing vestments, which prevented the public from recognizing them. In 1995 and again in 2011, the five largest national daily papers printed only three articles on Shinto relief work—the same number as those regarding Islam—out of a total of 102 articles. The *Asahi Newspaper* did not cover Shinto relief work at all in 2011. Most newspaper articles concerned Buddhism. The image of the Buddhist priest performing funerals or memorials for the dead typified newspaper portrayal of religions' relief work.[68]

By the late 1990s, some of the most influential newspapers already had established positions on religion, stances that had been adopted in part to distinguish themselves from their competitors. For example, the *Yomiuri Newspaper* had adopted a critical stance on religion in the aftermath of the Aum incident, with a particular focus on the failure in 1999 of more than one thousand religious corporations to submit financial information as required under the revised Religious Corporations Law. Letters to the editor supported the paper's position. Some local editions of the paper followed up with articles criticizing Buddhism, for the high cost of funerals, and shrine priests, for the high cost of talismans, but by 2005 the paper was tending toward a more positive view. From the mid-1990s, the *Asahi Newspaper* praised religious organizations for their fight to prevent constitutional revision, as well as their contributions to social welfare, human rights, and environmental issues. Letters to the editor supported that view, but also called for higher taxation of religious organizations. But the paper was also critical of religions for not taking a stronger stance against the US war in Iraq, and for exploiting the poor and was, in my impression, generally critical of Shinto.[69]

A religious corporation that ceases to function can lose its corporate status, so all temples, shrines, and churches in the disaster area are under pressure to prove that they continue to function. One of the first organizations to recognize this need was the Miyagi Prefectural Shrine Agency. It is expensive to erect a temporary shrine, and in some parts of the prefecture, construction was forbidden for a time. So they started in June 2011 by putting up pillars where a destroyed shrine had been, with the shrine's name on it, roping off the precincts with *shimenawa*, measures that did not conflict with the law. Later they were able to proceed to further reconstruction.[70]

There were fourteen shrines, forty-three temples, and five Christian churches within the contaminated area defined by a twenty-kilometer radius from the Fukushima nuclear plant that melted down. It is forbidden to approach any of them. Shrine personnel wanted badly to retrieve the *shintai* at least, but in some cases the object was a large boulder or stone, making it physically impossible. The Fukushima Prefectural Shrine Agency, as well as Buddhist groups, Tenrikyō, Konkōkyō, and others decided to seek compensation for damages from Tokyo Electric Power Company, the company that had managed the reactor. The company eventually included religious corporations among the organizations it undertook to compensate. However, compensation was limited to organizations that would rebuild where they were before, and that excluded all those in the contaminated area. Religious leaders including shrine priests protested that a shrine or temple would be necessary for the people forcibly relocated, in order for them to retain some sense of themselves as a community in exile.[71]

After the 1995 Hanshin-Awaji earthquake, local government associations set up private foundations to collect money, and a similar move to repair shrines arose after a major earthquake in Niigata. Because people also fear that taxes will rise to fund recovery, however, it is unlikely that the general public will support rebuilding shrines and temples with public funds. To overcome that obstacle, it would probably be necessary for the prefectures to state that temples and shrines and churches are vital to the welfare of the people and communities that are trying to rebuild.[72] For government to affirm the public significance of religion in such a way, however, would probably stimulate lawsuits.

Shinto in Popular Culture

Many researchers have approached Japanese popular culture in order to discover religious origins. While it is useful to know what traditions an author or filmmaker may be drawing on, however, research results are not the same thing as an audience's reaction. Investigating the reception of popular culture works is by no means a simple task. The vitality of popular culture resides in the interaction among an audience, a production, and the industries producing and marketing these works. Complicated loops link fans to authors and industries. In addition to commercialized narratives and images, "fan art" is a major area of popular creativity, as Internet sites like pixiv.net vividly show. Because I cannot hope to do justice to all the Shinto-related images, practices, and stories of popular culture in a compact treatment, to say nothing of their commercialization and distribution, I will concentrate mainly on the narrative dimension of selected works.[73]

It is rare for popular culture works to address Shinto in a sustained way. More frequent are entertaining references or images that enliven a story, or present striking visual effects. This is true of religious references in Japanese popular culture as a whole.[74] For this reason, it seems farfetched to understand popular culture works as reflecting Shinto (or any other religion) comprehensively. Instead, something about Shinto seems to spark either creative fantasy or provide an ideological soapbox.

There are innumerable manga and anime set in shrines, featuring *miko* with supernatural powers, or focusing the plot on a love story about *miko*; these are called "*miko* love manga" (*miko moe manga*). When a *torii* or shrine building appears in an anime, it signals the audience that they are about to be transported out of ordinary space and time, and into a zone of hitherto unknown possibilities. The popular animated series *Inuyasha* projects the hero and his compatriots into many fantastic lands but continually returns to a shrine as its "home base." The plot turns on the hero's need to reassemble the shards of a shattered jewel originally possessed by the shrine. The series *Asagiri no miko* concerns three sisters who are *miko*, and who use such shrine implements as *suzu* (bells on stalks) and *Ōnusa* (purifying wands) to fight wrongdoers in each episode.

A similar production, *Kamichū!* or, "A Kami as a Middle-School Student" concerns a middle school girl named Hitotsubashi Yurie, who suddenly becomes a Kami.[75] Each episode concerns her travels among the Kami as she tries to become a mature and powerful Kami herself. Two of her friends are *miko*, and one of them tries to capitalize on Yurie's special powers through moneymaking schemes for her family's impoverished shrine. Yurie often consults with this shrine's Kami, named

Yashima-sama, who is portrayed as an older teenager who wants to become a rock star. Other Kami are shown in the form of cartoon deer, butterflies, fish, foxes, and in human form. In episode 12, Yurie attends a "New Gods Seminar" at the Izumo Shrine, where Benzaiten appears as a Kami rock star giving a concert.[76]

Other anime, television series, and manga have led fans to try to ferret out the "real-life" prototype of shrines seen in popular culture productions. The Internet site "Punynari's Island Adventures" (https://punynari.wordpress.com) is devoted to such quests. A custom of "costume play" (*kosupure*) shrine visits has also arisen. Fans dress up as particular characters and visit the shrine featured in their favorite productions. *Sailor Moon* produced a fad resembling the *hayarigami* of the Edo period for the Hikawa Shrine in the Azabu area of Tokyo, where one of the main characters worked as a *miko*. In another case, the shrine previously served by Kōno Seizō, former president of Kokugakuin University, Washinomiya Shrine, also became an overnight fad for the fans of *Lucky Star*.[77]

Two *manga* concerning women at shrines depict their daily lives more realistically. The title of *Takamagahara ni kamu zumari masu* is taken from the opening lines of *norito*. The author, Shino Yukiko (b. 1958), observed at shrines in order to depict their daily routine faithfully. Her protagonist is a female shrine priest at a small Tokyo shrine, who wears male vestments and is often mistaken for a man. Tanaka Yuki (b. 1974), author of *Recommending Shrines* (*Jinja no Susume*), had some work experience in a shrine that served as the basis for her story about a Shinto priest-in-training who falls in love with a *miko*, who possesses the power to foretell the future through palmistry. The *manga* emphasizes the strict rules of deportment at shrines.[78]

In what follows I examine three works and their reception: a novel, titled *The Goddess Chronicle* (*Joshinki*),[79] by Kirino Natsuo; a *manga* by Kobayashi Yoshinori, called *On Yasukuni* (*Yasukuniron*)[80]; and an anime by Miyazaki Hayao, titled *Princess Mononoke (Mononoke Hime)*.[81] I chose these works because each has been seen as touching on Shinto in some way, and because each of the creators has an established fan base, making it possible to investigate audience reception. Each work has generated a mixture of positive and negative evaluations among fans. While exact figures are not available, it is apparent that each of the works has sold well and has circulated widely in Japanese society. *Princess Mononoke* was a blockbuster, and was the highest grossing movie in Japanese history through 1997. None of the authors attempts to transmit an understanding of Shinto as a whole. Kirino's novel is a reinterpretation of the myth of Izanami and Izanagi. Kobayashi's work is a zealous call to worship at the Yasukuni Shrine. Miyazaki's anime invents a variety of different kinds of Kami and looks back nostalgically to a golden age of environmental purity. While I believe that efforts to evaluate audience reception can produce important indicators, the potential for skewed results remains a danger. While we can reduce skewing by sampling audience reviews on a variety of Internet sites and blogs, it is likely that casual readers and viewers who do not react strongly one way or another to a production are unlikely to compose a review at all. Instead, review authors will be those with more extreme reactions or "axes to grind." It is important to temper our interpretation of results with that in mind.

Popular Books on Shinto

A 2007 study of popular books on Shinto found that most customers who recorded a "reader review" on Amazon.co.jp describe themselves as not well versed in Shinto or express surprise that they had no previous opportunity to learn about Shinto, for example:

> I always go to a shrine at New Years, but I really had no idea what Shinto is all about.
>
> Shinto is so formal and hard to understand that even after reading the book, I feel very distant from it.
>
> Even though I have some confidence in my ability to explain Buddhism, I was really puzzled by Shinto.
>
> Even though Shinto is all around me, I'm surprised at how little I know about it.[82]

The same study found that Hamuro Yoriaki (1927–2009), author of many nonfiction works introducing Shinto, is the highest-selling author of such books. He was a physician before becoming a shrine priest, by taking correspondence courses, eventually rising to such prestigious appointments as Head Priest at Hiraoka Shrine and the Kasuga Shrine. Reader-reviewers seem to like the fact that, like them, Hamuro initially lacked understanding of Shinto, and that he promotes Shinto as a part of Japanese ethnicity:

> [*The Heart of Shinto* (*Shinto no kokoro*)] reminds us of what it means to be Japanese, returning us to a perspective we had forgotten—Shinto—not religion but an unseen world.
>
> I do not believe in anything unscientific, but Professor Hamuro's handbook on Shinto, written while he was a physician of Western medicine, is extremely logical . . . with good explanations. It swept away the stereotypes I had as a person who is against religion. I believe that through this book I have come to understand the meaning of life a bit. Moreover, it has given me hope and courage. It is my Bible.[83]

The Goddess Chronicle differs from the books on Shinto mentioned earlier, because it is a work of fiction and does not attempt to introduce Shinto. Instead, it brings together a portrayal of Izanami's life in Yomi, the land of the dead, with a narrative concerning Namima, a woman from the impoverished Sea Snake Island (Umihebi shima), partially modeled on Kudakajima in the Okinawan island chain.

Plot Summary

Namima and her elder sister Kamikū were born to a family that always provided the island's religious leader called the Grand Oracle (*Ōmiko*), a woman who devotes her life to praying for the island's welfare, especially that of the men, who spend most of their lives fishing at sea. Kamikū and Namima were separated in childhood as Kamikū went to live with the reigning Grand Oracle to train to succeed her. Namima was forbidden to speak to Kamikū but served her by taking specially prepared foods to her every morning, to nourish her so that she could bear many daughters. Namima continued this service into her teenage years. She also was required to go to the edge of the Grand Oracle's compound every evening, where she would find the remains of the food delivered that morning wrapped in a leaf. She was to take the packet directly to a cliff overlooking the sea and throw it away, not eating any of it herself or allowing anyone else to partake. This seemed cruel to her, because the island was very poor, and it seemed a waste to throw away nourishing food when so many were hungry. One night, a man named Mahito ("true man") begged her for the leftovers to give to his ailing mother. His family was ostracized from the rest of the villagers because his mother had failed to produce a daughter, and now she was sick and pregnant again. Although Namima resisted at first, she fell in love with Mahito. When the Grand Oracle died, Namima learned that she also was to take on a role in the island's religious life. She was to guard the body of the deceased Grand Oracle as well as that of the deceased guardian of the dead, the Miko of Darkness. Kamikū and Namima were paired as yin and yang, life and death, with Kamikū the Grand Oracle and Namima as the Miko of Darkness. When the Grand Oracle died, the Miko of Darkness also had to die. This meant that Namima would be put to death when Kamikū died. Namima was forced to live in a tiny hut in a grove surrounding a cave where innumerable coffins were stored. She had to look into the coffins each day for twenty-nine days. As she tried to resign herself to this horrible life, she realized that she was pregnant although she was under a strict taboo against any contact with men. Mahito and Namima fled the island in a rickety boat, and Namima gave birth to a baby girl, Yayoi. Soon after the birth, Mahito murdered Namima, and the next thing she knew, she found herself in Yomi, where she became the servant of Izanami. Eventually Namima is briefly released from Yomi in the form of a wasp. She travels back to her island, discovers that Mahito has married her sister Kamikū and passed Yayoi off as his sister, to save his family from further ostracism. Namima the wasp stings him between the eyes, and he dies. When the two meet later in Yomi, Namima forgives him.

The book's second half largely concerns Izanami and Yomi. After Izanagi and Izanami separated at the passage from the human realm to Yomi, Izanami became a goddess of death, putting one thousand people to death each day, while on earth Izanagi traveled the world impregnating as many women as possible, to make up for the deaths Izanami

> causes. Izanami chooses those who are to die by scattering drops of water over a map of the world each day. The people touched by that water are the ones to die. However, Izanami's choices are not random. She tries to kill as many of Izanagi's lovers as possible. Namima's fate is to assist Izanami in this task. Eventually the narrative turns to Izanagi, who after millennia has only a dim recollection of Izanami. He only realizes, when a young servant notices the coincidence, that all his "wives" die shortly after his brief liaisons with them. Horrified, Izanagi and the servant kill each other so that Izanagi may become mortal, die, and go to Yomi where he can confront Izanami again. The result is that when the two meet again, Izanami agrees to spare Namima's daughter in exchange for the death of Izanagi, who dies a miserable and painful death in Yomi.

Izanagi is depicted as being "clueless" about his effects on the women he has loved; he is the quintessential narcissist, irresistibly handsome, never returning to any of the women from his past, though he sometimes recalls them fondly. He remains selfish to the end, saying to Izanami at the moment of his death, "I have accepted everything that came my way and lived life to the fullest." Izanami is so filled with bitterness and hatred toward him that she glows blue. Even after Izanagi dies, when Namima asks whether she will go on choosing who will die, she says that her bitterness will never abate, and that, "I will continue to resent, hate, and kill for all eternity."[84]

The novel ends as follows:

> This, then, is Izanami's story. She serves as the goddess of the Realm of the Dead, now and forever more. And all around her the grumbling of the restless spirits knows no end but grows and grows and grows. This, too, is beautiful and clear and as insubstantial as dust.... Izanami is without doubt a woman among women. The trials that she has borne are the trials all women must face.
>
> Revere the goddess!
>
> In the darkness of the underground palace, I secretly sing her praises.

Blogs and readers' reviews of this novel were posted mainly by fans of Kirino's previous mystery stories, such as *Out!*, a story of women night-shift workers who make boxed lunches. After one of the women kills her abusive husband, she and her friends cover up the crime by dismembering the body. Eventually they start to dispose of bodies for the mob. Kirino takes up such contemporary social problems as alienation between husbands and wives, parents and children, people caught in a spiral of debt, and the low wage work done by women. Compared to Kirino's usual mystery stories, *The Goddess Chronicle* is completely different. The following is a sampling of readers' reactions.

> When I consider that such beings exist in Yomi, I'm afraid of what will happen to me after I die. Am I the only one thinking this way?[85]

> Right from the beginning, I didn't care for *The Goddess Chronicle*, and although I kept reading, I don't feel as drawn in as [with Kirino's other books]. I kept thinking, 'Is this how it ends?'... Yes, this is what Kirino really thinks.[86]

> [The male] is superior while [the female] is regarded as base. Even in the world of the *Kojiki*, the goddess represents *yin*, while creation is regarded as solely the work of the god. This could be the basis for the recent declaration by the Governor of Osaka. However in this story, Izanami stands superior to Izanagi, and Namima kills Mahito. Kirino has surely portrayed women's essential strength and noble roles.[87]

> We have a woman who resists her fate but finally forgives the man she loves, though he betrayed her. Then there's Izanami, who takes revenge on Izanagi, who betrayed her. It's a kind of stereotyped portrayal of men and women, with a selfish man and a woman facing all kinds of difficulties... So women are weak for their forgiveness, while the one who won't forgive is in the right? Is this Kirino's notion of the ideal woman?[88]

The first two reactions focus on the bleak portrayal of life in Yomi, which makes them fearful and leaves them uneasy. The third and fourth take the book to be a parable about human men and women set in mythic time. The third draws a connection to a statement in May 2013 by Hashimoto Tōru, Governor of Osaka Prefecture, to the effect that the prostitution system of the Japanese military in the Pacific War was a necessary evil, ignoring its effects on the women dragooned into sexual slavery. The fourth statement interprets Kirino's portrayal of Izanami's eternal hatred as a veiled justification. None of the reader responses I found related the book to Shinto, or characterized its portrayal of the Kami in any way other than as an allegory about relations between men and women.

The second work to be considered here, *On Yasukuni*, by Kobayashi Yoshinori, a popular writer known for his right-wing views, has been called "religiously nationalistic manga."[89] The work is openly didactic, arguing that all Japanese should worship at the Yasukuni Shrine. The work has been advertised on the homepage of the Yasukuni Shrine, which constitutes an endorsement. Let us consider the work's treatment of the issue of separation of religion from state, treated in two pages of the work.

A figure wearing glasses and a black turtleneck sweater represents Kobayashi himself. The text of the manga constitutes a lecture with illustrations. The following is a translation of his speech:

> *Kobayashi*: The problem was Prime Minister Nakasone's tenth visit to the Yasukuni Shrine on August 15, 1985. Nakasone announced with great fanfare that as part of his "complete resolution of postwar politics" he would worship at Yasukuni Shrine, and he had held a consultation where legal

scholars debated this. The result was a determination that a prime minister's visit to this shrine is not a violation of the constitution. That's right, of course. Article 20 of the constitution declared a separation of religion from state, but there is no way the two can be completely separated. If there were a complete separation, then it would violate the constitution for the government to preserve shrines and temples as cultural properties, or to fund religious schools. It was the Occupation that put this stipulation in the Constitution of Japan, based on the US constitution, but all it means there is that the government can't support a specific sect of Christianity. Even in America it is taken for granted that the President is sworn in by a religious ritual of swearing on the Bible! When the *Asahi Newspaper* and other left-wing mass media put up a big campaign to oppose the Yasukuni Shrine and the Prime Minister's visit, Nakasone came up with something to placate the left wing temporarily. He started talking about a form of worship from which religious coloration was eliminated. He said he would not worship in the Shinto form of two bows, two claps, and one more bow.

There are two ways of thinking about separation of religion from state: as an absolute or limited separation. As I pointed out earlier, the absolute form is impossible. Almost all the countries that have separation of religion from state take the limited form, in which the state is only prohibited from proselytizing for some particular religion or participating in religion. However, Japan keeps on upholding a complete separation, resulting in weird feuds, claiming that it's a constitutional violation for the Police Agency to hold prayers for traffic safety, or for a public high school to have a *kamidana* in its martial arts hall, or for the city office to use a Daruma doll for a donation box.

It was the Supreme Court's verdict in the Tsu Grounds Purification Case that finally resolved all these problems legally. The city of Tsu in Mie Prefecture had used public funds to hold a Grounds Purification ceremony when it constructed a gymnasium. The Supreme Court held that it is impossible for there to be a total separation of religion from state, and that if one tried to implement such a thing it would result in irrational situations in social life. So they clearly upheld limited separation of religion from state. Besides that, the verdict stated that as long as there is no intention or effect of promoting religion, assisting it, encouraging it, interfering with it, or oppressing it, then the state and local organizations would participate in religion without violating the constitution. This came to be known as the Purpose and Effect standard, and they ruled that there had been no constitutional violation in the Tsu City case. Based on this verdict, there's absolutely no problem with the prime minister worshipping at Yasukuni. But in 1997, the Supreme Court's disastrous verdict in the Ehime Tamagushi case was issued. This was a lawsuit about the prefecture's payment for

> tamagushi for the Yasukuni Shrine and the Nation Protecting Shrine for the war dead from Ehime Prefecture. The verdict used the same wording as the Tsu City case and clearly upheld limited separation of religion from state [but found that the prefecture had violated the constitution].

Kobayashi ignores the split result of Nakasone's 1985 Advisory Committee on cabinet visits to Yasukuni. He critiques the 1997 Supreme Court verdict on a case from Ehime Prefecture, in which the prefectural governor had used public money for shrine offerings, referred to here as *tamagushi* (literally, a decorated sprig of the *sakaki* tree), both at the Yasukuni Shrine and the prefectural Nation-Protecting Shrine. The suit charged that this use of public funds violated the separation of religion from state. Though the plaintiffs lost several rounds in the lower courts, the Supreme Court upheld them in 1997, ruling that the governor's actions violated article 89. The court found that the placement of a *tamagushi* on a shrine altar is a religious act, and that the governor had done so with the purpose of supporting a religion, namely Shinto.

A vast number of readers have recorded their reactions in reader reviews and blog postings. On the Japanese Yahoo site, a group of readers conducted an extended exchange about the book in the form of an opinion questionnaire.[90] The following represents a small sample of responses recorded on the Japanese Amazon site:

> We have come to the point that there are lots of people who don't know of the existence of the Yasukuni Shrine and don't even know that Shinto exists. That's what this book says.... [Kobayashi] says that Yasukuni is a place for heightening the religious feeling that is indispensable to us as Japanese.... This country possesses Shinto.... We cannot separate ourselves from [it].... The mass media and the left wing that call for separation of religion from state are stepping on the hearts of those who have gone before. And I completely agree [with Kobayashi's criticism of the Tokyo War Crimes trials]. However, there's one problem: this book is extremely dangerous.... The author portrays the people he thinks are good as shining heroes (*pika pikaa-to!*), while he makes the people he thinks are bad out to be evil.... I'd like to ask him to [calm down], but if he were to do so, he'd lose his charm as Kobayashi Yoshinori.[91]

> It would be dangerous to swallow the account in this work whole. You have to remember that it's a manga. It's not a textbook.... It's a manga that tries to put across the author's self-righteous interpretation... It isn't a drama but a lecture with pictures.[92]

> This is a book in manga form that carefully describes the history and significance of the Yasukuni Shrine. At minimum, all the things you'd need to know in order to talk about the Yasukuni Shrine are covered. It's the most appropriate introduction for a non-specialist to gain that necessary knowledge.[93]

> This book forces us to recognize that those of us living in Japan today are standing on top of the self-sacrificing and suffering hearts of the many war dead, who loved their families and their country. Although the Yasukuni Shrine is the source of support of the hearts of the Japanese, I felt ashamed of myself for having only found out about Yasukuni through the mass media during the Koizumi administration.[94]

> I believe that the emperor is important as part of Japan's traditional culture. But while the emperor may be a Kami in religious terms, biologically he's an ordinary human being. I think it's weird to take the emperor system as a status system and force people to worship. Japan adopted State Shinto in the Meiji period, didn't recognize any god but the emperor, and stamped out other religions. Then they all shouted "Banzai for the emperor!" and went off to die in war... Isn't the Yasukuni Shrine, which was built in Meiji, a product of that time? In spite of that, Kobayashi responds to criticism of Yasukuni by bringing up Japan's polytheism from the ancient and medieval periods. This kind of argument is sleight of hand and looks like a double standard to me.[95]

> [When I think of] the ancestors who fought and died for Japan, I'm ashamed of myself, and it's deplorable. Why do the people of Japan today, the descendants of the people who gave their lives to protect the ancestral country, look down on them so much? It's because of the ignorance of our own history, and the anti-Japanese activities of China, Korea, and the left-wing media. Japan could be at war even now, and moreover we're getting beaten.[96]

As these readers' reviews show, Kobayashi's *On Yasukuni* provokes a spectrum of strong reactions. Even some of his supporters find him extreme, while others are moved to shame at their ignorance of Japanese history. Readers comment on Kobayashi's assertion that the affluence of contemporary Japan owes to the sacrifice of the war dead. Some find his argument compelling and express remorse that they had not realized their debt to the ancestors sooner, or that they had to find out about it from "left-wing media." Others find his argument unpersuasive and see the war dead as victims of the same militaristic attitude that Kobayashi promotes. Some readers find fault with Kobayashi for dressing up a political harrangue as a work of popular culture. Only the first writer drew a connection between Yasukuni and Shinto.

Princess Mononoke

Plot Summary:

> Set at an unspecified time in the remote past, the narrative opens when a horrifying monster attacks a village. Its surface is seething with wormlike beings in dark gray and blood red. Ashitaka, a young warrior, rides out on

an elk, addresses the monster as a Kami and begs it to desist. In the end he must shoot an arrow through its eye to stop it. As it lies dying, the wormlike covering falls away to reveal the Boar God, who has been driven mad by being shot with an iron ball. It curses Ashitaka, whose arm is marked and festering from contact with the wormlike things, that represent the boar's hatred of all humans. The village priestess charges Ashitaka to find out where the iron ball came from. His journey leads him deep into a primeval forest, alive with small spirits called Kodama. Eventually he comes to Iron Town, ruled by Lady Eboshi, who has cleared the forest to build an iron mine. She employs former prostitutes, whom she has bought out of sexual slavery, to power the furnace, and sufferers from Hansen's Disease, who are the gunsmiths of her industry. All the animals of the forest, including packs of monkeys and boars, are determined to get rid of Iron Town, because it is poisoning their habitat, and because they realize that if humans are allowed to reside in the forest, it will soon be destroyed. The animals are championed by the feral child Princess Mononoke, who has been raised by the gigantic wolf, Moro. Mononoke attacks Lady Eboshi's pack trains as they thread their way along narrow mountain paths. She is able to kill many men and oxen, laden with iron or the proceeds from its sale, sending them falling into a deep ravine. A corrupt *yamabushi* stalks the Kami of the Forest, the Deer God (Shishigami), hoping to behead it and thus put an end to the forest animals and Mononoke resisting the encroachment of Iron Town. He claims to have an imperial decree authorizing him to kill the Shishigami. The Shishigami has two forms. At night he becomes a huge, semi-transparent blue figure who walks in the forest, towering hundreds of meters above the treetops. When they sense his approach, the Kodama begin to rattle. At dawn, he changes into a deerlike creature, with a huge ruff of multiple horns. He has the power of life and death over all the beings of the forest. Thereafter, the plot develops through depictions of the antagonism between Iron Town and the forest creatures, as witnessed by Ashitaka.

As Jolyon Thomas has written, scholarship on the relation between Japanese popular culture and religion has concentrated overwhelmingly on Miyazaki's work, to the neglect of the vast majority of popular culture products.[97] The connection has been pursued even though Miyazaki himself rejects it and is highly critical of religion:

> Dogma inevitably will find corruption, and I've certainly never made religion a basis for my films. My own religion, if you can call it that, has no practice, no Bible, no saints, only a desire to keep certain places and my own self as pure and holy as possible. That kind of spirituality is very

> important to me. Obviously it's an essential value that cannot help but manifest itself in my films.[98]

That the author of *Princess Mononoke* discourages interpreting this film as religious has not deterred some of its audience from pursuing the connection. It is rumored among Miyazaki's fans that the island of Yakushima was the model for the anime's setting, and some have traveled there as if they were embarking on a religious pilgrimage.

> For part of the audience, the movie... promotes ritual action, as the posts on a Miyazaki fan board attest. In response to a post entitled "The Setting of *Princess Mononoke" (Mononoke hime no butaichi),* one person wrote, "I really went to Yakushima..., and it seemed as if Shishigamisama would really appear!" Another respondent wrote, "There [in Yakushima] people really believe in *Princess Mononoke*... [and the other animal gods]."[99]

Miyazaki's films convey his concern for the environment. Audiences understand his portrayal of primeval forests devastated by Iron Town as an obvious metaphor for the destruction of Japan's natural environment by industrialization, urbanization, indeed, by the processes of modernization as a whole.

> *Princess Mononoke* is a famous work about the antagonism between iron and the forest. The hero Ashitaka is a courageous traveler trying to find a path of coexistence between humanity and the forest.... The forests of Japan are in danger.[100]

As we have seen above, however, a didactic message runs the risk of audience rejection, and Miyazaki is no exception.

> Joining hands with environmentalists smells a little like a sermon. What is this film trying to say, "Cut it out! [*shizumari tamae!*]"? If it were possible to resolve the anger of nature so easily, this world would already be at peace! [Miyazaki's] worldview is growing smaller all the time, although he has the reputation for huge scale and fantasy. I'm disappointed.[101]
>
> Once you put the keywords of 'destruction of nature', 'coexistence', and 'environment' front and center, unfortunately the depth of the story is lost.[102]

Other audience reactions praise Miyazaki for the prominence of female protagonists in his works:

> I take my hat off [to Miyazaki] every time, for the way he has portrayed women. He can do this precisely because he really values women.[103]

As these comments suggest, Japanese audiences only rarely draw conclusions about Shinto from popular culture works, even though the productions suggest strong connections to scholars. But it may be that consumers who make that connection simply do not bother to post reviews. Audience reactions to works perceived as didactic are usually negative, unless the didactic character of the work is made plain by the author, as in the case of *On Yasukuni*. On the other hand, we have seen that many vehicles of popular culture, especially the manga and anime concerned with *miko* or set at shrines, keep images drawn from Shinto before the public in these various media formats, giving them an up-to-date appearance. Sometimes these works prompt an audience to visit a natural site or a particular shrine, sometimes dressed in costumes worn by anime or manga characters. Shinto institutions do not appear to be involved in the creation or promotion of these works, with the exception of the Yasukuni Shrine's endorsement of *On Yasukuni*.

Conclusion

From one perspective, Shinto today illustrates what appears to be an inexorable decline of religion across the developed world, at least as measured by sociological indicators. Japanese society's wholesale defection from religion after the Aum incident exacerbated declining rates of belief and observance of traditional customs that had begun in the 1950s. At the same time, however, it is important to balance statistical findings against other evidence. Customs like New Years visits to shrines mobilize the population on a scale rivaling the Edo period's *okage mairi*. In fact, in 2010, a year that by a traditional calculation would have been an *okage mairi* year, some 8,800,000 people visited the Ise Shrines. In 2013, some 14,200,000 people visited the Ise Shrines for the Vicennial Renewal, over 10 percent of the national population, the largest number ever to visit the shrines in a single year in recorded history.[104] Numbers like these suggest vitality, not decline.

On the other hand, a significant proportion of shrines have too little income to support basic costs, and priests are suffering as a result. Young men fear that they may be unable to support themselves if they enter the shrine priesthood. Others respond by offering new services and emphasizing Shinto's religious qualities. An indirect result of shrines' economic distress is a trend toward female succession in smaller shrines. Some priests complain that their national organization lacks creative leadership.

Japanese popular culture is awash in images drawn from Shinto, and these creations sell well and circulate widely, which means that the industries of popular culture will continue to produce them. Audiences are dazzled by technical wizardry and charmed by fantasy worlds populated with eccentric depictions of *miko*, Kami, and other things loosely connected with Shinto. The entertainment provided by these works is *asobi*—directly continuous with the combination of prayer and play that became conspicuous in the Edo period. These works spark new forms of creativity that contribute to Shinto's ongoing transformation. Some fans travel to shrines as "power spots," reminiscent of the Edo period's *hayarigami*. Yet we also find that critical audiences frequently ignore Shinto-derived content, regard it as mere window dressing, interpret it as allegory, or reject it as didactic.

While Shinto has been scrutinized in terms of its contribution to the public good, and while shrine priests find it important to uphold the image of shrines as "public" in various senses, society's understanding of "the public good" remains vague and undefined. Nevertheless, attempts to define Shinto's social contributions in terms of ritual's function to enhance social solidarity are gaining acceptance. But in any case, the idea that "all religions are as bad as Aum" has faded, and religions' responses to the Great East Japan Earthquake are beginning to counteract negative images of religion. Religions as a whole, including Shinto, have turned a corner as more positive images emerge from their contributions to the recovery. Contemporary Shinto is both contracting and expanding, but with substantial social support, much evidence of vigorous labor to preserve the tradition, and determined expressions of hope.

APPENDIX: SHRINE FUNDING

Table A.1 shows that the national budget for the Ise Shrines, the Imperial, and National shrines remained well below 500,000 yen annually until 1908, and the budget for almost all years from 1875 to 1908 had only a single category, suggesting that the appropriation was a matter of routine. Column A shows the regular appropriation for the Imperial Shrines and the National Shrines, while Column B shows appropriations for the Ise Shrines. Columns C and D show separate allocations for offerings (C, later folded into general appropriations) and preservation (D, ending in 1897). Column E was a fund devoted to expanding the Ise Shrine Office.[1] A small, but significant rise in the total budget occurred in 1908, taking the total above 500,000 yen for the first time. Japan's victory in the Russo-Japanese War stimulated the government to create a new fund for expanding the Ise Shrines.[2] That fund also assisted the Ise Shrines in the performance of their Vicennial Renewals in 1909, 1929, and the one planned for 1949 (postponed to 1953). This supplemental fund grew so large in some years as to exceed the government's regular appropriation for Ise and all the Imperial and National shrines combined. Columns F and G show the rapid increase in funding for the Meiji Shrine.

If we examine other categories of shrine-related expenses from the national budget, we can get a sense of the government's shifting priorities. Column H represents special allocations for repairs or refurbishing at the Imperial and National Shrines, often in response to fire damage. Column I shows that the government did not make regular appropriations for priests' professional development until 1915. This category doubled between 1918 and 1919, when the Shrine Bureau looked to shrine priests to help calm the Rice Rioters.[3]

Column J enumerates expenses the Shrine Bureau incurred in documenting the rituals and observances unique to particular shrines over the years 1926 to 1936. In the background of this new allocation lay shrine priests' anger over the Shrine Bureau's drive to homogenize and standardize all shrine practice. The Shrine Bureau evidently sought to counter negative criticism by publicizing documents relating to unusual practices at particular shrines in *The Journal*. Column K shows expenses related to ongoing research on the precincts of the Ise Shrines. Finally, Column L shows expenses to enlarge and refurbish the Kashihara Shrine and the nearby site that had been identified as the tomb of Emperor Jinmu, in order to accommodate huge crowds anticipated for the festivities of the 1940 observance of the empire's 2600th anniversary.

Table A.1 **National Shrine Budget, 1875–1939, in Yen**

Column	*A*	*B*	*C*	*D*	*E*	*F*	*G*	*H*	*I*	*J*	*K*	*L*	*M*
Year/ Expense	*Appropriation for Shrines from Ordinary Budget* (国庫歳出神社費)	*Appropriation for the Ise Shrines* (神宮費)	*Offering Fees to National Shrines' Annual Festivals* (国幣社例祭幣帛料)	*Preservation of old temples and shrines* (古社寺保存費)	*Expansion of Ise Shrine Office* (造神宮司庁)	*Construction of Meiji Shrine* (明治神宮造営)	*Construction of Meiji Shrine Outer Garden* (明治神宮外苑工事施行費)	*Special Appropriations for Shrines* (臨時神社費)	*Shrine Priests' Professional Development Research* (神職養成及神社調査費)	*Research on the Shrine System* (神社制度調査費)	*Research on Ise Shrine Facilities* (神宮関係施設調査費)	*Improvements to Kashihara Shrine and Walkway to Emp. Jinmu's Tomb*	*Total*
1875/M8	210,507	–	–	–	–	–	–	–	–	–	–	–	210,507
1876/M9	198,261	–	–	–	–	–	–	–	–	–	–	–	198,261
1877/M10	168,979	–	–	–	–	–	–	–	–	–	–	–	168,979
1878/M11	123,614	–	–	–	–	–	–	–	–	–	–	–	123,614
1879/M12	129,226	–	–	–	–	–	–	–	–	–	–	–	129,226
1880/M13	135,000	–	–	–	–	–	–	–	–	–	–	–	135,000
1881/M14	142,550	–	–	–	–	–	–	–	–	–	–	–	142,550
1882/M15	147,750	–	–	–	–	–	–	–	–	–	–	–	147,750
1883/M16	150,165	–	–	–	–	–	–	–	–	–	–	–	150,165
1884/M17	156,243	–	–	–	–	–	–	–	–	–	–	–	156,243
1885/M18	115,754	–	–	–	–	–	–	–	–	–	–	–	115,754
1886/M19	268,213	–	–	–	–	–	–	–	–	–	–	–	268,213
1887/M20	251,911	–	–	–	–	–	–	–	–	–	–	–	251,911
1888/M21	252,165	–	–	–	–	–	–	–	–	–	–	–	252,165

(*continued*)

Table A.1 **Continued**

Column	A	B	C	D	E	F	G	H	I	J	K	L	M
Year/ Expense	*Appropriation for Shrines from Ordinary Budget* (国庫歳出神社費)	*Appropriation for the Ise Shrines* (神宮費)	*Offering Fees to National Shrines' Annual Festivals* (国幣社例祭幣帛料)	*Preservation of old temples and shrines* (古社寺保存費)	*Expansion of Ise Shrine Office* (造神宮司庁)	*Construction of Meiji Shrine* (明治神宮造営)	*Construction of Meiji Shrine Outer Garden* (明治神宮外苑工事施行費)	*Special Appropriations for Shrines* (臨時神社費)	*Shrine Priests' Professional Development Research* (神職養成及神社調査費)	*Research on the Shrine System* (神社制度調査費)	*Research on Ise Shrine Facilities* (神宮関係施設調査費)	*Improvements to Kashihara Shrine and Walkway to Emp. Jinmu's Tomb*	*Total*
1889/M22	252,220	–	–	–	–	–	–	–	–	–	–	–	252,220
1890/M23	177,893	–	–	–	–	–	–	26,800	–	–	–	–	204,693
1891/M24	177,893	–	–	–	–	–	–	–	–	–	–	–	177,893
1892/M25	177,893	27,113	1,790	10,000	–	–	–	–	–	–	–	–	216,796
1893/M26	177,907	27,113	1,790	10,000	–	–	–	–	–	–	–	–	216,810
1894/M27	177,907	27,113	1,790	10,000	–	–	–	–	–	–	–	–	216,810
1895/M28	177,906	27,113	1,680	20,000	–	–	–	–	–	–	–	–	226,699
1896/M29	174,924	27,113	1,640	49,999	–	–	–	–	–	–	–	–	253,676
1897/M30	177,975	27,113	1,580	50,000	–	–	–	–	–	–	–	–	256,668
1898/M31	177,972	27,113	1,580		–	–	–	–	–	–	–	–	206,665
1899/M32	221,781	27,113	1,640		–	–	–	–	–	–	–	–	250,534
1900/M33	221,780	50,000	1,635		–	–	–	–	–	–	–	–	273,415
1901/M34	221,788	50,000	1,635		–	–	–	–	–	–	–	–	273,423
1902/M35	221,788	50,000	1,690		–	–	–	–	–	–	–	–	273,478
1903/M36	223,423	50,000			–	–	–	–	–	–	–	–	273,423

1904/M37	223,423	50,000	–	–	–	–	–	–	–	–	273,423
1905/M38	223,874	50,000	–	–	–	–	–	–	–	–	273,874
1906/M39	223,854	50,000	–	–	–	–	–	–	–	–	273,854
1907/M40	223,857	50,000	–	–	–	–	–	–	–	–	273,857
1908/M41	223,861	50,000	281,798	–	–	–	–	–	–	–	555,659
1909/M42	223,824	50,000	316,920	–	–	–	–	–	–	–	590,744
1910/M43	233,688	70,000	107,663	–	–	–	–	–	–	–	411,351
1911/M44	304,997	70,000	38,461	–	–	–	–	–	–	–	413,458
1912/T1	234,730	70,000	35,801	–	–	–	–	–	–	–	340,531
1913/T2	234,728	100,000	30,525	–	–	–	–	–	–	–	365,253
1914/T3	234,697	100,000	16,654	–	–	–	–	–	–	–	351,351
1915/T4	234,959	100,000	13,637	327,417	–	55,000	9,938	–	–	–	740,951
1916/T5	234,959	130,000	132,525	270,667	–	55,000	9,954	–	–	–	833,105
1917/T6	234,882	130,000	12,692	465,493	16,483	30,000	9,954	–	–	–	899,504
1918/T7	364,817	130,000	15,686	600,822	29,321	275,781	9,949	–	–	–	1,426,376
1919/T8	364,845	130,000	28,285	1,085,877	30,143	67,356	18,909	–	–	–	1,725,415
1920/T9	590,937	200,000	140,377	789,273	42,806	293,246	23,840	–	–	–	2,080,479
1921/T10	820,937	200,000	2,538,508	263,239	49,132	538,090	24,356	–	–	–	4,434,262
1922/T11	820,535	230,000	2,773,395	251,946	68,302	263,447	24,355	–	–	–	4,431,980
1923/T12	812,591	230,000	1,511,178	–	51,227	137,617	35,918	–	–	–	2,778,531
1924/T13	820,595	230,000	1,228,394	–	51,096	126,972	33,503	–	–	–	2,490,560
1925/T14	740,937	230,000	463,731	–	38,277	105,636	17,153	–	–	–	1,595,734

(continued)

Table A.1 **Continued**

Column	A	B	C	D	E	F	G	H	I	J	K	L	M
Year/ Expense	*Appropriation for Shrines from Ordinary Budget* (国庫歳出神社費)	*Appropriation for the Ise Shrines* (神宮費)	*Offering Fees to National Shrines' Annual Festivals* (国幣社例祭幣帛料)	*Preservation of old temples and shrines* (古社寺保存費)	*Expansion of Ise Shrine Office* (造神宮司庁)	*Construction of Meiji Shrine* (明治神宮造営)	*Construction of Meiji Shrine Outer Garden* (明治神宮外苑工事施行費)	*Special Appropriations for Shrines* (臨時神社費)	*Shrine Priests' Professional Development Research* (神職養成及神社調査費)	*Research on the Shrine System* (神社制度調査費)	*Research on Ise Shrine Facilities* (神宮関係施設調査費)	*Improvements to Kashihara Shrine and Walkway to Emp. Jinmu's Tomb*	*Total*
1926/T15	740,937	230,000			659,300	–	–	225,000	17,153	10,717	–	–	1,883,107
1927/S2	751,000	230,000			1,174,000	–	–	242,000	17,000	10,000	–	–	2,424,000
1928/S3	750,000	230,000			939,000	–	–	210,000	17,000	10,000	–	–	2,156,000
1929/S4	771,000	230,000			1,590,000	–	–	275,000	16,000	30,000	–	–	2,912,000
1930/S5	771,000	230,000			220,000	–	–	244,000	15,000	29,000	–	–	1,509,000
1931/S6	771,000	230,000			78,000	–	–	147,000	13,000	26,000	–	–	1,265,000
1932/S7	771,000	230,000			30,000	–	–	189,000	11,000	18,000	–	–	1,249,000
1933/S8	771,000	230,000			35,000	–	–	174,000	11,000	19,000	–	–	1,240,000
1934/S9	771,000	230,000			35,000	–	–	511,000	11,000	17,000	10,000	–	1,585,000
1935/S10	771,000	230,000			35,000	–	–	686,000	11,000	15,000	9,000	–	1,757,000
1936/S11	771,000	230,000			40,000	–	–	1,023,000	11,000	9,000	9,000	–	2,093,000
1937/S12	1,021,000	230,000			35,000	–	–	1,041,000	51,000	–	9,000	27,000	2,414,000
1938/S13	1,022,000	230,000			221,000	–	–	891,000	41,000	–	–	14,000	2,419,000
1939/S14	1,022,000	230,000			69,000	–	–	1,110,000	50,000	–	–	14,000	2,495,000

Source: Nihon Teikoku Tōkei Nenkan.

SELECTED LIST OF CHARACTERS

This list contains only significant terms used in the text. Some proper names are included, but only those that are not widely known. Most names of contemporary scholars cited are not included. Please note that there are multiple ways of writing Kami names (such as different renderings in *Kojiki* versus *Nihon shoki*), and many other terms related to Shinto may be written in various character combinations. The characters for items listed as such-and-such "shrine" in English are rendered here according to the Japanese title, which may be read as *jinga, jingū*, etc. Italics indicates the title of a written work.

Abe no Seimei 安倍晴明
Ahodarakyō 阿呆陀羅経
Ai no yama 間の山
Aisenji, Aizenji 愛染寺
Aizawa Seishisai 会沢正志斎
Aizu jinjashi 会津神社史
Akagi Tadaharu 赤木忠春
Akazawa Bunji 赤沢文治
Akitsumikami 現御神
Akurei 悪霊
Akusha 幄舎
Amaterasu Ōmikami 天照大御神
Amatsu tsumi 天津罪
Amatsukami 天津髪
Ame no iwato 天岩戸
Ame no koyane no Mikoto 天児屋命
Ame no nuhoko 天の瓊矛
Ame no Uzume no Mikoto 天鈿女命
Amenominakanushi no kami 天之御中主神
Anesaki Masaharu 姉崎正治
Aohitokusa 青人草
Aoi matsuri 葵祭
Aoyama Naomichi 青山直道
Araburu Kami 荒神
Arahito gami 現人神
Arai Hakuseki 新井白石
Arakida 荒木田
Arakida Hisaoyu 荒木田久老
Aramatsuri no Miya 荒祭宮
Ara-mitama 荒魂
Aruga Nagao 有賀長雄
Asagiri no miko 朝霧の巫女
Asano Wasaburō 浅野和三郎
Ashizu Uzuhiko 葦津 珍彦
Asobi 遊び

Asomi 朝臣
Asukayama 飛鳥山
Awa Odori 阿波踊り
Aya Uji 漢氏
Bakemono 化け物
Ban Nobutomo 伴信友
Bansei ikkei 万世一系
Bekkaku Kanpeisha 別格官幣社
Bekkakusha 別格社
Benzaiten 弁財天
Betsugū 別宮
Bettō 別当
Bikisho 鼻帰書
Bikuni 比丘尼
Bishamonten 毘沙門天
Bonjin 凡人
Bonshun 梵舜
Bonten 梵天
Buke shohatto 武家諸法度
Bunkateki shūkyō 文化的宗教
Bunrei 分霊
Bunshin 分心
Butsudan 仏壇
Chidorigafuchi 千鳥ケ淵
Chigi 千木
Chigo 稚児
Chihō kairyō undō 地方改良運動
Chingo kokka 鎮護国家
Chinkon kishin 鎮魂帰神
Chinkonsai 鎮魂祭
Chinreisha 鎮霊社
Chinzasai 鎮座祭
Chōgen 重源
Chokugansho 勅願所
Chokusai 勅祭
Chōnaikai 町内会
Chūjaku Gate 中雀門
Chūkyōin 中教院
Chūyūki 中右記
Dai Nihon Jingikai 大日本神祇会
Dai nihonshi 大日本史
Dai tōa sensō 大東亜戦争
Daibosatsu 大菩薩
Daigen sonjin 大元尊神
Daigokuden 大極殿
Daijingū 大神宮
Daijōkyū (Daijōgū) 大嘗宮
Daijōsai 大嘗祭
Daikoku 大黒
Daikyōin 大教院
Daimyō 大名
Daimyōjin 大明神
Dainichi 大日
Dainihon hennenshi 大日本編年史
Daiō 大王
Dairokuten Ma-ō 第六天魔王
Daishinpōshi 大神宝使
Dajōkan 太政官
Dakini shinten 荼枳尼真天
Dannaba 旦那場
Darani 陀羅尼
Dashi 山車
Datsu-e Ba 奪衣婆
Deguchi Nao 出口なお
Deguchi Onisaburō 出口王仁三郎
Dengaku 田楽
Dōkyō 道鏡
Dōtaku 銅鐸
Dōzasai 動座祭
Ebisu 恵比寿
Echizen gohō ikki 越前護法一揆
Edo meisho ki 江戸名所記

Edo shinbutsu gankake jūhōki 江戸神仏願掛重宝記
Ee ja naika ええじゃないか
Ehō mairi 恵方参り
Eirei ni Kotaeru Kai 英霊にこたえる会
Eirei no kenshō 英霊の顕彰
Eison 叡尊
Eitai Kagura 永代神楽
Ekōin 回向院
En no Gyōja (also, En no Ubasoku, En no Ozunu) 役行者
Endō tsugan 艶道通鑑
Engi 縁起
Engishiki 延喜式
Enma-ō 閻魔王
Ennen 延年
Ennichi 縁日
Fudoki 風土記
Fugeki 巫覡
Fujiwara Munetada 藤原宗忠
Fujiwara Sanesuke 藤原実資
Fujiwara Seika 藤原惺窩
Fujiwara Tadahira 藤原忠平
Fujiwara Takao 藤原孝夫
Fujiwara Teika 藤原定家
Fujiwara Tokihira 藤原時平
Fukko Shintō 復古神道
Fukuba Bisei 福羽美静
Fukurokuju 福禄寿
Furusato 故郷
Fūryū 風流
Fushimi Inari 伏見稲荷
Fusōkyō 扶桑教
Futsunushi no Kami 経津主神
Gaichi 外地
Gankake 願掛け
Garanjin 伽藍神
Gazu hyakki yakō 画図百鬼夜行
Geden 下殿
Gekū 外宮
Gekū gishikichō 外宮儀式帳
Gengō 元号
Genpon Sōgen Shintō 元本宗源神道
Genshisai 元始祭
Gion Matsuri 祇園祭
Gion Shrine 祇園社
Go-ō hōin 牛王宝印
Gobusho 五部書
Gohonsha 御本社
Gojisō 護持僧
Gojū soden 五重祖伝
Gokoku jinja 護国神社
Goma 護摩
Gongen 権現
Gōnō 豪農
Goryō 御霊
Goryō-e 御霊会
Goryōgū 御霊宮
Goseibai shikimoku 御成敗式目
Goshichinichi mishuhō (mishihō) 後七日御修法
Gozu Tennō 牛頭天王
Gozu Tennō engi 牛頭天王縁起
Gōshi 合祀
Gūji 宮司
Gyōhō jisō 行法事相
Hachiman 八幡
Hafuri 祝
Hagiwara Kaneyori 萩原兼従
Haibutsu kishaku 廃仏毀釈
Hakkō ichiu 八紘一宇
Hakodate Gokoku Jinja 函館護国神社
Hakone Gongen 箱根権現
Hakone Jinja 箱根神社

Hakusan (Shirayama) Hime Jinja 白山比咩神社

Hamuro Yoriaki 葉室 頼昭

Han 藩

Hanitsu Reijin 土津霊神

Haniwa 埴輪

Hanpei 班弊

Harae no ōnusa 祓の大幣

Haraibashira 払い柱

Hashimoto Tōru 橋下徹

Hasshinden 八神殿

Hata 秦

Hatsu miya mairi 初宮参り

Hatsumōde 初詣

Hatsuuma 初午

Hatto 法度

Hattori Ankyū 服部安休

Hattori Nakatsune 服部中庸

Hayarigami 流行神

Hayashi 囃子

Hayashi Razan 林羅山

Heian Jingū 平安神宮

Heihaku 幣帛

Hibutsu 秘仏

Hie Shrine 日吉大社

Hieda no Are (Pieda no Are) 稗田阿礼

Hijiri 聖

Hikawa Shrine 氷川神社

Himegami 姫神

Himiko 卑弥呼

Himorogi 神籬

Hiranuma Kiichirō 平沼騏一郎

Hiraoka Shrine 枚岡神社

Hirata Atsutane 平田篤胤

Hirata Kanetane 平田銕胤

Hiratsuka Tanabata 平塚七夕

Hitachi no Kuni Fudoki 常陸国風土記

Hitokotonushi no Kami 一言主神

Hitorigoto 独り言

Hōanden 奉安殿

Hōben 方便

Hogoshi 保護師

Hōhei 奉幣

Hōjō-e 放生会

Hokkaidō Jingū 北海道神宮

Hōkoku Jinja (also, Toyokuni Jinja) 豊国神社

Hōō 法王

Honchō jinja kō 本朝神社考

Hongaku 本覚

Honji 本寺

Honji-suijaku 本地垂跡

Honkyō 本教

Honkyō gaihen 本教外篇

Hoshina Masayuki 保科正之

Hotei 布袋

Hyakudo mairi 百度参り

Hyakuman Koku Matsuri 百万石祭り

Ibukinoya 気吹乃屋

Ichijō Kaneteru 一条兼輝

Ichinomiya 一宮

Ichinomiya sankeiki 一宮参詣記

Ijin 異神

Ikeda Mitsumasa 池田光政

Ikota Shrine, Ikeda Jinja 伊古太神社

Ikukunitama Jinja 生国魂神社

Ikuta Yorozu 生田万

Inari 稲荷

Inari oroshi 稲荷降ろし

Inari sage 稲荷下げ

Inari Taisha 稲荷大社

Inbe 斎部
Inbe Hironari 斎部広成
Inki 陰気
Inoue Masakane 井上正鉄
Inoue Tetsujirō 井上哲次郎
Inoue Tomoichi 井上友一
Inshi 淫祠
Ippin 一品
Ireisai 慰霊祭
Ise Jingū 伊勢神宮
Ise mairi okage no nikki 伊勢参りおかげの日記
Ise sangū meisho zue 伊勢参宮名所図絵
Ise-ya 伊勢屋
Ishida Baigan 石田梅岩
Ishida Kazuto 石田和外
Ishio Kansuke 石尾幹介
Isonokami no sasamegoto 石上私淑言
Itō Jinsai 伊藤仁斎
Itō Wakasa 伊藤若狭
Iwanagahime 磐長姫
Iwashimizu Hachimangū 石清水八幡宮
Iyahiko Shrine 弥彦神社
Izanagi no kami 伊邪那岐神
Izanami no kami 伊弉冉神
Izumo Fudoki 出雲風土記
Izumo Ōyashirokyō 出雲大社教
Jichikai 自治会
Jichinsai 地鎮祭
Jigyaku-teki 自虐的
Jihi 慈悲
Jika Shintōka 自家神道家
Jikkōkyō 実行教
Jimyōin 慈妙院
Jindai Izumo Chōsakai 神代出雲調査会
Jindai no maki fūyōshū 神代巻風葉集
Jingi 神祇
Jingi fuhai 神祇不拝
Jingi kanjō 神祇勧請
Jingi kanryō chōjō 神祇管領長上
Jingihaku 神器伯
Jingihaku 神祇伯
Jingiin 神祇院
Jingikan 神祇館
Jingiryō 神祇令
Jingishō 神祇省
Jingū Hōsaikai 神宮奉斎会
Jingūji 神宮寺
Jingūkyōkai 神宮教会
Jingūshichō 神宮司庁
Jinin (jinnin) 神人
Jinja chūshin shugi 神社中心主義
Jinja hi 神社費
Jinja Honchō 神社本庁
Jinja hongi 神社本義
Jinja kyōkai zasshi 神社協会雑誌
Jinja no Susume 神社のススメ
Jinja seido chōsakai 神社制度調査会
Jinja shinpō 神社新報
Jinjakyoku 神社局
Jinkonjiki 神今食
Jinmu Tennō 神武天皇
Jinmu Tennōsai 神武天皇祭
Jinmyōchō 神名帳
Jinnōshōtōki 神皇正統記
Jinpū Kōsha 神風講社
Jinshin War 壬申の乱
Jinshu 人種
Jissha 実社
Joshinki 女神記
Joya-sai 除夜祭

Jōgan gishiki 貞観儀式
Jōkei, also Gedatsu Shōnin 貞慶, 解脱上人
Jōkyū War 承久の乱
Jūhachi Shintō 十八神道
Junshi 殉死
Jurōjin 寿老神
Kada no Azumamaro 荷田春満
Kagura 神楽
Kaitaku Sanjin 開拓三神
Kaji 加持
Kakei Katsuhiko 筧克彦
Kamei Koremi 亀井茲監
Kami 神
Kami wa hirei o ukezu 神は非礼を受けず
Kamichū! 神中!
Kamidana 神棚
Kamikaze 神風
Kamimusubi no kami 神産巣日神
Kamo Mabuchi 賀茂真淵
Kamo Shrines 賀茂社
Kamunagara (kannagara) 随神
Kanbe 神戸
Kanda Matsuri 神田祭
Kanjō 勧請
Kannagara no michi 惟神の道
Kanname-sai 神嘗祭
Kannushi 神主
Kanpei Taisha 官幣大社
Kanpeisha 官幣社
Kansha 官社
Karagokoro 唐心
Kariya Ekisai 狩谷棭斎
Kashihara Jingū 橿原神宮
Kashikodokoro 賢所
Kasuga Daimyōjin 春日大明神
Kasuga Gongen Genki-emaki 春日権現験記絵巻
Kasuga Gongen Reigenki 春日権現霊験記
Kasuga Taisha 春日大社
Kasumi 霞
Katō Genchi 加藤玄智
Katō Hiroyuki 加藤弘之
Katsuogi 鰹木
Kawakami Tsuyako 河上艶子
Kaya Okinori 賀屋興宣
Keichū 契沖
Ken chiji 県知事
Kengyō 検校
Kenkin sengo 献芹詹語
Kenkoku Shinbyō 建国神廟
Kenshō 顕彰
Ketsudan 決断
Kidō 鬼道
Kigen 2600 nen shikiten 紀元2600年式典
Kigensetsu 紀元節
Kikke keifu den 吉家系譜伝
Kimon 崎門
Kinchū narabi ni kuge shohatto 禁中並公家諸法度
Kinensai (Toshigoi no matsuri) 祈年祭
Kirigami 切り紙
Kirikabu jinja 切り株神社
Kirino Natsuo 桐野夏生
Kishimojin 鬼子母神
Kishimoto Hideo 岸本英夫
Kishin 寄進
Kishōmon 起請文
Kitabatake Chikafusa 北畠親房
Kitagawa Morisada 喜田川守貞
Kitano Tenman Shrine 北野天満宮

Kitō 祈祷
Kitōdera 祈祷寺
Kobayashi Yoshinori 小林よしのり
Kōbe Matsuri 神戸祭り
Kofun 古墳
Kogaku 古学
Kogoshūi 古語拾遺
Kojiki 古事記
Kojikiden 古事記伝
Kokka kanri 国家管理
Kokka no sōshi 国家の宗祀
Kokka Shintō 国家神道
Kokkyō 国教
Kokoro 心
Kokubunji 国分寺
Kokubunniji 国分尼寺
Kokueki honron 国益本論
Kokugaku 国学
Kokuheisha 国幣社
Kokumin 国民
Kokumin dōtoku 国民道徳
Kokumin dōtoku gairon 国民道徳概論
Kokushi 国司
Kokutai 国体
Kokutai no Hongi 国体の本義
Kokuzō (kuni no miyatsuko) 国造
Konakamura Kiyonori 小中村清矩
Konkōkyō 金光教
Konoe Fumimaro 近衛文麿
Konohana Sakuyahime 木花咲耶姫
Konpira Gongen 金比羅権現
Konton 混沌
Konton no miya 混沌の宮
Koshiden 古史伝
Koshu kai 戸主会
Kosupure コスプレ
Kotodama 言霊
Kotohiragū 金刀比羅宮
Kō 講
Kō (also, ōyake, kimi) 公
Kōeki 公益
Kōeki hōjin 公益法人
Kōgi 公儀
Kōka san-nen no go teisho 弘化三年御定書
Kōkyō 公共
Kōmeitō 公明党
Kōminka 皇民化
Kōno Seizō 河野省三
Kōnomiya Hadaka matsuri 国府宮裸祭
Kōreiden 皇霊殿
Kōsai 公祭
Kōshiki sanpai 公式参拝
Kōshitsu tenpan 皇室典範
Kōtai Jingū 皇大神宮
Kōtai jingū gishikichō 皇大神宮儀式帳
Kōten Kōkyūjo 皇典講究所
Kumaso 熊襲
Kumazawa Banzan 熊沢蕃山
Kume Kunitake 久米邦武
Kunitama 国魂
Kunitokotachi no Kami 国之常立神
Kunitsu tsumi 国津罪
Kunitsukami 国津神
Kurayami Matsuri 暗闇祭り
Kuroda Toshio 黒田俊雄
Kurokawa Nō 黒川能
Kurozumi Munetada 黒住宗忠
Kurozumikyō 黒住教
Kusanagi no tsurugi 草薙剣
Kushi-mitama 奇御魂
Kusunoki Masashige 楠木正成
Kyōbushō 教部省
Kyōdo 郷土

Kyōdōshoku 教導職
Kyōgen 狂言
Kyōha Shintō 教派神道
Kyōka undō 教化運動
Kyōkai 教会
Kyūchū saishi 宮中祭祀
Lucky Star ラッキースター
Magatama 勾玉
Magatsuhi no Kami 禍津日神
Maichō Go-daihai 毎朝御代拝
Maichō shinpai shiki 毎朝神拝式
Majinai 禁厭
Makoto 誠
Mando Taikai 万灯大会
Mangan Zenji 満願禅師
Man'yōshū 万葉集
Mappō 末法
Massatsu hakase 抹殺博士
Masse 末世
Massha 末社
Masuho Zankō 増穂残口
Matarajin 摩多羅神
Matsudaira Nagayoshi 松平永芳
Matsuji 末寺
Matsuo Taseko 松尾多勢子
Matsuoka Obuchi 松岡雄淵
Matsurigoto-Hajime 政始
Matsuru 祭る
Meigetsuki 明月記
Meiji Jingū Hōsankai 明治神宮奉賛会
Meiji Seitoku Kinen Gakkai 明治聖徳記念学会
Meiroku zasshi 明六雑誌
Miare shinji 御阿礼神事
Michi 道
Michizure 道連れ
Michizure nen oboedome 道連年覚留め
Mifunashiro 御船代
Mi-kagura 御神楽
Mikannagi 御巫
Miko 巫女
Miko gami 御子神
Miko moe manga 巫女萌え漫画
Mikoshi 神輿
Mikumari Shrine 水分神社
Mimi-bukuro 耳袋
Minatogawa Shrine 湊川神社
Minhi 民費
Mino Mission 美濃ミッション
Minsei iin 民生委員
Minsha 民社
Minzoku 民族
Misai-e 御斎会
Misakibarai 御先払い
Mishōtai 御正体
Misogi 禊
Misogikyō 禊教
Mitama 御霊
Mitama hako 御霊箱
Mitama Matsuri みたままつり
Miya mandara 宮曼荼羅
Miyaji Naokazu 宮地直一
Miyadera 宮寺
Miyagomori 宮籠り
Miyaji 宮主
Miyanome Shrine 宮乃咩神社
Miyaoi Sadao 宮負定雄
Miyaza 宮座
Miyazaki Hayao 宮崎駿
Miyazaki Jingū 宮崎神宮
Miyoshi no Kiyoyuki 三善清行
Mizuno Rentarō 水野錬太郎
Mogari 殯
Mokuteki-kōka kijun 目的効果基準

Monjin 門人
Mono no aware 物の哀れ
Mononobe 物部
Mononoke 物の怪
Mononoke Hime もののけ姫
Monzeki 門跡
Monzenmachi 門前町
Mori Arinori 森有礼
Motoori Norinaga 本居宣長
Motoori Ōhira 本居大平
Mujū Ichien 無住一円
Mukakusha 無格社
Muku Jinja 椋神社
Mukyūki 無窮紀
Munetada Shrine 宗忠神社
Mura Chinju 村鎮守
Musubi 産霊
Musubi no Kami (Musuhi no Kami) 産霊神
Mutobe Yoshika 六人部是香
Myōbatsu 冥罰
Myōe 明恵
Myōjin 明神
Myōō 明王
Nagasaki Kunchi 長崎くんち
Nagoya Matsuri 名古屋祭り
Naichi 内地
Naikū 内宮
Naimushō 内務省
Naishōten 内掌典
Nakae Tōju 中江藤樹
Nakasone Yasuhiro 中曽根康弘
Nakatomi 中臣
Nakatomi Harae Kunge 中臣祓訓言
Nakatomi no Harae fūsuisō 中臣祓風水草
Nakaya Takafumi 中谷孝文
Nakaya Yasuko 中谷康子
Nakayama Miki 中山みき
Nakayama Tadayasu 中山忠能
Nan'yō Shrine 南洋神社
Naobi no Mitama 直毘霊
Naorai 直会
Nashimoto Morimasa 梨本守正
Ne no Katasu Kuni 根の堅洲国
Nebuta Matsuri ねぶた祭り
Negi 禰宜
Negi-ni 禰宜尼
Negishi Yasumori 根岸鎮衛
Nenbutsu 念仏
Nenjū gyōji 年中行事
Nichinichi kanai kokore no koto 日々家内心得の事
Nigi Hayahi no Mikoto 邇芸速日命
Nigi-mitama 和魂
Nihon damashii 日本魂
Nihon Izokukai 日本遺族会
Nihon Shūkyōsha Heiwa Kyōgikai 日本宗教者平和協議会
Nihon ryōiki 日本霊異記
Nihon shoki 日本書紀
Niinamesai 新嘗祭
Nijūnisha 二十二社
Ningen sengen 人間宣言
Ninigi no mikoto 瓊瓊杵尊
Ninomiya 二宮
Nippai 日拝
Nishi Amane 西周
Nishino Shrine 西野神社
Nisshin 日新
Nonomiya 野々宮
Norito 祝詞
Nukemairi 抜け参り
Nyoi hōju 如意宝珠

Ōdō 王道
Ogasawara Shōzō 小笠原省三
Ōgetsuhime no Kami 大宜津比売神
Ōgi Matsuri 王祇祭
Ōgimachi Kinmichi 正親町公通
Ogyū Sorai 荻生徂徠
Ōharae (Ōharai) 大祓え
Ōharae (Ōharai) no kotoba 大祓詞
Ōharano Shrine 大原野神社
Ohyakudo お百度
Oide Inari おいで稲荷
Ōji 王子
Ōji Inari 王子稲荷
Oka Kumaomi 岡熊臣
Okage mairi お陰参り
Okina Inari 翁稲荷
Ōkuni Takamasa 大国隆正
Ōkuninushi 大国主
Ōkunitama Jinja 大国魂神社
Ōmi Jingū 近江神宮
Ōmiwa Shrine 大神神社
Ōmononushi no Kami 大物主神
Ōmoto 大本
Ōnamuchi 大穴牟遅
Oni 鬼
Ōnin War 応仁の乱
Onjōji 園城寺
Ono Sokyō 小野祖教
Onshi (oshi) 御師
Ontakekyō 御嶽教
On'ryō 怨霊
On'yō-ryō 陰陽令
On'yōdō 陰陽道
Orita Toshihide 折田年秀
Ōsei fukko 王政復古
Oshihomimi no Mikoto 忍穂耳命
Oshirasu お白州
Ōtsu Jun'ichirō 大津淳一郎
Pekin Jinja 北京神社
Rakugo 落語
Reibutsu 霊物
Reijin 霊神
Reijingō 霊神号
Reiken 霊験
Reikiki kanjō 麗気記勧請
Reikiki 麗気記
Reisai 例祭
Reitaisai 例大祭
Reiyūkai Kyōdan 霊友会教団
Renmonkyō 蓮門教
Ri 理
Rigaku Shintō 理学神道
Rinji-sai 臨時祭
Rinnōji 輪王寺
Risshō Kōseikai 立正佼成会
Ritō shinchi Shintō 理当心地神道
Ritsuryō 律令
Rokkon shōjō harae 六根清浄祓
Rokusho no Miya (also, Rokushogū, Rokusho Myōjin) 六所宮
Ruijū jingi hongen 類聚神祇本源
Ryōbu Shintō 両部神道
Ryōkiden 綾綺殿
Ryōsai kenbo 良妻賢母
Saigū 斎宮
Saiin 斎院
Saijin ronsō 祭神論争
Saijōsho 斎場所
Sailor Moon セーラムーン
Saiō (itsuki no miya) 斎王
Saisei itchi 祭政一致
Saishu 祭主
Saitansai 歳旦祭
Sakaki 榊

Saki-mitama 幸魂
Sakuhō 冊封
Sandaikō 三大考
Sandan gyōji 三段行事
Sanjō Sanetsumu 三条実万
Sankyō itchi 三教一致
Sankyō Kaidō 三教会同
Sannō 山王
Sannō Ichijitsu Shintō 山王一実神道
Sannō Matsuri 山王祭
Sannō Reigenki 山王霊験記
Sannomiya 三宮
Sano Tsunehiko 佐野経彦
Sanrō 参籠
Sansha Takusen 三社託宣
Sanshu no ōharai 三種大祓
Saionji Kinhira 西園寺公衡
Sapporo Gokoku Jinja 札幌護国神社
Sapporo Sōreisha 札幌総霊社
Sarume 猿女
Sarutahiko 猿田彦
Satō Norio 佐藤範雄
Sawatari Masamori 猿渡昌盛
Seichō no Ie 生長の家
Seigitai 正義隊
Seirei 精霊
Seisen 聖戦
Seken 世間
Sendai kuji hongi 先代旧事本紀
Sendai Tanabata 仙台七夕
Senge Takatomi 千家尊福
Senkyō ibun 仙境異聞
Senn'yūji 泉涌寺
Senso 践祚
Sensōji 浅草寺
Sessha 摂社
Setsuwa 説話
Sezoku-nai shūkyō 世俗内宗教
Shajikyoku 社寺局
Shakai 社会
Shakai jigyō 社会事業
Shake 社家
Shaku nihongi 釈日本紀
Shasekishū 沙石集
Shasō 社僧
Shi (also, watakushi) 私
Shiba Takatsune 斯波高経
Shibun yōryō 紫文要領
Shichi Fukujin 七福神
Shichi-go-san 七五三
Shigeno Yasutsugu 重野安繹
Shihōhai 四方拝
Shika mandara 鹿曼荼羅
Shikinaisha 式内社
Shikinen Sengū 式年遷宮
Shimaji Mokurai 島地黙雷
Shimenawa 注連縄
Shin Nihon Shūkyō Dantai Rengōkai 新日本宗教団体連合会
Shin no mihashira 心御柱
Shinbatsu 神罰
Shinbutsu bunri 神仏分離
Shinbutsu Reijōkai 神仏霊場会
Shinden 神殿
Shinden 神田
Shin'en Kai 神苑会
Shingaku 心学
Shingikai 審議会
Shingun 神郡
Shinhen shūshin kyōkasho 新編修身教科書
Shinkaden 神嘉殿
Shinkō 信仰
Shinkoku 神国

Shinkyō soshiki monogatari 神教組織物語
Shinmei 神明
Shinmeisha 神明社
Shinmin no Michi 臣民の道
Shinmon 神文
Shino Yukiko 篠有紀子
Shinpen Musashi fudokikō 新編武蔵風土記稿
Shinpō 神宝
Shinpūren 神風連
Shinra Myōjin 新羅明神
Shinreigun 神霊軍
Shinrikyō 神理教
Shinron 新論
Shinryaku 侵略
Shinryaku sensō 侵略戦争
Shinryō 神領
Shinsen 神饌
Shinsen-heihaku 神饌幣帛
Shinshin 神心
Shinshoku 神職
Shinshutsu 進出
Shinshūkyō 神習教
Shintai 神体
Shintai hō 進退法
Shinto 神都
Shintō 神道
Shintō denju 神道傳授
Shintō gairon 神道概論
Shintō gobusho 神道五部書
Shintō jimukyoku 神道事務局
Shintō kanryō chōjō 神道管領長上
Shintō kōshaku 神道講釈
Shintō nonaka no shimizu 神道野中の清水
Shintō Seiji Renmei 神道政治連盟
Shintō Seinen Konwakai 神道青年懇話会
Shintō Shūseiha 神道修成派
Shintō Taikyō 神道大教
Shintō taii 神道大意
Shintō yuiitsu mondō sho 神道唯一問答書
Shintōgaku 神道学
Shintōka 神道家
Shintōkata 神道方
Shintokukai 神徳会
Shintōkyō 神道教
Shintōsha 神道者
Shintōshū 神道集
Shinza 神座
Shinzō 神像
Shirakawa 白川
Shishinden 紫宸殿
Shisō zasshiki 祠曹雑識
Shissō 執奏
Shitennō 四天王
Shitomi Kangetsu 蔀関月
Shizutani Gakkō 閑谷学校
Shosha negi kannushi hatto 諸社禰宜神主法度
Shōbatsu 賞罰
Shōen 荘園
Shōheikō 昌平黌
Shōjiki 正直
Shōkonjō 招魂場
Shōkyōin 小教院
Shoryō matsuri 諸霊祭
Shōten 掌典
Shōya 庄屋
Shōyūki 小右記
Shugendō 修験道
Shumisen 須弥山

Shunnichi Kō 春日講
Shunsai 旬祭
Shūkyō 宗教
Shūkyō hōjin 宗教法人
Shūkyō hōjin rei 宗教法人令
Shūkyō hōjinhō 宗教法人法
Shūkyōteki jinkaku ken 宗教的人格権
Shūshin 修身
Soga Umako 蘇我馬子
Sōja 総社
Sokui 即位
Sokui kanjō 即位勧請
Somin Shōrai 蘇民将来
Sonnō jōi 尊王攘夷
Sorachita Jinja 空知太神社
Sugawara Michizane 菅原道真
Suika shagō 垂加社号
Suika Shintō 垂加神道
Suki 主基
Susanoo no Mikoto 素戔嗚命
Suserihime 須世理姫
Suwa Shrine 諏訪神社
Suzuya 鈴屋
Sōbyō 宗廟
Sōdai 総代
Sōgen Shintō gojūroku den 宗源神道五十六伝
Sōgen Shintō gyōji 宗源神道行事
Sōgen senji 宗源宣旨
Sōka Gakkai 創価学会
Sūkeisha 崇敬者
Ta no kami 田の神
Tabisho 旅所
Tachibana Mitsuyoshi 橘三喜
Tado Jinja 多度神社
Tada Yoshitoshi 多田善俊
Taigenkyū 太元宮
Taika Reforms 大化の改新
Taikyō senpu undō 大教宣布運動
Taima-dera 当麻寺
Taisai 大祭
Taiseikyō 大成教
Taishaku-ten 帝釈天
Taishakyō 大社教
Taisō no rei 大喪の礼
Taiwan Jinja 台湾神社
Tajihi no Ayako 多治比文子
Takamagahara 高天原
Takamagahara ni kamu zumari masu 高天原に神留坐す
Takamimusubi no kami 高御産巣日神
Takashina Takakane 高階隆兼
Takemikazuchi 武甕槌
Takenouchi Shikibu 竹内式部
Takusen 託宣
Tama 霊
Tama no Mihashira 霊之真柱
Tamada Naganori 玉田永教
Tamagushi 玉串
Tamashii 魂
Tamatasuki 玉たすき
Tamayori Hime 玉依姫
Tamukeyama Hachimangū 手向山八幡宮
Tanaka Sen'ya 田中千弥
Tanaka Yoritsune 田中頼庸
Tanaka Yoshitō 田中義能
Tanaka Yuki 田中ユキ
Tatari 祟り
Tayasu Munetake 田安宗武
Teiki 帝紀
Tenbu 天部
Tenchō mukyū reki 天朝無窮暦
Tendō 天道

Tengu 天狗
Tengu zōshi 天狗草紙
Tenjin 天神
Tenjin chigi 天神地祇
Tenjin Matsuri 天神祭
Tenka 天下
Tenkai 天海
Tenman Daijizai Tenjin 天満大自在天神
Tenmei jikiju 天命直受
Tenmu Tennō 天武天皇
Tennō shinsai 天皇親祭
Tenrikyō 天理教
Tenrin shōō 転輪聖王
Tenshinkō 天心講
Tenshō Daijin 天照大神
Tensō 伝奏
Tōdaiji 東大寺
Tōgū Binden 東宮便殿
Tokoyo Nagatane 常世長胤
Tōkyō saiban shikan 東京裁判史観
Tōkyo Shōkonsha 東京招魂社
Tōkyōto Ireidō 東京都慰霊堂
Tōshō Daigongen 東照大権現
Tomobe Yasutaka 伴部安崇
Tonden-hei 屯田兵
Torii 鳥居
Toritsugi 取次
Toshigami 年神
Toyoda Mitsugi 豊田貢
Toyokawa Inari 豊川稲荷
Toyokuni Daimyōjin 豊国大明神
Toyomiyazaki bunko 豊宮崎文庫
Toyotamahime 豊玉姫
Toyouke no Ōkami 豊受大神
Tsubonomiya Shrine 坪の宮神社
Tsuchimikado 土御門
Tsuina 追儺
Tsukinamisai 月次祭
Tsukioka Yoshitoshi 月岡芳年
Tsukiyomi no Mikoto 月読命
Tsukuba Fujimaro 筑波藤麿
Tsumi 罪
Tsurugaoka Hachiman Shrine 鶴岡八幡宮
Tsutsushimi 慎み
Ubusuna shako denshō kōgi 産須那社古伝抄広義
Ubusunagami 産土神
Uden Shintō 烏伝神道
Ugajin 宇賀神
Uiyamabumi 初山踏
Uji 氏
Uji shūi monogatari 宇治拾遺物語
Ujigami 氏神
Ujiko shirabe 氏子調
Ukiyo doko 浮世床
Umeda Shinmeigū 梅田神明宮
Umetsuji Norikiyo 梅辻規清
Uneme 采女
Urabe 卜部
Urata Chōmin 浦田長民
Usa Jingū 宇佐神宮
Ushirodo 後戸
Wa 倭
Waka 和歌
Wakabayashi Kyōsai 若林強斎
Wake mitama 分霊
Wakō dōjin 和光同塵
Washinomiya Shrine 鷲宮神社
Watarai 度会
Watarai (Deguchi) Nobuyoshi 度会（出口）延佳
Watarai Hironori 度会弘乗

Watarai Ieyuki 度会家行
Yabusame 流鏑馬
Yaketsu 野決
Yaku barai 厄払い
Yakudoshi 厄年
Yama no kami 山の神
Yamabushi 山伏
Yamagata Aritomo 山県有朋
Yamatai 邪馬台
Yamato 大和
Yamato Hime 大和姫
Yamato Hime no mikoto seiki 倭姫命世記
Yamato shōgaku 倭小学
Yamato Takeru no Mikoto 日本武尊
Yamato ōken 大和王権
Yamazaki Ansai 山崎闇斎
Yano Harumichi 矢野玄道
Yasha 夜叉
Yashikigami 屋敷神
Yashiro 社
Yasukuni Jinja 靖国神社
Yasukuniron 靖国論
Yokohama Kōtai Jingū 横浜皇大神宮
Yomi 黄泉
Yo-ori 節折
Yorishiro 依代
Yosakoi Matsuri よさこい祭り
Yoshida Kanemi 吉田兼見
Yoshida Kanemigi 吉田兼右
Yoshida Kanetomo 吉田兼俱
Yoshikawa Koretaru 吉川惟足
Yoshimi Yukikazu 吉見幸和
Yudate kagura 湯立て神楽
Yuiitsu shinmei-zukuri 唯一神明造
Yuiitsu Shintō 唯一神道
Yuiitsu Shintō myōbō yōshū 唯一神道名法要集
Yuishiki 唯識
Yuki 悠紀
Yōfukki 陽復記
Yōhaisho 遥拝所
Yōkai 妖怪
Yōki 陽気
Yūmei 幽冥
Yūshūkan 遊就館
Yūtoku Inari 祐徳稲荷
Zaō Gongen 蔵王権現
Zenkoku joshi shinshoku kyōgikai 全国女子神職協議会
Zenkoku sen'yū rengōkai 全国戦友連合会
Zenkoku shinshokukai 全国神職会
Zenkoku shinshokukai kaihō 全国神職会会報
Zoku Shintō 俗神道
Zuishin Gate 隋神門
Zōjōji 増上寺
Zōka no sanshin 造化の三神

CHRONOLOGY

Commonly recognized periodizations are used here, though different disciplines vary in their terminology, sometimes overlapping, sometimes leaving gaps; in such cases, intervening years are set in brackets below.

YAYOI PERIOD (400 BCE–300 CE)

Rice cultivation and metallurgy begin.

Dōtaku, magatama appear.

Japanese rulers enter relations with Han China by around 200 BCE, based on trade in iron ingots and iron weapons; Japanese rulers receive "investiture" (*sakuhō*) from Chinese rulers.

The fall of the Han Dynasty in the late 3rd century destabilized the Korean Peninsula and caused a flow of immigrants into Japan that continued into the Nara period.

Queen Himiko's reign (?).

Chronicles of Wei (ca. 297).

The Yamato clan emerged, centered at Miwa, worshipping a Kami associated with Mt. Miwa, Ōmononushi (also called Ōnamuchi, Ōkuninushi).

KOFUN PERIOD (300–700)

Late 3rd–Early 4th Centuries	Formation of the Yamato State.
Mid-4th Century	The three Korean kingdoms went to war with each other; Wa allied with Paekche against Koguryŏ.
	Distinctions between "native" and "immigrant" clans emerged.

456–479	Putative reign of Yūryaku; Yūryaku was one of five "Kings of Wa" recognized by the Chinese monarch. Yūryaku ruled the Nara-Osaka area directly and made alliances with lesser rulers beyond that sphere.
	Appearance of clans with specializations relating to Kami ritual: The Mononobe managed an armory of weapons in Isonokami; they claimed descent from Nigihayahi no Mikoto.
	The Nakatomi supervised the production of *magatama* in Soga; they later took the name Fujiwara and claimed descent from Amenokoyane no Mikoto.
	The women of the Sarume clan practiced sacred dance and spirit possession; they claimed descent from Amenouzume no Mikoto.
	The Inbe (or Imibe) practiced abstinences and procured materials used in ritual; they claimed descent from Ame no Futodama no Mikoto.
	The Urabe practiced divination and later claimed descent from Amenokoyane no Mikoto.
Late 5th Century	The concept of *tenka* was known in Japan from at least the late 5th century.
6th Century	A group called the Hiokibe, associated with worship of solar deities, was sent out from Yamato to coordinate regional Kami rites with those of the court, spreading the Yamato clan's style of ritual far from the center of the country.
	Buddhism's influence over the court strengthened steadily from the 6th century.
Mid-6th Century	Yamato rule extends from Kyūshū through Kantō Plain.
	The appearance of the first permanent shrine buildings.
	The Yamato court officially incorporates Buddhist rituals into its ceremonial calendar.
552	The King of Paekche sends a Buddhist statue to the Yamato ruler Keitai.
584	Soga Umako builds a Buddhist chapel, installs a statue of Maitreya, Buddha of the Future, and has two women ordained as "nuns."
587	Yōmei converts to Buddhism with Soga support, leading to the rapid spread of Buddhism.
592–628	Suiko's reign.
592	The Soga clan, proponents of Buddhism, carry out a coup, putting Suiko on the throne. They destroyed the main line of the Mononobe clan. With this, Buddhism expands greatly. Temples replace *kofun*.

RITSURYŌ ERA (7th–9th Centuries) and NARA PERIOD (710–784) [794]

7th Century	Tokoyo no Kami cult appears.
603	Reorganization of the court, replacing the *kabane* ranking system with the cap-rank (*kan'i*) system.
604	Shōtoku Taishi's Seventeen-Article Constitution.
645	The Taika Reform initiates the Ritsuryō System, based on the example of the T'ang Dynasty.
647	Edict of 647, in which the term *kamunagara* "as a Kami would" is explained.
672	Jinshin War.
673–686	Tenmu's reign; the use of the term *tennō* for the sovereign begins.
	Great Purification rite established under Tenmu.
689	Kiyomihara Code—first mention of the Jingikan and *Jingiryō*.
690, 692	First Vicennial Renewals (*Shikinen Sengū*) of the Inner (690) and Outer (692) Shrines at Ise.
Late 7th	Founding of the Jingikan.
Century	The court dedicated a consecrated imperial princess (*saiō, itsuki no miya*) to serve at Ise, initiating a system that continued to the early 14th century.
701	Taihō Code.
712	Completion of *Kojiki*.
713	An edict required each province to compile *fudoki*, a cadastral survey including distinctive tales and legends.
718	Yōrō Code—established Kami Law (*Jingiryō*) and Regulations for Monks and Nuns (*Sōniryō*).
720	Completion of *Nihon shoki*.
724–749	Emperor Shōmu's reign.
734	Emperor Shōmu establishes a Buddhist chapel in the palace compound, called the Shingon'in, and a network of provincial temples (*kokubunji, kokubunniji*) headed by Tōdaiji in Nara.
743	Emperor Shōmu issues an edict calling for the construction of a 15-meter-high bronze sculpture of the Buddha Rushana.
768	The Dokyō Incident.
781–806	Emperor Kanmu's reign.

HEIAN PERIOD (784–1185)

798	The capital is moved to Heiankyō (Kyoto).
	After 798, provincial governors assume responsibility for the provincial shrines.

Early 9th Century	The Ritsuryō system begins to fall apart.
	Traditional mourning observances are replaced by the Buddhist practices of sutra chanting and offering incense before the corpse.
	Clans begin to construct *ujigami* shrines.
810	The court dedicates a consecrated imperial princess (*saiin*) to worship at the Kamo shrines, initiating a system that continued until the early 13th century. The annual festival of the Kamo shrines is made an official rite.
820	Dissolution of the Bureau of Yin and Yang (On'yōryō).
Late 9th Century	Beginning with Emperor Uda (r. 887–897), daily worship of the Ise deities on a stone platform at the Seiryōden hall of the palace becomes an established practice.
863	First recorded *goryō* meeting held.
872	*Jōgan gishiki* compiled.
887	The court begins approving the ordination of two monks each year dedicated to the service of the Sannō deities.
907	Fall of the T'ang Dynasty.
927	Compilation of *Engi Shiki*.
969–984	Emperor En'yū's reign; imperial processions to the Iwashimizu, Kamo, and Hirano Shrines become established practices. Offering of official tribute (*hōbei*) to the Twenty-One Shrines becomes customary.
Late 10th–mid-11th Century	Rise of the *jinin*.
1001	As of 1001, the Urabe House is allocated the position of second-in-command at the Jingikan.
1031	At the Tsukinamisai of the sixth month, the *Saiō* becomes possessed by the Aramitama of Amaterasu and proclaims an oracle complaining of the emperor's dismissive treatment of the Ise Shrines.
1052	*Mappō*, "The Latter days of the Dharma," believed to have begun this year.
Late 11th Century	The Jingikan loses control over official, public rites through the widened scope of imperial involvement in shrines to which the Jingikan has no connection.
	Miscellaneous appropriations of the Great Purification Rite.
1087–1192	Era of Cloister Government (government by cloistered emperors).
	Nakatomi no Harae Kunge promotes an analogy likening the Inner and Outer Shrines at Ise to the Diamond and Womb-world mandalas of esoteric Buddhism.

	Around this time, the total number of official shrines grows to twenty-two, giving rise to the expression, "Twenty-Two Shrines."
Early 12th Century	By the late 11th or 12th century, Buddhist enthronement rites incorporate symbolism likening the emperor to the cosmic Buddha Dainichi.
	New designations of provincial shrines as a province's "First Shrine," "Second Shrine," or "Third Shrine" emerge through pressure from provincial people for court recognition.
1150	Compilation of Ryōbu Shinto texts begins around this time.
1156	Emperor Go-Shirakawa issues an edict seeking to restrict the number of *jinin*.
1161	Headship of the Jingikan becomes hereditary in the Shirakawa family.

MEDIEVAL PERIOD (1185–1600)

1185–1333 [1336]	Kamakura Period.
Late 12th Century	Shrine mandalas begin to be produced.
1192–1333	Kamakura Shogunate.
1196	Sixty monks of Tōdaiji travel to Ise to perform a major ceremony to dedicate to the Ise Shrines a copy of the Greater Prajñāpāramitā Sutra, copied for this purpose by all the monks of Tōdaiji.
1199–1333	Hōjō Regency.
1232	*Goseibai shikimoku*, composed by Hōjō Yasutoki.
Late 13th Century	Compilation of *Shasekishū*.
	Urabe Kanekata compiles *Shaku nihongi*.
	The Five Books of Shinto (*Shintō gobusho*) circulate.
1274, 1281	Mongol Invasions.
1275	The imperial court raises the ranks of all Kami by one rank, in recognition of their role in warding off the first Mongol Invasion through their "divine wind."
1281	A Hall of the Eight Deities built at the Jingikan.
1330	Watarai Ieyuki composes *Ruijū jingi hongen*.
1333–1568	Muromachi Period (Ashikaga Shogunate).
1333–1336	Kenmu Restoration.
1336–1428	Period of Northern and Southern Courts.
1339	Kitabatake Chikafusa composes *Jinnō Shōtōki*.
1358	*Shintōshū* composed around this time.
15th Century	Court tribute to shrines ceases.

1457	First *okage mairi.*
1467–1477	Ōnin War.
1467/1493–1568 [1573]	Warring States (Sengoku) era.
1484	Yoshida Kanetomo completes *Yuiitsu Shintō Myōbō Yōshū* (The Essentials of the Name and Law of the One and Only Shinto).
1489	Outer Shrine forces burn the town of Uji.
Late 15th Century	Francis Xavier establishes Catholic missions in Japan.
1563	Vicennial Renewal held for the Outer Shrine at Ise after a hiatus of 129 years.
1585	Vicennial Renewal held for the Inner Shrine at Ise after a hiatus of 123 years.

AZUCHI-MOMOYAMA PERIOD 1568 [1573]–1600 [1603]

1585	Kanemi approaches future Emperor Go-Yōzei for permission to build a replica of the Hall of the Eight Deities at the Saijōsho.
1587	Hideyoshi issues an expulsion edict to the Christian missionaries.

EDO PERIOD (also known as the TOKUGAWA PERIOD or EARLY MODERN PERIOD) 1600 [1603]–1867 [1868]

Early Edo Period	Tokugawa Mitsukuni judges the *Sendai kuji hongi* to be a forgery.
1605	Ise *oshi* begin organizing pilgrimage associations.
1610	The shogunate reinstates the Vicennial Renewal and directs that the Yoshida House should conduct the related rite dispatching an Imperial Emissary to the Ise Shrines.
1637–1638	Shimabara Rebellion.
1644	Publication of a new version of the *Kojiki.*
1645–1648	Hayashi Razan's *Shintō denju* compiled.
1648	Revival of the library at the Outer Shrine at Ise.
1650	Deguchi Nobuyoshi's *Yōfukki* compiled.
	Okage mairi.
1655	Yamazaki Ansai's *Yamato shōgaku* compiled.

1662	*Edo meisho ki* declares the Ōji Inari Shrine the "big boss" of all Edo Inari shrines.
1665	The shogunate issues "Regulations Governing All Shinto Shrines, Senior Priests, and Other Shrine Functionaries" (*Shosha negi kannushi hatto*).
1666	Hoshina Masayuki has Yoshikawa Koretaru and Yamazaki Ansai survey the shrines of the Aizu domain.
	Creation of the Shintōkata post within the shogunal government.
	Deguchi Nobuyoshi's "A Record of Divine Marvels of the Grand Shrine of Ise" compiled.
1667	On the basis of the 1666 survey, Hoshina Masayuki abolishes numerous Aizu temples and shrines.
	Daijōsai is revived for Emperor Higashiyama, after a hiatus of 241 years.
1669	Hoshina Masayuki has Yoshikawa Koretaru and Yamazaki Ansai compile a history of Aizu shrines, *Aizu jinjashi.*
	Yoshikawa Koretaru bestows a "living shrine" name on Hoshina Masayuki, and later the same year a similar name for Yamazaki Ansai.
1675–1697	Shinto popularizer Tachibana Mitsuyoshi travels to the First Shrines of the country, compiling his *A Record of Pilgrimage to the First Shrines* (*Ichinomiya sankeiki*).
1680	Kamigamo Shrine's library established.
1685	Promulgation of a law prohibiting construction of new shrines.
1686	Revival of the library at the Inner Shrine at Ise.
1688	Revival of the library at the Kitano Tenmangū.
1705	*Okage mairi.*
	Kashima Shrine's library established.
1706	Watarai Hironori's *The Continuing Record of Divine Marvels of the Grand Shrine of Ise* compiled.
1715	Masuho Zankō's *Endō tsugan* compiled.
1718	*Okage mairi.*
1723	*Okage mairi.*
	Osaka's Sumiyoshi Shrine's library established.
1730s–1770s	The volume of publishing in Edo doubles, marking a publishing boom.
1732	Tomobe Yasutaka's *Shintō nonaka no shimizu* compiled.
1751–1764	The Okina Inari *hayarigami* craze.
1758	Hōreki Incident.
1763	Motoori Norinaga's *Essentials of the Tale of Genji* (*Shibun yōryō*) and *Personal Views on Poetry* (*Isonokami sasamegoto*) compiled.

1771	*Okage mairi.*
	Tsuda Kin'uemon Norinao's "Ise mairi okage no nikki" compiled.
1772–1781	Oide Inari incident.
1780s	Parts of Motoori Norinaga's *Kojikiden* begin to circulate.
1782	Founding of Motoori Norinaga's academy, the Suzuya.
1785	Tada Yoshitoshi's *Shintō benwaku* compiled.
1790	Publication of Motoori Norinaga's *Naobi no mitama.*
1791	Publication of Hattori Nakatsune's *Sandaikō.*
	The Yoshida House opens an office in Edo.
1795	Movements to protest against Buddhist funerals arise in Wakayama domain.
1797	Shitomi Kangetsu's *An Illustrated Guide to the Famous Sites of a Pilgrimage to Ise* (*Ise sangū meisho zue*) compiled.
1798	Completion of Motoori Norinaga's *Kojikiden.*
1804	The shogunate prohibits First Horse Day festivals for Inari.
1806	Hirata Atsutane opens his academy, Masugenoya, in Edo; compiles *Honkyō gaihen.*
1812	Hirata Atsutane's *Tama no mihashira* compiled.
1812–1826	Hirata Atsutane's *Koshiden* compiled.
1814	Kurozumi Munetada's first revelations.
1815	Kurozumi Munetada begins to issue certificates of discipleship (*shinmon*).
1818–1830	Disputes regarding Inari enshrinements.
1822	Hirata Atsutane begins interviewing Edo shaman, Takayama Torakichi.
1823	Hirata Atsutane presents copies of his work to Emperor Ninkō, through Mutobe Yoshika.
1825	Publication of Aizawa Seishisai's *New Theses.*
1829	Toyoda Mitsugi dies in prison.
1830	*Okage mairi.*
1832	Publication of Hirata Atsutane's *Tamatasuki.*
1833	Inoue Masakane's first revelations.
1834	Asadani Rōgu's *Shisō zasshiki* compiled.
1838	Tenrikyō founded by Nakayama Miki.
1839	The shogunate prohibits public worship at *yashikigami* shrines and construction of new shrines.
Early 1840s	Shogunal crackdown on assemblies for Shinto preaching and proselytizing (*Shintō kōshaku*).
1841	Hirata Atsutane banished from Edo.
	Inoue Masakane arrested; compiles *Shintō yuiitsu mondō sho.*
1843	Death of Hirata Atsutane.

1845 Inoue Masakane banished to Miyakejima.

1846 Kurozumi Munetada's "Rules of 1846" *(Kōka san-nen no go teisho)* compiled.

Umetsuji Norikiyo opens the Crow Garden (Sui-u-en) in the Ikenohata district of Edo.

1847 Umetsuji Norikiyo banished to Hajijōjima, where he dies in 1861.

1851 Akagi Tadaharu begins proselytizing for Kurozumikyō in Kyoto.

1852 *Tairyō Inari* craze.

1853 Kitagawa Morisada's *Morisada Mankō* compiled.

1856 The Yoshida House confers the Daimyōjin title on Kurozumi Munetada posthumously.

1862 The Munetada Shrine constructed in Kyoto.

1863 *Okage mairi.*

1865 The Munetada Shrine designated an imperial prayer shrine (*chokugansho*).

1867 "Anything Goes!"(*Eejanaika*).

MEIJI PERIOD (1868–1912)

1868–1869 Boshin War.

1868–1870 Meiji government arrests over 3,000 Hidden Christians in an attempt to stamp out Christianity and exalt Shinto.

1868 Order for the separation of Buddhas and Kami (*shinbutsu bunri rei*).

Buddhist priests prohibited from serving at shrines unless they became Shinto priests.

Buddhist priests in service at shrines forced to laicize or become shrine priests.

Shrine priests warned not to destroy temple property.

Nichirenshū ordered not to incorporate Amaterasu into its 30 protective deities (*sanjūbanjin*) or into mandala.

Hachiman shrines ordered to remove the "bodhisattva" suffix from the deity's name.

Establishment of the Department of Divinities (Jingikan) as central administrative unit for shrines; shrine priests put under its administration (thus severing them from foregoing administration by the Yoshida and Shirakawa Houses).

1869 The Tokyo Shōkonsha (later renamed Yasukuni Shrine) established to honor the spirits of those who had died on the imperial side in the struggles surrounding the Meiji Restoration.

Vicennial Renewal of the Ise Shrines.

1870 Great Proselytization Campaign begins (*taikyō senpū undō*); participants drawn from Buddhist and Shinto priests, actors, and others; worship facilities designated throughout the country.

Echizen Gohō Ikki.

1871 (11.17) Enthronement of Emperor Meiji.

Abolition of Shugendō.

Shrine and temple lands "returned" to the throne (*shajiryō jōchi rei*).

Department of Divinities demoted to Ministry of Divinities (Jingishō).

Unified system of shrine ranks established.

Shrines defined as providing the "rites of the nation" (*kokka no sōshi*).

Standard scale established for shrine priests' salaries.

Ise Shrines made head of all shrines; other reforms initiated at Ise.

Buddhist rites formerly performed in the imperial household are abolished.

1872 Ministry of Divinities abolished and its functions moved to the Ministry of Religion (*Kyōbushō*), established that year to manage the Great Proselytization Campaign.

Establishment of the Minatogawa Shrine.

1873 Salaries for priests of Prefectural Shrines and below abolished; thereafter, any salaries are provided by local communities.

Ban on Christianity lifted.

1875 Jōdo Shinshū withdraws from the Great Proselytization Campaign, effectively signaling the Campaign's failure.

1876 Shinpūren Rebellion.

1877–1878 Satsuma Rebellion.

1877 Abolition of the Ministry of Religion (Kyōbushō); administration of shrines and religions transferred to the Home Ministry.

1880 Sano Tsunehiko founds Shinrikyō.

Limited subsidies for shrines' preservation established, with the provision that public funding would eventually be phased out.

1881 All shrines and temples legally required to appoint a minimum of three stewards.

1884 Great Proselytization Campaign formally ends with abolition of the system of National Instructors.

1889 Promulgation of the Meiji Constitution, with provisions for limited freedom of religion.

Establishment of the Kashihara Shrine.

Vicennial Renewal of the Ise Shrines.

1890 Promulgation of the Imperial Rescript on Education.

1891 Tokyo Imperial University historian Kume Kunitake (1839–1931) publishes an article holding that Shinto represents the remains of

	an ancient worship of Heaven. After an outcry by "Shintoists," he is removed from his post in 1892.
	Uchimura Kanzō's "Disrespect Incident" provokes nationalist criticism of Christianity as unpatriotic.
1895	Establishment of Heian Jingū, commemorating the 1100th anniversary of the founding of Kyoto; Emperor Kanmu named the shrine's deity; Emperor Kōmei added in 1940.
1900	Taiwan Jinja established.
	Shrine Bureau (Jinjakyoku) established within the Home Ministry.
1904–1905	Russo-Japanese War.
1905–1910	Most shrine mergers occur in this period.
1908	Boshin Rescript: "It is now desired... that the shrines will be utilized in promoting the unification and administration of the country."
1909	Vicennial Renewal of the Ise Shrines.
1914	Shrines of all ranks are directed to conduct ceremonies corresponding to rites in the imperial palace, according to standardized procedures.
1915	(11.14) Enthronement of Emperor Taishō.
	Construction begins on the Meiji Shrine (completed in 1920).
1919	Chōsen Jingū built in Seoul, with Amaterasu and Emperor Meiji as its deities.
1921	First suppression of Ōmoto, on charges of violating the newspaper law and lèse majesté.
1928	(11.14) Enthronement of Emperor Shōwa.
1929	The Committee to Investigate the Shrine System was formed, attached to the Shrine Bureau.
	Vicennial Renewal of the Ise Shrines.
1935	Second suppression of Ōmoto.
1937	Publication of *Kokutai no Hongi*.
1938	The Shrine Bureau dissolves the Shrine Federation, as an austerity measure in support of Japan's "holy war" in China.
1940	Creation of the Jingiin.
	Celebration of the 2600th Anniversary of the Founding of Japan.
1945–1952	Allied Occupation.
1945	Japan signs the Potsdam Declaration.
	(12.15) Promulgation of the Shinto Directive.
1946	(1.1) Hirohito's "Declaration of Humanity."
	Establishment of NASS (Jinja Honchō).
1952	(6.2) Emperor Hirohito travels to the Ise Grand Shrines to announce the signing of the peace treaty and Japan's regaining of sovereignty.

1957	Yasukuni Shrine develops its own draft for a "Yasukuni Bill" and continues to issue calls for the shrine to remain a Shinto establishment under state support, reclassified as a "special corporation."
1959	Chidorigafuchi, an ossuary for the remains of unknown war dead, established near Yasukuni Shrine.
1969	Shinto Seiji Renmei established.
1969–1974	Over this period, the LDP submits a bill five times calling for restoration of public support to Yasukuni Shrine.
1975	Last imperial visit to Yasukuni Shrine.
1977	Supreme Court ruling on the Tsu Purification Ceremony Case.
1978	Yasukuni Shrine apotheosizes fourteen Class A war criminals.
1980	LDP Cabinet Secretary Miyazawa Kiichi makes public the party's view that any visit to the Yasukuni Shrine by the prime minister is unconstitutional.
1982	LDP forms a committee to study the Yasukuni issue, seeking to overturn its 1980 statement.
1985	Prime Minister Nakasone's visit to Yasukuni provokes unexpectedly strong opposition from China and S. Korea.
1988	Supreme Court finds against the plaintiff in the Self-Defense Force Apotheosis case.
1989	Emperor Hirohito dies.

HEISEI PERIOD (1989–present)

1990	(11.22) Enthronement of Heisei Emperor Akihito.
1990–1991	Japan experiences an economic "bubble" based on a rapid inflation of the price of land.
1991–present	Japan enters a long economic recession.
1995	Aum Shinrikyō Incident.
	Hanshin-Awaji earthquake.
1997	Ehime Tamagushi Case Supreme Court verdict.
1999	LDP Cabinet Secretary Nonaka proposes that the Class A war criminals be removed from Yasukuni Shrine, in preparation for giving the shrine state support.
2000	(5.15) Prime Minister Mori states that Japan is a "divine nation centered on the Emperor" (*Nihon wa tennō o chūshin to suru kami no kuni*) at a meeting of the League of Shintō Parliamentarians (Shintō Seiji Renmei).
	(5.17) In response to Prime Minister Mori's "divine nation" remark, Japan Conference of Religions for Peace (Nihon Shūkyōsha Heiwa Kaigi) demands his resignation.

2006 (7.20) The *Nihon Keizai Shinbun* releases a memo written by Grand Steward Tomita Tomohiko purportedly recording remarks by Hirohito to the effect that he ceased visiting Yasukuni Shrine after 1975 out of displeasure with the enshrinement of the 14 Class A war criminals.

(8.15) Prime Minister Koizumi Jun'ichirō visits Yasukuni Shrine on the anniversary of Japan's surrender, leading to harsh criticism from China and S. Korea.

(September) Yasukuni Shrine refuses a request to apotheosize a Japanese member of the Coast Guard, who was killed in 1950 as part of a secret minesweeping operation in support of the US military during the Korean War. The shrine explains that at present it does not enshrine anyone killed in conflicts subsequent to World War II.

2008 MEXT Minister Tokai Kisaburō voids the foregoing Occupation prohibition on school visits to Yasukuni Shrine.

2010 Supreme Court verdict in the Sorachita Shrine Case, Sunagawa City.

Supreme Court verdict in Hakusan Hime Jinja case.

ABBREVIATIONS

JJRS	*Japanese Journal of Religious Studies.*
JKZ	*Jinja kyōkai zasshi.*
KSDJ	*Kokushi daijiten,* accessed through Japan Knowledge.com: Encyclopedias, Dictionaries, and Databases, http://nrs.harvard.edu/urn-3:hul.eresource:japanknr.
NKBT	*Nihon koten bungaku taikei.* Tokyo: Iwanami shoten.
SJKBM	*Shintō jinbutsu kenkyū bunken mokuroku,* edited by Kokugakuin Daigaku Nihon bunka kenkyūjo. Tokyo: Kōbundō, 2000.
SSDJ	*Shintōshi daijiten,* edited by Sonoda Minoru and Hashimoto Masanori. Tokyo: Yoshikawa kōbunkan, 2004.
SJ	*Shintō jiten,* edited by Kokugakuin Daigaku Nihon Bunka Kenkyūjo. Tokyo: Kōbunkan, 1993.
ST	Shintō taikei hensankai, *Shintō taikei.* Tokyo: Shintō taikei hensankai, 1996–.
ZSKK	*Zenkoku shinshokukai kaihō.*

NOTES

Introduction

1. Ono Sokyō, *Shinto, The Kami Way: An Introduction to Shrine Shinto*, in collaboration with William P. Woodward (Rutland, Vermont and Tokyo: Charles E. Tuttle Company, 1962).
2. Ibid., 1.
3. Ibid., 3–4.
4. See, for example, Suzuki, Daisetz Teitarō, *Zen and Japanese Culture* (New York: Pantheon Books, 1959).
5. *Shintō no kiso chishiki to kiso mondai* (Tokyo: Jinja shinpōsha, 1963).
6. Kuroda Toshio, "Shinto in the History of Japanese Religion," *Journal of Japanese Studies* 7, no. 1 (1981): 1–21.

Chapter 1

1. Joan R. Piggott, *The Emergence of Japanese Kingship* (Stanford, CA: Stanford University Press, 1997).
2. See Inoue Nobutaka, "Introduction: What Is Shinto?," in *Shinto: A Short History*, by Inoue Nobutaka (ed.), Itō Satoshi, Endō Jun, Mori Mizue, trans. by Mark Teeuwen and John Breen (London: RoutledgeCurzon, 1998), 1–10; Mitsuhashi Tadashi, *Nihon kodai jingi seido no seisei to tenkai* (Kyoto: Hōzōkan, 2010); and Itō Satoshi, Endō Jun, Matsuo Kōichi, Mori Mizue, eds., *Shintō*, Nihonshi kohyakka (Tokyo: Tōkyōdō shuppan, 2002); Mori Mizue, "Ancient and Classical Japan: The Dawn of Shinto," in Inoue et al., *Shinto: A Short History*, 12–62.
3. Gina Barnes and Masaaki Okita review the major issues in the archaeological study of the Yayoi period and discuss major excavation sites in "Japanese Archaeology in the 1990s," *Journal of Archaeological Research* 7, no. 4 (1999): 349–95.
4. Norman Havens, "Shinto," in *Nanzan Guide to Japanese Religions*, ed. Paul Swanson and Clark Chilson (Honolulu: University of Hawai'i Press, 2006), 20; and Okada Shōji, "Kodai no Shintō," *SJ*, 5–9.
5. Havens, "Shinto," in Swanson and Chilson, *Nanzan Guide*, 19–20.
6. J. Edward Kidder, Jr., *Himiko and Japan's Elusive Chiefdom of Yamatai: Archaeology, History, and Mythology* (Honolulu: University of Hawai'i Press, 2007), 114.
7. Piggott, *Emergence of Japanese Kingship*, 21–25.
8. Theodore de Bary et al., eds. *Sources of Japanese Tradition*, vol. 1, 2nd ed. (New York: Columbia University Press, 2001), 7.
9. The topic of Himiko and the kingdom or chiefdom of Yamatai has been a major topic in the study of Japanese early history and religion. In addition to Piggott, *Emergence of Japanese Kingship*, and Kidder, *Himiko*, another recent Western-language treatment of the subject is

William Farris, *Sacred Texts and Buried Treasures: Issues in the Historical Archaeology of Ancient Japan* (Honolulu: University of Hawai'i Press, 1997), 5–54.

10. Piggott, *Emergence of Japanese Kingship*, 20–21. For a consideration of the arguments identifying Yoshinogari as Himiko's ceremonial center, see Farris, *Sacred Texts*, 39–42. Farris does not accept that identification, and the weight of current opinion seems to agree with him. According to Barnes and Okita, "Japanese Archaeology in the 1990s," recent scholarly opinion leans toward the view that Yamatai was somewhere near present-day Nara. For a critical assessment of the reconstruction of Yoshinogari, see Koji Mizoguchi, *Archaeology, Society and Identity in Modern Japan*. Cambridge Studies in Archaeology (Cambridge: Cambridge University Press, 2006), Kindle edition, location 94–274.
11. See Kidder, *Himiko*, 127–59, for a consideration of the religious and shamanic elements of Himiko's rule.
12. Fukunaga Shin'ya, Iwamoto Naofumi, Koyamada Kōichi et al., eds. *Shinpojiyumu sankakuen shinjūkyō* (Tokyo: Gakuseisha, 2003), 197ff. Also, see Kidder, *Himiko*, 160–84, for a detailed review of current scholarly opinion on ancient mirrors associated with Himiko.
13. For a study of the distribution of Chinese mirrors throughout East Asia in the second and third centuries, see Kanaseki Hiroshi, Arai Hiroshi, Sugaya Fuminori et al., *Kodai no kagami to higashi Ajia* (Tokyo: Gakuseisha, 2011). See also Fukunaga, Iwamoto, Koyamada et al., *Shinpojiyumu sankakuen shinjūkyō*, 197ff.; and Kidder, *Himiko*, 160–84, for a detailed review of current scholarly opinion on ancient mirrors associated with Himiko.
14. In *State Formation in Japan: Emergence of a 4th-Century Ruling Elite* (London: Routledge, 2006), chap. 5, Gina Barnes argues that the Hashihaka tumulus is the leading contender as Himiko's grave.
15. Piggott, *Emergence of Japanese Kingship*, 24ff.
16. Piggott, *Emergence of Japanese Kingship*, 29ff. For extensive review of current research on the Kofun period, see Habuta Yoshiyuki and Kamada Shūichi, eds., *Kofun jidai kenkyū no genjō to kadai*, 2 vols. (Tokyo: Dōseisha, 2012). On the Makimuku kofun, see Kidder, *Himiko*, 239–82.
17. See Joan Piggott, "Sacral Kingship and Confederacy in Early Izumo," *Monumenta Nipponica* 44, no. 1 (1989): 45–74; and Kidder, *Himiko*, 114–26.
18. Farris, *Sacred Texts and Buried Treasures*, 108–19.
19. Most *uji* were based in the Yamato area, but some, like the Imibe (or Inbe), had branches in distant territories, and others, such as the Izumo, were located outside Yamato. The *uji* chiefs managed the work performed by their subordinate groups, some of which could be located in separate villages.
20. Piggott, *Emergence of Japanese Kingship*, chap. 2.
21. On the Inariyama sword, its inscription, and its discovery, see Murayama Shichirō and Roy Andrew Miller, "The Inariyama Tumulus Sword Inscription," *Journal of Japanese Studies* 5, no. 2 (1979): 405–38. The inscription is also translated in Piggott, *Emergence of Japanese Kingship*, 54.
22. Ōba Iwao, Sugiyama Shigetsugu, and other scholars have argued that Okinoshima represents a distinct kind of ritual site. In their view, Okinoshima demonstrates an historical evolution of rites for the Kami during the Kofun period, divorced from death rites and graves. See Ōhira Shigeru, "Saishi iseki," in *Kofun jidai kenkyū no genjō to kadai*, ed. Habuta Yoshiyuki and Kameda Shūichi, (Tokyo: Dōseisha, 2012), 269–83.
23. Ibid.; Mori, "Dawn of Shinto," 39–41.
24. Piggott, *Emergence of Japanese Kingship*, 61–62. Mizoguchi Mutsuko asserts that originally the Yamato identified the male Kami Takamimusubi as their divine ancestor, only later substituting Amaterasu for him. See Mizoguchi Mutsuko, *Amaterasu no tanjō: Kodai ōken no genryū o saguru* (Tokyo: Iwanami shoten, 2009) and *Ōken shinwa no ningen kōzō: Takamimusubi to Amaterasu* (Tokyo: Yoshikawa Kōbunkan, 2000).
25. The evolution of the Yamato clan's religious authority is treated in Matsumae Takeshi, "Early Kami Worship," trans. Janet Goodwin, in *The Cambridge History of Japan*, vol. 1: *Ancient Japan*, ed. Delmer Brown (Cambridge: Cambridge University Press, 1993), 342–49. *Tenka* was also

pronounced as *ame ga shita* or *ame no shita* in ancient Japan. Watanabe Shin'ichirō, "Tenka no ideorogii kōzō," *Nihonshi kenkyū* 440 (April 1999): 36–49.

26. Some research suggests that succession rites for the new ruler were carried out on the flat surface of the rectangular portion. On ancient death ritual, see Gary Ebersole, *Ritual Poetry and the Politics of Death in Early Japan* (Princeton, NJ: Princeton University Press, 1989).
27. The name Hioki is composed of *hi* (sun) and *oki* (rising). *Be* were occupation-based groups attached to particular clans. Piggott, *Emergence of Japanese Kingship*, 73.
28. Piggott shows that the character and strength of Yamato hegemony varied over time in accord with changes in the balance of power among allied clans and with the changing geopolitics of Northeast Asia. Piggott, *Emergence of Japanese Kingship*, chaps. 2 and 3.
29. W. G. Aston, trans., *Nihongi: Chronicles of Japan from the Earliest Times to A.D. 697*, (Rutland, VT: C. E. Tuttle Co., 1972), bk. 2, 65; *Nihon shoki ge*, annotated by Sakamoto Tarō, Ienaga Saburō, Inoue Mitsusada, and Ōno Susumu, NKBT 68 (Tokyo: Iwanami shoten, 1967), 100–101.
30. Because no system for ordaining Buddhist clergy yet existed in Japan, this "ordination" was probably informal in nature.
31. The question whether Shōtoku actually existed has recently been vigorously debated by Ōyama Seiichi, in *"Shōtoku Taishi" no tanjō* (Tokyo: Yoshikawa Kōbunkan, 1999). Ōyama denies Shōtoku's historicity. His view is disputed by Morita Tei, in *Suiko-chō to Shōtoku Taishi* (Tokyo: Iwata shoin, 2005), and others. A recent study in English that uses accounts of Shōtoku to illuminate the roles of immigrant clans in early Japan is Michael I. Como, *Shōtoku: Ethnicity, Ritual, and Violence in the Japanese Buddhist Tradition* (New York: Oxford University Press, 2008).
32. Because the denial of Shōtoku's historicity undermined the image of an unbroken imperial line, when Tsuda Sōkichi first published his views in 1939, his work was banned. He was forced to resign his position at Waseda University, and he was accused of lèse-majesté. See Ienaga Saburō, *Tsuda Sōkichi no shisōshiteki kenkyū* (Tokyo: Iwanami shoten, 1988), esp. part 5.
33. It is notable also that use of the term *tennō* declined in the Heian period. See Yamaguchi Osamu, "Tennō shō no keifu," *Bukkyō Daigaku sōgō kenkyūjo kiyō* 2, special issue (March 1995): 96–118, noted by Luke Roberts on the PMJS (Premodern Japanese Studies) Listserve, October 22, 2015. See also Herman Ooms, *Imperial Politics and Symbolics in Ancient Japan: The Tenmu Dynasty, 650–800* (Honolulu: University of Hawai'i Press, 2009), 58, 64–65, 146. On Jitō as the first Japanese sovereign to be called *tennō* in her lifetime, see Piggott, *Emergence of Japanese Kingship*, 127. In China, the idea of an emperor having "the mandate of heaven" prevailed: he who could unseat the ruler of the day was held to have heaven's mandate to rule the land. Thus there were many examples in China of emperors and dynasties being overthrown, and of the victors claiming to hold the mandate of heaven. In Japan, by contrast, the idea of descent from the Kami, tracing back to Amaterasu in a single, unbroken line, became more prominent. This is not to say that there were not many succession disputes in Japan, and there was even a time when two rival courts claimed legitimacy, the period of Northern and Southern Courts (1336–1392). Nevertheless, as in China, the Japanese sovereign was expected to rule through the correct performance of ritual, the moral force of personal example, and by promoting peace and harmony in society by promulgating the calendar, establishing era names, and other civilizing actions. According to scholar of Daoism Fukunaga Mitsuji, the term *tennō* was originally a Daoist word signifying the highest leader of the Immortals. The Daoist term refers to a ruler who is the highest deity, and whose sovereignty is symbolized by regalia, such as a mirror and a sword. Use of this term in early Japan both signals the influence of Daoism on concepts of rulership and shows that the term inevitably brought with it Daoist conceptions. Significantly, the use of the term *tennō* shifted from designating a heavenly being to refer instead to a ruler of the earth in the seventh century, a usage adopted in Japan. This means that the conception of the sovereign changed from one who is the object of worship and ritual to one who presides over the performance of rites. See Fukunaga Mitsuji, *Dōkyō to kodai Nihon* (Kyoto: Jinbun shoin, 1987), 9–11, 17–18.

34. This legal model was further elaborated in the Kiyomihara Code of 689, where we find the first mention of the Council of Divinities, the Jingikan. The Taihō Code of 701 and the Yōrō Code of 718 (enacted in 757) further developed the system. The land was divided into "seven circuits" (*shichidō*), each of which was subdivided into provinces (*kuni*), and a provincial governor (*kokushi*) was appointed by the central government. The provinces were further divided into districts (*kōri* or *gun*), and each district was divided into villages (*sato, ri*). A census was taken every six years, and a portion of land was allotted for every man, woman, and child over six years old, the amount differing by sex and age. Redistribution of the land was carried out every six years (later, every twelve years). The Yamato court had been structured by clan groups called *uji*, and *be* (the occupational groups associated with the clans), but both *uji* and *be* were formally abolished with the Taika Reform. In the Ritsuryō system, the people were divided into two castes, the ordinary people (*ryōmin*, literally "good people") and the "vulgar" or "base" people (*senmin*). Each of these castes had subdivisions, and those at the bottom of the *senmin* were like slaves. The people were taxed on the production of crops, and there was also a head tax on adult males. The people were subject to corvée labor requirements, and adult males were required to do military service.
35. The Jingikan is believed to have had a precedent in the Saikan, a position charged with unifying solar cults as imperial protectors. The Saikan (a term that refers both to a position and its incumbent) is first mentioned in the reign of the sovereign Bidatsu (r. 572–585, or perhaps 538–585), as the supervisor of ritualists sent out to tame unruly provincial Kami. See Okada Seishi, *Kodai saishi no shiteki kenkyū* (Tokyo: Kōshobō, 1992), 11. The Taihō Code of 701 established the Jingikan. One example of the Jingikan's subordinate position within the governing system headed by the Council of State is that all the Jingikan's official correspondence had to be passed through the Dajōkan central admintrative body, the Benkan. See Aritomi Jun'ya, "Jingikan no tokushitsu: Chihō jinja gyōsei kara no kentō," *Hisutoria* 187 (Nov. 2003): 83–106.
36. The distinction between the heavenly and earthly Kami is not always clear, however. *Jingi* also came to be used as a general reference for all the Kami of Japan, and as a reference to ritual devoted to the Kami. On the meaning of the term *jingi*, see Mitsuhashi Tadashi, *Nihon kodai jingi seido no seisei to tenkai*, 54–58.
37. *Nihon shoki*, reign of Emperor Tenmu, seventh year: "This spring, as a preparation for worshipping the Gods of Heaven and Earth, a purification was held throughout the Empire. An abstinence palace was erected on the bank of the Kurahashi river," Aston, *Nihongi*, bk. 2, 338; NKBT 68, *Nihon shoki ge*, 431. Tenmu paid particular attention each year to the gods of rain and wind, enshrined at the Hirose Shrine (Hirose Jinja) and at the Tatsuta Shrine (Tatsuta Jinja), sending offerings through an emissary (*chokushi*) to their annual festivals each year. On the historical development of usage of the term *jingi*, see Mitsuhashi, *Nihon kodai jingi seido no seisei to tenkai*.
38. The codification of the Jingiryō in the early eighth century might be seen as a reaction to this earlier lack of systematization. See Mitsuhashi Tadashi, *Nihon kodai jingi seido no seisei to tenkai*, 54–58.
39. Mitsuhashi Tadashi, *Nihon kodai jingi seido no seisei to tenkai*, 15–18, 71–72. For an overview of current research regarding court ceremonial during the Ritsuryō era, see Suzuki Keiji, "Ritsuryō kokka to jingi, bukkyō," in *Kodai* 3, Iwanami kōza Nihon rekishi (Tokyo: Iwanami shoten, 2014), 285–320.
40. Thereafter the imperial court added a large number of other ceremonies to its official ritual calendar, to be discussed in subsequent chapters.
41. An English translation of *Jingiryō* is available in George Sansom, "Early Japanese Law and Administration, Part II," *Transactions of the Asiatic Society of Japan*, second series, 11 (1934): 117–49. For the original Japanese text with annotations, see Inoue Mitsusada et al., eds., *Ritsuryō*, Nihon shisō taikei 3 (Tokyo: Iwanami shoten, 1976), 211–15. A translation in modern Japanese is available at http://www.sol.dti.ne.jp/~hiromi/kansei/yoro.html.

42. Satō Masato, "Shinbutsu kakuri no yōin o meguru kōsatsu," *Shūkyō kenkyū* 81, no. 2: (2007), 152–53. Although a number of rituals in the Chinese *Book of Rites* were not mandated by Jingiryō, some of them were actually performed in Japan. For example, one of the Chinese rites omitted from Jingiryō was called *kōshi* and called for the emperor to go to the outskirts of the capital to perform worship of Heaven and Earth; Jinmu is said to have performed this rite on a round, raised earthen dais; later, Emperor Kanmu (r. 781–806) revived this ritual. Rites for Confucius were not incorporated into the Jingiryō, but they are known to have been performed in Japan as early as 701 and were revived by the shogunate and various domain lords during the Edo period. Kanmu twice offered animal sacrifice to Heaven on the winter solstice. See Ooms, *Imperial Politics*, 154. Animal sacrifice was repeatedly prohibited, but each repetition attested to the populace's continued attraction to the sacrifice of cattle and horses. See Araki Toshio, "Kodai kokka to minkan saishi," *Rekishigaku kenkyū* 560 (October 1986): 45–51.
43. Kansei taikan, ritsuryō kanseika no kanshoku ni kansuru rifarensu, http://www.sol.dti.ne.jp/hiromi/kansei/o_kan_jingi.html, accessed June 20, 2012.
44. Namiki Kazuko, "Saigusa no matsuri," *Encyclopedia of Shinto*, http://eos.kokugakuin.ac.jp/modules/xwords/entry-php?emtruID=879, accessed June 18, 2012.
45. Bock, Felicia, trans., *Engi-Shiki, Procedures of the Engi Era*, 2 vols. A Monumenta Nipponica Monograph (Tokyo: Sophia University, 1970, 1972), 1:16–24.
46. According to the *Engi-Shiki*, the Eight Deities were Kamimusubi no Kami, Takamimusubi no Kami, Tamatsume musubi no Kami, Ikumusubi no Kami, Tarumusubi no Kami, Ōmiyanome no Kami, Miketsukami, and Kotoshironushi no Kami.
47. *Kanbe* were households allotted to particular shrines by the court as cultivators whom the shrine could tax. Only a small minority of the larger shrines were connected to the court, or powerful families had them. They participated in shrine ceremonies by presenting offerings and also repaired shrines when they were damaged and did cleaning and other miscellaneous tasks. The *hafuri* were drawn from this group. The *kanbe* overlap with other categories, but the court's involvement in the original assignment of a group to a particular shrine is the *kanbe*'s distinguishing feature. The term can also be read as *kantomo*. See Ōzeki Kunio, "*Kanbe*," in *SJ*, 144.
48. The idea of ranking shrines is first mentioned in *Nihon shoki*, year seven of the legendary tenth sovereign Sūjin (Aston, *Nihongi*, bk. 1, 154; NKBT 67 *Nihon shoki jō*, 426, n. 10), where a distinction is made between *amatsu yashiro*, those enshrining heavenly deities, and *kunitsu yashiro*, those enshrining earthly deities; see Toki Masanori, "Shakaku," *SSDJ*, 468–69. The first mention of ranks actually bestowed on Kami was in 672, when Tenmu bestowed honors on three Kami to whom he attributed his victory in the Jinshin War. See Watanabe Naohiko, "Shinkai," *SSDJ*, 496–97; Aston, *Nihongi*, bk. 2, 318; NKBT 68 *Nihon shoki ge*, 405, n. 29.
49. The Nakatomi line later divided into two, and one of them became the Fujiwara clan. The Mononobe had died out.
50. The first credible documentary evidence of an actual appointment to this office is from 690 or 691. See Sakamoto Katsunari, "Jingikan no seiritsu ni tsuite no ichi kōsatsu," *Shintōgaku* 98 (1978): 40–44.
51. Okada Shōji, "The Development of State Ritual in Ancient Japan," *Acta Asiatica* 51 (1987): 26.
52. Odaira Mika, "Jingi saishi ni okeru josei shinshoku no hataraki," *Gakushūin Daigaku jinbun kagaku ronshū* 12 (2003): 41–67; and Odaira Mika, *Josei shinshoku no tanjō*, (Tokyo: Perikansha, 2009), 82–83; Bock, *Engi-Shiki*, 1:20–21.
53. The exact number and definition of *hyakkan* is vague, but it means "the numerous officials." Bock translates it as "all the civil officials," in *Engi-Shiki*, 1:59
54. Bock, *Engi-Shiki*, 1:62.
55. Hirai, Atsuko, *Government by Mourning: Death and Political Integration in Japan, 1603–1912* (Cambridge, MA: Harvard University Press, 2014), 24–25. The abstinences are detailed in articles 10 and 11 of Kami Law. Violation was punishable by flogging. "Total abstinence" on the fourth day required abstention from meat eating and sexual intercourse. See Bock, *Engi-Shiki*, vols. 1, 2.

56. For the order of ceremony, see Bock, *Engi-Shiki*, 1:61–64.
57. For the complete text of this *norito*, see Bock, *Engi-Shiki*, 2:66–70.
58. On the use of these sleeve-ties, see Bock, *Engi-Shiki*, 1:70n34.
59. *Ashihara no mizuho no kuni*, a name for the sovereign's realm. See Philippi, *Kojiki*, (Tokyo: University of Tokyo Press, 1968), bk. 1, chap. 38, 137n5.
60. *Man'yōshū* 13; see Ogasawara Kazuo, "Kotoage," *SSDJ*, 386. The expression *kotoage* may also be found in *Kojiki* (NKBT 39, n. 10) and *Fudoki* (NKBT 299, n. 10). See also "Kotoage," *Nihon kokugo daijiten*, accessed on Japan Knowledge.com, September 5, 2014.
61. Bock, *Engi-Shiki*, 1:62. While the offerings presented in the annual distributions were called *heihaku*, those presented by emissaries were called *hōhei* or *hōbei*.
62. Nishinomiya Hideki, *Ritsuryō kokka to jingi saishi seido no kenkyū* (Tokyo: Kōshobō, 2004), 22.
63. Mitsuhashi Tadashi, *Nihon kodai jingi seido no seisei to tenkai*, 71–72.
64. Okada Seishi, *Kodai saishi no shiteki kenkyū*, 15.
65. Okada Seishi, *Kodai ōken no saishi to shinwa* (Tokyo: Hanawa shobō, 1970), 139. Nakai Masataka agrees with this point but sees it as too broadly stated, developing more specific conclusions in Nakai Masataka, "Kodai kokka to jingi ideorogii: Daikai, Okada hōkoku ni yosete," *Rekishigaku kenkyū* 8, no. 363 (1970): 31–34.
66. Morita Tei, *Nihon kodai no seiji to shūkyō* (Tokyo: Yūzankaku, 1997), 247–58.
67. Itō et al., *Shintō*, 26.
68. Ogura Shigeji, "Kenkyū nōto: Hachi, kyū seiki ni okeru chihō jinja gyōsei no tenkai," *Shigaku zasshi* 10, no. 3 (1994): 390–415.
69. Okada Shōji holds that the Jingikan was effectively functioning through the Nara period (700–784), that is, roughly the whole eighth century. See Okada Shōji, "Development of State Ritual," 22–41.
70. Nishinomiya Hideki, *Ritsuryō kokka to jingi saishi seido no kenkyū*, 34–41. In a separate essay, Nishinomiya outlines the history of government agencies for shrine administration that preceded the Jingikan. See Nishinomiya Hideki, "Ritsuryō Jingikansei no seiritsu ni tsuite: Sono kōzō, kinō o chūshin to shite," *Hisutoria* 93 (1981): 22–42.
71. Mitsuhashi Tadashi, *Nihon kodai jingi seido no seisei to tenkai*, 71–72. The term *jingi* was invoked to suggest that Kami ritual had existed unchanged from time immemorial, but it is important to realize that this characterization represents *an ideal*, not historical reality. The Jingiryō itself represents an ideal, not a description of actual practice.
72. The first Chinese usage of the term *shendao* (J: *Shintō*) occurred in the Book of Changes, where it means "a mysterious way." Later the term comes to mean magic and magical techniques, or "the way to the graveyard," "the graveyard gate." It can also mean religion in general, according to Mitsuhashi Takeshi, "Kiki to Shintō to iu go," in *Kojiki no sekai*, ed. Kojiki Gakkai, Kojiki kenkyū taikei 11 (Tokyo: Takashina shobō, 1996), 103, 114.
73. Uses of *Shintō* in *Nihon shoki* are closely tied to the term *Nihon*, the text's preferred term for the realm ruled by the Japanese sovereign; ibid, 104. Terms used interchangeably with *Shintō* in *Nihon shoki* include *shinkyō* (the "teachings" of the Kami), *tendō* (the way of Heaven), *kodō* (the ancient way), and others. In some manuscripts it is apparent that the term was pronounced *jindō, shintau*, or *shindō*. See Mark Teeuwen, "From Jindō to Shintō: A Concept Takes Shape," *JJRS* 29, no. 3/4 (2002): 233–63.
74. Kuroda Toshio, "Shinto in the History of Japanese Religions," trans. James Dobbins, *Journal of Japanese Studies* 7, no. 1 (1981): 5.
75. Kuroda, "Shinto in the History of Japanese Religions," 4–5. See also Ooms, *Imperial Politics*, 57.
76. As Kuroda Toshio explains it,

> [I]t is clear that Shinto was another term for Daoism in China. . . . Moreover, as Daoist concepts and practices steadily passed into Japan between the first century A.D. and the period when the *Nihon shoki* was compiled, they no doubt exerted a considerable influence on the ceremonies and the beliefs of communal groups bound by blood ties or geographical proximity and on those which emerged around imperial authority. Among the many elements of

Daoist origin transmitted to Japan are the following: veneration of swords and mirrors as religious symbols; titles such as *mahito* or *shinjin* (Daoist meaning—perfected man, Japanese meaning—the highest of eight court ranks in ancient times which the emperor bestowed on his descendants), *hijiri* or *sen* (Daoist—immortal, Japanese—saint, emperor, or recluse), and *tennō* (Daoist—lord of the universe, Japanese—emperor); the cults of Polaris and the Big Dipper; terms associated with Ise Shrine, such as *jingū* (Daoist—a hall enshrining a deity, Japanese—Ise Shrine), *naikū* (Chinese—inner palace, Japanese—inner shrine at Ise), *gekū* (Chinese—detached palace, Japanese—outer shrine at Ise), and *taiichi* (Daoist—the undifferentiated origin of all things, Japanese—no longer in general use except at Ise Shrine where it has been used since ancient times on flags signifying Amaterasu Ōmikami); the concept of *daiwa* (meaning a state of ideal peace, but in Japan used to refer to Yamato, the center of the country); and the Daoist concept of immortality. (Kuroda, "Shinto in the History of Japanese Religions," 6–7).

77. See Inoue Hiroshi, *Nihon no jinja to Shintō* (Tokyo: Kōsō shobō, 2006), 118n14.
78. Teeuwen, "From Jindō to Shintō."
79. Ibid., 239.
80. Ibid., 239, 240.
81. Atsuko Hirai, *Government by Mourning*, 32, 33.
82. Tsuda Sōkichi, *Nihon no Shintō* Tsuda Sōkichi zenshū, vol. 9 (Tokyo: Iwanami shoten, 1964); Asoya Masahiko, *Shintō shisō no keisei* (Tokyo: Perikansha, 1985); Mitsuhashi Tadashi, *Nihon kodai jingi seido no saisei to tenkai*, 15–18.
83. Inoue Hiroshi, *Nihon no jinja to Shintō*, 56.
84. Itō et al., *Shintō*.
85. Inoue et al., *Shinto: A Short History*, 5.
86. Mori Mizue, "Ancient and Classical Japan, the Dawn of Shinto," in Inoue et al., *Shinto: A Short History*, 13.

Chapter 2

1. The discovery in 1979 of the grave inscription (*boshi*) of Ō no Yasumaro has strengthened scholarly belief that the preface of *Kojiki* indeed reflects the facts of its compilation. While the inscription would appear to confirm that Yasumaro was an historical personage, however, the inscription alone does not confirm the sequence of events set out in the preface. Scholars who believe that the preface was added in the ninth century include Ōba Iwao, *Kojiki seiritsu kō* (Tokyo: Daiwa shobō, 1975) and Miura Sukeyuki, *Kojiki o yominaosu* (Tokyo: Chikuma shobō, 2010), 261ff.
2. The preface to *Kojiki* is virtually the only extant source discussing the circumstances or process of the work's compilation.
3. See Kojiki Gakkai, ed., *Kojiki no kotoba*. Kojiki kenkyū taikei, vol. 10 (Tokyo: Takashina shoten, 1995), for discussion of issues arising from *Kojiki*'s origins in oral literature.
4. See Isomae Jun'ichi, *Japanese Mythology: Hermeneutics on Scripture*. Nichibunken Monograph Series (London and Oakville, CT: Equinox; Kyoto: International Research Center for Japanese Studies, 2009), 20; Tsuda Sōkichi, *Jindaishi no atarashii kenkyū* (Tokyo: Nishōdō, 1913), chap. 4; and Tsuda Sōkichi, *Kojiki oyobi Nihon shoki no shin kenkyū* (Tokyo: Rakuyōdō, 1919), chap. 5.
5. Kōnoshi Takamitsu, "Constructing Imperial Mythology: *Kojiki* and *Nihon shoki*," trans. Iori Joko, in *Inventing the Classics: Modernity, National Identity, and Japanese Literature*, ed. Haruo Shirane and Tomi Suzuki (Stanford, CA: Stanford University Press, 2000), 51–70.
6. This study of the *Kojiki* relies on the translation by Donald Philippi. See Donald Philippi, trans., *Kojiki* (Tokyo: University of Tokyo Press, 1968). When referring to the Japanese original, I

have used *Kojiki*, annotated by Takeda Yūkichi and Kurano Kenji, NKBT 1, *Kojiki* (Tokyo: Iwanami shoten, 1958); and a digital version from the Japanese Historical Text Initiative, University of California, Berkeley, http://sunsite.berkeley.edu/jhti/Kojiki.html. For a review of scholarship regarding the overall design and conceptualization of *Kojiki*, see Nishinomiya Kazutami, "Kojiki kenkyūshi: Shōwa gojūnen ikō," *Kojiki no kenkyūshi*, Kojiki kenkyū taikei 2: 313–16.

7. The following account of the main "plot" we find in ancient myth emphasizes *Kojiki*, a choice that requires explanation, because there are also good reasons why a researcher might give priority to *Nihon shoki*. Over the course of Japanese history, *Nihon shoki* has been regarded as more authoritative, especially in its historical sections. It has been the touchstone for the creation of much medieval ritual and thought concerning the Kami. As later chapters will show, *Nihon shoki* remained significant at court and was a foundational element of intellectual life. Yet its multiple versions make it unwieldy in the context of a treatment addressed to both general and specialist readers. Moreover, in modern and contemporary Shinto and Shinto scholarship, *Kojiki* has displaced *Nihon shoki*. This study seeks to present the past in a way that illuminates the present, even granting that this approach is open to criticism as presentist.
8. NKBT 1 *Kojiki*, 50–51. For a review of current trends in analysis of this sequence, see Nishinomiya, "Kojiki kenkyūshi: Shōwa gojūnen ikō," 317–20.
9. For a historical study of research on *Kojiki*, see Kojiki Gakkai, n. 3. A timeline encompassing only the most important works consumes sixty pages of this volume; Oikawa Chihaya, Taniguchi Masahiro, and Watanabe Masato, "Kojiki kenkyūshi nenpyō," in *Kojiki no kenkyūshi*, ed. Kojiki Gakkai (Tokyo: Takashina shoten, 1999), 339–409.
10. See W. G. Aston, trans., *Nihongi: Chronicles of Japan from the Earliest Times to A.D. 697* (Rutland, VT: Tuttle Co., 1972).
11. Quoted in Michael J. Puett, *To Become a God: Cosmology, Sacrifice, and Self-Divinization in Early China* (Cambridge, MA: Harvard University Press, 2002), 145.
12. Ibid., 1.
13. Ibid., 3.
14. NKBT 1 *Kojiki*, 52–67. Research on this sequence is extremely voluminous. For a classic study, see Mishina Akihide, *Kenkoku shinwaron, Mishina Akihide ronbunshū*, vol. 2 (Tokyo: Heibonsha, 1971).
15. Kōnoshi Takamitsu, "The Land of Yomi: On the Mythical World of the Kojiki," *JJRS* 11, no. 1 (1984): 57–76.
16. Research on Japanese myth from the perspective of gender studies remains scarce. See Saijō Tsutomu, "Sosō Amaterasu Ōkami no seisei," in *Josei to shūkyō*, ed. Sōgō Joseishi Kenkyūkai, Nihon joseishi ronshū 5 (Tokyo: Yoshikawa kōbunkan, 1998), 3–18; Allan G. Grapard, "Visions of Excess and Excess of Vision," Women and Transgression in Japanese Myth," *JJRS* 18, no. 1 (1991): 3–22.
17. NKBT 1 *Kojiki*, 68–91.
18. This obscure point of ancient divination was apparently confusing to the ancients as well. The *Nihon shoki* shows Susanoo's creations here as male deities and gives the fact that they were male as the reason he claimed victory (Aston, *Nihongi*, bk. 1, 40; NKBT 67 *Nihon shoki jō*, 104ff.
19. Some commentators believe that Amaterasu herself was injured or killed; Gary Ebersole (pers. corr., June 7, 2013). For example, see Yoshida Atsuhiko, *Girisha shinwa to Nihon shinwa: Hikaku shinwagaku no kokoromi* (Tokyo: Misuzu shobō, 1974), 37.
20. Gary Ebersole, *Ritual Poetry and the Politics of Death in Early Japan* (Princeton, NJ: Princeton University Press, 1989), chap. 2.
21. Yoshida Atsuhiko, n. 19, 37. Yoshida compares the cave myth to stories of Demeter, also identifying the figure of Baubo or Iambe as paralleling Ame no Uzume.
22. For a review of major studies of this myth, see Matsumura Takeo, *Nihon shinwa no kenkyū* (Tokyo: Baifūkan, 1955) vol. 3, 46–66.
23. NKBT 1 *Kojiki*, 91–111.

24. Philippi, *Kojiki*, chap. 19:10; NKBT 1 *Kojiki*, 87.
25. For detailed discussion of the origins of this myth, see Matsumura Takeo, n.22, vol. 3, chap. 10.
26. NKBT 1 *Kojiki*, 111–25. On the religious and political aspects of this sequence, see Matsumura Takeo, n.22, 3:485–98.
27. Philippi, *Kojiki*, chap. 37: 3; NKBT 1 *Kojiki*, 123.
28. NKBT 1 *Kojiki*, 125–31. It has become widely accepted that the Heavenly Descent myth reflects the enthronement rite Daijōsai (see chapter 3). See Tsuda Sōkichi, *Kojiki oyobi Nihon shoki no kenkyū* (Tokyo: Iwanami shoten, 1925).
29. Philippi, *Kojiki*, chap. 39:3; NKBT 1 *Kojiki*, 127.
30. Ame no Uzume later takes Sarutahiko's name, and her descendants are known as Sarume.
31. For the sake of brevity, I have omitted significant "subplots" of the tale, including the identity and failings of various messengers, as well as multiple versions of the way the last of these, Amewaka, was killed and his funeral conducted.
32. Matsumura Takeo, n.22, 3:510–17; Mishina Akihide, *Nissen shinwa densetsu no kenkyū, Mishina Akihide ronbunshū*, (Tokyo: Heibonsha, 1972), vol. 4, 240–46; Ōbayashi Tarō, *Higashi Ajia no ōken shinwa* (Tokyo: Kōbundō, 1984).
33. John Breen and Mark Teeuwen, *A New History of Shinto* (Malden, MA: Wiley-Blackwell, 2010), 30.
34. Takemikazuchi was born from the drops of blood falling from Izanagi's sword when he killed the fire deity.
35. *Kojiki*'s account of the negotiations with Ōkuninushi and his sons is considerably more complex than are the comparable *Nihon shoki* tales, in line with *Kojiki*'s greater emphasis on Izumo tales.
36. Philippi, *Kojiki*, 139n3.
37. *Kojiki*'s list of clan ancestors in this sequence parallels the list of those Kami responsible for enticing Amaterasu out of the Heavenly Rock Cave. By contrast, the *Nihon shoki* account includes four different versions, and Ame no Uzume is included only in one.
38. Philippi, *Kojiki* chap. 45: 6; NKBT 1 *Kojiki*, 145.
39. Ibid.
40. Hyman Kublin, *Japan: Selected Readings* (New York: Houghton Mifflin, 1968), 31–34. Available online at http://afe.easia.columbia.edu/japan/japanworkbook/traditional/shotoku.htm. Accessed June 4, 2012.
41. Three instances of 私 occur in *Nihon shoki*; only one appears in *Kojiki*. Mizubayashi Takeshi, "Waga kuni ni okeru kōshi kannen no rekishiteki tenkai," in *Nihonshi ni okeru kō to shi*, Rekishi to hōhō hensan iinkai, ed. (Tokyo: Aoki shoten, 1996), 110.
42. A useful summary of these debates may be found in Tanaka Sadaaki, "Kōshi no engen: Kiki no naka no kō to shi," *Rekishi hyōron* tsūgō 596 (December 1999): 2–16.
43. Ibid.
44. Yoshie Akiko, *Nihon kodai joseishi ron* (Tokyo: Yoshikawa kōbunkan, 2007), 217–18, 245–46, 254–56.
45. Philippi, *Kojiki*, chaps. 70–72; NKBT 1 *Kojiki*, 189–97.
46. The analysis presented here follows that in Tanaka Sadaaki, n. 42.
47. John R. Bentley, *The Authenticity of Sendai Kuji Hongi, A New Examination of Texts with a Translation and Commentary* (Leiden: Brill, 2006), 74–87, 163. Bentley advances the thesis that this work was a draft of *Nihon shoki*, but this provocative thesis has not yet received wide commentary and evaluation.
48. Ibid., 74.
49. Inbe Hironari, *Kogoshūi, Gleanings from Ancient Stories*, trans. Genchi Katō and Hikoshirō Hoshino (Tokyo: Meiji Japan Society, 1926).
50. Aoki Michiko, trans., *Izumo fudoki*, Monumenta Nipponica Monograph 44 (Tokyo: Sophia University Press, 1971).
51. Mark Funke, "Hitachi no Kuni Fudoki," *Monumenta Nipponica* 49, no. 1 (1994): 23.
52. Aoki, n. 50, 100.
53. Anders Carlqvist, "The Land-Pulling Myth and Some Aspects of Historical Reality," *JJRS* 37, no. 2 (2010): 185–222.

54. Matsumura Kazuo, "Kojiki," in *An Encyclopedia of Shinto*, ed. Norman Havens and Inoue Nobutaka, trans. Norman Havens, Institute for Japanese Culture and Classics (Tokyo: Kokugakuin University, 2001–6), http://eos.kokugakuin.ac.jp/modules/xwords/entry.php?entryID=1243. For extensive discussion of the stylistic differences between *Kojiki* and *Nihon shoki* in the context of the development of writing and literacy in ancient Japan, see David B. Lurie, *Realms of Literacy: Early Japan and the History of Writing* (Cambridge, MA: Harvard University Asia Center, 2011), chap. 5.
55. The six national histories chronicled the history of Japan until 887. They were *Nihon shoki*, covering the mythological period through 697 and completed in 720; *Shoku Nihongi*, covering 697 through 791 and completed in 797; *Nihon Kōki*, covering 792 through 833 and completed in 840; *Shoku Nihon Kōki*, covering 833 through 850 and completed in 869; *Nihon Montoku Tennō Jitsuroku*, covering 850 through 858 and completed in 879; and *Nihon Sandai Jitsuroku*, covering 858 through 887 and completed in 901.
56. See Mitani Eiichi, *Kojiki seiritsu no kenkyū* (Tokyo: Yūseidō, 1980), esp. pt. I, chap. 4.
57. Miura Sukeyuki, *Kojiki o yominaosu*, 53. According to Miura, tales of heroes killing multi-headed monsters are known throughout Eurasia. They are all tied to the origin of grain.
58. This name is one of several for the same Kami; others include Ashiharanoshikora, Yachihoko, and Utsushikunitama. It is likely that these names were attached to different territories that Ōkuninushi conquered.
59. Matsumura, n. 54.

Chapter 3

1. Okada Seishi, *Kodai ōken no saishi to shinwa* (Tokyo: Hanawa shobō, 1970), 139, 170–173.
2. Kase Naomi shows how Kami ranks were esteemed in ancient provincial shrines in "Kōwa go-nen kanshi ni miru Jingikan to chihō jinja to no kakawari," *Shintō kenkyū shūroku* 3 (2003): 35–49.
3. Okada Seishi, n. 1, 13–14.
4. Uno Yukio, "Kodai ni okeru seiji to shūkyō to no kankei: Jingikan no seiritsu o chūshin toshite," *Shichō* 45 (1952): 15–20.
5. In a limited sense, the rites of accession install a new emperor, but his transformation is not complete without the Daijōsai. Because Daijōsai is based on harvest ritual, it is invariably held in the eleventh month, on the lunar calendar. If the preceding emperor died and the new one acceded by the seventh month, the Daijōsai would be held in that year. But if those events occurred in the eighth month or later, the Daijōsai would not be held until the following year. In modern times, a mourning period of one year has also been added, moving enthronement to the second year after the previous emperor's death. *Nihon shoki* and other texts contain varying accounts of what items were presented to the new sovereign as his regalia. See Hashimoto Yoshihiko, *Nihon kodai no girei to tenseki* (Tokyo: Seishi shuppan, 1999), 6–12.
6. The rites of enthronement were first codified in the *Jōgan gishiki*, composed during the Jōgan era (859–876), believed to have consisted originally of ten volumes compiled beginning in late 872. For detailed discussion of this text and changes in the way the rites were performed, see Emura Hiroyuki, *Ritsuryō tennōsei saishi no kenkyū* (Tokyo: Kōshobō, 1996), 35–76; and Hashimoto Yoshihiko, n. 5, 1–30.
7. Emura, n. 6, 35–76; Hashimoto Yoshihiko, n. 5, 1–30.
8. Iwanaga Shōzō, "Daijōkyū idō ron," *Kyūshū Daigaku sōgō kenkyū hakubutsukan kenkyū hōkoku* 4 (2006): 99–132.
9. Emura, n. 6, 46.
10. Felicia Bock, trans. *Engi-Shiki: Procedures of the Engi Era, Books VI–X*, Monumenta Nipponica Monograph (Tokyo: Sophia University, 1972) 2: 92; quoted in Joan R. Piggott, *Emergence of Japanese Kingship* (Stanford, CA: Stanford University Press, 1997), 141.
11. Carmen Blacker, "The *Shinza* in the Daijōsai," *JJRS* 17, no. 2/3 (1990): 187.

12. Piggott, n. 10, 213–15.
13. W. G. Aston, trans. *Nihongi; Chronicles of Japan from the Earliest Times to A.D. 697*. With an introduction by Terence Barrow (Rutland, VT: C. E. Tuttle Co., 1972) 1:86.
14. Herman Ooms, *Imperial Politics and Symbolics in Ancient Japan: The Tenmu Dynasty, 650–800* (Honolulu: University of Hawai'i Press, 2009), 129.
15. Aston, n. 13, 2:321; Ooms, n. 14, 57–58, 107–11, 113.
16. Beginning episodically in 1288 and then consistently from 1382 to 1847, all emperors underwent the Buddhist *sokui kanjō* rite, making the sovereign a *cakravartin*. Ooms, n. 14, 130.
17. Emura, n. 6, 45–66.
18. See Gary Ebersole, *Ritual Poetry and the Politics of Death in Early Japan* (Princeton, NJ: Princeton University Press, 1989), 201–2, for discussion and analysis of the poem composed on Tenmu's death.
19. She was temporarily enshrined for around a year before the cremation. See Ebersole, n. 18, 201–2.
20. Nakazawa Nobuhiro, *Kyūchū saishi* (Tokyo: Dentensha, 2010), 98–100. Emperor Daigo had Buddhist rites at the eponymous temple Daigoji.
21. Her full name and title was Yamato no hime ohkimi; Aston, n. 13, bk 1, 176–77; NKBT 68, *Nihon shoki ge*, 367.
22. In principle, she would be the daughter or sister of the emperor, but in fact women of the court outside that category also served.
23. A similar appointment of an unmarried woman from the imperial court to serve as a priestess at the Kamo Shrine was also made from the ninth century, called the *saiin*. This practice ended in the thirteenth century.
24. For an overview of this system, see Furukawa Junichi, "Saigūryō ni kansuru kisoteki kōsatsu," in *Nihon ritsuryōsei ronshū*, ed. Sasayama Haruo Sensei kanreki kinenkai (Tokyo: Yoshikawa kōbunkan, 1993), 2:131–69; and Mayumi Tsunetada, "Saiō to uneme," *Shintōgaku* 98 (1978): 1–14.
25. Suzuki Yoshikazu, "Shikinen sengū," *SSDJ*, 449–450.
26. Okada Yoneo, "Jingū Shikinen sengū sei no sōshi," *Shintōshi kenkyū* 20 (1972): 2–7.
27. The rites listed in Table 3.1 are the main rituals, but in the modern period others have been added, allowing people living near the shrine and others who revere it to participate in the renewal.
28. Felicia Bock, trans. *Engi-Shiki: Procedures of the Engi Era, Books I–V*, Monumenta Nipponica Monograph (Tokyo: Sophia University, 1970), 1:133ff.
29. Ibid., 135–40.
30. "Tatari," *SJ*, 390; "Tatari," in *Nihonshi kōjien*, ed. Nihonshi kōjien henshū iinkai, (Tokyo: Yamakawa shuppansha, 1997), 1352. Other terms for *tatari* include *bachi* or *batsu*, *sawari*, and *togame*. In the Heian period the idea developed that human beings, the spirits of animals, and Buddhas, as well as Kami, can cause *tatari*. In the Heian period the idea that the spirits of human beings, living and dead, can cause *tatari*, led to the belief in *goryō* (see chapter 4).
31. This episode is discussed in Michael Como, *Weaving and Binding: Immigrant Gods and Female Immortals in Ancient Japan* (Honolulu: University of Hawai'i Press, 2009), 10–11.
32. Ooms discusses this episode in Ooms, n. 14, 165.
33. This incident is also discussed in Como, n. 31, 2–21.
34. Fujimori Kaoru, *Heian jidai no kyūtei saishi to Jingikan-jin*, 261–62.
35. Okada Shōji, *Heian jidai no kokka to saishi* (Tokyo: Zoku Gunsho Ruijū Kanseikai, 1994), 646–47, 676ff.
36. On Shōmu as a Buddhist monarch, see Piggott, n. 10, chap. 7.
37. Inoue Mitsusada, *Nihon kodai no kokka to bukkyō* (Tokyo: Iwanami shoten, 1971), 62–74; Richard Bowring, *The Religious Traditions of Japan, 500–1600* (Cambridge: Cambridge University Press, 2005), 78–85; Piggott, n. 10, 277.

38. *SJ*, 611.
39. Sugawara Ikuko, *Nihon kodai no minkan shūkyō* (Tokyo: Yoshikawa kōbunkan, 2003), 209–10.
40. Yamaori Tetsuo, ed. *Nihon shūkyōshi nenpyō*. (Tokyo: Kawade shobō shinsha, 2004), 45, 46, 47, 50.
41. Tsuji Zennosuke, *Nihon Bukkyōshi no kenkyū* (Tokyo: Kinkōdō shoseki, 1919), 1:58–67.
42. See, for example, Tamura Enchō, *Kodai Nihon no kokka to Bukkyō—Tōdaiji sōken no kenkyū* (Tokyo: Yoshikawa kōbunkan, 1999), pt. 1, chap. 2, sec. 2, "Hachiman Daijin to Bukkyō"; Wada Atsumu, *Nihon kodai no girei to saishi, shinkō* (Tokyo: Hanawa shobō, 1995), chap. 4, sec. 5, "Daibutsu zōryū to shinbutsu shūgō"; Nakai Shinkō, *Gyōki to kodai Bukkyō* (Tokyo: Nagata bunshōdō, 1991).
43. Ross Bender, "The Hachiman Cult and the Dōkyō Incident," *Monumenta Nipponica* 34, no. 2 (1979): 152.
44. Sugawara, n. 39, 212.
45. Bender, n. 43, 151.
46. Abe Ryūichi, *The Weaving of Mantra: Kūkai and the Construction of Esoteric Buddhist Discourse* (New York: Columbia University Press, 1999), 349–55.
47. Brian Ruppert, *Jewel in the Ashes: Buddha Relics and Power in Early Medieval Japan* (Cambridge, MA: Harvard East Asian Monographs, 2000), chap. 4. For a discussion of the extant paintings and scrolls illustrating these rites, see Elizabeth Lillehoj, *Art and Palace Politics in Early Modern Japan, 1580s–1680s* (Leiden: Brill, 2004), 108–111.
48. Quoted in Mark Teeuwen and Fabio Rambelli, introduction to *Buddhas and Kami in Japan: Honji Suijaku as a Combinatory Paradigm*, ed. Mark Teeuwen and Fabio Rambelli (London: RoutledgeCurzon, 2003), 10.
49. Teeuwen and Rambelli, n. 48, 20–21.
50. On the Dōkyō incident, see Bender, n. 43. Dōkyō's attempt to establish a Buddhist cult at Ise is outlined in John Breen and Mark Teeuwen, *A New History of Shinto* (Malden, MA: Wiley-Blackwell, 2010), 40.
51. Mori Mizue, "Ancient and Classical Japan: The Dawn of Shinto," in *Shinto: A Short History*, ed. Inoue Nobutaka, with Itō Satoshi, Endō Jun, and Mori Mizue, trans. Mark Teeuwen and John Breen (London: RoutledgeCurzon, 1998), 55.
52. Ibid., 53–54.
53. Ibid., 54. For a detailed study of the Kasuga Shrine, see Allan G. Grapard, *The Protocol of the Gods: A Study of the Kasuga Cult in Japanese History* (Berkeley: University of California Press, 1992).
54. Mori Mizue, n. 51, 54.
55. Ibid., 56–57.
56. Ibid.
57. Yoshii Yoshiaki, *Jinja seido shi no kenkyū* (Tokyo: Yūzankaku, 1935), 181–84, 199–204, 223.
58. Gradually the order of *kokuzō* died out except at Izumo, where it still persists, but a dual structure can still be found in many shrines.
59. Mori Mizue, n. 51, 45–46.
60. Itō Satoshi, Endō Jun, Matsuo Kōichi, and Mori Mizue, eds. *Shintō*. Nihonshi kohyakka (Tokyo: Tōkyōdō shuppan, 2002), 41; Yamamoto Nobuyoshi, "Jinin no seiritsu," in *Kannushi to jinin no shakaishi* Jinja shiryō kenkyūkai sōsho dai isshū (Kyoto: Shibunkaku shuppan, 1998), 3–57.
61. Suzuki Yoshikazu, "Saishu," *SSDJ*, 413–14.
62. Itō, Endō, Matsuo, and Mori, n. 60, 42–48.
63. Probably the reference to Izumo should simply be understood as a statement that this Kami came from somewhere else. Most provincial gods were classed with "Izumo," but this was entirely a conceptual, rhetorical move, since most of them actually had nothing to do with that region; see Okada Seishi, *Kodai saishi no shiteki kenkyū* (Tokyo: Kōshobō, 1992), 19–21.

64. There is another city in Hiroshima called Fuchū, and it likewise was the capital of the former Bingo Province. Other towns of the same name are found in Yamanashi and Shizuoka Prefectures. There was also a Fuchū-ken, and a Fuchū-han (in Tsushima).
65. Provincial governors were appointed to serve in Musashi beginning in 703 and continuing to 887.
66. Fuchū shishi hensan iinkai, ed., *Fuchū shishi* (Fuchū: Fuchū City, 1974), 1:200, 212.
67. There are several shrines known as Rokusho, "six-place." There are regional differences in the deities enshrined, but they are usually *sōja* connected with a *kokufu*. Besides Musashi, there are examples from Sagami, Hitachi, and Mutsu. They may be called Rokushogū, Sōja rokusho, Rokusho Myōjin, Rokusho Gongen, or Rokusho Daijingū. Shrines bearing such names are also mentioned in *Heike Monogatari* and *Azuma Kagami*. See "Rokusho," in *SDJ*, 1456; and Ashizu Motohiko and Umeda Yoshihiko, eds., *Shintō jiten* (Osaka: Hori shoten, 1968), 603.
68. Mori Mizue, n. 51, 50–51.
69. For a brief overview, see Itō Satoshi, "The Kami Merge with Buddhism" in *Shinto: A Short History*, ed. Inoue Nobutaka, with Itō Satoshi, Endō Jun, and Mori Mizue, trans. Mark Teeuwen and John Breen (London: RoutledgeCurzon, 1998), 65–66.
70. *Setsuwa* collections are numerous. Some of the most important are these:
Nihon ryōiki, by the monk Kyōkai, compiled in the early ninth century; *Sanbō-e kotoba*, compiled by Minamoto Tamenori in 984; *Shasekishū* [Collection of sand and pebbles], compiled by the monk Mujū Ichien in the mid- to late thirteenth century; *Konjaku monogatari*, compiler unknown, ca. 1120; and *Uji shūi monogatari*, compiler unknown, early thirteenth century. Among the later works, the influence of the earlier ones, especially *Nihon ryōiki*, can frequently be seen. A later work in this genre is *Shintōshū*, composed around 1358 by the Agui school of Tendai sect preachers. Besides *setsuwa*, this work contains many tales of the origins and history of temples and shrines, with an emphasis on famous shrines, such as Kitano Tenjin, Suwa Myōjin, Kumano, and other shrines. See Douglas E. Mills, *A Collection of Tales from Uji: A Study and Translation of Uji shūi monogatari* (Cambridge: Cambridge University Press, 1970), 1–4.
71. Nakamura Kyōko Motomochi, trans., *Miraculous Stories from the Japanese Buddhist Tradition: The Nihon ryōiki of the Monk Kyōkai* (Cambridge, MA: Harvard University Press, 1973), 3–9.
72. Mills, n. 70, 6.
73. Nakamura Kyōko, n. 71, 141.
74. Ibid., 141–42.
75. Ibid., 253–55.

Chapter 4

1. The main difference between the two is that *on'ryō* are the vengeful spirits of a human being, usually someone who has died but may also be the spirit of a living person, while the *goryō* category may encompass the *on'ryō* idea but also include disease gods.
2. Okada Shōji, *Heian jidai no kokka to saishi* (Tokyo: Zoku gunsho ruijū kansei kai, 1994), 676–78, and the chart on 682–83.
3. Allan G. Grapard's pathbreaking work in *The Protocol of the Gods* elaborated the concept of "combinatory" phenomena as an alternative to the older concept of syncretism. See Allan G. Grapard, *The Protocol of the Gods: A Study of the Kasuga Cult in Japanese History* (Berkeley: University of California Press, 1992), 73–99, and 208–15, on combinatory processes in the case of the Kasuga Shrine.
4. Felicia Bock, trans., *Engi-Shiki, Procedures of the Engi Era, Books I-V*, Monumenta Nipponica Monograph (Tokyo: Sophia University, 1970), 13–14. This passage is also quoted in Richard Bowring, *The Religious Traditions of Japan, 1500–1600*. Cambridge: Cambridge University Press, 2005), 1:189.

5. Itō Satoshi, Endō Jun, Matsuo Kōichi, and Mori Mizue, eds. *Shintō,* Nihonshi kohyakka (Tokyo: Tōkyōdō shuppan, 2002), 28.
6. As of 1165, some 101 shrines were being taxed for this purpose. Around the same time we see the first evidence of a district within Kyoto that was designated "Jingikan town" (*Jingikan machi*), producing income for the agency. The existence of three fourteenth-century Jingikan fiefs (*shōen*) has been documented. See Imae Hiromichi, "Jingikan," *KSDJ*, Japan Knowledge.com, accessed March 3, 2012.
7. Okada Shōji, "The Development of State Ritual in Ancient Japan," *Acta Asiatica* 51 (1987): 40.
8. Mitsuhashi Tadashi, "Chūseiteki shinshoku seido no keisei," *Shintō koten kenkyū: Kaihō* 1 (Oct. 1979): 38–42, 74.
9. On the twenty-two shrines, see Allan Grapard, "Institution, Ritual, and Ideology: The Twenty-Two Shrine Temple Multiplexes of Heian Japan." *History of Religions* 27, no. 3 (1988): 246–69.
10. Itō Satoshi, "The Kami Merge with Buddhism," in *Shinto: A Short History*, ed. by Inoue Nobutaka, with Itō Satoshi, Endō Jun, Mori Mizue, translated and adapted by Mark Teeuwen and John Breen (London: RoutledgeCurzon, 1998), 64–65.
11. Allan G. Grapard, "Religious Practices," in *The Cambridge History of Japan*, vol. 2: *Heian Japan*, ed. Donald H. Shively and William H. McCullough, (Cambridge: Cambridge University Press, 1999), 2:533, 550.
12. Bock, n. 4, 83.
13. Ibid., 88.
14. David Bialock, *Eccentric Spaces, Hidden Histories: Narrative, Ritual, and Royal Authority from the Chronicles of Japan to the Tale of the Heike* (Stanford, CA: Stanford University Press, 2007), 99.
15. "Fusō" is a Chinese term for Japan.
16. "Yu-yen" is the place where the sun sets.
17. Felicia Bock, translator, *Engi-Shiki, Procedures of the Engi Era, Books VI–X,* Monumenta Nipponica Monograph (Tokyo: Sophia University, 1972), 88–89.
18. Ibid.
19. Herman Ooms makes a similar point but with a different emphasis, asserting that "the Tenmu dynasty, unstable from its beginning, resorted to a number of legitimizing strategies." See Herman Ooms, *Imperial Politics and Symbolics in Ancient Japan: The Tenmu Dynasty, 650–800* (Honolulu: University of Hawai'i Press, 2009), 3.
20. Nishimuta Takao, *Norito gaisetsu* (Tokyo: Kokusho kankōkai, 1987), 4–5.
21. Mitsuhashi Tadashi, *Nihon kodai jingi seido no seisei to tenkai* (Kyoto: Hōzōkan, 2010), 209.
22. *Ayamachi okashikemu* is equivalent to modern *ayamattari okashitari. Ayamu* is to incur offense by inadvertence, while *okasu* is to commit a crime, or incur defilement by deliberate acts.
23. In this passage, the title "Sume-mima-no-mikoto" refers to the Heavenly Grandson, i.e., Ninigi.
24. *Amatsu norito no futo noritogoto*, lit., "the potent words for casting the spell of the heavenly formula."
25. From Bock, n. 17, 85–87.
26. Inoue Mitsusada, "Kodai ni okeru tsumi to seisai," *Nihon rekishi* 190 (1964): 2–18; Harashima Reiji, "Amatsutsumi, kunitsutsumi to sono shakai haikei," *Rekishigaku kenkyū* 290 (1964): 1–12; Umeda Yoshihiko, "Amatsustumi to kunitsutsumi: tsumi to kegare," *Shintōgaku* 65 (1970): 1–9.
27. Mitsuhashi Tadashi, n. 21, 212ff; Aston, *Nihongi*, bk. 2, 378; NKBT 68 *Nihon shoki ge*, 478.
28. This incident is discussed in Shinkawa Tokio, "Nihon kodai ni okeru Bukkyō to Dōkyō," in *Kodai bunka no tenkai to Dōkyō*, Senshū: Dōkyō to Nihon, ed. Noguchi Tetsurō and Nakamura Shōhachi (Tokyo: Yūzankaku, 1997), 3:51–83; and Shinkawa Tokio, *Dōkyō o meguru kōbō: Nihon no kunnō dōshi no hō o agamezu* (Tokyo: Taishūkan shoten, 1999).
29. Mitsuhashi Tadashi, n. 21, 3:224–26.
30. See Miyake Kazuo, *Kodai kokka no jingi to saishi* (Tokyo: Yoshikawa Kōbunkan, 1995), 197–205, for a table setting out 214 documented instances of performance of the rite.

31. Mitsuhashi Tadashi, *Heian jidai no shinkō to shūkyō girei* (Tokyo: Zoku Gunsho Ruijū Kanseikai, 2000), 233–42.
32. Grapard, n. 11, 2:529, 530, 534, 538.
33. Mitsuhashi Tadashi, n. 32, 245–51. See also Mitsuhashi Tadashi, n. 21, 247. On Kiyomori's use of the Great Purification Rite, see Okada Shōji, n. 2, 665–69. The idea that more recitations were more effective is similar to the idea that more recitations of various religious spells, such as *darani* and *nenbutsu*, had intensified effect.
34. Mitsuhashi Tadashi, n. 32, 48–59.
35. Nakano Hatano, "Iwashimizu Hachimangū," *SSDJ*, 96. The shrine's name is not found in the *Engi shiki*, perhaps because it was clear from the outset that the temple and shrine were inseparably linked. For extensive discussion of the ritual protocols used to "invite" a Kami to a new shrine, see Uejima Susumu, *Nihon chūsei shakai no keisei to ōken* (Nagoya: Nagoya Daigaku shuppankai, 2010), 109–11, 113–14, 390–92, 397–403.
36. The distinction between *jingūji* and *miyadera* often seems blurred and incomplete, even in recent reference works. Compare the descriptions in these two articles: Satō Mahito, "Jingūji," *SJ*, 108–9 and Murayama Shūichi, "Jingūji," *SSDJ*, 507–8.
37. Nakano Hatano, n. 36.
38. Murayama Shūichi and Toda Iwao, "Kamo Jinja," *SSDJ*, 237.
39. Ibid. In the Kamakura period, the family fissured into different branches. It died out in the sixteenth century, and its skills were taken up by the Tsuchimikado family.
40. Okada Shōji, "Miare no shinjin," *SSDJ*, 906–7.
41. Okada Shōji, n. 2, 95–99, 142–45.
42. Helen Craig McCullough, *Ōkagami, The Great Mirror: Fujiwara Michinaga (966–1027) and His Times; A Study and Translation* (Princeton, NJ: Princeton University Press, 1980), 191.
43. This discussion of imperial processions to shrines is based on Okada Shōji, n. 2, 362–68.
44. Mitsuhashi Tadashi, n. 32, 47–64.
45. Ibid., 70–98.
46. Mitsuhashi Tadashi, n. 8, 32–38.
47. Sagai Tatsuru, "Kamo-sha no norito to kaeshi norito," in *Kannushi to jinin no shakaishi*, ed. Hashimoto Masanobu and Yamamoto Nobuyoshi (Kyoto: Shibunkaku shuppan, 1998), 62.
48. The account that follows is adapted from "Shishi no tani," in Helen Craig McCullough, trans., *The Tale of the Heike* (Stanford, CA: Stanford University Press, 1988), 45–47.
49. New Major Counselor Narichika, third son of the late Naka no Mikado Middle Counselor Ienari.
50. Greater Prajñāparamita Sutra, Greater Perfection of Wisdom Sutra (also called Śatasāhasrikā Prajñāpāramitā Sūtra; J: *Dai-hannya kyō* 大般若経 or *Maka hannya haramitsu kyō* 摩訶般若波羅蜜経). This is the longest of the Perfection of Wisdom genre of sutras. *Prajñā* is "wisdom", and *pāramitā* is "perfection." The idea of the perfection of wisdom is a basic concept of Mahayana Buddhism. Practice of the perfection of wisdom is an essential element of the bodhisattva path. The concept and practice are described in the Perfection of Wisdom sutras, which are classified by their length. This is the longest, at 100,000 lines. *Prajñā* is wisdom based on the direct realization of such things as the four noble truths, impermanence, interdependent origination, non-self and emptiness. *Prajñā* is able to extinguish afflictions and bring about enlightenment.
51. Dakini Shinten, a female *yaksa* (J: *yasha*), a type of Indian deity believed to live in forests. On the one hand, Dakini Shinten are demonic spirits with power to harm humans; on the other, they were worshipped as gods of wealth. Rites for Dakini Shinten were believed to confer unlimited power. Dakini Shinten was believed to have the form of a fox and was equated with Inari Daimyōjin and Izuna Gongen.
52. The discussion of Sugawara Michizane is drawn from Robert Borgen, *Sugawara no Michizane and the Early Heian Court* (Honolulu: University of Hawai'i Press, 1994), 307–36.

53. Tokihira had his sister Yasuko marry the young Emperor Daigo; they had a son in 903, who was named crown prince, making Tokihira potentially an uncle of an emperor.
54. Neil McMullin, "On Placating the Gods and Pacifying the Populace: The Case of the Gion 'Goryō' Cult," *History of Religions* 27, no. 3 (1988): 270–93.
55. Moriya Takashi, "Toshi sairei to furyū: Sono rekishiteki henbō," in *Toshi to inaka: Machi no seikatsu bunka*, Nihon minzoku bunka taikei (Tokyo: Shōgakkan, 1985), 11:387–458.
56. Ibid., 11:400–401.
57. Mitsuhashi Tadashi, n. 32, 105–11.
58. Ibid., 120–131ff.
59. Ibid., 124–39. Regarding the practice of sutra recitation before the altars of the Kami, seen both in Munetada's and Teika's diaries, see Uejima Susumu, n. 35, 253–54; and Murayama Shūichi, "Shinzen dokkyō," in *Nihon bukkyōshi jiten*, Imaizumi Yoshio, ed. (Tokyo: Yoshikawa kōbunkan, 2005), 551. Known from the early eighth century, this practice spread widely and was adopted for many different Kami, not just the ones mentioned in these diaries. The Heart Sutra or variants of it were among the most frequently chosen texts. See Takafuji Harutoshi, "Shinzen dokkyō no ichi kōsatsu," *Shintōgaku* 94 (August 1977): 32–53, for a study of this practice from the standpoint of a Shinto historian.
60. Mitsuhashi Tadashi, n. 8, 74–75.
61. Jacob Raz, "Popular Entertainment and Politics: The Great Dengaku of 1096," *Monumenta Nipponica* 40, no. 3 (1985): 283–98.
62. Ibid., 289.
63. Adapted from ibid., 297–98.
64. For a general overview of *shōen*, see Kuroda Hideo, "Shōen," *Kokushi daijiten*, Japan Knowledge, June 24, 2015, http:Japanknowledge.com. See also Mikael Adolphson and Mark Ramseyer, "The Competitive Enforcement of Property Rights in Medieval Japan: The Role of Temples and Monasteries," *Journal of Economic Behavior and Organization* 71, no. 3 (2009): 660–68; Kuroda Toshio, *Jisha seiryoku* (Tokyo: Iwanami shinsho 117, 1980).
65. Yoshii Yoshiaki, *Jinja seido shi no kenkyū* (Tokyo: Yūzankaku, 1935), 181–84, 199–204, 223.
66. Yamamoto Nobuyoshi, "Jinin no seiritsu," in *Kannushi to jinin no shakaishi*, ed. Hashimoto Masanobu and Yamamoto Nobuyoshi (Kyoto: Shibunkaku shuppan, 1998), 6–7. We note that five out of the ten recorded incidents involved priests of the Ise Shrines. Of these, two were protests against the provincial governor. The cause of one (the incident in 1017) is obscure. In one, the priests united with the peasantry against new regulations, and one was an internal dispute between the priests and the peasants, on the one hand, against the Saishu, on the other.
67. Yamamoto Nobuyoshi, n. 67, 7–8.
68. Mark Teeuwen, "The Creation of a *Honji-Suijaku* Deity: Amaterasu as the Judge of the Dead," in *Buddhas and Kami in Japan: Honji Suijaku as a Combinatory Paradigm*, ed. Mark Teeuwen and Fabio Rambelli (London: RoutledgeCurzon, 2003), 127, 133–34. Teeuwen acknowledges relying for this material on Hayami Tasuku, *Heian kizoku shakai to bukkyō* (Tokyo: Yoshikawa Kōbunkan, 1975), 117–18; 120, 126.
69. Itō et al., n. 5, 28–29.
70. Kase Naomi, "Kōwa go-nen kanshi ni miru Jingikan to chihō jinja to no kakawari," *Shintō kenkyū shūroku* 3 (2003): 35–49.
71. Allan G. Grapard provides a concise history of the Hiei Shrines in "Linguistic Cubism: A Singularity of Pluralism in the Sannō Cult," *JJRS* 14, no. 2/3 (1987), 212–15. See also Kageyama Haruki and Murayama Shūichi, *Hieizan—sono shūkyō to rekishi* (Tokyo: NHK Books, 1970).
72. Itō Satoshi identifies the origin of this proliferation of deities in an ancient distinction between the Kami who are associated with rulership and others outside that group. Evil Kami existed outside the *honji-suijaku* framework and included evil spirits, ghosts, wandering spirits of the living and dead, and evil deities appearing in the form of poisonous snakes or ferocious beasts. See Itō Satoshi, "Shinbutsu shūgō riron no hen'yō," *Shūkyō kenkyū* 81, no. 2 (2007): 385.

73. Mark Teeuwen, n. 69, 127, 133–34. Teeuwen acknowledges relying on Hayami Tasuku, *Heian kizoku shakai to bukkyō*, 234–61.
74. This text was the *Sandai jitsuroku*. The idea of *honji-suijaku* had first emerged in Buddhist doctrinal discussion of the Lotus Sutra, in which its twenty-eight chapters were divided into two groups. The first fourteen chapters were described as the "trace gate" (*jakumon*), while the latter fourteen chapters were described as the "original gate" (*honmon*). The distinction sought to clarify the relation between the human, phenomenal Buddha Shakyamuni, on the one hand, and the original, cosmic, eternal Buddha Kuon Jitsujō, on the other. In India the distinction was also used to structure the understanding of the relation between Buddhist figures and Indian deities appropriated as protectors of Buddhism. Likewise, in China, the paradigm was used with respect to Buddhism's relation to Daoist figures.
75. Mark Teeuwen and Fabio Rambelli, "Introduction: Combinatory Religion and the Honji-Suijaku Paradigm in Pre-Modern Japan," in *Buddhas and Kami in Japan: Honji Suijaku as a Combinatory Paradigm*, ed. Mark Teeuwen and Fabio Rambelli (London: RoutledgeCurzon, 2003).
76. Itō Satoshi, n. 73, 385.
77. Teeuwen, Mark, "From Jindō to Shintō: A Concept Takes Shape," *JJRS* 29, no. 3/4 (2002): 248–51.
78. Ibid.
79. *Oxford English Dictionary*, s. v. "syncretism." (http://www.oed.com)
80. Fritz Graf, "Syncretism, Further Considerations," *Encyclopedia of Religion*, 2nd ed. (Detroit: Macmillan Reference USA, 2005), 13:8934–38.
81. Grapard, n. 11, 2:267–68.

Chapter 5

1. For a useful summary of these changes, see Satō Hirō, "Chūsei ni okeru kami kannen no hen'yō," in *Chūsei shinwa to jinji, Shintō sekai*, ed. Itō Satoshi (Tokyo: Chikurinsha, 2011), 10–32.
2. Abe Yasurō, "Shintō as Written Representation: The Phases and Shifts of Medieval Shintō Texts," *Cahiers d'Extrême-Asie* 16 (2006–7): 105.
3. See, for example, Kuroda Toshio, "The Discourse on the 'Land of the Kami' (*Shinkoku*) in Medieval Japan," *JJRS* 23, no. 3/4 (1996): 353–85.
4. Fabio Rambelli, "Re-positioning the Gods: 'Medieval Shinto' and the Origins of Non-Buddhist Discourses on the Kami," *Cahiers d'Extrême-Asie* 16 (2006–7): 306.
5. Yamaori Tetsuo, ed., *Nihon shūkyōshi nenpyō* (Tokyo: Kawade shobō shinsha, 2004), 141.
6. Ibid., 196.
7. Ibid., 195–98.
8. Ibid., 199–204.
9. Ibid., 198–210.
10. One *koku* is equal to about five bushels.
11. Yamaori, n. 5, 204, 207.
12. Ibid., 217.
13. Itō Satoshi, Endō Jun, Matsuo Kōichi, and Mori Mizue, eds. *Shintō*, Nihonshi kohyakka (Tokyo: Tōkyōdō shuppan, 2002), 148–49.
14. Ibid., 149–50.
15. Ōsumi Kazuo, "Shaku nihongi," *SSDJ*, 469; Itō et al., n. 13, 151.
16. Itō Satoshi, "Ise no Shintōsetsu no tenkai ni okeru Saidaijiryū no dōkō ni tsuite," *Shintō shūkyō* 153 (Dec. 1993): 70–105; see also Itō et al., n. 13, 151.
17. Abe Yasurō, *Chūsei Nihon no shūkyō tekusuto taikei* (Nagoya: Nagoya Daigaku shuppankai, 2013), 233.
18. Satō Hirō, *Kishōmon no seishinshi: Chūsei sekai no kami to hotoke* (Tokyo: Kōdansha, 2006), 65–73.
19. Ibid., 73.

20. Yamaori, n. 5, 202.
21. A common remedy used to treat a variety of illnesses in East Asia, moxibustion involves burning a small cone of incense on the skin.
22. Quoted in Satō Hirō, n. 18, 234.
23. I would like to thank Fabio Rambelli for helpful comments on an earlier draft of this discussion (pers. corr., June 13, 2013).
24. Satō Hirō, n. 18, 31. Another assessment of the deities seen in Satō's table of the deities invoked in oaths is seen in these comments by Fabio Rambelli:

    [H]ere we are dealing with different sets of deities: in the *Goseibai shikimoku* we find a hierarchical line, from the supreme Buddhist deity Brahma (Bonten), the head of the gods Indra (Taishakuten), the generals of the four directions (*shitennō*), down to the Japanese kami as avatars. In Shōson's vow, there are two hierarchies superimposed: one with Tenshō Daijin at the top and the kami underneath her; the other with the Daibutsu, the four heavenly kings on a cosmic level, Hachiman and the other light-dimming kami all over Japan, and the Nigatsudō Kannon in particular (very local). Conceptually and structurally, though, I don't see major differences between these two sets. (pers. corr., June 13, 2013).

25. Satō Hirō, n. 18, 32.
26. Chijiwa Itaru has made a comprehensive study of vows, collecting and categorizing a huge number of them. He disputes Satō's assertion of a hierarchy of deities, noting that such an impression arises only if one restricts the purview to a single type of vow. Based on a more wide-ranging survey of these documents, Chijiwa shows that the lists of divinities seen in vows reveals a striking local specificity, in which those prominent shrines, temples, and sculptures known to the writer, as well as the writer's *ujigami*, are the ones from which the writer typically anticipates punishment if he should break the vow. See Chijiwa Itaru, "Chūsei no kishōmon ni miru shinbutsu: Kishōmon jinmon kara zenkindai no hitobito no kami kannen o saguru kokoromi-1," *Nihon bunka to Shintō* 2 (2006): 135–55.
27. Mitsuhashi Tadashi, *Nihon kodai jingi seido no seisei to tenkai* (Kyoto: Hōzōkan, 2010), 251–53; "Nakatomi no harae kunge," *SJ*, 585.
28. Commenting on Ryōbu Shinto and texts from the Watarai lineage, Fabio Rambelli notes that the two are closely related, and that from one perspective the distinction between them is artificial:

    Since at least the Edo period, the cosmogonic texts generated within this environment have been divided into two different groups on the basis of the form of Shinto they allegedly represent, namely, Ryōbu Shinto on the one hand and Ise Shinto or Watarai Shinto on the other. In brief, "Ryōbu Shinto" refers to the discourses concerning the kami, primarily centered on the gods worshipped at the Ise shrines, developed in medieval and early modern Japan by Buddhist authors under a strong influence from esoteric Buddhism; "Ise Shinto," by contrast, refers to the discourses about the kami produced mainly by authors related to the Outer Shrine (Gekū) of Ise and its priestly family, the Watarai. Recent scholarship has questioned the validity of such a distinction for a number of reasons, including the fact that, especially in the medieval period, these two discourses were not clearly differentiated and authors often borrowed freely from texts belonging to both; Buddhist authors writing on Ise seem to have had access to Ise texts, and Watarai authors had a fairly good knowledge of Buddhist doctrines. Further, until the Edo period, if not later, people seem not to have shared a sense that Ise Shinto constituted the fountainhead of Shinto as a whole. (Fabio Rambelli "Before the First Buddha," *Monumenta Nipponica* 64, no. 2 [2009], 237–38.)

29. "Nakatomi no harae kunge," n. 27, 585.
30. Mark Teeuwen and Hendrik van der Veere, trans., *Nakatomi Harae Kunge: Purification and Enlightenment in Late-Heian Japan*, Buddhismus-Studien 1 (Munchen: Iudicium, 1998), 1–18.
31. Ibid., 55–91.

32. Uejima Susumu, *Nihon chūsei shakai no keisei to ōken* (Nagoya: Nagoya Daigaku shuppankai, 2010), 121–22.
33. Yamaori, *Nihon shūkyōshi nenpyō,* 199, 243. Chōgen's pilgrimage account was titled *Tōdaiji shuto sankei Ise Daijingūji-ki* (Record of a Tōdaiji pilgrim's pilgrimage to the Daijingūji of Ise). This work was followed by others, such as Tsūkai's *Daijingū sankeiki* [Record of a pilgrimage to the Ise Shrines] (1286). See also "Nakatomi no harae kunge," n. 27, 585; Itō Satoshi, "The Medieval Cult of Gyōki and Ise Shrines: Concerning the Narratives of Gyōki's Pilgrimage to Ise," *Cahiers d'Extrême-Asie* 16 (2006-2007): 49–70.
34. Uejima Susumu, n. 32, 127–28.
35. Yamaori, n. 5., 203. The tax was called *yakubukumai.*
36. Ibid., 215–16.
37. Ibid., 197.
38. For extensive treatment of the *Yaketsu,* see Abe Yasurō, n. 2, 99–110; and Abe Yasurō, n. 17, 436–44.
39. Abe Yasurō, n. 2, 99–110; Abe Yasurō, n. 17, 436–44.
40. Abe Yasurō, n. 2, 107–9; Abe Yasurō, n. 17, 444–49.
41. In this connection it should be mentioned that it was as recently as 2013 that the first comprehensive study of medieval Japanese religious texts, including *jingi* texts, was published by Abe Yasurō. See Abe Yasurō, n. 17.
42. Fabio Rambelli, "The Ritual World of Buddhist 'Shinto': The *Reikiki* and Initiations of Kami-Related Matters (*jingi kanjō*) in Late Medieval and Early-Modern Japan," *JJRS* 29, no. 3/4 (2002): 265–70.
43. Ibid., 270–73.
44. Uejima Susumu, n. 32, 79; Mark Teeuwen, "The Creation of a *Honji-Suijaku* Deity: Amaterasu as the Judge of the Dead," in *Buddhas and Kami in Japan: Honji Suijaku as a Combinatory Paradigm,* ed. Mark Teeuwen and Fabio Rambelli (London: RoutledgeCurzon, 2003),115–16; Satō Hirō, *Kishōmon no seishinshi,* 30–31.
45. Teeuwen, n. 44, 144.
46. Ibid., 144, n. 69.
47. Kuroda Toshio, n. 3, 371–73.
48. Satō Hirō, "*Shinbutsu Shūgō* and *Jingi Fuhai,*" 21coe.kokugakuin.ac.jp/articlesintranslation/pdf/07sato-en.pdf; originally published as "Shinbutsu shūgō to jingi fuhai," *2004 nendo Nihonshi kenkyūkai taikai tokushūgō* (March 2005): 22–40; Kuroda Toshio, n. 3, 359, 375–77.
49. Yamaori, n. 5, 238.
50. Ibid., 239.
51. Ibid., 243.
52. H. Paul Varley, trans., *A Chronicle of Gods and Sovereigns: Jinnō Shōtōki of Kitabatake Chikafusa* (New York: Columbia University Press, 1980), 49.
53. John S. Brownlee, review of H. Paul Varley, trans., *A Chronicle of Gods and Sovereigns: Jinnō Shōtōki of Kitabatake Chikafusa, Monumenta Nipponica* 36, no. 2, (1981): 207–8.
54. Michelle Marra, "The Conquest of Mappō: Jien and Kitabatake Chikafusa," *JJRS* 12, no. 4 (1985): 319–41. Chikafusa had to rebut the arguments of Jien, author of the historical work *Gukanshō,* who had argued that the regalia in use by medieval emperors were actually copies of the originals, which had been lost over the centuries in various wars, fires, and calamities. From a different perspective, we can see in these arguments about the regalia that the symbolic and conceptual significance of the emperor could be considered separately from the facts concerning any particular individual. Uejima Susumu, n. 32, 81.
55. Thomas D. Conlan, *From Sovereign to Symbol: An Age of Ritual Determinism in Fourteenth-Century Japan* (Oxford: Oxford University Press, 2011), 74–75.
56. Ibid., 9, 60, 79–82.
57. Ibid., 52–53, 64–65.
58. H. Paul Varley, n. 52, 59–60.
59. Conlan, n. 55, 62.

60. Mark Teeuwen, "Shintō Thought at the Ise Shrines," *Research Papers in Japanese Studies*, Cardiff Centre for Japanese Studies, No. 1 (1996), 28–29.
61. Kuroda Toshio, n. 3, 361.
62. Fabio Rambelli, "Before the First Buddha," *Monumenta Nipponica* 64, no. 2 (2009): 235.
63. Uejima Susumu, n. 5, 83–84, 95–97, 105.
64. Fabio Rambelli, n. 62, 235–62; quotations are on 238, 261–62.
65. See Haruko Wakabayashi, *The Seven Tengu Scrolls: Evil and the Rhetoric of Legitimacy in Medieval Japanese Buddhism* (Honolulu: University of Hawai'i Press, 2012).
66. Miyake Hitoshi, *Shintō to Shugendō: Minzoku shūkyō shisō no tenkai* (Tokyo: Shunbunsha, 2007), 72–79. Keikōin (?–1566) is also the name of the nun most closely associated with this fundraising campaign.
67. Allan Grapard, *The Protocol of the Gods: A Study of the Kasuga Cult in Japanese History* (Berkeley: University of California Press, 1992), 103–14.
68. See Mikael Adolphson, "Institutional Diversity and Religious Integration: The Establishment of Temple Networks in the Heian Age," in *Heian Japan, Centers and Peripheries*, ed. Mikael S. Adolphson, Edward Kamens, and Stacie Matsumoto (Honolulu: University of Hawai'i Press, 2007), 212–45.
69. Allan Grapard, "Medieval Shintō Boundaries: Real or Imaginary?" *Cahiers d'Extrême-Asie* 16 (2006–7): 8–9; Grapard, n. 67, 115.
70. Uno Hideo, "Rakuchū Hie jinin no sonzai keitai," in *Kannushi to jinin no shakaishi*, ed. Hashimoto Masanobu and Yamamoto Nobuyoshi (Kyoto: Shibunkaku shuppan, 1998), 125.
71. Kitai Toshio, "Iwashimizu Hachimangū jinin no keizai katsudō: mibun to shogyō," in ibid., 150–61.

Chapter 6

1. For a comprehensive study of rear and underground chambers, see Kuroda Ryūji, *Chūsei jisha shinkō no ba* (Tokyo: Shibunkaku shuppan, 1999). Regarding Taima-dera as the earliest example, see Suzuki Masataka, *Kami to hotoke no minzokugaku* (Tokyo: Yoshikawa Kōbunkan, 2001), 204–6.
2. Suzuki Masataka, n. 1, 208–9.
3. Ibid., 212ff.
4. Ibid., 222.
5. Kuroda Ryūji, *Chūsei jisha shinkō no ba*, 184–98; see also Suzuki Masataka, *Kami to hotoke no minzokugaku*, 216–17.
6. Suzuki Masataka, *Kami to hotoke no minzokugaku*, 217–18; Kuroda Ryūji, "Hie shichi sha honden no kōsei," *Nihon kenchiku gakkai ronbun hōkokusho* 317 (1982): 148–54.
7. For a comprehensive study of medieval "foreign gods," see Yamamoto Hiroko, *Ijin*, 2 vols. (Tokyo: Chikuma shobō, 2003).
8. Suzuki Masataka, *Kami to hotoke no minzokugaku*, 202–46. See also Kuroda, "Hie shichi sha honden no kōsei," 148–54.
9. Yamamoto Hiroko, *Chūsei Shintō* (Tokyo: Iwanami shinsho, 1998), 86–90.
10. Ibid., 101–9.
11. Ibid., 110.
12. "Matarajin" *SSDJ*, 894. While the deity seems to have originated in China, however, there are virtually no documents concerning Matarajin that predate the deity's arrival in Japan. See Suzuki Masataka, *Kami to hotoke no minzokugaku*, 264–65.
13. Suzuki Masataka, *Kami to hotoke no minzokugaku*, 264–67.
14. For comprehensive studies of Matarajin, see Suzuki Masataka, *Kami to hotoke no minzokugaku*, 263–337; Yamamoto Hiroko, *Ijin* (Tokyo: Chikuma shobō, 2003), 1:156–397; and William Bodiford, "Matara: A Dream King between Insight and Imagination," *Cahiers d'Extrême-Asie* 16 (2006–7): 233–62.

15. These rites were called *Jōgyōdō shushō-e*.
16. Suzuki Masataka, n. 1, 270–73.
17. Ibid., 324–25.
18. Fabio Rambelli, "Re-positioning the Gods: 'Medieval Shinto' and the Origins of Non-Buddhist Discourses on the Kami," *Cahiers d'Extrême-Asie* 16 (2006/7): 316.
19. Mitsuhashi Takeshi, *Nihonjin to fuku no kami: Shichifukujin to kōfukuron* (Tokyo: Maruzen, 2002); Tsuboi Naofusa, "Shichifukujin," *SSDJ*, 458–59.
20. Matsuo Kōichi, "Chūsei, Kasuga-sha jinin no geinō," in *Kannushi to jinin no shakaishi*, ed. by Hashimoto Masanobu and Yamamoto Nobuyoshi (Kyoto: Shibunkaku shuppan, 1998), 87–95.
21. Ibid., 101–5.
22. At the end of the medieval period, groups of *jinin* and *miko* began to travel to perform their music and dance. They formed associations with other popular entertainers of the period and in the Edo period influenced the formation of *kabuki* theater.
23. Nagasaka Ichirō, "Chōkoku ni arawasareta Kami no katachi," *Kami no sugata o arawasu*, Bukkyō bijutsu kenkyū Ueno kinen zaidan josei kenkyūkai hōkokusho 32 (2005): 1–4. See also Christine Guth, *Shinzo: Hachiman Imagery and Its Development* (Cambridge, MA: Council on East Asian Studies, Harvard University, 1985); and Kageyama Haruki, *The Arts of Shinto*, trans. Christine Guth (New York: Weatherhill, 1973), 15–22; Kageyama Haruki, *Shintō bijutsu* (Tokyo: Yūzankaku, 1973).
24. Kadoya Atsushi, "On the Formation of Shinto Icons," *Cahiers d'Extrême-Asie* 16 (2006/7): 156.
25. Yamaori Tetsuo, ed. *Nihon shūkyōshi nenpyō* (Tokyo: Kawade shobō shinsha, 2004), 228, 234.
26. See Kadoya Atsushi, "On the Formation of Shinto Icons," 158, for a concise typology of shrine mandala, according to the arrangement of deities within the painting.
27. Meri Arichi, "Sannō Miya Mandara: The Iconography of Pure Land on This Earth," *JJRS* 33, no. 2 (2006): 323.
28. Susan Tyler, "Honji Suijaku Faith," *JJRS* 16, no. 2/3 (1989): 229.
29. Arichi, "Sannō Miya Mandara," 322.
30. Allan Grapard, *The Protocol of the Gods: A Study of the Kasuga Cult in Japanese History* (Berkeley: University of California Press, 1992), 91.
31. See Royall Tyler, *The Miracles of the Kasuga Deity* (New York: Columbia University Press, 1990), 111–26.
32. Susan Tyler, "Honji Suijaku Faith," 229.
33. Arichi, "Sannō Miya Mandara," 325.
34. Grapard, n. 30, 212.
35. Ibid., 95–96.
36. Arichi, "Sannō Miya Mandara," 343.
37. The Saionji house was a collateral line of the Fujiwara house.
38. Tyler, n. 31, 13.
39. Ibid., 9, 58, 112–26.
40. Ibid., 9.
41. Ibid., 93–99.
42. The identity of this person is uncertain; see Royall Tyler, *Miracles of the Kasuga Deity*, 275n4.
43. Adapted from Royall Tyler, *Miracles of the Kasuga Deity*, 272–76.
44. Yamamoto Yōko, "Jinja engi emaki ni okeru kamigami no egakikata: ikanaru baai ni kami no sugata o arawasu koto o habakaru ka," in *Nihon bijutsu shūkō: Sasaki Kōzō Sensei koki kinen ronbunshū* (Tokyo: Meitoku shuppansha, 1998), 14–174.
45. Ibid., 157–58.
46. Ibid., 159–62.
47. Royall Tyler, *Miracles of the Kasuga Deity*, 18–20.
48. Kageyama Haruki, *Arts of Shinto*, 98–100.

49. Yamaori, *Nihon shūkyōshi nenpyō*, 243.
50. Robert E. Morrell, *Sand and Pebbles (Shasekishū): The Tales of Mujū Ichien, A Voice for Pluralism in Kamakura Buddhism* (Albany: State University of New York Press, 1985).
51. Ibid., 80–81.
52. Ibid., 73–74.
53. Sueki Fumihiko, *Chūsei no kami to hotoke*, Nihonshi rifuretto 32 (Tokyo: Yamakawa shuppansha, 2003), 38.
54. Robert E. Morrell, "Mujū Ichien's Shinto-Buddhist Syncretism: Shasekishū, Book I," *Monumenta Nipponica* 28, no. 4 (1973) : 463–64.
55. Ibid.
56. Yanase Kazuo, *Shaji engi no kenkyū* (Tokyo: Benseisha, 1998).
57. For a general survey of *engi* literature, see Sakurai Tokutarō, "Engi no ruikei to tenkai," in *Jisha engi*, Nihon shisō taikei 20 (Tokyo: Iwanami shoten, 1975), 445–78.
58. In other words, they did not ordinarily use the padded rice-straw *tatami* mats, living on a board floor most of the time (a mark of rustication) except when they were receiving guests.
59. "Kagami no Miya no koto," in *Shintōshū*, ed. Kishi Shōzō, Tōyō bunko 94 (Tokyo: Heibonsha, 1967), 155–58.
60. Yamaori, n. 25, 221.
61. Ibid., 241.
62. Ibid., 245.
63. Royall Tyler, *Miracles of the Kasuga Deity*, 147.
64. Adapted from Royall Tyler, *Miracles of the Kasuga Deity*, 148–51.

Chapter 7

1. Yamaori Tetsuo, ed., *Nihon shūkyōshi nenpyō* (Tokyo: Kawade shobō shinsha, 2004), 240.
2. Lee Butler, *Emperor and Aristocracy in Japan, 1467–1680: Resilience and Renewal*, Harvard East Asian Monographs 209 (Cambridge, MA: Harvard University Asia Center, 2002), 15, 32–38.
3. Ibid., 60–67, 141–44, 288.
4. Ibid., 23, 25, 46, 56–57, 78–81, 288.
5. Ibid., 60–7, 141–44, 288.
6. Allan Grapard, *The Protocol of the Gods: A Study of the Kasuga Cult in Japanese History* (Berkeley: University of California Press, 1992), 201–2.
7. Uejima Susumu, *Nihon chūsei shakai no keisei to ōken* (Nagoya: Nagoya Daigaku shuppankai, 2010), 300–301.
8. Yamaori, *Nihon shūkyōshi nenpyō*, 197–98; Butler, *Emperor and Aristocracy in Japan*, 288.
9. Yamaori, *Nihon shūkyōshi nenpyō*, 208, 224, 232.
10. Mark Teeuwen and Hendrik van der Veere, trans. *Nakatomi Harae Kunge: Purification and Enlightenment in Late-Heian Japan*. Buddhismus-Studien 1 (Munchen: Iudicium, 1998), 150, 163, 165. It was also during these years that the first records of pilgrimage fraternities emerged. Hagiwara's analysis shows that many "Shinmei" shrines dedicated to the Ise deities were established after the Ōnin War by warriors; Hagiwara Tatsuo, "Chūsei makki no jinja to kyōson kannushi-sō," in *Gendai Shintō kenkyū shūsei*, vol. 2, ed. Gendai Shintō kenkyū shūsei henshū iinkai (Tokyo: Jinja Honchō, Jinja Shinpōsha, 1998), 317–43.
11. Table: "Nihon shoki chūshakusho ichiran," *SSDJ*, 778–81.
12. Itō Satoshi, Endō Jun, Matsuo Kōichi, and Mori Mizue, eds. *Shintō*, Nihonshi kohyakka (Tokyo: Tōkyōdō shuppan, 2002), 152; Kamata Jun'ichi, *Shintō bunken* (Tokyo: Jinja shinpōsha, 1993), 255.
13. Itō et al., *Shintō*, 152.
14. Maeda Hiromi, "Imperial Authority and Local Shrines: The Yoshida House and the Creation of a Countrywide Shinto Institution in Early Modern Japan" (PhD diss., Harvard University, 2003), 26–29, 47–48.

15. Ibid., 28–31.
16. Ibid., 40–41, 61.
17. On the life of Yoshida Kanetomo, see Allan Grapard, "The Shinto of Yoshida Kanetomo," *Monumenta Nipponica* 47, no. 1 (1992): 40ff.
18. Demura Katsuaki, a leading scholar on the formation of Kanetomo's thought, believes that the Saijōsho was constructed in 1468. Demura Katsuaki, *Yoshida Shintō no kisoteki kenkyū* (Kyoto: Rinkawa shoten, 1997), 584–94. See also Maeda Hiromi, "Imperial Authority and Local Shrines," 41.
19. Hagiwara Tatsuo, *Chūsei saishi soshiki no kenkyū* (Tokyo: Yoshikawa kōbunkan, 1962), 391.
20. Inoue Tomokatsu, "Jingikan ryōchōjō-kō: Muromachi-ki no Yoshida-ke to jingikan," *Shūkyō kenkyū* 78, no. 1 (2004): 86.
21. Ibid., 350–51.
22. Miyaji Naokazu, *Shintōshi*, Miyaji Naokazu ronshū 5–8 (Tokyo: Sōyōsha, 1985), vol 3, 277, 367.
23. Ibid., 279–80.
24. "Yoshida Kanetomo," in *SJ*.
25. Modern scholars suspect that the edict was not genuine. See Maeda Hiromi, "Imperial Authority and Local Shrines," 41n55.
26. Inoue Tomokatsu, n. 20, 77.
27. Ibid.
28. Miyaji Naokazu, *Shintōshi*, 365.
29. Demura Katsuaki, *Yoshida Shintō no kisoteki kenkyū*, 584–94, and English summary 16–17.
30. Yoshida Kanetomo, "Yuiitsu shintō myōbō yōshū," trans. Allan Grapard, *Monumenta Nipponica* 47, no. 2 (1992): 144.
31. Yoshida Kanetomo, "Yuiitsu shintō myōbō yōshū," 157.
32. Maeda Hiromi, "Imperial Authority and Local Shrines," 33.
33. Yoshida Kanetomo, "Yuiitsu shintō myōbō yōshū," 138–39.
34. Okada Yoneo, *Shintō bunken gaisetsu* (Tokyo: Jinja Honchō, 1951, 6th ed. 1982) 142; Demura Katsuaki, *Yoshida Shintō no kisoteki kenkyū*, 584–94.
35. Yoshida Kanetomo, n. 30, 158.
36. Ibid., 143–44.
37. Ibid., 156–57.
38. Ibid., 154–55.
39. Kubota Osamu, *Chūsei Shintō no kenkyū* (Kyoto: Shintōshi gakkai, 1959), 139–59, particularly 150ff. See also Satō Hirō, "Chūsei ni okeru kami kannen no hen'yō," 24ff.; and Jihen, *Kuji hongi gengi* (1332), in *Chūsei Shintōron*, ed. Ōsumi Kazuo, Nihon shisō taikei 19 (Tokyo: Iwanami shoten, 1977), 135–80.
40. Maeda Hiromi, "Imperial Authority and Local Shrines," 55–56.
41. Miyaji Naokazu, *Shintōshi*, 3:268–69.
42. Maeda Hiromi, n. 14, 56.
43. Ibid., 42.
44. Miyaji Naokazu, n. 22, 3:157–58, 268–69.
45. Ibid., 3:268–70.
46. Maeda Hiromi, "Imperial Authority and Local Shrines," 42–43.
47. This report is said to have been prepared by Shirakawa Tadatomi; see Maeda Hiromi, "Imperial Authority and Local Shrines," 45n68.
48. In the meantime, on the twenty-ninth day of the eleventh month, Kanetomo conducted a Shinto initiation for Emperor Go-Tsuchimikado, transmitting to him the Eighteen-fold Shinto ritual; see Maeda Hiromi, "Imperial Authority and Local Shrines," 45. On the thirteenth day of the twelfth month, Kanetomo conducted a lecture on the Twenty-Two Shrines for the court. These activities show that he enjoyed the emperor's full support.
49. Miyaji Naokazu, *Shintōshi*, 3:271.

50. In fact, of course, Kanetomo had to have had a mirror and the other items he claimed were the Ise *shintai* made by some Kyoto craftsman.
51. Nevertheless, the Ise Shrines were sufficiently outraged to send a petition, though it was too late, and to exclude the Yoshida from acting as imperial emissary to any ceremony at Ise. See Miyaji Naokazu, *Shintōshi*, 3:274.
52. Ōsumi Kazuo, "Chūsei Shintōron no shisōteki ichi," in *Chūsei Shintōron*, ed. Ōsumi Kazuo, Nihon shisō taikei 19 (Tokyo: Iwanami shoten, 1977), 363.
53. Bernhard Scheid, "Reading the *Yuiitsu Shintō myōbō yōshū*: A Modern Exegesis of an Esoteric Shinto Text," in *Shinto: Ways of the Kami*, ed. John Breen and Mark Teeuwen (Honolulu: University of Hawai'i Press, 2000), 130–31.
54. Yoshida Kanetomo, "Yuiitsu shintō myōbō yōshū," 146. The proposition of an Eighteenfold Shinto suggests that Kanetomo used the term *Shinto* in more than one sense. As we saw above, he saw Shinto as a universal first principle of the cosmos, but in the context of ritual he speaks of multiple kinds of Shinto. See Scheid, "Reading the Yuiitsu Shintō myōbō yōshū," 123.
55. According to Bernhard Scheid, these Kami are selected arbitrarily from *Nihon shoki* and *Sendai Kuji Hongi*. Scheid, "Reading the Yuiitsu Shintō myōbō yōshū," 135.
56. Yoshida Kanetomo, n. 30, 151.
57. Ibid., 148.
58. Demura Katsuaki, "Yoshida Shintō ni okeru on'yūkyō no hiden-ge: Tokuni jūhachi Shintō gyōji no seiritsu ni tsuite," *Shintōshi kenkyū* 23, no. 3 (1975): 32–63. This article contains an exhaustive comparison of extant manuscripts detailing the separate steps to be followed in the Eighteenfold Shinto rite.
59. Yoshida Kanetomo, "Yuiitsu shintō myōbō yōshū," 145–46.
60. For the complete set of ritual actions comprising the Sōgen Shintō Rite, see Demura Katsuaki, *Yoshida Shintō no kisoteki kenkyū*, 296–364, esp. the summary listing on 360–63.
61. Demura Katsuaki, *Yoshida Shintō no kisoteki kenkyū*, 438.
62. For the complete set of ritual actions comprising the Yui Shintō Goma Rite, see Demura Katsuaki, *Yoshida Shintō no kisoteki kenkyū*, 365–439.
63. Scheid, "Reading the Yuiitsu Shintō myōbō yōshū," 138.
64. Demura Katsuaki, *Yoshida Shintō no kisoteki kenkyū*, 437.
65. Itō Satoshi, "Shinbutsu shūgō riron no hen'yō," *Shūkyō kenkyū* 81, no. 2 (2007): 385–409.
66. Ibid., 385–90.
67. Ibid., 390–91.
68. Ibid., 401–5.
69. Yamaori, *Nihon shūkyōshi nenpyō*, 319; Inoue Tomokatsu, "Jingikan ryōchōjō-kō," 82.
70. Ibid., 365. In Miyaji's view, Kanetomo took advantage of the court at a time of weakness, usurping authority that originally belonged only to the court.
71. Hagiwara Tatsuo, n. 19, 349–50.
72. Ibid., 397–406.
73. Maeda Hiromi, "Imperial Authority and Local Shrines," 50.
74. Hagiwara Tatsuo, *Chūsei saishi soshiki no kenkyū*, 683–84.
75. Maeda Hiromi, "Imperial Authority and Local Shrines," 62–68.
76. Hagiwara Tatsuo, n. 19, 681–83.
77. Ibid.
78. Miyaji Naokazu, *Shintōshi*, 3:379.
79. Hagiwara Tatsuo, *Chūsei saishi soshiki no kenkyū*, 685.
80. Maeda Hiromi, "Imperial Authority and Local Shrines," 51.
81. Miyaji Naokazu, *Shintōshi*, 3:378.
82. Hagiwara Tatsuo, *Chūsei saishi soshiki no kenkyū*, 682; Maeda Hiromi, "Imperial Authority and Local Shrines," 51. *Koku*: a unit of measurement for rice, equivalent to about five bushels; served as a basic measurement of value until the late nineteenth century.
83. Hagiwara Tatsuo, *Chūsei saishi soshiki no kenkyū*, 682.
84. Inoue Tomokatsu, "Jingikan ryōchōjō-kō," 91.

85. Maeda Hiromi, "Imperial Authority and Local Shrines," 51.
86. Mase Kumiko, "Jinja to tennō," in *Tennō to shakai shoshūdan*, ed. Nagahara Keiji, Kōza zen kindai no tennō, vol. 3 (Tokyo: Aoki Shoten, 1993), 242; Endō Jun, *Hirata Kokugaku to kinsei shakai* (Tokyo: Perikansha, 2008), 167.
87. Hagiwara Tatsuo, *Chūsei saishi soshiki no kenkyū*, 682.
88. Maeda Hiromi, "Imperial Authority and Local Shrines," 52–53.
89. Bonshun's diary covers the years 1583 to 1585 and 1596 to 1632; Hagiwara Tatsuo, *Chūsei saishi soshiki no kenkyū*, 685–93.
90. Maeda Hiromi, "Imperial Authority and Local Shrines," 53.
91. Ibid., 54.
92. Bonshun, *Bonshun nikki*; also known as *Shunkyūki*. See Bonshun, *Shunkyūki*, ed. Kamata Jun'ichi (Tokyo: Zoku Gunsho Ruijū kanseikai, 1970), 5:4–6. For extensive treatment of the events resulting in the decision that Bonshun would conduct this important ritual, see W. J. Boot, "The Death of a Shogun: Deification in Early Modern Japan," in *Shinto in History*, ed. John Breen and Mark Teeuwen (London: Curzon Press, 2000), 144–66. For a history of Shinto funeral rites, see Elizabeth Kenney, "Shinto Funerals in the Edo Period," *JJRS* 27, 3, no. 4 (2000): 243ff. Yoshida Kanemi's funeral in 1573 had included both Buddhist and Shinto rites.
93. Bonshun, *Shunkyūki*, 5:4–6; W. J. Boot, "The Death of a Shogun: Deification in Early Modern Japan." In *Shinto in History*, ed. John Breen and Mark Teeuwen (London: Curzon Press, 2000), 149–50.
94. Endō Jun, "The Early Modern Period," in *Shinto: A Short History*, edited by Inoue Nobutaka, Endō Jun, Mori Mizue, translated and adapted by Mark Teeuwen and John Breen (London: RoutledgeCurzon, 1998), 112.

Chapter 8

1. For a comprehensive study of the domains, see Harold Bolitho, "The *Han*," in *The Cambridge History of Japan*, ed. John Whitney Hall, vol. 4 (Cambridge: Cambridge University Press, 1991), 183–234.
2. Social discontent was manifested in different ways and on different scales, from "smashings" (*uchikowashi*) directed at local wealthy merchants to mass demonstrations against government policies (*ikki*). See A. James White, *Ikki: Social Conflict and Political Protest in Early Modern Japan* (Ithaca, NY: Cornell University Press, 1995).
3. *Encyclopedia of Japan*, s.v. "Kōgi," accessed through Japan Knowledge.com, October 9, 2014, http://japanknowledge.com/library/display/?lid=10800LW005710.
4. The particle *gi* in other contexts can refer to ritual and ceremonial.
5. Asao Naohiro, "Kōgi to bakuhan ryōshu sei," *Kōza Nihon rekishi* 5 (Tokyo: Tokyo Daigaku shuppankai, 1984–1985); Fukaya Katsumi, *Kinsei no kokka, shakai to tennō* (Tokyo: Azekura shobō, 1991); Fukaya Katsumi, "Kōgi" in *KDJ*, accessed on Japan Knowledge.com, http://japanknowledge.com/library/search/basic/?q1=公儀; Fujii Jōji, *Bakuhan ryōshu no kenryoku kōzō* (Tokyo: Iwanami shoten, 2002); Hashimoto Masanobu, *Kinsei kuge shakai no kenkyū* (Tokyo: Yoshikawa kōbunkan, 2002); "Kōgi," *Encyclopedia of Japan*, accessed on Japan Knowledge.com, http://japanknowledge.com/library/display/?lid=10800LW005710.
6. Bernhard Scheid, "Shinto as a Religion for the Warrior Class: The Case of Yoshikawa Koretaru," *JJRS* 29, no. 3/4 (2002): 301.
7. Beatrice Bodart-Bailey, "The Persecution of Confucianism in Early Tokugawa Japan," *Monumenta Nipponica* 48 (1993): 309.
8. Taniguchi Sumio, "Okayama hansei kakuritsuki ni okeru jisha seisaku," in *Chihō shakai to shūkyō no shiteki kenkyū*, ed. Ogura Toyofumi (Kyoto: Yanagihara shoten, 1963), 157–80.
9. Adapted from Kokugakuin University, *Encyclopedia of Shinto*, ed. Norman Havens and Inoue Nobutaka, trans. Norman Havens, Institute for Japanese Culture and Classics (Tokyo: Kokugakuin University, 2001–6).

10. Kiyohara Sadao, *Shintō shi* (Tokyo: Kōseikaku shoten, 1932), 650.
11. Maeda Hiromi, "Imperial Authority and Local Shrines: The Yoshida House and the Creation of a Countrywide Shinto Institution in Early Modern Japan" (PhD diss., Harvard University, 2003), 54.
12. Bob Wakabayashi, "In Name Only: Imperial Sovereignty in Early Modern Japan," *Journal of Japanese Studies* 17, no. 1 (1991): 31.
13. Helen Hardacre, *Religion and Society in Nineteenth-Century Japan: A Study of the Southern Kantō Region, Using Late Edo and Early Meiji Gazetteers*. Michigan Monograph Series in Japanese Studies 41 (Ann Arbor: Center for Japanese Studies, University of Michigan, 2002), 51.
14. Adapted from Maeda Hiromi, "Court Rank for Village Shrines: The Yoshida House's Interactions with Local Shrines During the Mid-Tokugawa Period," *Japanese Journal of Religious Studies* 29, no. 3/4 (2002): 331.
15. Ibid., 325.
16. Inoue Tomokatsu, *Kinsei no jinja to chōtei ken'i* (Tokyo: Yoshikawa Kōbunkan, 2007), 93.
17. Maeda Hiromi, "Court Rank for Village Shrines," 328, 331–32.
18. For detailed data on the expenses involved in acquiring these certificates, see Miyaji Harukuni, "Yoshida Shintō kaikyojō no juju ni tsuite," *Shintōgaku* 19 (1958): 58–65.
19. Maeda Hiromi, "Court Rank for Village Shrines," 332–33. During the entire Edo period, the court issued only sixty-seven such decrees. See Mase Kumiko, "Jinja to tennō," in *Zen kindai no tennō: Tennō to shakai shūdan*, ed. by Ishigami Eiichi et al. (Tokyo: Aoki Shoten, 1993), 227, referred to in Maeda Hiromi, "Imperial Authority and Local Shrines," 332.
20. Inoue Tomokatsu, *Kinsei no jinja to chōtei ken'i*, 181.
21. See Suzuki Rie, "Kinsei kōki, Shinshoku no zaikyō seikatsu to kōshō," *Hiroshima Daigaku daigakuin Kyōikugaku kenkyū kiyō* 58 (2009): 17–26, for analysis of the travel diary of a shrine priest from Hiroshima who journeyed to Kyoto five times between 1806 and 1848 to secure ritual certifications and titles for himself and his son.
22. Lee Butler, *Emperor and Aristocracy in Japan, 1467–1680: Resilience and Renewal*, Harvard East Asian Monographs, 209 (Cambridge, MA: Harvard University Asia Center, 2002), 198–211.
23. Ibid., 223.
24. Hashimoto Masanobu, n. 5, 853.
25. Ibid., 670–75, 698–99. The *sokui kanjō* in theory resulted in the emperor "becoming" the cosmic Buddha Dainichi after complicated ritual in which the emperor formed mudras (hand gestures) and pronounced mantras. The Nijō House had a special role in these rites and transmitted esoteric knowledge to the emperor in the form of *kirigami*.
26. Haga Shōji, "Meiji Jingikansei no seiritsu to kokka saishi no saihen," *Jinbun gakuhō* 50 (1981): chart on p. 41.
27. Takano Toshihiko, "Edo bakufu to jisha," in *Kōza Nihon rekishi* 5: Kinsei 1. ed. by Rekishigaku Kenkyūkai and Nihonshi Kenkyūkai (Tokyo Daigaku shuppankai, 1985), 88.
28. *SJ*, 233.
29. Fujii Sadafumi, *Kinsei ni okeru jingi shisō* (Tokyo: Shunbunsha, 1944), 110.
30. Mase Kumiko, "Jinja to tennō," 242.
31. Takano Toshihiko, "Edo bakufu to jisha," 87.
32. Mase Kumiko, n. 19, 221.
33. Ibid., 243.
34. Okada Shōji, "Chinkonsai," *SSDJ*. The Chinkonsai had fallen into disuse in the Sengoku era but was revived and performed within the Shirakawa residence.
35. Haga Shōji, "Meiji Jingikansei no seiritsu to kokka saishi no saihen," 34–36.
36. Taira Shigemichi, *Yoshikawa Shintō no kisoteki kenkyū* (Tokyo: Yoshikawa kōbunkan, 1966), 425.
37. Ibid., 418–21.
38. Ibid., 422–44.
39. Ibid., 418–24.

40. Mark Teeuwen, *Watarai Shinto: An Intellectual History of the Outer Shrine in Ise* (Leiden: Research School CNWS, 1996), 135.
41. Hayashi Razan, "Shintō denju," in *Kinsei Shintōron: Zenki kokugaku,* Nihon shisō taikei 39, ed. by Taira Shigemichi and Abe Akio (Tokyo: Iwanami shoten, 1972), 57. Sakai Tadakatsu (1587–1662) was a confidant of the third shogun Iemitsu and lord of Obama domain.
42. "Hayashi Razan," *SSDJ,* 819–20.
43. Taira, "Kinsei no Shintō shisō," in *Kinsei Shintōron: Zenki Kokugaku,* Nihon shisō taikei 39, ed. Taira Shigemichi and Abe Akio (Tokyo: Iwanami shoten, 1972), 518.
44. Edo-period Confucians were much influenced by the neo-Confucian philosophy of Zhu Xi (1130–1200) and explained that principle and *ki* were reality's basic components. *Ki* is an active, "generative" force, while principle represented the "rational and ethical order of all things." Most Edo-period Confucian thinkers believed the two to be inseparable, though each could be analyzed separately. James W. Heisig, Thomas P. Kasulis, and John C. Maraldo, eds., *Japanese Philosophy: A Sourcebook* (Honolulu: University of Hawai'i Press, 2011), 295, 1260.
45. Ibid., 12, 17.
46. Hayashi Razan, "Shintō denju," in Taira Shigemichi and Abe Akio, *Kinsei Shintōron,* 12–13.
47. Ibid., 13, 51. Mark Teeuwen provides extensive analysis of Razan's views on the Inner and Outer Shrines in Teeuwen, *Watarai Shinto,* 202–15, as well as the text of a report that Razan prepared in the context of a dispute between the two shrines. Teeuwen, *Watarai Shinto,* 406–12.
48. Hayashi Razan, "Shintō denju," in Taira Shigemichi and Abe Akio, *Kinsei Shintōron,* 13–14.
49. Translation by Kate Nakai, in Kate Nakai, "The Naturalization of Confucianism in Tokugawa Japan: The Problem of Sinocentrism," *Harvard Journal of Asiatic Studies* 40, no. 1 (1980): 161; see Hayashi Razan, "Shintō denju," in Taira Shigemichi and Abe Akio, *Kinsei Shintōron,* 19.
50. Hayashi Razan, "Shintō denju," in Taira Shigemichi and Abe Akio, *Kinsei Shintōron,* 19.
51. Teeuwen, *Watarai Shinto,* 109–16, 125, 391.
52. Taira, *Yoshikawa Shintō,* 425.
53. Deguchi Nobuyoshi, "Yōfukki," in *Kinsei Shintōron: Zenki kokugaku,* Nihon shisō taikei 39, ed. Taira Shigemichi and Abe Akio (Tokyo: Iwanami shoten, 1972), 86–117. See also Teeuwen, *Watarai Shinto,* 221–43; Taira, "Kinsei no Shintō shisō," in Taira Shigemichi and Abe Akio, *Kinsei Shintōron,* 537–40.
54. Taira Shigemichi, *Kinsei Nihon shisōshi* (Tokyo: Yoshikawa Kōbunkan, 1969), 17.
55. Ibid., 18–22.
56. Ibid., 17–27, 39–47.
57. Taira, *Yoshikawa Shintō,* 3–8.
58. Ibid., 9–17.
59. Ibid., 10–20.
60. Ibid., 116–19.
61. Ibid.
62. Ibid.
63. Ibid.
64. Ibid., 23, 481–482. Elaborating further on this theme, Koretaru held that the Heavenly Jeweled Spear punishes the wicked and increases the fortunes of the good. However, the spear is not merely a weapon; its jewel signifies that governance should be just. If governance is just but exercised only with metal, the people will merely fear it. The jewel also symbolizes mercy. When governance is exercised with both the jewel and the spear, the hearts of the people will be tranquil. The virtue of governance through the jewel is that the good will love virtue, and the wicked will cease wrongdoing. Koretaru finished by proclaiming that the ideal of Shinto governance was made manifest in the shogun's government.
65. Taira, *Kinsei Nihon shisōshi,* 17–27; Herman Ooms, *Tokugawa Ideology: Early Constructs, 1570–1680* (Princeton, NJ: Princeton University Press, 1985), 197–98.
66. Taira, *Kinsei Nihon shisōshi,* 34–35; Taira, *Yoshikawa Shintō,* 40–41.

67. Taira, *Yoshikawa Shintō*, 426–27.
68. See Ooms, *Tokugawa Ideology*, 225ff., on Ansai's other work for Masayuki, including a fifteen-point code of conduct for Masayuki's heirs.
69. For discussion of this work, see Ooms, *Tokugawa Ideology*, 216–21.
70. Ooms, *Tokugawa Ideology*, 222. Deguchi Nobuyoshi apparently initiated Ansai because Ansai had used his marital connection to the Kamo Shrine to secure a complete text of "Yamato Hime Seiki," one of the Five Books of *Watarai Shinto* that had been lost at Ise.
71. Taira, *Kinsei Nihon shisōshi*, 27; Yamaguchi Kōhei, ed. *Kinsei Aizu shi no kenkyū*, vol. 1 (Aizu City: Rekishi shunbunsha, 1978), 40–42. Masayuki had begun investigating the pedigrees of Aizu temples before Ansai and Koretaru came on the scene. He disliked Buddhism enough to have burned some Buddhist writings, placed restrictions on people taking the tonsure, and to have refused to receive a gift of writing from Ingen, the founder of the Ōbaku Zen school in Japan.
72. Taira, *Kinsei Nihon shisōshi*, 35; Taira, *Yoshikawa Shintō*, 30–31; Taira, "Kinsei no Shintō shisō," in Taira Shigemichi and Abe Akio, *Kinsei Shintōron*, 541–53. According to Taira, Koretaru did not initiate Ansai to the most secret teachings, though Ansai's disciples claimed otherwise.
73. Taira, *Yoshikawa Shintō*, 33. On Masayuki's funeral, see "Hoshina Masayuki sōgi kiroku" [1672], in *Shinsōsai shiryō shūsei*, ed. Asoya Masahiko and Tanuma Mayumi (Tokyo: Perikansha, 1995), 185–92, quoted in Elizabeth Kenney, "Shinto Funerals in the Edo Period," *JJRS* 27, no. 3/4 (2000), 258, n. 29.
74. Ooms, *Tokugawa Ideology*, 198; on the Shintōkata post, see Kiyohara Sadao, *Shintō Shi*, 505. The Shintōkata office after Koretaru was hereditary in the Yoshikawa line. It carried no regular political duties. The office holder had the name Genjūrō (源十朗) and could accumulate disciples by distributing a kind of certificate that was recognized by the shogunate.
75. Taira, *Yoshikawa Shintō*, 429. Although Yoshikawa influence faded from national prominence, Koretaru's descendants retained some influence in Aizu. Taira explains the complicated circumstances that prevented Koretaru from transmitting the Yoshida secrets back to the heir in this work (42–43). See also Mase Kumiko, "Jinja to tennō," 235.
76. Taira, *Yoshikawa Shintō*, 98–110, 414–15.
77. Taira, "Kinsei no Shintō shisō," in Taira Shigemichi and Abe Akio, *Kinsei Shintōron*, 545–46.
78. For extensive discussion of Ansai's Confucian writings, see Ooms, *Tokugawa Ideology*, chaps. 6 and 7.
79. Teeuwen, *Watarai Shinto*, 259.
80. Ooms, *Tokugawa Ideology*, 223.
81. "Suika Shintō," *SJ*.
82. See Yamazaki Ansai, "Jijushō," in Taira Shigemichi and Abe Akio, *Kinsei Shintōron*, 129–38.
83. See Yamazaki Ansai, "Suika shagō," in Taira Shigemichi and Abe Akio, *Kinsei Shintōron*, 119–28.
84. Yamazaki Ansai, "Jindaimaki kōgi," in Taira Shigemichi and Abe Akio, *Kinsei Shintōron*, 166–70.
85. Okada Shōji, "Reishagō, reijingō" in *SSDJ*, 1034; Ooms, *Tokugawa Ideology*, 230–32.
86. This work had been lost until recently, when a copy was discovered. See Isomae Jun'ichi and Ogura Shigeji, *Kinsei chōtei to Suika Shintō* (Tokyo: Perikansha, 2005), 139–78.
87. Takebe Toshio, "Ōgimachi Kinmichi," *SSDJ*, 142; Kobayashi Kenzō, "Ōgimachi Shintō," *SSDJ*, 147; Isomae and Ogura, *Kinsei chōtei to Suika Shintō*, 28–39.
88. Isomae and Ogura, n. 86, 45.
89. Ibid., 50–54.
90. Ibid., 146–55. Amano Sadakage, a fellow researcher of Yoshimi's, pointed out the strong Buddhist influence in Yoshida ritual procedure and how this contradicted many of their purist claims. Razan and others had made this criticism from a Confucian point of view. In fact, the point was so widely acknowledged that it had become a kind of conventional wisdom about the Yoshida.

91. Teeuwen, *Watarai Shinto*, 388–89.
92. Inoue Tomokatsu, *Kinsei no jinja to chōtei ken'i*, 181. See Maeda Hiromi, "Court Rank for Village Shrines," 332–33 for other criticism of the Yoshida certificates.
93. Inoue Tomokatsu, n. 16, 153.
94. Ibid., 152.
95. Ibid., 301.
96. See, for example, Nishida Kaoru, "Kinseiteki jinja shihai taisei to shake no kakuritsu ni tsuite" *Chihōshi kenkyū* 251 (1994): 22–39. Satō Masato presents intriguing cases from the Hie Shrines showing how shrine personnel, who were frequently Buddhist clerics, used Yoshida licenses to strengthen their positions in dealings with Enryakuji, the temple in control of these shrines, even though they were by no means committed to Yoshida Shinto as a doctrinal position. Satō Masato, "Kinsei shake no Yoshida Shintō juju: Hie shake no jirei o megutte" in *Kinsei no seishin seikatsu*, ed. Seishin Bunka Kenkyūjo (Yokohama: Ōkura Seishin Bunka Kenkyūjo, 1996), 253–301. Later in the period, the Yoshida faced competition from the Shirakawa House in licensing lower-ranking shrine personnel. See Hardacre, *Religion and Society in Nineteenth-Century Japan*, 95–104.
97. Maeda Tsutomu, "Kinsei Nihon ni okeru tennō ken'i no kōjō no riyū," *Nihon shisō shigaku* 32 (2000): 57–64.
98. "Hōreki, Meiwa jiken" in *KSDJ*, Japan Knowledge.com, accessed April 12, 2013, http://www.jkn21.com.ezp-prod1.hul.harvard.edu/body/display/.

Chapter 9

1. The population of Kyoto was about 400,000, with Osaka close behind at 350,000, while Nagoya and Kanazawa had more than 100,000 each, making them comparable to the great cities of Europe. Nishiyama Matsunosuke, *Edo Culture: Daily Life and Diversions in Urban Japan, 1600-1868*, trans. and ed. Gerald Groemer (Honolulu: University of Hawai'i Press, 1997), 23–52.
2. See Nobori Masao, "*Jinja bukkaku gankake jūhōki shohen* ni miru hokora to jibyō: Genze riyaku no fōkuroa," in *Minkan shinkō to minshū shūkyō*, ed. Miyata Noboru and Tsukamoto Manabu, Nihon rekishi minzoku ronshū 10 (Tokyo: Yoshikawa kōbunkan, 1994), 108–19.
3. Also transliterated as *Gazu hyakki yagyō*, quoted in Michael Dylan Foster, *Pandemonium and Parade: Japanese Monsters and the Culture of Yōkai* (Berkeley: University of California Press, 2009), 52–53.
4. Nam-lin Hur, *Prayer and Play in Late Tokugawa Japan: Asakusa Sensōji and Edo Society* (Cambridge, MA: Harvard University Asia Center, 2000), 83.
5. Miyata Noboru, "Inari shinkō no shintō to minshū," in *Inari shinkō*, vol. 3: *Minshū shūkyōshi sōsho*, ed. Naoe Hiroji (Tokyo: Yūzankaku, 1983), 137.
6. "Inari Taisha," *SSDJ*, 84–85; "Inari shinkō," in *Nihon dai hyakka zensho* (accessed on Japan Knowledge. japanknowledge.com.ezo-prod1.hul.harvard.edu/lib/display/?lid=1001000022060, May 21, 2013); Nakagawa Sagane, "Inari Worship in Early Modern Osaka," in *Osaka: The Merchants' Capital of Early Modern Japan*, ed. James L. McClain and Wakita Osamu (Ithaca, NY: Cornell University Press, 1999), 180.
7. Nam-lin Hur, *Prayer and Play in Late Tokugawa Japan*, 14–15; Miyata Noboru, *Edo no hayarigami* (Tokyo: Chikuma shobō, 1993), 133–34.
8. Nakagawa Sagane, "Inari Worship in Early Modern Osaka," 198–200.
9. Hagiwara Tatsuo, "Edo no Inari," in *Inari shinkō*, 155–59.
10. Kita-ku hensan chōsakai, *Kita-ku shi*, Tsūshi hen, Kinsei (Tokyo: Gyōsei, 1996), 195–98.
11. Ibid.
12. Yasuda Takehiro, *Rakugo jiten* (Tokyo: Seiabō, 1994), 88–89.
13. Miyata Noboru, *Edo no hayarigami*, 155. Inari worship sometimes took the form of healing cults.

14. Nakagawa Sagane, "Inari Worship in Early Modern Osaka," 199; Miyata Noboru, *Edo no hayarigami*, 28, 182ff.
15. On the life and thought of Tada Yoshitoshi, see "Tada Yoshitoshi" in *SSDJ*, 653; and Endō Jun, "Tada Yoshitoshi," in *Shintō jinbutsu kenkyū bunken mokuroku*, ed. Kokugakuin Daigaku Nihon Bunka Kenkyūjo (Tokyo: Kōbundō, 2000), 394–95.
16. Inoue Tomokatsu, "Shintōsha," in *Minkan ni ikiru shūkyōsha*, Kinsei no mibunteki shūhen, ed. Takano Toshihiko (Tokyo: Yoshikawa Kōbunkan, 2000), 18, 27.
17. Ibid., 20.
18. Ibid., 16, 22, 26.
19. Ibid., 25.
20. Hagiwara Tatsuo, "Edo no Inari," 157.
21. Miyata Noboru, *Edo no hayarigami*, 31–33.
22. Nakagawa Sagane, "Inari Worship in Early Modern Osaka," 192.
23. Miyata Noboru, "Inari shinkō no shintō to minshū," 3:146.
24. Mimeguri Inari and Teppōzu Inari were the *yokozuna*, or top-ranked, shrines, followed by Shimamori Inari and Shinzaki Inari as *ōzeki*, with Misaki Inari and Sugimori Inari as *komusubi*, followed down the list by ninety other Inari shrines ranked as *maegashira*, with further sub-rankings. Nishigaki Seiji, "Inari shinkō no shosō," in *Inari shinkō*, 3:166–69.
25. Nakagawa Sagane, n. 6, 190–91.
26. Ibid., 181–89.
27. Ibid., 194–97.
28. Yamaori, *Nihon shūkyōshi nenpyō*, 429, 436; Inoue Tomokatsu, "Shintōsha," 28.
29. Nakagawa Sagane, "Inari Worship in Early Modern Osaka," 192–97, 209.
30. For a review of scholarship on Japanese pilgrimage, see Ian Reader and Paul L. Swanson, "Editors' Introduction: Pilgrimage in the Japanese Religious Tradtion," in the *JJRS* special issue on this topic: *JJRS* 24, no. 3/4 (1997): 225–70. For earlier studies of pilgrimage in the Edo period, see Carmen Blacker, "The Religious Traveller in the Edo Period," *Modern Asian Studies* 18, no. 4 (1984): 593–608; Winston Davis, "Pilgrimage and World Renewal: A Study of Religious and Social Values in Tokugawa Japan," *History of Religions* 23, no. 2 (1983): 97–116 and 23, no. 3 (1984): 197–221; Maeda Takashi, *Junrei no shakaigaku* (Tokyo: Minerva shobō, 1971); Nathalie Kouamé, *Pèlerinage et societé dans le Japon des Tokugawa, la pèlerinage de Shikoku entre 1598 et 1868* (Paris: École française d'Extrême-Orient, 2001); and Laura Nenzi, *Excursions in Identity: Travel and the Intersection of Place, Gender, and Status in Edo Japan* (Honolulu: University of Hawai'i Press, 2008). For studies of women's travel and pilgrimage in the Edo period, see Anne Walthall, *The Weak Body of a Useless Woman: Matsuo Taseko and the Meiji Restoration* (Chicago: University of Chicago Press, 1998); Anne Walthall, "Writing about Pilgrimage, Exile, and Politics: Women's Travel Diaries in Late Edo-Period Japan," *Transactions of the Asiatic Society of Japan*, fifth series, 3 (2011): 29–50; and Shiba Keiko, *Literary Creations on the Road: Women's Travel Diaries in Early Modern Japan*, trans. Motoko Ezaki (Lanham, MD: University Press of America, 2012). On the relation between improvements in national infrastructure and increased pilgrimage, see Shinjō Tsunezō, *Shaji to kōtsū: Kumano mōde to Ise mairi* (Tokyo: Shibundō, 1960). For a general study of travel during the Edo period, see Constantine Vaporis, *Breaking Barriers: Travel and the State in Early Modern Japan* (Cambridge, MA: Harvard University Press, 1994).
31. *Kō* were formed for some common purpose, including but not limited to pilgrimage, such as pooling funds to support a shared undertaking or for some religious purpose, such as reciting the name of the Buddha Amida or the title of the Lotus Sutra, or to worship particular Kami, such as the Kami of the Rice Fields, the Mountain Kami, and others. Some confraternities worshipped Buddhist figures such as Kūkai, and others were organized for pilgrimage to such sacred mountains as Mt. Fuji, Kumano, Konpira, and Ōyama.
32. Deguchi Nobuyoshi, "*Ise Daijingū Jin'iki*, a Record of Divine Marvels of the Grand Shrine of Ise," trans. Norman Havens, *Transactions of the Institute for Japanese Culture and Classics* 74 September, 1994: (95) tale #41, 133–36.

33. Ibid., (95), 132–33.
34. Ibid., 128.
35. Ibid., 139–40.
36. Nishigaki Seiji, *O-ise mairi* (Tokyo: Iwanami shoten, 1983), 159.
37. Ibid., 100–103.
38. See Itō Satoshi, "Gekū Takakura-san jōdo kō," *Nihon bunka kenkyūjo kiyō* 83 (1999): 95–133.
39. Tada Yoshitoshi, "Miyakawa nikki" (1746), reprinted in Jingūshichō, *Jingū sanpaiki taisei*, Jingū sōsho 11 (Gifu: Seinō insatsu kabushiki kaisha, 1937), 252–56. See also Peter Knecht, "Ise *sankei mandara* and the Image of the Pure Land," *JJRS* 33, no. 2 (2006): 233–48.
40. On the surge in publishing, see Mary Elizabeth Berry, *Japan in Print: Information and Nation in the Early Modern Period* (Berkeley: University of California Press, 2006).
41. In its modern edition of 1919, the work is 695 pages in length, of which the sections on Ise occupy about 250 pages. The work includes hundreds of poems and nearly two hundred illustrations.
42. Shitomi Kangetsu, *Ise sangū meisho zue: 5 kan oyobi furoku, shūi*, annotated by Harada Kan (Tokyo: Dai Nihon meisho zue kankōkai, 1919), 400–406.
43. Ibid., 319–24 (illustrations separate two pages of text).
44. Shitomi's *Illustrated Guide* provides us with much valuable information that is not evident from examining Ise mandalas, including the name, function, and history of each structure, fence, gate, and *torii* on the grounds; architectural details; and the names of the deities enshrined there. It identifies the spots designated for Buddhist clerics and *yamabushi* to worship (and beyond which they weren't supposed to go, though this information contradicts the mandala, which show Buddhist figures at all locations except the inner sanctuaries of the two main shrines). It provides illustrations of rituals unique to Ise, such as the Kanname-sai and the Vicennial Renewal, as well as extended descriptions, with quotations from numerous historical texts. One of the distinctive ritual practitioners at Ise described in the guide was the *kora*, a young girl who offered food to the Kami each morning and night with her father; she was a daughter of the Mono Imi, one of the priests whose job it was to observe taboos strictly, and she continued this service from the age of eight or nine until menarche. Shitomi Kangetsu, n. 42, 307.
45. Ibid., 346.
46. Ibid., 325. The subsidiary shrines to be seen at Ise are, Shitomi writes, really satellites of their originals, whose true location is elsewhere. The small, hut-like establishments that pilgrims go around have been set up beside the main sanctuaries to save pilgrims the effort of traveling to their main sites.
47. Fujitani Toshio, *Okage mairi to eejanaika* (Tokyo: Iwanami shoten, 1968), 32.
48. In addition to the sources on *okage mairi* mentioned here, see Davis, "Pilgrimage and World Renewal"; and Laura Nenzi, "To Ise at All Costs: Religious and Economic Implications of Early Modern *Nukemairi*," *JJRS* 33, no. 1 (2006): 75–114.
49. Watarai Hironori, *Ise Daijingū Zoku Jin'iki* [The continuing record of divine marvels of the grand shrine of Ise], trans. Norman Havens. *Transactions of the Institute for Japanese Culture and Classics* 78 (September 1996): pp. 129/208–130/207. See also Nenzi, "To Ise At All Costs."
50. Mie ken, ed., *Mie kenshi*, Shiryō hen, Kinsei-4, part 1 (Tsu City: Gyōsei, 1998), 1026.
51. Watarai Hironori, "*Ise Daijingū Zoku Jin'iki*," 109/228–110/227.
52. Ibid., 95/242. On the economic implications of workers absconding on pilgrimage, see Nenzi, "To Ise at All Costs"; and Shinjō Tsunezō, *Shaji sankei no shakai keizaishiteki kenkyū* (Tokyo: Hanawa shobō, 1982).
53. This and similar stories are discussed in Nenzi, "To Ise at All Costs," 92.
54. Watarai Hironori, *Ise Daijingū Zoku Jin'iki*, 113/224.
55. Nenzi, "To Ise at All Costs," 80ff, 86–87.
56. Mie ken, ed., *Mie kenshi*, Shiryō hen, Kinsei-4, part 1, 1028.
57. "Meiwa nuke mairi kyakunansen ikken kakidome" in Mie ken, ed., *Mie kenshi*, Shiryō hen, Kinsei-4, part 1, 1030–38.

58. Fujitani Toshio, *Okage mairi to eejanaika*, fig. 1.
59. People living along the route gave the pilgrims rainwear and umbrellas. Osaka merchants (each one is named) gave the following as alms: 250,000 pairs of sandals, 12 *mon* given to each of 184,000 people; 16 *mon* given to each of 60,000 people; 120,000 umbrellas, bamboo staffs, 5,000 bushels of rice, 30 boats sent to transport pilgrims, gloves, oil; others went out to carry the sick and aged over mountain passes. In the fifth month, some 54,000 people showed up at the Outer Shrine. There were whole groups of women pilgrims traveling without men. On some days at least half of the pilgrims were women and children. *Oshi* provided palanquins, food, and porridge. Celebratory red rice was provided in front of the Outer Shrine. Everyone wanted to offer something. Many different alms groups were active. Osaka and Sakai seemed to be the places sending the most pilgrims. People were starving. Alms stations were set up in two nearby temples and a *gongen* shrine. Even dogs were observed going on pilgrimage, with talismans on their collars! People came out for a day's entertainment to watch the throngs of pilgrims passing by. Local residents and *oshi* provided money alms in huge amounts. The inns were completely overwhelmed, but they took people on a "sleep only" basis (without offering meals). Tsuda Kin'uemon Norinao, "Ise mairi okage no nikki," in *Sesō* part 1, ed. Tanigawa Ken'ichi, Nihon shomin seikatsu shiryō shūsei (Tokyo: San'ichi shobō, 1971), 12:103–23.
60. "Ise okage mairi jitsuroku kagami," in *Sesō* part 1, 12:123–27.
61. Ibid.
62. Laura Nenzi discusses the appearance of affluent pilgrims in "To Ise at All Costs," 96.
63. From *Nihon Kokugo daijiten*, Japan Knowledge. http://japanknowledge.com.ezp-prod1.hul.harvard.edu/lib/display/?lid=20020234b5653808IWoL, accessed October 22, 2014.

Chapter 10

1. Janine Sawada, *Practical Pursuits: Religion, Politics, and Personal Cultivation in Nineteenth-Century Japan* (Honolulu: University of Hawai'i Press, 2004), 3, 10.
2. Catherine Wessinger, "New Religious Movements," in *Encyclopedia of Religion*, 2nd ed., ed. Lindsay Jones (Detroit: Macmillan Reference USA), accessed at Gale Virtual Reference Library, 2005, vol. 10, 6512 Web. July 18, 2013. http://go.galegroup.com.ezp-prod1.hul.harvard.edu/ps/i.do?id=GALE%7CCX3424502234&v=2.1&u=camb55135&it=r&p=GVRL&sw=w&asid=117f32bbf241442de1c333ee899289c2
3. Ibid.
4. Helen Hardacre, *Kurozumikyō and the New Religions of Japan* (Princeton, NJ: Princeton University Press, 1986), 4–7.
5. Adapted from Mori Mizue, "Sansha Takusen," *Encyclopedia of Shinto*, http://eos.kokugakuin.ac.jp/modules/xwords/entry.php?entryID=1317, accessed November 20, 2014.
6. Brian Bocking, *The Oracles of the Three Shrines: Windows on Japanese Religion* (Richmond, Surrey: Curzon, 2001). See also Nishida Nagao, "Sanja takusen no seisaku," *Kokugaguin Zasshi* 47 (1939), revised edition in *Nihon Shintōshi kenkyū* 5, *Chūsei-hen* (2) 1978, quoted in Bocking, *Oracles of the Three Shrines*. In the late eighteenth century, Ise Sadatake (1717–1784), a scholar of ancient etiquette and deportment, criticized the Oracle of the Three Shrines as a fabrication by Yoshida Kanetomo, pointing out that the oracles were permeated with Buddhist influence, in a work titled *Sansha takusen kō*. See Mori Mizue, "Sanshatakusenkō," *Encyclopedia of Shinto*, http://eos.kokugakuin.ac.jp/modules/xwords/entry.php?entryID=1358, accessed November 20, 2014.
7. Mitsuyoshi occasionally refers to a Yoshida document concerning *ichinomiya*, which he evidently carried with him on his travels.
8. Mitsuyoshi sometimes conferred certificates of discipleship; an example from Okayama is included in Fujii Shun and Tanaka Shūji, eds., *Okayama-ken komonjo shū*, (1955; repr. Kyoto: Shibunka, 1981), document 304, 2:363.

9. Mitsuyoshi's maner of promoting the prayer can be known from his writings, such as *Shokoku Ichinomiya junkeiki* and *Yosashibumi*. He mainly preached on the Age of the Gods section of *Nihon shoki*, the Nakatomi Harae, and the Sansha Takusen. Often, he gave only a single lecture, but he also had a set of thirty lectures on the Age of the Gods. In one case, these lectures were delivered over a period of about three weeks. See Nagasawa Hiroko, "Shintō kōshaku," *SJ*, 567–68.
10. Tachibana Mitsuyoshi, "Ichinomiya sankeiki," in *Jingi zensho*, vol. 2, ed. Saeki Ariyoshi (Tokyo: Kōten kōkyūsho, 1908), 262–339. This version of the work has been edited and its original illustrations have been deleted. Interlinear notes by the editor provide notations on the subject of Mitsuyoshi's lectures at regional shrines, such as the Three Oracles, the Great Purification Prayer, or the Purification of the Six Roots Prayer.
11. Peter Nosco, "Masuho Zankō (1655–1742): A Shinto Popularizer between Nativism and National Learning," in *Confucianism and Tokugawa Culture*, ed. Peter Nosco (Princeton, NJ: Princeton University Press, 1984), 166–87.
12. Nagasawa Hiroko, "Shintō kōshaku," *SJ*, 567–68.
13. Tomobe's views on the afterlife and the connection to loyal service to the emperor are discussed in Maeda Tsutomu, "Kinsei Nihon ni okeru tennō ken'i no kōjō no riyū," *Nihon shisōshigaku* 32 (2000): 57–64.
14. Hikino Kyōsuke, "Shintō kōshakushi Tamada Naganori no shomin kyōka to jingi kanryōchō Yoshida ke," *Shūkyō kenkyū* 79, no. 4 (2006): 110–11.
15. Kōmoto Kazushi, *Kurozumikyō tokuhon* (Okayama: Kurozumikyō Nisshinsha, 1961), 126.
16. Translated in Hardacre, *Kurozumikyō and the New Religions of Japan*, 57.
17. Kurozumi Tadaaki, *Kurozumikyō kyōsoden*, 5th ed. (Okayama: Kurozumikyō Nisshinsha, 1976), 67.
18. Kurozumi Tadaaki, *Kyōsoden*, 62–64.
19. Kurozumi Muneyasu, ed., *Kurozumikyō kyōsho* (Okayama City: Kurozumikyō Nisshinsha, 1974), 441.
20. Ibid., 449.
21. Ibid., 441–43.
22. Sasaki Junnosuke, *Bakumatsu shakairon* (Tokyo: Kōshobō, 1969), 147–48; Shibata Hajime, *Kinsei gōnō no gakumon to shisō*, ed. Negishi Yōichi (Tokyo: Shinseisha, 1966), 150. Tetsuo Najita describes village headmen's sponsorship of the Hōtoku movement inspired by Ninomiya Sontoku (1787–1856) as an effort to reinvigorate the morale of their villages and thereby undercut the urge toward insurrection in *Ordinary Economies in Japan: A Historical Perspective 1750-1950* (Berkeley: University of California Press, 2009).
23. Shibata Hajime, *Kinsei gōnō no gakumon to shisō*, 157–60.
24. Ibid., 186–200.
25. Shōji Kichinosuke, *Kinsei minshū shisō no kenkyū* (Tokyo: Kōshobō, 1979), 172ff.
26. Kurozumi Muneyasu, *Kurozumikyō kyōsho*, 469.
27. Ronald Dore shows how a variety of preachers promoted obedience to authority in *Education in Tokugawa Japan* (Berkeley: University of California Press, 1965), 237–41.
28. Letter 166, quoted in Kurozumi Muneharu, "Kurozumikyō rikkyō 200-nen e no michi. Part 5: Kyōdan no seiritsu," *Nisshin* 2013.5: 23.
29. Kōmoto Kazunobu, *Akagi Tadaharu* (Okayama: Kurozumikyō Nisshinsha, 1980), 20–21.
30. For a discussion of Kōmei's many prayers to the Kami for Japan's deliverance from the foreign threat, see Fujita Satoru, *Bakumatsu no tennō* (Tokyo: Kōdansha, 1994), 149–50, 154–56.
31. Regarding relations between Kurozumikyō and the Kyoto aristocracy, see Mayumi Tsunetada, *Kōmei Tennō to Munetada Jinja* (Kyoto: Kyoto Kaguraoka Munetada Jinja, 1992).
32. On Akagi Tadaharu, see Kōmoto Kazunobu, *Akagi Tadaharu* (Okayama: Kurozumikyō Nisshinsha, 1980).
33. Ibid., 21–36.

34. Sakata Yasuyoshi, "Kaidai," in *Shoke Shinto* 2, Shintō taikei, Ronsetsuhen 28, ed. Kurozumi Tadaaki and Sakata Yasuyoshi (Tokyo: Shintō Taikei Hensankai, 1982), 9–10 (*NB*: volume lacks continuous pagination.)
35. Sawada, n. 1, 59–60.
36. Ibid., 69.
37. Inoue Masakane, "Yume monogatari," *Ikunshū* 1, in *Shoke Shinto* 2, 52–53.
38. Misogikyō retains a document from 1834 showing an affiliation with the Shirakawa, but the Shirakawa documents date from 1836. See Ogihara Minori, "Shirakawa-ke to Edo no monjin—Tenpo nenkan no Inoue Masakane entō o megutte," *Shintō shūkyō* 143 (1991): 49.
39. Demura Katsuaki, *Yoshida Shintō no kisoteki kenkyū*, 225–37.
40. Okada Shōji, "Sanshu no ōharae," *SSDJ*, 438. It is believed that the second part was deleted on the basis of Masuho Zankō's views.
41. Inoue Masakane, "Yuiitsu Shintō mondō sho," in *Shoke Shinto* 2, 3.
42. Sawada, *Practical Pursuits*, 68–70.
43. Sakata Yasuyoshi, "Kaidai," 14–15.
44. Ogihara Minori, "Shirakawa-ke to Edo no monjin," 43–69.
45. Sawada, *Practical Pursuits*, 63–64; Asō Shōichi, *Shintō-ka Inoue Masakane* (Tokyo: Shintō Chūkyōin, 1933), 36.
46. Ashida Ijin, ed., *Shinpen Musashi fudokikō*, Dai Nihon chishi taikei 13 (Tokyo: Yūzankaku, 1996), 7:137–38.
47. Taira Shigemichi, "Kamo no Norikiyo," *SSDJ*, 242–43; "Umetsuji Norikiyo," in *Shintō jinbutsu kenkyū bunken mokuroku*, ed. Kokugakuin Daigaku Nihon Bunka Kenkyūsho (Tokyo: Kōbunkan, 2000), 102–3; "Uden Shintō," in *Kokushi daijiten* online edition, accessed via Japan Knowledge. http://japanknowledge.com.ezp-prod1.hul.harvard.edu/lib/display/?lid=30010zz050960, July 16, 2013.
48. Suenaga Keiko, *Uden Shintō no kisoteki kenkyū* (Tokyo: Iwata shoin, 2001), 157–67.

Chapter 11

1. For a concise overview of interpretations of the appearance of Kokugaku, see Peter Nosco, "Masuho Zankō (1655–1742): A Shinto Popularizer between Nativism and National Learning," in *Confucianism and Tokugawa Culture*, ed. Peter Nosco (Princeton, NJ: Princeton University Press, 1984), 166–87.
2. On Ihara Saikaku's description of the no-good son, see Peter Nosco, *Remembering Paradise: Nativism and Nostalgia in Eighteenth Century Japan* (Cambridge, MA: Council on East Asian Studies, Harvard University Press, 1990), 30.
3. Nosco, *Remembering Paradise*, 34–40. For a general study of private academies during the Edo period, see Richard Rubinger, *Private Academies in Tokugawa Japan* (Princeton, NJ: Princeton University Press, 1982).
4. On the publishing revolution, see Mary Elizabeth Berry, *Japan in Print: Information and Nation in the Early Modern Period* (Berkeley: University of California Press, 2006); and Peter Kornicki, *The Book in Japan: A Cultural History from the Beginning to the Nineteenth Century* (Leiden: Brill, 1998; repr. Honolulu: University of Hawai'i Press, 2002), 171; Susan Burns, *Before the Nation: Kokugaku and the Imagining of Community in Early Modern Japan* (Durham, NC: Duke University Press, 2003), 27.
5. Koki Kinen Ono Noriaki Sensei Ronbunshū Kankōkai, ed., "Jinja bunko no kenkyū," in *Ono Noriaki toshokangaku ronbunshū: Koki kinen* (Kyoto: Koki Kinen Ono Noriaki Sensei Ronbunshū Kankōkai, 1978), 502–44.
6. Kornicki, *The Book in Japan*, 195, 198–99; 386–87. For a study of the books possessed at the end of the period by a lower-ranking priest (*shake*) of the Izumo Shrine, see Nakazawa Nobuhiro, "Tominaga Yoshihisa kyūzō 'Tatenosha shoseki mokuroku' no ichikōsatsu: Kinsei kōki no shake zōsho no ippan," *Kokugakuin Daigaku Nihon bunka kenkyūjo kiyō* 97 (2006): 87–115.

Nakazawa's study found that Tominaga Yoshihisa (1814–1880) owned over 400 titles in over 700 volumes, in addition to the books he had written himself. Although he eventually became an instructor to the Kitajima family, one of two *kokuzō* lines at the shrine, and thus cannot be considered "typical," the quantity and variety of his books reflected broad learning, including in history, literature, shrine affairs, studies of Izumo history and customs, numerous works by Kokugaku scholars, and other subjects. After the Meiji Restoration, Tominaga rose to become *gonnegi* of the Izumo Shrine. For an outline of his life and related research, see SJKBM, 463.

7. Burns, *Before the Nation*, 40.
8. Ibid., 50.
9. Endō Jun, "The Early Modern Period: In Search of a Shinto Identity," in *Shinto: A Short History*, ed. Inoue Nobutaka, Endō Jun, Mori Mizue, trans. Mark Teeuwen and John Breen (London: RoutledgeCurzon, 1998), 149.
10. On Motoori's early life, see Haga Noboru, *Motoori Norinaga: Kinsei Kokugaku no seiritsu*, Hito to rekishi, Nihon 22 (Tokyo: Shimizu shoin, 1972), 12–34, and, for Motoori's appreciation of Keichū, 56ff.; Nosco, *Remembering Paradise*, 159–67. For a selection of Motoori's writings in English translation, see "Motoori Norinaga," in *Japanese Philosophy: A Sourcebook*, ed. James W. Heisig, Thomas P. Kasulis, and John C. Maraldo (Honolulu: University of Hawai'i Press, 2011), 472–92. Motoori's complete works are collected in Motoori Norinaga, *Motoori Norinaga zenshū*, 23 vols. (Tokyo: Chikuma shobō, 1968–1993).
11. John R. Bentley, *Tamakatsuma: A Window into the Scholarship of Motoori Norinaga* (Ithaca NY: East Asia Program, Cornell University, 2013), 7.
12. Nosco, *Remembering Paradise*, 178–79.
13. Isomae Jun'ichi, *Japanese Mythology: Hermeneutics on Scripture* (Oakville, CT: Equinox Pub.; Kyoto: International Research Center for Japanese Studies [Nichibunken], 2009), 116.
14. Motoori Norinaga, *Kojikiden*, vol. 3, *Motoori Norinaga zenshū* (Tokyo: Chikuma shobō, 1968–1993), 135–36; translated in Stuart Picken, *Sourcebook in Shinto: Selected Documents*, Resources in Asian Philosophy and Religion (Westport, CT: Praeger, 2004), 200–201. The translation appearing here has been adapted from Picken.
15. Isomae, *Japanese Mythology*, 114–16.
16. Nishimura Sei and Motoori Norinaga, "The Way of the Gods, Motoori Norinaga's Naobi no Mitama," *Monumenta Nipponica* 46, no. 1 (1991): 31.
17. Ibid., 30.
18. Ibid., 34.
19. Ibid., 39.
20. Ibid., 33.
21. Ibid., 37.
22. Bentley, *Tamakatsuma*, 79.
23. Nishimura and Motoori, "Way of the Gods," 39–40.
24. Burns, *Before the Nation*, 1–2, 76. For discussion of Motoori's students, see Nosco, *Remembering Paradise*, 207–8. The largest occupational group of students were merchants (34 percent), followed by cultivators (23 percent, probably with a concentration of village officers or headmen), followed by samurai and shrine priests (each at 14 percent), and a small number of Buddhist clergy (5 percent). About 5 percent of Motoori's students were women.
25. Haga Noboru, "Bakumatsu ni okeru Motoori, Hirata gaku no keishō," *Tokyo kasei daigakuin daigaku kiyō* 35 (1995): 68.
26. Okanaka Masayuki, Suzuki Jun, and Nakamura Kazumoto, *Motoori Norinaga to Suzuya shachū 'Jugyō monjin seimei roku' no sōgōteki kenkyū* (Tokyo: Kinseisha, 1984), 385–87.
27. Mark Teeuwen, "Poetry, Sake, and Acrimony, Arakida Hisaoyu and the Kokugaku Movement," *Monumenta Nipponica* 53, no. 3 (1997): 296.
28. Okanaka, Suzuki, and Nakamura, *Motoori Norinaga to Suzuya shachū*, 356–58.
29. Nosco, *Remembering Paradise*, 192–93.
30. Nishimura and Motoori, "Way of the Gods," 37.

31. Nishimura Sei, "First Steps into the Mountains: Motoori Norinaga's Uiyamabumi," *Monumenta Nipponica* 42, no. 4 (1987): 463.
32. Nishimura and Motoori, "Way of the Gods," 28.
33. Teeuwen, n. 27, 306.
34. Ibid., 309.
35. Ibid., 320.
36. Ibid., 324.
37. For a selection of Atsutane's writings in English translation, see "Hirata Atsutane," in Heisig, Kasulis, and Maraldo, *Japanese Philosophy*, 509–22. For a succinct treatment of Atsutane's life, see Tahara Tsuguo, "Hirata Atsutane," *Nihon dai hyakka zensho*. For more extensive treatment, see Miki Shōtarō, *Hirata Atsutane no kenkyū* (Ise-shi: Shintōshi Gakkai, 1967), 1–45. Endō Jun provides a chronology of Atsutane's life and his school in *Hirata Kokugaku to kinsei shakai*, 313–48. The most comprehensive biographical study is Watanabe Kinzō, *Hirata Atsutane kenkyū* (Tokyo: Rokkō shobō, 1942). Since Watanabe's study, a large number of letters and other writings not available to him have been published. See Miyachi Masato, ed., "Hirata Kokugaku no saikentō 1," *Kokuritsu Rekishi Minzoku Hakubutsukan kenkyū kiyō* 122 (March 2005): 1–221; and three continuations of that study, also edited by Miyachi, in subsequent issues of the same journal, "Hirata Kokugaku no saikentō 2," *Kokuritsu Rekishi Minzoku Hakubutsukan kenkyū kiyō* 128 (March 2006): 1–503; "Hirata Kokugaku no saikentō 3," *Kokuritsu Rekishi Minzoku Hakubutsukan kenkyū kiyō* 146 (March 2009): 1–389; and "Hirata Kokugaku no saikentō 4," *Kokuritsu Rekishi Minzoku Hakubutsukan kenkyū kiyō* 159 (March 2010): 1–162. An index to this collection can be found in Kokuritsu Rekishi Minzoku Hakubutsukan, *Hirata Atsutane kankei shiryō mokuroku*, Kokuritsu Rekishi Minzoku Hakubutsukan shiryō mokuroku 6 (Tokyo: Kokuritsu Rekishi Minzoku Hakubutsukan, 2007). The most comprehensive collection of Hirata's writings is Hirata Atsutane and Zenshū Kankōkai, eds., *Shinshū Hirata Atsutane zenshū*, 21 vols. (Tokyo: Meichō shuppan, 1976–1981).
38. On *Senkyō ibun*, see Wilburn Hansen, *When Tengu Talk: Hirata Atsutane's Ethnography of the Other World* (Honolulu: University of Hawai'i Press, 2008).
39. Richard Devine, "Hirata Atsutane and Christian Sources," *Monumenta Nipponica* 36, no. 1 (1981): 37–54. On Atsutane's beliefs regarding Amenominakanushi, see Jinbo Kunio, "Hirata Atsutane Amenominakanushi shinkō no hensei to kakuritsu—jō," *Shintō shūkyō* 162 (March 1996): 43–73; and a continuation of that essay, Jinbo Kunio, "Hirata Atsutane Amenominakanushi shinkō no hensei to kakuritsu—ge," *Shintō shūkyō* 163 (June 1996): 59–85.
40. Miki Shōtarō, "Hirata Atsutane no 'Maichō shinpai shiki' ni tsuite," *Geirin* 17, no. 4 (1936): 129. On Atsutane's religious practices, see Watanabe Kinzō, *Hirata Atsutane kenkyū*, 208–24. Based on diary entries, Watanabe shows that Atsutane's personal faith was quite eclectic. Besides the Kami identified in the "Morning Prayers," he worshipped Tenjin, a dragon-snake deity called Ryūjajin (he was encouraged to worship this figure by a priest of the Izumo Shrine), the deified spirit of Taira Masakado, and miscellaneous folk deities such as the toilet god and the god of wells (he regarded wells as leading to the underworld). He also believed in ghosts, foxes transforming into people, and related ideas. While in Akita after his banishment from Edo, in 1843, he conducted a successful prayer healing (*kitō*).
41. H. D. Harootunian, *Things Seen and Unseen: Discourse and Ideology in Tokugawa Nativism* (Chicago: University of Chicago Press, 1988), 160, 190.
42. Mark McNally, *Proving the Way: Conflict and Practice in the History of Japanese Nativism* (Cambridge, MA: Harvard University Asia Center, 2005), 23–24.
43. Ibid., 93–96.
44. Ibid., 101–19.
45. Endō Jun, *Hirata Kokugaku to kinsei shakai* (Tokyo: Perikansha, 2008), 142–63.
46. Ibid., 120; quoting *Tama no Mihashira* in *Hirata Atsutane, Ban Nobutomo, Ōkuni Takamasa*, ed. Tahara Tsuguo, et al., Nihon shisō taikei 50 (Tokyo: Iwanami shoten, 1973), 109.

47. H. D. Harootunian, *Things Seen and Unseen*, 31–32.
48. *Tama no Mihashira*, in Tahara Tsuguo, *Hirata Atsutane, Ban Nobutomo, Ōkuni Takamasa*, 112, 121; also cited in McNally, *Proving the Way*.
49. Quoted in Wilburn Hansen, "The Medium Is the Message: Hirata Atsutane's Ethnography of the World Beyond," *History of Religions* 45, no. 2 (2006): 366. On the continuity of the dead and the living, see H. D. Harootunian, *Things Seen and Unseen*, 150–52. The main leaders of other academies devoted to studies of Norinaga's works were not convinced by Atsutane's arguments, and he was believed at the time to have lost the debate started by Nakatsune's work; McNally, *Proving the Way*, 130.
50. McNally, n. 42, 167–70.
51. Ibid., 181.
52. Hirata Atsutane, *Tamatasuki* in *Shinshū Hirata Atsutane zenshū*, vol. 6. For a brief outline of the prayers, see Endō Jun, *Hirata Kokugaku to kinsei shakai*, 143–45. Motoori Norinaga had written a text for daily prayers using almost the same title (only the final characters differed), and Atsutane was undoubtedly aware of this work. Motoori's composition differed in that it directed prayers to nineteen Kami, whereas Atsutane used twenty-eight. Atsutane's first draft of "Morning Prayers" was completed in 1816. It was revised several times, notably in 1824 (the year following Atsutane's visit to Norinaga's grave), in 1829, included in *Tamatasuki* with commentary and reissued in 1850. It continued to be published in different editions at least until the 1880s. On "Morning Prayers," see Miki Shōtarō, "Hirata Atsutane no 'Maichō shinpai shiki' ni tsuite," 128–51; and Watanabe Yutaka, "Hirata Atsutane no 'Maichō shinpai shiki,'" in *Takahara sensei kiju kinen kōgakukan ronshū* (Ise City: Kōgakukan Daigaku shuppan-bu, 1969); and Watanabe Yutaka, "Hirata Atsutane no Maichō shinpai shiki, tsuiho," *Shintōshi kenkyū* 19, no. 1 (1971): 31–49. Watanabe's 1971 study includes the text of the *norito*. A digital facsimile of an edition published in 1881, bearing a colophon by Atsutane dated 1811 and a preface dated 1850 is available through the National Diet Library of Japan: http://kindai.ndl.go.jp/BIImgFrame.php?JP_NUM=40043554&VOL_NUM=00000&KOMA=1&ITYPE=0). Atsutane noted that if time did not permit a complete recitation, then an abbreviated version would suffice, which would include prayers for the palace, the Kami of one's own *kamidana*, and the ancestors. The text was accompanied by phonetic reading guides (*furigana*), making it easy to read or recite.
53. The prayers repeatedly express gratitude to the Kami for all existence, from the body and its health to food, clothing, and shelter, and it is clear that Atsutane's followers were meant to cultivate this attitude as the basis of worship. Each section asks for continued blessing and protection, and it is clear that the Kami were believed to watch over those who worshipped them faithfully. All of the prayers adopt the characteristic lexicon of *norito* and a rhythmical style of repeated phrases that embellish and lengthen the recitation. See Miki Shōtarō, *Hirata Atsutane no kenkyū*, 312.
54. Miki Shōtarō, "Hirata Atsutane no 'Maichō shinpai shiki' ni tsuite," 139–45.
55. Endō Jun, "Early Modern Period: In Search of a Shinto Identity," 138–39; Endō Jun, "The Shinto Funeral Movement in Early Modern and Modern Japan," trans. Norman Havens, *Transactions of the Institute for Japanese Culture and Classics* 82 (1998): 1–31; Elizabeth Kenney, "Shinto Funerals in the Edo Period." Kenney's study contains detailed descriptions of Shinto funerals over several centuries, emphasizing the variety among them. The author includes commentary from one Shinto priest of the late Edo period, who found the emergence of Shinto funerals an abomination because of their novelty.
56. Endō Jun, *Hirata Kokugaku to kinsei shakai*, 156–57.
57. As explained in chapter 7, the shrines whose priests had been first licensed by the Yoshida in the medieval period were rather small institutions compared to the larger shrines with established priestly lineages. The larger ones rejected Yoshida authority over them and were granted exemptions from affiliating with them.
58. The Yoshida office opened in 1791; the Shirakawa office opened in 1802. Endō Jun, *Hirata Kokugaku to kinsei shakai*, 168, 181–82. On the Yoshida's office in Edo, see Sugiyama

Shigetsugu, "Yoshida-ke Kantō yakusho no sōritsu to shoki no katsudō," *Kokugakuin Daigaku Nihon bunka kenkyūjo kiyō* 45 (March 1980): 59–106.

59. For example, the Yoshida could not issue licenses to farmers or low-level shrine functionaries, such as *miko* and those who kept the shrine's keys, without special permission, and they had to seek the permission of the village headmen and the local shogunal supervisor (*daikan*) before issuing new licenses to provincial priests. The Shirakawa did not face such restrictions, and besides the full spectrum of customary ritualists and functionaries at shrines, they also issued licenses to shrine carpenters and the makers of sweets used in ceremonies. See Toki Masanori, "Kinsei no shinshoku soshiki—Musashi Kuni no jirei," *Kokugakuin Daigaku Nihon bunka kenkyūjo kiyō* 12 (March 1963): 232–33. For a listing of all the Shirakawa house affiliates, including their occupations, see Kondō Yoshihiro, *Shirakawa-ke monjinchō* (Osaka: Seibundō, 1972).
60. Endō Jun, *Hirata Kokugaku to kinsei shakai*, 175–76. In lectures delivered in 1811 and later collected as "On Vulgar Shinto" ("Zoku Shintō tai-i"), Atsutane had critiqued Ryōbu, Yuiitsu, and Confucian forms of Shinto as foreign in inspiration.
61. Endō Jun, *Hirata Kokugaku to kinsei shakai*, 182–83. For a discussion of Ikuta Yorozu in English, see H. D. Harootunian, *Things Seen and Unseen*, 235–43.
62. Endō Jun, *Hirata Kokugaku to kinsei shakai*, 176–78, 181.
63. Kobayashi Yūhachi, "Hakke Shintō to Hirata Atsutane—*Jingihaku-ke gakusoku* no sakusha oyobi sono seiritsu jiki ni tsuite," *Kōgakukan ronsō* 7, no. 6 (1974): 41–58; Endō Jun, *Hirata Kokugaku to kinsei shakai*, 211, 228–32.
64. Anne Walthall, "Off with Their Heads!": The Hirata Disciples and the Ashikaga Shoguns," *Monumenta Nipponica* 50, no. 2 (Summer 1995): 137, 141, 148; Anne Walthall, *The Weak Body of a Useless Woman: Matsuo Taseko and the Meiji Restoration* (Chicago: University of Chicago Press, 1998).
65. Ōkuni Takamasa, "Hongaku kyoyō," in Tahara Tsuguo, *Hirata Atsutane, Ban Nobutomo, Ōkuni Takamasa*, 412–16; McNally, *Proving the Way*, 198–99; see also Jennifer Robertson, "Sexy Rice: Plant Gender, Farm Manuals, and Grass-Roots Nativism," *Monumenta Nipponica* 39, no. 3 (1984): 233–60, esp., 239, 249, 254, 258.
66. On the symmetry of the thinking between nativists and the leaders of Shinto-derived new religious movements at the end of the Edo period, see Haga Noboru, "Bakumatsu henkakuki ni okeru kokugakusha no undō to rinri—tokuni yonaoshi jōkyū to kanren sasete," in *Kokugaku undo no shisō*, 670–71. On the common themes of late nativist writings from the Hirata school, see H. D. Harootunian, *Things Seen and Unseen*, 253–62, and chap. 6.
67. On the use of these terms, see Michael Wachutka, *Kokugaku in Meiji-Period Japan: The Modern Transformation of "National Learning" and the Formation of Scholarly Societies* (Leiden: Global Oriental, 2013), 1–4.
68. Haga Noboru, "Bakumatsu kokugaku no kenkyū," *Shigaku sensho* 1 (Tokyo: Kyōiku shuppan sentaa, 1980), 46, 51, 62, 74. See also Robertson, "Sexy Rice," 237–39, 252, 257–59; Helen Hardacre, "Creating State Shinto: The Great Promulgation Campaign and the New Religions," *JJRS* 12, no. 1 (Winter 1986): 36. H.D. Harootunian discusses Mutobe Yoshika's thought in *Things Seen and Unseen*, 235–43. For the text of Miyaoi Sadao's "Kokueki honron," see *Kokugaku undō no shisō*, 291–309. The text of Mutobe's "Ubusuna shako denshō kōgi" is available in the same volume, 221–30.
69. For discussion of the Hirata school's membership numbers, see Wachutka, *Kokugaku in Meiji-Period Japan*, 4.
70. Yano Harumichi, "Kenkin sengo," in *Kokugaku undō no shisō*, 547–85. On Yano's life and thought, see Kuwabara Megumi, "Bakumatsu kokugaku shisō ni okeru kokka kan, tennō kan," *Rekishigaku Kenkyū* 599 (1989): 10, 107–15. For discussion of "Kenkin sengo," see Wachutka, *Kokugaku in Meiji-Period Japan*, 21–26.
71. Sugata Masaaki, *Fukugan no Shintōka-tachi* (Tokyo: Hachiman shoten, 1987), 65–79. For an annotated version of Ōkuni's major works, see Tahara Tsuguo, *Hirata Atsutane, Ban Nobutomo,*

Ōkuni Takamasa, 401–517. For studies of Ōkuni in English, see H. D. Harootunian, *Things Seen and Unseen,* 376–94; John Breen, "Shintoists in Restoration Japan: Toward a Reassessment," *Modern Asian Studies* 24 (1990): 579–602; Wachutka, *Kokugaku in Meiji-Period Japan,* 4–7. On Ōkuni's change of attitude toward Christianity, see John Breen, "Accommodating the Alien: Ōkuni Takamasa and the Religion of Heaven," in *Religion in Japan: Arrows to Heaven and Earth,* ed. Peter F. Kornicki and Ian J. McMullen (Cambridge: Cambridge University Press, 1996), 170–97.

72. Haga Noboru, "Bakumatsu henkakuki ni okeru kokugakusha no undō to ronri," 701; Matsumoto Sannosuke, "Bakumatsu Kokugaku no shisōshiteki igi," in *Kokugaku undō no shisō,* 633–61. See also Endō Jun, "Early Modern Period: In Search of a Shinto Identity," 155–56.
73. For a detailed breakdown of the roles of the various aristocratic houses (including the division of labor between the Yoshida and Shirakawa Houses) and Buddhist temples in imperial ritual at the end of the period, see Haga Shōji, "Meiji Jingikansei no seiritsu to kokka saishi no saihen," *Jinbun gakuhō* 50 (1981): 34–36, 40–46. This study surveys various opinions about the ideal structure and functioning of the Jingikan, as well as provides a detailed chronology of the organization's re-establishment.
74. On Kōmei's revival of court ceremonies in the context of the foreign threat, see Mase Kumiko, "Jinja to tennō" and Fujita Satoru, *Bakumatsu no tennō* (Tokyo: Kōdansha, 1994), 154–55, and Haga Shōji, "Meiji Jingikansei no seiritsu to kokka saishi no saihen," 42–44.
75. Wachutka, *Kokugaku in Meiji-Period Japan,* 52–54.
76. Haga Shōji, "Meiji Jingikansei no seiritsu to kokka saishi no saihen," 56; Wachutka, *Kokugaku in Meiji-Period Japan,* 52–56.
77. "Anything Goes!" was concentrated in the central part of the main island, Honshū, and did not spread to the northeast or southern Kyūshū. Besides those mentioned here, incidents occurred in and around Edo, in present-day Gunma Prefecture, in central Japan (present-day Nagano and Fukui Prefectures), in the cities of Kyoto and Osaka, as far west as present-day Shimane and Fukuoka Prefectures. See Tamura Sadao, "Ee janaika no shodankai to denban chizu," *Kokusai kankei kenkyū* 28, no. 3 (2007): 113–33.
78. There are no comprehensive accounts from the time, only records specific to the author's location; the main ones are *Notes on Mysterious Happenings of Ise: Thanks Pilgrimage of the Keiō Era* (Keiō Ise okage kenbun shokoku fushigi no hikae) and *Bukō nenpyō.* Other than these, there are only scattered records from specific locales. See Fujitani Toshio, *Shintō shinkō to minshū, tennōsei* (Kyoto: Hōritsu bunkasha, 1980), 159–74; and George Wilson, "Ee ja nai ka on the Eve of the Meiji Restoration in Japan," *Semiotics* 70, no. 3/4 (1988): 301–19.
79. Fujitani Toshio, *Shintō shinkō to minshū, tennōsei,* 162.
80. From *Ikeda chōshi,* quoted in Fujitani, *Shintō shinkō to minshū, tennōsei,* 162.
81. From *Awa eejanaika,* quoted in Fujitani, *Shintō shinkō to minshū, tennōsei,* 165.
82. Endō, *Hirata kokugaku to kinsei shakai,* 230–37.

Chapter 12

1. Murakami Shigeyoshi, *Kokka Shintō* (Tokyo: Iwanami shinsho, 1970).
2. Shimazono Susumu, "State Shinto and the Religious Structure of Modern Japan," *Journal of the American Academy of Religion* 73, no. 4 (2005): 1077–98; Shimazono Susumu, "State Shinto in the Lives of the People: The Establishment of Emperor Worship, Modern Nationalism, and State Shinto in Late Meiji," *JJRS* 36, no. 1 (2009): 93–124: Shimazono Susumu, *Kokka Shintō to Nihonjin* (Tokyo: Iwanami shoten, 2010).
3. Inoue Hiroshi, *Nihon no jinja to "Shintō,"* (Tokyo: Azekura shobō, 2006), 256, quoted in Okuyama Michiaki, "State Shinto in Recent Japanese Scholarship," *Monumenta Nipponica* 66, no. 1 (2011): 135. See also Isomae Jun'ichi, "The Formative Process of State Shinto in Relation to the Westernization of Japan: The Concept of 'Religion' and 'Shinto,'" in *Religion and the Secular: Historical and Colonial Formations,* ed. Timothy Fitzgerald (London: Equinox,

2007), 93–101; and Isomae Jun'ichi, "Kokka Shintō to wa nanika," in *Nihon shisōshi handobukku*, ed. Karube Tadashi and Kataoka Ryū (Tokyo: Shinshōkan, 2008), 142–45.

4. Ashizu Uzuhiko, *Kokka Shinto to wa nan datta no ka* (Tokyo: Jinja Shinpōsha, 1987). Likewise, Ōhara Yasuo excoriated the Occupation for the Shinto Directive of December 1945, based on minute analysis of draft versions. See Ōhara Yasuo, *Shintō shirei no kenkyū* (Tokyo: Hara shobō, 1993).
5. See Sakamoto Koremaru, "'Kokka Shintō' kenkyū no yonjū nen," *Nihon shisōshi gaku* 42 (2010): 46–58; Nitta Hitoshi, "'Kokka Shintō' ron no keifu," part 1: *Kōgakkan ronsō* 32, no. 1 (February 1999): 1–36; and part 2: *Kōgakkan ronsō* 32, no. 2 (April 1999): 23–59.
6. Daniel Holtom, *Modern Japan and Shinto Nationalism: A Study of Present-Day Trends in Japanese Religions* (Chicago: University of Chicago Press, 1943). See also Ernst Lokowandt, *Die rechtliche Entwicklung des Staats-Shintō in der ersten Hälfte der Meiji-Zeit (1868-1890)* (Wien: Harrassowitz, 1978); and Helen Hardacre, *Shinto and the State, 1868-1988* (Princeton, NJ: Princeton University Press, 1989).
7. See Klaus Antoni, *Shintō & die Konzeption des japanischen Nationalwesens (kokutai): Der religiöse Traditionalismus in Neuzeit und Moderne Japans* (Leiden: Brill, 1998); and Walter Skya, *Japan's Holy War: The Ideology of Radical Shinto Ultranationalism* (Durham, NC: Duke University Press, 2009). Mark Teeuwen criticizes Antoni's approach in "State Shinto: An 'Independent Religion'?," *Monumenta Nipponica* 54, no. 1 (Spring 1999): 111–21.
8. John Breen and Mark Teeuwen, *A New History of Shinto*. Also see John Breen and Mark Teeuwen, eds., *Shinto in History: Ways of the Kami* (Honolulu: University of Hawai'i Press, 2000); and John Breen, ed. *Yasukuni, the War Dead, and the Struggle for Japan's Past* (New York: Columbia University Press, 2008); Bernhard Scheid, ed., *Kami Ways in Nationalist Territory: Shinto Studies in Prewar Japan and the West*, with Kate Wildman Nakai (Wien: Österreichische Akademie der Wissenschaften, 2013); Trent Maxey, *The "Greatest Problem": Religion and State Formation in Meiji Japan* (Cambridge, MA: Harvard University Asia Center, 2014).
9. Sheldon Garon, "State and Religion in Imperial Japan, 1912-1945," *Journal of Japanese Studies* 12, no. 2 (Summer 1986): 274.
10. Okuyama, "State Shinto in Recent Japanese Scholarship."
11. Umeda Yoshihiko, "Jinja seido enkakushi," in *Meiji ishin Shintō hyakunenshi*, ed. Shintō Bunkakai (Tokyo: Shintō Bunkakai, 1966), 1:160.
12. See Suga Kōji, "'Chōsen Jingū go saijin ronsō' saikaishaku no kokoromi: Jinja no 'dochakusei' to mōdanizumu no shiten kara," *Shūkyō to shakai* 5 (1999): 21–38; Fujimoto Yorio, "Shinshoku yōsei to shūkyō kyōiku: Sengo rokujū go nen no ayumi kara miru genjō to kadai" (Tokushū: Shūkyō no kyōiku to denshō) *Shūkyō kenkyū* 85, no. 2 (2011): 505–28.
13. John Breen, "Ideologues, Bureaucrats, and Priests: On 'Shinto' and 'Buddhism' in Early Meiji Japan," in Breen and Teeuwen, *Shinto in History*, 230–51.
14. Bob Wakabayashi, *Anti-Foreignism and Western Learning in Early-Modern Japan: The New Theses of 1825* (Cambridge, MA: Council on East Asian Studies, Harvard University, 1991), 52–54.
15. Ibid., 69–84.
16. Ibid., 90. Aizawa had studied Western history and had come to admire Peter the Great of Russia as a reformer who improved the lot of the peasantry by developing agriculture, providing education, and indoctrinating the people with Russian Orthodox teachings.
17. Ibid., 124, 129–30. The concept of *kokutai* originated in Chinese texts, but through extensive commentary in the late Edo and Meiji periods, it acquired distinctly new meanings associated with the goal of ensuring the spiritual unity of the Japanese people. *Kokutai* for Aizawa was the spiritual unity that was a nation's most essential element, without which it could not endure. To nurture and strengthen the *kokutai* was the aim of his ideas about indoctrinating the populace in a national teaching. Other Confucians who took it up included Kaibara Ekken, Yamaga Sokō, and Ogyū Sorai; it also figured importantly in Yamazaki Ansai's writings. See Matsumoto Takashi, "Kinsei ni okeru saisei itchi shisō no tenkai: Suika Shintō yori Mitogaku e," in Sakamoto Koremaru, *Kokka Shintō saikō: Saisei itchi kokka no kaisei to tenkai* (Tokyo: Kōbundō, 2006), 39–64.

18. *Yokoi Shōnan ikō*, Yamazaki Masatada, ed., 242–43, quoted in Wakabayashi, *Anti-Foreignism and Western Learning*, 142–43.
19. Mark McNally, *Proving the Way: Conflict and Practice in the History of Japanese Nativism* (Cambridge, MA: Harvard University Asia Center, 2005), 203.
20. This proclamation was called the Five-Article Vow, or the Charter Oath (Gokajō no go-seimon).
21. On the central role of Tsuwano figures in the early Meiji administration, see Sakamoto Ken'ichi, *Meiji Shintōshi no kenkyū* (Tokyo: Kokusho kankōkai, 1983), 377–467. On the importance attributed to personal imperial performance of ritual, see Takeda Hideaki, *Ishinki tennō saishi no kenkyū* (Tokyo: Taimeidō, 1996), 238–39; Odaira Mika, *Josei shinshoku no tanjō* (Tokyo: Perikansha, 2009), 192–95. To realize Ōkuni's vision of a Shinto purified of Buddhist influence, Ōkuni's disciple Fukuba Bisei had carried out Tsuwano's own "separation of Buddhas from Kami" in 1867. That campaign resulted in the closing and eradicating of many temples, forcibly laicizing the priests, and the destruction of much temple property. Fukuba, who later headed the Jingikan, drew fellow Ōkuni disciples into the organization, and thus directly brought Ōkuni's thought to bear on the new government.
22. Takeda, *Ishinki tennō saishi no kenkyū*, 240–50. Takeda introduces memorials written separately by Konakamura and Urata Nagatami that call for the Jingikan to be absorbed into the Dajōkan. Both placed greatest emphasis on the emperor's personal performance of state ritual; they did not want any agency acting as the emperor's proxy in the performance of ritual. Konakamura believed that the Jingikan could be abolished once shrines were constructed within the palace. Urata favored splitting off the indoctrination function of the Jingikan from the performance of state rites.
23. Takeda, *Ishinki tennō saishi no kenkyū*, 176–82. See also John Breen, "The Imperial Oath of April 1868: Ritual, Politics, and Power in the Restoration," *Monumenta Nipponica* 51, no. 4 (1996): 407–29.
24. Odaira, *Josei shinshoku no tanjō*, 204–13.
25. On the issues surrounding the cessation of Buddhist worship in the palace, see Sakamoto Ken'ichi, *Meiji Shintōshi no kenkyū*, 469–511; Murakami Shigeyoshi, *Tennō no saishi* (Tokyo: Iwanami shinsho 993, 1977), 59–60. Female members of the imperial house who had become nuns were permitted to remain in Buddhist orders.
26. Konakamura undertook a survey of the *shikinaisha* and consulted ancient sources to discover how imperial rites had been performed in antiquity; Fujita Hiromasa, "Meiji shonen no kokka saishi keisei to kokugakusha: Jingikan, Jingishō no kōshō sagyō o chūshin ni," *Kokugakuin daigaku Nihon bunka kenkyūjo kiyō* 97 (2006): 117–64.
27. Nakazawa Nobuhiro, *Kyūchū saishi* (Tokyo: Dentensha, 2010), 16–25. This custom was in abeyance between 1946 and the Shikinen Sengū of 1973. Since the loss of the sword in 1185, a lacquered sword has been used as its replacement.
28. For compact summary of palace ritual, see Nakazawa, *Kyūchū saishi*, 64–108. More detailed discussion is available in Yatsuka Kiyotsura, "Kōshitsu saishi hyakunenshi," in *Meiji ishin Shintō hyakunenshi* (Tokyo: Shintō Bunkakai, 1966), 1:49–155. Developing this calendar of imperial rites took several years, and even after its standardization, the separate ceremonies were subject to modification in ritual procedures and other matters.
29. Takeda, *Ishinki tennō saishi no kenkyū*, 253ff.
30. Ibid.
31. Breen, "Ideologues, Bureaucrats, and Priests," 231–35. For the text of this and subsequent edicts and laws concerning religion, up to around 1980, see Toyoda Takeshi, *Shūkyō seidoshi* (Tokyo: Yoshikawa Kōbunkan; 1982).
32. Tamamuro Fumio, *Shinbutsu bunri* (Tokyo: Kyōikusha, 1979); and Yasumaru Yoshio, *Kamigami no Meiji ishin*, Iwanami shinsho 103 (Tokyo: Iwanami shoten, 1980), 145–59. James Ketelaar has extensively examined the implications of these policies for Buddhism in *Of Heretics and Martyrs in Meiji Japan: Buddhism and Its Persecution* (Princeton, NJ: Princeton University Press, 1990). See also Tamamuro Fumio, "On the Suppression of Buddhism," in

New Directions in the Study of Meiji Japan, ed. Helen Hardacre with Adam Kern (Leiden: E. J. Brill, 1997), 499–505.

33. Allan Grapard, "Japan's Ignored Cultural Revolution: The Separation of Shinto and Buddhist Divinities in Meiji (*shinbutsu bunri*) and a Case Study: Tonomine," *History of Religions* 23 (February 1984): 240–65.
34. The most extensive collection of primary documents on *shinbutsu bunri* is Tsuji Zennosuke, Murakami Senshō, and Washio Junkei, eds., *Shinpen Meiji ishin shinbutsu bunri shiryō*, 10 vols. (Tokyo: Meichō shuppan, 2001); see also Tamamuro Fumio, ed., *Meiji shonen jiin meisaichō*, 2 vols. (Tokyo: Hatsubai Suzuwa shōten, 2008). For recent case studies, see Sarah Thal, *Rearranging the Landscape of the Gods: The Politics of a Pilgrimage Site in Japan, 1573-1912* (Chicago: University of Chicago Press, 2005), chaps. 5, 6; Barbara Ambros, *Emplacing a Pilgrimage: The Ōyama Cult and Regional Religion in Early Modern Japan* (Cambridge, MA: Harvard University Asia Center, 2008); Helen Hardacre, *Religion and Society in Nineteenth-Century Japan: A Study of the Southern Kantō Region, Using Late Edo and Early Meiji Gazetteers*, Michigan Monograph Series in Japanese Studies 41 (Ann Arbor: Center for Japanese Studies, University of Michigan, 2002).
35. Hardacre, *Religion and Society in Nineteenth-Century Japan*, 114–25, 186–90, and 96 table 6, 176 table 9.
36. Haga Noboru, *Meiji kokka to minshū* (Tokyo: Yūzankaku, 1974), 19.
37. "Naegi-han sōsai shobun," in *Shūkyō to kokka*, ed. Miyachi Masato and Yasumaru Yoshio, vol. 5 of *Nihon kindai shisō taikei* (Tokyo: Iwanami shoten, 1988), 119–24.
38. For a longer discussion of these "conversions," see Hardacre, *Religion and Society in Nineteenth-Century Japan*, chap. 6.
39. Yasumaru, *Kamigami no Meiji ishin*, 145–59; Miyachi Masato, "Kokka Shintō keisei katei no mondaiten," in Yasumaru and Miyachi, *Shūkyō to kokka*, 568.
40. Umeda Yoshihiko, "Jinja seido enkakushi," 164; Miyachi Masato, "Kokka Shintō keisei katei no mondaiten," in Yasumaru and Miyachi, *Shūkyō to kokka*, 569.
41. From 1868 to 1870, Urata held several posts in the government of the newly established Watarai Prefecture, which superseded the former town governments of Uji and Yamada. He later served in the Ise priesthood under Tanaka Yoritsune (1836–1897), who became Chief Priest in 1874.
42. Gomazuru Hiroyuki, Sakurai Katsunoshin, Suzuki Yoshikazu et al., "Jingū hyakunen no ayumi," in *Meiji ishin Shintō hyakunenshi*, vol. 1, ed. Shintō Bunkakai, 363–95 (Tokyo: Shintō Bunkakai, 1966). The number of priests rose to seventy-three in 1896, and to 195 in 1922.
43. Jingūshichō, *Jingū: Meiji hyakunenshi* (Ise-shi: Jingūshichō, 1968), 1:15ff., 65–71.
44. Fujitani Toshio, *Shintō shinkō to minshū, tennōsei* (Kyoto: Hōritsu bunkasha, 1980), 190–91. Mishima Michitsune (1835–1888), an official in the early government of Tokyo who later served in the Kyōbushō, had proposed that a golden pavilion be constructed on a hill in Tokyo to house the Ise deities, with symbols of each Buddhist sect ranged below it. See Tanigawa Yutaka, "Kyōiku, kyōka seisaku to shūkyō," in *Kin-gendai 1*, Iwanami kōza Nihon rekishi (Tokyo: Iwanami shoten, 2014), 15:271–306.
45. Gomazuru et al., "Jingū hyakunen no ayumi," 447–48. Construction of private structures of any kind was prohibited at Ise. Buildings regarded as inessential were razed. This cleared the precincts of miscellaneous structures for building pure fires, small dance stages for *kagura*, and the like. The stall-shrines around the main sanctuaries (*massha*) were cleared away.
46. Jingūshichō, *Jingū: Meiji hyakunenshi*, 1:192ff., 369. Area shrines were also affected by the Ise reforms, because up to the Meiji period there had been numerous shrines on Ise's sprawling landholdings in Watarai-gun, Taki-gun, Uno-gun, Shima-gun, Wakayama- and Tsu domains that were loosely affiliated with the Ise shrines. By the beginning of the Meiji period, they had come to function as tutelary shrines for the people living around them. The Ise reforms paralleled the changes in shrine deities resulting from the separation of Buddhism from the Kami. Near the Ise Shrines, there was a group of some eighteen Tennō shrines, most of which had been dedicated to the Ox-Headed God, Gozu Tennō, who was associated with disease. As of

1869, all of these shrines were required to oust Gozu Tennō and enshrine Susanoo instead. Likewise, there were some thirty-four shrines dedicated to Hachiōji, the Eight Princelings. Of these, nineteen were converted to the worship of the Ukei deities, a group of five male and three female Kami. This grouping derived from the exchange of vows between Amaterasu and Susanoo in ancient myth, in which they chewed up and spat out each other's emblems, resulting in the creation of five male and three female Kami (see chapter 2). There is virtually no evidence of popular worship of the Ukei deities before Meiji. See Sakurai Haruo, "Meiji shonen no jinja chōsaki ni okeru chiiki jinja no yōsu: Meiji 4-nen [1874] Toba-han 'Jinja torishirabe' no bunseki kara," *Jinja honchō kyōgaku kenkyūjo kiyō* 2 (1997): 26–31; and Sakurai Haruo, *Chiiki jinja no shūkyōgaku* (Tokyo: Kōbundō, 2010).

47. Miura Masayuki, *Jinja no honden: Kenchiku ni miru kami no kūkan*, Rekishi bunka raiburari 362 (Tokyo: Yoshikawa kōbunkan, 2013), 224–30. The standard blueprint called, not for a traditional style of shrine architecture, but instead for a *kirizuma zukuri* style, to which eaves (*hizashi*) were attached in the front. The supply of large Japanese cypress (*hinoki*) trees was quickly exhausted, prompting the use of Taiwan cypress, easily recognizable, as it turns darker than Japanese as it ages.
48. The thirteen families were the Senge, Kitajima, Ki, Kaneko, Kawabe, Chiaki, Totsu, Miyanari, Aso, Tsumori, Sawada, Matsuki, and Ono families. Yamaori Tetsuo, *Nihon shūkyōshi nenpyō*, 489.
49. The revolt was suppressed in only a day, but it sparked two similar rebellions in the same month, in the Akizuki domain of Fukuoka Prefecture and the Hagi Rebellion of Yamaguchi Prefecture. These also were suppressed almost immediately, and their leaders either committed suicide on the battlefield or were executed. The Satsuma Rebellion was the largest of these uprisings and was only put down after nearly eight months of fighting. Haga Noboru, *Henkakuki ni okeru Kokugaku* (Tokyo: San'yōsha, 1975), 258–60.
50. *Kokka no sōshi* had been taken from *The Classic of Filial Piety*, a Confucian text, and it was frequently used in subsequent government directives to the shrines, such as one that abolished hereditary succession to the shrine priesthood. On the standardization of shrine rites beginning in 1871, see *SJ*, 19.
51. The unranked shrines later became the target of a program of forced mergers with larger shrines (see chapter 13), often resulting in the razing of their buildings and confiscation of their property.
52. Umeda Yoshihiko, *Nihon shūkyō seidoshi* (Tokyo: Tōsen shuppan, 1971), 3:38. There were thought to be 87,558 temples.
53. Yasumaru Yoshio, *Kamigami no Meiji Ishin*, 131–34.
54. Yoneji Minoru, *Sonraku saishi to kokka tōsei* (Tokyo: Ochanomizu shobō, 1977), 23.
55. The edict was called the *Senpu taikyō mikotonori*, January 3, 1867.
56. The Jingishō has also been glossed in English as Ministry of Divinities, and Kyōbushō is sometimes glossed as Ministry of Religious Education.
57. Etō Shinpei (1834–1874) composed these tenets during his brief tenure at the Jingikan.
58. The term that was adopted for religion, *shūkyō*, literally meant the teachings (*kyō*) of a sect (*shū*). Prior to its adoption for translation purposes, it was used mainly as a technical term within Buddhism but was not a part of the vernacular language. The first use of *shūkyō* in a government document came in 1867, where it was used to refer to Christianity. In other words, a foreign-sounding term for *religion* first referred to a foreign religion, and in fact, strong associations linked *shūkyō* and Christianity for decades. Originating in this way, the term entered ordinary speech only slowly. It did not appear in early Meiji dictionaries; it first appeared in a book title in 1880. See Aihara Ichirōsuke, "Yakugo shūkyō no seiritsu," *Shūkyōgaku kiyō* 5 (1938): 1–5; Abe Yoshiya, "Religious Freedom under the Meiji Constitution," *Contemporary Religions in Japan* 10, no. 1/2 (1969): 60–62. On the views of religion expressed in the *Meiroku zasshi*, see Maxey, *"Greatest Problem,"* 97–102; and William R. Braisted, trans., *Meiroku zasshi: Journal of the Japanese Enlightenment* (Cambridge, MA: Harvard University Press, 1976), 59–60, 78.

59. Uno Masato, "Tokoyo Nagatane kōjutsu monjinra hikki, 'Shinkyō soshiki monogatari,'" *Nihon bunka kenkyūjo kiyō* 52 (May 1983): 207; Yasumaru Yoshio, *Kamigami no Meiji ishin*, 190.
60. For example, Buddhist and Shintō priests managed the Campaign in the Northeast and the northern Kantō Plain, unlike the case of Okayama, where the preachers from Kurozumikyō and Konkōkyō took an active role. On the operation of the Teaching Institutes in the Northeast, see Fujī Sadafumi, "Fukushima-ken chūkyōin no kenkyū," *Shintōgaku* 93 (May 1977): 1–22. Other studies of the Campaign by Fujī are available: see "Chūkyōin no kenkyū," *Shintōgaku* 91 (1976): 1–20; and "Yamagata-ken no chūkyōin," *Shintōgaku* 92 (1977): 1–14. See also Haga Shōji, *Meiji ishin to shūkyō* (Tokyo: Chikuma shobō, 1994), chap. 7; Toyota Takeshi, *Nihon shūkyo seido shi no kenkyū* (Tokyo: Kōseikaku, 1938), 206–7; Helen Hardacre, "Creating State Shinto: The Great Promulgation Campaign and the New Religions," *Japanese Journal of Religious Studies* 12, no. 1 (1986): 29–63.
61. The term *kyōdōshoku* can refer to the Instructors themselves or to the system of examinations. Although the government abandoned the Daikyōin in 1875, its activities did not cease but were transferred to the newly established Office of Shinto Affairs (Shintō Jimukyoku). Toyota Takeshi, *Nihon shūkyō seido shi no kenkyū*, 216. The top rank for Instructors, *daikyōsei*, was generally conferred automatically upon heads of sects and also upon *daimyō* and nobility who served at shrines.
62. The correct reading of his personal name is Yoshishizu, but most romanized works refer to him as Bisei, and I have adopted that usage.
63. Uno Masato, "Tokoyo Nagatane kōjutsu monjinra hikki, 'Shinkyō soshiki monogatari.'"
64. Yasumaru, *Kamigami no Meiji ishin*, 186ff.
65. Tokoyo Nagatane, "Shinkyō soshiki monogatari," annotated by Sakamoto Koremaru, in Yasumaru and Miyachi, *Shūkyō to kokka*, 5:361–422. Uno Masato, "Tokoyo Nagatane kōjutsu monjinra hikki, 'Shinkyō soshiki monogatari,'" 182, 194, 197, 200, 205.
66. Uno Masato, "Tokoyo Nagatane kōjutsu monjinra hikki, 'Shinkyō soshiki monogatari,'" 199.
67. This account is based on "Echizen gohō ikki" (1873), in Yasumaru and Miyachi, *Shūkyō to kokka*, 5:135–51.
68. A newly established penal provision allowed prefectural governors to carry out summary executions if in their judgment the preservation of the social order required such a step. It was sufficient to report the executions to Tokyo after the fact.
69. See Kodama Shiki, "Shimaji Mokurai," in *Shapers of Japanese Buddhism*, ed. Kashiwahara Yūsen and Sonoda Kōyū, trans. Gaynor Sekimori (Tokyo: Kōsei Publishing, 1994), 207–18; and Hans M. Kramer, "How Religion Came to Be Translated as *Shūkyō*: Shimaji Mokurai and the Appropriation of Religion in Early Meiji Japan," *Japan Review* 25 (2013): 89–111.
70. Kanzaki Issaku, *Meiji igo ni okeru Shintōshi no shosō* (Tokyo: Yoshikawa Kōbunkan, 1937), 253–54. Both organizations had variant names early in their histories; to avoid confusion, I refer to them throughout by the names they eventually settled on.
71. Uno Masato, n. 59, 236, 271–72.
72. Ibid., 229; Toyota, *Nihon shūkyō seido*, 207–9, 216; Nakajima Michio, "Taikyō senpu undō to saijin ronsō," *Nihonshi kenkyū* 126 (1972): 41.
73. Uno Masato, "Tokoyo Nagatane kōjutsu monjinra hikki, 'Shinkyō monogatari,'" 235–47.
74. Tanaka became Chief Priest of the Ise Grand Shrine in 1877.
75. Nakajima Michio, n. 72, 49.
76. Ibid., 34–38.
77. This deity appears prominently in book 1 of *Kojiki* as the son of Susanoo. See esp., chaps. 21–30.
78. Fujii Sadafumi, *Meiji kokugaku hassei shi no kenkyū* (Tokyo: Yoshikawa Kōbunkan, 1974), 1–3. Taishakyō was formed when Senge drew all the Izumo confraternities under a single umbrella in 1870.
79. A full record of these proceedings is recorded in Fujii, *Meiji kokugaku*.
80. See Inoue Nobutaka, "Shintō-kei kyōdan ni kansuru shūsenzen no kenkyū jōkyō ni tsuite," *Nihon bunka kenkyūjo kiyō* 51 (March 1983): 246–304.

81. Tokoyo records these protests in the "Shinkyō soshiki monogatari," 45, and they are also mentioned in diaries of such Instructors as Satō Norio. See Satō Norio, *Shinkō kaiyo rokujūgo-nen*, 2 vols. (Konkō Machi, Okayama Pref.: Konkōkyō, 1971).
82. The end came after Inoue Kowashi called for the elimination of the Campaign in an 1884 work titled, "Draft Opinion on the Elimination of the National Instructors" [Kyōdōshoku haishi iken an]. He recommended that the state no longer concern itself with the content of religious doctrine. Instead, government should show respect for the majority religious practices of the people, recognizing that religion could be used as a "tool" (*kigu*) for maintaining public order and manipulating public sentiment. See Nakajima Michio, "Meiji kokka to shūkyō: Inoue Kowashi no shūkyōkan, shūkyō seisaku no bunseki," *Rekishigaku kenkyū* 413 (1974): 40–42.
83. The terminology of Shinto-derived new religious movements and Shinto sects follows that set out by Inoue Nobutaka, though the typology seen in Table 12.2 differs in some respects. See Inoue Nobutaka, *Kyōha Shintō no keisei* (Tokyo: Kōbundō, 1991).
84. Hardacre, "Creating State Shinto," 55–58.
85. Inoue Nobutaka, "The Shinto World of the 1880s: Sano Tsunehiko, *A Journey to the East*," *Journal of the History of Religions* 27, no. 3 (1988): 342.
86. For a detailed study of Shinrikyō and its founder, see Inoue Nobutaka, "Shinto World of the 1880s.
87. Hardacre, n. 60
88. Ibid., 52n105.
89. Ibid., 60–62.
90. The term *sect* in Western scholarship on religion has tended to be used pejoratively, though that is not the intention here. In Weber and Troeltsch's usage, a *sect* is distinct from a *church* in that a church is a religious institution showing a high degree of integration with and acceptance by society. A sect is less well integrated and accepted in society, tending to be smaller and less structured. Sects frequently arise as schisms from churches, which tend to view the break-away group as heretical. The sect stands in opposition to the church's values and aims to live apart from society in order to achieve spiritual perfection. See Massimo Introvigne, "Cults and Sects," *Encyclopedia of Religion*, ed. Lindsay Jones, vol. 3, 2nd ed., (Detroit: Macmillan Reference USA, 2005), 2084–86. By contrast with this history of Western usage, among Japanese sociologists of religion, the term sect (*shūha*) is used to refer to a small religious organization that operates as a variant expression of a larger religion. Thus we can speak of a sect of Buddhism or Shinto without implications regarding the way it is integrated into society or viewed by the religion from which it derives.
91. See Inoue Nobutaka, *Kyōha Shintō no keisei*, 112–27.
92. Breen, "Ideologues, Bureaucrats, and Priests," 230–51.
93. Haga Noboru presents a fascinating case of this kind in Satō Kiyotomi from Mino. Satō expected that the fulfillment of the Restoration would make National Learning or Shinto the state religion, and to further that end he founded a school, preached vigorously, and promoted cults of local tutelary deities as a means to instill the populace with reverence for the Kami. See Haga Noboru, *Meiji kokka to minshū*, 28–49.
94. Helen Hardacre, "The Shintō Priesthood in Early Meiji Japan," *History of Religions* 27 (1988): 294–320.
95. Umeda Yoshihiko, "Jinja seido enkakushi," 218.
96. Tanaka Sen'ya, *Tanaka Sen'ya nikki* (Urawa: Saitama Shinbunsha shuppankyoku, 1977). The diary covers the years 1850 to 1898 and is composed of eight manuscripts, the last of which describes the Chichibu Uprising of 1884–1885.
97. Hardacre, "Shintō Priesthood in Early Meiji Japan," 313–17.
98. The changing relations between shrines and their supporting communities in the Meiji period, especially the resulting change in shrine festivals, is extensively discussed in Matsudaira Makoto, *Matsuri no bunka* (Tokyo: Yūhikaku, 1983).

99. See Okada Yoneo, "Jingū, Jinja sōkenshi," in *Meiji ishin Shintō hyakunenshi*, ed. Shintō Bunkakai (Tokyo: Shintō Bunkakai, 1966), 2:4–182. Okada lists thirty-six new shrines of this type; the first five were devoted to the apotheosized spirits of ancestors of the Shimazu clan of Satsuma. Treating these spirits as Kami can also be seen as a manifestation of Satsuma's anti-Buddhist stance, which entailed the rejection of Buddhist practices of ancestor worship.
100. For example, the Tokyo Daijingū, founded in 1872, was a newly established shrine, not a pre-existing shrine given a new name. Its buildings had previously been used by the Ise Shrines as a Tokyo office and also for Jingūkyōkai.
101. *Yōhaisho* were distinguished from shrines in that they held no consecrated object of worship, and usually they had no buildings, but were just spaces marked off by sacred ropes, containing a stone or stele inscribed with the name of the Ise Shrines.
102. Hardacre, *Shinto and the State, 1868-1988*, 87–89.
103. Also, on the occasion of the 400th and 500th anniversaries of his death, the Mito family held ceremonies to honor his memory.
104. Morita Yasunosuke, *Minatogawa jinja shi* (Kobe: Minatogawa Jinja, 1987), 1:119–52. Until 1871, the *ryō* was the common unit of currency, but after the promulgation of new currency laws that year, the *ryō* was exchanged for the *yen*, at the rate of one to one. I converted the pre-1871 construction costs to *yen* for convenience.
105. Haga Shōji makes a similar point in *Meiji ishin to shūkyō*, 410. Where the actual grave of the person(s) to be deified was known, the site might have had to be wrested from a Buddhist temple acting as a custodian up to that time. In Kusunoki's case, the solution was to perform a ceremony in which the spirits of Masashige and his fifteen kinsmen were symbolically separated from their graves at Kōgenji temple and transferred to the new shrine. Thereafter, Kusunoki's grave and the spot where he died, which were both immediately adjacent to the shrine, came under its administration. In 1885, a 550th anniversary celebration was held, and Emperor Meiji visited the shrine in 1888. These events were followed by a 600th anniversary celebration in 1935. See Sano Kazushi, "Minatogawa Jinja," *SJ*, 684.
106. The earliest sites of Kami worship appear to have been founded by mountain ascetics practicing a combination of esoteric Buddhism and reverence for the spirits of the mountain, whom they worshipped as *Gongen*.
107. By the mid-fifteenth century, the clan had twelve such shrines. Hokkaidō Jinjachōshi Henshū Iinkai, *Hokkaidō Jinjachōshi* (Sapporo: Hokkaidō Jinjachō, 1999), 1–5.
108. Ibid., 7–17. Matsumae strictly regulated its shrines in Hokkaidō. The domain required its residents to visit the shrines monthly, and shrine priests were expected to maintain close links with the Yoshida house, traveling to its Kyoto headquarters for instruction, at the villagers' expense. The Matsumae domain expanded its holdings in Hokkaidō by selling the rights to do business there, such as for fishing and shipping, charging fees that went to the domain. Both the domain and those who moved to Hokkaidō for business built shrines to protect their enterprises.
109. Ibid., 18; and Shintō taikei Jinja-hen 51, *Hokkaidō*. The decision to assign these three Kami to the territory was taken in the ninth month of 1869; "Hokkaidō Jingū," *SSDJ*, 885.
110. The settler-soldier system was first proposed by Kuroda Kiyotaka (1840–1900), a Satsuma samurai who fought in the Boshin and Seinan Wars, later becoming Governor of Hokkaidō. This system had origins in Han China, and there were parallel examples in Roman history.
111. Author's fieldwork, August 16–19, 2009.
112. The Sapporo Jinja was renamed Hokkaidō Jingū in 1964, when the spirit of Emperor Meiji was added to its deities. A recent collection of essays concerning this shrine is Hokkaidō Jingū, Kokugakuin Daigaku Kenkyū Kaihatsu Suishin Sentā, eds., *Hokkaidō Jingū kenkyū ronsō* (Tokyo: Kōbundō, 2014).
113. Author's fieldwork, August 16–19, 2009.
114. *Hokkaidō tōkeisho*, 1873–1883. Hokkaidō was not treated as a single prefecture until 1886; before that time, it was divided into a series of multiple, changing units.

115. Yasukuni Jinja, ed., *Yasukuni Jinja hyakunenshi, Jireki nenpyō* (Tokyo: Yasukuni Jinja, 1987), 14–72.
116. Jinja Honchō Kyōgaku Kenkyūjo, *Yasukuni Jinjashi* Kindai Jinja Gyōseishi Kenkyū sōsho IV (Tokyo: Bun'eisha, 2002), 88–89. The divinization ceremony proper was preceded by *shōkonshiki*, a ritual to "call the spirits." In darkness, with the representatives of the army and navy present, the Chief Ritualist, the Head Priest, and the other priests in attendance "called" the spirits to enter a container for the spirits of the dead called a *reisha* (霊舎). At this point, the spirits were referred to as *mitama*, a multivalent term that can mean either the spirit of a Kami or a spirit of the dead. The spirits were then purified, presented with food offerings and prayers praising their sacrifice, as a military ensemble played music. Then the container was carried into the shrine itself. The military men formed a line to escort the divine spirits to the Main Hall and install them there; the route was lined with an honor guard. For diagrams of the "spirit-calling garden," see Yasukuni Jinja, ed., *Yasukuni Jinja hyakunenshi, Shiryō hen jō* (Tokyo: Yasukuni Jinja, 1983), 505–11. Regarding imperial visits to Yasukuni, see Ōe Shinobu, *Yasukuni Jinja* (Tokyo: Iwanami shoten, 1984), 130–35.
117. Not all of those honored at Yasukuni are war dead, however. Although Yasukuni was in its infancy, it is not clear that any written code governed its choice of those to be enshrined, beyond the stipulation that they should have died on the imperial side in the struggles around the Meiji Restoration. At this time, twenty women and girls were enshrined. One of them had actually died in combat, but the others were apparently enshrined because they had been imprisoned or executed because of their connections to men who had died on the imperial side, as their wives, concubines, or children, including infants. The sword and mirror were gifts from the imperial house. Yasukuni Jinja, ed., *Yasukuni Jinja hyakunenshi, Shiryōhen chū* (Tokyo: Yasukuni Jinja, 1983), 38–40.
118. Yasukuni Jinja, *Yasukuni Jinja hyakunenshi, Jireki nenpyō*, 96–140.
119. The process by which the Ministries of Army and Navy compiled their list of those to be officially divinized is outlined in Tanaka Nobumasa, *Yasukuni no sengoshi*, Iwanami shinsho 788 (Tokyo: Iwanami shoten, 2002), 62. The ritual for divinizing spirits at Yasukuni is called *gōshisai* (合祀祭). The term means a ceremony or ritual (*-sai, matsuri*) to add (*gō-, awasu*) a deity (or deities) and worship (*-shi, matsuru*) them. Outside Yasukuni, deities are "added" in such cases as the merger of one shrine with another, or in Shinto funerals, at the end of which the purified spirit of the deceased is "added" or merged with the other ancestral spirits of the family as a Kami. Mogi Sada'atsu, "Shinsōsai," *SJ*, 296–98. Once enshrined, the spirits are so entirely subsumed within the collectivity of the shrine's deities that they no longer "belong to" their families. This makes sense if one recalls that the spirits enshrined at Yasukuni were assumed to be enshrined also at the prefectural Nation-Protecting Shrines, and most would also be enshrined in their families' Buddhist or Shinto altars as ancestral deities. Thus, their ritual treatment at Yasukuni was assumed to come *in addition to* the memorialization at the family and provincial levels, as the highest form of honor that a person might receive. At no time was survivors' consent for divinization sought, since there was no expectation that anyone would object. The public is not notified of those to be enshrined, either before or after the fact, though Yasukuni Shrine's published historical documents record the aggregate numbers enshrined. For a description of divinization ritual at Yasukuni by its former Head Priest, see Kamizaka Fuyuko and Yuzawa Tadashi, "Kamizaka Fuyuko renzoku taidan: Zen Gūji ni tou, Yasukuni Jinja no nazo," *Bungei shunju* 84, no. 11 (2006): 154–62.
120. Home Ministry funding for war memorial shrines ended in 1886, with the exception of occasional special appropriations. Tōyō Keizai Shinpōsha, *Meiji, Taishō zaisei shoran* (Tokyo: Tōyō Keizai Shinpōsha, 1926), see table 201 for Army Ministry funding of Yasukuni.
121. On Army funding, see Asakura Haruhiko, ed., *Kindaishi shiryō Rikugunshō Nisshi*, (Tokyo: Tōkyōdō shuppan, 1988-1989), 7:366. On the difficulties the shrine faced in dealing with inflexible income from the Army, see 8: 59, 89. For the liturgy for the Annual Festivals in early Meiji, see 6:454–56. From 1891, Yasukuni gained significant income from memorial

ceremonies performed annually in tandem with the Annual Festivals, sponsored by veterans' groups, town associations, and others wishing to have annual "masses for the dead" performed. Survivors would accumulate a fund, place it in trust, and pay Yasukuni to perform ceremonies using the interest generated. In 1891 such ceremonies garnered income of 136,753 yen, climbing to 474,592 yen in 1896, following the first Sino-Japanese War, and to 2,706,544 yen in 1906, after the Russo-Japanese War; see Jinja Honchō Kyōgaku Kenkyūjo, *Yasukuni Jinjashi*, 112.

122. Prefectural data may be drawn from *Nihon fuken minpi hyō: Meiji 6-9 nen*, reprinted in Meiji Bunken Shiryō Kankōkai, ed., *Meiji zenki sangyō hattatsu shi shiryō*, Bessatsu: dai 9-shū dai 5 (Tokyo: Meiji Bunken Shiryō Kankōkai, 1966). Prefectures were established in 1873, but redrawing of boundaries, mergers, renaming, and other reshuffling continued into the 1880s, so that these records are not completely consistent. Cities, towns, and villages were constituted as governing administrations from 1888. After that time, data on shrine funding by those administrations gradually becomes available in prefectural statistical yearbooks. Data for the interim years, from the late 1870s into the 1890s, are scarce and fragmentary. National-level shrine funding is recorded in the annual statistical compilation *Nihon teikoku tōkei nenkan* (Tokyo: Tōkei kyōkai), published from 1875.
123. While the prefectures contributed to the maintenance of the National Shrines, they provided salaries only for priests at Prefectural Shrines and shrines of lower ranks.
124. During these years, there were no special events to stimulate unusually large appropriations for shrines, such as the Vicennial Renewal of the Ise Shrines, enthronement ceremonies, or the birth of an imperial prince.
125. Quotation adapted from Abe Yoshiya, "Religious Freeedom under the Meiji Constitution," part 2, 91.
126. According to Trent Maxey, Ōtsu was the most effective of several politicians the priests cultivated, such as Hayakawa Ryūsuke (1853–1933), Maruyama Sakura (1840-1899), and Iwashita Masahira (1827–1900). See Maxey, *"Greatest Problem,"* 199.
127. The title of the lead editorial of an early issue of the shrine priests' journal vividly conveyed their sentiment: "What Are We Waiting For? We Must Swiftly Establish a Special Bureaucratic Unit for Shrines!" (Nanzo—Sumiyaka ni tokubetsu kanga o setchi sezaru) *ZSKK* 1, no. 4 (1899): 165–72.
128. The Diet took up proposals to revive the Jingikan and make it the supervisory body for Shinto in 1894, but when that attempt failed, the idea of reviving the Jingikan by name was dropped. A bill was eventually passed in 1896 calling for creation of a government organization dedicated to administer the shrines. See Maxey, *"Greatest Problem,"* 199–208. On Naimushō's administration of shrines, see Taigakai, ed., *Naimushōshi* (Tokyo: Chihō zaimu kyōkai, 1971), 2:1–61.
129. Liah Greenfeld, *Nationalism: Five Roads to Modernity* (Cambridge, MA: Harvard University Press, 1992), 77.

Chapter 13

1. Mitani Hiroshi and Yamaguchi Teruomi, *Jūkyū seiki Nihon no rekishi: Meiji ishin o kangaeru* (Tokyo: Hōsō Daigaku Kyōiku Shinkōkai, 2000), 175–79.
2. Nakajima Michio, "Shinto Deities That Crossed the Sea," *JJRS* 37, no. 1 (2010): 30. The shrine's Kami were Ōkunitama no Mikoto, Ōnamuchi no Mikoto, and Sukunabiko no Mikoto and a divinized Japanese military commander, Prince Kitashirakawa Yoshihisa (1847–1895), who had fought in Taiwan and later died of malaria. In 1944, Amaterasu was added to this list, and the shrine was renamed Taiwan Jingū. Regarding the Home Ministry's appropriation for the shrine, see Yamaguchi Teruomi, *Meiji kokka to shūkyō* (Tokyo: Tōkyō Daigaku shuppankai, 1999), 284. For the national government's annual allocations for shrines, see *Teikoku tōkei nenkan*, 1901; the figure for 1900 was 273,480 yen.

3. Kevin Doak delineates a variety of theories of ethnic nationalism in twentieth-century Japan, showing how they frequently challenged state views on the constitution of the nation in Kevin Doak, "What Is a Nation and Who Belongs? National Narratives and the Ethnic Imagination in Twentieth-Century Japan," *American Historical Review* 102, no. 2 (1997): 283–309. Carol Gluck has discussed how the imperial family's growing presence in relief and charitable projects, education, and the arts underlined the government's position that charity rather than public welfare should assume the financial burden in these areas. See Carol Gluck, *Japan's Modern Myths: Ideology in the Late Meiji Period* (Princeton, NJ: Princeton University Press, 1985).
4. In 1900, the first director of the museum of the Ministry of Education, Tanahashi Gentarō (1869–1961) proclaimed that *kyōdo* would serve as a kind of pedagogy to promote a sense of identity, an idea incorporated into the educational system in the 1910s and 1920s, culminating in a 1927 plan to create Kyōdo Museums throughout the nation, in which love of one's home place would be nurtured as a source of patriotism. See Noriko Aso, *Public Properties: Museums in Imperial Japan* (Durham, NC: Duke University Press, 2013), Kindle edition, location 2018–2024. Yamaguchi Teruomi explains how shrine priests at the beginning of the twentieth century hoped to become educators of society through popularizing shrine ceremonies and nurturing love of the home place. Yamaguchi Teruomi, *Meiji kokka to shūkyō*, 280.
5. Yoneji Minoru, *Sonraku saishi to kokka tōsei* (Tokyo: Ochanomizu shobō, 1977), 294.
6. Stefan Tanaka, *New Times in Modern Japan* (Princeton, NJ: Princeton University Press, 2009), 44–48.
7. Basil Hall Chamberlain, trans., *The Kojiki: Records of Ancient Matters*, with annotations by W. G. Aston, 2nd ed. (Rutland, VT: Tuttle, 1982); W. G. Aston, *Nihongi: Chronicles of Japan from the Earliest Times to A.D. 697*, 2nd ed. (Rutland, VT: Tuttle, 1972).
8. Margaret Mehl, "Scholarship and Ideology in Conflict: The Kume Affair," *Monumenta Nipponica* 48, no. 3 (1993): 339–41.
9. Kume Kunitake, "Shintō wa saiten no kozoku," *Shigaku zasshi* 2 (1891): 636–49; reprinted for a popular audience in *Shikai*, June 1892.
10. This summary is drawn from Mehl, "Scholarship and Ideology in Conflict," 341–42.
11. A variety of newspapers covered this incident; the coverage by the *Yomiuri shinbun* during March 1892 is representative and easily accessible. For an exhaustive listing of newspaper and journal articles that took up the topic at the time, see Kano Masanao and Imai Osamu, "Nihon kindai shisōshi no naka no Kume jiken," in *Kume Kunitake no kenkyū*, ed. Ōkubo Toshiaki, (Tokyo: Yoshikawa Kōbunkan, 1991), 201–316.
12. Miyachi Masato, *Tennōsei no seijishi-teki kenkyū* (Tokyo: Azekura shobō, 1981), part 2, chap. 2; Mehl also discusses Miyachi's interpretation in "Scholarship and Ideology in Conflict," 349–50; Akazawa Shirō, *Kindai Nihon no shisō dōin to shūkyō tōsei* (Tokyo: Azekura shobō, 1985), 51.
13. Miyachi Masato, *Tennōsei no seijishi-teki kenkyū*, 180–84; Mehl, "Scholarship and Ideology in Conflict," 347–48.
14. Richard Reitan, *Making a Moral Society: Ethics and the State in Meiji Japan* (Honolulu: University of Hawai'i Press, 2010), 115–33 (quotation on 133).
15. On the Boshin Rescript, which the press began to call "the diligence and frugality rescript," see Gluck, *Japan's Modern Myths*, 92.
16. Reitan, *Making a Moral Society*, 135–40 (Uchiyama is quoted on 135–36).
17. Isomae Jun'ichi, *Religious Discourse in Modern Japan: Religion, State, and Shinto*, trans. Galen Amstutz and Lynne E. Riggs, Nichibunken Monograph Series 17 (Leiden: Brill, 2014), 242–45 (the quotation is drawn from p. 243). Isomae discusses Tanaka Yoshitō in chapter 7. Tanaka and Katō will be discussed in greater detail later in this chapter. The third person appointed under the chair of Shinto studies was Miyaji Naokazu, who did not hold that Shinto was a religion; his career will also be discussed in the next chapter.

18. For Ōtsu's Diet discussion on this issue, see Yamaguchi Teruomi, *Meiji kokka to shūkyō*, 316–17. Aruga expounded his position in "Shintō kokkyō ron," *Tetsugaku zasshi* 280 (June 1910), also cited in Yamaguchi, *Meiji kokka to shūkyō*, 317; and in "Kokkyō to shite no Shintō," *ZSKK* 23 (1911): 13–19; and in a supplementary article of the same title in *ZSKK* 28 (1911): 219–23. A sample of the view that Shinto should be regarded as a religion may be consulted in Yamazaki Hifumi, "Nihon no kokkyō wa Shintō tarubeshi," *ZSKK* 4, no. 23 (1901): 344–47.
19. See Isomae, *Religious Discourse in Modern Japan*, 135–37 and Yamaguchi Teruomi, *Meiji kokka to shūkyō*, 322–24. The resolution is quoted in Sheldon Garon, *Molding Japanese Minds* (Princeton, NJ: Princeton University Press, 1997), 67.
20. See, for example, these four works by Tanaka Yoshitō: *Shintō jūsanpa no kenkyū* (Tokyo: Daiichi shobō, 1987), *Kurozumikyō no kenkyū* (Tokyo: Nihon Gakujutsu Kenkyūkai, 1932), *Tenrikyō no kenkyū* (Tokyo: Nihon Gakujutsu Kenkyūkai, 1933), and *Shintō shūseiha no kenkyū* (Tokyo: Nihon Gakujutsu Kenkyūkai, 1932), among other works.
21. *Shintō gairon* (Tokyo: Nihon Gakujutsu Kenkyūkai, 1936), 187, quoted in Isomae, *Religious Discourse in Modern Japan*, 249.
22. Tanaka Yoshitō, "Shin ki shūgō," *Shintōgaku zasshi* 13 (1932): 210, quoted in Isomae, *Religious Discourse in Modern Japan*, 252.
23. In his 1919 work *Shinto and the Kokutai* (*Waga kokutai to Shintō*), Katō wrote, "These days some people ignore the history of Shinto's development and give a twisted interpretation of shrines, separating Shinto from the sphere of religion and confining [Shinto] to the field of morality alone," quoted in Miyamoto Takashi, "Kindai shūkyōgakusha no Shintōkan," *Shintō shūkyō* 198 (2005): 99.
24. Naomi Hylkema-Vos, "Katō Genchi: A Neglected Pioneer in Comparative Religion," *JJRS* 17, no. 4 (1990): esp. 377–78.
25. For an overview of Katō's thought and writing, see Umeda Yoshihiko, "Katō Genchi," *Shintō shūkyō* 41 (1965): 82–88.
26. Katō Genchi, *Study of Shinto: The Religion of the Japanese Nation* (Tokyo: Zaidan hōjin Meiji seitoku kinen gakkai, 1926), 206–7, quoted in *Sources of Japanese Tradition: From Earliest Times to 1600*, ed. William Theodore DeBary (New York: Columbia University Press, 2001), 795.
27. The postwar history of the Annual Festival of Ōkunitama Shrine is the subject of chapter 15. On the history of the shrine and its festival in the Meiji period, see Komine Masaharu, *Musashi Fuchū shuku fudokikō: Shinpen Musashi fudokikō no genbun to sono kanren hosoku setsumei* (privately published in Fuchū by Meisei kikaku, 2003); and Suzuki Nobuhide, Kudo Yoshiaki, Miyauchi Satoshi, "Ōkunitama Jinja reitaisai 'Kurayami matsuri' no misakibarai taiko ni kansuru yōguron-teki kōsatsu," *Dezain-gaku kenkyū* 47, no. 6 (2001): 31–40. For more general information on the modern history of Fuchū, see Fuchū shishi hensan iinkai, ed., *Fuchū shishi*, vol. 2 (Fuchū: Fuchū City, 1974).
28. Sano Kazushi, "Heian Jingū," *SD*, 639. The spirit of Emperor Kōmei, father of the Meiji emperor, was added as a Kami of the shrine in 1938. The shrine was greatly expanded in 1940, for the celebrations marking the 2600th anniversary of the founding of the empire. Its annual festival, known as the Festival of the Ages, takes the form of a parade exhibiting the costumes of all historical eras from the time of Kanmu through the reign of Kōmei.
29. Shimizu Shigeatsu, "Sōken jinja no zōei to kindai Kyoto," in *Kindai nihon no rekishi koto: Koto to jōkamachi*, ed. Takagi Hiroshi (Kyoto: Shibunkaku shuppan, 2013), 104–5.
30. Material related here regarding the combination of groups that cooperated to realize the founding of the Heian Shrine is drawn from Kobayashi Takehiro, "Heian sento senhyakunen kinensai to Heian Jingū no sōken," *Nihonshi kenkyū* 538 (2007): 1–28.
31. See Soeda Yoshiya, *Naimushō no shakaishi* (Tokyo: Tokyo Daigaku shuppankai, 2007), 288. The Shrine Bureau did not supervise the staffing of shrines below the imperial and national levels. The first of the journals was managed by the National Association of Shrine Priests; it was succeeded by the second journal, which over time became a mouthpiece for the Shrine

Bureau, functioning mainly to communicate the bureau's directions to the shrine priests, whom it had dubbed the "Shrine Federation," though in fact its membership was essentially the same as that of the National Association of Shrine Priests. The Shrine Bureau dissolved the Shrine Federation in 1938, as an austerity measure in support of Japan's "holy war" (*seisen*) in China. See the announcement of the journal's abolition in Kodama Kyūichi, "Jinja Kyōkai no kaisan ni atari kaiin shokun ni tsugu," *Jinja kyōkai zasshi* 37, no. 7 (1938): 2–3.

32. The last of them, Iinuma Kazumi, went on to lead the Jingiin, which replaced the Shrine Bureau in 1940 (the Home Minister was the actual Chief of the Jingiin, an ex-officio appointment; the Vice-Chief's post was held by Iinuma, and this was the position that actually headed up the unit).
33. Kodama Kyūichi, who served as Shrine Bureau Chief from 1937 to 1939, had written a book on shrine administration in 1934. See Kodama Kyūichi, *Jinja gyōsei*, Jichi gyōsei sōsho 1 (Tokyo: Tokiwa shobō, 1934). Kodama went on to become best known for his work in the area of welfare.
34. Mizuno was one of the most powerful bureaucrats in the country and was also involved in party politics. He was the only Shrine Bureau Chief ever to become Home Minister. He later served as head of the National Association of Shrine Priests, from 1940. The bureau included clerical and accounting staff, and in some years there were one or more staff capable of evaluating shrines' archaeological materials and historical documents, especially in the context of applications from the shrines to raise their ranks. Some specialized staff members simultaneously held academic appointments, such as Miyaji Naokazu, a historian with wide-ranging skills in the evaluation of shrine related documents and materials. These specialized staff members were not career bureaucrats. The most numerous staff within the bureau were architects, builders, and shrine carpenters, grouped together into a distinct "technologists" office. The architects included some celebrated figures, such as Itō Chūta, who also built important new Buddhist temples.
35. The prefectures were divided into three classes, and the prestige, salaries, and responsibilities of each differed hugely. Predictably, the post of Tokyo *ken chiji* was the highest, and the prefectures that were far from the capital or lacking a large city were much less desirable and remunerative. Four Shrine Bureau Chiefs were assigned subsequent posts as the *chiji* of Tokyo, Kyoto, or Kanagawa. See Taigakai, ed., *Naimushō-shi* (Tokyo: Chihō zaimu kyōkai, 1971), 2:285. On the different salaries and benefits of the *ken chiji* at different prefectures, see Momose Takashi, *Naimushō: Meimon kanchō wa naze kaitai sareta ka?* (Tokyo: PHP shinsho, 2001).
36. Teikoku Chihō Gyōsei Gakkai, *Genkō jinja hōrei ruisan: kajo jizai* (Tokyo: Teikoku Chihō Gyōsei Gakkai, 1936), 338.
37. Iinuma's opinions on this issue are reported in Soeda Yoshiya, *Naimushō no shakaishi*, 596.
38. Naimushō Jinjakyoku, *Jinja ni kansuru tōkeisho* (Tokyo: Naimushō, 1933), 1.
39. Ariizumi Sadao, "Chihō kairyō undō," *Kokushi daijiten*; accessed through Japan Knowledge.com, at www.jkn21.com.ezp-prod1.hul.harvard.edu, accessed January 9, 2014.
40. Offerings were to be made by the administrative unit corresponding to the shrine's rank, so the prefectures were to provide for the Prefectural Shrines, the counties or cities for the District Shrines, and cities, towns, or villages for the village shrines. Terms of eligibility for "offerings" included being a *shikinaisha*, founding by imperial order, a documented instance of worship there by a member of the imperial family, *daimyō*, or military commander, possession of an official shrine history (*yuisho*), or some distinguished local significance. Yamaguchi Teruomi, *Meiji kokka to shūkyō*, 288–91; Wilbur M. Fridell, *Japanese Shrine Mergers 1906-1912: State Shinto Moves to the Grassroots* (Tokyo: Sophia University Press, 1973), 11–13.
41. Quoted in Kōmoto Mitsugi, "Jinja gōshi: Kokka Shintō-ka seisaku no tenkai," in *Kindai to no kaikō*, Nihonjin no shūkyō, Tamaru Noriyoshi, Miyata Noboru et. al., eds. (Tokyo: Kōsei shuppansha, 1973), 3:77.
42. Fridell, *Japanese Shrine Mergers*, 16.
43. See *ZSKK* 6 (January 1900): 19–22; *JKZ* 11 (May 1912): 48–50; and, "Jinja gappei to sonraku no henka: Hokusei chihō no jirei," *Kōgakukan daigaku kiyō* 14 (1976): 226.

44. Fridell, *Japanese Shrine Mergers*, 22–25.
45. Azegami Naoki, *"Mura no chinju" to senzen Nihon: Kokka Shintō no chiiki shakaishi* (Tokyo: Yūshisha, 2009), 45–77.
46. Tsukamoto Seiji, "Kome sōdō ni tsuki, toku ni shinshoku shokun ni nozomu," *JKZ* 17 (September 1918): 1–4. On the moral suasion campaigns following World War I, see Akazawa Shirō, *Kindai Nihon no shisō dōin to shūkyō tōsei*, 16–20. For a general study of moral suasion campaigns, see Garon, *Molding Japanese Minds*.
47. Takagi Hiroshi, *Kindai tennōsei no bunkashi teki kenkyū* (Tokyo: Kōsō shobō, 1997), 235–62.
48. Akazawa Shirō, "Hōanden," *Nihon daihyakka zensho*, accessed via Japan Knowledge.com. http://japanknowledge.com.ezp-prod1.hul.harvard.edu/lib/display/?lid=1001000211414,March 2, 2015.
49. Akazawa Shirō, n. 12, 16–18, 53, 62.
50. Ibid., 58–62.
51. Takase Yukie, "1930 nendai ni okeru shōgakkō kun'iku to jinja sanpai: Mino misshon jiken o jirei to shite," *Nihon no kyōiku shigaku: Kyōiku gakkai kiyō* 50 (October 2007): 58–70.
52. See, for example, "Kirisutokyō no san jido jinja sanpai o kyohi," *Yomiuri shinbun*, September 1, 1933, 7.
53. Following training at the Moody Bible Institute, Sadie Weidner traveled to Japan, in 1900, as a missionary for the German Reform Church and served as the head of Miyagi Gakuin Joshi Daigaku, a women's college in Miyagi Prefecture. The Mino Mission served widows, orphans, female-headed families, female factory workers, and Koreans residing in Japan. See Aso Tasuku, "Shūkyō shūdan o meguru haijo no jūsōsei to kokumin kokka," *Jinbun chirigakkai taikai kenkyū happyō yōshi* 2013, 50–51.
54. Takase Yukie, "1930 nendai ni okeru shōgakkō kun'iku to jinja sanpai."
55. Katō Genchi, *Shintō no saikakunin* (1935), quoted in Takase Yukie, "1930 nendai ni okeru shōgakkō kun'iku to jinja sanpai," 59.
56. Aso Tasuku, "Shūkyō shūdan o meguru haijo no jūsōsei to kokumin kokka," 51; Shimazono Susumu, *Kokka Shintō to Nihonjin*, Iwanami shinsho 1259 (Tokyo: Iwanami shoten, 2010), 146–55.
57. Inoue Nobutaka outlines the path to autonomy followed by each of the original thirteen organizations in *Kyōha Shintō no keisei* (Tokyo: Kōbundō, 1991), chap. 1. As he points out, research on these groups has lagged that concerning shrine Shinto, and many areas of research remain untouched. For a study of these groups' regional expansion, see Inoue Nobutaka, "Kyōha Shintō no chiikiteki tenkai to sono shakaiteki jōken," *Kokugakuin zasshi* 104 (November 2003): 342–59. Regarding the federation of Shinto sects, see Kinenshi hensan iinkai, ed., *Kyōha Shintō rengōkai hyakunenshi* (Place of publication unknown: Kyōha Shintō rengōkai, 1996), an online chronology of events relating to the sects, http://www.kyoharen.net/1541-.pdf, accessed March 2, 2015.
58. Inoue Nobutaka, *Kyōha Shintō no keisei*, 40–44. Tenrikyō made especially effective use of print media; see Ōya Wataru, *Kyōha Shintō to kindai Nihon: Tenrikyō no shiteki kōsatsu* (Osaka: Tōhō shuppan, 1992), chap. 2.
59. Ōya Wataru, *Kyōha Shintō to kindai Nihon*, 156–73; "Chōsen bōdō to kirisutokyō," *ZSKK*, 49 (March 1919): 42.
60. Helen Hardacre, "Asano Wasaburō and Japanese Spiritualism in Early Twentieth-Century Japan," in *Japan's Conflicting Modernities, Issues in Culture and Democracy, 1900-1930*, ed. Sharon A. Minichiello (Honolulu: University of Hawai'i Press, 1998), 133–53.
61. The shrine priests' association of Matsue City, in Shimane Prefecture, passed a resolution condemning Ōmoto and had it published in *Reports*. The association was horrified to discover that not only were the lower orders attracted, but even a middle-school teacher and graduate of Kokugakuin University (one of the Shinto universities), who should have known better, had quit his job and gone off to join Ōmoto. It was rumored that civil servants and even bankers had joined the ranks of this evil religion. Shrine priests' reaction to Ōmoto is set out in "Ōmotokyō to shinshoku ketsugi," *ZSKK* 49 (March 1919): 41–42. For analysis of the

religious world's near-universal damning of Ōmoto, see Sheldon Garon, "State and Religion in Imperial Japan, 1912–1945," *Journal of Japanese Studies* 12, no. 2 (1986): 273–302.

62. Helen Hardacre, *Shinto and the State, 1868-1988* (Princeton, NJ: Princeton University Press, 1989), 93–94.
63. The Meiji Shrine accounted for a major part of the Shrine Bureau's budget from 1915 through 1925. On the construction of this shrine, see Morioka Kiyomi, *Kindai no shūraku jinja to kokka tōsei*, Nihon shūkyōshi kenkyū sōsho (Tokyo: Yoshikawa kōbunkan, 1987), 268–69; and Sano Kazushi, "Meiji Jingū," *SJ* 686–7.
64. Morioka, *Kindai no shūraku jinja to kokka tōsei*, 270–71.
65. Azegami Naoki, *"Mura no chinju" to senzen Nihon*. Azegami presents extensive analysis of the situation of *minsha* priests in part II, chaps. 3–5. On the examination system, see 265–66.
66. *Minsha* priests began to argue for better treatment at the 1910 annual meeting of the national priests' association, Zenkoku Shinshokukai, continuing in subsequent years. Their resentment against the higher-ranked priests was palpable. See Azegami Naoki, n. 45, 120–53.
67. Ibid., 166–93. Activism by the young *minsha* priests resembles the Young Buddhist movement that roiled Japanese Buddhism in the late nineteenth and early twentieth century.
68. Inoue mentioned that already some eight hundred priests had taken the course, and that at the prefectural level there are now twenty-four training courses for shrine priests. Inoue Tomoichi, "Shinshoku shokun nimu nozomi" (Shinshoku yōseibu sotsugyōshiki kōen) *ZSKK* 34, no. 174 (1913): 339–51.
69. See, for example, Aoyama Yoshio, "Jinjahi tai-funō shobun ni tsuite," *ZSKK* 46 (August 1917): 85–87, a complaint against prefectures and municipalities that drag their feet on providing funding; Itogawa Genjirō, "Kibō," *ZSKK* 46 (August 1917): 87–88. Itogawa claims that the *ujiko* cannot be depended upon and that a law should be passed forcing them to pay for shrines' upkeep. The following two articles complain that while Imperial and National shrine priests' salaries are upgraded, there is *no* aid to lower-ranking priests: "Kankoku heisha shinshoku hōkyūrei no kaisei," *ZSKK* 47 (April 1918): 54ff.; Jingi Ōtsugi, "Fuken gōsonsha no shinshoku no hōkyū ni tsukite," *ZSKK* 50 (October 1919): 203–5. This editorial demands that the Home Ministry unify priests' salaries and require that they be paid regularly: "Ronsetsu: Shinshoku hōkyū rei o tōitsu shi, Naimushō rei ni yorite kōfu subeshi," *ZSKK* 49 (March 1919): 127–33.
70. Yamaguchi Teruomi, *Meiji kokka to shūkyō*, 279.
71. Data presented here concerning shrine funding at the prefectural level and below are based on a collection of records in the annual statistical yearbooks (*tōkeisho*) of each prefecture over the years 1875 through 1945. These works can be consulted at the prefectural libraries or at the National Diet Library (Digital Archive). To date I have collected the existing records for the following prefectures: Hokkaidō, Yamagata, Tokyo, Kanagawa, Kyoto, Hyogo, Shiga, Shizuoka, Wakayama, Kagawa, Okayama, Shimane, Hiroshima, Yamaguchi, Saga, Miyazaki, Fukuoka, Nagasaki, Mie, Osaka, Toyama, Ishikawa, and Fukui.
72. The Imperial Household Ministry collected these statistics over the years 1899 to 1914, but the record stops after 1914. The data were not published until 1993, and researchers have not yet mined them fully. The figures recorded are not included in the *Teikoku tōkei nenkan*, and it is not known whether the funds were drawn from the imperial house's annual allocation from the national budget or from its own assets. See Gotō Yasushi, "Kaidai: Tennōsei kenkyū to Teishitsu tōkeisho," in *Teishitsu tōkeisho* (Tokyo: Kashiwa shobō, 1993), 1:1–6.
73. "Shiryō," *JKZ* 32, no. 6 (June 1933): 15–28.
74. Kodama Kyūichi, *Jinja gyōsei*, 297.
75. Mitani and Yamaguchi, *Jūkyū seiki Nihon no rekishi*, 152–62 and table 12–1.
76. For an essay on the history of petroleum development in Niigata, see https://www.city.niigata.lg.jp/akiha/about/kankou/oil/heritage.files/11.pdf, accessed March 13, 2015. See also the website for Niigata's historical museum of petroleum development, "Sekiyū no sekaikan," http://www.shiteikanrisha.jp/sekiyu-sekaikan/ayumi.html, accessed March 13, 2015. http://www.shiteikanrisha.jp/sekiyu-sekaikan/

77. Matsubara Shūhei, compiler, *Konpira shomin shinkō shiryōshū, nenpyō* (Kotohira Town, Kagawa Prefecture: Kotohiragū shamusho, 1988), 91–92.
78. The shrine's historical documents have been published as Hakone Jinja shamusho, ed., *Hakone Jinja taikei*, 2 vols. (Hakone Jinja: Hakone Jinja shamusho, 1930–1935); see also, Hakone Jinja, *Hakone Jinja: Shinkō no rekishi to bunka* (Hakone Town: Hakone Jinja shamusho, 1989) for a chronology of major events in the shrine's history. On the growth of the Fujiya Hotel, see David Leheny, "'By Other Means': Tourism and Leisure in Pre-war Japan," *Social Science Japan Journal* 3, no. 2 (2000): 178.
79. For an early example, see "Ehime tsūshin," *ZSKK* 19 (January 1908): 65. "Taishō rokunen rokugatsu hokan rin kisoku kaisei ni yori jinja kyoka shirabe," *ZSKK* 50 (August 1918): 36–41, presents a list of fifty-three shrines that secured forest land for preservation.
80. For a collection of documents of petitions for the return of land, see Hakone Jinja shamusho, *Hakone Jinja taikei*, 1:102–201.
81. Nishikawa Masatami, "Kindai no shikinen sengū," *Shintōshi kenkyū* 20, no. 6 (1973): 94–109.
82. This is essentially the same strategy employed by the postwar bureaucracy in its many "advisory committees" (*shingikai*) attached to the separate ministries or the office of the prime minister.
83. Taigakai, *Naimushō-shi*, 2:12–14.
84. Wan-yao Chou, "The *Kōminka* Movement in Taiwan and Korea: Comparisons and Interpretations," in *The Japanese Wartime Empire, 1931-1945*, ed. Peter Duus, Ramon H. Myers, Mark Peattie, and Wan-yao Chou (Princeton, NJ: Princeton University Press, 1996), 41.
85. According to Mitani and Yamaguchi (*Jūkyū seiki Nihon no rekishi*, 182), the colonies differed significantly regarding the question whether the Meiji constitution or the census law applied. In Karafuto Japanese law applied. In the Kwangtung Leased Territories, the area retained some sovereignty, and the Japanese constitution was never applied; residents held Chinese citizenship. It was unclear whether the area was part of the "outer territories" or whether it was to be regarded as a colony. Taiwanese were treated as Japanese, and from 1899, the census laws even applied to them. Koreans were treated as Japanese, but the census law did not apply. Nan'yō differed yet again. But in spite of all these differences, most of the people in the Japanese empire were treated as Japanese subjects, though they did not have all the same rights and duties as Japanese did under the Meiji constitution.
86. Sagai Tatsuru, *Manshū no jinja kōbōshi: Nihonjin no iku tokoro jinja ari* (Tokyo: Fuyō shobō shuppan, 1998), 33.
87. On this incident, and on the thought of Ogasawara, see Suga Kōji, "A Concept of 'Overseas Shinto Shrines': A Pantheistic Attempt by Ogasawara Shōzō and Its Limitations," *JJRS* 37, no. 1 (2010): 47–74.
88. Quoted in Suga Kōji, *Kaigai no jinja* (Tokyo: Yumani Shobō, 2005), 192.
89. Chou, n. 84, 43.
90. Ibid.
91. John Owen Gauntlett, trans., *Kokutai no Hongi: Cardinal Principles of the National Entity of Japan*, ed. Robert King Hall (Cambridge, MA: Harvard University Press, 1949). See also the extensive discussion of this work by Walter Skya in *Japan's Holy War*, 262–96.
92. Soeda Yoshiya, *Naimushō no shakaishi*, 593.
93. Statistics regarding imperial funding for shrines are available only for a few years, but it is likely that they continued from the early Meiji period to 1945 and beyond. Table 13.2 shows that in 1910 imperial funding of shrines amounted to about 4 percent of the shrine fees paid in the same year from the national budget. In 1945 (table 13.3) the imperial house's contributions to shrines equaled about 5 percent of the national budget allocation, suggesting that a proportion around 4 or 5 percent represented a baseline.
94. Kenneth J. Ruoff, *Imperial Japan at Its Zenith: The Wartime Celebration of the Empire's 2600th Anniversary* (Ithaca, NY: Cornell University Press, 2010), 1–3.

95. Okada, "Shinto keikaku ni tsuite," 3–13; Taigakai, *Naimushōshi*, 205; Takagi Hiroshi, "Kindai shin'en shiron," *Rekishi hyōron* 573 (January, 1998): 16–27; John Breen, "Shintō monogatari: Meij-ki no Ise," in *Kindai Nihon no rekishi toshi: Koto to jōkamachi* (Kyoto: Shibunkaku shuppan, 2013), 351–83.
96. Shimasaki Tomomi and Sugawara Yōichi, "Kindai Ise no toshi seibi ni mukete no jimoto dōkō ni kansuru kenkyū," *Nihon kenchiku gakkai tōkai shibu kenkyū hōhokusho* 46 (February 2008): 749–52.
97. Narakenshi hensan iinkai, ed. *Jinja*, Narakenshi (Tokyo: Meichō shuppan, 1989), vol. 5, 385–87; Ruoff, *Imperial Japan at Its Zenith*, 4. An allied effort to refurbish and dignify the site identified as Jinmu's grave was also conducted. Following the Sino-Japanese War, in 1898 the grave was refurbished and enlarged, making a large enclosure with an outer wall, topped with a tile roof, an enlargement of the hill, extensive landscaping, and terracing at two levels interior to the outer wall, with *torii* as entrances to each level. The area thought to hold the tomb itself was shaped into a hexagon, but when new archaeological evidence made it clear that tombs of Jinmu's antiquity were round, this earthwork was reshaped into a circular form. See Mae Kei'ichi, *Nara: Tennō no daigawari gishiki to "kenkoku no seichi"* (Tokyo: Azumi no shobō, 1990), 30–34; and Takagi Hiroshi, "Kindai ni okeru shinwateki kodai no sōzō: Unebiyama, Jinmu ryō, Kashihara Jingū, san'i ittai no Jinmu seiseki," *Jinbun gakuhō* 83 (2000): 19–38.
98. NHK Sensō shōgen Archives (a digital archive of NHK films; cgi2.nhk.or.jp) contain numerous newsreel films relating to the events of the 2600th Anniversary, including a Tokyo City Festival held in the Outer Gardens of the Meiji Shrine and attended by 100,000 people, where a sacred flame from Kashihara Shrine was delivered to a soaring platform, symbolizing the continuity from Jinmu to Meiji. Smaller ceremonies and festivals are documented at numerous inner territory locations, as well as in Shanghai, Nanjing, Peking, and Canton. See also "Kigen 2600 nen kinen gyōji," Wikipedia (Japanese version), accessed March 10, 2015; and Walter Edwards, "Forging Tradition for a Holy War: The *Hakkō Ichiū* Tower in Miyazaki and Japanese Wartime Ideology," *Journal of Japanese Studies* 29 (2003): 289–324.
99. Imperial visits to Yasukuni were regularly documented by NHK newsreel broadcast; see for example NHK news broadcast 124 (October 20, 1942), http://cgi2.nhk.or.jp/shogenarchives/jpnews/movie.cgi?das_id=D0001300509_00000&seg_number=001, accessed March 11, 2015.
100. *Nisshin* 34, no. 1 (January 1942).
101. I have adapted this formulation of the tacit beliefs of Shinto in this period from Haga Shōji, *Meiji ishin to shūkyō* (Tokyo: Chikuma shobō, 1994), 410. Kōno Seizō comes close to expounding Haga's interpretation in Kōno Seizō, "Kannagara no michi," *Monumenta Nipponica* 3, no. 2 (1940): 381–82.
102. For convenience, I have used the following work as a primary reference for *kokutai* theology: Kiyohara Sadao, *Kokutai ronshi* (Tokyo: Naimushō Jinjakyoku, 1921).
103. Ibid., 325–26.
104. Kōno Seizō, "Kannagara no michi," 369.
105. Kiyohara Sadao, *Kokutai ronshi*, 354–57. Sectarian Shinto writers also adopted the idea of the family state as a unique property of *kokutai*. Satō Norio, longtime leader of Konkōkyō, writing in "Our Empire in World Upheaval" (*Sekai no dairan to waga teikoku*) claimed that the imperial house is like a head family (*honke*), to which subjects are related as branch families (*bunke*). The emperor is the father of the people, and the people are his children. Kiyohara Sadao, 335–36.

Chapter 14

1. Planning for the Occupation of Japan began in late 1943, when the State Department convened a group called the Inter-Divisional Area Committee on the Far East to plan postsurrender policies. This body worked intensively, meeting over 200 times by July 1945. Its

most important members were George H. Blakesley and a historian of Japan at Columbia University, Hugh Borton. "Shintō no tokken haishi, are kara jūgo nen," *Asahi shinbun*, August 2, 1959, 2. According to one popular account circulating within Japan, it was rumored at the end of the war that all shrine priests would be executed because of their close connections with the military.

2. Bunce, who had a PhD in history, had been an English teacher in a Japanese high school from 1936 to 1939, and was married to a woman whose parents were Protestant missionaries. See Mark Mullins, "How Yasukuni Shrine Survived the Occupation: A Critical Examination of Popular Claims," *Monumenta Nipponica* 65, no. 1 (2010): 108–10.
3. William P. Woodward, *The Allied Occupation of Japan 1945-1952 and Japanese Religions* (Leiden: E. J. Brill, 1972), 55.
4. The memo denied that Shinto was a state religion but proposed to renounce shrine rites that gave the appearance of state religion. The Imperial Rule Assistance League (also still in existence) would no longer carry out shrine worship or purifications. Shrine visits by school children would cease, and Shinto facilities would be removed from schools. Government offices would cease performing the Ōharai ritual. The memo proposed further that shrines would be treated as religious organizations. The Jingiin would be decreased in size. Jinja Honchō, *Jingiin shūsen shimatsu, Jinja no kokka kanri bunri shiryō* (Tokyo: Jinja Honchō, 1964), 7. As of 1940, the Jingiin had 195 staff, whereas in 1945, it had ninety-three. Imperial and National Shrine maintenance from public funds for building and maintenance would be decreased, noting that in 1940 the annual amount was 1,150,000 yen, and in 1945 it was 830,000 yen. The annual appropriations for these shrines would be reduced; from 1937 to 1945 it was 1,030,000 yen. This memo further noted that the Kōten Kōkyūjo was receiving 43,650 yen per year, and that Dai Nihon Jingikai received 30,000 yen from public funds.
5. Ibid., 8–9.
6. Or, under a scaled-back version, perhaps not *all* shrines, but only the Imperial or National Shrines, or, under a further diminished plan, perhaps only the Ise Grand Shrines would be described in terms of *kokka no sōshi*. Jinja Honchō, *Jinja no kokka kanri bunri shiryō*, 9–10.
7. Woodward, *Allied Occupation of Japan*, 59–60. Puzzled that the Jingiin "held aloof" for so long, Woodward suggests that perhaps its officials were waiting for Dyke to take the initiative to call on them.
8. Mullins, "How Yasukuni Shrine Survived the Occupation," 111–18.
9. See http://www2.kokugakuin.ac.jp/frontier/projects/miyaji.html, accessed August 4, 2010, for a chronology of Miyaji's life and career. Miyaji's complete works are collected in Miyaji Naokazu, *Miyaji Naokazu ronshū*.
10. Six days later, they were visited by the Vice Head Priest at Yasukuni, Yokoi Tokitsune, who told them of a plan to register Yasukuni as a religious corporation and to transform the shrine by creating an amusement center, with roller-skating, ping-pong, a merry-go-round, and a movie theater. In other words, the shrine indicated to the Occupation its willingness to transform itself dramatically, in a way that would mute its former military associations. Mullins, "How Yasukuni Shrine Survived the Occupation,"113–21.
11. Woodward, *Allied Occupation of Japan*, 69. Moreover, Bunce was unable to sample public opinion regarding the status of Shinto and shrines as part of the investigations that informed his drafting. The newspapers provided virtually no coverage of the question until Bunce was well along in composing the staff report and the directive. Even then, press coverage was largely devoted to the views of Shinto seen in the foreign papers. A single opinion piece appearing in the *Asahi* on November 12, by Takashima Beihō, a Buddhist leader known as a reformer, championed the idea that Shinto is not a religion. While Bunce undoubtedly was informed of this article, he had already rejected the author's position. Takashima Beihō, "Jinja wa shūkyō ni arazu," *Asahi shinbun*, November 12, 1945, 2. This article is translated in Wilhemus Creemers, *Shrine Shinto after World War II* (Leiden: E. J. Brill, 1968), 51–52.

12. The understanding that Bunce and other Occupation officials reached regarding Shinto can be seen both in the Shinto Directive and in the staff study that accompanied the directive. Whenever a directive was to be issued, a staff study of it was composed, a document that would explain its necessity and its aims to the Chief of Staff. Staff studies included whatever information would be needed in order to explain the directive to the Supreme Commander, as well as information necessary for the Japanese government to implement the directive. Woodward, n. 3, 322–41.
13. Ibid., 324.
14. Since the directive's formal title was "Abolition of Governmental Sponsorship, Support, Perpetuation, Control and Dissemination of State Shinto (*Kokka Shinto, Jinja Shinto*)" (SCAPIN 448 (CIE) 15 Dec 45 (AG 000.3), it is little wonder that it became known by the much simpler moniker "Shinto Directive." The full text is reproduced in Woodward, n. 3, appendix B: 5, 295–99.
15. Ibid., 298.
16. Ibid., 69.
17. Ibid., 69–72; 106–9.
18. The text of Kishimoto's broadcast is reprinted in Woodward, *Allied Occupation of Japan*, 347–50.
19. "Shintō to tennōsei," *Yomiuri shinbun*, December 18, 1945, 1.
20. Ōhara Yasuo, "Shintō shirei no sōgōteki hyōka," *Nihon bunka kenkyūjo kiyō* 71 (1993): 1–26.
21. Woodward, *Allied Occupation of Japan*, 129.
22. "Minshushugi to mikoshi," *Yomiuri shinbun*, October 26, 1948, 1.
23. Alfred Hussey Papers, University of Michigan Library, document 78-D-9-1.
24. Herbert Bix, *Hirohito and the Making of Modern Japan* (New York: HarperCollins, 2000), 561–62. *Jinja shinpō* has taken this position consistently. See "Ronsetsu: Chūkyō-shin kaikaku-an no hankyō," *Jinja shinpō*, June 28, 1971, 2; "Shuchō: Kyōiku chokugo kanpatsu hyakunen ni atatte," *Jinja shinpō*, November 2, 1990, 2; "Ronsetsu: Kyōiku chokugo hyaku nijūnen kawaranu omomi," *Jinja shinpō*, November 1, 2010, 2.
25. See these editorials: "Shasetsu: Kyūchū saishi wa kōji ka shiji ka," *Jinja shinpō*, October 20, 1952, 1; "Ronsetsu: Kōshitsu no go-keijin o aoide," *Jinja shinpō*, July 27, 1970, 1; "Ronsetsu: Tennō wa Amaterasu Ōmikami no shison ka," *Jinja shinpō*, March 29, 1971, 2; "Ronsetsu: Ichi seinen shinshoku no tōsho ni kotaete," *Jinja shinpō*, April 5, 1971, 2; and "Ronsetsu: Shinseiren to giin-kon: Yonjūnen no omomi to kongo no kadai," *Jinja shinpō*, June 7, 2010, 2.
26. In the interval between the actual drafting and the formal adoption of the constitution, the Diet discussed most of the articles in some detail, especially those dealing with sovereignty, the emperor, war renunciation, and new rights such as woman suffrage. In searching the digital record of all those deliberations, however, I was not able to locate a single discussion of article 20 or 89. I conclude from this that the legislators did not find the clauses problematic.
27. Woodward, *Allied Occupation of Japan*, 7, 41, and 82–102 for an account of the drafting and Diet adoption of the law. The Religious Juridical Persons Law superseded the Religious Corporations Ordinance (Shūkyō hōjin rei), which itself had superseded the prewar Religious Organizations Law (Shūkyō dantaihō).
28. Whereas religious bodies had been allowed to incorporate before the surrender, the process was one of application, followed by inspections and authorizations by government officials. By contrast, the process of incorporation under the 1951 law was simple registration, supplying documents showing that the organization was religious in character, met the financial standards of a corporation, had a governing board and an official representative, and a codified creed. In theory at least, the government body administering the law is not authorized to withhold corporate status if the applying organization has met the requisite standards. Ishimura Kōji, *Shūkyō hōjinsei to zeisei no arikata* (Kyoto: Hōritsu Bunkasha, 2006), 18–24.
29. See Helen Hardacre, *Shinto and the State, 1868-1988* (Princeton, NJ: Princeton University Press, 1989), 139.

30. "Shasetsu: Shūkyō hōjin hōan no ninshō seido," *Jinja shinpō*, January 29, 1951; "Shasetsu: Jinja to shūkyō," *Jinja shinpō*, March 5, 1951; "Shasetsu: Shūkyō hōjinhō ni saishite," *Jinja shinpō*, April 9, 1951.
31. Jinja Honchō, *Jinja Honchō jūnenshi* (Tokyo: Jinja Honchō, 1956), 68.
32. Creemers, *Shrine Shinto after World War II*, 70; Jinja Honchō, *Jinja Honchō jūnenshi*, 82–84.
33. A special issue of the Yomiuri newspaper was issued on December 3, and the matter was covered in several articles in the Yomiuri and the Asahi newspapers over the following weeks.
34. Kawata Sadao, "Nashimoto Morimasa," *Kokushi daijiten*, Yoshikawa kōbunkan, accessed May 2, 2105, on Japan Knowledge.com. See also Wikipedia, s.v., "Prince Nashimoto Morimasa," http://en.wikipedia.org/wiki/Prince_Nashimoto_Morimasa. An example of sympathetic press treatment can be seen in "O-kazari mo hanzainin ka: Nashimoto Miya, kono hi no go-shinkyō, AP kisha to no go-kaikendan," *Yomiuri shinbun*, December 4, 1945, 1.
35. Sasaki Ryū, "Mizuno Rentarō," *Kokushi daijiten*, Yoshikawa kōbunkan, accessed May 2, 2011, on Japan Knowledge.com; "Nyūjo, nyūjo enki shimei," *Yomiuri shinbun*, December 13, 1945.
36. Indictment from the International Military Tribunal for the Far East, World War II file, Bontecou Papers, Harry S. Truman Presidential Museum and Library, accessed online on May 3, 2011, at http://www.trumanlibrary.org/whistlestop/study_collections/nuremberg/documents/index.php?pagenumber=14&documentid=18-2&documentdate=0000-00-00&study collectionid=nuremberg&groupid=.
37. Adapted from Creemers, *Shrine Shinto after World War II*, 76; and Jinja Honchō, *Jinja Honchō jūnenshi*, 130.
38. From Jinja Honchō's website: www.jinjahoncho.or.jp, accessed April 3, 2015.
39. The Director's permission was required to move a shrine, change its name, change its deities, build or move subsidiary shrines in their precincts, and make other significant alterations (article 82). While member shrines bore a responsibility to support the association and its regional branches financially (article 84), a corresponding explication of what the shrines could expect the association to do for them was lacking in the charter. Jinja Honchō, *Jinja Honchō jūnenshi*, 113–30.
40. Creemers, *Shrine Shinto after World War II*, 55; Jinja Honchō, *Jinja Honchō jūnenshi*, table 9, 346–48.
41. These shrines are called "separately listed shrines" (*beppyō jinja*); shrines can apply for this status; Inoue Nobutaka, "Beppyō jinja," *SJ*, 188.
42. Shrines held a total of 72,280 acres as their precincts (*keidai*), the compounds where their main buildings stood. Fully half of that land was actually held by some 206 shrines, averaging 176 acres each. In addition to their precincts, shrines held a total of roughly 63,000 acres, mostly forests. Around half of that was held by 140 shrines, with 195 acres each, on average. The Ise Shrines held 15,000 acres of forest, while the Kirishima Shrine in Kyushu held nearly as much. Numerous shrines held arable land farmed by tenants. Some shrines that had mountain deities claimed entire mountains, and there were two shrines on Mt. Fuji that both laid claim to the mountain as a whole. As these figures suggest, there was a vast gap between a small number of shrines with large land holdings and the rest, which had little. The land held by shrines was an important source of income. Revenue from the sale of timber and rent from tenants allowed them to support daily operations, maintenance, and repairs without depending fully upon donations from supporters. Creemers, *Shrine Shinto after World War II*, 77–81; Woodward, *Allied Occupation of Japan*, 119–27; Togami Shūken, "Shajiryō kokuyūchi shobun no igi to eikyō," in *Senryō to Nihon shūkyō*, ed. Ikado Fujio (Tokyo: Miraisha, 1993), 239–63.
43. Woodward, *Allied Occupation of Japan 1945-1952*, 119–27.
44. "Shasetsu: Zenkoku jinja no shūchūteki kyōryoku," *Jinja shinpō*, July 15, 1946, 1; "Shasetsu: Keidaichi, hokanrin mondai," *Jinja shinpō*, July 29, 1946, 1; "Shasetsu: Shaji kōchi to shūkyō katsudō," *Jinja shinpō*, September 30, 1946, 1; "Shasetsu: Keidō wa narihibiku," *Jinja shinpō*, November 25, 1946, 1.

45. Essentially, this granted shrines an exception to the provisions on the separation of religion from state. The SCAP directive paved the way for the Diet to pass a law including the new provisions. The grant was conditional on the land having been in the shrine's possession before 1868. Lands customarily held by shrines but not directly involved in their religious functions might be purchased at half the market value if the land was not a revenue source. Revenue-producing land, such as forest and farmland, could be purchased on the open market. Shrines established after 1868 and the former Nation-Protecting Shrines were not eligible for this scheme, since their land had not been confiscated by the Meiji government, and because SCAP viewed these newer shrines as having been established for the promotion of nationalism and imperialism.
46. Jinja Honchō, *Jinja Honchō jūnenshi*, 153–57. The text of the SCAP directive is available in Woodward, *Allied Occupation of Japan*, appendix B: 8; "Shasetsu: Shūkyōjin no kenri to gimu," *Jinja shinpō*, September 15, 1947, 1.
47. Woodward, *Allied Occupation of Japan*, 162–63.
48. "Shasetsu: Shin shirei, shin tsūchō no shushi tettei ni tsuite," *Jinja shinpō*, August 5, 1946, 1.
49. *Nihon shoki* contains a reference to *jichinsai* for the fifth year of Jitō's reign (691), and the rite is included in *Engi shiki* and a variety of other *jingi* texts. Depending on the occasion, the offerings and items buried at the site may be numerous and elaborate, and may include human effigies, mirrors, swords, and other precious materials. In medieval times, there was a Buddhist version of *jichinsai*. In the late Edo period, *jichinsai* is thought to have become widespread, based on the increasing durability of houses; Hirai Naofusa, "Jichinsai," *SSDJ*, 459; "Iijima Yoshiharu, "Jichinsai," *Nihon rekishi daijiten*.
50. Tsukuba graduated from Gakushūin University, which was usual for the nobility, but whereas his peers almost always proceeded to a military career, he entered the graduate course in ancient Japanese history at Tokyo Imperial University. At thirty-five, he became a member of the House of Peers and in 1939, headed the committee to locate sites connected with Emperor Jinmu, in advance of the 1940 celebrations of the country's supposed 2600th anniversary of its founding. According to his son, Tsukuba Hisaharu, while in the Diet Fujimaro took a dislike to the military for their arrogance. For a genealogical chart explaining Tsukuba's imperial connections, see Mainichi Shinbun Yasukuni shuzaihan, *Yasukuni sengo hishi: A-kyū senpan o gōshi shita hito* (Tokyo: Mainichi Shinbun, 2007), 106–14.
51. The figures are drawn from the National Federation of War Comrades' website, http://www.senyu-ren.jp/BOKIN2.HTM. Smaller veterans' groups contribute to Yasukuni in less obvious ways, such as the National Solomon Islands Association (Zenkoku Soromon kai), composed of veterans of Guadalcanal and other battles in the Solomon Islands. Their main activity is the repatriation of the remains of Japanese troops lost in those conflicts. In 1998, they built their own memorial in the islands, with two priests from Yasukuni officiating. The Naniwa Club (Naniwa kai) is a group of veterans who also are alumni of the naval academy. Their blog is filled with reminiscences of the war, along with obituaries. They sponsor annual *ireisai* at Yasukuni, masses for the repose of the dead in a Shinto style. Veterans are also natural supporters of the Nation-Protecting Shrines, which continue to be directly linked to Yasukuni. Like Yasukuni, these shrines are now religious corporations. Their deities include each prefecture's war dead, who are also enshrined at Yasukuni, and some of these shrines also apotheosize members of the Self-Defense Force, the police, and firefighters. The priesthood of the Nation-Protecting Shrines formed an association in 1946, the Nation-Protecting Shrine Association (Zenkoku Gokoku Jinja kai), whose purpose is to maintain their connection to Yasukuni Shrine and to serve the spirits of the war dead. Yasukuni Jinja, *Furusato no gokoku jinja to Yasukuni Jinja* (Tokyo: Dentensha, 2007), 54–55.
52. Yanagita Kunio first broached the idea of a Shinto version of the popular Buddhist festival *obon*, and Vice Head Priest Yokoi took up the idea, patterned on the Buddhist festivals in late summer to welcome the ancestors back to their homes for an annual visit. Mainichi Shinbun Yasukuni shuzaihan, *Yasukuni sengo hishi*, 117–21.

53. Ceremonies like this had been an established part of shrine life in northeastern Japan, and when a relative of one of Yasukuni's enshrined war dead spirits requested that the shrine perform such a rite, the custom was adopted in Yasukuni. Tokita Hideyuki, "Yasukuni Jinja ni kansuru 11 no shitsumon," *Chūō kōron* (March, 2003): 156–61.
54. While these new ceremonies brought new revenue, they also diluted the shrine's wartime image as a place where the military and death in battle were glorified. Head Priest Tsukuba's personal beliefs played an important role in the transformation. He evidently saw Shinto as a religion and went to considerable lengths to represent Yasukuni Shrine in that light. In 1963, he and his wife participated in the Religionists' Mission to Abolish Nuclear Weapons (Kakuheiki kinshi shūkyōsha heiwa shisetsudan). He served as one of the Vice Leaders, sharing the role with two Buddhist leaders, the Abbott of Yakushiji and the head of Risshō Kōseikai, Niwano Nikkyō. Over a forty-one-day journey, this group visited ten countries and met with the pope, the head of the Russian Orthodox church, and the Archbishop of Canterbury, as well as Secretary-General U Thant of the United Nations. This experience fired Tsukuba's desire to send a message of peace to the world from Yasukuni. Mainichi shinbun, *Yasukuni shuzaihan, Yasukuni sengo hishi*, 130–32.
55. Mainichi shinbun, *Yasukuni shuzaihan, Yasukuni sengo hishi*, 103–5.
56. "Chinreisha kara mita Yasukuni Jinja: Hissori tessaku no naka," *Chūnichi web press*, August 12, 2006, accessed August 14, 2006, http://www.tokyo=np.co.jp/00/tplijp/2006812/mng______tokuho___00.shtml. It is so small (around 10 square meters) and set so deep within the bushes and trees that even people who operate stalls inside the shrine precincts are sometimes unaware of its existence.
57. An army SDF band performed, and there was a display of flags. The right-wing new religious movement Seichō no Ie participated, as did some 3,000 members of the Naval SDF. Crowds along the parade route waved the Japanese flag. A song composed for Kigensetsu was sung; "worship from afar" (*yōhai*) toward the palace and Kashihara Shrine (on the spot where Jinmu was putatively enthroned) was performed; resolutions to give the holiday legal status were read.
58. Jinja Honchō, *Jinja Honchō jūgonenshi* (Tokyo: Jinja Honchō, 1961), 1–6, 331–35.
59. "Ronsetsu: Kigensetsu fukkatsu no kangeki," *Jinja shinpō*, December 17, 1966, 1.
60. Tanaka Nobumasa, *Yasukuni no sengoshi* (Tokyo: Iwanami shinsho, 2002), 74–78.
61. Kaya Okinori (1899–1977) had served as Finance Minister in the Tōjō cabinet from 1941 to 1944, and because of his role in securing the financial base for Japan's wartime government, was convicted as a Class-A war criminal. Released in 1955, he served as Minister of Justice from 1963 to 1964.
62. Tanaka, n. 60, 78–82.
63. Ibid., 85.
64. Ibid., 83; Hardacre, *Shinto and the State, 1868-1988*, 145ff.
65. Hardacre, *Shinto and the State, 1868-1988*, 145ff.
66. Support for the Yasukuni Bill was a litmus test for Izokukai support to candidates for office; Tanaka Nobumasa, *Izoku to sengo* (Tokyo: Iwanami Shinsho, 1995), 198, 205ff.
67. "Ronsetsu: Yasukuni Hōan e saido no dōryoku o," *Jinja shinpō*, August 16, 1969, 1.
68. "Higashi Honganji ga kōgi: Yasukuni hōan no kyōkō saiketsu ni—Ingai no ugoki," *Yomiuri shinbun*, evening edition, April 13, 1974, 10; Tanaka Nobumasa, *Yasukuni no sengoshi*, 101–5.
69. "Ronsetsu: Yotō 300 giseki no sekinin," *Jinja shinpō*, January 25, 1971, 2.
70. Tanaka, *Yasukuni no sengoshi*, 107.
71. Franziska Seraphim, *War Memory and Social Politics in Japan, 1945-2000*, (Cambridge, MA: Harvard University Press, 2006), 241.
72. "Ronsetsu: Yasukuni mondai o aratamete kangaeru," *Jinja shinpō*, August 26, 1974, 2.
73. "Shushō sanpai 'shijin' no katachi," *Asahi shinbun*, August 15, 1975, 1.
74. "Ronsetsu: Yasukuni Jinja 'kōshiki sanpai' jitsugen no undō," *Jinja shinpō*, August 22, 1977, 2.
75. Quoted in Mainichi Shinbun Yasukuni shuzaihan, n. 50, 70.

76. Ibid.
77. "Ronsetsu: 'Eirei ni kotaeru kai' no undō," *Jinja shinpō*, May 2, 1977, 2.
78. Seraphim, *War Memory and Social Politics in Japan, 1945-2000*, 252ff.
79. "Jinja Shintō futō ni reigū, Kindai Shintōshi kenkyūka Ashizu Uzuhiko-san, Watashi no iibun," *Asahi shinbun*, evening ed., March 25, 1985, 5.
80. These groups also continued to stage public demonstrations and signature drives against state support for Yasukuni.
81. When the word *shinryaku* is used as a noun in contrast to the term *shinshutsu* (advance), it is usually translated as "invasion." When *shinryaku* is used as an adjective to describe war, it is translated as "aggressive." For a detailed examination of postwar textbooks and controversies surrounding them, see James J. Orr, *The Victim as Hero: Ideologies of Peace and National Identity in Postwar Japan* (Honolulu: University of Hawai'i Press, 2001), chap. 4.
82. "Ronsetsu: Kono mama de yoi ka, Nihon seinen no ishiki," *Jinja shinpō*, February 27, 1984, 1.
83. "Ronsetsu: Shōgaku kyōkasho mo 'shinryaku' isshoku ni," *Jinja shinpō*, July 15, 1985, 1.
84. Matsudaira was born in Fukui Prefecture and was descended from one of the wealthiest *daimyō* of the Edo period. One of his uncles was Tokugawa Yoshichika, first president of the Yasukuni Association (Yasukuni Kai), a powerful shrine support group. His father Yoshitami had served in the Imperial Household Ministry, rising to the position of Chamberlain to Emperor Taishō, and was deeply knowledgeable about all aspects of the imperial court and the imperial family. Yoshitami entrusted his son to Hiraizumi Kiyoshi (a right-wing historian who was also from Fukui) to mentor the young Nagayoshi as he studied for the Naval Academy examinations. Matsudaira came to revere Hiraizumi greatly. Failing to enter the Naval Academy, he matriculated at the Naval Engineering College (Kaigun Kikan Gakkō). Matsudaira served in the Imperial Navy, and after 1945, in the infantry SDF, later resigning because of illness, then taking up the headship of the Fukui Prefectural Local History Museum. Before becoming Head Priest of Yasukuni, he had neither priestly experience nor any education that had prepared him for the role. Although Matsudaira was initially reluctant to accept the post, former Supreme Court justice and the first head of the Association to Answer the War Dead, Ishida Kazuto, urged him to accept. Matsudaira reportedly discussed with Ishida his desire to enshrine the fourteen men who had been executed for Class-A war crimes, saying that the Japanese spirit could never be recovered unless the war crimes trials were repudiated. Ishida saw no legal barrier to this course of action and encouraged Matsudaira. See Matsudaira Nagayoshi, "Dare ga mitama o kegashita no ka? Yasukuni hōshi jūyonen no munen," 1997, http://homepage.mac.com/credo99/public_html/8.15/tono.html, accessed June 21, 2011.
85. "'Shinryaku sensō o mitometa shushō, Kanjichō hōchū o nentō? Kinrinkoku e no hairyo yūsen 'kenkyo ni uketomeru' shushō shūhen, Naikaku shijiritsu," *Asahi shinbun*, February 19, 1983, 3.
86. "Ronsetsu: Tokyo saiban shikan no kokufuku o," *Jinja shinpō*, March 27, 1983, 1.
87. Hardacre, *Shinto and the State, 1868-1988*, 150.
88. The report is reprinted in *Jurist* 848 (November 1985): 110–15.
89. Hardacre, *Shinto and the State, 1868-1988*, 151.
90. "The nature of the war of aggression must not be blurred 侵略战争的性质不容模糊," *People's Daily*, August 22, 1985, quoted in Xiaojun Chen, "Belated Criticism? Analysis of the Reasons for Chinese Government's Attitude toward Nakasone's Visit on August 15, 1985" (unpublished term paper, Harvard University, 2010).
91. Hardacre, *Shinto and the State, 1868-1988*, 151.
92. *Mainichi shinbun*, June 1, 1988, 1.
93. One of the associated issues was whose wishes should prevail in choosing how the dead are remembered. The wishes of Nakaya Takafumi's parents conflicted with his wife's beliefs; the parents were willing to have his spirit to be enshrined as a Kami. They were not Christians. The deceased himself had no strong religious commitment. In such a case, whose wishes should prevail? This question pitted the nuclear family against the more traditional *ie* form. While

the constitution and the postwar civil code recognized the nuclear family and did not confer recognition on the *ie*, many Japanese, across the religious spectrum, nevertheless continue to imbue the *ie* with religious significance. To them it is axiomatic that the parents' wishes should prevail over those of a wife.

94. Whether the court was aware of it or not, however, older traditions regarding memorials of the dead by occupational groups provide some justification for the court's reasoning. Groups formed by those following a shared occupation such as fishermen or craftsmen or people employed by the same corporation have typically held periodic memorials. The underlying assumption is that the living and dead are linked through their occupation, and that it is proper for occupational groups to honor them through religious rites, usually Buddhist ceremonies. Such associations would not typically inquire into the religious beliefs of the family members of the deceased but would instead consider that it is the prerogative of those who continue to pursue the same occupation to honor the dead with Buddhist masses. In the Nakaya case we can see an analogy between the SDF and an occupational group, given that the SDF is an all-volunteer force and constitutes the occupation of all its members.

Chapter 15

1. Sonoda Minoru, "Matsuri: Hyōshō no kōzō," in *Girei no kōzō*, Nihonjin no shūkyō 2, ed. Tamaru Noriyoshi, Muraoka Kū, and Miyata Noboru (Tokyo: Kōsei shuppan, 1972), 264.
2. Sonoda Minoru, "Matsuri: Hyōshō no kōzō."
3. Related synonymous verbs include *tsukaematsuru, itsukimatsuru*, and *iwaimatsuru*.
4. Sonoda Minoru, "Matsuri," *SSDJ*, 899–901.
5. "Matsuri," *SJ*, 212.
6. Ono Sokyō, *Shintō no kiso chishiki to kiso mondai* (Tokyo: Jinja shinpōsha, 1963), 283–84.
7. "Matsuri," in *SJ*. Synonyms for *matsuri* include the terms *saishi, sairei*, and *saigi*. Related terms include *saishiki* (the method for performing a *matsuri*, the steps or procedures carried out in the performance, or the order of those steps), *saiten* (a set form or format for presenting *saishi, sairei*, or *saigi*), *shinji* (an inclusive term incorporating all the separate ritual actions involved in rites for the Kami), and *gishiki* and *gyōji*, two synonymous terms meaning ceremonies performed according to established prescriptions.
8. In his authoritative work on basic concepts in Shinto, Ono Sokyō advances a variety of typologies of *matsuri*, drawing from historical texts such as the *Kojiki* and *Nihon shoki*. His work introduces further subdivisions beyond the five main purposes noted here, including praising the Kami, expressing one's feelings toward the Kami, expressing a sincere intention to fulfill the will of the Kami, soothing a Kami's displeasure, and making an announcement to the Kami. See Ono Sokyō, *Jinja Shintō no kiso chishiki to kiso mondai*, 215–16.
9. Sonoda Minoru, "Matsuri," *SSDJ*, 899–901.
10. For the details of this festival, see Mogi Sakae, *Matsuri denshōron* (Tokyo: Daimeidō, 1993), 224–331.
11. One of the largest civic pageants, the Kobe Matsuri, was founded through an initiative of the city government slightly later, in 1967, based on an earlier observance of 1933 called the Harbor Festival (Minato no Matsuri). Its main event is a parade that in 1982 included some ninety-four different dancing groups, bands, baton twirling groups, and children's *mikoshi*. Many of these groups are formed autonomously by companies, schools, workplaces, etc. The parade's composition, the route, and other details have changed greatly over the years. The highlight of the parade is the samba dancers who come at the end; many of them are foreigners. Twice in its history there have been major problems: in 1975 a group of *bōsōzoku* (young men on motorcycles who detach their mufflers and run red lights) monopolized the parade route on the night before the parade, making a great racket, starting fires, and intimidating people. A taxi was overturned and burned. The festival was canceled in 1995, but revived in 1996 and dedicated to those who had died in the catastrophic Hanshin earthquake of 1995.

See Anami Tōru, "Dentōteki matsuri no henbō to aratana matsuri no sōzō," in *Matsuri to ibento,* Gendai no sesō 5, ed. Komatsu Kazuhiko (Tokyo: Shōgakkan, 1997), 67–110.

12. Ibid.; Yoneyama Toshinao, "Kōbe matsuri ni tsuite," *Kikan jinruigaku* 18, no. 3 (1987): 4–11; Inoue Nobutaka, Kōmoto Mitsugu, Nakamaki Hirochika, et al., "A Festival with Anonymous Kami: The Kobe Matsuri," *JJRS* 6, no. 1/2 (1978): 163–85.
13. Many studies attest to the tendency of *matsuri* to exclude newcomers. See Arisue Ken, "Toshi sairei no jūsōteki kōzō," *Shakaigaku hyōron* 33, no. 4 (1983): 37–62; Nakamura Fumi, "Chichibu matsuri: Toshi no matsuri no shakai jinruigaku," *Kikan jinruigaku* 3 (1972): 149–90; Yoneyama Toshinao, *Gion matsuri* (Tokyo: Chūō Kōronsha, 1974).
14. Arisue, "Toshi sairei no jūsōteki kōzō," Nakamura Fumi, "Chichibu matsuri," Yoneyama Toshinao, *Gion matsuri.*
15. Ashida Tetsuro, "The Festival and Religion Boom: Irony of the Age of the Heart," in *Folk Beliefs in Modern Japan,* Contemporary Papers on Japanese Religions 3, ed. Inoue Nobutaka (Tokyo: Institute for Japanese Culture and Classics, Kokugakuin University, 1994), http://www2.kokugakuin.ac.jp/iicc/wp/cpir/folkbeliefs.
16. Ōtani Jun, "Kurokawa nō," *Shinpan nō, kyōgen jiten* (from the online database Japan Knowledge.com; accessed January 2, 2013). A full list of Japan's Intangible Folk Culture Assets may be found on Wikipedia, http://ja.wikipedia.org/wiki/%E6%B0%91%E4%BF%97%E6%96%87%E5%8C%96%E8%B2%A1.
17. See Matsudaira Makoto, "Gendai Kanda matsuri sokubun," *Kokuritsu minzoku hakubutsukan kenkyū hōkoku* 33 (1991): 75–94.
18. Matsudaira Makoto, "Gendai Kanda matsuri sokubun." Matsudaira notes in another essay that it is now common for outsiders to take major roles in festivals, as in the case of the Kōenji Awa Odori, a Tokyo dance festival based on the Tokushima Awa Odori. In this case, dance groups come from all over Eastern Japan. The dance groups may be from companies, religious groups, the handicapped, or other cities. There are no restrictions or limitations on their participation; they can expand and contract and come and go as they like, without forming ongoing bonds to the place where the festival is held. The length of time in which these people are all linked together is very short, lasting no longer than the time they are dancing. See Matsudaira Makoto, "Toshi shukusai no gendaiteki imi," *Toshi mondai* 90, no. 8 (1999): 3–12.
19. Takezawa Naoichirō, Fukuma Yūya, Minami Hirofumi, Komatsu Hideo, Toda Tetsurō, Shigenobu Yukihiko, Seki Kazutoshi, "Toshi sairei kenkyū no kadai to kanōsei," *1998 nendo waakushoppu hōkokusho* (Tokyo: Shūkyō to shakai gakkai, 1998).
20. Anami Tōru, "Dentōteki matsuri no henbō to aratana matsuri no sōzō."
21. The formal title of the "Matsuri Law" is *Chiiki dentō geinō-tō o katsuyo shita gyōji no jisshi ni yoru kankō oyobi tokutei chiiki shōkōgyō no shinkō ni kansuru hōritsu.*
22. Research in 2001 to observe the festival was supported by the Clark Fund (Harvard University) and the Edwin O. Reischauer Institute of Japanese Studies, Harvard University. Research conducted from 2003 to 2004 was funded under a Guggenheim Fellowship from the John Simon Guggenheim Memorial Foundation, with assistance from the Edwin O. Reischauer Institute of Japanese Studies, Harvard University.
23. The discussion here is not a comprehensive study of the Darkness Festival, but only those aspects of it that bear on Shinto's claims to represent a public phenomenon embodying indigenous tradition.
24. Komine Masaharu, *Musashi sōsha Ōkunitama Jinja taisai shi* (Privately published in Fuchū by Meisei kikaku, 2001), 108nn3–5.
25. Ibid., 108nn3–6.
26. A newspaper account of the 1938 festival described stone throwing as a common occurence when rival *mikoshi* encountered each other; Komine Masaharu, *Musashi sōsha Ōkunitama Jinja taisai shi.*, 108nn3–7.
27. The four wards take in the residences of the *shinjin* as well as the oldest residents.

28. There is a local legend holding that the assignment of a particular area to manage a particular set of *mikoshi* and drum was originally chosen by lot. See Komine Masaharu, *Musashi Fuchū shuku fudokikō: Shinpen Musashi fudokikō, no genbun to sono kanren hosoku setsumei* (unpublished manuscript, 2003).
29. Photographs from festivals prior to that time show men in unmatched, ordinary clothing, sometimes wearing helmets, carrying the *mikoshi*. It is thought that before 1945 the *mikoshi* bearers probably wore only a loincloth and a headband.
30. Though documentary evidence is lacking, it is not uncommon to see heavily tattooed men happily strolling through festivals. They sometimes extort money at the Darkness Festival by standing nonchalantly in a gate that *mikoshi* must pass through, in effect daring the *mikoshi* bearers to knock them out of the way. In this writer's experience, festival organizers generally pay them off rather than risk a violent confrontation. There is a local legend holding that a gambler boss, of the late nineteenth century, named Koganei Kōjirō broke up gangs of ruffians who had blocked the *mikoshi* from passing, and ever afterward *kō* from Koganei City have taken responsibility for clearing the road for the festival procession, most notably by sponsoring the Misakibarai Taiko. Mr. Mizukoshi and Mr. Kamoshita of the Koganei Kōjū, interview by the author, May 4, 2001.
31. In the "Reflection Meeting" (*hanseikai*) held regularly at the conclusion of the festival by representatives of the main organizers, the question how best to control the shadowy elements who manage the food and game stalls is a regular topic of discussion.
32. Mr. Tanaka Shigeo, President of the Miyamachi Ōhayashi Society, interview with author, May 10, 2001 (Fuchū City).
33. Similar decorations are used in Buddhist festivals of light, such as the Oeshiki ceremony in the Nichiren sects, held on the thirteenth day of the tenth month, to commemorate the day of Nichiren's death.
34. For example, the tradition of seven dances in the *Dōzasai*, which announces the imminent procession to the Kami, must be drastically shortened on a daytime schedule.
35. Sawatari Masamori, interview by the author, May 8, 2001 (Fuchū City).
36. Essentially, this was a process of persuading the other priests of the shrine, local shrine supporters, and city officials of the Police and Fire Departments, as well as the city Chamber of Commerce and tourism office.
37. The order of ritual for Annual Festivals was prescribed under prewar religious administration and subsequently modified by NASS, in 1948; this is the system that prevails today. The NASS modifications to the old system consisted principally of deleting the requirement that representatives of government participate, and that representatives of the national Shrine Bureau (after 1940, the Jingiin) would present offerings at the Annual Festivals of Imperial Shrines. Representatives of NASS took over the role of the former Shrine Bureau, and an association representative, called a *kenpeishi*, now presents these offerings. The *kenpeishi* attends wearing formal vestments, with an entourage to help him shoulder a large, wooden trunk filled with offerings. These changes did not substantially alter the order of ceremony.
38. The Review of the Horses is noted in the earliest record of the order of festival events, "Goyuisho narabini shahō teisho" (1775). See Miyake Hitoshi, "Fuchū Ōkunitama Jinja Kurayamisai ni okeru jizoku to hen'yō," *Kokugakuin zasshi* 102 (2001): 9.
39. Now there is a racetrack in that location.
40. When a Kami is invoked to be present, or invited to depart, when the doors of the Main Sanctuary are opened or closed, or when the Kami is departing in a portable shrine for a procession, a ritualist pronounces a long, drawn-out, loud "Ōoo" sound. It initiates that part of a rite at which a Kami is present. The *keihitsu* is pronounced as a sign of respect toward the Kami, and it also encourages all participants in the rite to show respect to the divine spirit. In the past, *keihitsu* was pronounced on the occasion of imperial processions also. Inoue Nobutaka, "Keihitsu," *SJ*, 235–36.
41. Sakamoto Koremaru and Ishii Kenji, eds., *Puresuteppu Shintōgaku* (Tokyo: Kōbundō, 2011), 115.

42. Announcer's script, received from Head Priest Sawatari.
43. To outside spectators not familiar with the festival, the Review of the Horses probably looks like a horse race, but it is not a contest of speed.
44. For another account of these ceremonies, see Mogi Sakae, *Matsuri denshōron*, 194–95; 201–4.
45. This writer's presence at the back of the Worship Hall to view and film this ceremony was met with some opposition by local men, but the Head Priest intervened to smooth things over.
46. Mogi Sakae, *Matsuri denshōron*, 198.
47. This ceremony is called *Goreisen no gi*.
48. This drum is too large to pass under the Chūjaku or Zuishin Gates, so it joins the procession just beyond the latter, coming in from the west side.
49. Sonoda Minoru, "Matsuri: Hyōshō no kōzō," 272–78.
50. Mr. Katō Shin'ichi, President, and Mr. Ishizaka Kōhei, Section Chief (Kachō) of the Fuchū City Tourism Office, interview by the author, April 7, 2004 (Fuchū City).
51. Nakasato Ryōhei, "Sairei ni okeru momegoto no shori to rūru: Kare wa naze nagurareta no ka," *Gendai minzokugaku kenkyū* 2 (2010): 41–56.
52. Ibid.
53. Ibid.
54. Festival organizers recognize the importance of informing themselves about how other festivals are managed. The Hōsankai (the overall supervising organization managing the accounts and activities of Ōkunitama Shrine) takes an annual trip to observe another successful festival. According to one interviewee, the purpose is to consider how they can best present the Darkness Festival to promote tourism.

Chapter 16

1. This material represents a paraphrase of Sonoda Minoru, "Jinja Shintō no shōraizō," *Jinja shinpō*, January 1, 1996, 1.
2. While *Jinja shinpō* would never criticize the emperor, it argues against his traveling to any place where an apology might be warranted, stating that he might be made a pawn in international relations, or that unscrupulous politicians might use him for political ends. See "Shuchō: Kaifu shushō no kutsujoku gaikō," *Jinja shinpō*, September 23, 1991, 2; "Shuchō: Sōru no ningyō funshō jiken ni tsuite," *Jinja shinpō*, February 3, 1992, 2; "Shuchō: Kyōdō sengen to go hōkan mondai," *Jinja shinpō*, October 26, 1998, 2; "Ronsetsu: On shushō hōnichi: yusurarenai heika no seiji riyō," *Jinja shinpō*, April 23, 2007, 2. Shintō Seiji Renmei also produced a position paper on this subject, reiterating *Jinja shinpō*'s warnings. The paper is discussed in Kenneth J. Ruoff, *The People's Emperor: Democracy and the Japanese Monarchy, 1945-1995* (Cambridge, MA: Harvard University Press, 2011), 154–55.
3. Helen Hardacre, "Tokyo Broadcasting and Aum Shinrikyo," *Nieman Reports* 51, no. 1 (Spring 1997): 66–69.
4. See, for example, Ishimura Kōji, "Kōeki hōjin seido kaikaku to shūkyō hōjin e no eikyō: 'Eiri hōjin nami kazei' e no tenkan to shūkyō hōjin e no hakyū mondai," *Shūkyō hō* 24 (2005): 21–56; Ishimura Kōji, *Shūkyō hōjinsei to zeisei no arikata* (Kyoto: Hōritsu Bunkasha, 2006), 18–24; and Tanaka Osamu, "Shūkyō hōjin to zeisei to no kankei: Kazei ga nai koto no imi," *Kyōbutsu* 88 (2010): 4–5.
5. On the legal issues surrounding pet funerals, see Miki Yoshikazu, "Shūkyō hōjin ni yoru petto kuyō no hi-shūeki jigyōsei," *Ritsumeikan hōgaku* 298 (2004): 406–17; on the two court verdicts, see Barbara Ambros, *Bones of Contention: Animals and Religion in Contemporary Japan* (Honolulu: University of Hawai'i Press, 2012), chap. 3.
6. Ishii Kenji, "Jinja Shintō wa suita shita no ka," in *Shintō wa doko e iku ka?*, ed. Ishii (Tokyo: Perikansha, 2010), 21–23.
7. Ochi Miwa, "Joshi shinshoku: Josei no shinshutsu wa aru no ka," in Ishii, *Shintō wa doko e iku ka?*, 100.

8. It is important to recognize that the term "Kami" is used both for the Kami of Shinto and as a name for the God of Christianity and Judaism, though the impact of Christians and Jews in these surveys is probably of no statistical significance.
9. Ishii Kenji, "Jinja Shintō wa suita shita no ka?," 21–23.
10. "Hatsumōde," *SD*, 302.
11. "Shichi-go-san," *SD*, 293.
12. "Yakudoshi," *SD*, 354–55.
13. Taguchi Yūko, "Hatsu miya mairi: Haha oyatachi kara kiita gendai no o-miya mairi," in Ishii Kenji, *Shintō wa doko e iku ka?*, 51–71.
14. Shūkyō jōhō risāchi sentā, *Jinja soshiki ni kansuru ankēto chōsa hōkokusho,* (Tokyo: Shūkyō jōhō risāchi sentā, 2003), 74.
15. Ibid., 75.
16. Ibid.
17. Ibid.
18. Ibid., 74–75.
19. Ibid., 25.
20. Ibid., 43–45.
21. Ibid., 32–34.
22. See the text of the Religious Corporations Law, section 3, articles 18–25, http://law.e-gov.go.jp/htmldata/S26/S26HO126.html, accessed August 9, 2013.
23. Shūkyō jōhō risāchi sentā, *Jinja soshiki ni kansuru ankēto chōsa hōkokusho*, 61.
24. The newsletter is called *Ōkunitama* and is published quarterly. The Ōkunitama Shrine's Hōsankai represents the most active form of shrine management by shrine stewards and other supporters.
25. Shūkyō jōhō risāchi sentā, n. 14, 63.
26. Ibid., 70.
27. Ibid., 71.
28. Ibid., 68.
29. Ibid., 69.
30. Ibid., 64.
31. Ibid., 68.
32. Ibid.
33. Andō Takayuki, "Seikyō bunri gensoku ni kansuru saikōsai no futatsu no hanketsu: Sunagawa seikyō bunri soshō hanketsu to Hakusan Hime Jinja taisai Hōsankai jiken hanketsu," *Kyūshū Kokusai Daigaku Hōgaku Ronshū* 17 (March 2011): 1–34.
34. Yamazaki Tomoya, "Ishikawa, Toyama hen: Hakusan shinkō to seikyō bunri gensoku," in *Chiiki ni manabu kenpō enshū*, ed. Arai Makoto, Kotani Junko, Yokodaidō Satoshi (Tokyo: Nihon hyōronsha, 2011), 74–75.
35. Ibid., 78–80.
36. Shūkyō jōhō risāchi sentā, n. 14, 77–78.
37. Ibid., 78.
38. Ibid.
39. The Head Priest of the Iwashimizu Hachiman Shrine sets out the organization's objectives: shinbutsureijou.net, accessed April 16, 2015.
40. Shūkyō jōhō risāchi sentā, n. 14, 78.
41. Ibid.
42. Ibid., 77–78.
43. Shibata Ryōichi, "Shin shinsōsai bochi no tanjō: Jinja wa shi to dō mukiau no ka," in Ishii, *Shintō wa doko e iku ka*, 72–92.
44. Besides graveyards constructed by shrines, there are also cases of graveyards that operate in a Shinto style and present themselves as extensions of such well-known shrines as the Izumo Shrine, but which in fact are separate commercial enterprises. Their advertisements can give

the impression that they have the imprimatur of the shrine, whether they do or not; one of these is the Shimane Sōreisha. See http://www.jinja.in/single/120800.html, accessed April 20, 2015.

45. See these sites for data on the proportion of weddings conducted in Shinto style: bridal-souken.net/data/trend2012/XY_MT12_release_00zenkoku.pdf/ and office-isc-wedding.sblo.jp/category/1139161-1.html.
46. See ja.wikipedia.org/wiki/伊勢山皇大神宮.
47. Ochi Miwa, "Joshi shinshoku: Josei no shinshutsu wa aru no ka," in Ishii, *Shintō wa doko e iku ka*, 99–102.
48. Ishii Kenji, "Yamaguchi-ken: Kōkeisha mondai jittai chōsa hōkokusho" (unpublished report, 2007).
49. Ishii Kenji, "Zentai tōgi," *Jinja Honchō sōgō kenkyūjo kiyō* 16 (2011): 190.
50. Ochi Miwa, "Joshi shinshoku," 110–11.
51. Two recent books by female priests provide much insight into their lives and the daily routine at shrines. See Okada Momoko, *Jinja wakaoku nikki* (Tokyo: Shōdensha, 2004) and Matsuoka Rie, *Jinja no musume ganbaru* (Tokyo: Hara shobō, 2004).
52. Okada Momoko, *Jinja wakaoku nikki*; Matsuoka Rie, *Jinja no musume ganbaru*.
53. Ochi Miwa, "Joshi shinshoku," 103–4.
54. Ishii Kenji, "Shūkyō dantai no kōeki katsudō: Kōekisei ni kansuru ichi kōsatsu," *Kokugakuin Daigaku daigakuin kiyō* Bungaku kenkyūka 39 (2007): 1–24.
55. Fujimoto Yorio, *Shintō to shakai jigyō no kindaishi* (Tokyo: Kōbundō, 2009), 1.
56. Inaba Keishin and Kurosaki Hiroyuki, eds., *Shinsai fukkō to shūkyō*, Sōsho: shūkyō to soshyaru kyapitaru, vol. 4. (Tokyo: Akashi shoten, 2013).
57. Fujimoto Yorio, *Shintō to shakai jigyō no kindaishi*.
58. Itai Masanari, *Sasaeai no Shintō bunka* (Tokyo: Kōbundō, 2011).
59. Yoshino Kōichi and Terazawa Shigenori, "Chiiki shakai ni okeru shūkyō no shakai kōken katsudō," in Inaba Keishin and Sakurai Yoshihide, eds. *Shakai kōken suru shūkyō* (Tokyo: Sekai shisōsha, 2009), 164, 173ff.
60. Sakurai Haruo, "Shintō: Tamen-teki na kachi o naiho suru sei naru hako," *Aera Mook 11: Shūkyōgaku ga wakaru* (Asahi shinbunsha, 1995), quoted in Fujimoto Yorio, *Shintō to shakai jigyō no kindaishi*, 465.
61. Fujimoto Yorio, "Jinja Shintō to shakai kōken no kakawari o kangaeru," in *Shakai kōken suru shūkyō*, 84–85.
62. See the website of the national association for chaplains, Kyōkaishi Renmei, http://kyoukaishi.server-shared.com/serviceindex1.html.
Fujimoto Yorio, *Shintō to shakai jigyō no kindaishi*, 557, Table 28.
63. Fujimoto Yorio, *Shintō to shakai jigyō no kindaishi*, 547–49.
64. http://www.jinjahoncho.or.jp/reconstruction/000080.html.
65. Fujiyama Midori, "Kokunai no shinsai hōdō ni mirareta shūkyō no yakuwari: Shūkyōsha ni yoru shien katsudō," *Shūkyō jōhō sentā* Kenkyūin repōto (2011). www.circam.jp/reports/02/detail/id=1998. See also Levi McLaughlin, "What Have Religious Groups Done after 3.11? Part 1: A Brief Survey of Religious Mobilization after the Great East Japan Earthquake Disasters," *Religion Compass* 7, no. 8 (2013): 294–308.
66. *Jinja shinpō*, August 1, 2011.
67. Fujiyama Midori, "Genpatsu ni taisuru shūkyōkai no kenkai," *Shūkyō jōhō sentā* Kenkyūin repōto" (2012), www.circam.jp/reports/02/detail/id=2012.
68. Fujiyama Midori, "Shūkyōkai no shinsai shien ga hōdō sarenai riyū 1: Hanshin, Higashi Nihon Daishinsai no hikaku yori," *Shūkyō jōhō sentā* Kenkyūin repōto (2011), www.circam.jp/reports/02/detail/id=2007.
69. Ibid.
70. *Jinja shinpō*, July 25, 2011.

71. A related issue concerns government-recognized cultural properties held by temples and shrines. The government provides compensation for damages by natural disaster to religious organizations. A recent case is the Itsukushima Shrine of Hiroshima, which in 2004 was badly damaged by a typhoon. The government provided 85 percent of the money needed for repairs, $6,715,000. While at least one of the shrines damaged on 3.11, Ōsaki Hachimangū in Sendai, has significant cultural properties, however, most of them do not.
72. Fujiyama Midori, "Shūkyōkai no shinsai fukkyū o kobamu seikyō bunri no kabe," *Shūkyō jōhō sentā* Kenkyūin repōto (2011), www.circam.jp/reports/02/detail/id=2009.
73. The research referenced here has been discussed in some detail by Jolyon Thomas in *Drawing on Tradition: Manga, Anime, and Religion in Contemporary Japan* (Honolulu: University of Hawai'i Press, 2012), 103–7.
74. Ibid., 14ff.
75. *Kamichū!* is short for *Kamisama de Chūgakusei*. The animated version was based on a manga of the same title, written by Hanaharu Naruko and published in two volumes from June 2005 to January 2007 in *Dengeki Daioh*. The anime version was created by the collaborative called Besamemūcho and was broadcast in sixteen episodes, from June through September 2005. The series was awarded the Japan Media Arts Festival Award for Excellence in 2005.
76. *Inuyasha, Asagiri no miko,* and *Kamichū!* are relatively uncomplicated, "vanilla" tales lacking elements of film noir or moral complexity. By contrast, *Higurashi When They Cry* (*Higurashi no Naku Koro ni*) concerns a cycle of murders in a fictional small town, as experienced by the local shrine *miko*. Originally released from 2002 to 2006 as eight video games, *Higurashi* spawned allied productions in various genres: manga, a novel, an animated television series, and several live-action films. See "Higurashi When They Cry," on Wikipedia (https://en.wikipedia.org/wiki/Higurashi_When_They_Cry) for plot summaries and over seventy references to Internet sites on which these productions can be accessed. I would like to thank Professor Alexander Zahlten (Harvard University) for helpful references and advice on these productions.
77. Ishii Kenji, "Anime no naka no dentō shūkyō," in *Gendai bunka no naka no shūkyō dentō Gendai shūkyō* 2011, 154–56.
78. *Jinja no susume*, eight issues published originally in *Gekkan afutanūn* (Kōdansha) 2004–2006, later as a book in four volumes from AfutanūnKC; *Takamagahara ni kami zumarimasu*, manga in nineteen issues, published in *Kiss* (Kōdansha, 2004); later published as a book in three volumes by Kōdansha. Also see Ishii, "Anime no naka no dentō shūkyō."
79. Kirino Natsuo, *Joshinki* (Tokyo: Kadokawa shoten, 2008).
80. Kobayashi Yoshinori, *Yasukuniron* (Tokyo: Gentōsha, 2005).
81. Miyazaki Hayao, *Mononoke Hime* (Tokyo: Ghibli Studio, 1997).
82. Sakamoto Naoko, "Shintō no ninkibon: Ureru "Shintō" hon no himitsu," in Ishii, *Shintō wa do e iku ka?*, 207.
83. Ibid., 211.
84. Adapted from Kirino Natsuo, *The Goddess Chronicle*, trans. Rebecca Copeland (Edinburgh, New York, and Melbourne: Canongate, 2012), 307; *Joshinki*, 258 (*kore kara mo urande nikunde koroshi tsukusu no da*).
85. Ariyoshi Hiroshi. Blog.goo.ne.jp/iruka-1967/e/e/, accessed August 12, 2013.
86. Blogs.yahoo.co.jp/chgyd212/10908407.html, accessed August 12, 2013.
87. Yamaguchi Hidekazu.Yamaguchihidekazu.com, May, 19, 2013, accessed August 12, 2013.
88. Amazon.jp site advertising Kirino's *Joshinki* and providing a variety of reader reviews. www.amazon.co.jp/product-revivews/4041000203/, accessed August 12, 2013.
89. Thomas, *Drawing on Tradition*, 84ff.
90. Yahoo.co.jp site providing reader reviews of Kobayashi Yoshinori, *Yasukuniron*. http://detail.chiebukuro.yahoo.co.jp/qa/question_detail/q10107936980, accessed April 21, 2015.
91. Chihō no Tenshō Daijin, March 1, 2012, on www.amazon.co.jp/product-reviews/434401023X/, accessed August 13, 2013.

92. Biri za kiddo, May 27, 2013, on www.amazon.co.jp/product-reviews/434401023X/, accessed August 13, 2013.
93. Hanabōzu, August 22, 2012, on www.amazon.co.jp/product-reviews/434401023X/, accessed August 13, 2013.
94. Asuran, August 9, 2012, on www.amazon.co.jp/product-reviews/434401023X/, accessed August 13, 2013.
95. Yamabuki Midori, March 9, 2013, on www.amazon.co.jp/product-reviews/434401023X/, accessed August 13, 2013.
96. Ritoru mi, February 9, 2013, on www.amazon.co.jp/product-reviews/434401023X/, accessed August 13, 2013.
97. For a review of scholarship linking Miyazaki's work with Shinto, see Jacqueline Berndt, "Considering Manga Discourse: Location, Ambiguity, Historicity," in *Japanese Visual Culture: Explorations in the World of Manga and Anime,* ed. Mark W. MacWilliams (Armonk, NY: M. E. Sharp, 2008), 295–310. An example of such scholarship is James W. Boyd and Tetsuya Nishimura, "Shinto Perspectives on Miyazaki's Anime Film *Spirited Away,*" *Journal of Religion and Film* 8, no. 2 (2004), http://www.unomaha.edu/jrf/Vol8No2/boydShinto.htm.
98. Miyazaki Hayao interview, in Elisabeth Vincentelli, "For a Japanese Animator, Grown-up Messages Are Kid Stuff," *Village Voice,* November 2, 1999, 44, quoted in Thomas, *Drawing on Tradition,* 110.
99. Thomas, *Drawing on Tradition,* 117.
100. Buriki Otoko, May 23, 2013, on www.amazon.co.jp/product-reviews/B00005Q413/, accessed August 12, 2013.
101. Harayasu (Nagoya), July 8, 2013, on www.amazon.co.jp/product-reviews/B00005Q413/, accessed August 12, 2013.
102. Sow-seed, June 17, 2013, on www.amazon.co.jp/product-reviews/B00005Q413/, accessed August 12, 2013.
103. Nirvanakamura, June 19, 2013, on www.amazon.co.jp/product-reviews/B00005Q413/, accessed August 12, 2013.
104. See Ise-shi sangyō kankōbu kankō kikakuka, "Heisei 25 nen Ise-shi kankō tōkei," 3, http://www.city.ise.mie.jp/secure/12124/25kankotoukei.pdf, accessed April 23, 2015.

Appendix

1. The Shrine Bureau linked itself to the Ise Shrines so that the Shrine Bureau Chief nominally headed an office at Ise devoted to expanding and upgrading its lands (Zō-Jingūshichō). The Jingūshichō had existed at Ise since the 1870s. It dwarfed the Shrine Bureau in terms of staff size. It appears that the main purpose of creating this link was to give the Shrine Bureau some nominal oversight of the Ise Shrines, especially the Vicennial Renewals held in 1909 and 1929. A second external unit linking the Shrine Bureau to the Ise Shrines, the Kanbesho, was formed for the distribution of Ise almanacs and talismans. A third external office was created to oversee the construction of the Meiji Shrine (Meiji Jingū zōei kyoku).
2. An ambitious plan to transform Ise into a "Kami Capital" (*shinto*) originated with a group of local boosters from the towns of Uji and Yamada. They bought up land around the Ise Shrines in 1886 and donated it to the shrines, so that the precincts could be expanded and cleared of private dwellings. Beginning in 1912, the government continued the expansion, and the transformation of private landholdings into public land dedicated to the Ise Shrines, with significant purchases in 1912, 1922, and 1934. The plan to make Ise Japan's "Kami Capital" was based on the expectation of major festivities in 1940 for the 2600th anniversary of the founding of the empire, as well as the hope of performing the Vicennial Renewal rites on a grand scale in 1949, by which time Japan would also have emerged victorious from its wars; see Okada Kaneyoshi, "Shinto keikaku nitsuite," *JKZ* 36, no. 5 (1937): 3–12.
3. Tsukamoto Seiji, "Kome sōjō nitsuki tokuni shinshoku shokun ni nozomu."

BIBLIOGRAPHY

Abe Ryūichi. *The Weaving of Mantra: Kūkai and the Construction of Esoteric Buddhist Discourse.* New York: Columbia University Press, 1999.

Abe Yasurō. *Chūsei Nihon no shūkyō tekusuto taikei.* Nagoya: Nagoya Daigaku shuppankai, 2013.

———. "Shintō as Written Representation: The Phases and Shifts of Medieval Shintō Texts." *Cahiers d'Extrême-Asie* 16 (2006/7): 91–117.

Abe Yoshiya. "Religious Freedom under the Meiji Constitution (continued)." *Contemporary Religions in Japan* 10, no. 1–2 (1969): 57–97.

Adolphson, Mikael. "Institutional Diversity and Religious Integration: The Establishment of Temple Networks in the Heian Age." In *Heian Japan, Centers and Peripheries,* edited by Mikael S. Adolphson, Edward Kamens, and Stacie Matsumoto, 212–45. Honolulu: University of Hawai'i Press, 2007.

Adolphson, Mikael, and Mark Ramseyer. "The Competitive Enforcement of Property Rights in Medieval Japan: The Role of Temples and Monasteries." *Journal of Economic Behavior and Organization* 71, no. 3 (2009): 660–668.

Aihara Ichirōsuke. "Yakugo shūkyō no seiritsu." *Shūkyōgaku kiyō* 5 (1938): 1–6.

Akazawa Shirō. "Hōanden." *Nihon daihyakka zensho.* Accessed via Japan Knowledge.com, March 2, 2015.

———. *Kindai Nihon no shisō dōin to shūkyō tōsei.* Tokyo: Kōsō shobō, 1985.

Ambros, Barbara. *Bones of Contention: Animals and Religion in Contemporary Japan.* Honolulu: University of Hawai'i Press, 2012.

———. *Emplacing a Pilgrimage: The Ōyama Cult and Regional Religion in Early Modern Japan.* Cambridge, MA: Harvard University Asia Center, 2008.

Andō Takayuki. "Seikyō bunri gensoku ni kansuru saikōsai no futatsu no hanketsu: Sunagawa seikyō bunri soshō hanketsu to Hakusan Hime Jinja taisai Hōsankai jiken hanketsu." *Kyūshū Kokusai Daigaku Hōgaku Ronshū* 17 (March 2011): 1–34.

Antoni, Klaus. *Shintō & die Konzeption des japanischen Nationalwesens (kokutai): Der religiöse Traditionalismus in Neuzeit und Moderne Japans.* Leiden: Brill, 1998.

Aoki, Michiko, trans. *Izumo fudoki.* Monumenta Nipponica Monograph 44. Tokyo: Sophia University Press, 1971.

Araki Toshio. "Kodai kokka to minkan saishi." *Rekishigaku kenkyū* 560 (October 1986): 45–51.

Arichi, Meri. "Sannō Miya Mandara: The Iconography of Pure Land on this Earth." *JJRS* 33, no. 2 (2006): 319–47.

Aritomi Jun'ya. "Jingikan no tokushitsu: Chihō jinja gyōsei kara no kentō." *Hisutoria* 187 (November 2003): 83–106.

Aruga Nagao. "Kokkyō to shite no Shintō" [Part 1]. *ZSKK* 23 (1911): 13–19.

———. "Kokkyō to shite no Shintō" [Part 2]. *ZSKK* 28 (1911): 219–23.

———. "Shintō kokkyō ron." *Tetsugaku zasshi* 280 (June, 1910): 1–27.

Asakura Haruhiko, ed. *Kindaishi shiryō Rikugunshō Nisshi*. 10 vols. Tokyo: Tōkyōdō shuppan, 1988–1989.

Asao Naohiro. "Kōgi to bakuhan ryōshu sei." In *Kōza Nihon rekishi* 5: Kinsei 1, edited by Rekishigaku Kenkyūkai and Nihonshi Kenkyūkai. 13 vols. Vol. 5, 35–66. Tokyo: Tokyo Daigaku shuppankai, 1985.

Ashida Ijin, ed. *Shinpen Musashi fudokikō*, Dai Nihon chishi taikei 13. Tokyo: Yūzankaku, 1996.

Ashizu Motohiko and Umeda Yoshihiko, eds. *Shintō jiten*. Osaka: Hori shoten, 1968.

Ashizu Uzuhiko. *Kokka Shintō to wa nan datta no ka*. Tokyo: Jinja Shinpōsha, 1987.

Aso, Noriko. *Public Properties: Museums in Imperial Japan*. Durham, NC: Duke University Press, 2013.

Aso Tasuku. "Shūkyō shūdan o meguru haijo no jūsōsei to kokumin kokka." *Jinbun chirigakkai taikai kenkyū happyō yōshi*, 2013, 50–51.

Asō Shōichi. *Shintō-ka Inoue Masakane*. Tokyo: Shintō Chūkyōin, 1933.

Asoya Masahiko. *Shintō shisō no keisei*. Tokyo: Perikansha, 1985.

Asoya Masahiko and Tanuma Mayumi, eds. *Shinsōsai shiryō shūsei*. Tokyo: Perikansha, 1995.

Aston, W. G., trans. *Nihongi; Chronicles of Japan from the Earliest Times to A.D. 697*. With an introduction by Terence Barrow. Rutland, VT: C. E. Tuttle Co., 1972.

Azegami Naoki. *"Mura no chinju" to senzen Nihon: Kokka Shintō no chiiki shakaishi*. Tokyo: Yūshisha, 2009.

Barnes, Gina. *State Formation in Japan: Emergence of a 4th Century Ruling Elite*. London: Routledge, 2006.

Barnes, Gina, and Masaaki Okita. "Japanese Archaeology in the 1990s." *Journal of Archaeological Research* 7, no. 4 (1999): 349–95.

Bender, Ross Lynn. "The Hachiman Cult and the Dōkyō Incident." *Monumenta Nipponica* 34, no. 2 (1979): 125–53.

Bentley, John R. *Tamakatsuma: A Window into the Scholarship of Motoori Norinaga*. Ithaca, NY: East Asia Program, Cornell University, 2013.

———. *The Authenticity of Sendai Kuji Hongi: A New Examination of Texts with a Translation and Commentary*. Leiden: Brill, 2006.

Berndt, Jacqueline. "Considering Manga Discourse: Location, Ambiguity, Historicity." In *Japanese Visual Culture: Explorations in the World of Manga and Anime*, edited by Mark W. MacWilliams, 295–310. Armonk, NY: M. E. Sharp, 2008.

Berry, Mary Elizabeth. *Japan in Print: Information and Nation in the Early Modern Period*. Berkeley: University of California Press, 2006.

Bialock, David. *Eccentric Spaces, Hidden Histories: Narrative, Ritual, and Royal Authority from the Chronicles of Japan to the Tale of the Heike*. Stanford, CA: Stanford University Press, 2007.

Bix, Herbert. *Hirohito and the Making of Modern Japan*. New York: HarperCollins, 2000.

Blacker, Carmen. "The Religious Traveller in the Edo Period." *Modern Asian Studies* 18, no. 4 (1984): 593–608.

———. "The *Shinza* in the *Daijōsai*—Throne, Bed, or Incubation Couch?" *JJRS* 17, no. 2–3 (1990): 180–97.

Bock, Felicia, trans. *Engi-Shiki, Procedures of the Engi Era*. 2 vols. A Monumenta Nipponica Monograph. Tokyo: Sophia University, 1970, 1972.

Bocking, Brian. *The Oracles of the Three Shrines: Windows on Japanese Religion*. Richmond, Surrey: Curzon, 2001.

Bodart-Bailey, Beatrice. "The Persecution of Confucianism in Early Tokugawa Japan." *Monumenta Nipponica* 48 (1993): 293–314.

Bodiford, William. "Matara: A Dream King between Insight and Imagination." *Cahiers d'Extrême-Asie* 16 (2006/7): 233–62.

Bolitho, Harold. "The *Han*." In *The Cambridge History of Japan*, edited by John Whitney Hall. Vol. 4, *Early Modern Japan*, 183–234. Cambridge: Cambridge University Press, 1991.

Bonshun. *Shunkyūki*. In *Zoku gunsho ruiju*, edited by Kamata Jun'ichi. 8 vols. Tokyo: Zoku Gunsho Ruiju Kanseikai, 1970.

Boot, W. J. "The Death of a Shogun: Deification in Early Modern Japan." In *Shinto in History*, edited by John Breen and Mark Teeuwen, 144–66. London: Curzon Press, 2000.

Borgen, Robert. *Sugawara no Michizane and the Early Heian Court*. Honolulu: University of Hawai'i Press, 1994. Originally published in 1986 by Harvard University Press, Cambridge, MA.

Bowring, Richard. *The Religious Traditions of Japan, 500–1600*. Cambridge: Cambridge University Press, 2005.

Boyd, James W., and Tetsuya Nishimura. "Shinto Perspectives on Miyazaki's Anime Film *Spirited Away*." *Journal of Religion and Film* 8, no. 2 (2004). http://www.unomaha.edu/jrf/Vol8No2/boydShinto.htm.

Braisted, William R., trans. *Meiroku zasshi: Journal of the Japanese Enlightenment*. Cambridge, MA: Harvard University Press, 1976.

Breen, John. "Accommodating the Alien: Ōkuni Takamasa and the Religion of Heaven." In *Religion in Japan: Arrows to Heaven and Earth*, edited by Peter F. Kornicki and Ian J. McMullen, 179–97. Cambridge: Cambridge University Press, 1996.

———. "Ideologues, Bureaucrats, and Priests: On 'Shinto' and 'Buddhism' in Early Meiji Japan." In *Shinto in History: Ways of the Kami*, edited by John Breen and Mark Teeuwen, 230–51. Honolulu: University of Hawai'i Press, 2000.

———. "Shintoists in Restoration Japan: Toward a Reassessment." *Modern Asian Studies* 24 (1990): 579–602.

———. "Shintō monogatari: Meiji-ki no Ise." In *Kindai Nihon no rekishi toshi: Koto to jōkamachi* (Kyoto: Shibunkaku shuppan, 2013), 351–83.

———. "The Imperial Oath of April 1868: Ritual, Politics, and Power in the Restoration." *Monumenta Nipponica* 51, no. 4 (1996): 407–29.

———, ed. *Yasukuni, the War Dead, and the Struggle for Japan's Past*. New York: Columbia University Press, 2008.

Breen, John, and Mark Teeuwen. *A New History of Shinto*. Malden, MA: Wiley-Blackwell, 2010.

Breen, John, and Mark Teeuwen, eds. *Shintō in History: Ways of the Kami*. Honolulu: University of Hawai'i Press, 2000.

Brown, Philip. *Central Authority and Local Autonomy in the Formation of Modern Japan*. Stanford, CA: Stanford University Press, 1993.

Brownlee, John. "The Jeweled Box Comb: Motoori Norinaga's 'Tamakushige.'" *Monumenta Nipponica* 43, no. 1 (1988): 35–44.

Brownlee, John S. Review of *A Chronicle of Gods and Sovereigns: Jinnō Shōtōki of Kitabatake Chikafusa*, by H. Paul Varley, trans. *Monumenta Nipponica* 36, no. 2 (1981): 207–8.

Burns, Susan. *Before the Nation: Kokugaku and the Imagining of Community in Early Modern Japan*. Durham, NC: Duke University Press, 2003.

Butler, Lee. *Emperor and Aristocracy in Japan, 1467–1680: Resilience and Renewal*. Harvard East Asian Monographs 209. Cambridge, MA: Harvard University Asia Center, 2002.

Carlqvist, Anders. "The Land-pulling Myth and Some Aspects of Historical Reality." *JJRS* 37, no. 2 (2010): 185–222.

Chamberlain, Basil Hall, trans. *Kojiki: Records of Ancient Matters*. 2nd ed. Annotated by W. G. Aston. Rutland, VT: Tuttle, 1982.

Chijiwa Itaru. "Chūsei no kishōmon ni miru shinbutsu: Kishōmon jinmon kara zenkindai no hitobito no kami kannen o saguru kokoromi-1." *Nihon bunka to Shintō* 2 (2006): 135–55.

Chou, Wan-yao. "The *Kōminka* Movement in Taiwan and Korea: Comparisons and Interpretations." In *The Japanese Wartime Empire, 1931–1945*, edited by Peter Duus, Ramon H. Myers, Mark Peattie, and Wan-yao Chou, 40–68. Princeton, NJ: Princeton University Press, 1996.

Como, Michael I. *Shōtoku: Ethnicity, Ritual, and Violence in the Japanese Buddhist Tradition*. New York: Oxford University Press, 2008.

———. *Weaving and Binding: Immigrant Gods and Female Immortals in Ancient Japan*. Honolulu: University of Hawai'i Press, 2009.

Conlan, Thomas D. *From Sovereign to Symbol: An Age of Ritual Determinism in Fourteenth-Century Japan*. Oxford: Oxford University Press, 2011.

Creemers, Wilhemus. *Shrine Shinto after World War II*. Leiden: E. J. Brill, 1968.

Daitō Takaaki. "Shintō kirigami to jishaken." In *Chūsei jisha no kūkan—tekusuto—gigei—Jishaken no pāsupekutibu*, edited by Ōhashi Naoyoshi, Fujimaki Kazuhiro, Takahashi Yūsuke, 155–68. Tokyo: Bensei shuppan, 2014.

Davis, Winston. "Pilgrimage and World Renewal: A Study of Religious and Social Values in Tokugawa Japan." *History of Religions* 23, no. 2 (1983): 97–116 and no. 3 (1984): 197–221.

de Bary, Theodore, et al., eds. *Sources of Japanese Tradition*. 2nd ed. New York: Columbia University Press, 2001.

Deguchi Nobuyoshi. "*Ise Daijingū Jin'iki*, a Record of Divine Marvels of the Grand Shrine of Ise." Translated by Norman Havens. *Transactions of the Institute for Japanese Culture and Classics* 74 (September 1994): (95) 328–(155) 268.

———. "Yōfukki." In *Kinsei Shintōron: Zenki kokugaku*, edited by Taira Shigemichi and Abe Akio. Nihon shisō taikei 39, 86–117. Tokyo: Iwanami shoten, 1972.

Demura Katsuaki. "Yoshida Shintō ni okeru on'yūkyō no hiden-ge: Tokuni jūhachi Shintō gyōji no seiritsu ni tsuite." *Shintōshi kenkyū* 23, no. 3 (1975): 32–63.

———. *Yoshida Shintō no kisoteki kenkyū*. Kyoto: Rinkawa shoten, 1997.

Devine, Richard. "Hirata Atsutane and Christian Sources." *Monumenta Nipponica* 36, no. 1 (1981): 37–54.

Doak, Kevin. "What Is a Nation and Who Belongs? National Narratives and the Ethnic Imagination in Twentieth-century Japan." *American Historical Review* 102, no. 2 (1997): 283–309.

Dore, Ronald. *Education in Tokugawa Japan*. Berkeley: University of California Press, 1965.

Ebersole, Gary. *Ritual Poetry and the Politics of Death in Early Japan*. Princeton, NJ: Princeton University Press, 1989.

"Echizen gohō ikki" (1873). In *Shūkyō to kokka*, edited by Miyachi Masato and Yasumaru Yoshio. Nihon kindai shisō taikei 5, 135–51. Tokyo: Iwanami shoten, 1988.

Edwards, Walter. "Forging Tradition for a Holy War: The *Hakkō Ichiū* Tower in Miyazaki and Japanese Wartime Ideology." *Journal of Japanese Studies* 29 (2003): 289–324.

Emura Hiroyuki. *Ritsuryō tennōsei saishi no kenkyū*. Tokyo: Kōshobō, 1996.

Endō Jun. "The Early Modern Period: In Search of a Shinto Identity." In *Shinto: A Short History*, edited by Inoue Nobutaka, Endō Jun, Mori Mizue, translated and adapted by Mark Teeuwen and John Breen, 108–58. London: RoutledgeCurzon, 1998.

———. *Hirata Kokugaku to kinsei shakai*. Tokyo: Perikansha, 2008.

———. "Tada Yoshitoshi." In *Shintō jinbutsu kenkyū bunken mokuroku*, edited by Kokugakuin Daigaku Nihon Bunka Kenkyūjo, 394–95. Tokyo: Kōbundō, 2000.

———. "The Shinto Funeral Movement in Early Modern and Modern Japan." Translated by Norman Havens. *Transactions of the Institute for Japanese Culture and Classics* 82 (September 1998): 1–31.

Farris, William. *Sacred Texts and Buried Treasures: Issues in the Historical Archaeology of Ancient Japan*. Honolulu: University of Hawai'i Press, 1997.

Foster, Michael Dylan. *Pandemonium and Parade: Japanese Monsters and the Culture of Yōkai*. Berkeley: University of California Press, 2009.

Fridell, Wilbur M. *Japanese Shrine Mergers 1906–1912: State Shinto Moves to the Grassroots*. Tokyo: Sophia University Press, 1973.

Fuchū shishi hensan iinkai, ed. *Fuchū shishi*. 2 vols. Fuchū: Fuchū City, 1974.

Fudoki. NKBT 299.

Fujii Jōji. *Bakuhan ryōshu no kenryoku kōzō*. Tokyo: Iwanami shoten, 2002.

Fujii Sadafumi. "Chūkyōin no kenkyū." *Shintōgaku* 91 (1976): 1–20.

———. "Fukushima-ken chūkyōin no kenkyū." *Shintōgaku* 93 (May 1977): 1–22.

———. *Kinsei ni okeru jingi shisō*. Tokyo: Shunbunsha, 1944.

———. *Meiji kokugaku hassei shi no kenkyū*. Tokyo: Yoshikawa Kōbunkan, 1974.

———. "Yamagata-ken no chūkyōin." *Shintōgaku* 92 (1977): 1–14.

Fujii Shun and Tanaka Shūji, eds. *Okayama-ken komonjo shū*. Kyoto: Shibunka, 1955.
Fujimori Kaoru. *Heian jidai no kyūtei saishi to Jingikan-jin*. Tokyo: Daimeidō, 2000.
Fujimoto Yorio. "Jinja Shintō to shakai kōken no kakawari o kangaeru." In *Shakai kōken suru shūkyō*, edited by Inaba Keishin and Sakurai Yoshihide, 83–105. Tokyo: Sekai shisōsha, 2009.
———. "Shinshoku yōsei to shūkyō kyōiku: Sengo rokujū go nen no ayumi kara miru genjō to kadai (Tokushū: Shūkyō no kyōiku to denshō)." *Shūkyō kenkyū* 85, no. 2 (2011): 505–28.
———. *Shintō to shakai jigyō no kindaishi*. Tokyo: Kōbundō, 2009.
Fujita Hiromasa. "Meiji shonen no kokka saishi keisei to kokugakusha—Jingikan, Jingishō no kōshō sagyō o chūshin ni." *Kokugakuin daigaku Nihon bunka kenkyūjo kiyō* 97 (2006): 117–64.
Fujita Satoru. *Bakumatsu no tennō*. Tokyo: Kōdansha, 1994.
Fujitani Toshio. *Okage mairi to eejanaika*. Tokyo: Iwanami shoten, 1968.
———. *Shintō shinkō to minshū, tennōsei*. Kyoto: Hōritsu bunkasha, 1980.
Fujiyama Midori. "Genpatsu ni taisuru shūkyōkai no kenkai. *Shūkyō jōhō sentā* Kenkyūin repōto." 2012. www.circam.jp/reports/02/detail/id=2012.
———. "Kokunai no shinsai hōdō ni mirareta shūkyō no yakuwari: Shūkyōsha ni yori shien katsudō." *Shūkyō jōhō sentā* Kenkyūin repōto, 2011. www.circam.jp/reports/02/detail/id=1998.
———. "Shūkyōkai no shinsai fukkyū o kobamu seikyō bunri no kabe." *Shūkyō jōhō sentā* Kenkyūin repōto, 2011. www.circam.jp/reports/02/detail/id=2009.
———. "Shūkyōkai no shinsai shien ga hōdō sarenai riyū 1: Hanshin, Higashi Nihon Daishinsai no hikaku yori." *Shūkyō jōhō sentā* Kenkyūin repōto, 2011. www.circam.jp/reports/02/detail/id=2007.
Fukaya Katsumi. *Kinsei no kokka, shakai to tennō*. Tokyo: Azekura shobō, 1991.
Fukunaga Mitsuji. *Dōkyō to kodai Nihon*. Kyoto: Jinbun shoin, 1987.
Fukunaga Shin'ya, Iwamoto Naofumi, Koyamada Kōichi et al., eds. *Shinpojiyumu sankakuen shinjūkyō*. Tokyo: Gakuseisha, 2003.
Funke, Mark. "Hitachi no Kuni Fudoki." *Monumenta Nipponica* 49, no. 1 (1994): 1–29.
Furukawa Junichi. "Saigūryō ni kansuru kisoteki kōsatsu." In *Nihon ritsuryōsei ronshū*, edited by Sasayama Haruo Sensei kanreki kinenkai, vol. 2, 131–169. Tokyo: Yoshikawa kōbunkan, 1993.
Garon, Sheldon. *Molding Japanese Minds*. Princeton, NJ: Princeton University Press, 1997.
———. "State and Religion in Imperial Japan, 1912–1945." *Journal of Japanese Studies* 12, no. 2 (1986): 273–302.
Gauntlett, John Owen, trans. *Kokutai no Hongi: Cardinal Principles of the National Entity of Japan*, edited by Robert King Hall. Cambridge, MA: Harvard University Press, 1949.
Gerhart, Karen. *The Eyes of Power: Art and Early Tokugawa Authority*. Honolulu: University of Hawai'i Press, 1999.
Gluck, Carol. *Japan's Modern Myths: Ideology in the Late Meiji Period*. Princeton, NJ: Princeton University Press, 1985.
Gomazuru Hiroyuki, Sakurai Katsunoshin, Suzuki Yoshikazu, et al. "Jingū hyakunen no ayumi." In *Meiji ishin Shintō hyakunenshi*, vol. 1, edited by Shintō Bunkakai, 363–510. Tokyo: Shintō bunkakai, 1966.
Gotō Yasushi "Kaidai: Tennōsei kenkyū to Teishitsu tōkeisho." In *Teishitsu tōkeisho*. 9 vols. Vol. 1, 1–6. Tokyo: Kashiwa shobō, 1993.
Graf, Fritz. "Syncretism, Further Considerations." *Encyclopedia of Religion*. Vol. 13, 8934–38. 2nd ed. Detroit: Macmillan Reference USA, 2005.
Grapard, Allan. "Japan's Ignored Cultural Revolution: The Separation of Shinto and Buddhist Divinities in Meiji (*shinbutsu bunri*) and a Case Study: Tonomine." *History of Religions* 23 (February 1984): 240–65.
———. "Institution, Ritual, and Ideology: The Twenty-Two Shrine Temple Multiplexes of Heian Japan." *History of Religions* 27, no. 3 (1988): 246–69.
———. "Linguistic Cubism: A Singularity of Pluralism in the Sannō Cult." *JJRS* 14, no. 2/3 (1987): 211–34.

———. "Medieval Shintō Boundaries: Real or Imaginary?," *Cahiers d'Extrême-Asie* 16 (2006–2007): 1–18.

———. *The Protocol of the Gods: A Study of the Kasuga Cult in Japanese History*. Berkeley: University of California Press, 1992.

———. "Religious Practices." In *The Cambridge History of Japan*. Vol. 2: *Heian Japan*, edited by Donald H. Shively and William H. McCullough, 550–75. Cambridge: Cambridge University Press, 1999.

———. "The Shinto of Yoshida Kanetomo." *Monumenta Nipponica* 47, no. 1 (1992): 27–58.

———. "Visions of Excess and Excess of Vision: Women and Transgression in Japanese Myth." *JJRS* 18, no. 1 (1991): 3–22.

Guth, Christine. *Shinzo: Hachiman Imagery and Its Development*. Harvard East Asian Monographs, 119. Cambridge, MA: Council on East Asian Studies and Harvard University, 1985.

Habuta Yoshiyuki, and Kamada Shūichi, eds., *Kofun jidai kenkyū no genjō to kadai*. 2 vols. Tokyo: Dōseisha, 2012.

Haga Noboru. "Bakumatsu henkakuki ni okeru kokugakusha no undō to rinri—tokuni yonaoshi jōkyū to kanren sasete." In *Kokugaku undō no shisō*, Nihon shisō taikei 51, edited by Haga Noboru and Matsumoto Sannosuke, 662–714. Tokyo: Iwanami shoten, 1971.

———. *Bakumatsu kokugaku no kenkyū*. Shigaku sensho 1. Tokyo: Kyōiku shuppan sentaa, 1980.

———. "Bakumatsu ni okeru Motoori, Hirata gaku no keishō." *Tokyo kasei daigakuin daigaku kiyō* 35 (1995): 1–60.

———. *Henkakuki ni okeru Kokugaku*. Tokyo: San'yōsha, 1975.

———. "Hirata Atsutane no gakumon no shakaiteki kiso—Edo no minzokuteki, fūzokuteki jijitsu to no kanren o chūshin to shite." *Rekishi jinrui* 10 (1982): 51–105.

———. *Meiji kokka to minshū*. Tokyo: Yūzankaku, 1974.

———. *Motoori Norinaga: Kinsei Kokugaku no seiritsu*. Hito to rekishi, Nihon 22. Tokyo: Shimizu shoin, 1972.

Haga Shōji. *Meiji ishin to shūkyō*. Tokyo: Chikuma shobō, 1994.

———. "Meiji Jingikansei no seiritsu to kokka saishi no saihen." *Jinbun gakuhō* 50 (1981): 27–84.

Hagiwara Tatsuo. "Chūsei makki no jinja to kyōson kannushi." In *Gendai Shintō kenkyū shūsei*, vol. 2, edited by Gendai Shintō kenkyū shūsei, henshū iinkai, 317–43. Tokyo: Jinja Honchō, Jinja Shinpōsha, 1998.

———. *Chūsei saishi soshiki no kenkyū*. Tokyo: Yoshikawa kōbunkan, 1962.

———. "Edo no Inari." In *Inari shinkō*, edited by Naoe Hiroji, 151–64. Minshū shūkyō shisōsho 3. Tokyo: Yūzankaku shuppan, 1983.

Hakone Jinja. *Hakone Jinja: Shinkō no rekishi to bunka*. Hakone Town: Hakone Jinja shamusho, 1989.

Hakone Jinja shamusho, ed., *Hakone Jinja taikei*. 2 vols. Hakone Jinja: Hakone Jinja shamusho, 1930–1935.

Hansen, Wilburn. "The Medium Is the Message: Hirata Atsutane's Ethnography of the World Beyond." *History of Religions* 45, no. 2 (2006): 337–72.

———. *When Tengu Talk: Hirata Atsutane's Ethnography of the Other World*. Honolulu: University of Hawai'i Press, 2008.

Harashima Reiji. "Amatsutsumi, kunitsutsumi to sono shakai haikei." *Rekishigaku kenkyū* 290 (1964): 1–12.

Hardacre, Helen. "Asano Wasaburō and Japanese Spiritualism in Early Twentieth-Century Japan." In *Japan's Conflicting Modernities, Issues in Culture and Democracy, 1900–1930*, edited by Sharon A. Minichiello, 133–53. Honolulu: University of Hawai'i Press, 1998.

———. "Creating State Shinto: The Great Promulgation Campaign and the New Religions." *JJRS* 12, no. 1 (1986): 29–63.

———. *Kurozumikyō and the New Religions of Japan*. Princeton, NJ: Princeton University Press, 1986.

———. *Religion and Society in Nineteenth-century Japan: A Study of the Southern Kantō Region, Using Late Edo and Early Meiji Gazetteers*. Michigan Monograph Series in Japanese Studies 41. Ann Arbor: Center for Japanese Studies, University of Michigan, 2002.

———. *Shinto and the State, 1868–1988*. Princeton, NJ: Princeton University Press, 1989.

———. "The Shintō Priesthood in Early Meiji Japan." *History of Religions* 27 (1988): 294–320.

Harootunian, H. D. *Things Seen and Unseen: Discourse and Ideology in Tokugawa Nativism*. Chicago: University of Chicago Press, 1988.

Hashimoto Masanobu. *Kinsei kuge shakai no kenkyū*. Tokyo: Yoshikawa kōbunkan, 2002.

Hashimoto Megumi. "1930 nendai Tōkyō-fu (Tōkyō-shi) shōgakkō no Ise sangū ryokō: Kibo kakudai no keika to unchin waribiki yōkyū." *Kyōikugaku kenkyū* 80, no. 1 (2013): 26–38.

Hashimoto Yoshihiko. *Nihon kodai no girei to tenseki*. Tokyo: Seishi shuppan, 1999.

Havens, Norman. "Shinto." In *Nanzan Guide to Japanese Religions*, edited by Paul Swanson and Clark Chilson, 14–37. Honolulu: University of Hawai'i Press, 2006.

Hayami Tasuku. *Heian kizoku shakai to bukkyō*. Tokyo: Yoshikawa Kōbunkan, 1975.

Hayashi Razan. "Shintō denju." In *Kinsei Shintōron: Zenki kokugaku*, edited by Taira Shigemichi and Abe Akio. Nihon shisō taikei 39. Tokyo: Iwanami shoten, 1972.

Heisig, James W., Thomas P. Kasulis, and John C. Maraldo, eds. *Japanese Philosophy: A Sourcebook*. Honolulu: University of Hawai'i Press, 2011.

Henry, Todd A. *Assimilating Seoul: Japanese Rule and the Politics of Public Space in Colonial Korea, 1910–1945*. Berkeley: University of California Press, 2014.

Higuchi Setsuko. "Hirata Atsutane to minshū no setten: Sosen sūhai no sekaikan." *Ryūkoku shidan* 73, 74 (1978): 253–69.

Hikino Kyōsuke. "Shintō kōshakushi Tamada Naganori no shomin kyōka to jingi kanryōchō Yoshida ke." *Shūkyō kenkyū* 79, no. 4 (2006): 110–11.

Hirai, Atsuko. *Government by Mourning: Death and Political Integration in Japan, 1603–1912*. Cambridge, MA: Harvard University Press, 2014.

Hirai Tarō. "Tokyo no Daijingū: Kahei no chikuseki, shōhi no ba toshite no 'ie' to sono hen'yō." *Senshū ningen kagaku ronshū* 1/2 Shakaigaku hen 1 (2011): 133–43.

Hirata Atsutane, and Zenshū Kankōkai, eds. *Shinshū Hirata Atsutane zenshū*. 21 vols. Tokyo: Meichō shuppan, 1976–81.

Hokkaidō Jingū and Kokugakuin Daigaku Kenkyū Kaihatsu Suishin Sentā, eds. *Hokkaidō Jingū kenkyū ronsō*. Tokyo: Kōbundō, 2014.

Hokkaidō Jinjachōshi Henshū Iinkai. *Hokkaidō Jinjachōshi*. Sapporo: Hokkaidō Jinjachō, 1999.

Hokkaidō sōgō seisakubu chiiki gyōseikyoku tōkeika, ed. *Hokkaidō tōkeisho*. Sapporo, Hokkaidō: 1873–1941.

Holtom, Daniel. *Modern Japan and Shinto Nationalism: A Study of Present-Day Trends in Japanese Religions*. Chicago: University of Chicago Press, 1943.

Hur, Nam-lin. *Prayer and Play in Late Tokugawa Japan: Asakusa Sensōji and Edo Society*. Cambridge, MA: Harvard University Asia Center, 2000.

Hylkema-Vos, Naomi. "Katō Genchi: A Neglected Pioneer in Comparative Religion." *JJRS* 17, no. 4 (1990): 375–395.

Ienaga Saburō. *Tsuda Sōkichi no shisōshiteki kenkyū*. Tokyo: Iwanami shoten, 1988.

Ikeda Genta. "Heian shoki ni okeru jingi shinkō no keitai." *Shintōgaku* 54 (1967): 1–21.

Inaba Keishin, and Kurosaki Hiroyuki, eds. *Shinsai fukkō to shūkyō*. Sōsho: shūkyō to soshyaru kyapitaru 4. Tokyo: Akashi shoten, 2012.

Inaba Keishin, and Sakurai Yoshihide, eds. *Shakai kōken suru shūkyō*. Kyoto: Sekai shisōsha, 2009.

Inbe Hironari. *Kogoshūi: Gleanings from Ancient Stories*. 3rd ed. Translated by Genchi Katō and Hikoshirō Hoshino. Tokyo: Meiji Japan Society, 1926.

Inoue Hiroshi. *Nihon no jinja to "Shintō."* Tokyo: Kōsō shobō, 2006.

Inoue Masakane. "Yuiitsu Shintō mondō sho." In *Shoke Shintō* 2, Shintō taikei, Ronsetsuhen 28, edited by Kurozumi Tadaaki and Sakata Yasuyoshi, 3. Tokyo: Shintō Taikei Hensankai, 1982.

———. "Yume monogatari." *Ikunshū* 1. In *Shoke Shintō* 2, Shintō taikei, Ronsetsuhen 28, edited by Kurozumi Tadaaki and Sakata Yasuyoshi, 52–53. Tokyo: Shintō Taikei Hensankai, 1982.

Inoue Mitsusada. "Kodai ni okeru tsumi to seisai." *Nihon rekishi* 190 (1964): 2–18.

———. *Nihon kodai no kokka to bukkyō*. Tokyo: Iwanami shoten, 1971.

Inoue Mitsusada et al., eds. *Ritsuryō*. Nihon shisō taikei 3. Tokyo: Iwanami shoten, 1976.

Inoue Nobutaka. "Hirata Atsutane to minshū kiso shinkō." *Shūkyō kenkyū* 51, no. 1 (1977): 21–42.

———. "Introduction: What Is Shinto?" In *Shinto: A Short History*, edited by Inoue Nobutaka, with Itō Satoshi, Endō Jun, and Mori Mizue, translated and adapted by Mark Teeuwen and John Breen, 1–10. London: RoutledgeCurzon, 1998.

———. "Kyōha Shintō no chiikiteki tenkai to sono shakaiteki jōken" *Kokugakuin zasshi* 104 (November 2003): 342–59.

———. *Kyōha Shintō no keisei*. Tokyo: Kōbundō, 1991.

———. "Shintō-kei kyōdan ni kansuru shūsenzen no kenkyū jōkyō ni tsuite." *Nihon bunka kenkyūjo kiyō* 51 (March 1983): 246–304.

———. "The Shinto World of the 1880s: Sano Tsunehiko's *A Journey to the East*." *History of Religions* 27, no. 3 (1988): 326–53.

Inoue Nobutaka, Itō Satoshi, Endō Jun, Mori Mizue. *Shinto: A Short History*. Translated and adapted by Mark Teeuwen and John Breen. London: RoutledgeCurzon, 1998.

Inoue Tomoichi. "Shinshoku shokun nimu nozomi" (Shinshoku yōseibu sotsugyōshiki kōen). *ZSKK* 34, no. 174 (1913): 339–51.

Inoue Tomokatsu. "Jingikan ryōchōjō-kō: Muromachi-ki no Yoshida-ke to jingikan." *Shūkyō kenkyū* 78, no. 1 (2004): 71–94.

———. *Kinsei no jinja to chōtei ken'i*. Tokyo: Yoshikawa Kōbunkan, 2007.

———. "Shintōsha." In *Minkan ni ikiru shūkyōsha*. Series: Kinsei no mibunteki shūhen, edited by Takano Toshihiko, 15–49. Tokyo: Yoshikawa Kōbunkan, 2000.

Introvigne, Massimo. "Cults and Sects." In *Encyclopedia of Religion*, 2nd ed., edited by Lindsay Jones, vol. 3, 2084–86. Detroit: Macmillan Reference USA, 2005.

Ise-shi sangyō kankōbu kankō kikakuka. "Heisei 25 nen Ise-shi kankō tōkei." http://www.city.ise.mie.jp/secure/12124/25kankotoukei.pdf. Accessed April 23, 2015.

Ishii Kenji. "Anime no naka no dentō shūkyō." In *Gendai bunka no naka no shūkyō dentō, Gendai shūkyō* 2011: 154–56.

———. "Jinja Shintō wa suita no ka." In *Shintō wa doko e iku ka?*,edited by Ishii Kenji, 11–30. Tokyo: Perikansha, 2010.

———, ed. *Shintō wa doko e iku ka?*, Tokyo: Perikansha, 2010.

———. "Shūkyō dantai no kōeki katsudō: Kōekisei ni kansuru ichi kōsatsu." *Kokugakuin Daigaku daigakuin kiyō*. Bungaku kenkyūka 39 (2007): 1–24.

———. "*Yamaguchi-ken: Kōkeisha mondai jittai chōsa hōkokusho*." Unpublished report, 2007.

———. "Zentai tōgi." (Dai nijūhachi kai Jinja Honchō Shintō kyōgaku kenkyū taikai hōkoku: Shinshoku kōkeisha mondai no genjō to kadai). *Jinja Honchō sōgō kenkyūjo kiyō* 16 (June 2011): 165–222.

Ishimura Kōji. "Kōeki hōjin seido kaikaku to shūkyō hōjin e no eikyō: 'Eiri hōjin nami kazei' e no tenkan to shūkyō hōjin e no hakyū mondai." *Shūkyō hō* 24 (2005): 21–56.

———. *Shūkyō hōjinsei to zeisei no arikata*. Kyoto: Hōritsu Bunkasha, 2006.

Isomae Jun'ichi. *Japanese Mythology: Hermeneutics on Scripture*. Oakville, CT: Equinox Pub.; Kyoto: International Research Center for Japanese Studies (Nichibunken), 2009.

———. "Kokka Shintō to wa nanika" in *Nihon shisōshi handobukku*, edited by Karube Tadashi and Kataoka Ryū, 142–45. Tokyo: Shinshōkan, 2008.

———. "The Formative Process of State Shinto in Relation to the Westernization of Japan: The Concept of 'Religion' and 'Shinto.'" In *Religion and the Secular: Historical and Colonial Formations*, edited by Timothy Fitzgerald, 93–101. London: Equinox, 2007.

———. *Religious Discourse in Modern Japan: Religion, State, and Shinto*. Translated by Galen Amstutz and Lynne E. Riggs. Nichibunken Monograph Series 17. Leiden: Brill, 2014.

Isomae Jun'ichi, and Ogura Shigeji. *Kinsei chōtei to Suika Shintō*. Tokyo: Perikansha, 2005.

Itai Masanari. *Sasaeai no Shintō bunka*. Tokyo: Kōbundō, 2011.

Itō Satoshi. "Gekū Takakura-san jōdo kō." *Nihon bunka kenkyūjo kiyō* 83 (1999): 95–133.

———. "Ise no Shintōsetsu no tenkai ni okeru Saidaijiryū no dōkō ni tsuite." *Shintō shūkyō* 153 (December 1993): 70–105.

———. "Shinbutsu shūgō riron no hen'yō." *Shūkyō kenkyū* 81, no. 2 (2007): 385–409.

———. "The Medieval Cult of Gyōki and Ise Shrines: Concerning the Narratives of Gyōki's Pilgrimage to Ise." *Cahiers d'Extrême-Asie* 16 (2006–2007): 49–70.

Itō Satoshi. "The Kami Merge with Buddhism." In *Shinto: A Short History*, edited by Inoue Nobutaka, with Itō Satoshi, Endō Jun, Mori Mizue, translated and adapted by Mark Teeuwen and John Breen, 63–107. London: RoutledgeCurzon, 1998.

Itō Satoshi, Endō Jun, Matsuo Kōichi, and Mori Mizue, eds. *Shintō*. Nihonshi kohyakka. Tokyo: Tōkyōdō shuppan, 2002.

Iwahashi Koyata. "Nakatomi to Imibe." *Kokugakuin zasshi* 20 (1967): 19–38.

Iwanaga Shōzō. "Daijōkyū idō ron." *Kyūshū Daigaku sōgō kenkyū hakubutsukan kenkyū hōkoku* 4 (2006): 99–132.

Jihen. "Kuji hongi gengi." In *Chūsei Shintōron*. Compiled by Ōsumi Kazuo. Nihon shisō taikei 19, 135–80. Tokyo: Iwanami shoten, 1977.

Jinbo Kunio. "Hirata Atsutane Amenominakanushi shinkō no hensei to kakuritsu—jō." *Shintō shūkyō* 162 (March 1996): 43–73.

———. "Hirata Atsutane Amenominakanushi shinkō no hensei to kakuritsu—ge." *Shintō shūkyō* 163 (June 1996): 59–85.

Jingūshichō. *Jingū: Meiji hyakunenshi*. 4 vols. Ise-shi: Jingūshichō, 1968.

Jinja Honchō. *Jingiin shūsen shimatsu, Jinja no kokka kanri bunri shiryō*. Tokyo: Jinja Honchō, 1964.

———. *Jinja Honchō jūnenshi*. Tokyo: Jinja Honchō, 1956.

———. *Jinja Honchō jūgonenshi*. Tokyo: Jinja Honchō, 1961.

Jinja Honchō Kyōgaku Kenkyūjo. *Yasukuni Jinjashi* Kindai. Jinja Gyōseishi Kenkyū sōsho IV. Tokyo: Bun'eisha, 2002.

Kadoya Atsushi. "On the Formation of Shinto Icons." *Cahiers d'Extrême-Asie* 16 (2006/7): 151–82.

Kageyama Haruki. *Shintō bijutsu*. Tokyo: Yūzankaku, 1973.

———. *The Arts of Shinto*, Translated and adapted by Christine Guth. New York: Weatherhill, 1973.

Kageyama Haruki and Murayama Shūichi. *Hieizan—sono shūkyō to rekishi*. Tokyo: NHK Books, 1970.

Kamata Jun'ichi. *Shintō bunken*. Tokyo: Jinja shinpōsha, 1993.

Kamizaka Fuyuko, and Yuzawa Tadashi. "Kamizaka Fuyuko renzoku taidan: Zen Gūji ni tou, Yasukuni Jinja no nazo." *Bungei shunju* 84, no. 11 (2006): 154–62.

Kanaseki Hiroshi, Arai Hiroshi, and Sugaya Fuminori. *Kodai no kagami to higashi Ajia*. Tokyo: Gakuseisha, 2011.

Kano Masanao and Imai Osamu. "Nihon kindai shisōshi no naka no Kume jiken." In *Kume Kunitake no kenkyū*, edited by Ōkubo Toshiaki, 201–316. Tokyo: Yoshikawa Kōbunkan, 1991.

Kanzaki Issaku. *Meiji igo ni okeru Shintōshi no shosō*. Tokyo: Yoshikawa Kōbunkan, 1937.

Kase Naomi. "Kōwa go-nen kanshi ni miru Jingikan to chihō jinja to no kakawari." *Shintō kenkyū shūroku* 3 (2003): 35–49.

Katō Genchi. *Study of Shinto: The Religion of the Japanese Nation*. Tokyo: Zaidan hōjin Meiji seitoku kinen gakkai, 1926.

———. *Waga kokutai to Shintō*. Tokyo: Kōdōkan, 1919.

Kenney, Elizabeth. "Shinto Funerals in the Edo Period." *JJRS* 27, no. 3/4 (2000): 239–71.

Ketelaar, James. *Of Heretics and Martyrs in Meiji Japan: Buddhism and Its Persecution*. Princeton, NJ: Princeton University Press, 1990.

Kidder, J. Edward, Jr. *Himiko and Japan's Elusive Chiefdom of Yamatai: Archaeology, History, and Mythology*. Honolulu: University of Hawai'i Press, 2007.

Kinsei hensan iinkai, ed. *Kyōha Shintō rengōkai hyakunenshi* Kyōha Shintō Rengōkai, 1996 http://www.kyoharen.net/1541-pdf.

Kirino Natsuo. *Joshinki*. Tokyo: Kadokawa shoten, 2008.

———. *The Goddess Chronicle*. Translated by Rebecca Copeland. Edinburgh, Scotland; New York; and Melbourne: Canongate, 2012.

Kishi Shōzō. *Shintōshū*. Tōyō bunko 94. Tokyo: Heibonsha, 1967.
Kitai Toshio. "Iwashimizu Hachimangū jinin no keizai katsudō: mibun to shogyō." In *Kannushi to jinnin no shakaishi*, edited by Hashimoto Masanobu and Yamamoto Nobuyoshi, 147–75. Kyoto: Shibunkaku shuppan, 1998.
Kita-ku hensan chōsakai. *Kita-ku shi* Tsūshi hen, Kinsei. Tokyo: Gyōsei, 1996.
Kiyohara Sadao. *Kokutai ronshi*. Tokyo: Naimushō Jinjakyoku, 1921.
———. *Shintō shi*. Tokyo: Kōseikaku shoten, 1932.
Knecht, Peter. "*Ise sankei mandara* and the Image of the Pure Land." *JJRS* 33, no. 2 (2006): 233–48.
Kobayashi Takehiro. "Heian sento senhyakunen kinensai to Heian Jingū no sōken." *Nihonshi kenkyū* 538 (2007): 1–28.
Kobayashi Yoshinori. *Yasukuniron*. Tokyo: Gentōsha, 2005.
Kobayashi Yūhachi. "Hakke Shintō to Hirata Atsutane—*Jingihakke gakusoku* no sakusha oyobi sono seiritsu jiki ni tsuite." *Kōgakukan ronsō* 7, no. 6 (1974): 41–58.
Kodama Kyūichi. *Jinja gyōsei*. Tokyo: Jiji gyōsei sōsho, 1934.
———. "Jinja Kyōkai no kaisan ni atari kaiin shokun ni tsugu." *JKZ* 37, no. 7 (1938): 2–3.
Kodama Shiki. "Shimaji Mokurai." In *Shapers of Japanese Buddhism*, edited by Kashiwahara Yūsen and Sonoda Kōyū, trans. Gaynor Sekimori, 207–18. Tokyo: Kōsei Publishing, 1994.
Kojiki. Annotated by Takeda Yūkichi and Kurano Kenji, NKBT 1. Tokyo: Iwanami shoten, 1958.
Kojiki Gakkai, ed. *Kojiki no kenkyūshi*. Tokyo: Takashina shoten, 1999.
———. *Kojiki no kotoba*. Kojiki kenkyū taikei, vol. 10. Tokyo: Takashina shoten, 1995.
Koki Kinen Ono Noriaki Sensei Ronbunshū Kankōkai, ed. "Jinja bunko no kenkyū." In *Ono Noriaki toshokangaku ronbunshū: Koki kinen*, 502–44. Kyoto: Koki Kinen Ono Noriaki Sensei Ronbunshū Kankōkai, 1978.
Kokuritsu Rekishi Minzoku Hakubutsukan. *Hirata Atsutane kankei shiryō mokuroku*. Kokuritsu Rekishi Minzoku Hakubutsukan shiryō mokuroku 6. Tokyo: Kokuritsu Rekishi Minzoku Hakubutsukan, 2007.
Komine Masaharu. *Musashi Fuchū shuku fudokikō: Shinpen Musashi fudokikō no genbun to sono kanren hosoku setsumei*. Privately published in Fuchū by Meisei kikaku, 2003.
———. *Musashi sōsha Ōkunitama Jinja taisai shi*. Privately published in Fuchū by Meisei kikaku, 2001.
Kōmoto Kazunobu. *Akagi Tadaharu*. Okayama: Kurozumikyō Nisshinsha, 1980.
———. *Kurozumikyō tokuhon*. Okayama: Kurozumikyō Nisshinsha, 1961.
Kōmoto Mitsugi. "Jinja gōshi: Kokka Shintō-ka seisaku no tenkai." In *Kindai to no kaikō* Nihonjin no shūkyō, vol. 3, edited by Tamaru Noriyoshi, Miyata Noboru, and Tamamuro Fumio. Tokyo: Kōsei shuppansha, 1973.
Kondō Yoshihiro. *Shirakawa-ke monjinchō*. Osaka: Seibundō, 1972.
Kōno Seizō. "Kannagara no michi." *Monumenta Nipponica* 3, no. 2 (1940): 369–91.
Kōnoshi Takamitsu. "Constructing Imperial Mythology: *Kojiki* and *Nihon shoki*." Translated by Iori Joko. In *Inventing the Classics: Modernity, National Identity, and Japanese Literature*, edited by Haruo Shirane and Tomi Suzuki, 51–70. Stanford, CA: Stanford University Press, 2000.
———. "The Land of Yomi: On the Mythical World of the Kojiki." *JJRS* 11, no. 1 (1984): 57–76.
Kornicki, Peter. *The Book in Japan: A Cultural History from the Beginning to the Nineteenth Century*. Leiden: Brill, 1998; paperback ed., Honolulu: University of Hawai'i Press, 2002.
Kouamé, Nathalie. *Pèlerinage et societé dans le Japon des Tokugawa, la pèlerinage de Shikoku entre 1598 et 1868*. Paris: École française d'Extrême-Orient, 2001.
Kramer, Hans M. "How Religion Came to Be Translated as *Shūkyō*: Shimaji Mokurai and the Appropriation of Religion in Early Meiji Japan." *Japan Review* 25 (2013): 89–111.
Kublin, Hyman. *Japan: Selected Readings*. New York: Houghton Mifflin, 1968.
Kubota Osamu. *Chūsei Shintō no kenkyū*. Kyoto: Shintōshi gakkai, 1959.
Kume Kunitake. "Shintō wa saiten no kozoku." *Shigaku zasshi* 2 (1891): 636–49.
Kuroda Ryūji. *Chūsei jisha shinkō no ba*. Tokyo: Shibunkaku shuppan, 1999.
———. "Hiei shichi sha honden no kōsei." *Nihon kenchiku gakkai ronbun hōkokusho* 317 (1982): 148–54.

Kuroda Toshio. *Jisha seiryoku*. Tokyo: Iwanami shinsho, 1980.

———. "Shinto in the History of Japanese Religions." Translated by James Dobbins and Suzanne Gay. *Journal of Japanese Studies* 7, no. 1 (1981): 1–21.

———. "The Discourse on the 'Land of the Kami' (*Shinkoku*) in Medieval Japan." *JJRS* 23, no. 3/4 (Fall 1996), 353–85.

Kurozumi Muneharu. "Kurozumikyō rikkyō 200-nen e no michi 5: Kyōdan no seiritsu." *Nisshin* (May 2013): 23–26.

Kurozumi Muneyasu, ed., *Kurozumikyō kyōsho*. Okayama City: Kurozumikyō Nisshinsha, 1974.

Kurozumi Tadaaki. *Kurozumikyō kyōsoden*. 5th ed. Okayama: Kurozumikyō Nisshinsha, 1976.

Kuwabara Megumi. "Bakumatsu kokugaku shisō ni okeru kokka kan, tennō kan." *Rekishigaku Kenkyū* 599 (October, 1989): 107–115.

Leheny, David. "'By Other Means': Tourism and Leisure in Pre-War Japan." *Social Science Japan Journal* 3, no. 2 (2000): 171–86.

Lillehoj, Elizabeth. *Art and Palace Politics in Early Modern Japan, 1580s–1680s*. Leiden: Brill, 2004.

Lokowandt, Ernst. *Die rechtliche Entwicklung des Staats-Shintō in der ersten Hälfte der Meiji-Zeit (1868–1890)*. Wien: Harrassowitz, 1978.

Lurie, David B. *Realms of Literacy: Early Japan and the History of Writing*. Cambridge, MA: Harvard University Asia Center, 2011.

Mae Kei'ichi. *Nara: Tennō no daigawari gishiki to "kenkoku no seichi."* Tokyo: Azumi no shobō, 1990.

Maeda Hiromi. "Court Rank for Village Shrines: The Yoshida House's Interactions with Local Shrines during the Mid-Tokugawa Period." *JJRS* 29, no. 3/4 (2002): 325–58.

———. "Imperial Authority and Local Shrines: The Yoshida House and the Creation of a Countrywide Shinto Institution in Early Modern Japan." PhD diss., Harvard University, 2003.

Maeda Takashi. *Junrei no shakaigaku*. Tokyo: Minerva shobō, 1971.

Maeda Tsutomu. "Hirata Atsutane no kōsetsu 'Ibuki oroshi' o chūshin ni." *Nihon bunka ronsō* 22 (March 2014): 37–55.

———. "Kinsei Nihon ni okeru tennō ken'i no kōjō no riyū." *Nihon shisō shigaku* 32 (2000): 57–64.

Mainichi Shinbun Yasukuni shuzaihan. *Yasukuni sengo hishi: A-kyū senpan o gōshi shita hito*. Tokyo: Mainichi Shinbun, 2007.

Mandair, Arvind-Pal S. *Religion and the Specter of the West: Sikhism, India, Postcoloniality, and the Politics of Translation*. New York: Columbia University Press, 2009.

Marra, Michelle. "The Conquest of Mappō: Jien and Kitabatake Chikafusa." *JJRS* 12, no. 4 (1985): 319–41.

Mase Kumiko. "Jinja to tennō." In *Zen kindai no tennō: Tennō to shakai shūdan*, edited by Ishigami Eiichi et al. Vol. 3, 217–46. Tokyo: Aoki Shoten, 1993.

Matsubara Shūhei, compiler. *Konpira shomin shinkō shiryōshū, nenpyō*. Kotohira Town, Kagawa Prefecture: Kotohiragū shamusho, 1988.

Matsudaira Makoto. *Matsuri no bunka*. Tokyo: Yūhikaku, 1983.

Matsumoto Sannosuke. "Bakumatsu Kokugaku no shisōshiteki igi." In *Kokugaku undō no shisō* Nihon shisō taikei 51, edited by Matsumoto Sannosuke and Haga Noboru, 633–61. Tokyo: Iwanami shoten, 1971.

———. "Kinsei ni okeru saisei itchi shisō no tenkai: Suika Shintō yori Mitogaku e." In *Kokka Shintō saikō: Saisei itchi kokka no kaisei to tenkai*, edited by Sakamoto Koremaru, 39–64. Tokyo: Kōbundō, 2006.

Matsumae Takeshi. "Early Kami Worship." Translated by Janet Goodwin. In *Cambridge History of Japan*. Vol 1: *Ancient Japan*, edited by Delmer Brown, 317–58. Cambridge: Cambridge University Press, 1993.

Matsumura Takeo. *Nihon shinwa no kenkyū*. 4 vols. Tokyo: Baifūkan, 1954–1958.

Matsuo Kōichi. "Chūsei, Kasuga-sha jinin no geinō." In *Kannushi to jinin no shakaishi*, edited by Hashimoto Masanobu and Yamamoto Nobuyoshi, 85–122. Kyoto: Shibunkaku shuppan, 1998.

Matsuoka Rie. *Jinja no musume ganbaru*. Tokyo: Hara shobō, 2004.

Maxey, Trent. *The "Greatest Problem": Religion and State Formation in Meiji Japan*. Cambridge, MA: Harvard University Asia Center, Harvard University Press, 2014.

Mayumi Tsunetada. *Kōmei Tennō to Munetada Jinja*. Kyoto: Kyoto Kaguraoka Munetada Jinja, 1992.

———. "Saiō to uneme." *Shintōgaku* 98 (1978): 1–14.

McCullough, Helen Craig, trans. *Ōkagami, The Great Mirror: Fujiwara Michinaga (966–1027) and His Times; A Study and Translation*. Princeton, NJ: Princeton University Press, 1980.

———. trans. *The Tale of the Heike*. Stanford, CA: Stanford University Press, 1988.

McLaughlin, Levi. "What Have Religious Groups Done after 3.11? Part 1: A Brief Survey of Religious Mobilization after the Great East Japan Earthquake Disasters." *Religion Compass* 7, no. 8 (2013): 294–308.

McMullin, Neil. "On Placating the Gods and Pacifying the Populace: The Case of the Gion 'Goryō' Cult." *History of Religions* 27, no. 3 (1988): 270–93.

McNally, Mark. *Proving the Way: Conflict and Practice in the History of Japanese Nativism*. Cambridge, MA: Harvard University Asia Center, 2005.

———. "The *Sandaikō* Debate: The Issue of Orthodoxy in Late Tokugawa Nativism." *JJRS* 29, no. 3/4 (2002): 359–78.

Mehl, Margaret. "Scholarship and Ideology in Conflict: The Kume Affair." *Monumenta Nipponica* 48, no. 3 (1993): 337–57.

———. "The Mid-Meiji 'History Boom': Professionalization of Historical Scholarship and Growing Pains of an Emerging Academic Discipline." *Japan Forum* 10, no. 1 (1998): 67–83.

Meiji Bunken Shiryō Kankōkai, ed. *Nihon fuken minpi hyō: Meiji 6-9 nen*, reprinted in *Meiji zenki sangyō hattatsu shi shiryō*, Bessatsu: dai 9-shū dai 5. Tokyo: Meiji Bunken Shiryō Kankōkai, 1966.

Mieda Akiko. *Hieizan to muromachi bakufu: Jisha to buke no Kyoto shihai*. Tokyo: Tokyo Daigaku shuppankai, 2011.

Mie ken, ed. *Mie kenshi* Shiryō hen, Kinsei-4, Part 1. Tsu City: Gyōsei, 1998.

Miki Shōtarō. *Hirata Atsutane no kenkyū*. Ise City: Shintōshi Gakkai, 1967.

———. "Hirata Atsutane no 'Maichō shinpai shiki' ni tsuite." *Geirin* 17, no. 4 (1936): 128–51.

Miki Yoshikazu. " Shūkyō hōjin ni yoru petto kuyō no hi-shūeki jigyōsei." *Ritsumeikan hōgaku* 298 (2004): 406–417.

Miller, Richard J. *Japan's First Bureaucracy: Study of Eighth-century Government*. Ithaca, NY: Cornell University China-Japan Program, 1979.

Mills, Douglas E. *A Collection of Tales from Uji: A Study and Translation of Uji shūi monogatari*. Cambridge: Cambridge University Press, 1970.

Mishina Akihide. *Kenkoku shinwa no shomondai, Mishina Akihide ronbunshū* vol. 2. Tokyo: Heibonsha, 1971.

———. *Nissen shinwa densetsu zōho, Mishina Akihide ronbunshū* vol. 4. Tokyo: Heibonsha, 1972.

Mitani Eiichi. *Kojiki seiritsu no kenkyū*. Tokyo: Yūseidō, 1980.

Mitani Hiroshi and Yamaguchi Teruomi. *Jūkyū-seiki Nihon no rekishi: Meiji ishin o kangaeru*. Tokyo: Hōsō Daigaku Kyōiku Shinkōkai, 2000.

Mitsuhashi Tadashi. "Chūseiteki shinshoku seido no keisei." *Shintō koten kenkyū: Kaihō* 1 (October 1979): 29–76.

———. *Heian jidai no shinkō to shūkyō girei*. Tokyo: Zoku Gunsho Ruijū Kanseikai, 2000.

———. *Nihon kodai jingi seido no seisei to tenkai*. Kyoto: Hōzōkan, 2010.

Mitsuhashi Takeshi. "Kiki to Shintō to iu go." In *Kojiki no sekai*, edited by Kojiki Gakkai, 99–124. Kojiki kenkyū taikei 11. Tokyo: Takashina shobō, 1996.

———. *Nihonjin to fuku no kami: Shichifukujin to kōfukuron*. Tokyo: Maruzen, 2002.

Miura Masayuki. *Jinja no honden: Kenchiku ni miru kami no kūkan*. Rekishi bunka raiburari 362. Tokyo: Yoshikawa kōbunkan, 2013.

Miura Sukeyuki. *Kojiki o yominaosu*. Tokyo: Chikuma shobō, 2010.

Miyachi Masato, ed. "Hirata Kokugaku no saikentō 1." *Kokuritsu Rekishi Minzoku Hakubutsukan kenkyū kiyō* 122 (March 2005): 1–221.

———. "Hirata Kokugaku no saikentō 2." *Kokuritsu Rekishi Minzoku Hakubutsukan kenkyū kiyō* 128 (March 2006): 1–503.

———. "Hirata Kokugaku no saikentō 3." *Kokuritsu Rekishi Minzoku Hakubutsukan kenkyū kiyō* 146 (March 2009): 1–389.

———. "Hirata Kokugaku no saikentō 4." *Kokuritsu Rekishi Minzoku Hakubutsukan kenkyū kiyō* 159 (March 2010): 1–162.

———. "Kokka Shintō keisei katei no mondaiten." In *Shūkyō to kokka*, edited by Yasumaru Yoshio and Miyachi Masato. *Nihon kindai shisō taikei*, vol. 5, 565–93. Tokyo: Iwanami shoten, 1988.

———. *Tennōsei no seijishi-teki kenkyū*. Tokyo: Azekura shobō, 1981.

Miyachi Masato and Yasumaru Yoshio, eds. *Shūkyō to kokka*. Nihon kindai shisō taikei, vol. 5. Tokyo: Iwanami shoten, 1988.

Miyaji Harukuni. "Yoshida Shintō kaikyojō no juju ni tsuite." *Shintōgaku* 19 (1958): 58–65.

Miyaji Naokazu. *Miyaji Naokazu ronshū*. 8 vols. Tokyo: Sōyōsha, 1985.

Miyake Hitoshi. *Shintō to Shugendō: Minzoku shūkyō shisō no tenkai*. Tokyo: Shunbunsha, 2007.

Miyake Kazuo. *Kodai kokka no jingi to saishi*. Tokyo: Yoshikawa Kōbunkan, 1995.

Miyamoto Takashi. "Kindai shūkyōgakusha no Shintōkan." *Shintō shūkyō* 198 (2005): 99–101.

Miyata Noboru. *Edo no hayarigami*. Tokyo: Chikuma shobō, 1993.

———. "Inari shinkō no shintō to minshū." In *Inari shinkō*. Vol. 3: *Minshū shūkyōshi sōsho*, ed. Naoe Hiroji, 137–50. Tokyo: Yūzankaku, 1983.

Miyazaki Fumiko. "Female Pilgrims and Mt. Fuji: Changing Perspectives on the Exclusion of Women." *Monumenta Nipponica* 60, no. 3 (Autumn 2005): 339–91.

Miyazaki Hayao. *Mononoke Hime*. Tokyo: Ghibli Studio, 1997.

Mizoguchi, Koji. *Archaeology, Society and Identity in Modern Japan*. Cambridge Studies in Archaeology. Cambridge: Cambridge University Press, 2006.

Mizoguchi Mutsuko. *Amaterasu no tanjō: Kodai ōken no genryū o saguru*. Tokyo: Iwanami shoten, 2009.

———. *Ōken shinwa no ningen kōzō: Takamimusubi to Amaterasu*. Tokyo: Yoshikawa Kōbunkan, 2000.

Mizubayashi Takeshi. "Waga kuni ni okeru kōshi kannen no rekishiteki tenkai." In *Nihonshi ni okeru kō to shi*, edited by Rekishi to hōhō hensan iinkai, 91–118. Tokyo: Aoki shoten, 1996.

Momose Takashi. *Naimushō: Meimon kanchō wa naze kaitai sareta ka?* Tokyo: PHP shinsho, 2001.

Mori Mizue. "Ancient and Classical Japan: The Dawn of Shinto." In *Shinto: A Short History*, edited by Inoue Nobutaka, with Itō Satoshi, Endō Jun, and Mori Mizue. Translated by Mark Teeuwen and John Breen, 12–62. London: RoutledgeCurzon, 1998.

Morioka Kiyomi. *Kindai no shūraku jinja to kokka tōsei*. Nihon shūkyōshi kenkyū sōsho. Tokyo: Yoshikawa kōbunkan, 1987.

Morita Tei. *Nihon kodai no seiji to shūkyō*. Tokyo: Yūzankaku, 1997.

———. *Suiko-chō to Shōtoku Taishi*. Tokyo: Iwata shoin, 2005.

Morita Yasunosuke. *Minatogawa jinja shi*. 2 vols. Kobe: Minatogawa Jinja, 1987.

Moriya Takashi. "Toshi sairei to furyū: Sono rekishiteki henbō." In *Toshi to inaka: Machi no seikatsu bunka*, 387–458. Nihon minzoku bunka taikei 11. Tokyo: Shōgakkan, 1985.

Morrell, Robert E. "Mujū Ichien's Shinto-Buddhist Syncretism: Shasekishū, Book I." *Monumenta Nipponica* 28, no. 4 (1973): 447–88.

———. *Sand and Pebbles (Shasekishū): The Tales of Mujū Ichien, a Voice for Pluralism in Kamakura Buddhism*. Albany: State University of New York Press, 1985.

Motoori Norinaga. *Kojikiden* Motoori Norinaga zenshū 1. Tokyo: Chikuma shobō, 1968–1993.

———. *Motoori Norinaga zenshū*. 23 vols. Tokyo: Chikuma shobō, 1968–1993.

———. "Tamakushige." Translated by John Brownlee. *Monumenta Nipponica* 43, no. 1 (1988): 45–61.

Mullins, Mark. "How Yasukuni Shrine Survived the Occupation: A Critical Examination of Popular Claims." *Monumenta Nipponica* 65, no. 1 (2010): 89–136.

Murakami Shigeyoshi. *Kokka Shintō*. Tokyo: Iwanami shinsho, 1970.

———. *Tennō no saishi*. Tokyo: Iwanami shinsho 993, 1977.

Murakami Yoshihide. "Taiwan ni okeru Tenrikyō no genjō." *Yamato bunka* 51 (1972): 69–77.

Murayama Shichirō, and Roy Andrew Miller. "The Inariyama Tumulus Sword Inscription." *Journal of Japanese Studies* 5, no. 2 (1979): 405–38.

Murayama Shūichi. "Shinzen dokkyō." *Nihon bukkyōshi jiten*, edited by Imaizumi Yoshio, 551. Tokyo: Yoshikawa kōbunkan, 2005.

"Naegi-han sōsai shobun." In *Shūkyō to kokka*, edited by Miyachi Masato and Yasumaru Yoshio. Nihon kindai shisō taikei, vol. 5, 119–24. Tokyo: Iwanami shoten, 1988.

Nagasaka Ichirō. "Chōkoku ni arawasareta Kami no katachi." *Kami no sugata o arawasu*. Bukkyō bijutsu kenkyū Ueno kinen zaidan josei kenkyūkai hōkokusho 32 (2005): 1–4.

Naimushō Jinjakyoku. *Jinja ni kansuru tōkeisho*. Tokyo: Naimushō, 1933.

Najita, Tetsuo. *Ordinary Economies in Japan: A Historical Perspective 1750–1950*. Berkeley: University of California Press, 2009.

Nakagawa Sagane. "Inari Worship in Early Modern Osaka." In *Osaka: The Merchants' Capital of Early Modern Japan*, edited by James L. McClain and Wakita Osamu, 180–212. Ithaca, NY: Cornell University Press, 1999.

Nakai, Kate Wildman. "The Naturalization of Confucianism in Tokugawa Japan: The Problem of Sinocentrism." *Harvard Journal of Asiatic Studies* 40, no. 1 (1980), 157–99.

Nakai Masataka. "Kodai kokka to jingi ideorogii: Taikai, Okada hōkoku ni yosetse." *Rekishigaku kenkyū* 8, no. 363 (1970): 31–34.

Nakai Shinkō. *Gyōki to kodai Bukkyō*. Tokyo: Nagata bunshōdō, 1991.

Nakajima Michio. "Meiji kokka to shūkyō: Inoue Kowashi no shūkyōkan, shūkyō seisaku no bunseki." *Rekishigaku kenkyū* 413 (1974): 29–43.

———. "Shinto Deities That Crossed the Sea." *JJRS* 37, no. 1 (2010): 21–46.

———. "Taikyō senpu undō to saijin ronsō." *Nihonshi kenkyū* 126 (1972): 26–67.

Nakamura, Kyōko Motomochi, trans. *Miraculous Stories from the Japanese Buddhist Tradition: The Nihon ryōiki of the Monk Kyōkai*. Cambridge, MA: Harvard University Press, 1973.

Nakazawa Nobuhiro. *Kyūchū saishi*. Tokyo: Dentensha, 2010.

———. "Tominaga Yoshihisa kyūzō 'Tatenosha shoseki mokuroku' no ichikōsatsu: Kinsei kōki no shake zōsho no ippan." *Kokugakuin Daigaku Nihon bunka kenkyūjo kiyō* 97 (2006): 87–115.

Narakenshi hensan iinkai, ed. *Jinja*, Narakenshi, vol. 5. Tokyo: Meichō shuppan, 1989.

Nenzi, Laura. *Excursions in Identity: Travel and the Intersection of Place, Gender, and Status in Edo Japan*. Honolulu: University of Hawai'i Press, 2008.

———. "To Ise at All Costs: Religious and Economic Implications of Early Modern *Nukemairi*." *JJRS* 33, no. 1 (2006): 75–114.

Nihon shoki jō, ge. Annotated by Sakamoto Tarō, Ienaga Saburō, Inoue Mitsusada, and Ōno Susumu. NKBT 67, 68. Tokyo: Iwanami shoten, 1967.

Nihon teikoku tōkei nenkan, ed. *Nihon teikoku tōkei nenkan*. Tokyo: Tōkei kyōkai, Sōrifu tōkei kyoku, 1875–1941.

Nishida Kaoru. "Kinseiteki Jinja shihai taisei to shake no kakuritsu ni tsuite." *Chihōshi kenkyū* 251 (1994): 22–39.

Nishida Nagao. "Sanja takusen no seisaku." *Kokugakuin zasshi* 47 (1939): 2–17.

Nishigaki Seiji. "Inari shinkō no shosō." In *Inari shinkō*. Vol. 3: *Minshū shūkyōshi sōsho*, edited by Naoe Hiroji. 165–73. Tokyo: Yūzankaku, 1983.

———. *O-ise mairi*. Tokyo: Iwanami shoten, 1983.

Nishikawa Masatami. "Kindai no shikinen sengū." *Shintōshi kenkyū* 20, no. 6 (1973): 94–109.

Nishimura Sei. "First Steps into the Mountains; Motoori Norinaga's Uiyamabumi." *Monumenta Nipponica* 42, no. 4 (1987): 449–55.

Nishimura Sei and Motoori Norinaga. "The Way of the Gods, Motoori Norinaga's Naobi no Mitama." *Monumenta Nipponica* 46, no. 1 (1991): 21–41.

Nishimuta Takao. *Norito gaisetsu*. Tokyo: Kokusho kankōkai, 1987.

Nishinomiya Hideki."Ritsuryō Jingikansei no seiritsu ni tsuite: Sono kōzō, kinō o chūshin to shite." *Hisutoria* 93 (1981): 22–42.

———. *Ritsuryō kokka to jingi saishi seido no kenkyū*. Tokyo: Kōshobō, 2004.

Nishinomiya Kazutami. "Kojiki kenkyūshi: Shōwa gojūnen ikō." In *Kojiki no kenkyūshi*, edited by Kojiki kenkyū taikei, vol. 2, 313–20. Tokyo: Takashina shoten, 1999.

Nishitsunoi Masayoshi. "Jingikan no saigi: Kinen, Tsukinami, Niiname." *Kokugakuin zasshi* 21 (1967): 1–26.

Nishiyama Matsunosuke. *Edo Culture: Daily Life and Diversions in Urban Japan, 1600–1868*, translated and edited by Gerald Groemer. Honolulu: University of Hawai'i Press, 1997.
Nitta Hitoshi. "'Kokka Shintō' ron no keifu." Part 1: *Kōgakkan ronsō* 32, no. 1 (1999): 1–36.
———. "'Kokka Shintō' ron no keifu." Part 2: *Kōgakkan ronsō* 32, no. 2 (1999): 23–59.
Nobori Masao. "*Jinja bukkaku gankake jūhōki shohen* ni miru hokora to jibyō: Genze riyaku no fōkuroa." In *Minkan shinkō to minshū shūkyō*, edited by Miyata Noboru and Tsukamoto Manabu, 108–119, Nihon rekishi minzoku ronshū 10. Tokyo: Yoshikawa kōbunkan, 1994.
Nosco, Peter Erling. "Confucianism and Shinto." In *RoutledgeCurzon Encyclopedia of Confucianism*. 2 vols., edited by Xinzhong Yao, 144–145. London: RoutledgeCurzon, 2003.
———. "Masuho Zankō (1655–1742): A Shinto Popularizer between Nativism and National Learning." In *Confucianism and Tokugawa Culture*, ed. Peter Nosco, 166–87. Princeton, NJ: Princeton University Press, 1984.
———. *Remembering Paradise: Nativism and Nostalgia in Eighteenth Century Japan*. Cambridge, MA: Council on East Asian Studies / Harvard University Press, 1990.
———. "Shinju funi (Shinto and Confucianism are not separate traditions)." In *RoutledgeCurzon Encyclopedia of Confucianism*. 2 vols., edited by Xinzhong Yao, 558–559. London: RoutledgeCurzon, 2003.
Ōba Iwao. *Kojiki seiritsu kō*. Tokyo: Daiwa shobō, 1975.
Ōbayashi Tarō. *Higashi Ajia no ōken shinwa*. Tokyo: Kōbundō, 1984.
Ochi Miwa. "Joshi shinshoku: Josei no shinshutsu wa aru no ka." In *Shintō wa doko e iku ka*, edited by Ishii Kenji, 93–112. Tokyo: Perikansha, 2010.
Odaira Mika. "Jingi saishi ni okeru josei shinshoku no hataraki." *Gakushūin Daigaku jinbun kagaku ronshū* 12 (2003): 41–67.
———. *Josei shinshoku no tanjō*. Tokyo: Perikansha, 2009.
Ōe Shinobu. *Yasukuni Jinja*. Tokyo: Iwanami shoten, 1984.
Ogihara Minori. "Shirakawa-ke to Edo no monjin—Tenpo nenkan no Inoue Masakane entō o megutte." *Shintō shūkyō* 143 (1991): 43–69.
Ogura Shigeji. "Kenkyū nōto: Hachi, kyū seiki ni okeru chihō jinja gyōsei no tenkai." *Shigaku zasshi* 10, no. 3 (March 1994): 390–415.
Ōhara Yasuo. *Shintō shirei no kenkyū*. Tokyo: Hara shobō, 1993.
———. "Shintō shirei no sōgōteki hyōka." *Nihon bunka kenkyūjo kiyō* 71 (1993): 1–26.
Ōhira Shigeru. "Saishi iseki." In *Kofun jidai kenkyū no genjō to kadai*, edited by Habuta Yoshiyuki and Kameda Shūichi, 269–283. Tokyo: Dōseisha, 2012.
Oikawa Chihaya, Taniguchi Masahiro, and Watanabe Masato. "Kojiki kenkyūshi nenpyō." In *Kojiki no kenkyūshi*, edited by Kojiki Gakkai, 339–409. Tokyo: Takashina shoten, 1999.
Okada Kaneyoshi. "Shintō keikaku ni tsuite," *JKZ* 36, no. 5 (1937): 3–13.
Okada Momoko. *Jinja wakaoku nikki*. Tokyo: Shōdensha, 2004.
Okada Seishi. *Kodai ōken no saishi to shinwa*. Tokyo: Hanawa shobō, 1970.
———. *Kodai saishi no shiteki kenkyū*. Tokyo: Kōshobō, 1992.
Okada Shōji. "Daijōsai: madoko-ofusuma-ron to shinza no imi." *Kokugakuin zasshi* 90, no. 12 (1989): 1–27.
———. *Heian jidai no kokka to saishi*. Tokyo: Zoku Gunsho Ruijū Kanseikai, 1994.
———. "Tennō to kamigami no junkangata saishi taikei—kodai no tatarigami" [The circular system of rites linking the emperor and the kami—menacing apparitions of the kami in antiquity]. *Shintō shūkyō* 199, no. 200 (2005): 73–88. The English translation is available online at http://21coe.kokugakuin.ac.jp/articlesintranslation/pdf/okada.pdf.
———. "The Development of State Ritual in Ancient Japan." *Acta Asiatica* 51 (1987): 22–41.
Okada Yoneo. "Jingū, Jinja sōkenshi." In *Meiji ishin Shintō hyakunenshi*, edited by Shintō Bunkakai, vol. 2, pp. 4–182. Tokyo: Shintō Bunkakai, 1966.
———. "Jingū Shikinen sengū sei no sōshi." *Shintōshi kenkyū* 20 (1972): 2–7.
———. *Shintō bunken gaisetsu*. Tokyo: Jinja Honchō, 1951; 6th ed. 1982.
Okanaka Masayuki, Suzuki Jun, and Nakamura Kazumoto. *Motoori Norinaga to Suzuya shachū 'Jugyō monjin seimei roku' no sōgōteki kenkyū*. Tokyo: Kinseisha, 1984.

Okuyama Michiaki. "State Shinto in Recent Japanese Scholarship." *Monumenta Nipponica* 66, no. 1 (2011): 123–45.

Ono Masaaki. "1930 nendai no go-shin'ei kanri genkakuka to gakkō gishiki: Tennō shinkō no kyōsei to gakkō kyōiku." *Kyōikugaku kenkyū* 74, no. 4 (December 2007): 542–553.

Ono Sokyō. *Shintō no kiso chishiki to kiso mondai.* Tokyo: Jinja shinpōsha, 1963.

———. *Shinto, The Kami Way: An Introduction to Shrine Shinto.* With William P. Woodward. Rutland, VT: Charles E. Tuttle Company, 1962.

Ooms, Herman. *Imperial Politics and Symbolics in Ancient Japan: The Tenmu Dynasty, 650–800.* Honolulu: University of Hawai'i Press, 2009.

———. *Tokugawa Ideology: Early Constructs, 1570–1680.* Princeton, NJ: Princeton University Press, 1985.

Orr, James J. *The Victim as Hero: Ideologies of Peace and National Identity in Postwar Japan.* Honolulu: University of Hawai'i Press, 2001.

Ōsumi Kazuo. "Chūsei Shintōron no shisōteki ichi." In *Chūsei Shintōron,* edited by Ōsumi Kazuo, 135–80. Nihon shisō taikei 19. Tokyo: Iwanami shoten, 1977.

Ōya Wataru. *Kyōha Shintō to kindai Nihon: Tenrikyō no shiteki kōsatsu.* Osaka: Tōhō shuppan, 1992.

Ōyama Seiichi. *"Shōtoku Taishi" no tanjō.* Tokyo: Yoshikawa Kōbunkan, 1999.

Philippi, Donald, trans. *Kojiki.* Tokyo: University of Tokyo Press, 1968.

Picken, Stuart. *Sourcebook in Shinto: Selected Documents.* Resources in Asian Philosophy and Religion. Westport, CT: Praeger, 2004.

Piggott, Joan. *The Emergence of Japanese Kingship.* Stanford, CA: Stanford University Press, 1997.

———. "Sacral Kingship and Confederacy in Early Izumo." *Monumenta Nipponica* 44, no. 1 (Spring 1989): 45–74.

Puett, Michael J. *To Become a God: Cosmology, Sacrifice, and Self-Divinization in Early China.* Cambridge, MA: Harvard University Press, 2002.

Rambelli, Fabio. "Before the First Buddha: Medieval Japanese Cosmogony and the Quest for the Primeval Kami." *Monumenta Nipponica* 64, no. 2 (2009): 235–71.

———. "Re-positioning the Gods: 'Medieval Shinto' and the Origins of Non-Buddhist Discourses on the Kami." *Cahiers d'Extrême-Asie* 16 (2006/7): 305–25.

———. "The Ritual World of Buddhist "Shinto": The *Reikiki* and Initiations of Kami-Related Matters (*jingi kanjō*) in Late Medieval and Early-Modern Japan." *JJRS* 29, no. 3–4 (2002): 353–85.

Raz, Jacob. "Popular Entertainment and Politics: The Great Dengaku of 1096." *Monumenta Nipponica* 40, no. 3 (1985): 283–298.

Reader, Ian, and Paul L. Swanson. "Editors' Introduction: Pilgrimage in the Japanese Religious Tradition." *JJRS* 24, no. 3–4 (1997): 225–70.

Reitan, Richard. *Making a Moral Society: Ethics and the State in Meiji Japan.* Honolulu: University of Hawai'i Press, 2010.

Robertson, Jennifer. "Sexy Rice: Plant Gender, Farm Manuals, and Grass-Roots Nativism." *Monumenta Nipponica* 39, no. 3 (1984): 233–60.

Rubinger, Richard. *Private Academies in Tokugawa Japan.* Princeton, NJ: Princeton University Press, 1982.

Ruoff, Kenneth J. *Imperial Japan at Its Zenith: The Wartime Celebration of the Empire's 2600th Anniversary.* Ithaca, NY: Cornell University Press, 2010.

———. *The People's Emperor: Democracy and the Japanese Monarchy, 1945–1995.* Cambridge, MA: Harvard University Press, 2001.

Ruppert, Brian. *Jewel in the Ashes: Buddha Relics and Power in Early Medieval Japan.* Cambridge, MA: Harvard East Asian Monographs, 2000.

———. "Royal Progresses to Shrines: Cloistered Sovereign, *Tennō,* and the Sacred Sites of Medieval Japan. *Cahiers d'Extrême-Asie* 16 (2006/7): 183–202.

Sagai Tatsuru. "Kamo-sha no norito to kaeshi norito." In *Kannushi to jinin no shakaishi,* edited by Hashimoto Masanobu and Yamamoto Nobuyoshi, 59–84. Kyoto: Shibunkaku shuppan, 1998.

———. *Manshū no jinja kōbōshi: Nihonjin no iku tokoro jinja ari.* Tokyo: Fuyō shobō shuppan, 1998.

Saigū Rekishi Hakubutsukan, ed. *Maboroshi no miya: Ise saigū*. Tokyo: Asashi shinbun, 1999.
Saijō Tsutomu. "Sosō Amaterasu Ōkami no seisei." In *Josei to shūkyō*, edited by Sōgō Joseishi Kenkyūkai, Nihon joseishi ronshū 5, 3–18. Tokyo: Yoshikawa kōbunkan, 1998.
Saitō Kōji. "Jūtaku kyojū yōshiki no kenkyū 10: Shintō shūraku no kyojū yōshiki—Miyazaki-ken Nishi Mera Mura chōsa yori." *Nihon kenchiku gakkai kita Kyūshū shibu kenkyū hōkoku* 36 (1997): 153–156.
Sakamoto Katsunari. "Jingikan no seiritsu ni tsuite no ichi kōsatsu." *Shintōgaku* 98 (1978): 40–44.
Sakamoto Ken'ichi. *Meiji Shintōshi no kenkyū*. Tokyo: Kokusho kankōkai, 1983.
Sakamoto Koremaru. "'Kokka Shintō' kenkyū no yonjū nen." *Nihon shisōshi gaku* 42 (2010): 46–58.
———. *Kokka Shintō saikō: Saisei itchi kokka no keisei to tenkai*. Tokyo: Kōbundō, 2006.
Sakamoto Naoko. "Shintō no ninkibon: Ureru 'Shintō' hon no himitsu." In *Shintō wa doko e iku ka?* edited by Ishii Kenji, 195–214. Tokyo: Perikansha, 2010.
Sakata Yasuyoshi. "Kaidai." In *Shoke Shintō* 2, Shintō taikei, Ronsetsuhen 28, edited by Kurozumi Tadaaki and Sakata Yasuyoshi, 9–28. Tokyo: Shintō Taikei Hensankai, 1982.
Sakurai Haruo. *Chiiki jinja no shūkyōgaku*. Tokyo: Kōbundō, 2010.
———. "Jinja gappei to sonraku no henka: Hokusei chihō no jirei." *Kōgakukan daigaku kiyō* 14 (1976): 221–41.
———. "Meiji shonen no jinja chōsaki ni okeru chiiki jinja no yōsu: Meiji 4-nen [1874] Toba-han 'Jinja torishirabe' no bunseki kara." *Jinja honchō kyōgaku kenkyūjo kiyō* 2 (1997): 17–58.
Sakurai Tokutarō. "Engi no ruikei to tenkai." In *Jisha engi*. Nihon shisō taikei 20, 445–78. Tokyo: Iwanami shoten, 1975.
Sakurai Yoshihide. "Gendai shūkyō ni shakai kōken o tō." In *Shakai kōken suru shūkyō*, edited by Inaba Keishin and Sakurai Yoshihide, 3–27. Kyoto: Sekai shisōsha, 2009.
Sansom, George. "Early Japanese Law and Administration, Part II." *Transactions of the Asiatic Society of Japan*. Second series. Vol. 11 (1934): 117–49.
Sasaki Junnosuke. *Bakumatsu shakairon*. Tokyo: Kōshobō, 1969.
Satō Hirō. "Chūsei ni okeru kami kannen no hen'yō." In *Chūsei shinwa to jingi, Shintō sekai*, edited by Itō Satoshi, 10–32. Tokyo: Chikurinsha, 2011.
———. "*Shinbutsu Shūgō* and *Jingi Fuhai*." https://21coe.kokugakuin.ac.jp/articlesintranslation/pdf/07sato-en.pdf. Originally published as "Shinbutsu shūgō to jingi fuhai." *2004 nendo Nihonshi kenkyūkai taikai tokushūgō* (March 2005): 22–40.
———. *Kishōmon no seishinshi: chūsei sekai no kami to hotoke*. Tokyo: Kōdansha, 2006.
Satō Masato. "Kinsei shake no Yoshida Shintō juju: Hie shake no jirei o megutte." In *Kinsei no seishin seikatsu*, edited by Seishin Bunka Kenkyūjo, 253–301. Yokohama: Ōkura Seishin Bunka Kenkyūjo, 1996.
———. "Shinbutsu kakuri no yōin o meguru kōsatsu." *Shūkyō kenkyū* 81, no. 2 (2007): 359–83.
Satō Norio. *Shinkō kaiyo rokujūgo-nen*. 2 vols. Konkō Machi, Okayama Pref.: Konkōkyō, 1971.
Sawada, Janine. *Practical Pursuits: Religion, Politics, and Personal Cultivation in Nineteenth-Century Japan*. Honolulu: University of Hawai'i Press, 2004.
Scheid, Bernhard. "Reading the *Yuiitsu Shintō myōbō yōshū*: A Modern Exegesis of an Esoteric Shinto Text." In *Shinto: Ways of the Kami*, edited by John Breen and Mark Teeuwen, 117–43. Honolulu: University of Hawai'i Press, 2000.
———. "Shinto as a Religion for the Warrior Class: The Case of Yoshikawa Koretaru." *JJRS* 29, no. 3-4 (2002): 299–324.
Scheid, Bernhard, ed., *Kami Ways in Nationalist Territory: Shinto Studies in Prewar Japan and the West*. With Kate Wildman Nakai. Wien: Österreichische Akademie der Wissenschaften, 2013.
Seidel, Anna. "Chronicle of Taoist Studies in the West, 1950–1990." *Cahiers d'Extrême Asie* 5 (1989): 223–347.
Seraphim, Franziska. *War Memory and Social Politics in Japan, 1945–2000*. Cambridge, MA: Harvard University Press, 2006.
Shiba Keiko. *Literary Creations on the Road: Women's Travel Diaries in Early Modern Japan*, translated by Motoda Ezaki. Lanham, MD: University Press of America, 2012.

Shibata Hajime. *Kinsei gōnō no gakumon to shisō*, edited by Negishi Yōichi. Tokyo: Shinseisha, 1966.
Shibata Ryōichi. "Shin shinsōsai bochi no tanjō: Jinja wa shi to dō mukiau no ka." In *Shintō wa doko e iku ka*, edited by Ishii Kenji, 72–92. Tokyo: Perikansha, 2010.
Shimasaki Tomomi and Sugawara Yōichi. "Kindai Ise no toshi seibi ni mukete no jimoto dōkō ni kansuru kenkyū." *Nihon kenchiku gakkai tōkai shibu kenkyū hōhokusho* 46 (February 2008): 749–52.
Shimazono Susumu. *Kokka Shintō to Nihonjin*. Tokyo: Iwanami shoten, 2010.
———. "State Shinto and the Religious Structure of Modern Japan." *Journal of the American Academy of Religion* 73, no. 4 (2005), 1077–98.
———. "State Shinto in the Lives of the People: The Establishment of Emperor Worship, Modern Nationalism, and State Shinto in Late Meiji." *JJRS* 36, no. 1 (2009): 93–124.
Shimizu Shigeatsu. "Sōken jinja no zōei to kindai Kyoto." In *Kindai nihon no rekishi koto: Koto to jōkamachi*, edited by Takagi Hiroshi, 93–113. Kyoto: Shibunkaku shuppan, 2013.
Shimonaka Yasaburō, ed. *Shintō daijiten shukusatsuban*. Kyoto: Rinkawa shoten, 1986.
Shinjō Tsunezō. *Shaji sankei no shakai keizaishiteki kenkyū*. Tokyo: Hanawa shobō, 1982.
———. *Shaji to kōtsū: Kumano mōde to Ise mairi*. Tokyo: Shibundō, 1960.
Shinkawa Tokio. *Dōkyō o meguru kōbō: Nihon no kunnō dōshi no hō o agamezu*. Tokyo: Taishūkan shoten, 1999.
———. "Nihon kodai ni okeru Bukkyō to Dōkyō." In *Kodai bunka no tenkai to Dōkyō*. Senshū: Dōkyō to Nihon, edited by Noguchi Tetsurō and Nakamura Shōhachi. Vol. 3, 51–83. Tokyo: Yūzankaku, 1997.
Shitomi Kangetsu. *Ise sangū meisho zue: 5 kan oyobi furoku, shūi*. Annotated by Harada Kan. Tokyo: Dai Nihon meisho zue kankōkai, 1919.
Shōji Kichinosuke. *Kinsei minshū shisō no kenkyū*. Tokyo: Kōshobō, 1979.
Shūkyō jōhō risāchi sentā. *Jinja soshiki ni kansuru ankēto chōsa hōkokusho*. Tokyo: Shūkyō jōhō risāchi sentā, 2003.
Skya, Walter. *Japan's Holy War: The Ideology of Radical Shinto Ultranationalism*. Durham, NC: Duke University Press, 2009.
Soeda Yoshiya. *Naimushō no shakaishi*. Tokyo: Tokyo Daigaku shuppankai, 2007.
Steele, M. William. *Alternative Narratives in Modern Japanese History*. London: RoutledgeCurzon, 2003.
Sueki Fumihiko. *Chūsei no kami to hotoke*. Nihonshi rifuretto 32. Tokyo: Yamakawa shuppansha, 2003.
Suenaga Keiko. *Uden Shintō no kisoteki kenkyū*. Tokyo: Iwata shoin, 2001.
Suga Kōji. "A Concept of 'Overseas Shinto Shrines': A Pantheistic Attempt by Ogasawara Shōzō and its Limitations." *JJRS* 37, no. 1 (2010): 47–74.
———. "'Chōsen Jingū go saijin ronsō' saikaishaku no kokoromi: Jinja no 'dochakusei' to mōdanizumu no shiten kara." *Shūkyō to shakai* 5 (1999): 21–38.
———. *Kaigai no jinja*. Tokyo: Yumani Shobō, 2005.
Sugata Masaaki. *Fukugan no Shintōka-tachi*. Tokyo: Hachiman shoten, 1987.
Sugawara Ikuko. *Nihon kodai no minkan shūkyō*. Tokyo: Yoshikawa kōbunkan, 2003.
Sugiyama Shigetsugu. "Yoshida-ke Kantō yakusho no sōritsu to shoki no katsudō." *Kokugakuin Daigaku Nihon bunka kenkyūjo kiyō* 45 (March 1980): 59–106.
Suzuki, Daisetz Teitarō. *Zen and Japanese Culture*. New York: Pantheon Books, 1959.
Suzuki Keiji, "Ritsuryō kokka to jingi, bukkyō." in *Kodai* 3 Iwanami kōza Nihon rekishi, 285–320. Tokyo: Iwanami shoten, 2014.
Suzuki Masataka. *Kami to hotoke no minzokugaku*. Tokyo: Yoshikawa Kōbunkan, 2001.
Suzuki Nobuhide, Kudo Yoshiaki, and Miyauchi Satoshi. "Ōkunitama Jinja reitaisai 'Kurayami matsuri' no misakibarai taiko ni kansuru yōguron-teki kōsatsu." *Dezain-gaku kenkyū* 47, no. 6 (March 2001): 31–40.
Suzuki Rie. "Kinsei kōki, shinshoku no zaikyō seikatsu to kōshō." *Hiroshima Daigaku daigakuin Kyōikugaku kenkyū kiyō* 58 (2009): 17–26.

Tachibana Mitsuyoshi. "Ichinomiya sankeiki." In *Jingi zensho*, vol. 2, edited by Saeki Ariyoshi. Tokyo: Kōten kōkyūsho, 1908.

Tada Yoshitoshi (a.k.a. Tada Nanrei). "Miyakawa nikki" (1746); reprinted in Jingūshichō, *Jingū sanpaiki taisei*. Jingū sōsho 11, 252–96. Gifu: Seinō insatsu kabushiki kaisha, 1937.

Taguchi Yūko. "Hatsu miya mairi." In *Shintō wa doko e iku ka*, edited by Ishii Kenji, 51–71. Tokyo: Perikansha, 2010.

Tahara Tsuguo. Haga Noboru et al., eds., *Hirata Atsutane, Ban Nobutomo, Ōkuni Takamasa* Nihon shisō taikei 50. Tokyo: Iwanami shoten, 1973.

Taigakai, ed. *Naimushōshi*. 2 vols. Tokyo: Chihō zaimu kyōkai, 1971.

Taira Shigemichi. *Kinsei Nihon shisōshi*. Tokyo: Yoshikawa kōbunkan, 1969.

———. "Kinsei no Shintō shisō." In *Kinsei Shintōron: Zenki Kokugaku*, annotated by Taira Shigemichi and Abe Akio, 507–88. Nihon shisō taikei 39. Tokyo: Iwanami shoten, 1972.

———. *Yoshikawa Shintō no kisoteki kenkyū*. Tokyo: Yoshikawa kōbunkan, 1966.

Takafuji Harutoshi. "Shinzen dokkyō no ichi kōsatsu." *Shintōgaku* 94 (1977): 32–53.

Takagi Hiroshi. "Kindai ni okeru shinwateki kodai no sōzō: Unebiyama, Jinmu ryō, Kashihara Jingū, san'i ittai no Jinmu seiseki." *Jinbun gakuhō* 83 (2000): 19–38.

———. "Kindai shin'en shiron." *Rekishi hyōron* 573 (January, 1998): 16–27.

———. *Kindai tennōsei no bunkashi teki kenkyū*. Tokyo: Kōsō shobō, 1997.

Takano Toshihiko. "Edo bakufu to jisha." In *Kōza Nihon rekishi* 5: Kinsei 1. edited by Rekishigaku Kenkyūkai and Nihonshi Kenkyūkai. 13 vols. Vol. Kinsei 1, 79–116. Tokyo: Tokyo Daigaku shuppankai, 1985.

Takase Yukie. "1930 nendai ni okeru shōgakkō kun'iku to jinja sanpai: Mino misshon jiken o jirei to shite." *Nihon no kyōiku shigaku: Kyōiku gakkai kiyō* 50 (October 2007): 58–70.

Takeda Hideaki. *Ishinki tennō saishi no kenkyū*. Tokyo: Daimeidō, 1996.

Tamamuro Fumio, ed. *Meiji shonen jiin meisaichō*. 2 vols. Tokyo: Hatsubai Suzuwa shoten, 2008.

———. "On the Suppression of Buddhism." In *New Directions in the Study of Meiji Japan*, edited by Helen Hardacre with Adam Kern, 499–505. Leiden: E. J. Brill, 1997.

———. *Shinbutsu bunri*. Tokyo: Kyōikusha, 1979.

Tamura Enchō. *Kodai Nihon no kokka to Bukkyō—Tōdaiji sōken no kenkyū*. Tokyo: Yoshikawa kōbunkan, 1999.

Tamura Sadao. "Eejanaika no shodankai to denban chizu." *Kokusai kankei kenkyū* 28, no. 3 (December 2007): 113–33.

Tanaka Nobumasa. *Izoku to sengo*. Tokyo: Iwanami Shinsho, 1995.

———. *Yasukuni no sengoshi*. Iwanami shinsho 788. Tokyo: Iwanami shoten, 2002.

Tanaka Osamu. "Shūkyō hōjin to zeisei to no kankei: Kazei ga nai koto no imi." *Kyōbutsu* 88 (2010): 4–5.

Tanaka Sadaaki. "Kōshi no engen: Kiki no naka no kō to shi." *Rekishi hyōron* tsūgō 596 (December 1999): 2–16.

Tanaka Sen'ya. *Tanaka Sen'ya nikki*. Urawa: Saitama Shinbunsha shuppankyoku, 1977.

Tanaka, Stephan. *New Times in Modern Japan*. Princeton, NJ: Princeton University Press, 2009.

Tanaka Yoshitō. *Kurozumikyō no kenkyū*. Tokyo: Nihon Gakujutsu Kenkyūkai, 1932.

———. "Shin ki shūgō" *Shintōgaku zasshi* 13 (1932): 203–210.

———. *Shintō gairon*. Tokyo: Nihon Gakujutsu Kenkyūkai, 1936.

———. *Shintō jūsanpa no kenkyū*. Tokyo: Daiichi shobō, reprinted 1987.

———. *Shintō shūseiha no kenkyū*. Tokyo: Nihon Gakujutsu Kenkyūkai, 1932.

———. *Tenrikyō no kenkyū*. Tokyo: Nihon Gakujutsu Kenkyūkai, 1933.

Tanigawa Yutaka. "Kyōiku, kyōka seisaku to shūkyō." In *Kin-gendai 1*, Iwanami kōza Nihon rekishi vol. 15, 271–306. Tokyo: Iwanami shoten, 2014.

Taniguchi Sumio. "Okayama hansei kakuritsuki ni okeru jisha seisaku." In *Chiiki shakai to shūkyō no shiteki kenkyū*, edited by Ogura Toyofumi, 157–80. Kyoto: Yanagihara shoten, 1963.

Teeuwen, Mark. "From Jindō to Shintō: A Concept Takes Shape." *JJRS* 29, no. 3/4 (2002): 233–63.

———. "Poetry, Sake, and Acrimony, Arakida Hisaoyu and the Kokugaku Movement." *Monumenta Nipponica* 52, no. 3 (1997): 295–325.
———. "Shintō Thought at the Ise Shrines." *Research Papers in Japanese Studies*, Cardiff Centre for Japanese Studies, no. 1 (1996): 23–40.
———. "State Shinto: An 'Independent Religion'"? *Monumenta Nipponica* 54, no. 1 (Spring 1999): 111–121.
———. "The Creation of a *Honji-Suijaku* Deity: Amaterasu as the Judge of the Dead." In *Buddhas and Kami in Japan: Honji Suijaku as a Combinatory Paradigm*, edited by Mark Teeuwen and Fabio Rambelli, 115–44. London and New York: RoutledgeCurzon, 2003.
———. *Watarai Shintō: An Intellectual History of the Outer Shrine in Ise*. Leiden: Research School CNWS, 1996.
Teeuwen, Mark, and Fabio Rambelli. "Introduction: Combinatory Religion and the Honji-Suijaku Paradigm in Pre-Modern Japan." In *Buddhas and Kami in Japan: Honji Suijaku as a Combinatory Paradigm*, edited by Mark Teeuwen and Fabio Rambelli, 1–53. London: RoutledgeCurzon, 2003.
Teeuwen, Mark, and Hendrik van der Veere, trans. *Nakatomi Harae Kunge: Purification and Enlightenment in Late-Heian Japan*. Buddhismus-Studien 1. Munchen: Iudicium, 1998.
Teikoku Chihō Gyōsei Gakkai. *Genkō jinja hōrei ruisan: kajo jizai*. Tokyo: Teikoku Chihō Gyōsei Gakkai, 1936.
Thal, Sarah. *Rearranging the Landscape of the Gods: The Politics of a Pilgrimage Site in Japan, 1573–1912*. Chicago: University of Chicago Press, 2005.
Thomas, Jolyon. *Drawing on Tradition: Manga, Anime, and Religion in Contemporary Japan*. Honolulu: University of Hawai'i Press, 2012.
Togami Shūken. "Shajiryō kokuyūchi shobun no igi to eikyō." In *Senryō to Nihon shūkyō*, edited by Ikado Fujio, 239–63. Tokyo: Miraisha, 1993.
Toki Masanori. "Kinsei no shinshoku soshiki—Musashi Kuni no jirei." *Kokugakuin Daigaku Nihon bunka kenkyūjo kiyō* 12 (March 1963): 191–254.
Tokita Hideyuki. "Yasukuni Jinja ni kansuru 11 no shitsumon." *Chūō kōron* (March 2003): 156–61.
Tokoyo Nagatane. "Shinkyō soshiki monogatari." Annotated by Sakamoto Koremaru. In *Shūkyō to kokka*, edited by Yasumaru Yoshio and Miyachi Masato, 361–422. Nihon kindai shisō taikei 5. Tokyo: Iwanami shoten, 1988.
Toyama Mitsuo. *Tenchi to Jitō*. Kōdansha gendai shinsho 2077. Tokyo: Kōdansha, 2010.
Tōyō Keizai Shinpōsha. *Meiji, Taishō zaisei shoran*. Tokyo: Tōyō Keizai Shinpōsha, 1926.
Toyoda Takeshi. *Shūkyō seidoshi*. Tokyo: Yoshikawa Kōbunkan, 1982.
Tsuchihashi Yutaka. "Nakatomi yogoto to Jitō-chō." *Bungaku* 54, no. 5 (1986): 1–18.
Tsuda Kin'uemon Norinao. "Ise mairi okage no nikki" (1771). In *Okage mairi*, in *Sesō*, Pt. 1; vol. 12 of Nihon shomin seikatsu shiryō shūsei, edited by Tanigawa Ken'ichi, 85–149. Tokyo: San'yōsha, 1971.
Tsuda Sōkichi. *Jindaishi no atarashii kenkyū*. Tokyo: Nishōdō, 1913.
———. *Kojiki oyobi Nihon shoki no shin kenkyū*. Tokyo: Iwanami shoten, 1925.
———. *Nihon no Shintō*. Tsuda Sōkichi zenshū. Vol. 9. Tokyo: Iwanami shoten, 1964.
Tsuji Zennosuke. *Nihon Bukkyōshi no kenkyū*. 2 vols. Tokyo: Kinkōdō shoseki, 1919.
Tsuji Zennosuke, Murakami Senshō, and Washio Junkei, eds. *Shinpen Meiji ishin shinbutsu bunri shiryō*. 10 vols. Tokyo: Meichō shuppan, 2001.
Tsukamoto Seiji. "Kome sōdō ni tsuki, toku ni shinshoku shokun ni nozomu." *JKZ* 17 (September 1918): 1–4.
Tyler, Royall. *The Miracles of the Kasuga Deity*. New York: Columbia University Press, 1990.
Tyler, Susan. "Honji Suijaku Faith." *JJRS* 16, no. 2/3 (1989): 227–50.
Tze, May Loo. *Heritage Politics: Shuri Castle and Okinawa's Incorporation into Modern Japan, 1879–2000*. Lanham, MD: Lexington Books, 2014.
Uejima Susumu. *Nihon chūsei shakai no keisei to ōken*. Nagoya: Nagoya Daigaku shuppankai, 2010.
Umeda Yoshihiko. "Amatsustumi to kunitsutsumi: tsumi to kegare." *Shintōgaku* 65 (1970): 1–9.

———. "Jinja seido enkakushi." In *Meiji ishin Shintō hyakunenshi*, edited by Shintō Bunkakai, vol. 1, 157–245. Tokyo: Shintō Bunkakai, 1966.

———. "Katō Genchi." *Shintō shūkyō* 41 (1965): 82–88.

———. *Nihon shūkyō seidoshi*. 3 vols. Tokyo: Tōsen shuppan, 1971.

Uno Hideo. "Rakuchū Hie jinin no sonzai keitai." In *Kannushi to jinin no shakaishi*, edited by Hashimoto Masanobu and Yamamoto Nobuyoshi, 123–46. Kyoto: Shibunkaku shuppan, 1998.

Uno Masato. "Tokoyo Nagatane kōjutsu monjinra hikki, 'Shinkyō soshiki monogatari.'" *Nihon bunka kenkyūjo kiyō* 52 (May 1983): 179–272.

Uno Yukio. "Kodai ni okeru seiji to shūkyō to no kankei: Jingikan no seiritsu o chūshin toshite." *Shichō* 45 (1952): 15–20.

Vaporis, Constantin. *Breaking Barriers: Travel and the State in Early Modern Japan*. Cambridge, MA: Harvard University Press, 1994.

Varley, H. Paul, trans. *A Chronicle of Gods and Sovereigns: Jinnō Shōtōki of Kitabatake Chikafusa*. New York: Columbia University Press, 1980.

Wachutka, Michael. *Kokugaku in Meiji-period Japan: The Modern Transformation of 'National Learning' and the Formation of Scholarly Societies*. Leiden: Global Oriental, 2013.

Wada Atsumu. *Nihon kodai no girei to saishi, shinkō*. Tokyo: Hanawa shobō, 1995.

Wakabayashi, Bob Tadashi. *Anti-foreignism and Western Learning in Early-modern Japan, the New Theses of 1825*. Cambridge, MA: Council on East Asian Studies, Harvard University, 1991.

———. "In Name Only: Imperial Sovereignty in Early Modern Japan." *Journal of Japanese Studies* 17, no. 1 (1991): 25–57.

Wakabayashi, Haruko. *The Seven Tengu Scrolls: Evil and the Rhetoric of Legitimacy in Medieval Japanese Buddhism*. Honolulu: University of Hawai'i Press, 2012.

Walthall, Anne. "Off with Their Heads!: The Hirata Disciples and the Ashikaga Shoguns." *Monumenta Nipponica* 50, no. 2 (Summer 1995): 137–70.

———. *The Weak Body of a Useless Woman: Matsuo Taseko and the Meiji Restoration*. Chicago: University of Chicago Press, 1998.

———. "Writing about Pilgrimage, Exile, and Politics: Women's Travel Diaries in Late Edo-period Japan." *Transactions of the Asiatic Society of Japan*. Fifth series 3 (2011): 29–50.

Watanabe Kinzō. *Hirata Atsutane kenkyū*. Tokyo: Rokkō shobō, 1942.

Watanabe Shin'ichirō. "Tenka no ideorogii kōzō." *Nihonshi kenkyū* 440 (April 1999): 36–49.

Watanabe Yutaka. "Hirata Atsutane no 'Maichō shinpai shiki.'" In *Takahara sensei kiju kinen kōgakuronshū*, edited by Tanaka Takashi, 495–515. Ise City: Kōgakukan Daigaku shuppanbu, 1969.

———. "Hirata Atsutane no Maichō shinpai shiki, tsuiho." *Shintōshi kenkyū* 19, no. 1 (1971): 31–49.

Watarai Hironori. *Ise Daijingū Zoku Jin'iki* [The continuing record of divine marvels of the grand shrine of Ise]. Annotated translation by Norman Havens. *Transactions of the Institute for Japanese Culture and Classics* 78 (September 1996): (75) 262–(135) 202.

Wessinger, Catherine. "New Religious Movements." In *Encyclopedia of Religion*, 2nd ed., edited by Lindsay Jones, vol. 10, 6512. Detroit: Macmillan Reference USA. Accessed from *Gale Virtual Reference Library*, 2005.

White, A. James. *Ikki: Social Conflict and Political Protest in Early Modern Japan*. Ithaca, NY: Cornell University Press, 1995.

Wilson, George. "Ee ja nai ka on the Eve of the Meiji Restoration in Japan." *Semiotica* 70, no. 3 (1988): 301–20.

Wilson, Noell. "Tokugawa Defense Redux: Organizational Failure in the Phaeton Incident of 1808." *Journal of Japanese Studies* 36, no. 1 (2009): 1–32.

Woodward, William P. *The Allied Occupation of Japan 1945–1952 and Japanese Religions*. Leiden: E. J. Brill, 1972.

Yamaguchi Kōhei, ed. *Kinsei Aizu shi no kenkyū*. Aizuwakamatsu City: Rekishi shunjusha, 1978.

Yamaguchi Osamu. "Tennō shō no keifu." *Bukkyō Daigaku sōgō kenkyūjo kiyō*. Special issue. 2 (March 1995): 96–118.

Yamaguchi Teruomi. *Meiji kokka to shūkyō*. Tokyo: Tōkyō Daigaku shuppankai, 1999.
Yamamoto Hiroko. *Chūsei Shintō*. Tokyo: Iwanami shinsho, 1998.
———. *Ijin*. 2 vols. Tokyo: Chikuma shobō, 2003.
Yamamoto Nobuyoshi. "Jinin no seiritsu." In *Kannushi to jinin no shakaishi*, edited by Hashimoto Masanobu and Yamamoto Nobuyoshi, 3–57. Kyoto: Shibunkaku shuppan, 1998.
Yamamoto Yōko. "Jinja engi emaki ni okeru kamigami no egakikata: ikanaru baai ni kami no sugata o arawasu koto o habakaru ka." In *Nihon bijutsu shūkō: Sasaki Kōzō Sensei koki kinen ronbunshū*, 14–174. Tokyo: Meitoku shuppansha, 1998.
Yamaori Tetsuo, ed. *Nihon shūkyōshi nenpyō*. Tokyo: Kawade shobō shinsha, 2004.
Yamazaki Ansai. "Jijusho." In *Kinsei Shintōron: Zenki Kokugaku*, annotated by Taira Shigemichi and Abe Akio, 129–138, Nihon shisō taikei 39. Tokyo: Iwanami shoten, 1972.
———. "Jindaimaki kōgi." In *Kinsei Shintōron: Zenki Kokugaku*, annotated by Taira Shigemichi and Abe Akio, 166–70, Nihon shisō taikei 39. Tokyo: Iwanami shoten, 1972.
———. "Suika shagō." In *Kinsei Shintōron: Zenki Kokugaku*, annotated by Taira Shigemichi and Abe Akio, 119–28, Nihon shisō taikei 39. Tokyo: Iwanami shoten, 1972.
Yamazaki Hifumi. "Nihon no kokkyō wa Shintō tarubeshi." *ZSK* 4, no. 23 (1901): 344–47.
Yamazaki Tomoya. "Ishikawa, Toyama hen: Hakusan shinkō to seikyō bunri gensoku." In *Chiiki ni manabu kenpō enshū*, edited by Arai Makoto, Kotani Junko, and Yokodaidō Satoshi, 72–81. Tokyo: Nihon hyōronsha, 2011.
Yanase Kazuo. *Shaji engi no kenkyū*. Tokyo: Benseisha, 1998.
Yano Ken'ichi. "Kodai ni okeru kokka to saigi." *Rekishigaku kenkyū* 560 (October 1986): 28–36.
Yasuda Takehiro. *Rakugo jiten*. Tokyo: Seiabō, 1994.
Yasukuni Jinja. *Furusato no gokoku jinja to Yasukuni Jinja*. Tokyo: Dentensha, 2007.
Yasukuni Jinja, ed. *Yasukuni Jinja hyakunenshi, Jireki nenpyō*. Tokyo: Yasukuni Jinja, 1987.
———. *Yasukuni Jinja hyakunenshi, Shiryōhen chū*. Tokyo: Yasukuni Jinja, 1983.
———. *Yasukuni Jinja hyakunenshi, Shiryōhen jō*. Tokyo: Yasukuni Jinja, 1983.
Yasumaru Yoshio. *Kamigami no Meiji ishin*. Iwanami shinsho 103. Tokyo: Iwanami shoten, 1980.
Yatsuka Kiyotsura. "Kōshitsu saishi hyakunenshi." In *Meiji ishin Shintō hyakunenshi*, vol. 1, edited by Shintō Bunkakai, 49–155. Tokyo: Shintō Bunkakai, 1966.
Yoneji Minoru. *Sonraku saishi to kokka tōsei*. Tokyo: Ochanomizu shobō, 1977.
Yoshida Atsuhiko. *Girisha shinwa to Nihon shinwa: Hikaku shinwagaku no kokoromi*. Tokyo: Misuzu shobō, 1974.
Yoshida Kanetomo. "Yuiitsu shintō myōbō yōshū." Translated by Allan Grapard. *Monumenta Nipponica* 47/2 (1992): 137–61.
Yoshida Nobuyuki. "Kōgi to chōnin mibun." *Rekishigaku kenkyū* (Bessatsu) (November, 1980): 96–111.
Yoshie Akiko. *Nihon kodai joseishi ron*. Tokyo: Yoshikawa kōbunkan, 2007.
Yoshie Takashi. "Saishi kūkan to shite no Jingikan." *Rekishi kenkyū* 42 (2004): 85–106.
Yoshii Yoshiaki. *Jinja seidoshi no kenkyū*. Tokyo: Yūzankaku, 1935.
Yoshino Kōichi and Terazawa Shigenori. "Chiiki shakai ni okeru shūkyō no shakai kōken katsudō." In *Shakai kōken suru shūkyō*, edited by Inaba Keishin and Sakurai Yoshihide, 160–81. Tokyo: Sekai shisōsha, 2009.

INDEX

Note: Page numbers in *italics* indicate illustrations; those with a *t* indicate tables.